Co
g

S

D

Published by Collins
An imprint of HarperCollins Publishers
Westerhill Road
Bishopbriggs
Glasgow G64 2QT

HarperCollins Publishers
1st Floor, Watermarque Building
Ringsend Road, Dublin 4, Ireland

Sixth Edition 2022

10 9 8 7 6 5 4 3 2 1

ISBN 978-0-00-852393-0

www.collins.co.uk/scrabble

Typeset by Davidson Publishing Solutions

Printed and bound in Italy by
Grafica Veneta S.p.A. Trebaseleghe (PD)

A catalogue record for this book is available from the British Library.

If you would like to comment on any aspect of this book, please contact us at the given address or online.
E-mail: puzzles@harpercollins.co.uk
facebook.com/collinsdictionary
@collinsdict

Acknowledgements
We would like to thank those authors and publishers who kindly gave permission for copyright material to be used in the Collins Corpus. We would also like to thank Times Newspapers Ltd for providing valuable data.

EDITOR
Mary O'Neill

COMPUTING SUPPORT
Agnieszka Urbanowicz

FOR THE PUBLISHER
Gerry Breslin, Kerry Ferguson

Introduction

The *Collins Gem Scrabble Dictionary* is the ideal reference book for people who play Scrabble for enjoyment, in a social or family setting. This dictionary includes words of up to seven letters in length from the 279,000-plus words in *Collins Official Scrabble Words 2022*, the definitive Scrabble word list. The concise definitions in the *Gem Scrabble Dictionary* – given for base forms of words where the meaning is not well-known or self-explanatory – allow players to check the meaning of words, as well as to use the book for settling arguments during games.

Because this dictionary is designed for family play, it does not include vulgar or offensive terms. The complete word list for tournaments and club competitions can be found in *Collins Official Scrabble Words 2022*, along with words of eight to fifteen letters.

How the word list is arranged

Words are listed in alphabetical order, although some inflected forms are included in the base form entry to save space. These appear in capitals, after the base form. If the inflected form is created by the simple addition of a letter or letters, then only these letters are shown, for example:

ABET, -S, -TED

If there is some other spelling change, then the whole inflected form is shown:

ABATE, -D, -S, ABATING

Inflected forms also have a separate entry in the alphabetical list if another word interrupts the alphabetical sequence:

AGENT, -ED, -S *n, vb*
AGENTRY *n* activity of an agent
AGENTS ▸ **agent**

Therefore, you should first scan the alphabetical list to check for a word; if the word is not included as a full entry in the alphabetical list, it may well appear as an inflected form beside its base form.

A black triangle symbol (▸) is used to refer readers to another related entry in the dictionary. Inflected, derived, and variant forms are referred back to the main entry in this way.

ALERTLY ▸ **alert**
ALCADE, -S *same as* ▸ **alcalde**

References to playable words longer than seven letters are also included. These longer words are introduced by a chevron symbol (>), which indicates the word is not within the scope of this book, but it is included in *Collins Official Scrabble Words 2022*.

Two-letter words

A sound knowledge of the 127 two-letter words is crucial to success in Scrabble. Where many inexperienced Scrabble players go wrong is that they think the longer a word is, the better it is to know, as it's likely to score more. In fact, the key to a good Scrabble vocabulary is a good knowledge of short words.

The reason for that is you can use the short words to 'hook' the word you want to play onto the board, allowing you to play parallel to another word, rather than always going through it crosswise. That way you will usually make more than one word on each shot, gaining you a higher score.

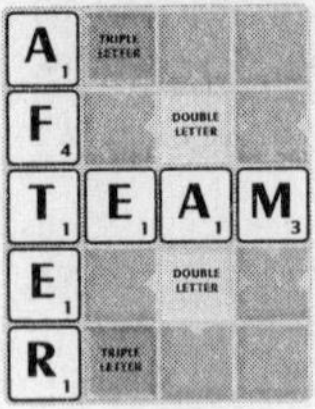

Notice how by using the same letters from your rack, you have scored seventeen more points. But notice also that little word **FA** which enabled you to fit the play in. And there we have the first, essential thing you have to know to improve your game: **all the allowable two-letter words**. Yes, all of them.

There are 127 of these to learn, but to make the list more manageable, you can divide them into three groups:

1. The ones you already know.
2. The ones you already know, but may not have realized were words.
3. The ones you probably don't know.

There are thirty-eight two-letter words which most people would know and which would appear in most dictionaries:

AH	AM	AN	AS	AT	AX	AY	BE	BY	DO	EH
GO	HA	HE	HI	HO	IF	IN	IS	IT	LA	LO
MA	ME	MY	NO	OF	OH	OK	ON	OR	OX	PA
SO	TO	UP	US	WE						

So straight away you only have eighty-nine new ones to learn. But it's not even as bad as that, because now we move on to the second group: the ones you know, but don't know you know.

These include:

Contractions

AD (advertisement)	**PO** (chamberpot)
MO (moment)	**RE** (concerning)
OP (operation)	**TA** (thank you)

Interjections and exclamations

AW	ER	EW	HM	MM	OI	OW	OY
SH	ST	UH	UM	UR	YA	YO	

Letters of the alphabet

AR	EF	EL	EM	EN	ES	EX

Then add in **ID** (a psychiatric term), **PI** (a Greek letter and mathematical term), and **YE** (the old form of **YOU**), and that's another thirty-one taken care of with no trouble at all.

Fifty-eight to go. These are the ones you probably don't know, so let's set them out where you can get the measure of them:

AA	AB	AE	AG	AI	AL	BA	BI	BO	CH	DA
DE	DI	EA	ED	EE	ET	FA	FE	FY	GI	GU
IO	JA	JO	KA	KI	KO	KY	LI	MI	MU	NA
NE	NU	NY	OB	OD	OE	OM	OO	OS	OU	PE
QI	SI	TE	TI	UG	UN	UT	WO	XI	XU	YU
ZA	ZE	ZO								

Once you're happy with the common two-letter words, have a go at mastering the unusual ones. These really are the essential first step to improving your game.

Special Scrabble words

To help family players learn and use some of the most useful words in the game, the *Collins Gem Scrabble Dictionary* includes a number of special panel entries, drawing attention to more than 200 words of particular interest or utility. For the most part these are words which are less likely to form part of a novice player's natural vocabulary, and the emphasis is on particularly useful three-letter words, on high probability seven-letter bonus words, on words that are especially useful when you have either too many vowels on your rack or too many consonants, and on selected shorter words that use the high-value consonants **J**, **K**, **Q**, **X** and **Z**. But just for fun we have also featured a few of the unusual and exciting words of the kind that Scrabble players dream about. Realistically, you may well never get the chance to play words like **ZOOTAXY**, **TZADDIQ** and **QUETZAL**. But imagine the thrill (and the score!) if you did...

The *Collins Gem Scrabble Dictionary* is designed to be useful to new players and Scrabble veterans alike – we hope you enjoy using it!

Abbreviations

adj	adjective
adv	adverb
Brit	*British*
conj	conjunction
det	determiner
E	East or eastern
eg	for example
esp	especially
interj	interjection
n	noun
N	North or northern
orig	originally
pl	plural
prep	preposition
pron	pronoun
S	South or southern
Scot	Scottish
sing	singular
usu	usually
vb	verb
W	West or western

Aa

AA, -S *n* volcanic rock
AAH, -ED, -ING, -S *vb* exclaim in pleasure
AAL, -S *n* small shrub or tree with yellow fruits

An **aal** is a South East Asian shrub, useful for getting rid of annoying multiples of A.

AALII, -S *n* bushy shrub

An **aalii** is a tropical shrub, great for getting rid of surplus As and Is.

AALS ▸ **aal**
AARGH *same as* ▸ **argh**
AARRGH *same as* ▸ **argh**
AARRGHH *same as* ▸ **argh**
AARTI, -S *n* Hindu ceremony
AAS ▸ **aa**
AB, -S *n* abdominal muscle
ABA, -S *n* type of Syrian cloth
ABAC, -S *n* mathematical diagram
ABACA, -S *n* species of banana
ABACI ▸ **abacus**
ABACK *adv*
ABACS ▸ **abac**
ABACTOR *n* cattle thief
ABACUS, ABACI *n*
ABAFT *adv* by the rear of (a ship) ▹ *adj* closer to the stern
ABAKA, -S *n* abaca
ABALONE *n*
ABAMP, -S *same as* > **abampere**
ABAND, -ED, -S *vb* abandon
ABANDON *vb, n*
ABANDS ▸ **aband**
ABAS ▸ **aba**
ABASE, -D, -S, ABASING *vb*
ABASER, -S ▸ **abase**
ABASES ▸ **abase**
ABASH, -ES *vb* cause to feel ill at ease
ABASHED *adj* embarrassed and ashamed
ABASHES ▸ **abash**
ABASIA, -S *n* disorder affecting ability to walk
ABASING ▸ **abase**
ABASK *adv* in pleasant warmth
ABATE, -D, -S, ABATING *vb*
ABATER, -S ▸ **abate**
ABATES ▸ **abate**
ABATING ▸ **abate**
ABATIS *n* rampart of felled trees
ABATOR, -S *n* person who effects an abatement
ABATTIS *same as* ▸ **abatis**
ABATTU *adj* dejected
ABATURE *n* trail left by hunted stag
ABAXIAL *adj* facing away from the axis
ABAXILE *adj* away from the axis
ABAYA, -S *n* Arab outer garment
ABB, -S *n* yarn used in weaving
ABBA, -S *n* Coptic bishop
ABBACY *n* office of abbot or abbess
ABBAS ▸ **abba**
ABBE, -S *n* French abbot
ABBED *adj* displaying strong abdominal muscles
ABBES ▸ **abbe**
ABBESS *n* nun in charge of a convent
ABBEY, -S *n*
ABBOT, -S *n*
ABBOTCY ▸ **abbot**
ABBOTS ▸ **abbot**
ABBS ▸ **abb**
ABCEE, -S *n* alphabet
ABDABS *n* highly nervous state
ABDOMEN *n*
ABDUCE, -D, -S *vb* abduct

ABDUCT, -S *vb*
ABEAM *adj* at right angles to a ship
ABEAR, -S, ABORE *vb* bear or behave
ABED *adv* in bed
ABEIGH *adv* aloof
ABELE, -S *n* white poplar tree
ABELIA, -S *n* garden plant with pink or white flowers
ABELIAN ▸ **abelia**
ABELIAS ▸ **abelia**
ABER, -S *n* estuary
ABET, -S, -TED *vb* help in wrongdoing
ABETTAL ▸ **abet**
ABETTED ▸ **abet**
ABETTER ▸ **abet**
ABETTOR ▸ **abet**
ABEYANT > **abeyance**
ABFARAD *n* unit of capacitance
ABHENRY *n* unit of inductance
ABHOR, -S *vb*
ABIDE, ABID, ABIDDEN, -D, -S *vb*
ABIDER, -S ▸ **abide**
ABIDES ▸ **abide**
ABIDING *adj* lasting ▹ *n* action of one who abides
ABIES, ABIETES *n* fir tree
ABIETIC *adj* as in **abietic acid** yellowish powder
ABIGAIL *n* a lady's maid
ABILITY *n*
ABIOSIS, ABIOSES *n* absence of life
ABIOTIC ▸ **abiosis**
ABITUR, -S *n* German examination
ABJECT, -S *adj* utterly miserable ▹ *vb* throw down
ABJOINT *vb* cut off
ABJURE, -D, -S *vb* deny or renounce on oath
ABJURER ▸ **abjure**
ABJURES ▸ **abjure**
ABLATE, -D, -S *vb* remove by ablation
ABLATOR *n* heat shield of a space craft
ABLAUT, -S *n* vowel gradation
ABLAZE *adj, adv*
ABLE, -R, -S, -ST, ABLING *adj, vb*
ABLED *adj*
ABLEISM *n*
ABLEIST ▸ **ableism**
ABLER ▸ **able**
ABLES ▸ **able**
ABLEST ▸ **able**
ABLET, -S *n* freshwater fish
ABLING ▸ **able**
ABLINGS *adv* possibly
ABLINS *adv* Scots word meaning perhaps
ABLOOM *adj* in flower
ABLOW *adj* blooming
ABLUENT *n* substance used for cleansing
ABLUSH *adj* blushing
ABLUTED *adj* washed thoroughly
ABLY *adv*
ABMHO, -S *n* unit of electrical conductance
ABOARD *adv, adj*
ABODE, -D, -S, ABODING *n* home, dwelling ▹ *vb* forebode
ABOHM, -S *n* unit of resistance
ABOIL *adj* boiling
ABOLISH *vb*
ABOLLA, -E, -S *n* Roman cloak
ABOMA, -S *n* South American snake
ABOMASA > **abomasum**
ABOMASI > **abomasus**
ABOON *Scots word for* ▸ **above**
ABORAL *adj* away from the mouth
ABORD, -ED, -S *vb* accost
ABORE ▸ **abear**
ABORNE *adj* Shakespearean form of auburn
ABORT, -ED, -S *vb, n*
ABORTEE *n* woman having an abortion
ABORTER ▸ **abort**
ABORTS ▸ **abort**
ABORTUS *n* aborted fetus
ABOUGHT ▸ **aby**
ABOULIA *same as* ▸ **abulia**
ABOULIC ▸ **aboulia**
ABOUND, -S *vb*
ABOUT *adv*
ABOUTS *prep* about
ABOVE, -S *adv, n*
ABRADE, -D, -S *vb* wear down by friction
ABRADER ▸ **abrade**
ABRADES ▸ **abrade**
ABRAID, -S *vb* awake
ABRAM *adj* auburn
ABRASAX *same as* ▸ **abraxas**
ABRAXAS *n* ancient charm composed of Greek letters
ABRAY, -ED, -S *vb* awake

ABRAZO, -S *n* embrace
ABREACT *vb* alleviate through abreaction
ABREAST *adj*
ABREGE, -S *n* abridgment
ABRI, -S *n* shelter or place of refuge, esp in wartime
ABRIDGE *vb*
ABRIM *adj* full to the brim
ABRIN, -S *n* poisonous compound
ABRIS ▸ **abri**
ABROACH *adj* (of a cask, barrel, etc) tapped
ABROAD, -S *adv, adj, n*
ABROOKE *vb* bear or tolerate
ABROSIA *n* condition involving refusal to eat
ABRUPT, -S *adj* sudden, unexpected ▹ *n* abyss
ABS ▸ **ab**
ABSCESS *n, vb*
ABSCIND *vb* cut off
ABSCISE *vb* separate or be separated by abscission
ABSCISS *same as* > **abscissa**
ABSCOND *vb*
ABSEIL, -S *vb, n*
ABSENCE *n*
ABSENT, -S *adj, vb*
ABSEY, -S *n* alphabet
ABSINTH *same as* > **absinthe**
ABSIT, -S *n* leave from college
ABSOLVE *vb*
ABSORB, -S *vb*
ABSTAIN *vb*
ABSURD, -S *adj, n*
ABTHANE *n* ancient Scottish church territory
ABUBBLE *adj* bubbling
ABULIA, -S *n* pathological inability to take decisions
ABULIC ▸ **abulia**
ABUNA, -S *n* male head of Ethiopian family
ABUNE *Scots word for* ▸ **above**
ABURST *adj* bursting
ABUSAGE *n* wrong use
ABUSE, -D, -S, ABUSING *vb, n*
ABUSER, -S ▸ **abuse**
ABUSES ▸ **abuse**
ABUSING ▸ **abuse**
ABUSION *n* wrong use or deception
ABUSIVE *adj*
ABUT, -S, -TED *vb* be next to or touching
ABUTTAL *same as* > **abutment**
ABUTTED ▸ **abut**
ABUTTER *n* owner of adjoining property
ABUZZ *adj*
ABVOLT, -S *n* unit of potential difference in the electromagnetic system
ABWATT, -S *n* unit of power
ABY, ABOUGHT, -ING, -S *vb* pay the penalty for

Remember this word can be expanded to **baby** and **gaby** and also to **abye** and **abys**.

ABYE, -ING, -S *same as* ▸ **aby**
ABYING ▸ **aby**
ABYS ▸ **aby**
ABYSM, -S *archaic word for* ▸ **abyss**
ABYSMAL *adj*
ABYSMS ▸ **abysm**
ABYSS, -ES *n*
ABYSSAL *adj* of the ocean depths
ABYSSES ▸ **abyss**
ACACIA, -S *n*
ACADEME *n* place of learning
ACADEMY *n*
ACAI, -S *n* berry
ACAJOU, -S *n* type of mahogany
ACALEPH *n* invertebrate
ACANTH, -S *n* acanthus
ACANTHA *n* thorn or prickle
ACANTHI > **acanthus**
ACANTHS ▸ **acanth**
ACAPNIA *n* lack of carbon dioxide
ACARI ▸ **acarus**
ACARIAN ▸ **acarus**
ACARID, -S *n* small arachnid ▹ *adj* of these arachnids
ACARINE *n* acarid
ACAROID *adj* resembling a mite
ACARUS, ACARI *n* type of mite
ACATER, -S *n* buyer of provisions
ACATES *n* provisions
ACATOUR *n* buyer of provisions
ACAUDAL *adj* having no tail
ACCA, -S *n* academic
ACCABLE *adj* dejected or beaten
ACCAS ▸ **acca**

ACCEDE, -D, -S *vb*
ACCEDER ▸ **accede**
ACCEDES ▸ **accede**
ACCEND, -S *vb* set alight
ACCENT, -S *n, vb*
ACCEPT, -S *vb*
ACCESS *n, vb*
ACCIDIA *same as* ▸ **accidie**
ACCIDIE *n* spiritual sloth
ACCINGE *vb* put a belt around
ACCITE, -D, -S *vb* summon
ACCLAIM *vb, n*
ACCLOY, -S *vb* choke or clog
ACCOAST *vb* accost
ACCOIED ▸ **accoy**
ACCOIL, -S *n* welcome ▹ *vb* gather together
ACCOMPT *vb* account
ACCORD, -S *n, vb*
ACCOST, -S *vb, n*
ACCOUNT *n, vb*
ACCOURT *vb* entertain
ACCOY, ACCOIED, -ED, -S *vb* soothe
ACCOYLD *vb* past tense of accoil
ACCOYS ▸ **accoy**
ACCRETE *vb* grow together
ACCREW, -S *vb* accrue
ACCRUAL *n* act of accruing
ACCRUE, -D, -S *vb* increase gradually
ACCURSE *vb* curse
ACCURST *same as* > **accursed**
ACCUSAL *n*
ACCUSE, -S *vb*
ACCUSED *n* person accused of a crime
ACCUSER ▸ **accuse**
ACCUSES ▸ **accuse**
ACE, -D, -S, ACING *n, adj, vb*
ACEDIA, -S *same as* ▸ **accidie**
ACEQUIA *n* irrigation ditch
ACER, -S *n* type of tree
ACERATE *same as* > **acerated**
ACERB, -ER *adj* bitter
ACERBIC *adj*
ACEROLA *n* cherry-like fruit
ACEROSE *adj* shaped like a needle
ACEROUS *same as* ▸ **acerose**
ACERS ▸ **acer**
ACES ▸ **ace**
ACETA ▸ **acetum**
ACETAL, -S *n* colourless liquid
ACETATE *n* salt or ester of acetic acid
ACETIC *adj* of or involving vinegar
ACETIFY *vb* become vinegar
ACETIN, -S *n* type of acetate
ACETONE *n* colourless liquid used as a solvent
ACETOSE *same as* ▸ **acetous**
ACETOUS *adj* containing acetic acid
ACETUM, ACETA *n* solution that has dilute acetic acid as solvent
ACETYL, -S *n* type of monovalent radical
ACH *interj* Scots expression of surprise
ACHAGE, -S *n* pain
ACHAR, -S *n* spicy pickle made from mango
ACHARNE *adj* furiously violent
ACHARS ▸ **achar**
ACHARYA *n* religious teacher and spiritual guide
ACHATES *same as* ▸ **acates**
ACHE, -D, -S *n, vb*
ACHENE, -S *n* type of fruit
ACHENIA > **achenium**
ACHES ▸ **ache**
ACHIER ▸ **achy**
ACHIEST ▸ **achy**
ACHIEVE *vb*
ACHING, -S ▸ **ache**
ACHIOTE *n* annatto
ACHIRAL *adj* of a tuber producing arrowroot
ACHKAN, -S *n* man's coat in India
ACHOLIA *n* bile condition
ACHOO, -S *n* sound of a sneeze
ACHY, ACHIER, ACHIEST *adj* affected by a continuous dull pain
ACICULA *n* needle-shaped part
ACID, -ER, -EST, -S *n, adj*
ACIDIC *adj*
ACIDIER ▸ **acidy**
ACIDIFY *vb* convert into acid
ACIDITY *n*
ACIDLY ▸ **acid**
ACIDS ▸ **acid**
ACIDY, ACIDIER *adj*
ACIFORM *adj* shaped like a needle
ACINAR *adj* of small sacs

ACING ▸ **ace**
ACINI ▸ **acinus**
ACINIC ▸ **acinus**
ACINOSE ▸ **acinus**
ACINOUS ▸ **acinus**
ACINUS, ACINI *n* part of a gland
ACKEE, -S *n* tropical tree
ACKER, -S *same as* ▸ **acca**
ACKNOW, ACKNEW, -N, -S *vb* recognize
ACLINIC *adj* unbending
ACMATIC *adj* highest or ultimate
ACME, -S *n* highest point of achievement or excellence
ACMIC *same as* ▸ **acmatic**
ACMITE, -S *n* chemical with pyramid-shaped crystals
ACNE, -S *n*
ACNED *adj* marked by acne
ACNES ▸ **acne**
ACNODAL ▸ **acnode**
ACNODE, -S *n* isolated point on the graph of a curve
ACOCK *adv* cocked
ACOLD *adj* feeling cold
ACOLYTE *n* follower or attendant
ACOLYTH *n* acolyte
ACONITE *n* poisonous plant with hoodlike flowers
ACORN, -S *n*
ACORNED *adj* covered with acorns
ACORNS ▸ **acorn**
ACOUCHI *n* South American rodent with a white-tipped tail
ACOUCHY *same as* ▸ **acouchi**
ACQUEST *n* something acquired
ACQUIRE *vb*
ACQUIS *n* as in **acquis communautaire** European Union laws
ACQUIST *n* acquisition
ACQUIT, -S *vb*
ACQUITE *vb* acquit
ACQUITS ▸ **acquit**
ACRASIA *n* lack of willpower
ACRASIN *n* chemical
ACRATIC ▸ **acrasia**
ACRAWL *adv* crawling
ACRE, -S *n*
ACREAGE *n, adj*
ACRED *adj* having acres of land
ACRES ▸ **acre**
ACRID, -ER *adj*
ACRIDIN *n* acridine
ACRIDLY ▸ **acrid**
ACRO, -S *n* event where acrobatic skiing moves are performed to music
ACROBAT *n*
ACROGEN *n* flowerless plant
ACROMIA > **acromion**
ACRONIC *adj* occurring at sunset
ACRONYM *n* word formed from the initial letters of other words, such as NASA
ACROS ▸ **acro**
ACROSS *adv*
ACROTER *n* plinth
ACROTIC *adj* of a surface
ACRYLIC *adj* (synthetic fibre, paint, etc) made from acrylic acid ▹ *n* synthetic fibre used for clothes and blankets
ACRYLYL *n* type of monovalent group
ACT, -ED, -S *n, vb*
ACTA *pl n* minutes of meeting
ACTABLE ▸ **act**
ACTANT, -S *n* noun phrase functioning as the agent of a verb
ACTED ▸ **act**
ACTIN, -S *n* protein
ACTINAL *adj* having tentacles
ACTING, -S *n, adj*
ACTINIA *n* type of sea anemone
ACTINIC *adj* (of radiation) producing a photochemical effect
ACTINON *same as* > **actinide**
ACTINS ▸ **actin**
ACTION, -S *n, vb*
ACTIVE, -S *adj, n*
ACTON, -S *n* jacket
ACTOR, -S *n*
ACTORLY *adj* characteristic of an actor
ACTORS ▸ **actor**
ACTRESS *n*
ACTS ▸ **act**
ACTUAL *adj*
ACTUALS *pl n* commercial commodities that can be bought and used
ACTUARY *n* statistician who calculates insurance risks
ACTUATE *vb* start up (a device)
ACTURE, -S *n* action

ACUATE, -D, -S *adj* sharply pointed ▷ *vb* sharpen
ACUITY *n* keenness of vision or thought
ACULEUS, ACULEI *n* prickle or spine, such as the thorn of a rose
ACUMEN, -S *n*
ACUSHLA *n* Irish endearment
ACUTE, -R, -S, -ST *adj*, *n*
ACUTELY ▶ **acute**
ACUTER ▶ **acute**
ACUTES ▶ **acute**
ACUTEST ▶ **acute**
ACYCLIC *adj* not cyclic
ACYL, -S *n* member of the monovalent group of atoms RCO-
ACYLATE *vb* add acyl group to
ACYLOIN *n* organic chemical compound
ACYLS ▶ **acyl**
AD, -S *n* advertisement
ADAGE, -S *n*
ADAGIAL ▶ **adage**
ADAGIO, -S *adv* (to be played) slowly and gracefully ▷ *n* movement or piece to be performed slowly
ADAMANT *adj*, *n*
ADAPT, -ED, -S *vb*
ADAPTER *same as* ▶ **adaptor**
ADAPTOR *n*
ADAPTS ▶ **adapt**
ADAW, -ED, -ING, -S *vb* subdue
ADAXIAL *adj* facing the axis
ADAYS *adv* daily
ADBOT, -S *n* spyware that collects information about a person to display targeted adverts
ADD, -ED, -S *vb*
ADDABLE ▶ **add**
ADDAX, -ES *n* antelope
ADDED ▶ **add**
ADDEDLY ▶ **add**
ADDEEM, -S *vb* adjudge
ADDEND, -S *n* any of a set of numbers that is to be added
ADDENDA > **addendum**
ADDENDS ▶ **addend**
ADDER, -S *n*
ADDIBLE *adj* addable
ADDICT, -S *n*, *vb*
ADDIES ▶ **addy**
ADDING, -S *n* act or instance of addition ▷ *adj* of, for, or relating to addition
ADDIO, -S *interj* farewell ▷ *n* cry of addio
ADDLE, -D, -S, ADDLING *vb* become muddled ▷ *adj* indicating a muddled state
ADDOOM, -S *vb* adjudge
ADDRESS, ADDREST *n*, *vb*
ADDS ▶ **add**
ADDUCE, -D, -S *vb* mention something as evidence or proof
ADDUCER ▶ **adduce**
ADDUCES ▶ **adduce**
ADDUCT, -S *vb* draw towards medial axis ▷ *n* compound
ADDY, ADDIES *n* email address
ADEEM, -ED, -S *vb* cancel
ADELGID *n* type of small sap-feeding insect
ADENINE *n* chemical
ADENOID *adj* of or resembling a gland
ADENOMA *n* tumour occurring in glandular tissue
ADENYL, -S *n* enzyme
ADEPT, -ER, -S *n*, *adj*
ADEPTLY ▶ **adept**
ADEPTS ▶ **adept**
ADERMIN *n* vitamin
ADHAN, -S *n* call to prayer
ADHARMA *n* wickedness
ADHERE, -D, -S *vb*
ADHERER ▶ **adhere**
ADHERES ▶ **adhere**
ADHIBIT *vb* administer or apply
ADIEU, -S, -X *n* goodbye

> Very useful when you want to say goodbye to a surplus of vowels. And remember its plural can be either **adieus** or **adieux**.

ADIOS, -ES *sentence substitute* Spanish for goodbye ▷ *n* goodbye
ADIPIC *adj* as in **adipic acid** crystalline solid used in the preparation of nylon
ADIPOSE *adj* of or containing fat ▷ *n* animal fat
ADIPOUS *adj* made of fat
ADIPSIA *n* complete lack of thirst

ADIT, -S *n* shaft into a mine, for access or drainage
ADJIGO, -S *n* SW Australian yam plant with edible tubers
ADJOIN, -S *vb*
ADJOINT *n* type of mathematical matrix
ADJOURN *vb*
ADJUDGE *vb*
ADJUNCT *n*
ADJURE, -D, -S *vb* command (to do)
ADJURER ▸ **adjure**
ADJURES ▸ **adjure**
ADJUROR ▸ **adjure**
ADJUST, -S *vb*
ADLAND, -S *n* advertising industry and the people who work in it
ADMAN, ADMEN *n* man who works in advertising
ADMASS *n* mass advertising
ADMEN ▸ **adman**
ADMIN, -S *n*
ADMIRAL *n*
ADMIRE, -D, -S *vb*
ADMIRER ▸ **admire**
ADMIRES ▸ **admire**
ADMIT, -S *vb*
ADMIX, -ED, -ES, -T *vb* mix or blend
ADNATE *adj* growing closely attached to an adjacent part or organ
ADNEXA *pl n* organs adjoining the uterus
ADNEXAL ▸ **adnexa**
ADNOUN, -S *n* adjective used as a noun
ADO, -S *n* fuss, trouble
ADOBE, -S *n* sun-dried brick
ADOBO, -S *n* Philippine dish
ADONIS *n* beautiful young man
ADONISE *vb* adorn
ADONIZE *vb* adorn
ADOORS *adv* at the door
ADOPT, -S *vb*
ADOPTED *adj* having been adopted
ADOPTEE *n*
ADOPTER *n*
ADOPTS ▸ **adopt**
ADORE, -D, -S *vb*
ADORER, -S ▸ **adore**
ADORES ▸ **adore**
ADORING *adj* displaying intense love
ADORN, -ED, -S *vb*
ADORNER ▸ **adorn**
ADORNS ▸ **adorn**
ADOS ▸ **ado**
ADOWN *adv* down
ADOZE *adv* asleep
ADPRESS *vb* press together
ADRAD *adj* afraid
ADRATE, -S *n* price or tariff that businesses pay to advertise
ADREAD, -S *vb* dread
ADRED *adj* filled with dread
ADRENAL *adj* near the kidneys ▹ *n* adrenal gland
ADRIFT *adv*
ADROIT *adj* quick and skilful
ADRY *adj* dry
ADS ▸ **ad**
ADSORB, -S *vb* condense to form a thin film
ADSPEAK *n* kind of language or jargon used in advertising or in advertisements
ADSUKI, -S *same as* ▸ **adzuki**
ADSUM *sentence substitute* I am present
ADUKI, -S *same as* ▸ **adzuki**
ADULATE *vb* flatter or praise obsequiously
ADULT, -S *adj, n*
ADULTLY ▸ **adult**
ADULTS ▸ **adult**
ADUNC *adj* hooked
ADUST, -ED, -S *vb* dry up or darken by heat
ADVANCE *vb, n, adj*
ADVECT, -S *vb* move horizontally in air
ADVENE, -D, -S *vb* add as extra
ADVENT, -S *n* arrival
ADVERB, -S *n*
ADVERSE *adj*
ADVERT, -S *n, vb*
ADVEW, -ED, -S *vb* look at
ADVICE, -S *n* recommendation as to what to do
ADVISE, -S *vb*
ADVISED *adj* considered, thought-out
ADVISEE *n* person receiving advice
ADVISER *n*
ADVISES ▸ **advise**
ADVISOR *same as* ▸ **adviser**
ADWARD, -S *vb* award
ADWARE, -S *n* computer software

ADWOMAN, ADWOMEN *n* woman working in advertising
ADYTUM, ADYTA *n* sacred place in ancient temples
ADZ *same as* ▸ **adze**

This is the American spelling of **adze**, and is one of the essential short words to know for using the Z.

ADZE, -D, -S, ADZING *n* woodworking tool ▹ *vb* use an adze
ADZUKI, -S *n* type of plant
AE *determiner* one
AECIA ▸ **aecium**
AECIAL ▸ **aecium**
AECIDIA > **aecidium**
AECIUM, AECIA *n* area of some fungi
AEDES *n* type of mosquito which transmits yellow fever and dengue
AEDILE, -S *n* magistrate of ancient Rome
AEDINE *adj* of a species of mosquito
AEFALD *adj* single
AEFAULD *adj* single
AEGIS, -ES *n* sponsorship, protection
AEMULE, -D, -S *vb* emulate
AENEOUS *adj* brass-coloured or greenish-gold
AENEUS *n* aquarium fish
AEOLIAN *adj* of or relating to the wind
AEON, -S *n* immeasurably long period of time

This little word gets played when you have too many vowels. And it has a partner **eoan**, meaning of the dawn: but beware, unlike **aeon**, it does not take a plural S.

AEONIAN *adj* everlasting
AEONIC ▸ **aeon**
AEONS ▸ **aeon**
AERADIO *n* radio system for pilots
AERATE, -D, -S *vb* put gas into (a liquid), as when making a fizzy drink
AERATOR ▸ **aerate**
AERIAL, -S *adj, n*
AERIE, -S *variant spelling (esp US) of* ▸ **eyrie**

This word for an eagle's nest is a great one for dealing with a surplus of vowels. And it has several variants: **aery, aiery, ayrie, eyrie** and **eyry**.

AERIED *adj* in a very high place
AERIER ▸ **aery**
AERIES ▸ **aerie**
AERIEST ▸ **aery**
AERIFY *vb* change or cause to change into a gas
AERILY ▸ **aery**
AERO, -S *n* aerodynamic vehicle or component
AEROBAT *n* person who does stunt flying
AEROBE, -S *n* organism that requires oxygen to survive
AEROBIA > **aerobium**
AEROBIC *adj* designed for or relating to aerobics
AEROBOT *n* unmanned aircraft used esp in space exploration
AEROBUS *n* monorail suspended by an overhead cable
AEROGEL *n* colloid
AEROS ▸ **aero**
AEROSAT *n* communications satellite
AEROSOL *n*
AERUGO, -S *(esp of old bronze) another name for* > **verdigris**
AERY, AERIER, AERIEST *adj* lofty, insubstantial, or visionary
AESC, -ES *n* rune
AESIR *pl n* Norse gods
AETATIS *adj* at the age of
AETHER, -S *same as* ▸ **ether**
AFALD *adj* single
AFAR, -S *adv, n*
AFARA, -S *n* African tree
AFARS ▸ **afar**
AFAWLD *adj* single
AFEAR, -S *vb* frighten
AFEARD *an archaic or dialect word for* ▸ **afraid**
AFEARED *same as* ▸ **afeard**
AFEARS ▸ **afear**
AFF *adv* off
AFFABLE *adj*

AFFABLY ▸ **affable**
AFFAIR *n*
AFFAIRE *n* love affair
AFFAIRS *pl n* personal or business interests
AFFEAR, -D, -S *vb* frighten
AFFEARE *vb* frighten
AFFEARS ▸ **affear**
AFFECT, -S *vb, n*
AFFEER, -S *vb* assess
AFFIANT *n* person who makes an affidavit
AFFICHE *n* poster
AFFIED ▸ **affy**
AFFIES ▸ **affy**
AFFINAL ▸ **affine**
AFFINE, -S *adj* involving transformations which preserve collinearity ▷ *n* relation by marriage
AFFINED *adj* closely related
AFFINES ▸ **affine**
AFFIRM, -S *vb*
AFFIX, -ED, -ES *vb, n*
AFFIXAL ▸ **affix**
AFFIXED ▸ **affix**
AFFIXER ▸ **affix**
AFFIXES ▸ **affix**
AFFLICT *vb*
AFFLUX *n* flowing towards a point
AFFOORD *vb* consent
AFFORCE *vb* strengthen
AFFORD, -S *vb*
AFFRAP, -S *vb* strike
AFFRAY, -S *n, vb*
AFFRET, -S *n* furious attack
AFFRONT *n, vb*
AFFY, AFFIED, AFFIES, -DE, -ING *vb* trust
AFGHAN, -S *n* type of blanket
AFGHANI *n* monetary unit of Afghanistan
AFGHANS ▸ **afghan**
AFIELD *adj* away from one's usual surroundings or home
AFIRE *adj* on fire
AFLAJ ▸ **falaj**
AFLAME *adj* burning
AFLOAT *adj, adv*
AFOCAL *adj* relating to a method for transferring an image without bringing it into focus
AFOOT *adj* happening, in operation ▷ *adv* happening
AFORE *adv* before
AFOUL *adj* in or into a state of difficulty, confusion, or conflict (with)
AFRAID *adj*
AFREET, -S *n* powerful evil demon or giant monster
AFRESH *adv* again, anew
AFRIT, -S *same as* ▸ **afreet**
AFRO, -S *n*
AFRONT *adv* in front
AFROS ▸ **afro**
AFT *adv* at or towards the rear of a ship or aircraft ▷ *adj* at or towards the rear of a ship or aircraft
AFTER *adv*
AFTERS *n* sweet course of a meal
AFTMOST *adj* furthest towards rear
AFTOSA, -S *n* foot-and-mouth disease
AG, -S *n* agriculture
AGA, -S *n* title of respect
AGACANT *adj* irritating
AGAIN *adv*
AGAINST *prep*
AGAMA, -S *n* small lizard
AGAMETE *n* reproductive cell
AGAMI, -S *n* South American bird
AGAMIC *adj* asexual
AGAMID, -S *same as* ▸ **agama**
AGAMIS ▸ **agami**
AGAMOID *n* lizard of the agamid type
AGAMONT *another name for* ▸ **schizont**
AGAMOUS *adj* without sex
AGAPE, AGAPAE, AGAPAI, -S *adj* (of the mouth) wide open ▷ *n* love feast among the early Christians
AGAPEIC ▸ **agape**
AGAPES ▸ **agape**
AGAR, -S *n* jelly-like substance obtained from seaweed and used as a thickener in food
AGARIC, -S *n* type of fungus
AGAROSE *n* gel used in chemistry
AGARS ▸ **agar**
AGAS ▸ **aga**
AGAST, -ED, -S *adj* aghast ▷ *vb* terrify or be terrified
AGATE, -S *n* semiprecious form of quartz with striped

colouring ▷ *adv* on the way
AGATISE *same as* ▶ **agatize**
AGATIZE *vb* turn into agate
AGATOID *adj* like agate
AGAVE, -S *n* tropical plant
AGAZE *adj* gazing at something
AGAZED *adj* amazed
AGE, -S *n, vb*
AGED *adj* old
AGEDLY ▶ **aged**
AGEE *adj* awry, crooked, or ajar ▷ *adv* awry
AGEING, -S *n* fact or process of growing old ▷ *adj* becoming or appearing older
AGEISM, -S *n* discrimination against people on the grounds of age
AGEIST, -S ▶ **ageism**
AGELAST *n* someone who never laughs
AGELESS *adj*
AGELONG *adj* lasting for a very long time
AGEMATE *n* person the same age as another person
AGEN *archaic form of* ▶ **again**
AGENCY *n*
AGENDA, -S *n*
AGENDER *adj* of a person who does not identify with a gender
AGENDUM *same as* ▶ **agenda**
AGENE, -S *n* chemical used to whiten flour
AGENISE *same as* ▶ **agenize**
AGENIZE *vb* whiten using agene
AGENT, -ED, -S *n, vb*
AGENTRY *n* activity of an agent
AGENTS ▶ **agent**
AGER, -S *n* something that ages
AGES ▶ **age**
AGEUSIA *n* lack of the sense of taste
AGGADA, -S, AGGADOT *n* explanation in Jewish literature
AGGADAH *same as* ▶ **aggada**
AGGADAS ▶ **aggada**
AGGADIC *adj* of aggada
AGGADOT ▶ **aggada**
AGGER *n* rampart
AGGERS *adj* aggressive
AGGIE, -S *n* American agricultural student
AGGRACE, AGRASTE *vb* add grace to
AGGRADE *vb* build up by the deposition of sediment
AGGRATE *vb* gratify
AGGRESS *vb* attack first or begin a quarrel
AGGRI *adj* of African beads
AGGRO, -S *n*
AGGRY *adj* of African beads
AGHA, -S *same as* ▶ **aga**
AGHAST *adj*
AGILA, -S *n* eaglewood
AGILE, -R, -ST *adj*
AGILELY ▶ **agile**
AGILER ▶ **agile**
AGILEST ▶ **agile**
AGILITY ▶ **agile**
AGIN *prep* against, opposed to
AGING, -S *same as* ▶ **ageing**
AGINNER *n* someone who is against something
AGIO, -S *n* difference between the nominal and actual values of a currency
AGISM, -S *same as* ▶ **ageism**
AGIST, -ED, -S *vb* care for and feed (cattle or horses) for payment
AGISTER *n* person who grazes cattle for money
AGISTOR *n* person who grazes cattle for money
AGISTS ▶ **agist**
AGITA, -S *n* acid indigestion
AGITANS *adj* as in **paralysis agitans** Parkinson's disease
AGITAS ▶ **agita**
AGITATE *vb*
AGITATO *adv* (to be performed) in an agitated manner
AGITPOP *n* use of pop music to promote political propaganda
AGLARE *adj* glaring
AGLEAM *adj* glowing
AGLEE *same as* ▶ **agley**
AGLET, -S *n* metal tag
AGLEY *adj* awry
AGLOO, -S *same as* ▶ **aglu**
AGLOW *adj*
AGLU, -S *n* breathing hole made in ice by a seal
AGLY *Scots word for* ▶ **wrong**

AGLYCON *n* chemical compound
AGMA, -S *n* symbol used to represent a velar nasal consonant
AGNAIL, -S *another name for* > **hangnail**
AGNAME, -S *n* name additional to first name and surname
AGNAMED *adj* having an agname
AGNAMES ▸ **agname**
AGNATE, -S *adj* related through a common male ancestor ▹ *n* descendant by male links from a common male ancestor
AGNATIC ▸ **agnate**
AGNISE, -D, -S *vb* acknowledge
AGNIZE, -D, -S *vb* acknowledge
AGNOMEN *n* name used by ancient Romans
AGNOSIA *n* loss of power to recognize familiar objects
AGNOSIC ▸ **agnosia**
AGO *adv*
AGOG *adj*
AGOGE, -S *n* ancient Greek melodic form
AGOGIC, -S *n* musical accent
AGOING *adj* moving
AGON, -ES, -S *n* ancient Greek festival
AGONAL *adj* of agony
AGONE *an archaic word for* ▸ **ago**
AGONES ▸ **agon**
AGONIC *adj* forming no angle
AGONIES ▸ **agony**
AGONISE *same as* ▸ **agonize**
AGONISM *n* struggle between opposing forces
AGONIST *n* any muscle that is opposed in action by another muscle
AGONIZE *vb*
AGONS ▸ **agon**
AGONY, AGONIES *n*
AGOOD *adv* seriously or earnestly
AGORA, -E, -S *n* place of assembly in ancient Greece
AGOROT *pl n* Israeli coins
AGOROTH *same as* ▸ **agorot**
AGOUTA, -S *n* Haitian rodent
AGOUTI, -S *n* rodent
AGOUTY *same as* ▸ **agouti**
AGRAFE, -S *same as* ▸ **agraffe**
AGRAFFE *n* loop and hook fastening
AGRAPHA > **agraphon**
AGRASTE ▸ **aggrace**
AGRAVIC *adj* of zero gravity
AGREE, -S *vb*
AGREED *adj*
AGREES ▸ **agree**
AGREGE, -S *n* winner in examination for university teaching post
AGRIA, -S *n* appearance of pustules
AGRIN, -S *adv* grinning ▹ *n* type of protein
AGRISE, -D, -S *vb* fill with fear
AGRIZE, -D, -S *vb* fill with fear
AGRO, -S *n* student of agriculture
AGROUND *adv, adj*
AGRYZE, -D, -S *vb* fill with fear
AGS ▸ **ag**
AGUE, -S *n* periodic fever with shivering
AGUED *adj* suffering from fever
AGUES ▸ **ague**
AGUISE, -D, -S *vb* dress
AGUISH ▸ **ague**
AGUIZE, -D, -S *vb* dress
AGUNA, AGUNOT, AGUNOTH *n* (in Jewish law) woman whose husband will not grant her a divorce
AGUNAH *same as* ▸ **aguna**
AGUNOT ▸ **aguna**
AGUNOTH ▸ **aguna**
AGUTI, -S *n* agouti
AGYRIA, -S *n* brain disease
AH, -ED, -ING, -S *interj* exclamation expressing surprise, joy etc ▹ *vb* say ah
AHA *interj* exclamation of triumph or surprise
AHCHOO *interj* sound made by someone sneezing
AHEAD *adv*
AHEAP *adv* in a heap
AHED ▸ **ah**
AHEIGHT *adv* at height
AHEM *interj* clearing of the throat in order to attract attention

AHENT *adv* behind
AHI, -S *n* yellowfin tuna

A very useful one to catch!

AHIGH *adv* at height
AHIMSA, -S *n* the law of reverence for every form of life
AHIND *adv* behind
AHING ▸ **ah**
AHINT *adv* behind
AHIS ▸ **ahi**
AHOLD *adv* holding
AHORSE *adv* on horseback
AHOY *interj*
AHS ▸ **ah**
AHULL *adv* with sails furled
AHUNGRY *adj* very hungry
AHURU, -S *n* type of small pink cod of SW Pacific waters
AI, -S *n* shaggy-coated slow-moving animal of South America
AIA, -S *n* female servant in E Asia
AIBLINS *Scots word for* ▸ **perhaps**
AID, -ED, -ING, -S *n, vb*
AIDA, -S *n* cotton fabric with a natural mesh
AIDANCE *n* help
AIDANT, -S *adj* helping ▹ *n* helper
AIDAS ▸ **aida**
AIDE, -S *n*
AIDED ▸ **aid**
AIDER, -S ▸ **aid**
AIDES ▸ **aide**
AIDFUL *adj* helpful
AIDING ▸ **aid**
AIDLESS *adj* without help
AIDMAN, AIDMEN *n* military medical assistant
AIDOI *adj* of the genitals
AIDOS *Greek word for* ▸ **shame**
AIDS ▸ **aid**
AIERY, AIERIES *n* eyrie
AIGA, -S *n* Māori word for family
AIGHT *adv* all right
AIGLET, -S *same as* ▸ **aglet**
AIGRET, -S *same as* > **aigrette**
AIKIDO, -S *n* Japanese self-defence
AIKONA *interj* South African expression meaning no
AIL, -ED, -S *vb*
AILANTO *n* Asian tree
AILED ▸ **ail**
AILERON *n* movable flap on an aircraft wing which controls rolling
AILETTE *n* shoulder armour
AILING *adj* sickly
AILMENT *n*
AILS ▸ **ail**
AIM, -ED, -ING, -S *vb, n*
AIMER, -S ▸ **aim**
AIMFUL *adj* with purpose or intention
AIMING ▸ **aim**
AIMLESS *adj*
AIMS ▸ **aim**
AIN, -S *variant of* ▸ **ayin**
AINE *adj* French word for elder (male)

Though it doesn't score much, it is useful to remember when you have too many vowels. And it can be extended to **ainee**, the feminine form.

AINEE *adj* French word for elder (female)
AINGA, -S *n* Māori word for village
AINS ▸ **ain**
AINSELL *n* Scots word meaning own self
AIOLI, -S *n* garlic mayonnaise
AIR, -ED *n, vb*
AIRBAG, -S *n*
AIRBALL *n* missed shot in basketball ▹ *vb* throw an airball
AIRBASE *n*
AIRBOAT *n* boat for use in swamps
AIRBUS *n* commercial passenger aircraft
AIRCON, -S *n* air conditioner
AIRCREW *n*
AIRDATE *n* date of a programme broadcast
AIRDROP *n* delivery of supplies by parachute ▹ *vb* deliver (supplies, etc) by an airdrop
AIRED ▸ **air**
AIRER, -S *n* device on which clothes are hung to dry
AIRFARE *n*
AIRFLOW *n*
AIRFOIL *same as* > **aerofoil**

AIRGAP, -S *n* gap between parts in an electrical machine
AIRGLOW *n* faint light in the night sky
AIRGUN, -S *n*
AIRHEAD *n* stupid person
AIRHOLE *n* hole that allows the passage of air
AIRIER ▶ **airy**
AIRIEST ▶ **airy**
AIRILY *adv* in a light-hearted and casual manner
AIRING, -S *n* exposure to air for drying or ventilation
AIRLESS *adj*
AIRLIFT *n, vb*
AIRLIKE ▶ **air**
AIRLINE *n*
AIRLOCK *n*
AIRMAIL *n, adj, vb*
AIRMAN, AIRMEN *n*
AIRN, -ED, -ING, -S *Scots word for* ▶ **iron**
AIRPARK *n* car park at airport
AIRPLAY *n*
AIRPORT *n*
AIRPOST *n* system of delivering mail by air
AIRPROX *n* near collision involving aircraft
AIRS *pl n* manners put on to impress people
AIRSHED *n* air over a particular geographical area
AIRSHIP *n*
AIRSHOT *n* shot that misses the ball completely
AIRSHOW *n*
AIRSICK *adj*
AIRSIDE *n* part of an airport nearest the aircraft
AIRSOME *adj* cold
AIRSTOP *n* helicopter landing-place
AIRT, -ED, -ING, -S *n* point of the compass ▷ *vb* direct
AIRTH, -ED, -S *same as* ▶ **airt**
AIRTIME *n*
AIRTING ▶ **airt**
AIRTRAM *n* cable car
AIRTS ▶ **airt**
AIRVAC, -S *n* evacuation by air ambulance
AIRWARD *adj* into air
AIRWAVE *n*
AIRWAY, -S *n*
AIRWISE *adv* towards the air
AIRY, AIRIER, AIRIEST *adj* well-ventilated
AIS ▶ **ai**
AISLE, -S *n*
AISLED ▶ **aisle**
AISLES ▶ **aisle**
AISLING *Irish word for* ▶ **dream**
AIT, -S *n* islet, esp in a river
AITCH, -ES *n* letter *h* or the sound represented by it
AITS ▶ **ait**
AITU, -S *n* half-human half-divine being

This demigod is often played to dispose of an excess of vowels.

AIVER, -S *n* working horse
AIYEE *interj* expressing alarm
AIZLE, -S *n* Scots word for hot ashes
AJAR *adv, adj*
AJEE *same as* ▶ **agee**

This Scots word meaning ajar is often useful for disposing of the J. It has an alternative spelling **agee**.

AJI, -ES, -S *n* type of spicy pepper
AJIVA, -S *n* Jainist term for a non-living thing
AJOWAN, -S *n* plant related to caraway
AJUGA, -S *n* garden plant
AJUTAGE *n* nozzle
AJWAN, -S *n* plant related to caraway
AKA, -S *n* type of New Zealand vine

One of the key short words when it comes to using the K.

AKATEA, -S *n* New Zealand vine with white flowers
AKE, -D, -S, AKING *vb* old spelling of ache
AKEAKE, -S *n* New Zealand tree
AKEBIA, -S *n* E Asian climbing plant
AKED ▶ **ake**
AKEDAH, -S *n* binding of Isaac in Bible
AKEE, -S *same as* ▶ **ackee**
AKELA, -S *n* adult leader of a pack of Cub Scouts

AKENE, -S *same as* ▸ **achene**
AKENIAL ▸ **akene**
AKES ▸ **ake**
AKHARA, -S *n* (in India) gymnasium
AKIMBO *adj*
AKIN *adj*
AKING ▸ **ake**
AKIRAHO *n* small New Zealand shrub with white flowers
AKITA, -S *n* large dog
AKKAS *slang word for* ▸ **money**
AKRASIA *n* weakness of will
AKRATIC ▸ **akrasia**
AKVAVIT *same as* ▸ **aquavit**
AL, -S *same as* ▸ **aal**
ALA, -E *n* winglike structure
ALAAP, -S *n* part of raga in Indian music
ALACK *archaic or poetic word for* ▸ **alas**
ALAE ▸ **ala**
ALALIA, -S *n* complete inability to speak
ALAMEDA *n* public walk lined with trees
ALAMO, -S *n* poplar tree
ALAMODE *n* soft light silk used for shawls and dresses, esp in the 19th century
ALAMORT *adj* exhausted and downcast
ALAMOS ▸ **alamo**
ALAN, -S *n* member of ancient European nomadic people
ALAND, -S *vb* come onto land
ALANE *Scots word for* ▸ **alone**
ALANG, -S *n* type of grass in Malaysia
ALANIN, -S *n* alanine
ALANINE *n* chemical
ALANINS ▸ **alanin**
ALANNAH *interj* term of endearment ▹ *n* cry of alannah
ALANS ▸ **alan**
ALANT, -S *n* flowering plant used in herbal medicine
ALANYL, -S *n* chemical found in proteins
ALAP, -S *n* Indian vocal music without words
ALAPA, -S *n* part of raga in Indian music
ALAPS ▸ **alap**
ALAR *adj* relating to, resembling, or having wings or alae
ALARM, -ED, -S *n, vb*
ALARUM, -S *n* alarm, esp a call to arms ▹ *vb* raise the alarm
ALARY *adj* of, relating to, or shaped like wings
ALAS *adv*
ALASKA, -S *n* dessert made of cake and ice cream
ALASTOR *n* avenging demon
ALATE, -S *adj* having wings or winglike extensions ▹ *n* winged insect
ALATED *adj* having wings
ALATES ▸ **alate**
ALATION *n* state of having wings
ALAY, -ED, -ING, -S *vb* allay
ALB, -S *n* long white robe worn by a Christian priest
ALBA, -S *n* song of lament
ALBATA, -S *n* variety of German silver consisting of nickel, copper, and zinc
ALBE *old word for* ▸ **albeit**
ALBEDO, -S *n* measure of intensity of reflected light
ALBEE *archaic form of* ▸ **albeit**
ALBEIT *conj*
ALBERGO *n* Italian word for inn
ALBERT, -S *n* watch chain
ALBINAL ▸ **albino**
ALBINIC ▸ **albino**
ALBINO, -S *n*
ALBITE, -S *n* type of mineral
ALBITIC ▸ **albite**
ALBIZIA *n* mimosa
ALBS ▸ **alb**
ALBUGO, -S *n* opacity of the cornea
ALBUM, -S *n*
ALBUMEN *same as* ▸ **albumin**
ALBUMIN *n* protein found in blood plasma, egg white, milk, and muscle
ALBUMS ▸ **album**
ALCADE, -S *same as* ▸ **alcalde**

ALCAIC, -S *n* verse consisting of strophes with four tetrametric lines
ALCAIDE *n* commander of a fortress or castle
ALCALDE *n* (in Spain and Spanish America) the mayor or chief magistrate in a town
ALCAYDE *n* alcaide
ALCAZAR *n* Moorish palace or fortress
ALCHEMY *n*
ALCHERA *n* mythical Golden Age
ALCHYMY *old spelling of* ▸ **alchemy**
ALCID, -S *n* bird of the auk family
ALCO, -S *same as* ▸ **alko**
ALCOHOL *n*
ALCOOL, -S *n* form of pure grain spirit distilled in Quebec
ALCOPOP *n*
ALCORZA *n* Spanish sweet
ALCOS ▸ **alco**
ALCOVE, -S *n*
ALCOVED *adj* with or in an alcove
ALCOVES ▸ **alcove**
ALDEA, -S *n* Spanish village
ALDER, -S *n* tree related to the birch
ALDERN *adj* made of alder wood
ALDERS ▸ **alder**
ALDOL, -S *n* colourless or yellowish oily liquid
ALDOSE, -S *n* type of sugar
ALDRIN, -S *n* brown to white poisonous crystalline solid
ALE, -S *n*
ALEC, -S *same as* ▸ **aleck**
ALECK, -S *n* irritatingly oversmart person
ALECOST *another name for* ▸ **costmary**
ALECS ▸ **alec**
ALEE *adj* on or towards the lee
ALEF, -S *n* first letter of Hebrew alphabet
ALEFT *adv* at or to left
ALEGAR, -S *n* malt vinegar
ALEGGE, -D, -S *vb* alleviate
ALEMBIC *n* anything that distils
ALENCON *n* elaborate lace worked on a hexagonal mesh
ALENGTH *adv* at length
ALEPH, -S *n* first letter in the Hebrew alphabet
ALEPINE *n* type of cloth
ALERCE, -S *n* wood of the sandarac tree
ALERION *n* eagle in heraldry
ALERT, -ED, -ER, -S *adj, n, vb*
ALERTLY ▸ **alert**
ALERTS ▸ **alert**
ALES ▸ **ale**
ALETHIC *adj* of philosophical concepts
ALEURON *n* outer layer of seeds
ALEVIN, -S *n* young fish, esp a young salmon or trout
ALEW, -S *n* cry to call hunting hounds
ALEWIFE *n* North American fish
ALEWS ▸ **alew**
ALEXIA, -S *n* disorder causing impaired ability to read
ALEXIC ▸ **alexia**
ALEXIN, -S *n* protein in blood serum
ALEXINE *same as* ▸ **alexin**
ALEXINS ▸ **alexin**
ALEYE, -D, -S, ALEYING *vb* allay
ALF, -S *n* uncultivated Australian
ALFA, -S *n* type of grass
ALFAKI, -S *same as* ▸ **alfaqui**
ALFALFA *n* kind of plant used to feed livestock
ALFAQUI *n* expert in Muslim law
ALFAS ▸ **alfa**
ALFEREZ *n* Spanish standard-bearer
ALFORJA *n* saddlebag made of leather or canvas
ALFREDO *adj* cooked with a cheese and egg sauce
ALFS ▸ **alf**
ALGA, -E, -S *n* multicellular organism
ALGAL ▸ **alga**
ALGAS ▸ **alga**
ALGATE *adv* anyway
ALGATES *adv* anyway
ALGEBRA *n*
ALGESES ▸ **algesis**
ALGESIA *n* capacity to feel pain
ALGESIC ▸ **algesia**
ALGESIS, ALGESES *n* feeling of pain

ALGETIC ▸ **algesia**
ALGID *adj* chilly or cold
ALGIN, -S *n* seaweed solution
ALGINIC *adj* as in **alginic acid** powdery substance extracted from kelp
ALGINS ▸ **algin**
ALGOID *adj* resembling or relating to algae
ALGOR, -S *n* chill
ALGUM, -S *n* type of wood mentioned in Bible
ALIAS, -ED, -ES *adv, n, vb*
ALIBI, -ED, -ES, -S *n, vb*
ALIBLE *adj* nourishing
ALICANT *n* wine from Alicante in Spain
ALIDAD, -S *same as* ▸ **alidade**
ALIDADE *n* surveying instrument
ALIDADS ▸ **alidad**
ALIEN, -ED, -S *adj, n, vb*
ALIENEE *n* person to whom a transfer of property is made
ALIENER ▸ **alien**
ALIENLY ▸ **alien**
ALIENOR *n* person who transfers property to another
ALIENS ▸ **alien**
ALIF, -S *n* first letter of Arabic alphabet
ALIFORM *adj* wing-shaped
ALIFS ▸ **alif**
ALIGHT, -S *vb, adj, adv*
ALIGN, -ED, -S *vb*
ALIGNER ▸ **align**
ALIGNS ▸ **align**
ALIKE *adj, adv*
ALIMENT *n* something that nourishes the body ▹ *vb* support or sustain
ALIMONY *n*
ALINE, -D, -S, ALINING *a rare spelling of* ▸ **align**
ALINER, -S ▸ **aline**
ALINES ▸ **aline**
ALINING ▸ **aline**
ALIPED, -S *n* bat-like creature ▹ *adj* having digits connected by a membrane
ALIQUOT *adj* of or denoting an exact divisor of a number ▹ *n* exact divisor
ALISMA, -S *n* marsh plant
ALISON, -S *same as* ▸ **alyssum**
ALIST *adj* leaning over
ALIT *rare past tense and past participle of* ▸ **alight**
ALIUNDE *adj* from a source under consideration
ALIVE *adj*
ALIYA, -S *same as* ▸ **aliyah**
ALIYAH, -S, ALIYOT, ALIYOTH *n* immigration to the Holy Land
ALIYAS ▸ **aliya**
ALIYOS *n* remission of sin in Jewish faith
ALIYOT ▸ **aliyah**
ALIYOTH ▸ **aliyah**
ALIZARI *n* madder plant from the Middle East
ALKALI, -S *n*
ALKALIC *adj* (of rocks) containing large amounts of alkalis
ALKALIN *adj* alkaline
ALKALIS ▸ **alkali**
ALKANE, -S *n* saturated hydrocarbon
ALKANET *n* European plant whose roots yield a red dye
ALKENE, -S *n* unsaturated hydrocarbon
ALKIE *same as* ▸ **alky**
ALKIES ▸ **alky**
ALKINE, -S *n* alkyne
ALKO, -S *n* slang word for alcoholic
ALKOXY *adj* of a type of chemical compound containing oxygen
ALKY, ALKIES *n* slang word for alcoholic
ALKYD, -S *n* synthetic resin
ALKYL, -S *n* type of monovalent radical
ALKYLIC ▸ **alkyl**
ALKYLS ▸ **alkyl**
ALKYNE, -S *n* any unsaturated aliphatic hydrocarbon
ALL, -S *adj, adv, n*
ALLAY, -ED, -S *vb*
ALLAYER ▸ **allay**
ALLAYS ▸ **allay**
ALLEDGE *vb* allege
ALLEE, -S *n* avenue
ALLEGE, -S *vb*
ALLEGED *adj* stated but not proved
ALLEGER ▸ **allege**
ALLEGES ▸ **allege**
ALLEGGE *vb* alleviate
ALLEGRO *adv* (to be played) in a brisk lively

manner ▷ *n* piece or passage to be performed in a brisk lively manner
ALLEL, -S *n* variant form of a gene
ALLELE, -S *n* variant form of a gene
ALLELIC ▶ allele
ALLELS ▶ allel
ALLERGY *n*
ALLEY, -S *n*
ALLEYED *adj* having alleys
ALLEYS ▶ alley
ALLHEAL *n* plant with reputed healing powers
ALLIAK, -S *n* Inuit sledge
ALLICE, -S *n* species of fish
ALLICIN *n* chemical found in garlic
ALLIED *adj*
ALLIES ▶ ally
ALLIS, -ES *n* species of fish
ALLIUM, -S *n* type of plant
ALLNESS *n* being all
ALLOBAR *n* form of an element
ALLOD, -S *same as* **> allodium**
ALLODIA > allodium
ALLODS ▶ allod
ALLONGE *n* paper extension to bill of exchange ▷ *vb* (in fencing) lunge
ALLONS *interj* French word meaning let's go
ALLONYM *n* name assumed by a person
ALLOT, -S *vb*
ALLOVER *n* fabric completely covered with a pattern
ALLOW, -ED, -S *vb*
ALLOXAN *n* chemical found in uric acid
ALLOY, -ED, -S *n, vb*
ALLS ▶ all
ALLSEED *n* type of plant
ALLUDE, -D, -S *vb*
ALLURE, -D, -S *n, vb*
ALLURER ▶ allure
ALLURES ▶ allure
ALLUVIA > alluvium
ALLY, ALLIES, -ING *vb, n*
ALLYL, -S *n* type of monovalent hydrocarbon
ALLYLIC ▶ allyl
ALLYLS ▶ allyl
ALLYOU *pron* all of you
ALMA, -S *same as* **▶ almah**
ALMAH, -S *n* (in Egypt) female entertainer
ALMAIN, -S *n* German dance
ALMANAC *n*
ALMAS ▶ alma
ALME, -S *same as* **▶ almeh**
ALMEH, -S *n* (in Egypt) female entertainer
ALMEMAR *n* area in a synagogue
ALMERY *n* cupboard for church vessels
ALMES ▶ alme
ALMIRAH *n* cupboard
ALMNER, -S *n* almoner
ALMOND, -S *n*
ALMONDY *adj* containing or resembling almond
ALMONER *n* formerly, a hospital social worker
ALMONRY *n* house of an almoner, usually the place where alms were given
ALMOST *adv*
ALMOUS *Scots word for* **▶ alms**
ALMS *pl n*
ALMSMAN, ALMSMEN *n* man who gives or receives alms
ALMUCE, -S *n* fur-lined hood or cape
ALMUD, -S *n* Spanish unit of measure
ALMUDE, -S *same as* **▶ almud**
ALMUDS ▶ almud
ALMUG, -S *n* type of wood mentioned in Bible
ALNAGE, -S *n* measurement in ells
ALNAGER *n* inspector of cloth
ALNAGES ▶ alnage
ALNICO, -S *n* alloy containing iron, nickel, and cobalt
ALOD, -S *n* feudal estate with no superior
ALODIA ▶ alodium
ALODIAL ▶ alodium
ALODIUM, ALODIA *same as* **> allodium**
ALODS ▶ alod
ALOE *n*
ALOED *adj* containing aloes
ALOES *another name for* **> eaglewood**
ALOETIC ▶ aloe
ALOFT *adv, adj*
ALOGIA, -S *n* inability to speak

ALOHA, -S *a Hawaiian word for* ▸ **hello**
ALOIN, -S *n* crystalline compound
ALONE *adv*
ALONELY ▸ **alone**
ALONG *adv*
ALONGST *adv*
ALOO, -S *n* (in Indian cookery) potato
ALOOF *adj*
ALOOFLY ▸ **aloof**
ALOOS ▸ **aloo**
ALOUD *adv, adj*
ALOW *adj* in or into the lower rigging of a vessel, near the deck
ALOWE *Scots word for* ▸ **ablaze**
ALP, -S *n*
ALPACA, -S *n*
ALPACCA *same as* ▸ **alpaca**
ALPEEN, -S *n* Irish cudgel
ALPHA, -S *n* first letter in the Greek alphabet
ALPHORN *n* wind instrument
ALPHYL, -S *n* univalent radical
ALPINE, -S *adj* of high mountains ▹ *n* mountain plant
ALPS ▸ **alp**
ALREADY *adv*
ALRIGHT *adj*
ALS ▸ **al**
ALSIKE, -S *n* clover native to Europe and Asia
ALSO *adv*
ALSOON *same as* ▸ **alsoone**
ALSOONE *adv* as soon
ALT, -S *n* octave directly above the treble staff
ALTAR, -S *n*
ALTER, -ED, -S *vb*
ALTERER ▸ **alter**
ALTERN *adj* alternate
ALTERNE *n* neighbouring but different plant group
ALTERS ▸ **alter**
ALTESSE *n* French word for highness
ALTEZA, -S *n* Spanish word for highness
ALTEZZA *n* Italian word for highness
ALTHAEA *n* type of plant
ALTHEA, -S *same as* ▸ **althaea**
ALTHO *conj* short form of although
ALTHORN *n* valved brass musical instrument
ALTO, -S *n* (singer with) the highest adult male voice ▹ *adj* denoting an instrument, singer, or voice with this range
ALTOIST *n* person who plays the alto saxophone
ALTOS ▸ **alto**
ALTS ▸ **alt**
ALU, -S *same as* ▸ **aloo**
ALUDEL, -S *n* pear-shaped vessel
ALULA, -E, -S *n* tuft of feathers
ALULAR ▸ **alula**
ALULAS ▸ **alula**
ALUM, -S *n* double sulphate of aluminium and potassium
ALUMIN, -S *same as* ▸ **alumina**
ALUMINA *n* aluminium oxide
ALUMINE *n* French word for alumina
ALUMINS ▸ **alumin**
ALUMISH *adj* like alum
ALUMIUM *old name for* > **aluminium**
ALUMNA, -E *n* female graduate of a school, college, etc
ALUMNUS, ALUMNI *n* graduate of a college
ALUMS ▸ **alum**
ALUNITE *n* white, grey, or reddish mineral
ALURE, -S *n* area behind battlements
ALUS ▸ **alu**
ALVAR, -S *n* area of exposed limestone
ALVEARY *n* beehive
ALVEOLE *n* alveolus
ALVEOLI > **alveolus**
ALVINE *adj* of or relating to the intestines or belly
ALWAY *same as* ▸ **always**
ALWAYS *adv*
ALYSSUM *n* garden plant with small yellow or white flowers
AM *vb* form of the present tense of *be*
AMA, -S *n* vessel for water
AMABILE *adj* sweet
AMADODA *pl n* South African word meaning grown men
AMADOU, -S *n* spongy substance made from fungi

AMAH, -S *n* (in East Asia, formerly) a nurse or maidservant
AMAIN *adv* with great strength, speed, or haste
AMAKOSI ▸ **inkhosi**
AMALGAM *n*
AMANDLA *n* political slogan calling for power to the Black population
AMANITA *n* type of fungus
AMARANT *n* amaranth
AMARNA *adj* pertaining to the reign of the Pharaoh Akhenaton
AMARONE *n* strong dry red Italian wine
AMAS ▸ **ama**
AMASS, -ED, -ES *vb*
AMASSER ▸ **amass**
AMASSES ▸ **amass**
AMATE, -D, -S, AMATING *vb* match
AMATEUR *n, adj*
AMATING ▸ **amate**
AMATIVE *a rare word for* ▸ **amorous**
AMATOL, -S *n* explosive mixture
AMATORY *adj* relating to love
AMAUT, -S *n* hooded coat worn by Inuit women
AMAUTI, -S *same as* ▸ **amaut**
AMAUTIK *same as* ▸ **amaut**
AMAUTIS ▸ **amauti**
AMAUTS ▸ **amaut**
AMAZE, -D, -S *vb*
AMAZING *adj* causing wonder or astonishment
AMAZON, -S *n* any tall, strong, or aggressive woman
AMBACH *same as* ▸ **ambatch**
AMBAGE, -S *n* ambiguity
AMBAN, -S *n* Chinese official
AMBARI, -S *same as* ▸ **ambary**
AMBARY *n* tropical Asian plant that yields a fibre similar to jute
AMBASSY *n* embassy
AMBATCH *n* tree or shrub
AMBEER, -S *n* saliva coloured by tobacco juice
AMBER, -S *n, adj*
AMBERED *adj* fixed in amber
AMBERS ▸ **amber**
AMBERY *adj* like amber ▹ *n* cupboard in the wall of a church
AMBIENT *adj, n*
AMBIT, -S *n* limits or boundary
AMBITTY *adj* crystalline and brittle
AMBLE, -D, -S *vb, n*
AMBLER, -S ▸ **amble**
AMBLES ▸ **amble**
AMBLING *n* walking at a leisurely pace
AMBO, -NES, -S *n* early Christian pulpit
AMBOINA *same as* ▸ **amboyna**
AMBONES ▸ **ambo**
AMBOS ▸ **ambo**
AMBOYNA *n* mottled curly-grained wood
AMBRIES ▸ **ambry**
AMBROID *same as* ▸ **amberoid**
AMBRY, AMBRIES *n* cupboard in the wall of a church
AMBSACE *n* double ace, the lowest throw at dice
AMBUSH *n, vb*
AME, -S *n* soul
AMEARST *old form of* ▸ **amerce**
AMEBA, -E, -S *same as* ▸ **amoeba**
AMEBAN ▸ **ameba**
AMEBAS ▸ **ameba**
AMEBEAN *same as* ▸ **amoebean**
AMEBIC ▸ **ameba**
AMEBOID *same as* ▸ **amoeboid**
AMEER, -S *n* (formerly) the ruler of Afghanistan
AMELIA, -S *n* congenital absence of arms or legs
AMEN, -ED, -ING, -S *n, vb*
AMENAGE *vb* tame
AMEND, -ED *vb*
AMENDE, -S *n* public apology
AMENDED ▸ **amend**
AMENDER ▸ **amend**
AMENDES ▸ **amende**
AMENDS *n* recompense for injury, insult, etc
AMENE *adj* pleasant
AMENED ▸ **amen**
AMENING ▸ **amen**
AMENITY *n*
AMENS ▸ **amen**
AMENT, -S *n* catkin
AMENTA ▸ **amentum**

AMENTAL ▸ **amentum**
AMENTIA *n* old word for congenital learning disability
AMENTS ▸ **ament**
AMENTUM, AMENTA *same as* ▸ **ament**
AMERCE, -D, -S *vb* punish by a fine
AMERCER ▸ **amerce**
AMERCES ▸ **amerce**
AMES ▸ **ame**
AMESACE *same as* ▸ **ambsace**
AMI *n* male friend
AMIA, -S *n* species of fish
AMIABLE *adj*
AMIABLY ▸ **amiable**
AMIAS ▸ **amia**
AMICE, -S *n* item of clothing
AMICUS, AMICI *n* Latin for friend
AMID *prep*
AMIDASE *n* enzyme
AMIDE, -S *n* type of organic compound
AMIDIC ▸ **amide**
AMIDIN, -S *n* form of starch
AMIDINE *n* crystalline compound
AMIDINS ▸ **amidin**
AMIDO *adj* containing amide
AMIDOL, -S *n* chemical used in developing photographs
AMIDONE *n* pain-killing drug
AMIDS *same as* ▸ **amid**
AMIDST *same as* ▸ **amid**
AMIE, -S *n* female friend
AMIGA, -S *n* female friend
AMIGO, -S *n* friend
AMILDAR *n* manager in India
AMIN, -S *same as* ▸ **amine**
AMINE, -S *n* chemical
AMINIC ▸ **amine**
AMINITY *n* amenity
AMINO, -S *n* type of organic compound present in amino acids
AMINS ▸ **amin**
AMIR, -S *n* (formerly) the ruler of Afghanistan
AMIRATE ▸ **amir**
AMIRS ▸ **amir**
AMIS, -ES *archaic form of* ▸ **amice**
AMISS, -ES *adv, adj, n*
AMITY, AMITIES *n* friendship
AMLA, -S *n* species of Indian tree
AMMAN, -S *same as* ▸ **amtman**
AMMETER *n* instrument for measuring electric current
AMMINE, -S *n* chemical compound
AMMINO *adj* containing ammonia molecules
AMMIRAL *old word for* ▸ **admiral**
AMMO, -S *n*
AMMON, -S *n* Asian wild sheep
AMMONAL *n* explosive
AMMONIA *n* strong-smelling alkaline gas containing hydrogen and nitrogen
AMMONIC *adj* of ammonia
AMMONO *adj* using ammonia
AMMONS ▸ **ammon**
AMMOS ▸ **ammo**
AMNESIA *n*
AMNESIC ▸ **amnesia**
AMNESTY *n, vb*
AMNIA ▸ **amnion**
AMNIC *adj* relating to amnion
AMNIO, -S *n* amniocentesis
AMNION, AMNIA, -S *n* innermost of two membranes enclosing an embryo
AMNIOS ▸ **amnio**
AMNIOTE *n* group of animals
AMOEBA, -E, -S *n* microscopic single-celled animal able to change its shape
AMOEBAN ▸ **amoeba**
AMOEBAS ▸ **amoeba**
AMOEBIC ▸ **amoeba**
AMOK, -S *n*
AMOKURA *n* type of sea bird
AMOLE, -S *n* American plant
AMOMUM, -S *n* plant of the ginger family
AMONG *prep*
AMONGST *same as* ▸ **among**
AMOOVE, -D, -S *vb* stir someone's emotions
AMORAL *adj*
AMORANT > **amorance**
AMORCE, -S *n* small percussion cap
AMORET, -S *n* sweetheart
AMORINO, AMORINI *same as* > **amoretto**

AMORISM ▸ **amorist**
AMORIST *n* lover or a writer about love
AMOROSO *adv* (to be played) lovingly ▹ *n* sherry
AMOROUS *adj*
AMORT *adj* in low spirits
AMOSITE *n* form of asbestos
AMOTION *n* act of removing
AMOUNT, -S *n, vb*
AMOUR, -S *n* love affair
AMOVE, -D, -S, AMOVING *vb* stir someone's emotions
AMOWT, -S *same as* ▸ **amaut**
AMP, -ED, -ING, -S *n* ampere ▹ *vb* excite or become excited
AMPASSY *n* ampersand
AMPED ▸ **amp**
AMPERE, -S *n* basic unit of electric current
AMPHORA *n* two-handled ancient Greek or Roman jar
AMPING ▸ **amp**
AMPLE, -R, -ST *adj*
AMPLIFY *vb*
AMPLY *adv* fully or generously
AMPOULE *n* small sealed glass vessel
AMPS ▸ **amp**
AMPUL, -S *n* ampoule
AMPULE, -S *same as* ▸ **ampoule**
AMPULLA *n* dilated end part of certain tubes in the body
AMPULS ▸ **ampul**
AMPUTEE *n* person who has had a limb amputated
AMREETA *same as* ▸ **amrita**
AMRIT, -S *n* liquid used in the Amrit Ceremony
AMRITA, -S *n* ambrosia of the gods that bestows immortality
AMRITS ▸ **amrit**
AMTMAN, -S *n* magistrate in parts of Europe
AMTRAC, -S *n* amphibious tracked vehicle
AMTRACK *same as* ▸ **amtrac**
AMTRACS ▸ **amtrac**
AMTRAK, -S *same as* ▸ **amtrac**
AMU, -S *n* unit of mass
AMUCK, -S *same as* ▸ **amok**
AMULET, -S *n* something carried or worn as a protection against evil
AMUS ▸ **amu**
AMUSE, -D, -S *vb*
AMUSER, -S ▸ **amuse**
AMUSES ▸ **amuse**
AMUSIA, -S *n* inability to recognize musical tones
AMUSIC ▸ **amusia**
AMUSING *adj* mildly entertaining
AMUSIVE *adj* deceptive
AMYGDAL *n* almond
AMYL, -S *n* chemical compound
AMYLASE *n* enzyme
AMYLENE *another name (no longer in technical usage) for* ▸ **pentene**
AMYLIC *adj* of or derived from amyl
AMYLOID *n* complex protein ▹ *adj* starchlike
AMYLOSE *n* type of chemical
AMYLS ▸ **amyl**
AMYLUM, -S *another name for* ▸ **starch**
AMYTAL, -S *n* as in **sodium amytal** type of sedative
AN *adj* form of *a* used before vowels ▹ *n* additional condition
ANA, -S *adv* in equal quantities ▹ *n* collection of reminiscences
ANABAS *n* type of fish
ANADEM, -S *n* garland for the head
ANAEMIA *n*
ANAEMIC *adj*
ANAGEN, -S *n* phase of hair growth
ANAGOGE *n* allegorical interpretation
ANAGOGY *same as* ▸ **anagoge**
ANAGRAM *n*
ANAL *adj*
ANALGIA *same as* > **analgesia**
ANALLY ▸ **anal**
ANALOG, -S *same as* > **analogue**
ANALOGA > **analogon**
ANALOGS ▸ **analog**
ANALOGY *n* similarity in some respects
ANALYSE *vb*
ANALYST *n*
ANALYTE *n* substance that is being analysed

ANALYZE *same as* ▸ **analyse**
ANAN *interj* expression of failure to understand
ANANA *n* pineapple

More than two As on your rack is bad news, but there are a number of short words that use three As, of which this word is one.

ANANAS *n* plant related to the pineapple
ANANDA, -S *n* Buddhist principle of extreme happiness
ANANKE, -S *n* unalterable necessity
ANAPEST *same as* > **anapaest**
ANAPHOR *n* word referring back to a previous word
ANARCH, -S *n* instigator or personification of anarchy
ANARCHY *n*
ANAS ▸ **ana**
ANATA, -S *n* Buddhist belief
ANATASE *n* rare blue or black mineral
ANATMAN *same as* ▸ **anata**
ANATOMY *n*
ANATTA, -S *n* annatto
ANATTO, -S *same as* ▸ **annatto**
ANAXIAL *adj* asymmetrical
ANBURY *n* soft spongy tumour occurring in horses and oxen
ANCE *dialect form of* ▸ **once**
ANCHO, -S *n* chilli pepper
ANCHOR *n, vb*
ANCHORS *pl n* brakes of a motor vehicle
ANCHOS ▸ **ancho**
ANCHOVY *n*
ANCHUSA *n* Eurasian plant
ANCIENT *adj, n*
ANCILE, ANCILIA *n* mythical Roman shield
ANCILLA *n* Latin word for servant
ANCLE, -S *old spelling of* ▸ **ankle**
ANCOME, -S *n* inflammation
ANCON *n* projecting bracket
ANCONAL ▸ **ancon**
ANCONE, -S *same as* ▸ **ancon**
ANCORA *adv* Italian for encore
ANCRESS *n* female anchorite
AND, -S *n* additional matter or problem
ANDANTE *adv* (to be played) moderately slowly ▹ *n* passage or piece to be performed moderately slowly
ANDIRON *n* iron stand for supporting logs in a fireplace
ANDRO, -S *n* type of hormone
ANDROID *n, adj*
ANDROS ▸ **andro**
ANDS ▸ **and**
ANDVILE *old form of* ▸ **anvil**
ANE, -S *Scots word for* ▸ **one**
ANEAR, -ED, -S *adv* nearly ▹ *vb* approach
ANEATH *Scots word for* ▸ **beneath**
ANELACE *same as* ▸ **anlace**
ANELE, -D, -S, ANELING *vb* anoint, esp to give extreme unction to
ANELLI *pl n* pasta shaped like small rings
ANEMIA, -S *n* anaemia
ANEMIC *same as* ▸ **anaemic**
ANEMONE *n* plant with white, purple, or red flowers
ANENST *dialect word for* ▸ **against**
ANENT *prep* Scots word meaning alongside
ANERGIA *n* anergy
ANERGIC ▸ **anergy**
ANERGY *n* lack of energy
ANERLY *Scots word for* ▸ **only**
ANEROID *adj* not containing a liquid ▹ *n* barometer that does not contain liquid
ANES ▸ **ane**
ANESTRA > **anestrum**
ANESTRI > **anestrus**
ANETHOL *n* substance derived from oil of anise
ANETIC *adj* medically soothing
ANEURIN *a less common name for* > **thiamine**
ANEW *adv*
ANGA, -S *n* part in Indian music

ANGAKOK *n* Inuit shaman
ANGARIA *n* species of shellfish
ANGARY *n* right to use the property of a neutral state during a war
ANGAS ▸ **anga**
ANGEKOK *n* Inuit shaman
ANGEL, -ED, -S *n, vb*
ANGELIC *adj*
ANGELS ▸ **angel**
ANGELUS *n* series of prayers
ANGER, -ED, -S *n, vb*
ANGERLY *adv* old form of angrily
ANGERS ▸ **anger**
ANGICO, -S *n* South American tree
ANGINA, -S *n*
ANGINAL ▸ **angina**
ANGINAS ▸ **angina**
ANGIOMA *n* tumour consisting of a mass of blood vessels or lymphatic vessels
ANGLE, -D, -S *n, vb*
ANGLER, -S *n*
ANGLES ▸ **angle**
ANGLICE *adv* in English
ANGLIFY *same as* > **anglicize**
ANGLING *n* art or sport of fishing with a hook and line
ANGLIST *same as* > **anglicist**
ANGLO, -S *n* White inhabitant of the US not of Latin extraction
ANGOLA *same as* ▸ **angora**
ANGORA, -S *n*
ANGRIER ▸ **angry**
ANGRIES ▸ **angry**
ANGRILY ▸ **angry**
ANGRY, ANGRIER, ANGRIES *adj* full of anger ▹ *n* angry person
ANGST, -S *n*
ANGSTY *adj* displaying angst
ANGUINE *adj* of, relating to, or similar to a snake
ANGUISH *n, vb*
ANGULAR *adj*
ANHINGA *n* type of bird
ANI, -S *n* tropical bird
ANICCA, -S *n* Buddhist belief
ANICUT, -S *n* dam in India
ANIGH *adv* near
ANIGHT *adv* at night
ANIL, -S *n* tropical shrub
ANILE *adj* of or like a feeble old woman
ANILIN, -S *n* aniline
ANILINE *n* colourless oily liquid
ANILINS ▸ **anilin**
ANILITY ▸ **anile**
ANILS ▸ **anil**
ANIMA, -S *n* feminine principle as present in the male unconscious
ANIMACY *n* state of being animate
ANIMAL, -S *n, adj*
ANIMAS ▸ **anima**
ANIMATE *vb, adj*
ANIMATO, ANIMATI *n* piece of music performed in a lively manner
ANIME, -S *n* type of Japanese animation
ANIMI ▸ **animus**
ANIMISM *n* belief that natural objects possess souls
ANIMIST ▸ **animism**
ANIMUS, ANIMI *n* hatred, animosity
ANION, -S *n* ion with negative charge
ANIONIC ▸ **anion**
ANIONS ▸ **anion**
ANIS ▸ **ani**
ANISE, -S *n* plant with liquorice-flavoured seeds
ANISEED *n*
ANISES ▸ **anise**
ANISIC ▸ **anise**
ANISOLE *n* colourless pleasant-smelling liquid used as a solvent
ANKER, -S *n* old liquid measure for wine
ANKH, -S *n* ancient Egyptian symbol
ANKLE, -D, -S, ANKLING *n, vb*
ANKLET, -S *n* ornamental chain worn round the ankle
ANKLING ▸ **ankle**
ANKLONG *n* Asian musical instrument
ANKLUNG *n* Asian musical instrument
ANKUS, -ES *n* stick used for goading elephants
ANKUSH *n* stick used for goading elephants
ANLACE, -S *n* medieval short dagger with a broad tapering blade
ANLAGE, -N, -S *n* organ or part in the earliest stage of development
ANLAS, -ES *same as* ▸ **anlace**

ANN, -S *n* old Scots word for a widow's pension
ANNA, -S *n* former Indian coin worth one sixteenth of a rupee
ANNAL, -S *n* recorded events of one year
ANNAS ▸ **anna**
ANNAT, -S *n* old Scots word for a widow's pension
ANNATES *pl n* money paid to the Pope
ANNATS ▸ **annat**
ANNATTA *n* annatto
ANNATTO *n* tropical tree
ANNEAL, -S *vb* toughen by heating and slow cooling ▹ *n* act of annealing
ANNELID *n* type of worm with a segmented body
ANNEX, -ED *vb* seize (territory)
ANNEXE, -S *n* extension to a building
ANNEXED ▸ **annex**
ANNEXES ▸ **annexe**
ANNICUT *n* dam in India
ANNO *adv* Latin for in the year
ANNONA, -S *n* American tree or shrub
ANNOY, -ED, -S *vb*
ANNOYER ▸ **annoy**
ANNOYS ▸ **annoy**
ANNS ▸ **ann**
ANNUAL, -S *adj, n*
ANNUITY *n*
ANNUL, -S *vb*
ANNULAR *adj* ring-shaped ▹ *n* ring finger
ANNULET *n* moulding in the form of a ring
ANNULI ▸ **annulus**
ANNULS ▸ **annul**
ANNULUS, ANNULI *n* area between two concentric circles
ANOA, -S *n* type of small cattle
ANOBIID *n* any type of beetle
ANODAL ▸ **anode**
ANODE, -S *n* positive electrode in a battery, valve, etc
ANODIC ▸ **anode**
ANODISE *same as* ▸ **anodize**
ANODIZE *vb* coat (metal) with a protective oxide film by electrolysis
ANODYNE *n, adj*
ANOESIS, ANOESES *n* feeling without understanding
ANOETIC ▸ **anoesis**
ANOINT, -S *vb*
ANOLE, -S *n* type of lizard
ANOLYTE *n* part of an electrolyte around an anode
ANOMALY *n*
ANOMIC ▸ **anomie**
ANOMIE, -S *n* lack of social or moral standards
ANOMY *same as* ▸ **anomie**
ANON *adv* in a short time, soon
ANONYM, -S *n* anonymous person or publication
ANONYMA *n* main vessel in the arterial network
ANONYMS ▸ **anonym**
ANOPIA, -S *n* inability to see
ANOPSIA *n* squint in which the eye turns upwards
ANORAK, -S *n*
ANOREXY *old name for* > **anorexia**
ANOSMIA *n* loss of the sense of smell
ANOSMIC ▸ **anosmia**
ANOTHER *adj*
ANOUGH *adj* old form of enough
ANOW *adj* old form of enough
ANOXIA, -S *n* lack or absence of oxygen
ANOXIC ▸ **anoxia**
ANS *pl n* as in **ifs and ans** things that might have happened, but which did not
ANSA, -E *n* either end of Saturn's rings
ANSATE *adj* having a handle or handle-like part
ANSATED *adj* ansate
ANSATZ *n* (in mathematics) assumption made to help solve a problem
ANSWER, -S *n, vb*
ANT, -S *n*
ANTA, -E, -S *n* pilaster
ANTACID *n* substance that counteracts acidity ▹ *adj* having the properties of this substance
ANTAE ▸ **anta**

ANTAR, -S *old word for* ▸ **cave**
ANTARA, -S *n* South American panpipes
ANTARS ▸ **antar**
ANTAS ▸ **anta**
ANTBEAR *n* aardvark
ANTBIRD *n* South American bird
ANTE, -D, -ED, -ING, -S *n* player's stake in poker ▹ *vb* place (one's stake) in poker
ANTEFIX *n* carved ornament
ANTEING ▸ **ante**
ANTENNA *n* insect's feeler
ANTES ▸ **ante**
ANTHEM, -S *n, vb*
ANTHER, -S *n* part of a flower's stamen containing pollen
ANTHILL *n* mound near an ants' nest
ANTHOID *adj* resembling a flower
ANTHRAX *n* dangerous disease of cattle and sheep, communicable to humans
ANTHRO, -S *n* short for anthropology
ANTI, -S *adj* opposed (to) ▹ *n* opponent of a party, policy, or attitude
ANTIAIR *adj* countering attack by aircraft or missile
ANTIAR, -S *another name for* ▸ **upas**
ANTIBUG *adj* acting against computer bugs
ANTIC *n* actor in a ludicrous or grotesque part ▹ *adj* fantastic
ANTICAL *adj* in front of or above another plant part
ANTICAR *adj* opposed to cars
ANTICK, -S *vb* perform antics
ANTICKE *archaic form of* ▸ **antique**
ANTICKS ▸ **antick**
ANTICLY *adv* grotesquely
ANTICS *pl n*
ANTIENT *old spelling of* ▸ **ancient**
ANTIFA, -S *n* antifascist organization
ANTIFAT *adj* acting to remove or prevent fat
ANTIFLU *adj* acting against influenza
ANTIFOG *adj* preventing the buildup of moisture on a surface
ANTIFUR *adj* opposed to the wearing of fur garments
ANTIGAY *adj* hostile to gay people
ANTIGEN *n* substance causing the blood to produce antibodies
ANTIGUN *adj* opposed to the possession of guns
ANTIJAM *adj* preventing jamming
ANTILOG *n* number whose logarithm to a given base is a given number
ANTIMAN *adj* hostile to men
ANTIMEN *adj* hostile to men
ANTING, -S *n* rubbing of ants by birds on their feathers
ANTIQUE *n, adj, vb*
ANTIRED *adj* of a particular colour of antiquark
ANTIS ▸ **anti**
ANTISAG *adj* preventing sagging
ANTITAX *adj* opposed to taxation
ANTIVAX *adj* opposed to vaccination
ANTIWAR *adj* opposed to war
ANTLER, -S *n*
ANTLIA, -E *n* butterfly proboscis
ANTLIKE *adj*
ANTLION *n* type of insect resembling a dragonfly
ANTONYM *n*
ANTRA ▸ **antrum**
ANTRAL ▸ **antrum**
ANTRE, -S *n* cavern or cave
ANTRUM, ANTRA, -S *n* natural cavity, esp in a bone
ANTS ▸ **ant**
ANTSY, ANTSIER *adj* restless, nervous, and impatient
ANURA *pl n* order of animals that comprises frogs and toads
ANURAL *adj* without a tail
ANURAN, -S *n* type of amphibian
ANURIA, -S *n* result of a kidney disorder
ANURIC ▸ **anuria**

ANUROUS *adj* lacking a tail
ANUS, -ES *n*
ANVIL, -ED, -S *n, vb*
ANXIETY *n*
ANXIOUS *adj*
ANY *adj, adv*
ANYBODY *n*
ANYHOW *adv*
ANYMORE *adv*
ANYON, -S *n* type of elementary particle
ANYONE, -S *pron, n*
ANYONS ▸ **anyon**
ANYROAD *a northern English dialect word for* ▸ **anyway**
ANYTIME *adv*
ANYWAY *adv*
ANYWAYS *nonstandard word for* ▸ **anyway**
ANYWHEN *adv* at any time
ANYWISE *adv* in any way or manner
ANZIANI *pl n* Italian word for councillors
AORIST, -S *n* tense of the verb in classical Greek
AORTA, -E, -S *n* main artery of the body, carrying oxygen-rich blood from the heart
AORTAL ▸ **aorta**
AORTAS ▸ **aorta**
AORTIC ▸ **aorta**
AOUDAD, -S *n* wild mountain sheep
APACE *adv* swiftly
APACHE, -S *n* Parisian gangster or ruffian
APADANA *n* ancient Persian palace hall
APAGE *interj* Greek word meaning go away
APAGOGE *n* reduction to absurdity
APAID ▸ **apay**
APANAGE *same as* > **appanage**
APAREJO *n* kind of packsaddle made of stuffed leather cushions
APART *adv*
APATHY *n*
APATITE *n* pale green to purple mineral, found in igneous rocks
APAY, APAID, -D, -ING, -S *vb* old word meaning satisfy
APE, -D, -S, APING *n, vb*
APEAK *adj* in a vertical or almost vertical position
APED ▸ **ape**
APEDOM, -S *n* state of being an ape
APEEK *adv* nautical word meaning vertically
APEHOOD *n* state of being an ape
APELIKE ▸ **ape**
APEMAN, APEMEN *n*
APEPSIA *n* digestive disorder
APEPSY *n* apepsia
APER, -S *n* person who apes
APERCU, -S *n* outline
APERIES ▸ **apery**
APERS ▸ **aper**
APERT *adj* open
APERY, APERIES *n* imitative behaviour
APES ▸ **ape**
APETALY > **apetalous**
APEX, -ES *n*
APGAR *n* as in **apgar score** system for determining the condition of an infant at birth
APHAGIA *n* refusal or inability to swallow
APHAKIA *n* absence of the lens of an eye
APHASIA *n* disorder causing loss of ability to communicate
APHASIC ▸ **aphasia**
APHELIA > **aphelion**
APHESIS, APHESES *n* gradual disappearance of an unstressed vowel at the beginning of a word
APHETIC ▸ **aphesis**
APHID, -S *n*
APHIDES ▸ **aphis**
APHIDS ▸ **aphid**
APHIS, APHIDES *n* type of aphid such as the blackfly
APHONIA *n* loss of the voice caused by damage to the vocal tract
APHONIC *adj* affected with aphonia ▹ *n* person affected with aphonia
APHONY *same as* ▸ **aphonia**
APHOTIC *adj* characterized by or growing in the absence of light
APHTHA, -E *n* small ulceration
APHYLLY > **aphyllous**
APIAN *adj* of, relating to, or resembling bees
APIARY *n*

APICAL, -S *adj* of, at, or being an apex ▷ *n* sound made with the tip of the tongue
APICES *plural of* ▸ **apex**
APICIAN *adj* of fine or dainty food
APICULI > **apiculus**
APIECE *adv* each
APIEZON *adj* as in **apiezon oil** oil left by distillation
APING ▸ **ape**
APIOL, -S *n* substance derived from parsley seeds
APISH *adj* stupid or foolish
APISHLY ▸ **apish**
APISM, -S *n* behaviour like an ape
APLANAT *n* aplanatic lens
APLASIA *n* congenital absence of an organ
APLENTY *adv*
APLITE, -S *n* type of igneous rock
APLITIC ▸ **aplite**
APLOMB, -S *n*
APNEA, -S *same as* ▸ **apnoea**
APNEAL ▸ **apnea**
APNEAS ▸ **apnea**
APNEIC ▸ **apnea**
APNOEA, -S *n* temporary inability to breathe
APNOEAL ▸ **apnoea**
APNOEAS ▸ **apnoea**
APNOEIC ▸ **apnoea**
APO, -S *n* type of protein
APOCARP *n* apocarpous gynoecium or fruit
APOCOPE *n* omission of the final sound or sounds of a word
APOD, -S *n* animal without feet
APODAL *adj* (of snakes, eels, etc) without feet
APODE, -S *n* animal without feet
APODOUS *same as* ▸ **apodal**
APODS ▸ **apod**
APOGAMY *n* type of reproduction in some ferns
APOGEAL ▸ **apogee**
APOGEAN ▸ **apogee**
APOGEE, -S *n* point of moon's orbit
APOGEIC ▸ **apogee**
APOLLO, -S *n* strikingly handsome youth
APOLOG, -S *same as* > **apologue**
APOLOGY *n*
APOLUNE *n* point in a lunar orbit
APOMICT *n* organism, esp a plant, produced by apomixis
APOOP *adv* on the poop deck
APOPLEX *vb* afflict with apoplexy
APORIA, -S *n* doubt, real or professed, about what to do or say
APORT *adj* on or towards the port side
APOS ▸ **apo**
APOSTIL *n* marginal note
APOSTLE *n*
APOTHEM *n* line from the centre of a polygon to one of its sides
APOZEM, -S *n* medicine dissolved in water
APP, -S *n* application program
APPAID ▸ **appay**
APPAIR, -S *vb* old form of impair
APPAL, -S *vb* dismay, terrify
APPALL, -S *same as* ▸ **appal**
APPALS ▸ **appal**
APPALTO, APPALTI *n* monopoly or contract
APPARAT *n* Communist Party organization
APPAREL *n, vb*
APPAY, APPAID, -D, -S *old word for* ▸ **satisfy**
APPEACH *old word for* ▸ **accuse**
APPEAL, -S *vb, n*
APPEAR, -S *vb*
APPEASE *vb*
APPEL, -S *n* stamp of the foot, used to warn of one's intent to attack
APPEND, -S *vb*
APPERIL *old word for* ▸ **peril**
APPLAUD *vb*
APPLE, -S *n*
APPLET, -S *n* computing program
APPLEY *adj* resembling or tasting like an apple
APPLIED *adj* (of a skill, science, etc) put to practical use
APPLIER ▸ **apply**
APPLY, APPLIES *vb*
APPOINT *vb*
APPORT, -S *n* production of objects at a seance

APPOSE, -D, -S *vb* place side by side or near to each other
APPOSER ▸ **appose**
APPOSES ▸ **appose**
APPRESS *vb* press together
APPRISE *vb* make aware (of)
APPRIZE *same as* ▸ **apprise**
APPRO, -S *n* approval
APPROOF *old word for* ▸ **trial**
APPROS ▸ **appro**
APPROVE *vb*
APPS ▸ **app**
APPUI, -S *n* support
APPUIED ▸ **appuy**
APPUIS ▸ **appui**
APPULSE *n* close approach of two celestial bodies
APPUY, APPUIED, -ED, -S *vb* support
APRAXIA *n* disorder impairing muscle movement
APRAXIC ▸ **apraxia**
APRES *prep* French word for after
APRICOT *n, adj*
APRON, -ED, -S *n, vb*
APROPOS *adj*
APROTIC *adj* (of solvents) neither accepting nor donating hydrogen ions
APSARAS *n* Hindu water sprite
APSE, -S *n* arched or domed recess, esp in a church
APSIDAL ▸ **apsis**
APSIS, APSIDES *n* point in the elliptical orbit of a planet or satellite
APSO, -S *n* Tibetan terrier
APT, -ED, -ER, -EST, -ING, -S *adj* having a specified tendency ▹ *vb* be fitting
APTAMER *n* artificially created DNA or RNA molecule
APTED ▸ **apt**
APTER ▸ **apt**
APTERAL *adj* (esp of a classical temple) not having columns at the sides
APTERIA > **apterium**
APTERYX *n* kiwi (the bird)
APTEST ▸ **apt**
APTING ▸ **apt**
APTLY ▸ **apt**
APTNESS ▸ **apt**
APTOTE, -S *n* noun without inflections
APTOTIC ▸ **aptote**
APTS ▸ **apt**
APYRASE *n* enzyme
AQUA, -E, -S *n* water

> This Latin word for water, together with its plural **aquae** or **aquas**, comes up over and over again.

AQUAFER *n* aquifer
AQUAFIT *n* type of aerobic exercise done in water
AQUARIA > **aquarium**
AQUAS ▸ **aqua**
AQUATIC *adj, n*
AQUAVIT *n* grain- or potato-based spirit
AQUEOUS *adj* of, like, or containing water
AQUIFER *n* deposit of rock containing water used to supply wells
AQUILON *n* name for the north wind
AQUIVER *adv* quivering
AR, -S *n* letter R
ARAARA, -S *another name for* > **trevally**
ARABA, -S *n* Asian carriage

> This is one of the short words that can help you deal with a surplus of As.

ARABESK *same as* > **arabesque**
ARABIC *adj* as in **gum arabic** gum exuded by certain acacia trees
ARABICA *n* high-quality coffee bean
ARABIN, -S *n* essence of gum arabic
ARABIS *n* type of plant
ARABISE *vb* make or become Arab
ARABIZE *vb* make or become Arab
ARABLE, -S *adj, n*
ARACHIS *n* Brazilian plant
ARAISE, -D, -S *vb* old form of raise
ARAK, -S *same as* ▸ **arrack**
ARALIA, -S *n* type of plant
ARAME, -S *n* Japanese edible seaweed
ARAMID, -S *n* synthetic fibre
ARANEID *n* member of the spider family
ARAR, -S *n* African tree
ARAROBA *n* Brazilian leguminous tree
ARARS ▸ **arar**

ARAWANA *n* tropical freshwater fish
ARAYSE, -D, -S *vb* old form of raise
ARB, -S *short for* **> arbitrage**
ARBA, -S *n* Asian carriage
ARBITER *n*
ARBLAST *n* arbalest
ARBOR, -ES, -S *n* revolving shaft or axle in a machine
ARBORED *adj* having arbors
ARBORES ▸ arbor
ARBORET *n* old name for an area planted with shrubs
ARBORIO *n* as in **arborio rice** variety of round-grain rice used for making risotto
ARBORS ▸ arbor
ARBOUR, -S *n* glade sheltered by trees
ARBS ▸ arb
ARBUTE, -S *old name for* **▸ arbutus**
ARBUTUS *n* evergreen shrub with strawberry-like berries
ARC, -ED, -KED, -S *n, vb*
ARCADE, -D, -S *n, vb*
ARCADIA *n* traditional idealized rural setting
ARCANA, -S *n* either of the two divisions of a pack of tarot cards
ARCANE *adj*
ARCANUM *n* profound secret or mystery known only to initiates
ARCED ▸ arc
ARCH, -ES, -EST *n, vb, adj*
ARCHAEA *n* order of prokaryotic microorganisms
ARCHAEI > archaeus
ARCHAIC *adj* ancient
ARCHEAN *same as* **> archaean**
ARCHED *adj* provided with or spanned by an arch or arches
ARCHEI ▸ archeus
ARCHER, -S *n*
ARCHERY *n*
ARCHES ▸ arch
ARCHEST ▸ arch
ARCHEUS, ARCHEI *n* spirit believed to inhabit a living thing
ARCHFOE *n* chief enemy
ARCHI ▸ arco
ARCHIL, -S *variant spelling of* **▸ orchil**
ARCHINE *n* Russian unit of length
ARCHING *n* arched part
ARCHIVE *n, vb*
ARCHLET *n* small arch
ARCHLY ▸ arch
ARCHON, -S *n* (in ancient Athens) one of the nine chief magistrates
ARCHWAY *n*
ARCING, -S *n* formation of an arc
ARCKED ▸ arc
ARCKING *n* formation of an arc
ARCMIN, -S *n* 1/60 of a degree of an angle
ARCO, ARCHI, -S *adv* musical direction meaning with bow ▹ *n* bow of a stringed instrument
ARCS ▸ arc
ARCSEC, -S *n* 1/3600 of a degree of an angle
ARCSINE *n* trigonometrical function
ARCTIC, -S *adj* very cold ▹ *n* high waterproof overshoe with buckles
ARCTIID *n* type of moth
ARCTOID *adj* like a bear
ARCUATE *adj* shaped or bent like an arc or bow
ARCUS, -ES *n* circle around the cornea of the eye
ARD, -S *n* primitive plough
ARDEB, -S *n* unit of dry measure
ARDENCY ▸ ardent
ARDENT *adj*
ARDOR, -S *same as* **▸ ardour**
ARDOUR, -S *n* passion
ARDRI, -S *n* Irish high king
ARDRIGH *n* Irish high king
ARDRIS ▸ ardri
ARDS ▸ ard
ARDUOUS *adj* hard to accomplish, strenuous
ARE, -S *n* unit of measure, 100 square metres ▹ *vb* form of the present tense of *be*
AREA, -E, -S *n*
AREACH *vb* old form of reach
AREAD, -S, ARED, AREDD *vb* old word meaning declare
AREAE ▸ area
AREAL ▸ area
AREALLY ▸ area

AREAR, -S *n* old form of arrear
AREAS ▸ **area**
AREAWAY *n* passageway
ARECA, -S *n* type of palm tree
ARED ▸ **aread**
AREDD ▸ **aread**
AREDE, -S, AREDING *vb* old word meaning declare
AREFY, AREFIED, AREFIES *vb* dry up
AREG *a plural of* ▸ **erg**
AREIC *adj* relating to area
ARENA, -S *n*
ARENE, -S *n* aromatic hydrocarbon
ARENITE *n* any arenaceous rock
ARENOSE *adj* sandy
ARENOUS *adj* sandy
AREOLA, -E, -S *n* small circular area
AREOLAR ▸ **areola**
AREOLAS ▸ **areola**
AREOLE, -S *n* space outlined on a surface
AREPA, -S *n* Colombian cornmeal cake
ARERE *adv* old word meaning backwards
ARES ▸ **are**
ARET, -S *vb* old word meaning entrust
ARETE, -S *n* sharp ridge separating two glacial valleys
ARETS ▸ **aret**
ARETT, -ED, -S *vb* old word meaning entrust
AREW *adv* old word meaning in a row
ARF, -S *n* barking sound
ARGAL, -S *same as* ▸ **argali**
ARGALA, -S *n* Indian stork
ARGALI, -S *n* wild sheep
ARGALS ▸ **argal**
ARGAN, -S *n* Moroccan tree
ARGAND, -S *n* lamp with a hollow circular wick
ARGANS ▸ **argan**
ARGENT, -S *n* silver
ARGH *interj* cry of pain
ARGHAN, -S *n* agave plant
ARGIL, -S *n* clay, esp potters' clay
ARGLE, -D, -S, ARGLING *vb* quarrel
ARGOL, -S *n* chemical compound
ARGON, -S *n* inert gas found in the air
ARGONON *n* inert gas
ARGONS ▸ **argon**
ARGOSY *n* large merchant ship
ARGOT, -S *n* slang or jargon
ARGOTIC ▸ **argot**
ARGOTS ▸ **argot**
ARGUE, -D, -S, ARGUING *vb*
ARGUER, -S ▸ **argue**
ARGUES ▸ **argue**
ARGUFY *vb* argue or quarrel, esp over something trivial
ARGUING ▸ **argue**
ARGULUS, ARGULI *n* parasite on fish
ARGUS, -ES *n* any of various brown butterflies
ARGUTE *adj* shrill or keen
ARGYLE, -S *adj* with a diamond-shaped pattern ▹ *n* sock with this pattern
ARGYLL, -S *n* sock with diamond pattern
ARGYRIA *n* staining of skin by exposure to silver
ARHAT, -S *n* Buddhist who has achieved enlightenment
ARIA, -S *n*
ARIARY *n* currency of Madagascar
ARIAS ▸ **aria**
ARID, -ER, -EST *adj*
ARIDITY ▸ **arid**
ARIDLY ▸ **arid**
ARIEL, -S *n* type of Arabian gazelle
ARIETTA *n* short aria
ARIETTE *same as* ▸ **arietta**
ARIGHT *adv* rightly
ARIKI, -S *n* Polynesian chief
ARIL, -S *n* appendage on certain seeds
ARILED *adj* having an aril
ARILLUS, ARILLI *n* aril
ARILS ▸ **aril**
ARIOSE *adj* songlike
ARIOSO, ARIOSI, -S *n* recitative with the lyrical quality of an aria
ARIOT *adv* riotously
ARIPPLE *adv* in ripples
ARISE, -N, -S, ARISING, AROSE *vb*
ARISH, -ES *n* field that has been mown
ARISING ▸ **arise**
ARISTA, -E, -S *n* stiff bristle

ARISTO, -S *n* aristocrat
ARK, -ED, -ING, -S *n, vb*
ARKITE, -S *n* passenger in ark
ARKOSE, -S *n* type of sandstone
ARKOSIC ▸ **arkose**
ARKS ▸ **ark**
ARLE, -D, -S, ARLING *vb* make a down payment
ARM, -S *n, vb*
ARMADA, -S *n*
ARMBAND *n*
ARMED *adj* equipped with or supported by arms, armour, etc
ARMER, -S ▸ **arm**
ARMERIA *n* generic name for the plant thrift
ARMERS ▸ **armer**
ARMET, -S *n* close-fitting medieval visored helmet with a neck guard
ARMFUL, -S, ARMSFUL *n*
ARMHOLE *n*
ARMIES ▸ **army**
ARMIGER *n* person entitled to bear heraldic arms
ARMIL, -S *n* bracelet
ARMILLA *n* bracelet
ARMILS ▸ **armil**
ARMING, -S *n* act of taking arms or providing with arms
ARMLESS ▸ **arm**
ARMLET, -S *n* band worn round the arm
ARMLIKE ▸ **arm**
ARMLOAD *n* amount carried in the arms
ARMLOCK *vb* grip someone's arms
ARMOIRE *n* large cabinet
ARMOR, -S *same as* ▸ **armour**
ARMORED *same as* > **armoured**
ARMORER *same as* > **armourer**
ARMORS ▸ **armor**
ARMORY *same as* ▸ **armoury**
ARMOUR, -S *n, vb*
ARMOURY *n*
ARMPIT, -S *n*
ARMREST *n*
ARMS ▸ **arm**
ARMSFUL ▸ **armful**
ARMURE, -S *n* silk or wool fabric with a small cobbled pattern
ARMY, ARMIES *n*
ARNA, -S *n* Indian water buffalo
ARNATTO *n* annatto
ARNICA, -S *n* temperate or Arctic plant
ARNOTTO *n* annatto
ARNUT, -S *n* plant with edible tubers
AROBA, -S *n* Asian carriage
AROHA, -S *n* love, compassion, or affection
AROID, -S *n* type of plant
AROINT, -S *vb* drive away
AROLLA, -S *n* European pine tree
AROMA, -S *n*
AROSE ▸ **arise**
AROUND *adv*
AROUSAL ▸ **arouse**
AROUSE, -D, -S *vb*
AROUSER ▸ **arouse**
AROUSES ▸ **arouse**
AROW *adv* in a row
AROWANA *n* tropical freshwater fish
AROYNT, -S *vb* old word meaning to drive away
ARPA, -S *n* website concerned with structure of the internet
ARPEN, -S *n* former French unit of length
ARPENT, -S *n* former French unit of length
ARRACK, -S *n* alcoholic drink distilled from grain or rice
ARRAH *interj* Irish exclamation
ARRAIGN *vb* bring (a prisoner) before a court to answer a charge
ARRANGE *vb*
ARRANT *adj* utter, downright
ARRAS, -ES *n* tapestry wall-hanging
ARRASED *adj* having an arras
ARRASES ▸ **arras**
ARRAY, -ED, -S *n, vb*
ARRAYAL ▸ **array**
ARRAYED ▸ **array**
ARRAYER ▸ **array**
ARRAYS ▸ **array**
ARREAR *n* singular of arrears
ARREARS *pl n*
ARRECT *adj* pricked up
ARREEDE *vb* old word meaning declare
ARREST, -S *vb, n*
ARRET, -S *n* judicial decision

ARRIAGE *n* Scottish feudal service
ARRIBA *interj* exclamation of pleasure or approval
ARRIDE, -D, -S *vb* old word meaning gratify
ARRIERE *adj* French word meaning old-fashioned
ARRIERO *n* mule driver
ARRIS, -ES *n* sharp edge at the meeting of two surfaces
ARRISH *n* corn stubble
ARRIVAL *n*
ARRIVE, -D, -S *vb*
ARRIVER ▸ **arrive**
ARRIVES ▸ **arrive**
ARROBA, -S *n* unit of weight in Spanish-speaking countries
ARROCES ▸ **arroz**
ARROW, -S *n*
ARROWED *adj* having an arrow pattern
ARROWS ▸ **arrow**
ARROWY *adj* like an arrow
ARROYO, -S *n* usually dry stream bed
ARROZ, ARROCES, -ES *n* Spanish word for rice, used in name of various dishes
ARS ▸ **ar**
ARSENAL *n*
ARSENIC *n, adj*
ARSENO *adj* containing arsenic
ARSES ▸ **arsis**
ARSHEEN *n* old measure of length in Russia
ARSHIN, -S *n* old measure of length in Russia
ARSHINE *n* old measure of length in Russia
ARSHINS ▸ **arshin**
ARSINE, -S *n* colourless poisonous gas
ARSINO *adj* containing arsine
ARSIS, ARSES *n* long or stressed syllable in a metrical foot
ARSON, -S *n*
ART, -S *n*
ARTAL *a plural of* ▸ **rotl**
ARTEL, -S *n* cooperative union
ARTERY *n*
ARTFUL *adj*
ARTI, -S *n* Hindu ritual performed in homes and temples
ARTIC, -S *n* articulated vehicle
ARTICLE *n, vb*
ARTICS ▸ **artic**
ARTIER ▸ **arty**
ARTIES ▸ **arty**
ARTIEST ▸ **arty**
ARTIGI, -S *n* kind of hooded coat worn in Canada
ARTILY ▸ **arty**
ARTIS ▸ **arti**
ARTISAN *n*
ARTIST, -S *n*
ARTISTE *n*
ARTISTS ▸ **artist**
ARTLESS *adj*
ARTS ▸ **art**
ARTSIE *n* arts student
ARTSIER ▸ **artsy**
ARTSIES ▸ **artsy**
ARTSMAN, ARTSMEN *old word for* > **craftsman**
ARTSY, ARTSIER, ARTSIES *adj* interested in the arts ▹ *n* person interested in the arts
ARTWORK *n*
ARTY, ARTIER, ARTIES, ARTIEST *adj* having an affected interest in art ▹ *n* person interested in art
ARUANA, -S *n* tropical freshwater fish
ARUGOLA *same as* ▸ **arugula**
ARUGULA *n* salad plant
ARUHE, -S *n* edible root of a fern
ARUM, -S *n* type of plant
ARUSPEX *variant spelling of* > **haruspex**
ARVAL *adj* of ploughed land
ARVEE, -S *n* short for recreational vehicle (RV)
ARVO, -S *n* afternoon
ARY *dialect form of* ▸ **any**
ARYL, -S *n* (in chemistry) an aromatic group
AS, -AR *adv* used to indicate amount or extent in comparisons ▹ *n* ancient Roman unit of weight
ASANA, -S *n* any of various postures in yoga
ASAR ▸ **as**
ASARUM, -S *n* dried strong-scented root
ASCARED *adj* afraid
ASCARID *n* type of parasitic nematode
ASCARIS *n* ascarid
ASCAUNT *adv* old word meaning slantwise
ASCEND, -S *vb*
ASCENT, -S *n*

ASCESIS, ASCESES *n* exercise of self-discipline
ASCETIC *adj* abstaining from worldly pleasures and comforts ▷ *n* person who abstains from worldly comforts and pleasures
ASCI ▶ **ascus**
ASCIAN, -S *n* person living in the tropics
ASCIDIA > **ascidium**
ASCITES *n* accumulation of serous fluid in the peritoneal cavity
ASCITIC ▶ **ascites**
ASCON, -S *n* type of sponge having an oval shape and a thin body wall
ASCONCE *adv* old form of askance
ASCONS ▶ **ascon**
ASCOT, -S *n* type of cravat
ASCRIBE *vb*
ASCUS, ASCI *n* saclike structure in fungi
ASDIC, -S *n* early form of sonar
ASEA *adv* towards the sea
ASEITY *n* existence derived from itself, having no other source
ASEPSIS, ASEPSES *n* aseptic condition
ASEPTIC *adj* free from harmful bacteria ▷ *n* aseptic substance
ASEXUAL *adj*
ASH, -ED, -ES, -ING *n*, *vb*
ASHAKE *adv* shaking
ASHAME, -S *vb*
ASHAMED *adj* feeling shame
ASHAMES ▶ **ashame**
ASHCAKE *n* cornmeal bread
ASHCAN, -S *n* large metal dustbin
ASHED ▶ **ash**
ASHEN *adj*
ASHERY *n* place where ashes are made
ASHES ▶ **ash**
ASHET, -S *n* shallow oval dish or large plate
ASHFALL *n* dropping of ash from a volcano
ASHIER ▶ **ashy**
ASHIEST ▶ **ashy**
ASHINE *adv* old word meaning shining
ASHING ▶ **ash**
ASHIVER *adv* shivering
ASHKEY, -S *n* winged fruit of the ash
ASHLAR, -S *n* block of hewn stone ▷ *vb* build with ashlars
ASHLER, -S *same as* ▶ **ashlar**
ASHLESS ▶ **ash**
ASHMAN, ASHMEN *n* man who shovels ashes
ASHORE *adv*, *adj*
ASHPAN, -S *n* pan or tray to catch ashes
ASHRAF *pl n* descendants of Muhammad
ASHRAM, -S *n* religious retreat where a Hindu holy man lives
ASHRAMA *n* stage in Hindu spiritual life
ASHRAMS ▶ **ashram**
ASHTRAY *n*
ASHY, ASHIER, ASHIEST *adj* pale greyish
ASIAGO, -S *n* type of cheese
ASIDE, -S *adv*, *n*
ASINICO *n* old Spanish word for fool
ASININE *adj* stupid, idiotic
ASK, -ED, -S *vb*
ASKANCE *adv*, *vb*
ASKANT, -S *same as* ▶ **askance**
ASKARI, -S *n* (in East Africa) a soldier or police officer
ASKED ▶ **ask**
ASKER, -S ▶ **ask**
ASKESIS, ASKESES *n* practice of self-discipline
ASKEW *adj*
ASKING, -S ▶ **ask**
ASKLENT *Scots word for* ▶ **aslant**
ASKOS, ASKOI *n* ancient Greek vase
ASKS ▶ **ask**
ASLAKE, -D, -S *vb* slake
ASLANT *adv* at a slant (to), slanting (across)
ASLEEP *adj*
ASLOPE *adj* sloping
ASLOSH *adj* awash
ASMEAR *adj* smeared
ASOCIAL *n* person who avoids social contact
ASP, -S *n* small poisonous snake
ASPECT, -S *n*, *vb*
ASPEN, -S *n* kind of poplar tree ▷ *adj* trembling
ASPER, -S *n* former Turkish monetary unit
ASPERGE *vb* sprinkle

ASPERS ▸ **asper**
ASPERSE *vb* spread false rumours about
ASPHALT *n, vb*
ASPHYXY *vb* smother, suffocate
ASPIC, -S *n*
ASPICK, -S *old word for* ▸ **asp**
ASPICS ▸ **aspic**
ASPIDIA > **aspidium**
ASPINE, -S *old word for* ▸ **aspen**
ASPIRE, -D, -S *vb*
ASPIRER ▸ **aspire**
ASPIRES ▸ **aspire**
ASPIRIN *n*
ASPIS, -ES *n* horned viper
ASPISH *adj* like an asp
ASPORT, -S *vb* old word meaning take away
ASPOUT *adv* spouting
ASPRAWL *adv* sprawling
ASPREAD *adv* spreading
ASPRO, -S *n* associate professor at an academic institution
ASPROUT *adv* sprouting
ASPS ▸ **asp**
ASQUAT *adv* squatting
ASQUINT *adj* with a glance from the corner of the eye
ASRAMA, -S *n* stage in Hindu spiritual life
ASS, -ES *n* donkey
ASSAGAI *same as* ▸ **assegai**
ASSAI, -S *adv* (usually preceded by a musical direction) very ▹ *n* Brazilian palm tree
ASSAIL, -S *vb*
ASSAIS ▸ **assai**
ASSAM, -S *n* (in Malaysia) tamarind as used in cooking
ASSART, -S *vb* clear ground for cultivation
ASSAULT *n, vb*
ASSAY, -ED, -S *n* analysis of a substance ▹ *vb* make such an analysis
ASSAYER ▸ **assay**
ASSAYS ▸ **assay**
ASSEGAI *n* slender spear used in S Africa ▹ *vb* spear with an assegai
ASSENT, -S *n, vb*
ASSERT, -S *vb*
ASSES ▸ **ass**
ASSESS *vb*
ASSET, -S *n*
ASSEVER *vb* old form of asseverate
ASSEZ *adv* (as part of a musical direction) fairly
ASSIEGE *vb* old form of besiege
ASSIGN, -S *vb, n*
ASSIST, -S *vb, n*
ASSIZE, -D, -S *n* sitting of a legislative assembly ▹ *vb* judge or assess
ASSIZER *n* weights and measures official
ASSIZES ▸ **assize**
ASSLIKE ▸ **ass**
ASSOIL, -S *vb* absolve
ASSORT, -S *vb* arrange or distribute equally
ASSOT, -S *vb* old word meaning make infatuated
ASSOTT *adj* besotted
ASSUAGE *vb* relieve (pain, grief, thirst, etc)
ASSUME, -S *vb*
ASSUMED *adj* false
ASSUMER ▸ **assume**
ASSUMES ▸ **assume**
ASSURE, -S *vb*
ASSURED *adj* confident ▹ *n* beneficiary under a life assurance policy
ASSURER ▸ **assure**
ASSURES ▸ **assure**
ASSUROR ▸ **assure**
ASSWAGE *old spelling of* ▸ **assuage**
ASTABLE *adj* not stable
ASTANGA *same as* > **ashtanga**
ASTARE *adv* staring
ASTART, -S *old word for* ▸ **start**
ASTASIA *n* inability to stand
ASTATIC *adj* not static
ASTATKI *n* fuel derived from petroleum
ASTEISM *n* use of irony
ASTELIC ▸ **astely**
ASTELY *n* lack of central cylinder in plants
ASTER, -S *n* plant with daisy-like flowers
ASTERIA *n* gemstone with starlike light effect
ASTERID *n* variety of flowering plant
ASTERN *adv* at or towards the stern of a ship ▹ *adj* at or towards the stern of a ship
ASTERS ▸ **aster**
ASTERT, -S *vb* start
ASTHENY *same as* > **asthenia**
ASTHMA, -S *n*
ASTHORE *n* Irish endearment

ASTILBE *n* type of plant
ASTIR *adj*
ASTONE, -D, -S *old form of* > **astonish**
ASTONY *old form of* > **astonish**
ASTOOP *adv* stooping
ASTOUND *vb*
ASTRAL, -S *adj* of stars ▷ *n* oil lamp
ASTRAND *adv* on the shore
ASTRAY *adv*
ASTRICT *vb* bind, confine, or constrict
ASTRIDE *adv, adj*
ASTROID *n* hypocycloid having four cusps
ASTRUT *adv* old word meaning in a protruding way
ASTUN, -S *vb* old form of astonish
ASTUTE, -R *adj*
ASTYLAR *adj* without columns or pilasters
ASUDDEN *adv* old form of suddenly
ASUNDER *adv, adj*
ASURA, -S *n* demon in Hindu mythology
ASWARM *adj* filled, esp with moving things
ASWAY *adv* swaying
ASWIM *adv* floating
ASWING *adv* swinging
ASWIRL *adv* swirling
ASWOON *adv* swooning
ASYLA ▶ **asylum**
ASYLEE, -S *n* person who is granted asylum
ASYLUM, ASYLA, -S *n*
AT, -S *n* Laotian monetary unit worth one hundredth of a kip
ATAATA, -S *n* grazing marine gastropod
ATABAL, -S *n* N African drum
ATABEG, -S *n* Turkish ruler
ATABEK, -S *same as* ▶ **atabeg**
ATABRIN *n* drug formerly used for treating malaria
ATACTIC *adj* attribute of a polymer
ATAGHAN *variant of* > **yataghan**
ATALAYA *n* watchtower in Spain
ATAMAN, -S *n* elected leader of the Cossacks
ATAP, -S *n* palm tree of S Asia
ATARAXY *same as* > **ataraxia**
ATAVIC ▶ **atavism**
ATAVISM *n* recurrence of a trait present in distant ancestors
ATAVIST ▶ **atavism**
ATAXIA, -S *n* lack of muscular coordination
ATAXIC, -S ▶ **ataxia**
ATAXY, ATAXIES *same as* ▶ **ataxia**
ATE ▶ **eat**
ATEBRIN *n* drug formerly used to treat malaria
ATELIC *adj* of action without end
ATELIER *n* workshop, artist's studio
ATEMOYA *n* tropical fruit tree
ATES *n* shop selling confectionery
ATHAME, -S *n* witch's ceremonial knife
ATHANOR *n* alchemist's furnace
ATHEISE *vb* speak atheistically
ATHEISM *n*
ATHEIST ▶ **atheism**
ATHEIZE *vb* speak atheistically
ATHEOUS *adj* without a belief in god
ATHIRST *adj* having an eager desire
ATHLETA *same as* ▶ **athlete**
ATHLETE *n*
ATHODYD *another name for* ▶ **ramjet**
ATHRILL *adv* feeling thrills
ATHROB *adv* throbbing
ATHWART *adv* transversely
ATIGI, -S *n* type of parka worn by the Inuit in Canada
ATILT *adj* in a tilted or inclined position
ATIMY, ATIMIES *n* loss of honour
ATINGLE *adv* tingling
ATISHOO *n* sound of a sneeze
ATLAS, -ES *n*
ATLATL, -S *n* Native American throwing stick
ATMA, -S *same as* ▶ **atman**
ATMAN, -S *n* personal soul or self
ATMAS ▶ **atma**
ATMOS, -ES *n* (short for) atmosphere
ATOC, -S *n* skunk
ATOCIA, -S *n* inability to have children

ATOCS ▸ **atoc**
ATOK, -S *n* skunk
ATOKAL *adj* having no children
ATOKE, -S *n* part of a worm
ATOKOUS *adj* having no children
ATOKS ▸ **atok**
ATOLL, -S *n*
ATOM, -S *n*
ATOMIC *adj*
ATOMICS *n* science of atoms
ATOMIES ▸ **atomy**
ATOMISE *same as* ▸ **atomize**
ATOMISM *n* ancient philosophical theory
ATOMIST ▸ **atomism**
ATOMIZE *vb*
ATOMS ▸ **atom**
ATOMY, ATOMIES *n* atom or minute particle
ATONAL *adj* (of music) not written in an established key
ATONE, -D, -S, ATONING *vb*
ATONER, -S ▸ **atone**
ATONES ▸ **atone**
ATONIA, -S *n* lack of normal muscle tone
ATONIC, -S *adj* carrying no stress ▹ *n* unaccented or unstressed syllable
ATONIES ▸ **atony**

The plural of **atony**, this is another of the most frequently played 7-letter bonus words that it is essential to know.

ATONING ▸ **atone**
ATONY, ATONIES *n* lack of normal tone or tension, as in muscles
ATOP *adv* on top
ATOPIC *adj* of or relating to hypersensitivity to certain allergens
ATOPY, ATOPIES *n* tendency to be hypersensitive to certain allergens
ATRESIA *n* absence of or unnatural narrowing of a body channel
ATRESIC ▸ **atresia**
ATRETIC ▸ **atresia**
ATRIA ▸ **atrium**
ATRIAL ▸ **atrium**
ATRIP *adj* (of an anchor) no longer caught on the bottom
ATRIUM, ATRIA, -S *n* upper chamber of either half of the heart
ATROPHY *n* wasting away of an organ or part ▹ *vb* (cause to) waste away
ATROPIA *same as* > **atropine**
ATROPIN *same as* > **atropine**
ATS ▸ **at**
ATT *n* old Siamese coin
ATTABOY *sentence substitute* expression of approval or exhortation
ATTACH *vb*
ATTACHE *n* specialist attached to a diplomatic mission
ATTACK, -S *vb, n*
ATTAIN, -S *vb*
ATTAINT *vb* pass judgment of death ▹ *n* dishonour
ATTAP, -S *n* palm tree of South Asia
ATTAR, -S *n* fragrant oil made from roses
ATTASK, -S, -T *old word for* > **criticize**
ATTEMPT *vb, n*
ATTEND, -S *vb*
ATTENT, -S *old word for* > **attention**
ATTEST, -S *vb*
ATTIC, -S *n*
ATTIRE, -D, -S *n, vb*
ATTONCE *adv* old word for at once
ATTONE, -D, -S *vb* old word meaning appease
ATTORN, -S *vb* acknowledge a new owner of land as one's landlord
ATTRACT *vb*
ATTRAP, -S *vb* adorn
ATTRIST *vb* old word meaning to sadden
ATTRIT, -S *vb* wear down or dispose of gradually
ATTRITE *vb* wear down
ATTRITS ▸ **attrit**
ATTUENT *adj* carrying out attuition
ATTUITE *vb* perceive by attuition
ATTUNE, -D, -S *vb* adjust or accustom (a person or thing)
ATUA, -S *n* spirit or demon
ATWAIN *adv* old word meaning into two parts

ATWEEL *Scots word for* ▸ **well**
ATWEEN *an archaic or Scots word for* ▸ **between**
ATWIXT *old word for* ▸ **between**
ATYPIC *adj* not typical
AUA, -S *n* yellow-eye mullet

This Māori word for a kind of mullet is very often played to balance a rack by getting rid of a surplus of vowels.

AUBADE, -S *n* song or poem greeting the dawn
AUBERGE *n* inn or tavern
AUBURN, -S *adj, n*
AUCEPS *n* old word for a person who catches hawks
AUCTION *n, vb*
AUCUBA, -S *n* Japanese laurel
AUDAD, -S *n* wild African sheep
AUDIAL *adj* of sound
AUDIBLE *adj, n, vb*
AUDIBLY ▸ **audible**
AUDIENT *n* person who hears
AUDILE, -S *n* person with a faculty for auditory imagery ▹ *adj* of or relating to such a person
AUDING, -S *n* practice of listening to try to understand
AUDIO, -S *adj, n*
AUDISM, -S *n* prejudice against deaf people
AUDIST, -S *n* person prejudiced against deaf people
AUDIT, -ED, -S *n, vb*
AUDITEE *n* one who is audited
AUDITOR *n* person qualified to audit accounts
AUDITS ▸ **audit**
AUE *interj* Māori exclamation

A Māori exclamation, so useful for getting rid of surplus vowels. But, unlike **aua**, it does not take an S.

AUF, -S *old word for* ▸ **oaf**
AUFGABE *n* word used in psychology to mean task
AUFS ▸ **auf**
AUGEND, -S *n* number to which a number is added
AUGER, -S *n* tool for boring holes
AUGH *interj* expressing frustration
AUGHT, -S *adv* in any least part ▹ *n* less common word for nought
AUGITE, -S *n* black or greenish-black mineral
AUGITIC ▸ **augite**
AUGMENT *vb, n*
AUGUR, -ED, -S *vb* be a sign of (future events) ▹ *n* religious official who interpreted omens
AUGURAL ▸ **augur**
AUGURED ▸ **augur**
AUGURER *old word for* ▸ **augur**
AUGURS ▸ **augur**
AUGURY *n* foretelling of the future
AUGUST, -S *adj* dignified and imposing ▹ *n* auguste
AUGUSTE *n* type of circus clown
AUGUSTS ▸ **august**
AUK, -S *n* sea bird with short wings
AUKLET, -S *n* type of small auk
AUKS ▸ **auk**
AULA, -S *n* hall
AULD, -ER, -EST *a Scots word for* ▸ **old**
AULIC *adj* relating to a royal court
AULNAGE *n* measurement in ells
AULOS, AULOI *n* ancient Greek pipe
AUMAIL, -S *old word for* ▸ **enamel**
AUMBRY *same as* ▸ **ambry**
AUMIL, -S *n* manager in India
AUNE, -S *n* old French measure of length
AUNT, -S *n*
AUNTER, -S *old word for* ▸ **adventure**
AUNTIE, -S *n*
AUNTLY *adj* of or like an aunt
AUNTS ▸ **aunt**
AUNTY *same as* ▸ **auntie**
AURA, -E, -S *n* distinctive air or quality of a person or thing
AURAL *adj* of or using the ears or hearing
AURALLY ▸ **aural**

AURAR *plural of* ▸ **eyrir**
AURAS ▸ **aura**
AURATE, -S *n* salt of auric acid
AURATED *adj* combined with auric acid
AURATES ▸ **aurate**
AUREATE *adj* covered with gold, gilded
AUREI ▸ **aureus**
AUREITY *n* attributes of gold
AURELIA *n* large jellyfish
AUREOLA *same as* ▸ **aureole**
AUREOLE *n* halo ▹ *vb* encircle
AURES ▸ **auris**
AUREUS, AUREI *n* gold coin of the Roman Empire
AURIC *adj* of or containing gold in the trivalent state
AURICLE *n* upper chamber of the heart
AURIFY *vb* turn into gold
AURIS, AURES *n* medical word for ear
AURIST, -S *n* former name for an audiologist
AUROCHS *n* recently extinct European wild ox
AURORA, -E, -S *n* bands of light seen in the sky
AURORAL ▸ **aurora**
AURORAS ▸ **aurora**
AUROUS *adj* of or containing gold, esp in the monovalent state
AURUM, -S *n* gold
AUSFORM *vb* temper steel
AUSPEX *same as* ▸ **augur**
AUSPICE *n* patronage or guidance
AUSTERE *adj*
AUSTRAL *adj* southern ▹ *n* former monetary unit of Argentina
AUSUBO, -S *n* tropical tree
AUTARCH *n* absolute ruler
AUTARKY *n* policy of economic self-sufficiency
AUTEUR, -S *n* director
AUTHOR, -S *n, vb*
AUTISM, -S *n*
AUTIST, -S *n* autistic person
AUTO, -ED, -ING, -S *n* automobile ▹ *vb* travel in an automobile
AUTOBUS *n* motor bus
AUTOCAR *n* motor car
AUTOCUE *n*
AUTOED ▸ **auto**
AUTOING ▸ **auto**
AUTOMAN, AUTOMEN *n* car manufacturer
AUTOMAT *n* vending machine
AUTOMEN ▸ **automan**
AUTONYM *n* writing published under the real name of an author
AUTOPEN *n* mechanical device used to produce imitation signatures
AUTOPSY *n* examination of a body to determine the cause of death
AUTOPUT *n* motorway in the former Yugoslavia
AUTOS ▸ **auto**
AUTOVAC *n* vacuum pump in a car petrol tank
AUTUMN, -S *n*
AUTUMNY *adj* like autumn
AUXESIS, AUXESES *n* increase in cell size without division
AUXETIC *n* something that promotes growth
AUXIN, -S *n* plant hormone that promotes growth
AUXINIC ▸ **auxin**
AUXINS ▸ **auxin**
AVA, -S *n* Polynesian shrub
AVAIL, -ED, -S *vb, n*
AVAILE, -S *old word for* ▸ **lower**
AVAILED ▸ **avail**
AVAILES ▸ **availe**
AVAILS ▸ **avail**
AVAL *adj* of a grandparent
AVALE, -D, -S, AVALING *old word for* ▸ **lower**
AVANT *prep* before
AVANTI *interj* forward!
AVARICE *n*
AVAS ▸ **ava**
AVAST *sentence substitute* stop! cease!
AVATAR, -S *n* appearance of a god in animal or human form
AVAUNT, -S *sentence substitute* go away! depart! ▹ *vb* go away; depart

AVE, -S *n* expression of welcome or farewell
AVEL, -S *variant of* ▸ **ovel**
AVELLAN *adj* of hazelnuts
AVELS ▸ **avel**
AVENGE, -D, -S *vb*
AVENGER ▸ **avenge**
AVENGES ▸ **avenge**
AVENIR, -S *n* future
AVENS, -ES *n* any of several temperate or Arctic rosaceous plants
AVENTRE *old word for* ▸ **thrust**
AVENUE, -S *n*
AVER, -RED, -S *vb* state to be true
AVERAGE *n, adj, vb*
AVERRED ▸ **aver**
AVERS ▸ **aver**
AVERSE *adj*
AVERT, -ED, -S *vb*
AVERTER ▸ **avert**
AVERTS ▸ **avert**
AVES ▸ **ave**
AVGAS, -ES *n* aviation fuel
AVIAN, -S *adj* of or like a bird ▹ *n* bird
AVIARY *n*
AVIATE, -D, -S *vb* pilot or fly in an aircraft
AVIATIC *adj* pertaining to aviation
AVIATOR *n*
AVID, -ER, -EST *adj*
AVIDIN, -S *n* protein found in egg white
AVIDITY *n* quality or state of being avid
AVIDLY ▸ **avid**
AVIETTE *n* aeroplane driven by human strength
AVIFORM *adj* like a bird
AVINE *adj* of birds
AVION, -S *n* aeroplane
AVIONIC > **avionics**
AVIONS ▸ **avion**
AVISE, -D, -S, AVISING *old word for* ▸ **advise**
AVISO, -S *n* boat carrying messages
AVITAL *adj* of a grandfather
AVIZE, -D, -S, AVIZING *old word for* ▸ **advise**
AVO, -S *n* Macao currency unit
AVOCADO *n*
AVOCET, -S *n* long-legged wading bird
AVODIRE *n* African tree
AVOID, -ED, -S *vb*
AVOIDER ▸ **avoid**
AVOIDS ▸ **avoid**
AVOS ▸ **avo**
AVOSET, -S *n* avocet
AVOUCH *vb* vouch for
AVOURE, -S *old word for* ▸ **avowal**
AVOW, -ING, -S *vb*
AVOWAL, -S ▸ **avow**
AVOWED *adj*
AVOWER, -S ▸ **avow**
AVOWING ▸ **avow**
AVOWRY *old word for* ▸ **avowal**
AVOWS ▸ **avow**
AVOYER, -S *n* former Swiss magistrate
AVRUGA, -S *n* herring roe
AVULSE, -D, -S *vb* take away by force
AVYZE, -D, -S, AVYZING *old word for* ▸ **advise**
AW *variant of* ▸ **all**
AWA *adv* Scots word for away
AWAIT, -ED, -S *vb*
AWAITER ▸ **await**
AWAITS ▸ **await**
AWAKE, -D, -S, AWOKE, AWOKEN *vb, adj*
AWAKEN, -S *vb* awake
AWAKES ▸ **awake**
AWAKING *n* emergence from sleep
AWARD, -ED, -S *vb, n*
AWARDEE ▸ **award**
AWARDER ▸ **award**
AWARDS ▸ **award**
AWARE, -R, -ST *adj*
AWARN, -ED, -S *vb* old form of warn
AWASH *adv, adj*
AWATCH *adv* watching
AWATO, -S *n* New Zealand caterpillar
AWAVE *adv* in waves
AWAY, -S *adv, adj, n*
AWAYDAY *n*
AWAYES *old word for* ▸ **away**
AWAYS ▸ **away**
AWDL, -S *n* traditional Welsh poem
AWE, -D, -ING, -S, AWING *n, vb*
AWEARY *old form of* ▸ **weary**
AWED ▸ **awe**
AWEE *adv* Scots word meaning for a short time
AWEEL *interj* Scots word meaning well
AWEIGH *adj* (of an anchor) no longer hooked onto the bottom
AWEING ▸ **awe**
AWELESS ▸ **awe**
AWES ▸ **awe**
AWESOME *adj*

AWETO, -S *n* New Zealand caterpillar
AWFUL *adj, adv*
AWFULLY *adv*
AWFY *adv* (Scots) awfully, extremely
AWHAPE, -D, -S *old word for* ▸ **amaze**
AWHATO, -S *n* New Zealand caterpillar
AWHEEL *adv* on wheels
AWHEELS *same as* ▸ **awheel**
AWHETO, -S *n* New Zealand caterpillar
AWHILE *adv*
AWHIRL *adv* whirling
AWING ▸ **awe**
AWK, -S *n* type of programming language

This provides a useful high-scoring outlet for what can be the awkward letters W and K.

AWKWARD *adj*
AWL, -S *n* pointed tool for piercing wood, leather, etc
AWLBIRD *n* woodpecker
AWLESS ▸ **awe**
AWLS ▸ **awl**
AWLWORT *n* type of aquatic plant
AWMOUS *Scots word for* ▸ **alms**
AWMRIE, -S *n* cupboard for church vessels
AWMRY *n* cupboard for church vessels
AWN, -S *n* bristle on certain grasses
AWNED ▸ **awn**
AWNER, -S *n* machine for removing awns
AWNIER ▸ **awny**
AWNIEST ▸ **awny**
AWNING, -S *n*
AWNLESS ▸ **awn**
AWNS ▸ **awn**
AWNY, AWNIER, AWNIEST *adj* having awns
AWOKE ▸ **awake**
AWOKEN ▸ **awake**
AWOL, -S *n* person who is absent without leave
AWORK *adv* old word meaning at work
AWRACK *adv* in wrecked condition
AWRONG *adv* old word meaning wrongly
AWRY *adj*
AWSOME *adj* old form of awesome
AX *same as* ▸ **axe**
AXAL *adj* of an axis
AXE, -D, AXING *n, vb*
AXEBIRD *n* nightjar
AXED ▸ **axe**
AXEL, -S *n* ice-skating movement
AXELIKE *adj* like an axe in form
AXELS ▸ **axel**
AXEMAN, AXEMEN *n* man who wields an axe, esp to cut down trees
AXENIC *adj* (of a biological culture) free from other microorganisms
AXES ▸ **axis**
AXIAL *adj* forming or of an axis
AXIALLY ▸ **axial**
AXIL, -S *n* angle where the stalk of a leaf joins a stem
AXILE *adj* of, relating to, or attached to the axis
AXILLA, -E, -S *n* area under a bird's wing
AXILLAR *same as* ▸ **axillary**
AXILLAS ▸ **axilla**
AXILS ▸ **axil**
AXING ▸ **axe**
AXINITE *n* crystalline substance
AXIOM, -S *n*
AXION, -S *n* type of hypothetical elementary particle
AXIS, AXES, -ES *n*
AXISED *adj* having an axis
AXISES ▸ **axis**
AXITE, -S *n* type of gunpowder
AXLE, -S *n*
AXLED *adj* having an axle
AXLES ▸ **axle**
AXLIKE ▸ **ax**
AXMAN, AXMEN *same as* ▸ **axeman**
AXOID, -S *n* type of curve
AXOLOTL *n* aquatic salamander of central America
AXON, -S *n* threadlike extension of a nerve cell
AXONAL ▸ **axon**
AXONE, -S *same as* ▸ **axon**
AXONEME *n* part of a cell consisting of proteins
AXONES ▸ **axone**

AXONIC ▸ **axon**
AXONS ▸ **axon**
AXSEED, -S *n* crown vetch
AY, -S *adv* ever ▹ *n* expression of agreement
AYAH, -S *n* Indian or Malay maidservant or nursemaid in former British Empire
AYAYA, -S *n* type of Inuit singing
AYE, -S *n, adv*
AYELP *adv* yelping
AYES ▸ **aye**
AYGRE *old word for* ▸ **eager**
AYIN, -S *n* 16th letter in the Hebrew alphabet
AYONT *adv* beyond
AYRE, -S *old word for* ▸ **air**
AYRIE, -S *old word for* ▸ **eyrie**
AYS ▸ **ay**
AYU, -S *n* small Japanese fish

This comes up quite often, being an extension of both **ay** and **yu**, showing how important it is to know those little 'hook' words.

AYWORD, -S *n* old word meaning byword
AZALEA, -S *n*
AZAN, -S *n* call to prayer
AZERTY *n* European version of keyboard
AZIDE, -S *n* type of chemical compound
AZIDO *adj* containing an azide
AZIMUTH *n* arc of the sky between the zenith and the horizon
AZINE, -S *n* organic compound
AZIONE, -S *n* musical drama
AZLON, -S *n* fibre made from protein
AZO *adj* of the divalent group -N:N-

Azo is a chemical term you will want to play often, but it does not take an S. It takes an N to form **azon**.

AZOIC *adj* without life
AZOLE, -S *n* organic compound
AZOLLA, -S *n* tropical water fern
AZON, -S *n* type of drawing paper
AZONAL *adj* not divided into zones
AZONIC *adj* not confined to a zone
AZONS ▸ **azon**
AZOTE, -S *an obsolete name for* > **nitrogen**
AZOTED *adj* old word meaning combined with nitrogen
AZOTES ▸ **azote**
AZOTH, -S *n* panacea postulated by Paracelsus
AZOTIC *adj* of, containing, or concerned with nitrogen
AZOTISE *same as* ▸ **azotize**
AZOTIZE *vb* combine or treat with nitrogen or a nitrogen compound
AZOTOUS *adj* containing nitrogen
AZUKI, -S *same as* ▸ **adzuki**
AZULEJO *n* Spanish porcelain tile

An **azulejo** is a kind of brightly coloured tile, beautiful in its combination of the J and Z.

AZURE, -S *n, adj*
AZUREAN *adj* azure
AZURES ▸ **azure**
AZURIES ▸ **azury**
AZURINE *n* blue dye
AZURITE *n* azure-blue mineral associated with copper deposits
AZURN *old word for* ▸ **azure**
AZURY, AZURIES *adj* bluish ▹ *n* bluish colour
AZYGIES ▸ **azygy**
AZYGOS *n* biological structure not in a pair
AZYGOUS *adj* developing or occurring singly
AZYGY, AZYGIES *n* state of not being joined in a pair
AZYM, -S *n* unleavened bread
AZYME, -S *same as* ▸ **azym**
AZYMITE *n* member of a church using unleavened bread in the Eucharist
AZYMOUS *adj* unleavened
AZYMS ▸ **azym**

Bb

BA, -S *n* symbol for the soul in Ancient Egyptian religion
BAA, -ED, -S *vb* make the characteristic bleating sound of a sheep ▷ *n* cry made by a sheep
BAAING, -S ▶ **baa**
BAAL, -IM, -S *n* any false god or idol
BAALISM ▶ **baal**
BAALS ▶ **baal**
BAAS ▶ **baa**
BABA, -S *n* small cake of leavened dough
BABACO, -S *n* greenish-yellow egg-shaped fruit
BABACU, -S *n* type of Brazilian palm tree
BABALAS *adj* South African word for drunk
BABAS ▶ **baba**
BABASSU *n* Brazilian palm tree with hard edible nuts
BABBITT *vb* line (a bearing) or face (a surface) with a similar soft alloy
BABBLE, -D, -S *vb, n*
BABBLER *n* person who babbles
BABBLES ▶ **babble**
BABBLY ▶ **babble**
BABE, -S *n*
BABEL, -S *n* confused mixture of noises or voices
BABES ▶ **babe**
BABESIA *n* parasite causing infection in cattle
BABICHE *n* thongs or lacings of rawhide
BABIED ▶ **baby**
BABIER ▶ **baby**
BABIES ▶ **baby**
BABIEST ▶ **baby**
BABKA, -S *n* cake
BABLAH, -S *n* fruit rind used as a dye
BABOO, -S *same as* ▶ **babu**
BABOOL, -S *n* type of acacia
BABOON, -S *n*
BABOOS ▶ **baboo**
BABOOSH *same as* > **babouche**
BABU, -S *n* title or form of address used in India
BABUCHE *same as* > **babouche**
BABUDOM ▶ **babu**
BABUISM ▶ **babu**
BABUL, -S *n* N African and Indian tree with small yellow flowers
BABUS ▶ **babu**
BABY, BABIED, BABIER, BABIES, BABIEST, -ING *n, adj, vb*
BABYISH ▶ **baby**
BABYSIT, BABYSAT *vb*
BAC, -S *n* baccalaureate
BACALAO *n* dried salt cod
BACCA, -E, -S *n* berry
BACCALA *same as* ▶ **bacalao**
BACCARA *same as* > **baccarat**
BACCARE *same as* ▶ **backare**
BACCAS ▶ **bacca**
BACCATE *adj* like a berry in form, texture, etc
BACCHIC *adj* riotously jovial
BACCHII > **bacchius**
BACCIES ▶ **baccy**
BACCO, -ES, -S *n* tobacco
BACCY, BACCIES *n* tobacco
BACH, -ED, -ES, -ING, -S *same as* ▶ **batch**
BACHA, -S *n* Indian English word for a young child
BACHATA *n* type of dance music originating in the Dominican Republic

BACHCHA *n* Indian English word for a young child
BACHED ▶ **bach**
BACHES ▶ **bach**
BACHING ▶ **bach**
BACHS ▶ **bach**
BACILLI > **bacillus**
BACK, -S *n, vb, adj, adv*
BACKARE *interj* instruction to keep one's distance; back off
BACKBAR *n* area behind a bar where bottles are stored
BACKBIT > **backbite**
BACKED *adj* having a back or backing
BACKER, -S *n*
BACKET, -S *n* shallow box
BACKFAT *n* layer of fat in animals between the skin and muscle
BACKFIT *vb* overhaul a nuclear power plant
BACKHOE *n* digger ▷ *vb* dig with a backhoe
BACKIE, -S *n* ride on the back of someone's bicycle
BACKING *n* support
BACKLIT *adj* illuminated from behind
BACKLOG *n*
BACKLOT *n* area outside a film or television studio used for outdoor filming
BACKOUT *n* instance of withdrawing (from an agreement, etc)
BACKS ▶ **back**
BACKSAW *n* small handsaw
BACKSET *n* reversal ▷ *vb* attack from the rear
BACKSEY *n* sirloin
BACKUP, -S *n* support or reinforcement
BACLAVA *same as* ▶ **baklava**
BACON, -S *n*
BACONER *n* pig that weighs between 83 and 101 kg, from which bacon is cut
BACONS ▶ **bacon**
BACS ▶ **bac**
BACULUM, BACULA *n* bony support in the penis of certain mammals
BAD, -DER, -DEST, -S *adj, n, adv*
BADDIE, -S *n*
BADDISH ▶ **bad**
BADDY *same as* ▶ **baddie**
BADE ▶ **bid**
BADGE, -D, -S, BADGING *n, vb*
BADGER, -S *n, vb*
BADGES ▶ **badge**
BADGING ▶ **badge**
BADIOUS *adj* chestnut; brownish-red
BADLAND > **badlands**
BADLY *adv* poorly
BADMAN, BADMEN *n* hired gunman, outlaw, or criminal
BADMASH *n* evil-doer ▷ *adj* naughty or bad
BADMEN ▶ **badman**
BADNESS ▶ **bad**
BADS ▶ **bad**
BADWARE *n* software designed to harm a computer system
BAE, -S *n* sweetheart
BAEL, -S *n* type of spiny Indian tree
BAES ▶ **bae**
BAETYL, -S *n* magical meteoric stone
BAFF, -ED, -ING, -S *vb* strike the ground with a golf club
BAFFIES *pl n* slippers
BAFFING ▶ **baff**
BAFFLE, -D, -S *vb, n*
BAFFLER ▶ **baffle**
BAFFLES ▶ **baffle**
BAFFS ▶ **baff**
BAFFY *n* obsolete golf club
BAFT, -S *n* coarse fabric
BAG, -GED, -S *n, vb*
BAGARRE *n* brawl
BAGASS *same as* ▶ **bagasse**
BAGASSE *n* pulp of sugar cane or similar plants
BAGEL, -ED, -S *n* hard ring-shaped bread roll ▷ *vb* win a tennis set by six games to love
BAGFUL, -S, BAGSFUL *n*
BAGGAGE *n*
BAGGED ▶ **bag**
BAGGER, -S *n* person who packs groceries
BAGGIE, -S *n* plastic bag
BAGGIER ▶ **baggy**
BAGGIES ▶ **baggie**
BAGGILY ▶ **baggy**
BAGGING *n* act of putting in a bag
BAGGIT, -S *n* salmon which has not yet spawned
BAGGY, BAGGIER *adj*
BAGH, -S *n* (in India and Pakistan) a garden

BAGIE, -S *n* turnip
BAGLESS *adj* (esp of a vacuum cleaner) not containing a bag
BAGLIKE ▶ **bag**
BAGMAN, BAGMEN *n* travelling salesman
BAGNIO, -S *n* bathing-house
BAGPIPE *vb*
BAGS ▶ **bag**
BAGSFUL ▶ **bagful**
BAGUET, -S *same as* > **baguette**
BAGUIO, -S *n* hurricane
BAGWASH *n* laundry that washes clothes without drying or pressing them
BAGWIG, -S *n* 18th-century wig with hair pushed back into a bag
BAGWORM *n* type of moth
BAH *interj* expression of contempt or disgust
BAHADA, -S *same as* ▶ **bajada**
BAHADUR *n* title formerly conferred by the British on distinguished Indians
BAHT, -S *n* standard monetary unit of Thailand, divided into 100 satang
BAHU, -S *n* (in India) daughter-in-law
BAHUT, -S *n* decorative cabinet
BAIDAR, -S *same as* > **baidarka**
BAIL, -ED, -ING, -S *n, vb*
BAILEE, -S *n* person to whom the possession of goods is transferred under a bailment
BAILER, -S ▶ **bail**
BAILEY, -S *n* outermost wall or court of a castle
BAILIE, -S *n* (in Scotland) a municipal magistrate
BAILIFF *n*
BAILING ▶ **bail**
BAILLI, -S *same as* ▶ **bailie**
BAILLIE *same as* ▶ **bailie**
BAILLIS ▶ **bailli**
BAILOR, -S *n* owner of goods entrusted to another under a bailment
BAILOUT *n* instance of helping (a person, organization, etc) out of a predicament
BAILS ▶ **bail**
BAININ, -S *n* Irish collarless jacket made of white wool
BAINITE *n* mixture of iron and iron carbide found in incompletely hardened steels
BAIRN, -S *n* child
BAIRNLY ▶ **bairn**
BAIRNS ▶ **bairn**
BAISA, -S *n* small unit of currency in Oman
BAIT, -ED, -S *n, vb*
BAITER, -S ▶ **bait**
BAITH *adj* both
BAITING *n*
BAITS ▶ **bait**
BAIZA, -S *n* Omani unit of currency
BAIZE, -D, -S, BAIZING *n, vb*
BAJADA, -S *n* sloping surface formed from rock deposits
BAJAN, -S *n* freshman at Aberdeen University
BAJRA, -S *n* Indian millet
BAJREE, -S *variant of* ▶ **bajra**
BAJRI, -S *variant of* ▶ **bajra**
BAJU, -S *n* Malay jacket
BAKE, -D, -N, -S *vb, n*
BAKEOFF *n*
BAKER, -S *n*
BAKERY *n*
BAKES ▶ **bake**
BAKGAT *adj* fine, excellent, marvellous
BAKING, -S *n* process of cooking bread, cakes, etc ▷ *adj* (esp of weather) very hot and dry
BAKKIE, -S *n* small truck
BAKLAVA *n* rich pastry of Middle Eastern origin
BAKLAWA *same as* ▶ **baklava**
BAL, -S *n* balmoral
BALADIN *n* dancer
BALAFON *n* type of W African xylophone
BALANCE *n, vb*
BALAS, -ES *n* red variety of spinel, used as a gemstone
BALATA, -S *n* tropical American tree yielding a latex-like sap
BALBOA, -S *n* standard currency unit of Panama
BALCONY *n*
BALD, -ED, -ER, -EST, -S *adj, vb*
BALDIE, -S *same as* ▶ **baldy**
BALDIER ▶ **baldy**

BALDIES ▸ **baldie**
BALDING *adj* becoming bald
BALDISH ▸ **bald**
BALDLY ▸ **bald**
BALDRIC *n* wide silk sash or leather belt worn across the body
BALDS ▸ **bald**
BALDY, BALDIER *adj* bald ▹ *n* bald person
BALE, -D, -S *same as* ▸ **bail**
BALEEN, -S *n* whalebone
BALEFUL *adj*
BALER, -S ▸ **bail**
BALES ▸ **bale**
BALING, -S *n* act of baling
BALISE, -S *n* electronic beacon used on a railway
BALISTA *same as* > **ballista**
BALK, -ED, -S *vb, n*
BALKER, -S ▸ **balk**
BALKIER ▸ **balky**
BALKILY ▸ **balky**
BALKING ▸ **balk**
BALKS ▸ **balk**
BALKY, BALKIER *adj* inclined to stop abruptly and unexpectedly
BALL, -ED *n, vb*
BALLAD, -S *n, vb*
BALLADE *n* verse form
BALLADS ▸ **ballad**
BALLAN, -S *n* species of fish
BALLANT *vb* write a ballad
BALLAST *n, vb*
BALLAT, -S *vb* write a ballad
BALLBOY *n*
BALLED ▸ **ball**
BALLER, -S *n* ball-game player
BALLET, -S *n, vb*
BALLIER ▸ **bally**
BALLIES ▸ **bally**
BALLING *n* formation of a ball
BALLIUM *same as* ▸ **bailey**
BALLON, -S *n* light, graceful quality
BALLOON *n, vb*
BALLOT, -S *n, vb*
BALLOW, -S *n* heavy club
BALLS *n* plural of ball
BALLUTE *n* inflatable balloon parachute
BALLY, BALLIER, BALLIES *adj* euphemism for bloody ▹ *n* exaggerated fuss
BALM, -ED, -ING, -S *n, vb*
BALMIER ▸ **balmy**
BALMILY ▸ **balmy**
BALMING ▸ **balm**
BALMS ▸ **balm**
BALMY, BALMIER *adj* (of weather) mild and pleasant
BALNEAL *adj* of or relating to baths or bathing
BALONEY *n*
BALOO, -S *n* bear
BALS ▸ **bal**
BALSA, -S *n*
BALSAM, -S *n, vb*
BALSAMY *adj* sweet-smelling
BALSAS ▸ **balsa**
BALTI, -S *n* spicy Indian dish served in a metal dish
BALTIC *adj* very cold
BALTIS ▸ **balti**
BALU, -S *same as* ▸ **baloo**
BALUN, -S *n* electrical device
BALUS ▸ **balu**
BAM, -MED, -MING, -S *vb* cheat
BAMBI, -S *n* born-again middle-aged biker
BAMBINO, BAMBINI *n* young child, esp an Italian one
BAMBIS ▸ **bambi**
BAMBOO, -S *n*
BAMMED ▸ **bam**
BAMMER, -S ▸ **bam**
BAMMING ▸ **bam**
BAMPOT, -S *n* fool
BAMS ▸ **bam**
BAN, -I, -NED *vb* prohibit or forbid officially ▹ *n* unit of currency in Romania and Moldova
BANAK, -S *n* type of Central American tree
BANAL, -ER *adj*
BANALLY ▸ **banal**
BANANA *n*
BANANAS *adj* crazy
BANC, -S *n* as in **in banc** sitting as a full court
BANCO, -S *n* call made in gambling games
BANCS ▸ **banc**
BAND, -ED, -S *n, vb*
BANDA, -S *n* African thatched hut
BANDAGE *n, vb*
BANDAID *adj* (of a solution or remedy) temporary
BANDANA *same as* > **bandanna**

BANDAR, -S *n* species of monkey
BANDARI *n* Indian English word for female monkey
BANDARS ▸ **bandar**
BANDAS ▸ **banda**
BANDBOX *n* lightweight usually cylindrical box for hats
BANDEAU *n* narrow ribbon worn round the head
BANDED ▸ **band**
BANDER, -S ▸ **band**
BANDH, -S *n* (in India) a general strike
BANDIED ▸ **bandy**
BANDIER ▸ **bandy**
BANDIES ▸ **bandy**
BANDING *n* practice of grouping schoolchildren according to ability
BANDIT, -S *n*
BANDITO *n* Mexican bandit
BANDITS ▸ **bandit**
BANDOG, -S *n* ferocious dog
BANDOOK *same as* ▸ **bundook**
BANDORA *same as* ▸ **bandore**
BANDORE *n* 16th-century musical instrument
BANDROL *same as* > **banderole**
BANDS ▸ **band**
BANDSAW *n* power saw with continuous blade ▹ *vb* cut with a bandsaw
BANDURA *n* type of lute
BANDY, BANDIED, BANDIER, BANDIES *adj, vb*
BANE, -D, -S, BANING *n* person or thing that causes misery or distress ▹ *vb* cause harm or distress to (someone)
BANEFUL *adj* destructive, poisonous, or fatal
BANES ▸ **bane**
BANG, -ED, -ING, -S *vb*
BANGER, -S *n*
BANGING ▸ **bang**
BANGKOK *n* type of straw hat
BANGLE, -S *n*
BANGLED ▸ **bangle**
BANGS ▸ **bang**
BANI ▸ **ban**
BANIA, -S *same as* ▸ **banyan**
BANIAN, -S *same as* ▸ **banyan**
BANIAS ▸ **bania**
BANING ▸ **bane**
BANISH *vb*
BANJAX *vb* ruin; destroy

Meaning to ruin or destroy, this is a great word to remember, with its high-scoring combination of J and X.

BANJO, -ES, -S *n* guitar-like musical instrument with a circular body
BANK, -ED, -S *n, vb*
BANKER, -S *n* manager or owner of a bank
BANKET, -S *n* gold-bearing conglomerate found in South Africa
BANKING ▸ **bank**
BANKIT, -S *same as* > **banquette**
BANKS ▸ **bank**
BANKSIA *n* Australian evergreen tree or shrub
BANNED ▸ **ban**
BANNER, -S *n, vb, adj*
BANNET, -S *n* bonnet
BANNING *n* act of banning
BANNOCK *n* round flat cake made from oatmeal or barley
BANNS *pl n* public declaration, esp in a church, of an intended marriage
BANOFFI *same as* > **banoffee**
BANQUET *n, vb*
BANS *same as* ▸ **banns**
BANSELA *same as* ▸ **bonsela**
BANSHEE *n*
BANSHIE *same as* ▸ **banshee**
BANT, -ED, -S *n* string ▹ *vb* tie with string
BANTAM, -S *n*
BANTED ▸ **bant**
BANTENG *n* wild ox
BANTER, -S *vb, n*
BANTIES ▸ **banty**
BANTING ▸ **bant**
BANTS ▸ **bant**
BANTY, BANTIES *n* bantam
BANYA, -S *n* traditional Russian steam bath
BANYAN, -S *n* Indian tree
BANYAS ▸ **banya**
BANZAI, -S *interj* patriotic cheer, battle cry, or salutation
BAO, -S *n* steamed dumpling
BAOBAB, -S *n* African tree with a thick trunk and angular branches

BAOS ▸ **bao**
BAP, -S *n*
BAPTISE *same as* ▸ **baptize**
BAPTISM *n*
BAPTIST *n*
BAPTIZE *vb*
BAPU, -S *n* spiritual father
BAR, -RED, -S *n, vb*
BARACAN *same as* > **barracan**
BARAZA, -S *n* place where public meetings are held
BARB, -ED, -ING, -S *n, vb*
BARBAL *adj* of a beard
BARBATE *adj* having tufts of long hairs
BARBE, -S *n* Waldensian missionary
BARBED ▸ **barb**
BARBEL, -S *n* long thin growth that hangs from the jaws of certain fishes, such as the carp
BARBELL *n* long metal rod to which heavy discs are attached at each end for weightlifting
BARBELS ▸ **barbel**
BARBER, -S *n, vb*
BARBES ▸ **barbe**
BARBET, -S *n* type of small tropical bird
BARBIE, -S *short for* > **barbecue**
BARBING ▸ **barb**
BARBOLA *n* creation of small models of flowers, etc from plastic paste
BARBOT, -S *same as* ▸ **burbot**
BARBS ▸ **barb**
BARBULE *n* very small barb
BARBUT, -S *n* open-faced helmet
BARBY *short for* > **barbecue**
BARCA, -S *n* boat
BARCHAN *n* crescent-shaped shifting sand dune
BARCODE *n*
BARD, -ING, -S *n, vb*
BARDE, -D, -S *same as* ▸ **bard**
BARDIC ▸ **bard**
BARDIE, -S *n* type of Australian grub
BARDIER ▸ **bardy**
BARDIES ▸ **bardie**
BARDING ▸ **bard**
BARDISM ▸ **bard**
BARDO, -S *n* (in Tibetan Buddhism) the state of the soul between its death and its rebirth
BARDS ▸ **bard**
BARDY, BARDIER ▸ **bard**
BARE, -D, -R, -S, -ST, BARING *adj, vb*
BAREFIT *Scots word for* > **barefoot**
BAREGE, -S *n* light silky gauze fabric made of wool ▷ *adj* made of such a fabric
BARELY *adv*
BARER ▸ **bare**
BARES ▸ **bare**
BAREST ▸ **bare**
BARF, -ED, -ING, -S *vb* vomit ▷ *n* act of vomiting
BARFI, -S *n* type of Indian dessert
BARFING ▸ **barf**
BARFIS ▸ **barfi**
BARFLY *n* person who frequents bars
BARFS ▸ **barf**
BARFUL *adj* presenting difficulties
BARGAIN *n, vb*
BARGE, -D, -S, BARGING *n, vb*
BARGEE, -S *n* person in charge of a barge
BARGES ▸ **barge**
BARGEST *same as* > **barghest**
BARGING ▸ **barge**
BARGOON *Canadian word for* ▸ **bargain**
BARHOP, -S *vb* visit several bars in succession
BARIC *adj* of or containing barium
BARILLA *n* impure mixture of sodium carbonate and sodium sulphate
BARING ▸ **bare**
BARISH *adj* quite thinly covered
BARISTA *n* person who makes and sells coffee in a coffee bar
BARITE, -S *n* colourless or white mineral
BARIUM, -S *n* soft white metallic element
BARK, -ED, -ING, -S *vb*
BARKAN, -S *same as* ▸ **barchan**
BARKED ▸ **bark**
BARKEEP *n* barkeeper
BARKEN, -S *vb* become dry with a bark-like outer layer
BARKER, -S *n* person at a fairground who calls

loudly to passers-by in order to attract customers
BARKHAN *same as* ▸ **barchan**
BARKIER ▸ **barky**
BARKING ▸ **bark**
BARKS ▸ **bark**
BARKY, BARKIER *adj* having the texture or appearance of bark
BARLESS ▸ **bar**
BARLEY, -S *n*
BARLOW, -S *n* type of strong knife
BARM, -S *n* yeasty froth on fermenting malt liquors
BARMAID *n*
BARMAN, BARMEN *same as* > **bartender**
BARMIE *same as* ▸ **barmy**
BARMIER ▸ **barmy**
BARMILY ▸ **barmy**
BARMKIN *n* protective wall around castle
BARMPOT *n* foolish person
BARMS ▸ **barm**
BARMY, BARMIER *adj*
BARN, -ED, -ING, -S *n, vb*
BARNET, -S *n* hair
BARNEY, -S *n* noisy fight or argument ▹ *vb* argue or quarrel
BARNIER ▸ **barny**
BARNING ▸ **barn**
BARNS ▸ **barn**
BARNY, BARNIER *adj* reminiscent of a barn
BAROCCO *same as* ▸ **baroque**
BAROCK, -S *same as* ▸ **baroque**
BAROLO, -S *n* red Italian wine
BARON, -S *n*
BARONET *n* man who holds the lowest hereditary British title
BARONG, -S *n* broad-bladed cleaver-like knife used in the Philippines
BARONNE *n* baroness
BARONS ▸ **baron**
BARONY *n* domain or rank of a baron
BAROQUE *n* style of art, architecture, or music ▹ *adj* ornate in style
BARP, -S *n* hillock or bank of stones
BARQUE, -S *n* sailing ship, esp one with three masts
BARRA, -S *n* barramundi
BARRACE *n* record of teams entering a sports contest
BARRACK *vb*
BARRAGE *n, vb*
BARRAS ▸ **barra**
BARRAT, -S *n* fraudulent dealings ▹ *vb* quarrel
BARRE, -ED, -S *n* rail at hip height used for ballet practice ▹ *vb* execute guitar chords by laying the index finger over some or all of the strings ▹ *adv* by using the barre
BARRED ▸ **bar**
BARREED ▸ **barre**
BARREL, -S *n, vb*
BARREN *adj*
BARRENS *pl n* (in North America) a stretch of land that is sparsely vegetated
BARRES ▸ **barre**
BARRET, -S *n* small flat cap resembling a biretta
BARRICO *n* small container for liquids
BARRIE *adj* dialect word for excellent
BARRIER *n, vb*
BARRIES ▸ **barry**
BARRING ▸ **bar**
BARRIO, -S *n* Spanish-speaking quarter in a town or city, esp in the US
BARRO *adj* embarrassing
BARROOM *n*
BARROW, -S *n*
BARRY, BARRIES *n* mistake or blunder ▹ *adj* dialect word for excellent
BARS ▸ **bar**
BARTEND *vb*
BARTER, -S *vb, n*
BARTON, -S *n* farmyard
BARTSIA *n* type of semiparasitic plant
BARWARE *n* glasses, etc used in a bar
BARWOOD *n* red wood from a small African tree
BARYE, -S *n* unit of pressure
BARYON, -S *n* elementary particle that has a mass greater than or equal to that of the proton
BARYTA, -S *same as* ▸ **barite**
BARYTE, -S *same as* ▸ **barite**
BARYTIC ▸ **baryta**

BARYTON *n* bass viol with sympathetic strings as well as its six main strings
BAS ▸ **ba**
BASAL *adj* of, at, or constituting a base
BASALLY ▸ **basal**
BASALT, -S *n*
BASAN, -S *n* sheepskin tanned in bark
BASANT, -S *n* Pakistani spring festival
BASCULE *n* drawbridge that operates by a counterbalanced weight
BASE, -D, -R, -ST, BASING *n, vb, adj*
BASEEJ *pl n* Iranian volunteer militia
BASELY ▸ **base**
BASEMAN, BASEMEN *n* fielder positioned near a base
BASEN *Spenserian spelling of* ▸ **basin**
BASENJI *n* small breed of dog
BASER ▸ **base**
BASES ▸ **basis**
BASEST ▸ **base**
BASH, -ED, -ES *vb, n*
BASHAW, -S *n* important or pompous person
BASHED ▸ **bash**
BASHER, -S ▸ **bash**
BASHES ▸ **bash**
BASHFUL *adj*
BASHING ▸ **bash**
BASHLIK *n* Caucasian hood
BASHLYK *same as* ▸ **bashlik**
BASHO *n* grand tournament in sumo wrestling
BASHTAG *n* (on Twitter) hashtag used for abusive comments
BASIC, -S *adj, n*
BASIDIA > **basidium**
BASIFY *vb* make basic
BASIJ *same as* ▸ **baseej**
BASIL, -S *n*
BASILAR *adj* of or situated at a base
BASILIC > **basilica**
BASILS ▸ **basil**
BASIN, -S *n*
BASINAL ▸ **basin**
BASINED ▸ **basin**
BASINET *n* close-fitting medieval helmet of light steel usually with a visor
BASING ▸ **base**
BASINS ▸ **basin**
BASION, -S *n* (in anatomy) midpoint on the forward border of the foramen magnum
BASIS, BASES *n*
BASK, -ED, -ING, -S *vb*
BASKET, -S *n*
BASKING ▸ **bask**
BASKS ▸ **bask**
BASMATI *n*
BASNET, -S *same as* ▸ **basinet**
BASOCHE *n* society of medieval French lawyers who performed comic plays
BASON, -S *same as* ▸ **basin**
BASQUE, -D, -S *n* tight-fitting bodice
BASS, -ED, -ES, -EST, -ING *n, adj, vb*
BASSE *same as* ▸ **bass**
BASSED ▸ **bass**
BASSER, -S *n* someone who plays bass guitar or double bass
BASSES ▸ **bass**
BASSEST ▸ **bass**
BASSET, -S *n* breed of hound ▹ *vb* (of rock) protrude through earth's surface
BASSETT *same as* ▸ **basset**
BASSI ▸ **basso**
BASSIER ▸ **bassy**
BASSING ▸ **bass**
BASSIST *n* player of a double bass, esp in a jazz band
BASSLY ▸ **bass**
BASSO, BASSI, -S *n* singer with a bass voice
BASSOON *n*
BASSOS ▸ **basso**
BASSY, BASSIER *adj* manifesting strong bass tones
BAST, -S *n* fibrous material used for making rope, matting, etc
BASTA *interj* enough; stop
BASTE, -D, -S *vb* moisten (meat) during cooking with hot fat
BASTER, -S ▸ **baste**
BASTES ▸ **baste**
BASTI, -S *n* (in India) a slum inhabited by poor people
BASTIDE *n* small isolated house in France
BASTILE *same as* > **bastille**
BASTING *n* loose temporary stitches

BASTION *n*
BASTIS ▸ **basti**
BASTLE, -S *n* fortified house
BASTO, -S *n* ace of clubs in certain card games
BASTS ▸ **bast**
BASUCO, -S *n* illegal cocaine-based drug
BAT, -S, -TED *n, vb*
BATABLE ▸ **bat**
BATARD, -S *n* canoe made of birchbark
BATATA, -S *n* sweet potato
BATAVIA *n* variety of lettuce with smooth pale green leaves
BATBOY, -S *n* boy who works at baseball games
BATCH, -ED, -ES *n, vb*
BATCHER ▸ **batch**
BATCHES ▸ **batch**
BATE, -D, -S, BATING *vb* (of hawks) to jump violently from a perch or the falconer's fist
BATEAU, -X *n* light flat-bottomed boat used on rivers in Canada and the northern US
BATED ▸ **bate**
BATES ▸ **bate**
BATFISH *n* type of angler fish with a flattened scaleless body
BATFOWL *vb* catch birds by temporarily blinding them with light
BATGIRL *n* girl who works at baseball games
BATH, -S *n, vb*
BATHE, -D, -S *vb*
BATHER ▸ **bathe**
BATHERS *pl n* swimming costume
BATHES ▸ **bathe**
BATHING *n* act of bathing
BATHMAT *n*
BATHMIC > **bathmism**
BATHOS *n* sudden change from a serious subject to a trivial one
BATHS ▸ **bath**
BATHTUB *n*
BATHYAL *adj* relating to an ocean depth of between 200 and 2000 metres
BATIK, -ED, -S *n* process of printing fabric using wax to cover areas not to be dyed ▹ *vb* treat material with this process
BATING ▸ **bate**
BATISTE *n* fine plain-weave cotton fabric
BATLER, -S *n* flat piece of wood for beating clothes, etc before washing
BATLET, -S *same as* ▸ **batler**
BATLIKE ▸ **bat**
BATMAN, BATMEN *n* male servant in the armed forces
BATON, -ED, -S *n, vb*
BATOON, -S *same as* ▸ **baton**
BATS ▸ **bat**
BATSMAN, BATSMEN *n*
BATT, -S *same as* ▸ **bat**
BATTA, -S *n* soldier's allowance
BATTEAU *same as* ▸ **bateau**
BATTED ▸ **bat**
BATTEL, -S *vb* make fertile
BATTEN, -S *n, vb*
BATTER, -S *vb, n*
BATTERO *n* heavy club
BATTERS ▸ **batter**
BATTERY *n, adj*
BATTIER ▸ **batty**
BATTIES ▸ **batty**
BATTIK, -S *same as* ▸ **batik**
BATTILL *vb* fatten an animal
BATTILY *adv* in an eccentric or crazy manner
BATTING *n* act of hitting with a bat
BATTLE, -D, -S *n, vb*
BATTLER ▸ **battle**
BATTLES ▸ **battle**
BATTS ▸ **batt**
BATTU *adj* (in ballet) involving a beating movement
BATTUE, -S *n* beating of woodland or cover to force game to flee in the direction of hunters
BATTUTA *n* (in music) a beat
BATTUTO *n* (in Italian cookery) selection of chopped herbs
BATTY, BATTIER, BATTIES *adj, n*
BATWING *adj* shaped like the wings of a bat, as a black tie, collar, etc
BAUBEE, -S *same as* ▸ **bawbee**
BAUBLE, -S *n*

BAUCHLE *vb* shuffle along
BAUD, -S *n* unit used to measure the speed of transmission of electronic data
BAUDRIC *same as* ▸ **baldric**
BAUDS ▸ **baud**
BAUERA, -S *n* small evergreen Australian shrub
BAUK, -ED, -ING, -S *same as* ▸ **balk**
BAULK, -ED, -S *same as* ▸ **balk**
BAULKER ▸ **baulk**
BAULKS ▸ **baulk**
BAULKY *same as* ▸ **balky**
BAUR, -S *n* humorous anecdote; joke
BAUSOND *adj* (of animal) dappled with white spots
BAUXITE *n*
BAVIN, -ED, -S *n* bundle of brushwood or firewood ▹ *vb* bind (brushwood or firewood) into bavins
BAWBEE, -S *n* former Scottish silver coin
BAWBLE, -S *same as* ▸ **bauble**
BAWCOCK *n* fine fellow
BAWDKIN *same as* > **baldachin**
BAWDRIC *n* heavy belt to support sword
BAWK, -S *n* type of Atlantic seabird
BAWL, -ED, -S *vb, n*
BAWLER, -S ▸ **bawl**
BAWLEY, -S *n* small fishing boat
BAWLING ▸ **bawl**
BAWLS ▸ **bawl**
BAWN, -S *n* fortified enclosure
BAWNEEN *same as* ▸ **bainin**
BAWNS ▸ **bawn**
BAWR, -S *same as* ▸ **baur**
BAWSUNT *adj* black and white in colour
BAWTIE, -S *n* Scots word for a dog
BAWTY *same as* ▸ **bawtie**
BAXTER, -S *old variant of* ▸ **baker**
BAY, -ED, -ER, -EST, -ING, -S *n* wide semicircular indentation of a shoreline ▹ *vb* howl in deep tones ▹ *adj* (esp of horses) of a reddish brown colour
BAYAMO, -S *n* Cuban strong wind
BAYARD, -S *n* bay horse
BAYE, -S *vb* bathe
BAYED ▸ **bay**
BAYER ▸ **bay**
BAYES ▸ **baye**
BAYEST ▸ **bay**
BAYING ▸ **bay**
BAYLE, -S *n* barrier
BAYMAN, BAYMEN *n* fisherman
BAYONET *n, vb*
BAYOU, -S *n* (in the southern US) a sluggish marshy tributary of a lake or river
BAYS ▸ **bay**
BAYSIDE *n* shore of a bay
BAYT, -ED, -ING, -S *same as* ▸ **bate**
BAYWOOD *n* light soft wood of a tropical American mahogany tree
BAYYAN, -S *n* Islamic declaration
BAZAAR, -S *n* sale in aid of charity
BAZAR, -S *same as* ▸ **bazaar**
BAZAZZ *same as* ▸ **pizzazz**
BAZOO, -S *a US slang word for* ▸ **mouth**
BAZOOKA *n*
BAZOOS ▸ **bazoo**
BAZOUKI *same as* > **bouzouki**
BAZZ, -ED, -ES, -ING *vb* throw (an object)
BAZZAZZ *same as* ▸ **pizzazz**
BAZZED ▸ **bazz**
BAZZES ▸ **bazz**
BAZZING ▸ **bazz**
BE *vb*
BEACH, -ED, -ES *n, vb*
BEACHY *adj* with gentle sandy slopes
BEACON, -S *n, vb*
BEAD, -ED, -S *n, vb*
BEADER, -S *n* person making things with beads
BEADIER ▸ **beady**
BEADILY ▸ **beady**
BEADING *n* strip of moulding used for edging furniture
BEADLE, -S *n* (formerly) a minor parish official who acted as an usher
BEADMAN, BEADMEN *same as* > **beadsman**
BEADS ▸ **bead**

BEADY, BEADIER *adj* small, round, and glittering
BEAGLE, -D, -S *n, vb*
BEAGLER *n* person who hunts with beagles
BEAGLES ▶ **beagle**
BEAK, -S *n*
BEAKED ▶ **beak**
BEAKER, -S *n*
BEAKIER ▶ **beaky**
BEAKS ▶ **beak**
BEAKY, BEAKIER ▶ **beak**
BEAL, -S *n* infected sore
BEALING *n* infected sore
BEALS ▶ **beal**
BEAM, -ED, -S *n, vb*
BEAMER, -S *n* full-pitched ball bowled at the batsman's head
BEAMIER ▶ **beamy**
BEAMILY ▶ **beam**
BEAMING ▶ **beam**
BEAMISH *adj* smiling
BEAMLET *n* small beam
BEAMS ▶ **beam**
BEAMY, BEAMIER ▶ **beam**
BEAN, -ED, -ING, -S *n, vb*
BEANBAG *n*
BEANED ▶ **bean**
BEANERY *n* cheap restaurant
BEANIE, -S *n* close-fitting woollen hat
BEANING ▶ **bean**
BEANO, -S *n* celebration or party
BEANS ▶ **bean**
BEANY *same as* ▶ **beanie**
BEAR, -ED, -S, BORNE *vb* support or hold up (something) ▷ *vb* lower the price of (a security) ▷ *n* type of omnivorous mammal
BEARCAT *n* lesser panda
BEARD, -ED, -S *n, vb*
BEARDIE *n* another name for bearded loach
BEARDS ▶ **beard**
BEARDY *adj* having a beard
BEARE, -S *same as* ▶ **bear**
BEARED ▶ **bear**
BEARER, -S *n*
BEARES ▶ **beare**
BEARHUG *n, vb*
BEARING ▶ **bear**
BEARISH *adj* like a bear
BEARPAW *n* paw of a bear
BEARS ▶ **bear**
BEAST, -ED, -S *n, vb*
BEASTIE *n*
BEASTLY *adj, adv*
BEASTS ▶ **beast**
BEAT, -EN, -S *vb, n, adj*
BEATBOX *n, vb*
BEATEN ▶ **beat**
BEATER, -S *n*
BEATH, -ED, -S *vb* dry; heat
BEATIER ▶ **beaty**
BEATIFY *vb* take first step towards making (a dead person) a saint
BEATING ▶ **beat**
BEATNIK *n* young person in the late 1950s who rebelled against conventional attitudes etc
BEATS ▶ **beat**
BEATY, BEATIER *adj* (of music) having a strong rhythm
BEAU, -S, -X *n* boyfriend or admirer
BEAUFET *same as* ▶ **buffet**
BEAUFIN *same as* ▶ **biffin**
BEAUISH *adj* vain and showy
BEAUS ▶ **beau**
BEAUT, -ER, -S *n* person or thing that is outstanding or distinctive ▷ *adj* good or excellent ▷ *interj* exclamation of joy or pleasure
BEAUTY *n, interj, vb*
BEAUX ▶ **beau**
BEAVER, -S *n, vb*
BEAVERY *n* place for keeping beavers
BEBEERU *n* tropical American tree
BEBLOOD *vb* stain with blood
BEBOP, -S *same as* ▶ **bop**
BEBUNG, -S *n* vibrato effect on clavichord
BECALL, -S *vb* use insulting words about someone
BECALM, -S *vb*
BECAME ▶ **become**
BECAP, -S *vb* put a cap on
BECASSE *n* woodcock
BECAUSE *conj*
BECHALK *vb* mark with chalk
BECHARM *vb* delight
BECK, -ED, -ING, -S *n* stream ▷ *vb* attract

someone's attention by nodding or gesturing
BECKE, -S *same as* ▸ **beak**
BECKED ▸ **beck**
BECKES ▸ **becke**
BECKET, -S *n* clevis forming part of one end of a sheave
BECKING ▸ **beck**
BECKON, -S *vb* summon with a gesture ▹ *n* summoning gesture
BECKS ▸ **beck**
BECLASP *vb* embrace
BECLOAK *vb* dress in cloak
BECLOG, -S *vb* put clogs on
BECLOUD *vb* cover or obscure with a cloud
BECLOWN *vb* clown around
BECOME, BECAME, -S *vb*
BECRAWL *vb* crawl all over
BECRIME *vb* make someone guilty of a crime
BECROWD *vb* crowd with something
BECRUST *vb* cover with crust
BECURL, -S *vb* curl
BECURSE, BECURST *vb* curse
BED, -DED, -S *n, vb*
BEDAD *interj* exclamation of affirmation
BEDAMN, -S *vb* damn
BEDASH *vb* sprinkle with liquid
BEDAUB, -S *vb* smear with something sticky or dirty
BEDAWIN *same as* ▸ **bedouin**
BEDAZE, -D, -S *vb* daze
BEDBATH *n*
BEDBUG, -S *n*
BEDDED ▸ **bed**
BEDDER, -S *n* (at some universities) college servant employed to keep students' rooms in order
BEDDING ▸ **bed**
BEDE, -S *n* prayer
BEDECK, -S *vb* cover with decorations
BEDEL, -S *archaic spelling of* ▸ **beadle**
BEDELL, -S *same as* ▸ **beadle**
BEDELS ▸ **bedel**
BEDEMAN, BEDEMEN *same as* > **beadsman**
BEDERAL *same as* ▸ **bedral**
BEDES ▸ **bede**
BEDEVIL *vb* harass, confuse, or torment
BEDEW, -ED, -S *vb* wet or cover with or as if with drops of dew
BEDFAST *an archaic word for* > **bedridden**
BEDGOWN *n* night dress
BEDHEAD *n* untidy state of the hair, esp caused by sleeping
BEDIDE ▸ **bedye**
BEDIGHT *vb* array or adorn ▹ *adj* adorned or bedecked
BEDIM, -S *vb* make dim
BEDIRTY *vb* make dirty
BEDIZEN *vb* dress or decorate gaudily
BEDLAM, -S *n*
BEDLAMP *n*
BEDLAMS ▸ **bedlam**
BEDLESS ▸ **bed**
BEDLIKE *adj* like a bed
BEDMATE *n* person who shares a bed
BEDOUIN *n* member of any of the nomadic tribes of Arabs
BEDPAN, -S *n*
BEDPOST *n*
BEDRAIL *n*
BEDRAL, -S *n* minor church official
BEDRAPE *vb* adorn
BEDREST *n* rest in bed, eg to recover from illness
BEDRID *same as* > **bedridden**
BEDROCK *n*
BEDROLL *n* portable roll of bedding
BEDROOM *n*
BEDROP, -S, -T *vb* drop on
BEDRUG, -S *vb* drug excessively
BEDS ▸ **bed**
BEDSIDE *n, adj*
BEDSIT, -S *n*
BEDSOCK *n* sock worn in bed
BEDSORE *n*
BEDTICK *n* case containing stuffing in mattress
BEDTIME *n*
BEDU *adj* relating to beduins
BEDUCK, -S *vb* duck under water
BEDUIN, -S *variant of* ▸ **bedouin**
BEDUMB, -S *vb* make dumb

BEDUNCE *vb* cause to look or feel foolish
BEDUNG, -S *vb* spread with dung
BEDUST, -S *vb* cover with dust
BEDWARD *adj* towards bed
BEDWARF *vb* hamper growth of
BEDYE, BEDYDE, -D, -S *vb* dye
BEE, -S *n* insect that makes wax and honey
BEEBEE, -S *n* air rifle
BEECH, -ES *n* tree with a smooth greyish bark
BEECHEN ▶ **beech**
BEECHES ▶ **beech**
BEECHY ▶ **beech**
BEEDI *n* Indian cigarette
BEEDIE, -S *same as* ▶ **beedi**
BEEF, -ED, -ING, -S, BEEVES *n, vb*
BEEFALO *n* cross between cow and buffalo
BEEFED ▶ **beef**
BEEFIER ▶ **beefy**
BEEFILY ▶ **beefy**
BEEFING ▶ **beef**
BEEFS ▶ **beef**
BEEFY, BEEFIER *adj* like beef
BEEGAH, -S *same as* ▶ **bigha**
BEEHIVE *n*
BEELIKE ▶ **bee**
BEELINE *n, vb*
BEEN *vb*
BEENAH, -S *n* understanding; insight
BEENTO, -S *n* W African word for a person who has lived in Britain ▷ *adj* of or relating to such a person
BEEP, -ED, -ING, -S *n, vb*
BEEPER, -S ▶ **beep**
BEEPING ▶ **beep**
BEEPS ▶ **beep**
BEER, -S *n*
BEERAGE *n* brewing industry
BEERIER ▶ **beery**
BEERILY ▶ **beery**
BEERMAT *n*
BEERNUT *n*
BEERS ▶ **beer**
BEERY, BEERIER *adj* smelling or tasting of beer
BEES ▶ **bee**
BEESOME *same as* ▶ **bisson**
BEESWAX *n* wax secreted by bees, used in polishes etc ▷ *vb* polish with such wax
BEET, -ED, -ING, -S *n* plant with an edible root and leaves ▷ *vb* improve or make better
BEETFLY *n* type of fly which is a common pest of beets and mangel-wurzels
BEETING ▶ **beet**
BEETLE, -D, -S *n, vb*
BEETLER *n* one who operates a beetling machine
BEETLES ▶ **beetle**
BEETS ▶ **beet**
BEEVES ▶ **beef**
BEEYARD *n* place where bees are kept
BEEZER, -S *n* person or chap ▷ *adj* excellent
BEFALL, -S, BEFELL *vb*
BEFANA, -S *n* Italian gift-bearing good fairy
BEFELD *archaic past participle of* ▶ **befall**
BEFELL ▶ **befall**
BEFFANA *same as* ▶ **befana**
BEFIT, -S *vb*
BEFLAG, -S *vb* decorate with flags
BEFLEA, -S *vb* infest with fleas
BEFLECK *vb* fleck
BEFLUM, -S *vb* fool; deceive
BEFOAM, -S *vb* cover with foam
BEFOG, -S *vb* surround with fog
BEFOOL, -S *vb* make a fool of
BEFORE *adv, prep*
BEFOUL, -S *vb* make dirty or foul
BEFRET, -S *vb* fret about something
BEG, -GED, -S *vb*
BEGAD *interj* emphatic exclamation
BEGALL, -S *vb* make sore by rubbing
BEGAN ▶ **begin**
BEGAR, -S *n* compulsory labour
BEGAT *archaic past tense of* ▶ **beget**
BEGAZE, -D, -S *vb* gaze about or around
BEGEM, -S *vb* decorate with gems
BEGET, -S, BEGOT *vb* cause or create
BEGGAR, -S *n, vb*
BEGGARY *n* extreme poverty or need

BEGGED ▸ **beg**
BEGGING ▸ **beg**
BEGHARD *n* member of a 13th century Christian brotherhood
BEGIFT, -S *vb* give a gift or gifts to
BEGILD, -S, BEGILT *vb* gild
BEGIN, BEGAN, -S, BEGUN *vb*
BEGINNE *same as* > **beginning**
BEGINS ▸ **begin**
BEGIRD, -S, BEGIRT *vb* surround
BEGLAD, -S *vb* make glad
BEGLOOM *vb* make gloomy
BEGNAW, -S *vb* gnaw at
BEGO, -ES, -ING, -NE, BEWENT *vb* harass; beset
BEGONIA *n*
BEGORAH *same as* ▸ **begorra**
BEGORED *adj* smeared with gore
BEGORRA *interj* emphatic exclamation, regarded as a characteristic utterance of Irish people
BEGOT ▸ **beget**
BEGRIM, -S *same as* ▸ **begrime**
BEGRIME *vb* make dirty
BEGRIMS ▸ **begrim**
BEGROAN *vb* groan at
BEGS ▸ **beg**
BEGUILE *vb* cheat or mislead
BEGUIN, -S *another name for* ▸ **beghard**
BEGUINE *n* S American dance
BEGUINS ▸ **beguin**
BEGULF, -S *vb* overwhelm
BEGUM, -S *n* Muslim woman of high rank
BEGUN ▸ **begin**
BEGUNK, -S *vb* delude; trick
BEHALF *n*
BEHAVE, -D, -S *vb*
BEHAVER ▸ **behave**
BEHAVES ▸ **behave**
BEHEAD, -S *vb*
BEHELD ▸ **behold**
BEHEST, -S *n*
BEHIGHT *vb* entrust
BEHIND, -S *adv, n, prep, adj*
BEHOLD, BEHELD, -S *vb*
BEHOOF, -S *n* advantage or profit
BEHOOVE *same as* ▸ **behove**
BEHOTE, -S *same as* ▸ **behight**
BEHOVE, -D, -S *vb* be necessary or fitting for
BEHOWL, -S *vb* howl at
BEIGE, -R, -S, -ST *adj, n*
BEIGEL, -S *same as* ▸ **bagel**
BEIGER ▸ **beige**
BEIGES ▸ **beige**
BEIGEST ▸ **beige**
BEIGIER ▸ **beigy**
BEIGNE, -S *variant of* ▸ **beignet**
BEIGNET *n* square deep-fried pastry served hot and sprinkled with icing sugar
BEIGY, BEIGIER ▸ **beige**
BEIN, -ED, -ING, -S *adj* financially comfortable ▹ *vb* fill
BEING, -S ▸ **be**
BEINING ▸ **bein**
BEINKED *adj* daubed with ink
BEINS ▸ **bein**
BEJADE, -D, -S *vb* jade; tire
BEJANT, -S *same as* ▸ **bajan**
BEJEWEL *vb* decorate with or as if with jewels
BEKAH, -S *n* half shekel
BEKISS *vb* smother with kisses
BEKNAVE *vb* treat as a knave
BEKNOT, -S *vb* tie a knot or knots in
BEKNOWN *adj* known about
BEL, -S *n* unit for comparing two power levels or measuring the intensity of a sound
BELABOR *same as* > **belabour**
BELACE, -D, -S *vb* decorate with lace
BELADY *vb* call a lady
BELAH, -S *n* Australian tree which yields a useful timber
BELAMY *n* close friend
BELAR, -S *same as* ▸ **belah**
BELATE, -S *vb* cause to be late
BELATED *adj*
BELATES ▸ **belate**
BELAUD, -S *vb* praise highly
BELAY, -ED, -S *vb* secure a line to a pin or cleat ▹ *n* attachment (of a climber) to a mountain

BELAYER ▸ **belay**
BELAYS ▸ **belay**
BELCH, -ED, -ES *vb, n*
BELCHER ▸ **belch**
BELCHES ▸ **belch**
BELDAM, -S *n* old woman, esp an ugly or malicious one
BELDAME *same as* ▸ **beldam**
BELDAMS ▸ **beldam**
BELEAP, -S, -T *vb* leap over
BELEE, -D, -S *vb* put on sheltered side
BELFRY *n*
BELGA, -S *n* former Belgian monetary unit worth five francs
BELGARD *n* kind gaze
BELGAS ▸ **belga**
BELIE, -D, -S, BELYING *vb* show to be untrue
BELIEF, -S *n*
BELIER, -S ▸ **belie**
BELIES ▸ **belie**
BELIEVE *vb*
BELIKE *adv* perhaps
BELIVE *adv* speedily
BELL, -ED, -S *n, vb*
BELLBOY *n* man or boy employed to carry luggage and answer calls for service
BELLE, -S *n* beautiful woman, esp the most attractive woman at a function
BELLED ▸ **bell**
BELLEEK *n* kind of thin fragile porcelain with a lustrous glaze
BELLES ▸ **belle**
BELLHOP *same as* ▸ **bellboy**
BELLIED ▸ **belly**
BELLIES ▸ **belly**
BELLING ▸ **bell**
BELLINI *n* Prosecco and peach cocktail
BELLMAN, BELLMEN *n* man who rings a bell, esp (formerly) a town crier
BELLOCK *vb* shout
BELLOW *vb, n*
BELLOWS *pl n* instrument for pumping a stream of air into something
BELLS ▸ **bell**
BELLY, BELLIED, BELLIES *n, vb*
BELON, -S *n* type of oyster
BELONG, -S *vb*
BELONS ▸ **belon**
BELOVE, -S *vb* love
BELOVED *adj* dearly loved ▹ *n* person dearly loved
BELOVES ▸ **belove**
BELOW *adv, prep*
BELOWS *same as* ▸ **bellows**
BELS ▸ **bel**
BELT, -ED, -S *n, vb*
BELTER, -S *n* outstanding person or event
BELTING *n* material used to make a belt or belts ▹ *adj* excellent
BELTMAN, BELTMEN *n* (formerly) a member of a beach life-saving team
BELTS ▸ **belt**
BELTWAY *n* people and institutions located in the area bounded by the Washington Beltway
BELUGA, -S *n* large white sturgeon
BELYING ▸ **belie**
BEMA, -S, -TA *n* speaker's platform in the assembly in ancient Athens
BEMAD, -S *vb* old word meaning cause to become mad
BEMADAM *vb* call a person madam
BEMADS ▸ **bemad**
BEMAS ▸ **bema**
BEMATA ▸ **bema**
BEMAUL, -S *vb* maul
BEMAZED *adj* amazed
BEMBEX *n* type of wasp
BEMBIX *same as* ▸ **bembex**
BEMEAN, -S, -T *a less common word for* ▸ **demean**
BEMEDAL *vb* decorate with medals
BEMETE, -D, -S *vb* measure
BEMIRE, -D, -S *vb* soil with or as if with mire
BEMIST, -S *vb* cloud with mist
BEMIX, -ED, -ES, -T *vb* mix thoroughly
BEMOAN, -S *vb*
BEMOCK, -S *vb* mock
BEMOIL, -S *vb* soil with mud
BEMOUTH *vb* endow with a mouth
BEMUD, -S *vb* cover with mud
BEMUSE, -S *vb*
BEMUSED *adj* puzzled or confused
BEMUSES ▸ **bemuse**

BEN, -S *n* mountain peak ▷ *adv* in ▷ *adj* inner
BENAME, -D, -S *an archaic word for* ▶ **name**
BENCH, -ED, -ES *n, vb*
BENCHER *n* member of the governing body of one of the Inns of Court
BENCHES ▶ **bench**
BENCHY *adj* (of a hillside) hollowed out in benches
BEND, -ED, -S *vb, n*
BENDAY, -S *vb* (printing) reproduce using the Benday technique
BENDED ▶ **bend**
BENDEE, -S *same as* ▶ **bendy**
BENDER, -S *n* makeshift shelter
BENDIER ▶ **bendy**
BENDING *n* curving action
BENDLET *n* narrow diagonal stripe on heraldic shield
BENDS ▶ **bend**
BENDY, BENDIER, -S *adj* flexible or pliable ▷ *n* okra
BENE, -S *n* blessing
BENEATH *prep, adv*
BENEFIC *adj* rare word for beneficent
BENEFIT *n, vb*
BENEMPT *a past participle of* ▶ **bename**
BENES ▶ **bene**
BENET, -S *vb* trap (something) in a net
BENGA, -S *n* type of Kenyan popular music featuring guitars
BENI, -S *n* sesame plant
BENIGHT *vb* shroud in darkness
BENIGN *adj*
BENIS ▶ **beni**
BENISON *n* blessing, esp a spoken one
BENJ, -ES *another word for* ▶ **bhang**
BENNE, -S *another name for* ▶ **sesame**
BENNET, -S *n* Eurasian and N African plant with yellow flowers
BENNI, -S *n* sesame
BENNIES ▶ **benny**
BENNIS ▶ **benni**
BENNY, BENNIES *n* US word for a man's overcoat
BENOMYL *n* fungicide
BENS ▶ **ben**
BENT, -S *adj, n*
BENTHAL ▶ **benthos**
BENTHIC ▶ **benthos**
BENTHON *same as* ▶ **benthos**
BENTHOS *n* animals and plants living at the bottom of a sea or lake
BENTIER ▶ **benty**
BENTO, -S *n* thin lightweight box used in Japanese cuisine
BENTS ▶ **bent**
BENTY, BENTIER *adj* covered with bentgrass
BENUMB, -S *vb* make numb or powerless
BENZAL, -S *n* transparent crystalline substance
BENZENE *n* flammable poisonous liquid used as a solvent, insecticide, etc
BENZIL, -S *n* yellow compound radical
BENZIN, -S *same as* ▶ **benzine**
BENZINE *n* volatile liquid used as a solvent
BENZINS ▶ **benzin**
BENZOIC *adj* of, containing, or derived from benzoic acid or benzoin
BENZOIN *n* gum resin used in ointments, perfume, etc
BENZOL, -S *n* crude form of benzene
BENZOLE *same as* ▶ **benzol**
BENZOLS ▶ **benzol**
BENZOYL *n* type of monovalent radical
BENZYL, -S *n* molecular fragment of certain alcohols and solvents
BEPAINT *vb* dye; paint
BEPAT, -S *vb* pat
BEPEARL *vb* decorate with pearls
BEPELT, -S *vb* pelt energetically
BEPITY *vb* feel great pity for
BEPROSE *vb* (of poetry) reduce to prose
BEPUFF, -S *vb* puff up
BEQUEST *n* legal gift of money or property by someone who has died
BERAKE, -D, -S *vb* rake thoroughly
BERATE, -D, -S *vb*
BERAY, -ED, -S *vb* soil; defile
BERBER, -S *same as* ▶ **berbere**

BERBERE *n* hot-tasting Ethiopian paste
BERBERS ▸ **berber**
BERBICE *n* as in **berbice chair** large armchair with long arms that can be folded inwards to act as leg rests
BERCEAU *n* arched trellis for climbing plants
BERE, -S *n* barley
BEREAVE *vb*
BEREFT *adj*
BERES ▸ **bere**
BERET, -S *n*
BERETTA *n* type of pistol
BERG, -S *n* iceberg
BERGALL *n* fish of the wrasse family
BERGAMA *n* type of Turkish rug
BERGEN, -S *n* large rucksack with a capacity of over 50 litres
BERGERE *n* type of French armchair
BERGS ▸ **berg**
BERGYLT *n* large northern marine food fish
BERHYME *vb* mention in poetry
BERIME, -D, -S *same as* ▸ **berhyme**
BERK, -S *n* stupid person
BERKO *adj* berserk
BERKS ▸ **berk**
BERLEY, -S *n* bait scattered on water to attract fish ▹ *vb* scatter (bait) on water
BERLIN, -S *n* fine wool yarn used for tapestry work, etc
BERLINE *same as* ▸ **berlin**
BERLINS ▸ **berlin**
BERM, -ED, -ING, -S *n* narrow grass strip between the road and the footpath in a residential area ▹ *vb* create a berm
BERME, -S *same as* ▸ **berm**
BERMED ▸ **berm**
BERMES ▸ **berme**
BERMING ▸ **berm**
BERMS ▸ **berm**
BEROB, -S *vb* rob
BEROBED *adj* wearing a robe
BEROBS ▸ **berob**
BERRET, -S *same as* ▸ **beret**
BERRY, BERRIED, BERRIES *n, vb*
BERSEEM *n* Mediterranean clover grown as a forage crop and to improve the soil
BERSERK *adj, n*
BERTH, -ED, -S *n, vb*
BERTHA, -S *n* type of lace collar
BERTHE, -S *n* type of lace collar
BERTHED ▸ **berth**
BERTHES ▸ **berthe**
BERTHS ▸ **berth**
BERYL, -S *n* hard transparent mineral
BES, -ES *variant of* ▸ **beth**
BESAINT *vb* give saint status to
BESANG ▸ **besing**
BESAT ▸ **besit**
BESAW ▸ **besee**
BESCOUR *vb* scour thoroughly
BESEE, BESAW, -N, -S *vb* provide for; mind
BESEECH *vb*
BESEEKE *archaic form of* ▸ **beseech**
BESEEM, -S *vb* be suitable for
BESEEN ▸ **besee**
BESEES ▸ **besee**
BESES ▸ **bes**
BESET, -S *vb*
BESHAME *vb* cause to feel shame
BESHINE, BESHONE *vb* illuminate
BESHOUT *vb* shout about
BESHREW *vb* wish evil on
BESIDE *prep*
BESIDES *prep, adv*
BESIEGE *vb*
BESIGH, -S *vb* sigh for
BESING, BESANG, -S, BESUNG *vb* sing about joyfully
BESIT, BESAT, -S *vb* suit; fit
BESLAVE *vb* treat as slave
BESLIME *vb* cover with slime
BESMEAR *vb* smear over
BESMILE *vb* smile on
BESMOKE *vb* blacken with smoke
BESMUT, -S *vb* blacken with smut
BESNOW, -S *vb* cover with snow
BESOIN, -S *n* need
BESOM, -ED, -S *n* broom made of twigs ▹ *vb* sweep with a besom

BESORT, -S *vb* fit
BESOT, -S *vb* make stupid or muddled
BESPAKE ▸ **bespeak**
BESPAT ▸ **bespit**
BESPATE ▸ **bespit**
BESPEAK, BESPAKE *vb* indicate or suggest
BESPEED, BESPED *vb* get on with (doing something)
BESPICE *vb* flavour with spices
BESPIT, BESPAT, BESPATE, -S *vb* cover with spittle
BESPOKE *adj*
BESPORT *vb* amuse oneself
BESPOT, -S *vb* mark with spots
BESPOUT *vb* speak pretentiously
BEST, -ED, -ING, -S *adj, adv, n, vb*
BESTAD *Spenserian form of* ▸ **bestead**
BESTAIN *vb* stain
BESTAR, -S *vb* decorate with stars
BESTEAD *vb* serve; assist ▹ *adj* beset (by)
BESTED ▸ **best**
BESTEST *adj* best
BESTI, -S *Indian English word for* ▸ **shame**
BESTIAL *adj*
BESTICK, BESTUCK *vb* cover with sharp points
BESTIE, -S *n* best friend
BESTILL *vb* cause to be still
BESTING ▸ **best**
BESTIR, -S *vb* cause (oneself) to become active
BESTIS ▸ **besti**
BESTORM *vb* assault
BESTOW, -S *vb*
BESTREW *vb* scatter or lie scattered over (a surface)
BESTRID > **bestride**
BESTROW *same as* ▸ **bestrew**
BESTS ▸ **best**
BESTUCK ▸ **bestick**
BESTUD, -S *vb* set with, or as with studs
BESUNG ▸ **besing**
BESWARM *vb* swarm over
BET, -S, -TED *n, vb*
BETA, -S *n* second letter in the Greek alphabet, a consonant, transliterated as *b*
BETAINE *n* sweet-tasting alkaloid that occurs in the sugar beet
BETAKE, -N, -S, BETOOK *vb* as in **betake oneself** go
BETAS ▸ **beta**
BETAXED *adj* burdened with taxes
BETCHA *interj* bet you
BETE, -D, -S, BETING *same as* ▸ **beet**
BETEEM, -S *vb* accord
BETEEME *same as* ▸ **beteem**
BETEEMS ▸ **beteem**
BETEL, -S *n* Asian climbing plant, the leaves and nuts of which can be chewed
BETES ▸ **bete**
BETH, -S *n* second letter of the Hebrew alphabet, transliterated as *b*
BETHANK *vb* thank
BETHEL, -S *n* seaman's chapel
BETHINK *vb* cause (oneself) to consider or meditate
BETHORN *vb* cover with thorns
BETHS ▸ **beth**
BETHUMB *vb* (of books) wear by handling
BETHUMP *vb* thump hard
BETIDE, BETID, -D, -S, BETIGHT *vb* happen (to)
BETIME, -D, -S *vb* befall
BETING ▸ **bete**
BETISE, -S *n* folly or lack of perception
BETITLE *vb* give title to
BETOIL, -S *vb* tire through hard work
BETOKEN *vb* indicate or signify
BETON, -S *n* concrete
BETONY *n* North American plant
BETOOK ▸ **betake**
BETOSS *vb* toss about
BETRAY, -S *vb*
BETREAD, BETROD *vb* tread over
BETRIM, -S *vb* decorate
BETROD ▸ **betread**
BETROTH *vb* promise to marry or to give in marriage
BETS ▸ **bet**
BETTA, -S *n* fighting fish
BETTED ▸ **bet**
BETTER, -S *adj, adv, vb*
BETTIES ▸ **betty**
BETTING ▸ **bet**

BETTONG *n* short-nosed rat kangaroo
BETTOR, -S *n* person who bets
BETTY, BETTIES *n* type of short crowbar
BETWEEN *adv, prep*
BETWIXT *adv*
BEURRE, -S *n* butter
BEVEL, -ED, -S *n* slanting edge ▷ *vb* slope
BEVELER ▸ **bevel**
BEVELS ▸ **bevel**
BEVER, -ED, -S *n* snack ▷ *vb* have a snack
BEVIES ▸ **bevy**
BEVOMIT *vb* vomit over
BEVOR, -S *n* armour protecting lower part of face
BEVUE, -S *n* careless error
BEVVY, BEVVIED, BEVVIES *n* alcoholic drink ▷ *vb* drink alcohol
BEVY, BEVIES *n* flock or group
BEWAIL, -S *vb* express great sorrow over
BEWARE, -D, -S *vb*
BEWEARY *vb* cause to be weary
BEWEEP, -S, BEWEPT *vb* express grief through weeping
BEWENT ▸ **bego**
BEWEPT ▸ **beweep**
BEWET, -S *vb* make wet
BEWIG, -S *vb* adorn with a wig
BEWITCH *vb* attract and fascinate
BEWORM, -S *vb* fill with worms
BEWORRY *vb* beset with worry
BEWRAP, -S, -T *vb* wrap up
BEWRAY, -S *an obsolete word for* ▸ **betray**
BEY, -S *n* title in the Ottoman Empire

A **bey** was an official in the Ottoman empire. If someone plays this remember that you can of course put an O in front of it to make **obey**.

BEYLIC, -S *n* province ruled over by a bey
BEYLIK, -S *same as* ▸ **beylic**
BEYOND, -S *prep* at or to a point on the other side of ▷ *adv* at or to the far side of something ▷ *n* unknown, esp life after death
BEYS ▸ **bey**
BEZ, -ES *n* part of a deer's horn

This word for the tine of a deer's horn is one of the essential short words for using the Z.

BEZANT, -S *n* medieval Byzantine gold coin
BEZAZZ *another word for* ▸ **pizzazz**
BEZEL, -S *n* sloping edge of a cutting tool
BEZES ▸ **bez**
BEZIL, -S *archaic word for* > **alcoholic**
BEZIQUE *n* card game for two or more players

This card game played with two decks of cards combines the Q and Z and would make a wonderful bonus word.

BEZOAR, -S *n* hard mass, such as a stone or hairball, in the stomach and intestines of animals
BEZZANT *same as* ▸ **bezant**
BEZZAZZ *same as* ▸ **bezazz**
BEZZIE, -S *n* best friend
BEZZLE, -D, -S *vb* waste (money)
BEZZY *same as* ▸ **bezzie**
BHAGEE, -S *same as* ▸ **bhaji**
BHAI, -S *n* Indian form of address for a man
BHAJAN, -S *n* singing of devotional songs and hymns
BHAJEE, -S *same as* ▸ **bhaji**
BHAJI, -A, -S *n* Indian deep-fried savoury of chopped vegetables in spiced batter
BHAKTA, -S *n* Hindu term for a devotee of God
BHAKTI, -S *n* loving devotion to God leading to nirvana
BHANG, -S *n* preparation of Indian hemp
BHANGRA *n* Punjabi folk music combined with elements of Western pop music

BHANGS ▸ **bhang**
BHARAL, -S *n* wild Himalayan sheep
BHAT, -S *n* currency of Thailand
BHAVAN, -S *n* (in India) a large house or building
BHAWAN, -S *same as* ▸ **bhavan**
BHEESTY *same as* ▸ **bhishti**
BHEL, -S *same as* ▸ **bael**
BHIKHU, -S *n* fully ordained Buddhist monk
BHINDI, -S *same as* ▸ **bindhi**
BHISHTI *n* (formerly in India) a water-carrier
BHISTEE *same as* ▸ **bhishti**
BHISTI, -S *same as* ▸ **bhishti**
BHISTIE *same as* ▸ **bhishti**
BHISTIS ▸ **bhisti**
BHOONA, -S *same as* ▸ **bhuna**
BHOOT, -S *same as* ▸ **bhut**
BHUNA, -S *n* Indian sauce
BHUT, -S *n* Hindu term for a type of ghost
BI *short for* > **bisexual**
BIALI, -S *same as* ▸ **bialy**
BIALIES ▸ **bialy**
BIALIS ▸ **biali**
BIALY, BIALIES, -S *n* type of bagel
BIAS, -ES *n, vb, adj, adv*
BIASED ▸ **bias**
BIASES ▸ **bias**
BIASING ▸ **bias**
BIASSED *same as* ▸ **biased**
BIASSES *same as* ▸ **biases**
BIAXAL *same as* ▸ **biaxial**
BIAXIAL *adj* (esp of a crystal) having two axes
BIB, -BED, -S *vb* drink
BIBASIC *adj* with two bases
BIBB, -S *n* wooden support on a mast for the trestletrees
BIBBED ▸ **bib**
BIBBER, -S *n* drinker
BIBBERY *n* drinking to excess
BIBBING *n* act of bibbing
BIBBLE, -S *n* pebble
BIBBS ▸ **bibb**
BIBCOCK *n* tap with a nozzle bent downwards
BIBE, -S *n* (in Newfoundland folklore) spirit whose wailing warns of a coming death
BIBELOT *n* attractive or curious trinket
BIBES ▸ **bibe**
BIBFUL, -S *n* as in **spill a bibful** divulge secrets
BIBLE, -S *n*
BIBLESS ▸ **bib**
BIBLIKE ▸ **bib**
BIBLIST *same as* > **biblicist**
BIBS ▸ **bib**
BICARB, -S *n* bicarbonate of soda
BICCY, BICCIES *n* biscuit
BICE, -S *n* medium blue colour
BICEP *same as* ▸ **biceps**
BICEPS *n*
BICES ▸ **bice**
BICHIR, -S *n* African freshwater fish with an elongated body
BICHORD *adj* having two strings for each note
BICKER, -S *vb, n*
BICKIE, -S *short for* ▸ **biscuit**
BICOLOR *same as* > **bicolour**
BICORN, -S *adj* having two horns or hornlike parts
BICORNE *same as* ▸ **bicorn**
BICORNS ▸ **bicorn**
BICRON, -S *n* billionth part of a metre
BICYCLE *n, vb*
BID, BADE, -DEN, -S *vb, n*
BIDARKA *same as* > **baidarka**
BIDDEN ▸ **bid**
BIDDER, -S ▸ **bid**
BIDDIES ▸ **biddy**
BIDDING ▸ **bid**
BIDDY, BIDDIES *n* woman, esp an old gossipy one
BIDE, -D, -S *vb* stay or continue
BIDENT, -S *n* instrument with two prongs
BIDER, -S ▸ **bide**
BIDES ▸ **bide**
BIDET, -S *n*
BIDI, -S *same as* ▸ **beedi**
BIDING, -S ▸ **bide**
BIDIS ▸ **bidi**
BIDON, -S *n* oil drum
BIDS ▸ **bid**
BIELD, -ED, -S *n* shelter ▹ *vb* shelter or take shelter

BIELDY *adj* sheltered
BIEN *adv* well
BIENNIA > **biennium**
BIER, -S *n* stand on which a body or coffin rests before burial
BIFACE, -S *n* prehistoric stone tool
BIFF, -ED, -ING, -S *n* blow with the fist ▷ *vb* give (someone) such a blow
BIFFER, -S *n* someone, such as a sportsperson, who has a reputation for hitting hard
BIFFIES ▶ **biffy**
BIFFIN, -S *n* variety of red cooking apple
BIFFING ▶ **biff**
BIFFINS ▶ **biffin**
BIFFO, -S *n* fighting or aggressive behaviour ▷ *adj* aggressive
BIFFS ▶ **biff**
BIFFY, BIFFIES *n* outdoor toilet
BIFID *adj* divided into two by a cleft in the middle
BIFIDA ▶ **bifidum**
BIFIDLY ▶ **bifid**
BIFIDUM, BIFIDA *n* type of bacterium
BIFIDUS *n* bacterium of the human digestive system
BIFILAR *adj* having two parallel threads, as in the suspension of certain measuring instruments
BIFLEX *adj* bent or flexed in two places
BIFOCAL *adj* having two different focuses
BIFOLD, -S *n* something folded in two places
BIFORM *adj* having or combining the characteristics of two forms, as a centaur
BIFTAH, -S *same as* ▶ **bifter**
BIFTER, -S *n* cigarette
BIG, -GED, -GER, -GEST, -S *adj, adv, vb*
BIGA, -E *n* chariot drawn by two horses
BIGAMY *n*
BIGENER *n* hybrid between individuals of different genera
BIGEYE, -S *n* type of red marine fish
BIGFOOT, BIGFEET *n* yeti ▷ *vb* throw one's weight around
BIGG, -S *n* type of barley
BIGGED ▶ **big**
BIGGER ▶ **big**
BIGGEST ▶ **big**
BIGGETY *adj* conceited
BIGGIE, -S *n* something big or important
BIGGIN, -S *n* plain close-fitting cap
BIGGING ▶ **big**
BIGGINS ▶ **biggin**
BIGGISH ▶ **big**
BIGGITY *adj* conceited
BIGGON, -S *same as* ▶ **biggin**
BIGGS ▶ **bigg**
BIGGY *same as* ▶ **biggie**
BIGHA, -S *n* in India, unit for measuring land
BIGHEAD *n*
BIGHORN *n* large wild mountain sheep
BIGHT, -ED, -S *n* long curved shoreline ▷ *vb* fasten or bind with a loop of rope
BIGLY ▶ **big**
BIGNESS ▶ **big**
BIGOS, -ES *n* Polish stew
BIGOT, -S *n*
BIGOTED ▶ **bigot**
BIGOTRY *n* attitudes, behaviour, or way of thinking of a bigot
BIGOTS ▶ **bigot**
BIGS ▶ **big**
BIGTIME *adj* important
BIGUINE *same as* ▶ **beguine**
BIGWIG, -S *n* important person
BIJOU, -S, -X *adj* (of a house) small but elegant ▷ *n* something small and delicately worked

A **bijou** is a French word for a jewel, and it is indeed a jewel to play, getting rid of awkward letters for a good score. And remember that the plural can be **bijous** or **bijoux**.

BIJURAL *adj* relating to two coexisting legal systems
BIKE, -D, -S *same as* ▶ **bicycle**
BIKER, -S *n*
BIKES ▶ **bike**
BIKEWAY *n* cycle lane
BIKIE, -S *n* member of a motorcycle gang
BIKING, -S ▶ **bike**
BIKINI, -S *n*
BIKKIE, -S *short for* ▶ **biscuit**

BILAYER *n* part of a cell membrane
BILBIES ▶ **bilby**
BILBO, -ES, -S *n* (formerly) a sword with a marked temper and elasticity
BILBOA, -S *same as* ▶ **bilbo**
BILBOES ▶ **bilbo**
BILBOS ▶ **bilbo**
BILBY, BILBIES *n* Australian marsupial with long pointed ears and grey fur
BILE, -D, -S, BILING *n, vb*
BILEVEL *n* hairstyle with two different lengths
BILGE, -D, -S, BILGING *n, vb*
BILGIER ▶ **bilgy**
BILGING ▶ **bilge**
BILGY, BILGIER ▶ **bilge**
BILIAN, -S *n* type of tree used for its wood
BILIARY *adj* of bile, the ducts that convey bile, or the gall bladder ▷ *n* disease found in dogs
BILIMBI *n* type of fruit-bearing tree
BILING ▶ **bile**
BILIOUS *adj* sick, nauseous
BILK, -ED, -ING, -S *vb* cheat, esp by not paying ▷ *n* swindle or cheat
BILKER, -S ▶ **bilk**
BILKING ▶ **bilk**
BILKS ▶ **bilk**
BILL, -ED, -S *n, vb*
BILLBUG *n* type of weevil
BILLED ▶ **bill**
BILLER, -S *n* stem of a plant
BILLET, -S *vb, n*
BILLIE *same as* ▶ **billy**
BILLIES ▶ **billy**
BILLING *n* prominence given in programmes, advertisements, etc, to performers or acts
BILLION *n, determiner*
BILLMAN, BILLMEN *n* person who uses a billhook
BILLON, -S *n* alloy consisting of gold or silver and a base metal
BILLOW, -S *n, vb*
BILLOWY *adj* full of or forming billows
BILLS ▶ **bill**
BILLY, BILLIES *n* metal can or pot for cooking on a camp fire
BILLYO *n* as in **like billyo** phrase used to emphasize or intensify something
BILLYOH *same as* ▶ **billyo**
BILOBAR *same as* > **bilobate**
BILOBED *same as* > **bilobate**
BILSTED *n* American gum tree
BILTONG *n* strips of dried meat
BIMA, -S *same as* ▶ **bema**
BIMAH, -S *same as* ▶ **bema**
BIMANAL *same as* > **bimanous**
BIMAS ▶ **bima**
BIMBLE *n* as in **bimble box** type of dense Australian tree
BIMBO, -ES, -S *n*
BIMETAL *n* material made from two sheets of metal
BIMINI, -S *n* type of awning for a yacht
BIMODAL *adj* having two modes
BIMORPH *n* assembly of piezoelectric crystals
BIN, -NED, -NING, -S *n, vb*
BINAL *adj* twofold
BINARY *adj, n*
BINATE *adj* occurring in two parts or in pairs
BIND, -S *vb, n*
BINDER, -S *n*
BINDERY *n* bookbindery
BINDHI, -S *same as* ▶ **bindi**
BINDI, -S *n* decorative dot worn in the middle of the forehead, esp by Hindu women
BINDING ▶ **bind**
BINDIS ▶ **bindi**
BINDLE, -S *n* small packet
BINDS ▶ **bind**
BINE, -S *n* climbing or twining stem of various plants
BINER, -S *n* clip used by climbers
BINES ▶ **bine**
BING, -S *n* heap or pile, esp of spoil from a mine
BINGE, -D, -S *n, vb*
BINGER, -S ▶ **binge**
BINGES ▶ **binge**
BINGIES ▶ **bingy**
BINGING *n* act of indulging in a binge

BINGLE, -D, -S *n* minor crash or upset, as in a car or on a surfboard ▷ *vb* layer (hair)
BINGO, -ED, -ES, -S *n* gambling game ▷ *sentence substitute* cry by the winner of a game of bingo ▷ *vb* (in Scrabble) play all seven of one's tiles in a single turn
BINGS ▶ **bing**
BINGY, BINGIES *Australian slang for* ▶ **stomach**
BINIOU, -S *n* small high-pitched Breton bagpipe
BINIT, -S *n* (computing) early form of bit
BINK, -S *n* ledge
BINMAN, BINMEN *another name for* ▶ **dustman**
BINNED ▶ **bin**
BINNING ▶ **bin**
BINOCLE *n* binocular-style telescope
BINOCS > **binocular**
BINS ▶ **bin**
BIO, -S *short for* > **biography**
BIOBANK *n* large store of human samples for medical research
BIOCHIP *n* small glass or silicon plate containing an array of biochemical molecules or structures
BIOCIDE *n* substance used to destroy living things
BIODATA *n* information regarding an individual's education and work history
BIODOT, -S *n* temperature-sensitive device stuck to the skin in order to monitor stress
BIOFACT *n* item of biological information
BIOFILM *n* thin layer of living organisms
BIOFUEL *n, vb*
BIOG, -S *short form of* > **biography**
BIOGAS *n*
BIOGEN, -S *n* hypothetical protein
BIOGENY *n* principle that a living organism must originate from a parent form similar to itself
BIOGS ▶ **biog**
BIOHERM *n* mound of material laid down by sedentary marine organisms
BIOLOGY *n*
BIOMASS *n* total number of living organisms in a given area
BIOME, -S *n* major ecological community
BIONIC *adj*
BIONICS *n* study of biological functions to create electronic versions
BIONOMY *n* laws of life
BIONT, -S *n* living thing
BIONTIC ▶ **biont**
BIONTS ▶ **biont**
BIOPHOR *n* hypothetical material particle
BIOPIC, -S *n* film based on the life of a famous person
BIOPLAY *n* play based on the life of a famous person
BIOPSIC ▶ **biopsy**
BIOPSY *n, vb*
BIOPTIC ▶ **biopsy**
BIOS ▶ **bio**
BIOTA, -S *n* plant and animal life of a particular region or period
BIOTECH *n*
BIOTIC, -S *adj* of or relating to living organisms ▷ *n* living organism
BIOTIN, -S *n* vitamin of the B complex, abundant in egg yolk and liver
BIOTITE *n* black or dark green mineral of the mica group
BIOTOPE *n* small area that supports its own distinctive community
BIOTRON *n* climate-control chamber
BIOTYPE *n* group of genetically identical plants within a species, produced by apomixis
BIPACK, -S *n* obsolete filming process
BIPARTY *adj* involving two parties
BIPED, -S *n, adj*
BIPEDAL *adj* having two feet
BIPEDS ▶ **biped**
BIPLANE *n*
BIPOD, -S *n* two-legged support or stand
BIPOLAR *adj* having two poles

BIPRISM *n* prism having a highly obtuse angle to facilitate beam splitting
BIRCH, -ED, -ES *n, vb*
BIRCHEN ▶ **birch**
BIRCHES ▶ **birch**
BIRCHIR *same as* ▶ **bichir**
BIRD, -ED, -S *n, vb*
BIRDDOG *n* dog used or trained to retrieve game birds
BIRDED ▶ **bird**
BIRDER, -S *n* birdwatcher
BIRDIE, -D, -S *n* score of one stroke under par for a hole ▷ *vb* play (a hole) in one stroke under par
BIRDING ▶ **bird**
BIRDMAN, BIRDMEN *n* man concerned with birds, such as a fowler or ornithologist
BIRDS ▶ **bird**
BIREME, -S *n* ancient galley having two banks of oars
BIRETTA *n* stiff square cap worn by the Catholic clergy
BIRIANI *same as* ▶ **biryani**
BIRK, -S *n* birch tree ▷ *adj* consisting or made of birch
BIRKEN *adj* relating to the birch tree
BIRKIE, -R, -S *n* spirited or lively person ▷ *adj* lively
BIRKS ▶ **birk**
BIRL, -ED, -S *same as* ▶ **burl**
BIRLE, -S *same as* ▶ **burl**
BIRLED ▶ **birl**
BIRLER, -S ▶ **birl**
BIRLES ▶ **birle**
BIRLING ▶ **birl**
BIRLINN *n* small Scottish book
BIRLS ▶ **birl**
BIRO, -S *n* tradename of a kind of ballpoint pen
BIRR, -ED, -ING, -S *vb* make or cause to make a whirring sound ▷ *n* whirring sound
BIRSE, -D, -S, BIRSING *n* bristle ▷ *vb* bruise
BIRSIER ▶ **birsy**
BIRSING ▶ **birse**
BIRSLE, -D, -S *vb* roast
BIRSY, BIRSIER *adj* bristly
BIRTH, -ED, -S *n, vb*
BIRTHER *n* person who believes Barack Obama was not born in the USA
BIRTHS ▶ **birth**
BIRYANI *n* Indian rice-based dish
BIS *adv* twice ▷ *sentence substitute* encore! again!
BISCUIT *n, adj*
BISE, -S *n* cold dry northerly wind
BISECT, -S *vb*
BISES ▶ **bise**
BISH, -ES *n* mistake
BISHOP, -S *n, vb*
BISK, -S *a less common spelling of* ▶ **bisque**
BISMAR, -S *n* type of weighing scale
BISMUTH *n* pinkish-white metallic element
BISNAGA *n* type of cactus
BISOM, -S *same as* ▶ **besom**
BISON, -S *same as* ▶ **buffalo**
BISQUE, -S *n* thick rich soup made from shellfish
BISSON, -S *adj* blind ▷ *vb* cause to be blind
BIST *a form of the second person singular of* ▶ **be**
BISTATE *adj* involving two states
BISTER, -S *same as* ▶ **bistre**
BISTORT *n* Eurasian plant with a spike of small pink flowers
BISTRE, -S *n* water-soluble pigment
BISTRED ▶ **bistre**
BISTRES ▶ **bistre**
BISTRO, -S *n*
BIT, -S *n*
BITABLE ▶ **bite**
BITCH, -ED, -ES *n, vb*
BITCHEN *same as* > **bitching**
BITCHES ▶ **bitch**
BITCHY *adj* spiteful or malicious
BITCOIN *n* type of digital currency
BITE, -S, BITTEN *vb, n*
BITER, -S ▶ **bite**
BITES ▶ **bite**
BITING, -S ▶ **bite**
BITLESS *adj* without a bit
BITMAP, -S *n* picture created by colour or shading on a visual display unit ▷ *vb* create a bitmap of

BITO, -S *n* African and Asian tree
BITONAL *adj* consisting of black and white tones
BITOS ▸ **bito**
BITOU *n* as in **bitou bush** type of sprawling woody shrub
BITRATE *n* rate of data processing
BITS ▸ **bit**
BITSER, -S *n* mongrel dog
BITSY, BITSIER *adj* very small
BITT, -ED, -S *n* strong post on the deck of a ship for securing lines ▹ *vb* secure (a line) by means of a bitt
BITTE *interj* you're welcome
BITTED ▸ **bitt**
BITTEN ▸ **bite**
BITTER *adj* having a sharp unpleasant taste ▹ *n* beer with a slightly bitter taste ▹ *adv* very ▹ *vb* make or become bitter
BITTERN *n* wading marsh bird with a booming call
BITTERS *pl n* bitter-tasting spirits flavoured with plant extracts
BITTIE, -S *n* small piece
BITTIER ▸ **bitty**
BITTIES ▸ **bittie**
BITTILY *adv* in a disjointed way
BITTING ▸ **bitt**
BITTOCK *n* small amount
BITTOR, -S *n* bittern
BITTOUR *same as* ▸ **bittor**
BITTS ▸ **bitt**
BITTUR, -S *same as* ▸ **bittor**
BITTY, BITTIER *adj* lacking unity, disjointed
BITUMED *adj* covered with bitumen
BITUMEN *n*
BITURBO *n* engine with two turbochargers
BITWISE *adj* relating to an operator in a programming language that manipulates bits
BIVALVE *adj* (of a marine mollusc) with two hinged segments to its shell ▹ *n* sea creature with a shell consisting of two hinged segments
BIVIA ▸ **bivium**
BIVINYL *another word for* > **butadiene**
BIVIOUS *adj* offering a choice of two different ways
BIVIUM, BIVIA *n* parting of ways
BIVOUAC *n* temporary camp in the open air ▹ *vb* camp in a bivouac
BIVVY, BIVVIED, BIVVIES *n* small tent or shelter ▹ *vb* camp in a bivouac
BIZ, -ZES *n* business
BIZARRE *adj, n*
BIZARRO *n* bizarre person
BIZAZZ *same as* ▸ **pizazz**
BIZE, -S *n* dry, cold wind in France
BIZJET, -S *n* small jet plane used by businesspeople
BIZNAGA *same as* ▸ **bisnaga**
BIZONAL ▸ **bizone**
BIZONE, -S *n* place comprising two zones
BIZZAZZ *n* combination of energy and style
BIZZES ▸ **biz**
BIZZIES ▸ **bizzy**
BIZZO, -S *n* empty and irrelevant talk or ideas
BIZZY, BIZZIES *n* slang word for a police officer
BLAB, -BED, -S *vb*
BLABBER *vb* talk without thinking ▹ *n* person who blabs
BLABBY *adj* talking too much; indiscreet
BLABS ▸ **blab**
BLACK, -ED, -ER, -S *adj, n, vb*
BLACKEN *vb*
BLACKER ▸ **black**
BLACKLY ▸ **black**
BLACKS ▸ **black**
BLAD, -DED, -S *same as* ▸ **blaud**
BLADDER *n*
BLADE, -S *n*
BLADED ▸ **blade**
BLADER, -S *n* person skating with in-line skates
BLADES ▸ **blade**
BLADIER ▸ **blady**
BLADING *n* act or instance of skating with in-line skates
BLADS ▸ **blad**
BLADY, BLADIER *adj* as in **blady grass** coarse leafy Australasian grass

BLAE, -R, -ST *adj* bluish-grey
BLAES *n* hardened clay or shale
BLAEST ▸ **blae**
BLAFF, -ED, -S *n* fish stew of the Caribbean ▹ *vb* make a barking noise
BLAG, -GED, -S *vb, n*
BLAGGER ▸ **blag**
BLAGS ▸ **blag**
BLAGUE, -S *n* pretentious but empty talk
BLAGUER ▸ **blague**
BLAGUES ▸ **blague**
BLAH, -ED, -ER, -EST, -ING, -S *n* worthless or silly talk ▹ *adj* uninteresting ▹ *vb* talk nonsense or boringly
BLAIN, -S *n* blister, blotch, or sore on the skin
BLAISE *same as* ▸ **blaes**
BLAIZE *same as* ▸ **blaes**
BLAM, -MED, -S *n* representation of the sound of a bullet being fired ▹ *vb* make the noise of a bullet being fired
BLAME, -S, BLAMING *vb, n*
BLAMED *euphemistic word for* ▸ **damned**
BLAMER, -S ▸ **blame**
BLAMES ▸ **blame**
BLAMING ▸ **blame**
BLAMMED ▸ **blam**
BLAMS ▸ **blam**
BLANCH *vb*
BLANCO, -S *n* whitening substance ▹ *vb* whiten (something) with blanco
BLAND, -ED, -ER, -S *adj, n, vb*
BLANDLY ▸ **bland**
BLANDS ▸ **bland**
BLANK, -ED, -ER, -S *adj, n, vb*
BLANKET *n, adj, vb*
BLANKIE *n* child's security blanket
BLANKLY ▸ **blank**
BLANKS ▸ **blank**
BLANKY *same as* ▸ **blankie**
BLARE, -D, -S, BLARING *vb, n*
BLARNEY *n* flattering talk ▹ *vb* cajole with flattery
BLART, -ED, -S *vb* sound loudly and harshly
BLASE *adj* indifferent or bored through familiarity
BLASH, -ED, -ES *n* splash ▹ *vb* splash (something) with liquid
BLASHY *adj* windy and rainy
BLAST, -S *n, vb, interj*
BLASTED *adv* extreme or extremely ▹ *adj* blighted or withered
BLASTER ▸ **blast**
BLASTIE *n* ugly creature
BLASTS ▸ **blast**
BLASTY *adj* gusty
BLAT, -S, -TED *vb* cry out or bleat like a sheep
BLATANT *adj*
BLATE, -D, -R, -S, -ST, BLATING *adj* shy; ill at ease ▹ *vb* babble (something)
BLATHER *vb, n*
BLATING ▸ **blate**
BLATS ▸ **blat**
BLATT, -S *n* newspaper
BLATTED ▸ **blat**
BLATTER *vb* prattle
BLATTS ▸ **blatt**
BLAUBOK *n* South African antelope
BLAUD, -ED, -S *vb* slap
BLAW, -ED, -ING, -N, -S *vb* Scots word for blow
BLAWORT *n* harebell
BLAWS ▸ **blaw**
BLAY, -S *n* small river fish
BLAZAR, -S *n* type of active galaxy
BLAZE, -D, BLAZING *n, vb*
BLAZER, -S *n* lightweight jacket, often in the colours of a school etc
BLAZES *pl n* hell
BLAZING ▸ **blaze**
BLAZON, -S *vb* proclaim publicly ▹ *n* coat of arms
BLEACH *vb, n*
BLEAK, -ER, -S *adj, n*
BLEAKLY ▸ **bleak**
BLEAKS ▸ **bleak**
BLEAKY *same as* ▸ **bleak**
BLEAR, -ED, -ER, -S *vb* make (eyes or sight) dim with or as if with tears ▹ *adj* bleary
BLEARY *adj* with eyes dimmed, as by tears or tiredness
BLEAT, -ED, -S *vb, n*
BLEATER ▸ **bleat**
BLEATS ▸ **bleat**
BLEB, -S *n* fluid-filled blister on the skin
BLEBBY ▸ **bleb**
BLEBS ▸ **bleb**

BLECH *interj* expressing disgust
BLED ▸ **bleed**
BLEE, -S *n* complexion; hue
BLEED, BLED, -S *vb*
BLEEDER *n* despicable person
BLEEDS ▸ **bleed**
BLEEP, -ED, -S *n, vb*
BLEEPER *n* small portable radio receiver that makes a bleeping signal
BLEEPS ▸ **bleep**
BLEES ▸ **blee**
BLELLUM *n* babbler; blusterer
BLEMISH *n, vb*
BLENCH *vb* shy away, as in fear
BLEND, -ED, -S *vb, n*
BLENDE, -S *n* mineral consisting mainly of zinc sulphide
BLENDED ▸ **blend**
BLENDER *n*
BLENDES ▸ **blende**
BLENDS ▸ **blend**
BLENNY *n* small fish with a tapering scaleless body
BLENT *a past participle of* ▸ **blend**
BLERT, -S *n* foolish person
BLESBOK *n* S African antelope
BLESS, -ES, BLEST *vb*
BLESSED *adj* made holy
BLESSER ▸ **bless**
BLESSES ▸ **bless**
BLEST ▸ **bless**
BLET, -S, -TED *n* state of decay in certain fruits, due to overripening ▹ *vb* go soft
BLETHER *same as* ▸ **blather**
BLETS ▸ **blet**
BLETTED ▸ **blet**
BLEW ▸ **blow**
BLEWART *same as* ▸ **blawort**
BLEWITS *n* type of edible fungus with a pale brown cap and a bluish stalk
BLEY, -S *same as* ▸ **blay**
BLIGHT, -S *n, vb*
BLIGHTY *n* home country; home leave
BLIKSEM *interj* South African expression of surprise
BLIMEY *interj* exclamation of surprise or annoyance
BLIMP, -ED, -S *n* small airship ▹ *vb* swell out
BLIMY *same as* ▸ **blimey**
BLIN, -NED, -S *Scots word for* ▸ **blind**
BLIND, -ED, -S *adj, vb, n*
BLINDER *n* outstanding performance
BLINDLY ▸ **blind**
BLINDS ▸ **blind**
BLING, -ED, -ER, -S *adj, n, vb*
BLINGY *same as* ▸ **bling**
BLINI *pl n* Russian pancakes made of buckwheat flour and yeast
BLINIS *same as* ▸ **blini**
BLINK, -ED, -S *vb, n*
BLINKER *vb* provide (a horse) with blinkers ▹ *n* flashing light for sending messages
BLINKS ▸ **blink**
BLINNED ▸ **blin**
BLINS ▸ **blin**
BLINTZ *n* thin pancake folded over a filling usually of apple, cream cheese, or meat
BLINTZE *same as* ▸ **blintz**
BLINY *same as* ▸ **blini**
BLIP, -PED, -S *n, vb*
BLISS, -ED, -ES *n, vb*
BLIST *archaic form of* ▸ **blessed**
BLISTER *n, vb*
BLIT, -S, -TED *vb* move (a block of data) in a computer's memory
BLITE, -S *n* type of herb
BLITHE *adj*
BLITHER *same as* ▸ **blather**
BLITS ▸ **blit**
BLITTED ▸ **blit**
BLITTER *n* circuit that transfers large amounts of data within a computer's memory
BLITZ, -ED, -ES *n, vb*
BLITZER ▸ **blitz**
BLITZES ▸ **blitz**
BLIVE *same as* ▸ **belive**
BLOAT, -S *vb* cause to swell, as with liquid or air ▹ *n* abnormal distention of the abdomen in cattle, sheep, etc
BLOATED *adj*
BLOATER *n* salted smoked herring
BLOATS ▸ **bloat**
BLOB, -BED, -S *n, vb*
BLOBBY ▸ **blob**
BLOBS ▸ **blob**
BLOC, -S *n*
BLOCK, -ED, -S *n, vb*

BLOCKER *n* person or thing that blocks
BLOCKIE *n* owner of a small property, esp a farm
BLOCKS ▶ **block**
BLOCKY *adj* like a block, esp in shape and solidity
BLOCS ▶ **bloc**
BLOG, -GED, -S *n, vb*
BLOGGER ▶ **blog**
BLOGGY *adj* characteristic of a blog
BLOGS ▶ **blog**
BLOKART *n* single-seat three-wheeled vehicle propelled by the wind
BLOKE, -S *n*
BLOKEY, BLOKIER *same as* > **blokeish**
BLOKISH *same as* > **blokeish**
BLOND, -S *adj, n*
BLONDE, -R, -S *adj, n*
BLONDS ▶ **blond**
BLOOD, -S *n, vb*
BLOODED *adj* (of horses, cattle, etc) of good breeding
BLOODS ▶ **blood**
BLOODY *adj* covered with blood ▷ *adv* extreme or extremely ▷ *vb* stain with blood
BLOOEY *adj* out of order; faulty
BLOOIE *same as* ▶ **blooey**
BLOOK, -S *n* book published on a blog
BLOOM, -S *n, vb*
BLOOMED *adj* (of a lens) coated to reduce light lost by reflection
BLOOMER *n* stupid mistake
BLOOMS ▶ **bloom**
BLOOMY *adj* having a fine whitish coating on the surface
BLOOP, -ED, -S *vb* (baseball) hit a ball into the air beyond the infield
BLOOPER *n*
BLOOPS ▶ **bloop**
BLOOPY *adj* (in baseball) relating to a ball hit into the air beyond the infield
BLOOSME *archaic form of* ▶ **blossom**
BLORE, -S *n* strong blast of wind
BLOSSOM *n, vb*
BLOT, -S, -TED *n, vb*
BLOTCH *n, vb*
BLOTCHY *adj* covered in or marked by blotches
BLOTS ▶ **blot**
BLOTTED ▶ **blot**
BLOTTER *n*
BLOTTO *adj* extremely drunk
BLOTTY *adj* covered in blots
BLOUBOK *same as* ▶ **blaubok**
BLOUSE, -D, -S *n, vb*
BLOUSON *n* short loose jacket with a tight waist
BLOUSY *adj* loose; blouse-like
BLOW, BLEW, -ED, -N, -S *vb, n*
BLOWBY, -S *n* leakage of gas past the piston of an engine at maximum pressure
BLOWED ▶ **blow**
BLOWER, -S *n* mechanical device, such as a fan, that blows
BLOWFLY *n* fly that lays its eggs in meat
BLOWGUN *same as* > **blowpipe**
BLOWIE, -S *n* bluebottle
BLOWIER ▶ **blowy**
BLOWIES ▶ **blowie**
BLOWING *n* moving of air
BLOWN ▶ **blow**
BLOWOFF *n* discharge of a surplus fluid
BLOWOUT *n* sudden loss of air in a tyre
BLOWS ▶ **blow**
BLOWSE, -S *n* large, red-faced woman
BLOWSED *same as* ▶ **blowsy**
BLOWSES ▶ **blowse**
BLOWSY *adj* fat, untidy, and red-faced
BLOWUP, -S *n* fit of temper
BLOWY, BLOWIER *adj* windy
BLOWZE, -S *variant of* ▶ **blowse**
BLOWZED *same as* ▶ **blowsy**
BLOWZES ▶ **blowze**
BLOWZY *same as* ▶ **blowsy**
BLUB, -BED, -S *a slang word for* ▶ **blubber**
BLUBBER *vb, adj, n*
BLUBS ▶ **blub**
BLUCHER *n* high shoe with laces over the tongue
BLUD, -S *n* slang term for a friend
BLUDE, -S *Scots form of* ▶ **blood**
BLUDGE, -D, -S *vb* evade work ▷ *n* easy task

BLUDGER *n* person who scrounges
BLUDGES ▶ **bludge**
BLUDIE, -R *Scots form of* ▶ **bloody**
BLUDS ▶ **blud**
BLUDY *same as* ▶ **bludie**
BLUE, -D, -R, -ST *n, adj, vb*
BLUECAP *another name for* ▶ **bluetit**
BLUED ▶ **blue**
BLUEFIN *another name for* ▶ **tunny**
BLUEGUM *n* widely cultivated Australian tree
BLUEING ▶ **blue**
BLUEISH *same as* ▶ **bluish**
BLUEJAY *n* N American jay
BLUELY ▶ **blue**
BLUER ▶ **blue**
BLUES *pl n* type of music
BLUEST ▶ **blue**
BLUESY ▶ **blues**
BLUET, -S *n* N American plant with small four-petalled blue flowers
BLUETIT *n*
BLUETS ▶ **bluet**
BLUETTE *n* short, brilliant piece of music
BLUEY, -S, BLUIER, BLUIEST *adj* bluish ▷ *n* informal Australian word meaning blanket
BLUFF, -ED, -S *vb, n, adj*
BLUFFER ▶ **bluff**
BLUFFLY ▶ **bluff**
BLUFFS ▶ **bluff**
BLUGGY *same as* ▶ **bloody**
BLUID, -S *Scots word for* ▶ **blood**
BLUIDY ▶ **bluid**
BLUIER ▶ **bluey**
BLUIEST ▶ **bluey**
BLUING, -S ▶ **blue**
BLUISH *adj* slightly blue
BLUME, -D, -S, BLUMING *Scots word for* ▶ **bloom**
BLUNDER *n, vb*
BLUNGE, -D, -S *vb* mix clay with water
BLUNGER *n* large vat in which the contents are mixed by rotating arms
BLUNGES ▶ **blunge**
BLUNK, -ED, -S *vb* ruin; botch
BLUNKER ▶ **blunk**
BLUNKS ▶ **blunk**
BLUNT, -ED, -ER, -S *adj, vb*
BLUNTLY ▶ **blunt**
BLUNTS ▶ **blunt**
BLUR, -RED, -S *vb, n*
BLURB, -ED, -S *n, vb*
BLURRED ▶ **blur**
BLURRY ▶ **blur**
BLURS ▶ **blur**
BLURT, -ED, -S *vb*
BLURTER ▶ **blurt**
BLURTS ▶ **blurt**
BLUSH, -ED, -ES *vb, n*
BLUSHER *n* cosmetic for giving the cheeks a rosy colour
BLUSHES ▶ **blush**
BLUSHET *n* modest young woman
BLUSTER *vb, n*
BLYPE, -S *n* piece of skin peeled off after sunburn
BO, -S *interj* exclamation uttered to startle or surprise someone ▷ *n* fellow, buddy
BOA, -S *n* large nonvenomous snake
BOAB, -S *short for* ▶ **baobab**
BOAK, -ED, -ING, -S *same as* ▶ **boke**
BOAR, -S *n*
BOARD, -ED, -S *n, vb*
BOARDER *n* person who pays rent for accommodation in someone else's home
BOARDS ▶ **board**
BOARISH *adj* coarse, cruel, or sensual
BOARS ▶ **boar**
BOART, -S *same as* ▶ **bort**
BOAS ▶ **boa**
BOAST, -ED, -S *vb, n*
BOASTER ▶ **boast**
BOASTS ▶ **boast**
BOAT, -ED, -S *n, vb*
BOATEL, -S *n* waterside hotel catering for boating people
BOATER, -S *n* flat straw hat
BOATFUL ▶ **boat**
BOATIE, -S *n* boating enthusiast
BOATING *n* rowing, sailing, or cruising in boats as a form of recreation
BOATMAN, BOATMEN *n* man who works on, hires out, or repairs boats
BOATS ▶ **boat**
BOB, -BED, -BING, -S *vb* move or cause to move up and down repeatedly ▷ *n* short abrupt movement, as of the head

BOBA, -S *n* type of Chinese tea
BOBAC, -S *same as* ▶ **bobak**
BOBAK, -S *n* type of marmot
BOBAS ▶ **boba**
BOBBED ▶ **bob**
BOBBER, -S *n* type of float for fishing
BOBBERY *n* mixed pack of hunting dogs ▷ *adj* noisy or excitable
BOBBIES ▶ **bobby**
BOBBIN, -S *n*
BOBBING ▶ **bob**
BOBBINS ▶ **bobbin**
BOBBISH *adj* cheery
BOBBLE, -D, -S *n, vb*
BOBBLY *adj* (of fabric) covered in small balls; worn
BOBBY, BOBBIES *n* slang word for a police officer
BOBCAT, -S *n* N American feline
BOBECHE *n* candle drip-catcher
BOBLET, -S *n* two-person bobsleigh
BOBO, -S *n* rich person who holds bohemian values
BOBOL, -S *n* type of fraud ▷ *vb* commit a bobol
BOBOS ▶ **bobo**
BOBOTIE *n* dish of curried mince
BOBS ▶ **bob**
BOBSLED *same as* > **bobsleigh**
BOBSTAY *n* stay between a bowsprit and the stem of a vessel
BOBTAIL *n* docked tail ▷ *adj* having the tail cut short ▷ *vb* dock the tail of
BOBWIG, -S *n* type of short wig
BOCAGE, -S *n* wooded countryside characteristic of northern France
BOCCA, -S *n* round opening of a glass-furnace
BOCCE, -S *same as* ▶ **boccie**
BOCCI, -S *same as* ▶ **boccie**
BOCCIA, -S *same as* ▶ **boccie**
BOCCIE, -S *n* Italian version of bowls
BOCCIS ▶ **bocci**
BOCK, -ED, -ING, -S *variant spelling of* ▶ **boke**
BOCKEDY *adj* (of a structure, piece of furniture, etc) unsteady
BOCKING ▶ **bock**
BOCKS ▶ **bock**
BOD, -S *n* person
BODACH, -S *n* old man
BODDLE, -S *same as* ▶ **bodle**
BODE, -D, -S *vb* portend or presage
BODEFUL *adj* portentous
BODEGA, -S *n* shop in a Spanish-speaking country that sells wine
BODES ▶ **bode**
BODGE, -D, -S, BODGING *vb* make a mess of
BODGER, -S *n* labourer who made chairs from felled trees
BODGES ▶ **bodge**
BODGIE, -R, -S *n* unruly or uncouth young man, esp in the 1950s ▷ *adj* inferior
BODGING ▶ **bodge**
BODHI, -S *n* as in **bodhi tree** holy tree of Buddhists
BODHRAN *n* shallow one-sided drum popular in Irish and Scottish folk music
BODICE, -S *n*
BODIED ▶ **body**
BODIES ▶ **body**
BODIKIN *n* little body
BODILY *adj* relating to the body ▷ *adv* by taking hold of the body
BODING, -S ▶ **bode**
BODKIN, -S *n* blunt large-eyed needle
BODLE, -S *n* small obsolete Scottish coin
BODRAG, -S *n* enemy attack
BODS ▶ **bod**
BODY, BODIED, BODIES, -ING *n, vb*
BODYMAN, BODYMEN *n* person who repairs car bodies
BOEP, -S *n* South African word for a big belly
BOERBUL *n* crossbred mastiff used esp as a watchdog
BOET, -S *n* brother
BOEUF, -S *n* as in **boeuf bourguignon** type of beef casserole
BOFF, -ED, -ING, -S *n* boffin ▷ *vb* hit
BOFFIN, -S *n* scientist or expert

BOFFING ▶ **boff**
BOFFINS ▶ **boffin**
BOFFINY *adj* like a boffin
BOFFO, -S *n* boffin
BOFFOLA *n* great success
BOFFOS ▶ **boffo**
BOFFS ▶ **boff**
BOG, -GED, -GING, -S *n, vb*
BOGAN, -S *n* youth who dresses and behaves rebelliously
BOGART, -S *vb* monopolize or keep to oneself selfishly
BOGBEAN *same as* > **buckbean**
BOGEY, -ED, -S *n* evil or mischievous spirit ▷ *vb* play (a hole) in one stroke over par
BOGGARD *same as* ▶ **boggart**
BOGGART *n* ghost or poltergeist
BOGGED ▶ **bog**
BOGGER, -S *n* lavatory
BOGGIER ▶ **boggy**
BOGGING ▶ **bog**
BOGGISH ▶ **bog**
BOGGLE, -D, -S *vb*
BOGGLER ▶ **boggle**
BOGGLES ▶ **boggle**
BOGGY, BOGGIER ▶ **bog**
BOGHEAD *adj* relating to variety of coal from which paraffin can be derived
BOGHOLE *n* natural hole of wet spongy ground
BOGIE, -D, -S *same as* ▶ **bogey**
BOGLAND *n* area of wetland
BOGLE, -D, -S, BOGLING *n* rhythmic dance performed to ragga music ▷ *vb* perform such a dance
BOGMAN, BOGMEN *n* body of a person found preserved in a peat bog
BOGOAK, -S *n* oak or other wood found preserved in peat bogs
BOGONG, -S *n* large nocturnal Australian moth
BOGS ▶ **bog**
BOGUE, -S *n* type of Mediterranean fish
BOGUS *adj*
BOGUSLY ▶ **bogus**
BOGWOOD *same as* ▶ **bogoak**
BOGY *same as* ▶ **bogey**
BOGYISM *same as* > **bogeyism**
BOGYMAN, BOGYMEN *same as* > **bogeyman**
BOH, -S *same as* ▶ **bo**
BOHEA, -S *n* black Chinese tea
BOHEMIA *n* area frequented by unconventional (esp creative) people
BOHO, -S *short for* > **bohemian**
BOHRIUM *n* element artificially produced in minute quantities
BOHS ▶ **boh**
BOIL, -ED, -S *vb, n*
BOILER, -S *n* piece of equipment which provides hot water
BOILERY *n* place where water is boiled to extract salt
BOILING *adj* very hot ▷ *n* sweet
BOILOFF *n* quantity of liquefied gases lost in evaporation
BOILS ▶ **boil**
BOING, -ED, -S *vb* rebound making a noise
BOINK, -ED, -S *same as* ▶ **boing**
BOITE, -S *n* artist's portfolio
BOK, -S *n* S African antelope

> This useful K word, meaning an antelope, can take quite a number of front extensions, forming words like **blesbok, bontbok, reitbok, rhebok**, and even, if you are lucky, **jambok** or **sjambok**.

BOKE, -D, -S, BOKING *vb* retch or vomit ▷ *n* retch
BOKEH, -S *n* blurred area of an image
BOKES ▶ **boke**
BOKING ▶ **boke**
BOKKEN, -S *n* wooden practice sword in kendo
BOKO, -S *slang word for* ▶ **nose**
BOKS ▶ **bok**
BOLA *n* missile used by gauchos and Indians of South America
BOLAR *adj* relating to clay
BOLAS, -ES *same as* ▶ **bola**

BOLD, -ED, -ER, -EST, -ING, -S *adj, n, vb*
BOLDEN, -S *vb* make bold
BOLDER ▶ **bold**
BOLDEST ▶ **bold**
BOLDING ▶ **bold**
BOLDLY ▶ **bold**
BOLDS ▶ **bold**
BOLE, -S *n* tree trunk
BOLERO, -S *n* (music for) traditional Spanish dance
BOLES ▶ **bole**
BOLETE, -S *same as* ▶ **boletus**
BOLETUS, BOLETI *n* type of fungus
BOLIDE, -S *n* large exceptionally bright meteor that often explodes
BOLINE, -S *n* (in Wicca) a knife
BOLIVAR *n* standard monetary unit of Venezuela, equal to 100 céntimos
BOLIVIA *n* type of woollen fabric
BOLL, -ED, -EN, -ING, -S *n* rounded seed capsule of cotton, flax, etc ▷ *vb* form into a boll
BOLLARD *n*
BOLLED ▶ **boll**
BOLLEN ▶ **boll**
BOLLING ▶ **boll**
BOLLS ▶ **boll**
BOLO, -S *n* large single-edged knife, originating in the Philippines
BOLOGNA *n* type of sausage
BOLONEY *variant spelling of* ▶ **baloney**
BOLOS ▶ **bolo**
BOLSHIE *adj* difficult or rebellious ▷ *n* any political radical
BOLSHY *same as* ▶ **bolshie**
BOLSON, -S *n* desert valley surrounded by mountains, with a shallow lake at the centre
BOLSTER *vb, n*
BOLT, -ED, -S *n, vb*
BOLTER, -S ▶ **bolt**
BOLTING ▶ **bolt**
BOLTS ▶ **bolt**
BOLUS, -ES *same as* ▶ **bole**
BOMA, -S *n* enclosure set up to protect a camp, herd of animals, etc
BOMB, -ED, -S *n, vb*
BOMBARD *vb, n*
BOMBAST *n* pompous language ▷ *vb* speak pompous language
BOMBAX *n* type of S American tree
BOMBE, -S *n* dessert of ice cream lined or filled with custard, cake crumbs, etc ▷ *adj* (of furniture) having a projecting swollen shape
BOMBED ▶ **bomb**
BOMBER, -S *n* aircraft that drops bombs
BOMBES ▶ **bombe**
BOMBING ▶ **bomb**
BOMBLET *n* small bomb
BOMBO, -S *same as* ▶ **bumbo**
BOMBORA *n* submerged reef
BOMBOS ▶ **bombo**
BOMBS ▶ **bomb**
BOMBYX *n* type of moth
BOMMIE, -S *n* outcrop of coral reef
BON *adj* good
BONA *pl n* goods
BONACI, -S *n* type of fish
BONAMIA *n* parasite
BONANZA *n* sudden good luck or wealth
BONASUS *n* European bison
BONBON, -S *n* sweet
BONCE, -S *n* head
BOND, -S *n, vb*
BONDAGE *n*
BONDED *adj* consisting of, secured by, or operating under a bond or bonds
BONDER, -S *same as* > **bondstone**
BONDING *n* process by which individuals become emotionally attached to one another
BONDMAN, BONDMEN *same as* > **bondsman**
BONDS ▶ **bond**
BONDUC, -S *n* type of North American tree
BONE, -D, -S *n, vb*
BONEBED *n* site where dinosaur fossils are found
BONED ▶ **bone**
BONER, -S *n* blunder
BONES ▶ **bone**
BONESET *n* N American plant with flat clusters of small white flowers

BONEY, -ER *same as* ▶ **bony**
BONFIRE *n*
BONG, -ED, -ING, -S *n* deep reverberating sound, as of a large bell ▷ *vb* make a deep reverberating sound
BONGO, -ES, -S *n* small drum played with the fingers
BONGS ▶ **bong**
BONHAM, -S *n* piglet
BONIATO *n* sweet potato
BONIE *same as* ▶ **bonny**
BONIER ▶ **bony**
BONIEST ▶ **bony**
BONING, -S ▶ **bone**
BONISM, -S *n* doctrine that the world is good, although not the best of all possible worlds
BONIST, -S ▶ **bonism**
BONITO, -S *n* small tuna-like marine food fish
BONJOUR *interj* hello
BONK, -ED, -S *vb* hit
BONKERS *adj* crazy
BONKING ▶ **bonk**
BONKS ▶ **bonk**
BONNE, -S *n* housemaid or female servant
BONNET, -S *n, vb*
BONNIE *same as* ▶ **bonny**
BONNIER ▶ **bonny**
BONNIES ▶ **bonny**
BONNILY ▶ **bonny**
BONNOCK *n* thick oatmeal cake
BONNY, BONNIER, BONNIES *adj, adv, n*
BONOBO, -S *n* type of anthropoid ape of central W Africa
BONSAI *n*
BONSELA *n* small gift of money
BONSOIR *interj* good evening
BONTBOK *n* antelope found in S Africa
BONUS, -ED, -ES *n, vb*
BONXIE, -S *n* great skua
BONY, BONIER, BONIEST *adj* having many bones
BONZA *same as* ▶ **bonzer**
BONZE, -S *n* Chinese or Japanese Buddhist priest or monk
BONZER *adj* excellent
BONZES ▶ **bonze**
BOO, -ED, -S *interj, vb*
BOOAI, -S *same as* ▶ **boohai**
BOOAY, -S *same as* ▶ **boohai**
BOOB, -ED, -ING, -S *n* foolish mistake ▷ *vb* make a foolish mistake ▷ *adj* of poor quality, similar to that provided in prison
BOOBIE *same as* ▶ **booby**
BOOBIES ▶ **booby**
BOOBING ▶ **boob**
BOOBIRD *n* person who boos
BOOBISH *adj* doltish
BOOBOO, -S *n* blunder
BOOBOOK *n* small spotted Australian brown owl
BOOBOOS ▶ **booboo**
BOOBS ▶ **boob**
BOOBY, BOOBIES *n* foolish person
BOOCOO, -S *same as* > **beaucoup**
BOODIE *n* type of kangaroo
BOODIED ▶ **boody**
BOODIES ▶ **boody**
BOODLE, -D, -S *n* money or valuables that are counterfeit or used as a bribe ▷ *vb* give or receive money corruptly or illegally
BOODLER ▶ **boodle**
BOODLES ▶ **boodle**
BOODY, BOODIED, BOODIES *vb* sulk
BOOED ▶ **boo**
BOOFY, BOOFIER *adj* muscular and strong but stupid
BOOGER, -S *n* piece of dried mucus from the nose
BOOGEY, -S *same as* ▶ **boogie**
BOOGIE, -D, -S *vb* dance to fast pop music ▷ *n* session of dancing to pop music
BOOGY *same as* ▶ **boogie**
BOOH, -ED, -ING, -S *same as* ▶ **boo**
BOOHAI, -S *n* as in **up the boohai** thoroughly lost
BOOHED ▶ **booh**
BOOHING ▶ **booh**
BOOHOO, -S *vb* sob or pretend to sob noisily ▷ *n* distressed or pretended sobbing
BOOHS ▶ **booh**
BOOING, -S *n* act of booing
BOOJUM, -S *n* American tree
BOOK, -ED, -S *n, vb*

BOOKBAG *n* bag for books
BOOKED ▶ **book**
BOOKEND *n*, *vb*
BOOKER, -S ▶ **book**
BOOKFUL ▶ **book**
BOOKIE, -S *short for* > **bookmaker**
BOOKIER ▶ **booky**
BOOKIES ▶ **bookie**
BOOKING *n* reservation, as of a table or seat
BOOKISH *adj* fond of reading
BOOKLET *n*
BOOKMAN, BOOKMEN *n* learned person
BOOKOO, -S *same as* ▶ **boocoo**
BOOKS ▶ **book**
BOOKSIE *same as* ▶ **booksy**
BOOKSY *adj* inclined to be bookish or literary
BOOKY, BOOKIER *adj* bookish
BOOL, -ED, -ING, -S *n* bowling ball ▷ *vb* play bowls
BOOM, -ED, -S *vb* make a loud deep echoing sound ▷ *n* loud deep echoing sound
BOOMBOX *n* portable stereo system
BOOMED ▶ **boom**
BOOMER, -S *n* large male kangaroo
BOOMIER ▶ **boomy**
BOOMING ▶ **boom**
BOOMKIN *n* short boom projecting from the deck of a ship
BOOMLET *n* small boom in business, birth rate, etc
BOOMS ▶ **boom**
BOOMY, BOOMIER *adj* characterized by heavy bass sound
BOON, -EST, -S *n*, *adj*
BOONER, -S *n* derogatory term for a young working-class person from Canberra
BOONEST ▶ **boon**
BOONIES *short form of* > **boondocks**
BOONS ▶ **boon**
BOOR, -S *n*
BOORD, -S *obsolete spelling of* ▶ **board**
BOORDE, -S *obsolete spelling of* ▶ **board**
BOORDS ▶ **boord**
BOORISH *adj* ill-mannered, clumsy, or insensitive
BOORKA, -S *same as* ▶ **burka**
BOORS ▶ **boor**
BOOS ▶ **boo**
BOOSE, -D, -S, BOOSING *same as* ▶ **booze**
BOOST, -ED, -S *n*, *vb*
BOOSTER *n* small additional injection of a vaccine
BOOSTS ▶ **boost**
BOOT, -ING, -S *n*, *vb*
BOOTCUT *adj* (of trousers) slightly flared at the bottom of the legs
BOOTED *adj* wearing boots
BOOTEE, -S *n* baby's soft shoe
BOOTERY *n* shop where boots and shoes are sold
BOOTH, -S *n*
BOOTIE *n* Royal Marine
BOOTIES ▶ **booty**
BOOTING ▶ **boot**
BOOTLEG *adj* produced, distributed, or sold illicitly ▷ *vb* make, carry, or sell (illicit goods) ▷ *n* something made or sold illicitly
BOOTS ▶ **boot**
BOOTY, BOOTIES *n*
BOOZE, -D, -S *n*, *vb*
BOOZER, -S *n*
BOOZES ▶ **booze**
BOOZEY *same as* ▶ **boozy**
BOOZIER ▶ **boozy**
BOOZILY ▶ **boozy**
BOOZING ▶ **booze**
BOOZY, BOOZIER *adj* inclined to or involving excessive drinking of alcohol
BOP, -PED, -PING, -S *vb*, *n*
BOPEEP, -S *n* quick look; peek
BOPPED ▶ **bop**
BOPPER, -S ▶ **bop**
BOPPIER ▶ **boppy**
BOPPING ▶ **bop**
BOPPISH *same as* ▶ **boppy**
BOPPY, BOPPIER *adj* resembling or suggesting bebop
BOPS ▶ **bop**
BOR, -S *n* neighbour
BORA, -S *n* Aboriginal Australian initiation ceremony
BORACES ▶ **borax**
BORACIC *same as* ▶ **boric**
BORAGE, -S *n* Mediterranean plant with star-shaped blue flowers
BORAK, -S *n* rubbish

BORAL, -S *n* type of fine powder
BORANE, -S *n* any compound of boron and hydrogen
BORAS ▸ **bora**
BORATE, -D, -S *n* salt or ester of boric acid ▹ *vb* treat with borax, boric acid, or borate
BORAX, BORACES, -ES *n* soluble white mineral occurring in alkaline soils and salt deposits
BORAZON *n* extremely hard form of boron nitride
BORD, -S *obsolete spelling of* ▸ **board**
BORDAR, -S *n* smallholder who held cottage in return for menial work
BORDE, -S *obsolete spelling of* ▸ **board**
BORDER, -S *n, vb*
BORDES ▸ **borde**
BORDS ▸ **bord**
BORDURE *n* outer edge of a shield, esp when decorated distinctively
BORE, -D, -S *vb*
BOREAL *adj* of or relating to the north or the north wind
BOREAS *n* name for the north wind
BORED ▸ **bore**
BOREDOM *n*
BOREE, -S *same as* ▸ **myall**
BOREEN, -S *n* country lane or narrow road
BOREES ▸ **boree**
BOREL, -S *adj* unlearned ▹ *n* boring tool
BORER, -S *n* machine or hand tool for boring holes
BORES ▸ **bore**
BORGO, -S *n* small attractive medieval village
BORIC *adj* of or containing boron
BORIDE, -S *n* compound in which boron is the most electronegative element
BORING, -S *n* act or process of making or enlarging a hole ▹ *adj* dull
BORK, -ED, -S *vb* dismiss from a job unfairly
BORKING *n* act of incorrectly configuring a device
BORKS ▸ **bork**
BORM, -ED, -ING, -S *vb* smear with paint, oil, etc
BORN *adj*
BORNA *n* as in **borna disease** viral disease found in mammals, esp horses
BORNE ▸ **bear**
BORNEOL *n* white solid terpene alcohol
BORNITE *n* type of mineral
BORNYL, -S *n* as in **bornyl alcohol** white solid alcohol from a Malaysian tree
BORON, -S *n* element used in hardening steel
BORONIA *n* Australian aromatic flowering shrub
BORONIC ▸ **boron**
BORONS ▸ **boron**
BOROUGH *n*
BORREL *adj* ignorant
BORRELL *same as* ▸ **borrel**
BORROW, -S *vb*
BORS ▸ **bor**
BORSCH *same as* ▸ **borscht**
BORSCHT *n* Russian soup based on beetroot
BORSHCH *same as* ▸ **borscht**
BORSHT, -S *same as* ▸ **borscht**
BORSIC, -S *n* composite material used in aviation
BORSTAL *n*
BORT, -S *n* inferior grade of diamond used for cutting and drilling
BORTIER ▸ **borty**
BORTS ▸ **bort**
BORTSCH *same as* ▸ **borscht**
BORTY, BORTIER ▸ **bort**
BORTZ, -ES *same as* ▸ **bort**
BORZOI, -S *n* tall dog with a long silky coat
BOS ▸ **bo**
BOSBOK, -S *same as* > **bushbuck**
BOSCAGE *n* mass of trees and shrubs
BOSH, -ES *n* empty talk, nonsense
BOSHBOK *same as* > **bushbuck**
BOSHES ▸ **bosh**
BOSHTA *same as* ▸ **boshter**
BOSHTER *adj* excellent

BOSIE, -S *n* (in cricket) another term for googly
BOSK, -S *n* small wood of bushes and small trees
BOSKAGE *same as* ▸ **boscage**
BOSKER *adj* excellent
BOSKET, -S *n* clump of small trees or bushes
BOSKIER ▸ **bosky**
BOSKS ▸ **bosk**
BOSKY, BOSKIER *adj* containing or consisting of bushes or thickets
BOSOM, -ED, -S *n, adj, vb*
BOSOMY *adj* (of a woman) having large breasts
BOSON, -S *n* type of elementary particle
BOSONIC ▸ **boson**
BOSONS ▸ **boson**
BOSQUE, -S *same as* ▸ **bosk**
BOSQUET *same as* ▸ **bosket**
BOSS, -ED, -ER, -ES, -EST *n, vb, adj*
BOSSDOM *n* bosses collectively
BOSSED ▸ **boss**
BOSSER ▸ **boss**
BOSSES ▸ **boss**
BOSSEST ▸ **boss**
BOSSET, -S *n* either of the rudimentary antlers found in young deer
BOSSIER ▸ **bossy**
BOSSIES ▸ **bossy**
BOSSILY ▸ **bossy**
BOSSING *n* act of shaping malleable metal
BOSSISM *n* domination of political organizations by bosses
BOSSY, BOSSIER, BOSSIES *adj, n*
BOSTON, -S *n* card game for four, played with two packs
BOSTRYX *n* phenomenon in which flowers develop on one side only
BOSUN, -S *same as* > **boatswain**
BOT, -TED, -TING *vb* scrounge
BOTA, -S *n* leather container
BOTANIC *same as* > **botanical**
BOTANY *n*
BOTARGO *n* relish consisting of the roe of mullet or tuna, salted and pressed into rolls
BOTAS ▸ **bota**
BOTCH, -ED, -ES *vb, n*
BOTCHER ▸ **botch**
BOTCHES ▸ **botch**
BOTCHY *adj* clumsily done or made
BOTE, -S *n* compensation given for injury or damage to property
BOTEL, -S *same as* ▸ **boatel**
BOTES ▸ **bote**
BOTFLY *n* type of stout-bodied hairy fly
BOTH *pron, adj, determiner*
BOTHAN, -S *n* unlicensed drinking house
BOTHER, -S *vb, n, interj*
BOTHIE *same as* ▸ **bothy**
BOTHIES ▸ **bothy**
BOTHOLE *n* hole made by the larva of the botfly
BOTHRIA > **bothrium**
BOTHY, BOTHIES *n* hut used for temporary shelter
BOTNET, -S *n* network of infected computers
BOTONE *adj* having lobes at the ends
BOTONEE *same as* ▸ **botone**
BOTOXED *adj* having had Botox treatment
BOTS *n* digestive disease of horses and some other animals
BOTT, -S *same as* ▸ **bot**
BOTTE, -S *n* thrust or hit
BOTTED ▸ **bot**
BOTTEGA *n* workshop; studio
BOTTES ▸ **botte**
BOTTIES ▸ **botty**
BOTTINE *n* light boot for women or children
BOTTING ▸ **bot**
BOTTLE, -D, -S *n, vb*
BOTTLER *n* exceptional person or thing
BOTTLES ▸ **bottle**
BOTTOM, -S *n, adj, vb*
BOTTONY *same as* ▸ **botone**
BOTTS ▸ **bott**
BOTTY, BOTTIES *n* diminutive for bottom
BOTULIN *n* potent toxin which causes botulism
BOUBOU, -S *n* long flowing garment
BOUCHE, -S *n* notch cut in the top corner of a shield

BOUCHEE *n* small pastry case filled with a savoury mixture
BOUCHES ▸ **bouche**
BOUCLE, -S *n* looped yarn giving a knobbly effect ▹ *adj* of or designating such a yarn or fabric
BOUCLEE *n* support for a cue in billiards using the hand
BOUCLES ▸ **boucle**
BOUDIN, -S *n* French version of a black pudding
BOUDOIR *n* woman's bedroom or private sitting room
BOUFFE, -S *n* type of light or satirical opera common in France during the 19th century
BOUGE, -D, -S, BOUGING *vb* move
BOUGET, -S *n* budget
BOUGH, -S *n*
BOUGHED ▸ **bough**
BOUGHS ▸ **bough**
BOUGHT, -S *n* curve
BOUGIE, -S *n* medical instrument
BOUGING ▸ **bouge**
BOUILLI *n* stew
BOUK, -S *n* bulk; volume
BOULDER *n, vb*
BOULE *same as* ▸ **boulle**
BOULES *n* game popular in France
BOULLE, -S *adj* relating to a type of marquetry much used on French furniture from the 17th century ▹ *n* something ornamented with such marquetry
BOULT, -ED, -S *same as* ▸ **bolt**
BOULTER ▸ **boult**
BOULTS ▸ **boult**
BOUN, -ED, -ING, -S *vb* prepare to go out
BOUNCE, -D, -S *vb, n*
BOUNCER *n* person employed at a nightclub etc to remove unwanted people
BOUNCES ▸ **bounce**
BOUNCY *adj* lively, exuberant, or self-confident
BOUND *vb, n, adj*
BOUNDED *adj* (of a set) having a bound
BOUNDEN *adj* morally obligatory
BOUNDER *n* morally reprehensible person
BOUNDS *pl n* limit
BOUNED ▸ **boun**
BOUNING ▸ **boun**
BOUNS ▸ **boun**
BOUNTY *n*
BOUQUET *n* bunch of flowers
BOURBON *n* whiskey made from maize
BOURD, -ED, -S *n* prank ▹ *vb* jest or joke
BOURDER *n* prankster
BOURDON *n* 16-foot organ stop of the stopped diapason type
BOURDS ▸ **bourd**
BOURG, -S *n* French market town, esp one beside a castle
BOURKHA *same as* ▸ **burka**
BOURLAW *same as* ▸ **byrlaw**
BOURN, -S *n* (in S Britain) stream
BOURNE, -S *same as* ▸ **bourn**
BOURNS ▸ **bourn**
BOURREE *n* traditional French dance in fast duple time
BOURSE, -S *n* stock exchange of continental Europe, esp Paris
BOURSIN *n* tradename of a smooth white creamy cheese, often flavoured with garlic
BOUSE, -D, -S, BOUSING *vb* raise or haul with a tackle
BOUSIER ▸ **bousy**
BOUSING ▸ **bouse**
BOUSY, BOUSIER *adj* drunken; boozy
BOUT, -S *n*
BOUTADE *n* outburst
BOUTON, -S *n* knob-shaped contact between nerve fibres
BOUTS ▸ **bout**
BOUVIER *n* large powerful dog
BOVATE, -S *n* obsolete measure of land
BOVID, -S *n* type of ruminant
BOVINE, -S *n*
BOVVER, -S *n* rowdiness, esp caused by gangs of teenage youths
BOW, -S *vb, n*
BOWAT, -S *n* lamp
BOWBENT *adj* bent; bow-like
BOWED *adj* lowered, bent forward, or curved

BOWEL, -ED, -S *n* intestine, esp the large intestine ▷ *vb* remove the bowels
BOWER, -ED, -S *n* shady leafy shelter ▷ *vb* surround as with a bower
BOWERY *n* farm
BOWES *poetic plural form of* ▸ **bough**
BOWET, -S *same as* ▸ **bowat**
BOWFIN, -S *n* N American freshwater fish
BOWGET, -S *obsolete variant of* ▸ **budget**
BOWHEAD *n* type of large-mouthed Arctic whale
BOWHUNT *vb* hunt using a bow and arrows
BOWIE *n* as in **bowie knife** type of hunting knife
BOWING, -S *n* musical technique
BOWKNOT *n* decorative knot usually having two loops and two loose ends
BOWL, -ED *n*, *vb*
BOWLDER *same as* ▸ **boulder**
BOWLED ▸ **bowl**
BOWLEG, -S *n* leg curving outwards like a bow between the ankle and the thigh
BOWLER, -S *n* player who sends a ball towards a batter
BOWLESS ▸ **bow**
BOWLFUL *same as* ▸ **bowl**
BOWLIKE ▸ **bow**
BOWLINE *n* line used to keep the sail taut against the wind
BOWLING *n* game in which bowls are rolled at a group of pins
BOWLS *n* game involving biased wooden bowls and a small bowl (the jack)
BOWMAN, BOWMEN *n* archer
BOWNE, -D, -S, BOWNING *same as* ▸ **boun**
BOWPOT, -S *same as* > **boughpot**
BOWR, -S *n* muscle
BOWS ▸ **bow**
BOWSAW, -S *n* saw with a thin blade in a bow-shaped frame
BOWSE, -D, -S, BOWSING *same as* ▸ **bouse**
BOWSER, -S *n* tanker containing fuel for aircraft, military vehicles, etc
BOWSES ▸ **bowse**
BOWSEY, -S *same as* ▸ **bowsie**
BOWSHOT *n* distance an arrow travels from the bow
BOWSIE, -S *n* low-class, mean or obstreperous person
BOWSING ▸ **bowse**
BOWSMAN, BOWSMEN *n* man who hunts using a bow and arrows
BOWWOOD *n* tree of the mulberry family, native to south-central US
BOWWOW, -S *n* imitation of the bark of a dog ▷ *vb* make a noise like a dog
BOWYANG *n* band worn round a trouser leg below the knee
BOWYER, -S *n* person who makes or sells archery bows
BOX, -ED, -ES *n* container with a firm flat base and sides ▷ *vb* put into a box
BOXBALL *n* street ball game
BOXCAR, -S *n* closed railway freight van
BOXED ▸ **box**
BOXEN *adj* made of boxwood
BOXER, -S *n* person who participates in the sport of boxing
BOXES ▸ **box**
BOXFISH *another name for* > **trunkfish**
BOXFUL, -S *same as* ▸ **box**
BOXHAUL *vb* method for bringing a square-rigged ship onto a new tack
BOXIER ▸ **boxy**
BOXIEST ▸ **boxy**
BOXILY ▸ **boxy**
BOXING, -S *n* sport of fighting with the fists
BOXLA, -S *n* type of lacrosse played indoors
BOXLIKE ▸ **box**
BOXPLOT *n* (in statistics) type of graph
BOXROOM *n*
BOXTY, BOXTIES *n* type of Irish potato pancake

BOXWOOD *n* hard yellow wood of the box tree, used to make tool handles, etc
BOXY, BOXIER, BOXIEST *adj* squarish or chunky
BOY, -ED, -ING, -S *n* male child ▷ *vb* act the part of a boy in a play
BOYAR, -S *n* member of an old order of Russian nobility
BOYARD, -S *same as* ▶ **boyar**
BOYARS ▶ **boyar**
BOYAU, -X *n* connecting trench
BOYCHIK *n* young boy
BOYCOTT *vb, n*
BOYED ▶ **boy**
BOYF, -S *n* boyfriend
BOYG, -S *n* troll-like mythical creature
BOYHOOD *n*
BOYING ▶ **boy**
BOYISH *adj*
BOYKIE, -S *n* chap or fellow
BOYLA, -S *n* Aboriginal Australian magician or medicine-man
BOYO, -S *n* boy or young man: often used in direct address
BOYS ▶ **boy**
BOYSY, BOYSIER *adj* suited to or typical of boys or young men
BOZO, -S *n* man, esp a stupid one
BRA *n* women's undergarment
BRAAI, -ED, -S *vb* grill or roast (meat) over open coals
BRAATA *n* small portion added to a purchase to encourage the customer to return
BRAATAS *same as* ▶ **braata**
BRABBLE *rare word for* > **squabble**
BRACCIO, BRACCIA *n* former unit of measurement of length
BRACE, -D *n, vb*
BRACER, -S *n* person or thing that braces
BRACERO *n* Mexican World War II labourer
BRACERS ▶ **bracer**
BRACES *pl n* pair of straps worn over the shoulders for holding up the trousers
BRACH, -ES, -S *n* female dog
BRACHAH, BRACHOT *n* blessing
BRACHES ▶ **brach**
BRACHET *same as* ▶ **brach**
BRACHIA > **brachium**
BRACHOT ▶ **brachah**
BRACHS ▶ **brach**
BRACING *adj* refreshing and invigorating ▷ *n* system of braces used to strengthen or support
BRACK, -S *same as* > **barmbrack**
BRACKEN *n*
BRACKET *n, vb*
BRACKS ▶ **brack**
BRACT, -S *n* leaf at the base of a flower
BRACTED ▶ **bract**
BRACTS ▶ **bract**
BRAD, -DED, -S *n* small tapered nail with a small head
BRADAWL *n* small boring tool
BRADDED ▶ **brad**
BRADOON *same as* ▶ **bridoon**
BRADS ▶ **brad**
BRAE, -S *n* hill or slope
BRAG, -GED, -S *vb* speak arrogantly and boastfully ▷ *n* boastful talk or behaviour ▷ *adj* boastful
BRAGGER ▶ **brag**
BRAGGY *adj* boastful
BRAGLY ▶ **brag**
BRAGS ▶ **brag**
BRAHMA, -S *n* breed of domestic fowl
BRAHMAN *n* member of the highest Hindu caste
BRAHMAS ▶ **brahma**
BRAHMIN *same as* ▶ **brahman**
BRAID, -S *vb, n, adj, adv*
BRAIDE *adj* given to deceit
BRAIDED *adj* flowing in several shallow interconnected channels
BRAIDER ▶ **braid**
BRAIDS ▶ **braid**
BRAIL, -ED, -S *n* one of several lines fastened to a fore-and-aft sail to aid in furling it ▷ *vb* furl (a fore-and-aft sail) using brails
BRAILLE *n* system of writing consisting of raised dots ▷ *vb* print or write using this method

BRAILS ▸ **brail**
BRAIN, -ED, -S *n, vb*
BRAINY *adj* clever
BRAIRD, -S *vb* appear as shoots
BRAISE, -D, -S *vb*
BRAIZE, -S *n* sea bream
BRAK, -S *n* crossbred dog ▹ *adj* (of water) slightly salty
BRAKE, -D, -S *n, vb*
BRAKIER ▸ **braky**
BRAKING *n* act of braking
BRAKS ▸ **brak**
BRAKY, BRAKIER *adj* brambly
BRALESS ▸ **bra**
BRAMBLE *n, vb*
BRAMBLY ▸ **bramble**
BRAME, -S *n* powerful feeling of emotion
BRAN, -NED, -S *n, vb*
BRANCH *n, vb*
BRANCHY ▸ **branch**
BRAND, -S *n, vb*
BRANDED *adj* identifiable as being the product of a particular company
BRANDER ▸ **brand**
BRANDS ▸ **brand**
BRANDY *n, vb*
BRANE, -S *n* hypothetical component of string theory
BRANGLE *vb* quarrel noisily
BRANK, -ED *vb* walk with a swaggering gait
BRANKS *pl n* (formerly) iron bridle used to restrain scolding women
BRANKY *adj* ostentatious
BRANLE, -S *n* old French country dance performed in a linked circle
BRANNED ▸ **bran**
BRANNER *n* person or machine that treats metal with bran
BRANNY *adj* having the appearance or texture of bran
BRANS ▸ **bran**
BRANSLE *another word for* ▸ **brantle**
BRANT, -S *n* type of small goose
BRANTLE *n* French country dance
BRANTS ▸ **brant**
BRAP *interj* exclamation used to imitate a burst of gunfire
BRAS, -ES *archaic form of* ▸ **brass**
BRASCO, -S *n* lavatory
BRASERO *n* metal grid for burning coals
BRASES ▸ **bras**
BRASH, -ED, -ER, -ES *adj, n, vb*
BRASHLY ▸ **brash**
BRASHY *adj* loosely fragmented
BRASIER *same as* ▸ **brazier**
BRASIL, -S *same as* ▸ **brazil**
BRASS, -ED, -ES *n, vb*
BRASSET *same as* > **brassart**
BRASSIE *n* former type of golf club
BRASSY *adj* showy and vulgar
BRAST, -S *same as* ▸ **burst**
BRAT, -S *n*
BRATTLE *vb* make a rattling sound
BRATTY ▸ **brat**
BRAUNCH *old variant of* ▸ **branch**
BRAVA, -S *n* professional assassin
BRAVADO *n, vb*
BRAVAS ▸ **brava**
BRAVE, -D, -S, -ST, BRAVING *adj, n, vb*
BRAVELY ▸ **brave**
BRAVER, -S ▸ **brave**
BRAVERY ▸ **brave**
BRAVES ▸ **brave**
BRAVEST ▸ **brave**
BRAVI ▸ **bravo**
BRAVING ▸ **brave**
BRAVO, BRAVI, -ED, -ES, -S *interj, n, vb*
BRAVURA, BRAVURE *n* display of boldness or daring
BRAW, -ER, -EST *adj* fine or excellent, esp in appearance or dress
BRAWL, -ED, -S *n, vb*
BRAWLER ▸ **brawl**
BRAWLIE *adj* in good health
BRAWLS ▸ **brawl**
BRAWLY ▸ **braw**
BRAWN, -S *n*
BRAWNED ▸ **brawn**
BRAWNS ▸ **brawn**
BRAWNY *adj* muscular and strong
BRAWS *pl n* fine apparel
BRAXY, BRAXIES *n* acute and usually fatal bacterial disease of sheep
BRAY, -ED, -ING, -S *vb* (of a donkey) utter its loud harsh sound

▷ *n* donkey's loud harsh sound
BRAYER, -S ▶ **bray**
BRAYING ▶ **bray**
BRAYS ▶ **bray**
BRAZA, -S *n* Spanish unit of measurement
BRAZE, -D, -S, BRAZING *vb* join (two metal surfaces) with brass ▷ *n* high-melting solder or alloy used in brazing
BRAZEN, -S *adj* shameless and bold ▷ *vb* face and overcome boldly or shamelessly
BRAZER, -S ▶ **braze**
BRAZES ▶ **braze**
BRAZIER *n* portable container for burning charcoal or coal
BRAZIL, -S *n* red wood used for cabinetwork
BRAZING ▶ **braze**
BREACH *n, vb*
BREAD, -ED, -S *n, vb*
BREADTH *n*
BREADY *adj* having the appearance or texture of bread
BREAK, -S, BROKEN *vb* separate into pieces ▷ *n* act of breaking
BREAKER *n* large wave
BREAKS ▶ **break**
BREAKUP *n* separation or disintegration
BREAM, -ED, -S *n, vb*
BREARE, -S *same as* ▶ **brier**
BREAST, -S *n, vb*
BREATH, -S *n*
BREATHE *vb*
BREATHS ▶ **breath**
BREATHY *adj* (of the speaking voice) accompanied by an audible emission of breath
BRECCIA *n* type of rock
BRECHAM *n* straw horse-collar
BRECHAN *same as* ▶ **brecham**
BRED, -S *n* person who lives in a small remote place
BREDE, -D, -S, BREDING *archaic spelling of* ▶ **braid**
BREDIE, -S *n* meat and vegetable stew
BREDING ▶ **brede**
BREDREN *same as* > **brethren**
BREDRIN *same as* > **brethren**
BREDS ▶ **bred**
BREE, -S *n* broth, stock, or juice
BREECH *n, vb*
BREED, -S *vb, n*
BREEDER *n* person who breeds plants or animals
BREEDS ▶ **breed**
BREEKS *pl n* trousers
BREEM *same as* ▶ **breme**
BREENGE *vb* lunge forward ▷ *n* violent movement
BREER, -ED, -S *another word for* ▶ **braird**
BREES ▶ **bree**
BREESE, -S *same as* ▶ **breeze**
BREEST, -S *Scot word for* ▶ **breast**
BREEZE, -D, -S *n, vb*
BREEZY *adj* windy
BREGMA, -S *n* point on the top of the skull
BREHON, -S *n* (formerly) judge in Ireland
BREI, -ING, -S *vb* speak with a uvular r, esp in Afrikaans
BREID, -S *n* bread
BREIING ▶ **brei**
BREINGE *same as* ▶ **breenge**
BREIS ▶ **brei**
BREIST, -S *Scot word for* ▶ **breast**
BREKKIE *same as* ▶ **brekky**
BREKKY *slang word for* > **breakfast**
BREME *adj* well-known
BREN, -S *n* type of machine gun ▷ *vb* burn
BRENNE, -S *vb* burn
BRENS ▶ **bren**
BRENT, -ER, -S *n* type of goose ▷ *adj* steep
BRER, -S *n* brother: usually prefixed to a name
BRERE, -S *same as* ▶ **brier**
BRERS ▶ **brer**
BRETON, -S *n* hat with an upturned brim and a rounded crown
BREVE, -S *n* accent placed over a vowel to indicate shortness
BREVET, -S *n* document entitling a commissioned officer to hold temporarily a higher military rank ▷ *vb* promote by brevet
BREVETE *adj* patented
BREVETS ▶ **brevet**

BREVIER *n* (formerly) size of printer's type approximately equal to 8 point
BREVIS *same as* ▸ **brewis**
BREVITY *n*
BREW, -ED, -S *vb, n*
BREWAGE *n* product of brewing
BREWED ▸ **brew**
BREWER, -S ▸ **brew**
BREWERY *n*
BREWING *n* quantity of a beverage brewed at one time
BREWIS *n* bread soaked in broth, gravy, etc
BREWPUB *n*
BREWS ▸ **brew**
BREWSKI *n* beer
BREY, -ED, -ING, -S *same as* ▸ **brei**
BRIAR, -S *n*
BRIARD, -S *n* medium-sized dog
BRIARED ▸ **briar**
BRIARS ▸ **briar**
BRIARY *adj* resembling or containing briar
BRIBE, -D, -S, BRIBING *vb, n*
BRIBEE, -S *n* one who is bribed
BRIBER, -S ▸ **bribe**
BRIBERY *n* process of giving or taking bribes
BRIBES ▸ **bribe**
BRIBING ▸ **bribe**
BRICHT *Scot word for* ▸ **bright**
BRICK, -ED, -S *n* (rectangular block of) baked clay used in building ▹ *vb* build, enclose, or fill with bricks
BRICKEN *adj* made of brick
BRICKIE *n* bricklayer
BRICKLE *variant of* ▸ **brittle**
BRICKS ▸ **brick**
BRICKY *adj* resembling brick
BRICOLE *n* billiards shot
BRIDAL, -S *adj* of a bride or a wedding ▹ *n* wedding or wedding feast
BRIDE, -D, -S, BRIDING *n, vb*
BRIDGE, -D, -S *n, vb*
BRIDIE, -S *n* semicircular pie containing meat and onions
BRIDING ▸ **bride**
BRIDLE, -D, -S *n* headgear for controlling a horse ▹ *vb* show anger or indignation
BRIDLER ▸ **bridle**
BRIDLES ▸ **bridle**
BRIDOON *n* horse's bit
BRIE, -S *same as* ▸ **bree**
BRIEF, -ED *adj, n, vb*
BRIEFER ▸ **brief**
BRIEFLY ▸ **brief**
BRIEFS *pl n* men's or women's underpants without legs
BRIER, -S *same as* ▸ **briar**
BRIERED ▸ **brier**
BRIERS ▸ **brier**
BRIERY ▸ **brier**
BRIES ▸ **brie**
BRIG, -S *n* two-masted square-rigged ship
BRIGADE *n, vb*
BRIGAND *n* bandit
BRIGHT *adj, adv*
BRIGHTS *pl n* high beam of the headlights of a motor vehicle
BRIGS ▸ **brig**
BRIGUE, -D, -S *vb* solicit
BRIK, -S *n* Tunisian pastry
BRIKI, -S *same as* ▸ **cezve**
BRIKS ▸ **brik**
BRILL, -ER, -S *n* type of European flatfish popular as a food fish ▹ *adj* brilliant
BRILLO, -S *n* tradename for a type of scouring pad impregnated with a detergent
BRILLS ▸ **brill**
BRIM, -MED, -S *n, vb*
BRIMFUL *adj* completely filled with
BRIMING *n* phosphorescence of sea
BRIMMED ▸ **brim**
BRIMMER *n* vessel, such as a glass or bowl, filled to the brim
BRIMS ▸ **brim**
BRIN, -S *n* thread of silk from silkworm
BRINDED *adj* streaky or patchy
BRINDLE *n* brindled animal
BRINE, -D, -S, BRINING *n, vb*
BRINER, -S ▸ **brine**
BRINES ▸ **brine**
BRING, -S, BROUGHT, BRUNG *vb*
BRINGER ▸ **bring**
BRINGS ▸ **bring**

BRINIER ▸ **briny**
BRINIES ▸ **briny**
BRINING ▸ **brine**
BRINISH ▸ **brine**
BRINJAL *n* dark purple tropical fruit, cooked and eaten as a vegetable
BRINK, -S *n*
BRINNY *n* stone, esp when thrown
BRINS ▸ **brin**
BRINY, BRINIER, BRINIES *adj* very salty ▹ *n* sea
BRIO, -S *n* liveliness
BRIOCHE *n* soft roll or loaf made from a very light yeast dough, sometimes mixed with currants
BRIONY *same as* ▸ **bryony**
BRIOS ▸ **brio**
BRIQUET *same as* > **briquette**
BRIS, -ES, -SES *n* ritual circumcision of male babies
BRISANT > **brisance**
BRISE *n* type of jump
BRISES ▸ **bris**
BRISK, -ED, -ER, -S *adj, vb*
BRISKEN *vb* make or become more lively or brisk
BRISKER ▸ **brisk**
BRISKET *n*
BRISKLY ▸ **brisk**
BRISKS ▸ **brisk**
BRISKY *another word for* ▸ **brisk**
BRISS *same as* ▸ **bris**
BRISSES ▸ **bris**
BRISTLE *n, vb*
BRISTLY ▸ **bristle**
BRISTOL *n* as in **bristol board** type of heavy cardboard
BRISURE *n* mark of cadency in heraldry
BRIT, -S *n* young of a herring, sprat, or similar fish
BRITH, -S *same as* ▸ **bris**
BRITS ▸ **brit**
BRITSKA *same as* ▸ **britzka**
BRITT, -S *n* young herring or sprat
BRITTLE *adj, vb, n*
BRITTLY ▸ **brittle**
BRITTS ▸ **britt**
BRITZKA *n* long horse-drawn carriage
BRIZE, -S *same as* ▸ **breeze**
BRO, -S *n* close male associate
BROACH *vb, n*
BROAD, -ER, -S *adj, n*
BROADAX *same as* > **broadaxe**
BROADEN *vb* make or become broad or broader
BROADER ▸ **broad**
BROADLY ▸ **broad**
BROADS ▸ **broad**
BROAST, -S *vb* cook by broiling and roasting
BROCADE *n, vb*
BROCAGE *another word for* > **brokerage**
BROCARD *n* basic principle of civil law
BROCH, -S *n* (in Scotland) a circular dry-stone tower large enough to serve as a fortified home
BROCHAN *n* type of thin porridge
BROCHE, -D, -S *adj* woven with a raised design, as brocade
BROCHO, -S *same as* ▸ **brachah**
BROCHS ▸ **broch**
BROCK, -S *n* badger
BROCKED *adj* having different colours
BROCKET *n* small tropical American deer with small unbranched antlers
BROCKIT *same as* ▸ **brocked**
BROCKS ▸ **brock**
BROCOLI *same as* > **broccoli**
BROD, -DED, -S *vb* prod
BRODDLE *vb* poke or pierce (something)
BRODKIN *same as* > **brodekin**
BRODS ▸ **brod**
BROG, -GED, -S *vb* prick with an awl
BROGAN, -S *n* heavy laced, usually ankle-high, work boot
BROGGED ▸ **brog**
BROGH, -S *same as* ▸ **broch**
BROGS ▸ **brog**
BROGUE, -S *n* gentle accent
BROIDER *archaic word for* > **embroider**
BROIL, -ED, -S *vb, n*
BROILER *n* young tender chicken for roasting
BROILS ▸ **broil**
BROKAGE *another word for* > **brokerage**

BROKE, -D, -S *vb* negotiate or deal
BROKEN ▶ **break**
BROKER, -S *n* agent who buys or sells goods, securities, etc ▷ *vb* act as a broker (in)
BROKERY *n* work done by a broker
BROKES ▶ **broke**
BROKING ▶ **broke**
BROLGA, -S *n* large grey Australian crane with a trumpeting call
BROLLY *n*
BROMAL, -S *n* synthetic liquid formerly used medicinally
BROMATE *same as* > **brominate**
BROME, -S *n* type of grass
BROMIC *adj* of or containing bromine in the trivalent or pentavalent state
BROMID, -S *same as* ▶ **bromide**
BROMIDE *n* chemical compound used in medicine and photography
BROMIDS ▶ **bromid**
BROMIN, -S *same as* ▶ **bromine**
BROMINE *n* dark red liquid element that gives off a pungent vapour
BROMINS ▶ **bromin**
BROMISE *same as* ▶ **bromize**
BROMISM *n* bromine poisoning
BROMIZE *vb* treat with bromine
BROMMER *n* S African word for bluebottle
BROMO, -S *n* something that contains bromide
BRONC, -S *same as* ▶ **bronco**
BRONCHI > **bronchus**
BRONCHO *same as* ▶ **bronco**
BRONCO, -S *n* (in the US) wild or partially tamed pony
BRONCS ▶ **bronc**
BROND, -S *n* piece of burning wood
BRONDE, -R, -S *adj* in a shade between blonde and brunette ▷ *n* woman with bronde hair
BRONDS ▶ **brond**
BRONZE, -D, -S *n, adj, vb*
BRONZEN *adj* made of or the colour of bronze
BRONZER *n* cosmetic applied to the skin to simulate a sun tan
BRONZES ▶ **bronze**
BRONZY ▶ **bronze**
BROO, -S *n* brow of hill
BROOCH *n, vb*
BROOD, -ED, -S *n, vb*
BROODER *n* structure used for rearing young chickens or other fowl
BROODS ▶ **brood**
BROODY *adj* moody and sullen
BROOK, -ED, -S *n, vb*
BROOKIE *n* brook trout
BROOKS ▶ **brook**
BROOL, -S *n* low roar
BROOM, -ED, -S *n* long-handled sweeping brush ▷ *vb* sweep with a broom
BROOMY *adj* covered with a growth of broom
BROOS ▶ **broo**
BROOSE, -S *n* race at a country wedding
BROS ▶ **bro**
BROSE, -S *n* oatmeal or pease porridge, sometimes with butter or fat added
BROSY, BROSIER *adj* smeared with porridge
BROTH, -S *n*
BROTHA, -S *n* informal term for an African-American man
BROTHER *n, interj, vb*
BROTHS ▶ **broth**
BROTHY *adj* having the appearance or texture of broth
BROUGH, -S *same as* ▶ **broch**
BROUGHT ▶ **bring**
BROUZE, -S *same as* ▶ **broose**
BROW, -S *n*
BROWED *adj* having a brow
BROWN, -ED, -S *n, adj, vb*
BROWNER *n* brown object
BROWNIE *n*
BROWNS ▶ **brown**
BROWNY ▶ **brown**
BROWS ▶ **brow**
BROWSE, -D, -S *vb, n*
BROWSER *n* software package that enables a user to read hypertext, esp on the internet
BROWSES ▶ **browse**
BROWST, -S *n* brewing (of ale, tea)

BROWSY ▸ **browse**
BRR *same as* ▸ **brrr**

This is useful if your consonant-heavy rack is giving you the shivers. And if you are even colder, **brrr** is available.

BRRR *interj* used to suggest shivering
BRU, -S *South African word for* ▸ **friend**
BRUCHID *n* type of beetle
BRUCIN, -S *same as* ▸ **brucine**
BRUCINE *n* bitter poisonous alkaloid resembling strychnine
BRUCINS ▸ **brucin**
BRUCITE *n* white translucent mineral
BRUCKLE *adj* brittle
BRUGH, -S *n* large house
BRUHAHA *same as* > **brouhaha**
BRUIN, -S *n* name for a bear, used in children's tales, fables, etc
BRUISE, -D, -S *n, vb*
BRUISER *n* strong tough person
BRUISES ▸ **bruise**
BRUIT, -ED, -S *vb* report ▹ *n* abnormal sound heard within the body
BRUITER ▸ **bruit**
BRUITS ▸ **bruit**
BRULE, -S *n* person of Native Canadian and French Canadian ancestry
BRULOT, -S *n* coffee-based alcoholic drink, served flaming
BRULYIE *same as* ▸ **brulzie**
BRULZIE *n* noisy dispute
BRUMAL *adj* of, characteristic of, or relating to winter
BRUMBY *n* wild horse
BRUME, -S *n* heavy mist or fog
BRUMMER *same as* ▸ **brommer**
BRUMOUS ▸ **brume**
BRUNCH *n, vb*
BRUNET, -S *n* boy or man with dark brown hair
BRUNG ▸ **bring**
BRUNT, -ED, -S *n* main force or shock of a blow, attack, etc ▹ *vb* suffer the main force or shock of a blow, attack, etc
BRUS ▸ **bru**
BRUSH, -ES *n, vb*
BRUSHED *adj* treated with a brushing process
BRUSHER ▸ **brush**
BRUSHES ▸ **brush**
BRUSHUP *n* the act or an instance of tidying one's appearance
BRUSHY *adj* like a brush
BRUSK, -ER *same as* ▸ **brusque**
BRUSQUE *adj* blunt or curt in manner or speech
BRUSSEN *adj* bold
BRUST, -S *same as* ▸ **burst**
BRUT, -S *adj* (of champagne or sparkling wine) very dry ▹ *n* very dry champagne
BRUTAL *adj*
BRUTE, -S, -ST *n, adj*
BRUTED ▸ **bruting**
BRUTELY ▸ **brute**
BRUTER, -S *n* diamond cutter
BRUTES ▸ **brute**
BRUTEST ▸ **brute**
BRUTIFY *less common word for* > **brutalize**
BRUTING *n* diamond cutting
BRUTISH *adj* of or like an animal
BRUTISM *n* stupidity; vulgarity
BRUTS ▸ **brut**
BRUX, -ED, -ES, -ING *vb* grind one's teeth
BRUXISM *n* habit of grinding the teeth, esp unconsciously
BRYONY *n* wild climbing hedge plant
BUAT, -S *same as* ▸ **bowat**
BUAZE, -S *n* fibrous African plant
BUB, -S *n* youngster
BUBA, -S *another name for* ▸ **yaws**
BUBAL, -S *n* type of antelope
BUBALE, -S *n* type of antelope
BUBALIS *same as* ▸ **bubal**
BUBALS ▸ **bubal**
BUBAS ▸ **buba**
BUBBE, -S *n* Yiddish word for grandmother
BUBBIE *same as* ▸ **bubbe**
BUBBLE, -D, -S *n, vb*
BUBBLER *n* drinking fountain
BUBBLES ▸ **bubble**

BUBBLY *adj* excited and lively ▷ *n* champagne
BUBINGA *n* reddish-brown wood from African tree
BUBKES *same as* ▶ **bubkis**
BUBKIS *n* nothing
BUBO, -ES *n* inflammation and swelling of a lymph node, esp in the armpit or groin
BUBOED ▶ **bubo**
BUBOES ▶ **bubo**
BUBONIC ▶ **bubo**
BUBS ▶ **bub**
BUBU, -S *same as* ▶ **boubou**
BUBUKLE *n* red spot on skin
BUBUS ▶ **bubu**
BUCARDO *n* type of Spanish mountain goat, recently extinct
BUCCAL *adj* of or relating to the cheek
BUCCINA *n* curved Roman horn
BUCHU, -S *n* S African shrub whose leaves are used as an antiseptic and diuretic
BUCK, -ED, -S *n, vb*
BUCKEEN *n* (in Ireland) poor young man who aspires to the habits and dress of the wealthy
BUCKER, -S ▶ **buck**
BUCKET, -S *n, vb*
BUCKEYE *n* N American tree with erect clusters of white or red flowers and prickly fruits
BUCKIE, -S *n* whelk or its shell
BUCKING ▶ **buck**
BUCKISH ▶ **buck**
BUCKLE, -D, -S *n, vb*
BUCKLER *n* small round shield worn on the forearm ▷ *vb* defend
BUCKLES ▶ **buckle**
BUCKO, -ES, -S *n* lively young fellow: often a term of address
BUCKRAM *n* cotton or linen cloth stiffened with size, etc ▷ *vb* stiffen with buckram
BUCKS ▶ **buck**
BUCKSAW *n* woodcutting saw
BUCKSOM *same as* ▶ **buxom**
BUCKU, -S *same as* ▶ **buchu**
BUCOLIC *adj* of the countryside or country life ▷ *n* pastoral poem
BUD, -DED, -S *n, vb*
BUDDER, -S ▶ **bud**
BUDDHA, -S *n* person who has achieved a state of perfect enlightenment
BUDDIED ▶ **buddy**
BUDDIER ▶ **buddy**
BUDDIES ▶ **buddy**
BUDDING ▶ **bud**
BUDDLE, -D, -S *n* sloping trough in which ore is washed ▷ *vb* wash (ore) in a buddle
BUDDY, BUDDIED, BUDDIER, BUDDIES *n* friend ▷ *vb* act as a friend to ▷ *adj* friendly
BUDGE, -D, -S, BUDGING *vb, n*
BUDGER, -S ▶ **budge**
BUDGERO *same as* ▶ **budgerow**
BUDGERS ▶ **budger**
BUDGES ▶ **budge**
BUDGET, -S *n, vb, adj*
BUDGIE, -S *n*
BUDGING ▶ **budge**
BUDLESS ▶ **bud**
BUDLIKE ▶ **bud**
BUDMASH *same as* ▶ **badmash**
BUDO, -S *n* combat and spirit in martial arts
BUDS ▶ **bud**
BUDWOOD *n* branch with buds that is used for grafting
BUDWORM *n* pest that eats tree leaves and buds
BUFF, -ED, -EST, -S *n, adj, vb*
BUFFA, -S *n* female comic part in an opera
BUFFALO *n* member of the cattle tribe ▷ *vb* confuse
BUFFAS ▶ **buffa**
BUFFE ▶ **buffo**
BUFFED ▶ **buff**
BUFFEL *adj* as in **buffel grass** grass used for pasture in Africa, India, and Australia
BUFFER, -S *vb*
BUFFEST ▶ **buff**
BUFFET, -S *n, vb*
BUFFI ▶ **buffo**
BUFFIER ▶ **buffy**
BUFFING *n* act of polishing
BUFFO, BUFFE, BUFFI, -S *n* (in Italian opera of the 18th century) comic part, esp one for a bass
BUFFOON *n*
BUFFOS ▶ **buffo**

BUFFS ▸ **buff**
BUFFY, BUFFIER *adj* having appearance or texture of buff
BUFO, -S *n* type of toad
BUG, -GED, -S *n, vb*
BUGABOO *n* imaginary source of fear
BUGBANE *n* European plant whose flowers are reputed to repel insects
BUGBEAR *n*
BUGEYE, -S *n* oyster-dredging boat
BUGGAN, -S *n* evil spirit
BUGGANE *same as* ▸ **buggan**
BUGGANS ▸ **buggan**
BUGGED ▸ **bug**
BUGGIER ▸ **buggy**
BUGGIES ▸ **buggy**
BUGGIN, -S *same as* ▸ **buggan**
BUGGING ▸ **bug**
BUGGINS ▸ **buggin**
BUGGY, BUGGIER, BUGGIES *n, adj*
BUGLE, -D, -S, BUGLING *n, vb*
BUGLER, -S ▸ **bugle**
BUGLES ▸ **bugle**
BUGLET, -S *n* small bugle
BUGLING ▸ **bugle**
BUGLOSS *n* hairy Eurasian plant with clusters of blue flowers
BUGONG, -S *same as* ▸ **bogong**
BUGOUT, -S *n* act of running away
BUGS ▸ **bug**
BUGSEED *n* form of tumbleweed
BUGSHA, -S *same as* ▸ **buqsha**
BUGWORT *another name for* ▸ **bugbane**
BUHL, -S *same as* ▸ **boulle**
BUHR, -S *same as* ▸ **burr**
BUHUND, -S *n* type of Norwegian dog
BUIBUI, -S *n* black cloth worn as a shawl by Muslim women
BUIK, -S *same as* ▸ **book**
BUILD, -ED, -S, BUILT *vb, n*
BUILDER *n* person who constructs houses and other buildings
BUILDS ▸ **build**
BUILDUP *n* gradual approach to a climax or critical point
BUILT ▸ **build**
BUIRDLY *adj* well-built
BUIST, -ED, -S *vb* brand sheep with an identification mark
BUKE, -S *same as* ▸ **book**
BUKSHEE *n* person in charge of paying wages
BUKSHI, -S *same as* ▸ **bukshee**
BULB, -ED, -ING, -S *n, vb*
BULBAR *adj* of or relating to a bulb, esp the medulla oblongata
BULBED ▸ **bulb**
BULBEL, -S *same as* ▸ **bulbil**
BULBIL, -S *n* small bulblike organ growing on plants such as the onion and tiger lily
BULBING ▸ **bulb**
BULBLET *n* small bulb at the base of a main bulb
BULBOUS *adj*
BULBS ▸ **bulb**
BULBUL, -S *n* songbird of tropical Africa and Asia
BULGAR, -S *same as* ▸ **bulgur**
BULGE, -D, -S *n, vb*
BULGER, -S ▸ **bulge**
BULGES ▸ **bulge**
BULGHUR *same as* ▸ **bulgur**
BULGIER ▸ **bulgy**
BULGINE *same as* > **bullgine**
BULGING *adj* curving outwards
BULGUR, -S *n* kind of dried cracked wheat
BULGY, BULGIER ▸ **bulge**
BULIMIA *n* eating disorder
BULIMIC ▸ **bulimia**
BULIMUS *n* terrestrial mollusc
BULIMY *same as* ▸ **bulimia**
BULK, -ED, -S *n, vb*
BULKAGE ▸ **bulk**
BULKED ▸ **bulk**
BULKER, -S *n* ship that carries bulk cargo
BULKIER ▸ **bulky**
BULKILY ▸ **bulky**
BULKING *n* expansion of excavated material to a greater volume
BULKS ▸ **bulk**
BULKY, BULKIER *adj* very large and massive, esp so as to be unwieldy
BULL, -ED, -S *n* male bovine animal ▷ *vb* raise the price of (a security)
BULLA, -E *n* leaden seal affixed to a papal bull

BULLACE *n* small Eurasian tree of which the damson is the cultivated form
BULLAE ▸ **bulla**
BULLARY *n* boilery for preparing salt
BULLATE *adj* puckered or blistered in appearance
BULLBAT *another name for* > **nighthawk**
BULLDOG *n*
BULLED ▸ **bull**
BULLER, -S *vb* make bubbling sound
BULLET, -S *n, vb*
BULLEY, -S *n* fishing boat with two masts
BULLIED ▸ **bully**
BULLIER ▸ **bully**
BULLIES ▸ **bully**
BULLING *n* act of raising the price of a security
BULLION *n*
BULLISH *adj* like a bull
BULLOCK *n, vb*
BULLOSA *adj* as in **epidermolysis bullosa** type of genetic skin disorder
BULLOUS *adj* blistered
BULLPEN *n* large cell where prisoners are confined together temporarily
BULLS ▸ **bull**
BULLY, BULLIED, BULLIER, BULLIES *n, vb, adj*
BULRUSH *n*
BULSE, -S *n* purse or bag for diamonds
BULWARK *n, vb*
BUM, -MED, -MEST, -MING, -S *n* loafer or idler ▹ *vb* get by begging ▹ *adj* of poor quality
BUMALO *same as* ▸ **bummalo**
BUMBAG, -S *n* small bag attached to a belt and worn round the waist
BUMBAZE *vb* confuse; bewilder
BUMBLE, -D, -S *vb, n*
BUMBLER ▸ **bumble**
BUMBLES ▸ **bumble**
BUMBO, -S *n* African tree
BUMBOAT *n* any small boat used for ferrying goods to a ship at anchor or at a mooring
BUMBOS ▸ **bumbo**
BUMELIA *n* thorny shrub
BUMF, -S *n* official documents or forms
BUMKIN, -S *same as* ▸ **bumpkin**
BUMMALO *n* Bombay duck
BUMMED ▸ **bum**
BUMMEL, -S *n* stroll
BUMMER, -S *n* unpleasant or disappointing experience
BUMMEST ▸ **bum**
BUMMING ▸ **bum**
BUMMLE, -D, -S *Scots variant of* ▸ **bumble**
BUMMOCK *n* submerged mass of ice projecting downwards
BUMP, -ED, -S *vb, n*
BUMPER, -S *n* bar on the front and back of a vehicle ▹ *adj* unusually large or abundant ▹ *vb* toast with a full drinking glass
BUMPH, -S *same as* ▸ **bumf**
BUMPIER ▸ **bumpy**
BUMPILY ▸ **bumpy**
BUMPING ▸ **bump**
BUMPKIN *n*
BUMPS ▸ **bump**
BUMPY, BUMPIER *adj* having an uneven surface
BUMS ▸ **bum**
BUMSTER *adj* (of trousers) cut very low at the hips
BUMWAD, -S *n* type of sketching paper
BUN, -S *n* small sweet bread roll or cake
BUNA, -S *n* synthetic rubber
BUNBURY *vb* make up a story to avoid an unwanted engagement
BUNCE, -D, -S, BUNCING *n* windfall; boom ▹ *vb* charge someone too much money
BUNCH, -ED *n, vb*
BUNCHER *n* person who groups things together
BUNCHES *pl n* hair tied into two sections
BUNCHY *adj* composed of or resembling bunches
BUNCING ▸ **bunce**
BUNCO, -ED, -ES, -S *n* swindle, esp one by confidence tricksters ▹ *vb* swindle
BUND, -E, -ED, -ING, -S *n* (in Germany)

confederation
▷ *vb* form into an embankment
BUNDH, -S *same as* ▶ **bandh**
BUNDIED ▶ **bundy**
BUNDIES ▶ **bundy**
BUNDING ▶ **bund**
BUNDIST ▶ **bund**
BUNDLE, -D, -S *n, vb*
BUNDLER ▶ **bundle**
BUNDLES ▶ **bundle**
BUNDOOK *n* rifle
BUNDS ▶ **bund**
BUNDT, -S *n* type of sweet cake
BUNDU, -S *n* largely uninhabited wild region far from towns
BUNDY, BUNDIED, BUNDIES *n* time clock at work ▷ *vb* register arrival or departure from work on a time clock
BUNG, -ED, -ING, -S *n, vb*
BUNGEE, -S *n* strong elastic cable
BUNGER, -S *n* firework
BUNGEY, -S *same as* ▶ **bungee**
BUNGIE, -S *same as* ▶ **bungee**
BUNGING ▶ **bung**
BUNGLE, -D, -S *vb, n*
BUNGLER ▶ **bungle**
BUNGLES ▶ **bungle**
BUNGS ▶ **bung**
BUNGY *same as* ▶ **bungee**
BUNHEAD *n* ballerina
BUNIA, -S *same as* ▶ **bunnia**
BUNION, -S *n*
BUNJE, -S *same as* ▶ **bungee**
BUNJEE, -S *same as* ▶ **bungee**
BUNJES ▶ **bunje**
BUNJIE, -S *same as* ▶ **bungee**
BUNJY *same as* ▶ **bungee**
BUNK, -ED, -ING, -S *n, vb*
BUNKER, -S *n, vb*
BUNKIE, -S *n* short for bunkhouse
BUNKING ▶ **bunk**
BUNKO, -ED, -S *same as* ▶ **bunco**
BUNKS ▶ **bunk**
BUNKUM, -S *n* nonsense
BUNN, -S *same as* ▶ **bun**
BUNNET, -S *same as* ▶ **bonnet**
BUNNIA, -S *n* Hindu shopkeeper
BUNNIES ▶ **bunny**
BUNNS ▶ **bunn**
BUNNY, BUNNIES *n*
BUNRAKU *n* Japanese puppet theatre
BUNS ▶ **bun**
BUNSEN, -S *n* as in **bunsen burner** gas burner used in scientific labs
BUNT, -ED, -S *vb* (of an animal) butt (something) with the head or horns ▷ *n* act or an instance of bunting
BUNTAL, -S *n* straw obtained from leaves of the talipot palm
BUNTED ▶ **bunt**
BUNTER, -S *n* batter who deliberately taps ball lightly
BUNTIER ▶ **bunty**
BUNTING *n*
BUNTS ▶ **bunt**
BUNTY, BUNTIER ▶ **bunt**
BUNYA, -S *n* tall dome-shaped Australian coniferous tree
BUNYIP, -S *n* legendary monster said to live in swamps and lakes
BUOY, -ED, -ING, -S *n, vb*
BUOYAGE *n* system of buoys
BUOYANT *adj*
BUOYED ▶ **buoy**
BUOYING ▶ **buoy**
BUOYS ▶ **buoy**
BUPKES *same as* ▶ **bupkis**
BUPKIS *n* nothing
BUPKUS *same as* ▶ **bupkis**
BUPPIE, -S *n* affluent young Black person
BUPPY *variant of* ▶ **buppie**
BUQSHA, -S *n* former Yemeni coin
BUR, -S *same as* ▶ **burr**
BURA, -S *same as* ▶ **buran**
BURAN, -S *n* blizzard, with the wind blowing from the north and reaching gale force
BURAS ▶ **bura**
BURB, -S *n* suburb
BURBLE, -D, -S *vb, n*
BURBLER ▶ **burble**
BURBLES ▶ **burble**
BURBLY *adj* burbling
BURBOT, -S *n* freshwater fish of the cod family that has barbels around its mouth
BURBS ▶ **burb**

BURD, -S *Scots form of* ▸ **bird**
BURDASH *n* fringed sash worn over a coat
BURDEN, -S *n, vb*
BURDIE, -S *Scots form of* ▸ **birdie**
BURDOCK *n* weed with prickly burrs
BURDS ▸ **burd**
BUREAU, -S, -X *n*
BURET, -S *same as* ▸ **burette**
BURETTE *n* glass tube for dispensing known volumes of fluids
BURFI, -S *same as* ▸ **barfi**
BURG, -S *n* fortified town
BURGAGE *n* type of tenure of land or tenement in a town or city
BURGEE, -S *n* triangular or swallow-tailed flag flown from the mast of a merchant ship
BURGEON *vb* develop or grow rapidly ▹ *n* bud of a plant
BURGER, -S *n*
BURGESS *n* (in England) citizen of a borough
BURGH, -S *n*
BURGHAL ▸ **burgh**
BURGHER *n* citizen
BURGHS ▸ **burgh**
BURGHUL *same as* ▸ **bulgur**
BURGLAR *n, vb*
BURGLE, -D, -S *vb* break into (a house, shop, etc)
BURGOO, -S *n* porridge
BURGOUT *same as* ▸ **burgoo**
BURGS ▸ **burg**
BURHEL, -S *same as* ▸ **bharal**
BURIAL, -S *n*
BURIED ▸ **bury**
BURIER, -S *n* person or thing that buries
BURIES ▸ **bury**
BURIN, -S *n* steel chisel used for engraving metal, wood, or marble
BURITI, -S *n* type of palm tree
BURK, -S *same as* ▸ **berk**
BURKA, -S *same as* ▸ **burqa**
BURKE, -D, -S, BURKING *vb* suppress or silence
BURKER, -S ▸ **burke**
BURKES ▸ **burke**
BURKHA, -S *same as* ▸ **burqa**
BURKING ▸ **burke**
BURKINI *n* swimming costume covering the whole body apart from the face, hands, and feet
BURKITE *n* murderer
BURKS ▸ **burk**
BURL, -ED, -ING, -S *n* small knot or lump in wool ▹ *vb* remove the burls from (cloth)
BURLAP, -S *n* coarse fabric woven from jute, hemp, or the like
BURLED ▸ **burl**
BURLER, -S ▸ **burl**
BURLESK *same as* > **burlesque**
BURLEY, -S *same as* ▸ **berley**
BURLIER ▸ **burly**
BURLIKE *adj* like a bur
BURLILY ▸ **burly**
BURLING ▸ **burl**
BURLS ▸ **burl**
BURLY, BURLIER *adj*
BURN, -ED, -S, -T *vb, n*
BURNER, -S *n* part of a stove or lamp that produces the flame
BURNET, -S *n* type of rose
BURNIE, -S *n* sideburn
BURNING ▸ **burn**
BURNISH *vb, n*
BURNOUS *n* long circular cloak with a hood, worn esp by Arabs
BURNOUT *n* failure of a mechanical device from excessive heating
BURNS ▸ **burn**
BURNT ▸ **burn**
BUROO, -S *n* informal Scottish or Irish name for an unemployment benefit office
BURP, -ED, -ING, -S *n, vb*
BURPEE, -S *n* type of physical exercise movement
BURPING ▸ **burp**
BURPS ▸ **burp**
BURQA, -S *n* garment worn by some Muslim women in public

This garment illustrates the fact that Q doesn't always have to be followed by U. It has several variants including **burka** and **burkha**.

BURR, -ED, -ING, -S *n* small rotary file ▹ *vb* form a rough edge on (a workpiece)

BURRATA *n* type of Italian cheese
BURRED ▶ **burr**
BURREL, -S *same as* ▶ **bharal**
BURRELL *variant of* ▶ **bharal**
BURRELS ▶ **burrel**
BURRER, -S *n* person who removes burrs
BURRHEL *same as* ▶ **bharal**
BURRIER ▶ **burry**
BURRING ▶ **burr**
BURRITO *n* tortilla folded over a filling of minced beef, chicken, cheese, or beans
BURRO, -S *n* donkey, esp one used as a pack animal
BURROW, -S *n, vb*
BURRS ▶ **burr**
BURRY, BURRIER *adj* full of or covered in burs
BURS ▶ **bur**
BURSA, -E, -S *n* small fluid-filled sac that reduces friction between movable parts of the body
BURSAL ▶ **bursa**
BURSAR, -S *n* treasurer of a school, college, or university
BURSARY *n*
BURSAS ▶ **bursa**
BURSATE ▶ **bursa**
BURSE, -S *n* flat case used at Mass as a container for the corporal
BURSEED *n* type of plant
BURSERA *adj* of a type of gum tree
BURSES ▶ **burse**
BURST, -ED, -EN, -S *vb, n, adj*
BURSTER ▶ **burst**
BURSTS ▶ **burst**
BURSTY *adj* occurring or happening in sudden bursts; irregular
BURTHEN *archaic word for* ▶ **burden**
BURTON, -S *n* type of hoisting tackle
BURWEED *n* any of various plants that bear burs, such as the burdock
BURY, BURIED, BURIES, -ING *vb* place in a grave
BUS, -ED, -ES, -SED, -SES *n, vb*
BUSBAR, -S *n* electrical conductor
BUSBIES ▶ **busby**
BUSBOY, -S *n* waiter's assistant
BUSBY, BUSBIES *n* tall fur hat worn by some soldiers
BUSED ▶ **bus**
BUSERA, -S *n* Ugandan alcoholic drink made from millet
BUSES ▶ **bus**
BUSGIRL *n* waiter's assistant
BUSH, -ES *n, vb*
BUSHED *adj* extremely tired
BUSHEL, -S *n* obsolete unit of measure equal to 8 gallons ▷ *vb* alter or mend (a garment)
BUSHER, -S ▶ **bush**
BUSHES ▶ **bush**
BUSHFLY *n* small black Australian fly
BUSHIDO *n* feudal code of the Japanese samurai
BUSHIE *same as* ▶ **bushy**
BUSHIER ▶ **bushy**
BUSHIES ▶ **bushy**
BUSHILY ▶ **bushy**
BUSHING *same as* ▶ **bush**
BUSHLOT *n* small wooded area of land
BUSHMAN, BUSHMEN *n*
BUSHPIG *n*
BUSHTIT *n* small grey active North American songbird
BUSHWA, -S *n* nonsense
BUSHWAH *same as* ▶ **bushwa**
BUSHWAS ▶ **bushwa**
BUSHY, BUSHIER, BUSHIES *adj* (of hair) thick and shaggy ▷ *n* person who lives in the bush
BUSIED ▶ **busy**
BUSIER ▶ **busy**
BUSIES ▶ **busy**
BUSIEST ▶ **busy**
BUSILY *adv* in a busy manner
BUSING, -S *n* act of transporting by bus from one area to another
BUSK, -ED, -S *vb, n*
BUSKER, -S ▶ **busk**
BUSKET, -S *n* bouquet
BUSKIN, -S *n* (formerly) sandal-like covering
BUSKING ▶ **busk**
BUSKINS ▶ **buskin**

BUSKS ▸ **busk**
BUSKY *same as* ▸ **bosky**
BUSLOAD *n*
BUSMAN, BUSMEN *n* person who drives a bus
BUSS *archaic or dialect word for* ▸ **kiss**
BUSSED ▸ **bus**
BUSSES ▸ **bus**
BUSSING *n* act of transporting by bus from one area to another
BUSSU, -S *n* type of palm tree
BUST, -ED, -S *n* chest of a human being ▹ *adj* broken ▹ *vb* burst or break
BUSTARD *n* type of bird
BUSTED ▸ **bust**
BUSTEE, -S *same as* ▸ **basti**
BUSTER, -S *n* person or thing destroying something as specified
BUSTI, -S *same as* ▸ **basti**
BUSTIC, -S *n* type of small American tree
BUSTIER *n* close-fitting strapless women's top
BUSTING ▸ **bust**
BUSTIS ▸ **busti**
BUSTLE, -D, -S *vb* hurry with a show of activity or energy ▹ *n* energetic and noisy activity
BUSTLER ▸ **bustle**
BUSTLES ▸ **bustle**
BUSTS ▸ **bust**
BUSTY *adj* (of a woman) having a prominent bust
BUSUUTI *n* garment worn by Ugandan women
BUSY, BUSIED, BUSIER, BUSIES, BUSIEST, -ING *adj, vb*
BUT, -S *prep, adv, n*
BUTANE, -S *n* gas used for fuel
BUTANOL *n* colourless substance
BUTCH, -ES *adj, n*
BUTCHER *n* person who slaughters animals or sells their meat ▹ *vb* kill and prepare (animals) for meat
BUTCHES ▸ **butch**
BUTE, -S *n* drug used in veterinary medicine
BUTENE, -S *n* pungent colourless gas
BUTEO, -S *n* type of American hawk
BUTES ▸ **bute**
BUTLE, -D, -S, BUTLING *vb* act as butler
BUTLER, -S *n, vb*
BUTLERY *n* butler's room
BUTLES ▸ **butle**
BUTLING ▸ **butle**
BUTMENT *same as* ▸ **abutment**
BUTOH, -S *n* style of contemporary Japanese dance
BUTS ▸ **but**
BUTT, -ED, -ING, -S *n, vb*
BUTTALS *pl n* abuttals
BUTTE, -S *n* isolated steep flat-topped hill
BUTTED ▸ **butt**
BUTTER, -S *n, vb*
BUTTERY *n* (in some universities) room in which food and drink are sold to students ▹ *adj* containing, like, or coated with butter
BUTTES ▸ **butte**
BUTTIES ▸ **butty**
BUTTING ▸ **butt**
BUTTLE, -D, -S *vb* act as butler
BUTTOCK *n, vb*
BUTTON *n, vb*
BUTTONS *n* page boy
BUTTONY *adj* having a lot of buttons
BUTTS ▸ **butt**
BUTTY, BUTTIES *n* sandwich
BUTUT, -S *n* Gambian monetary unit worth one hundredth of a dalasi
BUTYL, -S *n* substituent group of a certain carbon compound
BUTYRAL *n* type of resin
BUTYRIC *adj* as in **butyric acid** type of acid
BUTYRIN *n* colourless liquid found in butter
BUTYRYL *n* radical of butyric acid
BUVETTE *n* roadside café
BUXOM, -ER *adj*
BUXOMLY ▸ **buxom**
BUY, -S *vb, n*
BUYABLE ▸ **buy**
BUYBACK *n* repurchase by a company of some or all of its shares from an early investor
BUYER, -S *n* customer
BUYING, -S *n* act or instance of purchasing something

BUYOFF, -S *n* purchase
BUYOUT, -S *n* purchase of a company
BUYS ▶ **buy**
BUZUKI, -A, -S *same as* ▶ **bouzouki**
BUZZ, -ED, -ES *n, vb*
BUZZARD *n*
BUZZCUT *n* very short haircut
BUZZED ▶ **buzz**
BUZZER, -S *n* electronic device that produces a buzzing sound as a signal
BUZZES ▶ **buzz**
BUZZIER ▶ **buzzy**
BUZZING ▶ **buzz**
BUZZSAW *n*
BUZZWIG *n* bushy wig
BUZZY, BUZZIER *adj* making a buzzing sound
BWANA, -S *n* (in E Africa) master, often used as a respectful form of address
BWAZI, -S *same as* ▶ **buaze**
BY, -S *prep, adv, n*
BYCATCH *n* unwanted fish and sea animals caught along with the desired kind
BYCOKET *n* former Italian high-crowned hat
BYDE, -D, -S, BYDING *same as* ▶ **bide**
BYE, -S *n* situation where a player or team wins a round by having no opponent ▷ *interj* goodbye
BYELAW, -S *n* rule made by a local authority
BYES ▶ **bye**
BYGONE, -S *adj* past ▷ *n* article from a former time
BYKE, -D, -S, BYKING *n* wasp's nest ▷ *vb* swarm
BYLANE, -S *n* side lane or alley off a road
BYLAW, -S *n* rule made by a local authority
BYLINE, -D, -S *n* line under the title of a newspaper or magazine article giving the author's name ▷ *vb* give a byline to
BYLINER ▶ **byline**
BYLINES ▶ **byline**
BYLIVE *same as* ▶ **belive**
BYNAME, -S *n* nickname
BYNEMPT *archaic past participle of* ▶ **bename**
BYPASS, BYPAST *n, vb*
BYPATH, -S *n* little-used path or track, esp in the country
BYPLACE *n* private place
BYPLAY, -S *n* secondary action or talking carried on apart while the main action proceeds
BYRE, -S *n* shelter for cows
BYREMAN, BYREMEN *n* man who works in a byre
BYRES ▶ **byre**
BYRL, -ED, -ING, -S *same as* ▶ **birl**
BYRLADY *interj* archaic exclamation of surprise
BYRLAW, -S *same as* ▶ **bylaw**
BYRLED ▶ **byrl**
BYRLING ▶ **byrl**
BYRLS ▶ **byrl**
BYRNIE, -S *n* archaic word for coat of mail
BYROAD, -S *n* secondary or side road
BYROOM, -S *n* private room
BYS ▶ **by**
BYSSAL *adj* of mollusc's byssus
BYSSI ▶ **byssus**
BYSSINE *adj* made from flax
BYSSOID *adj* consisting of fine fibres
BYSSUS, BYSSI *n* mass of threads that attaches an animal to a hard surface
BYTALK, -S *n* trivial conversation
BYTE, -S *n* group of bits processed as one unit of data
BYWAY, -S *n* minor road
BYWONER *n* poor tenant-farmer
BYWORD, -S *n* person or thing regarded as a perfect example of something
BYWORK, -S *n* work done outside usual working hours
BYZANT, -S *same as* ▶ **bezant**

Cc

CAA, -ED, -ING, -S *a Scot word for* ▸ **call**
CAB, -BED, -BING, -S *n, vb*
CABA *same as* ▸ **cabas**
CABAL, -S *n, vb*
CABALA, -S *variant spelling of* > **kabbalah**
CABALS ▸ **cabal**
CABANA, -S *n* tent used as a dressing room by the sea
CABARET *n*
CABAS *n* small bag
CABBAGE *n, vb*
CABBAGY *adj* resembling cabbage
CABBALA *variant spelling of* > **kabbalah**
CABBED ▸ **cab**
CABBIE, -S *n*
CABBING ▸ **cab**
CABBY *same as* ▸ **cabbie**
CABER, -S *n* tree trunk tossed in competition at Highland games
CABEZON *n* large fish
CABILDO *n* Spanish municipal council
CABIN, -ED, -S *n, vb*
CABINET *n*
CABINS ▸ **cabin**
CABLE, -D, -S *n, vb*
CABLER, -S *n* cable broadcasting company
CABLES ▸ **cable**
CABLET, -S *n* small cable
CABLING ▸ **cable**
CABMAN, CABMEN *n* driver of a cab
CABOB, -S *vb* roast on a skewer
CABOC, -S *n* type of Scottish cheese
CABOMBA *n* type of aquatic plant
CABOOSE *n* guard's van on a train
CABOVER *n* truck or lorry in which the cab is over the engine
CABRE *adj* heraldic term designating an animal rearing
CABRIE, -S *n* pronghorn antelope
CABRIO, -S *short for* > **cabriolet**
CABRIT, -S *n* pronghorn antelope
CABS ▸ **cab**
CACAO, -S *same as* ▸ **cocoa**
CACHACA *n* white Brazilian rum made from sugar cane
CACHE, -D, -S, CACHING *n, vb*
CACHET, -S *n, vb*
CACHEXY *same as* > **cachexia**
CACHING ▸ **cache**
CACHOU, -S *same as* ▸ **catechu**
CACIQUE *n* Native American chief in a Spanish-speaking region
CACK, -ED, -ING, -S *n* slang word for nonsense ▹ *vb* slang word for defecate
CACKIER ▸ **cacky**
CACKING ▸ **cack**
CACKLE, -D, -S *vb, n*
CACKLER ▸ **cackle**
CACKLES ▸ **cackle**
CACKS ▸ **cack**
CACKY, CACKIER *adj* dirty or worthless
CACODYL *n* oily poisonous liquid with a strong garlic smell
CACOEPY *n* bad or mistaken pronunciation
CACOLET *n* seat fitted to the back of a mule
CACONYM *n* erroneous name
CACOON, -S *n* large seed of the sword-bean
CACTI ▸ **cactus**
CACTOID *adj* resembling a cactus
CACTUS, CACTI *n*
CACUMEN *n* apex

CAD, -S *n*
CADAGA, -S *n* eucalyptus tree
CADAGI, -S *same as* ▸ **cadaga**
CADAVER *n* corpse
CADDICE *same as* ▸ **caddis**
CADDIE, -D, -S *n, vb*
CADDIS *n* type of coarse woollen yarn, braid, or fabric
CADDISH ▸ **cad**
CADDY *same as* ▸ **caddie**
CADDYSS *same as* ▸ **caddis**
CADE, -S *n* juniper tree ▹ *adj* (of a young animal) left by its mother and reared by humans
CADEAU, -X *n* present
CADEE, -S *old form of* ▸ **cadet**
CADELLE *n* type of beetle that feeds on flour, grain, and other stored foods
CADENCE *n, vb*
CADENCY *same as* ▸ **cadence**
CADENT *adj* having cadence
CADENZA *n* complex solo passage in a piece of music
CADES ▸ **cade**
CADET, -S *n*
CADGE, -D, -S, CADGING *vb*
CADGER, -S *n* person who cadges
CADGES ▸ **cadge**
CADGIER ▸ **cadgy**
CADGING ▸ **cadge**
CADGY, CADGIER *adj* cheerful
CADI, -S *n* judge in a Muslim community
CADIE, -S *n* messenger
CADIS ▸ **cadi**
CADMIC ▸ **cadmium**
CADMIUM *n*
CADRANS *n* instrument used in gem cutting
CADRE, -S *n* group of people trained to form the core of a political or military unit
CADS ▸ **cad**
CADUAC, -S *n* windfall
CADUCEI > **caduceus**
CAECA ▸ **caecum**
CAECAL ▸ **caecum**
CAECUM, CAECA *n* pouch at the beginning of the large intestine
CAEOMA, -S *n* aecium in some rust fungi that has no surrounding membrane
CAERULE *same as* ▸ **cerule**
CAESAR, -S *n* any emperor, autocrat, dictator, or other powerful ruler
CAESE *interj* Shakespearean interjection
CAESIUM *n*
CAESTUS *same as* ▸ **cestus**
CAESURA *n* pause in a line of verse
CAF, -S *n* short for cafeteria
CAFARD, -S *n* feeling of severe depression
CAFE, -S *n*
CAFF, -S *n* café
CAFFEIN *same as* > **caffeine**
CAFFILA *n* caravan train
CAFFS ▸ **caff**
CAFILA, -S *same as* ▸ **caffila**
CAFS ▸ **caf**
CAFTAN, -S *same as* ▸ **kaftan**
CAG, -S *same as* ▸ **cagoule**
CAGANER *n* figure of a squatting defecating person
CAGE, -D, -S, CAGING *n, vb*
CAGEFUL *n* amount which fills a cage to capacity
CAGER, -S *n* basketball player
CAGES ▸ **cage**
CAGEY, CAGIER, CAGIEST *adj* reluctant to go into details
CAGILY ▸ **cagey**
CAGING ▸ **cage**
CAGMAG, -S *adj* done shoddily ▹ *vb* chat idly
CAGOT, -S *n* member of a class of French outcasts
CAGOUL, -S *same as* ▸ **cagoule**
CAGOULE *n*
CAGOULS ▸ **cagoul**
CAGS ▸ **cag**
CAGY *same as* ▸ **cagey**
CAHIER, -S *n* notebook
CAHOOT, -S *n*
CAHOUN, -S *n* type of S American palm tree
CAHOW, -S *n* Bermuda petrel
CAID, -S *n* Moroccan district administrator

CAILLE, -S *n* quail
CAIMAC, -S *same as* **> caimacam**
CAIMAN, -S *same as* **▶ cayman**
CAIN, -S *n* (in Scotland and Ireland) payment in kind
CAIQUE, -S *n* long narrow light rowing skiff used on the Bosporus
CAIRD, -S *n* travelling tinker
CAIRN, -S *n* mound of stones erected as a memorial or marker
CAIRNED *adj* marked by a cairn
CAIRNS ▶ cairn
CAIRNY *adj* covered with cairns
CAISSON *n* watertight enclosure pumped dry to enable construction work to be done
CAITIFF *n* cowardly or base person ▷ *adj* cowardly
CAITIVE *n* captive
CAJAPUT *same as* **▶ cajuput**
CAJEPUT *same as* **▶ cajuput**
CAJOLE, -D, -S *vb*
CAJOLER ▶ cajole
CAJOLES ▶ cajole
CAJON, -ES *n* Peruvian wooden box used as a drum
CAJUN *n* music of the Cajun people
CAJUPUT *n* small tree or shrub
CAKE, -D, -S *n, vb*
CAKEAGE *n* charge in a restaurant for serving cake brought in from outside
CAKEBOX *n* box for a cake
CAKED ▶ cake
CAKES ▶ cake
CAKEY ▶ cake
CAKIER ▶ caky
CAKIEST ▶ caky
CAKING, -S ▶ cake
CAKY, CAKIER, CAKIEST ▶ cake
CAL, -S *n* short for calorie
CALALOO *same as* **▶ calalu**
CALALU, -S *n* edible leaves of various plants
CALAMAR *n* any member of the squid family
CALAMUS, CALAMI *n* tropical Asian palm
CALANDO *adv* (to be performed) with gradually decreasing tone and speed
CALASH *n* horse-drawn carriage with low wheels and a folding top
CALATHI > calathus
CALCAR, -S *n* spur or spurlike process
CALCED *adj* wearing shoes
CALCES ▶ calx
CALCIC *adj* of, containing, or concerned with lime or calcium
CALCIFY *vb* harden by the depositing of calcium salts
CALCINE *vb* oxidize (a substance) by heating
CALCITE *n* colourless or white form of calcium carbonate
CALCIUM *n*
CALCULI > calculus
CALDERA *n* large basin-shaped crater at the top of a volcano
CALDRON *same as* **> cauldron**
CALECHE *variant of* **▶ calash**
CALEFY *vb* make warm
CALENDS *pl n* first day of each month in the ancient Roman calendar
CALESA, -S *n* horse-drawn buggy
CALF, -S, CALVES *n*
CALIBER *same as* **▶ calibre**
CALIBRE *n*
CALICES ▶ calix
CALICHE *n* bed of sand or clay in arid regions
CALICLE *same as* **▶ calycle**
CALICO, -S *n* white cotton fabric
CALID *adj* warm
CALIF, -S *same as* **▶ caliph**
CALIGO, -S *n* speck on the cornea causing poor vision
CALIMA, -S *n* Saharan dust-storm
CALIPEE *n* edible part of the turtle found next to the lower shell
CALIPER *same as* **> calliper**
CALIPH, -S *n* Muslim ruler

CALIVER *n* type of musket
CALIX, CALICES, -ES *n* cup
CALK, -ED, -S *same as* ▸ **caulk**
CALKER, -S ▸ **calk**
CALKIN, -S *same as* ▸ **calk**
CALKING ▸ **calk**
CALKINS ▸ **calkin**
CALKS ▸ **calk**
CALL, -ED, -S *vb, n*
CALLA, -S *n* S African plant with a white funnel-shaped spathe enclosing a yellow spadix
CALLAIS *n* type of green stone
CALLAN, -S *same as* ▸ **callant**
CALLANT *n* youth
CALLAS ▸ **calla**
CALLBOY *n* person who notifies actors when it is time to go on stage
CALLED ▸ **call**
CALLEE, -S *n* computer function being used
CALLER, -S *n* person or thing that calls, esp a person who makes a brief visit ▹ *adj* (of food, esp fish) fresh
CALLET, -S *n* scold
CALLID *adj* cunning
CALLING *n* vocation, profession
CALLOP, -S *n* edible Australian freshwater fish
CALLOSE *n* carbohydrate found in plants
CALLOUS *adj, vb*
CALLOUT *n* inset text within a printed article
CALLOW, -S *adj, n*
CALLS ▸ **call**
CALLUNA *n* type of heather
CALLUS *n* area of thick hardened skin ▹ *vb* produce or cause to produce a callus
CALM, -ED, -ER, -EST, -S *adj, n, vb*
CALMANT *n* sedative
CALMED ▸ **calm**
CALMER ▸ **calm**
CALMEST ▸ **calm**
CALMIER ▸ **calmy**
CALMING ▸ **calm**
CALMLY ▸ **calm**
CALMS ▸ **calm**
CALMY, CALMIER *adj* tranquil
CALO, -S *n* military servant
CALOMEL *n* colourless tasteless powder
CALORIC *adj* of heat or calories ▹ *n* hypothetical fluid formerly postulated as the embodiment of heat
CALORIE *n*
CALORY *same as* ▸ **calorie**
CALOS ▸ **calo**
CALOTTE *n* skullcap worn by Roman Catholic clergy
CALOYER *n* monk of the Greek Orthodox Church, esp of the Basilian Order
CALP, -S *n* type of limestone
CALPA, -S *n* Hindu unit of time
CALPAC, -S *n* large black brimless hat
CALPACK *same as* ▸ **calpac**
CALPACS ▸ **calpac**
CALPAIN *n* type of enzyme
CALPAS ▸ **calpa**
CALPS ▸ **calp**
CALQUE, -D, -S *same as* ▸ **caulk**
CALS ▸ **cal**
CALTHA, -S *n* marsh marigold
CALTRAP *same as* ▸ **caltrop**
CALTROP *n* floating Asian plant
CALUMBA *n* Mozambiquan root used for medicinal purposes
CALUMET *n* peace pipe
CALUMNY *n* false or malicious statement ▹ *vb* make a false or malicious statement about (a person)
CALVARY *n* representation of Christ's crucifixion
CALVE, -D, CALVING *vb* give birth to a calf
CALVER, -S *vb* prepare fish for cooking
CALVES ▸ **calf**
CALVING ▸ **calve**
CALX, CALCES, -ES *n* powdery metallic oxide formed when an ore or mineral is roasted
CALYCES ▸ **calyx**

CALYCLE *n* cup-shaped structure, as in the coral skeleton
CALYPSO *n*
CALYX, CALYCES, -ES *n* outer leaves that protect a flower bud
CALZONE, CALZONI *n* folded pizza filled with cheese, tomatoes, etc
CAM, -MED, -MING, -S *n* device that converts a circular motion to a to-and-fro motion ▷ *vb* furnish (a machine) with a cam
CAMA *n* hybrid offspring of a camel and a llama
CAMAIEU *n* cameo
CAMAIL, -S *n* covering of chain mail
CAMAN, -S *n* wooden stick used to hit the ball in shinty
CAMARON *n* shrimp
CAMAS, -ES *same as* ▶ **camass**
CAMASH *same as* ▶ **camass**
CAMASS *n* type of North American plant
CAMBER, -S *n, vb*
CAMBIA ▶ **cambium**
CAMBIAL ▶ **cambium**
CAMBISM ▶ **cambist**
CAMBIST *n* dealer or expert in foreign exchange
CAMBIUM, CAMBIA *n* meristem that increases the girth of stems and roots
CAMBOGE *n* type of gum resin
CAMBREL *variant of* ▶ **gambrel**
CAMBRIC *n* fine white linen fabric
CAMCORD *vb* film with a camcorder
CAME ▶ **come**
CAMEL, -S *n*
CAMELIA *same as* > **camellia**
CAMELID *adj* of or relating to camels ▷ *n* any animal of the camel family
CAMELOT *n* supposedly idyllic period or age
CAMELRY *n* troops mounted on camels
CAMELS ▶ **camel**
CAMEO, -ED, -S *n, vb*
CAMERA, -E, -S *n*
CAMERAL *adj* of or relating to a judicial or legislative chamber
CAMERAS ▶ **camera**
CAMES *pl n* pieces of lead used in lattice windows
CAMESE, -S *same as* ▶ **camise**
CAMI *n* camisole
CAMION, -S *n* lorry, or, esp formerly, a large dray
CAMIS *n* light robe
CAMISA, -S *n* smock
CAMISE, -S *n* loose light shirt, smock, or tunic originally worn in the Middle Ages
CAMISIA *n* surplice
CAMLET, -S *n* tough waterproof cloth
CAMMED ▶ **cam**
CAMMIE, -S *n* webcam award
CAMMING ▶ **cam**
CAMO, -S *n* short for camouflage
CAMOGIE *n* form of hurling played by women
CAMOODI *a Caribbean name for* > **anaconda**
CAMORRA *n* secret criminal group
CAMOS ▶ **camo**
CAMOTE, -S *n* type of sweet potato
CAMP, -ED, -EST, -S *vb, adj, n*
CAMPANA *n* bell or bell shape
CAMPED ▶ **camp**
CAMPER, -S *n*
CAMPERY *n* campness
CAMPEST ▶ **camp**
CAMPHOL *another word for* ▶ **borneol**
CAMPHOR *n*
CAMPI ▶ **campo**
CAMPIER ▶ **campy**
CAMPILY ▶ **campy**
CAMPING ▶ **camp**
CAMPION *n* red, pink, or white wild flower
CAMPLE, -D, -S *vb* argue
CAMPLY ▶ **camp**
CAMPO, CAMPI, -S *n* level or undulating savanna country
CAMPONG *n* in Malaysia, a village
CAMPOS ▶ **campo**
CAMPOUT *n* camping trip
CAMPS ▶ **camp**
CAMPUS *n, vb*
CAMPY, CAMPIER *adj* consciously artificial
CAMS ▶ **cam**
CAMSHO *adj* crooked
CAMUS, -ES *n* type of loose robe

CAMWOOD *n* W African leguminous tree
CAN, -NED, -S, COULD *vb* be able to ▷ *vb* put (food etc) into a can ▷ *n* metal container for food or liquids
CANADA, -S *n* canada goose
CANAKIN *same as* > **cannikin**
CANAL, -ED, -S *n, vb*
CANAPE, -S *n*
CANARD, -S *n* false report
CANARY *n, vb*
CANASTA *n* card game like rummy, played with two packs
CANBANK *n* container for receiving cans for recycling
CANCAN, -S *n* lively high-kicking dance performed by a female group
CANCEL, -S *vb, n*
CANCER, -S *n*
CANCHA, -S *n* toasted maize
CANDELA *n* unit of luminous intensity
CANDENT *adj* emitting light as a result of being heated to a high temperature
CANDID, -S *adj* honest and straightforward ▷ *n* unposed photograph
CANDIDA *n* yeastlike parasitic fungus
CANDIDS ▶ **candid**
CANDIE *n* South Indian unit of weight
CANDIED *adj* coated with sugar
CANDIES ▶ **candy**
CANDIRU *n* parasitic freshwater catfish of the Amazon region
CANDLE, -D, -S *n, vb*
CANDLER ▶ **candle**
CANDLES ▶ **candle**
CANDOCK *n* type of water lily
CANDOR, -S *same as* ▶ **candour**
CANDOUR *n* honesty and straightforwardness
CANDY, CANDIES *n, vb*
CANE, -D, -S *n, vb*
CANEH, -S *n* Hebrew unit of length
CANELLA *n* fragrant cinnamon-like inner bark of a Caribbean tree
CANER, -S ▶ **cane**
CANES ▶ **cane**
CANFUL, -S, CANSFUL *n* amount a can will hold
CANG, -S *same as* ▶ **cangue**
CANGLE, -D, -S *vb* wrangle
CANGS ▶ **cang**
CANGUE, -S *n* (formerly in China) a wooden collar worn as a punishment
CANID, -S *n* animal of the dog family
CANIER ▶ **cany**
CANIEST ▶ **cany**
CANIKIN *same as* > **cannikin**
CANINE, -S *adj, n*
CANING, -S *n* beating with a cane as a punishment
CANKER, -S *n* ulceration ▷ *vb* infect or become infected with or as if with canker
CANKERY *adj* like a canker
CANKLE, -S *n* thickened ankle on an overweight person
CANN, -S *vb* direct a ship's steering
CANNA, -S *n* type of tropical plant
CANNACH *n* cotton grass
CANNAE *vb* Scottish form of 'cannot'
CANNAS ▶ **canna**
CANNED ▶ **can**
CANNEL, -S *n* type of dull coal
CANNER, -S *n* person or organization whose job is to can foods
CANNERY *n* factory where food is canned
CANNIE *same as* ▶ **canny**
CANNIER ▶ **canny**
CANNILY ▶ **canny**
CANNING *n*
CANNOLI *n* Sicilian pudding of pasta shells filled with sweetened ricotta
CANNON, -S *n, vb*
CANNOT *vb* can not
CANNS ▶ **cann**
CANNULA *n* narrow tube for insertion into a bodily cavity
CANNY, CANNIER *adj, adv*
CANOE, -D, -S *n* light narrow open boat propelled by a paddle or paddles ▷ *vb* use a canoe

CANOER, -S ▸ **canoe**
CANOES ▸ **canoe**
CANOLA, -S *n* cooking oil extracted from a variety of rapeseed
CANON, -S *n*
CANONIC *same as* > **canonical**
CANONRY *n* office, benefice, or status of a canon
CANONS ▸ **canon**
CANOPIC *adj* of a type of ancient Egyptian vase
CANOPY *n, vb*
CANS ▸ **can**
CANSFUL ▸ **canful**
CANSO, -S *n* love song
CANST *vb* form of 'can' used with the pronoun *thou* or its relative form
CANT, -ED, -EST, -S *n* insincere talk ▹ *vb* use cant ▹ *adj* oblique
CANTAL, -S *n* French cheese
CANTALA *n* tropical American plant, the agave
CANTALS ▸ **cantal**
CANTAR, -S *variant form of* ▸ **kantar**
CANTATA *n* musical work consisting of arias, duets, and choruses
CANTATE *n* 98th psalm sung as a nonmetrical hymn
CANTDOG *same as* > **canthook**
CANTED ▸ **cant**
CANTEEN *n*
CANTER, -S *vb*
CANTEST ▸ **cant**
CANTHAL ▸ **canthus**
CANTHI ▸ **canthus**
CANTHIC *adj* relating to the canthus
CANTHUS, CANTHI *n* inner or outer corner or angle of the eye
CANTIC ▸ **cant**
CANTICO *vb* dance as part of an act of worship
CANTIER ▸ **canty**
CANTILY ▸ **canty**
CANTINA *n* bar or wine shop, esp in a Spanish-speaking country
CANTING ▸ **cant**
CANTION *n* song
CANTLE, -D, -S *n* back part of a saddle that slopes upwards ▹ *vb* set up, or stand, on high
CANTLET *n* piece
CANTO, -S *same as* ▸ **cantus**
CANTON, -S *n* political division of a country, esp Switzerland ▹ *vb* divide into cantons
CANTOR, -S *n* man employed to lead services in a synagogue
CANTOS ▸ **canto**
CANTRAP *same as* > **cantraip**
CANTRED *n* district comprising a hundred villages
CANTREF *same as* ▸ **cantred**
CANTRIP *n* magic spell ▹ *adj* (of an effect) produced by black magic
CANTS ▸ **cant**
CANTUS *n* medieval form of church singing
CANTY, CANTIER *adj* lively
CANULA, -E, -S *same as* ▸ **cannula**
CANULAR *adj* shaped like a cannula
CANULAS ▸ **canula**
CANVAS *n, vb*
CANVASS *vb, n*
CANY, CANIER, CANIEST *adj* cane-like
CANYON, -S *n*
CANZONA *n* type of 16th- or 17th-century contrapuntal music
CANZONE, CANZONI *n* Provençal or Italian lyric, often in praise of love or beauty
CAP, -PED, -S *n, vb*
CAPA, -S *n* type of Spanish cloak
CAPABLE *adj*
CAPABLY ▸ **capable**
CAPAS ▸ **capa**
CAPCOM, -S *n* flight controller who communicates with the crew of a spacecraft
CAPE, -D, -S, CAPING *n* short cloak ▹ *vb* cut and remove the hide of an animal
CAPEESH *same as* ▸ **capisce**
CAPELAN *another word for* ▸ **capelin**
CAPELET *n* small cape
CAPELIN *n* type of small marine food fish
CAPER, -ED *n, vb*
CAPERER ▸ **caper**

CAPERS *pl n* pickled flower buds of a Mediterranean shrub used in sauces
CAPES ▶ **cape**
CAPEX, -ES *n* capital expenditure
CAPFUL, -S *n* quantity held by a (usually bottle) cap
CAPH, -S *n* letter of the Hebrew alphabet
CAPI ▶ **capo**
CAPIAS *n* (formerly) a writ directing the arrest of a named person
CAPICHE *interj* do you understand?
CAPING ▶ **cape**
CAPISCE *interj* expression meaning *do you understand?*
CAPISH *interj* do you understand?
CAPITA ▶ **caput**
CAPITAL *n, adj*
CAPITAN *another name for* ▶ **hogfish**
CAPITOL *n* (in America) building housing the state legislature
CAPIZ, -ES *n* bivalve shell of a mollusc
CAPLE, -S *n* horse
CAPLESS ▶ **cap**
CAPLET, -S *n* medicinal tablet, usually oval in shape, coated in a soluble substance
CAPLIKE *adj* like a cap
CAPLIN, -S *same as* ▶ **capelin**
CAPO, CAPI, -S *n* device used to raise the pitch of a stringed instrument
CAPON, -S *n* cock fowl fattened for eating
CAPORAL *n* strong coarse dark tobacco
CAPOS ▶ **capo**
CAPOT, -S *n* winning of all the tricks by one player ▷ *vb* score a capot (against)
CAPOTE, -S *n* long cloak or soldier's coat, usually with a hood
CAPOTS ▶ **capot**
CAPOUCH *same as* ▶ **capuche**
CAPPED ▶ **cap**
CAPPER, -S ▶ **cap**
CAPPING ▶ **cap**
CAPRATE *n* any salt of capric acid
CAPRESE *n* salad of mozzarella, basil, and tomatoes
CAPRI *adj* as in **capri pants** women's tight-fitting trousers
CAPRIC *adj* (of a type of acid) smelling of goats
CAPRICE *n* whim
CAPRID, -S *n* any member of the goat family
CAPRIFY *vb* induce figs to ripen
CAPRINE *adj* of or resembling a goat
CAPRIS *pl n* women's tight-fitting trousers
CAPROCK *n* layer of rock that overlies a salt dome
CAPROIC *adj* as in **caproic acid** oily acid found in milk
CAPS ▶ **cap**
CAPSID, -S *n* outer protein coat of a mature virus
CAPSIZE *vb*
CAPSTAN *n* rotating cylinder round which a ship's rope is wound
CAPSULE *n, adj, vb*
CAPTAIN *n, vb*
CAPTAN, -S *n* type of fungicide
CAPTCHA *n* test in which the user of a website has to decipher a distorted image
CAPTION *n, vb*
CAPTIVE *n, adj, vb*
CAPTOR, -S *n*
CAPTURE *vb, n*
CAPUCHE *n* large hood or cowl, esp that worn by Capuchin friars
CAPUERA *variant of* > **capoeira**
CAPUL, -S *same as* ▶ **caple**
CAPUT, CAPITA *n* main or most prominent part of an organ or structure
CAR, -S *n* motor vehicle designed to carry a small number of people
CARABAO *n* water buffalo
CARABID *n* type of beetle
CARABIN *same as* ▶ **carbine**
CARACAL *n* lynx with reddish fur, which inhabits deserts of N Africa and S Asia
CARACK, -S *same as* ▶ **carrack**

CARACOL *same as* **> caracole**
CARACT, -S *n* sign or symbol
CARACUL *n* fur from the skins of newly born lambs of the karakul sheep
CARAFE, -S *n* glass bottle
CARAMBA *interj* Spanish interjection similar to 'wow!'
CARAMEL *n, vb*
CARANNA *n* gumlike substance
CARAP, -S *n* crabwood
CARAPAX *n* carapace
CARAPS ▸ carap
CARAT, -S *n* unit of weight of precious stones
CARATE, -S *n* tropical disease
CARATS ▸ carat
CARAUNA *same as* **▸ caranna**
CARAVAN *n, vb*
CARAVEL *n* two- or three-masted sailing ship
CARAWAY *n*
CARB, -S *n*
CARBARN *n* streetcar depot
CARBEEN *n* Australian eucalyptus tree
CARBENE *n* type of divalent free radical
CARBIDE *n* compound of carbon with a metal
CARBIES ▸ carby
CARBINE *n* light automatic rifle
CARBO, -S *n* carbohydrate
CARBON, -S *n*
CARBORA *n* former name for the koala
CARBOS ▸ carbo
CARBOY, -S *n* large bottle with a protective casing
CARBS ▸ carb
CARBY, CARBIES *n* short for carburettor
CARCAKE *n* (formerly, in Scotland) a cake traditionally made for Shrove Tuesday
CARCASE *same as* **▸ carcass**
CARCASS *n, vb*
CARCEL, -S *n* French unit of light
CARD, -ED, -S *n, vb*
CARDAN *n* as in **cardan joint** type of universal joint
CARDECU *n* old French coin (a quarter of a crown)
CARDED ▸ card
CARDER, -S ▸ card
CARDI, -S *n* cardigan
CARDIA, -E, -S *n* lower oesophageal sphincter
CARDIAC *adj, n*
CARDIAE ▸ cardia
CARDIAS ▸ cardia
CARDIE, -S *short for* **> cardigan**
CARDING ▸ card
CARDIO, -S *adj* exercising heart ▹ *n* cardiovascular exercise
CARDIS ▸ cardi
CARDON, -S *n* variety of cactus
CARDOON *n* thistle-like S European plant
CARDS ▸ card
CARDUUS *n* thistle
CARDY *short for* **> cardigan**
CARE, -D, -S *vb, n*
CAREEN, -S *vb* tilt over to one side
CAREER, -S *n, vb, adj*
CAREFUL *adj*
CAREME, -S *n* period of Lent
CARER, -S *n* person who looks after someone who is ill or old, often a relative
CARES ▸ care
CARESS *n, vb*
CARET, -S *n* proofreading symbol
CAREX, CARICES *n* any member of the sedge family
CARFARE *n* fare that a passenger is charged for a ride on a bus, etc
CARFAX *n* place where principal roads or streets intersect
CARFOX *same as* **▸ carfax**
CARFUL, -S *n* maximum number of people a car will hold
CARGO, -ED, -ES, -S *n, vb*
CARHOP, -S *n* waiter or waitress at a drive-in restaurant ▹ *vb* work as a carhop
CARIAMA *another word for* **▸ seriema**
CARIBE, -S *n* piranha
CARIBOO *same as* **▸ caribou**
CARIBOU *n*
CARICES ▸ carex
CARIED *adj* (of teeth) decayed

CARIERE *obsolete word for* ▸ **career**
CARIES *n* tooth decay
CARINA, -E, -S *n* keel-like part or ridge
CARINAL *adj* keel-like
CARINAS ▸ **carina**
CARING, -S *adj* feeling or showing care and compassion for other people ▹ *n* practice or profession of providing social or medical care
CARIOCA *n* Brazilian dance similar to the samba
CARIOLE *n* small open two-wheeled horse-drawn vehicle
CARIOSE *same as* ▸ **carious**
CARIOUS *adj* (of teeth or bone) affected with caries
CARITAS *n* divine love; charity
CARJACK *vb*
CARK, -ED, -ING, -S *vb* break down
CARL, -S *another word for* ▸ **churl**
CARLE, -S *same as* ▸ **carl**
CARLESS ▸ **car**
CARLIN, -S *same as* ▸ **carling**
CARLINE *same as* ▸ **carling**
CARLING *n* fore-and-aft beam in a vessel
CARLINS ▸ **carlin**
CARLISH *adj* churlish
CARLOAD *n*
CARLOCK *n* type of Russian isinglass
CARLOT, -S *n* boor
CARLS ▸ **carl**
CARMAN, CARMEN *n* man who drives a car or cart
CARMINE *adj* vivid red ▹ *n* vivid red colour, sometimes with a purplish tinge
CARN, -S *n* cairn
CARNAGE *n*
CARNAL, -S *adj* of a physical or sensual nature ▹ *vb* act in a carnal manner
CARNET, -S *n* type of customs licence
CARNEY, -S *same as* ▸ **carny**
CARNIE *same as* ▸ **carny**
CARNIED ▸ **carny**
CARNIER ▸ **carny**
CARNIES ▸ **carny**
CARNIFY *vb* be altered so as to resemble skeletal muscle
CARNOSE *adj* fleshy
CARNS ▸ **carn**
CARNY, CARNIED, CARNIER, CARNIES *vb* coax or cajole or act in a wheedling manner ▹ *n* person who works in a carnival ▹ *adj* sly
CARNYX *n* bronze Celtic war trumpet
CAROACH *same as* ▸ **caroche**
CAROB, -S *n* pod of a Mediterranean tree, used as a chocolate substitute
CAROCH *same as* ▸ **caroche**
CAROCHE *n* stately ceremonial carriage used in the 16th and 17th centuries
CAROL, -ED, -S *n, vb*
CAROLER ▸ **carol**
CAROLI ▸ **carolus**
CAROLS ▸ **carol**
CAROLUS, CAROLI *n* any of several coins struck in the reign of a king called Charles
CAROM, -ED, -S *n* shot in which the cue ball is caused to contact one object ball after another ▹ *vb* carambole
CAROMEL *vb* turn into caramel
CAROMS ▸ **carom**
CARON, -S *n* inverted circumflex
CAROTID *n* either of the two arteries supplying blood to the head ▹ *adj* of either of these arteries
CAROTIN *same as* ▸ **carotene**
CAROUSE *vb* have a merry drinking party
CARP, -ED, -S *n* large freshwater fish ▹ *vb* complain, find fault
CARPAL, -S *n* wrist bone
CARPALE *same as* ▸ **carpal**
CARPALS ▸ **carpal**
CARPED ▸ **carp**
CARPEL, -S *n* female reproductive organ of a flowering plant
CARPER, -S ▸ **carp**
CARPET, -S *n, vb*
CARPI ▸ **carpus**
CARPING *adj* tending to make petty complaints ▹ *n* petty complaint

CARPOOL *vb* share the use of a single car to travel to work or school
CARPORT *n*
CARPS ▸ **carp**
CARPUS, CARPI *n* set of eight bones of the wrist
CARR, -S *n* area of bog or fen in which scrub has become established
CARRACK *n* galleon used as a merchantman
CARRACT *same as* ▸ **carrack**
CARRAT, -S *same as* ▸ **carat**
CARRECT *same as* ▸ **carrack**
CARREL, -S *n* small individual study room or private desk
CARRELL *same as* ▸ **carrel**
CARRELS ▸ **carrel**
CARRICK *n* as in **carrick bend** type of knot
CARRIED ▸ **carry**
CARRIER *n*
CARRIES ▸ **carry**
CARRION *n*
CARROCH *variant of* ▸ **caroche**
CARROM, -S *same as* ▸ **carom**
CARRON *n* as in **carron oil** ointment of limewater and linseed oil
CARROT, -S *n*
CARROTY *adj* (of hair) reddish-orange
CARRS ▸ **carr**
CARRY, CARRIED, CARRIES *vb*
CARRYON *n* fuss or commotion
CARS ▸ **car**
CARSE, -S *n* riverside area of flat fertile alluvium
CARSEY, -S *slang word for* ▸ **toilet**
CARSICK *adj*
CART, -ED, -ING, -S *n, vb*
CARTA, -S *n* charter
CARTAGE *n* process or cost of carting
CARTAS ▸ **carta**
CARTE, -S *n* fencing position
CARTED ▸ **cart**
CARTEL, -S *n* association of competing firms formed to fix prices
CARTER, -S ▸ **cart**
CARTES ▸ **carte**
CARTFUL *n* amount a cart can hold
CARTING ▸ **cart**
CARTON, -S *n, vb*
CARTOON *n, vb*
CARTOP *adj* designed to be transported on top of a vehicle
CARTS ▸ **cart**
CARTWAY *n* way by which carts travel
CARVE, -D, -S *vb*
CARVEL, -S *same as* ▸ **caravel**
CARVEN *an archaic or literary past participle of* ▸ **carve**
CARVER, -S *n* carving knife
CARVERY *n* restaurant where customers pay a set price for unrestricted helpings
CARVES ▸ **carve**
CARVIES ▸ **carvy**
CARVING *n* figure or design produced by carving stone or wood
CARVY, CARVIES *n* caraway seed
CARWASH *n*
CASA, -S *n* house
CASABA, -S *n* kind of winter muskmelon
CASAS ▸ **casa**
CASAVA, -S *same as* ▸ **cassava**
CASBAH, -S *n* citadel of a N African city
CASCADE *n, vb*
CASCARA *n* bark of a N American shrub, used as a laxative
CASCO, -S *n* Argentinian homestead
CASE, -D, -S *n* instance, example ▹ *vb* inspect (a building) with the intention of burgling it
CASEASE *n* proteolytic enzyme
CASEATE *vb* undergo caseation
CASED ▸ **case**
CASEFY *vb* make or become similar to cheese
CASEIC *adj* relating to cheese
CASEIN, -S *n* phosphoprotein forming the basis of cheese
CASELAW *n* law established by previous cases
CASEMAN, CASEMEN *n* in printing, a person

who sets and corrects type
CASEMIX *n* mix or type of patients treated by a hospital or medical unit
CASEOSE *n* peptide produced by the peptic digestion of casein
CASEOUS *adj* of or like cheese
CASERN, -S *n* (formerly) a billet or accommodation for soldiers in a town
CASERNE *same as* ▸ **casern**
CASERNS ▸ **casern**
CASES ▸ **case**
CASETTE *variant of* > **cassette**
CASEVAC *vb* evacuate (a casualty) from a combat zone, usu by air
CASH, -ED, -ES, -ING *n, adj, vb*
CASHAW, -S *n* winter squash
CASHBOX *n* box for holding cash
CASHED ▸ **cash**
CASHES ▸ **cash**
CASHEW, -S *n*
CASHIER *n, vb*
CASHING ▸ **cash**
CASHOO, -S *n* catechu
CASING, -S *n* protective case, covering
CASINO, CASINI, -S *n*
CASITA, -S *n* small house
CASK, -ED, -ING, -S *n, vb*
CASKET, -S *n, vb*
CASKIER ▸ **casky**
CASKING ▸ **cask**
CASKS ▸ **cask**
CASKY, CASKIER *adj* (of wine) having a musty smell due to resting too long in the cask
CASPASE *n* type of enzyme
CASQUE, -S *n* helmet or a helmet-like process or structure
CASQUED ▸ **casque**
CASQUES ▸ **casque**
CASSABA *same as* ▸ **casaba**
CASSATA *n* ice cream usually containing nuts and candied fruit
CASSAVA *n* starch obtained from the roots of a tropical American plant, used to make tapioca
CASSENA *same as* ▸ **cassina**
CASSENE *same as* ▸ **cassina**
CASSIA, -S *n* tropical plant whose pods yield a mild laxative
CASSIE, -S *n* type of thorny shrub
CASSINA *n* American tree
CASSINE *same as* ▸ **cassina**
CASSINO *n* card game for two to four players
CASSIS *n* blackcurrant cordial
CASSOCK *n*
CASSONE *n* highly decorated Italian dowry chest
CASSPIR *n* armoured military vehicle
CAST, -S *n, vb*
CASTE, -S *n*
CASTED *adj* having a caste
CASTER, -S *n*
CASTES ▸ **caste**
CASTING ▸ **cast**
CASTLE, -S *n, vb*
CASTLED *adj* like a castle in construction
CASTLES ▸ **castle**
CASTOCK *n* kale stalk
CASTOFF *n* person or thing that has been discarded or abandoned
CASTOR, -S *same as* ▸ **caster**
CASTORY *n* dye derived from beaver pelts
CASTRAL *adj* relating to camps
CASTS ▸ **cast**
CASUAL, -S *adj, n*
CASUIST *n* person who attempts to resolve moral dilemmas
CASUS *n* event
CAT, -S, -TED, -TING *n* small domesticated furry mammal ▹ *vb* flog with a cat-'o-nine-tails
CATAGEN *n* phase of hair growth
CATALO, -S *same as* ▸ **cattalo**
CATALOG *same as* > **catalogue**
CATALOS ▸ **catalo**
CATALPA *n* tree of N America and Asia with bell-shaped whitish flowers
CATAPAN *n* governor in the Byzantine Empire
CATARRH *n*

CATASTA *n* platform on which slaves were presented for sale
CATAWBA *n* type of red North American grape
CATBIRD *n* North American songbird
CATBOAT *n* sailing vessel
CATCALL *n*, *vb*
CATCH, -ES, CAUGHT *vb*, *n*
CATCHED *rarely used past tense of* ▸ **catch**
CATCHEN *archaic form of* ▸ **catch**
CATCHER *n* person or thing that catches, esp in a game or sport
CATCHES ▸ **catch**
CATCHT *same as* ▸ **catched**
CATCHUP *variant spelling (esp US) of* ▸ **ketchup**
CATCHY *adj* (of a tune) pleasant and easily remembered
CATCLAW *n* type of shrub; black bead
CATCON, -S *n* catalytic converter
CATE *n* delicacy
CATECHU *n* astringent resinous substance
CATELOG *old form of* **> catalogue**
CATENA, -E, -S *n* connected series, esp of patristic comments on the Bible
CATER, -ED, -S *vb*
CATERAN *n* (formerly) a member of a band of brigands in the Scottish highlands
CATERED ▸ **cater**
CATERER *n* person whose job is to provide food for social events
CATERS ▸ **cater**
CATES *pl n* choice dainty food
CATFACE *n* deformity of the surface of a tree trunk, caused by fire or disease
CATFALL *n* line used as a tackle for hoisting an anchor to the cathead
CATFISH *vb*
CATFLAP *n*
CATFOOD *n*
CATGUT, -S *n* strong cord used to string musical instruments and sports rackets
CATHEAD *n* fitting at the bow of a vessel for securing the anchor when raised
CATHECT *vb* invest mental or emotional energy in
CATHODE *n*
CATHOLE *n* hole in a ship through which ropes are passed
CATHOOD *n* state of being a cat
CATION, -S *n* positively charged ion
CATJANG *n* tropical shrub
CATKIN, -S *n* drooping flower spike of certain trees
CATLIKE ▸ **cat**
CATLIN, -S *same as* ▸ **catling**
CATLING *n* long double-edged surgical knife for amputations
CATLINS ▸ **catlin**
CATMINT *n* Eurasian plant with scented leaves that attract cats
CATNAP, -S *vb*, *n*
CATNEP, -S *same as* ▸ **catmint**
CATNIP, -S *same as* ▸ **catmint**
CATS ▸ **cat**
CATSKIN *n* skin or fur of a cat
CATSPAW *n* person used by another as a tool
CATSUIT *n*
CATSUP, -S *variant (esp US) of* ▸ **ketchup**
CATTABU *n* cross between common cattle and zebu
CATTAIL *n* reed mace
CATTALO *n* hardy breed of cattle
CATTED ▸ **cat**
CATTERY *n* place where cats are bred or looked after
CATTIE *same as* ▸ **catty**
CATTIER ▸ **catty**
CATTIES ▸ **catty**
CATTILY ▸ **catty**
CATTING ▸ **cat**
CATTISH ▸ **cat**
CATTLE *pl n*
CATTY, CATTIER, CATTIES *adj* spiteful ▹ *n* unit of weight, used esp in China
CATWALK *n*
CATWORM *n* type of carnivorous worm
CAUCUS *n*, *vb*
CAUDA, -E *n* tail of an animal
CAUDAD *adv* towards the tail or posterior part

CAUDAE ▸ **cauda**
CAUDAL *adj* at or near an animal's tail
CAUDATE *adj* having a tail or a tail-like appendage ▹ *n* lizard-like amphibian
CAUDEX *n* thickened persistent stem base of some herbaceous perennial plants
CAUDLE, -D, -S *n* hot spiced wine drink made with gruel, formerly used medicinally ▹ *vb* make such a drink
CAUDRON *Spenserian spelling of* ▸ **cauldron**
CAUF, CAUVES *n* cage for holding live fish in the water
CAUGHT ▸ **catch**
CAUK, -S *n* type of barite
CAUKER, -S *n* one who caulks
CAUKS ▸ **cauk**
CAUL, -S *n* membrane sometimes covering a child's head at birth
CAULD, -ER, -S *a Scot word for* ▸ **cold**
CAULES ▸ **caulis**
CAULINE *adj* relating to or growing from a plant stem
CAULIS, CAULES *n* main stem of a plant
CAULK, -ED, -S *vb* fill in (cracks) with paste etc
CAULKER ▸ **caulk**
CAULKS ▸ **caulk**
CAULOME *n* plant's stem structure, considered as a whole
CAULS ▸ **caul**
CAUM, -ED, -ING, -S *same as* ▸ **cam**
CAUP, -S *n* type of quaich
CAURI, -S *n* former coin of Guinea
CAUSA, -E *n* reason or cause
CAUSAL, -S *adj* of or being a cause ▹ *n* something that suggests a cause
CAUSE, -D, -S, CAUSING *n, vb*
CAUSEN *old infinitive of* ▸ **cause**
CAUSER, -S ▸ **cause**
CAUSES ▸ **cause**
CAUSEY, -S *n* cobbled street ▹ *vb* cobble
CAUSING ▸ **cause**
CAUSTIC *adj, n*
CAUTEL, -S *n* craftiness
CAUTER, -S *n* cauterizing instrument
CAUTERY *n* coagulation of blood or destruction of body tissue by cauterizing
CAUTION *n, vb*
CAUVES ▸ **cauf**
CAVA, -S *n* Spanish sparkling wine
CAVALLA *n* type of tropical fish
CAVALLY *same as* ▸ **cavalla**
CAVALRY *n*
CAVAS ▸ **cava**
CAVASS *n* Turkish armed police officer
CAVE, -D, -S *n, vb*
CAVEAT, -S *n, vb*
CAVED ▸ **cave**
CAVEL, -S *n* drawing of lots among miners for an easy and profitable place at the coalface
CAVEMAN, CAVEMEN *n*
CAVEOLA *n* pit in a cell membrane
CAVER, -S ▸ **cave**
CAVERN, -S *n, vb*
CAVERS ▸ **caver**
CAVES ▸ **cave**
CAVETTO, CAVETTI *n* concave moulding, shaped to a quarter circle in cross section
CAVIAR, -S *n*
CAVIARE *same as* ▸ **caviar**
CAVIARS ▸ **caviar**
CAVIE *n* hen coop
CAVIER, -S *same as* ▸ **caviar**
CAVIES ▸ **cavy**
CAVIL, -ED, -S *vb* make petty objections ▹ *n* petty objection
CAVILER ▸ **cavil**
CAVILS ▸ **cavil**
CAVING, -S *n* sport of exploring caves
CAVITY *n*
CAVORT, -S *vb*
CAVY, CAVIES *n* type of small rodent
CAW, -ED, -S *n, vb*
CAWING, -S ▸ **caw**
CAWK, -S *same as* ▸ **cauk**
CAWKER, -S *n* metal projection on a horse's shoe to prevent slipping
CAWKS ▸ **cawk**
CAWS ▸ **caw**
CAXON, -S *n* type of wig

CAY, -S *n* low island or bank composed of sand and coral fragments
CAYENNE *n* very hot condiment
CAYMAN, -S *n* S American reptile similar to an alligator
CAYS ▸ **cay**
CAYUSE, -S *n* small pony used by Native Americans
CAZ *short for* ▸ **casual**

Caz is slang for casual, and is one of the essential short words for using the Z.

CAZH *adj* casual
CAZIQUE *same as* ▸ **cacique**

This word means a Native American chief, and its plural **caziques** was once played as a 9-timer (that is, a word spanning two triple-word squares) earning the highest score for a single word ever officially recorded in a game of Scrabble, 392 points.

CEAS *same as* ▸ **caese**
CEASE, -D, -S *vb*
CEASING ▸ **cease**
CEAZE, -D, -S, CEAZING *obsolete spelling of* ▸ **seize**
CEBID, -S *n* any member of the Cebidae family of New World monkeys
CEBOID, -S *same as* ▸ **cebid**
CECA ▸ **cecum**
CECAL ▸ **cecum**
CECALLY ▸ **cecum**
CECILS *pl n* fried meatballs
CECITIS *n* inflammation of the c(a)ecum
CECITY *n* rare word for blindness
CECUM, CECA *same as* ▸ **caecum**
CEDAR, -S *n, adj*
CEDARED *adj* covered with cedars
CEDARN *adj* relating to cedar
CEDARS ▸ **cedar**
CEDARY *adj* like cedar
CEDE, -D, -S, CEDING *vb*
CEDER, -S ▸ **cede**
CEDES ▸ **cede**
CEDI, -S *n* standard monetary unit of Ghana, divided into 100 pesewas
CEDILLA *n* character placed under a *c* in some languages
CEDING ▸ **cede**
CEDIS ▸ **cedi**
CEDRATE *n* citron
CEDRINE *adj* relating to cedar
CEDULA, -S *n* form of identification in Spanish-speaking countries
CEE, -S *n* third letter of the alphabet
CEIBA, -S *n* type of tropical tree
CEIL, -ED, -S *vb* line (a ceiling) with plaster, boarding, etc
CEILER, -S ▸ **ceil**
CEILI, -S *variant spelling of* ▸ **ceilidh**
CEILIDH *n* social gathering for singing and dancing
CEILING *n, vb*
CEILIS ▸ **ceili**
CEILS ▸ **ceil**
CEL, -S *short for* > **celluloid**
CELADON *n* type of porcelain having a greyish-green glaze: mainly Chinese
CELEB, -S *n*
CELERY *n*
CELESTA *n* instrument like a small piano
CELESTE *same as* ▸ **celesta**
CELIAC, -S *same as* ▸ **coeliac**
CELL, -S *n*
CELLA, -E *n* inner room of a classical temple
CELLAR, -S *n, vb*
CELLED *adj* cellular
CELLI ▸ **cello**
CELLING *n* formation of cells
CELLIST ▸ **cello**
CELLO, CELLI, -S *n*
CELLOSE *n* disaccharide obtained by the hydrolysis of cellulose by cellulase
CELLS ▸ **cell**
CELLULE *n* very small cell
CELOM, -S *same as* ▸ **coelom**
CELOMIC ▸ **celom**
CELOMS ▸ **celom**
CELOSIA *same as* > **cockscomb**
CELOTEX *n* tradename for a type of insulation board

CELS ▶ **cel**
CELT, -S *n* stone or metal axelike instrument with a bevelled edge
CEMBALO, CEMBALI *n* harpsichord
CEMBRA, -S *n* Swiss pine
CEMENT, -S *n, vb*
CEMENTA > **cementum**
CEMENTS ▶ **cement**
CENACLE *n* supper room, esp one on an upper floor
CENDRE *adj* ash-blond
CENOTE, -S *n* natural well formed by the collapse of an overlying limestone crust
CENS *n* type of annual property rent
CENSE, -D, -S, CENSING *vb* burn incense near or before (an altar, shrine, etc)
CENSER, -S *n* container for burning incense
CENSES ▶ **cense**
CENSING ▶ **cense**
CENSOR, -S *n, vb*
CENSUAL ▶ **census**
CENSURE *n, vb*
CENSUS *n, vb*
CENT, -S *n*
CENTAGE *n* rate per hundred
CENTAI ▶ **centas**
CENTAL, -S *n* unit of weight equal to 100 pounds (45.3 kilograms)
CENTARE *same as* > **centiare**
CENTAS, CENTAI, CENTU *n* former monetary unit of Lithuania
CENTAUR *n*
CENTAVO *n* monetary unit in many Latin American countries
CENTER, -S *same as* ▶ **centre**
CENTILE *n* (in statistics) another word for percentile
CENTIME *n* monetary unit worth one hundredth of a franc
CENTIMO *n* monetary unit of Costa Rica, Paraguay, Peru, and Venezuela
CENTNER *n* unit of weight equivalent to 100 pounds (45.3 kilograms)
CENTO, -S *n* piece of writing composed of quotations from other authors
CENTRA ▶ **centrum**
CENTRAL *adj, n*
CENTRE, -S *n, vb*
CENTRED *adj* mentally and emotionally confident, focused, and well-balanced
CENTRES ▶ **centre**
CENTRIC *adj* being central or having a centre
CENTRUM, CENTRA *n* main part or body of a vertebra
CENTRY *obsolete variant of* ▶ **sentry**
CENTS ▶ **cent**
CENTU ▶ **centas**
CENTUM, -S *adj* denoting or belonging to certain Indo-European languages ▷ *n* hundred
CENTURY *n*
CEORL, -S *n* freeman of the lowest class in Anglo-Saxon England
CEP, -S *another name for* ▶ **porcino**
CEPAGE, -S *n* grape variety or type of wine
CEPE, -S *another spelling of* ▶ **cep**
CEPHEID *n* type of variable star with a regular cycle of variations in luminosity
CEPS ▶ **cep**
CERAMAL *same as* ▶ **cermet**
CERAMIC *n, adj*
CERASIN *n* meta-arabinic acid
CERATE, -S *n* hard ointment or medicated paste
CERATED *adj* (of certain birds, such as the falcon) having a cere
CERATES ▶ **cerate**
CERATIN *same as* ▶ **keratin**
CERCAL *adj* of or relating to a tail
CERCI ▶ **cercus**
CERCIS *n* type of tree or shrub
CERCUS, CERCI *n* one of a pair of sensory appendages on some insects and other arthropods
CERE, -D, -S, CERING *n* soft waxy swelling at the base of the upper beak of a parrot ▷ *vb* wrap in a cerecloth
CEREAL, -S *n*
CEREBRA > **cerebrum**

CERED ▸ **cere**
CEREOUS *adj* waxlike
CERES ▸ **cere**
CERESIN *n* white wax extracted from ozocerite
CEREUS *n* type of tropical American cactus
CERGE, -S *n* large altar candle
CERIA, -S *n* ceric oxide
CERIC *adj* of or containing cerium in the tetravalent state
CERING ▸ **cere**
CERIPH, -S *same as* ▸ **serif**
CERISE, -S *adj* cherry-red ▹ *n* moderate to dark red colour
CERITE, -S *n* hydrous silicate of cerium
CERIUM, -S *n* steel-grey metallic element
CERMET, -S *n* material consisting of a metal matrix with ceramic particles disseminated through it
CERNE, -D, -S, CERNING *obsolete variant of* > **encircle**
CERO, -S *n* type of large food fish
CEROC, -S *n* dance combining many styles, including jive and salsa
CEROON, -S *n* hide-covered bale
CEROS ▸ **cero**
CEROTIC *adj* as in **cerotic acid** white insoluble odourless wax
CEROUS *adj* of or containing cerium in the trivalent state
CERRADO *n* vast area of tropical savanna in Brazil
CERRIAL *adj* relating to the cerris
CERRIS *n* Turkey oak
CERT, -S *n* certainty
CERTAIN *adj*
CERTES *adv* with certainty
CERTIE *n* as in **by my certie** assuredly
CERTIFY *vb*
CERTS ▸ **cert**
CERTY *n* as in **by my certy** assuredly
CERULE *adj* sky-blue
CERUMEN *n* wax secreted by glands in the external ear
CERUSE, -S *n* white lead
CERVEZA *n* Spanish word for beer
CERVID, -S *n* type of ruminant mammal characterized by the presence of antlers
CERVINE *adj* resembling or relating to a deer
CERVIX *n* narrow entrance of the womb
CESIOUS *same as* > **caesious**
CESIUM, -S *same as* ▸ **caesium**
CESS, -ED, -ES, -ING *n* any of several special taxes, such as a land tax in Scotland ▹ *vb* tax or assess for taxation
CESSE *obsolete variant of* ▸ **cease**
CESSED ▸ **cess**
CESSER, -S *n* coming to an end of a term interest or annuity
CESSES ▸ **cess**
CESSING ▸ **cess**
CESSION *n* ceding
CESSPIT *same as* > **cesspool**
CESTA, -S *n* in jai alai, the basket used to throw and catch the pelota
CESTI ▸ **cestus**
CESTODE *n* type of parasitic flatworm such as the tapeworms
CESTOI ▸ **cestos**
CESTOID *adj* (esp of tapeworms and similar animals) ribbon-like in form ▹ *n* ribbon-like worm
CESTOS, CESTOI *same as* ▸ **cestus**
CESTUI, -S *n* legal term to designate a person
CESTUS, CESTI *n* girdle of Aphrodite
CESURA, -E, -S *variant spelling of* ▸ **caesura**
CESURAL ▸ **cesura**
CESURAS ▸ **cesura**
CESURE, -S *same as* ▸ **caesura**
CETANE, -S *n* colourless liquid hydrocarbon, used as a solvent
CETE, -S *n* group of badgers
CETYL, -S *n* univalent alcohol radical
CEVICHE *n* Peruvian seafood dish
CEZVE, -S *n* small metal pot for brewing coffee

CH *pron* obsolete form of I
CHA, -S *n* tea
CHABLIS *n* dry white French wine
CHABOUK *n* type of whip
CHABUK, -S *same as* ▸ **chabouk**
CHACE, -D, -S, CHACING *obsolete variant of* ▸ **chase**
CHACHKA *n* cheap trinket
CHACING ▸ **chace**
CHACK, -ED, -S *vb* bite
CHACMA, -S *n* type of baboon with coarse greyish hair, living in S and E Africa
CHACO, -ES, -S *same as* ▸ **shako**
CHAD, -S *n* small pieces removed during the punching of holes in punch cards, printer paper, etc
CHADAR, -S *same as* ▸ **chuddar**
CHADDAR *same as* ▸ **chuddar**
CHADDOR *same as* ▸ **chuddar**
CHADO, -S *n* Japanese tea ceremony
CHADOR, -S *same as* ▸ **chuddar**
CHADOS ▸ **chado**
CHADRI *n* shroud which covers the body from head to foot
CHADS ▸ **chad**
CHAEBOL *n* large, usually family-owned, business group in South Korea
CHAETA, -E *n* a bristle on the body of an annelid
CHAETAL ▸ **chaeta**
CHAFE, -D, -S, CHAFING *vb*
CHAFER, -S *n* large beetle
CHAFES ▸ **chafe**
CHAFF, -ED, -S *n, vb*
CHAFFER *vb* haggle
CHAFFS ▸ **chaff**
CHAFFY ▸ **chaff**
CHAFING ▸ **chafe**
CHAFT, -S *n* jaw
CHAGAN, -S *n* Mongolian royal or imperial title
CHAGRIN *n, vb*
CHAI, -S *n* tea, esp as made in India with added spices
CHAIN, -ED, -S *n, vb*
CHAINE, -S *adj* (of a dance turn) producing a full rotation for every two steps taken ▹ *vb* produce a full rotation for every two steps taken
CHAINED ▸ **chain**
CHAINER *n* person who chains
CHAINES ▸ **chaine**
CHAINS ▸ **chain**
CHAIR, -ED, -S *n, vb*
CHAIS ▸ **chai**
CHAISE, -S *n* light horse-drawn carriage
CHAKRA, -S *n* (in yoga) any of the seven major energy centres in the body
CHAL, -S *n* in Romany, person or fellow
CHALAH, -S, CHALOT, CHALOTH *same as* ▸ **challah**
CHALAN, -S *vb* (in India) to cause an accused person to appear before a magistrate ▹ *n* invoice, pass, or voucher
CHALAZA *n* one of a pair of spiral threads holding the yolk of a bird's egg in position
CHALCID *n* type of tiny insect
CHALDER *n* former Scottish dry measure
CHALEH, -S *same as* ▸ **challah**
CHALET, -S *n* kind of Swiss wooden house with a steeply sloping roof
CHALICE *n*
CHALK, -ED, -S *n, vb*
CHALKY ▸ **chalk**
CHALLA, -S *same as* ▸ **challah**
CHALLAH, CHALLOT *n* type of bread
CHALLAN *same as* ▸ **chalan**
CHALLAS ▸ **challa**
CHALLIE *same as* ▸ **challis**
CHALLIS *n* lightweight plain-weave fabric
CHALLOT ▸ **challah**
CHALLY *same as* ▸ **challis**
CHALONE *n* any internal secretion that inhibits a physiological process or function
CHALOT ▸ **chalah**
CHALOTH ▸ **chalah**
CHALS ▸ **chal**
CHALUPA *n* Mexican dish

CHALUTZ *n* member of an organization of immigrants to Israeli agricultural settlements
CHAM, -S *an archaic word for* ▸ **khan**
CHAMADE *n* (formerly) a signal by drum or trumpet inviting an enemy to a parley
CHAMBER *n, vb*
CHAMBRE *adj* (of wine) at room temperature
CHAMETZ *n* leavened food which may not be eaten during Passover
CHAMFER *same as* ▸ **chase**
CHAMISA *n* American shrub
CHAMISE *same as* ▸ **chamiso**
CHAMISO *n* four-wing saltbush
CHAMLET *same as* ▸ **camlet**
CHAMMY *same as* ▸ **chamois**
CHAMOIS *n* small mountain antelope or a piece of leather from its skin, used for polishing ▹ *vb* polish with a chamois
CHAMOIX *same as* ▸ **chamois**
CHAMP, -ED, -S *vb*
CHAMPAC *n* type of tree
CHAMPAK *same as* ▸ **champac**
CHAMPAS *n* champagne
CHAMPED ▸ **champ**
CHAMPER ▸ **champ**
CHAMPS ▸ **champ**
CHAMPY *adj* (of earth) churned up (by cattle, for example)
CHAMS ▸ **cham**
CHANA, -S *n* (in Indian cookery) chickpeas
CHANCE, -D, -S *n, vb*
CHANCEL *n* part of a church containing the altar and choir
CHANCER *n* unscrupulous or dishonest opportunist
CHANCES ▸ **chance**
CHANCEY *same as* ▸ **chancy**
CHANCRE *n* small hard growth
CHANCY *adj* uncertain, risky
CHANG, -S *n* loud discordant noise
CHANGA *interj* in Indian English, an expression of approval or agreement
CHANGE, -D, -S *n, vb*
CHANGER ▸ **change**
CHANGES ▸ **change**
CHANGS ▸ **chang**
CHANK, -S *n* shell of several types of sea conch, used to make bracelets
CHANNEL *n, vb*
CHANNER *n* gravel
CHANOYO *variant of* ▸ **chado**
CHANOYU *same as* ▸ **chado**
CHANSON *n* song
CHANT, -ED, -S *vb, n*
CHANTER *n* (on bagpipes) pipe on which the melody is played
CHANTEY *the usual US spelling of* ▸ **shanty**
CHANTIE *n* chamber pot
CHANTOR *same as* ▸ **chanter**
CHANTRY *n* endowment for the singing of Masses for the founder
CHANTS ▸ **chant**
CHANTY *same as* ▸ **shanty**
CHAO *n* Vietnamese rice porridge
CHAOS, -ES *n*
CHAOTIC ▸ **chaos**
CHAP, -PED, -S *n, vb*
CHAPATI *n* (in Indian cookery) flat thin unleavened bread
CHAPE, -S *n* metal tip or trimming for a scabbard
CHAPEAU *n* hat
CHAPEL, -S *n*
CHAPES ▸ **chape**
CHAPESS *n* woman
CHAPKA, -S *same as* ▸ **czapka**
CHAPLET *n* garland for the head ▹ *vb* create a garland
CHAPMAN, CHAPMEN *n* travelling pedlar
CHAPPAL *n* one of a pair of sandals, usually of leather, worn in India
CHAPPED ▸ **chap**
CHAPPIE *n* man or boy
CHAPPY *adj* (of skin) chapped
CHAPS ▸ **chap**
CHAPT *adj* chapped
CHAPTER *n, vb*

CHAR, -RED, -S *vb* blacken by partial burning ▷ *n* charwoman
CHARA *n* type of green freshwater algae
CHARACT *n* distinctive mark
CHARADE *n*
CHARAS *another name for* ▶ **hashish**
CHARD, -S *n* variety of beet
CHARE, -D, -S, CHARING *same as* ▶ **char**
CHARET, -S *obsolete variant of* ▶ **chariot**
CHARGE, -D, -S *vb, n*
CHARGER *n* device for charging an accumulator
CHARGES ▶ **charge**
CHARIER ▶ **chary**
CHARILY *adv* cautiously
CHARING ▶ **chare**
CHARIOT *n, vb*
CHARISM *same as* > **charisma**
CHARITY *n*
CHARK, -ED, -S *vb* char
CHARKA, -S *same as* ▶ **charkha**
CHARKED ▶ **chark**
CHARKHA *n* (in India) a spinning wheel, esp for cotton
CHARKS ▶ **chark**
CHARLEY *n* as in **charley horse** muscle stiffness after strenuous exercise
CHARLIE *n* fool
CHARM, -S *n, vb*
CHARMED *adj* delighted or fascinated
CHARMER *n* attractive person
CHARMS ▶ **charm**
CHARNEL *adj* ghastly ▷ *n* ghastly thing
CHARPAI *same as* ▶ **charpoy**
CHARPIE *n* lint pieces used to make surgical dressings
CHARPOY *n* type of bedstead
CHARQUI *n* meat, esp beef, cut into strips and dried
CHARR, -S *same as* ▶ **char**
CHARRED ▶ **char**
CHARRO, -S *n* Mexican cowboy
CHARRS ▶ **charr**
CHARRY *adj* of or relating to charcoal
CHARS ▶ **char**
CHART, -ED, -S *n* graph, table, or diagram showing information ▷ *vb* plot the course of
CHARTA, -S *n* charter
CHARTED ▶ **chart**
CHARTER *n, vb*
CHARTS ▶ **chart**
CHARY, CHARIER *adj* wary, careful
CHAS ▶ **cha**
CHASE, -D, -S *vb, n*
CHASER, -S ▶ **chase**
CHASES ▶ **chase**
CHASING ▶ **chase**
CHASM, -S *n*
CHASMAL ▶ **chasm**
CHASMED ▶ **chasm**
CHASMIC ▶ **chasm**
CHASMS ▶ **chasm**
CHASMY *adj* full of chasms
CHASSE, -D, -S *n* one of a series of gliding steps in ballet ▷ *vb* perform either of these steps
CHASSIS *n* frame, wheels, and mechanical parts of a vehicle
CHASTE, -R *adj*
CHASTEN *vb* subdue by criticism
CHASTER ▶ **chaste**
CHAT, -S, -TED *n, vb*
CHATBOT *n* computer program that simulates conversation with human users over the internet
CHATEAU *n*
CHATON, -S *n* in jewellery, a stone with a reflective metal foil backing
CHATS ▶ **chat**
CHATTA, -S *n* umbrella
CHATTED ▶ **chat**
CHATTEL *n*
CHATTER *vb, n*
CHATTI, -S *n* (in India) earthenware pot
CHATTY *adj* (of a person) fond of friendly, informal conversation ▷ *n* (in India) earthenware pot
CHAUFE, -D, -S *obsolete variant of* ▶ **chafe**
CHAUFER *same as* > **chauffer**
CHAUFES ▶ **chaufe**
CHAUFF, -S *obsolete variant of* ▶ **chafe**
CHAUMER *n* chamber
CHAUNCE *archaic variant of* ▶ **chance**
CHAUNGE *archaic variant of* ▶ **change**

CHAUNT, -S *a less common variant of* ▸ **chant**
CHAUVIN *n* chauvinist
CHAV, -S *n* insulting word for a young working-class person who wears casual sports clothes
CHAVE *vb* old dialect term for 'I have'
CHAVISH ▸ **chav**
CHAVS ▸ **chav**
CHAVVY *adj* relating to or like a chav
CHAW, -ED, -ING, -S *vb* chew (tobacco), esp without swallowing it ▹ *n* something chewed, esp a plug of tobacco
CHAWER, -S ▸ **chaw**
CHAWING ▸ **chaw**
CHAWK, -S *n* jackdaw
CHAWS ▸ **chaw**
CHAY, -S *n* plant of the madder family
CHAYA, -S *same as* ▸ **chay**
CHAYOTE *n* tropical climbing plant
CHAYS ▸ **chay**
CHAZAN, -S *n* man employed to lead services in a synagogue
CHAZZAN *variant of* ▸ **chazan**
CHAZZEN *same as* ▸ **chazzan**
CHE *pron* dialectal form meaning 'I'
CHEAP, -ED, -ER, -S *adj, adv, n, vb*
CHEAPEN *vb* lower the reputation of
CHEAPER ▸ **cheap**
CHEAPIE *n* something inexpensive
CHEAPLY ▸ **cheap**
CHEAPO, -S *n* very cheap and possibly shoddy thing
CHEAPS ▸ **cheap**
CHEAPY *same as* ▸ **cheapie**
CHEAT, -ED, -S *vb, n*
CHEATER ▸ **cheat**
CHEATS ▸ **cheat**
CHEBEC, -S *n* type of boat
CHECHIA *n* Berber skullcap
CHECK, -ED, -S *vb, n*
CHECKER *same as* ▸ **chequer**
CHECKS ▸ **check**
CHECKUP *n*
CHECKY *adj* having squares of alternating tinctures or furs
CHEDDAR *n*
CHEDER, -S *n* Jewish religious education
CHEDITE *same as* > **cheddite**
CHEEK, -ED, -S *n, vb*
CHEEKY *adj* impudent, disrespectful
CHEEP, -ED, -S *n, vb*
CHEEPER ▸ **cheep**
CHEEPS ▸ **cheep**
CHEER, -ED *vb, n*
CHEERER ▸ **cheer**
CHEERIO *interj, n, sentence substitute*
CHEERLY *adv* cheerfully
CHEERO, -S *same as* ▸ **cheerio**
CHEERS *interj* drinking toast
CHEERY *adj* cheerful
CHEESE, -D, -S *n* food made from coagulated milk curd ▹ *vb* stop
CHEESY *adj* like cheese
CHEETAH *n*
CHEF, -ED, -FED, -ING, -S *n, vb*
CHEFDOM *n* state or condition of being a chef
CHEFED ▸ **chef**
CHEFFED ▸ **chef**
CHEFFY *adj* relating to or characteristic of chefs
CHEFING ▸ **chef**
CHEFS ▸ **chef**
CHEGOE, -S *same as* ▸ **chigger**
CHEKA, -S *n* secret police set up in Russia in 1917
CHEKIST *n* member of the cheka
CHELA, -E, -S *n* disciple of a religious teacher
CHELATE *n* coordination compound ▹ *adj* of or possessing chelae ▹ *vb* form a chelate
CHELLUP *n* noise
CHELOID *variant spelling of* ▸ **keloid**
CHELONE *n* hardy N American plant
CHELP, -ED, -S *vb* to chatter or speak out of turn
CHEM, -S *n* chemistry
CHEMIC, -S *vb* bleach ▹ *n* chemist
CHEMISE *n* woman's loose-fitting slip
CHEMISM *n* chemical action
CHEMIST *n*
CHEMMY *n* gambling card game

CHEMO, -S *n* short form of chemotherapy
CHEMS ▸ **chem**
CHENAR, -S *n* oriental plane tree
CHENET, -S *another word for* ▸ **genip**
CHENIX *n* ancient measure, slightly more than a quart
CHEQUE, -S *n*
CHEQUER *n* piece used in Chinese chequers ▹ *vb* make irregular in colour or character
CHEQUES ▸ **cheque**
CHEQUY *same as* ▸ **checky**
CHER *adj* dear or expensive
CHERE *feminine variant of* ▸ **cher**
CHERISH *vb*
CHEROOT *n* cigar with both ends cut flat
CHERRY *n, adj, vb*
CHERT, -S *n* microcrystalline form of silica
CHERTY ▸ **chert**
CHERUB, -S *n*
CHERUP, -S *same as* ▸ **chirrup**
CHERVIL *n* aniseed-flavoured herb
CHESIL, -S *n* gravel or shingle
CHESNUT *rare variant of* > **chestnut**
CHESS, -ES *n*
CHESSEL *n* mould used in cheese-making
CHESSES ▸ **chess**
CHEST, -ED, -S *n, vb*
CHESTY *adj* symptomatic of chest disease
CHETAH, -S *same as* ▸ **cheetah**
CHETH, -S *same as* ▸ **heth**
CHETNIK *n* member of a Serbian nationalist paramilitary group
CHETRUM *n* monetary unit in Bhutan
CHEVAL *n* as in **cheval glass** full-length mirror that can swivel
CHEVEN, -S *n* chub
CHEVET, -S *n* semicircular or polygonal east end of a church
CHEVIED ▸ **chevy**
CHEVIES ▸ **chevy**
CHEVIN, -S *same as* ▸ **cheven**
CHEVIOT *n* type of British sheep reared for its wool
CHEVRE, -S *n* any cheese made from goats' milk
CHEVRET *n* type of goats' cheese
CHEVRON *n, vb*
CHEVY, CHEVIED, CHEVIES *same as* ▸ **chivy**
CHEW, -ED, -ING, -S *vb, n*
CHEWER, -S ▸ **chew**
CHEWET, -S *n* type of meat pie
CHEWIE *n* chewing gum
CHEWIER ▸ **chewy**
CHEWIES ▸ **chewy**
CHEWING ▸ **chew**
CHEWINK *n* towhee
CHEWS ▸ **chew**
CHEWY, CHEWIER, CHEWIES *adj* requiring a lot of chewing ▹ *n* dog's rubber toy
CHEZ *prep* at the home of
CHI, -S *n* 22nd letter of the Greek alphabet

> **Chi** is a letter of the Greek alphabet. It can also be spelt **khi**.

CHIA, -S *n* plant of the mint family
CHIACK, -S *vb* tease or banter ▹ *n* good-humoured banter
CHIANTI *n* dry red Italian wine
CHIAO, -S *n* Chinese coin equal to one tenth of one yuan
CHIAS ▸ **chia**
CHIASM, -S *same as* ▸ **chiasma**
CHIASMA *n* crossing over of two anatomical structures
CHIASMI > **chiasmus**
CHIASMS ▸ **chiasm**
CHIAUS *same as* ▸ **chouse**
CHIB, -BED, -S *vb* in Scots English, stab or slash with a sharp weapon ▹ *n* sharp weapon
CHIBOL, -S *n* spring onion
CHIBOUK *n* Turkish tobacco pipe with an extremely long stem
CHIBS ▸ **chib**
CHIC, -ER, -EST, -S *adj, n*
CHICA, -S *n* Spanish girl or young woman
CHICANA *n* American female citizen of Mexican origin

CHICANE *n* obstacle in a motor-racing circuit ▷ *vb* deceive or trick by chicanery
CHICANO *n* American male citizen of Mexican origin
CHICAS ▶ **chica**
CHICER ▶ **chic**
CHICEST ▶ **chic**
CHICH, -ES *another word for* > **chickpea**
CHICHA, -S *n* Andean drink made from fermented maize
CHICHES ▶ **chich**
CHICHI, -S *adj* affectedly pretty or stylish ▷ *n* quality of being affectedly pretty or stylish
CHICK, -S *n*
CHICKEE *n* open-sided, thatched building on stilts
CHICKEN *n, adj, vb*
CHICKS ▶ **chick**
CHICLE, -S *n* gumlike substance obtained from the sapodilla
CHICLY ▶ **chic**
CHICO, -S *n* spiny chenopodiaceous shrub
CHICON, -S *same as* ▶ **chicory**
CHICORY *n*
CHICOS ▶ **chico**
CHICOT, -S *n* dead tree
CHICS ▶ **chic**
CHIDE, CHID, CHIDDEN, -D, -S, CHODE *vb* rebuke, scold
CHIDER, -S ▶ **chide**
CHIDES ▶ **chide**
CHIDING ▶ **chide**
CHIEF, -ER, -S *n, adj*
CHIEFLY *adv* especially ▷ *adj* of or relating to a chief or chieftain
CHIEFRY *same as* > **chiefery**
CHIEFS ▶ **chief**
CHIEL, -S *n* young man
CHIELD, -S *same as* ▶ **chiel**
CHIELS ▶ **chiel**
CHIFFON *n* fine see-through fabric ▷ *adj* made of chiffon
CHIGGER *n* parasitic larva of various mites
CHIGNON *n* knot of hair pinned up at the back of the head ▷ *vb* make a chignon
CHIGOE, -S *same as* ▶ **chigger**
CHIGRE, -S *same as* ▶ **chigger**
CHIK, -S *n* slatted blind
CHIKARA *n* Indian seven-stringed musical instrument
CHIKHOR *same as* ▶ **chukar**
CHIKOR, -S *same as* ▶ **chukar**
CHIKS ▶ **chik**
CHILD, -ED, -S *n* young human being ▷ *vb* give birth
CHILDE, -S *n* young man of noble birth
CHILDED ▶ **child**
CHILDER *dialect variant of* > **children**
CHILDES ▶ **childe**
CHILDLY ▶ **child**
CHILDS ▶ **child**
CHILE, -S *variant spelling of* ▶ **chilli**
CHILI, -ES, -S *same as* ▶ **chilli**
CHILIAD *n* group of one thousand
CHILIES ▶ **chili**
CHILIS ▶ **chili**
CHILL, -ED, -S *n, vb, adj*
CHILLAX *vb*
CHILLED ▶ **chill**
CHILLER *n* cooling or refrigerating device
CHILLI, -S *n* small red or green hot-tasting capsicum pod, used in cooking
CHILLS ▶ **chill**
CHILLUM *n* short pipe used for smoking
CHILLY *adj* moderately cold
CHIMAR, -S *same as* ▶ **chimere**
CHIMB, -S *same as* ▶ **chime**
CHIMBLY *same as* ▶ **chimney**
CHIMBS ▶ **chimb**
CHIME, -D, -S, CHIMING *n, vb*
CHIMER, -S ▶ **chime**
CHIMERA *n* unrealistic hope or idea
CHIMERE *n* gown worn by bishops
CHIMERS ▶ **chimer**
CHIMES ▶ **chime**
CHIMING ▶ **chime**
CHIMLA, -S *same as* ▶ **chimney**
CHIMLEY *same as* ▶ **chimney**
CHIMNEY *n, vb*
CHIMO *interj* Inuit greeting and toast
CHIMP, -S *n*
CHIN, -NED, -S *n, vb*

CHINA, -S *n*
CHINAR, -S *same as* ▸ **chenar**
CHINAS ▸ **china**
CHINCH *n* (S US) bedbug ▹ *vb* be frugal or miserly
CHINCHY *adj* tightfisted
CHINDIT *n* Allied soldier fighting behind the Japanese lines in Burma during World War II
CHINE, -D, -S, CHINING *same as* ▸ **chime**
CHINESE *adj* of or relating to China
CHING, -S *n* high-pitched ring or chime
CHINING ▸ **chine**
CHINK, -ED, -S *n*, *vb*
CHINNED ▸ **chin**
CHINO *n* durable cotton twill cloth
CHINOIS *n* conical sieve
CHINONE *n* benzoquinone
CHINOOK *n* wind found in the Rocky Mountains
CHINOS *pl n* trousers made of a kind of hard-wearing cotton
CHINS ▸ **chin**
CHINSE, -D, -S *vb* fill the seams of a boat
CHINTS *obsolete variant of* ▸ **chintz**
CHINTZ *n*
CHINTZY *adj* of or covered with chintz
CHINWAG *n* chat
CHIP, -PED, -S *n*, *vb*
CHIPPER *vb* chirp or chatter ▹ *adj* cheerful, lively
CHIPPIE *same as* ▸ **chippy**
CHIPPY *n* fish-and-chip shop ▹ *adj* resentful or oversensitive about being perceived as inferior
CHIPS ▸ **chip**
CHIPSET *n* highly integrated circuit on the motherboard of a computer
CHIRAL > **chirality**
CHIRK, -ED, -ER, -S *vb* creak, like a door ▹ *adj* high-spirited
CHIRL, -ED, -S *vb* warble
CHIRM, -ED, -S *n* chirping of birds ▹ *vb* (esp of a bird) to chirp
CHIRO, -S *n* informal name for chiropractor
CHIRP, -ED, -S *vb*, *n*
CHIRPER ▸ **chirp**
CHIRPS ▸ **chirp**
CHIRPY *adj* lively and cheerful
CHIRR, -ED, -S *vb* (esp of certain insects, such as crickets) to make a shrill trilled sound ▹ *n* sound of chirring
CHIRRE, -S *same as* ▸ **chirr**
CHIRRED ▸ **chirr**
CHIRREN *pl n* dialect form of children
CHIRRES ▸ **chirre**
CHIRRS ▸ **chirr**
CHIRRUP *vb*, *n*
CHIRT, -ED, -S *vb* squirt
CHIRU, -S *n* Tibetan antelope
CHIS ▸ **chi**
CHISEL, -S *n*, *vb*
CHIT, -S, -TED *n* short official note, such as a receipt ▹ *vb* sprout
CHITAL, -S *n* type of deer
CHITIN, -S *n* outer layer of the bodies of arthropods
CHITLIN *n* pig intestine cooked and served as a dish
CHITON, -S *n* (in ancient Greece and Rome) a loose woollen tunic
CHITS ▸ **chit**
CHITTED ▸ **chit**
CHITTER *vb* twitter or chirp
CHITTY *adj* childish ▹ *vb* sprout
CHIV, -S, -VED *n* knife ▹ *vb* stab (someone)
CHIVARI *same as* > **charivari**
CHIVE, -D, CHIVING *n* small Eurasian plant ▹ *vb* file or cut off
CHIVES *same as* ▸ **chive**
CHIVIED ▸ **chivy**
CHIVIES ▸ **chivy**
CHIVING ▸ **chive**
CHIVS ▸ **chiv**
CHIVVED ▸ **chiv**
CHIVVY *same as* ▸ **chivy**
CHIVY, CHIVIED, CHIVIES *vb* harass or nag ▹ *n* hunt
CHIZ, -ZED, -ZES *n* cheat ▹ *vb* cheat
CHIZZ *same as* ▸ **chiz**
CHIZZED ▸ **chiz**
CHIZZES ▸ **chiz**
CHLAMYS *n* woollen cloak worn by ancient Greek soldiers

CHLORAL *n* colourless oily liquid with a pungent odour
CHLORIC *adj* of or containing chlorine in the pentavalent state
CHLORID *n* type of chlorine compound
CHLORIN *same as* > **chlorine**
CHOANA, -E *n* posterior nasal aperture
CHOBDAR *n* in India and Nepal, king's macebearer or attendant
CHOC, -S *short form of* > **chocolate**
CHOCCY *n* chocolate ▹ *adj* made of, tasting of, smelling of, or resembling chocolate
CHOCHO, -S *same as* ▸ **chayote**
CHOCK, -ED, -S *n, vb, adv*
CHOCKER *adj* full up
CHOCKIE *n* chocolate ▹ *adj* like chocolate
CHOCKO, -S *same as* ▸ **choco**
CHOCKS ▸ **chock**
CHOCKY *n* chocolate ▹ *adj* like chocolate
CHOCO, -S *n* member of the Australian army
CHOCS ▸ **choc**
CHOCTAW *n* movement in ice-skating
CHODE ▸ **chide**
CHOENIX *same as* ▸ **chenix**
CHOG, -S *n* core of a piece of fruit
CHOICE, -R, -S *n, adj*
CHOIL, -S *n* end of a knife blade next to the handle
CHOIR, -ED, -S *n, vb*
CHOKE, -S, CHOKING *vb, n*
CHOKED *adj* disappointed or angry
CHOKER, -S *n* tight-fitting necklace
CHOKES ▸ **choke**
CHOKEY, -S, CHOKIER *n* slang word for prison ▹ *adj* involving, caused by, or causing choking
CHOKIES ▸ **choky**
CHOKING ▸ **choke**
CHOKO, -S *n* pear-shaped fruit of a tropical American vine, eaten as a vegetable
CHOKRA, -S *n* in India, a boy or young man
CHOKRI, -S *n* in India, a girl or young woman
CHOKY, CHOKIES *same as* ▸ **chokey**
CHOLA, -S *n* long, loose Sikh robe
CHOLATE *n* salt of cholic acid
CHOLENT *n* meal prepared on Friday and left to cook until eaten for Sabbath lunch
CHOLER, -S *n* bad temper
CHOLERA *n* serious infectious disease
CHOLERS ▸ **choler**
CHOLI, -S *n* short-sleeved bodice, as worn by Indian women
CHOLIC *adj* as in **cholic acid** crystalline acid found in bile
CHOLINE *n* colourless viscous soluble alkaline substance present in animal tissues
CHOLIS ▸ **choli**
CHOLLA, -S *n* type of spiny cactus
CHOLTRY *n* caravanserai
CHOMETZ *same as* ▸ **chametz**
CHOMMIE *n* (in informal South African English) friend
CHOMP, -ED, -S *vb, n*
CHOMPER ▸ **chomp**
CHOMPS ▸ **chomp**
CHON, -S *n* North and South Korean monetary unit
CHONDRE *another word for* > **chondrule**
CHONDRI > **chondrus**
CHONS ▸ **chon**
CHOOF, -ED, -S *vb* go away
CHOOK, -ED, -S *n* hen or chicken ▹ *vb* make the sound of a hen of chicken
CHOOKIE *same as* ▸ **chook**
CHOOKS ▸ **chook**
CHOOM, -S *n* Englishman
CHOON, -S *n* slang term for music that one likes
CHOOSE, -S, CHOSEN *vb*
CHOOSER ▸ **choose**
CHOOSES ▸ **choose**
CHOOSEY *same as* ▸ **choosy**
CHOOSY *adj* fussy, hard to please
CHOP, -PED, -S *vb, n*
CHOPIN, -S *same as* ▸ **chopine**

CHOPINE *n* sandal-like shoe popular in the 18th century
CHOPINS ▶ **chopin**
CHOPPED ▶ **chop**
CHOPPER *n*, *vb*
CHOPPY *adj* (of the sea) fairly rough
CHOPS ▶ **chop**
CHORAGI > **choragus**
CHORAL, -S *adj*, *n* slow stately hymn tune
CHORALE *n* slow stately hymn tune
CHORALS ▶ **choral**
CHORD, -S *n*, *vb*
CHORDA, -E *n* in anatomy, a cord
CHORDAL ▶ **chord**
CHORDED ▶ **chord**
CHORDS ▶ **chord**
CHORE, -D, -S, CHORING *n*, *vb*
CHOREA, -S *n* disorder of the nervous system
CHOREAL ▶ **chorea**
CHOREAS ▶ **chorea**
CHORED ▶ **chore**
CHOREE, -S *n* trochee
CHOREGI > **choregus**
CHOREIC ▶ **chorea**
CHORES ▶ **chore**
CHOREUS *same as* ▶ **choree**
CHORIA ▶ **chorion**
CHORIAL ▶ **chorion**
CHORIC *adj* in the manner of a chorus
CHORINE *n* young woman in a chorus line
CHORING ▶ **chore**
CHORION, CHORIA *n* outer membrane forming a sac around an embryo
CHORISM > **chorisis**
CHORIST *n* choir member
CHORIZO *n* kind of highly seasoned pork sausage of Spain or Mexico
CHOROID *adj* resembling the chorion, esp in being vascular ▷ *n* vascular membrane of the eyeball
CHORRIE *n* dilapidated old car
CHORTEN *n* Buddhist shrine
CHORTLE *vb*, *n*
CHORUS *n*, *vb*
CHOSE, -S *n* item of property
CHOSEN ▶ **choose**
CHOSES ▶ **chose**
CHOTA *adj* (in British Empire Indian usage) small
CHOTT, -S *variant spelling of* ▶ **shott**
CHOU, -X *n* type of cabbage
CHOUGH, -S *n* large black Eurasian and N African bird of the crow family
CHOUSE, -D, -S *vb* cheat
CHOUSER ▶ **chouse**
CHOUSES ▶ **chouse**
CHOUSH *n* Turkish messenger
CHOUT, -S *n* blackmail
CHOUX ▶ **chou**
CHOW, -ED, -ING, -S *n* thick-coated dog with a curled tail, orig from China ▷ *vb* eat
CHOWDER *n* thick soup containing clams or fish ▷ *vb* make a chowder of
CHOWED ▶ **chow**
CHOWING ▶ **chow**
CHOWK, -S *n* marketplace or market area
CHOWRI, -S *n* fly-whisk
CHOWRY *same as* ▶ **chowri**
CHOWS ▶ **chow**
CHOWSE, -D, -S *same as* ▶ **chouse**
CHRISM, -S *n* consecrated oil used for anointing in some churches
CHRISMA > **chrismon**
CHRISMS ▶ **chrism**
CHRISOM *same as* ▶ **chrism**
CHRISTY *n* skiing turn for stopping or changing direction quickly
CHROMA, -S *n* attribute of a colour
CHROME, -D, -S *n* anything plated with chromium ▷ *vb* plate with chromium ▷ *adj* of or having the appearance of chrome
CHROMEL *n* nickel-based alloy
CHROMES ▶ **chrome**
CHROMIC *adj* of or containing chromium in the trivalent state
CHROMO, -S *n* picture produced by lithography
CHROMY ▶ **chrome**
CHROMYL *n* type of divalent radical
CHRONIC *adj*, *n*

CHRONON *n* unit of time
CHUB, -S *n* European freshwater fish of the carp family
CHUBBY *adj*
CHUBS ▸ **chub**
CHUCK, -ED, -S *vb, n*
CHUCKER *n* person who throws something
CHUCKIE *n* small stone
CHUCKLE *vb, n*
CHUCKS ▸ **chuck**
CHUCKY *same as* ▸ **chuckie**
CHUDDAH *same as* ▸ **chuddar**
CHUDDAR *n* large shawl or veil
CHUDDER *same as* ▸ **chuddar**
CHUDDY *n* chewing gum
CHUFA, -S *n* type of sedge
CHUFF, -ER, -S *vb* (of a steam engine) move while making a puffing sound ▹ *n* puffing sound of or as if of a steam engine ▹ *adj* boorish
CHUFFED *adj* very pleased
CHUFFER ▸ **chuff**
CHUFFS ▸ **chuff**
CHUFFY *adj* boorish and surly
CHUG, -GED, -S *n, vb*
CHUGGER ▸ **chug**
CHUGS ▸ **chug**
CHUKAR, -S *n* common Indian partridge
CHUKKA, -S *n* period of play in polo
CHUKKAR *same as* ▸ **chukka**
CHUKKAS ▸ **chukka**
CHUKKER *same as* ▸ **chukka**
CHUKOR, -S *same as* ▸ **chukar**
CHUM, -MED, -S *n, vb*
CHUMASH *n* printed book containing one of the Five Books of Moses
CHUMLEY *same as* ▸ **chimney**
CHUMMED ▸ **chum**
CHUMMY *adj* friendly ▹ *n* chum
CHUMP, -ED, -S *n* stupid person ▹ *vb* chew noisily
CHUMS ▸ **chum**
CHUNDER *vb* slang word for vomit
CHUNK, -ED, -S *n, vb*
CHUNKY *adj* (of a person) broad and heavy
CHUNNEL *n* rail tunnel linking England and France
CHUNNER *same as* ▸ **chunter**
CHUNTER *vb* mutter or grumble incessantly in a meaningless fashion
CHUPATI *same as* > **chupatti**
CHUPPA, -S *variant of* ▸ **chuppah**
CHUPPAH, CHUPPOT *n* canopy under which a marriage is performed
CHUPPAS ▸ **chuppa**
CHUPPOT ▸ **chuppah**
CHUR *interj* expression of agreement
CHURCH *n, vb*
CHURCHY *adj* like a church, church service, etc
CHURL, -S *n* surly ill-bred person
CHURN, -ED, -S *n, vb*
CHURNER ▸ **churn**
CHURNS ▸ **churn**
CHURR, -ED, -S *same as* ▸ **chirr**
CHURRO, -S *n* Spanish dough stick snack
CHURRS ▸ **churr**
CHURRUS *n* hemp resin
CHUSE, -D, -S, CHUSING *obsolete variant of* ▸ **choose**
CHUT, -S *interj* expression of surprise or annoyance ▹ *n* such an expression
CHUTE, -D, -S, CHUTING *n, vb*
CHUTIST ▸ **chute**
CHUTNEE *same as* ▸ **chutney**
CHUTNEY *n*
CHUTS ▸ **chut**
CHUTZPA *same as* > **chutzpah**
CHYACK, -S *same as* ▸ **chiack**
CHYLDE *archaic word for* ▸ **child**
CHYLE, -S *n* milky fluid formed in the small intestine during digestion
CHYLIFY *vb* be turned into chyle
CHYLOUS ▸ **chyle**
CHYME, -S *n* partially digested food that leaves the stomach
CHYMIC, -S *same as* ▸ **chemic**

CHYMIFY *vb* form into chyme
CHYMIST *same as* ▸ **chemist**
CHYMOUS ▸ **chyme**
CHYND *adj* chined
CHYPRE, -S *n* perfume made from sandalwood
CHYRON, -S *n* caption superimposed on a TV screen
CHYTRID *n* variety of fungus
CIAO *an informal word for* ▸ **hello**
CIBOL, -S *same as* ▸ **chibol**
CIBORIA > **ciborium**
CIBOULE *same as* ▸ **chibol**
CICADA, -E, -S *n*
CICALA, -S, CICALE *same as* ▸ **cicada**
CICELY *n* type of plant
CICERO, -S *n* measure for type that is somewhat larger than the pica
CICHLID *n* type of tropical freshwater fish popular in aquariums
CICOREE *same as* ▸ **chicory**
CICUTA, -S *n* spotted hemlock
CID, -S *n* leader
CIDARIS *n* sea urchin
CIDE, -D, -S, CIDING *Shakespearean variant of* ▸ **decide**
CIDER, -S *n*
CIDERY *adj* like cider
CIDES ▸ **cide**
CIDING ▸ **cide**
CIDS ▸ **cid**
CIEL, -ED, -S *same as* ▸ **ceil**
CIELING *same as* ▸ **ceiling**
CIELS ▸ **ciel**
CIERGE, -S *same as* ▸ **cerge**
CIG, -S *same as* > **cigarette**
CIGAR, -S *n*
CIGARET *same as* > **cigarette**
CIGARS ▸ **cigar**
CIGGIE, -S *same as* > **cigarette**
CIGGY *same as* > **cigarette**
CIGS ▸ **cig**
CILIA ▸ **cilium**
CILIARY *adj* of or relating to cilia
CILIATE *n* type of protozoan
CILICE, -S *n* haircloth fabric or garment
CILIUM, CILIA *n* short thread projecting from a cell that causes movement
CILL, -S *variant spelling (used in the building industry) of* ▸ **sill**
CIMAR, -S *same as* ▸ **cymar**
CIMELIA *pl n* (especially, ecclesiastical) treasures
CIMEX, CIMICES *n* type of heteropterous insect, esp the bedbug
CIMIER, -S *n* crest of a helmet
CINCH, -ED, -ES *n* easy task ▹ *vb* fasten a girth around (a horse)
CINCT *adj* encircled
CINDER, -S *n, vb*
CINDERY *adj* covered in cinders
CINE, -S *n* as in **cine camera** camera able to film moving pictures
CINEAST *same as* > **cineaste**
CINEMA, -S *n*
CINEOL, -S *n* colourless oily liquid with a camphor-like odour and a spicy taste
CINEOLE *same as* ▸ **cineol**
CINEOLS ▸ **cineol**
CINEREA *n* grey matter of the brain and nervous system
CINERIN *n* either of two organic compounds used as insecticides
CINES ▸ **cine**
CINGULA > **cingulum**
CINQ, -S *n* number five
CINQUE, -S *n* number five in cards, dice, etc
CION, -S *same as* ▸ **scion**
CIPHER, -S *n, vb*
CIPHONY *n* ciphered telephony
CIPOLIN *n* Italian marble with alternating white and green streaks
CIPPUS, CIPPI *n* pillar bearing an inscription
CIRCA *prep*
CIRCAR, -S *n* in India, part of a province
CIRCLE, -D, -S *n, vb*
CIRCLER ▸ **circle**
CIRCLES ▸ **circle**
CIRCLET *n* circular ornament worn on the head

CIRCLIP *n* type of fastener
CIRCS *pl n* circumstances
CIRCUIT *n, vb*
CIRCUS *n*
CIRCUSY *adj* like a circus
CIRE, -S *adj* (of fabric) treated with a heat or wax process to make it smooth ▷ *n* such a surface on a fabric
CIRL, -S *n* bird belonging to the bunting family
CIRQUE, -S *n* steep-sided semicircular hollow found in mountainous areas
CIRRATE *adj* bearing or resembling cirri
CIRRI ▶ **cirrus**
CIRROSE *same as* ▶ **cirrate**
CIRROUS *same as* ▶ **cirrate**
CIRRUS, CIRRI *n* high wispy cloud
CIRSOID *adj* resembling a varix
CIS *adj* having two groups of atoms on the same side of a double bond
CISCO, -ES, -S *n* whitefish, esp the lake herring of cold deep lakes of North America
CISSIER ▶ **cissy**
CISSIES ▶ **cissy**
CISSING *n* appearance of pinholes, craters, etc, in paintwork
CISSOID *n* type of geometric curve
CISSUS *n* type of climbing plant
CISSY, CISSIER, CISSIES *same as* ▶ **sissy**
CIST, -S *n* wooden box for holding ritual objects used in ancient Rome and Greece
CISTED ▶ **cist**
CISTERN *n*
CISTIC *adj* cist-like
CISTRON *n* section of a chromosome that encodes a single polypeptide chain
CISTS ▶ **cist**
CISTUS *n* type of plant
CIT, -S *n* pejorative term for a town dweller
CITABLE ▶ **cite**
CITADEL *n*
CITAL, -S *n* court summons
CITATOR *n* legal publication
CITE, -D, -S, CITING *vb*
CITER, -S ▶ **cite**
CITES ▶ **cite**
CITESS *n* female cit
CITHARA *n* ancient stringed musical instrument
CITHER, -S *same as* ▶ **cittern**
CITHERN *same as* ▶ **cittern**
CITHERS ▶ **cither**
CITHREN *same as* ▶ **cithara**
CITIED *adj* having cities
CITIES ▶ **city**
CITIFY *vb* cause to conform to or adopt the customs, habits, or dress of city people
CITING ▶ **cite**
CITIZEN *n*
CITO *adv* swiftly
CITOLA, -S *same as* ▶ **citole**
CITOLE, -S *n* type of medieval stringed instrument
CITRAL, -S *n* volatile liquid with a lemon-like odour
CITRATE *n* any salt or ester of citric acid
CITRIC *adj* of or derived from citrus fruits or citric acid
CITRIN, -S *n* vitamin P
CITRINE *n* brownish-yellow variety of quartz: a gemstone
CITRINS ▶ **citrin**
CITRON, -S *n* lemon-like fruit of a small Asian tree
CITROUS *same as* ▶ **citrus**
CITRUS *n*
CITRUSY *same as* > **citrussy**
CITS ▶ **cit**
CITTERN *n* medieval stringed instrument
CITY, CITIES *n*
CITYFY *same as* ▶ **citify**
CIVE, -S *same as* ▶ **chive**
CIVET, -S *n* spotted catlike African mammal
CIVIC *adj*
CIVICS *n* study of the rights and responsibilities of citizenship
CIVIE, -S *same as* ▶ **civvy**
CIVIL *adj*
CIVILLY ▶ **civil**

CIVILS *n* civil engineering
CIVISM, -S *n* good citizenship
CIVVY, CIVVIES *n* civilian
CIZERS *archaic spelling of* > **scissors**
CLABBER *vb* cover with mud
CLACH, -ED, -ES, -S *n* stone ▷ *vb* kill by stoning
CLACHAN *n* small village
CLACHED ▸ **clach**
CLACHES ▸ **clach**
CLACHS ▸ **clach**
CLACK, -ED, -S *n* sound made by two hard objects striking each other ▷ *vb* make this sound
CLACKER *n* object that makes a clacking sound
CLACKS ▸ **clack**
CLAD, -S *vb*
CLADDED *adj* covered with cladding
CLADDER ▸ **clad**
CLADDIE *another name for* ▸ **korari**
CLADE, -S *n* group of organisms sharing a common ancestor
CLADISM ▸ **cladist**
CLADIST *n* proponent of cladistics
CLADODE *n* stem resembling and functioning as a leaf
CLADS ▸ **clad**
CLAES *Scots word for* ▸ **clothes**
CLAG, -GED, -S *n* sticky mud ▷ *vb* stick, as mud
CLAGGY *adj* stickily clinging, as mud
CLAGS ▸ **clag**
CLAIM, -ED, -S *vb, n*
CLAIMER ▸ **claim**
CLAIMS ▸ **claim**
CLAM, -MED, -S *n, vb*
CLAMANT *adj* noisy
CLAMBE *old variant of* ▸ **climb**
CLAMBER *vb, n*
CLAME, -S *archaic variant of* ▸ **claim**
CLAMMED ▸ **clam**
CLAMMER *n* person who gathers clams
CLAMMY *adj*
CLAMOR, -S *same as* ▸ **clamour**
CLAMOUR *n, vb*
CLAMP, -ED, -S *n, vb*
CLAMPER *n* spiked metal frame fastened to the sole of a shoe ▷ *vb* tread heavily
CLAMPS ▸ **clamp**
CLAMS ▸ **clam**
CLAN, -S *n*
CLANG, -ED, -S *vb, n*
CLANGER *n* obvious mistake
CLANGOR *same as* > **clangour**
CLANGS ▸ **clang**
CLANK, -ED, -S *n, vb*
CLANKY *adj* making clanking sounds
CLANS ▸ **clan**
CLAP, -PED, -S, -T *vb, n*
CLAPNET *n* net that can be closed instantly by pulling a string
CLAPPED ▸ **clap**
CLAPPER *n, vb*
CLAPS ▸ **clap**
CLAPT ▸ **clap**
CLAQUE, -S *n* group of people hired to applaud
CLAQUER *same as* > **claqueur**
CLAQUES ▸ **claque**
CLARAIN *n* one of the four major lithotypes of banded coal
CLARET, -S *n, adj, vb*
CLARIES ▸ **clary**
CLARIFY *vb* make (a matter) clear and unambiguous
CLARINO, CLARINI *adj* relating to a high passage for the trumpet in 18th-century music ▷ *n* high register of the trumpet
CLARION *n* obsolete high-pitched trumpet ▷ *adj* clear and ringing ▷ *vb* proclaim loudly
CLARITY *n*
CLARKIA *n* N American plant cultivated for its red, purple, or pink flowers
CLARO, -ES, -S *n* mild light-coloured cigar
CLART, -ED *vb* to dirty
CLARTS *pl n* lumps of mud, esp on shoes
CLARTY *adj* dirty, esp covered in mud
CLARY, CLARIES *n* European plant with aromatic leaves and blue flowers
CLASH, -ED, -ES *vb, n*
CLASHER ▸ **clash**
CLASHES ▸ **clash**
CLASP, -ED, -S *n, vb*
CLASPER ▸ **clasp**

CLASPS ▸ **clasp**
CLASPT *old inflection of* ▸ **clasp**
CLASS, -ED *n*, *vb*
CLASSER ▸ **class**
CLASSES ▸ **classis**
CLASSIC *adj*, *n*
CLASSIS, CLASSES *n* governing body of elders or pastors
CLASSON *n* elementary atomic particle
CLASSY *adj* stylish and elegant
CLAST, -S *n* fragment of a clastic rock
CLASTIC *adj* composed of fragments ▹ *n* clast
CLASTS ▸ **clast**
CLAT, -S, -TED *n* irksome or troublesome task ▹ *vb* scrape
CLATCH *vb* move making a squelching sound
CLATS ▸ **clat**
CLATTED ▸ **clat**
CLATTER *n*, *vb*
CLAUCHT *vb* seize by force
CLAUGHT *same as* ▸ **claucht**
CLAUSAL ▸ **clause**
CLAUSE, -S *n*
CLAUT, -ED, -S *same as* ▸ **clat**
CLAVATE *adj* shaped like a club with the thicker end uppermost
CLAVE, -S *n* one of a pair of hardwood sticks struck together to make a hollow sound
CLAVER, -S *vb* talk idly ▹ *n* idle talk
CLAVES ▸ **clave**
CLAVI ▸ **clavus**
CLAVIE, -S *n* tar-barrel traditionally set alight in Moray in Scotland on Hogmanay
CLAVIER *n* any keyboard instrument
CLAVIES ▸ **clavie**
CLAVIS *n* key
CLAVUS, CLAVI *n* corn on the toe
CLAW, -ED, -ING, -S *n*, *vb*
CLAWER, -S ▸ **claw**
CLAWING ▸ **claw**
CLAWS ▸ **claw**
CLAXON, -S *same as* ▸ **klaxon**
CLAY, -ED, -ING, -S *n*, *vb*
CLAYEY, CLAYIER ▸ **clay**
CLAYING ▸ **clay**
CLAYISH ▸ **clay**
CLAYPAN *n* layer of stiff impervious clay situated just below the surface of the ground
CLAYS ▸ **clay**
CLEAN, -ED, -S *adj*, *vb*, *adv*
CLEANER *n* person or thing that removes dirt
CLEANLY *adv* easily or smoothly ▹ *adj* habitually clean or neat
CLEANS ▸ **clean**
CLEANSE *vb*
CLEANUP *n* process of cleaning up or eliminating something
CLEAR, -ED, -S *adj*, *adv*, *vb*
CLEARER ▸ **clear**
CLEARLY *adv* in a clear, distinct, or obvious manner
CLEARS ▸ **clear**
CLEAT, -ED, -S *n* wedge ▹ *vb* supply or support with a cleat or cleats
CLEAVE, -D, -S, CLOVEN *vb* split apart ▹ *n* split
CLEAVER *n*
CLEAVES ▸ **cleave**
CLECHE *adj* (in heraldry) voided so that only a narrow border is visible
CLECK, -ED, -S *vb* (of birds) to hatch ▹ *n* piece of gossip
CLECKY ▸ **cleck**
CLEEK, -ED, -IT, -S *n* large hook, such as one used to land fish ▹ *vb* seize
CLEEP, -ED, -S *same as* ▸ **clepe**
CLEEVE, -S *n* cliff
CLEF, -S *n*
CLEFT, -ED, -S *vb*, *n*
CLEG, -S *another name for a* ▸ **horsefly**
CLEIK, -S *same as* ▸ **cleek**
CLEM, -MED, -S *vb* be hungry or cause to be hungry
CLEMENT *adj* (of weather) mild
CLEMMED ▸ **clem**
CLEMS ▸ **clem**
CLENCH *vb*, *n*
CLEOME, -S *n* type of herbaceous or shrubby plant
CLEPE, -D, -S, CLEPING, CLEPT *vb* call by the name of
CLERGY *n*
CLERIC, -S *n*
CLERID, -S *n* beetle that preys on other insects

CLERISY *n* learned or educated people
CLERK, -ED, -S *n, vb*
CLERKLY *adj* of or like a clerk ▷ *adv* in the manner of a clerk
CLERKS ▶ **clerk**
CLERUCH *n* settler in a cleruchy
CLEUCH, -S *same as* ▶ **clough**
CLEUGH, -S *same as* ▶ **clough**
CLEVE, -S *same as* ▶ **cleeve**
CLEVER *adj*
CLEVES ▶ **cleve**
CLEVIS *n* type of fastening used in agriculture
CLEW, -ED, -ING, -S *n* ball of thread, yarn, or twine ▷ *vb* coil or roll into a ball
CLICHE, -S *n* expression or idea that is no longer effective because of overuse ▷ *vb* use a cliché (in speech or writing)
CLICHED ▶ **cliche**
CLICHES ▶ **cliche**
CLICK, -ED, -S *n* short sharp sound ▷ *vb* make this sound
CLICKER ▶ **click**
CLICKET *vb* make a click
CLICKS ▶ **click**
CLIED ▶ **cly**
CLIENT, -S *n*
CLIES ▶ **cly**
CLIFF, -S *n, vb*
CLIFFED ▶ **cliff**
CLIFFS ▶ **cliff**
CLIFFY ▶ **cliff**
CLIFT, -S *same as* ▶ **cliff**
CLIFTED ▶ **clift**
CLIFTS ▶ **clift**
CLIFTY ▶ **clift**
CLIMATE *n, vb*
CLIMAX *n, vb*
CLIMB, -ED, -S *vb, n*
CLIMBER *n* person or thing that climbs
CLIMBS ▶ **climb**
CLIME, -S *n* place or its climate
CLINAL ▶ **cline**
CLINCH *vb, n*
CLINE, -S *n* variation within a species
CLING, -ED, -S, CLUNG *vb, n*
CLINGER ▶ **cling**
CLINGS ▶ **cling**
CLINGY ▶ **cling**
CLINIC, -S *n*
CLINK, -ED, -S *n, vb*
CLINKER *n* fused coal left over in a fire or furnace ▷ *vb* form clinker during burning
CLINKS ▶ **clink**
CLINT, -S *n* section of a limestone pavement separated from others by fissures
CLIP, -PED, -S *vb, n*
CLIPART *n* large collection of simple drawings stored in a computer
CLIPE, -D, -S, CLIPING *same as* ▶ **clype**
CLIPPED ▶ **clip**
CLIPPER *n*
CLIPPIE *n* bus conductress
CLIPS ▶ **clip**
CLIPT *old inflection of* ▶ **clip**
CLIQUE, -D, -S *n, vb*
CLIQUEY *adj* exclusive, confined to a small group
CLIQUY *same as* ▶ **cliquey**
CLITIC, -S *adj* (of a word) incapable of being stressed ▷ *n* clitic word
CLITTER *vb* make a shrill noise
CLIVERS *same as* ▶ **cleavers**
CLIVIA, -S *n* plant belonging to the Amaryllid family
CLOACA, -E, -S *n* body cavity in most animals
CLOACAL ▶ **cloaca**
CLOACAS ▶ **cloaca**
CLOAK, -ED, -S *n, vb*
CLOAM, -S *adj* made of clay or earthenware ▷ *n* clay or earthenware pots, dishes, etc, collectively
CLOBBER *vb, n*
CLOCHE, -S *n* cover to protect young plants
CLOCK, -ED, -S *n, vb*
CLOCKER ▶ **clock**
CLOCKS ▶ **clock**
CLOD, -DED, -S *n, vb*
CLODDY ▶ **clod**
CLODLY ▶ **clod**
CLODS ▶ **clod**
CLOFF, -S *n* cleft of a tree
CLOG, -GED, -S *vb* obstruct ▷ *n* wooden or wooden-soled shoe
CLOGGER *n* clogmaker
CLOGGY ▶ **clog**
CLOGS ▶ **clog**
CLOISON *n* partition

CLOKE, -D, -S, CLOKING *same as* ▸ **cloak**
CLOMB *a past tense and past participle of* ▸ **climb**
CLOMP, -ED, -S *same as* ▸ **clump**
CLON, -S *same as* ▸ **clone**
CLONAL ▸ **clone**
CLONE, -D, -S *n, vb*
CLONER, -S ▸ **clone**
CLONES ▸ **clone**
CLONIC ▸ **clonus**
CLONING ▸ **clone**
CLONISM *n* series of clonic spasms
CLONK, -ED, -S *vb* make a loud dull thud ▹ *n* loud thud
CLONKY *same as* ▸ **clunky**
CLONS ▸ **clon**
CLONUS *n* type of convulsion
CLOOP, -S *n* sound made when a cork is drawn from a bottle
CLOOT, -S *n* hoof
CLOOTIE *adj* as in **clootie dumpling** kind of dumpling
CLOOTS ▸ **cloot**
CLOP, -PED, -S *vb* make a sound as of a horse's hooves ▹ *n* sound of this nature
CLOQUE, -S *n* fabric with an embossed surface
CLOSE, -D, -S, -ST *vb, n, adj, adv*
CLOSELY ▸ **close**
CLOSER, -S ▸ **close**
CLOSES ▸ **close**
CLOSEST ▸ **close**
CLOSET, -S *n, adj, vb*
CLOSEUP *n* photo taken close to a subject
CLOSING ▸ **close**
CLOSURE *n, vb*
CLOT, -S, -TED *n* soft thick lump formed from liquid ▹ *vb* form soft thick lumps
CLOTBUR *n* burdock
CLOTE, -S *n* burdock
CLOTH, -S *n*
CLOTHE, -D *vb*
CLOTHES *pl n* garments
CLOTHS ▸ **cloth**
CLOTS ▸ **clot**
CLOTTED ▸ **clot**
CLOTTER *vb* to clot
CLOTTY *adj* full of clots
CLOTURE *n* closure in the US Senate ▹ *vb* end (debate) in the US Senate by cloture
CLOU, -S *n* crux; focus
CLOUD, -ED, -S *n, vb*
CLOUDY *adj* having a lot of clouds
CLOUGH, -S *n* gorge or narrow ravine
CLOUR, -ED, -S *vb* to thump or dent
CLOUS ▸ **clou**
CLOUT, -ED, -S *n, vb*
CLOUTER ▸ **clout**
CLOUTS ▸ **clout**
CLOVE, -S *n*
CLOVEN ▸ **cleave**
CLOVER, -S *n*
CLOVERY *adj* like clover
CLOVES ▸ **clove**
CLOVIS *n* as in **clovis point** flint projectile dating from the 10th millennium BC
CLOW, -ED, -ING, -S *n* clove ▹ *vb* rake with a fork
CLOWDER *n* collective term for a group of cats
CLOWED ▸ **clow**
CLOWING ▸ **clow**
CLOWN, -ED, -S *n, vb*
CLOWS ▸ **clow**
CLOY, -ED, -S *vb*
CLOYE, -S *vb* to claw
CLOYED ▸ **cloy**
CLOYES ▸ **cloye**
CLOYING *adj* sickeningly sweet
CLOYS ▸ **cloy**
CLOZE, -S *adj* as in **cloze test** test of the ability to understand text
CLUB, -BED, -S *n, vb*
CLUBBER *n* person who regularly frequents nightclubs
CLUBBY *adj* sociable, esp effusively so
CLUBMAN, CLUBMEN *n* man who is an enthusiastic member of a club or clubs
CLUBS ▸ **club**
CLUCK, -ED, -S *n, vb*
CLUCKER *n* chicken
CLUCKS ▸ **cluck**
CLUCKY *adj* wishing to have a baby
CLUDGIE *n* toilet
CLUE, -D, -ING, -S, CLUING *n, vb*
CLUEY, CLUIER, CLUIEST *adj* (Australian) well-informed and adroit
CLUING ▸ **clue**
CLUMBER *n* type of thickset spaniel
CLUMP, -ED, -S *n, vb*
CLUMPER *vb* walk heavily

CLUMPET *n* large chunk of floating ice
CLUMPS ▸ **clump**
CLUMPY ▸ **clump**
CLUMSY *adj*
CLUNCH *n* hardened clay
CLUNG ▸ **cling**
CLUNK, -ED, -S *n, vb*
CLUNKER *n* dilapidated old car or other machine
CLUNKS ▸ **clunk**
CLUNKY *adj* making a clunking noise
CLUPEID *n* type of fish
CLUSIA, -S *n* tree of the tropical American genus Clusia
CLUSTER *n, vb*
CLUTCH *vb, n*
CLUTCHY *adj* (of a person) tending to cling
CLUTTER *vb, n*
CLY, CLIED, CLIES, -ING *vb* steal or seize

A little word meaning to seize or steal, this can be useful when you are short of vowels.

CLYPE, -D, -S, CLYPING *vb* tell tales ▹ *n* person who tells tales
CLYPEAL ▸ **clypeus**
CLYPED ▸ **clype**
CLYPEI ▸ **clypeus**
CLYPES ▸ **clype**
CLYPEUS, CLYPEI *n* cuticular plate on the head of some insects
CLYPING ▸ **clype**
CLYSTER *a former name for an* ▸ **enema**
CNEMIAL ▸ **cnemis**
CNEMIS *n* shin or tibia
CNIDA, -E *n* stinging organ in jellyfish
COACH, -ED, -ES *n, vb*
COACHEE *n* person who receives training from a coach
COACHER ▸ **coach**
COACHES ▸ **coach**
COACHY *n* coachman ▹ *adj* resembling or pertaining to a coach
COACT, -ED, -S *vb* act together
COACTOR ▸ **coact**
COACTS ▸ **coact**
COADIES ▸ **coady**
COADMIT *vb* admit together
COADY, COADIES *n* sauce made from molasses
COAEVAL *n* contemporary
COAGENT > **coagency**
COAGULA > **coagulum**
COAITA, -S *n* spider monkey
COAL, -ED, -ING, -S *n, vb*
COALA, -S *same as* ▸ **koala**
COALBIN *n* bin for holding coal
COALBOX *n* box for holding coal
COALED ▸ **coal**
COALER, -S *n* ship, train, etc, used to carry or supply coal
COALIER ▸ **coaly**
COALIFY *vb* turn into coal
COALING ▸ **coal**
COALISE *vb* form a coalition
COALIZE *same as* ▸ **coalise**
COALMAN, COALMEN *n* man who delivers coal
COALPIT *n* pit from which coal is extracted
COALS ▸ **coal**
COALY, COALIER ▸ **coal**
COAMING *n* raised frame round a ship's hatchway for keeping out water
COANNEX *vb* annex with something else
COAPT, -ED, -S *vb* secure
COARB, -S *n* spiritual successor
COARSE, -R *adj*
COARSEN *vb* make or become coarse
COARSER ▸ **coarse**
COAST, -ED, -S *n, vb*
COASTAL ▸ **coast**
COASTED ▸ **coast**
COASTER *n* small mat placed under a glass
COASTS ▸ **coast**
COAT, -S *n, vb*
COATE, -S *same as* ▸ **quote**
COATED *adj* covered with an outer layer, film, etc
COATEE, -S *n* short coat, esp for a baby
COATER, -S *n* machine that applies a coating to something
COATES ▸ **coate**
COATI, -S *n* type of omnivorous mammal
COATING *n* covering layer
COATIS ▸ **coati**
COATS ▸ **coat**

COAX, -ED, -ES *vb*
COAXAL *same as* ▸ **coaxial**
COAXED ▸ **coax**
COAXER, -S ▸ **coax**
COAXES ▸ **coax**
COAXIAL *adj* (of a cable) transmitting by means of two concentric conductors separated by an insulator
COAXING *n* act of coaxing
COB, -BED, -BING, -S *n, vb*
COBAEA, -S *n* tropical climbing shrub
COBALT, -S *n*
COBB, -S *same as* ▸ **cob**
COBBED ▸ **cob**
COBBER, -S *n* friend
COBBIER ▸ **cobby**
COBBING ▸ **cob**
COBBLE, -D, -S *n, vb*
COBBLER *n* shoe mender
COBBLES ▸ **cobble**
COBBS ▸ **cobb**
COBBY, COBBIER *adj* short and stocky
COBIA, -S *n* large dark-striped game fish
COBLE, -S *n* small single-masted flat-bottomed fishing boat
COBLOAF *n* round loaf of bread
COBNUT, -S *another name for* > **hazelnut**
COBRA, -S *n*
COBRIC ▸ **cobra**
COBS ▸ **cob**
COBURG, -S *n* rounded loaf with a cross cut on the top
COBWEB, -S *n*
COBZA, -S *n* Romanian lute
COCA, -S *n* S American shrub
COCAIN, -S *same as* ▸ **cocaine**
COCAINE *n*
COCAINS ▸ **cocain**
COCAS ▸ **coca**
COCCAL ▸ **coccus**
COCCI ▸ **coccus**
COCCIC ▸ **coccus**
COCCID, -S *n* type of homopterous insect
COCCO, -S *n* taro
COCCOID ▸ **coccus**
COCCOS ▸ **cocco**
COCCOUS ▸ **coccus**
COCCUS, COCCI *n* any spherical or nearly spherical bacterium
COCCYX *n* bone at the base of the spinal column
COCH, -ES *obsolete variant of* ▸ **coach**
COCHAIR *vb* chair jointly
COCHES ▸ **coch**
COCHIN, -S *n* large breed of domestic fowl
COCHLEA *n* spiral tube in the internal ear
COCK, -ED, -ING, -S *n, vb*
COCKADE *n* feather or rosette worn on a hat as a badge
COCKED ▸ **cock**
COCKER, -S *n* devotee of cockfighting ▹ *vb* pamper or spoil by indulgence
COCKET, -S *n* document issued by a customs officer
COCKEYE *n* eye affected with strabismus or one that squints
COCKIER ▸ **cocky**
COCKIES ▸ **cocky**
COCKILY ▸ **cocky**
COCKING ▸ **cock**
COCKISH *adj* wanton
COCKLE, -D, -S *n, vb*
COCKLER *n* person employed to gather cockles
COCKLES ▸ **cockle**
COCKNEY *n, adj*
COCKPIT *n*
COCKS ▸ **cock**
COCKSHY *n* target aimed at in throwing games
COCKSY *adj* cocky
COCKY, COCKIER, COCKIES *adj* conceited and overconfident ▹ *n* farmer whose farm is regarded as small or of little account
COCO, -S *n* coconut palm
COCOA, -S *n*
COCOMAT *n* mat made from coconut fibre
COCONUT *n*
COCOON, -S *n, vb*
COCOPAN *n* (in South Africa) a small wagon running on narrow-gauge railway lines used in mines
COCOS ▸ **coco**
COCOTTE *n* small fireproof dish in which individual portions of food are cooked
COCOYAM *n* food plant of West Africa with edible underground stem

COCTILE *adj* made by exposing to heat
COCTION *n* boiling
COD, -DED, -DING, -S *n* large food fish of the North Atlantic ▷ *adj* having the character of an imitation or parody ▷ *vb* make fun of
CODA, -S *n* final part of a musical composition
CODABLE *adj* capable of being coded
CODAS ▸ **coda**
CODDED ▸ **cod**
CODDER, -S *n* cod fisherman or fishing boat
CODDING ▸ **cod**
CODDLE, -D, -S *vb* pamper, overprotect ▷ *n* stew made from ham and bacon scraps
CODDLER ▸ **coddle**
CODDLES ▸ **coddle**
CODE, -D, -S *n, vb*
CODEC, -S *n* set of electrical equipment
CODED ▸ **code**
CODEIA, -S *n* codeine
CODEIN, -S *same as* ▸ **codeine**
CODEINA *obsolete variant of* ▸ **codeine**
CODEINE *n* drug used as a painkiller
CODEINS ▸ **codein**
CODEN, -S *n* identification code assigned to a publication
CODER, -S *n* person or thing that codes
CODES ▸ **code**
CODETTA *n* short coda
CODEX, -ES, CODICES *n* volume of manuscripts of an ancient text
CODFISH *n* cod
CODGER, -S *n* old man
CODICES ▸ **codex**
CODICIL *n* addition to a will
CODIFY *vb*
CODILLA *n* coarse tow of hemp and flax
CODILLE *n* in the card game ombre, term indicating that the game is won
CODING, -S ▸ **code**
CODIST, -S *n* codifier
CODLIN, -S *same as* ▸ **codling**
CODLING *n* young cod
CODLINS ▸ **codlin**
CODON, -S *n* part of a DNA molecule
CODRIVE, CODROVE *vb* take alternate turns driving a car with another person
CODS ▸ **cod**
COED, -S *adj* educating boys and girls together ▷ *n* school or college that educates boys and girls together
COEDIT, -S *vb* edit (a book, newspaper, etc) jointly
COEDS ▸ **coed**
COEHORN *n* type of small artillery mortar
COELIAC *adj* of or relating to the abdomen ▷ *n* person who has coeliac disease
COELOM, -S *n* body cavity of many multicellular animals
COELOME *same as* ▸ **coelom**
COELOMS ▸ **coelom**
COEMPT, -S *vb* buy up something in its entirety
COENACT *vb* enact jointly
COENURE *variant form of* > **coenurus**
COENURI > **coenurus**
COEQUAL *n* equal ▷ *adj* of the same size, rank, etc
COERCE, -D, -S *vb*
COERCER ▸ **coerce**
COERCES ▸ **coerce**
COERECT *vb* erect together
COESITE *n* polymorph of silicon dioxide
COEVAL, -S *n* contemporary ▷ *adj* contemporary
COEXERT *vb* exert together
COEXIST *vb*
COFF, -ED, -ING, -S, COFT *vb* buy
COFFEE, -S *n, adj*
COFFER, -S *n, vb*
COFFIN, -S *n, vb*
COFFING ▸ **coff**
COFFINS ▸ **coffin**
COFFLE, -D, -S *n* (esp formerly) line of slaves, beasts, etc, fastened together ▷ *vb* fasten together in a coffle
COFFRET *n* small coffer
COFFS ▸ **coff**
COFOUND *vb* found jointly
COFT ▸ **coff**
COG, -GED, -S *n, vb*
COGENCE ▸ **cogent**

COGENCY ▶ **cogent**
COGENER *n* thing of the same kind
COGENT *adj* forcefully convincing
COGGED ▶ **cog**
COGGER, -S *n* deceiver
COGGIE, -S *n* quaich or drinking cup
COGGING ▶ **cog**
COGGLE, -D, -S *vb* wobble or rock
COGGLY ▶ **coggle**
COGIE, -S *same as* ▶ **coggie**
COGITO, -S *n* philosophical theory
COGNAC, -S *n*
COGNATE *adj* derived from a common original form ▷ *n* cognate word or language
COGNISE *same as* ▶ **cognize**
COGNIZE *vb* perceive, become aware of, or know
COGON, -S *n* type of coarse tropical grass used for thatching
COGS ▶ **cog**
COGUE, -S *n* wooden pail or drinking vessel
COGWAY, -S *n* rack railway
COHAB, -S *n* cohabitor
COHABIT *vb*
COHABS ▶ **cohab**
COHEAD, -S *vb* head jointly
COHEIR, -S *n* person who inherits jointly with others
COHEN, -S *same as* ▶ **kohen**
COHERE, -D, -S *vb* hold or stick together
COHERER *n* electrical component
COHERES ▶ **cohere**
COHIBIT *vb* restrain
COHO, -ES, -S *n* type of Pacific salmon
COHOE *same as* ▶ **coho**
COHOES ▶ **coho**
COHOG, -S *n* quahog, an edible clam
COHORN, -S *same as* ▶ **coehorn**
COHORT, -S *n* band of associates
COHOS ▶ **coho**
COHOSH *n* type of North American plant
COHOST, -S *vb* host jointly
COHUNE, -S *n* tropical feather palm
COIF, -FED, -ING, -S *vb* arrange the hair of ▷ *n* close-fitting cap worn in the Middle Ages
COIFED *adj* wearing a coif
COIFFE, -S *vb* coiffure
COIFFED ▶ **coif**
COIFFES ▶ **coiffe**
COIFING ▶ **coif**
COIFS ▶ **coif**
COIGN, -ED, -S *vb* wedge ▷ *n* quoin
COIGNE, -S *same as* ▶ **coign**
COIGNED ▶ **coign**
COIGNES ▶ **coigne**
COIGNS ▶ **coign**
COIL, -ED, -ING, -S *vb, n*
COILER, -S ▶ **coil**
COILING ▶ **coil**
COILS ▶ **coil**
COIN, -ED, -S *n, vb*
COINAGE *n* coins collectively
COINED ▶ **coin**
COINER, -S ▶ **coin**
COINFER *vb* infer jointly
COINING ▶ **coin**
COINOP *adj* (of a machine) operated by putting a coin in a slot
COINS ▶ **coin**
COINTER *vb* inter together
COIR, -S *n* coconut fibre, used for matting
COIT, -S *n* buttocks
COJOIN, -S *vb* conjoin
COKE, -D *n, vb*
COKES, -ES *n* fool
COKIER ▶ **coky**
COKIEST ▶ **coky**
COKING, -S *n* act of coking
COKY, COKIER, COKIEST *adj* like coke
COL, -S *n* high mountain pass
COLA, -S *n* dark brown fizzy soft drink
COLBY, COLBIES, -S *n* type of mild-tasting hard cheese
COLD, -ER, -EST, -S *adj, n*
COLDIE, -S *n* cold can or bottle of beer
COLDISH ▶ **cold**
COLDLY ▶ **cold**
COLDS ▶ **cold**
COLE, -S *same as* ▶ **cabbage**
COLEAD, -S, COLED *vb* lead together
COLES ▶ **cole**
COLETIT *n* coal tit
COLEUS *n* Old World plant

COLEY, -S *same as* > **coalfish**
COLIBRI *n* hummingbird
COLIC, -S *n* severe pains in the stomach and bowels
COLICIN *n* bactericidal protein
COLICKY *adj* relating to or suffering from colic
COLICS ▸ **colic**
COLIES ▸ **coly**
COLIN, -S *n* quail
COLITIC ▸ **colitis**
COLITIS *n* inflammation of the colon
COLL, -ED, -S *vb* embrace
COLLAB, -S *n* collaboration
COLLAGE *n* type of art form ▹ *vb* make a collage
COLLAR, -S *n, vb*
COLLARD *n* variety of cabbage with a crown of edible leaves
COLLARS ▸ **collar**
COLLATE *vb*
COLLECT *vb, n*
COLLED ▸ **coll**
COLLEEN *n* girl or young woman
COLLEGE *n*
COLLET, -S *n* (in a jewellery setting) a band or coronet-shaped claw that holds an individual stone ▹ *vb* mount in a collet
COLLIDE *vb*
COLLIE *n*
COLLIED ▸ **colly**
COLLIER *n* coal miner
COLLIES ▸ **colly**
COLLING *n* embrace
COLLINS *n* type of cocktail
COLLOID *n* suspension of particles in a solution ▹ *adj* relating to the gluelike material found in certain degenerating tissues
COLLOP, -S *n* small slice of meat
COLLS ▸ **coll**
COLLUDE *vb*
COLLY, COLLIED, COLLIES *n* soot or grime, such as coal dust ▹ *vb* begrime
COLOBI ▸ **colobus**
COLOBID *n* type of African monkey
COLOBUS, COLOBI *n* type of Old World monkey
COLOG, -S *n* logarithm of the reciprocal of a number
COLOGNE *n*
COLOGS ▸ **colog**
COLON, -S *n* punctuation mark (:)
COLONE, -S *variant of* ▸ **colon**
COLONEL *n*
COLONES ▸ **colone**
COLONI ▸ **colonus**
COLONIC *adj* of or relating to the colon ▹ *n* irrigation of the colon
COLONS ▸ **colon**
COLONUS, COLONI *n* ancient Roman farmer
COLONY *n*
COLOR, -S *same as* ▸ **colour**
COLORED *same as* > **coloured**
COLORER ▸ **color**
COLORS ▸ **color**
COLORY *adj* full of color
COLOSSI > **colossus**
COLOUR, -S *n, vb*
COLOURY *adj* possessing colour
COLS ▸ **col**
COLT, -ED, -ING, -S *n* young male horse ▹ *vb* to fool
COLTAN, -S *n* metallic ore
COLTED ▸ **colt**
COLTER, -S *same as* ▸ **coulter**
COLTING ▸ **colt**
COLTISH *adj* inexperienced
COLTS ▸ **colt**
COLUGO, -S *n* flying lemur
COLUMEL *n* in botany, the central column in a capsule
COLUMN, -S *n, vb*
COLURE, -S *n* either of two great circles on the celestial sphere
COLY, COLIES *n* S African arboreal bird
COLZA, -S *n* Eurasian plant with bright yellow flowers
COMA, -E, -S *n*
COMADE ▸ **comake**
COMAE ▸ **coma**
COMAKE, COMADE, -S *vb* make together
COMAKER ▸ **comake**
COMAKES ▸ **comake**
COMAL ▸ **coma**
COMARB, -S *same as* ▸ **coarb**

COMART, -S *n* covenant
COMAS ▸ **coma**
COMATE, -S *adj* having tufts of hair ▹ *n* companion
COMATIC ▸ **coma**
COMATIK *variant of* ▸ **komatik**
COMB, -ED, -ING, -S *n, vb*
COMBAT, -S *vb, n*
COMBE, -S *same as* ▸ **comb**
COMBED ▸ **comb**
COMBER, -S *n* long curling wave
COMBES ▸ **combe**
COMBI, -S *n* combination boiler
COMBIER ▸ **comby**
COMBIES ▸ **comby**
COMBINE *vb, n*
COMBING ▸ **comb**
COMBIS ▸ **combi**
COMBLE, -S *n* apex; zenith
COMBO, -S *n* small group of jazz musicians
COMBS ▸ **comb**
COMBUST *vb*
COMBY, COMBIER, COMBIES *adj* comb-like ▹ *n* combination boiler
COME, CAME, -S, -TH *vb*
COMEDIC *adj* of or relating to comedy
COMEDO, -S *the technical name for* > **blackhead**
COMEDY *n*
COMELY *adj* nice-looking
COMER, -S *n* person who comes
COMES ▸ **come**
COMET, -S *n*
COMETH ▸ **come**
COMETIC ▸ **comet**
COMETS ▸ **comet**
COMFIER ▸ **comfy**
COMFILY *adv* in a manner suggestive of or promoting comfort
COMFIT, -S *n* sugar-coated sweet
COMFORT *n, vb*
COMFREY *n* tall plant with bell-shaped flowers
COMFY, COMFIER *adj* comfortable
COMIC, -S *adj, n*
COMICAL *adj* amusing
COMICE, -S *n* kind of pear
COMICS ▸ **comic**
COMING, -S ▸ **come**
COMIQUE *n* comic actor
COMITAL *adj* relating to a count or earl
COMITIA *n* ancient Roman assembly
COMITY *n* friendly politeness, esp between different countries
COMIX *n* comic books in general
COMM *n* as in **comm badge** small wearable badge-shaped radio transmitter and receiver
COMMA, -S, -TA *n*
COMMAND *vb, n*
COMMAS ▸ **comma**
COMMATA ▸ **comma**
COMMEND *vb* praise
COMMENT *n, vb*
COMMER, -S *same as* ▸ **comer**
COMMERE *n* female compere
COMMERS ▸ **commer**
COMMIE, -S *n* communist
COMMIS *n* apprentice waiter or chef ▹ *adj* (of a waiter or chef) apprentice
COMMISH *n* commissioner
COMMIT, -S *vb*
COMMIX, -T *a rare word for* ▸ **mix**
COMMO, -S *short for* > **communist**
COMMODE *n* seat with a hinged flap concealing a chamber pot
COMMODO *same as* ▸ **comodo**
COMMON *adj, n, vb*
COMMONS *n* people not of noble birth viewed as forming a political order
COMMOS ▸ **commo**
COMMOT, -S *n* in medieval Wales, a division of land
COMMOTE *same as* ▸ **commot**
COMMOTS ▸ **commot**
COMMOVE *vb* disturb
COMMS *pl n* communications
COMMUNE *n, vb*
COMMUTE *vb, n*
COMMY *same as* ▸ **commie**
COMODO *adv* (to be performed) at a convenient relaxed speed
COMOSE *another word for* ▸ **comate**

COMOUS *adj* hairy
COMP, -ED, -S *n* person who sets and corrects type ▷ *vb* set or correct type
COMPACT *adj, n, vb*
COMPAGE *obsolete form of* > **compages**
COMPAND *vb* (of a transmitter signal) to compress before, and expand after, transmission
COMPANY *n, vb*
COMPARE *vb*
COMPART *vb* divide into parts
COMPAS *n* rhythm in flamenco
COMPASS *n, vb*
COMPAST *adj* rounded
COMPEAR *vb* in Scots law, to appear in court
COMPED ▸ **comp**
COMPEER *n* person of equal rank, status, or ability ▷ *vb* to equal
COMPEL, -S *vb*
COMPEND *n* compendium
COMPER, -S *n* person who regularly enters competitions
COMPERE *n, vb*
COMPERS ▸ **comper**
COMPETE *vb*
COMPILE *vb*
COMPING *n* act of comping
COMPLEX *adj, n, vb*
COMPLIN *same as* > **compline**
COMPLOT *n* plot or conspiracy ▷ *vb* plot together
COMPLY *vb*
COMPO, -S *n* mixture of materials, such as mortar, plaster, etc ▷ *adj* intended to last for several days
COMPONE *same as* ▸ **compony**
COMPONY *adj* made up of alternating metal and colour, colour and fur, or fur and metal
COMPORT *vb* behave (oneself) in a specified way
COMPOS ▸ **compo**
COMPOSE *vb*
COMPOST *n, vb*
COMPOT, -S *same as* ▸ **compote**
COMPOTE *n* fruit stewed with sugar
COMPOTS ▸ **compot**
COMPS ▸ **comp**
COMPT, -ED, -S *obsolete variant of* ▸ **count**
COMPTER *n* formerly, a prison
COMPTS ▸ **compt**
COMPUTE *vb, n*
COMRADE *n*
COMS *pl n* one-piece woollen undergarment with long sleeves and legs
COMSAT, -S *n* communications satellite
COMSYMP *n* disparaging term for a person sympathetic to communism
COMTE, -S *n* European noble
COMUS, -ES *n* wild party
CON, -NED, -S *vb* deceive, swindle ▷ *n* convict ▷ *prep* with
CONACRE *n* farming land let for a season or for eleven months ▷ *vb* let conacre
CONARIA > **conarium**
CONATUS *n* effort or striving of natural impulse
CONCAVE *adj, vb*
CONCEAL *vb*
CONCEDE *vb*
CONCEDO *interj* I allow; I concede (a point)
CONCEIT *n, vb*
CONCENT *n* concord, as of sounds, voices, etc
CONCEPT *n*
CONCERN *n, vb*
CONCERT *n*
CONCH, -S *same as* ▸ **concha**
CONCHA, -E, -S *n* any bodily organ or part resembling a shell in shape
CONCHAL ▸ **concha**
CONCHAS ▸ **concha**
CONCHE, -D, -S *n* machine used to make chocolate ▷ *vb* use a conche
CONCHIE *n* conscientious objector
CONCHO, -S *n* American metal ornament
CONCHS ▸ **conch**
CONCHY *same as* ▸ **conchie**
CONCISE *adj, vb*
CONCOCT *vb*
CONCORD *n* state of peaceful agreement, harmony ▷ *vb* agree

CONCREW *vb* grow together
CONCUPY *n* concupiscence
CONCUR, -S *vb*
CONCUSS *vb* injure (the brain) by a fall or blow
COND *old inflection of* ▸ **con**
CONDEMN *vb*
CONDER, -S *n* person who directs the steering of a vessel
CONDIE, -S *n* culvert; tunnel
CONDIGN *adj* (esp of a punishment) fitting
CONDO, -ES, -S *n* condominium
CONDOLE *vb* express sympathy with someone in grief, pain, etc
CONDONE *vb* overlook or forgive (wrongdoing)
CONDOR, -S *n* large vulture of S America
CONDOS ▸ **condo**
CONDUCE *vb* lead or contribute (to a result)
CONDUCT *n, vb*
CONDUIT *n*
CONDYLE *n* rounded projection on the articulating end of a bone
CONE, -D, -S, CONING *n* object with a circular base, tapering to a point ▹ *vb* shape like a cone or part of a cone
CONEY, -S *same as* ▸ **cony**
CONF, -S *n* online forum
CONFAB, -S *n* conversation ▹ *vb* converse
CONFECT *vb* prepare by combining ingredients
CONFER, -S *vb*
CONFESS *vb*
CONFEST *adj* admitted
CONFIDE *vb*
CONFINE *vb, n*
CONFIRM *vb*
CONFIT, -S *n* preserve
CONFIX *vb* fasten
CONFLUX *n* merging or following together, especially of rivers
CONFORM *vb*
CONFS ▸ **conf**
CONFUSE *vb*
CONFUTE *vb* prove wrong
CONGA, -ED, -S *n* dance performed by a number of people in single file ▹ *vb* dance the conga
CONGE, -D, -S *n* permission to depart or dismissal, esp when formal ▹ *vb* take one's leave
CONGEAL *vb*
CONGED ▸ **conge**
CONGEE, -D, -S *same as* ▸ **conge**
CONGER, -S *n* large sea eel
CONGES ▸ **conge**
CONGEST *vb*
CONGIUS, CONGII *n* unit of liquid measure equal to 1 imperial gallon
CONGO, -ES, -S *same as* ▸ **congou**
CONGOU, -S *n* kind of black tea from China
CONGREE *vb* agree
CONGRUE *vb* agree
CONI ▸ **conus**
CONIA, -S *same as* ▸ **coniine**
CONIC *adj* having the shape of a cone
CONICAL *adj* cone-shaped
CONICS *n* branch of geometry
CONIDIA > **conidium**
CONIES ▸ **cony**
CONIFER *n*
CONIINE *n* colourless poisonous soluble liquid alkaloid found in hemlock
CONIMA, -S *n* gum resin from the conium hemlock tree
CONIN, -S *same as* ▸ **coniine**
CONINE, -S *same as* ▸ **coniine**
CONING ▸ **cone**
CONINS ▸ **conin**
CONIUM, -S *n* umbelliferous plant, esp hemlock
CONJECT *vb* conjecture
CONJEE, -D, -S *n* gruel of boiled rice and water ▹ *vb* prepare as, or in, a conjee
CONJOIN *vb* join or become joined
CONJURE *vb*
CONJURY *n* magic
CONK, -ED, -ING, -S *n* nose ▹ *vb* strike (someone) on the head or nose
CONKER *n*
CONKERS *n* game played with conkers tied on strings
CONKIER ▸ **conky**

CONKING ▸ **conk**
CONKOUT *n* time when a machine stops working
CONKS ▸ **conk**
CONKY, CONKIER *adj* affected by the timber disease, conk
CONLANG *n* artificially constructed language
CONMAN, CONMEN *n*
CONN, -S *same as* ▸ **con**
CONNATE *adj* existing in a person or thing from birth
CONNE, -S *same as* ▸ **con**
CONNECT *vb*
CONNED ▸ **con**
CONNER, -S *same as* ▸ **conder**
CONNES ▸ **conne**
CONNIE, -S *n* tram or bus conductor
CONNING ▸ **con**
CONNIVE *vb*
CONNOR, -S *n* type of saltwater fish
CONNOTE *vb* imply or suggest
CONNS ▸ **conn**
CONOID, -S *n* geometric surface ▹ *adj* conical, cone-shaped
CONQUER *vb*
CONS ▸ **con**
CONSEIL *n* advice
CONSENT *n, vb*
CONSIGN *vb*
CONSIST *vb*
CONSOL *n* consolidated annuity, a former British government security
CONSOLE *vb, n*
CONSOLS ▸ **consol**
CONSORT *vb, n*
CONSPUE *vb* spit on with contempt
CONSTER *obsolete variant of* > **construe**
CONSUL, -S *n*
CONSULT *vb*
CONSUME *vb*
CONTACT *n, vb, interj*
CONTAIN *vb*
CONTE, -S *n* tale or short story, esp of adventure
CONTECK *n* contention
CONTEMN *vb* regard with contempt
CONTEND *vb*
CONTENT *n, adj, vb*
CONTES ▸ **conte**
CONTEST *n, vb*
CONTEXT *n*
CONTO, -S *n* former Portuguese monetary unit worth 1000 escudos
CONTORT *vb* twist out of shape
CONTOS ▸ **conto**
CONTOUR *n, vb*
CONTRA, -S *n* counter-argument
CONTRAT *old form of* > **contract**
CONTROL *n, vb*
CONTUND *vb* pummel
CONTUSE *vb* injure (the body) without breaking the skin
CONURE, -S *n* small American parrot
CONUS, CONI *n* any of several cone-shaped structures
CONVECT *vb* circulate hot air by convection
CONVENE *vb*
CONVENT *n, vb*
CONVERT *vb, n*
CONVEX *adj, vb*
CONVEY, -S *vb*
CONVICT *vb, n, adj*
CONVIVE *vb* feast together
CONVO, -S *n* conversation
CONVOKE *vb* call together
CONVOS ▸ **convo**
CONVOY, -S *n, vb*
CONY, CONIES *n* rabbit
COO, -ED, -S *vb* (of a dove or pigeon) make a soft murmuring sound ▹ *n* sound of cooing ▹ *interj* exclamation of surprise, awe, etc
COOCOO *old spelling of* ▸ **cuckoo**
COOED ▸ **coo**
COOEE, -D, -S *interj* call to attract attention ▹ *vb* utter this call ▹ *n* calling distance
COOER, -S ▸ **coo**
COOEY, -ED, -S *same as* ▸ **cooee**
COOF, -S *n* unintelligent person
COOING, -S ▸ **coo**
COOK, -ED, -S *vb, n*
COOKER, -S *n* apparatus for cooking heated by gas or electricity
COOKERY *n* art of cooking
COOKEY, -S *same as* ▸ **cookie**
COOKIE, -S *n*
COOKING ▸ **cook**

COOKOFF *n* cookery competition
COOKOUT *n* party where a meal is cooked and eaten out of doors
COOKS ▸ **cook**
COOKTOP *n* flat unit for cooking in saucepans or the top part of a stove
COOKY *same as* ▸ **cookie**
COOL, -ED, -EST, -S *adj, vb, n*
COOLANT *n*
COOLED ▸ **cool**
COOLER, -S *n* container for making or keeping things cool
COOLEST ▸ **cool**
COOLING *n* as in **regenerative cooling** method of cooling rocket combustion chambers
COOLISH ▸ **cool**
COOLIST *n* person who does not believe in global warming
COOLLY ▸ **cool**
COOLS ▸ **cool**
COOLTH, -S *n* coolness
COOM, -ED, -ING, -S *n* waste material ▹ *vb* blacken
COOMB, -S *n* short valley or deep hollow
COOMBE, -S *same as* ▸ **coomb**
COOMBS ▸ **coomb**
COOMED ▸ **coom**
COOMIER ▸ **coomy**
COOMING ▸ **coom**
COOMS ▸ **coom**
COOMY, COOMIER *adj* grimy
COONCAN *n* card game for two players, similar to rummy
COONDOG *n* dog trained to hunt raccoons
COONTIE *n* evergreen plant of S Florida
COONTY *same as* ▸ **coontie**
COOP, -ED, -ING, -S *n, vb*
COOPER, -S *n* person who makes or repairs barrels ▹ *vb* make or mend (barrels, casks, etc)
COOPERY *same as* > **cooperage**
COOPING ▸ **coop**
COOPS ▸ **coop**
COOPT, -ED, -S *vb* add (someone) to a group by the agreement of the existing members
COORIE, -D, -S *same as* ▸ **courie**
COOS ▸ **coo**
COOSEN, -S *same as* ▸ **cozen**
COOSER, -S *n* stallion
COOSIN, -S *same as* ▸ **cozen**
COOST *Scots form of* ▸ **cast**
COOT, -S *n* small black water bird
COOTCH *n* hiding place ▹ *vb* hide
COOTER, -S *n* type of freshwater turtle
COOTIE, -S *n* body louse
COOTS ▸ **coot**
COP, -PED, -PING, -S *same as* ▸ **copper**
COPAIBA *n* resin obtained from certain tropical trees
COPAIVA *same as* ▸ **copaiba**
COPAL, -S *n* resin used in varnishes
COPALM, -S *n* aromatic resin
COPALS ▸ **copal**
COPAY, -S *n* amount payable for treatment by person with medical insurance
COPE, -D, -S *vb, n*
COPECK, -S *same as* ▸ **kopeck**
COPED ▸ **cope**
COPEN, -S *n* shade of blue
COPEPOD *n* type of minute crustacean
COPER, -ED, -S *n* horse-dealer ▹ *vb* smuggle liquor to deep-sea fishermen
COPES ▸ **cope**
COPIED ▸ **copy**
COPIER, -S *n* machine that copies
COPIES ▸ **copy**
COPIHUE *n* Chilean bellflower
COPILOT *n* second pilot of an aircraft ▹ *vb* act as a copilot
COPING, -S *n* sloping top row of a wall
COPIOUS *adj*
COPITA, -S *n* tulip-shaped sherry glass
COPLOT, -S *vb* plot together
COPOUT, -S *n* act of avoiding responsibility
COPPED ▸ **cop**
COPPER, -S *n, adj, vb*
COPPERY *adj* like copper
COPPICE *n, vb*

COPPIES ▸ **coppy**
COPPIN, -S *n* ball of thread
COPPING ▸ **cop**
COPPINS ▸ **coppin**
COPPLE, -S *n* hill rising to a point
COPPRA, -S *same as* ▸ **copra**
COPPY, COPPIES *n* small wooden stool
COPRA, -S *n* dried oil-yielding kernel of the coconut
COPRAH, -S *same as* ▸ **copra**
COPRAS ▸ **copra**
COPS ▸ **cop**
COPSE, -D, -S, COPSING *same as* ▸ **coppice**
COPSHOP *n* police station
COPSIER ▸ **copsy**
COPSING ▸ **copse**
COPSY, COPSIER *adj* having copses
COPTER, -S *n* helicopter
COPULA, -E, -S *n* verb used to link the subject and complement of a sentence
COPULAR ▸ **copula**
COPULAS ▸ **copula**
COPY, COPIED, COPIES *n, vb*
COPYBOY *n* formerly, in journalism, young man who carried copy and ran errands
COPYCAT *n, vb*
COPYING *n* act of copying
COPYISM *n* slavish copying
COPYIST *n* person who makes written copies
COQUET, -S *vb* behave flirtatiously
COQUI, -S *n* type of tree-dwelling frog
COQUINA *n* soft limestone
COQUIS ▸ **coqui**
COQUITO *n* Chilean palm tree yielding edible nuts and a syrup
COR, -S *interj* exclamation of surprise, amazement, or admiration ▹ *n* Hebrew measure of dry weight
CORACLE *n*
CORAL, -S *n, adj*
CORALLA > **corallum**
CORALS ▸ **coral**
CORAM *prep* before, in the presence of
CORANTO *same as* > **courante**
CORBAN, -S *n* gift to God
CORBE, -S *obsolete variant of* ▸ **corbel**
CORBEAU *n* blackish green colour
CORBEIL *n* carved ornament in the form of a basket of fruit, flowers, etc
CORBEL, -S *n* stone or timber support sticking out of a wall ▹ *vb* lay (a stone or brick) so that it forms a corbel
CORBES ▸ **corbe**
CORBIE, -S *n* raven or crow
CORBINA *n* type of North American whiting
CORBY *same as* ▸ **corbie**
CORCASS *n* in Ireland, marshland
CORD *n, adj, vb*
CORDAGE *n* lines and rigging of a vessel
CORDATE *adj* heart-shaped
CORDED *adj* tied or fastened with cord
CORDER, -S ▸ **cord**
CORDIAL *adj, n*
CORDING ▸ **cord**
CORDITE *n* explosive used in guns and bombs
CORDOBA *n* standard monetary unit of Nicaragua
CORDON, -S *n, vb*
CORDS *pl n* trousers made of corduroy
CORE, -D, -S, CORING *n, vb*
COREIGN *vb* reign jointly
CORELLA *n* white Australian cockatoo
COREMIA > **coremium**
CORER, -S ▸ **core**
CORES ▸ **core**
CORF, CORVES *n* wagon or basket used formerly in mines
CORGI, -S *n*
CORIA ▸ **corium**
CORIES ▸ **cory**
CORING ▸ **core**
CORIOUS *adj* leathery
CORIUM, CORIA, -S *n* deep inner layer of the skin
CORIVAL *same as* > **corrival**
CORIXID *n* type of water bug

CORK, -S *n, vb, adj*
CORKAGE *n* restaurant's charge for serving wine bought elsewhere
CORKED *adj* (of wine) spoiled through having a decayed cork
CORKER, -S *n* splendid or outstanding person or thing
CORKIER ▶ **corky**
CORKING *adj* excellent
CORKIR, -S *n* lichen from which red or purple dye is made
CORKS ▶ **cork**
CORKY, CORKIER *same as* ▶ **corked**
CORM, -S *n* bulblike underground stem of certain plants
CORMEL, -S *n* new small corm arising from the base of a fully developed one
CORMLET *n* small corm
CORMOID *adj* like a corm
CORMOUS ▶ **corm**
CORMS ▶ **corm**
CORMUS *n* corm
CORN, -ING, -S *n, vb*
CORNAGE *n* rent fixed according to the number of horned cattle pastured
CORNCOB *n* core of an ear of maize, to which the kernels are attached
CORNEA, -E, -S *n*
CORNEAL ▶ **cornea**
CORNEAS ▶ **cornea**
CORNED *adj* preserved in salt or brine
CORNEL, -S *n* type of plant such as the dogwood and dwarf cornel
CORNER, -S *n, vb*
CORNET, -S *n*
CORNETT *n* musical instrument
CORNFED *adj*
CORNFLY *n* small fly
CORNI ▶ **corno**
CORNICE *n, vb*
CORNIER ▶ **corny**
CORNIFY *vb* turn soft tissue hard
CORNILY ▶ **corny**
CORNING ▶ **corn**
CORNIST *n* horn-player
CORNO, CORNI *n* French horn
CORNROW *n* hairstyle in which the hair is plaited in close parallel rows ▷ *vb* style the hair in a cornrow
CORNS ▶ **corn**
CORNU, -A *n* part or structure resembling a horn or having a hornlike pattern
CORNUAL ▶ **cornu**
CORNUS *n* any member of the genus Cornus, such as dogwood
CORNUTE *adj* having or resembling cornua
CORNY, CORNIER *adj* unoriginal or excessively sentimental
CORODY *n* feudal law
COROLLA *n* petals of a flower collectively
CORONA, -E, -S *n* ring of light round the moon or sun
CORONAL *n* circlet for the head ▷ *adj* of or relating to a corona or coronal
CORONAS ▶ **corona**
CORONEL *n* iron head of a tilting spear
CORONER *n*
CORONET *n*
CORONIS *n* symbol used in Greek writing
COROZO, -S *n* tropical American palm whose seeds yield a useful oil
CORPORA ▶ **corpus**
CORPS *n* military unit with a specific function
CORPSE, -D, -S *n* dead body ▷ *vb* laugh or cause to laugh involuntarily or inopportunely while on stage
CORPUS, CORPORA *n* collection of writings, esp by a single author
CORRADE *vb* erode by the abrasive action of rock particles
CORRAL, -S *n, vb*
CORREA, -S *n* Australian evergreen shrub with large showy tubular flowers
CORRECT *adj, vb*
CORRIDA *the Spanish word for* > **bullfight**
CORRIE, -S *same as* ▶ **cirque**
CORRODE *vb* eat or be eaten away by chemical action or rust
CORRODY *same as* ▶ **corody**
CORRUPT *adj, vb*
CORS ▶ **cor**

CORSAC, -S *n* type of fox of central Asia
CORSAGE *n* small bouquet worn on the bodice of a dress
CORSAIR *n* pirate
CORSE, -S *n* archaic word for corpse
CORSET, -S *n, vb*
CORSEY, -S *n* pavement or pathway
CORSITE *n* type of rock
CORSIVE *n* corrodent
CORSLET *same as* > **corselet**
CORSNED *n* ordeal to discover innocence or guilt
CORSO, -S *n* promenade
CORTEGE *n*
CORTEX *n* outer layer of the brain or other internal organ
CORTILE, CORTILI *n* open, internal courtyard
CORTIN, -S *n* adrenal cortex extract
CORTINA *n* weblike part of certain mushrooms
CORTINS ▸ **cortin**
CORULER *n* joint ruler
CORVEE, -S *n* day's unpaid labour owed by a feudal vassal to their lord
CORVES ▸ **corf**
CORVET, -S *same as* ▸ **curvet**
CORVID, -S *n* any member of the crow family
CORVINA *same as* ▸ **corbina**
CORVINE *adj* of, relating to, or resembling a crow
CORVUS *n* type of ancient hook
CORY, CORIES *n* catfish belonging to the South American Corydoras genus
CORYLUS *n* hazel genus
CORYMB, -S *n* flat-topped flower cluster
CORYPHE *n* leader of a Greek chorus
CORYZA, -S *n* acute inflammation in the nose
CORYZAL ▸ **coryza**
CORYZAS ▸ **coryza**
COS *same as* ▸ **cosine**
COSE, -D, -S, COSING *vb* get cosy
COSEC, -S *same as* > **cosecant**
COSECH, -S *n* hyperbolic cosecant
COSECS ▸ **cosec**
COSED ▸ **cose**
COSES ▸ **cose**
COSET, -S *n* mathematical set
COSEY, -S *n* tea cosy
COSH, -ED, -ES, -ING *n, vb*
COSHER, -S *vb* pamper or coddle
COSHERY *n* Irish chief's right to lodge at their tenants' houses
COSHES ▸ **cosh**
COSHING ▸ **cosh**
COSIE *same as* ▸ **cosy**
COSIED ▸ **cosy**
COSIER, -S *n* cobbler
COSIES ▸ **cosy**
COSIEST ▸ **cosy**
COSIGN, -S *vb* sign jointly
COSILY ▸ **cosy**
COSINE, -S *n* trigonometric function
COSING ▸ **cose**
COSMEA, -S *n* plant of the genus Cosmos
COSMIC *adj*
COSMID, -S *n* segment of DNA
COSMIN, -S *same as* ▸ **cosmine**
COSMINE *n* substance resembling dentine
COSMINS ▸ **cosmin**
COSMISM *n* Russian cultural and philosophical movement
COSMIST ▸ **cosmism**
COSMOID *adj* having two inner bony layers and a cosmine outer layer
COSMOS *n*
COSPLAY *n* recreational activity in which people interact while dressed as fictional characters
COSS, -ES *another name for* ▸ **kos**
COSSACK *n* Slavonic warrior-peasant
COSSES ▸ **coss**
COSSET, -S *vb, n*
COSSIE, -S *n* informal name for a swimming costume
COST, -ED, -S *n, vb*
COSTA, -E *n* riblike part, such as the midrib of a plant leaf

COSTAL, -S *n* strengthening rib of an insect's wing
COSTAR, -S *n* actor who shares the billing with another ▷ *vb* share the billing with another actor
COSTARD *n* English variety of apple tree
COSTARS ▶ **costar**
COSTATE *adj* having ribs
COSTE, -S *vb* draw near
COSTEAN *vb* mine for lodes
COSTED ▶ **cost**
COSTER, -S *n* person who sells fruit, vegetables etc from a barrow
COSTES ▶ **coste**
COSTING *n* as in **marginal costing** method of cost accounting
COSTIVE *adj* having or causing constipation
COSTLY *adj* expensive
COSTREL *n* flask, usually of earthenware or leather
COSTS ▶ **cost**
COSTUME *n, vb*
COSTUS *n* Himalayan herb with an aromatic root
COSY, COSIED, COSIES, COSIEST, -ING *adj, n, vb*
COT, -S, -TED, -TING *n* baby's bed with high sides ▷ *vb* entangle or become entangled
COTAN, -S *same as* > **cotangent**
COTE, -D, -S, COTING *same as* ▶ **cot**
COTEAU, -S, -X *n* hillside
COTED ▶ **cote**
COTERIE *n* exclusive group, clique
COTES ▶ **cote**
COTH, -S *n* hyperbolic cotangent
COTHURN *same as* > **cothurnus**
COTIDAL *adj* (of a line on a tidal chart) joining points at which high tide occurs simultaneously
COTIJA, -S *n* salty Mexican cheese
COTING ▶ **cote**
COTINGA *n* tropical bird
COTISE, -D, -S *same as* ▶ **cottise**
COTLAND *n* grounds that belong to a cotter
COTS ▶ **cot**
COTT, -S *same as* ▶ **cot**
COTTA, -E, -S *n* short surplice
COTTAGE *n*
COTTAR, -S *n* cottage-dwelling peasant
COTTAS ▶ **cotta**
COTTED ▶ **cot**
COTTER, -S *n* pin or wedge used to secure machine parts ▷ *vb* secure (two parts) with a cotter
COTTID, -S *n* type of fish typically with a large head, tapering body, and spiny fins
COTTIER *same as* ▶ **cottar**
COTTING ▶ **cot**
COTTISE *n* type of heraldic decoration ▷ *vb* (in heraldry) decorate with a cottise
COTTOID *adj* resembling a fish of the genus Cottus
COTTON, -S *n, vb*
COTTONY *adj* like cotton
COTTOWN *Scots variant of* ▶ **cotton**
COTTS ▶ **cott**
COTTUS *n* type of fish with four yellowish knobs on its head
COTWAL, -S *n* Indian police officer
COTYLE, COTYLAE, -S *n* cuplike cavity
COTYPE, -S *n* additional specimen in biological study
COUCAL, -S *n* type of ground-living bird of Africa, S Asia, and Australia, with long strong legs
COUCH, -ED, -ES *n, vb*
COUCHE *adj* in heraldry (of a shield), tilted
COUCHED ▶ **couch**
COUCHEE *n* reception held late at night
COUCHER ▶ **couch**
COUCHES ▶ **couch**
COUDE, -S *adj* relating to the construction of a reflecting telescope ▷ *n* type of reflecting telescope
COUGAN, -S *n* drunk and rowdy person
COUGAR, -S *n*
COUGH, -ED, -S *vb, n*
COUGHER ▶ **cough**
COUGHS ▶ **cough**
COUGUAR *same as* ▶ **cougar**

COULD ▸ **can**
COULDST *vb* form of 'could' used with the pronoun *thou* or its relative form
COULEE, -S *n* flow of molten lava
COULIS *n* thin purée of vegetables or fruit
COULOIR *n* deep gully on a mountain side, esp in the French Alps
COULOMB *n* SI unit of electric charge
COULTER *n* blade at the front of a ploughshare
COUNCIL *n, adj*
COUNSEL *n* advice or guidance ▹ *vb* give guidance to
COUNT, -ED, -S *vb, n*
COUNTER *n* long flat surface in a bank or shop ▹ *vb* oppose, retaliate against ▹ *adv* in the opposite direction
COUNTRY *n*
COUNTS ▸ **count**
COUNTY *n, adj*
COUP, -ED, -ING, -S *n* successful action ▹ *vb* turn or fall over
COUPE, -S *n* sports car with two doors and a sloping fixed roof
COUPED ▸ **coup**
COUPEE, -S *n* dance movement
COUPER, -S *n* dealer
COUPES ▸ **coupe**
COUPING ▸ **coup**
COUPLE, -D, -S *n, vb*
COUPLER *n* mechanical device
COUPLES ▸ **couple**
COUPLET *n*
COUPON, -S *n* piece of paper entitling the holder to a discount or gift
COUPS ▸ **coup**
COUPURE *n* entrenchment made by besieged forces behind a breach
COUR, -ING, -S *obsolete variant of* ▸ **cover**
COURAGE *n*
COURANT *n* old dance in quick triple time ▹ *adj* (of an animal) running
COURB, -ED, -S *vb* to bend
COURD *obsolete variant of* ▸ **covered**
COURE, -D, -S *obsolete variant of* ▸ **cover**
COURIE, -D, -S *vb* nestle or snuggle
COURIER *n* person employed to look after holidaymakers ▹ *vb* send (a parcel, letter, etc) by courier
COURIES ▸ **courie**
COURING ▸ **cour**
COURLAN *another name for* ▸ **limpkin**
COURS ▸ **cour**
COURSE, -D *n, vb*
COURSER *n* swift horse
COURSES *another word for* ▸ **menses**
COURT, -ED, -S *n, vb*
COURTER *n* suitor
COURTLY *adj* ceremoniously polite
COURTS ▸ **court**
COUSIN, -S *n*
COUTA, -S *n* traditional Australian sailing boat
COUTEAU *n* large two-edged knife used formerly as a weapon
COUTER, -S *n* armour designed to protect the elbow
COUTH, -ER, -S *adj* refined ▹ *n* refinement
COUTHIE *adj* sociable
COUTHS ▸ **couth**
COUTHY *same as* ▸ **couthie**
COUTIL, -S *n* type of tightly woven twill cloth
COUTURE *n* high-fashion designing and dressmaking ▹ *adj* relating to high fashion design and dress-making
COUVADE *n* custom in certain cultures relating to childbirth
COUVERT *another word for* ▸ **cover**
COUZIN, -S *n* South African word for a friend
COVARY *vb* vary together maintaining a certain mathematical relationship
COVE, -D, -S *n, vb*
COVELET *n* small cove
COVEN, -S *n* meeting of witches
COVENT, -S *same as* ▸ **convent**
COVER, -ED, -S *vb, n*
COVERER ▸ **cover**
COVERS ▸ **cover**
COVERT, -S *adj, n*
COVERUP *n* concealment of a mistake, crime, etc

COVES ▸ **cove**
COVET, -ED, -S *vb*
COVETER ▸ **covet**
COVETS ▸ **covet**
COVEY, -S *n* small flock of grouse or partridge
COVIN, -S *n* conspiracy between two or more persons
COVINE, -S *n* conspiracy between two or more persons
COVING, -S *same as* ▸ **cove**
COVINS ▸ **covin**
COVYNE, -S *same as* ▸ **covin**
COW, -ED, -ING, -S *n, vb*
COWAGE, -S *n* tropical climbing plant
COWAL, -S *n* shallow lake or swampy depression supporting vegetation
COWAN, -S *n* drystone waller
COWARD, -S *n* person who lacks courage ▹ *vb* show (someone) up to be a coward
COWBANE *n* poisonous marsh plant
COWBELL *n*
COWBIND *n* any of various bryony plants, esp the white bryony
COWBIRD *n* American oriole with a dark plumage and short bill
COWBOY, -S *n, vb*
COWED ▸ **cow**
COWEDLY ▸ **cow**
COWER, -ED, -S *vb*
COWFISH *n* type of trunkfish with hornlike spines over the eyes
COWFLAP *n* cow dung
COWFLOP *n* foxglove
COWGIRL *n*
COWHAGE *same as* ▸ **cowage**
COWHAND *same as* ▸ **cowboy**
COWHEEL *n* heel of a cow, used as a cooking ingredient
COWHERB *n* European plant with clusters of pink flowers
COWHERD *n*
COWHIDE *n, vb*
COWIER ▸ **cowy**
COWIEST ▸ **cowy**
COWING ▸ **cow**
COWISH *adj* cowardly ▹ *n* N American plant with an edible root
COWITCH *another name for* ▸ **cowage**
COWK, -ED, -ING, -S *vb* retch or feel nauseated
COWL, -S *same as* ▸ **cowling**
COWLED *adj* wearing a cowl
COWLICK *n* tuft of hair over the forehead
COWLIKE *adj* like a cow
COWLING *n* cover on an engine
COWLS ▸ **cowl**
COWMAN, COWMEN *n* man who owns cattle
COWP, -ED, -ING, -S *same as* ▸ **coup**
COWPAT, -S *n*
COWPEA, -S *n* type of tropical climbing plant
COWPED ▸ **cowp**
COWPIE, -S *n* cowpat
COWPING ▸ **cowp**
COWPLOP *n* cow dung
COWPOKE *n* cowboy
COWPOX *n* disease of cows
COWPS ▸ **cowp**
COWPUNK *n* music that combines country music and punk
COWRIE, -S *n* brightly marked sea shell
COWRITE, COWROTE *vb* write jointly
COWRY *same as* ▸ **cowrie**
COWS ▸ **cow**
COWSHED *n* byre
COWSKIN *same as* ▸ **cowhide**
COWSLIP *n* small yellow European wild flower
COWTOWN *n* rural town in a cattle-raising area
COWTREE *n* South American tree that produces latex
COWY, COWIER, COWIEST *adj* cowlike
COX, -ED, -ES, -ING *n, vb*
COXA, -E *n* technical name for the hipbone or hip joint
COXAL ▸ **coxa**
COXALGY *same as* > **coxalgia**
COXCOMB *same as* > **cockscomb**
COXED ▸ **cox**
COXES ▸ **cox**
COXIB, -S *n* anti-inflammatory drug
COXIER ▸ **coxy**
COXIEST ▸ **coxy**
COXING ▸ **cox**
COXITIS *n* inflammation of the hip joint

COXLESS ▶ **cox**
COXY, COXIER, COXIEST *adj* cocky
COY, -ED, -ER, -EST, -ING, -S *adj, vb*
COYAU, -S *n* type of steep roof
COYDOG, -S *n* cross between a coyote and a dog
COYED ▶ **coy**
COYER ▶ **coy**
COYEST ▶ **coy**
COYING ▶ **coy**
COYISH ▶ **coy**
COYLY ▶ **coy**
COYNESS ▶ **coy**
COYOTE, -S *n*
COYPOU, -S *same as* ▶ **coypu**
COYPU, -S *n* beaver-like aquatic rodent
COYS ▶ **coy**
COZ, -ZES *archaic word for* ▶ **cousin**

> **Coz** is an old word for **cousin**, and a good one to know for using the Z.

COZE, -D, -S, COZING *vb* to chat
COZEN, -ED, -S *vb* cheat, trick
COZENER ▶ **cozen**
COZENS ▶ **cozen**
COZES ▶ **coze**
COZEY, -S *n* tea cosy
COZIE *same as* ▶ **cozey**
COZIED ▶ **cozy**
COZIER, -S *n* cobbler
COZIES ▶ **cozy**
COZIEST ▶ **cozy**
COZILY ▶ **cozy**
COZING ▶ **coze**
COZY, COZIED, COZIES, COZIEST, -ING *same as* ▶ **cosy**
COZZES ▶ **coz**
COZZIE, -S *n* swimming costume
CRAAL, -ED, -S *n* enclosure for livestock ▷ *vb* enclose in a craal
CRAB, -BED, -S *n, vb*
CRABBER *n* crab fisherman
CRABBIT *adj* Scots word meaning bad-tempered
CRABBY *adj* bad-tempered
CRABS ▶ **crab**
CRACK, -S *vb, n, adj*
CRACKED *adj* damaged by cracking
CRACKER *n* thin dry biscuit
CRACKET *n* low stool, often one with three legs
CRACKIE *n* small mongrel dog
CRACKLE *vb* make small sharp popping noises ▷ *n* crackling sound
CRACKLY *adj* making a crackling sound
CRACKS ▶ **crack**
CRACKUP *n* collapse
CRACKY *adj* full of cracks ▷ *n* something that is full of cracks
CRACOWE *n* medieval shoe with a sharply pointed toe
CRADLE, -D, -S *n, vb*
CRADLER ▶ **cradle**
CRADLES ▶ **cradle**
CRAFT, -ED, -S *n, vb*
CRAFTER *n* person doing craftwork
CRAFTS ▶ **craft**
CRAFTY *adj* skilled in deception
CRAG, -S *n*
CRAGGED *same as* ▶ **craggy**
CRAGGER *n* member of a carbon reduction action group
CRAGGY *adj* having many crags
CRAGS ▶ **crag**
CRAIC, -S *n* Irish word meaning fun
CRAIG, -S *a Scot word for* ▶ **crag**
CRAKE, -D, -S, CRAKING *n* bird of the rail family, such as the corncrake ▷ *vb* to boast
CRAM, -MED, -S *vb, n*
CRAMBE, -S *n* any plant of the genus Crambe
CRAMBO, -S *n* word game
CRAME, -S *n* merchant's booth or stall
CRAMESY *same as* ▶ **cramoisy**
CRAMMED ▶ **cram**
CRAMMER *n* person or school that prepares pupils for an examination
CRAMP, -S *n, vb*
CRAMPED *adj* closed in
CRAMPER *n* brace for the feet in the sport of curling
CRAMPET *n* cramp iron
CRAMPIT *same as* ▶ **crampet**
CRAMPON *n* spiked plate strapped to a

boot for climbing on ice ▷ *vb* climb using crampons
CRAMPS ▶ **cramp**
CRAMPY *adj* affected with cramp
CRAMS ▶ **cram**
CRAN, -S *n* unit of capacity used for measuring fresh herring, equal to 37.5 gallons
CRANAGE *n* use of a crane
CRANCH *vb* to crunch
CRANE, -D, -S, CRANING *n, vb*
CRANIA ▶ **cranium**
CRANIAL *adj* of or relating to the skull
CRANING ▶ **crane**
CRANIUM, CRANIA *n*
CRANK, -ED, -ER, -S *n* arm projecting at right angles from a shaft ▷ *vb* turn with a crank ▷ *adj* (of a sailing vessel) easily keeled over by the wind
CRANKLE *vb* bend or wind
CRANKLY *adj* vigorously
CRANKS ▶ **crank**
CRANKY *same as* > **crankish**
CRANNOG *n* ancient Celtic lake or bog dwelling
CRANNY *n* narrow opening ▷ *vb* become full of crannies
CRANS ▶ **cran**
CRANTS *n* garland carried in front of a maiden's bier
CRAP *n* slang word for rubbish, nonsense
CRAPAUD *n* frog or toad
CRAPE, -D, -S, CRAPING *same as* ▶ **crepe**
CRAPIER ▶ **crapy**
CRAPING ▶ **crape**
CRAPLE, -S *same as* ▶ **grapple**
CRAPOLA *n* slang word for rubbish, nonsense
CRAPPIE *n* N American freshwater fish
CRAPPY *adj* slang word for worthless, of poor quality
CRAPS *pl n* game using two dice
CRAPY, CRAPIER ▶ **crape**
CRARE, -S *n* type of trading vessel
CRASES ▶ **crasis**
CRASH, -ED, -ES *n, vb, adj*
CRASHER ▶ **crash**
CRASHES ▶ **crash**
CRASIS, CRASES *n* fusion or contraction of two adjacent vowels into one
CRASS, -ER *adj* stupid and insensitive
CRASSLY ▶ **crass**
CRATCH *n* rack for holding fodder for cattle, etc
CRATE, -D, -S, CRATING *n, vb*
CRATER, -S *n, vb*
CRATES ▶ **crate**
CRATHUR *same as* ▶ **cratur**
CRATING ▶ **crate**
CRATON, -S *n* stable part of the earth's continental crust
CRATUR, -S *n* whisky or whiskey
CRAUNCH *same as* ▶ **crunch**
CRAVAT, -S *n* man's scarf worn like a tie ▷ *vb* wear a cravat
CRAVATE *same as* ▶ **cravat**
CRAVATS ▶ **cravat**
CRAVE, -D, -S *vb*
CRAVEN, -S *adj, n, vb*
CRAVER, -S ▶ **crave**
CRAVES ▶ **crave**
CRAVING *n* intense desire or longing
CRAW, -S *n* pouchlike part of a bird's oesophagus
CRAWDAD *n* crayfish
CRAWL, -ED, -S *vb, n*
CRAWLER *n* servile flatterer
CRAWLS ▶ **crawl**
CRAWLY *adj*
CRAWS ▶ **craw**
CRAY, -EST, -S *n* crayfish ▷ *adj* crazy
CRAYER, -S *same as* ▶ **crare**
CRAYEST ▶ **cray**
CRAYON, -S *n, vb*
CRAYS ▶ **cray**
CRAZE, -S *n, vb*
CRAZED *adj* wild and uncontrolled
CRAZES ▶ **craze**
CRAZIER ▶ **crazy**
CRAZIES ▶ **crazy**
CRAZILY ▶ **crazy**
CRAZING *n* act of crazing
CRAZY, CRAZIER, CRAZIES *adj* ridiculous ▷ *n* crazy person
CREACH, -S *same as* ▶ **creagh**

CREAGH, -S *n* foray
CREAK, -ED, -S *n, vb*
CREAKY ▶ **creak**
CREAM, -ED, -S *n, vb*
CREAMER *n* powdered milk substitute for use in coffee
CREAMS ▶ **cream**
CREAMY *adj* resembling cream in colour, taste, or consistency
CREANCE *n* long light cord used in falconry
CREANT *adj* formative
CREASE, -D, -S *n, vb*
CREASER ▶ **crease**
CREASES ▶ **crease**
CREASY ▶ **crease**
CREATE, -D, -S *vb*
CREATIC *adj* relating to flesh or meat
CREATIN *same as* ▶ **creatine**
CREATOR *n* person who creates
CRECHE, -S *n*
CRED, -S *n* short for credibility
CREDAL ▶ **creed**
CREDENT *adj* believing or believable
CREDIT *n, vb*
CREDITS *pl n* list of people responsible for the production of a film or TV programme
CREDO, -S *n*
CREDS ▶ **cred**
CREE, -ING, -S *vb* soften grain by boiling or soaking
CREED, -S *n*
CREEDAL ▶ **creed**
CREEDS ▶ **creed**
CREEING ▶ **cree**
CREEK, -S *n*
CREEKY *adj* abounding in creeks
CREEL, -ED, -S *n* wicker basket used by anglers ▷ *vb* to fish using creels
CREEP, -ED, -S, CREPT *vb, n*
CREEPER *n* creeping plant ▷ *vb* train a plant to creep
CREEPIE *n* low stool
CREEPS ▶ **creep**
CREEPY *adj* causing a feeling of fear or disgust
CREES ▶ **cree**
CREESE, -D, -S *same as* ▶ **kris**
CREESH *vb* lubricate
CREESHY *adj* greasy
CREM, -S *n* crematorium
CREMANT *adj* (of wine) moderately sparkling
CREMATE *vb* burn (a corpse) to ash
CREME, -S *n* cream
CREMINI *n* variety of mushroom
CREMONA *same as* ▶ **cromorna**
CREMOR, -S *n* thick creamy liquid
CREMS ▶ **crem**
CREMSIN *same as* ▶ **cremosin**
CRENA, -S *n* cleft or notch
CRENATE *adj* having a scalloped margin, as certain leaves
CRENEL, -S *n* opening formed in the top of a wall having slanting sides ▷ *vb* crenellate
CREOLE, -S *n, adj*
CREOSOL *n* insoluble oily liquid
CREPE, -D, -S, CREPING *n, vb*
CREPEY *same as* ▶ **crepy**
CREPIER ▶ **crepy**
CREPING ▶ **crepe**
CREPON, -S *n* thin material made of fine wool and/or silk
CREPS *pl n* slang term for training shoes
CREPT ▶ **creep**
CREPY, CREPIER *adj* (esp of the skin) having a dry wrinkled appearance like crepe
CRESOL, -S *n* aromatic compound
CRESS, -ES *n*
CRESSET *n* metal basket mounted on a pole
CRESSY ▶ **cress**
CREST, -ED, -S *n, vb*
CRESTA *adj* as in **cresta run** high-speed tobogganing down a steep narrow passage
CRESTAL ▶ **crystal**
CRESTED ▶ **crest**
CRESTON *n* hogback
CRESTS ▶ **crest**
CRESYL, -S *n* tolyl
CRETIC, -S *n* metrical foot
CRETIN, -S *n*
CRETISM *n* lying
CRETONS *pl n* spread made from pork fat and onions
CREVICE *n*
CREW, -ED, -ING, -S *n, vb*
CREWCUT *n* very short haircut

CREWE, -S *n* type of pot
CREWED ▸ **crew**
CREWEL, -S *n* fine worsted yarn used in embroidery ▹ *vb* embroider in crewel
CREWES ▸ **crewe**
CREWING ▸ **crew**
CREWMAN, CREWMEN *n* member of a ship's crew
CREWS ▸ **crew**
CRIA, -S *n* baby llama or alpaca
CRIANT *adj* garish
CRIAS ▸ **cria**
CRIB, -BED, -S *n, vb*
CRIBBER ▸ **crib**
CRIBBLE *vb* to sift
CRIBLE, -S *adj* dotted ▹ *n* method of engraving with holes or dots
CRIBS ▸ **crib**
CRICK, -ED, -S *n, vb*
CRICKET *n, vb*
CRICKEY *same as* ▸ **crikey**
CRICKS ▸ **crick**
CRICKY *same as* ▸ **crikey**
CRICOID *adj* of or relating to part of the larynx ▹ *n* this cartilage
CRIED ▸ **cry**
CRIER, -S *n* (formerly) official who made public announcements
CRIES ▸ **cry**
CRIKEY *interj* expression of surprise
CRIM, -S *short for* > **criminal**
CRIME, -D, -S, CRIMING *n, vb*
CRIMEN, CRIMINA *n* crime
CRIMES ▸ **crime**
CRIMINA ▸ **crimen**
CRIMINE *interj* expression of surprise
CRIMING ▸ **crime**
CRIMINI *same as* ▸ **crimine**
CRIMINY *same as* ▸ **crimine**
CRIMMER *variant spelling of* ▸ **krimmer**
CRIMP, -ED, -S *vb* fold or press into ridges ▹ *n* act or result of crimping
CRIMPER ▸ **crimp**
CRIMPLE *vb* crumple, wrinkle, or curl
CRIMPS ▸ **crimp**
CRIMPY ▸ **crimp**
CRIMS ▸ **crim**
CRIMSON *adj, n, vb*
CRINAL *adj* relating to the hair
CRINATE *adj* having hair
CRINE, -D, -S, CRINING *vb* to shrivel
CRINGE, -D, -S *vb, n*
CRINGER ▸ **cringe**
CRINGES ▸ **cringe**
CRINGEY *adj* causing the urge to cringe
CRINGLE *n* eye at the edge of a sail
CRINGY *same as* ▸ **cringey**
CRINING ▸ **crine**
CRINITE *adj* covered with soft hairs or tufts ▹ *n* sedimentary rock
CRINKLE *n, vb*
CRINKLY *adj* wrinkled ▹ *n* derogatory term for an old person
CRINOID *n* type of primitive echinoderm
CRINOSE *adj* hairy
CRINUM, -S *n* type of mostly tropical plant
CRIOLLO *n* native or inhabitant of Latin America of European descent ▹ *adj* of, relating to, or characteristic of a criollo or criollos
CRIOS, -ES *n* multicoloured woven woollen belt
CRIPE *variant of* ▸ **cripes**
CRIPES *interj* expression of surprise
CRIPPLE *vb*
CRIS *variant of* ▸ **kris**
CRISE *n* crisis
CRISES ▸ **crisis**
CRISIC *adj* relating to a crisis
CRISIS, CRISES *n*
CRISP, -S *adj, n, vb*
CRISPED *same as* > **crispate**
CRISPEN *vb* make crisp
CRISPER *n* compartment in a refrigerator
CRISPIN *n* cobbler
CRISPLY ▸ **crisp**
CRISPS ▸ **crisp**
CRISPY *adj* hard and crunchy
CRISSA ▸ **crissum**
CRISSAL ▸ **crissum**
CRISSUM, CRISSA *n* area or feathers surrounding the cloaca of a bird
CRISTA, -E *n* structure resembling a ridge or crest
CRIT, -S *short for* > **criticism**

CRITH, -S *n* unit of weight for gases
CRITIC, -S *n* professional judge of any of the arts
CRITS ▸ **crit**
CRITTER *a dialect word for* > **creature**
CRITTUR *same as* ▸ **critter**
CRIVENS *interj* expression of surprise
CROAK, -ED, -S *vb, n*
CROAKER *n* animal, bird, etc, that croaks
CROAKS ▸ **croak**
CROAKY ▸ **croak**
CROC, -S *short for* > **crocodile**
CROCEIN *n* any one of a group of red or orange acid azo dyes
CROCHE, -S *n* knob at the top of a deer's horn
CROCHET *vb* make by looping and intertwining yarn with a hooked needle ▹ *n* work made in this way
CROCI ▸ **crocus**
CROCINE *adj* relating to the crocus
CROCK, -S *n* earthenware pot or jar ▹ *vb* injure or cause to become weak
CROCKED *adj* injured
CROCKET *n* carved ornament in the form of a curled leaf or cusp
CROCKS ▸ **crock**
CROCS ▸ **croc**
CROCUS, CROCI *n*
CROFT, -ED, -S *n, vb*
CROFTER *n* owner or tenant of a small farm, esp in Scotland or northern England
CROFTS ▸ **croft**
CROG, -GED, -S *vb* ride on a bicycle as a passenger
CROGGY *n* ride on a bicycle as a passenger
CROGS ▸ **crog**
CROJIK, -S *n* triangular sail
CROMACK *same as* > **crummock**
CROMB, -ED, -S *same as* ▸ **crome**
CROMBEC *n* African bird with colourful plumage
CROMBED ▸ **cromb**
CROMBS ▸ **cromb**
CROME, -D, -S, CROMING *n* hook ▹ *vb* use a crome
CRON, -S *n* computer application that schedules tasks chronologically
CRONE, -S *n*
CRONET, -S *n* hair which grows over the top of a horse's hoof
CRONIES ▸ **crony**
CRONISH ▸ **crone**
CRONK, -ER *adj* unfit
CRONS ▸ **cron**
CRONY, CRONIES *n*
CROODLE *vb* nestle close
CROOK, -ER, -S *n* dishonest person ▹ *vb* bend or curve ▹ *adj* informal Australian word meaning ill
CROOKED *adj* bent or twisted
CROOKER ▸ **crook**
CROOKS ▸ **crook**
CROOL, -ED, -S *vb* spoil
CROON, -ED, -S *vb* sing, hum, or speak in a soft low tone ▹ *n* soft low singing or humming
CROONER ▸ **croon**
CROONS ▸ **croon**
CROONY *adj* singing like a crooner
CROOVE, -S *n* animal enclosure
CROP, -PED, -S *n, vb*
CROPFUL *n* quantity that can be held in the craw
CROPPED ▸ **crop**
CROPPER *n* person who cultivates or harvests a crop
CROPPIE *same as* ▸ **croppy**
CROPPY *n* rebel in the Irish rising of 1798
CROPS ▸ **crop**
CROQUET *n, vb*
CROQUIS *n* rough sketch
CRORE, -S *n* (in Indian English) ten million
CROSIER *n* staff carried by bishops as a symbol of pastoral office ▹ *vb* bear or carry such a staff
CROSS, -ED, -ES, CROST *vb, n, adj*
CROSSE *n* light staff used in playing lacrosse
CROSSED ▸ **cross**
CROSSER ▸ **cross**
CROSSES ▸ **cross**
CROSSLY ▸ **cross**
CROST ▸ **cross**
CROTAL, -S *n* any of various lichens used in dyeing wool

CROTALA > **crotalum**
CROTALE *n* type of small cymbal
CROTALS ▶ **crotal**
CROTCH *n* part of the body between the tops of the legs
CROTON, -S *n* type of shrub or tree, the seeds of which yield croton oil
CROTTLE *same as* ▶ **crotal**
CROUCH *vb, n*
CROUP, -ED, -S *n* throat disease of children, with a cough ▷ *vb* have croup
CROUPE, -S *same as* ▶ **croup**
CROUPED ▶ **croup**
CROUPER *obsolete variant of* ▶ **crupper**
CROUPES ▶ **croupe**
CROUPON *n* type of highly polished flexible leather
CROUPS ▶ **croup**
CROUPY ▶ **croup**
CROUSE *adj* lively, confident, or saucy
CROUT, -S *n* sauerkraut
CROUTE, -S *n* small round of toasted bread on which a savoury mixture is served
CROUTON *n*
CROUTS ▶ **crout**
CROW, -ED, -S *n, vb*
CROWBAR *n, vb*
CROWD, -ED, -S *n, vb*
CROWDER ▶ **crowd**
CROWDIE *n* porridge of meal and water
CROWDS ▶ **crowd**
CROWDY *same as* ▶ **crowdie**
CROWEA, -S *n* Australian shrub with pink flowers
CROWED ▶ **crow**
CROWER, -S ▶ **crow**
CROWING *n* act of crowing
CROWN, -ED, -S *n, vb*
CROWNER *n* promotional label
CROWNET *n* coronet
CROWNS ▶ **crown**
CROWS ▶ **crow**
CROZE, -S *n* recess cut at the end of a barrel or cask to receive the head
CROZER, -S *n* machine which cuts grooves in cask staves
CROZES ▶ **croze**
CROZIER *same as* ▶ **crosier**
CRU *n* (in France) a vineyard, group of vineyards, or wine-producing region
CRUBEEN *n* pig's trotter
CRUCES ▶ **crux**
CRUCIAL *adj*
CRUCIAN *n* European fish
CRUCIFY *vb*
CRUCK, -S *n* wooden timber supporting the end of certain roofs
CRUD, -DED, -S *n* sticky or encrusted substance ▷ *interj* expression of disgust, disappointment, etc ▷ *vb* cover with a sticky or encrusted substance
CRUDDLE *vb* curdle
CRUDDY *adj* dirty or unpleasant
CRUDE, -R, -S, -ST *adj, n*
CRUDELY ▶ **crude**
CRUDER ▶ **crude**
CRUDES ▶ **crude**
CRUDEST ▶ **crude**
CRUDIER ▶ **crudy**
CRUDITY ▶ **crude**
CRUDO, -S *n* sliced raw seafood
CRUDS ▶ **crud**
CRUDY, CRUDIER *adj* raw
CRUE, -S *obsolete variant of* ▶ **crew**
CRUEL, -ER *adj*
CRUELLS *same as* ▶ **cruels**
CRUELLY ▶ **cruel**
CRUELS *n* disease of cattle and sheep
CRUELTY *n* deliberate infliction of pain or suffering
CRUES ▶ **crue**
CRUET, -S *n*
CRUFT, -S *n* redundant technical hardware
CRUISE, -D, -S *n, vb*
CRUISER *n* fast warship
CRUISES ▶ **cruise**
CRUISEY *same as* ▶ **cruisy**
CRUISIE *same as* ▶ **cruizie**
CRUISY *adj* relaxed or easy-going
CRUIVE, -S *n* animal enclosure
CRUIZIE *n* oil lamp
CRULLER *n* light sweet ring-shaped cake, fried in deep fat
CRUMB, -ED *n, vb, adj*
CRUMBER ▶ **crumb**
CRUMBLE *vb* break into fragments ▷ *n*

pudding of stewed fruit with a crumbly topping
CRUMBLY *adj* easily crumbled or crumbling
CRUMBS *interj* expression of dismay or surprise
CRUMBUM *n* rogue
CRUMBY *adj* full of crumbs
CRUMEN, -S *n* deer's larmier or tear-pit
CRUMMIE *n* cow with a crumpled horn
CRUMMY *adj* of poor quality ▷ *n* lorry that carries loggers to work from their camp
CRUMP, -ED, -ER, -S *vb* thud or explode with a loud dull sound ▷ *n* crunching, thudding, or exploding noise ▷ *adj* crooked
CRUMPET *n*
CRUMPLE *vb* crush, crease ▷ *n* untidy crease or wrinkle
CRUMPLY ▸ **crumple**
CRUMPS ▸ **crump**
CRUMPY *adj* crisp
CRUNCH *vb, n*
CRUNCHY ▸ **crunch**
CRUNK, -S *n* form of hip-hop music originating in the Southern US
CRUNKED *adj* excited or intoxicated
CRUNKLE *Scots variant of* ▸ **crinkle**
CRUNKS ▸ **crunk**
CRUNODE *n* point at which two branches of a curve intersect
CRUOR, -ES, -S *n* blood clot
CRUPPER *n* strap that passes from the back of a saddle under a horse's tail
CRURA ▸ **crus**
CRURAL *adj* of or relating to the leg or thigh
CRUS, CRURA *n* leg, esp from the knee to the foot
CRUSADE *n, vb*
CRUSADO *n* former gold or silver coin of Portugal
CRUSE, -S *n* small earthenware jug or pot
CRUSET, -S *n* goldsmith's crucible
CRUSH, -ED, -ES *vb, n*
CRUSHER ▸ **crush**
CRUSHES ▸ **crush**
CRUSIAN *variant of* ▸ **crucian**
CRUSIE, -S *same as* ▸ **cruizie**
CRUSILY *adj* (in heraldry) strewn with crosses
CRUST, -ED, -S *n, vb*
CRUSTA, -E, -S *n* hard outer layer
CRUSTAL *adj* of or relating to the earth's crust
CRUSTAS ▸ **crusta**
CRUSTED ▸ **crust**
CRUSTS ▸ **crust**
CRUSTY *adj* having a crust ▷ *n* scruffy type of punk or hippy whose lifestyle involves travelling and squatting
CRUSY *same as* ▸ **cruizie**
CRUTCH *n, vb*
CRUVE, -S *same as* ▸ **cruive**
CRUX, CRUCES, -ES *n* crucial or decisive point
CRUZADO *same as* ▸ **crusado**
CRUZIE, -S *same as* ▸ **cruizie**
CRWTH, -S *n* ancient stringed instrument of Celtic origin

> This old Celtic musical instrument makes a fine tune when your rack is all consonants.

CRY, CRIED, CRIES *vb, n*
CRYBABY *n*
CRYER, -S *same as* ▸ **crier**
CRYING, -S ▸ **cry**
CRYOGEN *n* substance used to produce low temperatures
CRYONIC *adj* relating to or involving cryonics
CRYPT, -S *n*
CRYPTAL ▸ **crypt**
CRYPTIC *adj*
CRYPTO, -S *n* person who is a secret member of an organization or sect
CRYPTON *n* hypothetical particle
CRYPTOS ▸ **crypto**
CRYPTS ▸ **crypt**
CRYSTAL *n, adj*
CSARDAS *n* type of Hungarian folk dance
CTENE, -S *n* locomotor organ found in ctenophores (or comb jellies)

CTENOID *adj* toothed like a comb, as the scales of perches
CUATRO, -S *n* four-stringed guitar
CUB, -BED, -S *n, adj, vb*
CUBAGE, -S *same as* > **cubature**
CUBANE, -S *n* rare octahedral hydrocarbon
CUBBED ▶ **cub**
CUBBIER ▶ **cubby**
CUBBIES ▶ **cubby**
CUBBING ▶ **cub**
CUBBISH ▶ **cub**
CUBBY, CUBBIER, CUBBIES *n* cubbyhole ▷ *adj* short and plump
CUBE, -D, -S, CUBING *n, vb*
CUBEB, -S *n* SE Asian woody climbing plant with brownish berries
CUBED ▶ **cube**
CUBER, -S ▶ **cube**
CUBES ▶ **cube**
CUBHOOD *n* state of being a cub
CUBIC, -S *adj, n*
CUBICA, -S *n* fine shalloon-like fabric
CUBICAL *adj* of or related to volume
CUBICAS ▶ **cubica**
CUBICLE *n*
CUBICLY ▶ **cubic**
CUBICS ▶ **cubic**
CUBING ▶ **cube**
CUBISM, -S *n* style of art in which objects are represented by geometrical shapes
CUBIST, -S ▶ **cubism**
CUBIT, -S *n* old measure of length based on the length of the forearm
CUBITAL *adj* of or relating to the forearm
CUBITI ▶ **cubitus**
CUBITS ▶ **cubit**
CUBITUS, CUBITI *n* elbow
CUBLESS *adj* having no cubs
CUBOID, -S *adj* shaped like a cube ▷ *n* geometric solid whose six faces are rectangles
CUBS ▶ **cub**
CUCKING *adj* as in **cucking stool** stool in which suspected witches were tested
CUCKOO, -S *n, vb*
CUD, -S *n*
CUDBEAR *another name for* ▶ **orchil**
CUDDEN, -S *n* young coalfish
CUDDIE *same as* ▶ **cuddy**
CUDDIES ▶ **cuddy**
CUDDIN, -S *same as* ▶ **cudden**
CUDDLE, -D, -S *n* hug ▷ *vb* hold close
CUDDLER ▶ **cuddle**
CUDDLES ▶ **cuddle**
CUDDLY ▶ **cuddle**
CUDDY, CUDDIES *n* small cabin in a boat
CUDGEL, -S *n, vb*
CUDS ▶ **cud**
CUDWEED *n* type of temperate plant
CUE, -D, -S, CUING *n, vb*
CUEING, -S ▶ **cue**
CUEIST, -S *n* snooker or billiards player
CUES ▶ **cue**
CUESTA, -S *n* long low ridge with a steep scarp slope and a gentle back slope
CUFF, -ED, -ING, -S *n, vb*
CUFFIN, -S *n* man
CUFFING ▶ **cuff**
CUFFINS ▶ **cuffin**
CUFFLE, -D, -S *vb* scuffle
CUFFO *adv* free of charge
CUFFS ▶ **cuff**
CUIF, -S *same as* ▶ **coof**
CUING ▶ **cue**
CUIRASS *n* piece of armour covering the chest and back ▷ *vb* equip with a cuirass
CUISH, -ES *same as* ▶ **cuisse**
CUISINE *n*
CUISSE, -S *n* piece of armour for the thigh
CUISSER *same as* ▶ **cooser**
CUISSES ▶ **cuisse**
CUIT, -S *n* ankle
CUITER, -S *vb* pamper
CUITS ▶ **cuit**
CUITTLE *vb* wheedle
CUKE, -S *n* cucumber
CULCH, -ES *n* the basis of an oyster bed
CULCHIE *n* mildly derogatory Irish term for a country-dweller ▷ *adj* rough or unsophisticated
CULET, -S *n* flat face at the bottom of a gem
CULEX, -ES, CULICES *n* type of mosquito
CULICID *n* type of dipterous insect
CULL, -ED, -S *vb, n*
CULLAY, -S *n* soapbark tree
CULLED ▶ **cull**

CULLER, -S *n* person employed to cull animals
CULLET, -S *n* waste glass for melting down to be reused
CULLIED ▸ **cully**
CULLIES ▸ **cully**
CULLING ▸ **cull**
CULLION *n* rascal
CULLIS *same as* > **coulisse**
CULLS ▸ **cull**
CULLY, CULLIED, CULLIES *n* pal ▹ *vb* to trick
CULM, -ED, -ING, -S *n* coal-mine waste ▹ *vb* form a stalk or stem
CULMEN, CULMINA *n* summit
CULMING ▸ **culm**
CULMS ▸ **culm**
CULOTTE > **culottes**
CULPA, -E *n* act of neglect
CULPRIT *n*
CULSHIE *n* mildly derogatory Irish term for a country-dweller ▹ *adj* rough or unsophisticated
CULT, -S *n, adj*
CULTCH *same as* ▸ **culch**
CULTER, -S *same as* ▸ **coulter**
CULTI ▸ **cultus**
CULTIC *adj* of or relating to a religious cult
CULTIER ▸ **culty**
CULTISH *adj* intended to appeal to a small group of fashionable people
CULTISM ▸ **cult**
CULTIST ▸ **cult**
CULTS ▸ **cult**
CULTURE *n, vb*
CULTUS, CULTI *another word for* ▸ **cult**
CULTY, CULTIER *same as* ▸ **cultish**
CULVER, -S *an archaic or poetic name for* ▸ **pigeon**
CULVERT *n* drain under a road or railway ▹ *vb* direct water through a culvert
CUM *prep* with
CUMARIC ▸ **cumarin**
CUMARIN *same as* > **coumarin**
CUMBENT *adj* lying down
CUMBER, -S *vb* obstruct or hinder ▹ *n* hindrance or burden
CUMBIA, -S *n* Colombian style of music
CUMEC, -S *n* unit of volumetric rate of flow
CUMIN, -S *n*
CUMMER, -S *n* gossip
CUMMIN, -S *same as* ▸ **cumin**
CUMQUAT *same as* ▸ **kumquat**
CUMSHAW *n* (used, esp formerly, by beggars in Chinese ports) a present or tip
CUMULET *n* variety of domestic fancy pigeon
CUMULUS, CUMULI *n* thick white or dark grey cloud
CUNDY, CUNDIES *n* sewer
CUNEAL *same as* > **cuneiform**
CUNEATE *adj* wedge-shaped
CUNEI ▸ **cuneus**
CUNETTE *n* small trench dug in the main ditch of a fortification
CUNEUS, CUNEI *n* small wedge-shaped area of the cerebral cortex
CUNIT, -S *n* one hundred cubic feet
CUNNER, -S *n* fish of the wrasse family
CUNNING *adj* clever at deceiving ▹ *n* cleverness at deceiving
CUP, -PED, -S *n, vb*
CUPCAKE *n*
CUPEL, -ED, -S *n* refractory pot in which gold or silver is refined ▹ *vb* refine (gold or silver) by means of cupellation
CUPELER ▸ **cupel**
CUPELS ▸ **cupel**
CUPFUL, -S, CUPSFUL *n*
CUPGALL *n* gall found on oakleaves
CUPHEAD *n* type of bolt or rivet with a cup-shaped head
CUPID, -S *n* figure representing the Roman god of love
CUPLIKE ▸ **cup**
CUPMAN, CUPMEN *n* drinking companion
CUPOLA, -S *n* domed roof or ceiling ▹ *vb* provide with a cupola
CUPOLAR ▸ **cupola**
CUPOLAS ▸ **cupola**
CUPPA, -S *n* cup of tea
CUPPED ▸ **cup**

CUPPER, -S *same as* ▸ **cuppa**
CUPPIER ▸ **cuppy**
CUPPING ▸ **cup**
CUPPY, CUPPIER *adj* cup-shaped
CUPRIC *adj* of or containing copper in the divalent state
CUPRITE *n* red secondary mineral
CUPROUS *adj* of or containing copper in the monovalent state
CUPRUM, -S *an obsolete name for* ▸ **copper**
CUPS ▸ **cup**
CUPSFUL ▸ **cupful**
CUPULA, -E *n* dome-shaped structure
CUPULAR *same as* > **cupulate**
CUPULE, -S *n* cup-shaped part or structure
CUR, -S *n* mongrel dog
CURABLE *adj* capable of being cured
CURABLY ▸ **curable**
CURACAO *n* orange-flavoured liqueur
CURACOA *same as* ▸ **curacao**
CURACY *n* work or position of a curate
CURAGH, -S *same as* ▸ **currach**
CURARA, -S *same as* ▸ **curare**
CURARE, -S *n* poisonous resin of a S American tree
CURARI, -S *same as* ▸ **curare**
CURAT, -S *n* cuirass
CURATE, -D, -S *n* clergyman or clergywoman who assists a parish priest ▹ *vb* be in charge of (an art exhibition or museum)
CURATOR *n* person in charge of a museum or art gallery
CURATS ▸ **curat**
CURB, -ED, -S *n, vb*
CURBER, -S ▸ **curb**
CURBING *the US spelling of* ▸ **kerbing**
CURBS ▸ **curb**
CURCH, -ES *n* woman's plain cap or kerchief
CURCHEF *same as* ▸ **curch**
CURCHES ▸ **curch**
CURCUMA *n* type of tropical Asian tuberous plant
CURD, -ED, -ING, -S *n, vb*
CURDIER ▸ **curdy**
CURDING ▸ **curd**
CURDLE, -D, -S *vb*
CURDLER ▸ **curdle**
CURDLES ▸ **curdle**
CURDS ▸ **curd**
CURDY, CURDIER ▸ **curd**
CURE, -D, -S *vb, n*
CURER, -S ▸ **cure**
CURES ▸ **cure**
CURET, -S *same as* ▸ **curette**
CURETTE *n* surgical instrument for scraping tissue from body cavities ▹ *vb* scrape with a curette
CURF, -S *n* type of limestone
CURFEW, -S *n*
CURFS ▸ **curf**
CURIA, -E, -S *n* papal court and government of the Roman Catholic Church
CURIAL ▸ **curia**
CURIAS ▸ **curia**
CURIE, -S *n* standard unit of radioactivity
CURIET, -S *n* cuirass
CURING, -S *n* act of curing
CURIO, -S *n* rare or unusual object valued as a collector's item
CURIOSA *pl n* curiosities
CURIOUS *adj* eager to learn or know
CURITE, -S *n* oxide of uranium and lead
CURIUM, -S *n* radioactive element artificially produced from plutonium
CURL, -ED, -S *n, vb*
CURLER, -S *n* pin or small tube for curling hair
CURLEW, -S *n*
CURLI *pl n* curled hairlike processes on the surface of the E. coli bacterium
CURLIER ▸ **curly**
CURLIES *pl n* as in **have by the short and curlies** have completely in one's power
CURLILY ▸ **curly**
CURLING *n* game like bowls, played with heavy stones on ice
CURLS ▸ **curl**

CURLY, CURLIER *adj* tending to curl
CURN, -S *n* grain (of corn etc)
CURNEY *same as* ▸ **curny**
CURNIER ▸ **curny**
CURNS ▸ **curn**
CURNY, CURNIER *adj* granular
CURPEL, -S *same as* ▸ **crupper**
CURR, -ED, -ING, -S *vb* purr
CURRACH *a Scot or Irish name for* ▸ **coracle**
CURRAGH *same as* ▸ **currach**
CURRAN, -S *n* black bun
CURRANT *n*
CURRED ▸ **curr**
CURRENT *adj, n*
CURRIE *same as* ▸ **curry**
CURRIED ▸ **curry**
CURRIER *n* person who curries leather
CURRIES ▸ **curry**
CURRING ▸ **curr**
CURRISH *adj* of or like a cur
CURRS ▸ **curr**
CURRY, CURRIED, CURRIES *n, vb*
CURS ▸ **cur**
CURSAL ▸ **cursus**
CURSE, -S *vb, n*
CURSED ▸ **curse**
CURSER, -S ▸ **curse**
CURSES ▸ **curse**
CURSI ▸ **cursus**
CURSING ▸ **curse**
CURSIVE *n* handwriting done with joined letters ▹ *adj* of handwriting or print in which letters are joined in a flowing style
CURSOR, -S *n*
CURSORY *adj*
CURST *same as* ▸ **cursed**
CURSUS, CURSI *n* Neolithic parallel earthworks
CURT, -ER, -EST *adj*
CURTAIL *vb*
CURTAIN *n, vb*
CURTAL, -S *adj* cut short ▹ *n* animal whose tail has been docked
CURTANA *n* unpointed sword displayed at a coronation as an emblem of mercy
CURTATE *adj* shortened
CURTAXE *same as* > **curtalaxe**
CURTER ▸ **curt**
CURTEST ▸ **curt**
CURTESY *n* widower's life interest in his wife's estate
CURTLY ▸ **curt**
CURTSEY *same as* ▸ **curtsy**
CURTSY *n, vb*
CURULE *adj* (in ancient Rome) of the highest rank, esp one entitled to use a curule chair
CURVATE *adj* curved
CURVE, -D, -S, CURVING *n, vb*
CURVET, -S *n* horse's low leap with all four feet off the ground ▹ *vb* make such a leap
CURVEY *same as* ▸ **curvy**
CURVIER ▸ **curvy**
CURVING ▸ **curve**
CURVITY *n* curvedness
CURVY, CURVIER ▸ **curve**
CUSCUS *n* large Australian nocturnal possum
CUSEC, -S *n* unit of flow equal to 1 cubic foot per second
CUSH, -ES *n* cushion
CUSHAT, -S *n* wood pigeon
CUSHAW, -S *same as* ▸ **cashaw**
CUSHES ▸ **cush**
CUSHIE, -S *same as* ▸ **cushat**
CUSHIER ▸ **cushy**
CUSHIES ▸ **cushie**
CUSHILY ▸ **cushy**
CUSHION *n, vb*
CUSHTY *interj* exclamation of pleasure, agreement, approval, etc
CUSHY, CUSHIER *adj* easy
CUSK, -S *n* type of food fish of northern coastal waters, with a single long dorsal fin
CUSP, -S *n*
CUSPAL ▸ **cusp**
CUSPATE *adj* having a cusp or cusps
CUSPED *same as* ▸ **cuspate**
CUSPID, -S *n* tooth having one point
CUSPIER ▸ **cuspy**
CUSPIS *n* in anatomy, a tapering structure
CUSPS ▸ **cusp**
CUSPY, CUSPIER *adj* (of a computer program) well-designed and user-friendly

CUSS, -ES, -ING *n, vb*
CUSSED *adj* obstinate
CUSSER, -S *same as* ▶ **cooser**
CUSSES ▶ **cuss**
CUSSING ▶ **cuss**
CUSSO, -S *n* tree of the rose family
CUSTARD *n*
CUSTOCK *same as* ▶ **castock**
CUSTODE *n* custodian
CUSTODY *n*
CUSTOM *n, adj*
CUSTOMS *n* duty charged on imports or exports
CUSTOS *n* superior in the Franciscan religious order
CUSTREL *n* knave
CUSUM, -S *n* analysis technique used in statistics
CUT, -S *vb*
CUTAWAY *adj* (of a drawing or model) having part of the outside omitted to reveal the inside ▷ *n* man's coat cut diagonally from the front waist to the back of the knees
CUTBACK *n*
CUTBANK *n* steep banking at a bend in a river
CUTCH, -ES *same as* ▶ **catechu**
CUTCHA *adj* crude
CUTCHES ▶ **cutch**
CUTDOWN *n* decrease
CUTE, -R, -ST *adj*
CUTELY ▶ **cute**
CUTER ▶ **cute**
CUTES ▶ **cutis**
CUTESIE *same as* ▶ **cutesy**
CUTEST ▶ **cute**
CUTESY *adj* affectedly cute or coy
CUTEY, -S *same as* ▶ **cutie**
CUTICLE *n*
CUTIE, -S *n* person regarded as appealing or attractive
CUTIKIN *same as* > **cuitikin**
CUTIN, -S *n* waxy waterproof substance
CUTIS, CUTES, -ES *a technical name for the* ▶ **skin**
CUTLAS *same as* ▶ **cutlass**
CUTLASS *n*
CUTLER, -S *n* maker of cutlery
CUTLERY *n* knives, forks, and spoons
CUTLET, -S *n*
CUTLINE *n* caption
CUTOFF, -S *n*
CUTOUT, -S *n*
CUTOVER *n* transitional period in an IT system changeover
CUTS ▶ **cut**
CUTTAGE *n* propagation by using parts taken from growing plants
CUTTER, -S *n*
CUTTIER ▶ **cutty**
CUTTIES ▶ **cutty**
CUTTING ▶ **cut**
CUTTLE, -D, -S *vb* to whisper
CUTTO, -ES *n* large knife
CUTTOE *same as* ▶ **cutto**
CUTTOES ▶ **cutto**
CUTTY, CUTTIER, CUTTIES *adj* short or cut short ▷ *n* something cut short
CUTUP, -S *n* joker or prankster
CUTWORK *n* type of openwork embroidery
CUTWORM *n* caterpillar of various types of moth
CUVEE, -S *n* individual batch or blend of wine
CUVETTE *n* shallow dish or vessel for holding liquid
CUZ, -ES, -ZES *n* cousin

> **Cuz** is another word for **cousin**, great for using the Z.

CUZZIE, -S *n* close friend or family member
CWM, -S *same as* ▶ **cirque**

> **Cwm** is a Welsh word meaning a valley, a useful one to remember because it doesn't contain any vowels.

CWTCH, -ED, -ES *vb* cuddle or be cuddled

> This delightful Welsh word meaning to cuddle is not likely to come up, but it might just help you out of a tight spot one day when your rack is all consonants.

CYAN, -S *n* highly saturated green-blue ▷ *adj* of this colour
CYANATE *n* any salt or ester of cyanic acid
CYANIC *adj* as in **cyanic acid** colourless poisonous volatile liquid acid
CYANID, -S *same as* ▶ **cyanide**
CYANIDE *n* extremely poisonous chemical compound ▷ *vb* treat with cyanide
CYANIDS ▶ **cyanid**
CYANIN, -S *same as* ▶ **cyanine**
CYANINE *n* blue dye used in photography
CYANINS ▶ **cyanin**
CYANISE *same as* ▶ **cyanize**
CYANITE *variant spelling of* ▶ **kyanite**
CYANIZE *vb* turn into cyanide
CYANO *adj* containing cyanogen
CYANOSE *same as* > **cyanosis**
CYANS ▶ **cyan**
CYATHI ▶ **cyathus**
CYATHIA > **cyathium**
CYATHUS, CYATHI *n* ancient measure of wine
CYBER *adj*
CYBORG, -S *n*
CYBRID, -S *n* cytoplasmic hybrid
CYCAD, -S *n* type of tropical or subtropical plant
CYCAS, -ES *n* palm tree of the genus Cycas
CYCASIN *n* glucoside, toxic to mammals, occurring in cycads
CYCLASE *n* enzyme which acts as a catalyst in the formation of a cyclic compound
CYCLE, -D, -S *vb, n*
CYCLER, -S *same as* ▶ **cyclist**
CYCLERY *n* business dealing in bicycles and bicycle accessories
CYCLES ▶ **cycle**
CYCLIC *adj* recurring or revolving in cycles
CYCLIN, -S *n* type of protein
CYCLING ▶ **cycle**
CYCLINS ▶ **cyclin**
CYCLISE *same as* ▶ **cyclize**
CYCLIST *n*
CYCLIZE *vb* be cyclical
CYCLO, -S *n* type of rickshaw
CYCLOID *adj* resembling a circle ▷ *n* mathematical curve
CYCLONE *n*
CYCLOPS *n* type of copepod characterized by having one eye
CYCLOS ▶ **cyclo**
CYCLUS *n* cycle
CYDER, -S *same as* ▶ **cider**
CYESIS, CYESES *the technical name for* > **pregnancy**
CYGNET, -S *n*
CYLIX, CYLICES, CYLIKES *variant of* ▶ **kylix**
CYMA, -E, -S *n* moulding with a double curve, part concave and part convex
CYMAR, -S *n* woman's short fur-trimmed jacket, popular in the 17th and 18th centuries
CYMAS ▶ **cyma**
CYMATIA > **cymatium**
CYMBAL, -S *n*
CYMBALO *another name for* > **dulcimer**
CYMBALS ▶ **cymbal**
CYME, -S *n* type of flower cluster
CYMENE, -S *n* colourless insoluble liquid
CYMES ▶ **cyme**
CYMLIN, -S *same as* ▶ **cymling**
CYMLING *n* pattypan squash
CYMLINS ▶ **cymlin**
CYMOID *adj* resembling a cyme or cyma
CYMOL, -S *same as* ▶ **cymene**
CYMOSE *adj* having the characteristics of a cyme
CYMOUS *adj* relating to a cyme
CYNIC, -S *n, adj*
CYNICAL *adj* believing that people always act selfishly
CYNICS ▶ **cynic**
CYPHER, -S *same as* ▶ **cipher**
CYPRES *n* legal doctrine
CYPRESS *n*
CYPRIAN *n* licentious or profligate person
CYPRID, -S *n* small bivalve freshwater crustacean

CYPRINE *adj* relating to carp ▷ *n* type of silicate mineral
CYPRIS *n* small bivalve freshwater crustacean
CYPRUS *same as* ▶ **cypress**
CYPSELA *n* dry one-seeded fruit of the daisy and related plants
CYST, -S *n*
CYSTEIN *same as* > **cysteine**
CYSTIC *adj* of, relating to, or resembling a cyst
CYSTID, -S *n* fossil echinoderm of an extinct order of sea lilies
CYSTINE *n* sulphur-containing amino acid
CYSTOID *adj* resembling a cyst or bladder ▷ *n* tissue mass that resembles a cyst but lacks an outer membrane
CYSTS ▶ **cyst**
CYTASE, -S *n* cellulose-dissolving enzyme
CYTE, -S *n* biological cell
CYTISUS, CYTISI *n* any plant of the broom genus, Cytisus
CYTODE, -S *n* mass of protoplasm without a nucleus
CYTOID *adj* resembling a cell
CYTON, -S *n* main part of a neuron
CYTOSOL *n* solution in a biological cell
CZAPKA, -S *n* leather and felt peaked military helmet of Polish origin
CZAR, -S *n*
CZARDAS *n* Hungarian national dance of alternating slow and fast sections
CZARDOM ▶ **czar**
CZARINA *n*
CZARISM *n* system of government by a czar
CZARIST *n* supporter of a czar
CZARS ▶ **czar**

Dd

DA, -S *n* Burmese knife
DAAL, -S *n* (in Indian cookery) split pulses
DAB, -BED, -BING, -S *vb, n*
DABBA, -S *n* in Indian cookery, a round metal box used to transport hot food
DABBED ▸ **dab**
DABBER, -S *n* pad used by printers for applying ink by hand
DABBING ▸ **dab**
DABBITY *n* temporary tattoo
DABBLE, -D, -S *vb* be involved in something superficially
DABBLER ▸ **dabble**
DABBLES ▸ **dabble**
DABS ▸ **dab**
DABSTER *n* incompetent or amateurish worker
DACE, -S *n* small European freshwater fish
DACHA, -S *n* country cottage in Russia
DACITE, -S *n* volcanic rock
DACK, -ED, -ING, -S *vb* remove the trousers from (someone) by force
DACKER, -S *vb* walk slowly
DACKING ▸ **dack**
DACKS ▸ **dack**
DACOIT, -S *n* (in India and Myanmar) a member of a gang of armed robbers
DACOITY *n* (in India and Myanmar) robbery by an armed gang
DACRON, -S *n* US tradename for a synthetic polyester fibre or fabric
DACTYL, -S *n* metrical foot of three syllables, one long followed by two short
DACTYLI > **dactylus**
DACTYLS ▸ **dactyl**
DAD, -DED, -DING, -S *n* father ▹ *vb* act or treat as a father
DADA, -S *n* nihilistic artistic movement of the early 20th century
DADAISM *same as* ▸ **dada**
DADAIST ▸ **dada**
DADAS ▸ **dada**
DADBOD, -S *n* untoned male physique
DADDED ▸ **dad**
DADDIES ▸ **daddy**
DADDING ▸ **dad**
DADDLE, -D, -S *vb* walk unsteadily
DADDOCK *n* core of a dead tree
DADDY, DADDIES *n*
DADGUM *mild form of* ▸ **damned**
DADO, -ED, -ES, -ING, -S *n* lower part of an interior wall decorated differently from the upper part ▹ *vb* provide with a dado
DADS ▸ **dad**
DAE, -ING, -S *a Scot word for* ▸ **do**
DAEDAL *adj* skilful or intricate
DAEING ▸ **dae**
DAEMON, -S *same as* ▸ **demon**
DAES ▸ **dae**
DAFF, -ED, -S *vb* frolic
DAFFIER ▸ **daffy**
DAFFIES ▸ **daffy**
DAFFILY ▸ **daffy**
DAFFING ▸ **daff**
DAFFS ▸ **daff**
DAFFY, DAFFIER, DAFFIES *adj* daft ▹ *n* daffodil
DAFT, -ER, -EST *adj*
DAFTAR, -S *Indian word for* ▸ **office**
DAFTER ▸ **daft**
DAFTEST ▸ **daft**

DAFTIE, -S *n* foolish person
DAFTLY ▸ **daft**
DAG, -GED, -S *n* daglock ▹ *vb* cut daglocks from sheep
DAGABA, -S *n* dome-shaped Buddhist shrine
DAGGED ▸ **dag**
DAGGER, -S *n, vb*
DAGGIER ▸ **daggy**
DAGGING ▸ **dag**
DAGGLE, -D, -S *vb* trail through water
DAGGY, DAGGIER *adj* amusing
DAGLOCK *n* dung-caked lock of wool around the hindquarters of a sheep
DAGOBA, -S *n* dome-shaped Buddhist shrine
DAGS ▸ **dag**
DAGWOOD *n* European shrub
DAH, -S *n* long sound used in Morse code
DAHL, -S *same as* ▸ **dhal**
DAHLIA, -S *n*
DAHLS ▸ **dahl**
DAHOON, -S *n* evergreen shrub
DAHS ▸ **dah**
DAIDLE, -D, -S *vb* waddle about
DAIKER, -S *vb* walk slowly
DAIKO, -S *n* Japanese drum
DAIKON, -S *another name for* ▸ **mooli**
DAIKOS ▸ **daiko**
DAILY, DAILIES *adj, adv, n*
DAIMEN *adj* occasional
DAIMIO, -S *same as* ▸ **daimyo**
DAIMOKU *n* Nichiren Buddhist chant
DAIMON, -S *same as* ▸ **demon**
DAIMYO, -S *n* magnate in Japan from the 11th to the 19th century
DAINE, -D, -S, DAINING *vb* condescend
DAINT, -S *adj* dainty ▹ *n* dainty
DAINTY *adj, n*
DAIRY, DAIRIES *n, adj*
DAIS, -ES *n* raised platform in a hall, used by a speaker
DAISIED ▸ **daisy**
DAISY, DAISIES *n*
DAK *n* system of mail delivery or passenger transport

> A **dak** is an old mail or transport system, often useful for disposing of the K.

DAKER, -ED, -S *vb* walk slowly
DAKOIT, -S *same as* ▸ **dacoit**
DAKOITI *same as* ▸ **dakoit**
DAKOITS ▸ **dakoit**
DAKOITY *n* armed robbery
DAKS *an informal name for* > **trousers**
DAL, -S *same as* > **decalitre**
DALAPON *n* herbicide
DALASI, -S *n* standard monetary unit of The Gambia, divided into 100 bututs
DALE, -S *n*
DALED, -S *same as* ▸ **daleth**
DALEDH, -S *n* letter of the Hebrew alphabet
DALEDS ▸ **daled**
DALES ▸ **dale**
DALETH, -S *n* fourth letter of the Hebrew alphabet
DALGYTE *another name for* ▸ **bilby**
DALI, -S *n* type of tree
DALLES, DALLE *pl n* stretch of a river between high rock walls, with rapids and dangerous currents
DALLIED ▸ **dally**
DALLIER ▸ **dally**
DALLIES ▸ **dally**
DALLOP, -S *n* semisolid lump
DALLY, DALLIED, DALLIES *vb*
DALS ▸ **dal**
DALT, -S *n* foster child
DALTON, -S *n* atomic mass unit
DALTS ▸ **dalt**
DAM, -MED, -MING, -S *n, vb*
DAMAGE, -D *vb, n*
DAMAGER ▸ **damage**
DAMAGES *pl n* money awarded as compensation for injury or loss
DAMAN, -S *n* the Syrian rock hyrax
DAMAR, -S *same as* ▸ **dammar**
DAMASK, -S *n* fabric with a pattern woven into it, used for tablecloths etc ▹ *vb*

ornament (metal) by etching or inlaying, usually with gold or silver
DAMBROD *n* draughtboard
DAME, -S *n*
DAMFOOL *adj* foolish ▷ *n* foolish person
DAMIANA *n* herbal medicine
DAMMAR, -S *n* any of various resins obtained from SE Asian trees
DAMME *interj* exclamation of surprise
DAMMED ▶ **dam**
DAMMER, -S *same as* ▶ **dammar**
DAMMING ▶ **dam**
DAMMIT *interj* exclamation of surprise
DAMN, -ING, -S *interj, adj, adv, vb*
DAMNED *adj* condemned to hell ▷ *adv* extremely
DAMNER, -S *n* person who damns
DAMNEST *same as* ▶ **damnedest**
DAMNIFY *vb* cause loss or damage to (a person)
DAMNING ▶ **damn**
DAMNS ▶ **damn**
DAMOSEL *same as* ▶ **damsel**
DAMOZEL *n* young woman
DAMP, -ED, -EST, -S *adj, n, vb*
DAMPEN, -S *vb*
DAMPER, -S *n* movable plate to regulate the draught in a fire
DAMPEST ▶ **damp**
DAMPIER ▶ **dampy**
DAMPING *n* act of moistening
DAMPISH ▶ **damp**
DAMPLY ▶ **damp**
DAMPS ▶ **damp**
DAMPY, DAMPIER *adj* damp
DAMS ▶ **dam**
DAMSEL, -S *n*
DAMSON, -S *n*
DAN, -S *n* in judo, any of the 10 black-belt grades of proficiency
DANAZOL *n* synthetic male hormone
DANCE, -D, -S *vb, n*
DANCER, -S ▶ **dance**
DANCES ▶ **dance**
DANCEY, DANCIER *adj* of, relating to, or resembling dance music
DANCING ▶ **dance**
DANCY *adj* (of music) appropriate for dancing
DANDER, -S *n* stroll ▷ *vb* stroll
DANDIER ▶ **dandy**
DANDIES ▶ **dandy**
DANDIFY *vb* dress like or cause to resemble a dandy
DANDILY ▶ **dandy**
DANDLE, -D, -S *vb* move (a child) up and down on one's knee
DANDLER ▶ **dandle**
DANDLES ▶ **dandle**
DANDY, DANDIER, DANDIES *n, adj*
DANELAW *n* Danish law in parts of Anglo-Saxon England
DANG, -ED, -EST, -ING, -S *vb* euphemism for damn, meaning condemn ▷ *adj* euphemism for damn, meaning extreme
DANGER, -S *n, vb*
DANGEST ▶ **dang**
DANGING ▶ **dang**
DANGLE, -D, -S *vb* hang loosely ▷ *n* act of dangling or something that dangles
DANGLER ▶ **dangle**
DANGLES ▶ **dangle**
DANGLY ▶ **dangle**
DANGS ▶ **dang**
DANIO, -S *n* type of tropical freshwater fish
DANISH *n* sweet pastry
DANK, -ER, -EST, -S *adj, n*
DANKISH ▶ **dank**
DANKLY ▶ **dank**
DANKS ▶ **dank**
DANNY, DANNIES *n* hand (used esp when addressing children)
DANS ▶ **dan**
DANSAK, -S *n* type of Indian dish
DANSEUR *n* male ballet dancer
DANT, -ED, -ING, -S *vb* intimidate
DANTON, -S *same as* ▶ **daunton**
DANTS ▶ **dant**
DAP, -PED, -PING, -S *vb* engage in a type of fly fishing
DAPHNE, -S *n* ornamental Eurasian shrub
DAPHNIA *n* type of water flea

DAPHNID *n* water flea
DAPPED ▶ **dap**
DAPPER, -S *adj, n*
DAPPING ▶ **dap**
DAPPLE, -D, -S *vb* mark or become marked with spots or patches of a different colour ▷ *n* mottled or spotted markings ▷ *adj* marked with dapples or spots
DAPS ▶ **dap**
DAPSONE *n* antimicrobial drug
DAQUIRI *n* rum cocktail
DARAF, -S *n* unit of elastance equal to a reciprocal farad
DARB, -S *n* something excellent
DARBAR, -S *n* hall in a Sikh temple
DARBIES *pl n* handcuffs
DARBS ▶ **darb**
DARCY, DARCIES, -S *n* unit expressing the permeability coefficient of rock
DARE, -D, -S *vb, n*
DAREFUL *adj* daring
DARER, -S ▶ **dare**
DARES ▶ **dare**
DARESAY *vb* venture to say
DARG, -S *n* day's work
DARGA, -S *same as* ▶ **dargah**
DARGAH, -S *n* tomb of a Muslim saint
DARGAS ▶ **darga**
DARGLE, -S *n* wooded hollow
DARGS ▶ **darg**
DARI, -S *n* variety of sorghum
DARIC, -S *n* gold coin of ancient Persia
DARING, -S *adj* willing to take risks ▷ *n* courage to do dangerous things
DARIOLE *n* small cup-shaped mould
DARIS ▶ **dari**
DARK, -ED, -ER, -EST, -ING, -S *adj, n, vb*
DARKEN, -S *vb*
DARKER ▶ **dark**
DARKEST ▶ **dark**
DARKING ▶ **dark**
DARKISH ▶ **dark**
DARKLE, -D, -S *vb* grow dark
DARKLY ▶ **dark**
DARKNET *n* covert communication network on the internet
DARKS ▶ **dark**
DARLING *n, adj*
DARN, -S *vb, n*
DARNED *adj* damned
DARNEL, -S *n* weed that grows in grain fields
DARNER, -S ▶ **darn**
DARNEST *same as* > **darndest**
DARNING ▶ **darn**
DARNS ▶ **darn**
DAROGHA *n* in India, a manager
DARRAIN *vb* clear of guilt
DARRAYN *vb* clear of guilt
DARRE, -D, -S, DARRING *vb* archaic spelling of dare
DARSHAN *n* Hindu blessing
DART, -ED *n, vb*
DARTER, -S *n* type of aquatic bird
DARTING ▶ **dart**
DARTLE, -D, -S *vb* move swiftly
DARTRE, -S *n* skin disease
DARTS *n* game in which darts are thrown at a dartboard
DARZI, -S *n* tailor in India
DAS ▶ **da**
DASH, -ED, -ES *vb, n*
DASHCAM *n* video camera on a vehicle's dashboard
DASHED ▶ **dash**
DASHEEN *another name for* ▶ **taro**
DASHEKI *same as* ▶ **dashiki**
DASHER, -S *n*
DASHES ▶ **dash**
DASHI, -S *n* clear stock made from dried fish and kelp
DASHIER ▶ **dashy**
DASHIKI *n* large loose-fitting buttonless upper garment
DASHING *adj* stylish and attractive
DASHIS ▶ **dashi**
DASHPOT *n* device for damping vibrations
DASHY, DASHIER *adj* showy
DASSIE, -S *n* type of hoofed rodent-like animal
DASTARD *n* contemptible sneaking coward

DASYPOD *n* armadillo
DASYURE *n* small marsupial of Australia, New Guinea, and adjacent islands
DATA *n*
DATABLE ▶ **date**
DATABUS *n* pathway transferring data between computer parts
DATAL, -S *adj* slow-witted ▷ *n* day labour
DATARIA *n* Roman Catholic office
DATARY *n* head of the dataria
DATCHA, -S *same as* ▶ **dacha**
DATE, -S *n, vb*
DATED *adj* old-fashioned
DATEDLY ▶ **dated**
DATER, -S *n* person who dates
DATES ▶ **date**
DATING, -S *n* any of several techniques for establishing the age of objects
DATIVAL ▶ **dative**
DATIVE, -S *adj* denoting a grammatical case ▷ *n* grammatical case
DATO, -S *n* chief of any of certain Muslim tribes in the Philippine Islands
DATTO, -S *n* Datsun car
DATUM, -S *n* single piece of information in the form of a fact or statistic
DATURA, -S *n* type of plant
DATURIC ▶ **datura**
DAUB, -ED, -S *vb, n*
DAUBE, -S *n* braised meat stew
DAUBED ▶ **daub**
DAUBER, -S ▶ **daub**
DAUBERY *n* act or an instance of daubing
DAUBES ▶ **daube**
DAUBIER ▶ **dauby**
DAUBING ▶ **daub**
DAUBRY *n* unskilful painting
DAUBS ▶ **daub**
DAUBY, DAUBIER ▶ **daub**
DAUD, -ED, -ING, -S *n* lump or chunk of something ▷ *vb* (in dialect) whack
DAULT, -S *n* foster child
DAUNDER *vb* stroll
DAUNER, -S *vb* stroll
DAUNT, -ED, -S *vb* intimidate
DAUNTER ▶ **daunt**
DAUNTON *vb* dishearten
DAUNTS ▶ **daunt**
DAUPHIN *n* (formerly) eldest son of the king of France
DAUR, -ED, -ING, -S *a* *Scot word for* ▶ **dare**
DAUT, -ED, -ING, -S *vb* fondle
DAUTIE, -S *n* darling
DAUTING ▶ **daut**
DAUTS ▶ **daut**
DAVEN, -ED, -S *vb* pray
DAVIDIA *n* Chinese shrub
DAVIES ▶ **davy**
DAVIT, -S *n* crane, usu one of a pair, at a ship's side, for lowering and hoisting a lifeboat
DAVY, DAVIES *n* miner's safety lamp
DAW, -ED, -EN, -ING, -S *n* archaic, dialect, or poetic name for a jackdaw ▷ *vb* old word for dawn

> This is another name for a **jackdaw**. It is worth remembering that not only does this little word take D, K, N, S and T at the back, to make **dawd, dawk, dawn, daws** and **dawt**, but you can put an A on the front of it to make **adaw**.

DAWAH, -S *n* practice of educating non-Muslims about the message of Islam
DAWBAKE *n* foolish or slow-witted person
DAWBRY *n* unskilful painting
DAWCOCK *n* male jackdaw
DAWD, -ED, -ING, -S *vb* thump
DAWDLE, -D, -S *vb*
DAWDLER ▶ **dawdle**
DAWDLES ▶ **dawdle**
DAWDS ▶ **dawd**
DAWED ▶ **daw**
DAWEN ▶ **daw**
DAWING ▶ **daw**
DAWISH ▶ **daw**
DAWK, -S *same as* ▶ **dak**
DAWN, -ED, -S *n, vb*
DAWNER, -S *vb* stroll
DAWNEY *adj* (of a person) dull or slow
DAWNING ▶ **dawn**
DAWNS ▶ **dawn**

DAWS ▸ **daw**
DAWT, -ED, -ING, -S *vb* fondle
DAWTIE, -S *n* darling
DAWTING ▸ **dawt**
DAWTS ▸ **dawt**
DAY *n*
DAYAN, -IM, -S *n* senior rabbi, esp one who sits in a religious court
DAYBED, -S *n*
DAYBOAT *n* small sailing boat with no sleeping accommodation
DAYBOOK *n* book in which transactions are recorded as they occur
DAYBOY, -S *n* boy who attends a boarding school but returns home each evening
DAYCARE *n*
DAYCH, -ED, -ES *vb* thatch
DAYFLY *another name for* ▸ **mayfly**
DAYGIRL *n* girl who attends a boarding school but returns home each evening
DAYGLO *n* fluorescent colours
DAYGLOW *n* fluorescent colours
DAYLILY *n* any of various plants having lily-like flowers
DAYLIT > **daylight**
DAYLONG *adv* lasting the entire day
DAYMARE *n* bad dream during the day
DAYMARK *n* navigation aid
DAYNT, -S *adj* dainty ▹ *n* thing or condition that is extravagant or best
DAYPACK *n* small rucksack
DAYROOM *n*
DAYS *adv* during the day, esp regularly
DAYSACK *n* rucksack
DAYSAIL *vb* take a day trip on a sailing boat or yacht
DAYSIDE *n* side of a planet nearest the sun
DAYSMAN, DAYSMEN *n* umpire
DAYSTAR *a poetic word for* ▸ **sun**
DAYTALE *n* day labour
DAYTIME *n*
DAYWEAR *n* clothes for everyday or informal wear
DAYWORK *n*
DAZE, -D, -S, DAZING *vb, n*
DAZEDLY ▸ **daze**
DAZER, -S ▸ **daze**
DAZES ▸ **daze**
DAZING ▸ **daze**
DAZZLE, -D, -S *vb, n*
DAZZLER ▸ **dazzle**
DAZZLES ▸ **dazzle**
DE *prep* of or from
DEACON, -S *n, vb*
DEAD, -ED, -ERS, -EST, -ING, -S *adj, n, adv, vb*
DEADBOY *same as* ▸ **deadman**
DEADED ▸ **dead**
DEADEN, -S *vb*
DEADER *n* dead person
DEADERS ▸ **dead**
DEADEST ▸ **dead**
DEADEYE *n* either of two disclike blocks used to tighten a shroud on a boat
DEADING ▸ **dead**
DEADLY *adj* likely to cause death ▹ *adv* extremely
DEADMAN, DEADMEN *n* item used in construction
DEADPAN *adv* showing no emotion or expression ▹ *adj* deliberately emotionless ▹ *n* deadpan expression or manner
DEADS ▸ **dead**
DEAF, -ER, -EST *adj*
DEAFEN, -S *vb*
DEAFER ▸ **deaf**
DEAFEST ▸ **deaf**
DEAFISH ▸ **deaf**
DEAFLY ▸ **deaf**
DEAIR, -ED, -S *vb* remove air from
DEAL, -ING, -S, -T *n, vb, adj*
DEALATE *adj* (of insects) having lost their wings after mating ▹ *n* insect that has shed its wings
DEALER, -S *n* person whose business involves buying and selling
DEALIGN *vb* fall out of agreement with (a political party)
DEALING ▸ **deal**
DEALS ▸ **deal**
DEALT ▸ **deal**
DEAN, -ED, -ING, -S *n* chief administrative official of a college or university faculty

▷ *vb* punish (a student) by sending them to the dean
DEANER, -S *n* shilling
DEANERY *n* office or residence of a dean
DEANING ▶ **dean**
DEANS ▶ **dean**
DEAR, -ER, -S *n, adj*
DEARE, -D, -S, DEARING *vb* harm
DEARER ▶ **dear**
DEARES ▶ **deare**
DEAREST *n* term of affection
DEARIE *same as* ▶ **deary**
DEARIES ▶ **deary**
DEARING ▶ **deare**
DEARLY *adv* very much
DEARN, -ED, -S *vb* hide
DEARNLY ▶ **dearn**
DEARNS ▶ **dearn**
DEARS ▶ **dear**
DEARTH, -S *n*
DEARY, DEARIES *n* term of affection: now often sarcastic or facetious
DEASH, -ED, -ES *vb* remove ash from
DEASIL, -S *n* motion towards the sun
DEASIUL *n* motion towards the sun
DEASOIL *n* motion towards the sun
DEATH, -S *n*
DEATHLY *adv* like death ▷ *adj* resembling death
DEATHS ▶ **death**
DEATHY ▶ **death**
DEAVE, -D, -S, DEAVING *vb* deafen
DEAW, -ED, -ING, -S *n* archaic spelling of dew ▷ *vb* cover with dew
DEAWIE ▶ **deaw**
DEAWING ▶ **deaw**
DEAWS ▶ **deaw**
DEAWY ▶ **deaw**
DEB, -S *n* debutante
DEBACLE *n*
DEBAG, -S *vb* remove the trousers from (someone) by force
DEBAR, -S *vb* prevent, bar
DEBARK, -S *vb* remove the bark from (a tree)
DEBARS ▶ **debar**
DEBASE, -D, -S *vb* lower in value, quality, or character
DEBASER ▶ **debase**
DEBASES ▶ **debase**
DEBATE, -D, -S *n, vb*
DEBATER ▶ **debate**
DEBATES ▶ **debate**
DEBAUCH *vb* make (someone) bad or corrupt ▷ *n* instance or period of extreme dissipation
DEBBY, DEBBIER, DEBBIES *n* debutante ▷ *adj* of, or resembling a debutante
DEBE, -S *n* tin
DEBEAK, -S *vb* remove part of the beak of poultry
DEBEARD *vb* remove the beard from a mussel
DEBEL, -S *vb* beat in war
DEBES ▶ **debe**
DEBILE *adj* lacking strength
DEBIT, -ED, -S *n, vb*
DEBITOR *n* person in debt
DEBITS ▶ **debit**
DEBONE, -D, -S *vb* remove bones from
DEBONER ▶ **debone**
DEBONES ▶ **debone**
DEBOSH *vb* debauch
DEBOSS *vb* carve a design into
DEBOUCH *vb* move out from a narrow place to a wider one ▷ *n* outlet or passage, as for the exit of troops
DEBRIDE *vb* remove dead tissue from
DEBRIEF *vb*
DEBRIS *n*
DEBS ▶ **deb**
DEBT, -S *n*
DEBTED *adj* in debt
DEBTEE, -S *n* person owed a debt
DEBTOR, -S *n*
DEBTS ▶ **debt**
DEBUD, -S *same as* ▶ **disbud**
DEBUG, -S *vb* find and remove defects in (a computer program) ▷ *n* something that locates and removes defects in a device, system, etc
DEBUNK, -S *vb*
DEBUR, -S *vb* remove burs from
DEBURR, -S *vb* remove burrs from
DEBURS ▶ **debur**
DEBUS, -ED, -ES *vb* unload (goods) or (esp of troops) to alight from a motor vehicle
DEBUT, -ED, -S *n, vb*
DEBYE, -S *n* unit of electric dipole moment

DECAD, -S *n* ten years
DECADAL ▸ **decade**
DECADE, -S *n*
DECADS ▸ **decad**
DECAF, -S *n* decaffeinated coffee ▹ *adj* decaffeinated
DECAFF, -S *n* decaffeinated coffee
DECAFS ▸ **decaf**
DECAGON *n* geometric figure with ten faces
DECAL, -ED, -S *vb* transfer (a design) by decalcomania
DECALOG *same as* > **decalogue**
DECALS ▸ **decal**
DECAMP, -S *vb*
DECAN, -S *n* one of three divisions of a sign of the zodiac
DECANAL *adj* of or relating to a dean or deanery
DECANE, -S *n* liquid alkane hydrocarbon
DECANI *adj* to be sung by the decanal side of a choir
DECANS ▸ **decan**
DECANT, -S *vb* pour (a liquid) from one container to another
DECAPOD *n* creature, such as a crab, with five pairs of walking limbs ▹ *adj* of, relating to, or belonging to these creatures
DECARB, -S *vb* decarbonize
DECARE, -S *n* ten ares or 1000 square metres
DECAY, -ED, -S *vb, n*
DECAYER ▸ **decay**
DECAYS ▸ **decay**
DECCIE, -S *n* decoration
DECEASE *n*
DECEIT, -S *n*
DECEIVE *vb*
DECENCY *n*
DECENT *adj*
DECERN, -S *vb* decree or adjudge
DECIARE *n* one tenth of an are or 10 square metres
DECIBEL *n*
DECIDE, -S *vb*
DECIDED *adj* unmistakable
DECIDER *n* thing that determines who wins a match or championship
DECIDES ▸ **decide**
DECIDUA *n* membrane lining the uterus of some mammals during pregnancy
DECILE, -S *n* one of nine values of a variable divided into ten equal groups
DECIMAL *n, adj*
DECIME, -S *n* former French coin
DECK, -S *n, vb*
DECKED *adj* having a wooden deck or platform
DECKEL, -S *same as* ▸ **deckle**
DECKER, -S ▸ **deck**
DECKING *n* wooden platform in a garden
DECKLE, -D, -S *n* frame used to contain pulp on the mould in the making of handmade paper
DECKO, -ED, -S *n* look ▹ *vb* have a look
DECKS ▸ **deck**
DECLAIM *vb*
DECLARE *vb*
DECLASS *vb* lower in social status or position
DECLAW, -S *vb* remove claws from
DECLINE *vb, n*
DECO *adj* as in **art deco** style of art, jewellery, design, etc
DECOCT, -S *vb* extract the essence from (a substance) by boiling
DECODE, -D, -S *vb*
DECODER ▸ **decode**
DECODES ▸ **decode**
DECOKE, -D, -S *n* decarbonize
DECOLOR *vb* bleach
DECOR, -S *n* style in which a room or house is decorated
DECORUM *n*
DECOS *pl n* decorations
DECOY, -ED, -S *n* person or thing used to lure someone into danger ▹ *vb* lure away by means of a trick
DECOYER ▸ **decoy**
DECOYS ▸ **decoy**
DECREE, -D, -S *n, vb*
DECREER ▸ **decree**
DECREES ▸ **decree**
DECREET *n* final judgment or sentence of a court
DECREW, -S *vb* archaic word for decrease
DECRIAL ▸ **decry**
DECRIED ▸ **decry**
DECRIER ▸ **decry**

DECRIES ▸ **decry**
DECROWN *vb* depose
DECRY, DECRIED, DECRIES *vb*
DECRYPT *vb*
DECTET, -S *n* group of ten musicians
DECUMAN *n* large wave
DECUPLE *vb* increase by ten times ▹ *n* amount ten times as large as a given reference ▹ *adj* increasing tenfold
DECURIA *n* group of ten
DECURVE *vb* curve downwards
DECURY *n* (in ancient Rome) a body of ten men
DEDAL *same as* ▸ **daedal**
DEDANS *n* open gallery at the server's end of a real tennis court
DEDENDA > **dedendum**
DEDIMUS *n* document authorizing a person to act as a judge
DEDUCE, -D, -S *vb*
DEDUCT, -S *vb*
DEE, -ING, -S *a Scot word for* ▸ **die**
DEED, -ED, -ER, -EST, -ING, -S *n* something that is done ▹ *vb* convey or transfer (property) by deed ▹ *adj* Scots form of dead
DEEDFUL *adj* full of exploits
DEEDIER ▸ **deedy**
DEEDILY ▸ **deedy**
DEEDING ▸ **deed**
DEEDS ▸ **deed**
DEEDY, DEEDIER *adj* hard-working
DEEING ▸ **dee**
DEEJAY, -S *n* disc jockey ▹ *vb* work or act as a disc jockey
DEEK *interj* look at!
DEELY *adj* as in **deely boppers** hairband with two bobbing antennae-like attachments
DEEM, -ED, -ING, -S, DEMPT *vb*
DEEN, -S *n* din
DEEP, -ER, -EST, -S *adj* extending or situated far down, inwards, backwards, or sideways ▹ *n* any deep place on land or under water
DEEPEN, -S *vb*
DEEPER ▸ **deep**
DEEPEST ▸ **deep**
DEEPIE, -S *n* 3D film
DEEPLY ▸ **deep**
DEEPS ▸ **deep**
DEER, -S *n*
DEERE, -S *adj* serious ▹ *n* deer
DEERFLY *n* insect related to the horsefly
DEERLET *n* small deer
DEERS ▸ **deer**
DEES ▸ **dee**
DEET, -S *n* insect repellent
DEEV, -S *n* mythical monster
DEEVE, -D, -S, DEEVING *vb* deafen
DEEVS ▸ **deev**
DEEWAN, -S *n* chief of a village in India
DEF, -FER, -FEST *adj* very good
DEFACE, -D, -S *vb*
DEFACER ▸ **deface**
DEFACES ▸ **deface**
DEFAME, -D, -S *vb*
DEFAMER ▸ **defame**
DEFAMES ▸ **defame**
DEFANG, -S *vb* remove the fangs of
DEFAST *adj* old form of defaced
DEFASTE *adj* old form of defaced
DEFAT, -S *vb* remove fat from
DEFAULT *n, vb*
DEFEAT, -S *vb, n*
DEFECT, -S *n, vb*
DEFENCE *n, vb*
DEFEND, -S *vb*
DEFENSE *same as* ▸ **defence**
DEFER, -S *vb*
DEFFER ▸ **def**
DEFFEST ▸ **def**
DEFFLY *archaic form of* ▸ **deftly**
DEFFO *interj* informal word meaning definitely
DEFI, -S *n* challenge
DEFIANT *adj*
DEFICIT *n*
DEFIED ▸ **defy**
DEFIER, -S ▸ **defy**
DEFIES ▸ **defy**
DEFILE, -D, -S *vb, n*
DEFILER ▸ **defile**
DEFILES ▸ **defile**
DEFINE, -D, -S *vb*
DEFINER ▸ **define**
DEFINES ▸ **define**
DEFIS ▸ **defi**
DEFLATE *vb*
DEFLEA, -S *vb* remove fleas from
DEFLECT *vb*
DEFLEX *vb* turn downwards

DEFO *interj* informal word meaning definitely
DEFOAM, -S *vb* remove foam from
DEFOCUS *vb*
DEFOG, -S *vb* clear of vapour
DEFORCE *vb* withhold (property, esp land) wrongfully or by force from the rightful owner
DEFORM, -S *vb*
DEFOUL, -S *vb* defile
DEFRAG, -S *vb* defragment
DEFRAUD *vb*
DEFRAY, -S *vb* provide money for (costs or expenses)
DEFROCK *vb* deprive (a priest) of priestly status
DEFROST *vb*
DEFROZE > **defreeze**
DEFT, -ER, -EST *adj*
DEFTLY ▸ **deft**
DEFUEL, -S *vb* remove fuel from
DEFUNCT *adj, n*
DEFUND, -S *vb* stop funds to
DEFUSE, -D, -S *vb*
DEFUSER ▸ **defuse**
DEFUSES ▸ **defuse**
DEFUZE, -D, -S *same as* ▸ **defuse**
DEFY, DEFIED, DEFIES, -ING *vb*
DEG, -GED, -GING, -S *vb* water (a plant, etc)
DEGAGE *adj* unconstrained in manner
DEGAME, -S *n* tree of South and Central America
DEGAMI, -S *same as* ▸ **degame**
DEGAS, -ES *vb* remove gas from (a container, vacuum tube, liquid, adsorbent, etc)
DEGAUSS *vb* demagnetize
DEGERM, -S *vb* remove germs from
DEGGED ▸ **deg**
DEGGING ▸ **deg**
DEGLAZE *vb* dilute meat sediments in (a pan) in order to make a sauce or gravy
DEGOUT, -S *n* disgust ▹ *vb* cover (something) with gouts or drops of something
DEGRADE *vb*
DEGRAS *n* emulsion used for dressing hides
DEGREE, -S *n*
DEGREED *adj* having a degree
DEGREES ▸ **degree**
DEGS ▸ **deg**
DEGU, -S *n* small S American rodent
DEGUM, -S *vb* remove gum from
DEGUS ▸ **degu**
DEGUST, -S *vb* taste, esp with care or relish
DEHAIR, -S *vb* remove hair
DEHISCE *vb* (of the seed capsules of some plants) to burst open spontaneously
DEHORN, -S *vb* remove or prevent the growth of the horns of (cattle, sheep, or goats)
DEHORS *prep* apart from
DEHORT, -S *vb* dissuade
DEI ▸ **deus**
DEICE, -D, -S, DEICING *vb* free or be freed of ice
DEICER, -S ▸ **deice**
DEICES ▸ **deice**
DEICIDE *n* act of killing a god
DEICING ▸ **deice**
DEICTIC *adj* proving by direct argument ▹ *n* term whose reference depends on the context
DEID, -ER, -EST, -S *a Scot word for* ▸ **dead**
DEIF, -ER, -EST *a Scot word for* ▸ **deaf**
DEIFIC *adj* making divine or exalting to the position of a god
DEIFIED ▸ **deify**
DEIFIER ▸ **deify**
DEIFIES ▸ **deify**
DEIFORM *adj* having the form or appearance of a god
DEIFY, DEIFIED, DEIFIES *vb* treat or worship as a god
DEIGN, -ED, -S *vb*
DEIL, -S *a Scot word for* ▸ **devil**
DEINDEX *vb* cause to become no longer index-linked
DEISEAL *n* motion towards the sun
DEISM, -S *n* belief in God but not in divine revelation
DEIST, -S ▸ **deism**
DEISTIC ▸ **deism**
DEISTS ▸ **deist**
DEITY, DEITIES *n*

DEIXIS, DEIXES *n* use or reference of a deictic word
DEJECT, -S *vb, adj*
DEJECTA *pl n* waste products excreted from the body
DEJECTS ▶ **deject**
DEJEUNE *n* lunch
DEKARE, -S *n* unit of measurement equal to ten ares
DEKE, -D, -ING, -S, DEKING *vb* make a deceptive movement ▷ *n* deceptive movement
DEKKO, -ED, -S *n* look ▷ *vb* have a look
DEL, -S *n* differential operator
DELAINE *n* sheer wool or wool and cotton fabric
DELAPSE *vb* be inherited
DELATE, -D, -S *vb* (formerly) to bring a charge against
DELATOR ▶ **delate**
DELAY, -ED, -S *vb, n*
DELAYER ▶ **delay**
DELAYS ▶ **delay**
DELE, -D, -ING, -S *n* sign indicating that typeset matter is to be deleted ▷ *vb* mark (matter to be deleted) with a dele
DELEAD, -S *vb* remove lead from
DELEAVE *vb* separate copies
DELEBLE *adj* able to be deleted
DELED ▶ **dele**
DELEING ▶ **dele**
DELENDA *pl n* items for deleting
DELES ▶ **dele**
DELETE, -D, -S *vb*
DELF, -S *n* kind of earthenware
DELFT, -S *n* type of earthenware
DELI, -S *n*
DELIBLE *adj* able to be deleted
DELICE, -S *n* delicacy
DELICT, -S *n* wrongful act for which the person injured has the right to a civil remedy
DELIGHT *n, vb*
DELIME, -D, -S *vb* remove lime from
DELIMIT *vb* mark or lay down the limits of
DELINK, -S *vb* remove or break a link
DELIRIA > **delirium**
DELIS ▶ **deli**
DELISH *adj* delicious
DELIST, -S *vb* remove from a list
DELIVER *vb*
DELL, -S *n*
DELLIER ▶ **delly**
DELLIES ▶ **delly**
DELLS ▶ **dell**
DELLY, DELLIER, DELLIES *n* delicatessen ▷ *adj* full of dells
DELO, -S *an informal word for* > **delegate**
DELOPE, -D, -S *vb* shoot into the air
DELOS ▶ **delo**
DELOUSE *vb* rid (a person or animal) of lice
DELPH, -S *n* kind of earthenware
DELPHIC *adj* obscure or ambiguous
DELPHIN *n* fatty substance from dolphin oil
DELPHS ▶ **delph**
DELS ▶ **del**
DELT, -S *n* deltoid muscle
DELTA, -S *n*
DELTAIC ▶ **delta**
DELTAS ▶ **delta**
DELTIC ▶ **delta**
DELTOID *n* muscle acting to raise the arm ▷ *adj* shaped like a Greek capital delta
DELTS ▶ **delt**
DELUBRA > **delubrum**
DELUDE, -D, -S *vb* deceive
DELUDER ▶ **delude**
DELUDES ▶ **delude**
DELUGE, -D, -S *n, vb*
DELUXE *adj*
DELVE, -D, -S, DELVING *vb*
DELVER, -S ▶ **delve**
DELVES ▶ **delve**
DELVING ▶ **delve**
DEMAGOG *same as* > **demagogue**
DEMAIN, -S *n* demesne
DEMAINE *n* demesne
DEMAINS ▶ **demain**
DEMAN, -S *vb* reduce the workforce of (a plant, industry, etc)
DEMAND, -S *vb, n*
DEMANS ▶ **deman**
DEMARK, -S *vb* demarcate
DEMAST, -S *vb* remove the mast from
DEMAYNE *n* demesne
DEME, -S *n* (in preclassical Greece)

the territory inhabited by a tribe
DEMEAN, -S *vb*
DEMEANE *n* demesne
DEMEANS ▸ **demean**
DEMENT, -S *vb* deteriorate mentally, esp because of old age
DEMENTI *n* denial
DEMENTS ▸ **dement**
DEMERGE *vb* separate a company from another
DEMERIT *n* fault, disadvantage ▹ *vb* deserve
DEMERSE *vb* immerse
DEMES ▸ **deme**
DEMESNE *n* land surrounding a house
DEMETON *n* insecticide
DEMIC *adj* of population
DEMIES ▸ **demy**
DEMIGOD *n* being who is part mortal, part god
DEMINER *n* person who removes mines
DEMISE, -D, -S *n, vb*
DEMISS *adj* humble
DEMIST, -S *vb* remove condensation from (a windscreen)
DEMIT, -S *vb* resign (an office, position, etc)
DEMIVEG *n* person who eats poultry and fish, but no red meat ▹ *adj* denoting a person who eats poultry and fish, but no red meat
DEMO, -ED, -ING *n, vb*
DEMOB, -S *vb* demobilize
DEMODE *adj* out of fashion
DEMODED *adj* out of fashion
DEMOED ▸ **demo**
DEMOI ▸ **demos**
DEMOING ▸ **demo**
DEMON, -S *n*
DEMONIC *adj* evil
DEMONRY ▸ **demon**
DEMONS ▸ **demon**
DEMONYM *n* name for the inhabitants of a place
DEMOS, DEMOI, -ES *n* people of a nation regarded as a political unit
DEMOTE, -D, -S *vb* reduce in status or rank
DEMOTIC *adj* of the common people ▹ *n* demotic script of ancient Egypt
DEMOUNT *vb*
DEMPT ▸ **deem**
DEMUR, -S *vb* raise objections or show reluctance ▹ *n* act of demurring
DEMURE, -D, -R, -S *adj* quiet, reserved, and rather shy ▹ *vb* archaic word meaning to look demure
DEMURS ▸ **demur**
DEMY, DEMIES *n* size of printing paper, 17½ by 22½ inches (444.5 × 571.5 mm)
DEN, -NED, -NING, -S *n* home of a wild animal ▹ *vb* live in or as if in a den
DENAR, -I, -S *n* monetary unit of North Macedonia, divided into 100 deni
DENARII > **denarius**
DENARS ▸ **denar**
DENARY *same as* > **denarius**
DENAY, -ED, -S *vb* old form of deny
DENCH *adj* excellent
DENDRON *same as* > **dendrite**
DENE, -S *n* narrow wooded valley
DENET, -S *vb* remove from the former Net Book Agreement
DENGUE, -S *n* viral disease transmitted by mosquitoes
DENI, -S *n* monetary unit of North Macedonia
DENIAL, -S *n* statement that something is not true
DENIED ▸ **deny**
DENIER, -S *n* unit of weight used to measure the fineness of nylon or silk
DENIES ▸ **deny**
DENIM *n*
DENIMED *adj* wearing denim
DENIMS *pl n* jeans or overalls made of denim
DENIS ▸ **deni**
DENIZEN *n* inhabitant ▹ *vb* make a denizen
DENNED ▸ **den**
DENNET, -S *n* carriage for one horse
DENNING ▸ **den**
DENOTE, -D, -S *vb*
DENS ▸ **den**
DENSE, -R, -ST *adj*
DENSELY ▸ **dense**
DENSER ▸ **dense**
DENSEST ▸ **dense**
DENSIFY *vb* make or become dense

DENSITY *n* degree to which something is filled or occupied
DENT, -ED, -ING, -S *n, vb*
DENTAL, -S *adj* of teeth or dentistry ▷ *n* dental consonant
DENTARY *n* lower jawbone with teeth
DENTATE *adj* having teeth or toothlike notches
DENTED ▶ **dent**
DENTEL, -S *n* architectural ornament
DENTEX *n* large predatory fish
DENTIL, -S *n* architectural ornament
DENTIN, -S *same as* ▶ **dentine**
DENTINE *n* hard dense tissue forming the bulk of a tooth
DENTING ▶ **dent**
DENTINS ▶ **dentin**
DENTIST *n*
DENTOID *adj* resembling a tooth
DENTS ▶ **dent**
DENTURE *n*
DENUDE, -D, -S *vb* remove the covering or protection from
DENUDER ▶ **denude**
DENUDES ▶ **denude**
DENY, DENIED, DENIES, -ING *vb*
DEODAND *n* thing forfeited to charity because it has caused a death
DEODAR, -S *n* Himalayan cedar with drooping branches
DEODARA *same as* ▶ **deodar**
DEODARS ▶ **deodar**
DEODATE *n* offering to God
DEONTIC *n* ethical concept such as obligation or permissibility
DEORBIT *vb* go out of orbit
DEOXY *adj* having less oxygen than a specified related compound
DEP, -S *n* small shop where newspapers, sweets, soft drinks, etc are sold
DEPAINT *vb* depict
DEPART, -S *vb*
DEPECHE *n* message ▷ *vb* dispatch; rid oneself of
DEPEND, -S *vb* put trust (in)
DEPERM, -S *vb* demagnetize (a ship or submarine)
DEPICT, -S *vb*
DEPLANE *vb* disembark from an aeroplane
DEPLETE *vb*
DEPLORE *vb*
DEPLOY, -S *vb*
DEPLUME *vb* deprive of feathers
DEPONE, -D, -S *vb* declare (something) under oath
DEPORT, -S *vb*
DEPOSAL *n* deposition; giving of testimony under oath
DEPOSE, -D, -S *vb*
DEPOSER ▶ **depose**
DEPOSES ▶ **depose**
DEPOSIT *vb, n*
DEPOT, -S *n* building where goods or vehicles are kept when not in use ▷ *adj* (of a drug) designed for gradual release
DEPRAVE *vb* make morally bad
DEPRESS *vb* make sad
DEPRIME *vb* remove the primer from a device
DEPRIVE *vb*
DEPS ▶ **dep**
DEPSIDE *n* organic chemical compound
DEPTH, -S *n*
DEPUTE, -D, -S *vb* appoint (someone) to act on one's behalf ▷ *n* deputy
DEPUTY *n*
DEQUEUE *vb* remove (an item) from a queue of computing tasks
DERAIGN *vb* contest (a claim, suit, etc)
DERAIL, -S *vb*
DERANGE *vb* disturb the order or arrangement of
DERAT, -S *vb* remove rats from
DERATE, -D, -S *vb* assess the value of some types of property at a lower rate than others for local taxation
DERATS ▶ **derat**
DERAY, -ED, -S *vb* old word meanng go mad
DERBY, DERBIES *n* bowler hat
DERE, -D, -S, DERING *vb* injure

DERECHO *n* long, fast-moving line of severe storms
DERED ▸ **dere**
DERES ▸ **dere**
DERHAM, -S *same as* ▸ **dirham**
DERIDE, -D, -S *vb* treat with contempt or ridicule
DERIDER ▸ **deride**
DERIDES ▸ **deride**
DERIG, -S *vb* remove equipment from
DERING ▸ **dere**
DERIVE, -D, -S *vb*
DERIVER ▸ **derive**
DERIVES ▸ **derive**
DERM, -S *same as* ▸ **derma**
DERMA, -S *n* beef or fowl intestine used as a casing for certain dishes, esp kishke
DERMAL *adj* of or relating to the skin
DERMAS ▸ **derma**
DERMIC ▸ **dermis**
DERMIS *another name for* ▸ **corium**
DERMOID *adj* of or resembling skin ▹ *n* congenital cystic tumour whose walls are lined with epithelium
DERMS ▸ **derm**
DERN, -ED, -ING, -S *n* concealment ▹ *vb* keep hidden
DERNFUL *adj* sorrowful
DERNIER *adj* last
DERNIES ▸ **derny**
DERNING ▸ **dern**
DERNLY *adv* sorrowfully
DERNS ▸ **dern**
DERNY, DERNIES, -S *n* bicycle with a small motor
DERO, -S *n* vagrant or derelict
DERRICK *n* simple crane ▹ *vb* raise or lower the jib of (a crane)
DERRIES ▸ **derry**
DERRIS *n* woody climbing plant
DERRO, -S *n* vagrant or derelict
DERRY, DERRIES *n* derelict house, esp one used by tramps
DERTH, -S *same as* ▸ **dearth**
DERV, -S *n* diesel oil, when used for road transport
DERVISH *n*
DERVS ▸ **derv**
DESALT, -S *vb* desalinate
DESAND, -S *vb* remove sand from
DESCALE *vb* remove a hard coating from inside (a kettle or pipe)
DESCANT *n* tune played or sung above a basic melody ▹ *adj* denoting the highest member in a family of musical instruments ▹ *vb* compose or perform a descant (for a piece of music)
DESCEND *vb*
DESCENT *n*
DESCRY *vb* catch sight of
DESEED, -S *vb* remove the seeds from (eg a fruit)
DESERT, -S *n*, *vb*
DESERVE *vb*
DESHI, -S *same as* ▸ **desi**
DESI, -S *adj* (in Indian English) indigenous or local ▹ *n* (in Indian English) indigenous or local person
DESIGN, -S *vb*, *n*
DESINE, -D, -S *same as* ▸ **design**
DESIRE, -D, -S *vb*, *n*
DESIRER ▸ **desire**
DESIRES ▸ **desire**
DESIS ▸ **desi**
DESIST, -S *vb*
DESK, -S *n*
DESKILL *vb* mechanize or computerize (a job) thereby reducing the skill required to do it
DESKING *n* desks and related furnishings in a given space, eg an office
DESKMAN, DESKMEN *n* police officer in charge in police station
DESKS ▸ **desk**
DESKTOP *adj*, *n*
DESMAN, -S *n* either of two molelike amphibious mammals
DESMID, -S *n* type of mainly unicellular freshwater green alga
DESMINE *n* type of mineral
DESMOID *adj* resembling a tendon or ligament ▹ *n* very firm tumour of connective tissue
DESNOOD *vb* remove the snood of a turkey poult to reduce the risk of cannibalism

DESORB, -S *vb* change from an adsorbed state to a gaseous or liquid state
DESOXY *same as* ▸ **deoxy**
DESPAIR *n, vb*
DESPISE *vb*
DESPITE *prep, n, vb*
DESPOIL *vb*
DESPOND *vb* lose heart or hope
DESPOT, -S *n*
DESSE, -S *n* old word for desk
DESSERT *n*
DESSES ▸ **desse**
DESTAIN *vb* remove stain from
DESTINE *vb* set apart or appoint
DESTINY *n*
DESTOCK *vb* reduce the amount of stock
DESTROY *vb*
DESUGAR *vb* remove sugar from
DESYNE, -D, -S *same as* ▸ **design**
DETACH *vb*
DETAIL, -S *n, vb*
DETAIN, -S *vb*
DETECT, -S *vb*
DETENT, -S *n* mechanism to check movement in one direction only
DETENTE *n* easing of tension between nations
DETENTS ▸ **detent**
DETENU, -S *n* prisoner
DETENUE *n* female prisoner
DETENUS ▸ **detenu**
DETER, -S *vb*
DETERGE *vb* wash or wipe away
DETERS ▸ **deter**
DETEST, -S *vb*
DETICK, -S *vb* remove ticks from
DETINUE *n* action brought by a plaintiff to recover goods wrongfully detained
DETORT, -S *vb* twist or distort
DETOUR, -S *n, vb*
DETOX, -ED, -ES *n, vb*
DETRACT *vb*
DETRAIN *vb* leave or cause to leave a railway train, as passengers, etc
DETRUDE *vb* force down or thrust away or out
DETUNE, -D, -S *vb*
DEUCE, -S, DEUCING *vb* score deuce in tennis ▹ *n* score of forty all
DEUCED *adj* damned
DEUCES ▸ **deuce**
DEUCING ▸ **deuce**
DEUS, DEI, DI *n* god
DEUTON, -S *old form of* > **deuteron**
DEUTZIA *n* shrub with clusters of pink or white flowers
DEV, -S *same as* ▸ **deva**

Dev is a Sanskrit word for a deity; related words are **deev** and **deva**

DEVA, -S *n* (in Hinduism and Buddhism) divine being or god
DEVALL, -S *vb* Scots word meaning stop
DEVALUE *vb*
DEVAS ▸ **deva**
DEVEIN, -S *vb* remove vein from
DEVEL, -ED, -S *same as* ▸ **devvel**
DEVELOP *vb* grow or bring to a later, more elaborate, or more advanced stage
DEVELS ▸ **devel**
DEVEST, -S *variant spelling of* ▸ **divest**
DEVI, -S *n* Hindu goddess
DEVIANT *adj, n*
DEVIATE *vb*
DEVICE, -S *n*
DEVIL, -ED, -S *n, vb*
DEVILET *n* young devil
DEVILRY *n* mischievousness
DEVILS ▸ **devil**
DEVIOUS *adj*
DEVIS ▸ **devi**
DEVISAL *n* act of inventing, contriving, or devising
DEVISE, -D, -S *vb, n*
DEVISEE *n* person to whom property, esp realty, is devised by will
DEVISER ▸ **devise**
DEVISES ▸ **devise**
DEVISOR *n* person who devises property, esp realty, by will
DEVLING *n* young devil
DEVO, -S *n* short for devolution
DEVOICE *vb* make (a voiced speech sound) voiceless
DEVOID *adj*
DEVOIR, -S *n* duty
DEVOLVE *vb*

DEVON, -S *n* bland processed meat in sausage form, eaten cold in slices
DEVORE, -S *n* velvet fabric with a raised pattern
DEVOS ▸ **devo**
DEVOT, -S *n* devotee
DEVOTE, -S *vb*
DEVOTED *adj* showing loyalty or devotion
DEVOTEE *n*
DEVOTES ▸ **devote**
DEVOTS ▸ **devot**
DEVOUR, -S *vb*
DEVOUT *adj*
DEVS ▸ **dev**
DEVVEL, -S *vb* strike with blow
DEW, -ED, -ING, -S *n, vb*
DEWAN, -S *n* (formerly in India) the chief or finance minister of a state ruled by an Indian prince
DEWANI, -S *n* post of a dewan
DEWANNY *same as* ▸ **dewani**
DEWANS ▸ **dewan**
DEWAR, -S *n* type of vacuum flask
DEWATER *vb* remove water from
DEWAX, -ED, -ES *vb* remove wax from
DEWCLAW *n* nonfunctional claw on a dog's leg
DEWDROP *n*
DEWED ▸ **dew**
DEWFALL *n* formation of dew
DEWFULL *obsolete form of* ▸ **due**
DEWIER ▸ **dewy**
DEWIEST ▸ **dewy**
DEWILY ▸ **dewy**
DEWING ▸ **dew**
DEWITT, -S *vb* kill, esp hang unlawfully
DEWLAP, -S *n* loose fold of skin hanging under the throat in dogs, cattle, etc
DEWLAPT ▸ **dewlap**
DEWLESS ▸ **dew**
DEWOOL, -S *vb* remove wool from
DEWORM, -S *vb* rid of worms
DEWS ▸ **dew**
DEWY, DEWIER, DEWIEST *adj* moist with or as with dew
DEX, -ES *n* dextroamphetamine
DEXTER, -S *adj* of or on the right side of a shield, etc, from the bearer's point of view ▹ *n* small breed of beef cattle
DEXTRAL *n* right-handed person
DEXTRAN *n* polysaccharide compound
DEXTRIN *n* sticky substance obtained from starch
DEXTRO *adj* dextrorotatory or rotating to the right
DEY, -S *n* title given to commanders or governors of the Janissaries of Algiers
DEZINC, -S *vb* remove zinc from
DHABA, -S *n* roadside café in India
DHAK, -S *n* tropical Asian tree
DHAL, -S *n* curry made from lentils or beans
DHAMMA, -S *variant of* ▸ **dharma**
DHANSAK *n* any of a variety of Indian dishes
DHARMA, -S *n* moral law or behaviour
DHARMIC ▸ **dharma**
DHARNA, -S *n* (in India) a method of obtaining justice
DHIKR, -S *n* Sufi religious ceremony
DHIMMI, -S *n* non-Muslim living in a state governed by sharia law
DHOBI, -S *n* (in India, Malaya, East Africa, etc, esp formerly) a washerman
DHOL, -S *n* type of Indian drum
DHOLAK, -S *n* type of two-headed drum
DHOLE, -S *n* fierce canine mammal
DHOLL, -S *same as* ▸ **dhal**
DHOLS ▸ **dhol**
DHOOLY *same as* ▸ **doolie**
DHOORA, -S *same as* ▸ **durra**
DHOOTI, -S *same as* ▸ **dhoti**
DHOOTIE *same as* ▸ **dhoti**
DHOOTIS ▸ **dhooti**
DHOTI, -S *n* long loincloth worn by men in India
DHOURRA *same as* ▸ **durra**

DHOW, -S *n* Arab sailing ship
DHURNA, -S *same as* ▸ **dharna**
DHURRA, -S *same as* ▸ **durra**
DHURRIE *same as* ▸ **durrie**
DHUTI, -S *same as* ▸ **dhoti**
DHYANA, -S *n* type of Hindu meditation
DI ▸ **deus**
DIABASE *n* altered dolerite
DIABLE, -S *n* type of sauce
DIABOLO *n* game using a spinning top and a cord fastened to two sticks
DIACID, -S *n* lead plaster
DIACT, -S *same as* > **diactine**
DIADEM, -S *n* crown ▹ *vb* adorn or crown with or as with a diadem
DIADROM *n* complete course of pendulum
DIAGRAM *n* sketch showing the form or workings of something ▹ *vb* show in or as if in a diagram
DIAGRID *n* diagonal structure network
DIAL, -ED, -LED, -S *n*, *vb*
DIALECT *n*
DIALED ▸ **dial**
DIALER, -S ▸ **dial**
DIALING ▸ **dial**
DIALIST *n* dial-maker
DIALLED ▸ **dial**
DIALLEL *n* interbreeding among a group of parents ▹ *adj* (of lines) not parallel, meeting, or intersecting
DIALLER ▸ **dial**
DIALOG, -S *same as* > **dialogue**
DIALS ▸ **dial**
DIALYSE *vb* separate by dialysis
DIALYZE *same as* ▸ **dialyse**
DIAMIDE *n* compound containing two amido groups
DIAMIN, -S *same as* ▸ **diamine**
DIAMINE *n* any chemical compound containing two amino groups in its molecules
DIAMINS ▸ **diamin**
DIAMOND *n*, *adj*, *vb*
DIAMYL *adj* with two amyl groups
DIANDRY *n* practice of having two husbands
DIANE *adj* as in **steak diane** steak served in a rich sauce
DIANOIA *n* perception and experience regarded as lower modes of knowledge
DIAPASE *same as* > **diapason**
DIAPER, -S *n*, *vb*
DIAPIR, -S *n* type of geological formation
DIAPSID *n* reptile with two holes in rear of skull
DIARCH *adj* (of a vascular bundle) having two strands of xylem
DIARCHY *n* government by two states, individuals, etc
DIARIAL ▸ **diary**
DIARIAN ▸ **diary**
DIARIES ▸ **diary**
DIARISE *same as* ▸ **diarize**
DIARIST *n*
DIARIZE *vb*
DIARY, DIARIES *n*
DIASCIA *n* S African plant, usu with pink flowers
DIASTEM *same as* > **diastema**
DIASTER *n* stage in cell division
DIATOM, -S *n* microscopic unicellular alga
DIATRON *n* circuit that uses diodes
DIAXON, -S *n* bipolar cell
DIAZIN, -S *same as* ▸ **diazine**
DIAZINE *n* organic compound
DIAZINS ▸ **diazin**
DIAZO, -ES, -S *adj* relating to a method for reproducing documents ▹ *n* document produced by this method
DIAZOLE *n* type of organic compound
DIAZOS ▸ **diazo**
DIB, -BED, -BING, -S *vb* fish by allowing the bait to bob and dip on the surface
DIBASIC *adj* (of an acid) containing two acidic hydrogen atoms
DIBBED ▸ **dib**
DIBBER, -S *same as* ▸ **dibble**

DIBBING ▸ **dib**
DIBBLE, -D, -S *n* small gardening tool ▹ *vb* make a hole in (the ground) with a dibble
DIBBLER ▸ **dibble**
DIBBLES ▸ **dibble**
DIBBS *n* money
DIBBUK, -S *variant spelling of* ▸ **dybbuk**
DIBS ▸ **dib**
DIBUTYL *adj* with two butyl groups
DICAMBA *n* type of weedkiller
DICAST, -S *n* juror in ancient Athens
DICE, -D, -S *n*, *vb*
DICER, -S ▸ **dice**
DICES ▸ **dice**
DICEY, DICIER, DICIEST *adj* dangerous or risky
DICH *interj* archaic expression meaning 'may it do'
DICHORD *n* two-stringed musical instrument
DICHT, -ED, -S *vb* wipe
DICIER ▸ **dicey**
DICIEST ▸ **dicey**
DICING, -S ▸ **dice**
DICK, -S *n* fellow
DICKENS *n* euphemism for devil
DICKER, -S *vb* trade (goods) by bargaining ▹ *n* petty bargain or barter
DICKEY, -S *same as* ▸ **dicky**
DICKIE *same as* ▸ **dicky**
DICKIER ▸ **dicky**
DICKIES ▸ **dicky**
DICKS ▸ **dick**
DICKTY *same as* ▸ **dicty**
DICKY, DICKIER, DICKIES *n* false shirt front ▹ *adj* shaky or weak
DICLINY > **diclinous**
DICOT, -S *n* type of flowering plant
DICOTYL *n* type of flowering plant
DICT, -ED, -ING, -S *vb* dictate
DICTA ▸ **dictum**
DICTATE *vb* say aloud for someone else to write down ▹ *n* authoritative command
DICTED ▸ **dict**
DICTIER ▸ **dicty**
DICTING ▸ **dict**
DICTION *n*
DICTS ▸ **dict**
DICTUM, DICTA, -S *n* formal statement
DICTY, DICTIER *adj* conceited; snobbish
DICYCLY > **dicyclic**
DID ▸ **do**
DIDACT, -S *n* instructive person
DIDAKAI *same as* ▸ **didicoy**
DIDAKEI *same as* ▸ **didicoy**
DIDDER, -S *vb* shake with fear
DIDDIER ▸ **diddy**
DIDDIES ▸ **diddy**
DIDDLE, -D, -S *vb*
DIDDLER ▸ **diddle**
DIDDLES ▸ **diddle**
DIDDLEY *n* worthless amount
DIDDLY *n* worthless amount
DIDDUMS *interj* expression of sympathy, esp to a child
DIDDY, DIDDIER, DIDDIES *n* Scots word for a foolish person ▹ *adj* foolish
DIDICOI *same as* ▸ **didicoy**
DIDICOY *n* (in Britain) a person who lives like a Roma but is not a true one
DIDIE *same as* ▸ **didy**
DIDIES ▸ **didy**
DIDO, -ES, -S *n* antic
DIDST *form of the past tense of* ▸ **do**
DIDY, DIDIES *n* (US) child's word for nappy
DIDYMO, -S *n* class of algae
DIE, -D, -ING, -S *vb*, *n*
DIEB, -S *n* N African jackal
DIEBACK *n* disease of trees and shrubs ▹ *vb* (of plants) to suffer from dieback
DIEBS ▸ **dieb**
DIED ▸ **die**
DIEDRAL *same as* > **dihedral**
DIEDRE, -S *n* large shallow groove or corner in a rock face
DIEHARD *n* person who resists change
DIEING ▸ **die**
DIEL, -S *n* 24-hour period ▹ *adj* of or lasting for any 24-hour period
DIENE, -S *n* type of hydrocarbon

DIEOFF, -S *n* process of dying in large numbers
DIES ▶ **die**
DIESEL, -S *vb, n*
DIESIS, DIESES *n* printed symbol indicating a footnote
DIESTER *n* synthetic lubricant
DIET, -ED, -S *n, vb, adj*
DIETARY *adj, n*
DIETED ▶ **diet**
DIETER, -S ▶ **diet**
DIETHER *n* chemical compound
DIETHYL *adj* as in **diethyl ether** ether
DIETINE *n* low-ranking diet or assembly
DIETING ▶ **diet**
DIETIST *another word for* > **dietitian**
DIETS ▶ **diet**
DIF, -S *same as* ▶ **diff**
DIFF, -S *n* informal word meaning difference
DIFFER, -S *vb*
DIFFORM *adj* irregular in form
DIFFS ▶ **diff**
DIFFUSE *vb, adj*
DIFS ▶ **dif**
DIG, -GING, -S *vb, n*
DIGAMMA *n* obsolete letter of the Greek alphabet
DIGAMY *n* second marriage
DIGEST, -S *vb, n*
DIGGED *a past tense of* ▶ **dig**
DIGGER, -S *n*
DIGGING ▶ **dig**
DIGHT, -ED, -S *vb* adorn or equip, as for battle
DIGICAM *n* digital camera
DIGIT, -S *n*
DIGITAL *adj, n*
DIGITS ▶ **digit**
DIGLOT, -S *n* bilingual book
DIGLYPH *n* ornament in a Doric frieze with two grooves
DIGNIFY *vb*
DIGNITY *n*
DIGONAL *adj* of or relating to a symmetry operation
DIGOXIN *n* glycoside extracted from the leaves of the woolly foxglove
DIGRAPH *n* two letters used to represent a single sound
DIGRESS *vb*
DIGS ▶ **dig**
DIHEDRA > **dihedron**
DIKA, -S *n* wild mango
DIKAST, -S *same as* ▶ **dicast**
DIKDIK, -S *n* small African antelope
DIKE, -D, -S, DIKING *same as* ▶ **dyke**
DIKER, -S *n* builder of dikes
DIKES ▶ **dike**
DIKING ▶ **dike**
DIKKOP, -S *n* type of brownish shore bird with a large head and eyes
DIKTAT, -S *n* dictatorial decree
DILATE, -D, -S *vb*
DILATER *same as* ▶ **dilator**
DILATES ▶ **dilate**
DILATOR *n* something that dilates an object
DILEMMA *n*
DILL, -ED, -S *n* sweet-smelling herb ▷ *vb* flavour with dill
DILLI, -S *n* small bag, esp one made of plaited grass
DILLIER ▶ **dilly**
DILLIES ▶ **dilly**
DILLING ▶ **dill**
DILLIS ▶ **dilli**
DILLS ▶ **dill**
DILLY, DILLIER, DILLIES *adj* foolish ▷ *n* person or thing that is remarkable
DILUENT *adj* causing dilution or serving to dilute ▷ *n* substance used for or causing dilution
DILUTE, -D, -S *vb, adj*
DILUTEE ▶ **dilute**
DILUTER ▶ **dilute**
DILUTES ▶ **dilute**
DILUTOR *n* thing intended to have a diluting effect
DILUVIA > **diluvium**
DIM, -MED, -MEST, -S *adj, vb*
DIMBLE, -S *n* wooded hollow; dingle
DIMBO, -ES, -S *n* unintelligent person
DIME, -S *n*
DIMER, -S *n* type of molecule
DIMERIC *adj* of a dimer
DIMERS ▶ **dimer**
DIMES ▶ **dime**
DIMETER *n* type of verse

DIMITY *n* light strong cotton fabric with woven stripes or squares
DIMLY ▸ **dim**
DIMMED ▸ **dim**
DIMMER, -S ▸ **dim**
DIMMEST ▸ **dim**
DIMMING *n* as in **global dimming** decrease in the amount of sunlight reaching the earth
DIMMISH ▸ **dim**
DIMNESS ▸ **dim**
DIMORPH *n* either of two forms of a substance that exhibits dimorphism
DIMOUT, -S *n* reduction of lighting
DIMP, -S *n* in Northern English dialect, a cigarette butt
DIMPLE, -D, -S *n, vb*
DIMPLY ▸ **dimple**
DIMPS ▸ **dimp**
DIMPSY *n* twilight
DIMS ▸ **dim**
DIMWIT, -S *n*
DIMYARY *adj* with two adductor muscles
DIN, -NED, -NING, -S *n, vb*
DINAR, -S *n* monetary unit
DINDLE, -D, -S *another word for* ▸ **dinnle**
DINE, -D, -S *vb*
DINER, -S *n* person eating a meal
DINERIC *adj* of or concerned with the interface between immiscible liquids
DINERO, -S *n* money
DINERS ▸ **diner**
DINES ▸ **dine**
DINETTE *n* alcove or small area for use as a dining room
DINFUL *adj* noisy
DING, -S *n* small dent in a vehicle ▹ *vb* ring or cause to ring, esp with tedious repetition
DINGBAT *n* any unnamed object
DINGE, -D, DINGING *n* dent ▹ *vb* make a dent in (something)
DINGER, -S *n* (in baseball) home run
DINGES *n* jocular word for something whose name is unknown or forgotten
DINGEY, -S *same as* ▸ **dinghy**
DINGHY *n, vb*
DINGIED ▸ **dingy**
DINGIER ▸ **dingy**
DINGIES ▸ **dingy**
DINGILY ▸ **dingy**
DINGING ▸ **dinge**
DINGLE, -S *n* small wooded hollow or valley
DINGO, -ED, -ES, -S *n* Australian wild dog ▹ *vb* act in a cowardly manner
DINGS ▸ **ding**
DINGUS *same as* ▸ **dinges**
DINGY, DINGIED, DINGIER, DINGIES *adj* lacking light ▹ *vb* ignore or avoid a person or event
DINIC, -S *n* remedy for vertigo
DINING, -S *n* act of dining
DINITRO *adj* containing two nitro groups
DINK, -ED, -ER, -EST, -ING, -S *adj* neat or neatly dressed ▹ *vb* carry (a second person) on a horse, bicycle, etc ▹ *n* ball struck delicately
DINKEY, -S *n* small locomotive
DINKIE, -S *n* affluent married childless person ▹ *adj* designed for or appealing to dinkies
DINKIER ▸ **dinky**
DINKIES ▸ **dinkie**
DINKING ▸ **dink**
DINKLY *adj* neat
DINKS ▸ **dink**
DINKUM, -S *n* truth or genuineness
DINKY, DINKIER *adj* small and neat
DINMONT *n* neutered sheep
DINNA *vb* a Scots word for do not
DINNAE *vb* (Scots) do not
DINNED ▸ **din**
DINNER, -S *vb* dine ▹ *n* main meal of the day
DINNING ▸ **din**
DINNLE, -D, -S *vb* shake
DINO, -S *n* dinosaur
DINS ▸ **din**
DINT, -ED, -ING, -S *variant of* ▸ **dent**
DIOBOL, -S *n* ancient Greek coin
DIOCESE *n* district over which a bishop has control
DIODE, -S *n* semiconductor device

DIOECY *n* state of being dioecious
DIOL, -S *n* any of a class of alcohols that have two hydroxyl groups in each molecule
DIOPTER *same as* ▶ **dioptre**
DIOPTRE *n* unit for measuring the refractive power of a lens
DIORAMA *n* miniature three-dimensional scene
DIORISM *n* definition; clarity
DIORITE *n* dark coarse-grained igneous plutonic rock
DIOTA, -S *n* type of ancient vase
DIOXAN, -S *n* colourless insoluble toxic liquid
DIOXANE *same as* ▶ **dioxan**
DIOXANS ▶ **dioxan**
DIOXID, -S *same as* ▶ **dioxide**
DIOXIDE *n* oxide containing two oxygen atoms per molecule
DIOXIDS ▶ **dioxid**
DIOXIN, -S *n* poisonous chemical by-product of certain weedkillers
DIP, -PED, -S, -T *vb, n*
DIPHASE *adj* of, having, or concerned with two phases
DIPHONE *n* combination of two speech sounds
DIPLEX *adj* permitting simultaneous transmission in both directions
DIPLOE, -S *n* spongy bone separating the two layers of compact bone of the skull
DIPLOIC *adj* relating to a diploe
DIPLOID *adj* denoting a cell or organism with pairs of homologous chromosomes ▷ *n* diploid cell or organism
DIPLOMA *vb, n*
DIPLON, -S *another name for* ▶ **deuteron**
DIPLONT *n* animal or plant that has the diploid number of chromosomes in its somatic cells
DIPNET, -S *vb* fish using a fishing net on a pole
DIPNOAN *n* lungfish
DIPODIC ▶ **dipody**
DIPODY *n* metrical unit consisting of two feet
DIPOLAR ▶ **dipole**
DIPOLE, -S *n* two equal but opposite electric charges or magnetic poles separated by a small distance
DIPPED ▶ **dip**
DIPPER, -S *n* ladle used for dipping
DIPPIER ▶ **dippy**
DIPPING ▶ **dip**
DIPPY, DIPPIER *adj* odd, eccentric, or crazy
DIPS ▶ **dip**
DIPSAS *n* type of snake
DIPSO, -S *n* dipsomaniac
DIPT ▶ **dip**
DIPTERA *n* order of insects with two wings
DIPTYCA *same as* ▶ **diptych**
DIPTYCH *n* painting on two hinged panels
DIQUARK *n* particle in physics
DIQUAT, -S *n* type of herbicide
DIRAM, -S *n* money unit of Tajikistan
DIRDAM, -S *same as* ▶ **dirdum**
DIRDUM, -S *n* tumult
DIRE, -R, -ST *adj*
DIRECT, -S *adj, adv, vb*
DIREFUL *same as* ▶ **dire**
DIRELY ▶ **dire**
DIREMPT *vb* separate with force
DIRER ▶ **dire**
DIREST ▶ **dire**
DIRGE, -S *n*
DIRHAM, -S *n* standard monetary unit of Morocco
DIRHEM, -S *same as* ▶ **dirham**
DIRIGE, -S *n* dirge
DIRK, -ED, -ING, -S *n* dagger, formerly worn by Scottish Highlanders ▷ *vb* stab with a dirk
DIRKE, -S *variant of* ▶ **dirk**
DIRKED ▶ **dirk**
DIRKES ▶ **dirke**
DIRKING ▶ **dirk**
DIRKS ▶ **dirk**
DIRL, -ED, -ING, -S *vb* tingle; vibrate
DIRNDL, -S *n* full gathered skirt
DIRT, -ED, -ING, -S *vb, n*
DIRTBAG *n* filthy person
DIRTED ▶ **dirt**
DIRTIED ▶ **dirty**
DIRTIER ▶ **dirty**

DIRTIES ▶ **dirty**
DIRTILY ▶ **dirty**
DIRTING ▶ **dirt**
DIRTS ▶ **dirt**
DIRTY, DIRTIED, DIRTIER, DIRTIES *adj* covered or marked with dirt ▷ *vb* make dirty
DIS *same as* ▶ **diss**
DISA, -S *n* type of orchid
DISABLE *vb*
DISALLY *vb* separate
DISARM, -S *vb*
DISAS ▶ **disa**
DISAVOW *vb* deny connection with or responsibility for
DISBAND *vb*
DISBAR, -S *vb* deprive (a barrister) of the right to practise
DISBARK *same as* > **disembark**
DISBARS ▶ **disbar**
DISBUD, -S *vb* remove superfluous buds from (a plant, esp a fruit tree)
DISC, -ED, -ING, -S *n* flat circular object ▷ *vb* work (land) with a disc harrow
DISCAGE *vb* release from cage
DISCAL *adj* relating to or resembling a disc
DISCANT *same as* ▶ **descant**
DISCARD *vb, n*
DISCASE *vb* remove the case from
DISCED ▶ **disc**
DISCEPT *vb* discuss
DISCERN *vb*
DISCERP *vb* divide
DISCI ▶ **discus**
DISCIDE *vb* split
DISCING ▶ **disc**
DISCO, -ED, -ES, -S *vb, n*
DISCOER ▶ **disco**
DISCOES ▶ **disco**
DISCOID *adj* like a disc ▷ *n* disclike object
DISCORD *n* lack of agreement or harmony between people ▷ *vb* disagree
DISCOS ▶ **disco**
DISCS ▶ **disc**
DISCURE *old form of* > **discover**
DISCUS, DISCI *n*
DISCUSS *vb*
DISDAIN *n, vb*
DISEASE *vb, n*
DISEDGE *vb* render blunt
DISEUR, -S *n* (esp formerly) an actor who presents dramatic recitals
DISEUSE *n* (esp formerly) an actress who presents dramatic recitals
DISFAME *n* discredit ▷ *vb* throw into disrepute or remove fame (from)
DISFORM *vb* change form of
DISGEST *vb* digest
DISGOWN *vb* remove a gown from
DISGUST *n, vb*
DISH, -ES *n, vb*
DISHED *adj* shaped like a dish
DISHELM *vb* remove a helmet from
DISHES ▶ **dish**
DISHFUL *n*
DISHIER ▶ **dishy**
DISHING ▶ **dish**
DISHMOP *n* mop for cleaning dishes
DISHOME *vb* deprive of home
DISHORN *vb* remove the horns from
DISHPAN *n*
DISHRAG *n* dishcloth
DISHY, DISHIER *adj* good-looking
DISJECT *vb* break apart
DISJOIN *vb* disconnect or become disconnected
DISJUNE *n* breakfast ▷ *vb* breakfast
DISK, -ED, -ING, -S *same as* ▶ **disc**
DISKER, -S *n* person who breaks up earth with a type of farm implement
DISKING ▶ **disk**
DISKS ▶ **disk**
DISLEAF *vb* remove a leaf or leaves from
DISLEAL *archaic form of* > **disloyal**
DISLIKE *vb, n*
DISLIMB *vb* remove limbs from
DISLIMN *vb* efface
DISLINK *vb* disunite
DISLOAD *vb*
DISMAL *adj*
DISMALS *pl n* gloomy state of mind
DISMAN, -S *vb* remove men from
DISMASK *vb* remove a mask from
DISMAST *vb* break off the mast or masts of (a sailing vessel)

DISMAY, -S *vb, n*
DISMAYD *adj* word used by Spenser meaning misshapen
DISMAYL *vb* remove a coat of mail from
DISMAYS ▸ **dismay**
DISME, -S *old form of* ▸ **dime**
DISMISS *vb, sentence substitute*
DISNEST *vb* remove from a nest
DISOBEY *vb* neglect or refuse to obey
DISOMIC *adj* having an extra chromosome in the haploid state
DISOMY ▸ **disomic**
DISOWN, -S *vb*
DISPACE *vb* move or travel about
DISPARK *vb* release
DISPART *vb* separate
DISPEL, -S *vb*
DISPEND *vb* spend
DISPLAY *vb, n*
DISPLE, -D, -S *vb* punish
DISPONE *vb* transfer ownership
DISPORT *vb* indulge (oneself) in pleasure ▹ *n* amusement
DISPOSE *vb*
DISPOST *vb* remove from a post
DISPRAD *old form of* > **dispread**
DISPRED *old spelling of* > **dispread**
DISPUTE *n, vb*
DISRANK *vb* demote
DISRATE *vb* punish (an officer) by lowering in rank
DISROBE *vb*
DISROOT *vb* uproot
DISRUPT *vb*
DISS, -ED, -ES, -ING *vb* treat (a person) with contempt
DISSAVE *vb* spend savings
DISSEAT *vb* unseat
DISSECT *vb*
DISSED ▸ **diss**
DISSENT *vb, n*
DISSERT *vb* give or make a dissertation; dissertate
DISSES ▸ **diss**
DISSING ▸ **diss**
DISTAFF *n* rod on which wool etc is wound for spinning
DISTAIN *vb* stain; tarnish
DISTAL *adj* (of a bone, limb, etc) situated farthest from the point of attachment
DISTANT *adj*
DISTEND *vb*
DISTENT *adj* bloated; swollen ▹ *n* breadth; distension
DISTICH *n* unit of two verse lines
DISTIL, -S *vb*
DISTILL *same as* ▸ **distil**
DISTILS ▸ **distil**
DISTOME *n* parasitic flatworm
DISTORT *vb*
DISTRIX *n* splitting of the ends of hairs
DISTUNE *vb* cause to be out of tune
DISTURB *vb*
DISTYLE *n* temple with two columns
DISUSE, -S *vb, n*
DISUSED *adj* no longer used
DISUSES ▸ **disuse**
DISYOKE *vb* unyoke
DIT, -S, -TED, -TING, -TIT *vb* stop something happening ▹ *n* short sound used in the spoken representation of telegraphic codes
DITA, -S *n* tropical shrub
DITAL, -S *n* key for raising the pitch of a lute string
DITAS ▸ **dita**
DITCH, -ED, -ES *n, vb*
DITCHER ▸ **ditch**
DITCHES ▸ **ditch**
DITE, -D, -S, DITING *vb* set down in writing
DITHER, -S *vb, n*
DITHERY ▸ **dither**
DITHIOL *n* chemical compound
DITING ▸ **dite**
DITONE, -S *n* interval of two tones
DITS ▸ **dit**
DITSY, DITSIER *same as* ▸ **ditzy**
DITT, -S *same as* ▸ **dit**
DITTANY *n* aromatic plant
DITTAY, -S *n* accusation; charge
DITTED ▸ **dit**
DITTIED ▸ **ditty**
DITTIES ▸ **ditty**
DITTING ▸ **dit**
DITTIT ▸ **dit**
DITTO, -ED, -S *n* same ▹ *adv* in the same way ▹ *sentence substitute* used to avoid repeating or to confirm

agreement with an immediately preceding sentence ▷ *vb* copy
DITTS ▶ **ditt**
DITTY, DITTIED, DITTIES *vb* set to music ▷ *n* short simple poem or song
DITZ, -ES *n* silly scatterbrained person
DITZY, DITZIER *adj* silly and scatterbrained
DIURNAL *adj* happening during the day or daily ▷ *n* service book containing all the canonical hours except matins
DIURON, -S *n* type of herbicide
DIV, -S *n* dividend
DIVA, -S *n*
DIVAN, -S *n* low backless bed
DIVAS ▶ **diva**
DIVE, -D, -S *vb, n*
DIVER *n* person who works or explores underwater
DIVERGE *vb*
DIVERS *adj* various ▷ *determiner* various
DIVERSE *vb, adj*
DIVERT, -S *vb*
DIVES ▶ **dive**
DIVEST, -S *vb*
DIVI, -ED, -S *alternative spelling of* ▶ **divvy**
DIVIDE, -S *vb, n*
DIVIDED *adj* split
DIVIDER *n* screen used to divide a room into separate areas
DIVIDES ▶ **divide**
DIVIED ▶ **divi**
DIVINE, -D, -S *adj, vb, n*
DIVINER ▶ **divine**
DIVINES ▶ **divine**
DIVING, -S ▶ **dive**
DIVIS ▶ **divi**
DIVISIM *adv* separately
DIVISOR *n* number to be divided into another number
DIVNA *vb* do not
DIVO, -S *n* male diva
DIVORCE *n, vb*
DIVOS ▶ **divo**
DIVOT, -S *n*
DIVS ▶ **div**
DIVULGE *vb*
DIVULSE *vb* tear apart
DIVVY, DIVVIED, DIVVIER, DIVVIES *vb* divide and share ▷ *adj* dialect word for stupid
DIVYING *alternative present participle of* ▶ **divvy**
DIWAN, -S *same as* ▶ **dewan**
DIXI *interj* I have spoken
DIXIE, -S *n* large metal pot for cooking, brewing tea, etc
DIXIT, -S *n* statement
DIXY *same as* ▶ **dixie**
DIYA, -S *n* small oil lamp, usu made from clay
DIZAIN, -S *n* ten-line poem
DIZEN, -ED, -S *archaic word for* ▶ **bedizen**
DIZZARD *n* dunce
DIZZIED ▶ **dizzy**
DIZZIER ▶ **dizzy**
DIZZIES ▶ **dizzy**
DIZZILY ▶ **dizzy**
DIZZY, DIZZIED, DIZZIER, DIZZIES *adj, vb*
DJEBEL, -S *variant spelling of* ▶ **jebel**
DJEMBE, -S *n* W African drum
DJIBBA, -S *same as* ▶ **jubbah**
DJIBBAH *same as* ▶ **jubbah**
DJIBBAS ▶ **djibba**
DJIN, -S *same as* ▶ **jinn**
DJINNI, DJINN, DJINNS *same as* ▶ **jinni**
DJINNY *same as* ▶ **jinni**
DJINS ▶ **djin**
DO, DID, -EN, -ES, -EST, -ETH, -ING, -NE, -S *vb* perform or complete (a deed or action) ▷ *n* party, celebration
DOAB, -S *n* alluvial land between two converging rivers
DOABLE *adj* capable of being done
DOABS ▶ **doab**
DOAT, -ED, -S *same as* ▶ **dote**
DOATER, -S ▶ **doat**
DOATING ▶ **doat**
DOATS ▶ **doat**
DOB, -BED, -BING, -S *vb* as in **dob in** inform against or report
DOBBER, -S *n* informant or traitor
DOBBIE *same as* ▶ **dobby**
DOBBIES ▶ **dobby**
DOBBIN, -S *n* name for a horse
DOBBING ▶ **dob**
DOBBINS ▶ **dobbin**
DOBBY, DOBBIES *n* attachment to a loom, used in weaving small figures

DOBE, -S *same as* ▸ **adobe**
DOBHASH *n* interpreter
DOBLA, -S *n* medieval Spanish gold coin, probably worth 20 maravedis
DOBLON, -S *variant spelling of* > **doubloon**
DOBRA, -S *n* standard monetary unit of São Tomé e Principe
DOBRO, -S *n* type of acoustic guitar
DOBS ▸ **dob**
DOBSON, -S *n* larva of a dobsonfly
DOC, -S *same as* ▸ **doctor**
DOCENT, -S *n* voluntary worker who acts as a guide
DOCETIC *adj* believing that the humanity of Christ was apparent and not real
DOCHMII > **dochmius**
DOCHT ▸ **dow**
DOCIBLE *adj* easily tamed
DOCILE, -R *adj*
DOCK, -ED, -S *n, vb*
DOCKAGE *n* charge levied upon a vessel for using a dock
DOCKED ▸ **dock**
DOCKEN, -S *n* something of no value or importance
DOCKER, -S *n* person employed to load and unload ships
DOCKET, -S *n* label on a delivery, stating contents, delivery instructions, etc ▹ *vb* fix a docket to (a package or other delivery)
DOCKING ▸ **dock**
DOCKISE *same as* ▸ **dockize**
DOCKIZE *vb* convert into docks
DOCKS ▸ **dock**
DOCO, -S *n* documentary
DOCQUET *same as* ▸ **docket**
DOCS ▸ **doc**
DOCTOR, -S *n, vb*
DOCU, -S *n* documentary film
DOD, -DED, -DING, -S *vb* clip
DODDARD *adj* archaic word for missing branches; rotten ▹ *n* tree missing its top branches through rot
DODDED ▸ **dod**
DODDER, -S *vb* move unsteadily ▹ *n* type of rootless parasitic plant
DODDERY ▸ **dodder**
DODDIER ▸ **doddy**
DODDIES ▸ **doddy**
DODDING ▸ **dod**
DODDLE, -S *n* something easily accomplished
DODDY, DODDIER, DODDIES *n* bad mood ▹ *adj* sulky
DODGE, -D, -S *vb, n*
DODGEM, -S *n*
DODGER, -S *n* person who evades a responsibility or duty
DODGERY *n* deception
DODGES ▸ **dodge**
DODGIER ▸ **dodgy**
DODGING ▸ **dodge**
DODGY, DODGIER *adj* dangerous, risky
DODKIN, -S *n* coin of little value
DODMAN, -S *n* snail
DODO, -ES, -S *n*
DODOISM ▸ **dodo**
DODOS ▸ **dodo**
DODS ▸ **dod**
DOE *n* female deer, hare, or rabbit
DOEK, -S *n* square of cloth worn on the head by some African women
DOEN ▸ **do**
DOER, -S *n* active or energetic person
DOES ▸ **do**
DOESKIN *n* skin of a deer, lamb, or sheep
DOEST ▸ **do**
DOETH ▸ **do**
DOF *informal South African word for* ▸ **stupid**
DOFF, -ED, -ING, -S *vb*
DOFFER, -S ▸ **doff**
DOFFING ▸ **doff**
DOFFS ▸ **doff**
DOG, -S *n, vb*
DOGATE, -S *n* office of doge
DOGBANE *n* N American plant
DOGBOLT *n* bolt on a cannon
DOGCART *n* light horse-drawn two-wheeled cart
DOGDOM, -S *n* world of dogs
DOGE, -S *n* (formerly) chief magistrate of Venice or Genoa

DOGEAR, -S *vb* fold down the corner of (a page) ▷ *n* folded-down corner of a page
DOGEATE *n* office of doge
DOGEDOM *n* domain of a doge
DOGES ▶ **doge**
DOGEY, -S *same as* ▶ **dogie**
DOGFACE *n* WW2 US soldier
DOGFISH *n* small shark
DOGFOOD *n*
DOGFOX *n* male fox
DOGGED *adj* stubbornly determined
DOGGER, -S *n* Dutch fishing vessel with two masts
DOGGERY *n* surly behaviour
DOGGESS *n* female dog
DOGGIE *same as* ▶ **doggy**
DOGGIER ▶ **doggy**
DOGGIES ▶ **doggy**
DOGGING ▶ **dog**
DOGGISH *adj* of or like a dog
DOGGO *adv* in hiding and keeping quiet
DOGGONE *interj* exclamation of annoyance, disappointment, etc ▷ *vb* damn ▷ *adj* damnedest
DOGGREL *same as* > **doggerel**
DOGGY, DOGGIER, DOGGIES *n* child's word for a dog ▷ *adj* of or like a dog
DOGHOLE *n* squalid dwelling place
DOGIE, -S *n* motherless calf
DOGLEG, -S *n* sharp bend ▷ *vb* go off at an angle ▷ *adj* of or with the shape of a dogleg
DOGLIKE ▶ **dog**
DOGMA, -S, -TA *n*
DOGMAN, DOGMEN *n* person who directs a crane whilst riding on an object being lifted by it
DOGMAS ▶ **dogma**
DOGMATA ▶ **dogma**
DOGMEN ▶ **dogman**
DOGNAP, -S *vb* carry off and hold (a dog), usually for ransom
DOGPILE *n* pile of bodies formed by people jumping on top of each other
DOGREL, -S *n* doggerel
DOGS ▶ **dog**
DOGSHIP *n* condition of being a dog
DOGSHOW *n*
DOGSKIN *n* leather from a dog's skin
DOGSLED *n*
DOGTAIL *same as* > **dogstail**
DOGTOWN *n* community of prairie dogs
DOGTROT *n* gently paced trot
DOGVANE *n* light windvane mounted on the side of a vessel
DOGWOOD *n* type of tree or shrub
DOGY *same as* ▶ **dogie**
DOH, -S *n* in tonic sol-fa, the first degree of any major scale ▷ *interj* exclamation of annoyance when something goes wrong

This is one of the very useful short words denoting a note of the musical scale.

DOHYO, -S *n* sumo wrestling ring
DOILED *same as* ▶ **doilt**
DOILIED *adj* having a doily
DOILIES ▶ **doily**
DOILT, -ER *adj* foolish
DOILY, DOILIES *n*
DOING ▶ **do**
DOINGS *pl n* deeds or actions
DOIT, -S *n* former small copper coin of the Netherlands
DOITED *adj* foolish or childish, as from senility
DOITIT *same as* ▶ **doited**
DOITKIN *same as* ▶ **doit**
DOITS ▶ **doit**
DOJO, -S *n* room or hall for the practice of martial arts
DOL, -S *n* unit of pain intensity, as measured by dolorimetry
DOLCE, -S, DOLCI *n* dessert ▷ *adv* (to be performed) gently and sweetly
DOLE, -D, -S, DOLING *n, vb*
DOLEFUL *adj*
DOLENT *adj* sad
DOLENTE *adv* (to be performed) in a sorrowful manner

DOLES ▶ **dole**
DOLIA ▶ **dolium**
DOLINA, -S *same as* ▶ **doline**
DOLINE, -S *n* depression of the ground surface formed in limestone regions
DOLING ▶ **dole**
DOLIUM, DOLIA *n* genus of molluscs
DOLL, -ED, -ING, -S *n, vb*
DOLLAR, -S *n*
DOLLDOM ▶ **doll**
DOLLED ▶ **doll**
DOLLIED ▶ **dolly**
DOLLIER *n* person who operates a dolly
DOLLIES ▶ **dolly**
DOLLING ▶ **doll**
DOLLISH ▶ **doll**
DOLLOP, -S *n, vb*
DOLLS ▶ **doll**
DOLLY, DOLLIED, DOLLIES *adj* attractive and unintelligent ▷ *n* wheeled support for a camera ▷ *vb* wheel a camera on a dolly
DOLMA, -S *n* vine leaf stuffed with a filling of meat and rice
DOLMAN, -S *n* long Turkish outer robe
DOLMAS ▶ **dolma**
DOLMEN, -S *n* prehistoric monument
DOLOR, -S *same as* ▶ **dolour**
DOLOS, -SE *n* knucklebone of a sheep, buck, etc, used esp by diviners
DOLOUR, -S *n* grief or sorrow
DOLPHIN *n*
DOLS ▶ **dol**
DOLT, -S *n*
DOLTISH ▶ **dolt**
DOLTS ▶ **dolt**
DOM, -S *n* title given to various monks and to certain of the canons regular
DOMAIN, -S *n*
DOMAINE *n* French estate
DOMAINS ▶ **domain**
DOMAL *adj* of a house
DOMATIA > **domatium**
DOME, -D, -S, DOMING *n, vb*
DOMETT, -S *n* wool and cotton cloth
DOMIC *adj* dome-shaped
DOMICAL ▶ **dome**
DOMICIL *same as* > **domicile**
DOMIER ▶ **domy**
DOMIEST ▶ **domy**
DOMINE, -S *n* clergyman or clergywoman
DOMINEE *n* minister of the Dutch Reformed Church
DOMINES ▶ **domine**
DOMING ▶ **dome**
DOMINIE *n* minister, clergyman or clergywoman: also used as a term of address
DOMINO, -S *n*
DOMOIC *adj* as in **domoic acid** kind of amino acid
DOMS ▶ **dom**
DOMY, DOMIER, DOMIEST *adj* having a dome or domes
DON, -NED, -NING, -S *vb, n*
DONA, -S *n* Spanish woman
DONAH, -S *n* woman
DONAIR, -S *same as* ▶ **doner**
DONARY *n* thing given for holy use
DONAS ▶ **dona**
DONATE, -D, -S *vb*
DONATOR ▶ **donate**
DONDER, -S *vb* beat (someone) up ▷ *n* wretch
DONE ▶ **do**
DONEE, -S *n* person who receives a gift
DONEGAL *n* type of tweed
DONER, -S *n* kebab of grilled meat served in pitta bread
DONG, -ED, -ING, -S *n* deep reverberating sound of a large bell ▷ *vb* (of a bell) to make a deep reverberating sound
DONGA, -S *n* steep-sided gully created by soil erosion
DONGED ▶ **dong**
DONGING ▶ **dong**
DONGLE, -S *n* electronic device
DONGOLA *n* leather tanned using a particular method
DONGS ▶ **dong**
DONING, -S *n* act of giving blood
DONJON, -S *n* heavily fortified central tower of a castle
DONKEY, -S *n*

DONKO, -S *n* tearoom or cafeteria in a factory, wharf area, etc
DONNA, -S *n* Italian woman
DONNARD *same as* ▸ **donnert**
DONNART *same as* ▸ **donnert**
DONNAS ▸ **donna**
DONNAT, -S *n* lazy person
DONNE, -S *same as* ▸ **donnee**
DONNED ▸ **don**
DONNEE, -S *n* subject or theme
DONNERD *adj* stunned
DONNERT *adj* stunned
DONNES ▸ **donne**
DONNIES ▸ **donny**
DONNING ▸ **don**
DONNISH *adj* serious and academic
DONNISM *n* loftiness
DONNOT, -S *n* lazy person
DONNY, DONNIES *same as* ▸ **danny**
DONOR, -S *n*
DONS ▸ **don**
DONSHIP *n* state or condition of being a don
DONSIE, -R *adj* rather unwell
DONSY *same as* ▸ **donsie**
DONUT, -S *same as* > **doughnut**
DONZEL, -S *n* man of high birth
DOO, -S *a Scot word for* ▸ **dove**
DOOB, -S *n* type of Indian grass
DOOBIE, -S *same as* ▸ **doob**
DOOBREY *n* thingumabob
DOOBRIE *same as* ▸ **doobrey**
DOOBRY *n* thing whose name is unknown or forgotten
DOOBS ▸ **doob**
DOOCE, -D, -S, DOOCING *vb* dismiss (an employee) because of comments they have posted on the internet
DOOCOT, -S *n* dovecote
DOODAD, -S *same as* ▸ **doodah**
DOODAH, -S *n* unnamed thing
DOODIES ▸ **doody**
DOODLE, -D, -S *vb, n*
DOODLER ▸ **doodle**
DOODLES ▸ **doodle**
DOODOO, -S *n* excrement
DOODY, DOODIES *same as* ▸ **doodoo**
DOOFER, -S *n* thingamajig
DOOFUS *n* slow-witted or stupid person
DOOK, -ED, -ING, -S *n* wooden plug driven into a wall to hold a nail, screw, etc ▹ *vb* dip or plunge
DOOKET, -S *n* dovecote
DOOKING ▸ **dook**
DOOKS ▸ **dook**
DOOL, -S *n* boundary marker
DOOLAN, -S *n* New Zealand informal term for a Roman Catholic
DOOLE, -S *same as* ▸ **dool**
DOOLEE, -S *same as* ▸ **doolie**
DOOLES ▸ **doole**
DOOLIE, -S *n* enclosed couch on poles for carrying passengers
DOOLS ▸ **dool**
DOOLY *same as* ▸ **doolie**
DOOM, -ED, -ING, -S *n, vb*
DOOMFUL ▸ **doom**
DOOMIER ▸ **doomy**
DOOMILY ▸ **doomy**
DOOMING ▸ **doom**
DOOMS ▸ **doom**
DOOMY, DOOMIER *adj* despondent or pessimistic
DOON *same as* ▸ **down**
DOONA, -S *n* large quilt used as a bed cover
DOOR, -S *n*
DOORED *adj* having a door
DOORMAN, DOORMEN *n*
DOORMAT *n*
DOORMEN ▸ **doorman**
DOORN, -S *n* thorn
DOORS ▸ **door**
DOORWAY *n*
DOOS, -ES ▸ **doo**
DOOSRA, -S *n* type of delivery in cricket
DOOWOP, -S *n* style of singing in harmony
DOOZER, -S *same as* ▸ **doozy**
DOOZIE, -S *same as* ▸ **doozy**
DOOZY *n* something excellent
DOP, -PED, -S *n* small drink ▹ *vb* fail to reach the required standard in (an examination, course, etc)

DOPA, -S *n* precursor to dopamine
DOPANT, -S *n* element or compound used to produce an effect in a semiconductor
DOPAS ▸ **dopa**
DOPATTA *n* headscarf
DOPE, -D, -S, -ST *n, vb, adj*
DOPER, -S *n* person who administers dope
DOPES ▸ **dope**
DOPEST ▸ **dope**
DOPEY, DOPIER, DOPIEST *adj* half-asleep, drowsy
DOPIAZA *n* Indian meat or fish dish cooked in onion sauce
DOPIER ▸ **dopey**
DOPIEST ▸ **dopey**
DOPILY ▸ **dopey**
DOPING, -S ▸ **dope**
DOPPED ▸ **dop**
DOPPER, -S *n* member of an Afrikaner church which practises a strict Calvinism
DOPPIE, -S *n* cartridge case
DOPPING ▸ **dop**
DOPPIO, -S *n* double measure, esp of espresso coffee
DOPS ▸ **dop**
DOPY *same as* ▸ **dopey**
DOR, -RED, -RING, -S *n* European dung beetle ▹ *vb* mock
DORAD, -S *n* South American river fish
DORADO, -S *n* large marine percoid fish
DORADS ▸ **dorad**
DORB, -S *same as* ▸ **dorba**
DORBA, -S *n* stupid, inept, or clumsy person
DORBS ▸ **dorb**
DORBUG, -S *n* type of beetle
DORE, -S *n* walleye fish
DOREE, -S *n* walleye fish
DORES ▸ **dore**
DORHAWK *n* nightjar
DORIC *adj* rustic
DORIES ▸ **dory**
DORIS *n* woman
DORISE, -D, -S *same as* ▸ **dorize**
DORIZE, -D, -S *vb* become Doric
DORK, -S *n* stupid person
DORKIER ▸ **dorky**
DORKISH *adj* stupid or contemptible
DORKS ▸ **dork**
DORKY, DORKIER ▸ **dork**
DORLACH *n* quiver of arrows
DORM, -S *same as* > **dormitory**
DORMANT *n, adj*
DORMER, -S *n* window that sticks out from a sloping roof
DORMICE > **dormouse**
DORMIE *adj* (in golf) leading by as many holes as there are left
DORMIN, -S *n* hormone found in plants
DORMS ▸ **dorm**
DORMY *same as* ▸ **dormie**
DORNECK *same as* ▸ **dornick**
DORNICK *n* heavy damask cloth
DORNOCK *same as* ▸ **dornick**
DORP, -S *n* small town
DORPER, -S *n* breed of sheep
DORPS ▸ **dorp**
DORR, -S *same as* ▸ **dor**
DORRED ▸ **dor**
DORRING ▸ **dor**
DORRS ▸ **dorr**
DORS ▸ **dor**
DORSA ▸ **dorsum**
DORSAD *adj* towards the back or dorsal aspect
DORSAL, -S *adj, n*
DORSE, -S *n* type of small fish
DORSEL, -S *another word for* ▸ **dossal**
DORSER, -S *n* hanging tapestry
DORSES ▸ **dorse**
DORSUM, DORSA *n* the back
DORT, -ED, -ING, -S *vb* sulk
DORTER, -S *n* dormitory
DORTIER ▸ **dorty**
DORTING ▸ **dort**
DORTOUR *same as* ▸ **dorter**
DORTS ▸ **dort**
DORTY, DORTIER *adj* haughty, or sullen
DORY, DORIES *n* spiny-finned edible sea fish
DORYMAN, DORYMEN *n* person who fishes from a small boat called a dory
DOS ▸ **do**
DOSA, -I, -S *n* Indian pancake made from rice flour

DOSAGE, -S *same as* ▸ **dose**
DOSAI ▸ **dosa**
DOSAS ▸ **dosa**
DOSE, -D, -S, DOSING *n, vb*
DOSEH, -S *n* former Egyptian religious ceremony
DOSER, -S ▸ **dose**
DOSES ▸ **dose**
DOSH, -ES *n*
DOSHA, -S *n* (in Hinduism) any of the three energies believed to be in the body
DOSHES ▸ **dosh**
DOSING ▸ **dose**
DOSS, -ED, -ES, -ING *vb, n*
DOSSAL, -S *n* ornamental hanging used in churches
DOSSED ▸ **doss**
DOSSEL, -S *same as* ▸ **dossal**
DOSSER, -S *n* bag or basket for carrying objects on the back
DOSSES ▸ **doss**
DOSSIER *n* collection of documents about a subject or person
DOSSIL, -S *n* lint for dressing wound
DOSSING ▸ **doss**
DOST *a singular form of the present tense (indicative mood) of* ▸ **do**
DOT, -S, -TED, -TING *n, vb*
DOTAGE, -S *n*
DOTAL *adj* of a dowry
DOTANT, -S *another word for* ▸ **dotard**
DOTARD, -S *n* person who is feeble-minded through old age
DOTCOM, -S *n* company that does most of its business on the internet
DOTE, -D, -S *vb*
DOTER, -S ▸ **dote**
DOTES ▸ **dote**
DOTH *a singular form of the present tense of* ▸ **do**
DOTIER ▸ **doty**
DOTIEST ▸ **doty**
DOTING, -S ▸ **dote**
DOTISH *adj* foolish
DOTS ▸ **dot**
DOTTED ▸ **dot**
DOTTEL, -S *same as* ▸ **dottle**
DOTTER, -S ▸ **dot**
DOTTIER ▸ **dotty**
DOTTILY ▸ **dotty**
DOTTING ▸ **dot**
DOTTLE, -R, -S *n* tobacco left in a pipe after smoking ▹ *adj* relating to dottle
DOTTLED *adj* foolish
DOTTLER ▸ **dottle**
DOTTLES ▸ **dottle**
DOTTREL *same as* ▸ **dotterel**
DOTTY, DOTTIER *adj* rather eccentric
DOTY, DOTIER, DOTIEST *adj* (of wood) rotten
DOUANE, -S *n* customs house
DOUAR, -S *same as* ▸ **duar**
DOUBLE, -D, -S *adj, adv, n, vb*
DOUBLER ▸ **double**
DOUBLES ▸ **double**
DOUBLET *n* man's close-fitting jacket, with or without sleeves
DOUBLY *adv* in a greater degree, quantity, or measure
DOUBT, -ED, -S *n, vb*
DOUBTER ▸ **doubt**
DOUBTS ▸ **doubt**
DOUC, -S *n* Old World monkey
DOUCE, -R, -ST *adj* quiet
DOUCELY ▸ **douce**
DOUCER ▸ **douce**
DOUCEST ▸ **douce**
DOUCET, -S *n* former flute-like instrument
DOUCEUR *n* gratuity, tip, or bribe
DOUCHE, -D, -S *n* stream of water onto or into the body ▹ *vb* cleanse or treat by means of a douche
DOUCINE *n* type of moulding for a cornice
DOUCS ▸ **douc**
DOUGH, -S *n*
DOUGHT ▸ **dow**
DOUGHTY *adj* brave and determined
DOUGHY *adj* resembling dough in consistency, colour, etc
DOUK, -ED, -ING, -S *same as* ▸ **dook**
DOULA, -S *n* woman who supports families during pregnancy and childbirth
DOULEIA *same as* ▸ **dulia**

This word refers to the inferior veneration accorded to saints and angels, as distinct from **latria**, the veneration accorded to God alone, and is another of the few 7-letter words that use all five vowels. It's surprising how often you want to do this!

DOUM, -S *n* as in **doum palm** variety of palm tree
DOUMA, -S *same as* ▸ **duma**
DOUMS ▸ **doum**
DOUN *same as* ▸ **down**
DOUP, -S *n* bottom
DOUR, -ER, -EST *adj*
DOURA, -S *same as* ▸ **durra**
DOURAH, -S *same as* ▸ **durra**
DOURAS ▸ **doura**
DOURER ▸ **dour**
DOUREST ▸ **dour**
DOURINE *n* infectious disease of horses
DOURLY ▸ **dour**
DOUSE, -D, -S, DOUSING *vb, n*
DOUSER, -S ▸ **douse**
DOUSES ▸ **douse**
DOUSING ▸ **douse**
DOUT, -ED, -ING, -S *vb* extinguish
DOUTER, -S ▸ **dout**
DOUTING ▸ **dout**
DOUTS ▸ **dout**
DOUX *adj* sweet
DOVE, -D, -S, DOVING *vb* be semi-conscious ▹ *n* bird with a heavy body, small head, and short legs
DOVECOT *same as* > **dovecote**
DOVED ▸ **dove**
DOVEISH *adj* dovelike
DOVEKEY *same as* ▸ **dovekie**
DOVEKIE *n* small short-billed auk
DOVELET *n* small dove
DOVEN, -ED, -S *vb* pray
DOVER, -ED, -S *vb* doze ▹ *n* doze
DOVES ▸ **dove**
DOVIE, -R, -ST *Scots word for* ▸ **stupid**
DOVING ▸ **dove**
DOVISH ▸ **dove**
DOW, DOCHT, DOUGHT, -ED, -ING, -S *vb* archaic word meaning be of worth
DOWABLE *adj* capable of being endowed
DOWAGER *n* widow possessing property or a title obtained from her husband
DOWAR, -S *same as* ▸ **duar**
DOWD, -S *n* person who wears unfashionable clothes
DOWDIER ▸ **dowdy**
DOWDIES ▸ **dowdy**
DOWDILY ▸ **dowdy**
DOWDS ▸ **dowd**
DOWDY, DOWDIER, DOWDIES *adj, n*
DOWED ▸ **dow**
DOWEL, -ED, -S *n* wooden or metal peg used as a fastener ▹ *vb* join pieces of wood using dowels
DOWER, -ED, -S *n* life interest in a part of her husband's estate allotted to a widow by law ▹ *vb* endow
DOWERY *same as* ▸ **dowry**
DOWF *adj* dull; listless
DOWIE, -R, -ST *adj* dull and dreary
DOWING ▸ **dow**
DOWL, -S *n* fluff
DOWLAS *n* coarse fabric
DOWLE, -S *same as* ▸ **dowl**
DOWLIER ▸ **dowly**
DOWLNE, -S *n* obsolete word meaning down (feathers)
DOWLNEY ▸ **dowlne**
DOWLS ▸ **dowl**
DOWLY, DOWLIER *adj* dull
DOWN, -ED, -ING *adv, adj, vb, n*
DOWNA *obsolete Scots form of* ▸ **cannot**
DOWNBOW *n* (in music) a downward stroke of the bow across the strings
DOWNCRY *vb* denigrate or disparage
DOWNED ▸ **down**
DOWNER, -S *n* dispiriting experience
DOWNIER ▸ **downy**
DOWNIES ▸ **downy**
DOWNILY *adv* in a manner resembling or indicating a layer of soft fine feathers or hairs
DOWNING ▸ **down**
DOWNLOW *n* as in **on the downlow** not widely known
DOWNS *pl n* low grassy hills, esp in S England

DOWNY, DOWNIER, DOWNIES *adj* covered with soft fine hair or feathers ▷ *n* bed
DOWP, -S *same as* ▶ **doup**
DOWRY, DOWRIES *n*
DOWS ▶ **dow**
DOWSE, -D, -S *same as* ▶ **douse**
DOWSER, -S ▶ **dowse**
DOWSES ▶ **dowse**
DOWSET, -S *same as* ▶ **doucet**
DOWSING *n* act of dowsing
DOWT, -S *n* cigarette butt
DOX, -ED, -ES, -ING *vb* publish someone's personal information on the internet
DOXIE *same as* ▶ **doxy**
DOXIES ▶ **doxy**
DOXING ▶ **dox**
DOXY, DOXIES *n* opinion or doctrine, esp concerning religious matters
DOY, -S *n* beloved person: used esp as an endearment
DOYEN, -S *n* senior member of a group, profession, or society
DOYENNE ▶ **doyen**
DOYENS ▶ **doyen**
DOYLEY, -S *same as* ▶ **doily**
DOYLY, DOYLIES *same as* ▶ **doily**
DOYS ▶ **doy**
DOZE, -S *vb, n*
DOZED *adj* (of timber or rubber) rotten or decayed
DOZEN, -ED, -S *n* set of twelve ▷ *vb* stun
DOZENTH ▶ **dozen**
DOZER, -S ▶ **doze**
DOZES ▶ **doze**
DOZIER ▶ **dozy**
DOZIEST ▶ **dozy**
DOZILY ▶ **dozy**
DOZING, -S ▶ **doze**
DOZY, DOZIER, DOZIEST *adj* feeling sleepy
DRAB, -S *adj, n*
DRABBER *adj* more drab
DRABBET *n* yellowish-brown fabric of coarse linen
DRABBLE *vb* make or become wet or dirty
DRABBY *adj* slightly drab
DRABLER *same as* > **drabbler**
DRABLY ▶ **drab**
DRABS ▶ **drab**
DRAC *same as* ▶ **drack**
DRACENA *same as* > **dracaena**
DRACHM, -S *n* unit of liquid measure
DRACHMA *n* former monetary unit of Greece
DRACHMS ▶ **drachm**
DRACK *adj* unattractive
DRACO *n* as in **draco lizard** flying lizard
DRACONE *n* large container towed by a ship
DRAD *archaic past of* ▶ **dread**
DRAFF, -S *n* residue of husks used as a food for cattle
DRAFFY ▶ **draff**
DRAFT, -ED, -S *same as* ▶ **draught**
DRAFTEE *n* conscript
DRAFTER ▶ **draft**
DRAFTS ▶ **draft**
DRAFTY *same as* > **draughty**
DRAG, -GED, -S *vb, n*
DRAGEE, -S *n* sweet made of a nut, fruit, etc, coated with a hard sugar icing
DRAGGED ▶ **drag**
DRAGGER ▶ **drag**
DRAGGLE *vb* make or become wet or dirty by trailing on the ground
DRAGGY *adj* slow or boring
DRAGNET *n* net used to scour the bottom of a pond or river
DRAGON, -S *n*
DRAGOON *n, vb*
DRAGS ▶ **drag**
DRAGWAY *n* race course for drag racing
DRAIL, -ED, -S *n* weighted hook used in trolling ▷ *vb* fish with a drail
DRAIN, -ED, -S *n, vb*
DRAINER *n* person or thing that drains
DRAINS ▶ **drain**
DRAKE, -S *n*
DRAM, -MED, -S *n* small amount of a strong alcoholic drink, esp whisky ▷ *vb* drink a dram
DRAMA, -S *n*
DRAMADY *same as* ▶ **dramedy**
DRAMAS ▶ **drama**
DRAMEDY *n* television or film drama in which there are important elements of comedy

DRAMMED ▸ **dram**
DRAMS ▸ **dram**
DRANK ▸ **drink**
DRANT, -ED, -S *vb* drone
DRAP, -PED, -S *a Scot word for* ▸ **drop**
DRAPE, -D, DRAPING *vb, n*
DRAPER, -S *n* person who sells fabrics and sewing materials
DRAPERY *n* fabric or clothing arranged and draped
DRAPES *pl n* material hung at an opening or window to shut out light or to provide privacy
DRAPET, -S *n* cloth
DRAPEY *adj* hanging in loose folds
DRAPIER *n* draper
DRAPING ▸ **drape**
DRAPPED ▸ **drap**
DRAPPIE *n* little drop
DRAPPY *n* drop (of liquid)
DRAPS ▸ **drap**
DRASTIC *n* strong purgative ▹ *adj* strong and severe
DRAT, -S *interj* exclamation of annoyance ▹ *vb* curse
DRATTED *adj* wretched
DRAUGHT *vb, n, adj*
DRAUNT, -S *same as* ▸ **drant**
DRAVE *archaic past of* ▸ **drive**
DRAW, -N, -S, DREW *vb, n*
DRAWBAR *n* strong metal bar on a tractor, locomotive, etc
DRAWEE, -S *n* person or organization on which payment is drawn
DRAWER *n*
DRAWERS *pl n* undergarment worn on the lower part of the body
DRAWING ▸ **draw**
DRAWL, -ED, -S *vb, n*
DRAWLER ▸ **drawl**
DRAWLS ▸ **drawl**
DRAWLY ▸ **drawl**
DRAWN ▸ **draw**
DRAWS ▸ **draw**
DRAY, -ED, -ING, -S *vb* pull using cart ▹ *n* low cart used for carrying heavy loads
DRAYAGE *n* act of transporting something a short distance
DRAYED ▸ **dray**
DRAYING ▸ **dray**
DRAYMAN, DRAYMEN *n* driver of a dray
DRAYS ▸ **dray**
DREAD, -ED, -S *vb, n, adj*
DREADER ▸ **dread**
DREADLY ▸ **dread**
DREADS ▸ **dread**
DREAM, -ED, -S, -T *n, vb, adj*
DREAMER *n* person who dreams habitually
DREAMS ▸ **dream**
DREAMT ▸ **dream**
DREAMY *adj* vague or impractical
DREAR, -ER, -S *same as* ▸ **dreary**
DREARE, -S *obsolete form of* ▸ **drear**
DREARER ▸ **drear**
DREARES ▸ **dreare**
DREARS ▸ **drear**
DREARY *adj, n*
DRECK, -S *n* rubbish
DRECKY ▸ **dreck**
DREDGE, -D, -S *vb*
DREDGER *n* machine used to remove mud from a river bed or harbour
DREDGES ▸ **dredge**
DREE, -D, -ING, -R, -S, -ST *vb* endure ▹ *adj* dreary
DREG *n* small quantity
DREGGY *adj* like or full of dregs
DREGS *pl n*
DREICH *adj* dreary
DREIDEL *n* spinning top
DREIDL, -S *same as* ▸ **dreidel**
DREIGH *same as* ▸ **dreich**
DREK, -S *same as* ▸ **dreck**
DREKKY ▸ **drek**
DREKS ▸ **drek**
DRENCH *vb, n*
DRENT *obsolete word for* ▸ **drenched**
DRERE, -S *obsolete form of* ▸ **drear**
DRESS, -ED, -ES, DREST *n, vb, adj*
DRESSER *n* piece of furniture with shelves and cupboards
DRESSES ▸ **dress**
DRESSY *adj* (of clothes) elegant
DREST ▸ **dress**
DREVILL *n* offensive person
DREW ▸ **draw**
DREY, -S *n* squirrel's nest

DRIB, -BED, -S *vb* flow in drops
DRIBBER ▸ **drib**
DRIBBLE *vb, n*
DRIBBLY ▸ **dribble**
DRIBLET *n* small amount
DRIBS ▸ **drib**
DRICE, -S *n* pellets of frozen carbon dioxide
DRIED ▸ **dry**
DRIEGH *adj* dreary
DRIER, -S ▸ **dry**
DRIES ▸ **dry**
DRIEST ▸ **dry**
DRIFT, -ED, -S *vb, n*
DRIFTER *n* person who moves aimlessly from place to place or job to job
DRIFTS ▸ **drift**
DRIFTY ▸ **drift**
DRILL, -ED, -S *n, vb*
DRILLER ▸ **drill**
DRILLS ▸ **drill**
DRILY *adv* in a dry manner
DRINK, DRANK, -S *vb, n*
DRINKER *n* person who drinks
DRINKS ▸ **drink**
DRIP, -PED, -S, -T *vb, n*
DRIPPER ▸ **drip**
DRIPPY *adj* mawkish, insipid, or inane
DRIPS ▸ **drip**
DRIPT ▸ **drip**
DRIVE, -N, -S *vb, n*
DRIVEL, -S *n, vb*
DRIVEN ▸ **drive**
DRIVER, -S *n* person who drives a vehicle
DRIVES ▸ **drive**
DRIVING ▸ **drive**
DRIZZLE *n, vb*
DRIZZLY ▸ **drizzle**
DROGER, -S *n* long-masted boat
DROGHER *same as* ▸ **droger**
DROGUE, -S *n* any funnel-like device used as a sea anchor
DROGUET *n* woollen fabric
DROICH, -S *n* dwarf
DROICHY *adj* dwarfish
DROID, -S *same as* ▸ **android**
DROIL, -ED, -S *vb* carry out boring menial work
DROIT, -S *n* legal or moral right or claim
DROKE, -S *n* small group of trees
DROLE, -R, -S, -ST *adj* amusing ▹ *n* scoundrel
DROLL, -ED, -ER, -S *vb* speak wittily ▹ *adj* quaintly amusing
DROLLY ▸ **droll**
DROME, -S *same as* > **aerodrome**
DROMIC *adj* relating to a running track
DROMOI ▸ **dromos**
DROMON, -S *same as* ▸ **dromond**
DROMOND *n* sailing vessel of the 12th to 15th centuries
DROMONS ▸ **dromon**
DROMOS, DROMOI *n* Greek passageway
DRONE, -D, -S, DRONING *n, vb*
DRONER, -S ▸ **drone**
DRONES ▸ **drone**
DRONGO, -S *n* tropical songbird
DRONIER ▸ **drony**
DRONING ▸ **drone**
DRONISH ▸ **drone**
DRONY, DRONIER *adj* monotonous
DROOB, -S *n* pathetic person
DROOG, -S *n* ruffian
DROOK, -ED, -S *same as* ▸ **drouk**
DROOKIT *same as* ▸ **droukit**
DROOKS ▸ **drook**
DROOL, -ED, -S *vb* show excessive enthusiasm (for)
DROOLY *adj* tending to drool
DROOME, -S *obsolete form of* ▸ **drum**
DROOP, -ED, -S *vb* hang downwards loosely ▹ *n* act or state of drooping
DROOPY *adj* hanging or sagging downwards
DROP, -PED, -S, -T *vb, n*
DROPFLY *n* (in angling) an artificial fly
DROPLET *n*
DROPOUT *n*
DROPPED ▸ **drop**
DROPPER *n* small tube with a rubber part at one end
DROPPLE *n* trickle
DROPS ▸ **drop**
DROPSY *n* illness in which watery fluid collects in the body
DROPT ▸ **drop**
DROPTOP *n* convertible car
DROSERA *n* insectivorous plant
DROSHKY *n* four-wheeled carriage, formerly used in Russia

DROSKY *same as* ▸ **droshky**
DROSS, -ES *n*
DROSSY ▸ **dross**
DROSTDY *n* office of landdrost
DROUGHT *n*
DROUK, -ED, -S *vb* drench
DROUKIT *adj* drenched
DROUKS ▸ **drouk**
DROUTH, -S *same as* ▸ **drought**
DROUTHY *adj* thirsty or dry
DROVE, -D, -S *vb, n*
DROVER, -S *n* person who drives sheep or cattle
DROVES ▸ **drove**
DROVING ▸ **drove**
DROW, -S *n* sea fog
DROWN, -ED, -S *vb*
DROWND, -S *dialect form of* ▸ **drown**
DROWNED ▸ **drown**
DROWNER ▸ **drown**
DROWNS ▸ **drown**
DROWS ▸ **drow**
DROWSE, -D, -S *vb* be sleepy, dull, or sluggish ▹ *n* state of being drowsy
DROWSY *adj*
DRUB, -BED, -S *vb* beat as with a stick ▹ *n* blow, as from a stick
DRUBBER ▸ **drub**
DRUBS ▸ **drub**
DRUCKEN *adj* old word meaning drunken
DRUDGE, -D, -S *n, vb*
DRUDGER ▸ **drudge**
DRUDGES ▸ **drudge**
DRUG, -GED, -S *n, vb*
DRUGGER *n* druggist
DRUGGET *n* coarse fabric used as a protective floor-covering, etc
DRUGGY ▸ **drug**
DRUGS ▸ **drug**
DRUID, -S *n*
DRUIDIC ▸ **druid**
DRUIDRY ▸ **druid**
DRUIDS ▸ **druid**
DRUM, -MED, -S *n, vb*
DRUMBLE *vb* be inactive
DRUMLIN *n* streamlined mound of glacial drift
DRUMLY *adj* dismal; dreary
DRUMMED ▸ **drum**
DRUMMER *n* person who plays a drum or drums
DRUMMY *n* (in South Africa) drum majorette
DRUMS ▸ **drum**
DRUNK, -ER, -S *adj, n*
DRUNKEN *adj* drunk or frequently drunk
DRUNKER ▸ **drunk**
DRUNKS ▸ **drunk**
DRUPE, -S *n* fleshy fruit with a stone, such as the peach or cherry
DRUPEL, -S *same as* > **drupelet**
DRUPES ▸ **drupe**
DRUSE, -S *n* aggregate of small crystals within a cavity
DRUSEN *pl n* small deposits of material on the retina
DRUSES ▸ **druse**
DRUSY, DRUSIER *adj* made of tiny crystals
DRUTHER *n* preference
DRUXY, DRUXIER *adj* (of wood) having decayed white spots
DRY, DRIED, DRIES, DRIEST, -EST, -S *adj, vb*
DRYABLE ▸ **dry**
DRYAD, -ES, -S *n* wood nymph
DRYADIC ▸ **dryad**
DRYADS ▸ **dryad**
DRYAS *n* alpine plant with white flowers
DRYBEAT *vb* beat severely
DRYER, -S ▸ **dry**
DRYEST ▸ **dry**
DRYING, -S ▸ **dry**
DRYISH *adj* fairly dry
DRYLAND *n* arid area
DRYLOT, -S *n* livestock enclosure
DRYLY *same as* ▸ **drily**
DRYNESS ▸ **dry**
DRYS ▸ **dry**
DRYSUIT *n* waterproof rubber suit worn by divers
DRYWALL *n* wall built without mortar ▹ *vb* build a wall without mortar
DRYWELL *n* type of sewage disposal system
DSO, -S *same as* ▸ **zho**

A **dso** is a kind of Himalayan ox; the other forms are **dzo, zho, dzho** and **zo** and it's worth remembering all of them.

DSOBO, -S *same as* ▸ **zobo**
DSOMO, -S *same as* ▸ **zhomo**

DSOS ▶ **dso**
DUAD, -S *a rare word for* ▶ **pair**
DUAL, -LED, -S *adj* having two parts, functions, or aspects ▷ *n* dual number ▷ *vb* make (a road) into a dual carriageway
DUALIN, -S *n* explosive substance
DUALISE *same as* ▶ **dualize**
DUALISM *n* state of having two distinct parts
DUALIST ▶ **dualism**
DUALITY *n* state or quality of being two or in two parts
DUALIZE *vb* cause to have two parts
DUALLED ▶ **dual**
DUALLIE *n* pickup truck with dual rear tyres
DUALLY ▶ **dual**
DUALS ▶ **dual**
DUAN, -S *n* poem
DUAR, -S *n* Arab camp
DUARCHY *same as* ▶ **diarchy**
DUARS ▶ **duar**
DUB, -BED, -S *vb, n*
DUBBER, -S ▶ **dub**
DUBBIN, -S *n* thick grease applied to leather to soften and waterproof it ▷ *vb* apply dubbin to
DUBBING ▶ **dub**
DUBBINS ▶ **dubbin**
DUBBO, -S *adj* stupid ▷ *n* stupid person
DUBIETY *n* state of being doubtful
DUBIOUS *adj*
DUBNIUM *n* chemical element
DUBS ▶ **dub**
DUBSTEP *n* genre of electronic music
DUCAL *adj* of a duke
DUCALLY ▶ **ducal**
DUCAT, -S *n* former European gold or silver coin
DUCDAME *interj* Shakespearean nonsense word
DUCE, -S, DUCI *n* leader
DUCHESS *n, vb*
DUCHY, DUCHIES *n* territory of a duke or duchess
DUCI ▶ **duce**
DUCK, -ED, -S *n, vb*
DUCKER, -S ▶ **duck**
DUCKIE *same as* ▶ **ducky**
DUCKIER ▶ **ducky**
DUCKIES ▶ **ducky**
DUCKING ▶ **duck**
DUCKISH *n* twilight
DUCKPIN *n* short bowling pin
DUCKS ▶ **duck**
DUCKY, DUCKIER, DUCKIES *n* darling or dear ▷ *adj* delightful
DUCT, -ED, -S *vb, n*
DUCTAL ▶ **duct**
DUCTED ▶ **duct**
DUCTILE *adj* (of a metal) able to be shaped into sheets or wires
DUCTING ▶ **duct**
DUCTS ▶ **duct**
DUCTULE *n* small duct
DUD, -S *n, adj*
DUDDER, -S *n* door-to-door salesperson ▷ *vb* tremble or shudder
DUDDERY *n* place where old clothes are sold
DUDDIE, -R, -S *adj* ragged ▷ *n* friend or a chum
DUDDY *same as* ▶ **duddie**
DUDE, -D, -S, DUDING *vb* dress fashionably ▷ *n* man
DUDEEN, -S *n* clay pipe with a short stem
DUDES ▶ **dude**
DUDETTE *n* woman who behaves like a dude
DUDGEON *n* anger or resentment
DUDHEEN *n* type of pipe
DUDING ▶ **dude**
DUDISH ▶ **dude**
DUDISM, -S *n* being a dude
DUDS ▶ **dud**
DUE, -D, DUING *vb, adj, n, adv*
DUEFUL *adj* proper
DUEL, -ED, -LED, -S *n, vb*
DUELER, -S ▶ **duel**
DUELING ▶ **duel**
DUELIST ▶ **duel**
DUELLED ▶ **duel**
DUELLER ▶ **duel**
DUELLO, DUELLI, -S *n* art of duelling
DUELS ▶ **duel**
DUENDE, -S *n* Spanish goblin
DUENESS ▶ **due**
DUENNA, -S *n* (esp in Spain) woman acting as a chaperone to a young woman

DUES *pl n* membership fees
DUET, -ED, -ING, -S, -TED *n, vb*
DUETT, -S *same as* ▶ **duet**
DUETTED ▶ **duet**
DUETTO, DUETTI, -S *same as* ▶ **duet**
DUETTS ▶ **duett**
DUFF, -ED, -EST, -S *adj* broken or useless ▷ *vb* change the appearance of or give a false appearance to (old or stolen goods) ▷ *n* mishit golf shot
DUFFEL, -S *n*
DUFFER, -S *n*
DUFFEST ▶ **duff**
DUFFING ▶ **duff**
DUFFLE, -S *same as* ▶ **duffel**
DUFFS ▶ **duff**
DUFUS, -ES *same as* ▶ **doofus**
DUG, -S *Scottish word for* ▶ **dog**
DUGITE, -S *n* medium-sized Australian venomous snake
DUGONG, -S *n* whalelike mammal of tropical waters
DUGOUT, -S *n*
DUGS ▶ **dug**
DUH *interj* ironic response to a question or statement

This word provides a useful front hook to **uh**.

DUHKHA, -S *same as* ▶ **dukkha**
DUI ▶ **duo**
DUIKER, -S *n* small African antelope
DUING ▶ **due**
DUIT, -S *n* former Dutch coin
DUKA, -S *n* shop
DUKE, -D, DUKING *vb, n*
DUKEDOM *n*
DUKERY *n* duke's domain
DUKES *pl n* fists
DUKING ▶ **duke**
DUKKA, -S *n* mix of ground roast nuts and spices
DUKKAH, -S *same as* ▶ **dukka**
DUKKAS ▶ **dukka**
DUKKHA, -S *n* Buddhist belief that all things are suffering
DULCE, -S *n* sweet food or drink
DULCET, -S *adj* (of a sound) soothing or pleasant ▷ *n* soft organ stop
DULCIAN *n* precursor to the bassoon
DULCIFY *vb* make pleasant or agreeable
DULCITE *n* sweet substance
DULCOSE *another word for* ▶ **dulcite**
DULE, -S *n* suffering; misery
DULIA, -S *n* veneration accorded to saints
DULL, -ED, -ER, -EST, -ING, -S *adj, vb*
DULLARD *n*
DULLED ▶ **dull**
DULLER ▶ **dull**
DULLEST ▶ **dull**
DULLIER ▶ **dully**
DULLING ▶ **dull**
DULLISH ▶ **dull**
DULLS ▶ **dull**
DULLY, DULLIER ▶ **dull**
DULNESS ▶ **dull**
DULOSIS, DULOSES *n* behaviour where one species of ant forces members of another to work for them
DULOTIC ▶ **dulosis**
DULSE, -S *n* seaweed with large red edible fronds
DULY *adv* in a proper manner
DUM *adj* steamed
DUMA, -S *n* elective legislative assembly established by Tsar Nicholas II
DUMAIST *n* member of duma
DUMAS ▶ **duma**
DUMB, -ED, -ER, -EST, -ING, -S *vb, adj*
DUMBLY ▶ **dumb**
DUMBO, -S *n* unintelligent person
DUMBS ▶ **dumb**
DUMDUM, -S *n* soft-nosed bullet
DUMELA *sentence substitute* hello
DUMKA, -S, DUMKY *n* Slavonic lyrical song
DUMMY, DUMMIED, DUMMIER, DUMMIES *n, adj, vb*
DUMOSE *adj* bushlike
DUMOUS *same as* ▶ **dumose**
DUMP, -ED *vb, n*
DUMPBIN *n* unit in a bookshop displaying a

particular publisher's books
DUMPED ▸ **dump**
DUMPEE, -S *n* person dumped from a relationship
DUMPER, -S ▸ **dump**
DUMPIER ▸ **dumpy**
DUMPIES ▸ **dumpy**
DUMPILY ▸ **dumpy**
DUMPING ▸ **dump**
DUMPISH *same as* ▸ **dumpy**
DUMPLE, -D, -S *vb* form into a dumpling shape
DUMPS *pl n* state of melancholy
DUMPY, DUMPIER, DUMPIES *adj* short and plump ▹ *n* short, plump person
DUN, -NED, -NER, -NEST, -NING, -S *adj* brownish-grey ▹ *vb* demand payment from (a debtor) ▹ *n* demand for payment
DUNAM, -S *n* unit of area measurement
DUNCE, -S *n*
DUNCERY *n* duncelike behaviour
DUNCES ▸ **dunce**
DUNCH, -ED, -ES *vb* push against gently
DUNCISH *adj* duncelike
DUNDER, -S *n* cane juice lees
DUNE, -S *n*
DUNG, -ED, -ING, -S *n* faeces from animals such as cattle ▹ *vb* cover (ground) with manure
DUNGEON *vb, n*
DUNGER, -S *n* old decrepit car
DUNGIER ▸ **dungy**
DUNGING ▸ **dung**
DUNGS ▸ **dung**
DUNGY, DUNGIER ▸ **dung**
DUNITE, -S *n* ultrabasic igneous rock
DUNITIC ▸ **dunite**
DUNK, -ED, -S *vb*
DUNKER, -S ▸ **dunk**
DUNKING *n* act of dunking
DUNKS ▸ **dunk**
DUNLIN, -S *n* small sandpiper
DUNNAGE *n* loose material used for packing cargo
DUNNART *n* type of insectivorous marsupial
DUNNED ▸ **dun**
DUNNER ▸ **dun**
DUNNESS ▸ **dun**
DUNNEST ▸ **dun**
DUNNIER ▸ **dunny**
DUNNIES ▸ **dunny**
DUNNING ▸ **dun**
DUNNISH ▸ **dun**
DUNNITE *n* explosive containing ammonium picrate
DUNNO *vb* slang for don't know
DUNNOCK *n* hedge sparrow
DUNNY, DUNNIER, DUNNIES *n* in Australia, toilet ▹ *adj* like or relating to a dunny
DUNS ▸ **dun**
DUNSH, -ED, -ES *same as* ▸ **dunch**
DUNT, -ED, -ING, -S *n, vb*
DUO, DUI, -S *same as* ▸ **duet**
DUODENA > **duodenum**
DUOLOG, -S *same as* > **duologue**
DUOMO, DUOMI, -S *n* cathedral in Italy
DUOPOLY *n* situation when control of a commodity is vested in two producers or suppliers
DUOS ▸ **duo**
DUOTONE *n* process for producing halftone illustrations
DUP, -PED, -PING, -S *vb* open
DUPABLE ▸ **dupe**
DUPATTA *n* scarf worn in India
DUPE, -D, -S *vb, n*
DUPER, -S ▸ **dupe**
DUPERY ▸ **dupe**
DUPES ▸ **dupe**
DUPING, -S *n* act of duping
DUPION, -S *n* silk fabric made from the threads of double cocoons
DUPLE *adj* having two beats in a bar
DUPLET, -S *n* pair of electrons shared between two atoms in a covalent bond
DUPLEX *vb* duplicate ▹ *n* apartment on two floors ▹ *adj* having two parts
DUPLY, DUPLIED, DUPLIES *vb* give a second reply
DUPPED ▸ **dup**

DUPPIES ▸ **duppy**
DUPPING ▸ **dup**
DUPPY, DUPPIES *n* spirit or ghost
DUPS ▸ **dup**
DURA, -S *same as* ▸ **durra**
DURABLE *adj*
DURABLY ▸ **durable**
DURAL, -S *n* alloy of aluminium and copper
DURAMEN *another name for* ▸ **heartwood**
DURANCE *n* imprisonment
DURANT, -S *n* tough, leathery cloth
DURAS ▸ **dura**
DURBAR, -S *n* (formerly) the court of a native ruler or a governor in India
DURDUM, -S *same as* ▸ **dirdum**
DURE, -D, -S *vb* endure
DUREFUL *adj* lasting
DURES ▸ **dure**
DURESS *n*
DURESSE *same as* ▸ **duress**
DURGAH, -S *same as* ▸ **dargah**
DURGAN, -S *n* dwarf
DURGY, DURGIER *adj* dwarflike
DURIAN, -S *n* SE Asian tree with very large oval fruits
DURING *prep*
DURION, -S *same as* ▸ **durian**
DURMAST *n* large Eurasian oak tree with lobed leaves
DURN, -ING, -S *same as* ▸ **darn**
DURNED ▸ **durn**
DURNING ▸ **durn**
DURNS ▸ **durn**
DURO, -S *n* silver peso of Spain or Spanish America
DUROC, -S *n* breed of pig
DUROS ▸ **duro**
DUROY, -S *n* coarse woollen fabric
DURR, -S *same as* ▸ **durra**
DURRA, -S *n* Old World variety of sorghum
DURRIE *n* cotton carpet made in India, often in rectangular pieces fringed at the ends
DURRIES ▸ **durry**
DURRS ▸ **durr**
DURRY, DURRIES *n* cigarette
DURST *a past tense of* ▸ **dare**
DURUM, -S *n* variety of wheat
DURZI, -S *n* Indian tailor
DUSH, -ED, -ES, -ING *vb* strike hard
DUSK, -ED, -ER, -EST, -ING, -S *n* time just before nightfall, when it is almost dark ▹ *adj* shady ▹ *vb* make or become dark
DUSKEN, -S *vb* grow dark
DUSKER ▸ **dusk**
DUSKEST ▸ **dusk**
DUSKIER ▸ **dusky**
DUSKILY ▸ **dusky**
DUSKING ▸ **dusk**
DUSKISH ▸ **dusk**
DUSKLY ▸ **dusk**
DUSKS ▸ **dusk**
DUSKY, DUSKIER *adj* dark in colour
DUST, -ED, -S *n, vb*
DUSTBIN *n*
DUSTED ▸ **dust**
DUSTER, -S *n* cloth used for dusting
DUSTIER ▸ **dusty**
DUSTILY ▸ **dusty**
DUSTING ▸ **dust**
DUSTMAN, DUSTMEN *n*
DUSTOFF *n* casualty evacuation helicopter
DUSTPAN *n*
DUSTRAG *n* cloth for dusting
DUSTS ▸ **dust**
DUSTUP, -S *n* quarrel, fight, or argument
DUSTY, DUSTIER *adj* covered with dust
DUTCH, -ES *n* wife
DUTEOUS *adj* dutiful or obedient
DUTIED *adj* liable for duty
DUTIES ▸ **duty**
DUTIFUL *adj* doing what is expected
DUTY, DUTIES *n*
DUUMVIR *n* one of two coequal magistrates or officers
DUVET, -S *n* large quilt used as a bed cover
DUVETYN *n* soft napped velvety fabric of cotton, silk, wool, or rayon
DUX, -ES *n* (in Scottish and certain other schools) the top pupil in a class or school

A **dux** is a leader or top student, and is often useful for disposing of the X.

DUYKER, -S *same as* ▸ **duiker**
DVANDVA *n* class of compound words
DVORNIK *n* Russian doorkeeper
DWAAL, -S *n* state of absent-mindedness
DWALE, -S *n* deadly nightshade
DWALM, -ED, -S *same as* ▸ **dwam**
DWAM, -MED, -S *n* stupor or daydream ▹ *vb* faint or fall ill
DWANG, -S *n* short piece of wood inserted in a timber-framed wall
DWARF, -ED, -ER, -S, DWARVES *adj* undersized ▹ *n* person who is smaller than average ▹ *vb* cause (someone or something) to seem small by being much larger
DWAUM, -ED, -S *same as* ▸ **dwam**
DWEEB, -S *n* stupid or uninteresting person
DWEEBY *adj* like or typical of a dweeb
DWELL, -ED, -S, DWELT *vb, n*
DWELLER ▸ **dwell**
DWELLS ▸ **dwell**
DWELT ▸ **dwell**
DWILE, -S *n* floor cloth
DWINDLE *vb*
DWINE, -D, -S, DWINING *vb* languish
DYABLE ▸ **dye**
DYAD, -S *n* operator that is the unspecified product of two vectors
DYADIC, -S *adj* of or relating to a dyad ▹ *n* sum of a particular number of dyads
DYADS ▸ **dyad**
DYARCHY *same as* ▸ **diarchy**
DYBBUK, -S *n* (in Jewish folklore) the soul of a dead sinner possessing a living person's body
DYE, -D, -S *n, vb*
DYEABLE ▸ **dye**
DYED ▸ **dye**
DYEING, -S ▸ **dye**
DYELINE *same as* ▸ **diazo**
DYER, -S ▸ **dye**
DYES ▸ **dye**
DYESTER *n* dyer
DYEWEED *n* plant that produces dye
DYEWOOD *n* any wood from which dyes and pigments can be obtained
DYING, -S ▸ **die**
DYINGLY ▸ **die**
DYINGS ▸ **dying**
DYKE, -D, -S, DYKING *n, vb*
DYNAMIC *adj, n*
DYNAMO, -S *n*
DYNAST, -S *n* hereditary ruler
DYNASTY *n*
DYNE, -S *n* unit of force
DYNEIN, -S *n* class of proteins
DYNEL, -S *n* trade name for a synthetic fibre
DYNES ▸ **dyne**
DYNODE, -S *n* electrical component
DYSLOGY *n* uncomplimentary remarks
DYSODIL *n* yellow or green mineral
DYSPNEA *same as* ▸ **dyspnoea**
DYSURIA *n* difficult or painful urination
DYSURIC ▸ **dysuria**
DYSURY *same as* ▸ **dysuria**
DYVOUR, -S *n* debtor
DYVOURY *n* bankruptcy
DZEREN, -S *n* Chinese yellow antelope
DZHO, -S *same as* ▸ **zho**
DZO, -S *variant spelling of* ▸ **zo**

Ee

EA, -S *n* river
EACH *pron, determiner, adv*
EADISH *n* aftermath
EAGER, -ER, -S *adj* showing or feeling great desire, keen ▷ *n* eagre
EAGERLY ▶ **eager**
EAGERS ▶ **eager**
EAGLE, -D, -S, EAGLING *n, vb*
EAGLET, -S *n* young eagle
EAGLING ▶ **eagle**
EAGRE, -S *n* tidal bore, esp of the Humber or Severn estuaries
EALE, -D, -S, EALING *n* beast in Roman legend ▷ *vb* to ail
EAN, -ED, -ING, -S *vb* give birth
EANLING *n* newborn lamb
EANS ▶ **ean**
EAR, -S *n, vb*
EARACHE *n*
EARBALL *n* device used in acupressure
EARBASH *vb* talk incessantly
EARBOB, -S *n* earring
EARBUD, -S *n* small earphone
EARCON, -S *n* sound representing an object or event
EARD, -ED, -ING, -S *vb* bury
EARDROP *n* pendant earring
EARDRUM *n*
EARDS ▶ **eard**
EARED *adj* having an ear or ears
EARFLAP *n*
EARFUL, -S *n* scolding or telling-off
EARHOLE *n*
EARING, -S *n* line fastened to a corner of a sail for reefing
EARL, -S *n*
EARLAP, -S *same as* ▶ **earflap**
EARLDOM *n*
EARLESS ▶ **ear**
EARLIER ▶ **early**
EARLIES ▶ **early**
EARLIKE ▶ **ear**
EARLOBE *n*
EARLOCK *n* curl of hair close to ear
EARLS ▶ **earl**
EARLY, EARLIER, EARLIES *adv, adj, n*
EARMARK *vb, n*
EARMUFF *n*
EARN, -ED, -ING, -S, -T *vb*
EARNER, -S ▶ **earn**
EARNEST *adj, n*
EARNING ▶ **earn**
EARNS ▶ **earn**
EARNT ▶ **earn**
EARPICK *n* instrument for removing ear wax
EARPLUG *n*
EARRING *n*
EARS ▶ **ear**
EARSHOT *n*
EARST *adv* first; previously
EARTH, -ED, -S *n, vb*
EARTHEN *adj* made of baked clay or earth
EARTHLY *adj* conceivable or possible ▷ *n* chance
EARTHS ▶ **earth**
EARTHY *adj* coarse or crude
EARWAX *nontechnical name for* ▶ **cerumen**
EARWIG, -S *n, vb*
EARWORM *n* irritatingly catchy tune
EAS ▶ **ea**
EASE, -D, -S *n, vb*
EASEFUL *adj* characterized by or bringing ease
EASEL, -S *n*
EASELED *adj* mounted on an easel
EASELS ▶ **easel**
EASER, -S ▶ **ease**
EASES ▶ **ease**
EASIED ▶ **easy**

EASIER ▸ **easy**
EASIES ▸ **easy**
EASIEST ▸ **easy**
EASILY *adv*
EASING, -S *n* as in **quantitative easing** increasing the supply of money to stimulate the economy
EASLE, -S *n* hot ash
EASSEL *adv* easterly
EASSIL *adv* easterly
EAST, -ED, -S *n, adj, adv, vb*
EASTER, -S *n*
EASTERN *adj*
EASTERS ▸ **easter**
EASTING *n* net distance eastwards made by a vessel moving towards the east
EASTLIN *adj* easterly
EASTS ▸ **east**
EASY, EASIED, EASIER, EASIES, EASIEST, -ING *adj* not needing much work or effort ▹ *vb* stop rowing
EAT, ATE, -EN, -S *vb*
EATABLE *adj*
EATAGE, -S *n* grazing rights
EATCHE, -S *n* adze
EATEN ▸ **eat**
EATER, -S ▸ **eat**
EATERIE *same as* ▸ **eatery**
EATERS ▸ **eater**
EATERY *n* restaurant or eating house
EATH *adj* easy
EATHE *same as* ▸ **eath**
EATHLY ▸ **eath**
EATING, -S ▸ **eat**
EATS ▸ **eat**
EAU, -S, -X *same as* ▸ **ea**
EAVE, -S, EAVING *vb* give cover under the eaves of a building
EAVED *adj* having eaves
EAVES ▸ **eave**
EAVING ▸ **eave**
EBAUCHE *n* rough sketch
EBAYER, -S *n* any person who uses eBay
EBAYING *n* buying or selling using eBay
EBB, -ED, -ING, -S *vb, n*
EBBET, -S *n* type of newt
EBBING ▸ **ebb**
EBBLESS ▸ **ebb**
EBBS ▸ **ebb**
EBON, -S *poetic word for* ▸ **ebony**
EBONICS *n* dialect used by African-Americans
EBONIES ▸ **ebony**
EBONISE *same as* ▸ **ebonize**
EBONIST *n* carver of ebony
EBONITE *another name for* > **vulcanite**
EBONIZE *vb* stain or otherwise finish in imitation of ebony
EBONS ▸ **ebon**
EBONY, EBONIES *n, adj*
EBOOK, -S *n* book in electronic form
EBRIATE *adj* drunk
EBRIETY *n* drunkenness
EBRIOSE *adj* drunk
ECAD, -S *n* organism whose form has been affected by its environment
ECARTE, -S *n* card game for two, played with 32 cards and king high
ECBOLE, -S *n* digression
ECBOLIC *adj* inducing labour ▹ *n* drug or agent that induces labour
ECCE *interj* behold
ECCO *interj* look there
ECCRINE *adj* of or denoting glands that secrete externally
ECDEMIC *adj* not indigenous or endemic
ECDYSIS, ECDYSES *n* shedding of the cuticle in arthropods or the outer epidermal layer in reptiles
ECDYSON *same as* > **ecdysone**
ECESIC ▸ **ecesis**
ECESIS *n* establishment of a plant in a new environment
ECH *same as* ▸ **eche**
ECHAPPE *n* leap in ballet
ECHARD, -S *n* water that is present in the soil but cannot be utilized by plants
ECHE, -D, -S, ECHING *vb* eke out
ECHELLE *n* ladder; scale
ECHELON *n* level of power or responsibility ▹ *vb* assemble soldiers in rows
ECHES ▸ **eche**
ECHIDNA *n* spiny egg-laying mammal
ECHING ▸ **eche**
ECHINUS, ECHINI *n* ovolo moulding between the shaft and the abacus of a Doric column

ECHIUM, -S *n* type of Eurasian and African plant
ECHO, -ED, -ES, -ING, -S *n, vb*
ECHOER, -S ▸ **echo**
ECHOES ▸ **echo**
ECHOEY, ECHOIER *adj* producing echoes
ECHOIC *adj* characteristic of or resembling an echo
ECHOIER ▸ **echoey**
ECHOING ▸ **echo**
ECHOISE *same as* ▸ **echoize**
ECHOISM *n* onomatopoeia as a source of word formation
ECHOIST ▸ **echoism**
ECHOIZE *vb* repeat like an echo
ECHOS ▸ **echo**
ECHT *adj* real
ECLAIR, -S *n*
ECLAT, -S *n* brilliant success
ECLIPSE *n, vb*
ECLOGUE *n* pastoral or idyllic poem, usually in the form of a conversation or soliloquy
ECLOSE, -D, -S *vb* emerge
ECO, -S *n* ecology activist
ECOCIDE *n* total destruction of an area of the natural environment
ECOD *same as* ▸ **egad**
ECOGIFT *n* donation of land for environmental purposes
ECOLOGY *n*
ECOMAP, -S *n* diagram showing the links between an individual and their community
ECONOMY *n, adj*
ECONUT, -S *n* derogatory term for a keen environmentalist
ECORCHE *n* anatomical figure without the skin
ECOS ▸ **eco**
ECOTAGE *n* sabotage for ecological motives
ECOTONE *n* zone between two major ecological communities
ECOTOUR *n* holiday taking care not to damage environment ▹ *vb* take an ecotour
ECOTYPE *n* group of organisms in a species that have adapted to a particular environment
ECOZONE *n* large area with an ecosystem
ECRU, -S *n* greyish-yellow colour
ECSTASY *n*
ECTASES ▸ **ectasis**
ECTASIA *n* distension or dilation of a duct, vessel, or hollow viscus
ECTASIS, ECTASES *same as* ▸ **ectasia**
ECTATIC ▸ **ectasia**
ECTHYMA *n* local inflammation of the skin
ECTOPIA *n* congenital displacement of an organ or part
ECTOPIC ▸ **ectopia**
ECTOPY *same as* ▸ **ectopia**
ECTOZOA > **ectozoon**
ECTYPAL ▸ **ectype**
ECTYPE, -S *n* copy
ECU, -S *n* any of various former French gold or silver coins
ECUELLE *n* covered soup bowl with handles
ECUMENE *n* inhabited area of the world
ECURIE, -S *n* team of motor-racing cars
ECUS ▸ **ecu**
ECZEMA, -S *n*
ED, -S *n* editor
EDACITY > **edacious**
EDAMAME *n* Japanese dish of salted green soya beans
EDAPHIC *adj* of or relating to the physical and chemical conditions of the soil
EDDIED ▸ **eddy**
EDDIES ▸ **eddy**
EDDISH *n* pasture grass
EDDO, -ES *same as* ▸ **taro**
EDDY, EDDIED, EDDIES, -ING *n* circular movement of air, water, etc ▹ *vb* move with a circular motion
EDEMA, -S, -TA *same as* ▸ **oedema**
EDENIC *adj* delightful, like the Garden of Eden
EDENTAL *adj* having few or no teeth
EDGE, -D, -S *n, vb*
EDGER, -S ▸ **edge**
EDGES ▸ **edge**
EDGIER ▸ **edgy**
EDGIEST ▸ **edgy**
EDGILY ▸ **edgy**

EDGING, -S *n* anything placed along an edge to finish it ▷ *adj* relating to or used for making an edge
EDGY, EDGIER, EDGIEST *adj* nervous or irritable
EDH, -S *n* character of the runic alphabet
EDIBLE *adj*
EDIBLES *pl n* articles fit to eat
EDICT, -S *n*
EDICTAL ▶ **edict**
EDICTS ▶ **edict**
EDIFICE *n*
EDIFIED ▶ **edify**
EDIFIER ▶ **edify**
EDIFY, EDIFIED, EDIFIES *vb* improve morally by instruction
EDILE, -S *variant spelling of* ▶ **aedile**
EDIT, -ED, -S *vb, n*
EDITING ▶ **edit**
EDITION *n, vb*
EDITOR, -S *n*
EDITRIX *n* female editor
EDITS ▶ **edit**
EDS ▶ **ed**
EDUCATE *vb*
EDUCE, -D, -S, EDUCING *vb* evolve or develop
EDUCT, -S *n* substance separated from a mixture without chemical change
EDUCTOR ▶ **educe**
EDUCTS ▶ **educt**
EE, -N *Scots word for* ▶ **eye**
EECH, -ED, -ES, -ING *same as* ▶ **eche**
EEEW *interj* exclamation of disgust
EEJIT, -S *Scots and Irish word for* ▶ **idiot**
EEK *interj* indicating shock or fright
EEL, -S *n*
EELFARE *n* young eel
EELIER ▶ **eely**
EELIEST ▶ **eely**
EELING, -S *n* practice of catching eels
EELLIKE *adj* resembling an eel
EELPOUT *n* marine eel-like blennioid fish
EELS ▶ **eel**
EELWORM *n* any of various nematode worms
EELY, EELIER, EELIEST ▶ **eel**
EEN ▶ **ee**
EENSY, EENSIER *adj* very small
EERIE, -R, -ST *adj*
EERILY ▶ **eerie**
EERY *same as* ▶ **eerie**
EEVEN, -S *n* old form of evening
EEVN, -S *same as* ▶ **eeven**
EEVNING *n* old form of evening
EEVNS ▶ **eevn**
EEW *interj* exclamation of disgust
EF, -S *n* letter F
EFF, -ED, -S *vb* use bad language
EFFABLE *adj* capable of being expressed in words
EFFACE, -D, -S *vb* remove by rubbing
EFFACER ▶ **efface**
EFFACES ▶ **efface**
EFFECT *n, vb*
EFFECTS *pl n* personal belongings
EFFED ▶ **eff**
EFFEIR, -S *vb* suit
EFFENDI *n* (in the Ottoman Empire) a title of respect
EFFERE, -D, -S *same as* ▶ **effeir**
EFFETE *adj* powerless, feeble
EFFIGY *n*
EFFING, -S ▶ **eff**
EFFLUX *same as* > **effluence**
EFFORCE *vb* old word for force
EFFORT, -S *n*
EFFRAY, -S *archaic form of* ▶ **affray**
EFFS ▶ **eff**
EFFULGE *vb* radiate
EFFUSE, -D, -S *vb* pour or flow out ▷ *adj* (esp of an inflorescence) spreading out loosely
EFS ▶ **ef**
EFT, -S *n* dialect or archaic name for a newt ▷ *adv* again
EFTEST *adj* nearest at hand
EFTS ▶ **eft**
EFTSOON > **eftsoons**
EGAD, -S *n* mild oath or expression of surprise
EGAL *adj* equal
EGALITE *n* equality
EGALITY *n* equality
EGALLY ▶ **egal**
EGENCE, -S *n* need
EGENCY *same as* ▶ **egence**
EGER, -S *same as* ▶ **eagre**

EGEST, -ED, -S *vb* excrete (waste material)
EGESTA *pl n* anything egested, as waste material from the body
EGESTED ▸ **egest**
EGESTS ▸ **egest**
EGG, -ED, -ING, -S *n, vb*
EGGAR, -S *same as* ▸ **egger**
EGGCORN *n* misspelling caused by the mishearing of a word
EGGCUP, -S *n*
EGGED ▸ **egg**
EGGER, -S *n* moth with brown body and wings
EGGERY *n* place where eggs are laid
EGGHEAD *n*
EGGIER ▸ **eggy**
EGGIEST ▸ **eggy**
EGGING ▸ **egg**
EGGLER, -S *n* egg dealer: sometimes itinerant
EGGLESS ▸ **egg**
EGGLIKE *adj* like an egg
EGGMASS *n* intelligentsia
EGGNOG, -S *n*
EGGS ▸ **egg**
EGGWASH *n* beaten egg for brushing on pastry
EGGY, EGGIER, EGGIEST *adj* soaked in or tasting of egg
EGIS, -ES *rare spelling of* ▸ **aegis**
EGMA, -S *mispronunciation of* ▸ **enigma**
EGO, -S *n*
EGOISM, -S *n*
EGOIST, -S *n* person who is preoccupied with their own interests
EGOITY *n* essence of the ego
EGOLESS *adj* without an ego
EGOS ▸ **ego**
EGOSURF *vb* search for one's own name on the internet
EGOTISE *same as* ▸ **egotize**
EGOTISM *n*
EGOTIST *n* conceited boastful person
EGOTIZE *vb* talk or write in a self-important way
EGRESS *same as* > **emersion**
EGRET, -S *n* lesser white heron
EH, -ED, -ING, -S *interj* exclamation of surprise or inquiry ▹ *vb* say 'eh'
EIDE ▸ **eidos**
EIDENT *adj* diligent
EIDER, -S *n* Arctic duck
EIDETIC *adj* (of images) exceptionally vivid, allowing detailed recall of something ▹ *n* person with eidetic ability
EIDOLA ▸ **eidolon**
EIDOLIC ▸ **eidolon**
EIDOLON, EIDOLA *n* unsubstantial image
EIDOS, EIDE *n* intellectual character of a culture or a social group
EIGHT, -S *n*
EIGHTH, -S *n, adj*
EIGHTS ▸ **eight**
EIGHTVO *another word for* ▸ **octavo**
EIGHTY *n*
EIGNE *adj* firstborn
EIK, -ED, -ING, -S *variant form of* ▸ **eke**
EIKON, -ES, -S *variant spelling of* ▸ **icon**
EIKS ▸ **eik**
EILD, -S *n* old age
EILDING *n* fuel
EILDS ▸ **eild**
EINA *interj* exclamation of pain
EINE *pl n* eyes
EINKORN *n* variety of wheat of Greece and SW Asia
EIRACK, -S *n* young hen
EIRENIC *variant spelling of* ▸ **irenic**
EISEL, -S *n* vinegar
EISELL, -S *same as* ▸ **eisel**
EISELS ▸ **eisel**
EISH *interj* South African exclamation
EISWEIN *n* wine made from grapes frozen on the vine
EITHER *pron, adv, determiner*
EJECT, -ED, -S *vb*
EJECTA *pl n* matter thrown out by a volcano or during a meteorite impact
EJECTED ▸ **eject**
EJECTOR *n* person or thing that ejects
EJECTS ▸ **eject**
EJIDO, -S *n* communal farmland in Mexico
EKE, -D, -S, EKING *vb*

EKISTIC > **ekistics**
EKKA, -S *n* type of one-horse carriage
EKPWELE *n* former monetary unit of Equatorial Guinea
EKUELE *same as* ▸ **ekpwele**
EL, -S *n* American elevated railway
ELAIN, -S *same as* > **triolein**
ELAN, -S *n* style and vigour
ELANCE, -D, -S *vb* throw a lance
ELAND, -S *n* large antelope of southern Africa
ELANET, -S *n* bird of prey
ELANS ▸ **elan**
ELAPID, -S *n* mostly tropical type of venomous snake
ELAPINE *adj* of or like an elapid
ELAPSE, -D, -S *vb*
ELASTIC *adj, n*
ELASTIN *n* fibrous scleroprotein
ELATE, -S, ELATING *vb*
ELATED *adj* extremely happy and excited
ELATER, -S *n* elaterid beetle
ELATES ▸ **elate**
ELATING ▸ **elate**
ELATION *n* feeling of great happiness and excitement
ELATIVE *adj* denoting a grammatical case in Finnish and other languages ▹ *n* elative case
ELBOW, -ED, -S *n, vb*
ELCHEE, -S *n* ambassador
ELCHI, -S *same as* ▸ **elchee**
ELD, -S *n* old age
ELDER, -S *adj, n*
ELDERLY *adj* (fairly) old
ELDERS ▸ **elder**
ELDEST, -S *n* oldest child
ELDIN, -S *n* fuel
ELDING, -S *same as* ▸ **eldin**
ELDINS ▸ **eldin**
ELDRESS *n* woman elder
ELDRICH *same as* > **eldritch**
ELDS ▸ **eld**
ELECT, -ED, -S *vb, adj*
ELECTEE *n* someone who is elected
ELECTOR *n* someone who has the right to vote in an election
ELECTRO *vb* (in printing) make a metallic copy of a page
ELECTS ▸ **elect**
ELEGANT *adj*
ELEGIAC *adj* mournful or plaintive ▹ *n* elegiac couplet or stanza
ELEGIES ▸ **elegy**
ELEGISE *same as* ▸ **elegize**
ELEGIST ▸ **elegize**
ELEGIT, -S *n* writ delivering debtor's property to plaintiff
ELEGIZE *vb* compose an elegy or elegies (in memory of)
ELEGY, ELEGIES *n*
ELEMENT *n*
ELEMI, -S *n* fragrant resin obtained from various tropical trees
ELENCH, -S *n* refutation in logic
ELENCHI > **elenchus**
ELENCHS ▸ **elench**
ELEVATE *vb*
ELEVEN, -S *n*
ELEVON, -S *n* aircraft control surface usually fitted to tailless or delta-wing aircraft
ELF, -ED, -ING, -S, ELVES *n* (in folklore) small mischievous fairy ▹ *vb* entangle (esp hair)
ELFHOOD ▸ **elf**
ELFIN, -S *adj* small and delicate ▹ *n* young elf
ELFING ▸ **elf**
ELFINS ▸ **elfin**
ELFISH *adj* of, relating to, or like an elf or elves ▹ *n* supposed language of elves
ELFLAND *another name for* > **fairyland**
ELFLIKE ▸ **elf**
ELFLOCK *n* lock of hair
ELFS ▸ **elf**
ELHI *adj* informal US word meaning relating to elementary or high school
ELIAD, -S *n* glance
ELICHE, -S *n* pasta in the form of spirals
ELICIT, -S *vb*
ELIDE, -D, -S, ELIDING *vb* omit (a vowel or syllable) from a word
ELINT, -S *n* electronic intelligence

ELISION *n* omission of a vowel or syllable from a word
ELITE, -S *n, adj*
ELITISM *n* belief that society should be ruled by a small group of superior people
ELITIST ▸ **elitism**
ELIXIR, -S *n*
ELK, -S *n*
ELKHORN *n* as in **elkhorn fern** fern with a large leaf like an elk's horn
ELKS ▸ **elk**
ELL, -S *n* obsolete unit of length
ELLAGIC *adj* of an acid derived from gallnuts
ELLIPSE *n*
ELLOPS *same as* ▸ **elops**
ELLS ▸ **ell**
ELLWAND *n* stick for measuring lengths
ELM, -S *n*
ELMEN *adj* of or relating to elm trees
ELMIER ▸ **elmy**
ELMIEST ▸ **elmy**
ELMS ▸ **elm**
ELMWOOD *n* wood from an elm tree
ELMY, ELMIER, ELMIEST *adj* of or relating to elm trees
ELOCUTE *vb* speak as if practising elocution
ELODEA, -S *n* type of American plant
ELOGE, -S *same as* ▸ **eulogy**
ELOGIES ▸ **elogy**
ELOGIST ▸ **elogy**
ELOGIUM *same as* ▸ **eulogy**
ELOGY, ELOGIES *same as* ▸ **eulogy**
ELOIGN, -S *vb* remove (oneself, one's property, etc) to a distant place
ELOIN, -ED, -S *same as* ▸ **eloign**
ELOINER ▸ **eloin**
ELOINS ▸ **eloin**
ELOPE, -D, -S, ELOPING *vb*
ELOPER, -S ▸ **elope**
ELOPES ▸ **elope**
ELOPING ▸ **elope**
ELOPS, -ES *n* type of fish
ELPEE, -S *n* LP, long-playing record
ELS ▸ **el**
ELSE *adv*
ELSHIN, -S *n* cobbler's awl
ELSIN, -S *variant of* ▸ **elshin**
ELT, -S *n* young female pig
ELTCHI, -S *variant of* ▸ **elchee**
ELTS ▸ **elt**
ELUANT, -S *same as* ▸ **eluent**
ELUATE, -S *n* solution of adsorbed material obtained during the process of elution
ELUDE, -D, -S, ELUDING *vb*
ELUDER, -S ▸ **elude**
ELUDES ▸ **elude**
ELUDING ▸ **elude**
ELUENT, -S *n* solvent used for eluting
ELUSION ▸ **elude**
ELUSIVE *adj*
ELUSORY *adj* avoiding the issue
ELUTE, -D, -S, ELUTING *vb* wash out (a substance) by the action of a solvent
ELUTION ▸ **elute**
ELUTOR, -S ▸ **elute**
ELUVIA ▸ **eluvium**
ELUVIAL ▸ **eluvium**
ELUVIUM, ELUVIA *n* mass of sand, silt, etc
ELVAN, -S *n* type of rock
ELVEN *adj* like an elf
ELVER, -S *n* young eel
ELVES ▸ **elf**
ELVISH *same as* ▸ **elfish**
ELYSIAN *adj* delightful, blissful
ELYTRA ▸ **elytron**
ELYTRAL ▸ **elytron**
ELYTRON, ELYTRA *n* either of the horny front wings of beetles and some other insects
ELYTRUM *same as* ▸ **elytron**
EM, -S *n* square of a body of any size of type, used as a unit of measurement
EMACS, -EN *n* powerful computer program
EMAIL, -ED, -S *n, vb*
EMAILER ▸ **email**
EMAILS ▸ **email**
EMANANT ▸ **emanate**
EMANATE *vb*
EMBACE, -S *variant of* ▸ **embase**
EMBAIL, -S *vb* enclose in a circle
EMBALE, -D, -S *vb* bind
EMBALL, -S *vb* enclose in a circle
EMBALM, -S *vb*

EMBANK, -S *vb* protect, enclose, or confine with an embankment
EMBAR, -S *vb* close in with bars
EMBARGO *n, vb*
EMBARK, -S *vb*
EMBARS ▸ **embar**
EMBASE, -D, -S, EMBASTE *vb* degrade or debase
EMBASSY *n*
EMBASTE ▸ **embase**
EMBATHE *vb* bathe with water
EMBAY, -ED, -S *vb* form into a bay
EMBAYLD *archaic past form of* ▸ **embail**
EMBAYS ▸ **embay**
EMBED, -S *vb, n*
EMBER, -S *n*
EMBLAZE *vb* cause to light up
EMBLEM, -S *n, vb*
EMBLEMA *n* mosaic decoration
EMBLEMS ▸ **emblem**
EMBLIC, -S *n* type of Indian tree
EMBLOOM *vb* adorn with blooms
EMBODY *vb*
EMBOG, -S *vb* sink down into a bog
EMBOGUE *vb* go out through a narrow channel or passage
EMBOIL, -S *vb* enrage or be enraged
EMBOLI ▸ **embolus**
EMBOLIC *adj* of or relating to an embolus or embolism
EMBOLUS, EMBOLI *n* material that blocks a blood vessel
EMBOLY *n* infolding of an outer layer of cells so as to form a pocket in the surface
EMBOSK, -S *vb* hide or cover
EMBOSOM *vb* enclose or envelop, esp protectively
EMBOSS, EMBOST *vb*
EMBOUND *vb* surround or encircle
EMBOW, -ED, -S *vb* design or create (a structure) in the form of an arch or vault
EMBOWEL *vb* bury or embed deeply
EMBOWER *vb* enclose in or as in a bower
EMBOWS ▸ **embow**
EMBOX, -ED, -ES *vb* put in a box
EMBRACE *vb, n*
EMBRAID *vb* braid or interweave
EMBRAVE *vb* adorn or decorate
EMBREAD *vb* braid
EMBROIL *vb* involve (a person) in problems
EMBROWN *vb* make or become brown
EMBRUE, -D, -S *variant spelling of* ▸ **imbrue**
EMBRUTE *variant of* ▸ **imbrute**
EMBRYO, -S *n*
EMBRYON *variant of* ▸ **embryo**
EMBRYOS ▸ **embryo**
EMBUS, -ED, -ES *vb* cause (troops) to board a transport vehicle
EMBUSY *vb* keep occupied
EMCEE, -D, -S *n* master of ceremonies ▹ *vb* act as master of ceremonies (for or at)
EMDASH *n* long dash in punctuation
EME, -S *n* uncle
EMEER, -S *variant of* ▸ **emir**
EMEND, -ED, -S *vb* remove errors from
EMENDER ▸ **emend**
EMENDS ▸ **emend**
EMERALD *n, adj*
EMERG, -S *n* part of a hospital dealing with emergencies
EMERGE, -D, -S *vb*
EMERGS ▸ **emerg**
EMERIED ▸ **emery**
EMERIES ▸ **emery**
EMERITA *adj* retired, but retaining an honorary title ▹ *n* woman who is retired, but retains an honorary title
EMERITI > **emeritus**
EMEROD, -S *n* haemorrhoid
EMEROID *variant of* ▸ **emerod**
EMERSE *same as* ▸ **emersed**
EMERSED *adj* protruding above the surface of the water
EMERY, EMERIED, EMERIES *n* hard mineral used for smoothing and polishing ▹ *vb* apply emery to
EMES ▸ **eme**
EMESIS, EMESES *technical name for* > **vomiting**

EMETIC, -S *n* substance that causes vomiting ▷ *adj* causing vomiting
EMETIN, -S *same as* ▸ **emetine**
EMETINE *n* white bitter poisonous alkaloid
EMETINS ▸ **emetin**
EMEU, -S *variant of* ▸ **emu**
EMEUTE, -S *n* uprising or rebellion
EMIC, -S *adj* of or relating to a significant linguistic unit ▷ *n* emic viewpoint or approach
EMICANT ▸ **emicate**
EMICATE *vb* twinkle
EMICS ▸ **emic**
EMIGRE, -S *n* someone who has left his or her native country for political reasons
EMIGREE *n* female emigre
EMIGRES ▸ **emigre**
EMINENT *adj*
EMIR, -S *n* Muslim ruler
EMIRATE *n* emir's country
EMIRS ▸ **emir**
EMIT, -S, -TED *vb*
EMITTER *n* person or thing that emits
EMLETS *pl n* as in **blood-drop emlets** Chilean plant
EMMA, -S *n* former communications code for the letter M
EMMER, -S *n* variety of wheat
EMMESH *variant of* ▸ **enmesh**
EMMET, -S *n* tourist or holidaymaker
EMMEW, -ED, -S *vb* restrict
EMMOVE, -D, -S *vb* cause emotion in
EMMY, -S *n* award for outstanding television performances and productions
EMO, -S *n* type of music combining rock with emotional lyrics
EMOCORE *same as* ▸ **emo**
EMODIN, -S *n* chemical compound obtained from rhubarb root
EMOJI, -S *n* digital icon used in electronic communication
EMONG *variant of* ▸ **among**
EMONGES *variant of* ▸ **among**
EMONGST *variant of* ▸ **amongst**
EMOS ▸ **emo**
EMOTE, -D, -S, EMOTING *vb* display exaggerated emotion, as if acting
EMOTER, -S ▸ **emote**
EMOTES ▸ **emote**
EMOTING ▸ **emote**
EMOTION *n*
EMOTIVE *adj*
EMOVE, -D, -S, EMOVING *vb* cause to feel emotion
EMPAIRE *variant of* ▸ **impair**
EMPALE, -D, -S *less common spelling of* ▸ **impale**
EMPALER ▸ **empale**
EMPALES ▸ **empale**
EMPANEL *vb* enter on a list (names of persons to be summoned for jury service)
EMPARE, -D, -S *archaic variant of* ▸ **impair**
EMPARL, -S *variant of* ▸ **imparl**
EMPART, -S *variant of* ▸ **impart**
EMPATHY *n*
EMPAYRE *archaic variant of* ▸ **impair**
EMPEACH *variant of* ▸ **impeach**
EMPERCE *archaic variant of* > **empierce**
EMPEROR *n*
EMPERY *n* dominion or power
EMPIGHT *adj* attached or positioned ▷ *vb* attach or position
EMPIRE, -S *n*
EMPIRIC *n* person who relies on empirical methods
EMPLACE *vb* put in place or position
EMPLANE *vb* board or put on board an aeroplane
EMPLOY, -S *vb, n*
EMPLOYE *same as* > **employee**
EMPLOYS ▸ **employ**
EMPLUME *vb* put a plume on
EMPORIA > **emporium**
EMPOWER *vb*
EMPRESS *n*
EMPRISE *n* chivalrous or daring enterprise
EMPRIZE *variant of* ▸ **emprise**
EMPT, -ED, -ING, -S *vb* empty
EMPTIED ▸ **empty**

EMPTIER ▸ **empty**
EMPTIES ▸ **empty**
EMPTILY ▸ **empty**
EMPTING ▸ **empt**
EMPTINS *pl n* liquid leavening agent made from potatoes
EMPTION *n* process of buying something
EMPTS ▸ **empt**
EMPTY, EMPTIED, EMPTIES *adj, vb, n*
EMPUSA, -S *n* goblin in Greek mythology
EMPUSE, -S *variant of* ▸ **empusa**
EMPYEMA *n* collection of pus in a body cavity
EMS ▸ **em**
EMU, -S *n*
EMULATE *vb*
EMULE, -D, -S, EMULING *variant of* ▸ **emulate**
EMULGE, -D, -S *vb* remove liquid from
EMULING ▸ **emule**
EMULOUS *adj* desiring or aiming to equal or surpass another
EMULSIN *n* enzyme that is found in almonds
EMULSOR *n* device that emulsifies
EMUNGE, -D, -S *vb* clean or clear out
EMURE, -D, -S, EMURING *variant of* ▸ **immure**
EMUS ▸ **emu**
EMYD, -S *n* freshwater tortoise or terrapin
EMYDE, -S *same as* ▸ **emyd**
EMYDS ▸ **emyd**
EMYS *n* freshwater tortoise or terrapin
EN *n* unit of measurement, half the width of an em
ENABLE, -D, -S *vb*
ENABLER ▸ **enable**
ENABLES ▸ **enable**
ENACT, -ED, -S *vb*
ENACTOR ▸ **enact**
ENACTS ▸ **enact**
ENAMEL, -S *n, vb*
ENAMINE *n* type of unsaturated compound
ENAMOR, -S *same as* ▸ **enamour**
ENAMOUR *vb*
ENARCH *variant of* ▸ **inarch**
ENARM, -ED, -S *vb* provide with arms
ENATE, -S *adj* growing out or outwards ▹ *n* relative on the mother's side
ENATIC *adj* related on one's mother's side
ENATION ▸ **enate**
ENCAGE, -D, -S *vb* confine in or as in a cage
ENCALM, -S *vb* becalm, settle
ENCAMP, -S *vb* set up in a camp
ENCASE, -D, -S *vb* enclose or cover completely
ENCASH *vb* exchange (a cheque) for cash
ENCAVE, -D, -S *variant of* ▸ **incave**
ENCHAFE *vb* heat up
ENCHAIN *vb* bind with chains
ENCHANT *vb*
ENCHARM *vb* enchant
ENCHASE *less common word for* ▸ **chase**
ENCHEER *vb* cheer up
ENCINA, -S *n* type of oak
ENCINAL ▸ **encina**
ENCINAS ▸ **encina**
ENCLASP *vb* clasp
ENCLAVE *n, vb*
ENCLOSE *vb*
ENCLOUD *vb* hide with clouds
ENCODE, -D, -S *vb*
ENCODER ▸ **encode**
ENCODES ▸ **encode**
ENCOMIA > **encomium**
ENCORE, -D, -S *interj* again, once more ▹ *n* extra performance due to enthusiastic demand ▹ *vb* demand an extra or repeated performance
ENCRATY *n* control of one's desires, actions, etc
ENCRUST *vb*
ENCRYPT *vb* put (a message) into code
ENCYST, -S *vb* enclose or become enclosed by a cyst, thick membrane, or shell
END, -ED, -S *n, vb*
ENDARCH *adj* having the first-formed xylem internal to that formed later
ENDART, -S *variant of* ▸ **indart**
ENDASH *n* short dash in punctuation
ENDCAP, -S *n* display placed at the end of a shop aisle
ENDEAR, -S *vb* cause to be liked

ENDED ▸ **end**
ENDEMIC *adj* present within a particular area or group of people ▹ *n* endemic disease or plant
ENDER, -S ▸ **end**
ENDERON *variant of* ▸ **andiron**
ENDERS ▸ **ender**
ENDEW, -ED, -S *variant of* ▸ **endue**
ENDGAME *n*
ENDGATE *n* tailboard of a vehicle
ENDING, -S *n* last part or conclusion of something
ENDIRON *variant of* ▸ **andiron**
ENDITE, -D, -S *variant of* ▸ **indict**
ENDIVE, -S *n* curly-leaved plant used in salads
ENDLANG *variant of* ▸ **endlong**
ENDLEAF *n* endpaper in a book
ENDLESS *adj*
ENDLONG *adv* lengthways or on end
ENDMOST *adj* nearest the end
ENDNOTE *n* note at the end of a section of writing
ENDOGEN *n* plant that increases in size by internal growth
ENDOPOD *n* inner branch of a two-branched crustacean
ENDORSE *vb* give approval to
ENDOSS *vb* endorse
ENDOW, -ED, -S *vb*
ENDOWER ▸ **endow**
ENDOWS ▸ **endow**
ENDOZOA > **endozoon**
ENDPLAY *n* technique in card games ▹ *vb* force (an opponent) to make a particular lead near the end of a hand
ENDRIN, -S *n* type of insecticide
ENDS ▸ **end**
ENDSHIP *n* small village
ENDUE, -D, -S, ENDUING *vb* invest or provide, as with some quality or trait
ENDURE, -D, -S *vb* bear (hardship) patiently
ENDURER ▸ **endure**
ENDURES ▸ **endure**
ENDURO, -S *n* long-distance race for vehicles
ENDWAYS *adv* having the end forwards or upwards ▹ *adj* vertical or upright
ENDWISE *same as* ▸ **endways**
ENDYSIS, ENDYSES *n* formation of new layers of integument after ecdysis
ENDZONE *n* (in American football) area at either end of the playing field
ENE, -S *variant of* ▸ **even**
ENEMA, -S, -TA *n* medicine that helps to empty the bowels
ENEMY, ENEMIES *n, adj*
ENERGIC ▸ **energy**
ENERGID *n* nucleus and cytoplasm in a syncytium
ENERGY *n*
ENERVE, -D, -S *vb* enervate
ENES ▸ **ene**
ENEW, -ED, -ING, -S *vb* force a bird into water
ENFACE, -D, -S *vb* write, print, or stamp (something) on the face of (a document)
ENFANT, -S *n* French child
ENFELON *vb* infuriate
ENFEOFF *vb* invest (a person) with possession of a freehold estate in land
ENFEVER *vb* make feverish
ENFILED *adj* passed through
ENFIRE, -D, -S *vb* set alight
ENFIX, -ED, -ES *variant of* ▸ **infix**
ENFLAME *variant of* ▸ **inflame**
ENFLESH *vb* make flesh
ENFOLD, -S *vb*
ENFORCE *vb*
ENFORM, -S *variant of* ▸ **inform**
ENFRAME *vb* put inside a frame
ENFREE, -D, -S *vb* release, make free
ENFROZE > **enfreeze**
ENG, -S *another name for* ▸ **agma**
ENGAGE, -S *vb, adj*
ENGAGED *adj* pledged to be married
ENGAGEE *adj* (of a female artist) morally or politically committed to some ideology

ENGAGER ▸ **engage**
ENGAGES ▸ **engage**
ENGAOL, -S *vb* put into gaol
ENGILD, -S, ENGILT *vb* cover with or as if with gold
ENGINE, -D, -S *n, vb*
ENGINER ▸ **engine**
ENGINES ▸ **engine**
ENGIRD, -S, ENGIRT *vb* surround
ENGLISH *vb* put spin on a billiard ball
ENGLOBE *vb* surround as if in a globe
ENGLOOM *vb* make dull or dismal
ENGLUT, -S *vb* devour ravenously
ENGOBE, -S *n* liquid put on pottery before glazing
ENGORE, -D, -S *vb* pierce or wound
ENGORGE *vb* clog with blood
ENGRACE *vb* give grace to
ENGRAFF *variant of* ▸ **engraft**
ENGRAFT *vb* graft (a shoot, bud, etc) onto a stock
ENGRAIL *vb* decorate or mark with small carved notches
ENGRAIN *variant spelling of* ▸ **ingrain**
ENGRAM, -S *n* physical basis of an individual memory in the brain
ENGRASP *vb* grasp or seize
ENGRAVE *vb*
ENGROSS *vb*
ENGS ▸ **eng**
ENGUARD *vb* protect or defend
ENGULF, -S *vb* cover or surround completely
ENGULPH *variant of* ▸ **engulf**
ENHALO, -S *vb* surround with or as if with a halo
ENHANCE *vb*
ENIAC, -S *n* early type of computer built in the 1940s
ENIGMA, -S *n*
ENISLE, -D, -S *vb* put on or make into an island
ENJAMB, -S *vb* (of a line of verse) run over into the next line
ENJOIN, -S *vb* order (someone) to do something
ENJOY, -ED, -S *vb*
ENJOYER ▸ **enjoy**
ENJOYS ▸ **enjoy**
ENLACE, -D, -S *vb* bind or encircle with or as with laces
ENLARD, -S *vb* put lard on
ENLARGE *vb*
ENLEVE *adj* having been abducted
ENLIGHT, ENLIT *vb* light up
ENLINK, -S *vb* link together
ENLIST, -S *vb*
ENLIT ▸ **enlight**
ENLIVEN *vb*
ENLOCK, -S *vb* lock or secure
ENMESH *vb* catch or involve in or as if in a net or snare
ENMEW, -ED, -S *variant of* ▸ **emmew**
ENMITY *n* ill will, hatred
ENMOVE, -D, -S *variant of* ▸ **emmove**
ENNAGE, -S *n* number of ens in printed matter
ENNEAD, -S *n* group or series of nine
ENNOBLE *vb* make noble, elevate
ENNOG, -S *n* back alley
ENNUI, -ED, -S, ENNUYED *n* boredom, dissatisfaction ▷ *vb* bore
ENNUYE *adj* bored
ENNUYED ▸ **ennui**
ENNUYEE *same as* ▸ **ennuye**
ENODAL *adj* having no nodes
ENOKI, -S *variant of* > **enokitake**
ENOL, -S *n* type of organic compound
ENOLASE *n* type of enzyme
ENOLIC ▸ **enol**
ENOLOGY *usual US spelling of* > **oenology**
ENOLS ▸ **enol**
ENOMOTY *n* division of the Spartan army in ancient Greece
ENORM *variant of* > **enormous**
ENOSIS, ENOSES *n* union of Greece and Cyprus
ENOUGH, -S *adj, n, adv*
ENOUNCE *vb* enunciate
ENOW, -S *archaic word for* ▸ **enough**
ENPLANE *vb* board an aircraft

ENPRINT *n* standard photographic print
ENQUEUE *vb* add (an item) to a queue of computing tasks
ENQUIRE *same as* ▸ **inquire**
ENQUIRY ▸ **enquire**
ENRACE, -D, -S *vb* archaic word meaning to bring into a race (of people)
ENRAGE, -D, -S *vb*
ENRANGE *vb* arrange, organize
ENRANK, -S *vb* put in a row
ENRAPT > **enrapture**
ENRHEUM *vb* pass a cold on to
ENRICH *vb*
ENRING, -S *vb* put a ring round
ENRIVEN *adj* ripped
ENROBE, -D, -S *vb* dress in or as if in a robe
ENROBER ▸ **enrobe**
ENROBES ▸ **enrobe**
ENROL, -S *vb*
ENROLL, -S *same as* ▸ **enrol**
ENROLS ▸ **enrol**
ENROOT, -S *vb* establish (plants) by fixing their roots in the earth
ENROUGH *vb* roughen
ENROUND *vb* encircle
ENS, ENTIA *n* entity
ENSATE *adj* shaped like a sword
ENSEAL, -S *vb* seal up
ENSEAM, -S *vb* put a seam on
ENSEAR, -S *vb* dry
ENSERF, -S *vb* enslave
ENSEW, -ED, -S *variant of* ▸ **ensue**
ENSHELL *variant of* ▸ **inshell**
ENSIGN, -S *n* military officer ▹ *vb* mark with a sign
ENSILE, -D, -S *vb* store and preserve (green fodder) in an enclosed pit or silo
ENSKY, ENSKIED, ENSKIES, -ED *vb* put in the sky
ENSLAVE *vb*
ENSNARE *vb* catch in or as if in a snare
ENSNARL *vb* catch in or as if in a snarl
ENSOUL, -S *vb* endow with a soul
ENSTAMP *vb* imprint with a stamp
ENSTEEP *vb* soak in water
ENSTYLE *vb* give a name to
ENSUE, -D, -S *vb*
ENSUING *adj* following subsequently or in order
ENSUITE *n* bathroom attached to another room
ENSURE, -D, -S *vb* make certain or sure
ENSURER ▸ **ensure**
ENSURES ▸ **ensure**
ENSWEEP, ENSWEPT *vb* sweep across
ENTAIL, -S *vb, n*
ENTAME, -D, -S *vb* make tame
ENTASES ▸ **entasis**
ENTASIA *same as* ▸ **entasis**
ENTASIS, ENTASES *n* slightly convex curve given to the shaft of a structure
ENTAYLE *variant of* ▸ **entail**
ENTENTE *n* friendly understanding between nations
ENTER, -ED, -S *vb* come or go in
ENTERA ▸ **enteron**
ENTERAL *same as* ▸ **enteric**
ENTERED ▸ **enter**
ENTERER ▸ **enter**
ENTERIC *adj* intestinal ▹ *n* infectious disease of the intestines
ENTERON, ENTERA *n* alimentary canal
ENTERS ▸ **enter**
ENTETE *adj* obsessed
ENTETEE *variant of* ▸ **entete**
ENTHRAL *vb*
ENTHUSE *vb* (cause to) show enthusiasm
ENTIA ▸ **ens**

> This means entities, and because of the common letters it uses is one of the most frequently played 5-letter words, at least towards the end of the game.

ENTICE, -D, -S *vb*
ENTICER ▸ **entice**
ENTICES ▸ **entice**
ENTIRE, -S *adj, n*
ENTITLE *vb*
ENTITY *n*
ENTOIL, -S *archaic word for* ▸ **ensnare**

ENTOMB, -S *vb*
ENTOMIC *adj* denoting or relating to insects
ENTOPIC *adj* situated in its normal place or position
ENTOTIC *adj* of or relating to the inner ear
ENTOZOA > **entozoon**
ENTRAIL *vb* twist or entangle
ENTRAIN *vb* board or put aboard a train
ENTRALL *old variant of* > **entrails**
ENTRANT *n* person who enters a university, contest, etc
ENTRAP, -S *vb*
ENTREAT *vb* ask earnestly
ENTREE, -S *n* dish served before a main course
ENTREZ *interj* enter
ENTRIES ▸ **entry**
ENTRISM *variant of* > **entryism**
ENTRIST ▸ **entrism**
ENTROLD *adj* word used by Spenser meaning surrounded
ENTROPY *n* lack of organization
ENTRUST *vb*
ENTRY, ENTRIES *n, adj*
ENTS *pl n* (college) entertainments
ENTWINE *vb*
ENTWIST *vb* twist together or around
ENUF *common intentional literary misspelling of* ▸ **enough**
ENURE, -D, -S, ENURING *variant spelling of* ▸ **inure**
ENURN *same as* ▸ **inurn**
ENURNED *same as* ▸ **inurned**
ENURNS *same as* ▸ **inurns**
ENVAULT *vb* enclose in a vault; entomb
ENVELOP *vb*
ENVENOM *vb* fill or impregnate with venom
ENVIED ▸ **envy**
ENVIER, -S ▸ **envy**
ENVIES ▸ **envy**
ENVIOUS *adj* full of envy
ENVIRO, -S *n* environmentalist
ENVIRON *vb* encircle or surround
ENVIROS ▸ **enviro**
ENVOI, -S *same as* ▸ **envoy**
ENVOY, -S *n*
ENVY, ENVIED, ENVIES *n* feeling of discontent aroused by another's good fortune ▹ *vb* grudge (another's good fortune, success, or qualities)
ENVYING ▸ **envy**
ENWALL, -S *vb* wall in
ENWHEEL *archaic word for* > **encircle**
ENWIND, -S, ENWOUND *vb* wind or coil around
ENWOMB, -S *vb* enclose in or as if in a womb
ENWOUND ▸ **enwind**
ENWRAP, -S, -T *vb* wrap or cover up
ENZIAN, -S *n* gentian violet
ENZONE, -D, -S *vb* enclose in a zone
ENZYM, -S *same as* ▸ **enzyme**
ENZYME, -S *n*
ENZYMIC ▸ **enzyme**
ENZYMS ▸ **enzym**
EOAN *adj* of or relating to the dawn
EOBIONT *n* hypothetical chemical precursor of a living cell
EOCENE *adj* of, denoting, or formed in the second epoch of the Tertiary period
EOLIAN *adj* of or relating to the wind

6-letter words tend to be among the least known and least used, because they leave you at the mercy of the tile bag without scoring that extra 50 points you would get for using all 7 letters. This word, meaning relating to the wind, often comes in useful for dumping a surplus of vowels. Its alternative spelling **aeolian** is even better for this, and what's more will get you a bonus!

EOLITH, -S *n* stone used as a primitive tool in Eolithic times
EON, -S *n* immeasurably long period of time
EONIAN *adj* everlasting

EONISM, -S *n* adoption of female dress and behaviour by a male
EONS ▸ **eon**
EORL, -S *n* Anglo-Saxon nobleman
EOSIN, -S *n* red crystalline water-insoluble derivative of fluorescein
EOSINE, -S *same as* ▸ **eosin**
EOSINIC ▸ **eosin**
EOSINS ▸ **eosin**
EOTHEN *adv* from the East
EPACRID *n* type of heath-like plant
EPACRIS *n* genus of the epacrids
EPACT, -S *n* difference in time between the solar year and the lunar year
EPAGOGE *n* inductive reasoning
EPARCH, -S *n* bishop or metropolitan in charge of an eparchy
EPARCHY *n* diocese of the Eastern Christian Church
EPATANT *adj* startling or shocking
EPATER, -S *vb* startle or shock
EPAULE, -S *n* shoulder of a fortification
EPAULET *same as* > **epaulette**
EPAXIAL *adj* above the axis
EPAZOTE *n* type of herb
EPEE, -S *n* straight-bladed sword used in fencing
EPEEIST *n* one who uses or specializes in using an epee
EPEES ▸ **epee**
EPEIRA, -S *same as* ▸ **epeirid**
EPEIRIC *adj* in, of, or relating to a continent
EPEIRID *n* type of spider
EPERDU *adj* distracted
EPERDUE *adj* distracted
EPERGNE *n* ornamental centrepiece for a table
EPHA, -S *same as* ▸ **ephah**
EPHAH, -S *n* Hebrew unit of dry measure
EPHAS ▸ **epha**
EPHEBE, -S *n* (in ancient Greece) youth about to enter full citizenship
EPHEBI ▸ **ephebus**
EPHEBIC ▸ **ephebe**
EPHEBOS, EPHEBOI *same as* ▸ **ephebe**
EPHEBUS, EPHEBI *same as* ▸ **ephebe**
EPHEDRA *n* gymnosperm shrub
EPHELIS *n* freckle
EPHOD, -S *n* embroidered vestment worn by priests
EPHOR, -I, -S *n* one of a board of senior magistrates in several ancient Greek states
EPHORAL ▸ **ephor**
EPHORI ▸ **ephor**
EPHORS ▸ **ephor**
EPIBLEM *n* outermost cell layer of a root
EPIBOLY *n* process that occurs during gastrulation in vertebrates
EPIC, -S *n, adj*
EPICAL ▸ **epic**
EPICARP *n* outermost layer of the pericarp of fruits
EPICEDE *same as* > **epicedium**
EPICENE *adj* having the characteristics of both sexes; hermaphroditic ▹ *n* epicene person or creature
EPICIER *n* grocer
EPICISM *n* style or trope characteristic of epics
EPICIST *n* writer of epics
EPICS ▸ **epic**
EPICURE *n* person who enjoys good food and drink
EPIDERM *same as* > **epidermis**
EPIDOTE *n* green mineral
EPIGEAL *adj* of or relating to a form of seed germination
EPIGEAN *same as* ▸ **epigeal**
EPIGEIC *same as* ▸ **epigeal**
EPIGENE *adj* formed or taking place at or near the surface of the earth
EPIGON, -S *same as* ▸ **epigone**
EPIGONE, EPIGONI *n* inferior follower or imitator
EPIGONS ▸ **epigon**
EPIGRAM *n*
EPIGYNY > **epigynous**
EPILATE *vb* remove hair from
EPILOG, -S *same as* > **epilogue**

EPIMER, -S *n* isomer
EPIMERE *n* dorsal part of the mesoderm of a vertebrate embryo
EPIMERS ▸ **epimer**
EPINAOS, EPINAOI *n* rear vestibule
EPIPLOA > **epiploon**
EPISCIA *n* creeping plant
EPISODE *n*
EPISOME *n* unit of genetic material (DNA) in bacteria that can be replicated
EPISTLE *n*, *vb*
EPITAPH *n*, *vb*
EPITAXY *n* growth of a thin layer on the surface of a crystal
EPITHEM *n* external topical application
EPITHET *n*, *vb*
EPITOME *n*
EPITOPE *n* site on an antigen at which a specific antibody becomes attached
EPIZOA ▸ **epizoon**
EPIZOAN *same as* ▸ **epizoon**
EPIZOIC *adj* (of an animal or plant) growing or living on the exterior of a living animal
EPIZOON, EPIZOA *n* animal that lives on the body of another animal
EPOCH, -S *n*
EPOCHA, -S *same as* ▸ **epoch**
EPOCHAL ▸ **epoch**
EPOCHAS ▸ **epocha**
EPOCHS ▸ **epoch**
EPODE, -S *n* part of a lyric ode that follows the strophe and the antistrophe
EPODIC ▸ **epode**
EPONYM, -S *n* name derived from the name of a real or mythical person
EPONYMY *n* derivation of names of places, etc, from those of persons
EPOPEE, -S *n* epic poem
EPOPT, -S *n* one initiated into the Eleusinian mysteries, an ancient Greek festival
EPOS, -ES *n* body of poetry in which the tradition of a people is conveyed
EPOXIDE *n* chemical compound
EPOXY, EPOXIED, EPOXIES, -ED *adj* of or containing a specific type of chemical compound ▹ *n* epoxy resin ▹ *vb* glue with epoxy resin
EPRIS *adj* enamoured
EPRISE *feminine form of* ▸ **epris**
EPSILON *n* fifth letter of the Greek alphabet
EPUISE *adj* exhausted
EPUISEE *feminine form of* ▸ **epuise**
EPULARY *adj* of or relating to feasting
EPULIS *n* swelling of the gum
EPURATE *vb* purify
EPYLLIA > **epyllion**
EQUABLE *adj*
EQUABLY ▸ **equable**
EQUAL, -ED, -S *adj*, *n*, *vb*
EQUALI *pl n* pieces for a group of instruments of the same kind
EQUALLY ▸ **equal**
EQUALS ▸ **equal**
EQUANT, -S *n* circle in which a planet was formerly believed to move
EQUATE, -D, -S *vb*
EQUATOR *n*
EQUERRY *n* attendant to a member of a royal family
EQUES *n* (in ancient Rome) horseman
EQUID, -S *n* any animal of the horse family
EQUINAL *same as* ▸ **equine**
EQUINE, -S *adj*, *n*
EQUINIA *n* glanders
EQUINOX *n* time of year when day and night are of equal length
EQUIP, -S *vb*
EQUIPE, -S *n* (esp in motor racing) team
EQUIPS ▸ **equip**
EQUITES *pl n* cavalry
EQUITY *n*
ER *interj* sound made when hesitating in speech
ERA, -S *n* period of time considered as distinctive
ERASE, -D, -S, ERASING *vb*
ERASER, -S *n* object for erasing something written
ERASES ▸ **erase**
ERASING ▸ **erase**

ERASION *n* act of erasing

This means the act of erasing: not an exciting word, but its combination of common letters makes it one of the most frequently played 7-letter bonus words.

ERASURE *n* erasing
ERATHEM *n* stratum of rocks representing a specific geological era
ERBIA, -S *n* oxide of erbium
ERBIUM, -S *n* metallic element of the lanthanide series
ERE, -D, -S, ERING *prep* before ▷ *vb* plough
ERECT, -ED, -S *vb, adj*
ERECTER *same as* ▸ **erector**
ERECTLY ▸ **erect**
ERECTOR *n* any muscle that raises a part or makes it erect
ERECTS ▸ **erect**
ERED ▸ **ere**
ERELONG *adv* before long
EREMIC *adj* of or relating to deserts
EREMITE *n* Christian hermit
EREMURI > **eremurus**
ERENOW *adv* long before the present
EREPSIN *n* mixture of proteolytic enzymes secreted by the small intestine
ERES ▸ **ere**
ERETHIC > **erethism**
EREV, -S *n* day before
ERF, ERVEN *n* plot of land marked off for building purposes
ERG, -S *same as* > **ergometer**
ERGATE, -S *n* worker ant
ERGO, -S *same as* > **ergometer**
ERGODIC *adj* of or relating to the probability that any state will recur
ERGON, -S *n* work
ERGOS ▸ **ergo**
ERGOT, -S *n* fungal disease of cereal
ERGOTIC ▸ **ergot**
ERGOTS ▸ **ergot**
ERGS ▸ **erg**
ERHU, -S *n* Chinese two-stringed violin
ERIACH, -S *same as* ▸ **eric**
ERIC, -S *n* (in old Irish law) fine paid by a murderer to the family of his or her victim
ERICA, -S *n* genus of plants including heathers
ERICK, -S *same as* ▸ **eric**
ERICOID *adj* (of leaves) small and tough, resembling those of heather
ERICS ▸ **eric**
ERING ▸ **ere**
ERINGO, -S *same as* ▸ **eryngo**
ERINITE *n* arsenate of copper
ERINUS *n* type of plant
ERISTIC *adj* of, relating, or given to controversy or logical disputation ▷ *n* person who engages in logical disputes
ERK, -S *n* aircraftman or naval rating
ERLANG, -S *n* unit of traffic intensity in a telephone system
ERLKING *n* malevolent spirit who carries off children
ERM *interj* expression of hesitation
ERMELIN *n* ermine
ERMINE, -S *n*
ERMINED *adj* clad in the fur of the ermine
ERMINES ▸ **ermine**
ERN, -ED, -ING, -S *archaic variant of* ▸ **earn**
ERNE, -S *n* fish-eating (European) sea eagle
ERNED ▸ **ern**
ERNES ▸ **erne**
ERNING ▸ **ern**
ERNS ▸ **ern**
ERODE, -D, -S, ERODING *vb*
ERODENT ▸ **erode**
ERODES ▸ **erode**
ERODING ▸ **erode**
ERODIUM *n* type of geranium
EROS, -ES *n* love
EROSE *adj* jagged or uneven, as though gnawed or bitten
EROSELY ▸ **erose**
EROSES ▸ **eros**
EROSION *n*
EROSIVE ▸ **erosion**
EROTEMA *n* rhetorical question

EROTEME *same as* ▸ **erotema**
ERR, -ED, -S *vb*
ERRABLE *adj* capable of making a mistake
ERRANCY *n* state or an instance of erring or a tendency to err
ERRAND, -S *n*
ERRANT, -S *adj* behaving in a manner considered to be unacceptable ▹ *n* knight-errant
ERRATA ▸ **erratum**
ERRATIC *adj, n*
ERRATUM, ERRATA *n* error in writing or printing
ERRED ▸ **err**
ERRHINE *adj* causing nasal secretion ▹ *n* errhine drug or agent
ERRING, -S ▸ **err**
ERROR, -S *n*
ERRS ▸ **err**
ERS, -ES *same as* ▸ **ervil**
ERSATZ *adj* made in imitation ▹ *n* ersatz substance or article
ERSES ▸ **ers**
ERST *adv* long ago
ERUCIC *adj* as in **erucic acid** crystalline fatty acid
ERUCT, -ED, -S *vb* belch
ERUDITE *adj* having great academic knowledge ▹ *n* erudite person
ERUGO, -S *n* verdigris
ERUPT, -ED, -S *vb*
ERUV, -IM, -IN, -S *n* area within which certain activities forbidden to be done on the Sabbath are permitted
ERVEN ▸ **erf**
ERVIL, -S *n* type of vetch
ERYNGO, -S *n* type of plant with toothed or lobed leaves
ES, -ES *n* letter S
ESCALOP *another word for* ▸ **scallop**
ESCAPE, -D, -S *vb, n*
ESCAPEE *n* person who has escaped
ESCAPER ▸ **escape**
ESCAPES ▸ **escape**
ESCAR, -S *same as* ▸ **esker**
ESCARP, -S *n* inner side of a ditch separating besiegers and besieged ▹ *vb* make into a slope
ESCARS ▸ **escar**
ESCHAR, -S *n* dry scab or slough
ESCHEAT *n* possessions that become state property in the absence of an heir ▹ *vb* take such property
ESCHEW, -S *vb* abstain from, avoid
ESCOLAR *n* slender spiny-finned fish
ESCORT, -S *n, vb*
ESCOT, -ED, -S *vb* maintain
ESCRIBE *vb* make a mathematical drawing
ESCROC, -S *n* conman
ESCROL, -S *same as* ▸ **escroll**
ESCROLL *n* scroll
ESCROLS ▸ **escrol**
ESCROW, -S *n* item delivered to a third party pending fulfilment of a condition ▹ *vb* place (money, a document, etc) in escrow
ESCUAGE *(in medieval Europe) another word for* ▸ **scutage**
ESCUDO, -S *n* former monetary unit of Portugal
ESERINE *n* crystalline alkaloid
ESES ▸ **es**
ESILE, -S *n* vinegar
ESKAR, -S *same as* ▸ **esker**
ESKER, -S *n* long ridge of gravel, sand, etc
ESKY, ESKIES *n* portable insulated container
ESLOIN, -S *same as* ▸ **eloign**
ESLOYNE *same as* ▸ **eloign**
ESNE, -S *n* household slave
ESNECY *n* inheritance law
ESNES ▸ **esne**
ESOTERY ▸ **esoteric**
ESPADA, -S *n* sword
ESPANOL *n* Spanish person
ESPARTO *n* grass of S Europe and N Africa
ESPIAL, -S *n* act or fact of being seen or discovered
ESPIED ▸ **espy**
ESPIER, -S ▸ **espy**
ESPIES ▸ **espy**
ESPOIR, -S *n* category of wrestler
ESPOUSE *vb* adopt or give support to (a cause etc)
ESPRIT, -S *n* spirit, liveliness, or wit

ESPY, ESPIED, ESPIES, -ING *vb* catch sight of
ESQUIRE *n* courtesy title placed after a man's name ▷ *vb* escort
ESS, -ES *n* letter S
ESSAY, -ED, -S *n, vb*
ESSAYER ▶ **essay**
ESSAYS ▶ **essay**
ESSE *n* existence
ESSENCE *n*
ESSES ▶ **ess**
ESSIVE, -S *n* grammatical case
ESSOIN, -S *n* excuse ▷ *vb* excuse for not appearing in court
ESSOYNE *same as* ▶ **essoin**
EST, -S *n* treatment intended to help people towards psychological growth
ESTATE, -D, -S *n* landed property ▷ *vb* provide with an estate
ESTEEM, -S *n, vb*
ESTER, -S *n* chemical compound
ESTHETE *US spelling of* > **aesthete**
ESTIVAL *usual US spelling of* > **aestival**
ESTOC, -S *n* short stabbing sword
ESTOILE *n* heraldic star with wavy points
ESTOP, -S *vb* preclude by estoppel
ESTOVER *same as* > **estovers**
ESTRADE *n* dais or raised platform
ESTRAL *US spelling of* ▶ **oestral**
ESTRAY, -S *n* stray domestic animal of unknown ownership ▷ *vb* stray
ESTREAT *n* extract from a court record ▷ *vb* send an extract of a court record
ESTREPE *vb* lay waste
ESTRICH *n* obsolete word for ostrich
ESTRIN, -S *US spelling of* ▶ **oestrin**
ESTRIOL *usual US spelling of* > **oestriol**
ESTRO, -S *n* poetic inspiration
ESTRONE *usual US spelling of* > **oestrone**
ESTROS ▶ **estro**
ESTROUS ▶ **estrus**
ESTRUAL ▶ **estrus**
ESTRUM, -S *usual US spelling of* ▶ **oestrum**
ESTRUS *usual US spelling of* ▶ **oestrus**
ESTS ▶ **est**
ESTUARY *n*
ET *dialect past tense of* ▶ **eat**
ETA, -S *n* seventh letter in the Greek alphabet
ETACISM *n* pronunciation of eta as a long vowel sound
ETAERIO *n* aggregate fruit

This strange-looking word is a type of fruit, and because it uses the commonest letters it is, along with **otarine**, the most frequently played of all bonus words.

ETAGE, -S *n* floor in a multi-storey building
ETAGERE *n* stand with open shelves for displaying ornaments, etc
ETAGES ▶ **etage**
ETALAGE *n* display
ETALON, -S *n* device used in spectroscopy
ETAMIN, -S *same as* ▶ **etamine**
ETAMINE *n* cotton or worsted fabric of loose weave
ETAMINS ▶ **etamin**
ETAPE, -S *n* public storehouse
ETAS ▶ **eta**
ETAT, -S *n* state
ETATISM *same as* > **etatisme**
ETATIST > **etatisme**
ETATS ▶ **etat**
ETCH, -ED, -ES *vb* wear away or cut the surface of (metal, glass, etc) with acid
ETCHANT *n* any acid or corrosive used for etching
ETCHED ▶ **etch**
ETCHER, -S ▶ **etch**
ETCHES ▶ **etch**
ETCHING *n*
ETEN, -S *n* giant
ETERNAL *adj, n*
ETERNE *archaic or poetic word for* ▶ **eternal**
ETESIAN *adj* (of NW winds) recurring annually in the summer in the E Mediterranean ▷ *n* etesian wind
ETH, -S *same as* ▶ **edh**

ETHAL, -S *n* cetyl alcohol
ETHANAL *n* colourless volatile pungent liquid
ETHANE, -S *n* odourless flammable gas
ETHANOL *same as* ▸ **alcohol**
ETHE *adj* easy
ETHENE, -S *same as* > **ethylene**
ETHER, -S *n*
ETHERIC ▸ **ether**
ETHERS ▸ **ether**
ETHIC *n*
ETHICAL *adj*, *n*
ETHICS *n* code of behaviour
ETHINYL *same as* ▸ **ethynyl**
ETHION, -S *n* type of pesticide
ETHIOPS *n* dark-coloured chemical compound
ETHMOID *adj* denoting or relating to a specific bone of the skull ▹ *n* ethmoid bone
ETHNE ▸ **ethnos**
ETHNIC *adj*, *n*
ETHNOS, ETHNE *n* ethnic group
ETHOS, -ES *n*
ETHOXY *same as* ▸ **ethoxyl**
ETHOXYL *n* univalent radical
ETHS ▸ **eth**
ETHYL, -S *adj* type of chemical hydrocarbon group
ETHYLIC ▸ **ethyl**
ETHYLS ▸ **ethyl**
ETHYNE, -S *another name for* > **acetylene**
ETHYNYL *n* univalent radical
ETIC, -S *adj* relating to linguistic terms analysed without regard to structural function ▹ *n* etic approach or viewpoint
ETIOLIN *n* yellow pigment
ETNA, -S *n* container used to heat liquids
ETOILE, -S *n* star
ETOURDI *adj* foolish
ETRENNE *n* New Year's gift
ETRIER, -S *n* short portable ladder or set of webbing loops
ETTIN, -S *n* giant
ETTLE, -D, -S, ETTLING *vb* intend
ETUDE, -S *n* short musical composition for a solo instrument
ETUI, -S *n* small usually ornamented case
ETWEE, -S *same as* ▸ **etui**

E is a very desirable letter, but sometimes you can have too much of even this good thing. This word for a needle-case, a variant of **etui**, can help you dispose of a few of them.

ETYMA ▸ **etymon**
ETYMIC ▸ **etymon**
ETYMON, ETYMA, -S *n* earliest form of a word or morpheme from which another is derived
ETYPIC *adj* unable to conform to type
EUCAIN, -S *same as* ▸ **eucaine**
EUCAINE *n* crystalline optically active substance
EUCAINS ▸ **eucain**
EUCHRE, -D, -S *n* US and Canadian card game ▹ *vb* prevent (a player) from making their contracted tricks
EUCLASE *n* brittle green gem
EUCRITE *n* type of stony meteorite
EUDEMON *n* benevolent spirit or demon
EUGARIE *another name for* ▸ **pipi**
EUGE *interj* well done!
EUGENIA *n* plant of the clove family
EUGENIC > **eugenics**
EUGENOL *n* oily liquid used in perfumery
EUGH, -S *archaic form of* ▸ **yew**
EUGHEN *archaic form of* ▸ **yew**
EUGHS ▸ **eugh**
EUGLENA *n* type of freshwater unicellular organism
EUK, -ED, -ING, -S *vb* itch
EULOGIA *n* blessed bread

This is one of the few 7-letter words using all the vowels. What's more, it can take a plural in E as well as S, giving **eulogiae**, which can be great for getting you out of vowel trouble.

EULOGY *n*

EUMONG, -S *same as* ▸ **eumung**
EUMUNG, -S *n* any of various Australian acacias
EUNUCH, -S *n*
EUOI *n* cry of Bacchic frenzy

This is a cry expressing Bacchic frenzy, and is forever coming in useful to dispose of a surplus of vowels. It has the less commonly played but still useful variants **evoe, evhoe** and **evohe**.

EUOUAE, -S *n* mnemonic used in medieval music

This word is remarkable in that it contains no consonants. You will be surprised at how often you will be glad to play it!

EUPAD, -S *n* antiseptic powder
EUPEPSY *same as* > **eupepsia**
EUPHON, -S *n* glass harmonica
EUPHONY *n* pleasing sound
EUPHORY *same as* > **euphoria**
EUPHROE *n* wooden block through which the lines of a crowfoot are rove
EUPLOID *adj* having chromosomes in an exact multiple of the haploid number ▷ *n* euploid cell or individual
EUPNEA, -S *same as* ▸ **eupnoea**
EUPNEIC ▸ **eupnea**
EUPNOEA *n* normal relaxed breathing
EUREKA, -S *n*
EURIPUS, EURIPI *n* strait or channel with a strong current or tide
EURO, -S *n* unit of the single currency of the European Union
EUROKY *n* ability of an organism to live under different conditions
EUROPOP *n* type of pop music by European artists
EUROS ▸ **euro**
EURYOKY *same as* ▸ **euroky**
EUSOL, -S *n* solution of eupad in water
EUSTACY > **eustatic**
EUSTASY > **eustatic**
EUSTELE *n* central cylinder of a seed plant
EUSTYLE *n* building with columns optimally spaced
EUTAXIA *n* condition of being easily melted
EUTAXY *n* good order
EUTEXIA *same as* ▸ **eutaxia**
EUTROPY *n* chemical structure
EVACUEE *n* person evacuated from a place of danger
EVADE, -D, -S, EVADING *vb*
EVADER, -S ▸ **evade**
EVADES ▸ **evade**
EVADING ▸ **evade**
EVANGEL *n* gospel of Christianity
EVANISH *poetic word for* ▸ **vanish**
EVASION *n*
EVASIVE *adj* not straightforward
EVE, -S *n*
EVEJAR, -S *n* nightjar
EVEN, -ED, -EST *adj, adv, vb, n*
EVENER, -S ▸ **even**
EVENEST ▸ **even**
EVENING *n, adj*
EVENLY ▸ **even**
EVENS *adv* (of a bet) winning the same as the amount staked if successful
EVENT, -ED, -S *n, vb*
EVENTER > **eventing**
EVENTS ▸ **event**
EVER *adv* at any time
EVERNET *n* hypothetical form of internet
EVERT, -ED, -S *vb* turn (some bodily part) outwards or inside out
EVERTOR *n* any muscle that turns a part outwards
EVERTS ▸ **evert**
EVERY *adj*
EVES ▸ **eve**
EVET, -S *n* eft
EVHOE *interj* cry of Bacchic frenzy
EVICT, -ED, -S *vb*
EVICTEE ▸ **evict**
EVICTOR ▸ **evict**
EVICTS ▸ **evict**
EVIDENT *adj, n*
EVIL, -ER, -EST, -LER, -S *n, adj, adv*

EVILLY ▸ **evil**
EVILS ▸ **evil**
EVINCE, -D, -S *vb* make evident
EVIRATE *vb* deprive of strength or vigour
EVITATE *archaic word for* ▸ **avoid**
EVITE, -D, -S, EVITING *archaic word for* ▸ **avoid**
EVO, -S *informal word for* ▸ **evening**
EVOCATE *vb* evoke
EVOE *interj* cry of Bacchic frenzy
EVOHE *interj* cry of Bacchic frenzy
EVOKE, -D, -S, EVOKING *vb*
EVOKER, -S ▸ **evoke**
EVOKES ▸ **evoke**
EVOKING ▸ **evoke**
EVOLUE, -S *n* colonial term for an African educated according to European principles
EVOLUTE *n* geometric curve ▹ *adj* having the margins rolled outwards ▹ *vb* evolve
EVOLVE, -D, -S *vb*
EVOLVER ▸ **evolve**
EVOLVES ▸ **evolve**
EVOS ▸ **evo**
EVOVAE, -S *n* mnemonic used in medieval music
EVULSE, -D, -S *vb* extract by force
EVZONE, -S *n* soldier in an elite Greek infantry regiment
EW *interj* expression of disgust
EWE, -S *n*
EWER, -S *n* large jug with a wide mouth
EWES ▸ **ewe**
EWEST *Scots word for* ▸ **near**
EWFTES *Spenserian plural of* ▸ **eft**
EWGHEN *archaic form of* ▸ **yew**
EWHOW *interj* expression of pity or regret
EWK, -ED, -ING, -S *vb* itch

Ewk is a dialect word for **itch**. It's a handy little word and a good one to remember in case you end up with both K and W, and remember that it's a verb, so you can have **ewks, ewked** and **ewking**. It's also worth knowing its variants **euk, yeuk, youk, yuck** and **yuke**!

EWT, -S *archaic form of* ▸ **newt**
EX, -ED, -ES, -ING *prep* not including ▹ *n* former spouse, significant other, etc ▹ *vb* cross out or delete
EXABYTE *n* very large unit of computer memory
EXACT, -ED, -S *adj, vb*
EXACTA, -S *n* horse-racing bet
EXACTED ▸ **exact**
EXACTER ▸ **exact**
EXACTLY *adv, interj*
EXACTOR ▸ **exact**
EXACTS ▸ **exact**
EXACUM, -S *n* type of tropical plant
EXALT, -S *vb*
EXALTED *adj* high or elevated in rank, position, dignity, etc
EXALTER ▸ **exalt**
EXALTS ▸ **exalt**
EXAM, -S *n*
EXAMEN, -S *n* examination of conscience
EXAMINE *vb* look at closely
EXAMPLE *n*
EXAMS ▸ **exam**
EXAPTED *adj* biologically adapted
EXARATE *adj* (of the pupa of some insects) having legs, wings, antennae, etc, free and movable
EXARCH, -S *n* head of certain autonomous Orthodox Christian Churches ▹ *adj* (of a xylem strand) having the first-formed xylem external to that formed later
EXARCHY *same as* > **exarchate**
EXCAMB, -S *vb* exchange
EXCEED, -S *vb*
EXCEL, -S *vb*
EXCEPT, -S *prep, vb*
EXCERPT *n, vb*
EXCESS *n, vb*
EXCHEAT *same as* ▸ **escheat**
EXCIDE, -D, -S *vb* cut out
EXCIMER *n* excited dimer which would

remain dissociated in the ground state
EXCIPLE *n* part of a lichen
EXCISE, -D, -S *n, vb*
EXCITE, -S *vb*
EXCITED *adj* emotionally aroused, esp to pleasure or agitation
EXCITER *n* person or thing that excites
EXCITES ▸ **excite**
EXCITON *n* excited electron bound to the hole produced by its excitation
EXCITOR *n* type of nerve
EXCLAIM *vb*
EXCLAVE *n* territory owned by a country, but surrounded by another
EXCLUDE *vb*
EXCRETA *pl n* excrement
EXCRETE *vb*
EXCUDIT *sentence substitute* (named person) made this
EXCURSE *vb* wander
EXCUSAL ▸ **excuse**
EXCUSE, -D, -S *n, vb*
EXCUSER ▸ **excuse**
EXCUSES ▸ **excuse**
EXEAT, -S *n* leave of absence from school or some other institution
EXEC, -S *n* executive
EXECUTE *vb*
EXED ▸ **ex**
EXEDRA, -E, -S *n* building, room, portico, or apse containing a continuous bench
EXEEM, -ED, -S *same as* ▸ **exeme**
EXEGETE *n* person who practises exegesis
EXEME, -D, -S, EXEMING *vb* set free
EXEMPLA > **exemplum**
EXEMPLE *same as* ▸ **example**
EXEMPT, -S *adj, vb, n*
EXEQUY *n* funeral rite

Meaning a funeral rite, this word combines X and Q. Even better is its plural **exequies**, which would earn an extra 50 points for using all your tiles.

EXERGUE *n* space on the reverse of a coin or medal
EXERGY *n* maximum amount of useful work obtainable from a system
EXERT, -ED, -S *vb*
EXES ▸ **ex**
EXEUNT *vb* (they) go out
EXFIL, -S *vb* exfiltrate
EXHALE, -D, -S *vb*
EXHAUST *vb, n*
EXHEDRA *same as* ▸ **exedra**
EXHIBIT *vb, n*
EXHORT, -S *vb* urge earnestly
EXHUME, -D, -S *vb* dig up (something buried, esp a corpse)
EXHUMER ▸ **exhume**
EXHUMES ▸ **exhume**
EXIES *n* hysterics
EXIGENT *adj* urgent ▹ *n* emergency
EXILE, -D, -S, EXILING *n* prolonged, usu enforced, absence from one's country ▹ *vb* expel from one's country
EXILER, -S ▸ **exile**
EXILES ▸ **exile**
EXILIAN ▸ **exile**
EXILIC ▸ **exile**
EXILING ▸ **exile**
EXILITY *n* poverty or meagreness
EXINE, -S *n* outermost coat of a pollen grain or a spore
EXING ▸ **ex**
EXIST, -ED, -S *vb*
EXIT, -ED, -ING, -S *n, vb*
EXO *informal word for* > **excellent**

Exo is an informal Australian way of saying excellent. This is a great little word as it allows you to combine X with two of the most common tiles in the game, E and O.

EXOCARP *same as* ▸ **epicarp**
EXODE, -S *n* exodus
EXODERM *same as* > **ectoderm**
EXODES ▸ **exode**
EXODIC ▸ **exodus**
EXODIST ▸ **exodus**
EXODOS, EXODOI *n* (in Greek drama) concluding scene
EXODUS *n* departure of a large number of people

EXOGAMY *n* act of marrying a person from another tribe, clan, etc

EXOGEN, -S *n* type of plant

EXOME, -S *n* part of the genome consisting of exons

EXOMION *same as* ▸ **exomis**

EXOMIS *n* sleeveless jacket

EXON, -S *n* one of the officers who command the Yeomen of the Guard

EXONIC ▸ **exon**

EXONS ▸ **exon**

EXONYM, -S *n* name given to a place by foreigners

EXOPOD, -S *same as* > **exopodite**

EXORDIA > **exordium**

EXOSMIC > **exosmosis**

EXOTIC, -S *adj, n*

EXOTICA *pl n* (collection of) exotic objects

EXOTICS ▸ **exotic**

EXOTISM *n* something exotic

EXPAND, -S *vb*

EXPANSE *n* uninterrupted wide area

EXPAT, -S *n*

EXPECT, -S *vb*

EXPEL, -S *vb*

EXPEND, -S *vb*

EXPENSE *n, vb*

EXPERT, -S *n, adj, vb*

EXPIATE *vb* make amends for

EXPIRE, -D, -S *vb*

EXPIRER ▸ **expire**

EXPIRES ▸ **expire**

EXPIRY *n* end, esp of a contract period

EXPLAIN *vb*

EXPLANT *vb* transfer (living tissue) from its natural site to a new site or to a culture medium ▷ *n* piece of tissue treated in this way

EXPLODE *vb*

EXPLOIT *vb, n*

EXPLORE *vb*

EXPO, -S *n* exposition, large public exhibition

EXPORT, -S *n, vb*

EXPOS ▸ **expo**

EXPOSAL ▸ **expose**

EXPOSE, -S *vb, n*

EXPOSED *adj* not concealed

EXPOSER ▸ **expose**

EXPOSES ▸ **expose**

EXPOSIT *vb* state

EXPOUND *vb* explain in detail

EXPRESS *vb, adj, n, adv*

EXPUGN, -S *vb* storm

EXPULSE *vb* expel

EXPUNCT *vb* expunge

EXPUNGE *vb* delete, erase, blot out

EXPURGE *vb* purge

EXSCIND *vb* cut off or out

EXSECT, -S *vb* cut out

EXSERT, -S *vb* thrust out ▷ *adj* protruded or stretched out from (something)

EXTANT *adj* still existing

EXTASY *same as* ▸ **ecstasy**

EXTATIC *same as* > **ecstatic**

EXTEND, -S *vb*

EXTENSE *adj* extensive ▷ *n* extension; expanse

EXTENT, -S *n*

EXTERN, -S *n* person with an official connection to an institution but not residing in it

EXTERNE *same as* ▸ **extern**

EXTERNS ▸ **extern**

EXTINCT *adj, vb*

EXTINE, -S *same as* ▸ **exine**

EXTIRP, -S *vb* extirpate

EXTOL, -S *vb* praise highly

EXTOLD *archaic past participle of* ▸ **extol**

EXTOLL, -S *same as* ▸ **extol**

EXTOLS ▸ **extol**

EXTORT, -S *vb*

EXTRA, -S *adj* more than is usual, expected or needed ▷ *n* additional person or thing ▷ *adv* unusually or exceptionally

EXTRACT *vb* pull out by force ▷ *n* something extracted, such as a passage from a book etc

EXTRAIT *n* extract

EXTRAS ▸ **extra**

EXTREAT *n* extraction ▷ *vb* extract or eliminate (something)

EXTREMA > **extremum**

EXTREME *adj, n*

EXTROPY *n* supposition that human life will expand throughout the universe via technology

EXTRUDE *vb* squeeze or force out
EXUDATE *same as* **> exudation**
EXUDE, -D, -S, EXUDING *vb* (of a liquid or smell) seep or flow out slowly and steadily
EXUL, -LED, -S *vb* exile; banish
EXULT, -ED, -S *vb* be joyful or jubilant
EXURB, -S *n* residential area beyond suburbs
EXURBAN ▸ exurbia
EXURBIA *n* region outside the suburbs of a city
EXURBS ▸ exurb
EXUVIA, -E *n* something cast off
EXUVIAL ▸ exuvia
EXUVIUM *n* something cast off
EYALET, -S *n* province of Ottoman Empire
EYAS, -ES *n* nestling hawk or falcon
EYASS, -ES *same as* **▸ eyas**
EYE, -D, -ING, -S, EYING *n, vb*
EYEABLE *adj* pleasant to look at
EYEBALL *n, vb*
EYEBANK *n* place in which corneas are stored
EYEBAR, -S *n* bar with flattened ends with holes for connecting pins
EYEBATH *n* small cup for applying medication to the eye
EYEBEAM *n* glance
EYEBOLT *n* type of threaded bolt
EYEBROW *n, vb*
EYECUP, -S *same as* **▸ eyebath**
EYED ▸ eye
EYEFOLD *n* fold of skin above eye
EYEFUL, -S *n* view
EYEHOLE *n* hole through which something is passed
EYEHOOK *n* hook attached to a ring at the extremity of a rope or chain
EYEING ▸ eye
EYELASH *n*
EYELESS ▸ eye
EYELET, -S *n* small hole for a lace or cord to be passed through ▷ *vb* supply with an eyelet or eyelets
EYELIAD *same as* **> oeillade**
EYELID, -S *n*
EYELIFT *n* cosmetic surgery for eyes
EYELIKE ▸ eye
EYELINE *n* line of sight
EYEN *pl n* eyes
EYER, -S *n* someone who eyes
EYES ▸ eye
EYESHOT *n* range of vision
EYESOME *adj* attractive
EYESORE *n* ugly object
EYESPOT *n* small area of pigment
EYEWASH *n* nonsense
EYEWEAR *n* spectacles; glasses
EYEWINK *n* wink of the eye; instant
EYING ▸ eye
EYLIAD, -S *same as* **> oeillade**
EYNE *poetic plural of* **▸ eye**
EYOT, -S *n* island
EYRA, -S *n* reddish-brown variety of the jaguarondi
EYRE, -S *n* obsolete circuit court
EYRIE, -S *n* nest of an eagle
EYRIR *n* Icelandic monetary unit
EYRY *same as* **▸ eyrie**
EZINE, -S *n* magazine available only in electronic form

Ff

FA, -S *same as* ▸ **fah**
FAA, -ING, -N, -S *Scot word for* ▸ **fall**
FAB, -BER, -BEST, -S *adj* excellent ▹ *n* fabrication
FABBY, FABBIER *same as* ▸ **fab**
FABLE, -S *n, vb*
FABLED *adj* made famous in legend
FABLER, -S ▸ **fable**
FABLES ▸ **fable**
FABLET, -S *n* large smartphone able to perform many of the functions of a tablet computer
FABLIAU *n* comic, usually ribald verse tale
FABLING ▸ **fable**
FABRIC, -S *n, vb*
FABS ▸ **fab**
FABULAR *adj* relating to fables
FACADE, -S *n*
FACE, -D, -S *n, vb*
FACEBAR *n* wrestling hold
FACED ▸ **face**
FACEMAN, FACEMEN *n* miner who works at the coalface
FACEOFF *n* confrontation
FACER, -S *n* difficulty or problem
FACES ▸ **face**
FACET, -ED, -S *n, vb*
FACETE *adj* witty and humorous
FACETED ▸ **facet**
FACETS ▸ **facet**
FACEUP *adj* with the face or surface exposed
FACIA, -E, -S *same as* ▸ **fascia**
FACIAL, -S *adj* of or relating to the face ▹ *n* beauty treatment for the face
FACIAS ▸ **facia**
FACIEND *n* multiplicand
FACIES *n* general form and appearance
FACILE *adj* (of a remark, argument, etc) lacking depth
FACING, -S *n* lining or covering for decoration or reinforcement
FACONNE *adj* denoting a fabric with the design woven in ▹ *n* such a fabric
FACT, -S *n*
FACTA ▸ **factum**
FACTFUL ▸ **fact**
FACTICE *n* soft rubbery material
FACTION *n*
FACTIS *variant of* ▸ **factice**
FACTIVE *adj* giving rise to the presupposition that a sentence is true
FACTOID *n* piece of unreliable information believed to be true
FACTOR, -S *n, vb*
FACTORY *n*
FACTS ▸ **fact**
FACTUAL *adj*
FACTUM, FACTA, -S *n* something done, deed
FACTURE *n* construction
FACULA, -E *n* any of the bright areas on the sun's surface
FACULAR ▸ **facula**
FACULTY *n*
FAD, -S *n*
FADABLE ▸ **fade**
FADAISE *n* silly remark
FADDIER ▸ **faddy**
FADDISH ▸ **fad**
FADDISM ▸ **fad**
FADDIST ▸ **fad**
FADDLE, -D, -S *vb* mess around, toy with
FADDY, FADDIER *adj*
FADE, -D, -S *vb, n*
FADEDLY ▸ **fade**
FADEIN, -S *n* gradual appearance of an image on film

FADEOUT *n* gradual disappearance of an image on film
FADER, -S ▸ **fade**
FADES ▸ **fade**
FADEUR, -S *n* blandness, insipidness
FADGE, -D, -S, FADGING *vb* agree ▹ *n* package of wool in a wool-bale
FADIER ▸ **fady**
FADIEST ▸ **fady**
FADING, -S *n* variation in strength of received radio signals
FADLIKE ▸ **fad**
FADO, -S *n* type of melancholy Portuguese folk song
FADS ▸ **fad**
FADY, FADIER, FADIEST *adj* faded
FAE *Scot word for* ▸ **from**
FAECAL *adj*
FAECES *pl n*
FAENA, -S *n* matador's final actions before the kill
FAERIE, -S *n* land of fairies
FAERY *same as* ▸ **faerie**
FAFF, -ED, -ING, -S *vb* dither or fuss
FAFFIER ▸ **faffy**
FAFFING ▸ **faff**
FAFFS ▸ **faff**
FAFFY, FAFFIER *adj* awkward and time-consuming to do or use
FAG, -GED, -S *n, vb*
FAGGING ▸ **fag**
FAGIN, -S *n* criminal
FAGOTTO, FAGOTTI *n* bassoon
FAGS ▸ **fag**
FAH, -S *n* (in tonic sol-fa) fourth degree of any major scale
FAHLERZ *n* copper ore
FAHLORE *n* copper ore
FAHS ▸ **fah**
FAIBLE, -S *variant of* ▸ **foible**
FAIENCE *n* tin-glazed earthenware
FAIK, -ED, -ING, -S *vb* Scots word meaning fold
FAIKES *n* sandy rock
FAIKING ▸ **faik**
FAIKS ▸ **faik**
FAIL, -ED, -S *vb, n*
FAILING *n* weak point ▹ *prep* in the absence of
FAILLE, -S *n* soft light ribbed fabric of silk, rayon, or taffeta
FAILS ▸ **fail**
FAILURE *n*
FAIN, -ED, -ER, -EST, -ING, -S *adv* gladly ▹ *adj* willing or eager ▹ *vb* desire
FAINE, -S *variant of* ▸ **fain**
FAINED ▸ **fain**
FAINER ▸ **fain**
FAINES ▸ **faine**
FAINEST ▸ **fain**
FAINING ▸ **fain**
FAINLY ▸ **fain**
FAINNE, -S *n* badge worn by advocates of the Irish language
FAINS ▸ **fain**
FAINT, -ED, -S *adj, vb, n*
FAINTER ▸ **faint**
FAINTLY ▸ **faint**
FAINTS ▸ **faint**
FAINTY ▸ **faint**
FAIR, -ED, -ER, -EST, -S *adj* unbiased and reasonable ▹ *adv* fairly ▹ *n* travelling entertainment ▹ *vb* join together to form a smooth shape
FAIRIER ▸ **fairy**
FAIRIES ▸ **fairy**
FAIRILY ▸ **fairy**
FAIRING *n* structure fitted round part of a vehicle to reduce drag
FAIRISH *adj*
FAIRLY *adv* moderately
FAIRS ▸ **fair**
FAIRWAY *n* area between the tee and the green
FAIRY, FAIRIER, FAIRIES *n* imaginary small creature ▹ *adj* of or relating to a fairy or fairies
FAITH, -S *n*
FAITHED *adj* having faith or a faith
FAITHER *Scot word for* ▸ **father**
FAITHS ▸ **faith**
FAITOR, -S *n* impostor
FAITOUR *n* impostor
FAIX *interj* have faith
FAJITAS, FAJITA *pl n* Mexican dish
FAKE, -D, -S, -ST, FAKING *vb, n, adj*
FAKEER, -S *same as* ▸ **fakir**
FAKER, -S ▸ **fake**
FAKERY ▸ **fake**
FAKES ▸ **fake**
FAKEST ▸ **fake**
FAKEY, -S, FAKIER, FAKIEST *adj* (of a skateboarding manoeuvre) travelling

backwards ▷ *n* skateboarding position in which the skateboarder faces backwards
FAKIE, -S *same as* ▸ **fakey**
FAKIER ▸ **fakey**
FAKIES ▸ **fakie**
FAKIEST ▸ **fakey**
FAKING ▸ **fake**
FAKIR, -S *n* Muslim who spurns worldly possessions
FALAFEL *n* ball or cake made from chickpeas
FALAJ, AFLAJ *n* kind of irrigation channel in ancient Oman
FALBALA *n* gathered flounce, frill, or ruffle
FALCADE *n* movement of a horse
FALCATE *adj* shaped like a sickle
FALCES ▸ **falx**
FALCON, -S *n*
FALCULA *n* sharp curved claw, esp of a bird
FALDAGE *n* feudal right
FALL, -EN, -S *vb, n*
FALLACY *n*
FALLAL, -S *n* showy ornament, trinket, or article of dress
FALLEN ▸ **fall**
FALLER, -S *n* any device that falls or operates machinery by falling
FALLING ▸ **fall**
FALLOFF *n* decline or drop
FALLOUT *n* descent of solid material in the atmosphere onto the earth
FALLOW, -S *adj* (of land) ploughed but left unseeded to regain fertility ▷ *n* land treated in this way ▷ *vb* leave (land) unseeded after ploughing and harrowing it
FALLS ▸ **fall**
FALSE, -D, -R, -S, -ST, FALSING *adj* not true or correct ▷ *adv* in a false or dishonest manner ▷ *vb* falsify
FALSELY ▸ **false**
FALSER ▸ **false**
FALSERS *pl n* colloquial term for false teeth
FALSES ▸ **false**
FALSEST ▸ **false**
FALSIE, -S *n* pad used to enlarge breast shape
FALSIFY *vb*
FALSING ▸ **false**
FALSISH ▸ **false**
FALSISM ▸ **false**
FALSITY *n* state of being false
FALTER, -S *vb, n*
FALX, FALCES *n* sickle-shaped anatomical structure
FAME, -D, -S, FAMING *n* state of being widely recognized ▷ *vb* make known or famous
FAMILLE *n* type of Chinese porcelain
FAMILY *n, adj*
FAMINE, -S *n*
FAMING ▸ **fame**
FAMISH *vb*
FAMOUS *adj* very well-known ▷ *vb* make famous
FAMULUS, FAMULI *n* (formerly) the attendant of a sorcerer or scholar
FAN, -NED, -S *n, vb*
FANAL, -S *n* lighthouse
FANATIC *n, adj*
FANBASE *n* body of admirers
FANBOY, -S *n* obsessive fan of a subject or hobby
FANCIED *adj* imaginary
FANCIER *n* person interested in plants or animals
FANCIES ▸ **fancy**
FANCIFY *vb* make more beautiful
FANCILY ▸ **fancy**
FANCY, FANCIES *adj, n, vb*
FAND, -ED, -ING, -S *vb* old word meaning try
FANDOM, -S *n* collectively, the fans of a sport, pastime or person
FANDS ▸ **fand**
FANE, -S *n* temple or shrine
FANEGA, -S *n* Spanish unit of measurement
FANES ▸ **fane**
FANFARE *n, vb*
FANFIC, -S *n* fiction based on work by other authors
FANFOLD *vb* fold (paper) like a fan
FANG, -ED, -ING, -S *n* snake's tooth which injects poison ▷ *vb* dialect word meaning seize
FANGA, -S *same as* ▸ **fanega**

FANGED ▸ **fang**
FANGING ▸ **fang**
FANGIRL *n* enthusiastic female devotee of something
FANGLE, -D, -S *vb* fashion
FANGO, -S *n* mud from thermal springs in Italy
FANGS ▸ **fang**
FANION, -S *n* small flag used by surveyors
FANJET, -S *same as* > **turbofan**
FANK, -ED, -ING, -S *n* sheep pen ▹ *vb* put sheep in a pen
FANKLE, -D, -S *vb* entangle ▹ *n* tangle
FANKS ▸ **fank**
FANLIKE ▸ **fan**
FANNED ▸ **fan**
FANNEL, -S *n* ecclesiastical vestment
FANNELL *variant of* ▸ **fannel**
FANNELS ▸ **fannel**
FANNER, -S ▸ **fan**
FANNING ▸ **fan**
FANO, -S *same as* ▸ **fanon**
FANON, -S *n* collar-shaped vestment
FANOS ▸ **fano**
FANS ▸ **fan**
FANSITE *n* website aimed at fans of a celebrity, film, etc
FANSUB, -S *n* fan-produced subtitling of films
FANTAD, -S *n* nervous, agitated state
FANTAIL *n* small New Zealand bird with a tail like a fan
FANTASM *archaic spelling of* > **phantasm**
FANTAST *n* dreamer or visionary
FANTASY *n, adj, vb*
FANTEEG *n* nervous, agitated state
FANTOD, -S *n* crotchety or faddish behaviour
FANTOM, -S *archaic spelling of* ▸ **phantom**
FANUM, -S *n* temple
FANWISE *adj* like a fan
FANWORT *n* aquatic plant
FANZINE *n* magazine produced by fans
FAP *adj* drunk
FAQIR, -S *same as* ▸ **fakir**

> Meaning a Hindu ascetic, this is one of those invaluable words allowing you to play the Q without a U. It can also be spelt **fakeer, fakir** and **faquir**.

FAQUIR, -S *variant of* ▸ **faqir**
FAR, -RED, -RING, -S, -THER *adv* at, to, or from a great distance ▹ *adj* remote in space or time ▹ *vb* go far
FARAD, -S *n* unit of electrical capacitance
FARADAY *n* quantity of electricity
FARADIC *adj* of an intermittent asymmetric alternating current
FARADS ▸ **farad**
FARAND *adj* pleasant or attractive in manner or appearance
FARANG, -S *n* (in Thailand) a foreigner
FARAWAY *adj*
FARCE, -D, -S *n* boisterous comedy ▹ *vb* enliven (a speech, etc) with jokes
FARCER, -S *same as* ▸ **farceur**
FARCES ▸ **farce**
FARCEUR *n* writer of or performer in farces
FARCI *adj* (of food) stuffed
FARCIE *same as* ▸ **farci**
FARCIED *adj* afflicted with farcy
FARCIES ▸ **farcy**
FARCIFY *vb* turn into a farce
FARCIN, -S *n* bacterial disease of horses
FARCING ▸ **farce**
FARCINS ▸ **farcin**
FARCY, FARCIES *n* bacterial disease of horses
FARD, -ED, -S *n* paint for the face, esp white paint ▹ *vb* paint (the face) with fard
FARDAGE *n* material laid beneath or between cargo
FARDED ▸ **fard**
FARDEL, -S *n* bundle or burden
FARDEN, -S *n* farthing
FARDING ▸ **fard**
FARDS ▸ **fard**
FARE, -D, -S, FARING *n, vb*
FAREBOX *n* box where money for bus fares is placed
FARED ▸ **fare**

FARER, -S ▶ **fare**
FARES ▶ **fare**
FARFAL, -S *same as* ▶ **falafel**
FARFEL, -S *same as* ▶ **falafel**
FARFET *adj* far-fetched
FARINA, -S *n* flour or meal made from any kind of cereal grain
FARING ▶ **fare**
FARINHA *n* cassava meal
FARL, -S *n* thin cake of oatmeal, often triangular in shape
FARLE, -S *same as* ▶ **farl**
FARLS ▶ **farl**
FARM, -S *n, vb*
FARMED *adj* (of fish or game) reared on a farm
FARMER, -S *n*
FARMERY *n* farm buildings
FARMING *n* business or skill of agriculture
FARMOST *adj* most distant
FARMS ▶ **farm**
FARNESS ▶ **far**
FARO, -S *n* gambling game
FARRAGO *n* jumbled mixture of things
FARRAND *variant of* ▶ **farand**
FARRANT *variant of* ▶ **farand**
FARRED ▶ **far**
FARREN, -S *n* allotted ground
FARRIER *n* person who shoes horses
FARRING ▶ **far**
FARRO, -S *n* variety of wheat
FARROW, -S *n* litter of piglets ▷ *vb* (of a sow) give birth ▷ *adj* (of a cow) not calving in a given year
FARRUCA *n* flamenco dance performed by men
FARS ▶ **far**
FARSE, -D, -S, FARSING *vb* insert into
FARSIDE *n* part of the Moon facing away from the Earth
FARSING ▶ **farse**
FART, -ED, -ING, -S *n, vb*
FARTHEL *same as* ▶ **farl**
FARTHER ▶ **far**
FARTING ▶ **fart**
FARTLEK *n* in sport, another name for interval training
FARTS ▶ **fart**
FAS ▶ **fa**
FASCES *pl n* (in ancient Rome) a bundle of rods containing an axe
FASCI ▶ **fascio**
FASCIA, -E, -S *n* outer surface of a dashboard
FASCIAL ▶ **fascia**
FASCIAS ▶ **fascia**
FASCINE *n* bundle of long sticks used in construction
FASCIO, FASCI *n* political group
FASCISM *n* right-wing totalitarian political system
FASCIST *n, adj*
FASH, -ED, -ES, -ING *n* worry ▷ *vb* trouble
FASHERY *n* difficulty, trouble
FASHES ▶ **fash**
FASHING ▶ **fash**
FASHION *n, vb*
FAST, -ED, -EST, -S *adj* (capable of) acting or moving quickly ▷ *adv* quickly ▷ *vb* go without food, esp for religious reasons ▷ *n* period of fasting
FASTEN, -S *vb*
FASTER, -S ▶ **fast**
FASTEST ▶ **fast**
FASTI *pl n* in ancient Rome, business days
FASTIE, -S *n* deceitful act
FASTING ▶ **fast**
FASTISH ▶ **fast**
FASTLY ▶ **fast**
FASTS ▶ **fast**
FAT, -S, -TED, -TER, -TEST, -TING *adj, n, vb*
FATAL *adj*
FATALLY *adv*
FATBACK *n* fat from the upper part of a side of pork
FATBERG *n* large mass of fat in a sewer
FATBIRD *n* nocturnal bird
FATE, -S, FATING *n, vb*
FATED *adj* destined
FATEFUL *adj*
FATES ▶ **fate**
FATHEAD *n* stupid person
FATHER, -S *n, vb*
FATHOM, -S *n* unit of length ▷ *vb* understand
FATIDIC *adj* prophetic
FATIGUE *n, vb*
FATING ▶ **fate**
FATLESS ▶ **fat**
FATLIKE ▶ **fat**

FATLING *n* young farm animal fattened for killing
FATLY ▸ **fat**
FATNESS ▸ **fat**
FATS ▸ **fat**
FATSIA, -S *n* type of shrub
FATSO, -ES, -S *n* disparaging term for a fat person
FATTED ▸ **fat**
FATTEN, -S *vb*
FATTER ▸ **fat**
FATTEST ▸ **fat**
FATTIER ▸ **fatty**
FATTIES ▸ **fatty**
FATTILY ▸ **fatty**
FATTING ▸ **fat**
FATTISH ▸ **fat**
FATTISM *n* discrimination on the basis of weight
FATTIST ▸ **fattism**
FATTY, FATTIER, FATTIES *adj, n*
FATUITY *n* foolish thoughtlessness
FATUOUS *adj* foolish
FATWA, -ED, -S *n* religious decree issued by a Muslim leader ▹ *vb* issue a fatwa
FATWAH, -S *same as* ▸ **fatwa**
FATWAS ▸ **fatwa**
FATWOOD *n* wood used for kindling
FAUCAL, -S *adj* of or relating to the fauces
FAUCES *n* area of the mouth
FAUCET, -S *n* tap
FAUCHON *variant of* > **fauchion**
FAUCIAL *same as* ▸ **faucal**
FAUGH *interj* exclamation of disgust, scorn, etc
FAULD, -S *n* piece of armour
FAULT, -ED, -S *n, vb*
FAULTY *adj*
FAUN, -S *n* (in Roman legend) mythological creature
FAUNA, -E, -S *n* animals of a given place or time
FAUNAL ▸ **fauna**
FAUNAS ▸ **fauna**
FAUNIST ▸ **fauna**
FAUNS ▸ **faun**
FAUNULA *n* fauna of a small single environment
FAUNULE *same as* ▸ **faunula**
FAUR, -ER, -EST *Scot word for* ▸ **far**
FAURD *adj* favoured
FAURER ▸ **faur**
FAUREST ▸ **faur**
FAUT, -ED, -ING, -S *Scot word for* ▸ **fault**
FAUTOR, -S *n* patron
FAUTS ▸ **faut**
FAUVE, -S *adj* of the style of the Fauve art movement ▹ *n* member of the Fauve art movement
FAUVISM ▸ **fauve**
FAUVIST *n* artist following the Fauve style of painting
FAUX *adj* false
FAVA, -S *n* type of bean
FAVE, -R, -S, -ST *short for* > **favourite**
FAVEL, -S *adj* (of a horse) fallow-coloured ▹ *n* fallow-coloured horse
FAVELA, -S *n* (in Brazil) a shanty or shantytown
FAVELL *variant of* ▸ **favel**
FAVELLA *n* group of spores
FAVELS ▸ **favel**
FAVER ▸ **fave**
FAVES ▸ **fave**
FAVEST ▸ **fave**
FAVICON *n* icon displayed before a website's URL
FAVISM, -S *n* type of anaemia
FAVOR, -ED, -S *same as* ▸ **favour**
FAVORER ▸ **favour**
FAVORS ▸ **favor**
FAVOSE *same as* > **faveolate**
FAVOUR, -S *n, vb*
FAVOUS *adj* resembling honeycomb
FAVRILE *n* type of iridescent glass
FAVUS, -ES *n* infectious fungal skin disease
FAW, -S *n* old word for an itinerant person

A **faw** is a person with an itinerant lifestyle, a good word for taking advantage of a nearby bonus square.

FAWN, -ED, -S *n* young deer ▹ *adj* light yellowish-brown ▹ *vb* seek attention from (someone) by insincere flattery
FAWNER, -S ▸ **fawn**
FAWNIER ▸ **fawny**
FAWNING ▸ **fawn**
FAWNS ▸ **fawn**

FAWNY, FAWNIER *adj* of a fawn colour
FAWS ▶ **faw**
FAX, -ED, -ES, -ING *n, vb*
FAXABLE *adj* able to be faxed
FAXED ▶ **fax**
FAXES ▶ **fax**
FAXING ▶ **fax**
FAY, -ED, -ER, -EST, -ING, -S *n* fairy or sprite ▷ *adj* of or resembling a fay ▷ *vb* fit or be fitted closely or tightly

A **fay** is a fairy, but it can also be a verb meaning to fit closely. It has an older variant **fey**. Both are useful high-scoring short words.

FAYENCE *variant of* ▶ **faience**
FAYER ▶ **fay**
FAYEST ▶ **fay**
FAYING ▶ **fay**
FAYNE, -D, -S, FAYNING *archaic spelling of* ▶ **feign**
FAYRE, -S *pseudo-archaic spelling of* ▶ **fair**
FAYS ▶ **fay**
FAZE, -S, FAZING *vb* disconcert or fluster
FAZED ▶ **faze**
FAZENDA *n* large estate or ranch
FAZES ▶ **faze**
FAZING ▶ **faze**
FE, -S *n* variant of Hebrew letter *pe*, transliterated as *f*
FEAGUE, -D, -S *vb* whip or beat
FEAL, -ED, -ING, -S *vb* conceal
FEALTY *n* (in feudal society) subordinate's loyalty
FEAR, -ED, -ING, -S *n, vb*
FEARE, -S *n* companion
FEARED ▶ **fear**
FEARER, -S ▶ **fear**
FEARES ▶ **feare**
FEARFUL *adj*
FEARING ▶ **fear**
FEARS ▶ **fear**
FEART *adj* (Scots) afraid
FEASE, -D, -S, FEASING *vb* perform an act
FEAST, -ED, -S *n, vb*
FEASTER ▶ **feast**
FEASTS ▶ **feast**
FEAT, -ED, -ER, -EST, -ING, -S *n* remarkable, skilful, or daring action ▷ *adj* neat ▷ *vb* make neat
FEATHER *n, vb*
FEATING ▶ **feat**
FEATLY ▶ **feat**
FEATOUS *variant of* > **feateous**
FEATS ▶ **feat**
FEATURE *n, vb*
FEAZE, -D, -S, FEAZING *same as* ▶ **feeze**
FEBRILE *adj* very active and nervous
FECAL *same as* ▶ **faecal**
FECES *same as* ▶ **faeces**
FECHT, -S *Scot word for* ▶ **fight**
FECHTER ▶ **fecht**
FECHTS ▶ **fecht**
FECIAL, -S *adj* heraldic
FECIT *vb* (he or she) made it
FECKLY *adv* dialect word meaning mostly
FECULA, -E, -S *n* type of starch
FECUND *adj* fertile
FED, -S *n* FBI agent
FEDARIE *n* old word for an accomplice
FEDAYEE *n* (in Arab states) a commando
FEDERAL *adj, n*
FEDEX, -ED, -ES *vb* send by FedEx
FEDORA, -S *n* soft hat with a brim
FEDS ▶ **fed**
FEE, -ING, -S *n, vb*
FEEB, -S *n* contemptible person
FEEBLE, -D, -R, -S *adj* lacking physical or mental power ▷ *vb* make feeble
FEEBLY ▶ **feeble**
FEEBS ▶ **feeb**
FEED, -ING, -S *vb, n*
FEEDBAG *n* any bag in which feed for livestock is sacked
FEEDBOX *n* trough, manger
FEEDER, -S *n* baby's bib
FEEDING ▶ **feed**
FEEDLOT *n* area where livestock are fattened rapidly
FEEDS ▶ **feed**
FEEING ▶ **fee**
FEEL, -S *vb, n*
FEELBAD *adj* inducing feelings of unhappiness
FEELER, -S *n*
FEELESS ▶ **fee**
FEELING ▶ **feel**
FEELS ▶ **feel**
FEEN, -S *n* in Irish dialect, an informal word for 'man'
FEER, -ED, -S *vb* make a furrow

FEERIE, -S *n* fairyland
FEERIN, -S *n* furrow
FEERING ▶ **feer**
FEERINS ▶ **feerin**
FEERS ▶ **feer**
FEES ▶ **fee**
FEESE, -D, -S, FEESING *vb* perturb
FEET ▶ **foot**
FEEZE, -D, -S, FEEZING *vb* beat ▷ *n* rush
FEG, -S *same as* ▶ **fig**
FEGARY *variant of* ▶ **vagary**
FEGS ▶ **feg**
FEH, -S *same as* ▶ **fe**
FEHM, -E *n* medieval German court
FEHMIC ▶ **fehm**
FEHS ▶ **feh**
FEIGN, -ED, -S *vb* pretend
FEIGNER ▶ **feign**
FEIGNS ▶ **feign**
FEIJOA, -S *n* evergreen myrtaceous shrub of S America
FEINT, -ED, -ER *n, vb, adj*
FEINTS *pl n* leavings of the second distillation of Scotch malt whisky
FEIRIE, -R *adj* nimble
FEIS *n* Irish music and dance festival
FEIST, -S *n* small aggressive dog
FEISTY *adj* showing courage or spirit
FELAFEL *same as* ▶ **falafel**
FELICIA *n* type of African herb
FELID, -S *n* any animal belonging to the cat family
FELINE, -S *adj* of cats ▷ *n* member of the cat family
FELL, -ED, -EST, -S *vb* cut or knock down ▷ *adj* cruel or deadly
FELLA, -S *nonstandard variant of* ▶ **fellow**
FELLAH, -S *n* peasant in Arab countries
FELLAS ▶ **fella**
FELLED ▶ **fell**
FELLER, -S *n* person or thing that fells
FELLEST ▶ **fell**
FELLIES ▶ **felly**
FELLING ▶ **fell**
FELLOE, -S *n* (segment of) the rim of a wheel
FELLOW, -S *n, adj, vb*
FELLS ▶ **fell**
FELLY, FELLIES *same as* ▶ **felloe**
FELON, -S *n* (formerly) person guilty of a felony ▷ *adj* evil
FELONRY *n* felons collectively
FELONS ▶ **felon**
FELONY *n* serious crime
FELSIC *adj* relating to igneous rock
FELSITE *n* any fine-grained igneous rock
FELSPAR *same as* > **feldspar**
FELT, -ED, -S *n, vb*
FELTER, -S *vb* mat together
FELTIER ▶ **felty**
FELTING *n* felted material
FELTS ▶ **felt**
FELTY, FELTIER ▶ **felt**
FELUCCA *n* narrow lateen-rigged vessel
FELWORT *n* type of plant
FEM, -S *n* type of igneous rock
FEMAL, -S *archaic variant of* ▶ **female**
FEMALE, -S *adj, n*
FEMALS ▶ **femal**
FEME, -S *n* woman or wife
FEMINAL *adj* feminine, female
FEMINIE *n* women collectively
FEMITER *variant of* > **fumitory**
FEMME, -S *n* woman or wife
FEMMY, FEMMIER *adj* markedly or exaggeratedly feminine
FEMORA ▶ **femur**
FEMORAL *adj* of the thigh
FEMS ▶ **fem**
FEMUR, FEMORA, -S *n* thighbone
FEN, -S *n* low-lying flat marshy land
FENAGLE *variant of* ▶ **finagle**
FENCE, -D, -S *n, vb*
FENCER, -S *n*
FENCES ▶ **fence**
FENCING *n* sport of fighting with swords
FEND, -ED, -ING, -S *vb, n*
FENDER, -S *n* low metal frame in front of a fireplace
FENDIER ▶ **fendy**
FENDING ▶ **fend**
FENDS ▶ **fend**
FENDY, FENDIER *adj* thrifty
FENI, -S *n* Goan alcoholic drink

FENING, -A, -S *n* small currency unit of Bosnia-Herzegovina
FENIS ▶ **feni**
FENITAR *variant of* > **fumitory**
FENKS *n* whale blubber
FENLAND ▶ **fen**
FENMAN, FENMEN ▶ **fen**
FENNEC, -S *n* type of nocturnal desert fox
FENNEL, -S *n* fragrant plant
FENNIER ▶ **fenny**
FENNIES ▶ **fenny**
FENNING *same as* ▶ **fening**
FENNISH ▶ **fen**
FENNY, FENNIER, FENNIES *adj* boggy or marshy ▷ *n* feni
FENS ▶ **fen**
FENT, -S *n* piece of waste fabric
FENURON *n* type of herbicide
FEOD, -S *same as* ▶ **feud**
FEODAL ▶ **feod**
FEODARY ▶ **feod**
FEODS ▶ **feod**
FEOFF, -ED, -S *same as* ▶ **fief**
FEOFFEE *n* (in feudal society) a vassal granted a fief by their lord
FEOFFER ▶ **feoff**
FEOFFOR ▶ **feoff**
FEOFFS ▶ **feoff**
FER *same as* ▶ **far**
FERAL, -S *adj* wild ▷ *n* person who displays such tendencies and appearance
FERBAM, -S *n* powder used as a fungicide
FERE, -R, -S, -ST *n* companion ▷ *adj* fierce
FERIA, -E, -S *n* weekday on which no feast occurs
FERIAL *adj* of or relating to a feria
FERIAS ▶ **feria**
FERINE *same as* ▶ **feral**
FERITY ▶ **feral**
FERLIE *same as* ▶ **ferly**
FERLY, FERLIED, FERLIER, FERLIES *adj* wonderful ▷ *n* wonder ▷ *vb* wonder
FERM, -S *variant of* ▶ **farm**
FERMATA, FERMATE *another word for* ▶ **pause**
FERMENT *n, vb*
FERMI, -S *n* unit of length
FERMION *n* type of particle
FERMIS ▶ **fermi**
FERMIUM *n* chemical element
FERMS ▶ **ferm**
FERN, -S *n*
FERNERY *n* place where ferns are grown
FERNIER ▶ **ferny**
FERNING *n* production of a fern-like pattern
FERNS ▶ **fern**
FERNY, FERNIER ▶ **fern**
FERRATE *n* type of salt
FERREL, -S *variant of* ▶ **ferrule**
FERRET, -S *n, vb*
FERRETY *adj* like a ferret
FERRIC *adj* of or containing iron
FERRIED ▶ **ferry**
FERRIES ▶ **ferry**
FERRITE *n* type of ceramic compound
FERROUS *adj* of or containing iron in the divalent state
FERRUGO *n* disease affecting plants
FERRULE *n* metal cap to strengthen the end of a stick ▷ *vb* equip (a stick, etc) with a ferrule
FERRUM, -S *Latin word for* ▶ **iron**
FERRY, FERRIED, FERRIES *n, vb*
FERTILE *adj*
FERULA, -E, -S *n* large Mediterranean plant
FERULE, -D, -S *same as* ▶ **ferrule**
FERVENT *adj*
FERVID *same as* ▶ **fervent**
FERVOR, -S *same as* ▶ **fervour**
FERVOUR *n*
FES ▶ **fe**
FESCUE, -S *n* pasture and lawn grass with stiff narrow leaves
FESS, -ED, -ING *vb* confess
FESSE, -S *n* horizontal band across a shield
FESSED ▶ **fess**
FESSES ▶ **fesse**
FESSING ▶ **fess**
FEST, -S *n* event at which the emphasis is on a particular activity
FESTA, -S *n* festival
FESTAL, -S *adj* festive ▷ *n* festivity
FESTAS ▶ **festa**
FESTER, -S *vb, n*

FESTIER ▸ **festy**
FESTIVE *adj*
FESTOON *vb, n*
FESTS ▸ **fest**
FESTY, FESTIER *adj* dirty
FET, -S, -TED, -TING *vb* fetch
FETA, -S *n* white salty Greek cheese
FETAL *adj* of, relating to, or resembling a fetus
FETAS ▸ **feta**
FETCH, -ED, -ES *vb, n*
FETCHER *n* person or animal that fetches
FETCHES ▸ **fetch**
FETE, -D, -S, FETING *n, vb*
FETIAL, -S *n* ancient Roman herald
FETICH *same as* ▸ **fetish**
FETICHE *variant of* ▸ **fetich**
FETID, -ER *adj* stinking
FETIDLY ▸ **fetid**
FETING ▸ **fete**
FETISH *n*
FETLOCK *n* projection behind and above a horse's hoof
FETOR, -S *n* stale or putrid odour
FETS ▸ **fet**
FETT, -S *variant of* ▸ **fet**
FETTA, -S *variant of* ▸ **feta**
FETTED ▸ **fet**
FETTER, -S *n* chain or shackle for the foot ▹ *vb* restrict
FETTING ▸ **fet**
FETTLE, -D, -S *same as* ▸ **fettling**
FETTLER *n* person employed to maintain railway tracks
FETTLES ▸ **fettle**
FETTS ▸ **fett**
FETUS, -ES *n*
FETWA, -S *variant of* ▸ **fatwa**
FEU, -ED, -ING, -S *n* (in Scotland) type of rent ▹ *vb* grant land to a person who pays a feu
FEUAR, -S *n* tenant of a feu
FEUD, -ED, -S *n, vb*
FEUDAL *adj* of or like feudalism
FEUDARY *n* holder of land through feudal right
FEUDED ▸ **feud**
FEUDING ▸ **feud**
FEUDIST *n* person who takes part in a feud or quarrel
FEUDS ▸ **feud**
FEUED ▸ **feu**
FEUING ▸ **feu**
FEUS ▸ **feu**
FEUTRE, -D, -S *vb* place in a resting position
FEVER, -S *n, vb*
FEVERED ▸ **fever**
FEVERS ▸ **fever**
FEW, -ER, -EST, -S *adj, n*
FEWMET, -S *variant of* ▸ **fumet**
FEWNESS ▸ **few**
FEWS ▸ **few**
FEWTER, -S *variant of* ▸ **feutre**
FEY, -ED, -ER, -EST, -ING, -S *adj* whimsically strange ▹ *vb* clean out
FEYLY ▸ **fey**
FEYNESS ▸ **fey**
FEYS ▸ **fey**
FEZ, -ES, -ZES *n* brimless tasselled cap, orig from Turkey
FEZZED *adj* wearing a fez
FEZZES ▸ **fez**
FEZZY ▸ **fez**
FIACRE, -S *n* small four-wheeled horse-drawn carriage
FIANCE, -S *n*
FIANCEE *n*
FIANCES ▸ **fiance**
FIAR *n* property owner
FIARS *n* legally fixed price of corn
FIASCO, FIASCHI, -S *n*
FIAT, -ED, -ING, -S *n* arbitrary order ▹ *vb* issue a fiat
FIAUNT, -S *n* warrant issued to the Irish Court of Chancery
FIB, -BED, -BING, -S *n, vb*
FIBBER, -S ▸ **fib**
FIBBERY ▸ **fib**
FIBBING ▸ **fib**
FIBER, -S *same as* ▸ **fibre**
FIBERED ▸ **fibre**
FIBERS ▸ **fiber**
FIBRATE *n* drug used to lower fat levels in the body
FIBRE, -S *n*
FIBRED ▸ **fibre**
FIBRES ▸ **fibre**
FIBRIL, -S *n* small fibre
FIBRIN, -S *n* white insoluble elastic protein
FIBRO, -S *n* mixture of cement and asbestos fibre
FIBROID *adj* (of structures or tissues) containing or resembling fibres ▹ *n* benign tumour composed of fibrous connective tissue

FIBROIN *n* tough elastic protein
FIBROMA *n* type of benign tumour
FIBROS ▸ **fibro**
FIBROSE *vb* become fibrous
FIBROUS *adj* consisting of, containing, or resembling fibres
FIBS ▸ **fib**
FIBSTER *n* fibber
FIBULA, -E, -S *n* slender outer bone of the lower leg
FIBULAR ▸ **fibula**
FIBULAS ▸ **fibula**
FICAIN, -S *n* cysteine proteinase isolated from the latex of figs
FICE, -S *n* small aggressive dog
FICHE, -S *n* film for storing publications in miniature
FICHU, -S *n* woman's shawl or scarf
FICIN, -S *n* enzyme
FICKLE, -D, -R, -S *adj* changeable, inconstant ▹ *vb* puzzle
FICKLY ▸ **fickle**
FICO, -ES, -S *n* worthless trifle
FICTILE *adj* moulded or capable of being moulded from clay
FICTION *n*
FICTIVE *adj* of, relating to, or able to create fiction
FICTOR, -S *n* sculptor
FICUS, -ES *n* type of plant
FID, -S *n* spike for separating strands of rope in splicing
FIDDLE, -D, -S *n, vb*
FIDDLER *n*
FIDDLES ▸ **fiddle**
FIDDLEY *n* vertical space above a vessel's engine room
FIDDLY *adj*
FIDEISM *n* theological doctrine
FIDEIST ▸ **fideism**
FIDES *n* faith or trust
FIDGE, -D, -S, FIDGING *obsolete word for* ▸ **fidget**
FIDGET, -S *vb, n*
FIDGETY ▸ **fidget**
FIDGING ▸ **fidge**
FIDIBUS *n* spill for lighting a candle or pipe
FIDO, -S *n* generic term for a dog
FIDS ▸ **fid**
FIE, -ST *same as* ▸ **fey**
FIEF, -S *n* land granted by a lord in return for war service
FIEFDOM *n* (in Feudal Europe) the property owned by a lord
FIEFS ▸ **fief**
FIELD, -ED, -S *n, vb*
FIELDER *n*
FIELDS ▸ **field**
FIEND, -S *n* evil spirit
FIENT, -S *n* fiend
FIER, -S *same as* ▸ **fere**
FIERCE, -R *adj*
FIERE, -S *same as* ▸ **fere**
FIERIER ▸ **fiery**
FIERILY ▸ **fiery**
FIERS ▸ **fier**
FIERY, FIERIER *adj*
FIEST ▸ **fie**
FIESTA, -S *n*
FIFE, -D, -S, FIFING *n* small high-pitched flute ▹ *vb* play (music) on a fife
FIFER, -S ▸ **fife**
FIFES ▸ **fife**
FIFI, -S *n* mountaineering hook
FIFING ▸ **fife**
FIFIS ▸ **fifi**
FIFTEEN *n*
FIFTH, -S *n, adj*
FIFTHLY *adv* in the fifth place or position
FIFTHS ▸ **fifth**
FIFTY, FIFTIES *n*
FIG, -GED, -GING, -S *n* soft pear-shaped fruit ▹ *vb* dress (up) or rig (out)
FIGGERY *n* adornment, ornament
FIGGIER ▸ **figgy**
FIGGING ▸ **fig**
FIGGY, FIGGIER *adj* tasting like figs
FIGHT, -S, FOUGHT *vb, n*
FIGHTER *n*
FIGHTS ▸ **fight**
FIGJAM, -S *n* very conceited person
FIGLIKE *adj* like a fig
FIGMENT *n*
FIGO, -S *variant of* ▸ **fico**
FIGS ▸ **fig**
FIGTREE *n* tree that produces figs
FIGURAL *adj* composed of or relating to human or animal figures
FIGURE, -S *n, vb*
FIGURED *adj* decorated with a design
FIGURER ▸ **figure**
FIGURES ▸ **figure**

FIGWORT *n* plant with small brown or greenish flowers
FIKE, -D, -S, FIKING *vb* fidget
FIKERY *n* fuss
FIKES ▸ **fike**
FIKIER ▸ **fiky**
FIKIEST ▸ **fiky**
FIKING ▸ **fike**
FIKISH *adj* fussy
FIKY, FIKIER, FIKIEST *adj* fussy
FIL *same as* ▸ **fils**
FILA ▸ **filum**
FILABEG *variant of* ▸ **filibeg**
FILACER *n* formerly, English legal officer
FILAR *adj* of thread
FILAREE *n* type of storksbill, a weed
FILARIA *n* type of parasitic nematode worm
FILASSE *n* vegetable fibre such as jute
FILAZER *variant of* ▸ **filacer**
FILBERD *variant of* ▸ **filbert**
FILBERT *n* hazelnut
FILCH, -ED, -ES *vb* steal (small amounts)
FILCHER ▸ **filch**
FILCHES ▸ **filch**
FILE, -D, -S, FILING *n, vb*
FILEMOT *n* type of brown colour
FILER, -S ▸ **file**
FILES ▸ **file**
FILET, -ED, -S *variant of* ▸ **fillet**
FILFOT, -S *variant of* ▸ **fylfot**
FILIAL *adj* of or befitting a son or daughter
FILIATE *vb* fix judicially the paternity of (a child)
FILIBEG *n* kilt worn by Scottish Highlanders
FILII ▸ **filius**

This plural of **filius**, a Latin word for son, is the only 5-letter word that lets you get rid of three Is!

FILING ▸ **file**
FILINGS *pl n* shavings removed by a file
FILIUS, FILII *n* son
FILK, -S *n* parodic type of folk music with science fiction lyrics
FILL, -ED, -S *vb*
FILLE, -S *n* girl
FILLED ▸ **fill**
FILLER, -S *n*
FILLES ▸ **fille**
FILLET, -S *n, vb*
FILLIES ▸ **filly**
FILLING *n* substance that fills a gap or cavity ▹ *adj* (of food) substantial and satisfying
FILLIP, -S *n* something that adds stimulation or enjoyment ▹ *vb* stimulate or excite
FILLO, -S *variant of* ▸ **filo**
FILLS ▸ **fill**
FILLY, FILLIES *n*
FILM, -ED, -S *n, vb, adj*
FILMDOM *n* cinema industry
FILMED ▸ **film**
FILMER, -S *n* film-maker
FILMI *adj* of or relating to Indian films
FILMIC *adj* of or suggestive of films or the cinema
FILMIER ▸ **filmy**
FILMILY ▸ **filmy**
FILMING *n* act of photographing with a video camera
FILMISH ▸ **film**
FILMS ▸ **film**
FILMSET *vb* set (type matter) by filmsetting
FILMY, FILMIER *adj*
FILO, -S *n* type of flaky Greek pastry in very thin sheets
FILOSE *adj* resembling a thread or threadlike process
FILS *n* monetary unit of Bahrain, Iraq, Jordan, and Kuwait
FILTER, -S *n, vb*
FILTH, -S *n*
FILTHY *adj, adv*
FILTRE *adj* as in **cafe filtre** a strong black filtered coffee
FILUM, FILA *n* any threadlike structure or part
FIMBLE, -S *n* male plant of the hemp
FIMBRIA *n* fringe or fringelike margin or border
FIN, -NED, -NING, -S *n* any of the appendages of some aquatic animals ▹ *vb* provide with fins
FINABLE *adj* liable to a fine
FINAGLE *vb* get or achieve by craftiness or trickery

FINAL *adj, n*
FINALE, -S *n*
FINALIS *n* musical finishing note
FINALLY *adv*
FINALS *pl n* deciding part of a competition
FINANCE *vb, n*
FINBACK *another name for* ▶ **rorqual**
FINCA, -S *n* Spanish villa
FINCH, -ES *n*
FINCHED *adj* with streaks or spots on the back
FINCHES ▶ **finch**
FIND, -S *vb, n*
FINDER, -S *n* small telescope fitted to a larger one
FINDING ▶ **find**
FINDRAM *variant of* ▶ **finnan**
FINDS ▶ **find**
FINE, -D, -S *adj, n, vb*
FINEER, -S *variant of* ▶ **veneer**
FINEISH ▶ **fine**
FINELY *adv*
FINER, -S ▶ **fine**
FINERY *n*
FINES ▶ **fine**
FINESSE *n, vb*
FINEST, -S *n* (in the US) police of a particular city
FINFISH *n* fish with fins, as opposed to shellfish
FINFOOT *n* type of aquatic bird
FINGAN, -S *variant of* ▶ **finjan**
FINGER, -S *n, vb*
FINI *n* end; finish
FINIAL, -S *n* ornament at the apex of a gable or spire
FINICAL *another word for* ▶ **finicky**
FINICKY *adj*
FINIKIN *variant of* ▶ **finicky**
FINING, -S *n* process of removing bubbles from molten glass
FINIS, -ES *n* end; finish
FINISH *vb, n*
FINITE, -S *adj* having limits in space, time, or size ▷ *n* verb limited by person, number, tense or mood
FINITO *adj* finished
FINJAN, -S *n* small, handleless coffee cup
FINK, -ED, -ING, -S *n* strikebreaker ▷ *vb* inform (on someone), as to the police
FINLESS ▶ **fin**
FINLIKE ▶ **fin**
FINLIT, -S *n* understanding of the concepts associated with finance
FINMARK *n* former monetary unit of Finland
FINNAC, -S *variant of* ▶ **finnock**
FINNACK *variant of* ▶ **finnock**
FINNACS ▶ **finnac**
FINNAN, -S *n* smoked haddock
FINNED ▶ **fin**
FINNER, -S *another name for* ▶ **rorqual**
FINNIER ▶ **finny**
FINNING ▶ **fin**
FINNOCK *n* young sea trout on its first return to fresh water
FINNSKO *variant of* > **finnesko**
FINNY, FINNIER *adj* relating to or containing many fishes
FINO, -S *n* very dry sherry
FINS ▶ **fin**
FINSKO *variant of* > **finnesko**
FINTECH *n* financial services technology
FIORD, -S *same as* ▶ **fjord**
FIORIN, -S *n* type of temperate perennial grass
FIPPLE, -S *n* wooden plug forming a flue in the end of a pipe
FIQH, -S *n* Islamic jurisprudence
FIQUE, -S *n* hemp
FIR, -S *n*
FIRE, -D, -S *n, vb*
FIREARM *n*
FIREBOX *n* furnace chamber of a boiler in a steam locomotive
FIREBUG *n* person who deliberately sets fire to property
FIRED ▶ **fire**
FIREDOG *n* either of two metal stands supporting logs in a fire
FIREFLY *n*
FIRELIT *adj* lit by firelight
FIREMAN, FIREMEN *n*
FIREPAN *n* metal container for a fire in a room
FIREPIT *n* hole dug in the ground for a fire

FIREPOT *n* Chinese fondue-like cooking pot
FIRER, -S ▸ **fire**
FIRES ▸ **fire**
FIRIE, -S *n* in Australian English, informal word for a firefighter
FIRING, -S *n* discharge of a firearm
FIRK, -ED, -ING, -S *vb* beat
FIRKIN, -S *n* small wooden barrel or similar container
FIRKING ▸ **firk**
FIRKINS ▸ **firkin**
FIRKS ▸ **firk**
FIRLOT, -S *n* unit of measurement for grain
FIRM, -ED, -EST, -ING, -S *adj, adv, vb, n*
FIRMAN, -S *n* edict of a sultan
FIRMED ▸ **firm**
FIRMER, -S ▸ **firm**
FIRMEST ▸ **firm**
FIRMING ▸ **firm**
FIRMLY ▸ **firm**
FIRMS ▸ **firm**
FIRN, -S *another name for* ▸ **neve**
FIRRIER ▸ **firry**
FIRRING *n* wooden battens used in building construction
FIRRY, FIRRIER *adj* of, relating to, or made from fir trees
FIRS ▸ **fir**
FIRST *adj, n, adv*
FIRSTLY *adv* coming before other points, questions, etc
FIRSTS *pl n* saleable goods of the highest quality
FIRTH, -S *n* narrow inlet of the sea, esp in Scotland
FIRWOOD *n* wood of the fir tree
FISC, -S *n* state or royal treasury
FISCAL, -S *adj, n*
FISCS ▸ **fisc**
FISGIG, -S *variant of* ▸ **fishgig**
FISH, -ED, -ES *n* cold-blooded vertebrate with gills, that lives in water ▹ *vb* try to catch fish
FISHER, -S *n* fisherman
FISHERY *n* area of the sea used for fishing
FISHES ▸ **fish**
FISHEYE *n* type of lens
FISHFUL *adj* teeming with fish
FISHGIG *n* pole with barbed prongs for impaling fish
FISHIER ▸ **fishy**
FISHIFY *vb* change into fish
FISHILY ▸ **fishy**
FISHING *n*
FISHNET *n* open mesh fabric resembling netting
FISHWAY *n* fish ladder
FISHY, FISHIER *adj*
FISK, -ED, -ING, -S *vb* frisk
FISSATE ▸ **fissile**
FISSILE *adj* capable of undergoing nuclear fission
FISSION *n* splitting
FISSIVE ▸ **fissile**
FISSLE, -D, -S *vb* rustle
FISSURE *n* long narrow cleft or crack ▹ *vb* crack or split apart
FIST, -ED, -S *n, vb*
FISTFUL *n* quantity that can be held in a fist or hand
FISTIC *adj* of or relating to fisticuffs or boxing
FISTIER ▸ **fisty**
FISTING *n* act of fisting
FISTS ▸ **fist**
FISTULA *n* long narrow ulcer
FISTY, FISTIER ▸ **fist**
FIT, -S, -TED, -TEST, -TING *vb, adj, n*
FITCH, -ES *n* fur of the polecat or ferret
FITCHE *adj* pointed
FITCHEE *variant of* ▸ **fitche**
FITCHES ▸ **fitch**
FITCHET *same as* ▸ **fitch**
FITCHEW *archaic name for* ▸ **polecat**
FITCHY *variant of* ▸ **fitche**
FITFUL *adj*
FITLY, FITLIER *adv* in a proper manner or place or at a proper time
FITMENT *n* accessory attached to a machine
FITNA, -S *n* state of trouble or chaos
FITNESS *n*
FITS ▸ **fit**
FITT, -S *n* song
FITTE, -S *variant of* ▸ **fitt**
FITTED ▸ **fit**
FITTER, -S ▸ **fit**
FITTES ▸ **fitte**
FITTEST ▸ **fit**
FITTING ▸ **fit**
FITTS ▸ **fitt**

FIVE *n*
FIVEPIN > **fivepins**
FIVER, -S *n*
FIVES *n* ball game resembling squash
FIX, -ES *vb, n*
FIXABLE ▸ **fix**
FIXATE, -D, -S *vb* become or cause to become fixed
FIXATIF *variant of* > **fixative**
FIXED *adj* attached or placed so as to be immovable
FIXEDLY ▸ **fixed**
FIXER, -S *n* solution used to make a photographic image permanent
FIXES ▸ **fix**
FIXING *n* means of attaching one thing to another
FIXINGS *pl n* apparatus or equipment
FIXIT, -S *n* solution to a complex problem ▹ *adj* that fixes things
FIXITY *n* state of being fixed
FIXIVE ▸ **fix**
FIXT *adj* fixed
FIXTURE *n* permanently fitted piece of household equipment
FIXURE, -S *n* firmness
FIZ *variant of* ▸ **fizz**
FIZGIG, -S *vb* inform on someone to the police
FIZZ, -ED, -ES, -ING *vb, n*
FIZZEN, -S *variant of* ▸ **foison**
FIZZER, -S *n* anything that fizzes
FIZZES ▸ **fizz**
FIZZGIG *variant of* ▸ **fishgig**
FIZZIER ▸ **fizzy**
FIZZILY *adv* in a fizzy manner
FIZZING ▸ **fizz**
FIZZLE, -D, -S *vb, n*
FIZZY, FIZZIER ▸ **fizz**
FJELD, -S *n* high rocky plateau
FJORD, -S *n* long narrow inlet of the sea between cliffs
FJORDIC ▸ **fjord**
FJORDS ▸ **fjord**
FLAB, -S *n*
FLABBY *adj*
FLABS ▸ **flab**
FLACCID *adj* soft and limp
FLACK, -ED, -S *vb* flap
FLACKER *vb* flap
FLACKET *n* flagon ▹ *vb* flap or flutter about
FLACKS ▸ **flack**
FLACON, -S *n* small stoppered bottle or flask
FLAFF, -ED, -S *vb* flap
FLAFFER *vb* flutter
FLAFFS ▸ **flaff**
FLAG, -GED, -S *n, vb*
FLAGGER ▸ **flag**
FLAGGY *adj* drooping
FLAGMAN, FLAGMEN *n* person who has charge of a flag
FLAGON, -S *n* wide bottle
FLAGS ▸ **flag**
FLAIL, -ED, -S *vb, n*
FLAIR, -S *n* natural ability
FLAK, -S *n* anti-aircraft fire
FLAKE, -D, -S, FLAKING *n, vb*
FLAKER, -S ▸ **flake**
FLAKES ▸ **flake**
FLAKEY *same as* ▸ **flaky**
FLAKIER ▸ **flaky**
FLAKIES *pl n* dandruff
FLAKILY ▸ **flaky**
FLAKING ▸ **flake**
FLAKS ▸ **flak**
FLAKY, FLAKIER *adj*
FLAM, -MED, -S *n* falsehood, deception, or sham ▹ *vb* cheat or deceive
FLAMBE, -S *vb* cook or serve (food) in flaming brandy ▹ *adj* (of food) served in flaming brandy
FLAMBEE *same as* ▸ **flambe**
FLAMBES ▸ **flambe**
FLAME, -D, -S *n, vb*
FLAMEN, -S *n* (in ancient Rome) type of priest
FLAMER, -S ▸ **flame**
FLAMES ▸ **flame**
FLAMFEW *n* fantastic trifle
FLAMIER ▸ **flamy**
FLAMING *adj* burning with flames ▹ *adv* extremely
FLAMM, -S *variant of* ▸ **flam**
FLAMMED ▸ **flam**
FLAMMS ▸ **flamm**
FLAMS ▸ **flam**
FLAMY, FLAMIER ▸ **flame**
FLAN, -S *n*
FLANCH *variant of* ▸ **flaunch**
FLANE, -D, FLANING *vb* walk idly, saunter

FLANES ▸ **flane**
FLANEUR *n* idler or loafer
FLANGE, -S *n* projecting rim or collar ▹ *vb* attach or provide (a component) with a flange
FLANGED ▸ **flange**
FLANGER ▸ **flange**
FLANGES ▸ **flange**
FLANING ▸ **flane**
FLANK, -ED, -S *n, vb*
FLANKEN *n* cut of beef
FLANKER *n* one of a detachment of soldiers guarding the flanks
FLANKS ▸ **flank**
FLANNEL *n, vb*
FLANNEN *adj* made of flannel
FLANNIE *same as* ▸ **flanny**
FLANNY *n* shirt made of flannel
FLANS ▸ **flan**
FLAP, -PED, -S *vb, n*
FLAPPER *n*
FLAPPY *adj* loose
FLAPS ▸ **flap**
FLARE, -D, FLARING *vb, n*
FLARES *pl n* trousers with legs that widen below the knee
FLAREUP *n* outbreak of something
FLARIER ▸ **flary**
FLARING ▸ **flare**
FLARY, FLARIER *adj* flare-like
FLASER, -S *n* type of sedimentary structure in rock
FLASH, -ED, -ES *n, adj, vb*
FLASHER ▸ **flash**
FLASHES ▸ **flash**
FLASHY *adj*
FLASK, -S *n* flat bottle
FLASKET *n* long shallow basket
FLASKS ▸ **flask**
FLAT, -S, -TED *adj* level and horizontal ▹ *adv* in or into a flat position ▹ *n* flat surface ▹ *vb* live in a flat
FLATBED *n* type of printing machine
FLATCAP *n* Elizabethan man's hat
FLATCAR *n* railway goods wagon without raised sides
FLATLET *n* small flat
FLATLY ▸ **flat**
FLATS ▸ **flat**
FLATTED ▸ **flat**
FLATTEN *vb* make or become flat or flatter
FLATTER *vb*
FLATTIE *n* flat tyre
FLATTOP *n* informal name for an aircraft carrier
FLATTY *n* flat shoe
FLATUS *n* gas generated in the alimentary canal
FLAUGHT *vb* flutter
FLAUNCH *n* cement or mortar slope to throw off water ▹ *vb* cause to slope in this manner
FLAUNE, -S *variant of* ▸ **flam**
FLAUNT, -S *vb, n*
FLAUNTY *adj* characterized by or inclined to ostentatious display
FLAUTA, -S *n* tortilla rolled around a filling
FLAVA, -S *n* individual style
FLAVIN, -S *n* heterocyclic ketone
FLAVINE *same as* ▸ **flavin**
FLAVINS ▸ **flavin**
FLAVONE *n* crystalline compound occurring in plants
FLAVOR, -S *same as* ▸ **flavour**
FLAVORY *adj* flavoursome
FLAVOUR *n, vb*
FLAW, -ED, -ING, -S *n, vb*
FLAWIER ▸ **flawy**
FLAWING ▸ **flaw**
FLAWN, -S *variant of* ▸ **flam**
FLAWS ▸ **flaw**
FLAWY, FLAWIER ▸ **flaw**
FLAX, -ES *n*
FLAXEN *adj*
FLAXES ▸ **flax**
FLAXY, FLAXIER *same as* ▸ **flaxen**
FLAY, -ED, -ING, -S *vb* remove the skin from
FLAYER, -S ▸ **flay**
FLAYING ▸ **flay**
FLAYS ▸ **flay**
FLEA, -S *n*
FLEABAG *n* dirty or unkempt person, esp a woman
FLEADH, -S *n* festival of Irish music, dancing, and culture
FLEAM, -S *n* lancet used for letting blood
FLEAPIT *n* shabby cinema or theatre
FLEAS ▸ **flea**
FLECHE, -S *n* slender spire

FLECK, -ED, -S *n, vb*
FLECKER *same as* ▸ **fleck**
FLECKS ▸ **fleck**
FLECKY ▸ **fleck**
FLED ▸ **flee**
FLEDGE, -D, -S *vb* feed and care for (a young bird) until it is able to fly
FLEDGY *adj* feathery or feathered
FLEE, FLED, -ING, -S *vb*
FLEECE, -D, -S *n, vb*
FLEECER ▸ **fleece**
FLEECES ▸ **fleece**
FLEECH *vb* flatter
FLEECIE *n* person who collects fleeces for baling
FLEECY *adj* made of or like fleece ▹ *n* person who collects fleeces for baling
FLEEING ▸ **flee**
FLEEK *n* as in **on fleek** stylish, on trend
FLEEKS *same as* ▸ **fleek**
FLEER, -ED, -S *vb* grin or laugh at ▹ *n* derisory glance or grin
FLEERER ▸ **fleer**
FLEERS ▸ **fleer**
FLEES ▸ **flee**
FLEET, -ED, -S *n* number of warships organized as a unit ▹ *adj* swift in movement ▹ *vb* move rapidly
FLEETER *n* person who sails with a fleet of ships
FLEETLY ▸ **fleet**
FLEETS ▸ **fleet**
FLEG, -GED, -S *vb* scare
FLEHMEN *vb* (of mammal) grimace
FLEME, -D, -S, FLEMIT *vb* drive out
FLEMING *n* inhabitant of Flanders or a Flemish-speaking Belgian
FLEMISH *vb* stow (a rope) in a Flemish coil
FLEMIT ▸ **fleme**
FLENCH *same as* ▸ **flense**
FLENSE, -D, -S *vb* strip (a whale, seal, etc) of (its blubber or skin)
FLENSER ▸ **flense**
FLENSES ▸ **flense**
FLESH, -ED, -ES *n, vb*
FLESHER *n* person or machine that fleshes hides or skins
FLESHES ▸ **flesh**
FLESHLY *adj* fleshy; fat
FLESHY *adj* plump
FLETCH *same as* ▸ **fledge**
FLETTON *n* type of brick
FLEUR, -S *n* flower emblem used in heraldry
FLEURET *same as* > **fleurette**
FLEURON *n* decorative piece of pastry
FLEURS ▸ **fleur**
FLEURY *same as* ▸ **flory**
FLEW ▸ **fly**
FLEWED *adj* having large flews
FLEWS *pl n* upper lip of a bloodhound or similar dog
FLEX, -ED, -ES, -ING *n, vb*
FLEXI, -S *n* flexitime
FLEXILE *same as* > **flexible**
FLEXING ▸ **flex**
FLEXION *n* act of bending a joint or limb
FLEXIS ▸ **flexi**
FLEXO, -S *n* flexography
FLEXOR, -S *n* type of muscle
FLEXOS ▸ **flexo**
FLEXURE *n* act of flexing or the state of being flexed
FLEY, -ED, -ING, -S *vb* be afraid or cause to be afraid
FLIC, -S *n* French police officer
FLICK, -ED, -S *vb, n*
FLICKER *vb, n*
FLICKS ▸ **flick**
FLICS ▸ **flic**
FLIED ▸ **fly**
FLIER, -S ▸ **fly**
FLIES ▸ **fly**
FLIEST ▸ **fly**
FLIGHT, -S *n, vb*
FLIGHTY *adj*
FLIM, -S *n* five-pound note
FLIMP, -ED, -S *vb* steal
FLIMS ▸ **flim**
FLIMSY *adj, n*
FLINCH *vb* draw back suddenly
FLINDER *n* fragment ▹ *vb* scamper about flutteringly
FLING, -S, FLUNG *vb, n*
FLINGER ▸ **fling**
FLINGS ▸ **fling**
FLINT, -ED, -S *n, vb*
FLINTY *adj* cruel
FLIP, -PED, -S *vb, n, adj*
FLIPPER *n*
FLIPPY *adj* (of clothes) moving to and fro as the wearer walks
FLIPS ▸ **flip**

FLIR, -S *n* forward looking infrared radar
FLIRT, -ED, -S *vb, n*
FLIRTER ▶ **flirt**
FLIRTS ▶ **flirt**
FLIRTY ▶ **flirt**
FLISK, -ED, -S *vb* skip
FLISKY ▶ **flisk**
FLIT, -S, -TED *vb, n*
FLITCH *n* side of pork salted and cured ▷ *vb* cut (a tree trunk) into pieces of timber
FLITE, -D, -S, FLITING *vb* scold or rail at ▷ *n* dispute or scolding
FLITS ▶ **flit**
FLITT, -S *adj* fleet ▷ *vb* to flit
FLITTED ▶ **flit**
FLITTER ▶ **flit**
FLITTS ▶ **flitt**
FLIVVER *n* old, cheap, or battered car
FLIX, -ED, -ES, -ING *n* fur ▷ *vb* have fur
FLOAT, -ED *vb, n*
FLOATEL *same as* ▶ **flotel**
FLOATER *n*
FLOATS *pl n* footlights
FLOATY *adj*
FLOB, -BED, -S *vb* spit
FLOC, -S *same as* ▶ **flock**
FLOCCED ▶ **floc**
FLOCCUS, FLOCCI *n* downy or woolly covering ▷ *adj* (of a cloud) having the appearance of woolly tufts
FLOCK, -ED, -S *n, vb, adj*
FLOCKY ▶ **flock**
FLOCS ▶ **floc**
FLOE, -S *n* sheet of floating ice
FLOG, -GED, -S *vb*
FLOGGER ▶ **flog**
FLOGS ▶ **flog**
FLOKATI *n* Greek hand-woven shaggy woollen rug
FLONG, -S *n* material used for making moulds in stereotyping
FLOOD, -ED, -S *n, vb*
FLOODER ▶ **flood**
FLOODS ▶ **flood**
FLOOEY *adj* awry
FLOOIE *same as* ▶ **flooey**
FLOOR, -ED, -S *n, vb*
FLOORER *n* coup de grâce
FLOORS ▶ **floor**
FLOP, -PED, -S *vb, n*
FLOPPER ▶ **flop**
FLOPPY *adj, n*
FLOPS ▶ **flop**
FLOR, -S *n* type of yeast
FLORA, -E, -S *n* plants of a given place or time
FLORAL, -S *adj, n*
FLORAS ▶ **flora**
FLOREAT *vb* may (a person, institution, etc) flourish
FLORET, -S *n*
FLORID *adj* with a red or flushed complexion
FLORIER ▶ **flory**
FLORIN, -S *n* former British and Australian coin
FLORIST *n*
FLORS ▶ **flor**
FLORUIT *prep* (he or she) flourished in ▷ *n* such a period in a person's life
FLORULA *n* flora of a small single environment
FLORULE *same as* ▶ **florula**
FLORY, FLORIER *adj* containing a fleur-de-lys
FLOSH, -ES *n* hopper-shaped box
FLOSS, -ED, -ES *n, vb*
FLOSSER ▶ **floss**
FLOSSES ▶ **floss**
FLOSSIE *variant of* ▶ **flossy**
FLOSSY *adj*
FLOTA, -S *n* formerly, Spanish commercial fleet
FLOTAGE *n* act or state of floating
FLOTANT *adj* in heraldry, flying in the air
FLOTAS ▶ **flota**
FLOTE, -D, -S, FLOTING *n* aquatic perennial grass ▷ *vb* skim (eg milk)
FLOTEL, -S *n* (in the oil industry) rig or boat used as accommodation
FLOTES ▶ **flote**
FLOTING ▶ **flote**
FLOTSAM *n* floating wreckage
FLOUNCE *vb, n*
FLOUNCY ▶ **flounce**
FLOUR, -ED, -S *n, vb*
FLOURY ▶ **flour**
FLOUSE, -D, -S *vb* splash
FLOUSH *variant of* ▶ **flouse**
FLOUT, -ED, -S *vb*
FLOUTER ▶ **flout**
FLOUTS ▶ **flout**
FLOW, -ED, -ING, -S *vb, n*
FLOWAGE *n* act of overflowing or the

state of having overflowed
FLOWED ▸ **flow**
FLOWER, -S *n, vb*
FLOWERY *adj*
FLOWING ▸ **flow**
FLOWN ▸ **fly**
FLOWS ▸ **flow**
FLOX *adj* as in **flox silk** type of silk
FLU, -S *n*
FLUATE, -S *n* fluoride
FLUB, -BED, -S *vb* bungle
FLUBBER ▸ **flub**
FLUBDUB *n* bunkum
FLUBS ▸ **flub**
FLUE, -S *n* passage or pipe for smoke or hot air
FLUED *adj* having a flue
FLUENCE *n* particle or energy density
FLUENCY *n*
FLUENT, -S *adj, n*
FLUERIC *adj* of or relating to fluidics
FLUES ▸ **flue**
FLUEY, FLUIER, FLUIEST *adj* involved in, caused by, or like influenza
FLUFF, -ED, -S *n, vb*
FLUFFER *n* person employed on a railway to clear the tracks
FLUFFS ▸ **fluff**
FLUFFY *adj*
FLUGEL, -S *n* grand piano or harpsichord
FLUID, -S *n, adj*
FLUIDAL ▸ **fluid**
FLUIDIC > **fluidics**
FLUIDLY ▸ **fluid**
FLUIDS ▸ **fluid**
FLUIER ▸ **fluey**
FLUIEST ▸ **fluey**
FLUISH ▸ **flu**
FLUKE, -D, -S, FLUKING *n* accidental stroke of luck ▹ *vb* gain, make, or hit by a fluke
FLUKEY *same as* ▸ **fluky**
FLUKIER ▸ **fluky**
FLUKILY ▸ **fluky**
FLUKING ▸ **fluke**
FLUKY, FLUKIER *adj* done or gained by an accident
FLUME, -D, -S, FLUMING *n* narrow sloping channel for water ▹ *vb* transport (logs) in a flume
FLUMMOX *vb* puzzle or confuse
FLUMP, -ED, -S *vb* move or fall heavily
FLUNG ▸ **fling**
FLUNK, -ED, -S *vb* fail ▹ *n* low grade below the pass standard
FLUNKER ▸ **flunk**
FLUNKEY *same as* ▸ **flunky**
FLUNKIE *same as* ▸ **flunky**
FLUNKS ▸ **flunk**
FLUNKY *n* servile person
FLUOR, -S *same as* > **fluorspar**
FLUORIC *adj* of, concerned with, or produced from fluorine or fluorspar
FLUORID *same as* > **fluoride**
FLUORIN *same as* > **fluorine**
FLUORS ▸ **fluor**
FLURR, -ED, -S *vb* scatter
FLURRY *n, vb*
FLUS ▸ **flu**
FLUSH, -ED, -ES *vb, n, adj, adv*
FLUSHER ▸ **flush**
FLUSHES ▸ **flush**
FLUSHY *adj* ruddy
FLUSTER *vb, n*
FLUTE, -S *n, vb*
FLUTED *adj* having decorative grooves
FLUTER, -S *n* craftsperson who makes flutes or fluting
FLUTES ▸ **flute**
FLUTEY, FLUTIER *adj* resembling a flute in sound
FLUTINA *n* type of accordion
FLUTING *n* design of decorative grooves
FLUTIST *same as* > **flautist**
FLUTTER *vb* flap ▹ *n* flapping movement
FLUTY ▸ **flute**
FLUVIAL *adj* of rivers
FLUX, -ED, -ES, -ING *n, vb*
FLUXION *n* rate of change of a function
FLUXIVE ▸ **flux**
FLUYT, -S *n* Dutch sailing ship
FLY, FLEW, FLIED, FLIES, FLIEST, FLOWN, -EST *vb, n, adj*
FLYABLE ▸ **fly**
FLYAWAY *adj* (of hair) very fine and soft ▹ *n* person who is frivolous or flighty
FLYBACK *n* item of electrical equipment
FLYBANE *n* type of campion

FLYBELT *n* strip of tsetse-infested land
FLYBLOW, FLYBLEW *vb* contaminate ▷ *n* egg or young larva of a blowfly
FLYBOAT *n* any small swift boat
FLYBOOK *n* small case or wallet for storing artificial flies
FLYBOY, -S *n* air force pilot
FLYBY, -S *n* flight past a particular position or target
FLYER, -S ▶ **fly**
FLYEST ▶ **fly**
FLYHAND *n* device on a printing press
FLYING, -S ▶ **fly**
FLYLEAF *n* blank leaf at the beginning or end of a book
FLYLESS ▶ **fly**
FLYLINE *n* type of line used in fly fishing
FLYMAN, FLYMEN *n* stagehand
FLYOFF, -S *n* all water transferred from the earth to the atmosphere
FLYOVER *n* road passing over another by a bridge
FLYPAST *n* ceremonial flight of aircraft over a given area
FLYPE, -D, -S, FLYPING *vb* fold back
FLYSCH *n* type of marine sedimentary facies
FLYTE, -D, -S *same as* ▶ **flite**
FLYTIER *n* person who makes their own fishing flies
FLYTING ▶ **flyte**
FLYTRAP *n* any of various insectivorous plants
FLYWAY, -S *n* usual route used by birds when migrating
FOAL, -ED, -S *n, vb*
FOALING *n* act of giving birth to a foal
FOALS ▶ **foal**
FOAM, -ED, -S *n, vb*
FOAMER, -S *n* (possibly obsessive) enthusiast
FOAMIER ▶ **foamy**
FOAMILY ▶ **foamy**
FOAMING ▶ **foam**
FOAMS ▶ **foam**
FOAMY, FOAMIER *adj*
FOB, -BED, -BING, -S *n* short watch chain ▷ *vb* cheat
FOCAL *adj* of or at a focus
FOCALLY ▶ **focal**
FOCUS, FOCI, -ED, -ES *n, vb*
FOCUSER ▶ **focus**
FOCUSES ▶ **focus**
FODDER, -S *n, vb*
FODGEL *adj* buxom
FOE, -S *n* enemy, opponent
FOEFIE *adj* as in **foefie slide** rope along which a person may traverse on a pulley
FOEHN, -S *same as* ▶ **fohn**
FOEMAN, FOEMEN *n* enemy in war
FOEN *same as* ▶ **foe**
FOES ▶ **foe**
FOETAL *same as* ▶ **fetal**
FOETID *same as* ▶ **fetid**
FOETOR, -S *same as* ▶ **fetor**
FOETUS *same as* ▶ **fetus**
FOG, -GED, -S *n, vb*
FOGASH *n* type of Hungarian pikeperch
FOGBOW, -S *n* faint arc of light sometimes seen in a fog bank
FOGDOG, -S *n* spot sometimes seen in fog near the horizon
FOGEY, -S *n* old-fashioned person
FOGGAGE *n* grass grown for winter grazing
FOGGED ▶ **fog**
FOGGER, -S *n* device that generates a fog
FOGGIER ▶ **foggy**
FOGGILY ▶ **fog**
FOGGING *n* act of fogging
FOGGY, FOGGIER ▶ **fog**
FOGHORN *n* large horn sounded to warn ships in fog
FOGIE, -S *variant of* ▶ **fogey**
FOGLE, -S *n* silk handkerchief
FOGLESS ▶ **fog**
FOGMAN, FOGMEN *n* person in charge of railway fog-signals
FOGOU, -S *n* subterranean building found in Cornwall
FOGRAM, -S *n* fogey
FOGS ▶ **fog**
FOGY *same as* ▶ **fogey**
FOGYDOM ▶ **fogy**
FOGYISH ▶ **fogy**

FOGYISM ▸ **fogy**
FOH *interj* expression of disgust
FOHN, -S *n* type of warm dry wind
FOIBLE, -S *n* minor weakness or slight peculiarity
FOID, -S *n* rock-forming mineral similar to feldspar
FOIL, -ED, -S *vb, n*
FOILING ▸ **foil**
FOILIST *n* person who fences with a foil
FOILS ▸ **foil**
FOIN, -ED, -ING, -S *n* thrust or lunge with a weapon ▹ *vb* thrust with a weapon
FOISON, -S *n* plentiful supply or yield
FOIST, -ED, -S *vb* force or impose on
FOISTER ▸ **foist**
FOISTS ▸ **foist**
FOLACIN *n* folic acid
FOLATE, -S *n* folic acid
FOLD, -ED, -ING, -S *vb, n*
FOLDER, -S *n*
FOLDING ▸ **fold**
FOLDOUT *another name for* > **gatefold**
FOLDS ▸ **fold**
FOLDUP, -S *n* something that folds up
FOLEY, -S *n* footsteps editor
FOLIA ▸ **folium**
FOLIAGE *n* leaves
FOLIAR *adj* of or relating to a leaf or leaves
FOLIATE *adj* relating to, possessing, or resembling leaves ▹ *vb* ornament with foliage or with leaf forms such as foils
FOLIC *adj* as in **folic acid** any of a group of vitamins of the B complex
FOLIE, -S *n* madness
FOLIO, -ED, -S *n* sheet of paper folded in half to make two leaves of a book ▹ *adj* of or made in the largest book size ▹ *vb* number the leaves of (a book) consecutively
FOLIOLE *n* part of a compound leaf
FOLIOS ▸ **folio**
FOLIOSE *adj* leaf-bearing
FOLIOUS *adj* leaf-bearing
FOLIUM, FOLIA, -S *n* plane geometrical curve
FOLK, -S *n, adj*
FOLKIE, -R, -S *n* devotee of folk music ▹ *adj* of or relating to folk music
FOLKISH ▸ **folk**
FOLKMOT *same as* > **folkmoot**
FOLKS ▸ **folk**
FOLKSY *adj* simple and unpretentious
FOLKWAY *singular form of* > **folkways**
FOLKY *same as* ▸ **folkie**
FOLLES ▸ **follis**
FOLLIED ▸ **folly**
FOLLIES ▸ **folly**
FOLLIS, FOLLES *n* Roman coin
FOLLOW, -S *vb*
FOLLY, FOLLIED, FOLLIES *n* foolishness ▹ *vb* behave foolishly
FOMENT, -S *vb* encourage or stir up (trouble)
FOMES, FOMITES *n* any material that may harbour pathogens
FOMITE *same as* ▸ **fomes**
FOMITES ▸ **fomes**
FON, -NED, -NING, -S *vb* compel
FOND, -ED, -ER, -EST, -ING, -S *adj* tender, loving ▹ *n* background of a design, as in lace ▹ *vb* dote
FONDA, -S *n* Spanish hotel
FONDANT *n* (sweet made from) flavoured paste of sugar and water ▹ *adj* (of a colour) soft
FONDAS ▸ **fonda**
FONDED ▸ **fond**
FONDER ▸ **fond**
FONDEST ▸ **fond**
FONDING ▸ **fond**
FONDLE, -D, -S *vb* caress
FONDLER ▸ **fondle**
FONDLES ▸ **fondle**
FONDLY ▸ **fond**
FONDS ▸ **fond**
FONDU, -S *n* ballet movement
FONDUE, -D, -S *n* Swiss dish ▹ *vb* cook and serve (food) as a fondue
FONDUS ▸ **fondu**
FONE, -S *n* informal spelling of telephone

FONLY *adv* foolishly
FONNED ▸ **fon**
FONNING ▸ **fon**
FONS ▸ **fon**
FONT, -S *n*
FONTAL ▸ **font**
FONTINA *n* mild Italian cheese
FONTLET ▸ **font**
FONTS ▸ **font**
FOO, -S *n* temporary computer variable or file
FOOBAR *same as* ▸ **fubar**
FOOD, -S *n*
FOODERY *n* restaurant
FOODFUL *adj* supplying abundant food
FOODIE, -S *n* gourmet
FOODISM *n* enthusiasm for and interest in good food
FOODOIR *n* book or blog that combines a personal memoir with recipes
FOODS ▸ **food**
FOODY *same as* ▸ **foodie**
FOOL, -ED, -S *n, vb*
FOOLERY *n* foolish behaviour
FOOLING ▸ **fool**
FOOLISH *adj*
FOOLS ▸ **fool**
FOOS ▸ **foo**
FOOT, FEET, -ED *n, vb*
FOOTAGE *n*
FOOTBAG *n* sport of keeping a beanbag off the ground by kicking it
FOOTBAR *n* any bar used by the foot
FOOTBED *n* insole in a boot or shoe
FOOTBOY *n* boy servant
FOOTED ▸ **foot**
FOOTER, -S *n* person who goes on foot ▹ *vb* potter
FOOTIE, -S *same as* ▸ **footy**
FOOTIER ▸ **footy**
FOOTIES ▸ **footie**
FOOTING *n* basis or foundation
FOOTLE, -D, -S *vb* loiter aimlessly ▹ *n* foolishness
FOOTLER ▸ **footle**
FOOTLES ▸ **footle**
FOOTMAN, FOOTMEN *n* male servant in uniform
FOOTPAD *n* highwayman, on foot rather than horseback
FOOTRA, -S *variant of* ▸ **foutra**
FOOTS *pl n* sediment that accumulates at the bottom of a vessel
FOOTSAL *n* type of indoor football with five players on each side
FOOTSIE *n* flirtation involving the touching together of feet
FOOTSY *variant of* ▸ **footsie**
FOOTWAY *n* way or path for pedestrians
FOOTY, FOOTIER *n* football ▹ *adj* mean
FOOZLE, -D, -S *vb* bungle (a shot) ▹ *n* bungled shot
FOOZLER ▸ **foozle**
FOOZLES ▸ **foozle**
FOP, -PED, -PING, -S *n* man excessively concerned with fashion ▹ *vb* act like a fop
FOPLING *n* vain affected dandy
FOPPED ▸ **fop**
FOPPERY *n* clothes, affectations, etc of or befitting a fop
FOPPING ▸ **fop**
FOPPISH ▸ **fop**
FOPS ▸ **fop**
FOR *prep*
FORA ▸ **forum**
FORAGE, -D, -S *vb, n*
FORAGER ▸ **forage**
FORAGES ▸ **forage**
FORAM, -S *n* marine protozoan
FORAMEN *n* natural hole
FORAMS ▸ **foram**
FORANE *adj* as in **vicar forane** type of Roman Catholic priest
FORAY, -ED, -S *n* brief raid or attack ▹ *vb* raid or ravage (a town, district, etc)
FORAYER ▸ **foray**
FORAYS ▸ **foray**
FORB, -S *n* any herbaceous plant that is not a grass
FORBAD ▸ **forbid**
FORBADE ▸ **forbid**
FORBEAR, FORBARE *vb* cease or refrain (from doing something)
FORBID, FORBAD, FORBADE, -S *vb* prohibit, refuse to allow
FORBODE *vb* obsolete word meaning forbid

▷ *n* obsolete word meaning forbidding
FORBORE *past tense of* ▶ **forbear**
FORBS ▶ **forb**
FORBY *adv* besides
FORBYE *same as* ▶ **forby**
FORCAT, -S *n* convict or galley slave
FORCE, -S, FORCING *n, vb*
FORCED *adj* compulsory
FORCEPS *pl n* surgical pincers
FORCER, -S ▶ **force**
FORCES ▶ **force**
FORCING ▶ **force**
FORD, -ED, -ING, -S *n, vb*
FORDID ▶ **fordo**
FORDING ▶ **ford**
FORDO, FORDID, -ES, -NE *vb* destroy
FORDS ▶ **ford**
FORE, -S *adj, n, interj*
FOREARM *n* arm from the wrist to the elbow ▷ *vb* prepare beforehand
FOREBAY *n* reservoir or canal
FOREBY *variant of* ▶ **forby**
FOREBYE *variant of* ▶ **forby**
FORECAR *n* vehicle attached to a motorcycle
FOREDO, FOREDID *same as* ▶ **fordo**
FOREGO *same as* ▶ **forgo**
FOREGUT *n* anterior part of the digestive tract of vertebrates
FOREIGN *adj*
FOREL, -S *vb* cover (a book) with parchment
FORELAY *archaic word for* ▶ **ambush**
FORELEG *n* either of the front legs of an animal
FORELIE *vb* lie in front of
FORELS ▶ **forel**
FOREMAN, FOREMEN *n*
FOREPAW *n* either of the front feet of a land mammal
FORERUN, FORERAN *vb* serve as a herald for
FORES ▶ **fore**
FORESAW ▶ **foresee**
FORESAY *vb* foretell
FORESEE, FORESAW *vb*
FOREST, -S *n, vb*
FORETOP *n* platform at the top of the foremast
FOREVER *adv, n*
FOREX, -ES *n* foreign exchange
FORFAIR *vb* perish
FORFEIT *n, vb, adj*
FORFEND *vb* protect or secure
FORFEX *n* pair of pincers, esp the paired terminal appendages of an earwig
FORGAT *past tense of* ▶ **forget**
FORGAVE ▶ **forgive**
FORGE, -D, -S *n, vb*
FORGER, -S ▶ **forge**
FORGERY *n*
FORGES ▶ **forge**
FORGET, -S *vb*
FORGING *n* process of producing a metal component by hammering
FORGIVE, FORGAVE *vb*
FORGO, -ES, -NE *vb* do without or give up
FORGOER ▶ **forgo**
FORGOES ▶ **forgo**
FORGONE ▶ **forgo**
FORGOT *past tense of* ▶ **forget**
FORHENT *variant of* ▶ **forehent**
FORHOO, -S *vb* forsake
FORHOW, -S *variant of* ▶ **forhoo**
FORINT, -S *n* standard monetary unit of Hungary
FORK, -ING, -S *n, vb*
FORKED *adj* having a fork or forklike parts
FORKER, -S ▶ **fork**
FORKFUL ▶ **fork**
FORKIER ▶ **forky**
FORKING ▶ **fork**
FORKS ▶ **fork**
FORKY, FORKIER *adj* forked
FORLANA *n* Venetian dance
FORLEND, FORLENT *variant of* ▶ **forelend**
FORLESE, FORLORE *vb* lose, forsake
FORLORN *adj, n*
FORM, -ED, -S *n* shape or appearance ▷ *vb* give a (particular) shape to or take a (particular) shape
FORMAL, -S *adj, n*
FORMANT *n* any of several frequency ranges
FORMAT, -S *n, vb*
FORMATE *n* type of salt or ester of formic acid ▷ *vb* fly aircraft in formation

FORMATS ▸ **format**
FORME, -S *n* type matter assembled and ready for printing
FORMED ▸ **form**
FORMEE, -S *n* type of heraldic cross
FORMER, -S *adj, n*
FORMES ▸ **forme**
FORMFUL *adj* imaginative
FORMIC *adj* of, relating to, or derived from ants
FORMICA *n* tradename for any of various laminated plastic sheets
FORMING ▸ **form**
FORMOL, -S *same as* > **formalin**
FORMS ▸ **form**
FORMULA *n*
FORMYL, -S *n* the monovalent group CHO-
FORNENT *variant of* > **fornenst**
FORNIX *n* any archlike structure
FORPET, -S *n* quarter of a peck (measure)
FORPINE *vb* waste away
FORPIT, -S *variant of* ▸ **forpet**
FORRAD, -S *adv* Scots word for forward ▷ *n* forward
FORRAY, -S *archaic variant of* ▸ **foray**
FORREN *adj* old word for foreign
FORRIT *adv* Scots word for forward(s)
FORSAID ▸ **forsay**
FORSAKE *vb*
FORSAY, FORSAID, -S *vb* renounce
FORSLOE *variant of* ▸ **forslow**
FORSLOW *vb* hinder
FORSOOK *past tense of* ▸ **forsake**
FORT, -ED, -ING, -S *n* fortified building or place ▷ *vb* fortify
FORTE *n* thing at which a person excels ▷ *adv* loudly
FORTED ▸ **fort**
FORTES ▸ **fortis**
FORTH *adv, prep*
FORTHY *adv* old word for therefore
FORTIES ▸ **forty**
FORTIFY *vb* make (a place) defensible, as by building walls
FORTING ▸ **fort**
FORTIS, FORTES *adj* (of a consonant) articulated with considerable muscular tension ▷ *n* type of consonantal pronunciation
FORTLET ▸ **fort**
FORTS ▸ **fort**
FORTUNE *n, vb*
FORTY, FORTIES *n*
FORUM, FORA, -S *n*
FORWARD *same as* > **forwards**
FORWARN *archaic word for* ▸ **forbid**
FORWENT *past tense of* ▸ **forgo**
FORWHY *adv* for what reason
FORWORN *adj* weary
FORZA, FORZE *n* force
FORZATO, FORZATI *variant of* > **forzando**
FORZE ▸ **forza**
FOSS *same as* ▸ **fosse**
FOSSA, -E, -S *n* anatomical depression, trench, or hollow area
FOSSATE *adj* having cavities or depressions
FOSSE, -S *n* ditch or moat, esp one dug as a fortification
FOSSED *adj* having a ditch or moat
FOSSES ▸ **fosse**
FOSSICK *vb* search, esp for gold or precious stones
FOSSIL, -S *n, adj*
FOSSOR, -S *n* grave digger
FOSSULA *n* small fossa
FOSTER, -S *vb, adj*
FOTHER, -S *vb* stop a leak in a ship's hull
FOU, -ER, -EST, -S *adj* full ▷ *n* bushel
FOUAT, -S *n* succulent pink-flowered plant
FOUD, -S *n* sheriff in Orkney and Shetland
FOUDRIE *n* foud's district or office
FOUDS ▸ **foud**
FOUER ▸ **fou**
FOUEST ▸ **fou**
FOUET, -S *n* archaic word for a whip
FOUETTE *n* step in ballet
FOUGADE *n* booby-trapped pit or type of mine
FOUGHT ▸ **fight**
FOUGHTY *adj* musty
FOUL, -ED, -ER, -EST, -S *adj, n, vb*
FOULARD *n* soft light fabric

FOULDER *vb* flash like lightning
FOULE, -S *n* type of woollen cloth
FOULED ▸ **foul**
FOULER ▸ **foul**
FOULES ▸ **foule**
FOULEST ▸ **foul**
FOULIE, -S *n* bad mood
FOULING ▸ **foul**
FOULLY ▸ **foul**
FOULS ▸ **foul**
FOUMART *former name for the* ▸ **polecat**
FOUND, -ED, -S *vb*
FOUNDER *vb, n*
FOUNDRY *n*
FOUNDS ▸ **found**
FOUNT, -S *same as* ▸ **font**
FOUR, -S *n*
FOURGON *n* long covered wagon
FOURS ▸ **four**
FOURSES *n* snack eaten at four o'clock
FOURTH, -S *n, adj*
FOUS ▸ **fou**
FOUSSA, -S *n* Madagascan civet-like animal
FOUSTY *archaic variant of* ▸ **fusty**
FOUTER, -S *same as* ▸ **footer**
FOUTH, -S *n* abundance
FOUTRA, -S *n* fig; expression of contempt
FOUTRE, -D, -S *same as* ▸ **footer**
FOVEA, -E, -S *n* any small pit in the surface of a bodily organ or part
FOVEAL ▸ **fovea**
FOVEAS ▸ **fovea**
FOVEATE ▸ **fovea**
FOVEOLA *n* small fovea
FOVEOLE *same as* ▸ **foveola**
FOWL, -ED, -S *n, vb*
FOWLER, -S ▸ **fowling**
FOWLING *n* shooting or trapping of birds for sport or as a livelihood
FOWLPOX *n* viral infection of poultry and other birds
FOWLS ▸ **fowl**
FOWTH, -S *variant of* ▸ **fouth**
FOX, -ED, -ES *n, vb*
FOXFIRE *n* glow emitted by certain fungi
FOXFISH *n* type of shark
FOXHOLE *n* small pit dug for protection
FOXHUNT *n, vb*
FOXIE, -S *n* fox terrier
FOXIER ▸ **foxy**
FOXIES ▸ **foxie**
FOXIEST ▸ **foxy**
FOXILY ▸ **foxy**
FOXING, -S *n* piece of leather used on part of the upper of a shoe
FOXLIKE ▸ **fox**
FOXSHIP *n* cunning
FOXSKIN *adj* made from the skin of a fox ▹ *n* skin of a fox
FOXTAIL *n* type of grass
FOXTROT *n, vb*
FOXY, FOXIER, FOXIEST *adj* of or like a fox, esp in craftiness
FOY, -S *n* loyalty

This unusual word for loyalty can be a good scorer.

FOYBOAT *n* small rowing boat
FOYER, -S *n*
FOYLE, -D, -S, FOYLING *variant of* ▸ **foil**
FOYNE, -D, -S, FOYNING *variant of* ▸ **foin**
FOYS ▸ **foy**
FOZY, FOZIER, FOZIEST *adj* spongy
FRA, -S *n* brother: a title given to an Italian monk or friar
FRAB, -BED, -S *vb* nag
FRABBIT *adj* peevish
FRABS ▸ **frab**
FRACAS *n* noisy quarrel
FRACK, -ED, -S *adj* bold ▹ *vb* release oil or gas from rock by fracking
FRACKER *n* individual or company which engages in fracking
FRACKS ▸ **frack**
FRACT, -ED, -S *vb* break
FRACTAL *n* mathematically repeating structure ▹ *adj* relating to or involving fractals
FRACTED ▸ **fract**
FRACTI ▸ **fractus**
FRACTS ▸ **fract**
FRACTUR *variant of* ▸ **fraktur**
FRACTUS, FRACTI *n* ragged-shaped cloud formation
FRAE *Scot word for* ▸ **from**
FRAENUM, FRAENA *n* fold of membrane or skin that supports an organ
FRAG, -GED, -S *vb* kill or wound (a fellow soldier

or superior officer) deliberately
FRAGILE *adj*
FRAGOR, -S *n* sudden sound
FRAGS ▶ **frag**
FRAIL, -ER, -S *adj, n*
FRAILLY ▶ **frail**
FRAILS ▶ **frail**
FRAILTY *n*
FRAIM, -S *n* stranger
FRAISE, -D, -S *n* neck ruff worn during the 16th century ▷ *vb* provide a rampart with a palisade
FRAKTUR *n* style of typeface
FRAME, -D, -S *n, vb*
FRAMER, -S ▶ **frame**
FRAMES ▶ **frame**
FRAMING *n* frame, framework, or system of frames
FRAMPAL *same as* > **frampold**
FRANC, -S *n* monetary unit
FRANCO *adj* post-free
FRANCS ▶ **franc**
FRANION *n* lover, paramour
FRANK, -ED, -S *adj, n, vb*
FRANKER ▶ **frank**
FRANKLY *adv* in truth
FRANKS ▶ **frank**
FRANKUM *n* spruce resin
FRANTIC *adj*
FRANZY *adj* irritable
FRAP, -PED, -S *vb* lash down or together
FRAPE *adj* tightly bound
FRAPPE, -S *adj* (of drinks) chilled ▷ *n* type of drink
FRAPPED ▶ **frap**
FRAPPEE *same as* ▶ **frappe**
FRAPPES ▶ **frappe**
FRAPS ▶ **frap**
FRAS ▶ **fra**
FRASS, -ES *n* refuse left by insects and insect larvae
FRAT, -S *n* member of a fraternity
FRATCH *n* quarrel
FRATCHY *adj* quarrelsome
FRATE, FRATI *n* friar
FRATER, -S *n* mendicant friar or a lay brother in a monastery or priory
FRATERY ▶ **frater**
FRATI ▶ **frate**
FRATRY ▶ **frater**
FRATS ▶ **frat**
FRAU, -S *n* married German woman
FRAUD, -S *n*
FRAUGHT *adj* tense or anxious ▷ *vb* archaic word for load ▷ *n* archaic word for freight
FRAUS ▶ **frau**
FRAWZEY *n* celebration
FRAY, -ED, -S *n* noisy quarrel or conflict ▷ *vb* make or become ragged at the edge
FRAYING ▶ **fray**
FRAYS ▶ **fray**
FRAZIL, -S *n* small pieces of ice that form in turbulently moving water
FRAZZLE *n* exhausted state ▷ *vb* tire out
FREAK, -ED, -S *n, adj, vb*
FREAKY *adj*
FRECKLE *n, vb*
FRECKLY ▶ **freckle**
FREE, -D, -ING, -S, -ST *adj, vb*
FREEBEE *variant of* ▶ **freebie**
FREEBIE *n* something provided without charge ▷ *adj* without charge
FREED ▶ **free**
FREEDOM *n* right of unrestricted use or access
FREEGAN *n* person who avoids buying consumer goods
FREEING ▶ **free**
FREEKEH *n* type of cereal
FREELY ▶ **free**
FREEMAN, FREEMEN *n* person who has been given the freedom of a city
FREER, -S *n* liberator
FREES ▶ **free**
FREESIA *n* plant with fragrant tubular flowers
FREEST ▶ **free**
FREET, -S *n* omen or superstition
FREETY *adj* superstitious
FREEWAY *n* motorway
FREEZE, -S, FROZE, FROZEN *vb, n*
FREEZER *n*
FREEZES ▶ **freeze**
FREIGHT *n, vb*
FREIT, -S *variant of* ▶ **freet**
FREITY *adj* superstitious
FREMD, -S *n* strange person or thing

FREMIT, -S *same as* ▸ **fremd**
FRENA ▸ **frenum**
FRENCH *vb* cut (food) into thin strips
FRENEMY *n* supposed friend who behaves in a treacherous manner
FRENNE, -S *variant of* ▸ **fremd**
FRENULA > **frenulum**
FRENUM, FRENA, -S *same as* ▸ **fraenum**
FRENZY *n, vb*
FREON, -S *n* tradename for an aerosol refrigerant
FRERE, -S *n* friar
FRESCO, -S *n* watercolour painting done on wet plaster ▹ *vb* paint a fresco
FRESH, -ED, -ES *adj* newly made, acquired, etc ▹ *adv* recently ▹ *vb* freshen
FRESHEN *vb*
FRESHER *n* first-year student
FRESHES ▸ **fresh**
FRESHET *n* sudden overflowing of a river
FRESHIE *n* (in Australia) freshwater crocodile
FRESHLY ▸ **fresh**
FRESNEL *n* unit of frequency
FRET, -S, -TED *vb, n*
FRETFUL *adj* irritable
FRETS ▸ **fret**
FRETSAW *n* fine saw with a narrow blade, used for fretwork
FRETTED ▸ **fret**
FRETTER ▸ **fret**
FRETTY *adj* decorated with frets
FRIABLE *adj* easily crumbled
FRIAND, -S *n* small almond cake
FRIANDE *variant of* ▸ **friand**
FRIANDS ▸ **friand**
FRIAR, -S *n*
FRIARLY ▸ **friar**
FRIARS ▸ **friar**
FRIARY *n* house of friars
FRIB, -S *n* piece of wool removed from a fleece during classing
FRIBBLE *vb* fritter away ▹ *n* wasteful or frivolous person or action ▹ *adj* frivolous
FRIBS ▸ **frib**
FRICHT, -S *vb* Scots word for frighten
FRICOT, -S *n* Acadian stew of potatoes and meat or fish
FRIDGE, -D, -S *n* apparatus in which food and drinks are kept cool ▹ *vb* archaic word for chafe
FRIED ▸ **fry**
FRIEND, -S *n, vb*
FRIER, -S *same as* ▸ **fryer**
FRIES ▸ **fry**
FRIEZE, -D, -S *n* ornamental band on a wall ▹ *vb* give a nap to (cloth)
FRIG, -ES, -GED, -S *vb* behave foolishly or aimlessly ▹ *n* fridge
FRIGATE *n* medium-sized fast warship
FRIGES ▸ **frig**
FRIGGED ▸ **frig**
FRIGGER ▸ **frig**
FRIGHT, -S *n*
FRIGID *adj*
FRIGOT, -S *variant of* ▸ **frigate**
FRIGS ▸ **frig**
FRIJOL *n* variety of bean
FRIJOLE *variant of* ▸ **frijol**
FRILL, -ED, -S *n, vb*
FRILLER ▸ **frill**
FRILLS ▸ **frill**
FRILLY *adj*
FRINGE, -D, -S *n, vb, adj*
FRINGY *adj* having a fringe
FRIPON, -S *n* rogue
FRIPPER *n* dealer in old clothes
FRIPPET *n* frivolous or flamboyant young woman
FRIS, -ES *n* fine frieze-like fabric
FRISBEE *n*
FRISE *n* fabric with a long nap used for upholstery and rugs
FRISEE, -S *n* endive
FRISES ▸ **fris**
FRISEUR *n* hairdresser
FRISK, -ED, -S *vb, n*
FRISKA, -S *n* (in Hungarian music) the fast movement of a piece
FRISKED ▸ **frisk**
FRISKER ▸ **frisk**
FRISKET *n* part of a hand printing press
FRISKS ▸ **frisk**
FRISKY *adj*
FRISSON *n* shiver of fear or excitement
FRIST, -ED, -S *archaic word for* > **postpone**

FRISURE *n* styling the hair into curls
FRIT, -S, -TED *n* basic materials for making glass, glazes for pottery, etc ▷ *vb* fuse (materials) in making frit
FRITES *pl n* chipped potatoes
FRITFLY *n* type of small black fly
FRITH, -S *same as* ▶ **firth**
FRITS ▶ **frit**
FRITT, -S *same as* ▶ **frit**
FRITTED ▶ **frit**
FRITTER *n, vb*
FRITTS ▶ **fritt**
FRITURE *archaic word for* ▶ **fritter**
FRITZ, -ED, -ES *n* as in **on the fritz** in a state of disrepair ▷ *vb* (of an appliance, etc) become broken or start malfunctioning
FRIVOL, -S *vb* behave frivolously
FRIZ *variant of* ▶ **frizz**
FRIZADO *n* fine frieze-like fabric
FRIZE, -D, -S, FRIZING *n* coarse woollen fabric ▷ *vb* freeze
FRIZER, -S *n* person who gives nap to cloth
FRIZES ▶ **frize**
FRIZING ▶ **frize**
FRIZZ, -ED, -ES *vb, n*
FRIZZER ▶ **frizz**
FRIZZES ▶ **frizz**
FRIZZLE *vb* cook or heat until crisp and shrivelled ▷ *n* tight curl
FRIZZLY ▶ **frizzle**
FRIZZY *adj*
FRO, -S *adv* away ▷ *n* afro
FROCK, -ED, -S *n, vb*
FROE, -S *n* cutting tool
FROG, -S *n* type of amphibian
FROGBIT *n* floating aquatic Eurasian plant
FROGEYE *n* plant disease
FROGGED *adj* decorated with frogging
FROGGY *adj* like a frog
FROGLET *n* young frog
FROGMAN, FROGMEN *n*
FROGS ▶ **frog**
FROING, -S *n* as in **toing and froing** going back and forth
FROISE, -S *n* kind of pancake
FROLIC, -S *vb, n, adj*
FROM *prep*
FROMAGE *n* as in **fromage frais** low-fat soft cheese
FROND, -S *n* long leaf or leaflike part of a fern, palm, or seaweed
FRONDED *adj* having fronds
FRONDS ▶ **frond**
FRONS, FRONTES *n* plate on the head of some insects
FRONT, -ED, -S *n, adj, vb*
FRONTAL *adj, n*
FRONTED ▶ **front**
FRONTER *n* front side
FRONTES ▶ **frons**
FRONTON *n* wall against which pelota or jai alai is played
FRONTS ▶ **front**
FRORE *adj* very cold or frosty
FROREN *variant of* ▶ **frore**
FRORN *variant of* ▶ **frore**
FRORNE *variant of* ▶ **frore**
FRORY *variant of* ▶ **frore**
FROS ▶ **fro**
FROSH, -ES *n* freshman
FROST, -S *n, vb*
FROSTED *adj* (of glass) having a rough surface to make it opaque ▷ *n* type of ice cream dish
FROSTS ▶ **frost**
FROSTY *adj*
FROTH, -ED, -S *n, vb*
FROTHER ▶ **froth**
FROTHS ▶ **froth**
FROTHY ▶ **froth**
FROUGHY *adj* rancid
FROUNCE *vb* wrinkle
FROUZY *same as* ▶ **frowzy**
FROW, -S *same as* ▶ **froe**
FROWARD *adj* obstinate
FROWIE, -R *variant of* ▶ **froughy**
FROWN, -ED, -S *vb, n*
FROWNER ▶ **frown**
FROWNS ▶ **frown**
FROWNY *adj* displaying a frown
FROWS ▶ **frow**
FROWST, -S *n* hot and stale atmosphere ▷ *vb* abandon oneself to such an atmosphere
FROWSTY *adj* stale or musty
FROWSY *same as* ▶ **frowzy**
FROWY *variant of* ▶ **froughy**
FROWZY *adj* dirty or unkempt
FROZE ▶ **freeze**
FROZEN ▶ **freeze**
FRUCTAN *n* type of polymer of fructose
FRUCTED *adj* fruit-bearing

FRUG, -GED, -S *vb* perform the frug, a 1960s dance
FRUGAL *adj*
FRUGGED ▸ **frug**
FRUGS ▸ **frug**
FRUICT, -S *obsolete variant of* ▸ **fruit**
FRUIT, -ED, -S *n, vb*
FRUITER *n* fruit grower
FRUITS ▸ **fruit**
FRUITY *adj*
FRUMP, -ED, -S *n* dowdy person ▹ *vb* mock or taunt
FRUMPLE *vb* wrinkle or crumple
FRUMPS ▸ **frump**
FRUMPY *adj*
FRUSH, -ED, -ES *vb* break into pieces
FRUST, -S *n* fragment
FRUSTA ▸ **frustum**
FRUSTS ▸ **frust**
FRUSTUM, FRUSTA *n* part of a solid between the base and a plane parallel to the base
FRUTEX *n* shrub
FRUTIFY *vb* malapropism for notify
FRY, FRIED, FRIES *vb, n*
FRYABLE ▸ **fry**
FRYER, -S *n*
FRYING, -S ▸ **fry**
FRYPAN, -S *n* long-handled shallow pan used for frying
FUB, -BED, -BING, -S *vb* cheat
FUBAR *adj* irreparably damaged or bungled
FUBBED ▸ **fub**
FUBBERY *n* cheating
FUBBIER ▸ **fubby**
FUBBING ▸ **fub**
FUBBY, FUBBIER *adj* short and stout
FUBS ▸ **fub**
FUBSY, FUBSIER *adj* short and stout
FUCHSIA *n* ornamental shrub
FUCHSIN *n* greenish crystalline substance
FUCI ▸ **fucus**
FUCOID, -S *n* type of seaweed
FUCOSE, -S *n* aldose
FUCOUS *same as* > **fucoidal**
FUCUS, FUCI, -ES *n* type of seaweed
FUCUSED *adj* archaic word meaning made up with cosmetics
FUCUSES ▸ **fucus**
FUD, -S *n* rabbit's tail
FUDDIER ▸ **fuddy**
FUDDIES ▸ **fuddy**
FUDDLE, -D, -S *vb* cause to be intoxicated or confused ▹ *n* confused state
FUDDLER ▸ **fuddle**
FUDDLES ▸ **fuddle**
FUDDY, FUDDIER, FUDDIES *n* old-fashioned person ▹ *adj* old-fashioned
FUDGE, -D, -S, FUDGING *n, vb, interj*
FUDGIER ▸ **fudgy**
FUDGING ▸ **fudge**
FUDGY, FUDGIER *adj* resembling or containing fudge
FUDS ▸ **fud**
FUEHRER *n* leader: applied esp to Adolf Hitler
FUEL, -ED, -ING, -LED, -S *n, vb*
FUELER, -S ▸ **fuel**
FUELING ▸ **fuel**
FUELLED ▸ **fuel**
FUELLER ▸ **fuel**
FUELS ▸ **fuel**
FUERO, -S *n* Spanish code of laws
FUFF, -ED, -ING, -S *vb* puff
FUFFIER ▸ **fuffy**
FUFFING ▸ **fuff**
FUFFS ▸ **fuff**
FUFFY, FUFFIER *adj* puffy
FUG, -GED, -GING, -S *n* hot stale atmosphere ▹ *vb* sit in a fug
FUGAL *adj* of, relating to, or in the style of a fugue
FUGALLY ▸ **fugal**
FUGATO, -S *adj* in the manner or style of a fugue ▹ *n* movement, section, or piece in this style
FUGGED ▸ **fug**
FUGGIER ▸ **fuggy**
FUGGILY ▸ **fug**
FUGGING ▸ **fug**
FUGGY, FUGGIER ▸ **fug**
FUGIE, -S *n* runaway
FUGIO, -S *n* former US copper coin
FUGLE, -D, -S, FUGLING *vb* act as a fugleman
FUGS ▸ **fug**
FUGU, -S *n* puffer fish

U is not normally a desirable letter to have on your rack unless you happen to have the Q, and two Us can be trouble. This Japanese fish can help you out.

FUGUE, -D, -S, FUGUING *n* type of musical composition ▷ *vb* be in a dreamlike, altered state of consciousness
FUGUIST *n* composer of fugues
FUGUS ▶ fugu
FUHRER, -S *same as* ▶ fuehrer
FUJI, -S *n* type of African music
FULCRUM, FULCRA *n*
FULFIL, -S *vb*
FULFILL *same as* ▶ fulfil
FULFILS ▶ fulfil
FULGENT *adj* shining brilliantly
FULGID *same as* ▶ fulgent
FULGOR, -S *n* brilliance
FULGOUR *variant of* ▶ fulgor
FULHAM, -S *n* loaded die
FULL, -ED, -EST, -ING, -S *adj* containing as much or as many as possible ▷ *adv* completely ▷ *vb* clean, shrink, and press cloth
FULLAGE *n* price charged for fulling cloth
FULLAM, -S *variant of* ▶ fulham
FULLAN, -S *variant of* ▶ fulham
FULLED ▶ full
FULLER, -S *n* person who fulls cloth for a living ▷ *vb* forge (a groove) or caulk (a riveted joint)
FULLERY *n* place where fulling is carried out
FULLEST ▶ full
FULLING ▶ full
FULLISH ▶ full
FULLS ▶ full
FULLY *adv*
FULMAR, -S *n* Arctic sea bird
FULMINE *vb* fulminate
FULNESS ▶ full
FULSOME *adj*
FULVID *variant of* ▶ fulvous
FULVOUS *adj* of a dull brownish-yellow colour
FUM, -S *n* phoenix, in Chinese mythology
FUMADO, -S *n* salted, smoked fish
FUMAGE, -S *n* tax on hearths
FUMARIC *adj* as in **fumaric acid** colourless crystalline acid
FUMBLE, -D, -S *vb, n*
FUMBLER ▶ fumble
FUMBLES ▶ fumble
FUME, -S, FUMING *vb*
FUMED *adj* (of wood) having been exposed to ammonia fumes
FUMER, -S ▶ fume
FUMES ▶ fume
FUMET, -S *n* liquor from cooking fish, meat, or game
FUMETTE *variant of* ▶ fumet
FUMETTO, FUMETTI *n* speech balloon in a comic or cartoon
FUMIER ▶ fumy
FUMIEST ▶ fumy
FUMING ▶ fume
FUMOUS ▶ fume
FUMS ▶ fum
FUMULUS, FUMULI *n* smokelike cloud
FUMY, FUMIER, FUMIEST ▶ fume
FUN, -NED, -NER, -NEST, -NING, -S *n* enjoyment or amusement ▷ *vb* trick ▷ *adj* providing amusement or entertainment
FUNCKIA *n* ornamental plant
FUNCTOR *n* performer of a function
FUND, -ED *n, vb*
FUNDER, -S ▶ fund
FUNDI, -S *n* expert or boffin
FUNDIC ▶ fundus
FUNDIE, -S *n* fundamentalist
FUNDING ▶ fund
FUNDIS ▶ fundi
FUNDS *pl n* money that is readily available
FUNDUS *n* base of an organ
FUNDY *n* fundamentalist
FUNEBRE *adj* funereal or mournful
FUNERAL *n*
FUNEST *adj* lamentable
FUNFAIR *n*
FUNFEST *n* enjoyable time
FUNG, -S *same as* ▶ funk
FUNGAL, -S *adj, n*
FUNGI ▶ fungus
FUNGIC ▶ fungus
FUNGO, -ED, -ES, -S *n* in baseball, act of tossing and hitting the ball ▷ *vb* toss and hit a ball
FUNGOID *adj* resembling a fungus

FUNGOS ▸ **fungo**
FUNGOUS *adj* appearing and spreading quickly like a fungus
FUNGS ▸ **fung**
FUNGUS, FUNGI *n*
FUNICLE *n* stalk that attaches an ovule to the wall of the ovary
FUNK, -ED, -ING, -S *n, vb*
FUNKER, -S ▸ **funk**
FUNKIA, -S *n* ornamental plant
FUNKIER ▸ **funky**
FUNKILY ▸ **funky**
FUNKING ▸ **funk**
FUNKS ▸ **funk**
FUNKY, FUNKIER *adj*
FUNNED ▸ **fun**
FUNNEL, -S *n, vb*
FUNNER ▸ **fun**
FUNNEST ▸ **fun**
FUNNIER ▸ **funny**
FUNNIES *pl n* comic strips in a newspaper
FUNNILY ▸ **funny**
FUNNING ▸ **fun**
FUNNY, FUNNIER *adj, n*
FUNPLEX *n* large amusement centre
FUNS ▸ **fun**
FUNSTER *n* funnyman or funnywoman
FUR, -S *n, vb*
FURAL, -S *same as* > **furfural**
FURAN, -S *n* colourless liquid used as a solvent
FURANE, -S *variant of* ▸ **furan**
FURANS ▸ **furan**
FURBALL *n* ball of fur regurgitated by an animal
FURBISH *vb* smarten up
FURCA, -E *n* any forklike structure, esp in insects
FURCAL ▸ **furca**
FURCATE *vb* divide into two parts ▹ *adj* forked, branching
FURCULA *n* any forklike part or organ
FURDER *same as* ▸ **further**
FUREUR, -S *n* rage or anger
FURFAIR *variant of* ▸ **furfur**
FURFUR, -S *n* scurf or scaling of the skin
FURIES ▸ **fury**
FURIOSO *adv* in a frantically rushing manner ▹ *n* passage or piece to be performed in this way
FURIOUS *adj* very angry
FURKID, -S *n* companion animal
FURL, -ED, -ING, -S *vb, n*
FURLANA *variant of* ▸ **forlana**
FURLED ▸ **furl**
FURLER, -S ▸ **furl**
FURLESS ▸ **fur**
FURLIKE *adj* like fur
FURLING ▸ **furl**
FURLONG *n* unit of length
FURLS ▸ **furl**
FURMETY *same as* > **frumenty**
FURMITY *same as* > **frumenty**
FURNACE *n, vb*
FURNISH *vb* provide with furniture
FUROL, -S *variant of* ▸ **fural**
FUROLE, -S *variant of* ▸ **fural**
FUROLS ▸ **furol**
FUROR, -S *same as* ▸ **furore**
FURORE, -S *n*
FURORS ▸ **furor**
FURPHY *n* rumour or fictitious story
FURR, -S *vb* old word meaning furrow
FURRED *same as* ▸ **furry**
FURRIER *n* dealer in furs
FURRIES ▸ **furry**
FURRILY ▸ **furry**
FURRING ▸ **fur**
FURROW, -S *n, vb*
FURROWY *adj* having furrows
FURRS ▸ **furr**
FURRY, FURRIES *adj, n*
FURS ▸ **fur**
FURTH *adv* Scots word meaning out
FURTHER *adv, adj, vb*
FURTIVE *adj*
FURY, FURIES *n*
FURZE, -S *n* gorse
FURZY, FURZIER ▸ **furze**
FUSAIN, -S *n* fine charcoal pencil
FUSARIA > **fusarium**
FUSAROL *variant of* > **fusarole**
FUSBALL *same as* > **foosball**
FUSC *adj* dark brown
FUSCOUS *adj* of a brownish-grey colour
FUSE, -D, -S, FUSING *n, vb*
FUSEE, -S *n* (in early clocks and watches) a spirally grooved spindle

FUSEL, -S *n* mixture of amyl alcohols, propanol, and butanol
FUSES ▸ **fuse**
FUSHION *n* spirit
FUSIBLE *adj* capable of being melted
FUSIBLY ▸ **fusible**
FUSIDIC *adj* as in **fusidic acid** kind of acid
FUSIL, -S *n* light flintlock musket
FUSILE *adj* easily melted
FUSILLI *n* spiral-shaped pasta
FUSILS ▸ **fusil**
FUSING ▸ **fuse**
FUSION, -S *n, adj*
FUSK, -ED, -ING, -S *vb* obtain data from (a website) by using hacking software
FUSKER, -S *vb* obtain data from (a website) by using hacking software
FUSKING ▸ **fusk**
FUSKS ▸ **fusk**
FUSS, -ED, -ES, -ING *n, vb*
FUSSER, -S ▸ **fuss**
FUSSES ▸ **fuss**
FUSSIER ▸ **fussy**
FUSSILY ▸ **fussy**
FUSSING ▸ **fuss**
FUSSPOT *n*
FUSSY, FUSSIER *adj*
FUST, -ED, -ING, -S *vb* become mouldy
FUSTET, -S *n* wood of the Venetian sumach shrub
FUSTIAN *n* (formerly) a hard-wearing fabric of cotton mixed with flax or wool ▹ *adj* cheap
FUSTIC, -S *n* large tropical American tree
FUSTIER ▸ **fusty**
FUSTILY ▸ **fusty**
FUSTING ▸ **fust**
FUSTOC, -S *variant of* ▸ **fustic**
FUSTS ▸ **fust**
FUSTY, FUSTIER *adj* stale-smelling
FUSUMA, -S *n* Japanese sliding door
FUTCHEL *n* timber support in a carriage
FUTHARC *same as* ▸ **futhark**
FUTHARK *n* phonetic alphabet consisting of runes
FUTHORC *same as* ▸ **futhark**
FUTHORK *same as* ▸ **futhark**
FUTILE, -R *adj*
FUTON, -S *n* Japanese-style bed
FUTSAL, -S *n* form of association football
FUTTOCK *n* one of the ribs in the frame of a wooden vessel
FUTURAL *adj* relating to the future
FUTURE *n, adj*
FUTURES *pl n* type of commodity trading
FUTZ, -ED, -ES, -ING *vb* fritter time away
FUZE, -D, -S, FUZING *same as* ▸ **fuse**
FUZEE, -S *same as* ▸ **fusee**
FUZES ▸ **fuze**
FUZIL, -S *variant of* ▸ **fusil**
FUZING ▸ **fuze**
FUZZ, -ED, -ES, -ING *n, vb*
FUZZBOX *n* device that distorts sound
FUZZED ▸ **fuzz**
FUZZES ▸ **fuzz**
FUZZIER ▸ **fuzzy**
FUZZILY ▸ **fuzzy**
FUZZING ▸ **fuzz**
FUZZLE, -D, -S *vb* make drunk
FUZZY, FUZZIER *adj*
FY *interj* exclamation of disapproval
FYCE, -S *variant of* ▸ **fice**
FYKE, -D, -S, FYKING *n* fish trap ▹ *vb* catch fish in this manner
FYLE, -S *variant of* ▸ **file**
FYLFOT, -S *rare word for* > **swastika**
FYNBOS *n* area of low-growing, evergreen vegetation
FYRD, -S *n* militia of an Anglo-Saxon shire
FYTTE, -S *n* section of a song

Gg

GAB, -BED, -BING, -S *vb* talk or chatter ▷ *n* mechanical device
GABBA, -S *n* type of electronic dance music
GABBARD *same as* ▶ **gabbart**
GABBART *n* Scottish sailing barge
GABBAS ▶ **gabba**
GABBED ▶ **gab**
GABBER, -S ▶ **gab**
GABBIER ▶ **gabby**
GABBING ▶ **gab**
GABBLE, -D, -S *vb, n*
GABBLER ▶ **gabble**
GABBLES ▶ **gabble**
GABBRO, -S *n* dark basic plutonic igneous rock
GABBY, GABBIER *adj* talkative
GABELLE *n* salt tax levied until 1790
GABFEST *n* prolonged gossiping or conversation
GABIES ▶ **gaby**
GABION, -S *n* cylindrical metal container filled with stones
GABLE, -S *n*
GABLED ▶ **gable**
GABLES ▶ **gable**
GABLET, -S *n* small gable
GABLING ▶ **gable**
GABNASH *n* chatter
GABOON, -S *n* dark wood
GABS ▶ **gab**
GABY, GABIES *n* unintelligent person
GACH, -ED, -ES, -ING *vb* behave boastfully
GACHER, -S *n* person who boasts
GACHES ▶ **gach**
GACHING ▶ **gach**
GAD, -DED, -DING, -S *vb* go about in search of pleasure ▷ *n* carefree adventure
GADDER, -S ▶ **gad**
GADDI, -S *n* cushioned Indian throne
GADDING ▶ **gad**
GADDIS ▶ **gaddi**
GADE, -S *same as* ▶ **gad**
GADFLY *n*
GADGE, -S *n* man
GADGET, -S *n*
GADGETY *adj* characterized by gadgets
GADGIE, -S *n* fellow
GADI, -S *n* cushioned Indian throne
GADID, -S *n* type of marine fish
GADIS ▶ **gadi**
GADJE, -S *same as* ▶ **gadgie**
GADJO, -S *same as* ▶ **gorgio**
GADLING *n* vagabond
GADMAN, GADMEN *n* person who drives animals
GADOID, -S *adj* of the cod family of marine fishes ▷ *n* gadoid fish
GADROON *n* type of decorative moulding
GADS ▶ **gad**
GADSMAN, GADSMEN *n* person who drives animals
GADSO *n* archaic expression of surprise
GADWALL *n* type of duck related to the mallard
GAE, -D, -ING, -N, -S *Scot word for* ▶ **go**
GAFF, -ED, -S *n* stick with an iron hook for landing large fish ▷ *vb* hook or land (a fish) with a gaff
GAFFE, -S *n*
GAFFED ▶ **gaff**
GAFFER, -S *n*
GAFFES ▶ **gaffe**
GAFFING ▶ **gaff**
GAFFS ▶ **gaff**
GAG, -GED, -GING, -S *vb, n*
GAGA *adj* senile

GAGAKU, -S *n* type of traditional Japanese music
GAGE, -D, -S, GAGING *vb* gauge ▷ *n* (formerly) an object thrown down as a challenge to fight
GAGER, -S *same as* ▶ **gauger**
GAGES ▶ **gage**
GAGGED ▶ **gag**
GAGGER, -S *n* person or thing that gags
GAGGERY *n* practice of telling jokes
GAGGING ▶ **gag**
GAGGLE, -D, -S *n, vb*
GAGING ▶ **gage**
GAGMAN, GAGMEN *n* person who writes gags for a comedian
GAGS ▶ **gag**
GAGSTER *n* standup comedian
GAHNITE *n* dark green mineral
GAID, -S *same as* ▶ **gad**
GAIETY *n*
GAIJIN *n* (in Japan) a foreigner
GAILY *adv* merrily
GAIN, -ED, -EST, -ING *vb, n, adj*
GAINER, -S *n* person or thing that gains
GAINEST ▶ **gain**
GAINFUL *adj*
GAINING ▶ **gain**
GAINLY *adj* graceful or well-formed ▷ *adv* conveniently or suitably
GAINS *pl n* profits or winnings
GAINSAY *vb* deny or contradict
GAINST *short for* ▶ **against**
GAIR, -S *n* strip of green grass on a hillside
GAIT, -ED, -ING, -S *n, vb*
GAITA, -S *n* type of bagpipe
GAITED ▶ **gait**
GAITER, -S *n* cloth or leather covering for the lower leg
GAITING ▶ **gait**
GAITS ▶ **gait**
GAITT, -S *Scots word for* ▶ **gate**
GAJO, -S *same as* ▶ **gorgio**
GAL, -S *n*
GALA, -S *n*
GALABEA *same as* > **djellaba**
GALABIA *same as* > **djellaba**
GALAGE, -S *same as* ▶ **galosh**
GALAGO, -S *another name for* > **bushbaby**
GALAH, -S *n* Australian cockatoo
GALANGA *same as* > **galingale**
GALANT, -S *n* 18th-century style of music
GALANTY *n* as in **galanty show** pantomime shadow play
GALAS ▶ **gala**
GALATEA *n* strong twill-weave cotton fabric
GALAX, -ES *n* coltsfoot
GALAXY *n*
GALE, -D, -S, GALING *n, vb*
GALEA, -E, -S *n* part or organ shaped like a helmet
GALEATE ▶ **galea**
GALED ▶ **gale**
GALENA, -S *n* soft bluish-grey mineral
GALENIC ▶ **galena**
GALERE, -S *n* group of people having a common interest
GALES ▶ **gale**
GALETTE *n* type of savoury pancake
GALILEE *n* type of porch or chapel
GALING ▶ **gale**
GALIOT, -S *n* small swift galley
GALIPOT *n* resin obtained from several species of pine
GALL, -ED, -S *n, vb*
GALLANT *adj, n, vb*
GALLATE *n* salt of gallic acid
GALLED ▶ **gall**
GALLEIN *n* type of dyestuff
GALLEON *n*
GALLERY *n, vb*
GALLET, -S *vb* use mixture to support a roof-slate
GALLETA *n* low-growing, coarse grass
GALLETS ▶ **gallet**
GALLEY, -S *n*
GALLFLY *n* any of several small insects
GALLIC *adj* of or containing gallium
GALLICA *n* variety of rose
GALLIED ▶ **gally**
GALLIER ▶ **gally**
GALLIES ▶ **gally**
GALLING *adj* annoying or bitterly humiliating

GALLIOT *same as* ▸ **galiot**
GALLISE *same as* ▸ **gallize**
GALLIUM *n* soft grey metallic element
GALLIZE *vb* add water and sugar to increase the quantity of wine produced
GALLNUT *n* type of plant gall that resembles a nut
GALLOCK *adj* left-handed
GALLON, -S *n* liquid measure of eight pints, equal to 4.55 litres
GALLOON *n* narrow band of cord, gold braid, etc
GALLOOT *same as* ▸ **galoot**
GALLOP, -S *n, vb*
GALLOUS *adj* of or containing gallium in the divalent state
GALLOW *vb* frighten
GALLOWS *n* wooden structure used for hanging criminals
GALLS ▸ **gall**
GALLUS *adj* bold
GALLY, GALLIED, GALLIER, GALLIES *vb* frighten ▹ *adj* (of land) damp or barren
GALOCHE *same as* ▸ **galosh**
GALOOT, -S *n* clumsy or uncouth person
GALOP, -ED, -S *n* 19th-century dance in quick duple time ▹ *vb* dance a galop
GALOPIN *n* boy who ran errands for a cook
GALOPS ▸ **galop**
GALORE, -S *adj* in abundance ▹ *n* abundance
GALOSH *n* waterproof overshoe ▹ *vb* cover with galoshes
GALOSHE *same as* ▸ **galosh**
GALS ▸ **gal**
GALUMPH *vb*
GALUT, -S *same as* ▸ **galuth**
GALUTH, -S *n* exile of Jews from Palestine
GALUTS ▸ **galut**
GALVO, -S *n* instrument for measuring electric current
GALYAC, -S *same as* ▸ **galyak**
GALYAK, -S *n* smooth glossy fur
GAM, -MED, -MING, -S *n* school of whales ▹ *vb* (of whales) form a school
GAMA, -S *n* tall perennial grass
GAMASH *n* type of gaiter
GAMAY, -S *n* red grape variety
GAMB, -S *n* in heraldry, the whole foreleg of a beast
GAMBA, -S *n* second-largest member of the viol family
GAMBADE *same as* ▸ **gambado**
GAMBADO *n* leap or gambol; caper ▹ *vb* perform a gambado
GAMBAS ▸ **gamba**
GAMBE, -S *same as* ▸ **gamb**
GAMBET, -S *n* tattler
GAMBIA, -S *same as* ▸ **gambier**
GAMBIER *n* astringent resinous substance
GAMBIR, -S *same as* ▸ **gambier**
GAMBIST *n* person who plays the (viola da) gamba
GAMBIT, -S *n, vb*
GAMBLE, -D, -S *vb, n*
GAMBLER ▸ **gamble**
GAMBLES ▸ **gamble**
GAMBO, -ES, -S *n* farm cart
GAMBOGE *n* gum resin
GAMBOL, -S *vb, n*
GAMBOS ▸ **gambo**
GAMBREL *n* hock of a horse or similar animal
GAMBS ▸ **gamb**
GAME, -D, -S, -ST *n, vb, adj*
GAMEBAG *n* bag for carrying hunted game birds
GAMED ▸ **game**
GAMELAN *n* type of percussion orchestra
GAMELY *adv* in a brave or sporting manner
GAMER, -S *n* person who plays computer games
GAMES ▸ **game**
GAMEST ▸ **game**
GAMESY *adj* sporty
GAMETAL ▸ **gamete**
GAMETE, -S *n* reproductive cell
GAMETIC ▸ **gamete**
GAMEY, GAMIER, GAMIEST *adj* having the smell or flavour of game

GAMGEE *n* as in **gamgee tissue** type of wound-dressing
GAMIC *adj* (esp of reproduction) requiring the fusion of gametes
GAMIER ▸ **gamey**
GAMIEST ▸ **gamey**
GAMIFY *vb* add gamelike elements to a task to encourage participation
GAMILY ▸ **gamey**
GAMIN, -S *n* street urchin
GAMINE, -S *n* slim boyish young woman
GAMING, -S *n* playing games
GAMINS ▸ **gamin**
GAMMA, -S *n* third letter of the Greek alphabet
GAMME, -S *n* musical scale
GAMMED ▸ **gam**
GAMMER, -S *n* dialect word for an old woman
GAMMES ▸ **gamme**
GAMMIER ▸ **gammy**
GAMMING ▸ **gam**
GAMMOCK *vb* clown around
GAMMON, -S *n, vb*
GAMMY, GAMMIER *adj* (of the leg) lame
GAMONE, -S *n* chemical used by gametes
GAMP, -S *n* umbrella
GAMPISH *adj* bulging
GAMPS ▸ **gamp**
GAMS ▸ **gam**
GAMUT, -S *n*
GAMY *same as* ▸ **gamey**
GAN, -NED, -NING, -S *vb* go
GANACHE *n* rich icing or filling
GANCH, -ED, -ES *vb* impale
GANDER, -S *n, vb*
GANDY *adj* as in **gandy dancer** railway track maintenance worker
GANE ▸ **go**
GANEF, -S *n* unscrupulous opportunist
GANEV, -S *same as* ▸ **ganef**
GANG, -ED, -S *n, vb*
GANGBO, -S *n* order restricting the activities of a gang member
GANGED ▸ **gang**
GANGER, -S *n* foreman of a gang of labourers
GANGING ▸ **gang**
GANGLE, -D, -S *vb* move awkwardly
GANGLIA > **ganglion**
GANGLY *same as* > **gangling**
GANGREL *n* wandering beggar
GANGS ▸ **gang**
GANGSTA *n* member of a street gang
GANGUE, -S *n* valueless material in an ore
GANGWAY *same as* > **gangplank**
GANNED ▸ **gan**
GANNET, -S *n*
GANNING ▸ **gan**
GANOF, -S *same as* ▸ **ganef**
GANOID, -S *adj* of the scales of certain fishes ▷ *n* ganoid fish
GANOIN, -S *n* outer layer of fish scales
GANOINE *same as* ▸ **ganoin**
GANOINS ▸ **ganoin**
GANS ▸ **gan**
GANSEY, -S *n* jersey or pullover
GANT, -ED, -ING, -S *vb* yawn
GANTLET *n* section of a railway where two tracks overlap ▷ *vb* make railway tracks form a gantlet
GANTRY *n*
GANTS ▸ **gant**
GAOL, -ED, -ING, -S *same as* ▸ **jail**
GAOLER, -S ▸ **gaol**
GAOLING ▸ **gaol**
GAOLS ▸ **gaol**
GAP, -PED, -S *n*
GAPE, -D *vb, n*
GAPER, -S *n* person or thing that gapes
GAPES *n* disease of young domestic fowl
GAPIER ▸ **gapy**
GAPIEST ▸ **gapy**
GAPING, -S *adj* wide open ▷ *n* state of having a gaping mouth
GAPLESS ▸ **gap**
GAPO, -S *n* (in S America) forest near a river
GAPOSIS *n* gap between closed fastenings on a garment
GAPPED ▸ **gap**
GAPPER, -S *n* person taking a year out of education
GAPPIER ▸ **gappy**
GAPPING *n* the act of taking a gap year

GAPPY, GAPPIER ▶ **gap**
GAPS ▶ **gap**
GAPY, GAPIER, GAPIEST ▶ **gape**
GAR, -RED, -RING, -S *vb* Scots word meaning compel
GARAGE, -D, -S *n, vb*
GARAGEY *adj* (of music) in a garage style
GARB, -ED, -ING, -S *n, vb*
GARBAGE *n*
GARBAGY *adj* like garbage
GARBE, -S *n* in heraldry, a wheat-sheaf
GARBED ▶ **garb**
GARBES ▶ **garbe**
GARBING ▶ **garb**
GARBLE, -S *vb, n*
GARBLED *adj* (of a story etc) jumbled and confused
GARBLER ▶ **garble**
GARBLES ▶ **garble**
GARBO, -S *n* dustman
GARBOIL *n* confusion or disturbance
GARBOS ▶ **garbo**
GARBS ▶ **garb**
GARBURE *n* thick soup from France
GARCON, -S *n* waiter
GARDA, -I *n* member of the Irish police force
GARDANT *same as* > **guardant**
GARDEN, -S *n, vb*
GARE, -S *n* filth ▷ *adj* greedy; covetous
GARFISH *same as* ▶ **garpike**
GARGET, -S *n* inflammation of the mammary gland
GARGETY ▶ **garget**
GARGLE, -D, -S *vb, n*
GARGLER ▶ **gargle**
GARGLES ▶ **gargle**
GARI, -S *n* thinly sliced pickled ginger
GARIAL, -S *same as* ▶ **gavial**
GARIGUE *n* open shrubby vegetation of dry Mediterranean regions
GARIS ▶ **gari**
GARISH *adj, vb*
GARJAN, -S *same as* ▶ **gurjun**
GARLAND *n, vb*
GARLIC, -S *n*
GARMENT *n, vb*
GARMS *pl n* clothing
GARNER, -S *vb, n*
GARNET, -S *n*
GARNI *adj* garnished
GARNISH *vb, n*
GAROTE, -D, -S *same as* > **garrotte**
GAROTTE *same as* > **garrotte**
GAROUPA *same as* ▶ **groper**
GARPIKE *n* primitive freshwater bony fish
GARRAN, -S *same as* ▶ **garron**
GARRE, -S *vb* compel
GARRED ▶ **gar**
GARRES ▶ **garre**
GARRET, -S *n* attic in a house
GARRING ▶ **gar**
GARRON, -S *n* small sturdy pony
GARROT, -S *n* goldeneye duck
GARROTE *same as* > **garrotte**
GARROTS ▶ **garrot**
GARRYA, -S *n* catkin-bearing evergreen shrub
GARS ▶ **gar**
GART *a past tense of* ▶ **gar**
GARTER, -S *n, vb*
GARTH, -S *n* courtyard surrounded by a cloister
GARUDA, -S *n* Hindu god
GARUM, -S *n* fermented fish sauce
GARVEY, -S *n* small flat-bottomed yacht
GARVIE, -S *n* sprat
GARVOCK *n* sprat
GAS, -ES, -SED, -SES *n, vb*
GASAHOL *n* mixture of petrol and alcohol used as fuel
GASBAG, -S *n* person who talks too much ▷ *vb* talk in a voluble way
GASCON, -S *n* boaster
GASEITY *n* state of being gaseous
GASEOUS *adj*
GASES ▶ **gas**
GASH, -ED, -ER, -ES, -EST, -ING *vb, n, adj*
GASHFUL *adj* full of gashes
GASHING ▶ **gash**
GASHLY *adv* wittily ▷ *adj* hideous; ghastly
GASIFY *vb* change into a gas
GASKET, -S *n*
GASKIN, -S *n* lower part of a horse's thigh
GASKING *same as* ▶ **gasket**

GASKINS ▸ **gaskin**
GASLESS ▸ **gas**
GASLIT *adj* lit by gas
GASMAN, GASMEN *n*
GASOHOL *n* mixture of petrol and alcohol used as fuel
GASP, -ED, -S *vb, n*
GASPER, -S *n* person who gasps
GASPIER ▸ **gaspy**
GASPING ▸ **gasp**
GASPS ▸ **gasp**
GASPY, GASPIER ▸ **gasp**
GASSED ▸ **gas**
GASSER, -S *n* drilling or well that yields natural gas
GASSES ▸ **gas**
GASSIER ▸ **gassy**
GASSILY ▸ **gassy**
GASSING ▸ **gas**
GASSY, GASSIER *adj* filled with gas
GAST, -ED, -ING, -S *vb* old word for frighten
GASTER, -S *vb* old word for frighten
GASTING ▸ **gast**
GASTRAL *adj* relating to the stomach
GASTREA *same as* > **gastraea**
GASTRIC *adj*
GASTRIN *n* polypeptide hormone
GASTS ▸ **gast**
GAT, -S *n* pistol or revolver
GATCH, -ED, -ES *vb* behave boastfully
GATCHER *n* person who boasts
GATCHES ▸ **gatch**
GATE, -D, -S, GATING *n, vb*
GATEAU, -S, -X *n*
GATED ▸ **gate**
GATELEG *n* table having hinged legs that swing out
GATEMAN, GATEMEN *n* gatekeeper
GATER, -S *variant of* ▸ **gator**
GATES ▸ **gate**
GATEWAY *n*
GATH, -S *n* (in Indian music) second section of a raga
GATHER, -S *vb, n*
GATHS ▸ **gath**
GATING, -S ▸ **gate**
GATLING *n* as in **gatling gun** kind of machine-gun
GATOR, -S *short form of* > **alligator**
GATS ▸ **gat**
GATVOL *adj* in South African English, fed up
GAU, -S *n* district set up by the Nazi Party
GAUCH *vb* behave boastfully
GAUCHE, -D, -S *adj* socially awkward ▹ *vb* make gauche
GAUCHER *n* gauche person
GAUCHES ▸ **gauche**
GAUCHO, -S *n*
GAUCIE *variant of* ▸ **gaucy**
GAUCY, GAUCIER *adj* plump or jolly
GAUD, -ED, -ING, -S *n* article of cheap finery ▹ *vb* decorate gaudily
GAUDERY *n* cheap finery or display
GAUDGIE *same as* ▸ **gadgie**
GAUDIER ▸ **gaudy**
GAUDIES ▸ **gaudy**
GAUDILY ▸ **gaudy**
GAUDING ▸ **gaud**
GAUDS ▸ **gaud**
GAUDY, GAUDIER, GAUDIES *adj, n*
GAUFER, -S *n* wafer
GAUFFER *same as* ▸ **goffer**
GAUFRE, -S *same as* ▸ **gaufer**
GAUGE, -D, -S *vb, n, adj*
GAUGER, -S *n* person or thing that gauges
GAUGES ▸ **gauge**
GAUGING ▸ **gauge**
GAUJE, -S *same as* ▸ **gadgie**
GAULT, -S *n* stiff compact clay or thick heavy clayey soil
GAULTER *n* person who digs gault
GAULTS ▸ **gault**
GAUM, -ED, -ING, -S *vb* understand
GAUMIER ▸ **gaumy**
GAUMING ▸ **gaum**
GAUMS ▸ **gaum**
GAUMY, GAUMIER *adj* clogged
GAUN ▸ **go**
GAUNCH *same as* ▸ **ganch**
GAUNT, -ED, -ER, -S *adj* lean and haggard ▹ *vb* yawn
GAUNTLY ▸ **gaunt**
GAUNTRY *same as* ▸ **gantry**
GAUNTS ▸ **gaunt**
GAUP, -ED, -ING, -S *same as* ▸ **gawp**
GAUPER, -S ▸ **gaup**
GAUPING ▸ **gaup**

GAUPS ▶ **gaup**
GAUPUS *same as* ▶ **gawpus**
GAUR, -S *n* large wild member of the cattle tribe
GAUS ▶ **gau**
GAUSS, -ES *n* unit of magnetic flux density
GAUZE, -S *n*
GAUZIER ▶ **gauzy**
GAUZILY ▶ **gauzy**
GAUZY, GAUZIER *adj* resembling gauze
GAVAGE, -S *n* forced feeding by means of a tube
GAVE ▶ **give**
GAVEL, -ED, -S *n, vb*
GAVIAL, -S *n* as in **false gavial** small crocodile
GAVOT, -S *same as* ▶ **gavotte**
GAVOTTE *n* old formal dance ▷ *vb* dance a gavotte
GAW, -S *n* as in **weather gaw** partial rainbow
GAWCY, GAWCIER *same as* ▶ **gaucy**
GAWD, -S *same as* ▶ **gaud**
GAWK, -ED, -ING, -S *vb*
GAWKER, -S ▶ **gawk**
GAWKIER ▶ **gawky**
GAWKIES ▶ **gawky**
GAWKILY ▶ **gawky**
GAWKING ▶ **gawk**
GAWKISH *same as* ▶ **gawky**
GAWKS ▶ **gawk**
GAWKY, GAWKIER, GAWKIES *adj* clumsy or awkward ▷ *n* clumsy or awkward person
GAWMOGE *n* clownish person
GAWP, -ED, -ING, -S *vb*
GAWPER, -S ▶ **gawp**
GAWPING ▶ **gawp**
GAWPS ▶ **gawp**
GAWPUS *n* silly person
GAWS ▶ **gaw**
GAWSIE, -R *same as* ▶ **gaucy**
GAWSY *same as* ▶ **gaucy**
GAY, -ER, -EST, -S *adj, n*
GAYAL, -S *n* type of ox
GAYDAR, -S *n* supposed ability to recognize if another person is gay
GAYER ▶ **gay**
GAYEST ▶ **gay**
GAYETY *same as* ▶ **gaiety**
GAYLY ▶ **gay**
GAYNESS ▶ **gay**
GAYS ▶ **gay**
GAYSOME *adj* full of merriment
GAZABO, -S *n* fellow or companion
GAZAL, -S *same as* ▶ **ghazal**
GAZANG, -S *vb* inconvenience a buyer by declining to sell a house just before the purchase is completed
GAZANIA *n* S African plant
GAZAR, -S *n* type of silk cloth
GAZE, -D, -S *vb, n*
GAZEBO, -S *n*
GAZED ▶ **gaze**
GAZEFUL *adj* gazing
GAZELLE *n*
GAZER, -S ▶ **gaze**
GAZES ▶ **gaze**
GAZETTE *n* official publication containing announcements ▷ *vb* announce or report (facts or an event) in a gazette
GAZIER ▶ **gazy**
GAZIEST ▶ **gazy**
GAZING, -S ▶ **gaze**
GAZON, -S *n* sod used to cover a parapet in a fortification
GAZOO, -S *n* kazoo
GAZOOKA *same as* ▶ **gazoo**
GAZOON, -S *same as* ▶ **gazon**
GAZOOS ▶ **gazoo**
GAZUMP, -S *vb, n*
GAZY, GAZIER, GAZIEST *adj* prone to gazing
GEAL, -ED, -ING, -S *vb* congeal
GEALOUS *Spenserian spelling of* ▶ **jealous**
GEALS ▶ **geal**
GEAN, -S *n* white-flowered tree
GEAR, -ED, -S *n, vb*
GEARBOX *n*
GEARE, -S *Spenserian spelling of* ▶ **jeer**
GEARED ▶ **gear**
GEARES ▶ **geare**
GEARING *n* system of gears designed to transmit motion
GEARS ▶ **gear**
GEASON *adj* wonderful
GEAT, -S *n* in casting, the channel which leads to a mould
GEBUR, -S *n* tenant farmer
GECK, -ED, -ING, -S *vb* beguile

GECKO, -ES, -S *n*
GECKS ▶ **geck**
GED, -S *Scots word for* ▶ **pike**
GEDACT, -S *n* flutelike stopped metal diapason organ pipe
GEDDIT *interj* exclamation meaning *do you understand it?*
GEDECKT *same as* ▶ **gedact**
GEDS ▶ **ged**
GEE, -D, -ING, -S *interj* mild exclamation of surprise, admiration, etc ▷ *vb* move (an animal, esp a horse) ahead
GEEBUNG *n* Australian tree or shrub
GEECHEE *n* speaker of a dialect found in an area of the southern US
GEED ▶ **gee**
GEEGAW, -S *same as* ▶ **gewgaw**
GEEING ▶ **gee**
GEEK, -S *n*
GEEKDOM ▶ **geek**
GEEKED *adj* highly excited
GEEKERY *n* preoccupation with, or great knowledge about, a specialized subject
GEEKIER ▶ **geeky**
GEEKISH *adj* of or like a geek
GEEKISM *n* preoccupation with subjects generally considered unfashionable or boring
GEEKS ▶ **geek**
GEEKY, GEEKIER *adj* of or like a geek
GEELBEK *n* edible marine fish
GEEP, -S *n* cross between a goat and a sheep
GEES ▶ **gee**
GEESE ▶ **goose**
GEEST, -S *n* area of heathland in N Germany and adjacent areas
GEEZ *interj* expression of surprise
GEEZAH, -S *variant spelling of* ▶ **geezer**
GEEZER, -S *n*
GEFILTE *adj* as in **gefilte fish** dish of fish stuffed with various ingredients
GEGGIE, -S *Scottish slang word for* ▶ **mouth**
GEISHA, -S *n*
GEIST, -S *n* spirit
GEIT, -ED, -ING, -S *n* border on clothing ▷ *vb* put a border on (an article of clothing)
GEL, -LED, -LING, -S *n, vb*
GELABLE *adj* capable of forming a gel
GELADA, -S *n* NE African baboon
GELANDE *adj* as in **gelande jump** jump made in downhill skiing
GELANT, -S *same as* ▶ **gellant**
GELATE, -D, -S *vb* form a gel
GELATI, -S *n* layered dessert
GELATIN *same as* > **gelatine**
GELATIS ▶ **gelati**
GELATO, -S *n* Italian ice cream
GELCAP, -S *n* medicine enclosed in gelatine
GELCOAT *n* thin layer of gel or resin applied to a surface
GELD, -ED, -S *vb* emasculate; weaken ▷ *n* tax on land in Anglo-Saxon and Norman England
GELDER, -S ▶ **geld**
GELDING ▶ **geld**
GELDS ▶ **geld**
GELEE, -S *n* jelly
GELID, -ER *adj* very cold, icy, or frosty
GELIDLY ▶ **gelid**
GELLANT *n* substance that causes gelling
GELLED ▶ **gel**
GELLIES ▶ **gelly**
GELLING ▶ **gel**
GELLY, GELLIES *same as* > **gelignite**
GELOSY *Spenserian spelling of* > **jealousy**
GELS ▶ **gel**
GELT, -S *n* money
GEM, -MED, -MING, -S *n, vb*
GEMCLIP *n* paperclip
GEMEL, -S *n* in heraldry, either of a pair of parallel bars
GEMFISH *n* Australian food fish with a delicate flavour
GEMINAL *adj* occurring in pairs
GEMINI *n* expression of surprise

GEMINY *n* pair
GEMLIKE ▶ **gem**
GEMMA, -E *n* reproductive structure in liverworts, mosses, etc
GEMMAN, GEMMEN *dialect form of* > **gentleman**
GEMMATE *adj* (of some plants and animals) having gemmae ▷ *vb* produce or reproduce by gemmae
GEMMED ▶ **gem**
GEMMEN ▶ **gemman**
GEMMERY *n* gems collectively
GEMMIER ▶ **gemmy**
GEMMILY ▶ **gem**
GEMMING ▶ **gem**
GEMMULE *n* bud
GEMMY, GEMMIER ▶ **gem**
GEMONY *same as* ▶ **jiminy**
GEMOT, -S *n* (in Anglo-Saxon England) a legal or administrative assembly
GEMOTE, -S *same as* ▶ **gemot**
GEMOTS ▶ **gemot**
GEMS ▶ **gem**
GEMSBOK *same as* ▶ **oryx**
GEN, -NED, -NING *n* information ▷ *vb* gain information
GENA, -S *n* cheek
GENAL ▶ **gena**
GENAPPE *n* smooth worsted yarn used for braid, etc
GENAS ▶ **gena**
GENDER, -S *n, vb*
GENE, -S *n*
GENERA ▶ **genus**
GENERAL *adj, n, vb*
GENERIC *adj* of a class, group, or genus ▷ *n* drug, food product, etc that does not have a trademark
GENES ▶ **gene**
GENESIS, GENESES *n*
GENET, -S *n* type of agile catlike mammal
GENETIC *adj*
GENETS ▶ **genet**
GENETTE *same as* ▶ **genet**
GENEVA, -S *n* gin
GENIAL *adj*
GENIC *adj* of or relating to a gene or genes
GENIE, -S *n*
GENII ▶ **genius**
GENIP, -S *same as* ▶ **genipap**
GENIPAP *n* evergreen Caribbean tree
GENIPS ▶ **genip**
GENISTA *n* any member of the broom family
GENITAL *adj*
GENITOR *n* biological father
GENIUS, GENII *n*
GENIZAH, GENIZOT *n* repository for sacred objects which may not be destroyed
GENLOCK *n* generator locking device ▷ *vb* activate a genlock
GENNED ▶ **gen**
GENNEL, -S *same as* ▶ **ginnel**
GENNET, -S *n* female donkey or ass
GENNIES ▶ **genny**
GENNING ▶ **gen**
GENNY, GENNIES *same as* ▶ **genoa**
GENOA, -S *n* large triangular jib sail
GENOISE *n* rich sponge cake
GENOM, -S *same as* ▶ **genome**
GENOME, -S *n* all the genetic material in an organism
GENOMIC ▶ **genome**
GENOMS ▶ **genom**
GENRE, -S *n*
GENRO, -S *n* group of Japanese statesmen
GENS, GENTES *n* (in ancient Rome) a group of aristocratic families
GENSENG *same as* ▶ **ginseng**
GENT *n*
GENTEEL *adj*
GENTES ▶ **gens**
GENTIAN *n* mountain plant with deep blue flowers
GENTIER ▶ **genty**
GENTIL *adj* gentle
GENTILE *n* non-Jewish person ▷ *adj* used to designate a place or the inhabitants of a place
GENTLE, -D, -R, -S *adj, vb, n*
GENTLY ▶ **gentle**
GENTOO, -S *n* grey-backed penguin
GENTRY *n*
GENTS *n* men's public toilet
GENTY, GENTIER *adj* neat

GENU, -A *n* any knee-like bend in a structure or part
GENUINE *adj* not fake, authentic
GENUS, GENERA, -ES *n* group of animals or plants
GEO, -S *n* (esp in Shetland) a small fjord or gully
GEOCODE *vb* assign geographical coordinates to a physical location using a digital code
GEODATA *n* information about geographical location held in a digital format
GEODE, -S *n* cavity within a rock mass or nodule
GEODESY *n* study of the shape and size of the earth
GEODIC ▸ **geode**
GEODUCK *n* king clam
GEOFACT *n* rock shaped by natural forces
GEOGENY *same as* ▸ **geogony**
GEOGONY *n* science of the earth's formation
GEOID, -S *n* hypothetical surface
GEOIDAL ▸ **geoid**
GEOIDS ▸ **geoid**
GEOLOGY *n*
GEOMANT *n* geomancer
GEORGIC *adj* agricultural ▹ *n* poem about rural or agricultural life
GEOS ▸ **geo**
GEOTAG, -S *n* geographical co-ordinates digitally applied to data ▹ *vb* apply a geotag to data
GER, -S *n* portable Mongolian dwelling
GERAH, -S *n* ancient Hebrew unit of weight
GERBE, -S *same as* ▸ **garbe**
GERBERA *n* type of plant
GERBES ▸ **gerbe**
GERBIL, -S *n*
GERE, -S *Spenserian spelling of* ▸ **gear**
GERENT, -S *n* person who rules or manages
GERENUK *n* slender antelope
GERES ▸ **gere**
GERLE, -S *Spenserian spelling of* ▸ **girl**
GERM, -ED, -ING, -S *n, vb*
GERMAIN *same as* ▸ **germen**
GERMAN, -S *n* type of dance ▹ *adj* having the same parents as oneself
GERMANE *adj* relevant
GERMANS ▸ **german**
GERMED ▸ **germ**
GERMEN, -S, GERMINA *n* cells that gives rise to the germ cells
GERMIER ▸ **germy**
GERMIN, -S *same as* ▸ **germen**
GERMINA ▸ **germen**
GERMING ▸ **germ**
GERMINS ▸ **germin**
GERMS ▸ **germ**
GERMY, GERMIER *adj* full of germs
GERNE, -D, -S, GERNING *vb* grin
GERS ▸ **ger**
GERT *adv* in dialect, great or very big
GERTCHA *interj* get out of here!
GERUND, -S *n* noun formed from a verb
GESSE, -D, -S, GESSING *Spenserian spelling of* ▸ **guess**
GESSO, -ED, -ES *n* plaster used for painting or in sculpture ▹ *vb* apply gesso to
GEST, -S *n* notable deed or exploit
GESTALT *n* perceptual pattern or structure
GESTANT *adj* laden
GESTAPO *n*
GESTATE *vb* carry (young) in the uterus during pregnancy
GESTE, -S *same as* ▸ **gest**
GESTIC *adj* consisting of gestures
GESTS ▸ **gest**
GESTURE *n, vb*
GET, -S, GOT *vb*
GETA, -S *n* type of Japanese wooden sandal
GETABLE ▸ **get**
GETAS ▸ **geta**
GETAWAY *n*
GETOUT, -S *n* excuse to get out of doing something
GETS ▸ **get**
GETTER, -S *n* person or thing that gets ▹ *vb* remove (a gas) by the action of a getter
GETTING ▸ **get**

GETUP, -S *n* outfit
GEUM, -S *n* type of herbaceous plant
GEWGAW, -S *n* showy but valueless trinket ▷ *adj* showy and valueless
GEY, -ER, -EST *adv* extremely ▷ *adj* gallant
GEYAN *adv* somewhat
GEYER ▶ **gey**
GEYEST ▶ **gey**
GEYSER, -S *n, vb*
GHARIAL *same as* ▶ **gavial**
GHARRI, -S *same as* ▶ **gharry**
GHARRY *n* (in India) horse-drawn vehicle
GHAST, -ED, -S *vb* terrify
GHASTLY *adj, adv*
GHASTS ▶ **ghast**
GHAT, -S *n* (in India) set of steps leading down to a river
GHAUT, -S *n* small cleft in a hill
GHAZAL, -S *n* Arabic love poem
GHAZEL, -S *same as* ▶ **ghazal**
GHAZI, -ES, -S *n* Muslim fighter against infidels
GHEE, -S *n* (in Indian cookery) clarified butter
GHERAO, -S *n* form of industrial action in India ▷ *vb* trap an employer in his or her office, to indicate the workforce's discontent
GHERKIN *n*
GHESSE, -D, -S, GHEST *Spenserian spelling of* ▶ **guess**
GHETTO, -S *n, vb*
GHI, -S *same as* ▶ **ghee**
GHIBLI, -S *n* fiercely hot wind of North Africa
GHILGAI *same as* ▶ **gilgai**
GHILLIE *n* (in Scotland) attendant for hunting or fishing ▷ *vb* act as a ghillie
GHIS ▶ **ghi**
GHOST, -ED, -S *n, vb*
GHOSTLY *adj* frightening in appearance or effect
GHOSTS ▶ **ghost**
GHOSTY *adj* pertaining to ghosts
GHOUL, -S *n*
GHOULIE *n* goblin
GHOULS ▶ **ghoul**
GHRELIN *n* hormone that stimulates appetite
GHUBAR *adj* as in **ghubar numeral** type of numeral
GHYLL, -S *same as* ▶ **gill**
GI, -S *n* white suit worn in martial arts
GIANT, -S *n, adj*
GIANTLY *adj* giantlike
GIANTRY *n* collective term for giants
GIANTS ▶ **giant**
GIARDIA *n* species of parasite
GIB, -BED, -BING, -S *n* metal wedge, pad, or thrust bearing ▷ *vb* fasten or supply with a gib
GIBBER, -S *vb* speak or utter rapidly and unintelligibly ▷ *n* boulder
GIBBET, -S *n* gallows for displaying executed criminals ▷ *vb* put to death by hanging on a gibbet
GIBBING ▶ **gib**
GIBBON, -S *n*
GIBBOSE *same as* ▶ **gibbous**
GIBBOUS *adj* (of the moon) between half and fully illuminated
GIBE, -D, -S, GIBING *vb* make jeering or scoffing remarks (at) ▷ *n* derisive or provoking remark
GIBEL, -S *n* Prussian carp
GIBER, -S ▶ **gibe**
GIBES ▶ **gibe**
GIBING ▶ **gibe**
GIBLET ▶ **giblets**
GIBLETS *pl n* gizzard, liver, heart, and neck of a fowl
GIBLI, -S *same as* ▶ **ghibli**
GIBS ▶ **gib**
GIBSON, -S *n* martini garnished with onion
GIBUS, -ES *n* collapsible top hat
GID, -S *n* disease of sheep
GIDDAP *interj* exclamation used to make a horse go faster
GIDDAY *interj* expression of greeting
GIDDIED ▶ **giddy**
GIDDIER ▶ **giddy**
GIDDIES ▶ **giddy**
GIDDILY ▶ **giddy**
GIDDUP *same as* ▶ **giddyup**

GIDDY, GIDDIED, GIDDIER, GIDDIES *adj* having or causing a feeling of dizziness ▷ *vb* make giddy
GIDDYAP *same as* ▶ **giddyup**
GIDDYUP *interj* exclamation used to make a horse go faster
GIDGEE, -S *n* small acacia tree
GIDJEE, -S *same as* ▶ **gidgee**
GIDS ▶ **gid**
GIE, -D, -ING, -N, -S *Scot word for* ▶ **give**
GIF, -S *n* file held in GIF format
GIFT, -S *n, vb*
GIFTED *adj* talented
GIFTEE, -S *n* person given a gift
GIFTING *n* act of gifting
GIFTS ▶ **gift**
GIG, -GED, -GING, -S *n, vb*
GIGA, -S, GIGHE *same as* ▶ **gigue**
GIGABIT *n* unit of information in computing
GIGAS ▶ **giga**
GIGATON *n* unit of explosive force
GIGGED ▶ **gig**
GIGGING ▶ **gig**
GIGGIT, -S *vb* move quickly
GIGGLE, -D, -S *vb, n*
GIGGLER ▶ **giggle**
GIGGLES ▶ **giggle**
GIGGLY ▶ **giggle**
GIGHE ▶ **giga**
GIGLET, -S *n* flighty girl
GIGLOT, -S *same as* ▶ **giglet**
GIGMAN, GIGMEN *n* one who places great importance on respectability
GIGOT, -S *n* leg of lamb or mutton
GIGS ▶ **gig**
GIGUE, -S *n* piece of music incorporated into the classical suite
GILA, -S *n* large venomous brightly coloured lizard
GILBERT *n* unit of magnetomotive force
GILCUP, -S *same as* ▶ **giltcup**
GILD, -ED, -S *vb*
GILDEN *adj* gilded
GILDER, -S ▶ **gild**
GILDING ▶ **gild**
GILDS ▶ **gild**
GILET, -S *n* waist- or hip-length garment
GILGAI, -S *n* natural water hole
GILGIE, -S *n* type of freshwater crayfish
GILL, -ED, -ING *n, vb*
GILLER, -S ▶ **gill**
GILLET, -S *n* mare
GILLIE, -D, -S *n* (in Scotland) attendant for hunting or fishing ▷ *vb* act as a gillie
GILLING ▶ **gill**
GILLION *n* (no longer in technical use) one thousand million
GILLNET *n* net designed to catch fish by the gills ▷ *vb* fish using a gillnet
GILLS *pl n* breathing organs in fish and other water creatures
GILLY *same as* ▶ **gillie**
GILPEY, -S *n* mischievous, frolicsome boy or girl
GILPY, GILPIES *same as* ▶ **gilpey**
GILT, -S *n*
GILTCUP *n* buttercup
GILTS ▶ **gilt**
GIMBAL *vb* support on gimbals
GIMBALS *pl n* set of pivoted rings
GIMEL, -S *n* third letter of the Hebrew alphabet
GIMLET, -S *n, adj, vb*
GIMMAL, -S *n* ring composed of interlocking rings ▷ *vb* provide with gimmals
GIMME, -S *interj* give me! ▷ *n* something easily obtained
GIMMER, -S *n* year-old ewe
GIMMES ▶ **gimme**
GIMMICK *n* something designed to attract attention ▷ *vb* make gimmicky
GIMMIE, -S *n* very short putt in golf
GIMMOR, -S *n* mechanical device
GIMP, -ED, -ING, -S *n* tapelike trimming of silk, wool, or cotton, often stiffened with wire ▷ *vb* slang term for limp
GIMPIER ▶ **gimpy**
GIMPING ▶ **gimp**
GIMPS ▶ **gimp**
GIMPY, GIMPIER *same as* ▶ **gammy**
GIN, -NED, -S *n, vb*

GINCH, -ES *same as* ▶ **gitch**
GING, -S *n* child's catapult
GINGAL, -S *n* type of musket mounted on a swivel
GINGALL *same as* ▶ **gingal**
GINGALS ▶ **gingal**
GINGE, -S *n* person with ginger hair
GINGELI *same as* ▶ **gingili**
GINGELY *same as* ▶ **gingili**
GINGER, -S *n, adj, vb*
GINGERY *adj* like or tasting of ginger
GINGES ▶ **ginge**
GINGHAM *n*
GINGILI *n* oil obtained from sesame seeds
GINGIVA *same as* ▶ **gum**
GINGKO, -S *same as* ▶ **ginkgo**
GINGLE, -S *same as* ▶ **jingle**
GINGS ▶ **ging**
GINK, -S *n* man or boy
GINKGO, -S *n* ornamental Chinese tree
GINKS ▶ **gink**
GINN *same as* ▶ **jinn**
GINNED ▶ **gin**
GINNEL, -S *n* narrow passageway between buildings
GINNER, -S ▶ **gin**
GINNERY *another word for* ▶ **ginhouse**
GINNIER ▶ **ginny**
GINNING ▶ **gin**
GINNY, GINNIER *adj* relating to the spirit gin
GINS ▶ **gin**
GINSENG *n*
GINSHOP *n* tavern
GIO, -S *same as* ▶ **geo**
GIOCOSO *adv* (of music) to be expressed joyfully or playfully
GIOS ▶ **gio**
GIP, -S *vb* clean fish before curing
GIPON, -S *another word for* ▶ **jupon**
GIPPED ▶ **gip**
GIPPER, -S ▶ **gip**
GIPPIES ▶ **gippy**
GIPPING ▶ **gip**
GIPPY, GIPPIES *n* starling
GIPS ▶ **gip**
GIPSEN, -S *obsolete word for* ▶ **gypsy**
GIPSY, GIPSIED, GIPSIES *n* member of a nomadic people ▷ *vb* live like a gipsy
GIRAFFE *n*
GIRASOL *n* type of opal
GIRD, -ED, -S *vb* put a belt round ▷ *n* blow or stroke
GIRDER, -S *n*
GIRDING ▶ **gird**
GIRDLE, -D, -S *n, vb*
GIRDLER *n* person or thing that girdles
GIRDLES ▶ **girdle**
GIRDS ▶ **gird**
GIRKIN, -S *same as* ▶ **gherkin**
GIRL, -S *n*
GIRLIE, -S *adj, n*
GIRLIER ▶ **girly**
GIRLIES ▶ **girlie**
GIRLISH *adj*
GIRLOND *obsolete word for* ▶ **garland**
GIRLS ▶ **girl**
GIRLY, GIRLIER *same as* ▶ **girlie**
GIRN, -ED, -ING, -S *vb* grimace or snarl
GIRNEL, -S *n* large chest for storing meal
GIRNER, -S ▶ **girn**
GIRNIE, -R *adj* peevish
GIRNING ▶ **girn**
GIRNS ▶ **girn**
GIRO, -S *n* system of transferring money
GIROLLE *n* chanterelle mushroom
GIRON, -S *n* part of a heraldic shield
GIRONIC ▶ **giron**
GIRONNY *adj* divided into segments from the fesse point
GIRONS ▶ **giron**
GIROS ▶ **giro**
GIROSOL *same as* ▶ **girasol**
GIRR, -S *same as* ▶ **gird**
GIRSH, -ES *n* currency unit of Saudi Arabia
GIRT, -ED, -ING, -S *vb* gird; bind
GIRTH, -ED, -S *n, vb*
GIRTING ▶ **girt**
GIRTS ▶ **girt**
GIS ▶ **gi**
GISARME *n* long-shafted battle-axe
GISMO, -S *same as* ▶ **gizmo**
GIST, -S *n*
GIT, -S, -TED, -TING *vb*
GITANA, -S *n* Romany woman from Spain
GITANO, -S *n* Romany man from Spain
GITCH, -ES *n* underwear

GITE, -S *n* self-catering holiday cottage for let in France
GITS ▶ **git**
GITTED ▶ **git**
GITTERN *n* obsolete medieval instrument ▷ *vb* play the gittern
GITTIN *n* Jewish divorce
GITTING ▶ **git**
GIUST, -ED, -S *same as* ▶ **joust**
GIUSTO *adv* as observed strictly
GIUSTS ▶ **giust**
GIVABLE ▶ **give**
GIVE, GAVE, -S *vb, n*
GIVED *same as* ▶ **gyved**
GIVEN, -S *n* assumed fact
GIVER, -S ▶ **give**
GIVES ▶ **give**
GIVING, -S ▶ **give**
GIZMO, -S *n*
GIZZ, -ES *n* wig
GIZZARD *n*
GIZZEN, -S *vb* (of wood) to warp
GIZZES ▶ **gizz**
GJETOST *n* type of Norwegian cheese
GJU, -S *n* type of violin used in Shetland

This unusual word for a Shetland fiddle is great for disposing of awkward letters for a good score.

GLACE, -D, -ED, -S *adj* preserved in a thick sugary syrup ▷ *vb* ice or candy (cakes, fruits, etc)
GLACIAL *adj* of ice or glaciers ▷ *n* ice age
GLACIER *n*
GLACIS *n* slight incline
GLAD, -DED, -DER, -S *adj, vb, n*
GLADDEN *vb*
GLADDER ▶ **glad**
GLADDIE *n* gladiolus
GLADDON *n* stinking iris
GLADE, -S *n*
GLADFUL *adj* full of gladness
GLADIER ▶ **glady**
GLADIUS *n* short sword used by Roman legionaries
GLADLY ▶ **glad**
GLADS ▶ **glad**
GLADY, GLADIER ▶ **glade**
GLAIK, -S *n* prank
GLAIKET *same as* ▶ **glaikit**
GLAIKIT *adj* foolish
GLAIKS ▶ **glaik**
GLAIR, -ED, -S *n* white of egg ▷ *vb* apply glair to (something)
GLAIRE, -S *same as* ▶ **glair**
GLAIRED ▶ **glair**
GLAIRES ▶ **glaire**
GLAIRIN *n* viscous mineral deposit
GLAIRS ▶ **glair**
GLAIRY ▶ **glair**
GLAIVE, -S *archaic word for* ▶ **sword**
GLAIVED *adj* armed with a sword
GLAIVES ▶ **glaive**
GLAM, -MED, -MER, -S *n* magical illusion ▷ *vb* make oneself look glamorous ▷ *adj* glamorous
GLAMMY *adj* glamorous
GLAMOR, -S *same as* ▶ **glamour**
GLAMOUR *n, vb*
GLAMS ▶ **glam**
GLANCE, -D, -S *vb, n*
GLANCER *n* log or pole used to protect trees from damage
GLANCES ▶ **glance**
GLAND, -S *n*
GLANDES ▶ **glans**
GLANDS ▶ **gland**
GLANS, GLANDES *n* any small rounded body or glandlike mass
GLARE, -D, -S *vb, n, adj*
GLAREAL *adj* (of a plant) growing in cultivated land
GLARED ▶ **glare**
GLARES ▶ **glare**
GLARIER ▶ **glary**
GLARING *adj* conspicuous
GLARY, GLARIER ▶ **glare**
GLASS, -ED *n, vb*
GLASSEN *adj* glassy
GLASSES *pl n* pair of lenses for correcting faulty vision
GLASSIE *same as* ▶ **glassy**
GLASSY *adj* like glass ▷ *n* glass marble
GLAUM, -ED, -S *vb* snatch
GLAUR, -S *n* mud or mire
GLAURY ▶ **glaur**
GLAZE, -D, -S *vb, n*
GLAZEN *adj* glazed
GLAZER, -S ▶ **glaze**
GLAZES ▶ **glaze**
GLAZIER *n*
GLAZILY ▶ **glaze**

GLAZING *n* surface of a glazed object
GLAZY ▶ **glaze**
GLEAM, -ED, -S *n, vb*
GLEAMER *n* mirror used to cheat in card games
GLEAMS ▶ **gleam**
GLEAMY ▶ **gleam**
GLEAN, -ED, -S *vb*
GLEANER ▶ **glean**
GLEANS ▶ **glean**
GLEAVE, -S *archaic word for* ▶ **sword**
GLEBA, -E *n* mass of spores
GLEBE, -S *n* land granted to a member of the clergy
GLEBIER ▶ **gleby**
GLEBOUS *adj* gleby
GLEBY, GLEBIER *adj* relating to a glebe
GLED, -S *n* red kite (bird)
GLEDE, -S *same as* ▶ **gled**
GLEDGE, -D, -S *vb* glance sideways
GLEDS ▶ **gled**
GLEE, -ING, -S *n, vb*
GLEED, -S *n* burning ember or hot coal
GLEEFUL *adj* merry or joyful
GLEEING ▶ **glee**
GLEEK, -ED, -S *vb* jeer
GLEEMAN, GLEEMEN *n* minstrel
GLEENIE *n* guinea fowl
GLEES ▶ **glee**
GLEG, -GER *adj* quick
GLEGLY ▶ **gleg**
GLEI, -S *same as* ▶ **gley**
GLEN, -S *n*
GLENOID *adj* resembling or having a shallow cavity ▷ *n* shallow cavity
GLENS ▶ **glen**
GLENT, -ED, -S *same as* ▶ **glint**
GLEY, -ED, -S *n* bluish-grey compact sticky soil ▷ *vb* squint
GLEYING ▶ **gley**
GLEYS ▶ **gley**
GLIA, -S *n* web of tissue that supports nerve cells
GLIADIN *n* protein of cereals with a high proline content
GLIAL ▶ **glia**
GLIAS ▶ **glia**
GLIB, -BED, -BER, -S *adj, vb*
GLIBLY ▶ **glib**
GLIBS ▶ **glib**
GLID, -DER *adj* moving smoothly and easily
GLIDE, -D, -S, GLODE *vb, n*
GLIDER, -S *n* flying phalanger
GLIDES ▶ **glide**
GLIDING *n* sport of flying gliders
GLIFF, -S *n* slap
GLIFT, -S *n* moment
GLIKE, -S *same as* ▶ **gleek**
GLIM, -S *n* light or lamp
GLIME, -D, -S, GLIMING *vb* glance sideways
GLIMMER *vb, n*
GLIMPSE *n, vb*
GLIMS ▶ **glim**
GLINT, -ED, -S *vb, n*
GLINTY ▶ **glint**
GLIOMA, -S *n* tumour of the brain and spinal cord
GLIOSIS, GLIOSES *n* process leading to scarring in the nervous system
GLISK, -S *n* glimpse
GLISSE, -S *n* type of dance step
GLISTEN *vb, n*
GLISTER *archaic word for* ▶ **glitter**
GLIT, -S *n* slimy matter
GLITCH *n*
GLITCHY ▶ **glitch**
GLITS ▶ **glit**
GLITTER *vb, n*
GLITZ, -ED, -ES *n, vb*
GLITZY *adj* showily attractive
GLOAM, -S *n* dusk
GLOAT, -ED, -S *vb, n*
GLOATER ▶ **gloat**
GLOATS ▶ **gloat**
GLOB, -S *n* rounded mass of thick fluid
GLOBAL *adj*
GLOBATE *adj* shaped like a globe
GLOBBY *adj* thick and lumpy
GLOBE, -D, -S, GLOBING *n, vb*
GLOBI ▶ **globus**
GLOBIER ▶ **globy**
GLOBIN, -S *n* protein component of haemoglobin
GLOBING ▶ **globe**
GLOBINS ▶ **globin**
GLOBOID *adj* shaped approximately like a globe ▷ *n* globoid body
GLOBOSE *adj* spherical or approximately spherical ▷ *n* globose object
GLOBOUS *same as* ▶ **globose**
GLOBS ▶ **glob**
GLOBULE *n*
GLOBUS, GLOBI *n* any spherelike structure

GLOBY, GLOBIER *adj* round
GLOCHID *n* barbed spine on a plant
GLODE ▶ **glide**
GLOGG, -S *n* hot alcoholic mixed drink
GLOIRE, -S *n* glory
GLOM, -MED, -S *vb* attach oneself to or associate oneself with
GLOMERA ▶ **glomus**
GLOMMED ▶ **glom**
GLOMS ▶ **glom**
GLOMUS, GLOMERA *n* small anastomosis in an artery or vein
GLONOIN *n* nitroglycerin
GLOOM, -ED, -S *n, vb*
GLOOMY *adj* despairing or sad
GLOOP, -ED, -S *vb* cover with a viscous substance
GLOOPY ▶ **gloop**
GLOP, -PED, -S *vb* cover with a viscous substance
GLOPPY ▶ **glop**
GLOPS ▶ **glop**
GLORIA, -S *n* silk, wool, cotton, or nylon fabric
GLORIED ▶ **glory**
GLORIES ▶ **glory**
GLORIFY *vb*
GLORY, GLORIED, GLORIES *n, vb*
GLOSS, -ED, -ES *n, vb*
GLOSSA, -E, -S *n* paired tonguelike lobe in the labium of an insect
GLOSSAL ▶ **glossa**
GLOSSAS ▶ **glossa**
GLOSSED ▶ **gloss**
GLOSSER ▶ **gloss**
GLOSSES ▶ **gloss**
GLOSSY *adj* smooth and shiny ▷ *n* expensively produced magazine
GLOST, -S *n* lead glaze used for pottery
GLOTTAL *adj* of the glottis
GLOTTIC *adj* of or relating to the tongue or the glottis
GLOTTIS *n* vocal cords and the space between them
GLOUT, -ED, -S *vb* look sullen
GLOVE, -S *n*
GLOVED ▶ **glove**
GLOVER, -S *n* person who makes or sells gloves
GLOVES ▶ **glove**
GLOVING ▶ **glove**
GLOW, -ED, -S *vb, n*
GLOWER, -S *n* scowl ▷ *vb* stare angrily
GLOWFLY *n* firefly
GLOWING *adj* full of praise
GLOWS ▶ **glow**
GLOZE, -D, -S *vb* explain away ▷ *n* flattery or deceit
GLOZING ▶ **gloze**
GLUCAN, -S *n* any polysaccharide consisting of a polymer of glucose
GLUCINA *n* oxide of glucinum
GLUCOSE *n*
GLUE, -D, -ING, -S, GLUIER, GLUIEST, GLUING *n, vb*
GLUEISH *same as* ▶ **gluish**
GLUEPOT *n*
GLUER, -S ▶ **glue**
GLUES ▶ **glue**
GLUEY ▶ **glue**
GLUG, -GED, -S *n, vb*
GLUIER ▶ **glue**
GLUIEST ▶ **glue**
GLUILY ▶ **glue**
GLUING ▶ **glue**
GLUISH *adj* having the properties of glue
GLUM, -MER *adj*
GLUME, -S *n* one of a pair of dry membranous bracts in grasses
GLUMLY ▶ **glum**
GLUMMER ▶ **glum**
GLUMPS *n* state of sulking
GLUMPY *adj* sullen
GLUMS *n* gloomy feelings
GLUNCH *vb* look sullen
GLUON, -S *n* hypothetical particle
GLURGE, -S *n* stories supposed to be true but often fabricated
GLUT, -S, -TED *n, vb*
GLUTAEI > **glutaeus**
GLUTCH *vb* swallow
GLUTE, -S *same as* ▶ **gluteus**
GLUTEAL ▶ **gluteus**
GLUTEI ▶ **gluteus**
GLUTEN, -S *n* protein found in cereal grain
GLUTES ▶ **glute**
GLUTEUS, GLUTEI *n* any of the three muscles of the buttock
GLUTS ▶ **glut**
GLUTTED ▶ **glut**
GLUTTON *n*
GLYCAN, -S *n* polysaccharide

GLYCIN, -S *same as* ▸ **glycine**
GLYCINE *n* nonessential amino acid
GLYCINS ▸ **glycin**
GLYCOL, -S *n* another name (not in technical usage) for a diol
GLYCOSE *n* any of various monosaccharides
GLYCYL, -S *n* radical of glycine
GLYPH, -S *n* carved channel or groove
GLYPHIC ▸ **glyph**
GLYPHS ▸ **glyph**
GLYPTAL *n* alkyd resin
GLYPTIC *adj* of or relating to engraving or carving
GNAMMA *variant of* ▸ **namma**
GNAR, -RED, -S *same as* ▸ **gnarl**
GNARL, -S *n, vb*
GNARLED *adj* rough, twisted, and knobbly
GNARLS ▸ **gnarl**
GNARLY *adj* good
GNARR, -S *same as* ▸ **gnarl**
GNARRED ▸ **gnar**
GNARRS ▸ **gnarr**
GNARS ▸ **gnar**
GNASH, -ED, -ES *vb, n*
GNASHER *n* tooth
GNASHES ▸ **gnash**
GNAT, -S *n*
GNATHAL *same as* ▸ **gnathic**
GNATHIC *adj* of or relating to the jaw
GNATS ▸ **gnat**
GNATTY *adj* infested with gnats
GNAW, -ED, -N, -S *vb* bite or chew steadily ▹ *n* act or an instance of gnawing
GNAWER, -S ▸ **gnaw**
GNAWING ▸ **gnaw**
GNAWN ▸ **gnaw**
GNAWS ▸ **gnaw**
GNEISS *n* coarse-grained metamorphic rock
GNOCCHI *n* dumplings
GNOME, GNOMAE, -S *n*
GNOMIC *adj* of pithy sayings
GNOMISH ▸ **gnome**
GNOMIST *n* writer of pithy sayings
GNOMON, -S *n* stationary arm on a sundial
GNOSIS, GNOSES *n* supposedly revealed knowledge of spiritual truths
GNOSTIC *adj* of, relating to, or possessing knowledge ▹ *n* one who knows
GNOW, -S *n* Australian wild bird
GNU, -S *n*
GO, GANE, GAUN, -ES, -NE, -S *vb, n*
GOA, -S *n* Tibetan gazelle
GOAD, -ED, -ING, -S *vb, n*
GOAF, -S *n* waste left in old mine workings
GOAL, -ED, -ING, -S *n, vb*
GOALIE, -S *n*
GOALING ▸ **goal**
GOALS ▸ **goal**
GOANNA, -S *n* large Australian lizard
GOARY *variant spelling of* ▸ **gory**
GOAS ▸ **goa**
GOAT, -S *n*
GOATEE, -S *n* pointed tuft-like beard
GOATEED ▸ **goatee**
GOATEES ▸ **goatee**
GOATIER ▸ **goaty**

This means more like a goat: it may seem a silly sort of word but because it uses such common letters the chance to play it as a bonus comes up very frequently.

GOATIES ▸ **goaty**
GOATISH *adj* of, like, or relating to a goat
GOATS ▸ **goat**
GOATSE, -S *n* deliberately offensive image placed maliciously into a website
GOATY, GOATIER, GOATIES *n* pointed tuft-like beard ▹ *adj* resembling a goat
GOB, -BED, -BING, -S *n, vb*
GOBAN, -S *n* board on which go is played
GOBANG, -S *n* Japanese board-game
GOBANS ▸ **goban**
GOBAR *adj* as in **gobar numeral** kind of numeral
GOBBED ▸ **gob**
GOBBET, -S *n* lump, esp of food
GOBBI ▸ **gobbo**
GOBBIER ▸ **gobby**
GOBBING ▸ **gob**
GOBBLE, -D, -S *vb, n, interj*

GOBBLER *n* turkey
GOBBLES ▶ **gobble**
GOBBO, GOBBI *n* hunchback
GOBBY, GOBBIER *adj* loudmouthed and offensive
GOBI, -S *n* (in Indian cookery) cauliflower
GOBIES ▶ **goby**
GOBIID, -S *n* small spiny-finned fish
GOBIOID *n* type of spiny-finned fish
GOBIS ▶ **gobi**
GOBLET, -S *n*
GOBLIN, -S *n*
GOBO, -ES, -S *n* shield placed around a microphone
GOBONEE *same as* ▶ **gobony**
GOBONY *adj* in heraldry, composed of a row of small, alternately coloured, squares
GOBOS ▶ **gobo**
GOBS ▶ **gob**
GOBURRA *n* kookaburra
GOBY, GOBIES *n* small spiny-finned fish
GOD, -DED, -DING, -S *n, vb*
GODDEN, -S *n* evening greeting
GODDESS *n*
GODDING ▶ **god**
GODET, -S *n* triangular piece of material inserted into a garment
GODETIA *n* plant with showy flowers
GODETS ▶ **godet**
GODHEAD *n* essential nature and condition of being a god
GODHOOD *n* state of being divine
GODLESS *adj*
GODLIER ▶ **godly**
GODLIKE *adj*
GODLILY ▶ **godly**
GODLING *n* little god
GODLY, GODLIER *adj* devout or pious
GODOWN, -S *n* (in East Asia and India) a warehouse
GODROON *same as* ▶ **gadroon**
GODS ▶ **god**
GODSEND *n*
GODSHIP *n* divinity
GODSO *same as* ▶ **gadso**
GODSON, -S *n* male godchild
GODWARD *adv* towards God
GODWIT, -S *n* shore bird with long legs and an upturned bill
GOE *same as* ▶ **go**
GOEL, -S *n* in Jewish law, a blood-avenger
GOER, -S *n* person who attends something regularly
GOES ▶ **go**
GOEST *vb* archaic 2nd person sing present of go
GOETH *vb* archaic 3rd person sing present of go
GOETIC ▶ **goety**
GOETY, GOETIES *n* witchcraft
GOEY, GOIER, GOIEST *adj* go-ahead
GOFER, -S *n* employee or assistant performing menial tasks
GOFF, -ED, -ING, -S *obsolete variant of* ▶ **golf**
GOFFER, -S *vb* press pleats into (a frill) ▷ *n* ornamental frill made by pressing pleats
GOFFING ▶ **goff**
GOFFS ▶ **goff**
GOGGA, -S *n* any small insect
GOGGLE, -D, -S *vb, n*
GOGGLER *n* big-eyed scad
GOGGLES ▶ **goggle**
GOGGLY ▶ **goggle**
GOGLET, -S *n* long-necked water-cooling vessel
GOGO, -S *n* disco
GOIER ▶ **goey**
GOIEST ▶ **goey**
GOING, -S ▶ **go**
GOITER, -S *same as* ▶ **goitre**
GOITRE, -S *n* swelling of the thyroid gland in the neck
GOITRED ▶ **goitre**
GOITRES ▶ **goitre**
GOJI, -S *same as* > **wolfberry**
GOLD, -ER, -EST, -S *n, adj*
GOLDBUG *n* American beetle with a bright metallic lustre
GOLDEN, -S *adj* made of gold ▷ *vb* gild
GOLDER ▶ **gold**
GOLDEST ▶ **gold**
GOLDEYE *n* N American fish
GOLDIER ▶ **goldy**
GOLDIES ▶ **goldy**

GOLDISH ▸ **gold**
GOLDS ▸ **gold**
GOLDY, GOLDIER, GOLDIES *adj* gold-like ▹ *n* goldfinch
GOLE, -S *obsolete spelling of* ▸ **goal**
GOLEM, -S *n* (in Jewish legend) artificially created human
GOLES ▸ **gole**
GOLF, -ED, -S *n, vb*
GOLFER, -S *n* person who plays golf
GOLFING ▸ **golf**
GOLFS ▸ **golf**
GOLIARD *n* one of a number of wandering scholars
GOLIAS *vb* behave outrageously
GOLIATH *n*
GOLLAN, -S *n* yellow flower
GOLLAND *same as* ▸ **gollan**
GOLLANS ▸ **gollan**
GOLLAR, -S *same as* ▸ **goller**
GOLLER, -S *vb* roar
GOLLIED ▸ **golly**
GOLLIES ▸ **golly**
GOLLOP, -S *vb* eat or drink (something) quickly or greedily
GOLLY, GOLLIED, GOLLIES *interj* exclamation of mild surprise ▹ *vb* spit
GOLOSH *same as* ▸ **galosh**
GOLOSHE *same as* ▸ **galosh**
GOLP, -S *same as* ▸ **golpe**
GOLPE, -S *n* in heraldry, a purple circle
GOLPS ▸ **golp**
GOMBEEN *n* usury
GOMBO, -S *same as* ▸ **gumbo**
GOMBRO, -S *same as* ▸ **gumbo**
GOMER, -S *n* unwanted hospital patient
GOMERAL *same as* ▸ **gomeril**
GOMEREL *same as* ▸ **gomeril**
GOMERIL *n* Scots word for a slow-witted person
GOMERS ▸ **gomer**
GOMOKU, -S *another word for* ▸ **gobang**
GOMPA, -S *n* Tibetan monastery
GOMUTI, -S *n* feather palm tree
GOMUTO, -S *same as* ▸ **gomuti**
GON, -S *n* geometrical grade
GONAD, -S *n* organ producing reproductive cells
GONADAL ▸ **gonad**
GONADIC ▸ **gonad**
GONADS ▸ **gonad**
GONCH, -ES *same as* ▸ **gitch**
GONDOLA *n*
GONE ▸ **go**
GONEF, -S *same as* ▸ **ganef**
GONER, -S *n* person or thing beyond help or recovery
GONG, -ED, -ING, -S *n, vb*
GONGYO, -S *n* Buddhist ceremony
GONIA ▸ **gonion**
GONIDIA > **gonidium**
GONIDIC > **gonidium**
GONIF, -S *same as* ▸ **ganef**
GONIFF, -S *same as* ▸ **ganef**
GONIFS ▸ **gonif**
GONION, GONIA *n* point or apex of the angle of the lower jaw
GONIUM *n* immature reproductive cell
GONK, -S *n* stuffed toy, often used as a mascot
GONNA *vb* going to
GONOF, -S *same as* ▸ **ganef**
GONOPH, -S *same as* ▸ **ganef**
GONOPOD *n* either of the reproductive organs of insects
GONS ▸ **gon**
GONYS, -ES *n* lower outline of a bird's bill
GONZO, -S *adj* wild or crazy ▹ *n* wild or crazy person
GOO, -S *n* sticky substance
GOOBER, -S *another name for* ▸ **peanut**
GOOBY, GOOBIES *n* spittle
GOOD, -S *adj, n*
GOODBY, -S *same as* ▸ **goodbye**
GOODBYE *n, interj, sentence substitute*
GOODBYS ▸ **goodby**
GOODIE *same as* ▸ **goody**
GOODIER ▸ **goody**
GOODIES ▸ **goody**
GOODISH ▸ **good**
GOODLY *adj* considerable

GOODMAN, GOODMEN *n* husband
GOODS ▶ **good**
GOODY, GOODIER, GOODIES *n* hero in a book or film ▷ *interj* child's exclamation of pleasure ▷ *adj* smug and sanctimonious
GOOEY, GOOIER, GOOIEST *adj* sticky and soft
GOOF, -ED, -ING, -S *n* mistake ▷ *vb* make a mistake
GOOFIER ▶ **goofy**
GOOFILY ▶ **goofy**
GOOFING ▶ **goof**
GOOFS ▶ **goof**
GOOFUS *n* slow-witted or stupid person
GOOFY, GOOFIER *adj*
GOOG, -S *n* egg
GOOGLE, -D, -S *vb* search on the internet using a search engine
GOOGLY *n* ball that spins unexpectedly on the bounce
GOOGOL, -S *n* number shown as one followed by 100 zeros
GOOGS ▶ **goog**
GOOIER ▶ **gooey**
GOOIEST ▶ **gooey**
GOOILY ▶ **gooey**
GOOK, -S *n* sticky, messy substance
GOOKIER ▶ **gooky**
GOOKS ▶ **gook**
GOOKY, GOOKIER *adj* sticky and messy
GOOL, -S *n* corn marigold
GOOLD, -S *Scots word for* ▶ **gold**
GOOLS ▶ **gool**
GOOMBAH *n* patron or mentor
GOOMBAY *n* Bahamian soft drink
GOON, -S *n* person hired to commit violent acts
GOONDA, -S *n* (in India) habitual criminal
GOONERY *n* behaviour typical of goons
GOONEY, -S *n* albatross
GOONIE, -S *Scots word for a* ▶ **gown**
GOONIER ▶ **goony**
GOONIES ▶ **goonie**
GOONS ▶ **goon**
GOONY, GOONIER ▶ **goon**
GOOP, -S *n* sticky or semiliquid substance
GOOPED *adj* as in **gooped up** sticky with goop
GOOPIER ▶ **goopy**
GOOPS ▶ **goop**
GOOPY, GOOPIER ▶ **goop**
GOOR, -S *same as* ▶ **gur**
GOORAL, -S *same as* ▶ **goral**
GOORIE, -S *same as* ▶ **kuri**
GOOROO, -S *same as* ▶ **guru**
GOORS ▶ **goor**
GOORY *same as* ▶ **kuri**
GOOS ▶ **goo**
GOOSE, GEESE, -D, -S, GOOSING *n, vb*
GOOSERY *n* place for keeping geese
GOOSES ▶ **goose**
GOOSEY, -S *same as* ▶ **goosy**
GOOSIER ▶ **goosy**
GOOSIES ▶ **goosy**
GOOSING ▶ **goose**
GOOSY, GOOSIER, GOOSIES *adj* of or like a goose ▷ *n* goose
GOPAK, -S *n* Russian peasant dance
GOPHER, -S *n* American burrowing rodent ▷ *vb* burrow
GOPIK, -S *n* money unit of Azerbaijan
GOPURA, -S *n* gateway tower of an Indian temple
GOPURAM *same as* ▶ **gopura**
GOPURAS ▶ **gopura**
GOR, -S *interj* God! ▷ *n* seagull
GORA, -S *n* (in Indian English) White or fair-skinned male
GORAL, -S *n* small S Asian goat antelope
GORAMY *same as* ▶ **gourami**
GORAS ▶ **gora**
GORCOCK *n* male of the red grouse
GORCROW *n* carrion crow
GORDITA *n* small thick tortilla
GORE, -D, -S *n, vb*
GORGE, -D, -S, GORGING *n, vb*
GORGER, -S ▶ **gorge**
GORGES ▶ **gorge**
GORGET, -S *n* collar-like piece of armour
GORGIA, -S *n* improvised sung passage
GORGING ▶ **gorge**

GORGIO, -S *n* word used by Roma people for a non-Roma
GORGON, -S *n* terrifying or repulsive woman
GORHEN, -S *n* female red grouse
GORI, -S *n* (in Indian English) white or fair-skinned female
GORIER ▶ **gory**
GORIEST ▶ **gory**
GORILLA *n* largest of the apes, found in Africa
GORILY ▶ **gory**
GORING, -S ▶ **gore**
GORIS ▶ **gori**
GORM, -ED, -ING, -S *n* foolish person ▷ *vb* understand
GORMAND *same as* > **gourmand**
GORMED ▶ **gorm**
GORMIER ▶ **gormy**
GORMING ▶ **gorm**
GORMS ▶ **gorm**
GORMY, GORMIER *adj* gormless
GORP, -ED, -ING, -S *same as* ▶ **gawp**
GORS ▶ **gor**
GORSE, -S *n*
GORSEDD *n* meeting held daily before an eisteddfod
GORSES ▶ **gorse**
GORSIER ▶ **gorsy**
GORSOON *n* young boy
GORSY, GORSIER ▶ **gorse**
GORY, GORIER, GORIEST *adj*
GOS ▶ **go**
GOSH *interj*
GOSHAWK *n* large hawk
GOSHT, -S *n* Indian meat dish
GOSLET, -S *n* pygmy goose
GOSLING *n*
GOSPEL, -S *n, adj, vb*
GOSPODA > **gospodin**
GOSPORT *n* aeroplane communication device
GOSS, -ED, -ING *vb* spit
GOSSAN, -S *n* oxidized portion of a mineral vein in rock
GOSSE, -S *variant of* ▶ **gorse**
GOSSED ▶ **goss**
GOSSES ▶ **gosse**
GOSSIB, -S *n* gossip
GOSSING ▶ **goss**
GOSSIP, -S *n, vb*
GOSSIPY *adj* tending to gossip
GOSSOON *n* young boy
GOSTER, -S *vb* laugh uncontrollably
GOT ▶ **get**
GOTCH, -ES *same as* ▶ **gitch**
GOTCHA, -S *adj* as in **gotcha lizard** Australian name for a crocodile
GOTCHES ▶ **gotch**
GOTH, -S *n* aficionado of goth music and fashion
GOTHIC, -S *adj* relating to a literary style characterized by gloom and the supernatural ▷ *n* family of heavy script typefaces
GOTHIER ▶ **gothy**
GOTHITE *same as* > **goethite**
GOTHS ▶ **goth**
GOTHY, GOTHIER *adj* characteristic of goth music and fashion
GOTTA *vb* got to
GOTTEN *a past participle of* ▶ **get**
GOUACHE *n* (painting using) watercolours mixed with glue
GOUGE, -D, -S, GOUGING *vb, n*
GOUGER, -S *n* person or tool that gouges
GOUGERE *n* choux pastry flavoured with cheese
GOUGERS ▶ **gouger**
GOUGES ▶ **gouge**
GOUGING ▶ **gouge**
GOUJON, -S *n* small strip of food
GOUK, -S *same as* ▶ **gowk**
GOULASH *n* rich stew seasoned with paprika
GOURA, -S *n* large, crested ground pigeon found in New Guinea
GOURAMI *n* large SE Asian labyrinth fish
GOURAS ▶ **goura**
GOURD, -S *n* fleshy fruit of a climbing plant
GOURDE, -S *n* standard monetary unit of Haiti
GOURDS ▶ **gourd**
GOURDY *adj* (of horses) swollen-legged
GOURMET *n*
GOUSTY *adj* dismal
GOUT, -S *n*
GOUTFLY *n* fly whose larvae infect crops
GOUTIER ▶ **gouty**
GOUTILY ▶ **gouty**
GOUTS ▶ **gout**

GOUTTE, -S *n* (in heraldry) the shape of a drop of liquid
GOUTY, GOUTIER *adj* having the disease gout
GOV, -S *n* boss
GOVERN, -S *vb, n*
GOVS ▶ **gov**
GOWAN, -S *n* any of various yellow or white field flowers
GOWANED ▶ **gowan**
GOWANS ▶ **gowan**
GOWANY ▶ **gowan**
GOWD, -ER, -EST, -S *Scots word for* ▶ **gold**
GOWF, -ED, -ING, -S *vb* strike
GOWFER, -S ▶ **gowf**
GOWFING ▶ **gowf**
GOWFS ▶ **gowf**
GOWK, -S *n* stupid person
GOWL, -ED, -ING, -S *n* substance in the corner of the eyes after sleep ▷ *vb* howl
GOWLAN, -S *same as* ▶ **gollan**
GOWLAND *same as* ▶ **gollan**
GOWLANS ▶ **gowlan**
GOWLED ▶ **gowl**
GOWLING ▶ **gowl**
GOWLS ▶ **gowl**
GOWN, -ED, -ING, -S *n* woman's long formal dress ▷ *vb* supply with or dress in a gown
GOWNBOY *n* foundationer schoolboy who wears a gown
GOWNED ▶ **gown**
GOWNING ▶ **gown**
GOWNMAN, GOWNMEN *n* professional person who wears a gown
GOWNS ▶ **gown**
GOWPEN, -S *n* pair of cupped hands
GOX, -ES *n* gaseous oxygen

Gox is gaseous oxygen, especially useful if you can use it to hit a bonus square.

GOYLE, -S *n* ravine
GOZZAN, -S *same as* ▶ **gossan**
GRAAL, -S *n* holy grail
GRAB, -BED, -S *vb, n*
GRABBER ▶ **grab**
GRABBLE *vb* scratch or feel about with the hands
GRABBY *adj* greedy or selfish
GRABEN, -S *n* elongated trough of land
GRABS ▶ **grab**
GRACE, -D, -S, GRACING *n* beauty and elegance ▷ *vb* honour
GRACILE *adj* gracefully thin or slender
GRACING ▶ **grace**
GRACKLE *n* American songbird with a dark iridescent plumage
GRAD, -S *n* graduate
GRADATE *vb* change or cause to change imperceptibly
GRADDAN *vb* dress corn
GRADE, -D, -S, GRADING *n, vb*
GRADELY *adj* fine
GRADER, -S *n* person or thing that grades
GRADES ▶ **grade**
GRADIN, -S *n* ledge above or behind an altar
GRADINE *same as* ▶ **gradin**
GRADING ▶ **grade**
GRADINO, GRADINI *n* work of art that decorates an altar gradin
GRADINS ▶ **gradin**
GRADS ▶ **grad**
GRADUAL *adj, n*
GRADUS *n* book of études or other musical exercises
GRAFF, -ED, -S *same as* ▶ **graft**
GRAFT, -ED, -S *n, vb*
GRAFTER ▶ **graft**
GRAFTS ▶ **graft**
GRAHAM, -S *n* cracker made of graham flour
GRAIL, -S *n*
GRAILE, -S *same as* ▶ **grail**
GRAILS ▶ **grail**
GRAIN, -ED, -S *n, vb*
GRAINE, -S *n* eggs of the silkworm
GRAINED ▶ **grain**
GRAINER ▶ **grain**
GRAINES ▶ **graine**
GRAINS ▶ **grain**
GRAINY *adj* resembling, full of, or composed of grain
GRAIP, -S *n* long-handled gardening fork
GRAITH, -S *vb* clothe
GRAKLE, -S *same as* ▶ **grackle**

GRAM, -S *n*
GRAMA, -S *n* type of grass
GRAMARY *same as* > **gramarye**
GRAMAS ▶ **grama**
GRAMASH *n* type of gaiter
GRAME, -S *n* sorrow
GRAMMA, -S *n* pasture grass of the South American plains
GRAMMAR *n* branch of linguistics
GRAMMAS ▶ **gramma**
GRAMME, -S *same as* ▶ **gram**
GRAMP, -S *n* grandfather
GRAMPA, -S *variant of* ▶ **grandpa**
GRAMPS ▶ **gramp**
GRAMPUS *n* dolphin-like mammal
GRAMPY *n* grandfather
GRAMS ▶ **gram**
GRAN, -S *n*
GRANA ▶ **granum**
GRANARY *n*
GRAND, -ER, -S *adj*, *n*
GRANDAD *n*
GRANDAM *n* archaic word for grandmother
GRANDE *feminine form of* ▶ **grand**
GRANDEE *n* Spanish nobleman of the highest rank
GRANDER ▶ **grand**
GRANDLY ▶ **grand**
GRANDMA *n*
GRANDPA *n*
GRANDS ▶ **grand**
GRANFER *n* grandfather
GRANGE, -S *n*
GRANGER *n* keeper or member of a grange
GRANGES ▶ **grange**
GRANITA *n* Italian iced drink
GRANITE *n*
GRANNAM *n* old woman
GRANNIE *same as* ▶ **granny**
GRANNOM *n* type of caddis fly used as a bait by anglers
GRANNY *n*, *vb*
GRANOLA *n* muesli-like breakfast cereal
GRANS ▶ **gran**
GRANT, -ED, -S *vb*, *n*
GRANTEE *n* person to whom a grant is made
GRANTER ▶ **grant**
GRANTOR *n* person who makes a grant
GRANTS ▶ **grant**
GRANULE *n* small grain
GRANUM, GRANA, -S *n* membrane layer in a chloroplast
GRAPE, -D, GRAPING *n*, *vb*
GRAPERY *n* building where grapes are grown
GRAPES *n* abnormal growth on the fetlock of a horse
GRAPEY ▶ **grape**
GRAPH, -ED, -S *n*, *vb*
GRAPHIC *adj*
GRAPHS ▶ **graph**
GRAPIER ▶ **grapy**
GRAPING ▶ **grape**
GRAPLE, -S *same as* ▶ **grapple**
GRAPLIN *same as* ▶ **grapnel**
GRAPNEL *n* device with several hooks
GRAPPA, -S *n* type of Italian brandy
GRAPPLE *vb*, *n*
GRAPY, GRAPIER ▶ **grape**
GRASP, -ED, -S *vb*, *n*
GRASPER ▶ **grasp**
GRASPS ▶ **grasp**
GRASS, -ED, -ES *n*, *vb*
GRASSER *n* police informant
GRASSES ▶ **grass**
GRASSUM *n* in Scots law, sum paid when taking a lease
GRASSY *adj* covered with, containing, or resembling grass
GRASTE *archaic past participle of* ▶ **grace**
GRAT ▶ **greet**
GRATE, -D, -S *vb*, *n*
GRATER, -S *n* tool with a sharp surface for grating food
GRATES ▶ **grate**
GRATIFY *vb*, *adj*
GRATIN, -S *n* crust of browned breadcrumbs
GRATINE *adj* cooked au gratin
GRATING *adj* harsh or rasping ▷ *n* framework of metal bars covering an opening
GRATINS ▶ **gratin**
GRATIS *adj*
GRAUNCH *vb* crush or destroy
GRAUPEL *n* soft hail or snow pellets
GRAV, -S *n* unit of acceleration
GRAVE, -D, -N, -S, -ST *n*, *adj*, *vb*, *adv*

GRAVEL, -S *n* mixture of small stones and coarse sand ▷ *vb* cover with gravel
GRAVELY ▶ **grave**
GRAVEN ▶ **grave**
GRAVER, -S *n* tool for engraving
GRAVES ▶ **grave**
GRAVEST ▶ **grave**
GRAVID *adj* pregnant
GRAVIDA *n* pregnant woman
GRAVIES ▶ **gravy**
GRAVING ▶ **grave**
GRAVIS *adj* as in **myasthenia gravis** chronic muscle-weakening disease
GRAVITY *n*
GRAVLAX *n* dry-cured salmon
GRAVS ▶ **grav**
GRAVURE *n* method of intaglio printing
GRAVY, GRAVIES *n*
GRAWLIX *n* sequence of symbols used in text to replace profanity
GRAY, -ED, -ER, -EST, -ING, -S *same as* ▶ **grey**
GRAYFLY *n* trumpet fly
GRAYHEN *n* female of the black grouse
GRAYING ▶ **gray**
GRAYISH ▶ **gray**
GRAYLAG *same as* ▶ **greylag**
GRAYLE, -S *n* holy grail
GRAYLY ▶ **gray**
GRAYOUT *n* impairment of vision due to lack of oxygen
GRAYS ▶ **gray**
GRAZE, -D, -S *vb, n*
GRAZER, -S ▶ **graze**
GRAZES ▶ **graze**
GRAZIER *n* person who feeds cattle for market
GRAZING *n* land on which grass for livestock is grown
GREASE, -D, -S *n, vb*
GREASER *n* mechanic, esp of motor vehicles
GREASES ▶ **grease**
GREASY *adj* covered with or containing grease ▷ *n* shearer
GREAT, -ER, -S *adj, n*
GREATEN *vb* make or become great
GREATER ▶ **great**
GREATLY ▶ **great**
GREATS ▶ **great**
GREAVE *n* piece of armour for the shin ▷ *vb* grieve
GREAVED ▶ **greave**
GREAVES *pl n* residue left after the rendering of tallow
GREBE, -S *n*
GREBO, -ES, -S *same as* ▶ **greebo**
GRECE, -S *n* flight of steps
GRECIAN *same as* ▶ **grece**
GRECISE *same as* > **graecize**
GRECIZE *same as* > **graecize**
GRECQUE *n* ornament of Greek origin
GREE, -ING, -S *n* superiority or victory ▷ *vb* come or cause to come to agreement or harmony
GREEBO, -S *n* unkempt or dirty-looking rock music fan
GREECE, -S *same as* ▶ **grece**
GREED, -S *n*
GREEDY *adj* having an excessive desire for something
GREEING ▶ **gree**
GREEK, -ED *vb* represent text as grey lines on a computer screen
GREEN, -ED, -S *adj, n, vb*
GREENER *n* recent immigrant
GREENIE *n* conservationist
GREENLY ▶ **green**
GREENS ▶ **green**
GREENTH *n* greenness
GREENY ▶ **green**
GREES ▶ **gree**
GREESE, -S *same as* ▶ **grece**
GREET, GRAT, -ED, -S, GRUTTEN *vb, n*
GREETE, -S *same as* ▶ **greet**
GREETED ▶ **greet**
GREETER *n* person who greets people
GREETES ▶ **greete**
GREETS ▶ **greet**
GREGALE *n* northeasterly wind occurring in the Mediterranean
GREGE, -D, -S, GREGING *vb* make heavy
GREGO, -S *n* short, thick jacket
GREIGE, -S *adj* (of a fabric or material) not yet dyed ▷ *n* unbleached or undyed cloth or yarn
GREIN, -ED, -S *vb* desire fervently

GREISEN *n* light-coloured metamorphic rock
GREISLY *same as* ▸ **grisly**
GREMIAL *n* cloth spread on the lap of a bishop during Mass
GREMLIN *n*
GREMMIE *n* young surfer
GREMMY *same as* ▸ **gremmie**
GREN, -NED, -S *same as* ▸ **grin**
GRENADE *n*
GRENNED ▸ **gren**
GRENS ▸ **gren**
GRESE, -S *same as* ▸ **grece**
GREVE, -S *same as* ▸ **greave**
GREW, -ED, -ING, -S *vb* shudder
GREX, -ES *n* group of plants
GREY, -ED, -ER, -EST, -S *adj, n, vb*
GREYHEN *n* female of the black grouse
GREYING ▸ **grey**
GREYISH ▸ **grey**
GREYLAG *n* large grey goose
GREYLY ▸ **grey**
GREYS ▸ **grey**
GRIBBLE *n* type of small marine crustacean
GRICE, -D, -S *vb* collect objects concerned with railways ▹ *n* object collected or place visited by a railway enthusiast
GRICER, -S ▸ **grice**
GRICES ▸ **grice**
GRICING ▸ **grice**
GRID, -DED, -S *n* network of horizontal and vertical lines, bars, etc ▹ *vb* form a grid pattern
GRIDDER *n* American football player
GRIDDLE *n, vb*
GRIDE, -D, -S, GRIDING *vb* grate or scrape harshly ▹ *n* harsh or piercing sound
GRIDS ▸ **grid**
GRIECE, -D, -S *same as* ▸ **grece**
GRIEF, -S *n*
GRIEFER *n* online gamer who spoils the game for others on purpose
GRIEFS ▸ **grief**
GRIESIE *same as* ▸ **grisy**
GRIESLY *same as* ▸ **grisy**
GRIESY *same as* ▸ **grisy**
GRIEVE, -D, -S *vb, n*
GRIEVER ▸ **grieve**
GRIEVES ▸ **grieve**
GRIFF, -S *n* information
GRIFFE, -S *n* carved ornament at the base of a column
GRIFFIN *n*
GRIFFON *same as* ▸ **griffin**
GRIFFS ▸ **griff**
GRIFT, -ED, -S *vb* swindle
GRIFTER ▸ **grift**
GRIFTS ▸ **grift**
GRIG, -GED, -S *n* young eel ▹ *vb* fish for grigs
GRIGRI, -S *n* African talisman, amulet, or charm
GRIGS ▸ **grig**
GRIKE, -S *n* fissure in rock
GRILL, -S *n, vb*
GRILLE, -S *n* grating over an opening
GRILLED *adj* cooked on a grill or gridiron
GRILLER ▸ **grill**
GRILLES ▸ **grille**
GRILLS ▸ **grill**
GRILSE, -S *n* salmon on its first return from the sea to fresh water
GRIM, -MER *adj*
GRIMACE *n, vb*
GRIME, -D, -S, GRIMING *n, vb*
GRIMIER ▸ **grimy**
GRIMILY ▸ **grime**
GRIMING ▸ **grime**
GRIMLY ▸ **grim**
GRIMMER ▸ **grim**
GRIMY, GRIMIER ▸ **grime**
GRIN, -NED, -S *vb, n*
GRINCH *n* person whose attitude has a dispiriting effect
GRIND, -S *vb, n*
GRINDED *obsolete past participle of* ▸ **grind**
GRINDER *n* device for grinding substances
GRINDS ▸ **grind**
GRINNED ▸ **grin**
GRINNER ▸ **grin**
GRINS ▸ **grin**
GRIOT, -S *n* (in W Africa) member of a caste recording tribal history
GRIP, -PED, -S *n, vb*
GRIPE, -D, -S *vb, n*
GRIPER, -S ▸ **gripe**
GRIPES ▸ **gripe**
GRIPEY, GRIPIER *adj* causing gripes

GRIPING *n* act of griping
GRIPLE *same as* ▸ **gripple**
GRIPMAN, GRIPMEN *n* cable-car operator
GRIPPE, -S *former name for* > **influenza**
GRIPPED ▸ **grip**
GRIPPER ▸ **grip**
GRIPPES ▸ **grippe**
GRIPPLE *adj* greedy ▹ *n* hook
GRIPPY *adj* having grip
GRIPS ▸ **grip**
GRIPT *archaic variant of* ▸ **gripped**
GRIPY *same as* ▸ **gripey**
GRIS *same as* ▸ **grece**
GRISE, -D, -S, GRISING *vb* shudder
GRISELY *same as* ▸ **grisly**
GRISES ▸ **grise**
GRISING ▸ **grise**
GRISKIN *n* lean part of a loin of pork
GRISLED *another word for* > **grizzled**
GRISLY *adj, n*
GRISON, -S *n* type of mammal
GRIST, -S *n*
GRISTER *n* device for grinding grain
GRISTLE *n* tough stringy animal tissue found in meat
GRISTLY ▸ **gristle**
GRISTS ▸ **grist**
GRISY *adj* grim
GRIT, -S, -TED *n, vb, adj*
GRITH, -S *n* security or peace guaranteed for a period of time
GRITS ▸ **grit**
GRITTED ▸ **grit**
GRITTER *n* vehicle that spreads grit on the roads
GRITTY *adj* courageous and tough
GRIVET, -S *n* E African monkey
GRIZ, -ZES *n* grizzly bear
GRIZE, -S *same as* ▸ **grece**
GRIZZES ▸ **griz**
GRIZZLE *vb* whine or complain ▹ *n* grey colour
GRIZZLY *n, adj*
GROAN, -ED, -S *n, vb*
GROANER *n* person or thing that groans
GROANS ▸ **groan**
GROAT *n* fourpenny piece
GROATS *pl n* hulled and crushed grain of various cereals
GROCER, -S *n*
GROCERY *n* business or premises of a grocer
GROCKED *same as* ▸ **grokked**
GROCKLE *n* tourist in SW England
GRODY, GRODIER *adj* unpleasant
GROG, -GED, -S *n, vb*
GROGGY *adj* faint, shaky, or dizzy
GROGRAM *n* coarse fabric
GROGS ▸ **grog**
GROIN, -ED, -S *n* place where the legs join the abdomen ▹ *vb* construct with curved arrises
GROK, -ED, -ING, -KED, -S *vb* understand completely and intuitively
GROMA, -S *n* Roman surveying instrument
GROMET, -S *same as* ▸ **grommet**
GROMMET *n* ring or eyelet
GRONE, -D, -S, GRONING *obsolete word for* ▸ **groan**
GROOF, -S *n* face, or front of the body
GROOLY *adj* gruesome
GROOM, -ED, -S *n, vb*
GROOMER ▸ **groom**
GROOMS ▸ **groom**
GROOVE, -D, -S *n*
GROOVER *n* device that makes grooves
GROOVES ▸ **groove**
GROOVY *adj* attractive or exciting
GROPE, -D, -S, GROPING *vb, n*
GROPER, -S *n* type of large fish of warm and tropical seas
GROPES ▸ **grope**
GROPING ▸ **grope**
GROSER, -S *n* gooseberry
GROSERT *another word for* ▸ **groser**
GROSET, -S *another word for* ▸ **groser**
GROSS, -ED, -ES *adj, n, vb, interj*
GROSSER ▸ **gross**
GROSSES ▸ **gross**
GROSSLY ▸ **gross**
GROSZ, -E, -Y *n* Polish monetary unit
GROT, -S *n* rubbish
GROTTO, -S *n*
GROTTY *adj*

GROUCH *vb* grumble or complain ▷ *n* person who is always complaining
GROUCHY *adj* bad-tempered
GROUF, -S *same as* ▶ **groof**
GROUGH, -S *n* natural channel or fissure in a peat moor
GROUND, -S *n, adj, vb*
GROUP, -ED, -S *n, vb*
GROUPER *n* large edible sea fish
GROUPIE *n* ardent fan of a celebrity or of a sport or activity
GROUPS ▶ **group**
GROUPY *same as* ▶ **groupie**
GROUSE, -D, -S *n, vb, adj*
GROUSER ▶ **grouse**
GROUSES ▶ **grouse**
GROUT, -ED *n, vb*
GROUTER ▶ **grout**
GROUTS *pl n* sediment or grounds
GROUTY *adj* sullen or surly
GROVE, -S *n*
GROVED ▶ **grove**
GROVEL, -S *vb*
GROVES ▶ **grove**
GROVET, -S *n* wrestling hold
GROVY, GROVIER *adj* like a grove
GROW, -N, -S *vb*
GROWER, -S *n* person who grows plants
GROWING ▶ **grow**
GROWL, -ED, -S *vb, n*
GROWLER *n* person, animal, or thing that growls
GROWLS ▶ **growl**
GROWLY ▶ **growl**
GROWN ▶ **grow**
GROWNUP *n*
GROWS ▶ **grow**
GROWTH, -S *n, adj*
GROWTHY *adj* rapid-growing
GROYNE, -S *n* wall built out from the shore to control erosion
GROZING *adj* as in **grozing iron** iron for smoothing joints between lead pipes
GRR *interj* expressing anger or annoyance
GRRL, -S *n* as in **riot grrl** young woman who enjoys feminist punk rock

This slang term for a young woman who likes feminist punk can come in useful when you are short of vowels. And it can also be spelt **grrrl**.

GRRRL, -S *same as* ▶ **grrl**
GRUB, -BED, -S *n, vb*
GRUBBER *n* person who grubs
GRUBBLE *same as* ▶ **grabble**
GRUBBY *adj* dirty
GRUBS ▶ **grub**
GRUDGE, -D, -S *vb, n, adj*
GRUDGER ▶ **grudge**
GRUDGES ▶ **grudge**
GRUE, -D, -ING, -S, GRUING *n* shiver or shudder ▷ *vb* shiver or shudder
GRUEL, -ED, -S *n, vb*
GRUELER ▶ **gruel**
GRUELS ▶ **gruel**
GRUES ▶ **grue**
GRUFE, -S *same as* ▶ **groof**
GRUFF, -ED, -ER, -S *adj, vb*
GRUFFLY ▶ **gruff**
GRUFFS ▶ **gruff**
GRUFFY *adj* gruff
GRUFTED *adj* dirty
GRUGRU, -S *n* tropical American palm
GRUING ▶ **grue**
GRUM, -MER *adj* surly
GRUMBLE *vb, n*
GRUMBLY ▶ **grumble**
GRUME, -S *n* clot
GRUMLY ▶ **grum**
GRUMMER ▶ **grum**
GRUMMET *same as* ▶ **grommet**
GRUMOSE *same as* ▶ **grumous**
GRUMOUS *adj* (esp of plant parts) consisting of granular tissue
GRUMP, -ED, -S *n* surly or bad-tempered person ▷ *vb* complain or grumble
GRUMPH, -S *vb* grunt
GRUMPHY *same as* > **grumphie**
GRUMPS ▶ **grump**
GRUMPY *adj* bad-tempered ▷ *n* bad-tempered person
GRUND *n* as in **grund mail** payment for right of burial
GRUNGE, -S *n* style of rock music with a distorted guitar sound
GRUNGER *n* fan of grunge music
GRUNGES ▶ **grunge**

GRUNGEY *adj* messy or dirty
GRUNGY *adj* messy or dirty
GRUNION *n* Californian marine fish that spawns on beaches
GRUNT, -ED, -S *vb, n*
GRUNTER *n* person or animal that grunts, esp a pig
GRUNTLE *vb* grunt or groan
GRUNTS ▸ **grunt**
GRUSHIE *adj* healthy and strong
GRUTCH *vb* grudge
GRUTTEN ▸ **greet**
GRUYERE *n* hard flat whole-milk cheese with holes
GRYCE, -S *same as* ▸ **grice**
GRYDE, -D, -S, GRYDING *same as* ▸ **gride**
GRYESY *adj* grey
GRYFON, -S *same as* ▸ **griffin**
GRYKE, -S *same as* ▸ **grike**
GRYPE, -S *same as* ▸ **gripe**
GRYPHON *same as* ▸ **griffin**
GRYPT *archaic form of* ▸ **gripped**
GRYSBOK *n* small antelope
GRYSELY *same as* ▸ **grisly**
GRYSIE *same as* ▸ **grisy**
GU, -S *same as* ▸ **gju**
GUACO, -S *n* any of several plants used as an antidote to snakebite
GUAIAC, -S *same as* > **guaiacum**
GUAN, -S *n* type of bird of Central and S America
GUANA, -S *another word for* ▸ **iguana**
GUANACO *n* S American animal related to the llama
GUANAS ▸ **guana**
GUANASE *n* type of enzyme
GUANAY, -S *n* type of cormorant
GUANGO, -S *n* rain tree
GUANIN, -S *same as* ▸ **guanine**
GUANINE *n* white almost insoluble compound
GUANINS ▸ **guanin**
GUANO, -S *n* dried sea-bird manure
GUANS ▸ **guan**
GUANXI, -S *n* Chinese social concept
GUAR, -S *n* Indian plant
GUARANA *n* type of shrub native to Venezuela
GUARANI *n* standard monetary unit of Paraguay
GUARD, -S *vb, n*
GUARDED *adj* cautious or noncommittal
GUARDEE *n* guardsman
GUARDER ▸ **guard**
GUARDS ▸ **guard**
GUARISH *vb* heal
GUARS ▸ **guar**
GUAVA, -S *n*
GUAYULE *n* bushy shrub of the southwestern US
GUB, -BED, -BING, -S *n* Scots word for mouth ▹ *vb* hit or defeat
GUBBAH, -S *same as* ▸ **gub**
GUBBED ▸ **gub**
GUBBING ▸ **gub**
GUBBINS *n* object of little or no value
GUBS ▸ **gub**
GUCK, -S *n* slimy matter
GUCKIER ▸ **gucky**
GUCKS ▸ **guck**
GUCKY, GUCKIER *adj* slimy and mucky
GUDDLE, -D, -S *vb* catch (fish) with the hands ▹ *n* muddle
GUDE *Scots word for* ▸ **good**
GUDEMAN, GUDEMEN *n* male householder
GUDES *n* goods
GUDGEON *n* small freshwater fish ▹ *vb* trick or cheat
GUE, -S *same as* ▸ **gju**
GUELDER *adj* as in **guelder rose** kind of shrub
GUENON, -S *n* slender Old World monkey
GUERDON *n* reward or payment ▹ *vb* give a guerdon to
GUEREZA *n* handsome colobus monkey
GUERITE *n* turret used by a sentry
GUES ▸ **gue**
GUESS, -ED, -ES *vb, n*
GUESSER ▸ **guess**
GUESSES ▸ **guess**
GUEST, -ED, -S *n, vb*
GUESTEN *vb* stay as a guest in someone's house

GUESTS ▶ **guest**
GUFF, -S *n* nonsense
GUFFAW, -S *n, vb*
GUFFIE, -S *Scots word for* ▶ **pig**
GUFFS ▶ **guff**
GUGA, -S *n* gannet chick
GUGGLE, -D, -S *vb* drink making a gurgling sound
GUGLET, -S *same as* ▶ **goglet**
GUICHET *n* grating, hatch, or small opening in a wall
GUID *Scot word for* ▶ **good**
GUIDAGE *n* guidance
GUIDE, -D, -S *n, vb*
GUIDER, -S ▶ **guide**
GUIDES ▶ **guide**
GUIDING ▶ **guide**
GUIDON, -S *n* small pennant
GUIDS *pl n* Scots word for possessions
GUILD, -S *n*
GUILDER *n* former monetary unit of the Netherlands
GUILDRY *n* in Scotland, corporation of merchants
GUILDS ▶ **guild**
GUILE, -D, -S, GUILING *n, vb*
GUILER, -S *n* deceiver
GUILES ▶ **guile**
GUILING ▶ **guile**
GUILT, -ED, -S *n, vb*
GUILTY *adj* responsible for an offence or misdeed
GUIMP, -S *same as* ▶ **guimpe**
GUIMPE, -D, -S *n* short blouse worn under a pinafore dress ▷ *vb* make with gimp
GUIMPS ▶ **guimp**
GUINEA, -S *n*
GUINEP, -S *n* type of tropical American tree
GUIPURE *n* heavy lace
GUIRO, -S *n* percussion instrument made from a hollow gourd
GUISARD *n* guiser
GUISE, -D, -S *n, vb*
GUISER, -S *n* mummer, esp at Christmas or Halloween revels
GUISES ▶ **guise**
GUISING ▶ **guise**
GUITAR, -S *n*
GUIZER, -S *same as* ▶ **guiser**
GUL, -S *n* design used in Turkoman carpets
GULA, -S *n* gluttony
GULAG, -S *n* forced-labour camp
GULAR, -S *adj* of or situated in the throat or oesophagus ▷ *n* throat or oesophagus
GULAS ▶ **gula**
GULCH, -ED, -ES *n* deep narrow valley ▷ *vb* swallow fast
GULDEN, -S *same as* ▶ **guilder**
GULE *Scots word for* > **marigold**
GULES *n* red in heraldry
GULET, -S *n* wooden Turkish sailing boat
GULF, -ED, -ING, -S *n, vb*
GULFIER ▶ **gulfy**
GULFING ▶ **gulf**
GULFS ▶ **gulf**
GULFY, GULFIER ▶ **gulf**
GULL, -ED, -ING, -S *n, vb*
GULLER, -S *n* deceiver
GULLERY *n* breeding-place for gulls
GULLET, -S *n*
GULLEY, -S *same as* ▶ **gully**
GULLIED ▶ **gully**
GULLIES ▶ **gully**
GULLING ▶ **gull**
GULLISH *adj* stupid
GULLS ▶ **gull**
GULLY, GULLIED, GULLIES *n, vb*
GULP, -ED, -ING, -S *vb, n*
GULPER, -S ▶ **gulp**
GULPH, -S *archaic word for* ▶ **gulf**
GULPIER ▶ **gulpy**
GULPING ▶ **gulp**
GULPS ▶ **gulp**
GULPY, GULPIER ▶ **gulp**
GULS ▶ **gul**
GULY *adj* relating to gules
GUM, -MED, -S *n, vb*
GUMBALL *n* round piece of chewing gum
GUMBO, -S *n* soup or stew thickened with okra pods
GUMBOIL *n* abscess on the gum
GUMBOOT *n*
GUMBOS ▶ **gumbo**
GUMDROP *n*
GUMLESS ▶ **gum**
GUMLIKE ▶ **gum**
GUMLINE *n* line where gums meet teeth
GUMMA, -S, -TA *n* rubbery tumour
GUMMED ▶ **gum**
GUMMER, -S *n* punch-cutting tool

GUMMI, -S *n* gelatin-based flavoured sweet
GUMMIER ▶ **gummy**
GUMMIES ▶ **gummy**
GUMMILY ▶ **gummy**
GUMMING ▶ **gum**
GUMMIS ▶ **gummi**
GUMMITE *n* orange or yellowish amorphous secondary mineral
GUMMOSE *same as* ▶ **gummous**
GUMMOUS *adj* resembling or consisting of gum
GUMMY, GUMMIER, GUMMIES *adj* toothless ▷ *n* type of small crustacean-eating shark
GUMNUT, -S *n* hardened seed container of the gumtree
GUMP, -ED, -ING, -S *vb* guddle
GUMS ▶ **gum**
GUMSHOE *n* waterproof overshoe ▷ *vb* act stealthily
GUMTREE *n* any of various trees that yield gum
GUMWEED *n* any of several yellow-flowered plants
GUMWOOD *same as* ▶ **gumtree**
GUN, -NED, -NEN, -S *n, vb*
GUNBOAT *n*
GUNDIES ▶ **gundy**
GUNDOG, -S *n*
GUNDY, GUNDIES *n* toffee
GUNFIRE *n*
GUNG *adj* as in **gung ho** extremely or excessively enthusiastic about something
GUNGE, -D, -S, GUNGING *n, vb*
GUNGIER ▶ **gungy**
GUNGING ▶ **gunge**
GUNGY, GUNGIER ▶ **gunge**
GUNITE, -S *n* mortar sprayed in a very dense concrete layer
GUNK, -ED, -ING, -S *n* slimy or filthy substance ▷ *vb* cover with gunk
GUNKIER ▶ **gunky**
GUNKING ▶ **gunk**
GUNKS ▶ **gunk**
GUNKY, GUNKIER ▶ **gunk**
GUNLESS ▶ **gun**
GUNLOCK *n* mechanism in some firearms
GUNMAN, GUNMEN *n*
GUNNAGE *n* number of guns carried by a warship
GUNNED ▶ **gun**
GUNNEL, -S *same as* ▶ **gunwale**
GUNNEN ▶ **gun**
GUNNER, -S *n*
GUNNERA *n* type of herbaceous plant
GUNNERS ▶ **gunner**
GUNNERY *n* use or science of large guns
GUNNIES ▶ **gunny**
GUNNING ▶ **gun**
GUNNY, GUNNIES *n* strong coarse fabric used for sacks
GUNPLAY *n* use of firearms, as by criminals
GUNPORT *n* porthole or other opening for a gun
GUNROOM *n* room where guns are stored
GUNS ▶ **gun**
GUNSEL, -S *n* criminal who carries a gun
GUNSHIP *n*
GUNSHOT *n*
GUNTER, -S *n* type of gaffing
GUNWALE *n* top of a ship's side
GUNYAH, -S *n* hut or shelter in the bush
GUP, -S *n* gossip
GUPPY, GUPPIES *n* small colourful aquarium fish
GUPS ▶ **gup**
GUQIN, -S *n* type of Chinese zither
GUR, -S *n* unrefined cane sugar
GURAMI, -S *same as* ▶ **gourami**
GURDY, GURDIES *n* winch on a fishing boat
GURGE, -D, -S, GURGING *vb* swallow up
GURGLE, -D, -S *n* bubbling noise ▷ *vb* (of water) to make low bubbling noises when flowing
GURGLET *same as* ▶ **goglet**
GURGLY *adj* making gurgling sounds
GURJUN, -S *n* S or SE Asian tree that yields a resin

GURL, -ED, -ING, -S *vb* snarl
GURLET, -S *n* type of pickaxe
GURLIER ▶ **gurly**
GURLING ▶ **gurl**
GURLS ▶ **gurl**
GURLY, GURLIER *adj* stormy
GURN, -ED, -ING, -S *variant spelling of* ▶ **girn**
GURNARD *n* spiny armour-headed sea fish
GURNED ▶ **gurn**
GURNET, -S *same as* ▶ **gurnard**
GURNEY, -S *n* wheeled stretcher for transporting hospital patients
GURNING ▶ **gurn**
GURNS ▶ **gurn**
GURRAH, -S *n* type of coarse muslin
GURRIER *n* tough, ill-mannered person
GURRY, GURRIES *n* dog-fight
GURS ▶ **gur**
GURSH, -ES *n* unit of currency in Saudi Arabia
GURU, -S *n*
GURUDOM *n* state of being a guru
GURUISM ▶ **guru**
GURUS ▶ **guru**
GUS ▶ **gu**
GUSH, -ED, -ES, -ING *vb, n*
GUSHER, -S *n* spurting oil well
GUSHES ▶ **gush**
GUSHIER ▶ **gushy**
GUSHILY ▶ **gushy**
GUSHING ▶ **gush**
GUSHY, GUSHIER *adj* displaying excessive sentimentality
GUSLA, -S *n* Balkan single-stringed musical instrument
GUSLAR, -S *n* player of the gusla
GUSLAS ▶ **gusla**
GUSLE, -S *same as* ▶ **gusla**
GUSLI, -S *n* Russian harp-like musical instrument
GUSSET, -S *n* piece of material sewn into a garment to strengthen it ▷ *vb* put a gusset in (a garment)
GUSSIE *n* young pig
GUSSY, GUSSIED, GUSSIES *vb* dress elaborately
GUST, -ED, -ING, -S *n, vb*
GUSTFUL *adj* tasty
GUSTIE *adj* tasty
GUSTIER ▶ **gusty**
GUSTILY ▶ **gusty**
GUSTING ▶ **gust**
GUSTO, -ES, -S *n*
GUSTS ▶ **gust**
GUSTY, GUSTIER *adj* windy and blustery
GUT, -TED, -TING *n, vb, adj*
GUTCHER *n* grandfather
GUTFUL, -S *n* bellyful
GUTLESS *adj*
GUTLIKE ▶ **gut**
GUTROT, -S *n* upset stomach
GUTS, -ED, -ES, -ING *vb* devour greedily
GUTSER, -S *n* as in **come a gutser** fall heavily to the ground
GUTSES ▶ **guts**
GUTSFUL *n* bellyful
GUTSIER ▶ **gutsy**
GUTSILY ▶ **gutsy**
GUTSING ▶ **guts**
GUTSY, GUTSIER *adj* courageous
GUTTA, -E, -S *n* small drop-like ornament
GUTTATE *adj* covered with small drops or drop-like markings ▷ *vb* exude droplets of liquid
GUTTED ▶ **gut**
GUTTER, -S *n, vb*
GUTTERY *adj* vulgar
GUTTIER ▶ **gutty**
GUTTIES ▶ **gutty**
GUTTING ▶ **gut**
GUTTLE, -D, -S *vb* eat greedily
GUTTLER ▶ **guttle**
GUTTLES ▶ **guttle**
GUTTY, GUTTIER, GUTTIES *n* urchin or delinquent ▷ *adj* courageous
GUTZER, -S *n* bad fall
GUV, -S *informal name for* > **governor**
GUY, -ED, -ING, -S *n, vb*
GUYLE, -D, -S, GUYLING *same as* ▶ **guile**
GUYLER, -S ▶ **guyle**
GUYLES ▶ **guyle**
GUYLINE *n* guy rope
GUYLING ▶ **guyle**
GUYOT, -S *n* flat-topped submarine mountain
GUYS ▶ **guy**
GUYSE, -S *same as* ▶ **guise**
GUZZLE, -D, -S *vb*
GUZZLER *n* person or thing that guzzles

GUZZLES ▶ **guzzle**
GWEDUC, -S *same as* ▶ **geoduck**
GWEDUCK *same as* ▶ **geoduck**
GWEDUCS ▶ **gweduc**
GWINE *dialect form of* ▶ **going**
GWINIAD *n* type of freshwater white fish
GWYNIAD *n* type of freshwater white fish
GYAL, -S *same as* ▶ **gayal**
GYAN, -S *n* (in Indian English) knowledge
GYBE, -D, -S, GYBING *vb* (of a sail) swing suddenly from one side to the other ▷ *n* instance of gybing
GYELD, -S *old form of* ▶ **guild**
GYLDEN *old form of* ▶ **golden**
GYM, -S *n*
GYMBAL, -S *same as* ▶ **gimbal**
GYMMAL, -S *same as* ▶ **gimmal**
GYMNAST *n*
GYMNIC *adj* gymnastic
GYMP, -ED, -ING, -S *same as* ▶ **gimp**
GYMPIE, -S *n* tall tree with stinging hairs on its leaves
GYMPING ▶ **gymp**
GYMPS ▶ **gymp**
GYMS ▶ **gym**
GYMSLIP *n* tunic or pinafore formerly worn by schoolgirls
GYMSUIT *n* costume worn for gymnastics
GYNAE, -S *adj* gynaecological ▷ *n* gynaecology
GYNECIA > **gynecium**
GYNECIC *adj* relating to the female sex
GYNIE, -S *n* gynaecology
GYNNEY, -S *n* guinea hen
GYNNY, GYNNIES *same as* ▶ **gynney**
GYNO, -S *n* gynaecologist
GYNY *n* gynaecology
GYOZA, -S *n* Japanese fried dumpling
GYP, -S *n* slang word for severe pain

This little word, meaning severe pain, can be useful when you are short of vowels.

GYPLURE *n* synthetic version of a gypsy moth pheromone
GYPO, -S *n* small-scale independent logger
GYPPIE *same as* ▶ **gippy**
GYPPY, GYPPIES *same as* ▶ **gippy**
GYPS ▶ **gyp**
GYPSIED ▶ **gypsy**
GYPSIES ▶ **gypsy**
GYPSUM, -S *n* chalklike mineral
GYPSY, GYPSIED, GYPSIES *n, vb*
GYRAL *adj* having a circular, spiral, or rotating motion
GYRALLY ▶ **gyral**
GYRANT *adj* gyrating
GYRASE, -S *n* topoisomerase enzyme
GYRATE, -D, -S *vb* rotate or spiral about a point or axis ▷ *adj* curved or coiled into a circle
GYRATOR *n* electronic circuit that inverts the impedance
GYRE, -D, -S, GYRING *n* circular or spiral movement or path ▷ *vb* whirl
GYRENE, -S *n* nickname for a member of the US Marine Corps
GYRES ▶ **gyre**
GYRI ▶ **gyrus**
GYRING ▶ **gyre**
GYRO, -S *n* gyrocompass
GYROCAR *n* two-wheeled car
GYRON, -S *same as* ▶ **giron**
GYRONIC ▶ **gyron**
GYRONNY *same as* ▶ **gironny**
GYRONS ▶ **gyron**
GYROS ▶ **gyro**
GYROSE *adj* marked with sinuous lines
GYROUS *adj* marked with sinuous lines
GYRUS, GYRI, -ES *n* convolution
GYTE, -S *n* Scots word for a spoilt child
GYTRASH *n* spirit that haunts lonely roads
GYTTJA, -S *n* sediment on a lake bottom
GYVE, -D, -S, GYVING *vb* shackle or fetter ▷ *n* fetter

Hh

HA *interj* exclamation of triumph, surprise, or scorn
HAAF, -S *n* fishing ground off the Shetland and Orkney Islands
HAAR, -S *n* cold sea mist or fog off the North Sea
HABDABS *n* highly nervous state
HABILE *adj* skilful
HABIT, -S *n, vb*
HABITAN *same as* > **habitant**
HABITAT *n*
HABITED *adj* dressed in a habit
HABITS ▶ **habit**
HABITUE *n* frequent visitor to a place
HABITUS *n* general physical state
HABLE *old form of* ▶ **able**
HABOOB, -S *n* sandstorm
HABU, -S *n* large venomous snake
HACEK, -S *n* pronunciation symbol in Slavonic language
HACHIS *n* hash (the dish)
HACHURE *n* shading drawn on a map to indicate steepness of a hill ▷ *vb* mark or show by hachures
HACK, -ED, -S *vb, n, adj*
HACKBUT *another word for* > **arquebus**
HACKED ▶ **hack**
HACKEE, -S *n* chipmunk
HACKER, -S *n* computer enthusiast
HACKERY *n* journalism
HACKIE, -S *n* US word meaning cab driver
HACKING ▶ **hack**
HACKLE, -D *same as* ▶ **heckle**
HACKLER ▶ **hackle**
HACKLES *pl n* hairs which rise in response to emotion
HACKLET *n* kittiwake
HACKLY *adj* rough or jagged
HACKMAN, HACKMEN *n* taxi driver
HACKNEY *n* taxi ▷ *vb* make commonplace and banal by too frequent use
HACKS ▶ **hack**
HACKSAW *n, vb*
HAD, -DEN, -DING, -S *vb* Scots form of hold
HADAL *adj* denoting very deep zones of the oceans
HADARIM ▶ **heder**
HADAWAY *sentence substitute* exclamation urging the hearer to refrain from delay
HADDEN ▶ **had**
HADDEST *same as* ▶ **hadst**
HADDIE, -S *n* finnan haddock
HADDING ▶ **had**
HADDOCK *n*
HADE, -D, -S, HADING *n* angle made to the vertical by the plane of a fault or vein ▷ *vb* incline from the vertical
HADEDAH *n* large grey-green S African ibis
HADES ▶ **hade**
HADING ▶ **hade**
HADITH, -S *n* body of tradition about Muhammad and his followers
HADJ, -ES *same as* ▶ **hajj**
HADJEE, -S *same as* ▶ **hadji**
HADJES ▶ **hadj**
HADJI, -S *same as* ▶ **hajji**
HADROME *n* part of xylem
HADRON, -S *n* type of elementary particle
HADS ▶ **had**

HADST *singular form of the past tense (indicative mood) of* ▸ **have**
HAE, -D, -ING, -N, -S *Scot variant of* ▸ **have**
HAEM, -S *n* red organic pigment containing ferrous iron
HAEMAL *adj* of the blood
HAEMIC *same as* > **haematic**
HAEMIN, -S *n* haematin chloride
HAEMOID *same as* > **haematoid**
HAEMONY *n* plant mentioned in Milton's poetry
HAEMS ▸ **haem**
HAEN ▸ **hae**
HAERES *same as* ▸ **heres**
HAES ▸ **hae**
HAET, -S *n* whit
HAFF, -S *n* lagoon
HAFFET, -S *n* side of head
HAFFIT, -S *same as* ▸ **haffet**
HAFFLIN *same as* > **halfling**
HAFFS ▸ **haff**
HAFIZ, -ES *n* title for a person who knows the Koran by heart
HAFNIUM *n* metallic element found in zirconium ores
HAFT, -ED, -ING, -S *n* handle of an axe, knife, or dagger ▹ *vb* provide with a haft
HAFTARA *same as* > **haftarah**
HAFTED ▸ **haft**
HAFTER, -S ▸ **haft**
HAFTING ▸ **haft**
HAFTS ▸ **haft**
HAG, -GED, -GING, -S *n, vb*
HAGADIC *same as* > **haggadic**
HAGBOLT *same as* > **hackbolt**
HAGBORN *adj* born of a witch
HAGBUSH *same as* > **arquebus**
HAGBUT, -S *same as* > **arquebus**
HAGDEN, -S *same as* > **hackbolt**
HAGDON, -S *same as* > **hackbolt**
HAGDOWN *same as* > **hackbolt**
HAGFISH *n* any of various primitive eel-like vertebrates
HAGG, -S *n* boggy place
HAGGADA *same as* > **haggadah**
HAGGARD *adj, n*
HAGGED ▸ **hag**
HAGGING ▸ **hag**
HAGGIS *n*
HAGGISH ▸ **hag**
HAGGLE, -D, -S *vb*
HAGGLER ▸ **haggle**
HAGGLES ▸ **haggle**
HAGGS ▸ **hagg**
HAGLET, -S *same as* ▸ **hacklet**
HAGLIKE ▸ **hag**
HAGRIDE, HAGRODE *vb* torment or obsess
HAGS ▸ **hag**
HAH, -S *same as* ▸ **ha**
HAHA, -S *n* wall or other boundary marker that is set in a ditch
HAHNIUM *n* transuranic element
HAHS ▸ **hah**
HAICK, -S *same as* ▸ **haik**
HAIDUK, -S *n* rural brigand
HAIK, -A, -S *n* Arab's outer garment
HAIKAI *same as* ▸ **haiku**
HAIKS ▸ **haik**
HAIKU, -S *n* Japanese verse form in 17 syllables
HAIL, -ED, -ING, -S *n, vb, sentence substitute*
HAILER, -S ▸ **hail**
HAILIER ▸ **haily**
HAILING ▸ **hail**
HAILS ▸ **hail**
HAILY, HAILIER ▸ **hail**
HAIMISH *same as* ▸ **heimish**
HAIN, -ED, -S *vb* Scots word meaning save
HAINCH *Scots form of* ▸ **haunch**
HAINED ▸ **hain**
HAINING ▸ **hain**
HAINS ▸ **hain**
HAINT, -S *same as* ▸ **haunt**
HAIQUE, -S *same as* ▸ **haik**
HAIR, -ING, -S *n, vb*
HAIRCAP *n* type of moss
HAIRCUT *n*
HAIRDO, -S *n*
HAIRED *adj* with hair
HAIRIER ▸ **hairy**
HAIRIF, -S *another name for* > **cleavers**
HAIRILY *adv* in a hairy manner
HAIRING ▸ **hair**
HAIRNET *n*
HAIRPIN *n*
HAIRS ▸ **hair**
HAIRST, -S *Scots form of* ▸ **harvest**

HAIRY, HAIRIER *adj* covered with hair
HAITH *interj* Scots oath
HAJ, -ES *same as* ▸ **hadj**

A **haj** is a Muslim pilgrimage to Mecca, and one of the key words to remember for using the J. It can also be spelt **hadj** or **hajj**, and one who makes a haj is called a **hadjee, hadji, haji** or **hajji**.

HAJI, -S *same as* ▸ **hajji**
HAJJ, -ES *n* pilgrimage a Muslim makes to Mecca
HAJJAH, -S *n* Muslim woman who has made a pilgrimage to Mecca
HAJJES ▸ **hajj**
HAJJI, -S *n* Muslim who has made a pilgrimage to Mecca
HAKA, -S *n* ceremonial Māori dance with chanting
HAKAM, -S *n* text written by a rabbi
HAKARI, -S *n* Māori ritual feast
HAKAS ▸ **haka**
HAKE, -S *n*
HAKEA, -S *n* Australian tree or shrub with hard woody fruit
HAKEEM, -S *same as* ▸ **hakim**
HAKES ▸ **hake**
HAKIM, -S *n* Muslim judge, ruler, or administrator
HAKU, -S *in New Zealand English, same as* > **kingfish**
HALACHA *n* Jewish religious law
HALAKAH *same as* ▸ **halacha**
HALAKHA *same as* ▸ **halacha**
HALAKIC ▸ **halakha**
HALAL, -S *n, adj, vb*
HALALA, -S *n* money unit in Saudi Arabia
HALALAH *same as* ▸ **halala**
HALALAS ▸ **halala**
HALALS ▸ **halal**
HALAVAH *same as* ▸ **halvah**
HALBERD *n* spear with an axe blade
HALBERT *same as* ▸ **halberd**
HALCYON *adj* peaceful and happy ▹ *n* mythological bird
HALE, -D, -S, -ST, HALING *adj, vb*
HALER, -S, -U *same as* ▸ **heller**
HALES ▸ **hale**
HALEST ▸ **hale**
HALF, -S *n, adj, adv*
HALFA, -S *n* African grass
HALFEN *same as* ▸ **half**
HALFLIN *same as* > **halfling**
HALFS ▸ **half**
HALFWAY *adj*
HALFWIT *n*
HALIBUT *n*
HALID, -S *same as* ▸ **halide**
HALIDE, -S *n* binary compound
HALIDOM *n* holy place or thing
HALIDS ▸ **halid**
HALIER, -S *n* former currency unit of Slovakia
HALIMOT *n* court held by lord
HALING ▸ **hale**
HALITE, -S *n* colourless or white mineral
HALITUS *n* vapour
HALL, -S *n*
HALLAH, -S, HALLOT *variant spelling of* ▸ **challah**
HALLAL, -S *same as* ▸ **halal**
HALLALI *n* bugle call
HALLALS ▸ **hallal**
HALLAN, -S *n* partition in cottage
HALLEL, -S *n* (in Judaism) section of the liturgy
HALLIAN *same as* ▸ **hallion**
HALLING *n* Norwegian country dance
HALLION *n* lout
HALLO, -ED, -ES, -S *same as* ▸ **halloo**
HALLOA, -S *same as* ▸ **halloo**
HALLOED ▸ **hallo**
HALLOES ▸ **hallo**
HALLOO, -S *interj* shout used to call hounds at a hunt ▹ *n* shout of 'halloo' ▹ *vb* shout (something) to (someone)
HALLOS ▸ **hallo**
HALLOT ▸ **hallah**
HALLOTH *same as* ▸ **challah**
HALLOW, -S *vb* consecrate or set apart as being holy
HALLS ▸ **hall**

HALLUX *n* first digit on the hind foot of an animal
HALLWAY *n*
HALLYON *same as* ▸ **hallion**
HALM, -S *same as* ▸ **haulm**
HALMA, -S *n* board game
HALMS ▸ **halm**
HALO, -ED, -ES, -ING, -S *n, vb*
HALOGEN *n* any of a group of nonmetallic elements
HALOID, -S *adj* resembling or derived from a halogen ▹ *n* compound containing halogen atoms in its molecules
HALOING ▸ **halo**
HALON, -S *n* any of a class of chemical compounds
HALOS ▸ **halo**
HALOUMI *same as* > **halloumi**
HALSE, -D, -S, HALSING *vb* embrace
HALSER, -S ▸ **halse**
HALSES ▸ **halse**
HALSING ▸ **halse**
HALT, -ED, -S *vb, n, adj*
HALTER, -S *n* strap round a horse's head with a rope to lead it with ▹ *vb* put a halter on (a horse)
HALTERE *n* one of a pair of modified hind wings in dipterous insects
HALTERS ▸ **halter**
HALTING ▸ **halt**
HALTS ▸ **halt**
HALUTZ *variant spelling of* ▸ **chalutz**
HALVA, -S *same as* ▸ **halvah**
HALVAH, -S *n* E Mediterranean, Middle Eastern, or Indian sweetmeat
HALVAS ▸ **halva**
HALVE, -D, -S *vb* divide in half
HALVER, -S ▸ **halve**
HALVES ▸ **halve**
HALVING *n* act of halving
HALWA, -S *n* type of sweet Indian dish
HALYARD *n* rope for raising a ship's sail or flag
HAM, -MED, -MING, -S *n* smoked or salted meat from a pig's thigh ▹ *vb* overact
HAMADA, -S *n* rocky plateau in desert
HAMAL, -S *n* (in Middle Eastern countries) a porter or servant
HAMATE, -S *adj* hook-shaped ▹ *n* small bone in the wrist
HAMATSA *n* Native Canadian dance
HAMAUL, -S *same as* ▸ **hamal**
HAMBLE, -D, -S *vb* mutilate
HAMBONE *vb* strike body to provide percussion
HAMBURG *same as* > **hamburger**
HAME, -D, -S, HAMING *n* Scots word for home ▹ *vb* to home
HAMFAT, -S *n* mediocre performer
HAMING ▸ **hame**
HAMLET, -S *n* small village
HAMMADA *same as* ▸ **hamada**
HAMMAL, -S *same as* ▸ **hamal**
HAMMAM, -S *n* bathing establishment
HAMMED ▸ **ham**
HAMMER, -S *n* tool ▹ *vb* hit (as if) with a hammer
HAMMIER ▸ **hammy**
HAMMIES ▸ **hammy**
HAMMILY ▸ **hammy**
HAMMING ▸ **ham**
HAMMOCK *same as* ▸ **hummock**
HAMMY, HAMMIER, HAMMIES *adj* (of an actor) overacting or tending to overact ▹ *n* hamstring
HAMOSE *adj* shaped like a hook
HAMOUS *same as* ▸ **hamose**
HAMPER, -S *vb, n*
HAMS ▸ **ham**
HAMSTER *n*
HAMULAR ▸ **hamulus**
HAMULUS, HAMULI *n* biological attribute
HAMZA, -S *n* sign used in Arabic to represent the glottal stop
HAMZAH, -S *same as* ▸ **hamza**
HAMZAS ▸ **hamza**
HAN *archaic inflected form of* ▸ **have**
HANAP, -S *n* medieval drinking cup

HANAPER *n* small wickerwork basket
HANAPS ▸ **hanap**
HANCE, -S *same as* ▸ **haunch**
HANCH, -ED, -ES *vb* try to bite
HAND, -ED, -ING, -S *n* part of the body at the end of the arm ▷ *vb* pass, give
HANDAX *n* small axe held in one hand
HANDAXE *same as* ▸ **handax**
HANDBAG *n*
HANDCAR *n* small railway vehicle
HANDED ▸ **hand**
HANDER, -S ▸ **hand**
HANDFED > **handfeed**
HANDFUL *n*
HANDGUN *n*
HANDIER ▸ **handy**
HANDILY *adv* in a handy way or manner
HANDING ▸ **hand**
HANDISM *n* discrimination against left- or right-handed people
HANDJAR *n* Persian dagger
HANDLE, -D, -S *n, vb*
HANDLER *n* person who controls an animal
HANDLES ▸ **handle**
HANDOFF *n* (in rugby) act of warding off an opposing player
HANDOUT *n*
HANDS ▸ **hand**
HANDSAW *n*
HANDSEL *n* gift for good luck ▷ *vb* give a handsel to (a person)
HANDSET *n*
HANDSY *adj* engaging in unwanted physical contact
HANDY, HANDIER *adj* convenient, useful
HANG, -ED, -S, HUNG *vb*
HANGAR, -S *n* large shed for storing aircraft ▷ *vb* put in a hangar
HANGDOG *adj* guilty, ashamed ▷ *n* furtive or sneaky person
HANGED ▸ **hang**
HANGER, -S *n*
HANGI, -S *n* Māori oven
HANGING ▸ **hang**
HANGIS ▸ **hangi**
HANGMAN, HANGMEN *n*
HANGOUT *n* place where one lives or that one frequently visits
HANGRY *adj* irritable as a result of feeling hungry
HANGS ▸ **hang**
HANGTAG *n* attached label
HANGUL, -S *n* alphabetic scheme used in Korean
HANGUP, -S *n* emotional or psychological problem
HANIWA, -S *n* Japanese funeral offering
HANJAR, -S *same as* ▸ **handjar**
HANK, -ED, -ING, -S *n* coil, esp of yarn ▷ *vb* attach (a sail) to a stay by hanks
HANKER, -S *vb*
HANKIE *same as* ▸ **hanky**
HANKIES ▸ **hanky**
HANKING ▸ **hank**
HANKS ▸ **hank**
HANKY, HANKIES *n*
HANSA, -S *same as* ▸ **hanse**
HANSE, -S *n* medieval guild of merchants
HANSEL, -S *same as* ▸ **handsel**
HANSES ▸ **hanse**
HANSOM, -S *n* two-wheeled one-horse carriage
HANT, -ED, -ING, -S *same as* ▸ **haunt**
HANTLE, -S *n* good deal
HANTS ▸ **hant**
HANUMAN *n* type of monkey
HAO, -S *n* monetary unit of Vietnam
HAOMA, -S *n* type of ritual drink
HAOS ▸ **hao**
HAP, -PED, -PING, -S *n* luck ▷ *vb* cover up
HAPAX, -ES *n* word that appears once in a work of literature
HAPKIDO *n* Korean martial art
HAPLESS *adj*
HAPLITE *variant of* ▸ **aplite**
HAPLOID *adj* denoting a cell or organism with unpaired chromosomes ▷ *n* haploid cell or organism
HAPLONT *n* organism with a haploid number of chromosomes
HAPLY *archaic word for* ▸ **perhaps**
HAPPED ▸ **hap**
HAPPEN, -S *vb*

HAPPI, -S *n* type of loose Japanese coat
HAPPIED ▸ **happy**
HAPPIER ▸ **happy**
HAPPIES ▸ **happy**
HAPPILY ▸ **happy**
HAPPING ▸ **hap**
HAPPIS ▸ **happi**
HAPPY, HAPPIED, HAPPIER, HAPPIES *adj, vb*
HAPS ▸ **hap**
HAPTEN, -S *n* incomplete antigen
HAPTENE *same as* ▸ **hapten**
HAPTENS ▸ **hapten**
HAPTIC *adj* relating to or based on the sense of touch
HAPTICS *n* science of sense of touch
HAPU, -S *n* subtribe
HAPUKA, -S *another name for* ▸ **groper**
HAPUKU, -S *same as* ▸ **hapuka**
HAPUS ▸ **hapu**
HARAAM *same as* ▸ **haram**
HARAM, -S *n* anything that is forbidden by Islamic law
HARASS *vb*
HARBOR, -S *same as* ▸ **harbour**
HARBOUR *n, vb*
HARD, -ER, -EST *adj, adv*
HARDASS *n* tough person
HARDBAG *n* rigid container on a motorcycle
HARDEN, -S *vb* make or become hard ▹ *n* rough fabric made from hards
HARDER ▸ **hard**
HARDEST ▸ **hard**
HARDHAT *n* hat made of a hard material for protection ▹ *adj* typical of construction workers
HARDIER ▸ **hardy**
HARDIES ▸ **hardy**
HARDILY *adv* in a hardy manner
HARDISH ▸ **hard**
HARDLY *adv*
HARDMAN, HARDMEN *n* tough, ruthless, or violent man
HARDOKE *n* burdock
HARDPAN *n* hard impervious layer of clay below the soil
HARDS *pl n* coarse fibres and other refuse from flax and hemp
HARDSET *adj*
HARDTOP *n* car equipped with a metal or plastic roof
HARDY, HARDIER, HARDIES *adj, n*
HARE, -D, -S, HARING *n* animal like a large rabbit, with longer ears and legs ▹ *vb* run (away) quickly
HARELD, -S *n* long-tailed duck
HARES ▸ **hare**
HARIANA *n* Indian breed of cattle
HARICOT *n*
HARIJAN *n* member of an Indian caste
HARING ▸ **hare**
HARIRA, -S *n* Moroccan soup
HARISH *adj* like hare
HARISSA *n* hot paste
HARK, -ED, -ING, -S *vb* listen
HARKEN, -S *same as* ▸ **hearken**
HARKING ▸ **hark**
HARKS ▸ **hark**
HARL, -ED, -S *same as* ▸ **herl**
HARLING ▸ **harl**
HARLS ▸ **harl**
HARM, -ED, -ING, -S *vb* injure physically, mentally, or morally ▹ *n* physical, mental, or moral injury
HARMALA *n* African plant
HARMAN, -S *n* constable
HARMED ▸ **harm**
HARMEL, -S *same as* ▸ **harmala**
HARMER, -S ▸ **harm**
HARMFUL *adj*
HARMIN, -S *same as* > **harmalin**
HARMINE *same as* > **harmalin**
HARMING ▸ **harm**
HARMINS ▸ **harmin**
HARMONY *n*
HARMOST *n* Spartan governor
HARMS ▸ **harm**
HARN, -S *n* coarse linen
HARNESS *n, vb*
HARNS ▸ **harn**
HARO, -S *interj* cry meaning alas ▹ *n* cry of 'haro'
HAROSET *n* Jewish dish eaten at Passover
HARP, -ED, -ING, -S *n, vb*
HARPER, -S ▸ **harp**
HARPIES ▸ **harpy**

HARPIN *n* type of protein
HARPING ▶ **harp**
HARPINS *same as* > **harpings**
HARPIST ▶ **harp**
HARPOON *n, vb*
HARPS ▶ **harp**
HARPY, HARPIES *n* nasty or bad-tempered woman
HARRIED ▶ **harry**
HARRIER *n*
HARRIES ▶ **harry**
HARROW, -S *n, vb*
HARRY, HARRIED, HARRIES *vb*
HARSH, -ED, -ER, -ES *adj, vb*
HARSHEN *vb* make harsh
HARSHER ▶ **harsh**
HARSHES ▶ **harsh**
HARSHLY ▶ **harsh**
HARSLET *same as* ▶ **haslet**
HART, -S *n* adult male deer
HARTAL, -S *n* (in India) closing shops or suspending work
HARTELY *archaic spelling of* > **heartily**
HARTEN, -S *same as* ▶ **hearten**
HARTS ▶ **hart**
HARUMPH *same as* > **harrumph**
HARVEST *n, vb*
HAS ▶ **have**
HASH, -ED, -ES, -ING *n, vb*
HASHIER ▶ **hashy**
HASHING ▶ **hash**
HASHISH *n*
HASHTAG *n*
HASHY, HASHIER ▶ **hash**
HASK, -S *n* archaic name for a basket for transporting fish
HASLET, -S *n* loaf of cooked minced pig's offal, eaten cold
HASP, -ED, -ING, -S *n* type of fastening ▷ *vb* secure (a door, window, etc) with a hasp
HASS, -ES *n* as in **white hass** oatmeal pudding made with sheep's gullet
HASSAR, -S *n* South American catfish
HASSEL, -S *variant of* ▶ **hassle**
HASSES ▶ **hass**
HASSIUM *n* chemical element
HASSLE, -D, -S *n, vb*
HASSOCK *n*
HAST *singular form of the present tense (indicative mood) of* ▶ **have**
HASTA *Spanish for* ▶ **until**
HASTATE *adj* shaped like a spear
HASTE, -D, -S *n, vb*
HASTEN, -S *vb* (cause to) hurry
HASTES ▶ **haste**
HASTIER ▶ **hasty**
HASTILY ▶ **hasty**
HASTING ▶ **haste**
HASTY, HASTIER *adj* (too) quick
HAT, -S, -TED *n* covering for the head, often with a brim ▷ *vb* supply (a person) with a hat or put a hat on (someone)
HATABLE ▶ **hate**
HATBAND *n*
HATBOX *n*
HATCH, -ED, -ES *vb, n*
HATCHEL *same as* ▶ **heckle**
HATCHER ▶ **hatch**
HATCHES ▶ **hatch**
HATCHET *n* small axe
HATE, -D, -S, HATING *vb, n*
HATEFUL *adj*
HATER, -S ▶ **hate**
HATES ▶ **hate**
HATFUL, -S, HATSFUL *n* amount a hat will hold
HATH *form of the present tense (indicative mood) of* ▶ **have**
HATHA *n* as in **hatha yoga** form of yoga
HATING ▶ **hate**
HATLESS ▶ **hat**
HATLIKE ▶ **hat**
HATPEG, -S *n* peg to hang hat on
HATPIN, -S *n*
HATRACK *n* rack for hanging hats on
HATRED, -S *n* intense dislike
HATS ▶ **hat**
HATSFUL ▶ **hatful**
HATTED ▶ **hat**
HATTER, -S *n* person who makes and sells hats ▷ *vb* annoy
HATTING ▶ **hat**
HATTOCK *n* small hat
HAUBERK *n* long sleeveless coat of mail
HAUBOIS *same as* ▶ **hautboy**
HAUD, -ING, -S, HUDDEN *Scot word for* ▶ **hold**

HAUF, -S *Scot word for* ▶ **half**
HAUGH, -S *n* low-lying often alluvial riverside meadow
HAUGHT *same as* ▶ **haughty**
HAUGHTY *adj*
HAUL, -ED, -S *vb, n*
HAULAGE *n*
HAULD, -S *Scots word for* ▶ **hold**
HAULED ▶ **haul**
HAULER, -S *same as* ▶ **haulier**
HAULIER *n*
HAULING *n* act of hauling
HAULM, -S *n* stalks of beans, peas, or potatoes collectively
HAULMY *adj* having haulms
HAULOUT *n* act of hauling a boat out of water
HAULS ▶ **haul**
HAULST *same as* ▶ **halse**
HAULT *same as* ▶ **haughty**
HAUN, -S *n* Scot word for hand
HAUNCH *n, vb*
HAUNS ▶ **haun**
HAUNT, -S *vb, n*
HAUNTED *adj* frequented by ghosts
HAUNTER ▶ **haunt**
HAUNTS ▶ **haunt**
HAUSE, -D, -S, HAUSING *same as* ▶ **halse**
HAUSEN, -S *n* variety of sturgeon
HAUSES ▶ **hause**
HAUSING ▶ **hause**
HAUT, -ER, -EST *same as* ▶ **haughty**
HAUTBOY *n* type of strawberry
HAUTE *adj* French word meaning high
HAUTER ▶ **haut**
HAUTEST ▶ **haut**
HAUTEUR *n* haughtiness
HAUYNE, -S *n* blue mineral containing calcium
HAVARTI *n* Danish cheese
HAVE, HAS, -S *vb, n*
HAVEN, -ED, -S *n, vb*
HAVEOUR *same as* ▶ **havior**
HAVER, -ED, -S *vb* talk nonsense ▷ *n* nonsense
HAVEREL *n* fool
HAVERS ▶ **haver**
HAVES ▶ **have**
HAVING, -S ▶ **have**
HAVIOR, -S *same as* ▶ **haviour**
HAVIOUR *n* possession
HAVOC, -S *n, vb*
HAW, -ED, -ING, -S *n* hawthorn berry ▷ *vb* make an inarticulate utterance
HAWALA, -S *n* Middle Eastern system of money transfer
HAWBUCK *n* bumpkin
HAWED ▶ **haw**
HAWING ▶ **haw**
HAWK, -ED, -S *n, vb*
HAWKBIT *n* any of three perennial plants
HAWKED ▶ **hawk**
HAWKER, -S *n* travelling salesperson
HAWKEY, -S *same as* ▶ **hockey**
HAWKIE, -S *n* cow with white stripe on face
HAWKING *another name for* ▶ **falconry**
HAWKISH *adj* favouring the use of force rather than diplomacy
HAWKIT *adj* having a white streak
HAWKS ▶ **hawk**
HAWM, -ED, -ING, -S *vb* be idle and relaxed
HAWS ▶ **haw**
HAWSE, -D, -S, HAWSING *vb* of boats, pitch violently when at anchor
HAWSER, -S *n* large rope used on a ship
HAWSES ▶ **hawse**
HAWSING ▶ **hawse**
HAY, -ED, -S *n, vb*
HAYBAND *n* rope made by twisting hay together
HAYBOX *n* airtight box used to keep partially cooked food warm
HAYCOCK *n* pile of hay left until dry enough to move
HAYED ▶ **hay**
HAYER, -S *n* person who makes hay
HAYEY, HAYIER, HAYIEST ▶ **hay**
HAYFORK *n*
HAYIER ▶ **hayey**
HAYIEST ▶ **hayey**
HAYING, -S ▶ **hay**
HAYLAGE *n* type of hay for animal fodder
HAYLE, -S *n* welfare
HAYLOFT *n*
HAYMOW, -S *n* part of a barn where hay is stored

HAYRACK *n* rack for holding hay for feeding to animals
HAYRAKE *n* large rake used to collect hay
HAYRICK *same as* > **haystack**
HAYRIDE *n* pleasure trip in hay wagon
HAYS ▸ **hay**
HAYSEED *n* seeds or fragments of grass or straw
HAYSEL, -S *n* season for making hay
HAYWARD *n* parish officer in charge of enclosures and fences
HAYWIRE *adj, n*
HAZAN, -IM, -S *n* man employed to lead services in a synagogue
HAZARD, -S *n, vb*
HAZE, -D, -S *n, vb*
HAZEL, -S *n, adj*
HAZELLY ▸ **hazel**
HAZELS ▸ **hazel**
HAZER, -S ▸ **haze**
HAZES ▸ **haze**
HAZIER ▸ **hazy**
HAZIEST ▸ **hazy**
HAZILY ▸ **hazy**
HAZING, -S ▸ **haze**
HAZMAT, -S *n* hazardous material
HAZY, HAZIER, HAZIEST *adj* not clear, misty
HAZZAN, -S *same as* ▸ **hazan**
HE, -S *pron* male person or animal ▹ *n* male person or animal ▹ *interj* expression of amusement or derision
HEAD *n, adj, vb*
HEADAGE *n* payment to farmer based on animals owned
HEADED *adj* having a head or heads
HEADEND *n* facility from which cable television is transmitted
HEADER, -S *n* striking a ball with the head
HEADFUL *n* amount head will hold
HEADIER ▸ **heady**
HEADILY ▸ **heady**
HEADING *same as* ▸ **head**
HEADMAN, HEADMEN *n* chief or leader
HEADPIN *another word for* ▸ **kingpin**
HEADRIG *n* edge of ploughed field
HEADS *adv* with the side of a coin with a head on it uppermost
HEADSET *n*
HEADWAY *same as* > **headroom**
HEADY, HEADIER *adj* intoxicating or exciting
HEAL, -ED, -S *vb* make or become well
HEALD, -ED, -S *same as* ▸ **heddle**
HEALED ▸ **heal**
HEALEE, -S *n* person who is being healed
HEALER, -S ▸ **heal**
HEALING ▸ **heal**
HEALS ▸ **heal**
HEALTH, -S *n, interj*
HEALTHY *adj* having good health
HEAME *old form of* ▸ **home**
HEAP, -ED, -S *n, vb*
HEAPER, -S ▸ **heap**
HEAPIER ▸ **heapy**
HEAPING *adj* (of a spoonful) heaped
HEAPS ▸ **heap**
HEAPY, HEAPIER *adj* having many heaps
HEAR, -S *vb* perceive (a sound) by ear
HEARD, -S *same as* ▸ **herd**
HEARE, -S *old form of* ▸ **hair**
HEARER, -S ▸ **hear**
HEARES ▸ **heare**
HEARIE *old form of* ▸ **hairy**
HEARING ▸ **hear**
HEARKEN *vb* listen
HEARS ▸ **hear**
HEARSAY *n*
HEARSE, -D, -S *n, vb*
HEARSY *adj* like a hearse
HEART, -ED *n, vb*
HEARTEN *vb* encourage, make cheerful
HEARTH, -S *n*
HEARTLY *adv* vigorously
HEARTS *n* card game
HEARTY *adj* substantial, nourishing ▹ *n* comrade, esp a sailor
HEAST, -S *same as* ▸ **hest**
HEASTE, -S *same as* ▸ **hest**
HEASTS ▸ **heast**
HEAT, -S *vb, n*
HEATED *adj* angry and excited
HEATER, -S *n* device for supplying heat

HEATH, -S *n*
HEATHEN *n, adj*
HEATHER *n, adj*
HEATHS ▸ **heath**
HEATHY ▸ **heath**
HEATING *n* device or system for supplying heat
HEATS ▸ **heat**
HEAUME, -S *n* large helmet reaching the shoulders
HEAVE, -D, -S, HOVEN *vb, n*
HEAVEN, -S *n* place believed to be the home of God
HEAVER, -S ▸ **heave**
HEAVES ▸ **heave**
HEAVIER ▸ **heavy**
HEAVIES ▸ **heavy**
HEAVILY ▸ **heavy**
HEAVING ▸ **heave**
HEAVY, HEAVIER, HEAVIES *adj* of great weight ▹ *n* person hired to threaten violence
HEBE, -S *n* any of various flowering shrubs
HEBEN, -S *old form of* ▸ **ebony**
HEBENON *n* source of poison
HEBENS ▸ **heben**
HEBES ▸ **hebe**
HEBETIC *adj* of or relating to puberty
HEBONA, -S *same as* ▸ **hebenon**
HECH *interj* expression of surprise
HECHT, -S *same as* ▸ **hight**
HECK, -S *interj* mild exclamation of surprise, irritation, etc ▹ *n* frame for obstructing the passage of fish in a river
HECKLE, -D, -S *vb, n*
HECKLER ▸ **heckle**
HECKLES ▸ **heckle**
HECKS ▸ **heck**
HECKUVA *adj* heck of a
HECTARE *n*
HECTIC, -S *adj* rushed or busy ▹ *n* hectic fever or flush
HECTOR, -S *vb, n*
HEDARIM *same as* ▸ **hadarim**
HEDDLE, -D, -S *n* frame on a loom ▹ *vb* pass thread through a heddle
HEDER, HADARIM, -S *variant spelling of* ▸ **cheder**
HEDERA, -S *n* ivy
HEDERAL ▸ **hedera**
HEDERAS ▸ **hedera**
HEDERS ▸ **heder**
HEDGE, -D, -S *n, vb*
HEDGER, -S ▸ **hedge**
HEDGES ▸ **hedge**
HEDGIER ▸ **hedgy**
HEDGING ▸ **hedge**
HEDGY, HEDGIER ▸ **hedge**
HEDONIC > **hedonism**
HEED, -ED, -ING, -S *n, vb*
HEEDER, -S ▸ **heed**
HEEDFUL ▸ **heed**
HEEDIER ▸ **heedy**
HEEDING ▸ **heed**
HEEDS ▸ **heed**
HEEDY, HEEDIER *adj* heedful; attentive
HEEHAW, -S *interj* representation of the braying sound of a donkey ▹ *vb* make braying sound
HEEL, -ED, -S *n, vb*
HEELBAR *n* small shop where shoes are repaired
HEELED ▸ **heel**
HEELER, -S *n* dog that herds cattle by biting at their heels
HEELING ▸ **heel**
HEELS ▸ **heel**
HEELTAP *n* layer of leather, etc, in the heel of a shoe
HEEZE, -D, -S, HEEZING *Scots word for* ▸ **hoist**
HEEZIE, -S *n* act of lifting
HEEZING ▸ **heeze**
HEFT, -ED, -ING, -S *vb* assess the weight of (something) by lifting ▹ *n* weight
HEFTE *same as* ▸ **heave**
HEFTED ▸ **heft**
HEFTER, -S ▸ **heft**
HEFTIER ▸ **hefty**
HEFTILY ▸ **hefty**
HEFTING ▸ **heft**
HEFTS ▸ **heft**
HEFTY, HEFTIER *adj* large, heavy, or strong
HEGARI, -S *n* African sorghum
HEGEMON *n* person in authority
HEGIRA, -S *n* emigration escape or flight
HEGUMEN *n* head of a monastery of the Eastern Church
HEH, -S *interj* exclamation of surprise or inquiry

HEID, -S *Scot word for* ▸ **head**
HEIDUC, -S *n* Hungarian guerilla warrior
HEIFER, -S *n*
HEIGH *same as* ▸ **hey**
HEIGHT, -S *n*
HEIGHTH *obsolete form of* ▸ **height**
HEIGHTS ▸ **height**
HEIL, -ED, -ING, -S *vb* give a German greeting
HEIMISH *adj* comfortable
HEINIE, -S *n* buttocks
HEINOUS *adj*
HEIR, -ED, -ING, -S *n, vb*
HEIRDOM *n* succession by right of blood
HEIRED ▸ **heir**
HEIRESS *n*
HEIRING ▸ **heir**
HEIRS ▸ **heir**
HEISHI *n* Native American shell jewellery
HEIST, -ED, -S *n* robbery ▹ *vb* steal or burgle
HEISTER ▸ **heist**
HEISTS ▸ **heist**
HEITIKI *n* Māori neck ornament of greenstone
HEJAB, -S *same as* ▸ **hijab**
HEJIRA, -S *same as* ▸ **hegira**
HEJRA, -S *same as* ▸ **hegira**
HEKTARE *same as* ▸ **hectare**
HELCOID *adj* having ulcers
HELD ▸ **hold**
HELE, -D, -S, HELING *vb* as in **hele in** insert (cuttings, etc) into soil
HELIAC *same as* > **heliacal**
HELIAST *n* ancient Greek juror
HELIBUS *n* helicopter carrying passengers
HELICAL *adj* spiral
HELICES ▸ **helix**
HELICON *n* bass tuba
HELIMAN, HELIMEN *n* helicopter pilot
HELING ▸ **hele**
HELIO, -S *n* instrument for sending messages in Morse code
HELIPAD *n* place for helicopters to land and take off
HELISKI *vb* ski down a mountain after ascending it by helicopter
HELIUM, -S *n*
HELIX, HELICES, -ES *n* spiral
HELL, -ED, -ING, -S *n, vb*
HELLBOX *n* (in printing) container for broken type
HELLCAT *n* spiteful fierce-tempered woman
HELLED ▸ **hell**
HELLER, -S *n* monetary unit of the Czech Republic
HELLERI *n* Central American fish
HELLERS ▸ **heller**
HELLERY *n* wild or mischievous behaviour
HELLIER *n* slater
HELLING ▸ **hell**
HELLION *n* rough or rowdy person, esp a child
HELLISH *adj, adv*
HELLO, -ED, -ES, -S *interj, n, sentence substitute, vb*
HELLOVA *same as* ▸ **helluva**
HELLS ▸ **hell**
HELLUVA *adj* phonetic representation of 'hell of a'
HELM, -ED, -ING, -S *n, vb*
HELMER, -S *n* film director
HELMET, -S *n*
HELMING ▸ **helm**
HELMS ▸ **helm**
HELO, -S *n* helicopter
HELOT, -S *n* serf or slave
HELOTRY *n* serfdom or slavery
HELOTS ▸ **helot**
HELP, -ED, -S *vb, n*
HELPER, -S ▸ **help**
HELPFUL *adj* giving help
HELPING *n* single portion of food
HELPS ▸ **help**
HELVE, -D, -S, HELVING *n* handle of a hand tool such as an axe or pick ▹ *vb* fit a helve to (a tool)
HEM, -MED, -MING, -S *n, vb*
HEMAGOG *same as* > **hemagogue**
HEMAL *same as* ▸ **haemal**
HEMATAL *same as* ▸ **hemal**
HEMATIC *same as* > **haematic**
HEMATIN *same as* > **haematin**
HEME, -S *same as* ▸ **haem**

HEMIC *same as* > **haematic**
HEMIN, -S *same as* ▸ **haemin**
HEMINA, -S *n* old liquid measure
HEMINS ▸ **hemin**
HEMIOLA *n* rhythmic device
HEMIONE *same as* > **hemionus**
HEMIPOD *same as* > **hemipode**
HEMLINE *n*
HEMLOCK *n*
HEMMED ▸ **hem**
HEMMER, -S *n* attachment on a sewing machine for hemming
HEMMING ▸ **hem**
HEMOID *same as* > **haematoid**
HEMP, -S *n*
HEMPEN ▸ **hemp**
HEMPIE *variant of* ▸ **hempy**
HEMPIER ▸ **hempy**
HEMPIES ▸ **hempy**
HEMPS ▸ **hemp**
HEMPY, HEMPIER, HEMPIES *adj* of or like hemp ▹ *n* rogue
HEMS ▸ **hem**
HEN, -NED, -NING, -S *n, vb*
HENBANE *n* poisonous plant with sticky hairy leaves
HENBIT, -S *n* European plant with small dark red flowers
HENCE *adv, interj*
HENCH, -ER *adj* fit and muscular
HENCOOP *n* cage for poultry
HEND, -ED, -ING, -S *vb* seize
HENGE, -S *n* monument from the Neolithic and Bronze Ages
HENLEY, -S *n* type of sweater
HENLIKE ▸ **hen**
HENNA, -ED, -S *n, vb*
HENNED ▸ **hen**
HENNER, -S *n* challenge
HENNERY *n* place or farm for keeping poultry
HENNIER ▸ **henny**
HENNIES ▸ **henny**
HENNIN, -S *n* former women's hat
HENNING ▸ **hen**
HENNINS ▸ **hennin**
HENNISH ▸ **hen**
HENNY, HENNIER, HENNIES *adj* like a hen ▹ *n* cock that looks like a hen
HENOTIC *adj* acting to reconcile
HENPECK *vb* (of a woman) to harass or torment (a man)
HENRY, HENRIES, -S *n* unit of electrical inductance
HENS ▸ **hen**
HENT, -ED, -ING, -S *vb* seize ▹ *n* anything that has been grasped, esp by the mind
HEP, -PER, -PEST, -S *adj* aware of or following the latest trends ▹ *n* fact of being hep
HEPAR, -S *n* compound containing sulphur
HEPARIN *n* polysaccharide present in most body tissues
HEPARS ▸ **hepar**
HEPATIC *adj* of the liver ▹ *n* any of various drugs for use in treating diseases of the liver
HEPCAT, -S *n* person who is hep
HEPPER ▸ **hep**
HEPPEST ▸ **hep**
HEPS ▸ **hep**
HEPSTER *same as* ▸ **hipster**
HEPT *archaic spelling of* ▸ **heaped**
HEPTAD, -S *n* group or series of seven
HEPTANE *n* alkane found in petroleum
HEPTOSE *n* any monosaccharide with seven carbon atoms per molecule
HER *pron, adj, determiner*
HERALD, -S *n, vb*
HERB, -S *n*
HERBAGE *n* herbaceous plants collectively
HERBAL, -S *adj* of or relating to herbs, usually culinary or medicinal herbs ▹ *n* book describing and listing the properties of plants
HERBAR, -S *same as* ▸ **herbary**
HERBARY *n* herb garden
HERBED *adj* flavoured with herbs
HERBIER ▸ **herby**
HERBIST *same as* > **herbalist**
HERBLET *n* little herb

HERBOSE *same as* ▸ **herbous**
HERBOUS *adj* with abundance of herbs
HERBS ▸ **herb**
HERBY, HERBIER *adj* abounding in herbs
HERD, -ED, -S *n, vb*
HERDBOY *n* boy who looks after herd
HERDED ▸ **herd**
HERDEN, -S *n* type of coarse cloth
HERDER, -S *same as* > **herdsman**
HERDESS *n* female herder
HERDIC, -S *n* small horse-drawn carriage
HERDING *n* act of herding
HERDMAN, HERDMEN *same as* > **herdsman**
HERDS ▸ **herd**
HERE *adv*
HEREAT *adv* because of this
HEREBY *adv* by means of or as a result of this
HEREDES ▸ **heres**
HEREIN *adv* in this place, matter, or document
HEREOF *adv* of or concerning this
HEREON *archaic word for* > **hereupon**
HERES, HEREDES *n* heir
HERESY *n*
HERETIC *n*
HERETO *adv* this place, matter, or document
HERIED ▸ **hery**
HERIES ▸ **hery**
HERIOT, -S *n* (in medieval England) a death duty paid to the lord
HERISSE *adj* with bristles
HERITOR *n* person who inherits
HERL, -S *n* barb or barbs of a feather
HERLING *n* Scots word for a type of fish
HERLS ▸ **herl**
HERM, -S *n* (in ancient Greece) a stone head of Hermes
HERMA, -E, -I *same as* ▸ **herm**
HERMIT, -S *n* person living in solitude, esp for religious reasons
HERMS ▸ **herm**
HERN, -S *archaic or dialect word for* ▸ **heron**
HERNIA, -E, -S *n* medical problem
HERNIAL ▸ **hernia**
HERNIAS ▸ **hernia**
HERNS ▸ **hern**
HERO, -ES, -S *n*
HEROIC *adj*
HEROICS *pl n*
HEROIN, -S *n*
HEROINE *n*
HEROINS ▸ **heroin**
HEROISE *same as* ▸ **heroize**
HEROISM *n*
HEROIZE *vb* make into hero
HERON, -S *n*
HERONRY *n* colony of breeding herons
HERONS ▸ **heron**
HEROON, -S *n* temple or monument dedicated to a hero
HEROS ▸ **hero**
HERPES *n* any of several inflammatory skin diseases
HERRIED ▸ **herry**
HERRIES ▸ **herry**
HERRING *n*
HERRY, HERRIED, HERRIES *vb* harry
HERS *pron* something belonging to her
HERSALL *n* rehearsal
HERSE, -S *n*
HERSED *adj* arranged like a harrow
HERSELF *pron*
HERSES ▸ **herse**
HERSHIP *n* act of plundering
HERTZ, -ES *n* unit of frequency
HERY, HERIED, HERIES, -ING *vb* praise
HERYE, -D, -S *same as* ▸ **hery**
HERYING ▸ **hery**
HES ▸ **he**
HESP, -ED, -ING, -S *same as* ▸ **hasp**
HESSIAN *n*
HESSITE *n* black or grey metallic mineral
HEST, -S *archaic word for* ▸ **behest**
HET *adj* Scots word for hot
HETE, -S, HETING *same as* ▸ **hight**
HETH, -S *n* eighth letter of the Hebrew alphabet
HETHER *same as* ▸ **hither**
HETHS ▸ **heth**
HETING ▸ **hete**
HETMAN, -S, HETMEN *another word for* ▸ **ataman**

HEUCH, -S *Scots word for* ▸ **crag**
HEUGH, -S *same as* ▸ **heuch**
HEUREKA *same as* ▸ **eureka**
HEURISM *n* use of logic
HEVEA, -S *n* rubber-producing South American tree
HEW, -ED, -N, -S *vb* cut with an axe
HEWABLE ▸ **hew**
HEWED ▸ **hew**
HEWER, -S ▸ **hew**
HEWGH *interj* sound made to imitate the flight of an arrow
HEWING, -S ▸ **hew**
HEWN ▸ **hew**
HEWS ▸ **hew**
HEX, -ED, -ES *adj* of or relating to hexadecimal notation ▹ *n* evil spell ▹ *vb* bewitch

This word meaning to bewitch is a really useful one for using the X.

HEXACT, -S *n* part of a sponge with six rays
HEXAD, -S *n* group or series of six
HEXADE, -S *same as* ▸ **hexad**
HEXADIC ▸ **hexad**
HEXADS ▸ **hexad**
HEXAGON *n*
HEXANE, -S *n* liquid alkane existing in five isomeric forms
HEXAPLA *n* edition of the Old Testament
HEXAPOD *n* six-footed arthropod
HEXARCH *adj* (of a plant) with six veins
HEXED ▸ **hex**
HEXENE, -S *same as* > **hexylene**
HEXER, -S ▸ **hex**
HEXEREI *n* witchcraft
HEXERS ▸ **hexer**
HEXES ▸ **hex**
HEXING, -S ▸ **hex**
HEXONE, -S *n* colourless insoluble liquid ketone
HEXOSAN *n* form of polysaccharide
HEXOSE, -S *n* monosaccharide, such as glucose
HEXYL, -S *n* chemical compound
HEXYLIC ▸ **hexyl**
HEXYLS ▸ **hexyl**
HEY, -ED, -ING, -S *interj, vb*
HEYDAY, -S *n* time of greatest success, prime
HEYDEY, -S *variant of* ▸ **heyday**
HEYDUCK *same as* ▸ **haiduk**
HEYED ▸ **hey**
HEYING ▸ **hey**
HEYS ▸ **hey**
HI *interj* hello
HIANT *adj* gaping
HIATAL ▸ **hiatus**
HIATUS *n*
HIBACHI *n* portable brazier for heating and cooking food
HIC *interj* representation of the sound of a hiccup
HICATEE *same as* > **hiccatee**
HICCUP, -S *n, vb*
HICCUPY *adj* tending to hiccup
HICK, -ER, -EST, -S *n, adj*
HICKEY, -S *n* object or gadget
HICKIE, -S *same as* ▸ **hickey**
HICKISH ▸ **hick**
HICKORY *n*
HICKS ▸ **hick**
HID ▸ **hide**
HIDABLE ▸ **hide**
HIDAGE, -S *n* former tax on land
HIDALGA *n* Spanish noblewoman
HIDALGO *n* member of the lower nobility in Spain
HIDDEN ▸ **hide**
HIDDER, -S *n* young ram
HIDE, HID, HIDDEN, -D, -S *vb, n*
HIDEOUS *adj*
HIDEOUT *n*
HIDER, -S ▸ **hide**
HIDES ▸ **hide**
HIDING, -S ▸ **hide**
HIDLING *n* hiding place
HIDLINS *same as* > **hidlings**
HIE, -D, -ING, -S, HYING *vb* hurry
HIELAND *adj* characteristic of Highlanders
HIEMAL *less common word for* > **hibernal**
HIEMS *n* winter
HIES ▸ **hie**
HIGGLE, -D, -S *less common word for* ▸ **haggle**
HIGGLER ▸ **higgle**
HIGGLES ▸ **higgle**
HIGH, -ED, -EST, -ING, -S *adj* being a relatively

great distance from top to bottom; tall ▷ *adv* at or to a height ▷ *n* high place or level ▷ *vb* hie
HIGHBOY *n* tall chest of drawers in two sections
HIGHED ▶ **high**
HIGHER, -S *n* advanced level of the Scottish Certificate of Education ▷ *vb* raise up
HIGHEST ▶ **high**
HIGHING ▶ **high**
HIGHISH ▶ **high**
HIGHLY *adv* extremely
HIGHMAN, HIGHMEN *n* dice weighted to make it fall in particular way
HIGHS ▶ **high**
HIGHT, -ED, -S, HOTE, HOTEN *vb* archaic word for name or call
HIGHTH, -S *old form of* ▶ **height**
HIGHTOP *n* top of ship's mast
HIGHTS ▶ **hight**
HIGHWAY *n*
HIJAB, -S *n* covering for the head and face
HIJACK, -S *vb* seize control of (an aircraft or other vehicle) while travelling ▷ *n* instance of hijacking
HIJINKS *n* lively enjoyment
HIJRA, -S *same as* ▶ **hijrah**
HIJRAH, -S *same as* ▶ **hegira**
HIJRAS ▶ **hijra**
HIKE, -D, -S *n, vb*
HIKER, -S ▶ **hike**
HIKES ▶ **hike**
HIKING, -S *n* sport of taking long walks in the country
HIKOI, -ED, -S *n* walk or march, esp a Māori protest march ▷ *vb* take part in such a march
HILA ▶ **hilum**
HILAR ▶ **hilus**
HILCH, -ED, -ES *vb* hobble
HILD *same as* ▶ **hold**
HILDING *n* coward
HILI ▶ **hilus**
HILL, -ED, -ING, -S *n, vb*
HILLER, -S ▶ **hill**
HILLIER ▶ **hilly**
HILLING ▶ **hill**
HILLMEN *same as* > **hillfolk**
HILLO, -ED, -ES, -S *same as* ▶ **hello**
HILLOA, -S *same as* ▶ **halloa**
HILLOCK *n*
HILLOED ▶ **hillo**
HILLOES ▶ **hillo**
HILLOS ▶ **hillo**
HILLS ▶ **hill**
HILLTOP *n*
HILLY, HILLIER ▶ **hill**
HILT, -ED, -ING, -S *n, vb*
HILUM, HILA *n* scar on a seed
HILUS, HILI *rare word for* ▶ **hilum**
HIM, -S *pron, n*
HIMATIA > **himation**
HIMBO, -S *n* derogatory term for an attractive but empty-headed man
HIMS ▶ **him**
HIMSELF *pron*
HIN, -S *n* Hebrew unit of capacity
HINAU, -S *n* New Zealand tree
HIND, -S *adj, n*
HINDER, -S *vb, adj*
HINDGUT *n* part of the vertebrate digestive tract
HINDLEG *n*
HINDS ▶ **hind**
HING, -S *n* asafoetida
HINGE, -D, -S, HINGING *n* device for holding two parts so one can swing freely ▷ *vb* depend (on)
HINGER, -S *n* tool for making hinges
HINGES ▶ **hinge**
HINGING ▶ **hinge**
HINGS ▶ **hing**
HINKY, HINKIER *adj* strange
HINNIE *n* sweetheart
HINNY, HINNIED, HINNIES *n* offspring of a male horse and a female donkey ▷ *vb* whinny
HINS ▶ **hin**
HINT, -ED, -S *n* indirect suggestion ▷ *vb* suggest indirectly
HINTER, -S ▶ **hint**
HINTING ▶ **hint**
HINTS ▶ **hint**
HIOI, -S *n* New Zealand plant of the mint family
HIP, -PER, -PEST, -S *n, adj, interj*
HIPBONE *n*
HIPLESS ▶ **hip**
HIPLIKE ▶ **hip**

HIPLINE *n* widest part of a person's hips
HIPLY ▸ **hip**
HIPNESS ▸ **hip**
HIPPED *adj* having a hip or hips
HIPPEN, -S *n* baby's nappy
HIPPER ▸ **hip**
HIPPEST ▸ **hip**
HIPPIC *adj* of horses
HIPPIE *same as* ▸ **hippy**
HIPPIER ▸ **hippy**
HIPPIES ▸ **hippy**
HIPPIN, -S *same as* ▸ **hippen**
HIPPING *same as* ▸ **hippen**
HIPPINS ▸ **hippin**
HIPPISH *adj* in low spirits
HIPPO, -S *n*
HIPPUS *n* spasm of eye
HIPPY, HIPPIER, HIPPIES *n, adj*
HIPS ▸ **hip**
HIPSHOT *adj* having a dislocated hip
HIPSTER *n* enthusiast of modern jazz
HIPT *old form of* ▸ **hipped**
HIRABLE ▸ **hire**
HIRAGE, -S *n* fee for hiring
HIRCINE *adj* of or like a goat, esp in smell
HIRE, -D, -S *vb, n*
HIREAGE *same as* ▸ **hirage**
HIRED ▸ **hire**
HIREE, -S *n* hired person
HIRER, -S ▸ **hire**
HIRES ▸ **hire**
HIRING, -S ▸ **hire**
HIRLING *n* Scots word for a type of fish
HIRPLE, -D, -S *vb* limp ▹ *n* limping gait
HIRSEL, -S *vb* sort into groups
HIRSLE, -D, -S *vb* wriggle or fidget
HIRSTIE *adj* dry
HIRSUTE *adj* hairy
HIRUDIN *n* anticoagulant
HIS *adj*
HISH, -ED, -ES, -ING *same as* ▸ **hiss**
HISN *dialect form of* ▸ **his**
HISPID *adj* covered with stiff hairs or bristles
HISS, -ED, -ES *n, vb, interj*
HISSELF *dialect form of* ▸ **himself**
HISSER, -S ▸ **hiss**
HISSES ▸ **hiss**
HISSIER ▸ **hissy**
HISSIES ▸ **hissy**
HISSING ▸ **hiss**
HISSY, HISSIER, HISSIES *n* temper tantrum ▹ *adj* having the sound of a hiss
HIST, -ED, -ING, -S *interj* exclamation used to attract attention ▹ *vb* make hist sound
HISTIE *same as* ▸ **hirstie**
HISTING ▸ **hist**
HISTOID *adj* (esp of a tumour)
HISTONE *n* any of a group of proteins present in cell nuclei
HISTORY *n*
HISTRIO *n* actor
HISTS ▸ **hist**
HIT, -S, -TING *vb, n*
HITCH, -ED, -ES *n, vb*
HITCHER ▸ **hitch**
HITCHES ▸ **hitch**
HITCHY ▸ **hitch**
HITHE, -S *n* small harbour
HITHER, -S *adv, vb*
HITHES ▸ **hithe**
HITLESS ▸ **hit**
HITMAN, HITMEN *n*
HITS ▸ **hit**
HITTER, -S *n* boxer who has a hard punch rather than skill or finesse
HITTING ▸ **hit**
HIVE, -D, HIVING *n, vb*
HIVER, -S *n* person who keeps beehives
HIVES *n* allergic reaction
HIVING ▸ **hive**
HIYA *sentence substitute* informal term of greeting
HIZEN, -S *n* type of Japanese porcelain
HIZZ, -ED, -ES, -ING *same as* ▸ **hiss**
HM *interj* sound made to express hesitation or doubt
HMM *same as* ▸ **hm**

This variant of **hm**, like its shorter form, can be useful when you have a shortage of vowels.

HMMM *interj* expressing thoughtful consideration
HO, -ING, -S *interj* imitation or representation of the sound of a deep laugh ▹ *n* cry of 'ho' ▹ *vb* halt
HOA, -ED, -ING, -S *same as* ▸ **ho**

HOAGIE, -S *n* sandwich made with long bread roll
HOAGY *same as* ▸ **hoagie**
HOAING ▸ **hoa**
HOAR, -ED, -ING, -S *adj* covered with hoarfrost ▹ *vb* make hoary
HOARD, -ED, -S *n, vb*
HOARDER ▸ **hoard**
HOARDS ▸ **hoard**
HOARED ▸ **hoar**
HOARIER ▸ **hoary**
HOARILY ▸ **hoary**
HOARING ▸ **hoar**
HOARS ▸ **hoar**
HOARSE, -R *adj*
HOARSEN *vb* make or become hoarse
HOARSER ▸ **hoarse**
HOARY, HOARIER *adj* grey or white(-haired)
HOAS ▸ **hoa**
HOAST, -ED, -S *n* cough ▹ *vb* cough
HOATZIN *n* South American bird
HOAX, -ED, -ES, -ING *n, vb*
HOAXER, -S ▸ **hoax**
HOAXES ▸ **hoax**
HOAXING ▸ **hoax**
HOB, -BED, -BING, -S *n, vb*
HOBBER, -S *n* machine used in making gears
HOBBIES ▸ **hobby**
HOBBING ▸ **hob**
HOBBISH *adj* like a clown
HOBBIT, -S *n* one of an imaginary race of half-size people
HOBBLE, -D, -S *vb, n*
HOBBLER ▸ **hobble**
HOBBLES ▸ **hobble**
HOBBY, HOBBIES *n* activity pursued in one's spare time
HOBDAY, -S *vb* alleviate a breathing problem in certain horses
HOBJOB, -S *vb* do odd jobs
HOBLIKE ▸ **hob**
HOBNAIL *n* short nail with a large head for protecting soles ▹ *vb* provide with hobnails
HOBNOB, -S *vb*
HOBO, -ED, -ES, -ING, -S *n, vb*
HOBODOM ▸ **hobo**
HOBOED ▸ **hobo**
HOBOES ▸ **hobo**
HOBOING ▸ **hobo**
HOBOISM ▸ **hobo**
HOBOS ▸ **hobo**
HOBS ▸ **hob**
HOC *adj* Latin for this
HOCK, -ED, -ING, -S *n, vb*
HOCKER, -S ▸ **hock**
HOCKEY, -S *n*
HOCKING ▸ **hock**
HOCKLE, -D, -S *vb* spit
HOCKS ▸ **hock**
HOCUS, -ED, -ES *vb* take in
HOD, -DED, -DING, -S *n* open wooden box attached to a pole ▹ *vb* bob up and down
HODAD, -S *n* person who pretends to be a surfer
HODADDY *same as* ▸ **hodad**
HODADS ▸ **hodad**
HODDED ▸ **hod**
HODDEN, -S *n* coarse homespun cloth
HODDIN, -S *same as* ▸ **hodden**
HODDING ▸ **hod**
HODDINS ▸ **hoddin**
HODDLE, -D, -S *vb* waddle
HODJA, -S *n* respectful Turkish form of address
HODMAN, HODMEN *n* hod carrier
HODS ▸ **hod**
HOE, -D, -ING, -S *n, vb*
HOECAKE *n* maize cake
HOED ▸ **hoe**
HOEDOWN *n* boisterous square dance
HOEING ▸ **hoe**
HOELIKE ▸ **hoe**
HOER, -S ▸ **hoe**
HOES ▸ **hoe**
HOG, -GED, -S *n, vb*
HOGAN, -S *n* wooden dwelling covered with earth
HOGBACK *n* narrow ridge of steeply inclined rock strata
HOGEN, -S *n* strong alcoholic drink
HOGFISH *n* type of fish
HOGG, -S *same as* ▸ **hog**
HOGGED ▸ **hog**
HOGGER, -S ▸ **hog**
HOGGERY *n* hogs collectively
HOGGET, -S *n* young sheep that has yet to be sheared
HOGGIN, -S *n* finely sifted gravel
HOGGING *same as* ▸ **hoggin**
HOGGINS ▸ **hoggin**
HOGGISH *adj* selfish, gluttonous, or dirty

HOGGS ▶ **hogg**
HOGH, -S *n* ridge of land
HOGHOOD *n* condition of being hog
HOGHS ▶ **hogh**
HOGLIKE ▶ **hog**
HOGMANE *n* short stiff mane
HOGNOSE *n* as in **hognose snake** puff adder
HOGNUT, -S *another name for* ▶ **pignut**
HOGS ▶ **hog**
HOGTIE, -D, -S *vb* tie together the legs or the arms and legs of
HOGWARD *n* person looking after hogs
HOGWASH *n* nonsense
HOGWEED *n* any of several umbelliferous plants
HOH, -ED, -ING, -S *same as* ▶ **ho**
HOHA *adj* bored or annoyed
HOHED ▶ **hoh**
HOHING ▶ **hoh**
HOHS ▶ **hoh**
HOI, -ED, -ING, -S *same as* ▶ **hoy**
HOICK, -ED *vb* raise abruptly and sharply
HOICKS *interj* cry used to encourage hounds to hunt ▷ *vb* shout hoicks
HOIDEN, -S *same as* ▶ **hoyden**
HOIED ▶ **hoi**
HOIING ▶ **hoi**
HOIK, -ED, -ING, -S *same as* ▶ **hoick**
HOING ▶ **ho**
HOIS ▶ **hoi**
HOISE, -D, -S, HOISING *same as* ▶ **hoist**
HOISIN, -S *n* Chinese sweet spicy sauce
HOISING ▶ **hoise**
HOISINS ▶ **hoisin**
HOIST, -ED, -S *vb, n*
HOISTER ▶ **hoist**
HOISTS ▶ **hoist**
HOKA, -S *n* red cod
HOKE, -D, -S, HOKING *vb* overplay (a part, etc)
HOKEY, HOKIER, HOKIEST *adj* corny
HOKI, -S *n* fish of New Zealand waters
HOKIER ▶ **hokey**
HOKIEST ▶ **hokey**
HOKILY ▶ **hokey**
HOKING ▶ **hoke**
HOKIS ▶ **hoki**
HOKKU *same as* ▶ **haiku**
HOKONUI *n* illicit whisky
HOKUM, -S *n* rubbish, nonsense
HOLARD, -S *n* amount of water contained in soil
HOLD, HELD, -S *vb, n*
HOLDALL *n*
HOLDEN *past participle of* ▶ **hold**
HOLDER, -S *n* person or thing that holds
HOLDING ▶ **hold**
HOLDOUT *n* (in US English) person who refuses to change
HOLDS ▶ **hold**
HOLDUP, -S *n* robbery, esp an armed one
HOLE, -D, -S *n, vb*
HOLESOM *same as* > **holesome**
HOLEY, -ER *adj* full of holes
HOLIBUT *same as* ▶ **halibut**
HOLIDAY *n, vb*
HOLIER ▶ **holy**
HOLIES ▶ **holy**
HOLIEST ▶ **holy**
HOLILY *adv* in a holy, devout, or sacred manner
HOLING, -S ▶ **hole**
HOLISM, -S *n* view that a whole is greater than the sum of its parts
HOLIST, -S ▶ **holism**
HOLK, -ED, -ING, -S *vb* dig
HOLLA, -ED, -S *same as* ▶ **hollo**
HOLLAND *n* coarse linen cloth, used esp for furnishing
HOLLAS ▶ **holla**
HOLLER, -S *n, vb*
HOLLIES ▶ **holly**
HOLLO, -ED, -ES, -S *interj* cry for attention, or of encouragement ▷ *vb* shout
HOLLOA, -S *same as* ▶ **hollo**
HOLLOED ▶ **hollo**
HOLLOES ▶ **hollo**
HOLLOO, -S *same as* ▶ **halloo**
HOLLOS ▶ **hollo**
HOLLOW, -S *adj* having a hole or space inside ▷ *n* cavity or space ▷ *vb* form a hollow in
HOLLY, HOLLIES *n*
HOLM, -S *n* island in a river, lake, or estuary
HOLME, -S *same as* ▶ **holm**

HOLMIA, -S *n* oxide of holmium
HOLMIC *adj* of or containing holmium
HOLMIUM *n* silver-white metallic element
HOLMS ▶ **holm**
HOLO, -S *n* short for hologram
HOLON, -S *n* autonomous self-reliant unit, esp in manufacturing
HOLONIC ▶ **holon**
HOLONS ▶ **holon**
HOLOS ▶ **holo**
HOLP *past tense of* ▶ **help**
HOLPEN *past participle of* ▶ **help**
HOLS *pl n* holidays
HOLSTER *n, vb*
HOLT, -S *n* otter's lair
HOLY, HOLIER, HOLIES, HOLIEST *adj, n*
HOLYDAM *same as* ▶ **halidom**
HOLYDAY *n* day on which a religious festival is observed
HOM, -S *n* sacred plant of the Parsees and ancient Persians
HOMA, -S *same as* ▶ **hom**
HOMAGE, -D, -S *n, vb*
HOMAGER ▶ **homage**
HOMAGES ▶ **homage**
HOMAS ▶ **homa**
HOMBRE, -S *slang word for* ▶ **man**
HOMBURG *n* man's soft felt hat
HOME, -D, -S *n, adj, adv, vb*
HOMEBOY *n* close friend
HOMED ▶ **home**
HOMELY *adj* simple, ordinary, and comfortable
HOMELYN *n* species of ray
HOMER, -ED, -S *n* homing pigeon ▷ *vb* score a home run in baseball
HOMERIC *adj* grand or heroic
HOMERS ▶ **homer**
HOMES ▶ **home**
HOMEY, -S *same as* ▶ **homy**
HOMIE, -S *short for* ▶ **homeboy**
HOMIER ▶ **homy**
HOMIES ▶ **homie**
HOMIEST ▶ **homy**
HOMILY *n*
HOMINES ▶ **homo**
HOMING, -S *adj* relating to the ability to return home after travelling ▷ *n* ability to return home after travelling
HOMINID *n* humankind or any extinct forerunner of humankind ▷ *adj* of or belonging to this family
HOMININ *n* member of a zoological family
HOMINY *n* coarsely ground maize
HOMME, -S *French word for* ▶ **man**
HOMMOCK *same as* ▶ **hummock**
HOMMOS *same as* ▶ **hummus**
HOMO, HOMINES, -S *n* homogenized milk
HOMOLOG *same as* ▶ **homologue**
HOMONYM *n* word that is spelt the same as another
HOMOS ▶ **homo**
HOMS ▶ **hom**
HOMY, HOMIER, HOMIEST *adj* like a home
HON, -S *short for* ▶ **honey**
HONAN, -S *n* silk fabric of rough weave
HONCHO, -S *n* person in charge ▷ *vb* supervise or be in charge of
HOND, -S *old form of* ▶ **hand**
HONDA, -S *n* loop used to make a lasso
HONDLE, -D, -S *vb* negotiate on price
HONDS ▶ **hond**
HONE, -D, -S, HONING *vb* sharpen ▷ *n* fine whetstone used for sharpening edged tools and knives
HONER, -S ▶ **hone**
HONES ▶ **hone**
HONEST *adj*
HONESTY *n* quality of being honest
HONEY, -ED, -S *n, vb*
HONG, -ING, -S *n* (in China) a factory, warehouse, etc ▷ *vb* archaic form of hang
HONGI, -ED, -ES, -S *n* Māori greeting in which people touch noses ▷ *vb* touch noses

HONGING ▸ **hong**
HONGIS ▸ **hongi**
HONGS ▸ **hong**
HONIED *same as* ▸ **honeyed**
HONING ▸ **hone**
HONK, -ED, -ING, -S *n* sound made by a car horn ▹ *vb* (cause to) make this sound
HONKER, -S *n* person or thing that honks
HONKING ▸ **honk**
HONKS ▸ **honk**
HONOR, -ED *same as* ▸ **honour**
HONOREE *same as* > **honorand**
HONORER ▸ **honour**
HONORS *same as* ▸ **honours**
HONOUR, -S *n, vb*
HONS ▸ **hon**
HOO *interj* expression of joy, excitement, etc
HOOCH, -ES *n* alcoholic drink, esp illicitly distilled spirits
HOOCHIE *n* immoral woman
HOOD, -ING, -S *n, vb*
HOODED *adj* (of a garment) having a hood
HOODIA, -S *n* any of several southern African succulent plants
HOODIE, -S *n* hooded sweatshirt
HOODIER ▸ **hoody**
HOODIES ▸ **hoodie**
HOODING ▸ **hood**
HOODLUM *n*
HOODMAN, HOODMEN *n* man wearing a hood
HOODOO, -S *n, vb*
HOODS ▸ **hood**
HOODY, HOODIER ▸ **hood**
HOOEY, -S *n* nonsense ▹ *interj* nonsense
HOOF, -ING, -S, HOOVES *n, vb*
HOOFED *adj* having a hoof or hoofs
HOOFER, -S *n* professional dancer
HOOFING ▸ **hoof**
HOOFROT *n* disease of hoof
HOOFS ▸ **hoof**
HOOK, -S *n, vb*
HOOKA, -S *same as* ▸ **hookah**
HOOKAH, -S *n* water-pipe for smoking tobacco
HOOKAS ▸ **hooka**
HOOKED *adj* bent like a hook
HOOKER, -S *n* person or thing that hooks
HOOKEY, -S *same as* ▸ **hooky**
HOOKIER ▸ **hooky**
HOOKIES ▸ **hooky**
HOOKING *n* act of hooking
HOOKLET *n* little hook
HOOKS ▸ **hook**
HOOKUP, -S *n* contact of an aircraft with the hose of a tanker aircraft
HOOKY, HOOKIER, HOOKIES *n* truancy, usually from school ▹ *adj* hooklike
HOOLEY, -S *n* lively party
HOOLIE, -S *same as* ▸ **hooley**
HOOLIER ▸ **hooly**
HOOLIES ▸ **hoolie**
HOOLOCK *n* Indian gibbon
HOOLY, HOOLIER *adj* careful or gentle
HOON, -ED, -ING, -S *n* loutish youth who drives irresponsibly ▹ *vb* drive irresponsibly
HOOP, -ED, -ING, -S *n, vb*
HOOPER, -S *rare word for* ▸ **cooper**
HOOPING ▸ **hoop**
HOOPLA, -S *n*
HOOPOE, -S *n* bird with a pinkish-brown plumage
HOOPOO, -S *same as* ▸ **hoopoe**
HOOPS ▸ **hoop**
HOOR, -S *n* unpleasant or difficult thing
HOORAH, -S *same as* ▸ **hurrah**
HOORAY, -S *same as* ▸ **hurrah**
HOORD, -S *same as* ▸ **hoard**
HOOROO, -S *n* cheer of joy or victory ▹ *vb* shout 'hooroo'
HOORS ▸ **hoor**
HOOSGOW *same as* ▸ **jail**
HOOSH, -ED, -ES *vb* shoo away
HOOT, -ED, -ING *n, vb, interj*
HOOTCH *same as* ▸ **hooch**
HOOTED ▸ **hoot**
HOOTER, -S *n* device that hoots
HOOTIER ▸ **hooty**
HOOTING ▸ **hoot**

HOOTS *same as* ▶ **hoot**
HOOTY, HOOTIER ▶ **hoot**
HOOVE, -D, HOOVING *same as* ▶ **heave**
HOOVEN ▶ **hoove**
HOOVER, -S *vb*
HOOVES ▶ **hoof**
HOOVING ▶ **hoove**
HOP, -PED, -S *vb* jump on one foot ▷ *n* instance of hopping
HOPAK, -S *n* type of Ukrainian dance
HOPBIND *n* stalk of the hop
HOPBINE *same as* ▶ **hopbind**
HOPDOG, -S *n* species of caterpillar
HOPE, -D, -S, HOPING *vb, n*
HOPEFUL *adj, n*
HOPER, -S ▶ **hope**
HOPES ▶ **hope**
HOPING ▶ **hope**
HOPLITE *n* (in ancient Greece) a heavily armed infantryman
HOPPED ▶ **hop**
HOPPER, -S *n* container for storing substances
HOPPIER ▶ **hoppy**
HOPPING ▶ **hop**
HOPPLE, -D, -S *same as* ▶ **hobble**
HOPPLER ▶ **hopple**
HOPPLES ▶ **hopple**
HOPPUS *adj* as in **hoppus foot** unit of volume for round timber
HOPPY, HOPPIER *adj* tasting of hops
HOPS ▶ **hop**
HOPSACK *n* roughly woven fabric
HOPTOAD *n* toad
HORA, -S *n* traditional Israeli or Romanian circle dance
HORAH, -S *same as* ▶ **hora**
HORAL *less common word for* ▶ **hourly**
HORARY *adj* relating to the hours
HORAS ▶ **hora**
HORDE, -D, -S, HORDING *n* large crowd ▷ *vb* form, move in, or live in a horde
HORDEIN *n* simple protein, rich in proline, that occurs in barley
HORDES ▶ **horde**
HORDING ▶ **horde**
HORDOCK *same as* ▶ **hardoke**
HORE *same as* ▶ **hoar**
HORIZON *n*
HORK, -ED, -ING, -S *vb* spit
HORKEY, -S *same as* ▶ **hockey**
HORKING ▶ **hork**
HORKS ▶ **hork**
HORME, -S *n* (in Jungian psychology) fundamental vital energy
HORMIC ▶ **horme**
HORMONE *n*
HORN, -S *n, vb*
HORNBUG *n* stag beetle
HORNED *adj* having a horn, horns, or hornlike parts
HORNER, -S *n* dealer in horn
HORNET, -S *n*
HORNFUL *n* amount a horn will hold
HORNIER ▶ **horny**
HORNILY ▶ **horny**
HORNING ▶ **horn**
HORNISH *adj* like horn
HORNIST *n* horn player
HORNITO *n* small vent in volcano
HORNLET *n* small horn
HORNS ▶ **horn**
HORNY, HORNIER *adj* of or like horn
HOROEKA *n* New Zealand tree
HORRENT *adj* bristling
HORRID *adj*
HORRIFY *vb*
HORROR *n, adj*
HORRORS *pl n* fit of misery or anxiety ▷ *interj* expression of dismay, sometimes facetious
HORS *prep* as in **hors d'oeuvre** appetizer
HORSE, -D, -S *n, vb*
HORSEY, HORSIER *adj* very keen on horses
HORSIE, -S *n* child's word for a horse
HORSIER ▶ **horsey**
HORSIES ▶ **horsie**
HORSILY ▶ **horsey**
HORSING ▶ **horse**
HORST, -S *n* ridge of land
HORSTE, -S *variant of* ▶ **horst**
HORSTS ▶ **horst**
HORSY *same as* ▶ **horsey**
HOS ▶ **ho**
HOSANNA *interj* exclamation of praise to God ▷ *n* act of

crying 'hosanna' ▷ *vb* cry hosanna
HOSE, -D, -N, -S, HOSING *n, vb*
HOSEL, -S *n* socket in head of golf club
HOSEMAN, HOSEMEN *n* firefighter in charge of a hose
HOSEN ▸ **hose**
HOSER, -S *n* person who swindles or deceives others
HOSES ▸ **hose**
HOSEY, -ED, -S *vb* claim possession
HOSIER, -S *n* person who sells stockings, etc
HOSIERY *n*
HOSING ▸ **hose**
HOSPICE *n*
HOSS, -ES *n* horse
HOST, -ED, -S *n, vb*
HOSTA, -S *n* ornamental plant
HOSTAGE *n*
HOSTAS ▸ **hosta**
HOSTED ▸ **host**
HOSTEL, -S *n, vb*
HOSTESS *n, vb*
HOSTIE, -S *n* informal Australian word for an air hostess
HOSTILE *adj, n*
HOSTING ▸ **host**
HOSTLER *another name (esp Brit) for* ▸ **ostler**
HOSTLY ▸ **host**
HOSTRY *n* lodging
HOSTS ▸ **host**
HOT, -S, -TED, -TEST *adj, vb*
HOTBED, -S *n* any place encouraging a particular activity
HOTBOX *n* container maintained at a high temperature to heat its contents
HOTCAKE *n* pancake
HOTCH, -ED, -ES *vb* jog
HOTDOG, -S *vb*
HOTE ▸ **hight**
HOTEL, -S *n*
HOTEN ▸ **hight**
HOTFOOT *adv* quickly and eagerly ▷ *vb* move quickly
HOTHEAD *n*
HOTLINE *n*
HOTLINK *n* area on website connecting to another site
HOTLY ▸ **hot**
HOTNESS ▸ **hot**
HOTPOT, -S *n*
HOTROD, -S *n*
HOTS ▸ **hot**
HOTSHOT *n*
HOTSPOT *n* place where wireless broadband is provided
HOTSPUR *n* impetuous or fiery person
HOTTED ▸ **hot**
HOTTER, -S *vb* simmer
HOTTEST ▸ **hot**
HOTTIE, -S *n* attractive person
HOTTING *n* stealing fast cars to put on a show of skilful driving
HOTTISH *adj* fairly hot
HOTTY *same as* ▸ **hottie**
HOUDAH, -S *same as* ▸ **howdah**
HOUDAN, -S *n* breed of light domestic fowl
HOUF, -ED, -ING, -S *same as* ▸ **howf**
HOUFF, -ED, -S *same as* ▸ **howf**
HOUFING ▸ **houf**
HOUFS ▸ **houf**
HOUGH, -ED, -S *n* in Scotland, a cut of meat corresponding to shin ▷ *vb* hamstring (cattle, horses, etc)
HOUHERE *n* small evergreen New Zealand tree
HOUMMOS *same as* ▸ **hummus**
HOUMOUS *same as* ▸ **hummus**
HOUMUS *same as* ▸ **hummus**
HOUND, -ED, -S *n, vb*
HOUNDER ▸ **hound**
HOUNDS ▸ **hound**
HOUNGAN *n* voodoo priest
HOUR *n*
HOURI, -S *n* any of the nymphs of paradise
HOURLY *adv* (happening) every hour ▷ *adj* of, occurring, or done once every hour ▷ *n* something that is done by the hour
HOURS *pl n* indefinite time
HOUSE, -D, -S *n, vb*
HOUSEL, -S *vb* give the Eucharist to (someone)
HOUSER, -S ▸ **house**
HOUSES ▸ **house**
HOUSEY, HOUSIER *adj* of or like house music
HOUSING *n* (providing of) houses
HOUT, -ED, -S *same as* ▸ **hoot**
HOUTING *n* type of fish
HOUTS ▸ **hout**
HOVE, -D, -S, HOVING *vb* swell

HOVEA, -S *n* Australian plant with purple flowers
HOVED ▸ **hove**
HOVEL, -ED, -S *n* small dirty house or hut ▹ *vb* shelter or be sheltered in a hovel
HOVEN ▸ **heave**
HOVER, -ED, -S *vb, n*
HOVERER ▸ **hover**
HOVERS ▸ **hover**
HOVES ▸ **hove**
HOVING ▸ **hove**
HOW, -S *adv, n, sentence substitute*
HOWBE *same as* ▸ **howbeit**
HOWBEIT *adv* in archaic usage, however
HOWDAH, -S *n* canopied seat on an elephant's back
HOWDIE *n* midwife
HOWDY, HOWDIED, HOWDIES *vb* greet someone
HOWE, -S *n* depression in the earth's surface
HOWEVER *adv*
HOWF, -ED, -ING, -S *n* haunt, esp a public house ▹ *vb* visit a place frequently
HOWFF, -ED, -S *vb* visit a place frequently
HOWFING ▸ **howf**
HOWFS ▸ **howf**
HOWK, -ED, -ING, -S *vb* dig (out or up)
HOWKER, -S ▸ **howk**
HOWKING ▸ **howk**
HOWKS ▸ **howk**
HOWL, -ED, -S *n, vb*
HOWLER, -S *n* stupid mistake
HOWLET, -S *another word for* ▸ **owl**
HOWLING *adj* great ▹ *n* act of wailing
HOWLS ▸ **howl**
HOWRE, -S *same as* ▸ **hour**
HOWS ▸ **how**
HOWSO *same as* ▸ **howsoever**
HOWZAT *interj* cry in cricket appealing for dismissal of batsman
HOWZIT *informal word for* ▸ **hello**
HOX, -ED, -ES, -ING *vb* hamstring

This is a word found in Shakespeare's plays, and it means to cut a horse's hamstring. It's one of the many short words with X that can get you a high score.

HOY, -ED, -ING, -S *interj* cry used to attract someone's attention ▹ *n* freight barge ▹ *vb* drive animal with cry
HOYA, -S *n* any of various E Asian or Australian plants
HOYDEN, -S *n* wild or boisterous girl ▹ *vb* behave like a hoyden
HOYED ▸ **hoy**
HOYING ▸ **hoy**
HOYLE, -S *n* archer's mark used as a target
HOYS ▸ **hoy**
HRYVNA, -S *n* standard monetary unit of Ukraine
HRYVNIA *same as* ▸ **hryvna**
HRYVNYA *same as* ▸ **hryvna**
HUANACO *same as* ▸ **guanaco**
HUB, -S *n*
HUBBIES ▸ **hubby**
HUBBLY *adj* having an irregular surface
HUBBUB, -S *n*
HUBBY, HUBBIES *n* husband
HUBCAP, -S *n*
HUBLESS *adj* without a hub
HUBRIS *n*
HUBS ▸ **hub**
HUCK, -ED, -ING, -S *same as* ▸ **huckaback**
HUCKERY *adj* ugly
HUCKING ▸ **huck**
HUCKLE, -D, -S *n* hip or haunch ▹ *vb* force out or arrest roughly
HUCKS ▸ **huck**
HUDDEN ▸ **haud**
HUDDLE, -D, -S *vb, n*
HUDDLER ▸ **huddle**
HUDDLES ▸ **huddle**
HUDDUP *interj* get up
HUDNA, -S *n* truce or ceasefire for a fixed duration
HUDUD, -S *n* set of laws and punishments in the Koran
HUE, -S *n* colour, shade
HUED *adj* having a hue or colour as specified
HUELESS ▸ **hue**
HUER, -S *n* pilchard fisherman
HUES ▸ **hue**
HUFF, -ED, -S *n* passing mood of anger or resentment ▹ *vb* blow or puff heavily

HUFFER, -S ▸ **huffing**
HUFFIER ▸ **huffy**
HUFFILY ▸ **huff**
HUFFING *n* practice of inhaling fumes for intoxicating effects
HUFFISH ▸ **huff**
HUFFKIN *n* type of muffin
HUFFS ▸ **huff**
HUFFY, HUFFIER ▸ **huff**
HUG, -GED, -GING, -S *vb, n*
HUGE, -R, -ST *adj*
HUGELY *adv* very much
HUGEOUS *same as* ▸ **huge**
HUGER ▸ **huge**
HUGEST ▸ **huge**
HUGGED ▸ **hug**
HUGGER, -S ▸ **hug**
HUGGIER ▸ **huggy**
HUGGING ▸ **hug**
HUGGY, HUGGIER *adj* sensitive and caring
HUGS ▸ **hug**
HUGY *same as* ▸ **huge**
HUH *interj* exclamation of derision or inquiry
HUHU, -S *n* type of hairy New Zealand beetle
HUI, -S *n* meeting of Māori people
HUIA, -S *n* extinct bird of New Zealand
HUIC *interj* in hunting, a call to hounds
HUIPIL, -S *n* Mayan woman's blouse
HUIS ▸ **hui**
HUITAIN *n* verse of eighteen lines
HULA, -S *n* swaying Hawaiian dance
HULE, -S *same as* ▸ **ule**
HULK, -ED, -S *n* body of an abandoned ship ▹ *vb* move clumsily
HULKIER ▸ **hulky**
HULKING *adj* bulky, unwieldy
HULKS ▸ **hulk**
HULKY, HULKIER *same as* ▸ **hulking**
HULL, -ED, -ING, -S *n* main body of a boat ▹ *vb* remove the hulls from
HULLER, -S ▸ **hull**
HULLIER ▸ **hully**
HULLING ▸ **hull**
HULLO, -ED, -ES, -S *same as* ▸ **hello**
HULLOA, -S *same as* ▸ **halloa**
HULLOED ▸ **hullo**
HULLOES ▸ **hullo**
HULLOO, -S *same as* ▸ **halloo**
HULLOS ▸ **hullo**
HULLS ▸ **hull**
HULLY, HULLIER *adj* having husks
HUM, -MED, -S *vb, n*
HUMA, -S *n* mythical bird
HUMAN, -S *adj, n*
HUMANE, -R *adj*
HUMANLY *adv* by human powers or means
HUMANS ▸ **human**
HUMAS ▸ **huma**
HUMATE, -S *n* decomposed plants used as fertilizer
HUMBLE, -D, -S *adj, vb*
HUMBLER ▸ **humble**
HUMBLES ▸ **humble**
HUMBLY ▸ **humble**
HUMBUG, -S *n, vb*
HUMBUZZ *n* type of beetle
HUMDRUM *adj* ordinary, dull ▹ *n* monotonous routine, task, or person
HUMECT, -S *vb* make moist
HUMEFY *same as* ▸ **humify**
HUMERAL *adj* of or relating to the humerus ▹ *n* silk shawl worn by a priest at High Mass; humeral veil
HUMERUS, HUMERI *n* bone from the shoulder to the elbow
HUMF, -ED, -ING, -S *same as* ▸ **humph**
HUMHUM, -S *n* Indian cotton cloth
HUMIC *adj* of, derived from, or resembling humus
HUMID, -ER *adj*
HUMIDEX *n* system of measuring discomfort
HUMIDLY ▸ **humid**
HUMIDOR *n* humid place for storing cigars, tobacco, etc
HUMIFY *vb* convert or be converted into humus
HUMINT, -S *n* human intelligence
HUMITE, -S *n* mineral containing magnesium
HUMLIE, -S *n* hornless cow
HUMMAUM *same as* ▸ **hammam**
HUMMED ▸ **hum**
HUMMEL, -S *adj* (of cattle) hornless ▹ *vb* remove horns from
HUMMER, -S ▸ **hum**
HUMMING ▸ **hum**
HUMMLE *adj* as in **hummle bonnet** type of Scottish cap
HUMMOCK *n* very small hill ▹ *vb* form

into a hummock or hummocks
HUMMUM, -S *same as* ▶ **hammam**
HUMMUS *n* creamy dip
HUMOGEN *n* type of fertilizer
HUMOR, -ED, -S *same as* ▶ **humour**
HUMORAL *adj* denoting or relating to a type of immunity
HUMORED ▶ **humor**
HUMORS ▶ **humor**
HUMOUR, -S *n, vb*
HUMOUS *same as* ▶ **humus**
HUMP, -ED, -ING, -S *n, vb*
HUMPEN, -S *n* old German drinking glass
HUMPER, -S ▶ **hump**
HUMPH, -ED, -S *interj* exclamation of annoyance or scepticism ▷ *vb* exclaim humph
HUMPIER ▶ **humpy**
HUMPIES ▶ **humpy**
HUMPING ▶ **hump**
HUMPS ▶ **hump**
HUMPTY *n* low padded seat
HUMPY, HUMPIER, HUMPIES *adj* full of humps ▷ *n* primitive hut
HUMS ▶ **hum**
HUMUS, -ES *n* decomposing matter in the soil
HUMUSY *adj* like humus
HUMVEE, -S *n* military vehicle
HUN, -S *n* member of any of several nomadic peoples
HUNCH, -ED, -ES *n, vb*
HUNDRED *n, adj*
HUNG ▶ **hang**
HUNGAN, -S *same as* ▶ **houngan**
HUNGER, -S *n, vb*
HUNGRY *adj* desiring food
HUNH *same as* ▶ **huh**
HUNK *n*
HUNKER *vb* squat
HUNKERS *pl n* haunches
HUNKIER ▶ **hunky**
HUNKS, -ES *n* grumpy person
HUNKY, HUNKIER *adj* excellent
HUNNISH ▶ **hun**
HUNS ▶ **hun**
HUNT, -S *vb, n*
HUNTED *adj* harassed and worn
HUNTER, -S *n* person or animal that hunts wild animals
HUNTING *n* pursuit and killing or capture of wild animals
HUNTS ▶ **hunt**
HUP, -PED, -PING, -S *vb* cry hup to get a horse to move
HUPIRO, -S *in New Zealand English, same as* > **stinkwood**
HUPPAH, -S, HUPPOT *variant spelling of* ▶ **chuppah**
HUPPED ▶ **hup**
HUPPING ▶ **hup**
HUPPOT ▶ **huppah**
HUPPOTH *same as* ▶ **huppot**
HUPS ▶ **hup**
HURDEN, -S *same as* ▶ **harden**
HURDIES *pl n* buttocks or haunches
HURDLE, -D, -S *n, vb*
HURDLER ▶ **hurdle**
HURDLES ▶ **hurdle**
HURDS *same as* ▶ **hards**
HURL, -ED, -S *vb* throw or utter forcefully ▷ *n* act or an instance of hurling
HURLBAT *same as* > **whirlbat**
HURLED ▶ **hurl**
HURLER, -S ▶ **hurl**
HURLEY, -S *n* another word for the game of hurling
HURLIES ▶ **hurly**
HURLING *n* Irish game like hockey
HURLS ▶ **hurl**
HURLY, HURLIES *n* wheeled barrow
HURRA, -ED, -S *same as* ▶ **hurrah**
HURRAH, -S *interj* exclamation of joy or applause ▷ *n* cheer of joy or victory ▷ *vb* shout 'hurrah'
HURRAS ▶ **hurra**
HURRAY, -S *same as* ▶ **hurrah**
HURRIED *adj* done quickly or too quickly
HURRIER ▶ **hurry**
HURRY, HURRIES *vb, n*
HURST, -S *n* wood
HURT, -ING, -S *vb, n, adj*
HURTER, -S ▶ **hurt**
HURTFUL *adj*
HURTING ▶ **hurt**
HURTLE, -D, -S *vb* move quickly or violently
HURTS ▶ **hurt**
HUSBAND *n, vb*
HUSH, -ES, -ING *vb, n, interj*
HUSHABY *interj* used in quietening a baby or

child to sleep ▷ *n* lullaby ▷ *vb* quieten to sleep
HUSHED ▸ **hush**
HUSHER, -S *same as* ▸ **usher**
HUSHES ▸ **hush**
HUSHFUL *adj* quiet
HUSHIER ▸ **hushy**
HUSHING ▸ **hush**
HUSHY, HUSHIER *adj* secret
HUSK, -ED, -S *n, vb*
HUSKER, -S ▸ **husk**
HUSKIER ▸ **husky**
HUSKIES ▸ **husky**
HUSKILY ▸ **husky**
HUSKING ▸ **husk**
HUSKS ▸ **husk**
HUSKY, HUSKIER, HUSKIES *adj, n*
HUSO, -S *n* sturgeon
HUSS, -ES *n* flesh of the European dogfish
HUSSAR, -S *n* lightly armed cavalry soldier
HUSSES ▸ **huss**
HUSSIF, -S *n* sewing kit
HUSTLE, -D, -S *vb, n*
HUSTLER ▸ **hustle**
HUSTLES ▸ **hustle**
HUSWIFE *same as* > **housewife**
HUT, -S, -TED *n, vb*
HUTCH, -ED, -ES *n, vb*
HUTCHIE *n* temporary shelter
HUTIA, -S *n* rodent native to the Caribbean
HUTLIKE ▸ **hut**
HUTMENT *n* number or group of huts
HUTS ▸ **hut**
HUTTED ▸ **hut**
HUTTING ▸ **hut**
HUTZPA, -S *same as* ▸ **hutzpah**
HUTZPAH *variant spelling of* > **chutzpah**
HUTZPAS ▸ **hutzpa**
HUZOOR, -S *n* person of rank in India
HUZZA, -ED, -S *same as* ▸ **huzzah**
HUZZAH, -S *archaic word for* ▸ **hurrah**
HUZZAS ▸ **huzza**
HWAN *another name for* ▸ **won**
HWYL, -S *n* emotional fervour, as in the recitation of poetry

This Welsh word can come in very useful for dealing with a consonant-heavy rack.

HYACINE *same as* > **hyacinth**
HYAENA, -S *same as* ▸ **hyena**
HYAENIC ▸ **hyaena**
HYALIN, -S *n* glassy translucent substance
HYALINE *adj* clear and translucent, with no fibres or granules ▷ *n* glassy transparent surface
HYALINS ▸ **hyalin**
HYALITE *n* clear and colourless variety of opal in globular form
HYALOID *adj* clear and transparent ▷ *n* delicate transparent membrane
HYBRID, -S *n, adj*
HYBRIS *same as* ▸ **hubris**
HYDATID *n* cyst containing tapeworm larvae
HYDRA, -E, -S *n* mythical many-headed water serpent
HYDRANT *n* outlet from a water main with a nozzle for a hose
HYDRAS ▸ **hydra**
HYDRASE *n* enzyme that removes water
HYDRATE *n* chemical compound of water with another substance ▷ *vb* treat or impregnate with water
HYDRIA, -E *n* (in ancient Greece and Rome) a large water jar
HYDRIC *adj* of or containing hydrogen
HYDRID, -S *same as* ▸ **hydroid**
HYDRIDE *n* compound of hydrogen with another element
HYDRIDS ▸ **hydrid**
HYDRO, -S *n* hotel offering facilities for hydropathy ▷ *adj* short for hydroelectric
HYDROID *adj* of an order of colonial hydrozoan coelenterates ▷ *n* hydroid colony or individual
HYDROMA *same as* ▸ **hygroma**
HYDROPS *n* anaemia in a fetus
HYDROS ▸ **hydro**
HYDROUS *adj* containing water
HYDROXY *adj* of a type of chemical compound
HYDYNE, -S *n* type of rocket fuel

HYE, -D, -ING, -S *same as* ▸ **hie**
HYEN, -S *same as* ▸ **hyena**
HYENA, -S *n* scavenging doglike mammal of Africa and S Asia
HYENIC ▸ **hyena**
HYENINE *adj* of hyenas
HYENOID *adj* of or like hyenas
HYENS ▸ **hyen**
HYES ▸ **hye**
HYETAL *adj* of or relating to rain, rainfall, or rainy regions
HYGEIST *same as* > **hygienist**
HYGGE, -S *n* Danish practice that promotes wellbeing
HYGIENE *n*
HYGROMA *n* swelling soft tissue that occurs over a joint
HYING ▸ **hie**
HYKE, -S *same as* ▸ **haik**
HYLA, -S *n* type of tropical American tree frog
HYLDING *same as* ▸ **hilding**
HYLE, -S *n* wood
HYLEG, -S *n* dominant planet when someone is born
HYLES ▸ **hyle**
HYLIC *adj* solid
HYLISM, -S *same as* > **hylicism**
HYLIST, -S ▸ **hylism**
HYLOIST *n* materialist
HYMEN, -S *n* membrane partly covering the vaginal opening
HYMENAL ▸ **hymen**
HYMENIA > **hymenium**
HYMENS ▸ **hymen**
HYMN, -ED, -ING, -S *n, vb*
HYMNAL, -S *n* book of hymns ▹ *adj* of, relating to, or characteristic of hymns
HYMNARY *same as* ▸ **hymnal**
HYMNED ▸ **hymn**
HYMNIC ▸ **hymn**
HYMNING ▸ **hymn**
HYMNIST *n* person who composes hymns
HYMNODY *n* composition or singing of hymns
HYMNS ▸ **hymn**
HYNDE, -S *same as* ▸ **hind**
HYOID, -S *adj* of or relating to the hyoid bone ▹ *n* horseshoe-shaped bone
HYOIDAL *adj* of or relating to the hyoid bone
HYOIDS ▸ **hyoid**
HYP, -PED, -PING, -S *n* short for hypotenuse ▹ *vb* offend
HYPATE, -S *n* string of lyre
HYPE, -D, -S *n, vb*
HYPER, -ER, -S *n* excitable person ▹ *adj* excitable
HYPERON *n* any baryon that is not a nucleon
HYPERS ▸ **hyper**
HYPES ▸ **hype**
HYPHA, -E *n* any of the filaments in the mycelium of a fungus
HYPHAL ▸ **hypha**
HYPHEN, -S *n, vb*
HYPHY, HYPHIES *n* type of hip-hop music
HYPING, -S ▸ **hype**
HYPNIC, -S *n* sleeping drug
HYPNOID *adj* of or relating to a state resembling sleep
HYPNONE *n* sleeping drug
HYPNUM, -S *n* species of moss
HYPO, -ED, -ING, -S *vb* inject with a hypodermic syringe
HYPOGEA > **hypogeum**
HYPOID, -S *adj* as in **hypoid gear** type of gear ▹ *n* hypoid gear
HYPOING ▸ **hypo**
HYPONEA *same as* > **hypopnea**
HYPONYM *n* word whose meaning is included as part of another
HYPOS ▸ **hypo**
HYPOXIA *n* deficiency in oxygen delivery
HYPOXIC ▸ **hypoxia**
HYPPED ▸ **hyp**
HYPPING ▸ **hyp**
HYPS ▸ **hyp**
HYPURAL *adj* below the tail
HYRAX, HYRACES, -ES *n* type of hoofed rodent-like animal of Africa and Asia
HYSON, -S *n* Chinese green tea
HYSSOP, -S *n* sweet-smelling herb used in folk medicine
HYTE *adj* crazy
HYTHE, -S *same as* ▸ **hithe**

Ii

IAMB, -S *n* metrical foot of two syllables
IAMBI ▸ **iambus**
IAMBIC, -S *adj* written in a type of metrical unit ▹ *n* iambic foot, line, or stanza
IAMBIST *n* one who writes iambs
IAMBS ▸ **iamb**
IAMBUS, IAMBI *same as* ▸ **iamb**
IATRIC *adj* relating to medicine or physicians
IBADAH, IBADAT *n* following of Islamic beliefs and practices
IBERIS *n* plant with white or purple flowers
IBEX, -ES, IBICES *n* wild goat
IBIDEM *adv* in the same place
IBIS, -ES *n* large wading bird with long legs
IBRIK, -S *same as* ▸ **cezve**
ICE, -S *n, vb*
ICEBALL *n* ball of ice
ICEBERG *n*
ICEBOAT *n* boat that breaks up bodies of ice in water ▹ *vb* pilot an iceboat
ICEBOX *n* refrigerator
ICECAP, -S *n*
ICED *adj* covered with icing
ICEFALL *n* part of a glacier
ICEFISH *vb* fish through a hole in the ice on a lake
ICELESS ▸ **ice**
ICELIKE ▸ **ice**
ICEMAN, ICEMEN *n* person who sells or delivers ice
ICEPACK *n*
ICER, -S *n* person who ices cakes
ICES ▸ **ice**
ICEWINE *n* dessert wine made from grapes that have frozen before being harvested
ICEWORM *n* small worm found in glaciers
ICH, -ED, -ES, -ING, -S *archaic form of* ▸ **eke**

> A Shakespearean spelling of **eke**, this is a useful little word worth remembering because of its unusual combination of letters and relatively high score.

ICHABOD *interj* the glory has departed
ICHED ▸ **ich**
ICHES ▸ **ich**
ICHING ▸ **ich**
ICHNITE *n* trace fossil
ICHOR, -S *n* fluid said to flow in the veins of the gods
ICHS ▸ **ich**
ICHTHIC *same as* > **ichthyic**
ICHTHYS *n* early Christian emblem
ICICLE, -S *n*
ICICLED *adj* covered with icicles
ICICLES ▸ **icicle**
ICIER ▸ **icy**
ICIEST ▸ **icy**
ICILY *adv* in an icy or reserved manner
ICINESS *n* condition of being icy or very cold
ICING, -S *n* mixture used to decorate cakes
ICK, -S *interj* expression of disgust ▹ *n* something sticky

> An interjection expressing disgust, this is one of the highest-scoring 3-letter words beginning with I. It can also take a Y to make **icky**.

ICKER, -S *n* ear of corn

ICKIER ▸ **icky**
ICKIEST ▸ **icky**
ICKILY ▸ **icky**
ICKLE, -R, -ST *ironically childish word for* ▸ **little**
ICKS ▸ **ick**
ICKY, ICKIER, ICKIEST *adj* sticky
ICON, -S *n*
ICONES *archaic form of* ▸ **icons**
ICONIC *adj* relating to the character of an icon
ICONIFY *vb* render as an icon
ICONISE *same as* ▸ **iconize**
ICONIZE *vb* render as an icon
ICONS ▸ **icon**
ICTAL ▸ **ictus**
ICTERIC ▸ **icterus**
ICTERID *n* bird of the oriole family
ICTERUS *n* yellowing of plant leaves
ICTIC ▸ **ictus**
ICTUS, -ES *n* metrical or rhythmic stress in verse feet
ICY, ICIER, ICIEST *adj* very cold
ID, -S *n* mind's instinctive unconscious energies
IDANT, -S *n* chromosome
IDE *n* silver orfe fish
IDEA, -S *n*
IDEAED *adj* expressing a particular idea
IDEAL, -S *adj, n*
IDEALLY ▸ **ideal**
IDEALS ▸ **ideal**
IDEAS ▸ **idea**
IDEATA ▸ **ideatum**
IDEATE, -D, -S *vb* form or have an idea of
IDEATUM, IDEATA *n* objective reality
IDEE, -S *n* idea
IDEM *adj* same
IDENT, -S *n* short visual image that works as a logo
IDENTIC *adj* having the same intention regarding another power
IDENTS ▸ **ident**
IDES *n* specific date of each month in the Roman calendar
IDIOCY *n*
IDIOM, -S *n*
IDIOT, -S *n*
IDIOTCY *same as* ▸ **idiocy**
IDIOTIC *adj* of or resembling an idiot
IDIOTS ▸ **idiot**
IDLE, -D, -S, -ST, IDLING *adj, vb*
IDLER, -S *n* person who idles
IDLES ▸ **idle**
IDLESSE *poetic word for* > **idleness**
IDLEST ▸ **idle**
IDLING ▸ **idle**
IDLY ▸ **idle**
IDOL, -S *n*
IDOLA ▸ **idolum**
IDOLISE *same as* ▸ **idolize**
IDOLISM ▸ **idol**
IDOLIST ▸ **idolize**
IDOLIZE *vb*
IDOLON *n* mental picture
IDOLS ▸ **idol**
IDOLUM, IDOLA *n* mental picture
IDS ▸ **id**
IDYL, -S *same as* ▸ **idyll**
IDYLIST *same as* > **idyllist**
IDYLL, -S *n*
IDYLLIC *adj* of or relating to an idyll
IDYLLS ▸ **idyll**
IDYLS ▸ **idyl**
IF, -S *n*
IFF *conj* in logic, a shortened form of if and only if

> This word is one of the highest-scoring 3-letter words beginning with I, and of course provides a useful extension to **if**.

IFFIER ▸ **iffy**
IFFIEST ▸ **iffy**
IFFILY *adv* in an iffy manner
IFFY, IFFIER, IFFIEST *adj* doubtful, uncertain
IFS ▸ **if**
IFTAR, -S *n* meal eaten by Muslims
IGAD *same as* ▸ **egad**
IGAPO, -S *n* flooded forest
IGARAPE *n* canoe route
IGG, -ED, -ING, -S *vb* antagonize
IGLOO, -S *n*
IGLU, -S *same as* ▸ **igloo**
IGNARO, -S *n* ignoramus
IGNATIA *n* dried seed
IGNEOUS *adj* (of rock) formed as molten rock cools
IGNIFY *vb* turn into fire

IGNITE, -D, -S *vb*
IGNITER *n* person or thing that ignites
IGNITES ▸ **ignite**
IGNITOR *same as* ▸ **igniter**
IGNOBLE *adj*
IGNOBLY ▸ **ignoble**
IGNOMY *Shakespearean variant of* > **ignominy**
IGNORE, -D, -S *vb, n*
IGNORER ▸ **ignore**
IGNORES ▸ **ignore**
IGUANA, -S *n*
IGUANID *same as* ▸ **iguana**
IHRAM, -S *n* white robes worn by Muslim pilgrims to Mecca
IJTIHAD *n* effort of deriving a legal ruling from the Koran
IKAN, -S *n* (in Malaysia) fish
IKAT, -S *n* method of creating patterns in fabric
IKEBANA *n* Japanese art of flower arrangement
IKON, -S *same as* ▸ **icon**
ILEA ▸ **ileum**

This is the plural of **ileum**, part of the small intestine, and is often useful as a rack-balancing play when you have too many vowels.

ILEAC *adj* of or relating to the ileum
ILEAL *same as* ▸ **ileac**
ILEITIS *n* inflammation of the ileum
ILEUM, ILEA *n* lowest part of the small intestine
ILEUS, -ES *n* obstruction of the intestine
ILEX, -ES, ILICES *n* any of a genus of trees or shrubs that includes holly
ILIA ▸ **ilium**
ILIAC *adj* of or relating to the ilium
ILIACUS, ILIACI *n* muscle near the ilium
ILIAD, -S *n* epic poem
ILIAL ▸ **ilium**
ILICES ▸ **ilex**
ILIUM, ILIA *n* part of the hipbone
ILK, -S *n*
ILKA *determiner* Scots word meaning each
ILKADAY *n* Scots word for a weekday
ILKS ▸ **ilk**
ILL, -ER, -EST, -S *adj, n, adv*
ILLAPSE *vb* slide in
ILLEGAL *adj, n*
ILLER ▸ **ill**
ILLEST ▸ **ill**
ILLIAD, -S *n* wink
ILLICIT *adj*
ILLIPE, -S *n* Asian tree
ILLITE, -S *n* clay mineral of the mica group
ILLITIC ▸ **illite**
ILLNESS *n*
ILLOGIC *n* reasoning characterized by lack of logic
ILLS ▸ **ill**
ILLTH, -S *n* condition of poverty or misery
ILLUDE, -D, -S *vb* trick or deceive
ILLUME, -D, -S *vb* illuminate
ILLUPI, -S *same as* ▸ **illipe**
ILLUVIA > **illuvium**
ILLY *adv* badly
IMAGE, -D, -S *n, vb*
IMAGER, -S *n* device that produces images
IMAGERY *n* images collectively, esp in the arts
IMAGES ▸ **image**
IMAGINE *vb, sentence substitute*
IMAGING ▸ **image**
IMAGISM *n* poetic movement
IMAGIST ▸ **imagism**
IMAGO, -ES, -S *n* mature adult insect
IMAM, -S *n* leader of prayers in a mosque
IMAMATE *n* region or territory governed by an imam
IMAMS ▸ **imam**
IMARET, -S *n* (in Turkey) a hospice for pilgrims or travellers
IMARI, -S *n* Japanese porcelain
IMAUM, -S *same as* ▸ **imam**
IMBALM, -S *same as* ▸ **embalm**
IMBAR, -S *vb* bar in
IMBARK, -S *vb* cover in bark
IMBARS ▸ **imbar**
IMBASE, -D, -S *vb* degrade
IMBATHE *vb* bathe

IMBED, -S *same as* ▸ **embed**
IMBIBE, -D, -S *vb*
IMBIBER ▸ **imbibe**
IMBIBES ▸ **imbibe**
IMBIZO, -S *n* meeting in S Africa
IMBLAZE *vb* depict heraldically
IMBODY *same as* ▸ **embody**
IMBOSK, -S *vb* conceal
IMBOSOM *vb* hold in one's heart
IMBOSS *same as* ▸ **emboss**
IMBOWER *vb* enclose in a bower
IMBRAST *Spenserian past participle of* ▸ **embrace**
IMBREX *n* curved tile
IMBROWN *vb* make brown
IMBRUE, -D, -S *vb* stain, esp with blood
IMBRUTE *vb* reduce to a bestial state
IMBUE, -D, -S, IMBUING *vb*
IMBURSE *vb* pay
IMID, -S *n* immunomodulatory drug
IMIDE, -S *n* any of a class of organic compounds
IMIDIC ▸ **imide**
IMIDO ▸ **imide**
IMIDS ▸ **imid**
IMINE, -S *n* any of a class of organic compounds
IMINO ▸ **imine**
IMITANT *same as* > **imitation**
IMITATE *vb*
IMMANE *adj* monstrous
IMMASK, -S *vb* disguise
IMMENSE *adj*
IMMERGE *archaic word for* ▸ **immerse**
IMMERSE *vb*
IMMESH *variant of* ▸ **enmesh**
IMMEW, -ED, -S *vb* confine
IMMIES ▸ **immy**
IMMIT, -S *vb* insert
IMMIX, -ED, -ES *vb* mix in
IMMORAL *adj*
IMMUNE, -R, -S *adj, n*
IMMURE, -D, -S *vb* imprison
IMMY, IMMIES *n* image-orthicon camera
IMP, -ED, -S *n* (in folklore) creature with magical powers ▹ *vb* method of repairing the wing of a hawk or falcon
IMPACT, -S *n, vb*
IMPAINT *vb* paint
IMPAIR, -S *vb*
IMPALA, -S *n* southern African antelope
IMPALE, -D, -S *vb*
IMPALER ▸ **impale**
IMPALES ▸ **impale**
IMPANEL *variant spelling (esp US) of* ▸ **empanel**
IMPARK, -S *vb* make into a park
IMPARL, -S *vb* parley
IMPART, -S *vb* communicate (information)
IMPASSE *n*
IMPASTE *vb* apply paint thickly to
IMPASTO *n* technique of applying paint thickly ▹ *vb* apply impasto
IMPAVE, -D, -S *vb* set in a pavement
IMPAVID *adj* fearless
IMPAWN, -S *vb* pawn
IMPEACH *vb*
IMPEARL *vb* adorn with pearls
IMPED ▸ **imp**
IMPEDE, -D, -S *vb*
IMPEDER ▸ **impede**
IMPEDES ▸ **impede**
IMPEDOR *n* component that offers impedance
IMPEL, -S *vb*
IMPEND, -S *vb* be about to happen
IMPERIA > **imperium**
IMPERIL *vb*
IMPETUS *n*
IMPHEE, -S *n* African sorghum plant
IMPI, -ES, -S *n* group of Zulu warriors
IMPIETY *n*
IMPING, -S ▸ **imp**
IMPINGE *vb*
IMPINGS ▸ **imping**
IMPIOUS *adj*
IMPIS ▸ **impi**
IMPISH *adj* mischievous
IMPLANT *n, vb*
IMPLATE *vb* sheathe
IMPLEAD *vb* sue or prosecute
IMPLED ▸ **implead**
IMPLETE *vb* fill
IMPLEX *n* part of an arthropod
IMPLIED *adj* hinted at or suggested

IMPLIES ▸ **imply**
IMPLODE *vb*
IMPLORE *vb*
IMPLY, IMPLIES *vb*
IMPONE, -D, -S *vb* impose
IMPORT, -S *vb, n*
IMPOSE, -D, -S *vb*
IMPOSER ▸ **impose**
IMPOSES ▸ **impose**
IMPOSEX *n* acquisition by female organisms of male characteristics
IMPOST, -S *n* tax, esp a customs duty ▹ *vb* classify (imported goods) according to the duty payable on them
IMPOT, -S *n* slang term for the act of imposing
IMPOUND *vb*
IMPOWER *less common spelling of* ▸ **empower**
IMPREGN *vb* impregnate
IMPRESA *n* heraldic device
IMPRESE *same as* ▸ **impresa**
IMPRESS *vb, n*
IMPREST *n* fund of cash used to pay incidental expenses
IMPRINT *n, vb*
IMPRO, -S *n* short for improvisation
IMPROV, -S *n* improvisational comedy
IMPROVE *vb*
IMPROVS ▸ **improv**
IMPS ▸ **imp**
IMPUGN, -S *vb* challenge the truth or validity of
IMPULSE *vb, n*
IMPURE, -R *adj*
IMPUTE, -D, -S *vb* attribute responsibility to
IMPUTER ▸ **impute**
IMPUTES ▸ **impute**
IMSHI *interj* go away!
IMSHY *same as* ▸ **imshi**
IN, -NED, -S *prep* indicating position inside, state or situation, etc ▹ *adv* indicating position inside, entry into, etc ▹ *adj* fashionable ▹ *n* way of approaching or befriending a person ▹ *vb* take in
INANE, -R, -S, -ST *adj* senseless, silly ▹ *n* something that is inane
INANELY ▸ **inane**
INANER ▸ **inane**
INANES ▸ **inane**
INANEST ▸ **inane**
INANGA, -S *n* common type of New Zealand grass tree
INANITY *n* lack of intelligence or imagination
INAPT, -ER *adj* not apt or fitting
INAPTLY ▸ **inapt**
INARCH *vb* graft (a plant)
INARM, -ED, -S *vb* embrace
INBEING *n* existence in something else
INBENT *adj* bent inwards
INBOARD *adj* (of a boat's engine) inside the hull ▹ *adv* within the sides of or towards the centre of a vessel or aircraft
INBORN *adj* existing from birth, natural
INBOUND *vb* pass into the playing area from outside it ▹ *adj* coming in
INBOX, -ES *n* folder which stores incoming email messages
INBREAK *n* breaking in
INBRED, -S *n, adj*
INBREED *vb* breed from closely related individuals
INBRING *vb* bring in
INBUILT *adj* present from the start
INBURST *n* irruption ▹ *vb* burst in
INBY *adv* into the house or an inner room ▹ *adj* located near or nearest to the house
INBYE *adv* near the house
INCAGE, -D, -S *vb* confine in or as in a cage
INCANT, -S *vb* chant (a spell)
INCASE, -D, -S *variant spelling of* ▸ **encase**
INCAVE, -D, -S *vb* hide
INCAVO, INCAVI *n* incised part of a carving
INCEDE, -D, -S *vb* advance
INCENSE *vb, n*
INCENT, -S *vb* provide incentive

INCEPT, -S *vb* (of organisms) to ingest (food) ▷ *n* rudimentary organ
INCH, -ED, -ES, -ING *n, vb*
INCHASE *same as* ▶ **enchase**
INCHED ▶ **inch**
INCHER, -S *n* something measuring given amount of inches
INCHES ▶ **inch**
INCHING ▶ **inch**
INCHPIN *n* cervine sweetbread
INCIPIT *n* Latin introductory phrase
INCISAL *adj* relating to the cutting edge of incisors and cuspids
INCISE, -D, -S *vb* cut into with a sharp tool
INCISOR *n*
INCITE, -D, -S *vb*
INCITER ▶ **incite**
INCITES ▶ **incite**
INCIVIL *archaic form of* ▶ **uncivil**
INCLASP *vb* clasp
INCLE, -S *same as* ▶ **inkle**
INCLINE *vb* lean, slope ▷ *n* slope
INCLIP, -S *vb* embrace
INCLOSE *less common spelling of* ▶ **enclose**
INCLUDE *vb*
INCOG, -S *n* incognito
INCOME, -S *n*
INCOMER *n* person who comes to a place in which they were not born
INCOMES ▶ **income**
INCONIE *adj* fine or delicate
INCONNU *n* whitefish of Arctic waters
INCONY *adj* fine or delicate
INCROSS *n* variation produced by inbreeding ▷ *vb* produce by inbreeding
INCRUST *same as* ▶ **encrust**
INCUBUS, INCUBI *n* (in folklore) type of demon
INCUDAL ▶ **incus**
INCUDES ▶ **incus**
INCULT *adj* (of land) uncultivated
INCUR, -S *vb* cause (something unpleasant) to happen
INCURVE *vb* curve or cause to curve inwards
INCUS, INCUDES *n* bone in the ear of mammals
INCUSE, -D, -S *n* design stamped or hammered onto a coin ▷ *vb* impress (a design) in a coin ▷ *adj* stamped or hammered onto a coin
INCUT, -S *adj* cut or etched in ▷ *n* indent in rock used as a foothold
INDABA, -S *n* (among South Africans) a meeting to discuss a serious topic
INDAMIN *same as* > **indamine**
INDART, -S *vb* dart in
INDEED *adv, interj*
INDEEDY *interj* indeed
INDENE, -S *n* colourless liquid hydrocarbon
INDENT, -S *vb*
INDEW, -ED, -S *same as* ▶ **indue**
INDEX, -ED, -ES *n, vb*
INDEXAL ▶ **index**
INDEXED ▶ **index**
INDEXER ▶ **index**
INDEXES ▶ **index**
INDIA, -S *n* code word for the letter I
INDICAN *n* compound secreted in the urine
INDICES *plural of* ▶ **index**
INDICIA > **indicium**
INDICT, -S *vb*
INDIE, -S *adj* (of rock music) released by an independent record label ▷ *n* independent record company
INDIGEN *same as* > **indigene**
INDIGN *adj* undeserving
INDIGO, -S *adj, n*
INDITE, -D, -S *vb* write
INDITER ▶ **indite**
INDITES ▶ **indite**
INDIUM, -S *n* soft silvery-white metallic element
INDOL, -S *same as* ▶ **indole**
INDOLE, -S *n* crystalline heterocyclic compound
INDOLS ▶ **indol**
INDOOR *adj*
INDOORS *adv*
INDORSE *variant spelling of* ▶ **endorse**
INDOW, -ED, -S *archaic variant of* ▶ **endow**
INDOXYL *n* water-soluble crystalline compound
INDRAFT *same as* > **indraught**

INDRAWN *adj* drawn or pulled in
INDRI *same as* ▸ **indris**
INDRIS *n* large lemuroid primate
INDUCE, -D, -S *vb*
INDUCER ▸ **induce**
INDUCES ▸ **induce**
INDUCT, -S *vb*
INDUE, -D, -S, INDUING *variant spelling of* ▸ **endue**
INDULGE *vb*
INDULIN *same as* > **induline**
INDULT, -S *n* type of faculty granted by the Holy See
INDUNA, -S *n* (in South Africa) a Black African overseer
INDUSIA > **indusium**
INDWELL, INDWELT *vb* (of a spirit, principle, etc) to inhabit
INDYREF *n* independence referendum
INEARTH *poetic word for* ▸ **bury**
INEDITA *pl n* unpublished writings
INEPT, -ER *adj*
INEPTLY ▸ **inept**
INERM *adj* without thorns
INERT, -ER, -S *n, adj*
INERTIA *n*

This is not the easiest of words to see in play, but its combination of common letters makes it one of the most frequently played 7-letter bonuses, while its plurals, which can be **inertiae** or **inertias**, are among the 8-letter bonus words that come up most often.

INERTLY ▸ **inert**
INERTS ▸ **inert**
INEXACT *adj* not exact or accurate
INFALL, -S *vb* move towards (something) under the influence of gravity
INFAME, -D, -S *vb* defame
INFAMY *n*
INFANCY *n*
INFANT, -S *n, adj*
INFANTA *n* (formerly) daughter of a king of Spain or Portugal
INFANTE *n* (formerly) any son of a king of Spain or Portugal, except the heir to the throne
INFANTS ▸ **infant**
INFARCT *n* localized area of dead tissue ▹ *vb* obstruct the blood supply to part of a body
INFARE, -S *vb* enter
INFAUNA *n* fauna that lives in ocean and river beds
INFAUST *adj* unlucky
INFECT, -S *vb, adj*
INFEED, -S *n* action of supplying a machine with a material
INFEFT, -S *vb* give possession of heritable property
INFELT *adj* heartfelt
INFEOFF *same as* ▸ **enfeoff**
INFER, -S *vb*
INFERE *adv* together
INFERNO *n*
INFERS ▸ **infer**
INFEST, -S *vb*
INFIDEL *n* person with no religion ▹ *adj* of unbelievers or unbelief
INFIELD *n* area of the field near the pitch
INFIGHT *vb*
INFILL, -S *vb* fill in ▹ *n* act of filling or closing gaps in something
INFIMUM, INFIMA *n* greatest lower bound
INFIRM, -S *vb, adj*
INFIX, -ED, -ES *vb* fix firmly in ▹ *n* affix inserted into the middle of a word
INFLAME *vb*
INFLATE *vb*
INFLECT *vb* change (the voice) in tone or pitch
INFLICT *vb*
INFLOW, -S *n, vb*
INFLUX *n*
INFO, -S *n* information
INFOLD, -S *variant spelling of* ▸ **enfold**
INFORCE *same as* ▸ **enforce**
INFORM, -S *vb, adj*
INFOS ▸ **info**
INFRA *adv* (esp in textual annotation) below
INFRACT *vb* violate or break (a law, an agreement, etc)
INFULA *same as* ▸ **infulae**

INFULAE *pl n* two ribbons hanging from a bishop's mitre
INFUSE, -D, -S *vb*
INFUSER *n* any device used to make an infusion
INFUSES ▸ **infuse**
ING, -S *n* meadow near a river
INGAN, -S *Scots word for* ▸ **onion**
INGATE, -S *n* entrance
INGENER *Shakespearean form of* > **engineer**
INGENU, -S *n* artless or inexperienced boy or young man
INGENUE *n* inexperienced girl or young woman
INGENUS ▸ **ingenu**
INGEST, -S *vb* take (food or liquid) into the body
INGESTA *pl n* nourishment taken through the mouth
INGESTS ▸ **ingest**
INGINE, -S *n* genius
INGLE, -S *n* fire in a room or a fireplace
INGLOBE *vb* shape as a sphere
INGO, -ES *n* revelation
INGOING *same as* ▸ **ingo**
INGOT, -ED, -S *n* oblong block of cast metal ▹ *vb* shape (metal) into ingots
INGRAFT *variant spelling of* ▸ **engraft**
INGRAIN *vb* impress deeply on the mind or nature ▹ *adj* (of carpets) made of fibre that is dyed before being spun ▹ *n* carpet made from ingrained yarn
INGRAM, -S *adj* ignorant ▹ *n* ignorant person
INGRATE *n* ungrateful person ▹ *adj* ungrateful
INGRESS *n* entrance
INGROSS *archaic form of* ▸ **engross**
INGROUP *n* highly cohesive and relatively closed social group
INGROWN *adj* grown abnormally into the flesh
INGRUM, -S *adj* ignorant ▹ *n* ignorant person
INGS ▸ **ing**
INGULF, -S *variant spelling of* ▸ **engulf**
INGULPH *archaic form of* ▸ **engulf**
INHABIT *vb*
INHALE, -D, -S *vb* breathe in (air, smoke, etc)
INHALER *n* container for an inhalant
INHALES ▸ **inhale**
INHAUL, -S *n* line for hauling in a sail
INHAUST *vb* drink in
INHERCE *same as* > **inhearse**
INHERE, -D, -S *vb* be an inseparable part (of)
INHERIT *vb*
INHIBIN *n* peptide hormone
INHIBIT *vb*
INHOOP, -S *vb* confine
INHUMAN *adj*
INHUME, -D, -S *vb* inter
INHUMER ▸ **inhume**
INHUMES ▸ **inhume**
INION, INIA, -S *n* most prominent point at the back of the head
INISLE, -D, -S *vb* put on or make into an island
INITIAL *adj, n, vb*
INJECT, -S *vb*
INJELLY *vb* place in jelly
INJERA, -S *n* white Ethiopian flatbread, similar to a crepe
INJOINT *vb* join
INJUNCT *vb* issue a legal injunction against (a person)
INJURE, -D, -S *vb*
INJURER ▸ **injure**
INJURES ▸ **injure**
INJURY *n* physical hurt
INK, -ED, -ING, -S *n, vb*
INKBLOT *n*
INKED ▸ **ink**
INKER, -S ▸ **ink**
INKHORN *n* (formerly) a small portable container for ink
INKHOSI, AMAKOSI *n* Zulu clan chief
INKIER ▸ **inky**
INKIEST ▸ **inky**
INKING ▸ **ink**
INKJET, -S *adj* of a method of printing ▹ *n* inkjet printer
INKLE, -D, -S *n* kind of linen tape used for trimmings ▹ *vb* hint
INKLESS ▸ **ink**
INKLIKE ▸ **ink**
INKLING *n*
INKOSI, -S *same as* ▸ **inkhosi**

INKPAD, -S *n* pad used for rubber-stamping or fingerprinting
INKPOT, -S *n* ink-bottle
INKS ▸ **ink**
INKSPOT *n* ink stain
INKWELL *n*
INKWOOD *n* type of tree
INKY, INKIER, INKIEST *adj* dark or black
INLACE, -D, -S *variant spelling of* ▸ **enlace**
INLAID ▸ **inlay**
INLAND, -S *adv, adj, n*
INLAY, INLAID, -S *n* inlaid substance or pattern ▹ *vb* decorate by inserting wooden pieces
INLAYER ▸ **inlay**
INLAYS ▸ **inlay**
INLET, -S *n* water extending from the sea into the land ▹ *vb* insert or inlay
INLIER, -S *n* outcrop of rocks surrounded by younger rocks
INLOCK, -S *vb* lock up
INLY *adv* inwardly
INLYING *adj* situated within or inside
INMATE, -S *n*
INMESH *variant spelling of* ▸ **enmesh**
INMOST *adj* innermost
INN, -S *n* pub or small hotel, esp in the country ▹ *vb* stay at an inn
INNAGE, -S *n* type of measurement
INNARDS *pl n*
INNATE *adj*
INNED ▸ **in**
INNER, -S *adj* happening or located inside ▹ *n* red innermost ring on a target
INNERLY ▸ **inner**
INNERS ▸ **inner**
INNERVE *vb* supply with nervous energy
INNING, -S *n* division of baseball match
INNIT *interj* isn't it
INNLESS *adj* without inns
INNS ▸ **inn**
INNYARD *n* courtyard of an inn
INOCULA > **inoculum**
INORB, -ED, -S *vb* enclose in or as if in an orb
INOSINE *n* type of molecule making up cell
INOSITE *same as* > **inositol**
INPHASE *adj* in the same phase
INPOUR, -S *vb* pour in
INPUT, -S *n, vb*
INQILAB *n* (in India, Pakistan, etc) revolution
INQUERE *Spenserian form of* ▸ **inquire**
INQUEST *n* official inquiry into a sudden death
INQUIET *vb* disturb
INQUIRE *vb*
INQUIRY *n* question
INRO *n* Japanese seal-box
INROAD, -S *n* invasion or hostile attack
INRUN, -S *n* slope down which ski jumpers ski
INRUSH *n* sudden and overwhelming inward flow
INS ▸ **in**
INSANE, -R *adj*
INSANIE *n* insanity
INSCAPE *n* essential inner nature of a person, etc
INSCULP *vb* engrave
INSEAM, -S *vb* contain
INSECT, -S *n*
INSEEM, -S *vb* cover with grease
INSERT, -S *vb, n*
INSET, -S *n* small picture inserted within a larger one ▹ *vb* place in or within ▹ *adj* decorated with something inserted
INSHELL *vb* retreat, as into a shell
INSHIP, -S *vb* travel or send by ship
INSHORE *adj, adv*
INSIDE, -S *prep, adj, adv, n*
INSIDER *n* someone who has privileged knowledge
INSIDES ▸ **inside**
INSIGHT *n*
INSIGNE *same as* > **insignia**
INSINEW *vb* connect or strengthen, as with sinews
INSIPID *adj*
INSIST, -S *vb*
INSNARE *less common spelling of* ▸ **ensnare**
INSOFAR *adv* to the extent
INSOLE, -S *n* inner sole of a shoe or boot

INSOOTH *adv* indeed
INSOUL, -S *variant of* ▸ **ensoul**
INSPAN, -S *vb* harness (animals) to (a vehicle)
INSPECT *vb*
INSPIRE *vb*
INSPO, -S *n* source of inspiration
INSTAL, -S *same as* ▸ **install**
INSTALL *vb*
INSTALS ▸ **instal**
INSTANT *n, adj*
INSTAR, -S *vb* decorate with stars ▹ *n* stage in the development of an insect
INSTATE *vb* place in a position or office
INSTEAD *adv*
INSTEP, -S *n*
INSTIL, -S *vb*
INSTILL *same as* ▸ **instil**
INSTILS ▸ **instil**
INSULA, -E *n* pyramid-shaped area of the brain
INSULAR *adj* not open to new ideas, narrow-minded ▹ *n* islander
INSULIN *n*
INSULSE *adj* stupid
INSULT, -S *vb, n*
INSURE, -S *vb*
INSURED *adj* covered by insurance ▹ *n* those covered by an insurance policy
INSURER *n* person or company that sells insurance
INSURES ▸ **insure**
INSWEPT *adj* narrowed towards the front
INSWING *n* type of movement of a bowled cricket ball
INTACT *adj*
INTAGLI > **intaglio**
INTAKE, -S *n*
INTEGER *n* positive or negative whole number or zero
INTEL, -S *n* US military intelligence
INTEND, -S *vb*
INTENSE *adj*
INTENT, -S *n, adj*
INTER, -S *vb*
INTERIM *adj, n, adv*
INTERN, -S *vb, n*
INTERNE *same as* ▸ **intern**
INTERNS ▸ **intern**
INTERS ▸ **inter**
INTHRAL *archaic form of* ▸ **enthral**
INTI, -S *n* former monetary unit of Peru
INTIL *Scot form of* ▸ **into**
INTIMA, -E, -S *n* innermost layer of an organ or part
INTIMAL ▸ **intima**
INTIMAS ▸ **intima**
INTIME *adj* intimate
INTINE, -S *n* inner wall of a pollen grain or a spore
INTIRE *archaic form of* ▸ **entire**
INTIS ▸ **inti**
INTITLE *archaic form of* ▸ **entitle**
INTO *prep*
INTOED *adj* having inward-turning toes
INTOMB, -S *same as* ▸ **entomb**
INTONE, -D, -S *vb* speak or recite in an unvarying tone of voice
INTONER ▸ **intone**
INTONES ▸ **intone**
INTORT, -S *vb* twist inward
INTOWN *adj* infield
INTRA *prep* within
INTRADA *n* prelude
INTRANT *n* one who enters
INTREAT *archaic spelling of* ▸ **entreat**
INTRO, -S *n* introduction
INTROFY *vb* increase the wetting properties
INTROIT *n* short prayer said or sung
INTROLD *variant of* ▸ **entrold**
INTRON, -S *n* stretch of DNA
INTROS ▸ **intro**
INTRUDE *vb*
INTRUST *same as* ▸ **entrust**
INTUIT, -S *vb* know or discover by intuition
INTURN, -S *n* inward turn
INTUSE, -S *n* contusion
INTWINE *less common spelling of* ▸ **entwine**
INTWIST *vb* twist together
INUKSUK *same as* > **inukshuk**
INULA, -S *n* plant of the elecampane genus
INULASE *n* enzyme
INULIN, -S *n* fructose polysaccharide

INURE, -D, -S, INURING *vb* cause to accept or become hardened to
INURN, -ED, -S *vb* place (esp cremated ashes) in an urn
INUST *adj* burnt in
INUTILE *adj* useless
INVADE, -D, -S *vb*
INVADER ▶ **invade**
INVADES ▶ **invade**
INVALID *n, vb, adj*
INVAR, -S *n* alloy made from iron and nickel
INVEIGH *vb* criticize strongly
INVENIT *sentence substitute* (he or she) designed it
INVENT, -S *vb*
INVERSE *vb, adj, n*
INVERT, -S *vb*
INVEST, -S *vb*
INVEXED *adj* concave
INVIOUS *adj* without paths or roads
INVITAL *adj* not vital
INVITE, -D, -S *vb, n*
INVITEE *n* one who is invited
INVITER ▶ **invite**
INVITES ▶ **invite**
INVOICE *n, vb*
INVOKE, -D, -S *vb*
INVOKER ▶ **invoke**
INVOKES ▶ **invoke**
INVOLVE *vb*
INWALL, -S *vb* surround with a wall
INWARD *adj* directed towards the middle ▷ *adv* towards the inside or middle ▷ *n* inward part
INWARDS *adv* towards the inside or middle of something
INWEAVE, INWOVE, INWOVEN *vb* weave together
INWICK, -S *vb* perform a type of curling stroke
INWIND, -S, INWOUND *vb* wind or coil around
INWIT, -S *n* conscience
INWITH *adv* within
INWITS ▶ **inwit**
INWORK, -S *vb* work in
INWORN *adj* worn in
INWOUND ▶ **inwind**
INWOVE ▶ **inweave**
INWOVEN ▶ **inweave**
INWRAP, -S, -T *less common spelling of* ▶ **enwrap**
INYALA, -S *n* antelope
IO, -S *interj* exclamation of triumph ▷ *n* cry of 'io'
IODATE, -D, -S *same as* ▶ **iodize**
IODIC *adj* of or containing iodine
IODID, -S *same as* ▶ **iodide**
IODIDE, -S *n* chemical compound
IODIDS ▶ **iodid**
IODIN, -S *same as* ▶ **iodine**
IODINE, -S *n*
IODINS ▶ **iodin**
IODISE, -D, -S *same as* ▶ **iodize**
IODISER ▶ **iodise**
IODISES ▶ **iodise**
IODISM, -S *n* poisoning caused by iodine or its compounds
IODIZE, -D, -S *vb* treat with iodine
IODIZER ▶ **iodize**
IODIZES ▶ **iodize**
IODOUS *adj* of or containing iodine
IODURET *n* iodide
IOLITE, -S *n* grey or violet-blue dichroic mineral
ION, -S *n*
IONIC *adj* of or in the form of ions
IONICS *pl n* study of ions
IONISE, -D, -S *same as* ▶ **ionize**
IONISER *same as* ▶ **ionizer**
IONISES ▶ **ionise**
IONIUM, -S *n* naturally occurring radioisotope of thorium
IONIZE, -D, -S *vb* change into ions
IONIZER *n* person or thing that ionizes
IONIZES ▶ **ionize**
IONOGEN *n* compound that exists as ions when dissolved
IONOMER *n* type of thermoplastic
IONONE, -S *n* yellowish liquid mixture
IONS ▶ **ion**
IOS ▶ **io**
IOTA, -S *n* ninth letter in the Greek alphabet

This word for a Greek letter is another of those that come in handy when you are trying to rid your rack of too many vowels.

IPECAC, -S *n* type of S American shrub

IPOMOEA *n* convolvulaceous plant
IPPON, -S *n* winning point awarded in a judo or karate competition
IRACUND *adj* easily angered
IRADE, -S *n* written edict of a Muslim ruler
IRATE, -R, -ST *adj*
IRATELY ▶ **irate**
IRATER ▶ **irate**
IRATEST ▶ **irate**
IRE, -D, -S, IRING *vb* anger ▷ *n* anger
IREFUL ▶ **ire**
IRELESS ▶ **ire**
IRENIC *adj* tending to conciliate or promote peace
IRENICS *n* branch of theology
IRES ▶ **ire**
IRID, -S *n* type of iris
IRIDAL ▶ **irid**
IRIDEAL ▶ **irid**
IRIDES ▶ **iris**
IRIDIAL ▶ **irid**
IRIDIAN ▶ **irid**
IRIDIC *adj* of or containing iridium
IRIDISE *vb* make iridescent
IRIDIUM *n* very hard corrosion-resistant metal
IRIDIZE *vb* make iridescent
IRIDS ▶ **irid**
IRING ▶ **ire**
IRIS, IRIDES, -ED, -ES, -ING *n* part of the eye ▷ *vb* display iridescence
IRISATE *vb* make iridescent
IRISED ▶ **iris**
IRISES ▶ **iris**
IRISING ▶ **iris**
IRITIC ▶ **iritis**
IRITIS *n* inflammation of the iris of the eye

Since a plague of Is tends to afflict every Scrabble player's rack at regular intervals, it is well worth knowing words like this one, which use several of the wretched letter!

IRK, -ED, -ING, -S *vb*
IRKSOME *adj* irritating, annoying
IROKO, -S *n* tropical African hardwood tree
IRON, -ED, -S *n, adj, vb*
IRONE, -S *n* fragrant liquid

You may surprise your opponent by adding an E to **iron** if you know this word for a kind of aromatic oil.

IRONED ▶ **iron**
IRONER, -S ▶ **iron**
IRONES ▶ **irone**
IRONIC *adj* using irony
IRONIER ▶ **irony**
IRONIES ▶ **irony**
IRONING *n* clothes to be ironed
IRONISE *same as* ▶ **ironize**
IRONIST ▶ **ironize**
IRONIZE *vb* use or indulge in irony
IRONMAN, IRONMEN *n* very strong man
IRONS ▶ **iron**
IRONY, IRONIER, IRONIES *n* grammatical device ▷ *adj* of, resembling, or containing iron
IRREAL *adj* unreal
IRRUPT, -S *vb* enter forcibly or suddenly
IS *vb* form of the present tense of *be*
ISABEL, -S *n* brown yellow colour
ISAGOGE *n* academic introduction
ISATIN, -S *n* yellowish-red crystalline compound
ISATINE *same as* ▶ **isatin**
ISATINS ▶ **isatin**
ISBA, -S *n* log hut
ISCHIA ▶ **ischium**
ISCHIAL ▶ **ischium**
ISCHIUM, ISCHIA *n* part of the hipbone
ISH, -ES *n* issue

An **ish** is a word for an issue in Scots law. If you have I, S and H on your rack, remember that as well as adding **ish** to the end of many words, you can also play those letters as a word in its own right.

ISIT *sentence substitute* expression used in response to a statement
ISLAND, -S *n, vb*
ISLE, -D, -S, ISLING *vb* make an isle of ▷ *n* island
ISLEMAN, ISLEMEN *n* islander
ISLES ▶ **isle**

ISLET, -S *n* small island
ISLETED *adj* having islets
ISLETS ▶ **islet**
ISLING ▶ **isle**
ISM, -S *n* doctrine, system, or practice

While **ism** can be added to the ends of many words as a suffix, it's worth remembering as a word in its own right.

ISMATIC *adj* following fashionable doctrines
ISMS ▶ **ism**
ISNA *vb* is not
ISNAE *same as* ▶ **isna**
ISO, -S *n* short segment of film that can be replayed easily
ISOAMYL *n* as in **isoamyl acetate** colourless volatile compound
ISOBAR, -S *n* line on a map connecting areas of equal atmospheric pressure
ISOBARE *same as* ▶ **isobar**
ISOBARS ▶ **isobar**
ISOBASE *n* line connecting points of equal land upheaval
ISOBATH *n* line on a map connecting points of equal depth of water
ISOCHOR *n* line on a graph showing variation of a fluid's temperature and pressure
ISODICA > **isodicon**
ISODOMA > **isodomon**
ISODONT *n* animal in which the teeth are of similar size
ISODOSE *n* dose of radiation applied in radiotherapy
ISOETES *n* quillwort
ISOFORM *n* protein similar in function but not form to another
ISOGAMY *n* fusion of similar gametes
ISOGENY > **isogenous**
ISOGON, -S *n* equiangular polygon
ISOGONE *same as* > **isogonic**
ISOGONS ▶ **isogon**
ISOGONY > **isogonic**
ISOGRAM *same as* > **isopleth**
ISOGRIV *n* line on a map connecting points of equal angular bearing
ISOHEL, -S *n* line on a map connecting places with equal sunshine
ISOHYET *n* line on a map connecting places with equal rainfall
ISOKONT *same as* > **isokontan**
ISOLATE *vb*, *n*
ISOLEAD *n* line on a ballistic graph
ISOLEX *n* line on map showing where a particular word is used
ISOLINE *same as* > **isopleth**
ISOLOG > **isologous**
ISOLOGS > **isologous**
ISOMER, -S *n* compound that has the same molecular formula as another
ISOMERE *same as* ▶ **isomer**
ISOMERS ▶ **isomer**
ISONOME *n* line on a map showing equal abundance of a species
ISONOMY *n* equality before the law of the citizens of a state
ISOPACH *n* line on a map connecting places with equal rock thickness
ISOPOD, -S *n* type of crustacean ▷ *adj* of this type of crustacean
ISOS ▶ **iso**
ISOSPIN *n* number used to classify elementary particles
ISOTACH *n* line on a map connecting points of equal wind speed
ISOTONE *n* atom with same number of neutrons as another
ISOTOPE *n*
ISOTOPY ▶ **isotope**
ISOTRON *n* device for separating small quantities of isotopes
ISOTYPE *n* pictorial presentation of statistical information
ISOZYME *n* variant of an enzyme
ISSEI, -S *n* first-generation Japanese immigrant
ISSUANT *adj* emerging or issuing

ISSUE, -D, -S, ISSUING *n, vb*
ISSUER, -S ▶ **issue**
ISSUES ▶ **issue**
ISSUING ▶ **issue**
ISTANA, -S *n* (in Malaysia) a royal palace
ISTHMI ▶ **isthmus**
ISTHMIC ▶ **isthmus**
ISTHMUS, ISTHMI *n* narrow strip of land connecting two areas of land
ISTLE, -S *n* fibre obtained from various agave and yucca trees
IT *pron, n*
ITA, -S *n* type of palm
ITACISM *n* pronunciation of the Greek letter eta
ITALIC, -S *adj, n*
ITAS ▶ **ita**
ITCH, -ED, -ES *n, vb*
ITCHIER ▶ **itchy**
ITCHILY ▶ **itch**
ITCHING ▶ **itch**
ITCHY, ITCHIER ▶ **itch**
ITEM, -ED, -ING, -S *n* single thing in a list or collection ▷ *adv* likewise ▷ *vb* itemize
ITEMISE *same as* ▶ **itemize**
ITEMIZE *vb* make a list of
ITEMS ▶ **item**
ITERANT ▶ **iterate**
ITERATE *vb* repeat
ITERUM *adv* again
ITHER *Scot word for* ▶ **other**
ITS *pron* belonging to it ▷ *adj* of or belonging to it
ITSELF *pron*
IURE *adv* by law
IVIED *adj* covered with ivy
IVIES ▶ **ivy**
IVORIED ▶ **ivory**
IVORIER ▶ **ivory**
IVORIES *pl n* keys of a piano
IVORIST *n* worker in ivory
IVORY, IVORIER *n, adj*
IVRESSE *n* drunkenness
IVY, IVIES *n*
IVYLEAF *adj* as in **ivyleaf geranium** type of geranium plant
IVYLIKE ▶ **ivy**
IWI *n* Māori tribe

This Māori word for a tribe is a great one for getting rid of an awkward combination of letters.

IWIS *archaic word for* > **certainly**
IXIA, -S *n* southern African plant
IXNAY *interj* nix
IXODID, -S *n* hard-bodied tick
IXORA, -S *n* flowering shrub
IXTLE, -S *same as* ▶ **istle**
IZAR, -S *n* long garment worn by Muslim women
IZARD, -S *n* type of goat-antelope
IZARS ▶ **izar**
IZZARD, -S *n* letter Z
IZZAT, -S *n* honour or prestige

Jj

JA *interj* yes ▷ *sentence substitute* yes
JAB, -BED, -BING, -S *vb, n*
JABBER, -S *vb, n*
JABBING ▶ **jab**
JABBLE, -D, -S *vb* ripple
JABERS *interj* Irish exclamation
JABIRU, -S *n* large white-and-black Australian stork
JABOT, -S *n* frill or ruffle on the front of a blouse or shirt
JABS ▶ **jab**
JACAL, -ES, -S *n* Mexican daub hut
JACAMAR *n* tropical American bird with an iridescent plumage
JACANA, -S *n* long-legged long-toed bird
JACARE, -S *another name for* ▶ **cayman**
JACCHUS *n* small monkey
JACENT *adj* lying
JACINTH *another name for* > **hyacinth**
JACK, -ED *n, vb*
JACKAL, -S *n, vb*
JACKASS *n* fool
JACKDAW *n*
JACKED ▶ **jack**
JACKEEN *n* slick self-assertive lower-class Dubliner
JACKER, -S *n* labourer
JACKET, -S *n, vb*
JACKIES ▶ **jacky**
JACKING ▶ **jack**
JACKLEG *n* unskilled worker
JACKMAN, JACKMEN *n* retainer
JACKPOT *n, vb*
JACKS *n* type of game
JACKY, JACKIES *n* old slang word for gin
JACOBIN *n* variety of fancy pigeon
JACOBUS *n* former English gold coin
JACONET *n* light cotton fabric
JACUZZI *n* type of bath or pool
JADE, -S, JADING *n, adj, vb*
JADED *adj* tired and unenthusiastic
JADEDLY ▶ **jaded**
JADEITE *n* usually green or white mineral
JADERY *n* shrewishness
JADES ▶ **jade**
JADING ▶ **jade**
JADISH ▶ **jade**
JADITIC ▶ **jade**
JAEGER, -S *n* German or Austrian marksman
JAFFA, -S *n* (in cricket) well-bowled ball
JAG, -GING, -S *n* period of uncontrolled indulgence in an activity ▷ *vb* cut unevenly
JAGA, -ED, -ING, -S *n* guard ▷ *vb* guard or watch
JAGER, -S *same as* ▶ **jaeger**
JAGG, -S *same as* ▶ **jag**
JAGGARY *same as* ▶ **jaggery**
JAGGED ▶ **jag**
JAGGER, -S *n*
JAGGERY *n* coarse brown sugar
JAGGIER ▶ **jaggy**
JAGGIES ▶ **jaggy**
JAGGING ▶ **jag**
JAGGS ▶ **jagg**
JAGGY, JAGGIER, JAGGIES *adj* prickly ▷ *n* jagged computer image
JAGHIR, -S *n* Indian regional governance
JAGHIRE *n* Indian regional governance
JAGHIRS ▶ **jaghir**
JAGIR, -S *n* Indian regional governance
JAGLESS ▶ **jag**

JAGRA, -S *n* Hindu festival
JAGS ▶ **jag**
JAGUAR, -S *n*
JAI *interj* victory (to)
JAIL, -ED, -ING, -S *n, vb*
JAILER, -S *n*
JAILING ▶ **jail**
JAILOR, -S *same as* ▶ **jailer**
JAILS ▶ **jail**
JAK, -S *same as* ▶ **jack**
JAKE, -R, -ST *adj* slang word meaning all right
JAKES, -ES *n* toilet; lavatory
JAKEST ▶ **jake**
JAKEY, -S *n* derogatory Scots word for a homeless alcoholic person
JAKS ▶ **jak**
JALABIB ▶ **jilbab**
JALAP, -S *n* Mexican convolvulaceous plant
JALAPIC ▶ **jalap**
JALAPIN *n* purgative resin
JALAPS ▶ **jalap**
JALEBI, -S *n* type of Asian sweet fried snack
JALLEBI *same as* ▶ **jalebi**
JALOP, -S *same as* ▶ **jalap**
JALOPPY *same as* ▶ **jalopy**
JALOPS ▶ **jalop**
JALOPY *n*
JALOUSE *vb* suspect
JAM, -MED, -S *vb, n*
JAMAAT, -S *n* Islamic council
JAMADAR *n* Indian army officer
JAMB, -ED, -ING, -S *n* side post of a door or window frame ▷ *vb* climb up a crack in rock
JAMBART *same as* ▶ **greave**
JAMBE, -S *same as* ▶ **jamb**
JAMBEAU, JAMBEUX *another word for* ▶ **greave**
JAMBED ▶ **jamb**
JAMBEE, -S *n* light cane
JAMBER, -S *same as* ▶ **greave**
JAMBES ▶ **jambe**
JAMBEUX ▶ **jambeau**
JAMBIER *n* greave
JAMBING ▶ **jamb**
JAMBIYA *n* curved dagger
JAMBO *sentence substitute* E African salutation
JAMBOK, -S *same as* ▶ **sjambok**
JAMBONE *n* type of play in the card game euchre
JAMBOOL *same as* > **jambolan**
JAMBS ▶ **jamb**
JAMBU, -S *same as* > **jambolan**
JAMBUL, -S *same as* > **jambolan**
JAMBUS ▶ **jambu**
JAMDANI *n* patterned muslin
JAMES, -ES *n* jemmy
JAMJAR, -S *n*
JAMLIKE ▶ **jam**
JAMMED ▶ **jam**
JAMMER, -S ▶ **jam**
JAMMIER ▶ **jammy**
JAMMIES *informal word for* ▶ **pyjamas**
JAMMING ▶ **jam**
JAMMY, JAMMIER *adj* lucky
JAMON *n* as in **jamon serrano** cured ham from Spain
JAMPAN, -S *n* type of sedan chair used in India
JAMPANI *same as* > **jampanee**
JAMPANS ▶ **jampan**
JAMPOT, -S *n*
JAMS ▶ **jam**
JANE, -S *n* girl or woman
JANGLE, -D, -S *vb, n*
JANGLER ▶ **jangle**
JANGLES ▶ **jangle**
JANGLY *adj* making a jangling sound
JANITOR *n*
JANIZAR *same as* > **janissary**

This is an old word for a Turkish soldier, combining J and Z. If your opponent plays it, remember that you can add not only an S to it to form the plural, but also a Y, making the variant spelling **janizary**.

JANKER, -S *n* device for transporting logs
JANN, -S *n* lesser jinn
JANNEY, -S *vb* act as a disguised reveller at Christmas
JANNIED ▶ **janny**
JANNIES ▶ **janny**

JANNOCK *same as* ▸**jonnock**
JANNS ▸**jann**
JANNY, JANNIED, JANNIES *n* janitor ▹*vb* work as a janitor
JANSKY, -S *n* unit of flux density
JANTEE *archaic version of* ▸**jaunty**
JANTY, JANTIER, JANTIES *n* petty officer ▹*adj* (in archaic usage) jaunty
JAPAN, -S *n* very hard varnish, usu black ▹*vb* cover with this varnish ▹*adj* relating to or varnished with japan
JAPE, -D, -S *n, vb*
JAPER, -S ▸**jape**
JAPERY ▸**jape**
JAPES ▸**jape**
JAPING, -S ▸**jape**
JAR, -RED, -S *n, vb*
JARFUL, -S, JARSFUL *same as* ▸**jar**
JARGON, -S *n, vb*
JARGONY *adj* full of jargon
JARGOON *same as* ▸**jargon**
JARHEAD *n* US Marine
JARINA, -S *n* South American palm tree
JARK, -S *n* seal or pass
JARKMAN, JARKMEN *n* forger of passes or licences
JARKS ▸**jark**
JARL, -S *n* Scandinavian chieftain or noble
JARLDOM ▸**jarl**
JARLS ▸**jarl**
JAROOL, -S *n* Indian tree
JARP, -ED, -ING, -S *vb* strike or smash
JARRAH, -S *n* Australian eucalypt yielding valuable timber
JARRED ▸**jar**
JARRING ▸**jar**
JARS ▸**jar**
JARSFUL ▸**jarful**
JARTA, -S *n* heart
JARUL, -S *variant of* ▸**jarool**
JARVEY, -S *n* hackney coachman
JARVIE, -S *same as* ▸**jarvey**
JASEY, -S *n* wig
JASIES ▸**jasy**
JASMIN, -S *same as* ▸**jasmine**
JASMINE *n*
JASMINS ▸**jasmin**
JASP, -S *another word for* ▸**jasper**
JASPE, -S *adj* resembling jasper ▹*n* subtly striped woven fabric
JASPER, -S *n* variety of quartz
JASPERY *adj* resembling jasper
JASPES ▸**jaspe**
JASPIS *archaic word for* ▸**jasper**
JASPS ▸**jasp**
JASS, -ES *obsolete variant of* ▸**jazz**
JASSID, -S *n* leafhopper
JASY, JASIES *n* wig
JATAKA, -S *n* text describing the birth of Buddha
JATO, -S *n* jet-assisted takeoff
JAUK, -ED, -ING, -S *vb* dawdle
JAUNCE, -D, -S *vb* prance
JAUNSE, -D, -S *same as* ▸**jaunce**
JAUNT, -ED, -S *n, vb*
JAUNTEE *old spelling of* ▸**jaunty**
JAUNTIE *old spelling of* ▸**jaunty**
JAUNTS ▸**jaunt**
JAUNTY *adj* sprightly and cheerful ▹*n* master-at-arms on a naval ship
JAUP, -ED, -ING, -S *same as* ▸**jarp**
JAVA, -S *n* coffee or a variety of it
JAVEL, -S *adj* as in **javel water** bleach or disinfectant
JAVELIN *n, vb*
JAVELLE *adj* as in **javelle water** bleach or disinfectant
JAVELS ▸**javel**
JAW, -ED, -S *n, vb*
JAWAN, -S *n* (in India) a soldier
JAWARI, -S *n* variety of sorghum
JAWBONE *n, vb*
JAWBOX *n* metal sink

> This Scots word for a metal sink combines the J and X, and of course its plural **jawboxes**, earning an extra 50 points, would be even better.

JAWED ▸**jaw**
JAWFALL *n* dejection
JAWHOLE *n* cesspit
JAWING, -S ▸**jaw**
JAWLESS ▸**jaw**

JAWLIKE ▸**jaw**
JAWLINE *n*
JAWS ▸**jaw**
JAY, -S *n* type of bird
JAYBIRD *n*
JAYCEE, -S *n* member of a Junior Chamber of Commerce
JAYGEE, -S *n* lieutenant junior grade in the US army
JAYS ▸**jay**
JAYVEE, -S *n* junior varsity sports team
JAYWALK *vb*
JAZY, JAZIES *n* wig

This means a wig and is a wonderfully useful little word, combining J and Z for a high score.

JAZZ, -ED, -ES, -ING *n, vb*
JAZZBO, -S *n* jazz musician or fan
JAZZED ▸**jazz**
JAZZER, -S ▸**jazz**
JAZZES ▸**jazz**
JAZZIER ▸**jazzy**
JAZZILY ▸**jazzy**
JAZZING ▸**jazz**
JAZZMAN ▸**jazz**
JAZZMEN ▸**jazz**
JAZZY, JAZZIER *adj* flashy or showy
JEALOUS *adj*
JEAN *n* tough twill-weave cotton fabric
JEANED *adj* wearing jeans
JEANS *pl n* casual denim trousers
JEAT, -S *n* jet
JEBEL, -S *n* hill or mountain in an Arab country
JEDI, -S *n* person claiming to live according to the Jedi philosophy
JEE, -D, -ING, -S *variant of* ▸**gee**
JEEL, -ED, -ING, -S *vb* make into jelly
JEELIE *same as* ▸**jeely**
JEELIED ▸**jeely**
JEELIES ▸**jeely**
JEELING ▸**jeel**
JEELS ▸**jeel**
JEELY, JEELIED, JEELIES *n* jelly ▹*vb* make into jelly
JEEP, -ED, -ING, -S *n* small military four-wheel drive road vehicle ▹*vb* travel in a jeep
JEEPERS *interj*
JEEPING ▸**jeep**
JEEPNEY *n* Filipino bus converted from a jeep
JEEPS ▸**jeep**
JEER, -ED, -S *vb, n*
JEERER, -S ▸**jeer**
JEERING ▸**jeer**
JEERS ▸**jeer**
JEES ▸**jee**
JEESLY *same as* ▸**jeezly**
JEEZ *interj* expression of surprise or irritation
JEEZE *same as* ▸**jeez**
JEEZELY *same as* ▸**jeezly**
JEEZLY *adj* used as an intensifier
JEFE, -S *n* (in Spanish-speaking countries) a military or political leader
JEFF, -ED, -ING, -S *vb* downsize or close down (an organization)
JEHAD, -S *same as* ▸**jihad**
JEHADI, -S *same as* ▸**jihadi**
JEHADS ▸**jehad**
JEHU, -S *n* fast driver
JEJUNA ▸**jejunum**
JEJUNAL ▸**jejunum**
JEJUNE *adj* simple or naive
JEJUNUM, JEJUNA *n* part of the small intestine
JELAB, -S *same as* ▸**jellaba**
JELL, -ED, -ING, -S *vb* form into a jelly-like substance
JELLABA *n* loose robe with a hood
JELLED ▸**jell**
JELLIED ▸**jelly**
JELLIES ▸**jelly**
JELLIFY *vb* make into or become jelly
JELLING ▸**jell**
JELLO, -S *n* (in US English) type of dessert
JELLS ▸**jell**
JELLY, JELLIED, JELLIES *n, vb*
JEMADAR *n* native officer serving as a mercenary in India
JEMBE, -S *n* hoe
JEMIDAR *same as* ▸**jemadar**
JEMIMA, -S *n* boot with elastic sides
JEMMY, JEMMIED, JEMMIER, JEMMIES *n, vb, adj*
JENNET, -S *n* female donkey or ass
JENNY, JENNIES *same as* ▸**jennet**

JEOFAIL *n* oversight in legal pleading
JEON, -S *n* Korean pancake
JEOPARD *vb* put in jeopardy
JERBIL, -S *variant spelling of* ▸ **gerbil**
JERBOA, -S *n* small mouselike rodent with long hind legs
JEREED, -S *same as* ▸ **jerid**
JERID, -S *n* wooden javelin
JERK, -ED, -S *vb, n*
JERKER, -S ▸ **jerk**
JERKIER ▸ **jerky**
JERKIES ▸ **jerky**
JERKILY ▸ **jerky**
JERKIN, -S *n*
JERKING ▸ **jerk**
JERKINS ▸ **jerkin**
JERKS ▸ **jerk**
JERKY, JERKIER, JERKIES *adj* characterized by jerks ▹ *n* type of cured meat
JERQUE, -D, -S *vb* search for contraband

To **jerque** is to search a vessel for stolen goods, and if you have the right additional letters to make **jerqued, jerquer, jerques** or **jerquing**, using all your letters, you would get a really great score.

JERQUER ▸ **jerque**
JERQUES ▸ **jerque**
JERREED *variant spelling of* ▸ **jerid**
JERRID, -S *n* blunt javelin
JERRY, JERRIES *short for* > **jeroboam**
JERSEY, -S *n*
JESS, -ED, -ES, -ING *n* short leather strap used in falconry ▹ *vb* put jesses on (a hawk or falcon)
JESSAMY *n* fop
JESSANT *adj* emerging
JESSE *same as* ▸ **jess**
JESSED ▸ **jess**
JESSES ▸ **jess**
JESSING ▸ **jess**
JEST, -ED, -S *vb, n*
JESTEE, -S *n* person about whom a joke is made
JESTER, -S *n*
JESTFUL ▸ **jest**
JESTING ▸ **jest**
JESTS ▸ **jest**
JESUS *n* French paper size
JET, -S, -TED, -TING *n, vb*
JETBEAD *n* ornamental shrub
JETE, -S *n* dance step
JETFOIL *n*
JETLAG, -S *n*
JETLIKE ▸ **jet**
JETON, -S *n* gambling chip
JETPACK *n*
JETPORT *n* airport for jet planes
JETS ▸ **jet**
JETSAM, -S *n*
JETSOM, -S *same as* ▸ **jetsam**
JETSON, -S *archaic form of* ▸ **jetsam**
JETTED ▸ **jet**
JETTIED ▸ **jetty**
JETTIER ▸ **jetty**
JETTIES ▸ **jetty**
JETTING ▸ **jet**
JETTON, -S *n* counter or token
JETTY, JETTIED, JETTIER, JETTIES *n* small pier ▹ *adj* of or resembling jet, esp in colour or polish ▹ *vb* equip with a cantilevered floor
JETWAY, -S *n* tradename of device used in airports
JEU, -X *n* game

Jeu is the French word for game or play. The plural form, **jeux**, is a great little word, using both J and X, particularly if you can play it on a double- or triple-word square.

JEUNE *adj* young
JEUX ▸ **jeu**
JEWEL, -ED, -S *n, vb*
JEWELER *same as* > **jeweller**
JEWELRY *same as* > **jewellery**
JEWELS ▸ **jewel**
JEWFISH *n* old-fashioned name for a type of freshwater catfish
JEWIE, -S *n* informal Australian word for a jewfish
JEZAIL, -S *n* Afghan musket

A **jezail** is a kind of Afghan musket, and if you have an S to go with it, earning the extra 50 points, so much the better.

JEZEBEL *n* shameless or scheming woman
JHALA, -S *n* Indian musical style
JHATKA, -S *n* slaughter of animals for food according to Sikh law
JIAO, -S *n* Chinese currency unit
JIB, -S *same as* ▸ **jibe**
JIBB, -ED, -S *same as* ▸ **jibe**
JIBBA, -S *n* long, loose coat worn by Muslim men
JIBBAH, -S *same as* ▸ **jubbah**
JIBBAS ▸ **jibba**
JIBBED ▸ **jibb**
JIBBER, -S *variant of* ▸ **gibber**
JIBBING ▸ **jibb**
JIBBONS *pl n* spring onions
JIBBOOM *n* spar forming an extension of the bowsprit
JIBBS ▸ **jibb**
JIBE, -D, -S, JIBING *vb, n*
JIBER, -S ▸ **jibe**
JIBES ▸ **jibe**
JIBING ▸ **jibe**
JIBS ▸ **jib**
JICAMA, -S *n* pale brown turnip
JIFF, -S *same as* ▸ **jiffy**
JIFFIES ▸ **jiffy**
JIFFS ▸ **jiff**
JIFFY, JIFFIES *n*
JIG, -GED, -S *n, vb*
JIGGER, -S *n* small whisky glass ▹ *vb* interfere or alter
JIGGIER ▸ **jiggy**
JIGGING ▸ **jig**
JIGGISH ▸ **jig**
JIGGLE, -D, -S *vb, n*
JIGGLY ▸ **jiggle**
JIGGY, JIGGIER *adj* resembling a jig
JIGLIKE ▸ **jig**
JIGOT, -S *same as* ▸ **gigot**
JIGS ▸ **jig**
JIGSAW, -N, -S *n, vb*
JIHAD, -S *n*
JIHADI, -S *n*
JIHADS ▸ **jihad**
JILBAB, JALABIB, -S *n* long robe worn by Muslim women
JILGIE, -S *n* freshwater crayfish
JILL, -S *variant spelling of* ▸ **gill**
JILLET, -S *n* flighty or capricious woman
JILLION *n* extremely large number or amount
JILLS ▸ **jill**
JILT, -ED, -ING, -S *vb, n*
JILTER, -S ▸ **jilt**
JILTING ▸ **jilt**
JILTS ▸ **jilt**
JIMINY *interj* expression of surprise
JIMJAMS, JIMJAM *pl n* state of nervous tension, excitement, or anxiety
JIMMIE *same as* ▸ **jimmy**
JIMMIED ▸ **jimmy**
JIMMIES ▸ **jimmy**
JIMMINY *interj* expression of surprise
JIMMY, JIMMIED, JIMMIES *same as* ▸ **jemmy**
JIMP, -ER, -EST *adj* handsome
JIMPIER ▸ **jimpy**
JIMPLY *adv* neatly
JIMPSON *same as* ▸ **jimson**
JIMPY, JIMPIER *adj* neat and tidy
JIMSON, -S *n* as in **jimson weed** type of poisonous plant
JIN, -S *n* Chinese unit of weight
JINGAL, -S *n* swivel-mounted gun
JINGALL *same as* ▸ **jingal**
JINGALS ▸ **jingal**
JINGKO *same as* ▸ **gingko**
JINGLE, -D, -S *n, vb*
JINGLER ▸ **jingle**
JINGLES ▸ **jingle**
JINGLET *n* sleigh-bell clapper
JINGLY ▸ **jingle**
JINGO, -ES *n* loud and bellicose patriot; chauvinism
JINJILI *n* type of sesame
JINK, -ED, -ING, -S *vb, n*
JINKER, -S *n* vehicle for transporting timber ▹ *vb* carry or transport in a jinker
JINKING ▸ **jink**
JINKS ▸ **jink**
JINN, -S *n* spirit in Muslim mythology
JINNE *interj* South African exclamation
JINNEE *same as* ▸ **jinni**
JINNI, -S *n* spirit in Muslim mythology
JINNS ▸ **jinn**
JINS ▸ **jin**
JINX, -ED, -ES, -ING *n, vb*
JIPYAPA *same as* ▸ **jipijapa**
JIRBLE, -D, -S *vb* pour carelessly

JIRD, -S *n* gerbil
JIRGA, -S *n* Afghan council
JIRRE *same as* ▸**jinne**
JITNEY, -S *n* small cheap bus
JITTER, -S *vb*
JITTERY *adj* nervous
JIVE, -D, -S, -ST, JIVING *n, vb, adj*
JIVEASS *adj* misleading or phoney ▹ *n* person who loves fun and excitement
JIVED ▸**jive**
JIVER, -S ▸**jive**
JIVES ▸**jive**
JIVEST ▸**jive**
JIVEY, JIVIER, JIVIEST *adj* jazzy; lively
JIVING ▸**jive**
JIVY *same as* ▸**jivey**
JIZ *n* wig

When you find yourself with J and Z but nothing else that looks promising, there may well be an I on the board around which you can form **jiz**, which means a wig.

JIZZ, -ES *n* term for the characteristics that identify a particular species of bird or plant
JNANA, -S *n* type of yoga
JO *n* Scots word for sweetheart
JOANNA, -S *n* piano
JOANNES *same as* >**johannes**
JOB, -BED, -S *n, vb*
JOBBER, -S *n* person who jobs
JOBBERY *n* practice of making private profit out of a public office
JOBBIE, -S *n* referring to a thing usually specified in the preceding part of a sentence
JOBBING *adj* doing individual jobs for payment ▹ *n* act of seeking work
JOBE, -D, -S, JOBING *vb* scold
JOBLESS *pl n, adj*
JOBNAME *n* title of position
JOBS ▸**job**
JOCK, -S *n* athlete
JOCKDOM *n* world of male athletes
JOCKEY, -S *n* person who rides horses in races ▹ *vb* ride (a horse) in a race
JOCKIER ▸**jocky**
JOCKISH *adj* macho
JOCKNEY *n* the Scots dialect influenced by cockney speech patterns
JOCKO, -S *n* chimpanzee
JOCKS ▸**jock**
JOCKY, JOCKIER *adj* indicating or appropriate to a male athlete
JOCO, -S *adj* relaxed ▹ *n* joke
JOCOSE, -R *adj* playful or humorous
JOCULAR *adj*
JOCUND *adj* merry or cheerful
JODEL, -S *same as* ▸**yodel**
JODHPUR *n*
JOE, -S *same as* ▸**jo**
JOEY, -S *n* young kangaroo
JOG, -GED, -S *vb, n*
JOGGER, -S *n*
JOGGING ▸**jog**
JOGGLE, -D, -S *vb* shake or move jerkily ▹ *n* act of joggling
JOGGLER ▸**joggle**
JOGGLES ▸**joggle**
JOGS ▸**jog**
JOGTROT *n* easy bouncy gait ▹ *vb* move at a jogtrot
JOHN, -S *n* toilet
JOHNNIE *same as* ▸**johnny**
JOHNNY *n* chap
JOHNS ▸**john**
JOIN, -ED, -S *vb, n*
JOINDER *n* act of joining, esp in legal contexts
JOINED ▸**join**
JOINER, -S *n*
JOINERY *n* joiner's work
JOINING ▸**join**
JOINS ▸**join**
JOINT, -S *adj, n, vb*
JOINTED *adj* having a joint or joints
JOINTER *n* tool for pointing mortar joints
JOINTLY ▸**joint**
JOINTS ▸**joint**
JOIST, -ED, -S *n* horizontal beam ▹ *vb* construct (a floor, roof, etc) with joists
JOJOBA, -S *n* shrub of SW North America

JOKE, -D, -S *n, vb*
JOKER, -S *n*
JOKES ▸ **joke**
JOKEY, JOKIER, JOKIEST *adj* intended as a joke
JOKILY ▸ **joke**
JOKING, -S *n* act of joking
JOKOL *Shetland word for* ▸ **yes**
JOKY *same as* ▸ **jokey**
JOL, -LED, -LING, -S *n* party ▹ *vb* have a good time
JOLE, -D, -S, JOLING *vb* knock
JOLL, -S *variant of* ▸ **jole**
JOLLED ▸ **jol**
JOLLER, -S *n* person who has a good time
JOLLEY, -S *same as* ▸ **jolly**
JOLLIED ▸ **jolly**
JOLLIER *n* joker
JOLLIES ▸ **jolly**
JOLLIFY *vb* be or cause to be jolly
JOLLILY ▸ **jolly**
JOLLING ▸ **jol**
JOLLITY *n*
JOLLOF *adj* as in **jollof rice** W African dish made from rice and meat or fish
JOLLOP, -S *n* cream or unguent
JOLLS ▸ **joll**
JOLLY, JOLLIED, JOLLIES *adj* full of good humour ▹ *adv* extremely ▹ *vb* try to make or keep (someone) cheerful ▹ *n* festivity or celebration
JOLLYER ▸ **jolly**
JOLS ▸ **jol**
JOLT, -ED, -S *n, vb*
JOLTER, -S ▸ **jolt**
JOLTIER ▸ **jolty**
JOLTILY ▸ **jolt**
JOLTING *n* act of jolting
JOLTS ▸ **jolt**
JOLTY, JOLTIER ▸ **jolt**
JOMO, -S *same as* ▸ **zo**
JOMON, -S *n* particular era in Japanese history
JOMOS ▸ **jomo**
JONES, -ED, -ES *vb* desire
JONG, -S *n* friend, often used in direct address
JONNOCK *adj* genuine ▹ *adv* honestly
JONQUIL *n* fragrant narcissus
JONTY, JONTIES *n* petty officer
JOOK, -ED, -ING, -S *vb* poke or puncture (the skin) ▹ *n* jab or the resulting wound
JOOKERY *n* mischief
JOOKING ▸ **jook**
JOOKS ▸ **jook**
JOR, -S *n* movement in Indian music
JORAM, -S *same as* ▸ **jorum**
JORDAN, -S *n* chamber pot
JORS ▸ **jor**
JORUM, -S *n* large drinking bowl or vessel or its contents
JOSEPH, -S *n* woman's floor-length riding coat
JOSH, -ED, -ES *vb, n*
JOSHER, -S ▸ **josh**
JOSHES ▸ **josh**
JOSHING *n* act of joshing
JOSKIN, -S *n* bumpkin
JOSS, -ES *n* Chinese deity
JOSSER, -S *n* unintelligent person
JOSSES ▸ **joss**
JOSTLE, -D, -S *vb, n*
JOSTLER ▸ **jostle**
JOSTLES ▸ **jostle**
JOT, -S, -TED *vb, n*
JOTA, -S *n* Spanish dance
JOTS ▸ **jot**
JOTTED ▸ **jot**
JOTTER, -S *n*
JOTTIER ▸ **jotty**
JOTTING ▸ **jot**
JOTTY, JOTTIER ▸ **jot**
JOTUN, -S *n* giant
JOTUNN, -S *same as* ▸ **jotun**
JOTUNS ▸ **jotun**
JOUAL, -S *n* nonstandard variety of Canadian French
JOUGS *pl n* iron ring for restraining an offender
JOUK, -ED, -ING, -S *vb* duck or dodge ▹ *n* sudden evasive movement
JOUKERY *same as* ▸ **jookery**
JOUKING ▸ **jouk**
JOUKS ▸ **jouk**
JOULE, -D, -S, JOULING *n* unit of work or energy ▹ *vb* knock
JOUNCE, -D, -S *vb* shake or jolt or cause to shake or jolt ▹ *n* jolting movement
JOUNCY ▸ **jounce**
JOUR, -S *n* day
JOURNAL *n, vb*
JOURNEY *n, vb*
JOURNO, -S *n* journalist

JOURS ▸ **jour**
JOUST, -ED, -S *n, vb*
JOUSTER ▸ **joust**
JOUSTS ▸ **joust**
JOVIAL *adj*
JOW, -ED, -ING, -S *vb* ring (a bell)
JOWAR, -S *n* variety of sorghum
JOWARI, -S *same as* ▸ **jowar**
JOWARS ▸ **jowar**
JOWED ▸ **jow**
JOWING ▸ **jow**
JOWL, -ING, -S *n* lower jaw ▹ *vb* knock
JOWLED ▸ **jowl**
JOWLER, -S *n* dog with prominent jowls
JOWLIER ▸ **jowly**
JOWLING ▸ **jowl**
JOWLS ▸ **jowl**
JOWLY, JOWLIER ▸ **jowl**
JOWS ▸ **jow**
JOY, -ED, -ING, -S *n* feeling of great delight or pleasure ▹ *vb* feel joy
JOYANCE *n* joyous feeling or festivity
JOYED ▸ **joy**
JOYFUL *adj*
JOYING ▸ **joy**
JOYLESS *adj*
JOYOUS *adj*
JOYPAD, -S *n* computer games console
JOYRIDE, JOYRODE *n, vb*
JOYS ▸ **joy**
JUBA, -S *n* lively African-American dance
JUBATE *adj* possessing a mane
JUBBAH, -S *n* long loose outer garment with wide sleeves
JUBE, -S *n* part of a church or cathedral
JUBHAH, -S *same as* ▸ **jubbah**
JUBILE, -S *same as* ▸ **jubilee**
JUBILEE *n*
JUBILES ▸ **jubile**
JUCO, -S *n* junior college in America
JUD, -S *n* large block of coal
JUDAS, -ES *n* peephole
JUDDER, -S *vb, n*
JUDDERY *adj* shaky
JUDGE, -D, -S *n, vb*
JUDGER, -S ▸ **judge**
JUDGES ▸ **judge**
JUDGEY *adj* tending to be judgmental
JUDGIER ▸ **judgy**
JUDGING *n* act of judging
JUDGY, JUDGIER *adj* tending to be judgmental
JUDIES ▸ **judy**
JUDO, -S *n* type of sport
JUDOGI, -S *n* white two-piece cotton costume
JUDOIST ▸ **judo**
JUDOKA, -S *n* competitor or expert in judo
JUDOS ▸ **judo**
JUDS ▸ **jud**
JUDY, JUDIES *n* woman
JUG, -GED, -GING, -S *n, vb*
JUGA ▸ **jugum**
JUGAAD, -S *n* (in Indian English) problem-solving
JUGAL, -S *adj* of or relating to the zygomatic bone ▹ *n* cheekbone
JUGATE *adj* having parts arranged in pairs
JUGFUL, -S, JUGSFUL *same as* ▸ **jug**
JUGGED ▸ **jug**
JUGGING ▸ **jug**
JUGGINS *n* silly person
JUGGLE, -D, -S *vb, n*
JUGGLER *n*
JUGGLES ▸ **juggle**
JUGHEAD *n* clumsy person
JUGLET, -S *n* small jug
JUGS ▸ **jug**
JUGSFUL ▸ **jugful**
JUGULA ▸ **jugulum**
JUGULAR *n*
JUGULUM, JUGULA *n* lower throat
JUGUM, JUGA, -S *n* part of an insect's forewing
JUICE, -D, -S, JUICING *n, vb*
JUICER, -S *n*
JUICES ▸ **juice**
JUICIER ▸ **juicy**
JUICILY ▸ **juicy**
JUICING ▸ **juice**
JUICY, JUICIER *adj*
JUJITSU *n* Japanese martial art
JUJU, -S *n* W African magic charm or fetish
JUJUBE, -S *n* chewy sweet made of flavoured gelatine
JUJUISM ▸ **juju**
JUJUIST ▸ **juju**
JUJUS ▸ **juju**
JUJUTSU *same as* ▸ **jujitsu**

JUKE, -D, -S, JUKING *vb* dance or play dance music
JUKEBOX *n*
JUKED ▶ **juke**
JUKES ▶ **juke**
JUKING ▶ **juke**
JUKSKEI *n* type of game
JUKU, -S *n* Japanese martial art
JULEP, -S *n* sweet alcoholic drink
JULIET, -S *n* code word for the letter J
JUMAR, -ED, -S *n* climbing tool ▷ *vb* climb (up a fixed rope) using jumars
JUMART, -S *n* mythical offspring of a bull and a mare
JUMBAL, -S *same as* ▶ **jumble**
JUMBIE, -S *n* Caribbean ghost
JUMBLE, -D, -S *n, vb*
JUMBLER ▶ **jumble**
JUMBLES ▶ **jumble**
JUMBLY ▶ **jumble**
JUMBO, -S *adj, n*
JUMBUCK *n* sheep
JUMBY *n* Caribbean ghost
JUMELLE *n* paired objects
JUMP, -ED, -S *vb, n*
JUMPER, -S *n*
JUMPIER ▶ **jumpy**
JUMPILY ▶ **jumpy**
JUMPING ▶ **jump**
JUMPOFF *n* round in a showjumping contest
JUMPS ▶ **jump**
JUMPY, JUMPIER *adj* nervous
JUN *variant of* ▶ **chon**
JUNCATE *same as* ▶ **junket**
JUNCO, -ES, -S *n* North American bunting
JUNCUS *n* type of rush
JUNGLE, -S *n*
JUNGLED *adj* covered with jungle
JUNGLES ▶ **jungle**
JUNGLI, -S *n* uncultured person
JUNGLY ▶ **jungle**
JUNIOR, -S *adj, n, vb*
JUNIPER *n*
JUNK, -ED, -ING, -S *n, vb*
JUNKER, -S *n* (formerly) young German nobleman
JUNKET, -S *n, vb*
JUNKIE, -S *n*
JUNKIER ▶ **junky**
JUNKIES ▶ **junkie**
JUNKING ▶ **junk**
JUNKMAN, JUNKMEN *n* man who trades in discarded items
JUNKS ▶ **junk**
JUNKY, JUNKIER *adj* of low quality
JUNTA, -S *n*
JUNTO, -S *same as* ▶ **junta**
JUPATI, -S *n* type of palm tree
JUPE, -S *n* sleeveless jacket
JUPON, -S *n* short sleeveless padded garment
JURA ▶ **jus**
JURAL *adj* of or relating to law or to the administration of justice
JURALLY ▶ **jural**
JURANT, -S *n* person taking oath
JURAT, -S *n* statement at the foot of an affidavit
JURE, -S *adv* by legal right ▷ *n* legal right
JUREL, -S *n* edible fish
JURES ▶ **jure**
JURIDIC *same as* ▶ **juridical**
JURIED ▶ **jury**
JURIES ▶ **jury**
JURIST, -S *n* expert in law
JUROR, -S *n*
JURY, JURIED, JURIES, -ING *n* group of people sworn to deliver a verdict in a court of law ▷ *adj* makeshift ▷ *vb* evaluate by jury
JURYMAN, JURYMEN *n* member of a jury, esp a man
JUS, JURA *n* right, power, or authority
JUSSIVE *n* mood of verbs used for giving orders; imperative
JUST, -ED, -EST, -ING *adv* very recently ▷ *adj* fair or impartial in action or judgment ▷ *vb* joust
JUSTER, -S ▶ **just**
JUSTEST ▶ **just**
JUSTICE *n*
JUSTIFY *vb*
JUSTING ▶ **just**
JUSTLE, -D, -S *less common word for* ▶ **jostle**
JUSTLY ▶ **just**
JUSTS *same as* ▶ **joust**
JUT, -S, -TED, -TING *vb, n*

JUTE, -S *n* plant fibre, used for rope, canvas, etc
JUTS ▶ **jut**
JUTTED ▶ **jut**
JUTTIED ▶ **jutty**
JUTTIER ▶ **jutty**
JUTTIES ▶ **jutty**
JUTTING ▶ **jut**
JUTTY, JUTTIED, JUTTIER, JUTTIES *vb* project beyond ▷ *adj* characterized by jutting
JUVE, -S *same as* > **juvenile**
JUVENAL *variant spelling (esp US) of* > **juvenile**
JUVES ▶ **juve**
JUVIE, -S *n* juvenile detention centre
JYMOLD *adj* having a hinge
JYNX, -ES *n* wryneck

This unusual word, another name for the bird known as a wryneck, is unique in combining J, Y and X without using any vowels.

Kk

KA, -ING, -S *n* (in ancient Egypt) type of spirit ▷ *vb* (in archaic usage) help
KAAL *adj* naked
KAAMA, -S *n* large African antelope with lyre-shaped horns
KAAS *n* Dutch cabinet or wardrobe
KAB, -S *variant spelling of* ▶ **cab**
KABAB, -S *same as* ▶ **kebab**
KABADDI *n* type of game
KABAKA, -S *n* any of the former rulers of the Baganda people
KABALA, -S *same as* > **kabbalah**
KABAR, -S *archaic form of* ▶ **caber**
KABAYA, -S *n* tunic
KABBALA *same as* > **kabbalah**
KABELE, -S *same as* ▶ **kebele**
KABIKI, -S *n* fruit tree found in India
KABOB, -S *same as* ▶ **kebab**
KABOCHA *n* type of Japanese pumpkin
KABOOM, -S *n*
KABS ▶ **kab**
KABUKI, -S *n* form of Japanese drama
KACCHA, -S *n* trousers worn traditionally by Sikhs
KACHA *adj* crude
KACHCHA *same as* ▶ **kacha**
KACHERI *same as* > **kachahri**
KACHINA *n* type of supernatural being
KACHORI *n* balls of fried dough with various fillings, eaten as a snack
KACK, -S *same as* ▶ **cack**
KADAI, -S *same as* ▶ **karahi**
KADDISH *n* ancient Jewish liturgical prayer
KADE, -S *same as* ▶ **ked**
KADI, -S *variant spelling of* ▶ **cadi**
KAE, -D, -ING, -S *n* dialect word for jackdaw or jay ▷ *vb* (in archaic usage) help
KAF, -S *n* letter of the Hebrew alphabet
KAFILA, -S *n* caravan
KAFS ▶ **kaf**
KAFTAN, -S *n*
KAGO, -S *n* Japanese sedan chair
KAGOOL, -S *variant spelling of* ▶ **cagoule**
KAGOS ▶ **kago**
KAGOUL, -S *variant spelling of* ▶ **cagoule**
KAGOULE *same as* ▶ **kagoul**
KAGOULS ▶ **kagoul**
KAGU, -S *n* crested nocturnal bird
KAHAL, -S *n* Jewish community
KAHAWAI *n* food and game fish of New Zealand
KAHUNA, -S *n* Hawaiian priest, shaman, or expert
KAI, -S *n* food
KAIAK, -ED, -S *same as* ▶ **kayak**
KAID, -S *n* North African chieftain or leader
KAIE, -S *archaic form of* ▶ **key**
KAIF, -S *same as* ▶ **kif**
KAIK, -S *same as* ▶ **kainga**
KAIKA, -S *same as* ▶ **kainga**
KAIKAI, -S *n* food
KAIKAS ▶ **kaika**
KAIKS ▶ **kaik**
KAIL, -S *same as* ▶ **kale**
KAIM, -S *same as* ▶ **kame**

KAIN, -S *variant spelling of* ▸ **cain**
KAING ▸ **ka**
KAINGA, -S *n* (in New Zealand) a Māori village or small settlement
KAINIT, -S *same as* ▸ **kainite**
KAINITE *n* white mineral
KAINITS ▸ **kainit**
KAINS ▸ **kain**
KAIS ▸ **kai**
KAISER, -S *n*
KAIZEN, -S *n* type of philosophy
KAJAWAH *n* type of seat or pannier used on a camel
KAJEPUT *n* variety of Australian melaleuca
KAKA, -S *n* parrot of New Zealand
KAKAPO, -S *n* nocturnal New Zealand parrot
KAKAS ▸ **kaka**
KAKI, -S *n* Asian persimmon tree
KAKIVAK *n* fish spear used by Inuit people
KAKODYL *variant spelling of* ▸ **cacodyl**
KAKURO, -S *n* crossword-style puzzle with numbers
KALAM, -S *n* discussion and debate
KALE, -S *n*
KALENDS *same as* ▸ **calends**
KALES ▸ **kale**
KALI, -S *another name for* ▸ **saltwort**
KALIAN, -S *another name for* ▸ **hookah**
KALIF, -S *variant spelling of* ▸ **caliph**
KALIMBA *n* musical instrument
KALIPH, -S *variant spelling of* ▸ **caliph**
KALIS ▸ **kali**
KALIUM, -S *n* Latin for potassium
KALMIA, -S *n* evergreen ericaceous shrub
KALONG, -S *n* fruit bat
KALOOKI *n* card game
KALPA, -S *n* period in Hindu cosmology
KALPAC, -S *variant spelling of* ▸ **calpac**
KALPAK, -S *variant spelling of* ▸ **calpac**
KALPAS ▸ **kalpa**
KALPIS *n* Greek water jar
KALUKI, -S *same as* ▸ **kalooki**
KAM *Shakespearean word for* ▸ **crooked**
KAMA, -S *n* large African antelope with lyre-shaped horns
KAMAHI, -S *n* hardwood tree
KAMALA, -S *n* S Asian tree
KAMAS ▸ **kama**
KAME, -S *n* irregular mound of gravel, sand, etc
KAMEES *same as* ▸ **kameez**
KAMEEZ *n* long tunic
KAMELA, -S *same as* ▸ **kamala**
KAMERAD *interj* shout of surrender ▷ *vb* surrender
KAMES ▸ **kame**
KAMI *n* divine being or spiritual force in Shinto
KAMICHI *n* South American bird
KAMIK, -S *n* traditional Inuit boot
KAMILA, -S *same as* ▸ **kamala**
KAMIS, -ES *same as* ▸ **kameez**
KAMME *same as* ▸ **kam**
KAMOTIK *n* type of Inuit sledge
KAMOTIQ *same as* ▸ **kamotik**
KAMPONG *n* (in Malaysia) village
KAMSEEN *same as* ▸ **khamsin**
KAMSIN, -S *same as* ▸ **kamseen**
KANA, -S *n* Japanese syllabary
KANAE, -S *n* grey mullet
KANAS ▸ **kana**
KANBAN, -S *n* just-in-time manufacturing process
KANDY, KANDIES *same as* ▸ **candie**
KANE, -S *n* Hawaiian man or boy
KANEH, -S *n* 6-cubit Hebrew measure
KANES ▸ **kane**
KANG, -S *n* Chinese heatable platform
KANGA, -S *n* piece of gaily decorated thin cotton cloth
KANGHA, -S *n* comb traditionally worn by Sikhs
KANGS ▸ **kang**
KANJI, -S *n* Japanese writing system

KANS, -ES *n* Indian wild sugar cane
KANT, -ED, -ING, -S *archaic spelling of* ▸ **cant**
KANTAR, -S *n* unit of weight
KANTED ▸ **kant**
KANTELA *same as* ▸ **kantele**
KANTELE *n* Finnish stringed instrument
KANTEN, -S *same as* ▸ **agar**
KANTHA, -S *n* Bengali embroidered quilt
KANTING ▸ **kant**
KANTS ▸ **kant**
KANUKA, -S *n* New Zealand myrtaceous tree
KANZU, -S *n* long garment
KAOLIN, -S *n* fine white clay
KAOLINE *same as* ▸ **kaolin**
KAOLINS ▸ **kaolin**
KAON, -S *n* type of meson
KAONIC ▸ **kaon**
KAONS ▸ **kaon**
KAPA, -S *n* Hawaiian cloth made from beaten mulberry bark
KAPEYKA, KAPEEK *n* small currency unit of Belarus
KAPH, -S *n* 11th letter of the Hebrew alphabet
KAPOK, -S *n* fluffy fibre
KAPOW, -S *n*
KAPPA, -S *n* tenth letter in the Greek alphabet
KAPU, -S *n* (in Hawaii) system of rules for daily life
KAPUKA, -S *same as* > **broadleaf**
KAPUS ▸ **kapu**
KAPUT *adj* ruined or broken
KAPUTT *same as* ▸ **kaput**
KARA, -S *n* steel bangle traditionally worn by Sikhs
KARAHI, -S *n* type of wok
KARAISM *n* beliefs and doctrines of a Jewish sect
KARAIT, -S *same as* ▸ **krait**
KARAKA, -S *n* New Zealand tree
KARAKIA *n* prayer
KARAKUL *n* sheep of central Asia
KARAMU, -S *n* small New Zealand tree
KARANGA *n* call or chant of welcome, sung by a female elder ▹ *vb* perform a karanga
KARAOKE *n*
KARAS ▸ **kara**
KARAT, -S *n* measure of the proportion of gold in an alloy
KARATE, -S *n*
KARATS ▸ **karat**
KARENGO *n* edible type of Pacific seaweed
KARITE, -S *n* shea tree
KARK, -ED, -ING, -S *variant spelling of* ▸ **cark**
KARMA, -S *n*
KARMIC ▸ **karma**
KARN, -S *old word for* ▸ **cairn**
KARO, -S *n* small New Zealand tree or shrub
KAROO, -S *n* high arid plateau
KARORO, -S *n* large seagull
KAROS ▸ **karo**
KAROSHI *n* (in Japan) death caused by overwork
KAROSS *n* type of blanket
KARRI, -S *n* Australian eucalypt
KARROO, -S *same as* ▸ **karoo**
KARSEY, -S *variant spelling of* ▸ **khazi**
KARSIES ▸ **karsy**
KARST, -S *n* characteristic scenery of a limestone region
KARSTIC ▸ **karst**
KARSTS ▸ **karst**
KARSY, KARSIES *variant spelling of* ▸ **khazi**
KART, -S *n*
KARTER, -S ▸ **kart**
KARTING ▸ **kart**
KARTS ▸ **kart**
KARYON, -S *n* nucleus of a cell
KARZY, KARZIES *variant spelling of* ▸ **khazi**
KAS ▸ **ka**
KASBAH, -S *n*
KASHA, -S *n* dish originating in Eastern Europe
KASHER, -S *vb* make fit for use
KASHMIR *variant spelling of* > **cashmere**
KASHRUS *same as* > **kashruth**
KASHRUT *same as* > **kashruth**

KASME *interj* (in Indian English) I swear
KAT, -S *same as* ▸ **khat**
KATA, -S *n* form of exercise
KATAL, -S *n* SI unit of catalytic activity
KATANA, -S *n* Japanese samurai sword
KATAS ▸ **kata**
KATCINA *variant spelling of* ▸ **kachina**
KATHAK, -S *n* form of dancing
KATHODE *variant spelling of* ▸ **cathode**
KATHUMP *n* sound of a dull heavy blow
KATI, -S *variant spelling of* ▸ **catty**
KATION, -S *variant spelling of* ▸ **cation**
KATIPO, -S *n* small poisonous New Zealand spider
KATIS ▸ **kati**
KATORGA *n* type of labour camp
KATS ▸ **kat**
KATSINA *n* (among the Hopi) doll representing spirit messengers
KATSURA *n* Asian tree
KATTI, -S *variant spelling of* ▸ **catty**
KATYDID *n* large green grasshopper of N America
KAUGH, -S *same as* ▸ **kiaugh**
KAUPAPA *n* strategy, policy, or cause
KAURI, -S *n* large New Zealand conifer
KAURIES ▸ **kaury**
KAURIS ▸ **kauri**
KAURU, -S *n* edible stem of the cabbage tree
KAURY, KAURIES *variant spelling of* ▸ **kauri**
KAVA, -S *n* Polynesian shrub
KAVAL, -S *n* type of flute played in the Balkans
KAVAS ▸ **kava**
KAVASS *n* armed Turkish constable
KAW, -ED, -ING, -S *variant spelling of* ▸ **caw**
KAWA, -S *n* protocol or etiquette
KAWAII, -S *n* (in Japan) quality of being lovable or cute
KAWAS ▸ **kawa**
KAWAU, -S *n* New Zealand name for black shag
KAWED ▸ **kaw**
KAWING ▸ **kaw**
KAWS ▸ **kaw**
KAY, -S *n* name of the letter K
KAYAK, -ED, -S *n, vb*
KAYAKER ▸ **kayak**
KAYAKS ▸ **kayak**
KAYLE *n* one of a set of ninepins
KAYLES *pl n* ninepins
KAYLIED *adj* intoxicated or drunk
KAYO, -ED, -ES, -S *another term for* ▸ **knockout**
KAYOING ▸ **kayo**
KAYOS ▸ **kayo**
KAYS ▸ **kay**
KAZI, -S *variant spelling of* ▸ **khazi**
KAZOO, -S *n*
KBAR, -S *n* kilobar
KEA, -S *n* large brownish-green parrot of New Zealand
KEASAR, -S *archaic variant of* ▸ **kaiser**
KEAVIE, -S *n* archaic or dialect word for a type of crab
KEB, -BED, -BING, -S *vb* Scots word meaning miscarry or reject a lamb
KEBAB, -S *n, vb*
KEBAR, -S *n* Scots word for beam or rafter
KEBBED ▸ **keb**
KEBBIE, -S *n* Scots word for shepherd's crook
KEBBING ▸ **keb**
KEBBOCK *n* Scots word for a cheese
KEBBUCK *same as* ▸ **kebbock**
KEBELE, -S *n* Ethiopian local council
KEBLAH, -S *same as* ▸ **kiblah**
KEBOB, -S *same as* ▸ **kebab**
KEBS ▸ **keb**
KECK, -ED, -ING *vb* retch or feel nausea
KECKLE, -D, -S *Scots variant of* ▸ **cackle**
KECKS, -ES *n* trousers
KECKSY *n* dialect word meaning hollow plant stalk
KED, -S *n* as in **sheep ked** sheep tick
KEDDAH, -S *same as* ▸ **kheda**
KEDGE, -D, -S, KEDGING *vb* move (a ship) using

cable attached to an anchor ▷ *n* light anchor used for kedging
KEDGER, -S *n* small anchor
KEDGES ▶ **kedge**
KEDGIER ▶ **kedgy**
KEDGING ▶ **kedge**
KEDGY, KEDGIER *adj* dialect word for happy or lively
KEDS ▶ **ked**
KEECH, -ES *n* old word for lump of fat
KEEF, -S *same as* ▶ **kif**
KEEK, -ED, -ING, -S *Scot word for* ▶ **peep**
KEEKER, -S ▶ **keek**
KEEKING ▶ **keek**
KEEKS ▶ **keek**
KEEL, -ED, -S *n, vb*
KEELAGE *n* fee charged by certain ports
KEELED ▶ **keel**
KEELER, -S *n* bargeman
KEELIE, -S *n* kestrel
KEELING ▶ **keel**
KEELMAN, KEELMEN *n* bargeman
KEELS ▶ **keel**
KEELSON *n* part of a ship
KEEMA, -S *n* (in Indian cookery) minced meat
KEEN, -ED, -EST, -S *adj, vb, n*
KEENER, -S ▶ **keen**
KEENEST ▶ **keen**
KEENING ▶ **keen**
KEENLY ▶ **keen**
KEENO, -S *same as* ▶ **keno**
KEENS ▶ **keen**
KEEP, -S, KEPT *vb, n*
KEEPER, -S *n*
KEEPING ▶ **keep**
KEEPNET *n* cylindrical net used to keep fish alive
KEEPS ▶ **keep**
KEESTER *same as* ▶ **keister**
KEET, -S *short for* > **parakeet**
KEEVE, -S *n* tub or vat
KEF, -S *same as* ▶ **kif**
KEFFEL, -S *dialect word for* ▶ **horse**
KEFIR, -S *n* effervescent drink
KEFS ▶ **kef**
KEG, -GED, -GING, -S *n, vb*
KEGELER *same as* ▶ **kegler**
KEGGED ▶ **keg**
KEGGER, -S ▶ **keg**
KEGGING ▶ **keg**
KEGLER, -S *n* participant in a game of tenpin bowling
KEGLING *n* bowling
KEGS ▶ **keg**
KEHUA, -S *n* ghost or spirit
KEIGHT ▶ **ketch**
KEIR, -S *same as* ▶ **kier**
KEIREN, -S *n* type of track cycling event
KEIRIN, -S *n* cycling race originating in Japan
KEIRS ▶ **keir**
KEISTER *n* rump
KEITLOA *n* type of rhinoceros
KEKENO, -S *n* New Zealand fur seal
KEKS *same as* ▶ **kecks**
KEKSYE, -S *same as* ▶ **kex**
KELEP, -S *n* large ant found in Central and South America
KELIM, -S *same as* ▶ **kilim**
KELL, -S *dialect word for* ▶ **hairnet**
KELLAUT *same as* ▶ **khilat**
KELLIES ▶ **kelly**
KELLS ▶ **kell**
KELLY, KELLIES *n* part of a drill system
KELOID, -S *n* type of scar tissue
KELP, -ED, -ING, -S *n, vb*
KELPER, -S *n* Falkland Islander
KELPIE, -S *n* Australian sheepdog
KELPING ▶ **kelp**
KELPS ▶ **kelp**
KELPY *same as* ▶ **kelpie**
KELSON, -S *same as* ▶ **keelson**
KELT, -S *n* salmon that has recently spawned
KELTER, -S *same as* ▶ **kilter**
KELTIE *variant spelling of* ▶ **kelty**
KELTIES ▶ **kelty**
KELTS ▶ **kelt**
KELTY, KELTIES *n* old Scots word for a drink imposed on someone not thought to be drinking enough
KELVIN, -S *n* SI unit of temperature
KEMB, -ED, -ING, -S *old word for* ▶ **comb**
KEMBLA, -S *n* small change
KEMBO, -ED, -S *same as* ▶ **kimbo**

KEMBS ▸ **kemb**
KEMP, -ED, -S *n* coarse hair or strand of hair ▹ *vb* dialect word meaning to compete or try to come first
KEMPER, -S ▸ **kemp**
KEMPIER ▸ **kempy**
KEMPING ▸ **kemp**
KEMPLE, -S *n* variable Scottish measure for hay or straw
KEMPS ▸ **kemp**
KEMPT *adj* (of hair) tidy
KEMPY, KEMPIER ▸ **kemp**
KEN, -NED, -S *vb, n*
KENAF, -S *another name for* ▸ **ambary**
KENCH, -ES *n* bin for salting and preserving fish
KENDO, -S *n* Japanese sport of fencing using wooden staves
KENNED ▸ **ken**
KENNEL, -S *n, vb*
KENNER, -S ▸ **ken**
KENNET, -S *n* old word for a small hunting dog
KENNETT *vb* spoil or destroy ruthlessly
KENNING ▸ **ken**
KENO, -S *n* game of chance similar to bingo
KENOSIS, KENOSES *n* Christ's renunciation of certain divine attributes
KENOTIC ▸ **kenosis**
KENS ▸ **ken**
KENT, -ED, -ING, -S *dialect word for* ▸ **punt**
KENTE, -S *n* brightly coloured handwoven cloth
KENTED ▸ **kent**
KENTES ▸ **kente**
KENTIA, -S *n* plant name
KENTING ▸ **kent**
KENTS ▸ **kent**
KEP, -PED, -PEN, -PING, -PIT, -S, KIPPEN *vb* catch
KEPHIR, -S *same as* ▸ **kefir**
KEPI, -S *n* French military cap with a flat top and a horizontal peak
KEPPED ▸ **kep**
KEPPEN ▸ **kep**
KEPPING ▸ **kep**
KEPPIT ▸ **kep**
KEPS ▸ **kep**
KEPT ▸ **keep**
KERAMIC *rare variant of* ▸ **ceramic**
KERATIN *n* fibrous protein found in the hair and nails
KERB, -ED, -S *n, vb*
KERBAYA *n* blouse worn by Malay women
KERBED ▸ **kerb**
KERBING *n* material used for a kerb
KERBS ▸ **kerb**
KERCHOO *interj* atishoo
KEREL, -S *n* chap or fellow
KERERU, -S *n* New Zealand pigeon
KERF, -ED, -ING, -S *n* cut made by a saw, an axe, etc ▹ *vb* cut
KERKY, KERKIER *adj* stupid
KERMA, -S *n* quantity of radiation
KERMES *n* dried bodies of female scale insects
KERMESS *same as* ▸ **kermis**
KERMIS *n* (formerly) annual country festival or carnival
KERMODE *n* type of black bear found in Canada
KERN, -S *n* projection of a printed character ▹ *vb* furnish (a typeface) with a kern
KERNE, -D, -S *same as* ▸ **kern**
KERNEL, -S *n* seed of a nut, cereal, or fruit stone ▹ *vb* form kernels
KERNES ▸ **kerne**
KERNING *n* provision of kerns in printing
KERNISH *adj* resembling an armed foot soldier or peasant
KERNITE *n* light soft colourless or white mineral
KERNS ▸ **kern**
KERO, -S *short for* ▸ **kerosene**
KEROGEN *n* material that produces hydrocarbons when heated
KEROS ▸ **kero**
KERRIA, -S *n* type of shrub with yellow flowers
KERRY, KERRIES *n* breed of dairy cattle
KERSEY, -S *n* smooth woollen cloth
KERVE, -D, -S, KERVING *dialect word for* ▸ **carve**

KERYGMA *n* Christian gospel
KESAR, -S *old variant of* ▸ **kaiser**
KESH, -ES *n* beard and uncut hair traditionally worn by Sikhs
KEST, -ING, -S *old form of* ▸ **cast**
KESTREL *n*
KESTS ▸ **kest**
KET, -S *n* dialect word for carrion
KETA, -S *n* type of salmon
KETAINE *adj* in poor taste
KETAS ▸ **keta**
KETCH, KEIGHT, -ES *n* two-masted sailing vessel ▹ *vb* (in archaic usage) catch
KETCHUP *n*
KETE, -S *n* basket woven from flax
KETENE, -S *n* colourless irritating toxic gas
KETES ▸ **kete**
KETMIA, -S *n* as in **bladder ketmia** plant with pale yellow flowers
KETO *adj* as in **keto form** form of tautomeric compounds
KETOL, -S *n* nitrogenous substance
KETONE, -S *n* type of organic solvent
KETONIC ▸ **ketone**
KETOSE *n* any monosaccharide that contains a ketone group
KETOSIS, KETOSES *n* high concentration of ketone bodies in the blood
KETOTIC ▸ **ketosis**
KETS ▸ **ket**
KETTLE, -D, -S *n, vb*
KETUBAH, KETUBOT *n* Jewish marriage contract
KEVEL, -S *n* strong bitt or bollard for securing heavy hawsers
KEVIL, -S *old variant of* ▸ **kevel**
KEWL, -ER, -EST *nonstandard variant spelling of* ▸ **cool**
KEWPIE, -S *n* type of brightly coloured doll
KEX, -ES *n* any of several hollow-stemmed umbelliferous plants

This is another of the great high-scoring 3-letter words that use X.

KEY, -ED, -EST *n, adj, vb*
KEYCARD *n*
KEYED ▸ **key**
KEYER, -S *n* device that keys signals or information into a device or computing system
KEYEST ▸ **key**
KEYHOLE *n*
KEYING, -S ▸ **key**
KEYLESS ▸ **key**
KEYLINE *n* outline image on artwork or plans to show where it is to be placed
KEYNOTE *adj, n, vb*
KEYPAD, -S *n*
KEYPAL, -S *n* person one regularly exchanges emails with for fun
KEYRING *n*
KEYS *interj* children's cry for truce
KEYSET, -S *n* set of computer keys used for a particular purpose
KEYSTER *same as* ▸ **keister**
KEYWAY, -S *n* engineering device
KEYWORD *n* word or phrase used to find something on a computer
KGOTLA, -S *n* (in South African English) meeting place
KHADDAR *n* cotton cloth
KHADI, -S *same as* ▸ **khaddar**
KHAF, -S *n* letter of the Hebrew alphabet
KHAKI, -S *adj* dull yellowish-brown ▹ *n* fabric of this colour used for military uniforms
KHALAT, -S *same as* ▸ **khilat**
KHALIF, -S *variant spelling of* ▸ **caliph**
KHALIFA *same as* ▸ **caliph**
KHALIFS ▸ **khalif**
KHAMSIN *n* hot southerly wind
KHAN, -S *n* title of respect in Afghanistan and central Asia

KHANATE *n* territory ruled by a khan
KHANDA, -S *n* double-edged sword
KHANGA, -S *same as* ▸ **kanga**
KHANJAR *n* type of dagger
KHANS ▸ **khan**
KHANUM, -S *feminine form of* ▸ **khan**
KHAPH, -S *n* letter of the Hebrew alphabet
KHARIF, -S *n* crop harvested at the beginning of winter
KHAT, -S *n* white-flowered evergreen shrub
KHAYA, -S *n* type of African tree
KHAYAL, -S *n* kind of Indian classical vocal music
KHAYAS ▸ **khaya**
KHAZEN, -S *same as* ▸ **chazan**
KHAZI, -S *n* lavatory
KHEDA, -S *n* enclosure used to capture wild elephants
KHEDAH, -S *same as* ▸ **kheda**
KHEDAS ▸ **kheda**
KHEDIVA *n* khedive's wife
KHEDIVE *n* viceroy of Egypt under Ottoman suzerainty
KHET, -S *n* Thai district
KHETH, -S *same as* ▸ **heth**
KHETS ▸ **khet**
KHI, -S *n* letter of the Greek alphabet

This is a letter of the Greek alphabet, also spelt **chi**. It is worth remembering as one of the higher-scoring 3-letter words starting with K.

KHILAT, -S *n* (in the Middle East) gift given to someone as a mark of honour
KHILIM, -S *same as* ▸ **kilim**
KHIMAR, -S *n* type of headscarf worn by Muslim women
KHIRKAH *n* dervish's woollen or cotton outer garment
KHIS ▸ **khi**
KHODJA, -S *same as* ▸ **khoja**
KHOJA, -S *n* teacher in a Muslim school
KHOR, -S *n* watercourse
KHOTBAH *same as* ▸ **khutbah**
KHOTBEH *same as* ▸ **khutbah**
KHOUM, -S *n* Mauritanian monetary unit
KHUD, -S *n* Indian ravine
KHURTA, -S *same as* ▸ **kurta**
KHUTBAH *n* sermon in a Mosque, especially on a Friday
KI, -S *n* vital energy
KIAAT, -S *n* tropical African leguminous tree
KIACK, -S *n* N American fish of the herring family
KIANG, -S *n* variety of wild ass
KIAUGH, -S *n* (in Scots) anxiety
KIBBE, -S *n* Middle Eastern dish
KIBBEH, -S *same as* ▸ **kibbe**
KIBBES ▸ **kibbe**
KIBBI, -S *same as* ▸ **kibbe**
KIBBITZ *same as* ▸ **kibitz**
KIBBLE, -D, -S *n* bucket used in wells or in mining for hoisting ▹ *vb* grind into small pieces
KIBBUTZ *n*
KIBE, -S *n* chilblain
KIBEI, -S *n* someone of Japanese ancestry born in the US and educated in Japan
KIBES ▸ **kibe**
KIBITKA *n* (in Russia) covered sledge or wagon
KIBITZ *vb* interfere or offer unwanted advice
KIBLA, -S *same as* ▸ **kiblah**
KIBLAH, -S *n* direction of Mecca
KIBLAS ▸ **kibla**
KIBOSH *vb* put a stop to
KICK, -ED, -S *vb, n*
KICKBOX *vb* box with hands and feet
KICKED ▸ **kick**
KICKER, -S *n*
KICKIER ▸ **kicky**
KICKING *n* act of kicking
KICKOFF *n*
KICKOUT *n* (in basketball) instance of kicking the ball

KICKS ▸ **kick**
KICKUP, -S *n* fuss
KICKY, KICKIER *adj* excitingly unusual and different
KID, -DED, -S *n, vb, adj*
KIDDER, -S ▸ **kid**
KIDDIE *same as* ▸ **kiddy**
KIDDIED ▸ **kiddy**
KIDDIER *n* old word for a market trader
KIDDIES ▸ **kiddy**
KIDDING *n* act of kidding
KIDDISH ▸ **kid**
KIDDLE, -S *n* device for catching fish in a river or in the sea
KIDDO, -ES, -S *n* very informal term of address for a young person
KIDDUSH *n* (in Judaism) special blessing
KIDDY, KIDDIED, KIDDIES *n* affectionate word for a child ▹ *vb* tease or deceive
KIDEL, -S *same as* ▸ **kiddle**
KIDGE *dialect word for* ▸ **lively**
KIDGIE, -R *adj* dialect word for friendly and welcoming
KIDLET, -S *n* humorous word for small child
KIDLIKE ▸ **kid**
KIDLING *n* young kid
KIDLIT, -S *n* children's literature
KIDNAP, -S *vb*
KIDNEY, -S *n*
KIDS ▸ **kid**
KIDSKIN *n* soft smooth leather
KIDULT, -S *n, adj*
KIDVID, -S *n* informal word for children's video or television
KIEF, -S *same as* ▸ **kif**
KIEKIE, -S *n* climbing bush plant of New Zealand
KIER, -S *n* vat in which cloth is bleached
KIERIE, -S *n* South African cudgel
KIERS ▸ **kier**
KIESTER *same as* ▸ **keister**
KIEV, -S *n* type of chicken dish
KIEVE, -S *same as* ▸ **keeve**
KIEVS ▸ **kiev**
KIF, -S *n* marijuana
KIFF *adj* South African slang for excellent
KIFS ▸ **kif**
KIGHT, -S *n* archaic spelling of kite, the bird of prey
KIKOI, -S *n* piece of cotton cloth
KIKUMON *n* emblem of the imperial family of Japan
KIKUYU, -S *n* type of grass
KILD *old spelling of* ▸ **killed**
KILERG, -S *n* 1000 ergs
KILEY, -S *same as* ▸ **kylie**
KILIM, -S *n* pileless woven rug
KILL, -ED, -S *vb, n*
KILLAS *n* Cornish clay slate
KILLCOW *n* important person
KILLDEE *same as* ▸ **killdeer**
KILLED ▸ **kill**
KILLER, -S *n*
KILLICK *n* small anchor, esp one made of a heavy stone
KILLIE, -S *same as* ▸ **killifish**
KILLING *adj* very tiring ▹ *n* sudden financial success
KILLJOY *n*
KILLOCK *same as* ▸ **killick**
KILLS ▸ **kill**
KILLUT, -S *same as* ▸ **khilat**
KILN, -ED, -ING, -S *n, vb*
KILO, -S *n* code word for the letter *k*
KILOBAR *n* 1000 bars
KILOBIT *n* 1024 bits
KILORAD *n* 1000 rads
KILOS ▸ **kilo**
KILOTON *n* one thousand tons
KILP, -S *dialect form of* ▸ **kelp**
KILT, -S *n, vb*
KILTED ▸ **kilt**
KILTER, -S *n*
KILTIE, -S *n* someone wearing a kilt
KILTING ▸ **kilt**
KILTS ▸ **kilt**
KILTY *same as* ▸ **kiltie**
KIMBO, -ED, -S *vb* place akimbo
KIMCHEE *same as* ▸ **kimchi**
KIMCHI, -S *n* Korean dish
KIMMER, -S *same as* ▸ **cummer**
KIMONO, -S *n*

KIN, -S *n, adj*
KINA, -S *n* standard monetary unit of Papua New Guinea
KINARA, -S *n* African candle holder
KINAS ▸ **kina**
KINASE, -S *n* type of enzyme
KINCHIN *old slang word for* ▸ **child**
KINCOB, -S *n* fine silk fabric
KIND, -ED, -EST, -ING, -S *adj, n, vb*
KINDA *adv* very informal shortening of kind of
KINDED ▸ **kind**
KINDER, -S *adj* more kind ▹ *n* kindergarten or nursery school
KINDEST ▸ **kind**
KINDIE *same as* ▸ **kindy**
KINDIES ▸ **kindy**
KINDING ▸ **kind**
KINDLE, -D, -S *vb* set (a fire) alight
KINDLER ▸ **kindle**
KINDLES ▸ **kindle**
KINDLY *adj, adv*
KINDRED *adj, n*
KINDS ▸ **kind**
KINDY, KINDIES *n* kindergarten
KINE, -S *pl n* cows or cattle ▹ *n* Japanese pestle
KINEMA, -S *same as* ▸ **cinema**
KINES ▸ **kine**
KINESES ▸ **kinesis**
KINESIC *adj* of or relating to kinesics
KINESIS, KINESES *n* movement of an organism
KINETIC *adj*
KINETIN *n* plant hormone
KINFOLK *another word for* > **kinsfolk**
KING, -ED, -ING, -S *n, vb*
KINGCUP *n* yellow-flowered plant
KINGDOM *n*
KINGED ▸ **king**
KINGING ▸ **king**
KINGLE, -S *n* Scots word for a type of hard rock
KINGLET *n* king of a small or insignificant territory
KINGLY *adj, adv*
KINGPIN *n*
KINGS ▸ **king**
KININ, -S *n* type of polypeptide
KINK, -ED, -ING, -S *n, vb*
KINKIER ▸ **kinky**
KINKILY ▸ **kinky**
KINKING ▸ **kink**
KINKLE, -S *n* little kink
KINKS ▸ **kink**
KINKY, KINKIER *adj* tightly curled or looped
KINLESS *adj* without any relatives
KINO, -S *same as* ▸ **keno**
KINONE, -S *n* benzoquinone
KINOS ▸ **kino**
KINRED, -S *old form of* ▸ **kindred**
KINS ▸ **kin**
KINSHIP *n*
KINSMAN, KINSMEN *n*
KIORE, -S *n* small brown rat native to New Zealand
KIOSK, -S *n*
KIP, -PED, -PING, -S *vb* sleep ▹ *n* sleep or slumber
KIPE, -S *n* dialect word for a basket for catching fish
KIPP, -S *uncommon variant of* ▸ **kip**
KIPPA, -S *n* skullcap worn by male Jews
KIPPAGE *n* Scots word for a state of anger or excitement
KIPPAH, -S *same as* ▸ **kippa**
KIPPAS ▸ **kippa**
KIPPED ▸ **kip**
KIPPEN ▸ **kep**
KIPPER, -S *n, vb*
KIPPING ▸ **kip**
KIPPS ▸ **kipp**
KIPS ▸ **kip**
KIPSKIN *same as* ▸ **kip**
KIPUNJI *n* Tanzanian species of monkey
KIR, -S *n* drink made from dry white wine and cassis
KIRANA, -S *n* small family-owned shop in India
KIRBEH, -S *n* leather bottle
KIRBY *n* as in **kirby grip** type of hairgrip
KIRIMON *n* Japanese imperial crest
KIRK, -ED, -S *Scot word for* ▸ **church**
KIRKING ▸ **kirk**
KIRKMAN, KIRKMEN *n* member or strong upholder of the Kirk
KIRKS ▸ **kirk**
KIRKTON *n* village or town with a parish church
KIRMESS *same as* ▸ **kermis**

KIRN, -ED, -ING, -S *dialect word for* ▸ **churn**
KIRPAN, -S *n* short sword traditionally carried by Sikhs
KIRRI, -S *n* South African cudgel
KIRS ▸ **kir**
KIRSCH *n* cherry brandy
KIRTAN, -S *n* devotional singing
KIRTLE, -D, -S *n* woman's skirt or dress ▹ *vb* dress with a kirtle
KIS ▸ **ki**
KISAN, -S *n* peasant or farmer
KISH, -ES *n* graphite formed on the surface of molten iron
KISHKA, -S *same as* ▸ **kishke**
KISHKE, -S *n* stuffed beef or fowl intestine, boiled and roasted
KISMAT, -S *same as* ▸ **kismet**
KISMET, -S *n* fate or destiny
KISS, -ED, -ES, -ING *vb, n*
KISSEL, -S *n* Russian dessert
KISSER, -S *n*
KISSES ▸ **kiss**
KISSIER ▸ **kissy**
KISSING ▸ **kiss**
KISSY, KISSIER *adj*
KIST, -ED, -ING, -S *n* large wooden chest ▹ *vb* place in a coffin
KISTFUL ▸ **kist**
KISTING ▸ **kist**
KISTS ▸ **kist**
KIT, -S, -TED, -TING *n, vb*
KITBAG, -S *n*
KITCHEN *n, vb*
KITE, -D, -S *n, vb*
KITENGE *n* thick cotton cloth
KITER, -S ▸ **kite**
KITES ▸ **kite**
KITH, -S *n*
KITHARA *variant of* ▸ **cithara**
KITHE, -D, -S, KITHING *same as* ▸ **kythe**
KITHS ▸ **kith**
KITING, -S ▸ **kite**
KITLING *dialect word for* ▸ **kitten**
KITS ▸ **kit**
KITSCH *n, adj*
KITSCHY ▸ **kitsch**
KITSET, -S *n* New Zealand word for furniture supplied in pieces
KITTED ▸ **kit**
KITTEL, -S *n* white garment worn for certain Jewish rituals or burial
KITTEN, -S *n, vb*
KITTENY *adj* like a kitten
KITTIES ▸ **kitty**
KITTING ▸ **kit**
KITTLE, -D, -R, -S *adj* capricious and unpredictable ▹ *vb* be troublesome or puzzling to (someone)
KITTLY *Scots word for* > **ticklish**
KITTUL, -S *n* type of palm from which jaggery sugar comes
KITTY, KITTIES *n*
KITUL, -S *same as* ▸ **kittul**
KIVA, -S *n* large room in a Pueblo village
KIWI, -S *n*
KLANG, -S *n* (in music) kind of tone
KLAP, -PED, -S *vb* slap or spank
KLATCH *n* gathering, especially over coffee
KLATSCH *same as* ▸ **klatch**
KLAVERN *n* local Ku Klux Klan group
KLAVIER *same as* ▸ **clavier**
KLAXON, -S *n, vb*
KLEAGLE *n* person with a particular rank in the Ku Klux Klan
KLEENEX *n* tradename for a kind of tissue
KLEPHT, -S *n* group of Greeks
KLEPTO, -S *n* compulsive thief
KLETT, -S *n* lightweight climbing boot
KLEZMER *n* Jewish folk musician
KLICK, -S *n* kilometre
KLIEG, -S *n* as in **klieg light** intense carbon-arc light
KLIK, -S *US military slang word for* > **kilometre**
KLINKER *n* type of brick used in paving
KLIPDAS *n* rock hyrax
KLISTER *n* type of ski dressing for improving grip on snow
KLONG, -S *n* type of canal in Thailand
KLOOCH *same as* > **kloochman**
KLOOF, -S *n* mountain pass or gorge

KLOOTCH *same as* ▸ **kloochman**
KLUDGE, -D, -S *n* untidy solution ▹ *vb* cobble something together
KLUDGEY ▸ **kludge**
KLUDGY ▸ **kludge**
KLUGE, -D, -S, KLUGING *same as* ▸ **kludge**
KLUTZ, -ES *n* clumsy or stupid person
KLUTZY ▸ **klutz**
KNACK, -S *n, vb*
KNACKED *adj* broken or worn out
KNACKER *n, vb*
KNACKS ▸ **knack**
KNACKY *adj* old or dialect word for cunning or artful
KNAG, -S *n* knot in wood
KNAGGY *adj* knotty
KNAGS ▸ **knag**
KNAIDEL *same as* ▸ **kneidel**
KNAP, -PED, -S *n* crest of a hill ▹ *vb* hit, hammer, or chip
KNAPPER ▸ **knap**
KNAPPLE *old word for* ▸ **nibble**
KNAPS ▸ **knap**
KNAR, -S *old spelling of* ▸ **gnar**
KNARL, -S *old spelling of* ▸ **gnarl**
KNARLY *same as* ▸ **gnarly**
KNARRED ▸ **knar**
KNARRY ▸ **knar**
KNARS ▸ **knar**
KNAUR, -S *variant form of* ▸ **knur**
KNAVE, -S *n*
KNAVERY *n*
KNAVES ▸ **knave**
KNAVISH ▸ **knave**
KNAWE, -S *same as* ▸ **knawel**
KNAWEL, -S *n* type of Old World plant
KNAWES ▸ **knawe**
KNEAD, -ED, -S *vb*
KNEADER ▸ **knead**
KNEADS ▸ **knead**
KNEE, -D, -ING, -S *n, vb*
KNEECAP *nontechnical name for* ▸ **patella**
KNEED ▸ **knee**
KNEEING ▸ **knee**
KNEEL, -ED, -S, KNELT *vb, n*
KNEELER ▸ **kneel**
KNEELS ▸ **kneel**
KNEEPAD *n*
KNEEPAN *another word for* ▸ **patella**
KNEES ▸ **knee**
KNEIDEL *n* (in Jewish cookery) small dumpling
KNELL, -ED, -S *n, vb*
KNELT ▸ **kneel**
KNESSET *n* parliament or assembly
KNEVELL *vb* old Scots word meaning beat
KNEW ▸ **know**
KNICKER *adj* of or relating to knickers
KNICKS *pl n* knickers
KNIFE, -D, -S, KNIVES *n, vb*
KNIFER, -S ▸ **knife**
KNIFES ▸ **knife**
KNIFING ▸ **knife**
KNIGHT, -S *n, vb*
KNISH, -ES *n* type of dish
KNIT, -S, -TED *vb, n*
KNITCH *dialect word for* ▸ **bundle**
KNITS ▸ **knit**
KNITTED ▸ **knit**
KNITTER ▸ **knit**
KNITTLE *n* old word for string or cord
KNIVE, -D, KNIVING *rare variant of* ▸ **knife**
KNIVES ▸ **knife**
KNIVING ▸ **knive**
KNOB, -BED, -S *n* rounded projection, such as a switch on a radio ▹ *vb* supply with knobs
KNOBBER *n* two-year-old male deer
KNOBBLE *n* small knob ▹ *vb* dialect word meaning strike
KNOBBLY *adj*
KNOBBY ▸ **knob**
KNOBS ▸ **knob**
KNOCK, -ED, -S *vb, n*
KNOCKER *n*
KNOCKS ▸ **knock**
KNOLL, -ED, -S *n* small rounded hill ▹ *vb* (in archaic or dialect usage) knell
KNOLLER ▸ **knoll**
KNOLLS ▸ **knoll**
KNOLLY ▸ **knoll**
KNOP, -S *n* knob, esp an ornamental one
KNOPPED ▸ **knop**
KNOPS ▸ **knop**
KNOSP, -S *n* budlike architectural feature
KNOT, -S, -TED *n, vb*
KNOTTER ▸ **knot**
KNOTTY *adj* full of knots
KNOUT, -ED, -S *n* stout whip ▹ *vb* whip
KNOW, KNEW, -S *vb* be or feel certain of the

truth of (information etc)
KNOWE, -S *same as* ▸ **knoll**
KNOWER, -S ▸ **know**
KNOWES ▸ **knowe**
KNOWHOW *n*
KNOWING ▸ **know**
KNOWN, -S *n* fact or something that is known
KNOWS ▸ **know**
KNUB, -S *dialect word for* ▸ **knob**
KNUBBLE *vb* dialect word for beat or pound using one's fists
KNUBBLY *adj* having small lumps or protuberances
KNUBBY *adj* knub
KNUBS ▸ **knub**
KNUCKLE *n, vb*
KNUCKLY ▸ **knuckle**
KNUR, -S *n* knot or protuberance in a tree trunk or in wood
KNURL, -ED, -S *n* small ridge, often one of a series ▹ *vb* impress with a series of fine ridges or serrations
KNURLY *rare word for* ▸ **gnarled**
KNURR, -S *same as* ▸ **knur**
KNURS ▸ **knur**
KNUT, -S *n* dandy
KO *n* (in New Zealand) traditional digging tool
KOA, -S *n* Hawaiian leguminous tree
KOALA, -S *n*
KOAN, -S *n* (in Zen Buddhism) problem that admits no logical solution
KOAS ▸ **koa**
KOB, -S *n* any of several species of antelope
KOBAN, -S *n* old oval-shaped Japanese gold coin
KOBANG, -S *same as* ▸ **koban**
KOBANS ▸ **koban**
KOBO, -S *n* Nigerian monetary unit
KOBOLD, -S *n* mischievous household sprite
KOBOS ▸ **kobo**
KOBS ▸ **kob**
KOCHIA, -S *n* any of several plants whose foliage turns dark red
KOEKOEA *n* long-tailed cuckoo of New Zealand
KOEL, -S *n* any of several parasitic cuckoos
KOFF, -S *n* Dutch masted merchant vessel
KOFTA, -S *n* Indian dish
KOFTGAR *n* (in India) person skilled at inlaying steel with gold
KOGAL, -S *n* (in Japan) trendy teenage girl
KOHA, -S *n* gift or donation, esp of cash
KOHANIM ▸ **kohen**
KOHAS ▸ **koha**
KOHEN, KOHANIM *n* member of the Jewish priestly caste
KOHL, -S *n* cosmetic powder
KOI, -S *n* any of various ornamental forms of the common carp
KOINE, -S *n* common language among speakers of different languages
KOIS ▸ **koi**
KOJI, -S *n* Japanese steamed rice
KOKA, -S *n* former type of score in judo
KOKAKO, -S *n* type of crow
KOKAM, -S *same as* ▸ **kokum**
KOKANEE *n* type of freshwater salmon
KOKAS ▸ **koka**
KOKER, -S *n* Guyanese sluice
KOKIRI, -S *n* type of rough-skinned New Zealand triggerfish
KOKOBEH *adj* (of certain fruit) having a rough skin
KOKOPU, -S *n* any of several small freshwater fish of New Zealand
KOKOWAI *n* type of clay
KOKRA, -S *n* type of wood
KOKUM, -S *n* tropical tree
KOLA, -S *n* as in **kola nut** caffeine-containing seed used in medicine and soft drinks
KOLACKY *n* sweet bun with a fruit, jam, or nut filling
KOLAS ▸ **kola**
KOLBASI *same as* > **kolbassi**
KOLHOZ, -Y *same as* ▸ **kolkhoz**

KOLKHOS *same as* ▸ **kolkhoz**
KOLKHOZ *n* (formerly) collective farm in the Soviet Union
KOLKOZ, -Y *same as* ▸ **kolkhoz**
KOLO, -S *n* Serbian folk dance
KOMATIK *n* type of sledge
KOMBU, -S *n* dark brown seaweed
KON, -D, -NING, -S *old word for* ▸ **know**
KONAKI, -S *same as* ▸ **koneke**
KONBU, -S *same as* ▸ **kombu**
KOND ▸ **kon**
KONDO, -S *n* (in Uganda) thief or armed robber
KONEKE, -S *n* type of farm vehicle
KONFYT, -S *n* South African fruit preserve
KONGONI *n* E African hartbeest
KONINI, -S *n* edible dark purple berry
KONK, -ED, -ING, -S *same as* ▸ **conk**
KONNING ▸ **kon**
KONS ▸ **kon**
KOODOO, -S *same as* ▸ **kudu**
KOOK, -ED, -ING, -S *n* eccentric person ▹ *vb* dialect word for vanish
KOOKIE *same as* ▸ **kooky**
KOOKIER ▸ **kooky**
KOOKILY ▸ **kooky**
KOOKING ▸ **kook**
KOOKS ▸ **kook**
KOOKUM, -S *same as* ▸ **kokum**
KOOKY, KOOKIER *adj*
KOOLAH, -S *old form of* ▸ **koala**
KOORI, -ES, -S *n* Aboriginal Australian
KOP, -S *n* prominent isolated hill or mountain in southern Africa
KOPECK, -S *n* former Russian monetary unit
KOPEK, -S *same as* ▸ **kopeck**
KOPH, -S *n* 19th letter in the Hebrew alphabet
KOPIYKA, KOPIYKY, KOPIYOK *n* monetary unit of Ukraine
KOPJE, -S *n* small hill
KOPPA, -S *n* consonantal letter in the Greek alphabet
KOPPIE, -S *same as* ▸ **kopje**
KOPS ▸ **kop**
KOR, -S *n* ancient Hebrew unit of capacity
KORA, -S *n* West African instrument
KORAI ▸ **kore**
KORARI, -S *n* native New Zealand flax plant
KORAS ▸ **kora**
KORAT, -S *n* as in **korat cat** rare blue-grey breed of cat
KORE, KORAI, -S *n* ancient Greek statue of a young woman wearing clothes
KORERO, -S *n* talk or discussion ▹ *vb* speak or converse
KORES ▸ **kore**
KORKIR, -S *n* variety of lichen used in dyeing
KORMA, -S *n* type of mild Indian dish
KORO, -S *n* elderly Māori man
KORORA, -S *n* small New Zealand penguin
KOROS ▸ **koro**
KOROWAI *n* decorative woven cloak worn by a Māori chief
KORS ▸ **kor**
KORU, -S *n* stylized curved pattern used esp in carving
KORUNA, KORUN, -S, KORUNY *n* standard monetary unit of the Czech Republic
KORUS ▸ **koru**
KOS, -ES *n* Indian unit of distance
KOSHER, -S *adj, n, vb*
KOSMOS *variant form of* ▸ **cosmos**
KOSS, -ES *same as* ▸ **kos**
KOTARE, -S *n* small greenish-blue kingfisher
KOTCH, -ED, -ES *vb* South African slang for vomit
KOTO, -S *n* Japanese stringed instrument
KOTOW, -ED, -S *same as* ▸ **kowtow**
KOTOWER ▸ **kotow**
KOTOWS ▸ **kotow**
KOTUKU, -S *n* type of white heron
KOTWAL, -S *n* senior police officer or magistrate in an Indian town

KOULAN, -S *same as* ▸ **kulan**
KOUMIS *same as* ▸ **kumiss**
KOUMISS *same as* ▸ **kumiss**
KOUMYS *same as* ▸ **kumiss**
KOUMYSS *same as* ▸ **kumiss**
KOUPREY *n* large wild SE Asian ox
KOURA, -S *n* New Zealand freshwater crayfish
KOUROS, KOUROI *n* ancient Greek statue of a young man
KOUSSO, -S *n* Abyssinian tree
KOW, -S *old variant of* ▸ **cow**

> This old or dialect variant of **cow** scores well for a 3-letter word, and can be a good one to form when playing in more than one direction.

KOWHAI, -S *n* New Zealand tree
KOWS ▸ **kow**
KOWTOW, -S *vb* be servile (towards) ▷ *n* act of kowtowing
KRAAL, -ED, -S *n* S African village surrounded by a strong fence ▷ *adj* denoting or relating to the tribal aspects of the Black African way of life ▷ *vb* enclose (livestock) in a kraal
KRAB, -S *same as* > **karabiner**
KRAFT, -S *n* strong wrapping paper
KRAI, -S *n* administrative division of Russia
KRAIT, -S *n* brightly coloured venomous snake of S and SE Asia
KRAKEN, -S *n* legendary sea monster
KRANG, -S *n* dead whale from which the blubber has been removed
KRANS, -ES *n* sheer rock face
KRANTZ *same as* ▸ **krans**
KRANZ, -ES *same as* ▸ **krans**
KRATER, -S *same as* ▸ **crater**
KRAUT, -S *n* sauerkraut
KRAY, -S *same as* ▸ **krai**
KREEP, -S *n* lunar substance
KREESE, -D, -S *same as* ▸ **kris**
KREMLIN *n* citadel of any Russian city
KRENG, -S *same as* ▸ **krang**
KREUZER *same as* > **kreutzer**
KREWE, -S *n* club taking part in New Orleans carnival parade
KRILL, -S *n*
KRIMMER *n* tightly curled light grey fur
KRIS, -ED, -ES, -ING *n* type of Malayan and Indonesian knife ▷ *vb* stab or slash with a kris
KRONA, KRONOR, KRONUR *n* standard monetary unit of Sweden
KRONE, -N, -R *n* standard monetary unit of Norway and Denmark
KRONOR ▸ **krona**
KRONUR ▸ **krona**
KROON, -I, -S *n* former monetary unit of Estonia
KRUBI, -S *n* aroid plant with an unpleasant smell
KRUBUT, -S *same as* ▸ **krubi**
KRULLER *variant spelling of* ▸ **cruller**
KRUMPER > **krumping**
KRUNK, -S *n* style of hip-hop music
KRUNKED *same as* ▸ **crunked**
KRUNKS ▸ **krunk**
KRYPSIS, KRYPSES *n* idea that Christ made secret use of his divine attributes
KRYPTON *n* colourless gas
KRYTRON *n* type of fast electronic gas-discharge switch
KSAR, -S *old form of* ▸ **tsar**
KUBASA, -S *same as* > **kielbasa**
KUBIE, -S *n* Ukrainian roll filled with kielbasa
KUCCHA, -S *same as* ▸ **kaccha**
KUCHCHA *same as* ▸ **kacha**
KUCHEN, -S *n* breadlike cake

KUDLIK, -S *n* Inuit soapstone seal-oil lamp
KUDO *variant of* ▸ **kudos**
KUDOS, -ES *n* fame or credit
KUDU, -S *n* African antelope with spiral horns
KUDZU, -S *n* hairy leguminous climbing plant
KUE, -S *n* name of the letter Q
KUEH *n* (in Malaysia) any cake of Malay, Chinese, or Indian origin
KUES ▸ **kue**
KUFI, -S *n* cap for Muslim man
KUFIYAH *same as* > **keffiyeh**
KUGEL, -S *n* baked pudding in traditional Jewish cooking
KUIA, -S *n* Māori female elder or elderly woman
KUKRI, -S *n* heavy, curved knife used by Gurkhas
KUKU, -S *n* mussel
KULA, -S *n* ceremonial gift exchange among islanders in the W Pacific
KULAK, -I, -S *n* (formerly) property-owning Russian peasant
KULAN, -S *n* Asiatic wild ass
KULAS ▸ **kula**
KULBASA *same as* > **kielbasa**
KULFI, -S *n* Indian dessert
KULTUR, -S *n* German civilization
KUMARA, -S *n* tropical root vegetable with yellow flesh
KUMARI, -S *n* (in Indian English) maiden
KUMERA, -S *same as* ▸ **kumara**
KUMIS, -ES *same as* ▸ **kumiss**
KUMISS *n* drink made from fermented mare's or other milk
KUMITE, -S *n* freestyle sparring or fighting
KUMKUM, -S *n* red pigment used by Hindu women to make a mark on the forehead
KUMMEL, -S *n* German liqueur
KUMQUAT *n*
KUMYS, -ES *same as* ▸ **kumiss**
KUNA, KUNE *n* standard monetary unit of Croatia
KUNJOOS *adj* (in Indian English) mean or stingy
KUNKAR, -S *n* type of limestone
KUNKUR, -S *same as* ▸ **kunkar**
KUNZITE *n* variety of the mineral spodumene
KURBASH *vb* whip with a hide whip
KURGAN, -S *n* Russian burial mound
KURI, -S *n* mongrel dog
KURRE, -S *old variant of* ▸ **cur**
KURSAAL *n* public room at a health resort
KURTA, -S *n* long loose garment
KURU, -S *n* degenerative disease of the nervous system

This word for a kind of sickness found in New Guinea can give you something to play when you have two Us to dispose of.

KURUSH *n* small currency unit of Turkey
KURVEY, -S *vb* (in old South African English) transport goods by ox cart
KUSSO, -S *variant spelling of* ▸ **kousso**
KUTA, -S *n* (in Indian English) male dog
KUTCH, -ES *same as* ▸ **catechu**
KUTCHA *adj* makeshift or not solid
KUTCHES ▸ **kutch**
KUTI, -S *n* (in Indian English) female dog
KUTU, -S *n* body louse
KUVASZ *n* breed of dog from Hungary
KUZU, -S *same as* ▸ **kudzu**

A Japanese climbing plant, this can be a great word for getting a high score out of a difficult rack.

KVAS, -ES *same as* ▸ **kvass**
KVASS, -ES *n* alcoholic drink

KVELL, -ED, -S *vb* US word meaning be happy
KVETCH *vb* complain or grumble
KVETCHY *adj* tending to grumble or complain
KWACHA, -S *n* standard monetary unit of Zambia
KWAITO, -S *n* type of South African pop music
KWANZA, -S *n* standard monetary unit of Angola
KWELA, -S *n* type of pop music
KY *pl n* Scots word for cows
KYACK, -S *n* type of pannier
KYAK, -S *same as* ▸ **kayak**
KYANG, -S *same as* ▸ **kiang**
KYANISE *same as* ▸ **kyanize**
KYANITE *n* grey, green, or blue mineral
KYANIZE *vb* treat (timber) with corrosive sublimate
KYAR, -S *same as* ▸ **coir**
KYAT, -S *n* standard monetary unit of Myanmar
KYBO, -S *n* temporary lavatory used when camping
KYBOSH *same as* ▸ **kibosh**
KYDST ▸ **kythe**
KYE, -S *n* Korean fundraising meeting
KYLE, -S *n* narrow strait or channel
KYLICES ▸ **kylix**
KYLIE, -S *n* type of boomerang
KYLIKES ▸ **kylix**
KYLIN, -S *n* (in Chinese art) mythical animal
KYLIX, KYLICES, KYLIKES, -ES *n* drinking vessel used in ancient Greece
KYLOE, -S *n* breed of beef cattle
KYND, -ED, -ING, -S *old variant of* ▸ **kind**
KYNDE, -S *old variant of* ▸ **kind**
KYNDED ▸ **kynd**
KYNDES ▸ **kynde**
KYNDING ▸ **kynd**
KYNDS ▸ **kynd**
KYNE *pl n* archaic word for cows
KYOGEN, -S *n* type of Japanese drama
KYPE, -S *n* hook on the lower jaw of a mature male salmon
KYRIE, -S *n* type of prayer
KYTE, -S *n* belly
KYTHE, KYDST, -D, -S, KYTHING *vb* appear
KYU, -S *n* (in judo) one of the five student grades

This means a novice grade in judo, and its unusual combination of letters makes it a useful word to remember when you have an unpromising set of letters on your rack.

Ll

LA, -S *n* the sixth note of the musical scale
LAAGER, -S *n* (in Africa) a camp defended by a circular formation of wagons ▷ *vb* form (wagons) into a laager
LAARI, -S *same as* ▶ **lari**
LAB, -S *n* laboratory
LABARUM, LABARA *n* standard carried in Christian processions
LABDA, -S *same as* ▶ **lambda**
LABEL, -ED, -S *n*, *vb*
LABELER ▶ **label**
LABELLA > **labellum**
LABELS ▶ **label**
LABIA ▶ **labium**
LABIAL, -S *adj* of the lips ▷ *n* speech sound that involves the lips
LABIATE *n* plant with a two-lipped flower
LABILE *adj* (of a compound) prone to chemical change
LABIS, -ES *n* spoon used to give the Eucharist to communicants
LABIUM, LABIA *n* lip or liplike structure
LABLAB, -S *n* twining leguminous plant
LABNEH, -S *n* Mediterranean soft cheese
LABOR, -S *same as* ▶ **labour**
LABORED *same as* > **laboured**
LABORER *same as* > **labourer**
LABORS ▶ **labor**
LABOUR, -S *n*, *vb*
LABRA ▶ **labrum**
LABRAL *adj* of or like a lip
LABRET, -S *n* piece of bone or shell
LABRID, -S *same as* ▶ **labroid**
LABROID *n* type of fish ▷ *adj* of or relating to such fish
LABROSE *adj* thick-lipped
LABRUM, LABRA, -S *n* lip or liplike part
LABRYS *n* type of axe
LABS ▶ **lab**
LAC, -S *same as* ▶ **lakh**
LACE, -D, -S *n*, *vb*
LACER, -S ▶ **lace**
LACES ▶ **lace**
LACET, -S *n* braided work in lace
LACEY *same as* ▶ **lacy**
LACHES *n* unreasonable delay in pursuing a legal remedy
LACIER ▶ **lacy**
LACIEST ▶ **lacy**
LACILY ▶ **lacy**
LACING, -S ▶ **lace**
LACINIA *n* narrow fringe on petal
LACK, -ED, -ING, -S *n*, *vb*
LACKER, -S *variant spelling of* ▶ **lacquer**
LACKEY, -S *n*, *vb*
LACKING ▶ **lack**
LACKS ▶ **lack**
LACMUS *n* old form of litmus
LACONIC *adj*
LACQUER *n*, *vb*
LACQUEY *same as* ▶ **lackey**
LACS ▶ **lac**
LACTAM, -S *n* any of a group of inner amides
LACTARY *adj* relating to milk
LACTASE *n* any of a group of enzymes that hydrolyse lactose to glucose and galactose
LACTATE *vb* secrete milk ▷ *n* ester or salt of lactic acid
LACTEAL *adj* of or like milk ▷ *n* any of the lymphatic vessels that convey chyle from the small intestine to the blood

LACTEAN *another word for* > **lacteous**
LACTIC *adj* of or derived from milk
LACTONE *n* any of a class of organic compounds
LACTOSE *n* white crystalline sugar found in milk
LACUNA, -E, -S *n* gap or missing part, esp in a document or series
LACUNAL ▸ **lacuna**
LACUNAR *n* ceiling, soffit, or vault having coffers ▹ *adj* having a lacuna
LACUNAS ▸ **lacuna**
LACUNE, -S *n* hiatus
LACY, LACIER, LACIEST *adj* fine, like lace
LAD, -S *n*
LADANUM *same as* > **labdanum**
LADDER, -S *n, vb*
LADDERY *adj* (of tights) laddered
LADDIE, -S *n*
LADDIER ▸ **laddy**
LADDIES ▸ **laddie**
LADDISH *adj*
LADDISM *n*
LADDY, LADDIER *adj* laddish
LADE, -D, -S *vb* put cargo on board ▹ *n* watercourse
LADEN, -ED, -S *adj* loaded ▹ *vb* load with cargo
LADER, -S ▸ **lade**
LADES ▸ **lade**
LADETTE *n*
LADHOOD ▸ **lad**
LADIES *n* women's public toilet
LADIFY *same as* ▸ **ladyfy**
LADING, -S ▸ **lade**
LADINO, -S *n* Italian variety of white clover
LADLE, -D, -S, LADLING *n, vb*
LADLER, -S *n* person who serves with a ladle
LADLES ▸ **ladle**
LADLING ▸ **ladle**
LADRON, -S *same as* ▸ **ladrone**
LADRONE *n* thief
LADRONS ▸ **ladron**
LADS ▸ **lad**
LADY *n, adj*
LADYBUG *same as* > **ladybird**
LADYCOW *another word for* > **ladybird**
LADYFLY *another word for* > **ladybird**
LADYFY *vb* make a lady of (someone)
LADYISH ▸ **lady**
LADYISM ▸ **lady**
LADYKIN *n* endearing form of 'lady'
LAER, -ED, -ING, -S *another word for* ▸ **laager**
LAESIE *old form of* ▸ **lazy**
LAETARE *n* fourth Sunday of Lent
LAEVO *adj* on the left
LAG, -GED, -S *vb, n*
LAGAN, -S *n* goods or wreckage on the sea bed
LAGENA, -S *n* bottle with a narrow neck
LAGEND, -S *same as* ▸ **lagan**
LAGER, -ED, -S *n, vb*
LAGGARD *n, adj*
LAGGED ▸ **lag**
LAGGEN, -S *n* spar of a barrel
LAGGER, -S *n* person who lags pipes
LAGGIN, -S *same as* ▸ **laggen**
LAGGING ▸ **lag**
LAGGINS ▸ **laggin**
LAGOON, -S *n*
LAGS ▸ **lag**
LAGUNA, -S *n* lagoon
LAGUNE, -S *same as* ▸ **lagoon**
LAH, -S *n* (in tonic sol-fa) sixth degree of any major scale
LAHAL, -S *n* game played by native peoples of the Pacific Northwest
LAHAR, -S *n* landslide of volcanic debris and water
LAHS ▸ **lah**
LAIC, -S *adj* laical ▹ *n* layman
LAICAL *adj* secular
LAICH, -S *n* low-lying piece of land
LAICISE *same as* ▸ **laicize**
LAICISM ▸ **laic**
LAICITY *n* state of being laical
LAICIZE *vb* remove ecclesiastical status from
LAICS ▸ **laic**
LAID, -ED, -ING, -S *Scots form of* ▸ **load**
LAIDLY *adj* very ugly

LAIDS ▸ **laid**
LAIGH, -ER, -S *adj* low-lying ▹ *n* area of low-lying ground
LAIK, -ED, -ING, -S *vb* play (a game, etc)
LAIKA, -S *n* type of small dog
LAIKED ▸ **laik**
LAIKER, -S ▸ **laik**
LAIKING ▸ **laik**
LAIKS ▸ **laik**
LAIN ▸ **lay**
LAIPSE, -D, -S *vb* beat soundly
LAIR, -ED, -ING, -S *n, vb*
LAIRAGE *n* accommodation for farm animals
LAIRD, -S *n*
LAIRDLY *adj* pertaining to lairds
LAIRDS ▸ **laird**
LAIRED ▸ **lair**
LAIRIER ▸ **lairy**
LAIRING ▸ **lair**
LAIRISE *same as* ▸ **lairize**
LAIRIZE *vb* show off
LAIRS ▸ **lair**
LAIRY, LAIRIER *adj* gaudy or flashy
LAISSE, -S *n* type of rhyme scheme
LAITH *Scots form of* ▸ **loath**
LAITHLY *same as* ▸ **laidly**
LAITY, LAITIES *n* non-clergy
LAKE, -D, -S *n, vb*
LAKEBED *n*
LAKED ▸ **lake**
LAKELET *n*
LAKER, -S *n* lake cargo vessel
LAKES ▸ **lake**
LAKH, -S *n* (in India) 100 000, esp referring to this sum of rupees
LAKIER ▸ **laky**
LAKIEST ▸ **laky**
LAKIN, -S *short form of* ▸ **ladykin**
LAKING, -S ▸ **lake**
LAKINS ▸ **lakin**
LAKISH *adj* similar to poetry of Lake poets
LAKSA, -S *n* (in Malaysia) Chinese dish of rice noodles in curry or hot soup
LAKY, LAKIER, LAKIEST *adj* of the reddish colour of the pigment lake
LALANG, -S *n* coarse weedy Malaysian grass
LALDIE, -S *n* great gusto
LALDY *same as* ▸ **laldie**
LALIQUE *n* ornamental glass
LALL, -ED, -S *vb* make imperfect 'l' or 'r' sounds
LALLAN, -S *n* literary version of the English spoken in Lowland Scotland
LALLAND *same as* ▸ **lallan**
LALLANS ▸ **lallan**
LALLED ▸ **lall**
LALLING ▸ **lall**
LALLS ▸ **lall**
LAM, -MED, -S *vb* attack vigorously
LAMA, -S *n* Buddhist priest in Tibet or Mongolia
LAMB, -ED, -S *n, vb*
LAMBADA *n* type of Brazilian dance
LAMBAST *vb*
LAMBDA, -S *n* 11th letter of the Greek alphabet
LAMBED ▸ **lamb**
LAMBENT *adj* (of a flame) flickering softly
LAMBER, -S *n* person that attends to lambing ewes
LAMBERT *n* cgs unit of illumination, equal to 1 lumen per square centimetre
LAMBIE, -S *same as* ▸ **lambkin**
LAMBIER ▸ **lamby**
LAMBIES ▸ **lambie**
LAMBING *n* birth of lambs at the end of winter
LAMBKIN *n* young lamb
LAMBOYS *n* skirt-like piece of armour made from metal strips
LAMBS ▸ **lamb**
LAMBY, LAMBIER *adj* lamb-like
LAME, -R, -S, -ST, LAMING *adj, vb, n*
LAMED, -S *n* 12th letter in the Hebrew alphabet
LAMEDH, -S *same as* ▸ **lamed**
LAMEDS ▸ **lamed**
LAMELLA *n* thin layer, plate, etc, like the calcified layers of which bone is formed
LAMELY ▸ **lame**
LAMENT, -S *vb, n*
LAMER ▸ **lame**
LAMES ▸ **lame**
LAMEST ▸ **lame**

LAMETER *Scots form of* ▸ **lamiger**
LAMIA, -E, -S *n* female monster with a snake's body and a woman's head
LAMIGER *n* disabled person
LAMINA, -E, -S *n* thin plate, esp of bone or mineral
LAMINAL *n* consonant articulated with blade of tongue
LAMINAR ▸ **lamina**
LAMINAS ▸ **lamina**
LAMING ▸ **lame**
LAMININ *n* type of protein
LAMISH *adj* rather lame
LAMITER *same as* ▸ **lameter**
LAMMED ▸ **lam**
LAMMER, -S *Scots word for* ▸ **amber**
LAMMIE *same as* ▸ **lammy**
LAMMIES ▸ **lammy**
LAMMING ▸ **lam**
LAMMY, LAMMIES *n* thick woollen jumper
LAMP, -ED, -S *n, vb*
LAMPAD, -S *n* candlestick
LAMPAS *n* swelling of the mucous membrane of the hard palate of horses
LAMPED ▸ **lamp**
LAMPER, -S *n* lamprey
LAMPERN *n* migratory European lamprey
LAMPERS ▸ **lamper**
LAMPING ▸ **lamp**
LAMPION *n* oil-burning lamp
LAMPLIT *adj* lit by lamps
LAMPOON *n, vb*
LAMPREY *n*
LAMPS ▸ **lamp**
LAMPUKA *same as* ▸ **lampuki**
LAMPUKI *n* type of fish
LAMS ▸ **lam**
LAMSTER *n* fugitive
LANA, -S *n* wood from genipap tree
LANAI, -S *Hawaiian word for* ▸ **veranda**
LANAS ▸ **lana**
LANATE *adj* having or consisting of a woolly covering of hairs
LANATED *same as* ▸ **lanate**
LANCE, -D, -S, LANCING *n, vb*
LANCER *n* formerly, cavalry soldier armed with a lance
LANCERS *n* quadrille for eight or sixteen couples
LANCES ▸ **lance**
LANCET, -S *n*
LANCH, -ED, -ES *obsolete form of* ▸ **launch**
LANCING ▸ **lance**
LAND *n, vb*
LANDAU, -S *n* four-wheeled carriage with two folding hoods
LANDE, -S *n* type of moorland in SW France
LANDED *adj* possessing or consisting of lands
LANDER, -S *n* spacecraft which lands on a planet or other body
LANDES ▸ **lande**
LANDING *n* floor area at the top of a flight of stairs
LANDLER *n* Austrian country dance
LANDMAN, LANDMEN *n* person who lives and works on land
LANDS *pl n* holdings in land
LANE, -S *n*
LANELY *Scots form of* ▸ **lonely**
LANES ▸ **lane**
LANEWAY *n* lane
LANG, -EST *Scot word for* ▸ **long**
LANGAHA *n* type of Madagascan snake
LANGAR, -S *n* dining hall in a gurdwara
LANGER *adj* comparative form of lang
LANGEST ▸ **lang**
LANGLEY *n* unit of solar radiation
LANGREL *same as* > **langrage**
LANGUE, -S *n* language considered as an abstract system
LANGUED *adj* having a tongue
LANGUES ▸ **langue**
LANGUET *n* anything resembling a tongue
LANGUID *adj*
LANGUOR *n* dreamy relaxation
LANGUR, -S *n* type of arboreal Old World monkey
LANIARD *same as* ▸ **lanyard**

LANIARY *adj* adapted for tearing ▷ *n* tooth adapted for tearing
LANITAL *n* fibre used in production of synthetic wool
LANK, -ED, -ER, -EST, -ING, -S *adj* straight and limp ▷ *vb* become lank
LANKIER ▶ **lanky**
LANKILY ▶ **lanky**
LANKING ▶ **lank**
LANKLY ▶ **lank**
LANKS ▶ **lank**
LANKY, LANKIER *adj* tall and thin
LANNER, -S *n* large falcon
LANOLIN *n*
LANOSE *same as* ▶ **lanate**
LANT, -S *n* stale urine
LANTANA *n* shrub with orange or yellow flowers
LANTERN *n, vb*
LANTS ▶ **lant**
LANUGO, -S *n* layer of fine hairs, esp the covering of the human fetus before birth
LANX *n* dish; plate
LANYARD *n*
LAOGAI, -S *n* forced labour camp in China
LAP, -PED, -S *n, vb*
LAPDOG, -S *n*
LAPEL, -S *n*
LAPELED ▶ **lapel**
LAPELS ▶ **lapel**
LAPFUL, -S *same as* ▶ **lap**
LAPHELD *adj* small enough to be used on one's lap
LAPIDES ▶ **lapis**
LAPILLI > **lapillus**
LAPIN, -S *n* rabbit fur
LAPIS, LAPIDES, -ES *n* as in **lapis lazuli** brilliant blue mineral gemstone
LAPJE, -S *same as* ▶ **lappie**
LAPPED ▶ **lap**
LAPPEL, -S *same as* ▶ **lapel**
LAPPER, -S *n* one that laps ▷ *vb* curdle
LAPPET, -S *n* small hanging flap
LAPPIE, -S *n* rag
LAPPING ▶ **lap**
LAPS ▶ **lap**
LAPSANG *n* Chinese tea
LAPSE, -D, -S, LAPSING *n, vb*
LAPSER, -S ▶ **lapse**
LAPSES ▶ **lapse**
LAPSING ▶ **lapse**
LAPSUS *n* lapse or error
LAPTOP, -S *adj, n*
LAPTRAY *n* tray with a cushioned underside
LAPWING *n* plover with a tuft of feathers on the head
LAPWORK *n* work with lapping edges
LAR, -S *n* boy or young man
LARCENY *n* theft
LARCH, -ES *n*
LARCHEN *adj* of larch
LARCHES ▶ **larch**
LARD, -ED, -ING, -S *n, vb*
LARDER, -S *n*
LARDIER ▶ **lardy**
LARDING ▶ **lard**
LARDON, -S *n* strip or cube of fat or bacon used in larding meat
LARDOON *same as* ▶ **lardon**
LARDS ▶ **lard**
LARDY, LARDIER *adj* fat
LARE, -S *another word for* ▶ **lore**
LAREE, -S *n* Asian fish-hook
LARES ▶ **lare**
LARGE, -R, -S, -ST *adj, n*
LARGELY *adv* principally
LARGEN, -S *another word for* ▶ **enlarge**
LARGER ▶ **large**
LARGES ▶ **large**
LARGESS *same as* > **largesse**
LARGEST ▶ **large**
LARGISH *adj* fairly large
LARGO, -S *adv* in a slow and dignified manner ▷ *n* performance piece in a slow manner
LARI, -S *n* monetary unit of Georgia
LARIAT, -S *n* lasso ▷ *vb* tether with lariat
LARIGAN *n* type of tanned moccasin boot
LARINE *adj* of, relating to, or resembling a gull
LARIS ▶ **lari**
LARK, -ED, -ING, -S *n, vb*
LARKER, -S ▶ **lark**
LARKIER ▶ **larky**
LARKING ▶ **lark**
LARKISH ▶ **lark**
LARKS ▶ **lark**
LARKY, LARKIER *adj* frolicsome
LARMIER *n* pouch under lower eyelid of deer
LARN, -ED, -ING, -S, -T *vb* learn

LARNAX *n* terracotta coffin
LARNED ▸ **larn**
LARNEY, LARNIER *n* South African word for a rich person ▹ *adj* (of clothes) smart
LARNING ▸ **larn**
LARNS ▸ **larn**
LARNT ▸ **larn**
LAROID *adj* relating to Larus genus of gull family
LARRUP, -S *vb* beat or flog
LARS ▸ **lar**
LARUM, -S *archaic word for* ▸ **alarm**
LARVA, -E, -S *n*
LARVAL ▸ **larva**
LARVAS ▸ **larva**
LARVATE *adj* masked; concealed
LARYNX *n*
LAS ▸ **la**
LASAGNA *same as* ▸ **lasagne**
LASAGNE *n*
LASCAR, -S *n* Indian or SE Asian sailor
LASE, -D, -S *vb* be capable of acting as a laser
LASER, -ED, -S *n, vb*
LASES ▸ **lase**
LASH, -ED, -ES, -ING *n, vb*
LASHER, -S ▸ **lash**
LASHES ▸ **lash**
LASHING ▸ **lash**
LASHINS *variant of* ▸ **lashings**
LASHKAR *n* troop of Indian men with weapons
LASING, -S ▸ **lase**
LASKET, -S *n* loop at the foot of a sail onto which an extra sail may be fastened
LASQUE, -S *n* flat-cut diamond
LASS, -ES *n*
LASSI, -S *n* cold drink made of yoghurt or buttermilk, flavoured with sugar, salt, or spice
LASSIE, -S *n*
LASSIS ▸ **lassi**
LASSO, -ED, -ES, -S *n, vb*
LASSOCK *another word for* ▸ **lass**
LASSOED ▸ **lasso**
LASSOER ▸ **lasso**
LASSOES ▸ **lasso**
LASSOS ▸ **lasso**
LASSU, -S *n* slow part of csárdás folk dance
LASSY *n* short for molasses
LAST, -ED, -S *adv, adj, n, vb*
LASTAGE *n* space for storing goods in ship
LASTED ▸ **last**
LASTER, -S ▸ **last**
LASTING *adj* remaining effective for a long time ▹ *n* strong durable fabric used for shoe uppers, etc
LASTLY *adv* at the end or at the last point
LASTS ▸ **last**
LAT, -I, -S *n* former coin of Latvia
LATAH, -S *n* psychological condition
LATAKIA *n* Turkish tobacco
LATCH, -ED, -ES *n, vb*
LATCHET *n* shoe fastening
LATE *adj, adv*
LATED *archaic word for* ▸ **belated**
LATEEN, -S *adj* of a rig with a triangular sail bent to a yard hoisted to the head of a low mast
LATELY *adv* in recent times
LATEN, -ED, -S *vb* become or cause to become late
LATENCE ▸ **latent**
LATENCY ▸ **latent**
LATENED ▸ **laten**
LATENS ▸ **laten**
LATENT, -S *adj, n*
LATER *adv* afterwards
LATERAD *adv* towards the side
LATERAL *adj* of or relating to the side or sides ▹ *n* lateral object, part, passage, or movement ▹ *vb* pass laterally
LATEST, -S *n* the most recent news
LATEX, -ES, LATICES *n*
LATH, -S *n* thin strip of wood ▹ *vb* attach laths to
LATHE, -D, -S *n, vb*
LATHEE, -S *same as* ▸ **lathi**
LATHEN *adj* covered with laths
LATHER, -S *n, vb*
LATHERY ▸ **lather**
LATHES ▸ **lathe**
LATHI, -S *n* long heavy wooden stick used as a weapon in India

LATHIER ▸ **lathy**
LATHING ▸ **lathe**
LATHIS ▸ **lathi**
LATHS ▸ **lath**
LATHY, LATHIER *adj* resembling a lath, esp in being tall and thin
LATI ▸ **lat**
LATICES ▸ **latex**
LATIGO, -S *n* strap on horse's saddle
LATILLA *n* stick making up part of ceiling
LATINA, -S *n* American female citizen of Latin American origin
LATINO, -S *n* American male citizen of Latin American origin
LATISH *adv* rather late ▹ *adj* rather late
LATITAT *n* writ presuming that person accused was hiding
LATKE, -S *n* crispy Jewish pancake
LATOSOL *n* type of deep, well-drained soil
LATRANT *adj* barking
LATRIA, -S *n* adoration that may be offered to God alone
LATRINE *n*
LATRON, -S *n* bandit
LATS ▸ **lat**
LATTE, -S *n*
LATTEN, -S *n* metal or alloy, esp brass, made in thin sheets
LATTER, -S *adj, n*
LATTES ▸ **latte**
LATTICE *n, vb*
LATTIN, -S *n* brass alloy beaten into a thin sheet
LATU, -S *n* type of edible Asian seaweed
LAUAN, -S *n* type of wood used in furniture-making
LAUCH, -S, LEUCH, LEUCHEN, LEUGH, LEUGHEN *Scots form of* ▸ **laugh**
LAUD, -ED, -ING *vb, n*
LAUDER, -S ▸ **laud**
LAUDING ▸ **laud**
LAUDS *n* traditional morning prayer of the Western Church
LAUF, -S *n* run in bobsleighing
LAUGH, -ED, -S *vb, n*
LAUGHER ▸ **laugh**
LAUGHS ▸ **laugh**
LAUGHY *adj* laughing a lot
LAUNCE, -D, -S *old form of* ▸ **lance**
LAUNCH *vb, n*
LAUND, -S *n* open grassy space
LAUNDER *vb, n*
LAUNDRY *n*
LAUNDS ▸ **laund**
LAURA, -E, -S *n* group of monastic cells
LAUREL, -S *n* glossy-leaved shrub, bay tree ▹ *vb* crown with laurel
LAURIC *adj* as in **lauric acid** dodecanoic acid
LAURYL, -S *n* as in **lauryl alcohol** crystalline solid used to make detergents
LAUWINE *n* avalanche
LAV, -S *short for* > **lavatory**
LAVA, -S *n*
LAVABO, -S *n* ritual washing of priest's hands at Mass
LAVAGE, -S *n* washing out of a hollow organ
LAVAL *adj* of or relating to lava
LAVAS ▸ **lava**
LAVASH *n* Armenian flat bread
LAVE, -D, -S, LAVING *archaic word for* ▸ **wash**
LAVEER, -S *vb* (in sailing) tack
LAVER, -S *n* priest's basin for ritual ablutions
LAVES ▸ **lave**
LAVING ▸ **lave**
LAVISH *adj, vb*
LAVOLT, -S *same as* ▸ **lavolta**
LAVOLTA *n* old Italian dance ▹ *vb* dance the lavolta
LAVOLTS ▸ **lavolt**
LAVRA, -S *same as* ▸ **laura**
LAVROCK *same as* > **laverock**
LAVS ▸ **lav**
LAVVY, LAVVIES *n* lavatory
LAW, -ED, -ER, -EST, -S *n, vb, adj*
LAWBOOK *n* book on subject of law
LAWED ▸ **law**
LAWER ▸ **law**
LAWEST ▸ **law**
LAWFARE *n* use of the law by a country against its enemies
LAWFUL *adj*
LAWIN, -S *n* bill or reckoning

LAWINE, -S *n* avalanche
LAWING, -S *same as* ▸ **lawin**
LAWINS ▸ **lawin**
LAWK *interj* used to show surprise
LAWKS *same as* ▸ **lawk**
LAWLAND *same as* ▸ **lowland**
LAWLESS *adj*
LAWLIKE ▸ **law**
LAWMAN, LAWMEN *n*
LAWN, -ING, -S *n, vb*
LAWNED *adj* having a lawn
LAWNIER ▸ **lawny**
LAWNING ▸ **lawn**
LAWNS ▸ **lawn**
LAWNY, LAWNIER ▸ **lawn**
LAWS ▸ **law**
LAWSUIT *n*
LAWYER, -S *n, vb*
LAX, -ED, -ER, -ES, -EST, -ING *adj, vb*
LAXATOR *n* muscle that loosens body part
LAXED ▸ **lax**
LAXER ▸ **lax**
LAXES ▸ **lax**
LAXEST ▸ **lax**
LAXING ▸ **lax**
LAXISM, -S ▸ **laxist**
LAXIST, -S *n* lenient or tolerant person
LAXITY ▸ **lax**
LAXLY ▸ **lax**
LAXNESS ▸ **lax**
LAY, LAIN, -ED, -S *vb*
LAYAWAY *n* merchandise reserved for future delivery
LAYBACK *n* technique for climbing cracks ▹ *vb* use layback technique
LAYDEEZ *pl n* jocular spelling of ladies
LAYED ▸ **lay**
LAYER, -ED, -S *n* single thickness of some substance ▹ *vb* form a layer
LAYETTE *n* clothes for a newborn baby
LAYIN, -S *n* basketball score
LAYING, -S ▸ **lay**
LAYINS ▸ **layin**
LAYLOCK *old form of* ▸ **lilac**
LAYMAN, LAYMEN *n*
LAYOFF, -S *n* act of suspending employees
LAYOUT, -S *n* arrangement, esp of printing matter
LAYOVER *n* break in a journey
LAYS ▸ **lay**
LAYTIME *n* time allowed for loading cargo
LAYUP, -S *n* period of incapacity through illness
LAZAR, -S *n*
LAZARET *same as* ▸ **lazaretto**
LAZARS ▸ **lazar**
LAZE, -D, -S, LAZING *vb, n*
LAZIED ▸ **lazy**
LAZIER ▸ **lazy**
LAZIES ▸ **lazy**
LAZIEST ▸ **lazy**
LAZILY ▸ **lazy**
LAZING ▸ **laze**
LAZO, -ED, -ES, -ING, -S *another word for* ▸ **lasso**
LAZULI, -S *n* lapis lazuli
LAZY, LAZIED, LAZIER, LAZIES, LAZIEST, -ING *vb, adj*
LAZYISH ▸ **lazy**
LAZZO, LAZZI *n* comic routine in the commedia dell'arte
LEA, -S *n* meadow
LEACH, -ED, -ES *vb, n*
LEACHER ▸ **leach**
LEACHES ▸ **leach**
LEACHY *adj* porous
LEAD, -S, LED *vb, n, adj*
LEADED *adj* (of windows) made from many small panes of glass held together by lead strips
LEADEN, -S *adj* heavy or sluggish ▹ *vb* become or cause to become leaden
LEADER, -S *n*
LEADIER ▸ **leady**
LEADING ▸ **lead**
LEADMAN, LEADMEN *n* man who leads
LEADOFF *n* initial move
LEADS ▸ **lead**
LEADY, LEADIER *adj* like lead
LEAF, -ED, -ING, -S, LEAVES *n, vb*
LEAFAGE *n* leaves of plants
LEAFBUD *n* bud producing leaves rather than flowers
LEAFED ▸ **leaf**
LEAFERY *n* foliage
LEAFIER ▸ **leafy**
LEAFING ▸ **leaf**
LEAFLET *n, vb*
LEAFS ▸ **leaf**
LEAFY, LEAFIER *adj* covered with leaves

LEAGUE, -D, -S *n*
LEAGUER *vb* harass; beset ▷ *n* encampment, esp of besiegers
LEAGUES ▶ **league**
LEAK, -ED, -ING, -S *n, vb*
LEAKAGE *n*
LEAKED ▶ **leak**
LEAKER, -S ▶ **leak**
LEAKIER ▶ **leaky**
LEAKILY ▶ **leaky**
LEAKING ▶ **leak**
LEAKS ▶ **leak**
LEAKY, LEAKIER *adj* leaking
LEAL, -ER, -EST *adj* loyal
LEALLY ▶ **leal**
LEALTY ▶ **leal**
LEAM, -ED, -ING, -S *vb* shine
LEAN, -ED, -EST, -S, -T *vb, adj, n*
LEANER, -S ▶ **lean**
LEANEST ▶ **lean**
LEANING ▶ **lean**
LEANLY ▶ **lean**
LEANS ▶ **lean**
LEANT ▶ **lean**
LEANY *old form of* ▶ **lean**
LEAP, -ED, -ING, -S, -T *vb, n*
LEAPER, -S ▶ **leap**
LEAPING ▶ **leap**
LEAPS ▶ **leap**
LEAPT ▶ **leap**
LEAR, -ED, -ING, -S *vb* instruct
LEARE, -S *same as* ▶ **lear**
LEARED ▶ **lear**
LEARES ▶ **leare**
LEARIER ▶ **leary**
LEARING ▶ **lear**
LEARN, -ED, -S, -T *vb*
LEARNER *n* someone who is learning something
LEARNS ▶ **learn**
LEARNT ▶ **learn**
LEARS ▶ **lear**
LEARY, LEARIER *same as* ▶ **leery**
LEAS ▶ **lea**
LEASE, -D, -S *n, vb*
LEASER, -S ▶ **lease**
LEASES ▶ **lease**
LEASH, -ED, -ES *n, vb*
LEASING ▶ **lease**
LEASOW, -S *vb* pasture
LEASOWE *same as* ▶ **leasow**
LEASOWS ▶ **leasow**
LEAST, -S *n, adj, n, adv*
LEASURE *old form of* ▶ **leisure**
LEAT, -S *n* trench or ditch that conveys water to a mill wheel
LEATHER *n, adj, vb*
LEATS ▶ **leat**
LEAVE, LEAVING *vb, n*
LEAVED *adj* with leaves
LEAVEN, -S *n* substance that causes dough to rise ▷ *vb* raise with leaven
LEAVER, -S ▶ **leave**
LEAVES ▶ **leaf**
LEAVIER ▶ **leavy**
LEAVING ▶ **leave**
LEAVY, LEAVIER *same as* ▶ **leafy**
LEAZE, -S *same as* ▶ **lease**
LEBBEK, -S *n* type of timber tree
LEBEN, -S *n* semiliquid food made from curdled milk
LECCY, LECCIES *n* electricity
LECHAIM *interj* drinking toast ▷ *n* drink for a toast
LECHWE, -S *n* African antelope
LECTERN *n* reading desk
LECTIN, -S *n* type of protein
LECTION *n* variant reading of a passage in a text
LECTOR, -S *n* university lecturer
LECTURE *n, vb*
LECTURN *old form of* ▶ **lectern**
LECYTHI > **lecythus**
LED ▶ **lead**
LEDDEN, -S *n* language; speech
LEDE, -S *n* introductory part of a news story
LEDGE, -S *n*
LEDGED ▶ **ledge**
LEDGER, -S *n* book of debit and credit accounts ▷ *vb* fish using a wire trace while the bait floats freely and the weight sinks
LEDGES ▶ **ledge**
LEDGY, LEDGIER ▶ **ledge**
LEDUM, -S *n* evergreen shrub
LEE, -D, -ING *n* sheltered side ▷ *vb* (Scots) lie
LEEAR, -S *Scots form of* ▶ **liar**
LEECH, -ED, -ES *n, vb*
LEECHEE *same as* ▶ **litchi**
LEECHES ▶ **leech**
LEED ▶ **lee**
LEEING ▶ **lee**
LEEK, -S *n*

LEEP, -ED, -ING, -S *vb* boil; scald
LEER, -ED, -S *vb, n*
LEERIER ▸ **leery**
LEERILY ▸ **leery**
LEERING ▸ **leer**
LEERS ▸ **leer**
LEERY, LEERIER *adj* suspicious or wary (of)
LEES *pl n* sediment of wine
LEESE, -S, LEESING *old form of* ▸ **loose**
LEET, -S *n* shortlist
LEETLE *form of* ▸ **little**
LEETS ▸ **leet**
LEEWARD *n, adv, adj*
LEEWAY, -S *n*
LEEZE *adj* as in **leeze me** Scots for lief is me, an expression of affection
LEFT, -ER, -EST, -S *adj, n*
LEFTE *old past tense of* ▸ **lift**
LEFTER ▸ **left**
LEFTEST ▸ **left**
LEFTIE *same as* ▸ **lefty**
LEFTIES ▸ **lefty**
LEFTISH ▸ **left**
LEFTISM ▸ **leftist**
LEFTIST *adj, n*
LEFTS ▸ **left**
LEFTY, LEFTIES *n*
LEG, -S *n*
LEGACY *n*
LEGAL, -S *adj, n*
LEGALLY ▸ **legal**
LEGALS ▸ **legal**
LEGATE, -D, -S *n* messenger or representative, esp from the Pope ▹ *vb* leave as legacy
LEGATEE *n* recipient of a legacy
LEGATES ▸ **legate**
LEGATO, -S *adv* smoothly ▹ *n* playing with no gaps between notes
LEGATOR *n* person who gives a legacy or makes a bequest
LEGATOS ▸ **legato**
LEGEND, -S *n*
LEGER, -S *variant of* ▸ **ledger**
LEGES ▸ **lex**
LEGGE, -S *vb* lighten or lessen
LEGGED ▸ **leg**
LEGGER, -S *n* person who moves barge through tunnel using legs
LEGGES ▸ **legge**
LEGGIE, -S *n* leg spin bowler
LEGGIER ▸ **leggy**
LEGGIES ▸ **leggie**
LEGGIN, -S *same as* ▸ **legging**
LEGGING *n* extra outer covering for the lower leg
LEGGINS ▸ **leggin**
LEGGISM *n* blacklegging
LEGGO *sentence substitute* let go!
LEGGY, LEGGIER *adj* having long legs
LEGHOLD *n* type of animal trap that clamps down on the animal's leg
LEGHORN *n* Italian wheat straw woven into hats
LEGIBLE *adj*
LEGIBLY ▸ **legible**
LEGION, -S *n, adj*
LEGIST, -S *n* legal mind
LEGIT, -S *n* legitimate drama ▹ *adj* legitimate
LEGITIM *n* inheritance due to children from father
LEGITS ▸ **legit**
LEGLAN, -S *same as* ▸ **leglin**
LEGLEN, -S *same as* ▸ **leglin**
LEGLESS *adj* without legs
LEGLET, -S *n* leg jewellery
LEGLIKE ▸ **leg**
LEGLIN, -S *n* milk-pail
LEGMAN, LEGMEN *n* newsman who reports from the scene
LEGONG, -S *n* Indonesian dance
LEGROOM *n*
LEGS ▸ **leg**
LEGSIDE *n* part of a cricket field to the left of a right-handed batsman as they face the bowler
LEGUAAN *n* S African lizard
LEGUAN, -S *same as* ▸ **leguaan**
LEGUME, -S *n*
LEGUMIN *n* protein from leguminous plants
LEGWEAR *n*
LEGWORK *n*
LEHAIM, -S *same as* ▸ **lechaim**
LEHAYIM *same as* ▸ **lehaim**

LEHR, -S *n* long tunnel-shaped oven used for annealing glass
LEHUA, -S *n* flower of Hawaii
LEI, -S *n* Hawaiian garland
LEIDGER *same as* ▸ **ledger**
LEIGER, -S *same as* ▸ **ledger**
LEIPOA, -S *n* Australian bird
LEIR, -ED, -ING, -S *same as* ▸ **lear**
LEIS ▸ **lei**
LEISH, -ER *adj* agile
LEISLER *n* small bat
LEISTER *n* pronged fishing spear ▹ *vb* spear with a leister
LEISURE *n, vb*
LEK, -KED, -S, -U *n* bird display area ▹ *vb* gather at lek
LEKE *old form of* ▸ **leak**
LEKKED ▸ **lek**
LEKKER *adj* attractive or nice
LEKKING ▸ **lek**
LEKS ▸ **lek**
LEKU ▸ **lek**
LEKVAR, -S *n* prune or apricot pie filling
LEKYTHI > **lekythos**
LEMAN, -S *n* beloved
LEME, -D, -S, LEMING *same as* ▸ **leam**
LEMEL, -S *n* metal filings
LEMES ▸ **leme**
LEMING ▸ **leme**
LEMMA, -S, -TA *n* word in its citation form
LEMME *vb* (short for) let me
LEMMING *n*
LEMON, -ED, -S *n, adj, vb*
LEMONY *adj* like a lemon
LEMPIRA *n* monetary unit of Honduras
LEMUR, -S *n*
LEMURES *pl n* spirits of the dead
LEMURS ▸ **lemur**
LEND, -S, LENT *vb*
LENDER, -S ▸ **lend**
LENDING ▸ **lend**
LENDS ▸ **lend**
LENES ▸ **lenis**
LENG, -ED, -ER, -EST, -ING, -S *vb* linger ▹ *adj* long
LENGTH, -S *n*
LENGTHY *adj* very long
LENIENT *adj, n*
LENIFY *vb* make lenient
LENIS, LENES *adj* pronounced with little muscular tension ▹ *n* consonant like this
LENITE, -D, -S *vb* undergo lenition
LENITY *n* mercy or clemency
LENO, -S *n* weave in which the warp yarns are twisted in pairs between the weft
LENS, -ES *n*
LENSE *same as* ▸ **lens**
LENSED *adj* incorporating a lens
LENSES ▸ **lens**
LENSING *n* materials which colour and diffuse light
LENSMAN, LENSMEN *n* camera operator
LENT ▸ **lend**
LENTEN *adj* of or relating to Lent
LENTI ▸ **lento**
LENTIC *adj* of, relating to, or inhabiting still water
LENTIGO *technical name for a* ▸ **freckle**
LENTIL, -S *n*
LENTISC *same as* ▸ **lentisk**
LENTISK *n* mastic tree
LENTO, LENTI, -S *adv* slowly ▹ *n* movement or passage performed slowly
LENTOID *adj* lentiform ▹ *n* lentiform object
LENTOR, -S *n* lethargy
LENTOS ▸ **lento**
LENTOUS *adj* lethargic
LENVOY, -S *another word for* ▸ **envoy**
LEONE, -S *n* monetary unit of Sierra Leone
LEONINE *adj* like a lion
LEOPARD *n*
LEOTARD *n*
LEP, -PED, -PING, -S, -T *dialect word for* ▸ **leap**
LEPER, -S *n*
LEPID *adj* amusing
LEPORID *adj* of the family of mammals including rabbits and hares ▹ *n* any animal belonging to this family
LEPPED ▸ **lep**
LEPPING ▸ **lep**
LEPRA, -S *n* leprosy
LEPROSE *adj* having or denoting a whitish scurfy surface
LEPROSY *n* disease attacking the nerves and skin

LEPROUS *adj* having leprosy
LEPS ▸ **lep**
LEPT ▸ **lep**
LEPTA ▸ **lepton**
LEPTIN, -S *n* protein that regulates the amount of fat in the body
LEPTOME *n* tissue of plant conducting food
LEPTON, LEPTA, -S *n* any of a group of elementary particles with weak interactions
LEQUEAR *same as* ▸ **lacunar**
LERE, -D, -S, LERING *same as* ▸ **lear**
LERP, -S *n* crystallized honeydew
LESBIAN *n* homosexual woman ▹ *adj* of homosexual women
LESBIC *adj* relating to lesbians
LESION, -S *n* change in an organ of the body caused by injury ▹ *vb* cause lesions
LESS, -ES *n, adj, pron, adv, prep*
LESSEE, -S *n* person to whom a lease is granted
LESSEN, -S *vb*
LESSER *adj*
LESSES ▸ **less**
LESSON, -S *n, vb*
LESSOR, -S *n* person who grants a lease of property
LEST, -ED, -ING, -S *conj* so as to prevent any possibility that ▹ *vb* listen
LESULA, -S *n* species of monkey inhabiting forests in DR Congo
LET, -S, -TED *n* act of letting property ▹ *vb* obstruct
LETCHED ▸ **letch**
LETCHES ▸ **letch**
LETDOWN *n*
LETHAL, -S *adj, n*
LETHE, -S *n* forgetfulness
LETHEAN ▸ **lethe**
LETHEE, -S *n* life-blood
LETHES ▸ **lethe**
LETHIED *adj* forgetful
LETOUT, -S *n* circumstance that serves as an excuse not to do something
LETS ▸ **let**
LETTED ▸ **let**
LETTER *n, vb*
LETTERN *another word for* ▸ **lectern**
LETTERS *pl n* literary knowledge
LETTING ▸ **let**
LETTRE, -S *n* letter
LETTUCE *n*
LETUP, -S *n* lessening or abatement
LEU *n* monetary unit of Romania
LEUCH ▸ **lauch**
LEUCHEN ▸ **lauch**
LEUCIN, -S *same as* ▸ **leucine**
LEUCINE *n* essential amino acid
LEUCINS ▸ **leucin**
LEUCISM *n* condition causing pale discoloration of hair or skin
LEUCITE *n* grey or white mineral
LEUCO *n* as in **leuco base** colourless compound
LEUCOMA *n* white opaque scar of the cornea
LEUCON, -S *n* type of sponge
LEUD, -ES, -S *Scots word for* ▸ **breadth**
LEUGH ▸ **lauch**
LEUGHEN ▸ **lauch**
LEUKOMA *same as* ▸ **leucoma**
LEUKON, -S *n* white blood cell count
LEV, -A, -S *n* monetary unit of Bulgaria
LEVANT, -S *n* leather made from the skins of goats, sheep, or seals ▹ *vb* bolt or abscond
LEVATOR *n* muscle that raises a part of the body
LEVE, -S *same as* ▸ **lief**
LEVEE, -D, -S *n* natural or artificial river embankment ▹ *vb* go to the reception of
LEVEL, -ED, -S *adj, vb, n*
LEVELER *same as* ▸ **leveller**
LEVELLY ▸ **level**
LEVELS ▸ **level**
LEVER, -ED, -S *n, vb*
LEVERET *n* young hare
LEVERS ▸ **lever**
LEVES ▸ **leve**
LEVIED ▸ **levy**
LEVIER, -S ▸ **levy**
LEVIES ▸ **levy**
LEVIN, -S *archaic word for* ▸ **lightning**
LEVIS *pl n* jeans

LEVITE, -S *n* Christian clergyman or clergywoman
LEVITIC ▸ **levite**
LEVITY *n*
LEVO *adj* anticlockwise
LEVS ▸ **lev**
LEVULIN *n* substance obtained from certain bulbs
LEVY, LEVIED, LEVIES, -ING *vb, n*
LEW *adj* tepid
LEWDSBY *another word for* > **lewdster**
LEWIS, -ES *n* lifting device for heavy stone or concrete blocks
LEWISIA *n* type of herb
LEX, LEGES, -ES *n* system or body of laws
LEXEME, -S *n* minimal meaningful unit of language
LEXEMIC ▸ **lexeme**
LEXES ▸ **lex**
LEXICA ▸ **lexicon**
LEXICAL *adj* relating to the vocabulary of a language
LEXICON, LEXICA *n* dictionary
LEXIS, -ES *n* totality of vocabulary in a language
LEY, -S *n* land under grass
LI *n* Chinese measurement of distance
LIABLE *adj*
LIAISE, -D, -S *vb*
LIAISON *n*
LIANA, -S *n* climbing plant
LIANE, -S *same as* ▸ **liana**
LIANG, -S *n* Chinese unit of weight
LIANOID ▸ **liana**
LIAR, -S *n*
LIARD, -S *adj* grey ▹ *n* former small coin
LIARS ▸ **liar**
LIART *Scots form of* ▸ **liard**
LIAS, -ES *n* lowest series of rocks of the Jurassic system
LIASSIC *adj* relating to the earliest epoch of the Jurassic period
LIATRIS *n* North American plant with white flowers
LIB, -BED, -BING, -S *n* informal word for liberation ▹ *vb* geld
LIBANT *adj* touching lightly
LIBATE, -D, -S *vb* offer as gift to the gods
LIBBARD *another word for* ▸ **leopard**
LIBBED ▸ **lib**
LIBBER, -S *n* liberationist
LIBBING ▸ **lib**
LIBEL, -ED, -S *n, vb*
LIBELEE *same as* > **libellee**
LIBELER ▸ **libel**
LIBELS ▸ **libel**
LIBER, -S, LIBRI *n* tome or book
LIBERAL *adj, n*
LIBERO, -S *another name for* ▸ **sweeper**
LIBERS ▸ **liber**
LIBERTY *n*
LIBIDO, -S *n* psychic energy
LIBKEN, -S *n* lodging
LIBLAB, -S *n* 19th century British liberal
LIBRA, -E, -S *n* ancient Roman unit of weight
LIBRARY *n*
LIBRAS ▸ **libra**
LIBRATE *vb* oscillate or waver
LIBRI ▸ **liber**
LIBS ▸ **lib**
LICE ▸ **louse**
LICENCE *n, vb*
LICENSE *vb*
LICENTE *adj* permitted; allowed
LICH, -ES *n* dead body
LICHEE, -S *same as* ▸ **litchi**
LICHEN, -S *n, vb*
LICHES ▸ **lich**
LICHI, -S *same as* ▸ **litchi**
LICHT, -ED, -ER, -S *Scot word for* ▸ **light**
LICHTLY *vb* Scots word meaning treat discourteously
LICHTS ▸ **licht**
LICHWAY *n* path used to carry coffin into church
LICIT *adj* lawful, permitted
LICITLY ▸ **licit**
LICK, -ED, -S *vb* pass the tongue over ▹ *n* licking
LICKER, -S ▸ **lick**
LICKING *n* beating
LICKS ▸ **lick**
LICTOR, -S *n* one of a group of ancient Roman officials
LID, -S *n*
LIDAR, -S *n* radar-type instrument
LIDDED ▸ **lid**

LIDDING *n* lids
LIDGER, -S *variant form of* ▸ **ledger**
LIDLESS *adj* having no lid or top
LIDO, -S *n* open-air centre for swimming and water sports
LIDS ▸ **lid**
LIE, -S *vb, n*
LIED, -ER *n* setting for solo voice and piano of a poem
LIEF, -ER, -EST, -S *adv* gladly ▹ *adj* ready ▹ *n* beloved person
LIEFLY ▸ **lief**
LIEFS ▸ **lief**
LIEGE, -S *adj* bound to give or receive feudal service ▹ *n* lord
LIEGER, -S *same as* ▸ **ledger**
LIEGES ▸ **liege**
LIEN, -S *n* right to hold another's property until a debt is paid
LIENAL *adj* of or relating to the spleen
LIENEE, -S *n* person against whom a lien has been placed
LIENOR, -S *n* person who holds a lien
LIENS ▸ **lien**
LIER, -S *n* person who lies down
LIERNE, -S *n* short secondary rib that connects intersections of the primary ribs
LIERS ▸ **lier**
LIES ▸ **lie**
LIEU, -S *n* stead
LIEVE, -R, -S, -ST *same as* ▸ **leve**
LIFE, LIVES *n*
LIFEFUL *adj* full of life
LIFER, -S *n* prisoner sentenced to imprisonment for life
LIFES *pl n* as in **still lifes** paintings or drawings of inanimate objects
LIFEWAY *n* way of life
LIFT, -ED, -ING, -S *vb, n*
LIFTBOY *n* person who operates a lift
LIFTED ▸ **lift**
LIFTER, -S ▸ **lift**
LIFTING ▸ **lift**
LIFTMAN, LIFTMEN *same as* ▸ **liftboy**
LIFTOFF *n* moment a rocket leaves the ground ▹ *vb* (of a rocket) to leave its launch pad
LIFTS ▸ **lift**
LIFULL *obsolete form of* ▸ **lifeful**
LIG, -GED, -S *n* function with free entertainment and refreshments ▹ *vb* attend such a function
LIGAN, -S *same as* ▸ **lagan**
LIGAND, -S *n* atom, molecule, radical, or ion forming a complex with a central atom
LIGANS ▸ **ligan**
LIGASE, -S *n* any of a class of enzymes
LIGATE, -D, -S *vb* tie up or constrict (something) with a ligature
LIGER, -S *n* hybrid offspring of a female tiger and a male lion
LIGGE, -S *obsolete form of* ▸ **lie**
LIGGED ▸ **lig**
LIGGER, -S ▸ **lig**
LIGGES ▸ **ligge**
LIGGING ▸ **lig**
LIGHT, -ED, -S *n, adj, vb, adv*
LIGHTEN *vb*
LIGHTER *n, vb*
LIGHTLY *adv* in a light way ▹ *vb* belittle
LIGHTS ▸ **light**
LIGNAGE *another word for* ▸ **lineage**
LIGNAN, -S *n* beneficial substance found in plants
LIGNE, -S *n* unit of measurement
LIGNIFY *vb* become woody with the deposition of lignin in cell walls
LIGNIN, -S *n* complex polymer occurring in certain plant cell walls making the plant rigid
LIGNITE *n* woody textured rock used as fuel
LIGNOSE *n* explosive compound
LIGNUM, -S *n* wood
LIGROIN *n* volatile fraction of petroleum
LIGS ▸ **lig**
LIGULA, -E, -S *same as* ▸ **ligule**
LIGULAR ▸ **ligula**
LIGULAS ▸ **ligula**
LIGULE, -S *n* membranous outgrowth between the leaf blade and sheath

LIGURE, -S *n* any of the 12 precious stones used in the breastplates of high priests
LIKABLE *adj* easy to like
LIKABLY ▸ **likable**
LIKE, -D, -S, -ST *adj, vb, n*
LIKELY *adj, adv*
LIKEN, -ED, -S *vb* compare
LIKER, -S ▸ **like**
LIKES ▸ **like**
LIKEST ▸ **like**
LIKIN, -S *n* historically, Chinese tax
LIKING, -S *n* fondness
LIKINS ▸ **likin**
LIKUTA *n* coin in the former Zaïre
LILAC, -S *n, adj*
LILIED *adj* decorated with lilies
LILIES ▸ **lily**
LILL, -ED, -ING, -S *obsolete form of* ▸ **loll**
LILO, -S *n* inflatable mattress
LILT, -ED, -S *n, vb*
LILTING ▸ **lilt**
LILTS ▸ **lilt**
LILY, LILIES *n* plant which has large, often white, flowers
LIMA, -S *n* type of edible bean
LIMACEL *n* small shell inside some kinds of slug
LIMACES ▸ **limax**
LIMACON *n* heart-shaped curve
LIMAIL, -S *same as* ▸ **lemel**
LIMAN, -S *n* lagoon
LIMAS ▸ **lima**
LIMAX, LIMACES *n* slug
LIMB, -ED, -ING, -S *n, vb*
LIMBA, -S *n* type of African tree
LIMBATE *adj* having an edge or border of a different colour from the rest
LIMBEC, -S *obsolete form of* ▸ **alembic**
LIMBECK *obsolete form of* ▸ **alembic**
LIMBECS ▸ **limbec**
LIMBED ▸ **limb**
LIMBER, -S *vb, adj, n*
LIMBI ▸ **limbus**
LIMBIC ▸ **limbus**
LIMBIER ▸ **limby**
LIMBING ▸ **limb**
LIMBO, -ED, -ES, -S *n, vb*
LIMBOUS *adj* with overlapping edges
LIMBS ▸ **limb**
LIMBUS, LIMBI *n* border
LIMBY, LIMBIER *adj* with long legs, stem, branches, etc
LIME, -D *n, vb, adj*
LIMEADE *n*
LIMED ▸ **lime**
LIMELIT > **limelight**
LIMEN, -S, LIMINA *another term for* > **threshold**
LIMEPIT *n*
LIMES, LIMITES *n* fortified boundary of the Roman Empire
LIMEY, -S *n* British person ▹ *adj* British
LIMIER ▸ **limy**
LIMIEST ▸ **limy**
LIMINA ▸ **limen**
LIMINAL *adj* relating to the point beyond which a sensation becomes too faint to be experienced
LIMING, -S ▸ **lime**
LIMIT, -S *n, vb*
LIMITED *adj* having a limit ▹ *n* limited train, bus, etc
LIMITER *n* thing that limits something
LIMITES ▸ **limes**
LIMITS ▸ **limit**
LIMMA, -S *n* semitone
LIMMER, -S *n* scoundrel
LIMN, -ED, -ING, -S *vb* represent in drawing or painting
LIMNER, -S ▸ **limn**
LIMNIC *adj* relating to lakes
LIMNING ▸ **limn**
LIMNS ▸ **limn**
LIMO, -S *short for* > **limousine**
LIMOSIS, LIMOSES *n* excessive hunger
LIMOUS *adj* muddy
LIMP, -ED, -EST, -S *vb, n, adj*
LIMPA, -S *n* type of rye bread
LIMPED ▸ **limp**
LIMPER, -S ▸ **limp**
LIMPEST ▸ **limp**
LIMPET, -S *n, adj*
LIMPID *adj* clear or transparent
LIMPING ▸ **limp**
LIMPKIN *n* rail-like wading bird
LIMPLY ▸ **limp**
LIMPS ▸ **limp**
LIMPSEY *same as* ▸ **limpsy**
LIMPSY *adj* limp
LIMULUS, LIMULI *n* horseshoe crab
LIMY, LIMIER, LIMIEST *adj* of, like, or smeared with birdlime

LIN, -NED, -NING, -S *vb* cease
LINABLE ▶ **line**
LINAC, -S *n* linear accelerator
LINAGE, -S *n* number of lines in written or printed matter
LINALOL *same as* > **linalool**
LINCH, -ES *n* ledge
LINCHET *another word for* ▶ **linch**
LINCTUS *n* cough medicine
LIND, -S *variant of* ▶ **linden**
LINDANE *n* white poisonous crystalline powder
LINDEN, -S *n* large tree with heart-shaped leaves and fragrant yellowish flowers
LINDIED ▶ **lindy**
LINDIES ▶ **lindy**
LINDS ▶ **lind**
LINDY, LINDIED, LINDIES *n* lively dance ▷ *vb* perform the lindy
LINE, -D, -S *n, vb*
LINEAGE *n* descent from an ancestor
LINEAL *adj* in direct line of descent
LINEAR *adj*
LINEATE *adj* marked with lines
LINECUT *n* method of relief printing
LINED ▶ **line**
LINEMAN, LINEMEN *same as* > **linesman**
LINEN, -S *n* cloth or thread made from flax
LINENY *adj* like linen
LINER, -S *n*
LINES ▶ **line**
LINEUP, -S *n*
LINEY ▶ **line**
LING, -S *n* slender food fish
LINGA, -S *same as* ▶ **lingam**
LINGAM, -S *n* (in Sanskrit) masculine gender
LINGAS ▶ **linga**
LINGCOD *n* type of food fish
LINGEL, -S *n* shoemaker's thread
LINGER, -S *vb* delay or prolong departure
LINGIER ▶ **lingy**
LINGLE, -S *same as* ▶ **lingel**
LINGO, -ES, -S *n*
LINGOT, -S *n* ingot
LINGS ▶ **ling**
LINGUA, -E, -S *n* any tongue-like structure
LINGUAL *adj* of the tongue ▷ *n* lingual consonant
LINGUAS ▶ **lingua**
LINGULA *n* small tongue
LINGY, LINGIER *adj* heather-covered
LINHAY, -S *n* farm building with an open front
LINIER ▶ **liny**
LINIEST ▶ **liny**
LININ, -S *n* network of viscous material in the nucleus of a cell
LINING, -S *n* layer of cloth attached to the inside of a garment etc
LININS ▶ **linin**
LINISH *vb* polish metal
LINK, -ED, -ING, -S *n, vb*
LINKAGE *n*
LINKBOY *n* (formerly) a boy who carried a torch for pedestrians in dark streets
LINKED ▶ **link**
LINKER, -S *n* person or thing that links
LINKIER ▶ **linky**
LINKING ▶ **link**
LINKMAN, LINKMEN *same as* ▶ **linkboy**
LINKROT *n* state of having expired hyperlinks on a website
LINKS ▶ **link**
LINKUP, -S *n*
LINKY, LINKIER *adj* (of countryside) consisting of links
LINN, -S *n* waterfall or a pool at the foot of it
LINNED ▶ **lin**
LINNET, -S *n* songbird of the finch family
LINNEY, -S *same as* ▶ **linhay**
LINNIES ▶ **linny**
LINNING ▶ **lin**
LINNS ▶ **linn**
LINNY, LINNIES *same as* ▶ **linhay**
LINO, -S *same as* > **linoleum**
LINOCUT *n* design cut in relief in lino mounted on a block of wood
LINOS ▶ **lino**
LINS ▶ **lin**
LINSANG *n* any of several forest-dwelling viverrine mammals
LINSEED *n*

LINSEY, -S *n* type of cloth
LINT, -S *n, vb*
LINTED *adj* having lint
LINTEL, -S *n*
LINTER, -S *n* machine for stripping the short fibres of ginned cotton seeds
LINTIE, -S *Scot word for* ▸ **linnet**
LINTIER ▸ **linty**
LINTIES ▸ **lintie**
LINTING *n* process of making lint
LINTOL, -S *same as* ▸ **lintel**
LINTS ▸ **lint**
LINTY, LINTIER ▸ **lint**
LINUM, -S *n* type of plant of temperate regions
LINURON *n* type of herbicide
LINUX, -ES *n* nonproprietary computer operating system
LINY, LINIER, LINIEST ▸ **line**
LION, -S *n*
LIONCEL *n* (in heraldry) small lion
LIONEL, -S *same as* ▸ **lioncel**
LIONESS *n*
LIONET, -S *n* young lion
LIONISE *same as* ▸ **lionize**
LIONISM *n* the condition of being treated as a celebrity
LIONIZE *vb*
LIONLY *adj* like a lion
LIONS ▸ **lion**
LIP, -PED, -S *n, vb*
LIPA, -S *n* monetary unit of Croatia
LIPASE, -S *n* any of a group of enzymes that digest fat
LIPE, -S *n* lurching or jerking movement
LIPEMIA *same as* > **lipaemia**
LIPES ▸ **lipe**
LIPID, -S *n* any of a group of organic compounds including fats, oils, waxes, and sterols
LIPIDE, -S *same as* ▸ **lipid**
LIPIDIC ▸ **lipid**
LIPIDS ▸ **lipid**
LIPIN, -S *n* family of nuclear proteins
LIPLESS ▸ **lip**
LIPLIKE ▸ **lip**
LIPO, -S *n* liposuction
LIPOIC *adj* as in **lipoic acid** sulphur-containing fatty acid
LIPOID, -S *n* fatlike substance, such as wax
LIPOMA, -S *n* benign tumour composed of fatty tissue
LIPOS ▸ **lipo**
LIPPED ▸ **lip**
LIPPEN, -S *vb* trust
LIPPER, -S *Scots word for* ▸ **ripple**
LIPPIE *variant of* ▸ **lippy**
LIPPIER ▸ **lippy**
LIPPIES ▸ **lippy**
LIPPING ▸ **lip**
LIPPY, LIPPIER, LIPPIES *adj* insolent or cheeky ▹ *n* lipstick
LIPREAD *vb*
LIPS ▸ **lip**
LIPURIA *n* presence of fat in the urine
LIQUATE *vb* separate one component of by heating until the more fusible part melts
LIQUEFY *vb* become liquid
LIQUEUR *n, vb*
LIQUID, -S *n, adj*
LIQUIDY *adj* having the nature of liquid
LIQUIFY *same as* ▸ **liquefy**
LIQUOR, -S *n, vb*
LIRA, -S, LIRE, LIRI, LIROT, LIROTH *n* monetary unit of Turkey, Malta, and formerly of Italy
LIRIOPE *n* grasslike plant
LIRK, -ED, -ING, -S *vb* wrinkle
LIROT ▸ **lira**
LIROTH ▸ **lira**
LIS, -SES *n* fleur-de-lis
LISENTE ▸ **sente**
LISK, -S *Yorkshire dialect for* ▸ **groin**
LISLE, -S *n* strong fine cotton thread or fabric
LISP, -ED, -S *n, vb*
LISPER, -S ▸ **lisp**
LISPING ▸ **lisp**
LISPS ▸ **lisp**
LISPUND *same as* > **lispound**
LISSES ▸ **lis**
LISSOM *adj* supple, agile
LISSOME *same as* ▸ **lissom**
LIST, -ED, -ETH *n, vb*
LISTBOX *n* small box on a computer screen,

showing a list of options
LISTED ▸ **list**
LISTEE, -S *n* person on list
LISTEL, -S *another name for* ▸ **fillet**
LISTEN, -S *vb*
LISTER, -S *n* plough that throws soil to the sides of a central furrow
LISTETH ▸ **list**
LISTFUL *adj* paying attention
LISTING *n* list or an entry in a list
LISTS *pl n* field of combat in a tournament
LIT, -S *n* archaic word for dye or colouring
LITAI ▸ **litas**
LITANY *n*
LITAS, LITAI, LITU *n* monetary unit of Lithuania
LITCHI, -S *n* Chinese tree with round edible fruits
LITE, -D, -S, -ST, LITING *same as* ▸ **light**
LITER, -S *same as* ▸ **litre**
LITERAL *adj, n*
LITERS ▸ **liter**
LITES ▸ **lite**
LITEST ▸ **lite**
LITH, -S *n* limb or joint
LITHATE *n* salt of uric acid
LITHE, -D, -R, -S, -ST, LITHING *adj* flexible or supple, pliant ▹ *vb* listen
LITHELY ▸ **lithe**
LITHER ▸ **lithe**
LITHES ▸ **lithe**
LITHEST ▸ **lithe**
LITHIA, -S *n* lithium present in mineral waters as lithium salts
LITHIC *adj* of stone
LITHIFY *vb* turn into rock
LITHING ▸ **lithe**
LITHITE *n* part of cell with sensory element
LITHIUM *n* chemical element, the lightest known metal
LITHO, -ED, -ES, -S *n* lithography ▹ *vb* print using lithography
LITHOID *adj* resembling rock
LITHOPS *n* fleshy-leaved plant
LITHOS ▸ **litho**
LITHS ▸ **lith**
LITING ▸ **lite**
LITMUS *n* soluble powder obtained from lichens
LITORAL *same as* > **littoral**
LITOTES *n* ironical understatement used for effect
LITOTIC ▸ **litotes**
LITRE, -S *n*
LITS ▸ **lit**
LITTEN *adj* lighted
LITTER, -S *n, vb*
LITTERY *adj* covered in litter
LITTLE, -R, -S *adj, adv, n*
LITTLIE *n* young child
LITTLIN *same as* > **littling**
LITU ▸ **litas**
LITURGY *n*
LITUUS *n* curved trumpet
LIVABLE *adj*
LIVE, -D, -ST *vb, adj, adv*
LIVEDO, -S *n* reddish discoloured patch on the skin
LIVELOD *n* livelihood
LIVELY *adj*
LIVEN, -ED, -S *vb*
LIVENER ▸ **liven**
LIVENS ▸ **liven**
LIVER, -S *n*
LIVERED *adj* having liver
LIVERS ▸ **liver**
LIVERY *n, adj*
LIVES ▸ **life**
LIVEST ▸ **live**
LIVEYER *n* (in Newfoundland) a full-time resident
LIVID, -ER *adj*
LIVIDLY ▸ **livid**
LIVIER, -S *same as* ▸ **liveyer**
LIVING, -S *adj* possessing life, not dead or inanimate ▹ *n* means whereby one lives
LIVOR, -S *another word for* > **lividity**
LIVRE, -S *n* former French unit of money of account
LIVYER, -S *same as* ▸ **liveyer**
LIXIVIA > **lixivium**
LIZARD, -S *n*
LIZZIE, -S *n* as in **tin lizzie** old or decrepit car
LLAMA, -S *n* woolly animal of the camel family

LLANERO *n* native of llanos
LLANO, -S *n* extensive grassy treeless plain
LO *interj* look!
LOACH, -ES *n* carplike fish
LOAD *n, vb*
LOADED *adj* containing a hidden trap
LOADEN, -S *vb* load
LOADER, -S *n* person who loads a gun or other firearm
LOADING *n* load or burden
LOADS *pl n* lots or a lot
LOAF, -ED, -S, LOAVES *n, vb*
LOAFER, -S *n* idler
LOAFING ▸ loaf
LOAFS ▸ loaf
LOAM, -ED, -ING, -S *n* fertile soil ▹ *vb* cover, treat, or fill with loam
LOAMIER ▸ loamy
LOAMING ▸ loam
LOAMS ▸ loam
LOAMY, LOAMIER ▸ loam
LOAN, -ED, -ING, -S *n, vb*
LOANEE, -S *n* sportsperson who is loaned out
LOANER, -S ▸ loan
LOANING ▸ loan
LOANS ▸ loan
LOAST ▸ lose
LOATH *adj* unwilling or reluctant (to)
LOATHE, -D, -S *vb* hate
LOATHER ▸ loathe
LOATHES ▸ loathe
LOATHLY *adj* loathsome
LOATHY *obsolete form of* **> loathsome**
LOAVE, -D, LOAVING *vb* form a loaf
LOAVES ▸ loaf
LOAVING ▸ loave
LOB, -BED, -BING, -S *n, vb*
LOBAR *adj* of or affecting a lobe
LOBATE *adj* with or like lobes
LOBATED *same as* **▸ lobate**
LOBBED ▸ lob
LOBBER, -S *n* one who lobs
LOBBIED ▸ lobby
LOBBIES ▸ lobby
LOBBING ▸ lob
LOBBY, LOBBIED, LOBBIES *n, vb*
LOBBYER ▸ lobby
LOBE, -S *n*
LOBED ▸ lobe
LOBEFIN *n* type of fish
LOBELET *n* small lobe
LOBELIA *n* garden plant
LOBES ▸ lobe
LOBI ▸ lobus
LOBING, -S *n* formation of lobes
LOBIPED *adj* with lobed toes
LOBO, -S *n* timber wolf
LOBOLA, -S *n* (in African custom) price paid by a bridegroom's family to his bride's family
LOBOLO, -S *same as* **▸ lobola**
LOBOS ▸ lobo
LOBOSE *another word for* **▸ lobate**
LOBS ▸ lob
LOBSTER *n, vb*
LOBTAIL *vb* (of a whale) hit a surface of water with the tail
LOBULAR ▸ lobule
LOBULE, -S *n* small lobe or a subdivision of a lobe
LOBULUS, LOBULI *n* small lobe
LOBUS, LOBI *n* lobe
LOBWORM *same as* **▸ lugworm**
LOCA ▸ locus
LOCAL, -S *adj, n*
LOCALE, -S *n*
LOCALLY *adv* within a particular area or place
LOCALS ▸ local
LOCATE, -D, -S *vb* discover the whereabouts of
LOCATER ▸ locate
LOCATES ▸ locate
LOCATOR *n* part of index that shows where to find information
LOCH, -S *n* lake
LOCHAN, -S *n* small inland loch
LOCHE, -S *n* freshwater fish of the cod family
LOCHS ▸ loch
LOCI ▸ locus
LOCIE, -S *n* type of logging engine
LOCK, -ED, -S *n, vb*
LOCKAGE *n* system of locks in a canal
LOCKBOX *n* system of collecting funds from companies by banks
LOCKED ▸ lock
LOCKER, -S *n*
LOCKET, -S *n*

LOCKFUL *n* sufficient to fill a canal lock
LOCKING ▶ **lock**
LOCKJAW *n*
LOCKMAN, LOCKMEN *n* lock-keeper
LOCKNUT *n* nut screwed down on a primary nut to stop it from loosening
LOCKOUT *n*
LOCKRAM *n* type of linen cloth
LOCKS ▶ **lock**
LOCKSET *n* hardware used to lock door
LOCKUP, -S *n*
LOCO, -ED, -ES, -ING, -S *n* locomotive ▷ *vb* poison with locoweed
LOCOISM *n* disease of cattle, sheep, and horses caused by eating locoweed
LOCOMAN, LOCOMEN *n* railwayman
LOCOS ▶ **loco**
LOCULAR *adj* divided into compartments by septa
LOCULE, -S *n* any of the chambers of an ovary or anther
LOCULED *adj* having locules
LOCULES ▶ **locule**
LOCULUS, LOCULI *same as* ▶ **locule**
LOCUM, -S *n* temporary stand-in for a doctor, or clergyman or clergywoman
LOCUS, LOCA, LOCI *n* area or place where something happens
LOCUST, -S *n, vb*
LOCUSTA *n* flower cluster unit in grasses
LOCUSTS ▶ **locust**
LOD, -S *n* type of logarithm
LODE, -S *n*
LODEN, -S *n* thick waterproof, woollen cloth
LODES ▶ **lode**
LODGE, -D, -S *n, vb*
LODGER, -S *n* tenant
LODGES ▶ **lodge**
LODGING *n* temporary residence
LODS ▶ **lod**
LOERIE, -S *same as* ▶ **lourie**
LOESS, -ES *n* fine-grained soil
LOESSAL ▶ **loess**
LOESSES ▶ **loess**
LOESSIC *adj* relating to or consisting of loess
LOFT, -ED, -ING, -S *n, vb*
LOFTER, -S *n* former type of golf club
LOFTIER ▶ **lofty**
LOFTILY ▶ **lofty**
LOFTING ▶ **loft**
LOFTS ▶ **loft**
LOFTY, LOFTIER *adj* of great height
LOG, -GED, -S *n, vb*
LOGAN, -S *another name for* ▶ **bogan**
LOGANIA *n* type of Australian plant
LOGANS ▶ **logan**
LOGBOOK *n*
LOGE, -S *n* small enclosure or box in a theatre or opera house
LOGGAT, -S *n* small piece of wood
LOGGED ▶ **log**
LOGGER, -S *n*
LOGGETS *n* old-fashioned game played with sticks
LOGGIA, -S, LOGGIE *n* covered gallery at the side of a building
LOGGIER ▶ **loggy**
LOGGING ▶ **log**
LOGGISH ▶ **log**
LOGGY, LOGGIER *adj* sluggish
LOGIA ▶ **logion**
LOGIC, -S *n*
LOGICAL *adj* of logic
LOGICS ▶ **logic**
LOGIE, -S *n* fireplace of a kiln
LOGIER ▶ **logy**
LOGIES ▶ **logie**
LOGIEST ▶ **logy**
LOGILY ▶ **logy**
LOGIN, -S *n* process by which a computer user logs on
LOGION, LOGIA, -S *n* saying of Christ regarded as authentic
LOGJAM, -S *n, vb*
LOGLINE *n* synopsis of screenplay
LOGLOG, -S *n* logarithm of a logarithm (in equations, etc)
LOGO *same as* > **logotype**
LOGOED *adj* having a logo
LOGOFF, -S *n* process by which a computer user logs out
LOGOI ▶ **logos**
LOGON, -S *variant of* ▶ **login**

LOGOS, LOGOI *n* reason expressed in words and things, argument, or justification
LOGOUT, -S *variant of* ▸ **logoff**
LOGROLL *vb* procure the passage of (legislation) by trading votes
LOGS ▸ **log**
LOGWAY, -S *another name for* ▸ **gangway**
LOGWOOD *n* tree of the Caribbean and Central America
LOGY, LOGIER, LOGIEST *adj* dull or listless
LOHAN, -S *another word for* ▸ **arhat**
LOIASIS, LOIASES *n* disease caused by a tropical eye worm
LOID, -ED, -ING, -S *vb* open (a lock) using a celluloid strip
LOIN *n*
LOINS *pl n* hips and the inner surface of the legs
LOIPE, -N *n* cross-country skiing track
LOIR, -S *n* large dormouse
LOITER, -S *vb*
LOKE, -S *n* track
LOKSHEN *pl n* noodles
LOLIGO, -S *n* type of squid
LOLIUM, -S *n* type of grass
LOLL, -ED, -ING, -S *vb* lounge lazily ▹ *n* act or instance of lolling
LOLLER, -S ▸ **loll**
LOLLIES ▸ **lolly**
LOLLING ▸ **loll**
LOLLOP, -S *vb* move clumsily
LOLLOPY *adj* moving with a lollop
LOLLS ▸ **loll**
LOLLY, LOLLIES *n*
LOLOG, -S *same as* ▸ **loglog**
LOLZ *same as* ▸ **lulz**
LOMA, -S, -TA *n* lobe
LOME, -S, LOMING *n* fertile soil ▹ *vb* cover with lome
LOMED ▸ **lome**
LOMEIN, -S *n* Chinese dish
LOMENT, -S *n* pod of certain leguminous plants
LOMENTA > **lomentum**
LOMENTS ▸ **loment**
LOMES ▸ **lome**
LOMING ▸ **lome**
LOMPISH *another word for* ▸ **lumpish**
LONE *adj*
LONELY *adj* sad because alone
LONER, -S *n* solitary person
LONG, -ED, -EST *adj, adv, vb*
LONGA, -S *n* long note
LONGAN, -S *n* sapindaceous tree of tropical and subtropical Asia
LONGAS ▸ **longa**
LONGBOW *n*
LONGE, -S *n* rope used in training a horse ▹ *vb* train using a longe
LONGED ▸ **long**
LONGER, -S *n* line of barrels on a ship
LONGES ▸ **longe**
LONGEST ▸ **long**
LONGIES *n* long johns
LONGING *n* yearning ▹ *adj* having or showing desire
LONGISH *adj* rather long
LONGLY ▸ **long**
LONGS *pl n* full-length trousers
LOO, -ED, -ING, -S *n* toilet ▹ *vb* Scots word meaning love
LOOBIER ▸ **looby**
LOOBIES ▸ **looby**
LOOBILY ▸ **looby**
LOOBY, LOOBIER, LOOBIES *adj* foolish ▹ *n* foolish or stupid person
LOOED ▸ **loo**
LOOEY, -S *n* lieutenant
LOOF, -S, LOOVES *n* part of ship's side
LOOFA, -S *same as* ▸ **loofah**
LOOFAH, -S *n*
LOOFAS ▸ **loofa**
LOOFFUL *n* handful
LOOFS ▸ **loof**
LOOGIE, -S *n* lump of spit and phlegm
LOOIE, -S *same as* ▸ **looey**
LOOING ▸ **loo**
LOOK, -ED, -ING, -S *vb, n*
LOOKER, -S *n* person who looks
LOOKIE *interj* look (over here)
LOOKING ▸ **look**
LOOKISM *n* discrimination because of appearance

LOOKIST ▶ **lookism**
LOOKIT *interj* look at this
LOOKOUT *n, vb*
LOOKS ▶ **look**
LOOKUP, -S *n* act of looking up information
LOOKY *same as* ▶ **lookie**
LOOM, -ED, -ING, -S *n, vb*
LOON, -S *n* diving bird
LOONEY, -S *same as* ▶ **loony**
LOONIE *n* Canadian dollar coin
LOONIER ▶ **loony**
LOONIES ▶ **loony**
LOONILY ▶ **loony**
LOONING *n* cry of the loon
LOONS ▶ **loon**
LOONY, LOONIER, LOONIES *adj, n*
LOOP, -ED, -S *n, vb*
LOOPER, -S *n* person or thing that loops or makes loops
LOOPIER ▶ **loopy**
LOOPILY ▶ **loopy**
LOOPING ▶ **loop**
LOOPS ▶ **loop**
LOOPY, LOOPIER *adj* curly or twisted
LOOR *a Scots form of* ▶ **lief**
LOORD, -S *obsolete word for* ▶ **lout**
LOOS ▶ **loo**
LOOSE, -D, -R, -S, -ST *adj, adv, vb*
LOOSELY ▶ **loose**
LOOSEN, -S *vb*
LOOSER ▶ **loose**
LOOSES ▶ **loose**
LOOSEST ▶ **loose**
LOOSIE *n* informal word for loose forward
LOOSIES *pl n* cigarettes sold individually
LOOSING *n* celebration of one's 21st birthday
LOOT, -ED, -S, LUTTEN *vb, n*
LOOTEN *Scots past form of* ▶ **let**
LOOTER, -S ▶ **loot**
LOOTING ▶ **loot**
LOOTS ▶ **loot**
LOOVES ▶ **loof**
LOP, -PED, -S *vb, n*
LOPE, -D, -S, LOPING *vb, n*
LOPER, -S ▶ **lope**
LOPES ▶ **lope**
LOPING ▶ **lope**
LOPPED ▶ **lop**
LOPPER, -S *n* tool for lopping ▷ *vb* curdle
LOPPET, -S *n* long-distance cross-country ski race
LOPPIER ▶ **loppy**
LOPPIES ▶ **loppy**
LOPPING ▶ **lop**
LOPPY, LOPPIER, LOPPIES *adj* floppy ▷ *n* ranch hand
LOPS ▶ **lop**
LOQUAT, -S *n* ornamental evergreen rosaceous tree
LOR *interj* exclamation of surprise or dismay
LORAL *adj* of part of side of bird's head
LORAN, -S *n* radio navigation system operating over long distances
LORATE *adj* like a strap
LORCHA, -S *n* junk-rigged vessel
LORD, -ED, -S *n, vb*
LORDING *n* gentleman
LORDKIN *n* little lord
LORDLY *adj* imperious, proud ▷ *adv* in the manner of a lord
LORDOMA *same as* ▶ **lordosis**
LORDS ▶ **lord**
LORDY *interj* exclamation of surprise or dismay
LORE, -S *n* body of traditions
LOREAL *adj* concerning or relating to lore
LOREL, -S *another word for* ▶ **losel**
LORES ▶ **lore**
LORGNON *n* monocle or pair of spectacles
LORIC, -S *same as* ▶ **lorica**
LORICA, -E, -S *n* hard outer covering of rotifers, ciliate protozoans, and similar organisms
LORICS ▶ **loric**
LORIES ▶ **lory**
LORIMER *n* (formerly) a person who made bits and spurs
LORINER *same as* ▶ **lorimer**
LORING, -S *n* teaching
LORIOT, -S *n* golden oriole (bird)
LORIS, -ES *n* any of several prosimian primates
LORN, -ER, -EST *adj* forsaken or wretched
LORRELL *obsolete word for* ▶ **losel**

LORRY, LORRIES *n*
LORY, LORIES *n* small parrot of Australia and Indonesia
LOS *n* approval
LOSABLE ▶ **lose**
LOSE, LOAST, -D, -S *vb* part with
LOSEL, -S *n* worthless person ▷ *adj* worthless
LOSEN *same as* ▶ **lose**
LOSER, -S *n* person or thing that loses
LOSES ▶ **lose**
LOSH *interj* lord
LOSING *adj* unprofitable; failing
LOSINGS *pl n* losses
LOSS, -ES *n*
LOSSY, LOSSIER *adj* designed to have a high attenuation
LOST *adj*
LOT, -S, -TED, -TING *pron, n, vb*
LOTA, -S *n* globular water container
LOTAH, -S *same as* ▶ **lota**
LOTAS ▶ **lota**
LOTE, -S *another word for* ▶ **lotus**
LOTH, -ER, -EST *same as* ▶ **loath**
LOTI *n* monetary unit of Lesotho
LOTIC *adj* of communities living in rapidly flowing water
LOTION, -S *n*
LOTO *same as* ▶ **lotto**
LOTOS, -ES *same as* ▶ **lotus**
LOTS ▶ **lot**
LOTSA *determiner* lots of
LOTTA *determiner* lot of
LOTTE, -S *n* type of fish
LOTTED ▶ **lot**
LOTTER, -S *n* someone who works an allotment
LOTTERY *n*
LOTTES ▶ **lotte**
LOTTING ▶ **lot**
LOTTO, -S *n*
LOTUS, -ES *n*
LOU, -ED, -ING, -S *Scot word for* ▶ **love**
LOUCHE, -R *adj* shifty
LOUD, -ER, -EST *adj*
LOUDEN, -S *vb*
LOUDER ▶ **loud**
LOUDEST ▶ **loud**
LOUDISH *adj* fairly loud
LOUDLY ▶ **loud**
LOUED ▶ **lou**
LOUGH, -S *n* loch
LOUIE, -S *same as* ▶ **looey**
LOUING ▶ **lou**
LOUIS *n* former French gold coin
LOUMA, -S *n* market in developing countries
LOUN, -ED, -ING, -S *same as* ▶ **lown**
LOUND, -ED, -S *same as* ▶ **loun**
LOUNDER *vb* beat severely
LOUNDS ▶ **lound**
LOUNED ▶ **loun**
LOUNGE, -D, -S *n, vb*
LOUNGER *n* extending chair
LOUNGES ▶ **lounge**
LOUNGEY *adj* suggestive of a lounge bar or easy-listening music
LOUNGY *adj* casual; relaxed
LOUNING ▶ **loun**
LOUNS ▶ **loun**
LOUP, -ED, -EN, -ING, -IT, -S *Scot word for* ▶ **leap**
LOUPE, -S *n* magnifying glass used by jewellers, horologists, etc
LOUPED ▶ **loup**
LOUPEN ▶ **loup**
LOUPES ▶ **loupe**
LOUPING ▶ **loup**
LOUPIT ▶ **loup**
LOUPS ▶ **loup**
LOUR, -ED, -S *vb* be overcast ▷ *n* menacing scowl
LOURE, -S *n* slow, former French dance
LOURED ▶ **lour**
LOURES ▶ **loure**
LOURIE, -S *n* type of African bird
LOURIER ▶ **loury**
LOURIES ▶ **lourie**
LOURING ▶ **lour**
LOURS ▶ **lour**
LOURY, LOURIER *adj* sombre
LOUS ▶ **lou**
LOUSE, LICE, -D, -S *n, vb*
LOUSER, -S *n* mean nasty person
LOUSES ▶ **louse**
LOUSIER ▶ **lousy**
LOUSILY ▶ **lousy**
LOUSING *n* act or instance of removing lice
LOUSY, LOUSIER *adj*
LOUT, -ED, -ING, -S *n, vb*
LOUTERY *n* crude or boorish behaviour
LOUTING ▶ **lout**
LOUTISH *adj* of a lout
LOUTS ▶ **lout**
LOUVAR, -S *n* large silvery whalelike scombroid fish

LOUVER, -S *same as* ▶ **louvre**
LOUVRE, -S *n*
LOUVRED *adj* having louvres
LOUVRES ▶ **louvre**
LOVABLE *adj*
LOVABLY ▶ **lovable**
LOVAGE, -S *n* European plant used for flavouring food
LOVAT, -S *n* yellowish-or bluish-green mixture in tweeds
LOVE, -D, -S *vb, n*
LOVEBUG *n* small US flying insect
LOVED ▶ **love**
LOVELY *adj* very attractive ▷ *n* attractive woman
LOVER, -S *n* person who loves something or someone
LOVERED *adj* having a lover
LOVERLY *adj* like a lover
LOVERS ▶ **lover**
LOVES ▶ **love**
LOVEY, -S, LOVIER, LOVIEST *adj* loving; affectionate ▷ *n* affectionate person
LOVIE, -S *n* beloved person
LOVIER ▶ **lovey**
LOVIES ▶ **lovie**
LOVIEST ▶ **lovey**
LOVING, -S *adj* affectionate, tender ▷ *n* state of being in love
LOW, -ED, -EST, -S *adj, adv, n, vb*
LOWAN, -S *n* type of Australian bird
LOWBALL *vb* deliberately under-charge
LOWBORN *adj* of ignoble or common parentage
LOWBOY, -S *n* table fitted with drawers
LOWBRED *same as* ▶ **lowborn**
LOWBROW *adj, n*
LOWBUSH *n* type of blueberry bush
LOWDOWN *n*
LOWE, -S *variant of* ▶ **low**
LOWED ▶ **low**
LOWER, -ED, -S *adj* below one or more other things ▷ *vb* cause or allow to move down
LOWERY *adj* sombre
LOWES ▶ **lowe**
LOWEST ▶ **low**
LOWING, -S ▶ **low**
LOWISH ▶ **low**
LOWLAND *n, adj*
LOWLIER ▶ **lowly**
LOWLIFE *n*
LOWLILY ▶ **lowly**
LOWLY, LOWLIER *adj* modest, humble ▷ *adv* in a low or lowly manner
LOWN, -ED, -ING, -S *vb* calm
LOWND, -ED, -S *same as* ▶ **lown**
LOWNE, -S *same as* ▶ **loon**
LOWNED ▶ **lown**
LOWNES ▶ **lowne**
LOWNESS ▶ **low**
LOWNING ▶ **lown**
LOWNS ▶ **lown**
LOWP, -ED, -ING, -S *same as* ▶ **loup**
LOWPASS *adj* (of a filter) transmitting frequencies below a certain value
LOWPED ▶ **lowp**
LOWPING ▶ **lowp**
LOWPS ▶ **lowp**
LOWRIE *another name for* ▶ **lory**
LOWRY, LOWRIES *another name for* ▶ **lory**
LOWS ▶ **low**
LOWSE, -D, -R, -S, -ST, LOWSING *vb* release or loose ▷ *adj* loose
LOWSIT ▶ **lowse**
LOWT, -ED, -ING, -S *same as* ▶ **lout**
LOWVELD *n* low ground in S Africa
LOX, -ED, -ES, -ING *vb* load fuel tanks of spacecraft with liquid oxygen ▷ *n* kind of smoked salmon

A good word when you have an X to dispose of.

LOXYGEN *n* liquid oxygen
LOY, -S *n* narrow spade with a single footrest
LOYAL, -ER *adj* faithful
LOYALLY ▶ **loyal**
LOYALTY *n*
LOYS ▶ **loy**
LOZELL, -S *obsolete form of* ▶ **losel**
LOZEN, -S *n* window pane
LOZENGE *n*
LOZENGY *adj* divided by diagonal lines to form a lattice

LOZENS ▶ **lozen**
LUACH, LUCHOT, LUCHOTH *n* Jewish calendar
LUAU, -S *n* feast of Hawaiian food
LUBBARD *same as* ▶ **lubber**
LUBBER, -S *n* big, awkward, or stupid person
LUBE, -D, -S, LUBING *n* lubricating oil ▷ *vb* lubricate with oil
LUBFISH *n* type of fish
LUBING ▶ **lube**
LUBRIC *adj* slippery
LUCARNE *n* type of dormer window
LUCE, -S *another name for* ▶ **pike**
LUCENCE ▶ **lucent**
LUCENCY ▶ **lucent**
LUCENT *adj* brilliant
LUCERN, -S *same as* ▶ **lucerne**
LUCERNE *n* alfalfa
LUCERNS ▶ **lucern**
LUCES ▶ **luce**
LUCHOT ▶ **luach**
LUCHOTH ▶ **luach**
LUCID, -ER *adj*
LUCIDLY ▶ **lucid**
LUCIFER *n* friction match
LUCIGEN *n* type of lamp
LUCITE, -S *n* type of transparent acrylic-based plastic
LUCK, -ED, -ING, -S *n, vb*
LUCKEN *adj* shut
LUCKIE *same as* ▶ **lucky**
LUCKIER ▶ **lucky**
LUCKIES ▶ **lucky**
LUCKILY ▶ **lucky**
LUCKING ▶ **luck**
LUCKS ▶ **luck**
LUCKY, LUCKIER, LUCKIES *adj* having or bringing good luck ▷ *n* old woman
LUCRE, -S *n* money or wealth
LUCUMA, -S *n* S American tree
LUCUMO, -S *n* Etruscan king
LUD, -S *n* lord ▷ *interj* exclamation of dismay or surprise
LUDIC *adj* playful
LUDO, -S *n* game played with dice and counters on a board
LUDS ▶ **lud**
LUDSHIP ▶ **lud**
LUES *n* pestilence
LUETIC, -S ▶ **lues**
LUFF, -ED, -ING, -S *vb* sail (a ship) towards the wind ▷ *n* leading edge of a fore-and-aft sail
LUFFA, -S *same as* ▶ **loofah**
LUFFED ▶ **luff**
LUFFING ▶ **luff**
LUFFS ▶ **luff**
LUG, -GED, -GING, -S *vb, n*
LUGE, -D, -S *n* racing toboggan ▷ *vb* ride on a luge
LUGEING ▶ **luge**
LUGER, -S *n* pistol
LUGES ▶ **luge**
LUGGAGE *n*
LUGGED ▶ **lug**
LUGGER, -S *n* small working boat with an oblong sail
LUGGIE, -S *n* wooden bowl
LUGGING ▶ **lug**
LUGHOLE *informal word for* ▶ **ear**
LUGING, -S ▶ **luge**
LUGS ▶ **lug**
LUGSAIL *n* four-sided sail
LUGWORM *n* large worm used as bait
LUIT, -EN *Scots past form of* ▶ **let**
LUKE *variant of* ▶ **lukewarm**
LULIBUB *obsolete form of* ▶ **lollipop**
LULL, -ED, -ING, -S *vb, n*
LULLABY *n, vb*
LULLED ▶ **lull**
LULLER, -S ▶ **lull**
LULLING ▶ **lull**
LULLS ▶ **lull**
LULU, -S *n* person or thing deemed to be outstanding
LULZ *pl n* laughs at someone else's or one's own expense
LUM, -S *n* chimney
LUMA, -S *n* monetary unit of Armenia
LUMBAGO *n* pain in the lower back
LUMBANG *n* type of tree
LUMBAR, -S *adj* of the part of the body between the lowest ribs and the hipbones ▷ *n* old-fashioned kind of ship
LUMBER, -S *n, vb*
LUMBUS, LUMBI *n* part of the lower back and sides between the pelvis and the ribs

LUMEN, -S, LUMINA *n* derived SI unit of luminous flux
LUMENAL ▸ **lumen**
LUMENS ▸ **lumen**
LUMINA ▸ **lumen**
LUMINAL ▸ **lumen**
LUMINE, -D, -S *vb* illuminate
LUMME *interj* exclamation of surprise or dismay
LUMMIER ▸ **lummy**
LUMMOX *n* clumsy person
LUMMY, LUMMIER *interj* exclamation of surprise ▹ *adj* excellent
LUMP, -ED, -ING, -S *n, vb*
LUMPEN, -S *adj* stupid or unthinking ▹ *n* member of underclass
LUMPER, -S *n* stevedore
LUMPIA, -S *n* type of Indonesian spring roll
LUMPIER ▸ **lumpy**
LUMPILY ▸ **lumpy**
LUMPING ▸ **lump**
LUMPISH *adj* stupid or clumsy
LUMPKIN *n* lout
LUMPS ▸ **lump**
LUMPY, LUMPIER *adj* full of lumps
LUMS ▸ **lum**
LUN, -S *n* sheltered spot
LUNA, -S *n* large American moth
LUNACY *n*
LUNAR, -S *adj, n*
LUNARY *n* moonwort herb
LUNAS ▸ **luna**
LUNATE, -S *adj* shaped like a crescent ▹ *n* crescent-shaped bone forming part of the wrist
LUNATED *variant of* ▸ **lunate**
LUNATES ▸ **lunate**
LUNATIC *adj, n*
LUNCH, -ED, -ES *n, vb*
LUNCHER ▸ **lunch**
LUNCHES ▸ **lunch**
LUNE, -S *same as* ▸ **lunette**
LUNET, -S *n* small moon or satellite
LUNETTE *n* anything that is shaped like a crescent
LUNG, -S *n*
LUNGAN, -S *same as* ▸ **longan**
LUNGE, -D, -S, LUNGING *n* sudden forward motion ▹ *vb* move with or make a lunge
LUNGEE, -S *same as* ▸ **lungi**
LUNGER, -S ▸ **lunge**
LUNGES ▸ **lunge**
LUNGFUL ▸ **lung**
LUNGI, -S *n* cotton cloth worn as a loincloth, sash, or turban
LUNGIE, -S *n* guillemot
LUNGING ▸ **lunge**
LUNGIS ▸ **lungi**
LUNGS ▸ **lung**
LUNGYI, -S *same as* ▸ **lungi**
LUNIER ▸ **luny**
LUNIES ▸ **luny**
LUNIEST ▸ **luny**
LUNK, -S *n* awkward person
LUNKER, -S *n* very large fish
LUNKS ▸ **lunk**
LUNS ▸ **lun**
LUNT, -ED, -ING, -S *vb* produce smoke
LUNULA, -E *n* white area at base of the fingernail
LUNULAR *same as* > **lunulate**
LUNULE, -S *same as* ▸ **lunula**
LUNY, LUNIER, LUNIES, LUNIEST *same as* ▸ **loony**
LUNYIE, -S *same as* ▸ **lungie**
LUPIN, -S *n* garden plant
LUPINE, -S *adj* like a wolf ▹ *n* lupin
LUPINS ▸ **lupin**
LUPOID *adj* having lupus
LUPOUS *adj* relating to lupus
LUPPEN *Scots past form of* ▸ **leap**
LUPULIN *n* resinous powder extracted from the hop plant
LUPUS, -ES *n* ulcerous skin disease
LUR, -S *n* large bronze musical horn
LURCH, -ED, -ES *vb, n*
LURCHER *n* crossbred dog trained to hunt silently
LURCHES ▸ **lurch**
LURDAN, -S *n* stupid or dull person ▹ *adj* dull or stupid
LURDANE *same as* ▸ **lurdan**
LURDANS ▸ **lurdan**
LURDEN, -S *same as* ▸ **lurdan**

LURE, -D, -S, LURING *vb, n*
LURER, -S ▸ **lure**
LURES ▸ **lure**
LUREX, -ES *n* thin glittery thread
LURGI, -S *same as* ▸ **lurgy**
LURGIES ▸ **lurgy**
LURGIS ▸ **lurgi**
LURGY, LURGIES *n* any undetermined illness
LURID, -ER *adj*
LURIDLY ▸ **lurid**
LURING, -S ▸ **lure**
LURK, -ED, -S *vb*
LURKER, -S ▸ **lurk**
LURKING *adj* lingering
LURKS ▸ **lurk**
LURRY, LURRIES *n* confused jumble
LURS ▸ **lur**
LURVE, -S *n* love
LUSER, -S *n* humorous term for computer user
LUSH, -ED, -ES, -EST, -ING *adj, n, vb*
LUSHER, -S *adj* more lush ▹ *n* drunkard
LUSHES ▸ **lush**
LUSHEST ▸ **lush**
LUSHIER ▸ **lushy**
LUSHIES ▸ **lushy**
LUSHING ▸ **lush**
LUSHLY ▸ **lush**
LUSHY, LUSHIER, LUSHIES *adj* slightly intoxicated ▹ *n* drunkard
LUSK, -ED, -ING, -S *vb* lounge around
LUSKISH *adj* lazy
LUSKS ▸ **lusk**
LUST, -ED, -ING, -S *n, vb*
LUSTER, -S *same as* ▸ **lustre**
LUSTICK *obsolete word for* ▸ **lusty**
LUSTIER ▸ **lusty**
LUSTILY ▸ **lusty**
LUSTING ▸ **lust**
LUSTRA ▸ **lustrum**
LUSTRAL *adj* of or relating to a ceremony of purification
LUSTRE, -D, -S *n, vb*
LUSTRUM, LUSTRA *n* period of five years
LUSTS ▸ **lust**
LUSTY, LUSTIER *adj* vigorous, healthy
LUSUS, -ES *n* freak, mutant
LUTE, -D, -S *n, vb*
LUTEA *adj* yellow
LUTEAL *adj* relating to the development of the corpus luteum
LUTED ▸ **lute**
LUTEIN, -S *n* xanthophyll pigment
LUTEOUS *adj* of a greenish-yellow colour
LUTER, -S *n* lute player
LUTES ▸ **lute**
LUTEUM *adj* yellow
LUTFISK *same as* > **lutefisk**
LUTHERN *another name for* ▸ **dormer**
LUTHIER *n* lute-maker
LUTING, -S *n* cement and clay
LUTIST, -S *same as* > **lutenist**
LUTITE, -S *another name for* ▸ **pelite**
LUTTEN ▸ **loot**
LUTZ, -ES *n* skating jump
LUV, -S, -VED, -VING *n* love ▹ *vb* love
LUVVIE, -S *n* person who is involved in acting or the theatre
LUVVING ▸ **luv**
LUVVY *same as* ▸ **luvvie**
LUX, -ED, -ES, -ING *n* unit of illumination ▹ *vb* clean with a vacuum cleaner

One of the key words using X.

LUXATE, -D, -S *vb* put (a shoulder, knee, etc) out of joint
LUXE, -R, -ST *adj* luxurious
LUXED ▸ **lux**
LUXER ▸ **luxe**
LUXES ▸ **lux**
LUXEST ▸ **luxe**
LUXING ▸ **lux**
LUXURY *n, adj*
LUZ, -ZES *n* supposedly indestructible bone of the human body

This very unusual word is very useful for playing the Z.

LUZERN, -S *n* alfalfa
LUZZES ▸ **luz**
LWEI, -S *n* Angolan monetary unit
LYAM, -S *n* leash
LYARD *same as* ▸ **liard**
LYART *same as* ▸ **liard**
LYASE, -S *n* any enzyme that catalyses the separation of two parts of a molecule
LYCEA ▸ **lyceum**
LYCEE, -S *n* secondary school
LYCEUM, LYCEA, -S *n* public building for concerts
LYCH, -ES *same as* ▸ **lich**

LYCHEE, -S *same as* ▶ **litchi**
LYCHES ▶ **lych**
LYCHNIS *n* plant with red, pink, or white flowers
LYCOPOD *n* type of moss
LYCRA, -S *n*
LYDDITE *n* explosive consisting chiefly of fused picric acid
LYE, -S *n* caustic solution
LYFULL *obsolete form of* ▶ **lifeful**
LYING, -S ▶ **lie**
LYINGLY ▶ **lie**
LYINGS ▶ **lying**
LYM, -S *obsolete form of* ▶ **lyam**
LYME, -S *n* as in **lyme grass** type of perennial dune grass
LYMITER *same as* ▶ **limiter**
LYMPH *n* colourless bodily fluid
LYMPHAD *n* ancient rowing boat
LYMPHS ▶ **lymph**
LYMS ▶ **lym**
LYNAGE, -S *obsolete form of* ▶ **lineage**
LYNCEAN *adj* of a lynx
LYNCH, -ED, -ES *vb* put to death without a trial
LYNCHER ▶ **lynch**
LYNCHES ▶ **lynch**
LYNCHET *n* ridge formed by ploughing a hillside
LYNE, -S *n* flax
LYNX, -ES *n*
LYOPHIL *same as* > **lyophilic**
LYRA *n* as in **lyra viol** lutelike musical instrument
LYRATE *adj* shaped like a lyre
LYRATED *same as* ▶ **lyrate**
LYRE, -S *n* ancient musical instrument
LYRIC, -S *adj*, *n*
LYRICAL *same as* ▶ **lyric**
LYRICON *n* wind synthesizer
LYRICS ▶ **lyric**
LYRISM, -S *n* art or technique of playing the lyre
LYRIST, -S *same as* > **lyricist**
LYSATE, -S *n* material formed by lysis
LYSE, -D, LYSING *vb* undergo lysis
LYSES ▶ **lysis**
LYSIN, -S *n* group of antibodies that dissolve cells
LYSINE, -S *n* essential amino acid that occurs in proteins
LYSING ▶ **lyse**
LYSINS ▶ **lysin**
LYSIS, LYSES *n* destruction of cells by a lysin
LYSOGEN *n* lysis-inducing agent
LYSOL, -S *n* antiseptic solution
LYSSA, -S *less common word for* ▶ **rabies**
LYTE, -D, -S, LYTING *vb* dismount
LYTHE, -S *n* type of fish
LYTHRUM *n* genus of plants including loosestrife
LYTIC *adj* relating to, causing, or resulting from lysis
LYTING ▶ **lyte**
LYTTA, -E, -S *n* mass of cartilage under the tongue in carnivores

Mm

MA, -S *n* mother
MAA, -ED, -ING *vb* (of goats) bleat
MAAR, -E, -S *n* coneless volcanic crater
MAAS, -ES *n* thick soured milk
MAATJES *n* pickled herring
MABE, -S *n* type of pearl
MABELA, -S *n* ground sorghum
MABES ▸ **mabe**
MAC, -S *n* macintosh
MACA, -S *n* type of plant
MACABER *same as* ▸ **macabre**
MACABRE *adj*
MACACO, -S *n* type of lemur
MACADAM *n* type of road surface
MACAQUE *n* monkey of Asia and Africa
MACARON *n* small meringue cake
MACAS ▸ **maca**
MACAW, -S *n*
MACCHIA, MACCHIE *n* thicket in Italy
MACE, -D, -S, MACING *n, vb*
MACER, -S *n* macebearer, esp (in Scotland) an official who acts as usher in a court of law
MACERAL *n* any of the organic units that constitute coal
MACERS ▸ **macer**
MACES ▸ **mace**
MACH, -S *n* ratio of the speed of a body in a particular medium to the speed of sound in that medium
MACHACA *n* Mexican dish of shredded dried beef
MACHAIR *n* (in the western Highlands of Scotland) a strip of sandy, grassy land
MACHAN, -S *n* (in India) a raised platform used in tiger hunting
MACHE, -S *n* papier-mâché
MACHER, -S *n* important or influential person
MACHES ▸ **mache**
MACHETE *n*
MACHI *n* as in **machi chips** in Indian English, fish and chips
MACHINE *n, vb*
MACHO, -S *adj, n*
MACHREE *n* Irish form of address meaning my dear
MACHS ▸ **mach**
MACHZOR *n* Jewish prayer book
MACING ▸ **mace**
MACK, -S *same as* ▸ **mac**
MACKLE, -D, -S *n* blurred impression ▹ *vb* mend hurriedly or in a makeshift way
MACKS ▸ **mack**
MACLE, -S *n* crystal consisting of two parts
MACLED ▸ **macle**
MACLES ▸ **macle**
MACON, -S *n* wine from the Mâcon area
MACOYA, -S *n* South American tree
MACRAME *n* ornamental work of knotted cord
MACRAMI *same as* ▸ **macrame**
MACRO, -S *n* close-up lens
MACRON, -S *n* mark placed over a letter to represent a long vowel
MACROS ▸ **macro**
MACS ▸ **mac**
MACULA, -E, -S *n* small spot like a freckle
MACULAR ▸ **macula**
MACULAS ▸ **macula**
MACULE, -S *same as* ▸ **mackle**

MACULED ▸ **macule**
MACULES ▸ **macule**
MACUMBA *n* religious cult in Brazil
MAD, -DED, -DEST, -DING, -S *adj* mentally deranged ▹ *vb* make mad
MADAFU, -S *n* coconut milk
MADAM, -ED, -S *n* polite term of address for a woman ▹ *vb* call someone madam
MADAME, -S *n*
MADAMED ▸ **madam**
MADAMES ▸ **madame**
MADAMS ▸ **madam**
MADCAP, -S *adj, n*
MADDED ▸ **mad**
MADDEN, -S *vb*
MADDER, -S *n* type of rose
MADDEST ▸ **mad**
MADDING ▸ **mad**
MADDISH ▸ **mad**
MADDOCK *same as* ▸ **mattock**
MADE ▸ **make**
MADEFY *vb* make moist
MADEIRA *n*
MADGE, -S *n* type of hammer
MADID *adj* wet
MADISON *n* type of cycle relay race
MADLING *n* foolish person
MADLY *adv* with great speed and energy
MADMAN, MADMEN *n*
MADNESS *n*
MADONNA *n*
MADOQUA *n* Ethiopian antelope
MADRAS *n*
MADRASA *same as* > **madrasah**
MADRE, -S *Spanish word for* ▸ **mother**
MADRONA *n* N American evergreen tree or shrub
MADRONE *same as* ▸ **madrona**
MADRONO *same as* ▸ **madrona**
MADS ▸ **mad**
MADTOM, -S *n* species of catfish
MADURO, -S *adj* (of cigars) dark and strong ▹ *n* cigar of this type
MADWORT *n* low-growing Eurasian plant with small blue flowers
MADZOON *same as* ▸ **matzoon**
MAE, -S *adj* more
MAELID, -S *n* mythical spirit of apple tree
MAENAD, -S *n* female disciple of Dionysus
MAERL, -S *n* type of red coralline algae
MAES ▸ **mae**
MAESTRO, MAESTRI *n*
MAFFIA, -S *same as* ▸ **mafia**
MAFFICK *vb* celebrate extravagantly and publicly
MAFFLED *adj* baffled
MAFFLIN *n* half-witted person
MAFIA, -S *n*
MAFIC, -S *n* minerals present in igneous rock
MAFIOSO, MAFIOSI *n* member of the Mafia
MAFTED *adj* suffering under oppressive heat
MAFTIR, -S *n* final section of the weekly Torah reading
MAG, -GED, -GING, -S *vb* talk ▹ *n* talk
MAGALOG *same as* > **magalogue**
MAGE, -S *archaic word for* > **magician**
MAGENTA *adj, n*
MAGES ▸ **mage**
MAGG, -S *same as* ▸ **mag**
MAGGED ▸ **mag**
MAGGIE, -S *n* magpie
MAGGING ▸ **mag**
MAGGOT, -S *n*
MAGGOTY *adj* relating to, resembling, or ridden with maggots
MAGGS ▸ **magg**
MAGI ▸ **magus**
MAGIAN, -S ▸ **magus**
MAGIC, -S *n, vb, adj*
MAGICAL ▸ **magic**
MAGICS ▸ **magic**
MAGILP, -S *same as* ▸ **megilp**
MAGISM, -S ▸ **magus**
MAGLEV, -S *n* type of high-speed train
MAGMA, -S, -TA *n* molten rock inside the earth's crust
MAGNATE *n* influential or wealthy person, esp in industry
MAGNES *n* magnetic iron ore
MAGNET, -S *n*
MAGNETO *n* apparatus for ignition in an internal-combustion engine
MAGNETS ▸ **magnet**

MAGNIFY *vb*
MAGNON, -S *n* short for Cro-Magnon
MAGNOX *n* alloy used in fuel elements of some nuclear reactors
MAGNUM, -S *n*
MAGNUS *adj* as in **magnus hitch** knot similar to a clove hitch but having one more turn
MAGOT, -S *n* Chinese or Japanese figurine in a crouching position, usually grotesque
MAGPIE, -S *n*
MAGS ▸ **mag**
MAGSMAN, MAGSMEN *n* raconteur
MAGUEY, -S *n* tropical American agave plant
MAGUS, MAGI *n* Zoroastrian priest of the ancient Medes and Persians
MAGYAR *adj* of or relating to a style of sleeve
MAHA *n* as in **maha yoga** form of yoga
MAHANT, -S *n* chief priest in a Hindu temple
MAHATMA *n*
MAHEWU, -S *n* (in South Africa) fermented liquid meal porridge
MAHJONG *n* game of Chinese origin, using tiles
MAHMAL, -S *n* litter used in Muslim ceremony
MAHOE, -S *n* New Zealand tree
MAHONIA *n* Asian and American evergreen shrub
MAHOUT, -S *n* (in India) elephant driver or keeper
MAHSEER *n* large freshwater Indian fish
MAHSIR, -S *same as* ▸ **mahseer**
MAHUA, -S *n* Indian tree
MAHUANG *n* herbal medicine from shrub
MAHUAS ▸ **mahua**
MAHWA, -S *same as* ▸ **mahua**
MAHZOR, -S *same as* ▸ **machzor**
MAID, -ED, -ING, -S *n*, *vb*
MAIDAN, -S *n* (in Pakistan, India, etc) open area
MAIDED ▸ **maid**
MAIDEN, -S *n*, *adj*
MAIDING ▸ **maid**
MAIDISH ▸ **maid**
MAIDISM *n* pellagra
MAIDS ▸ **maid**
MAIGRE, -S *adj* not containing meat ▹ *n* species of fish
MAIHEM, -S *same as* ▸ **mayhem**
MAIK, -S *n* old halfpenny
MAIKO, -S *n* apprentice geisha
MAIKS ▸ **maik**
MAIL, -ED, -ING, -S *n*, *vb*
MAILBAG *n*
MAILBOX *n*
MAILCAR *same as* > **mailcoach**
MAILE, -S *n* halfpenny
MAILED ▸ **mail**
MAILER, -S *n* person who addresses or mails letters, etc
MAILES ▸ **maile**
MAILING ▸ **mail**
MAILL, -S *n* Scots word meaning rent
MAILLOT *n* tights worn for ballet, gymnastics, etc
MAILLS ▸ **maill**
MAILMAN, MAILMEN *n*
MAILS ▸ **mail**
MAILVAN *n*
MAIM, -ED, -S *vb*, *n*
MAIMER, -S ▸ **maim**
MAIMING ▸ **maim**
MAIMS ▸ **maim**
MAIN, -ED, -ER, -EST, -ING, -S *adj* chief or principal ▹ *n* principal pipe or line carrying water, gas, or electricity ▹ *vb* lower sails
MAINLY *adv* for the most part, chiefly
MAINOR, -S *n* act of doing something
MAINOUR *same as* ▸ **mainor**
MAINS ▸ **main**
MAINTOP *n* top or platform at the head of the mainmast
MAIR, -S *Scots form of* ▸ **more**
MAIRE, -S *n* New Zealand tree
MAIRS ▸ **mair**
MAISE, -S *n* measure of herring
MAIST, -S *Scot word for* ▸ **most**
MAISTER *Scots word for* ▸ **master**

MAISTRY ▸ **maister**
MAISTS ▸ **maist**
MAIZE, -S *n*
MAJAGUA *same as* ▸ **mahoe**
MAJESTY *n*
MAJLIS *n* (in Arab countries) an assembly
MAJOR, -ED, -S *adj, n, vb*
MAJORAT *n* estate, the right to which is that of the first born child of a family
MAJORED ▸ **major**
MAJORLY *adv* very
MAJORS ▸ **major**
MAK, -S *Scot word for* ▸ **make**
MAKABLE ▸ **make**
MAKAR, -S *same as* ▸ **maker**
MAKE, MADE, -S, MAKING *vb, n*
MAKER, -S *n* person or company that makes something
MAKES ▸ **make**
MAKEUP, -S *n*
MAKHANI *n* Indian dish made with butter or ghee ▹ *adj* denoting such a dish
MAKI, -S *n* in Japanese cuisine, rice and other ingredients wrapped in a short seaweed roll
MAKING ▸ **make**
MAKINGS *pl n* potentials, qualities, or materials
MAKIS ▸ **maki**
MAKO, -S *n* powerful shark of the Atlantic and Pacific Oceans
MAKS ▸ **mak**
MAKUTA *plural of* ▸ **likuta**
MAKUTU, -S *n* Polynesian witchcraft ▹ *vb* cast a spell on
MAL, -S *n* illness
MALA, -S *n* string of beads or knots, used in praying and meditating
MALACCA *n* stem of the rattan palm
MALACIA *n* softening of an organ or tissue
MALADY *n* disease or illness
MALAISE *n*
MALAM, -S *same as* ▸ **mallam**
MALANGA *same as* ▸ **cocoyam**
MALAR, -S *n* cheekbone ▹ *adj* of or relating to the cheek or cheekbone
MALARIA *n*
MALARKY *same as* > **malarkey**
MALARS ▸ **malar**
MALAS ▸ **mala**
MALATE, -S *n* any salt or ester of malic acid
MALAX, -ED, -ES *vb* soften
MALE, -S *adj, n*
MALEATE *n* any salt or ester of maleic acid
MALEFIC *adj* causing evil
MALEIC *adj* as in **maleic acid** colourless soluble crystalline substance
MALES ▸ **male**
MALFED *adj* having malfunctioned
MALGRE, -D, -S *same as* ▸ **maugre**
MALI, -S *n* member of an Indian caste
MALIBU *n* as in **malibu board** lightweight surfboard
MALIC *adj* as in **malic acid** colourless crystalline compound occurring in apples
MALICE, -D, -S *n, vb*
MALICHO *n* mischief
MALIGN, -S *vb, adj*
MALIK, -S *n* person of authority in India
MALINE, -S *n* stiff net
MALIS ▸ **mali**
MALISM, -S *n* belief that evil dominates world
MALISON *archaic or poetic word for* ▸ **curse**
MALIST ▸ **malism**
MALKIN, -S *archaic or dialect name for a* ▸ **cat**
MALL, -ED, -S *n* street or shopping area closed to vehicles ▹ *vb* maul
MALLAM, -S *n* (in W Africa) expert in the Koran
MALLARD *n*
MALLED ▸ **mall**
MALLEE, -S *n* low-growing eucalypt in dry regions
MALLEI ▸ **malleus**
MALLET, -S *n*
MALLEUS, MALLEI *n* small bone in the middle ear
MALLING ▸ **mall**
MALLOW, -S *n*
MALLS ▸ **mall**
MALM, -S *n* soft greyish limestone that crumbles easily

MALMAG, -S *n* Asian monkey
MALMIER ▸ **malmy**
MALMS ▸ **malm**
MALMSEY *n* sweet Madeira wine
MALMY, MALMIER *adj* looking like malm
MALODOR *same as* > **malodour**
MALONIC *adj* as in **malonic acid** colourless crystalline compound
MALOTI *plural of* ▸ **loti**
MALS ▸ **mal**
MALT, -S *n, vb*
MALTASE *n* enzyme that hydrolyses maltose to glucose
MALTED, -S *n* malted milk drink
MALTESE *adj* as in **maltese cross** cross-shaped part of a film projector
MALTHA, -S *n* any of various naturally occurring mixtures of hydrocarbons
MALTIER ▸ **malty**
MALTING *n* building in which malt is made or stored
MALTMAN, MALTMEN *same as* > **maltster**
MALTOL, -S *n* food additive
MALTOSE *n*
MALTS ▸ **malt**
MALTY, MALTIER *adj* of, like, or containing malt
MALUS, -ES *n* financial penalty incurred by an investor
MALVA, -S *n* mallow plant
MALWA, -S *n* Ugandan drink brewed from millet
MALWARE *n*
MALWAS ▸ **malwa**
MAM, -S *same as* ▸ **mother**
MAMA, -S *n*
MAMAGUY *vb* deceive or tease ▹ *n* deception or flattery
MAMAKAU *same as* ▸ **mamaku**
MAMAKO, -S *same as* ▸ **mamaku**
MAMAKU, -S *n* tall edible New Zealand tree fern
MAMAS ▸ **mama**
MAMASAN *n* (in Japan) woman in a position of authority
MAMBA, -S *n*
MAMBO, -ED, -ES, -S *n, vb*
MAMEE, -S *same as* ▸ **mamey**
MAMELON *n* small rounded hillock
MAMEY, -ES, -S *n* tropical tree
MAMIE, -S *n* tropical tree
MAMILLA *n* nipple or teat
MAMLUK, -S *same as* > **mameluke**
MAMMA, -E, -S *n* buxom and voluptuous woman
MAMMAL, -S *n*
MAMMARY *adj, n*
MAMMAS ▸ **mamma**
MAMMATE *adj* having breasts
MAMMATI > **mammatus**
MAMMEE, -S *same as* ▸ **mamey**
MAMMER, -S *vb* hesitate
MAMMET, -S *same as* ▸ **maumet**
MAMMEY, -S *same as* ▸ **mamey**
MAMMIE *same as* ▸ **mammy**
MAMMIES ▸ **mammy**
MAMMOCK *n* fragment ▹ *vb* tear or shred
MAMMON, -S *n* wealth regarded as a source of evil
MAMMOTH *n, adj*
MAMMY, MAMMIES *same as* ▸ **mother**
MAMPARA *n* foolish person, idiot
MAMPOER *n* home-distilled brandy
MAMS ▸ **mam**
MAN, -D, -NED, -NING, -S, MEN *n, vb*
MANA, -S *n* authority, influence
MANACLE *vb, n*
MANAGE, -D, -S *vb*
MANAGER *n* person in charge of a business, institution, actor, sports team, etc
MANAGES ▸ **manage**
MANAIA, -S *n* figure in Māori carving
MANAKIN *same as* ▸ **manikin**
MANANA, -S *n* tomorrow ▹ *adv* tomorrow
MANAS ▸ **mana**

MANAT, -S *n* standard monetary unit of Azerbaijan
MANATEE *n* large tropical plant-eating aquatic mammal
MANATI, -S *same as* ▸ **manatee**
MANATS ▸ **manat**
MANATU, -S *n* large flowering deciduous New Zealand tree
MANAWA, -S *in New Zealand, same as* > **mangrove**
MANBAG, -S *n*
MANBAND *n* boy band whose members have reached maturity
MANCALA *n* African and Asian board game
MANCHE, -S *n* long sleeve
MANCHET *n* type of bread
MANCUS *n* former English coin
MAND ▸ **man**
MANDALA *n* circular design symbolizing the universe
MANDATE *n, vb*
MANDI, -S *n* (in India) a big market
MANDIOC *same as* ▸ **manioc**
MANDIR, -S *n* Hindu or Jain temple
MANDIRA *same as* ▸ **mandir**
MANDIRS ▸ **mandir**
MANDIS ▸ **mandi**
MANDOLA *n* early type of mandolin
MANDOM, -S *n* mankind
MANDORA *n* ancestor of mandolin
MANDREL *n* shaft on which work is held in a lathe
MANDRIL *same as* ▸ **mandrel**
MANE *n*
MANEB, -S *n* powdered fungicide
MANED ▸ **mane**
MANEGE, -D, -S *n* art of training horses and riders ▹ *vb* train horse
MANEH, -S *same as* ▸ **mina**
MANENT ▸ **manet**
MANES *pl n* spirits of the dead, often revered as minor deities
MANET, MANENT *vb* theatre direction, remain on stage
MANFUL *adj*
MANG, -ED, -ING, -S *vb* speak
MANGA, -S *n* type of Japanese comic book
MANGABY *same as* > **mangabey**
MANGAL, -S *n* Turkish brazier
MANGAS ▸ **manga**
MANGE, -S *n*
MANGEAO *n* small New Zealand tree with glossy leaves
MANGED ▸ **mang**
MANGEL, -S *n* Eurasian variety of the beet plant
MANGER, -S *n*
MANGES ▸ **mange**
MANGEY *same as* ▸ **mangy**
MANGIER ▸ **mangy**
MANGILY ▸ **mangy**
MANGING ▸ **mang**
MANGLE, -D, -S *vb, n*
MANGLER ▸ **mangle**
MANGLES ▸ **mangle**
MANGO, -ES, -S *n*
MANGOLD *n* type of root vegetable
MANGOS ▸ **mango**
MANGS ▸ **mang**
MANGY, MANGIER *adj*
MANHOLE *n*
MANHOOD *n*
MANHUNT *n*
MANI *n* place to pray
MANIA, -S *n*
MANIAC, -S *n*
MANIAS ▸ **mania**
MANIC, -S *adj, n*
MANIES ▸ **many**
MANIHOC *variation of* ▸ **manioc**
MANIHOT *n* tropical American plant
MANIKIN *n* little man or dwarf
MANILA, -S *n*
MANILLA *n* early currency in W Africa in the form of a small bracelet
MANILLE *n* (in ombre and quadrille) the second best trump
MANIOC, -S *same as* ▸ **cassava**
MANIOCA *same as* ▸ **manioc**
MANIOCS ▸ **manioc**
MANIPLE *n* (in ancient Rome) a unit of 120 to 200 foot soldiers
MANIS, -ES *n* pangolin
MANITO, -S *same as* ▸ **manitou**

MANITOU *n* Native American deified spirit or force
MANITU, -S *same as* ▶ **manitou**
MANJACK *n* single individual
MANKIER ▶ **manky**
MANKIND *n*
MANKINI *n* man's revealing swimming costume
MANKY, MANKIER *adj* worthless, rotten, or in bad taste
MANLESS ▶ **man**
MANLIER ▶ **manly**
MANLIKE *adj* resembling or befitting a man
MANLILY ▶ **manly**
MANLY, MANLIER *adj* (possessing qualities) appropriate to a man
MANMADE *adj*
MANNA, -S *n* miraculous food which sustained the Israelites in the wilderness
MANNAN, -S *n* drug derived from mannose
MANNAS ▶ **manna**
MANNED ▶ **man**
MANNER *n*
MANNERS *pl n* person's social conduct
MANNING ▶ **man**
MANNISH *adj* like a man
MANNITE *same as* > **mannitol**
MANNOSE *n* hexose sugar
MANO, -ES, -S *n* stone for grinding grain
MANOAO, -S *n* New Zealand shrub
MANOES ▶ **mano**
MANOR, -S *n*
MANOS ▶ **mano**
MANPACK *n* load carried by one person
MANQUE, -S *adj* would-be ▷ *n* section on a roulette table
MANRED, -S *n* homage
MANRENT *same as* ▶ **manred**
MANROPE *n* rope railing
MANS ▶ **man**
MANSARD *n* type of sloping roof
MANSE, -S *n* house provided for a minister in some religious denominations
MANSION *n*
MANTA, -S *n* type of large ray with very wide winglike pectoral fins
MANTEAU *n* cloak or mantle
MANTEEL *n* cloak
MANTEL, -S *n* structure round a fireplace ▷ *vb* construct a mantel
MANTES ▶ **mantis**
MANTIC *adj* of or relating to divination and prophecy
MANTID, -S *same as* ▶ **mantis**
MANTIES ▶ **manty**
MANTIS, MANTES *n*
MANTLE, -D, -S *same as* ▶ **mantel**
MANTLET *same as* > **mantelet**
MANTO, -ES, -S *same as* ▶ **manteau**
MANTRA, -S *n*
MANTRAM *same as* ▶ **mantra**
MANTRAP *n*
MANTRAS ▶ **mantra**
MANTRIC ▶ **mantra**
MANTUA, -S *n* loose gown of the 17th and 18th centuries
MANTY, MANTIES *Scots variant of* ▶ **mantua**
MANUAL, -S *adj, n*
MANUARY *same as* ▶ **manual**
MANUKA, -S *n* New Zealand tree
MANUL, -S *n* Asian wildcat
MANUMEA *n* pigeon of Samoa
MANUMIT *vb* free from slavery
MANURE, -D, -S *n, vb*
MANURER ▶ **manure**
MANURES ▶ **manure**
MANUS *n* wrist and hand
MANWARD *adv* towards humankind
MANWISE *adv* in a human way
MANY, MANIES *adj* numerous ▷ *n* large number
MANYATA *same as* > **manyatta**
MAOMAO, -S *n* fish of New Zealand seas
MAORMOR *same as* ▶ **mormaor**
MAP, -PED, -S *n, vb*
MAPAU, -S *n* small New Zealand tree
MAPLE, -S *n*
MAPLESS ▶ **map**
MAPLIKE ▶ **map**
MAPPED ▶ **map**

MAPPER, -S ▸ **map**
MAPPERY *n* making of maps
MAPPING ▸ **map**
MAPPIST ▸ **map**
MAPS ▸ **map**
MAPWISE *adv* like map
MAQUI *n* Chilean shrub
MAQUILA *n* US-owned factory in Mexico
MAQUIS *n* French underground movement in World War II
MAR, -D, -RED, -RING, -S *vb* spoil or impair ▹ *n* disfiguring mark
MARA, -S *n* harelike S American rodent
MARABI, -S *n* kind of music popular in S African townships in the 1930s
MARABOU *n* large black-and-white African stork
MARACA, -S *n* shaken percussion instrument
MARAE, -S *n* enclosed space in front of a Māori meeting house
MARAH, -S *n* bitterness
MARAKA ▸ **marka**
MARANTA *n* tropical American plant
MARARI, -S *n* eel-like blennioid food fish
MARAS ▸ **mara**
MARASCA *n* European cherry tree with red acid-tasting fruit
MARAUD, -S *vb* wander or raid in search of plunder
MARBLE, -D *n*, *vb*
MARBLER ▸ **marble**
MARBLES *n* game in which marble balls are rolled at one another
MARBLY ▸ **marble**
MARC, -S *n* remains of grapes or other fruit that have been pressed for wine-making
MARCATO *adj* (of notes) heavily accented ▹ *adv* with each note heavily accented ▹ *n* heavily accented note
MARCEL, -S *n* hairstyle characterized by repeated regular waves ▹ *vb* make such waves in (the hair)
MARCH, -ED, -ES *vb*, *n*
MARCHEN *n* German story
MARCHER *n* person who marches
MARCHES ▸ **march**
MARCONI *vb* communicate by wireless
MARCS ▸ **marc**
MARD ▸ **mar**
MARDY, MARDIED, MARDIER, MARDIES *adj* (of a child) spoilt ▹ *vb* behave in mardy way
MARE, -S, MARIA *n*
MAREMMA, MAREMME *n* marshy unhealthy region near the shore, esp in Italy
MARENGO *adj* browned in oil and cooked with tomatoes, mushrooms, garlic, wine, etc
MARERO, -S *n* member of a C American organized criminal gang
MARES ▸ **mare**
MARG, -S *short for* ▸ **margarine**
MARGATE *n* greyish fish of W Atlantic
MARGAY, -S *n* feline mammal of Central and S America
MARGE, -S *n* margarine
MARGENT *same as* ▸ **margin**
MARGES ▸ **marge**
MARGIN, -S *n*, *vb*
MARGOSA *n* Indian tree
MARGS ▸ **marg**
MARIA ▸ **mare**
MARID, -S *n* spirit in Muslim mythology
MARIES ▸ **mary**
MARIMBA *n* Latin American percussion instrument
MARINA, -S *n*
MARINE, -S *adj*, *n*
MARINER *n* sailor
MARINES ▸ **marine**
MARISH *n* marsh
MARITAL *adj*
MARK, -S *n*, *vb*
MARKA, MARAKA, -S *n* unit of currency introduced as an interim currency in Bosnia-Herzegovina
MARKED *adj* noticeable
MARKER, -S *n* object used to show the position of something
MARKET, -S *n*, *vb*
MARKHOR *n* large wild Himalayan goat
MARKING *n* arrangement of

colours on an animal or plant
MARKKA, -A, -S *n* former standard monetary unit of Finland
MARKMAN, MARKMEN *n* person owning land
MARKS ▸ **mark**
MARKUP, -S *n*
MARL, -ED, -S *n* soil formed of clay and lime, used as fertilizer ▹ *vb* fertilize (land) with marl
MARLE, -S *same as* ▸ **marvel**
MARLED ▸ **marl**
MARLES ▸ **marle**
MARLIER ▸ **marly**
MARLIN, -S *same as* ▸ **marline**
MARLINE *n* light rope, usually tarred, made of two strands laid left-handed
MARLING *same as* ▸ **marline**
MARLINS ▸ **marlin**
MARLITE *n* type of marl that contains clay and calcium carbonate
MARLS ▸ **marl**
MARLY, MARLIER *adj* marl-like
MARM, -S *same as* ▸ **madam**
MARMEM *n* as in **marmem alloy** type of alloy
MARMITE *n*
MARMOSE *n* South American opossum
MARMOT, -S *n* burrowing rodent
MARMS ▸ **marm**
MARON, -S *n* freshwater crustacean
MAROON, -S *adj, vb, n*
MAROR, -S *n* Jewish ceremonial dish of bitter herbs
MARPLOT *n* person who spoils a plot
MARQUE, -S *n* brand of product, esp of a car
MARQUEE *n*
MARQUES ▸ **marque**
MARQUIS *n*
MARRA, -S *n* (in N England) friend
MARRAM, -S *n* as in **marram grass** any of several grasses that grow on sandy shores
MARRANO *n* Spanish or Portuguese Jew of the late Middle Ages who was converted to Christianity
MARRAS ▸ **marra**
MARRED ▸ **mar**
MARRELS *same as* ▸ **merils**
MARRER, -S ▸ **mar**
MARRI, -S *n* W Australian eucalyptus
MARRIED ▸ **marry**
MARRIER ▸ **marry**
MARRIES ▸ **marry**
MARRING ▸ **mar**
MARRIS ▸ **marri**
MARRON, -S *n* large edible sweet chestnut
MARROW, -S *n, vb*
MARROWY *adj* full of marrow
MARRUM, -S *same as* ▸ **marram**
MARRY, MARRIED, MARRIES *vb, interj*
MARS ▸ **mar**
MARSALA *n* dark sweet dessert wine made in Sicily
MARSE, -S *same as* ▸ **master**
MARSH, -ES *n*
MARSHAL *n, vb*
MARSHED *adj* having a marsh
MARSHES ▸ **marsh**
MARSHY *adj* of, involving, or like a marsh
MART, -ED, -ING, -S *n* market ▹ *vb* sell or trade
MARTEL, -S *n* hammer-shaped weapon ▹ *vb* use such a weapon
MARTEN, -S *n* weasel-like animal
MARTEXT *n* preacher who makes many mistakes
MARTIAL *adj*
MARTIAN *n*
MARTIN, -S *n* bird with a slightly forked tail
MARTING ▸ **mart**
MARTINI *n* cocktail of vermouth and gin
MARTINS ▸ **martin**
MARTLET *n* footless bird often found in coats of arms
MARTS ▸ **mart**
MARTYR, -S *n, vb*
MARTYRY *n* shrine or chapel erected in honour of a martyr
MARVEL, -S *vb, n*
MARVER, -S *vb* roll molten glass on slab

MARVY, MARVIER *shortened form of* > **marvelous**
MARY, MARIES *n* woman
MARYBUD *n* bud of marigold
MAS ▶ **ma**
MASA, -S *n* Mexican maize dough
MASALA, -S *n* mixture of spices ground into a paste ▷ *adj* spicy
MASAS ▶ **masa**
MASCARA *n*
MASCLE, -S *n* charge consisting of a lozenge with a lozenge-shaped hole in the middle
MASCLED ▶ **mascle**
MASCLES ▶ **mascle**
MASCON, -S *n* any of several lunar regions of high gravity
MASCOT, -S *n*
MASCULY ▶ **mascle**
MASE, -D, -S, MASING *vb* function as maser
MASER, -S *n* device for amplifying microwaves
MASES ▶ **mase**
MASH, -ED, -ES *n, vb*
MASHER, -S ▶ **mash**
MASHES ▶ **mash**
MASHIE, -S *n* former golf club, used for approach shots
MASHIER ▶ **mashy**
MASHIES ▶ **mashie**
MASHING ▶ **mash**
MASHLAM *same as* ▶ **maslin**
MASHLIM *same as* ▶ **maslin**
MASHLIN *same as* ▶ **maslin**
MASHLUM *same as* ▶ **maslin**
MASHMAN, MASHMEN *n* brewery worker
MASHUA, -S *n* South American plant
MASHUP, -S *n* piece of music in which a producer or DJ blends together two or more tracks
MASHY, MASHIER *adj* like mash
MASING ▶ **mase**
MASJID, -S *same as* ▶ **mosque**
MASK, -S *n, vb*
MASKED *adj* disguised or covered by or as if by a mask
MASKEG, -S *n* North American bog
MASKER, -S *n* person who wears a mask or takes part in a masque
MASKING *n* act or practice of masking
MASKS ▶ **mask**
MASLIN, -S *n* mixture of wheat, rye or other grain
MASON, -ED, -S *n* person who works with stone ▷ *vb* construct or strengthen with masonry
MASONIC *adj*
MASONRY *n* stonework
MASONS ▶ **mason**
MASQUE, -S *n*
MASQUER *same as* ▶ **masker**
MASQUES ▶ **masque**
MASS, -ING *n, adj, vb*
MASSA, -S *old fashioned variant of* ▶ **master**
MASSAGE *n, vb*
MASSAS ▶ **massa**
MASSE *n* billiard stroke that makes the ball move in a curve around another ball
MASSED ▶ **mass**
MASSES *pl n* body of common people
MASSEUR *n*
MASSIER ▶ **massy**
MASSIF, -S *n* connected group of mountains
MASSING ▶ **mass**
MASSIVE *adj, n*
MASSY, MASSIER *literary word for* ▶ **massive**
MAST, -ED, -ING, -S *n, vb*
MASTABA *n* mud-brick superstructure above tombs in ancient Egypt
MASTED ▶ **mast**
MASTER, -S *n, vb*
MASTERY *n* expertise
MASTFUL ▶ **mast**
MASTIC, -S *n* gum obtained from certain trees
MASTICH *same as* ▶ **mastic**
MASTICS ▶ **mastic**
MASTIER ▶ **masty**
MASTIFF *n* large dog
MASTING ▶ **mast**
MASTIX *n* type of gum
MASTOID *n* projection of the bone behind the ear ▷ *adj* shaped like a nipple or breast
MASTS ▶ **mast**
MASTY, MASTIER ▶ **mast**

MASU, -S *n* Japanese salmon
MASULA, -S *same as* > **masoolah**
MASUS ▸ **masu**
MAT, -S, -TED *n, vb, adj*
MATADOR *n*
MATAI, -S *n* New Zealand tree, the wood of which is used for timber for building
MATATA, -S *same as* > **fernbird**
MATATU, -S *n* type of shared taxi used in Kenya
MATCH, -ED, -ES *n, vb*
MATCHA, -S *n* Japanese green tea
MATCHED ▸ **match**
MATCHER ▸ **match**
MATCHES ▸ **match**
MATCHET *same as* ▸ **machete**
MATCHUP *n*
MATE, -D, -S *n, vb*
MATELOT *n* sailor
MATER, -S, MATRES *n*
MATES ▸ **mate**
MATEY, -S, MATIER, MATIES, MATIEST *adj, n*
MATH *same as* ▸ **maths**
MATHS *n*
MATICO, -S *n* Peruvian shrub
MATIER ▸ **matey**
MATIES ▸ **matey**
MATIEST ▸ **matey**
MATILDA *n* bushman's swag
MATILY ▸ **matey**
MATIN *adj* of or relating to matins
MATINAL *same as* ▸ **matin**
MATINEE *n*
MATING, -S ▸ **mate**
MATINS *pl n* early morning church service
MATIPO, -S *n* New Zealand shrub
MATJES *same as* ▸ **maatjes**
MATLESS ▸ **mat**
MATLO, -S *same as* ▸ **matelot**
MATLOW, -S *same as* ▸ **matelot**
MATOKE, -S *n* (in Uganda) the flesh of bananas, boiled and mashed as a food
MATOOKE *same as* ▸ **matoke**
MATRASS *n* long-necked glass flask
MATRES ▸ **mater**
MATRIC, -S *n* matriculation
MATRICE *same as* ▸ **matrix**
MATRICS ▸ **matric**
MATRIX *n*
MATRON, -S *n*
MATROSS *n* gunner's assistant
MATS ▸ **mat**
MATSAH, -S *same as* ▸ **matzo**
MATSURI *n* Japanese religious ceremony
MATT, -S *adj, n*
MATTE, -S *same as* ▸ **matt**
MATTED ▸ **mat**
MATTER, -S *n, vb*
MATTERY *adj* containing pus
MATTES ▸ **matte**
MATTIE, -S *n* young herring
MATTIFY *vb* make (the skin of the face) less oily or shiny using cosmetics
MATTIN *same as* ▸ **matin**
MATTING ▸ **mat**
MATTINS *same as* ▸ **matins**
MATTOCK *n* large pick with one of its blade ends flattened for loosening soil
MATTOID *n* person displaying eccentric behaviour
MATTS ▸ **matt**
MATURE, -D, -S *adj, vb*
MATURER ▸ **mature**
MATURES ▸ **mature**
MATWEED *n* grass found on moors
MATY *same as* ▸ **matey**
MATZA, -S *same as* ▸ **matzo**
MATZAH, -S *same as* ▸ **matzo**
MATZAS ▸ **matza**
MATZO, -S, -T *n* large very thin biscuit of unleavened bread
MATZOH, -S, MATZOTH *same as* ▸ **matzo**
MATZOON *n* fermented milk product similar to yogurt
MATZOS ▸ **matzo**
MATZOT ▸ **matzo**
MATZOTH ▸ **matzoh**
MAUBY, MAUBIES *n* Caribbean bittersweet drink
MAUD, -S *n* shawl or rug of grey wool plaid
MAUDLIN *adj*
MAUDS ▸ **maud**

MAUGER *same as* ▸ **maugre**
MAUGRE, -D, -S *prep* in spite of ▹ *vb* behave spitefully towards
MAUL, -ED, -S *vb, n*
MAULER ▸ **maul**
MAULERS *pl n* hands
MAULGRE *same as* ▸ **maugre**
MAULING *n* act of mauling
MAULS ▸ **maul**
MAULVI, -S *n* expert in Islamic law
MAUMET, -S *n* false god
MAUN *dialect word for* ▸ **must**
MAUND, -ED, -S *n* unit of weight used in Asia ▹ *vb* beg
MAUNDER *vb*
MAUNDS ▸ **maund**
MAUNDY *n* ceremonial washing of the feet of poor people
MAUNGY *adj* (esp of a child) sulky, bad-tempered, or peevish
MAUNNA *vb* Scots term meaning must not
MAURI, -S *n* soul
MAUSY, MAUSIER *adj* foggy; misty
MAUT, -S *same as* ▸ **mahout**
MAUTHER *n* girl or young woman
MAUTS ▸ **maut**
MAUVAIS *adj* bad
MAUVE, -R, -S, -ST *adj, n*
MAUVEIN *same as* > **mauveine**
MAUVER ▸ **mauve**
MAUVES ▸ **mauve**
MAUVEST ▸ **mauve**
MAUVIN, -S *same as* > **mauveine**
MAUVINE *same as* > **mauveine**
MAUVINS ▸ **mauvin**
MAUZY, MAUZIER *adj* foggy; misty
MAVEN, -S *n* expert or connoisseur
MAVIE, -S *n* type of thrush
MAVIN, -S *same as* ▸ **maven**
MAVIS, -ES *n* song thrush
MAW, -ED, -ING, -S *n* animal's mouth, throat, or stomach ▹ *vb* eat or bite
MAWGER *adj* (of persons or animals) thin or lean
MAWING ▸ **maw**
MAWK, -S *n* maggot
MAWKIER ▸ **mawky**
MAWKISH *adj*
MAWKS ▸ **mawk**
MAWKY, MAWKIER ▸ **mawk**
MAWMET, -S *same as* ▸ **maumet**
MAWN, -S *n* measure of capacity
MAWPUS *same as* ▸ **mopus**
MAWR, -S *same as* ▸ **mauther**
MAWS ▸ **maw**
MAWSEED *n* poppy seed
MAWTHER *same as* ▸ **mauther**
MAX, -ED, -ES, -ING *vb* reach the full extent

Max is a short form of **maximum**, and can also be a verb giving **maxed, maxes** and **maxing**. Another of the key words using X, and it can be extended to **maxi**.

MAXI, -S *adj* (of a garment) very long ▹ *n* type of large racing yacht
MAXILLA *n* upper jawbone of a vertebrate
MAXIM, -S *n*
MAXIMA ▸ **maximum**
MAXIMAL *adj* maximum ▹ *n* maximum
MAXIMIN *n* highest of a set of minimum values
MAXIMS ▸ **maxim**
MAXIMUM, MAXIMA *n, adj*
MAXIMUS *n* method rung on twelve bells
MAXING ▸ **max**
MAXIS ▸ **maxi**
MAXIXE, -S *n* Brazilian dance in duple time
MAXWELL *n* cgs unit of magnetic flux
MAY, -ED, -ING, -S, MIGHTST, MOUGHT *vb* used as an auxiliary to express possibility, permission, opportunity, etc ▹ *vb* gather may (hawthorn)
MAYA, -S *n* illusion, esp the material world of the senses regarded as illusory
MAYAN ▸ **maya**

MAYAS ▸ **maya**
MAYBE, -S *adv, sentence substitute, n*
MAYBIRD *n* American songbird
MAYBUSH *n* flowering shrub
MAYDAY, -S *n*
MAYED ▸ **may**
MAYEST *same as* ▸ **mayst**
MAYFISH *n* type of N American fish
MAYFLY *n*
MAYHAP *archaic word for* ▸ **perhaps**
MAYHEM, -S *n*
MAYING, -S ▸ **may**
MAYO, -S *n* mayonnaise
MAYOR, -S *n*
MAYORAL ▸ **mayor**
MAYORS ▸ **mayor**
MAYOS ▸ **mayo**
MAYPOLE *n*
MAYPOP, -S *n* American wild flower
MAYS ▸ **may**
MAYST *singular form of the present tense of* ▸ **may**
MAYSTER *same as* ▸ **master**
MAYVIN, -S *same as* ▸ **maven**
MAYWEED *n* widespread Eurasian weedy plant
MAZARD, -S *same as* ▸ **mazer**
MAZE, -D, -S, MAZING *n*
MAZEDLY *adv* in a bewildered way
MAZEFUL ▸ **maze**
MAZER, -S *n* large hardwood drinking bowl
MAZES ▸ **maze**
MAZEY *adj* dizzy
MAZHBI, -S *n* low-caste Sikh
MAZIER ▸ **mazy**
MAZIEST ▸ **mazy**
MAZILY ▸ **mazy**
MAZING ▸ **maze**
MAZOUT, -S *same as* ▸ **mazut**
MAZUMA, -S *n* money
MAZURKA *n* lively Polish dance
MAZUT, -S *n* residue left after distillation of petrol
MAZY, MAZIER, MAZIEST *adj* of or like a maze
MAZZARD *same as* ▸ **mazard**
MBIRA, -S *n* African musical instrument
ME, -S *n* (in tonic sol-fa) third degree of any major scale ▹ *pron* refers to the speaker or writer
MEACOCK *n* timid person
MEAD, -S *n*
MEADOW, -S *n*
MEADOWY *adj* consisting of meadows
MEADS ▸ **mead**
MEAGER *same as* ▸ **meagre**
MEAGRE, -R, -S *adj, n*
MEAL, -ED, -ING, -S *n, vb*
MEALER, -S *n* person eating but not lodging at boarding house
MEALIE, -S *n* maize
MEALIER ▸ **mealy**
MEALIES ▸ **mealie**
MEALING ▸ **meal**
MEALS ▸ **meal**
MEALY, MEALIER *adj* resembling meal
MEAN, -EST, -S, -T *vb, adj, n*
MEANDER *vb, n*
MEANE, -D, -S *vb* moan
MEANER, -S ▸ **mean**
MEANES ▸ **meane**
MEANEST ▸ **mean**
MEANIE, -S *n* unkind or miserly person
MEANING *n* what something means
MEANLY ▸ **mean**
MEANS ▸ **mean**
MEANT ▸ **mean**
MEANY *same as* ▸ **meanie**
MEARE, -S *same as* ▸ **mere**
MEARING *adj* forming boundary
MEASE, -D, -S, MEASING *vb* assuage
MEASLE *vb* infect with measles
MEASLED *adj* (of cattle, sheep, or pigs) infested with tapeworm larvae
MEASLES *n*
MEASLY *adj* meagre
MEASURE *n, vb*
MEAT, -S *n*
MEATAL ▸ **meatus**
MEATAXE *n* meat cleaver
MEATED *adj* fattened
MEATH, -S *same as* ▸ **mead**
MEATHE, -S *same as* ▸ **mead**
MEATHS ▸ **meath**
MEATIER ▸ **meaty**
MEATILY ▸ **meaty**

MEATMAN, MEATMEN *n* meat seller
MEATS ▸ **meat**
MEATUS *n* natural opening or channel
MEATY, MEATIER *adj* (tasting) of or like meat
MEAWES *same as* ▸ **mews**
MEAZEL, -S *same as* ▸ **mesel**
MEBOS, -ES *n* South African dish of dried apricots
MECCA, -S *n*
MECH, -S *n* mechanic
MECHOUI *n* Canadian dish of meat roasted on a spit
MECHS ▸ **mech**
MECK, -S *same as* ▸ **maik**
MECONIC *adj* derived from poppies
MECONIN *n* substance found in opium
MED, -S *n* doctor
MEDACCA *n* Japanese freshwater fish
MEDAKA, -S *same as* ▸ **medacca**
MEDAL, -ED, -S *n, vb*
MEDALET *n* small medal
MEDALS ▸ **medal**
MEDDLE, -D, -S *vb*
MEDDLER ▸ **meddle**
MEDDLES ▸ **meddle**
MEDEVAC *n* evacuation of casualties ▹ *vb* transport (a wounded or sick person) to hospital
MEDFLY *n* Mediterranean fruit fly
MEDIA, -E, -S *n*
MEDIACY *n* quality or state of being mediate
MEDIAD *adj* situated near the median line or plane of an organism
MEDIAE ▸ **media**
MEDIAL, -S *adj* of or in the middle ▹ *n* speech sound between being fortis and lenis
MEDIAN, -S *n, adj*
MEDIANT *n* third degree of a major or minor scale
MEDIAS ▸ **media**
MEDIATE *vb* intervene in a dispute to bring about agreement ▹ *adj* occurring as a result of or dependent upon mediation
MEDIC, -S *n*
MEDICAL *adj, n*
MEDICK, -S *n* type of small leguminous plant with yellow or purple flowers
MEDICO, -S *n* doctor or medical student
MEDICS ▸ **medic**
MEDIGAP *n* private health insurance
MEDII ▸ **medius**
MEDINA, -S *n* ancient quarter of North African city
MEDIUM *adj, n*
MEDIUMS *pl n* medium-dated gilt-edged securities
MEDIUS, MEDII *n* middle finger
MEDIVAC *variant spelling of* ▸ **medevac**
MEDLAR, -S *n* apple-like fruit of a small tree
MEDLE, -D, -S, MEDLING *same as* ▸ **meddle**
MEDLEY, -S *n* miscellaneous mixture ▹ *adj* of, being, or relating to a mixture or variety
MEDLING ▸ **medle**
MEDRESA *same as* > **madrasah**
MEDRESE *same as* > **madrasah**
MEDS ▸ **med**
MEDULLA *n* marrow, pith, or inner tissue
MEDUSA, -E, -S *n* jellyfish
MEDUSAL ▸ **medusa**
MEDUSAN ▸ **medusa**
MEDUSAS ▸ **medusa**
MEE, -S *n* Malaysian noodle dish
MEED, -S *n* recompense
MEEK, -ER, -EST *adj*
MEEKEN, -S *vb* make meek
MEEKER ▸ **meek**
MEEKEST ▸ **meek**
MEEKLY ▸ **meek**
MEEMIE, -S *n* attack of hysteria
MEER, -ED, -ING, -S *same as* ▸ **mere**
MEERCAT *same as* ▸ **meerkat**
MEERED ▸ **meer**
MEERING ▸ **meer**
MEERKAT *n* S African mongoose
MEERS ▸ **meer**
MEES ▸ **mee**
MEET, -EST, -S *vb* come together (with) ▹ *n* meeting, esp a sports meeting ▹ *adj* fit or suitable

MEETER, -S ▸ **meet**
MEETEST ▸ **meet**
MEETING ▸ **meet**
MEETLY ▸ **meet**
MEETS ▸ **meet**
MEFF, -S *dialect word for* ▸ **tramp**
MEG, -S *short for* > **megabyte**
MEGA *adj* extremely good, great, or successful
MEGABAR *n* unit of million bars
MEGABIT *n*
MEGAFOG *n* amplified fog signal
MEGAHIT *n* great success
MEGAPOD *same as* > **megapode**
MEGARA ▸ **megaron**
MEGARAD *n* unit of million rads
MEGARON, MEGARA *n* tripartite rectangular room, found in Bronze Age Greece and Asia Minor
MEGASS *another name for* ▸ **bagasse**
MEGASSE *same as* ▸ **megass**
MEGATON *n*
MEGILLA *same as* > **megillah**
MEGILP, -S *n* oil-painting medium of linseed oil mixed with mastic varnish or turpentine
MEGILPH *same as* ▸ **megilp**
MEGILPS ▸ **megilp**
MEGOHM, -S *n* one million ohms
MEGRIM *n* caprice
MEGRIMS *n* period of low spirits
MEGS ▸ **meg**
MEH *interj* expression of indifference or boredom
MEHNDI, -S *n* (esp in India) the practice of painting designs on the hands, feet, etc using henna
MEIKLE *adj* Scots word meaning large
MEIN, -ED, -ING, -S *Scots word for* ▸ **moan**
MEINEY, -S *same as* ▸ **meiny**
MEINIE *same as* ▸ **meiny**
MEINIES ▸ **meiny**
MEINING ▸ **mein**
MEINS ▸ **mein**
MEINT *same as* ▸ **ming**
MEINY, MEINIES *n* retinue or household
MEIOSIS, MEIOSES *n* type of cell division
MEIOTIC ▸ **meiosis**
MEISHI, -S *n* business card in Japan
MEISTER *n* person who excels at a particular activity
MEITH, -S *n* landmark
MEJLIS *same as* ▸ **majlis**
MEKKA, -S *same as* ▸ **mecca**
MEL, -S *n* pure form of honey
MELA, -S *n* Indian cultural or religious fair or festival
MELAENA *n* medical condition
MELAMED *n* Hebrew teacher
MELANGE *n* mixture
MELANIC *adj* relating to melanism or melanosis ▹ *n* darker form of creature
MELANIN *n* dark pigment found in the hair, skin, and eyes
MELANO, -S *n* person with extremely dark skin
MELAS ▸ **mela**
MELBA *adj* relating to a type of dessert sauce or toast
MELD, -ED, -ING, -S *vb, n*
MELDER, -S ▸ **meld**
MELDING ▸ **meld**
MELDS ▸ **meld**
MELEE, -S *n* noisy confused fight or crowd
MELENA, -S *n* excrement stained by blood
MELIC, -S *adj* (of poetry, esp ancient Greek lyric poems) intended to be sung ▹ *n* type of grass
MELICK, -S *n* either of two pale green perennial grasses
MELICS ▸ **melic**
MELIK, -S *same as* ▸ **malik**
MELILOT *n* plant with small white or yellow fragrant flowers
MELISMA *n* expressive vocal phrase or passage consisting of several notes sung to one syllable
MELL, -ED, -ING, -S *vb* mix

MELLAY, -S *same as* ▶ **melee**
MELLED ▶ **mell**
MELLING ▶ **mell**
MELLITE *n* soft yellow mineral
MELLOW, -S *adj, vb*
MELLOWY *adj* mellow
MELLS ▶ **mell**
MELODIA *same as* ▶ **melodica**
MELODIC *adj* of melody
MELODY *n*
MELOID, -S *n* type of long-legged beetle
MELON, -S *n*
MELONY *adj* like a melon
MELS ▶ **mel**
MELT, -ED, -S, MOLTEN *vb, n*
MELTAGE *n* process or result of melting or the amount melted
MELTED ▶ **melt**
MELTEMI *n* northerly wind in the northeast Mediterranean
MELTER, -S ▶ **melt**
MELTIER ▶ **melty**
MELTING ▶ **melt**
MELTITH *n* meal
MELTON, -S *n* heavy smooth woollen fabric with a short nap, used esp for overcoats
MELTS ▶ **melt**
MELTY, MELTIER *adj* tending to melt
MEM, -S *n* 13th letter in the Hebrew alphabet, transliterated as *m*
MEMBER, -S *n, adj*
MEMBRAL *adj* of limbs
MEME, -S *n* idea or element of social behaviour
MEMENTO *n*
MEMES ▶ **meme**
MEMETIC *adj* of or relating to a meme
MEMO, -S *n*
MEMOIR *n*
MEMOIRS *pl n* collection of reminiscences about a period or series of events
MEMORY *n*
MEMOS ▶ **memo**
MEMS ▶ **mem**
MEN ▶ **man**
MENACE, -D, -S *n, vb*
MENACER ▶ **menace**
MENACES ▶ **menace**
MENAD, -S *same as* ▶ **maenad**
MENAGE, -D, -S *old form of* ▶ **manage**
MENAZON *n* type of insecticide
MEND, -ED, -S *vb, n*
MENDER, -S ▶ **mend**
MENDIGO *n* Spanish beggar or vagrant
MENDING *n* something to be mended, esp clothes
MENDS ▶ **mend**
MENE, -D, -S, MENING *Scots form of* ▶ **moan**
MENEER, -S *n* S African title of address
MENES ▶ **mene**
MENFOLK *pl n*
MENG, -ED, -ING, -S *vb* mix
MENGE, -S *same as* ▶ **meng**
MENGED ▶ **meng**
MENGES ▶ **menge**
MENGING ▶ **meng**
MENGS ▶ **meng**
MENHIR, -S *n* single upright prehistoric stone
MENIAL, -S *adj, n*
MENING ▶ **mene**
MENINX *n* one of three membranes that envelop the brain and spinal cord
MENISCI ▶ **meniscus**
MENO *adv* musical instruction indicating 'less'
MENORAH *n* seven-branched candelabrum used as an emblem of Judaism
MENSA, -S *n* faint constellation in the S hemisphere
MENSAE *n* star of the mensa constellation
MENSAL *adj* monthly
MENSAS ▶ **mensa**
MENSCH *n* decent person
MENSCHY *adj* decent
MENSE, -D, MENSING *vb* grace
MENSES *n* menstruation
MENSH, -ED, -ES *vb* mention
MENSHEN *n* Chinese door god
MENSHES ▶ **mensh**
MENSING ▶ **mense**
MENSUAL *same as* ▶ **mensal**
MENT *same as* ▶ **ming**
MENTA ▶ **mentum**
MENTAL *adj*
MENTEE, -S *n* person trained by mentor
MENTHOL *n* organic compound found in peppermint

MENTION *vb, n*
MENTO, -S *n* Jamaican song
MENTOR, -S *n* adviser or guide ▷ *vb* act as a mentor to (someone)
MENTOS ▸ **mento**
MENTUM, MENTA *n* chin
MENU, -S *n* list of dishes to be served, or from which to order
MENUDO, -S *n* Mexican soup
MENUS ▸ **menu**
MENYIE, -S *same as* ▸ **meinie**
MEOU, -ED, -ING, -S *same as* ▸ **meow**
MEOW, -ED, -ING, -S *vb, interj*
MERANTI *n* wood from any of several Malaysian trees
MERC, -ES, -S *n* mercenary
MERCADO *n* market
MERCAT, -S *Scots word for* ▸ **market**
MERCER, -S *n* dealer in textile fabrics and fine cloth
MERCERY ▸ **mercer**
MERCES ▸ **merc**
MERCH, -ES *n* merchandise
MERCHET *n* type of fine paid by feudal tenant to his lord
MERCIES ▸ **mercy**
MERCIFY *vb* show mercy to
MERCS ▸ **merc**
MERCURY *n*
MERCY, MERCIES *n*
MERDE, -S *French word for* > **excrement**
MERE, -R, -S, -ST, MERING *adj* nothing more than ▷ *n* lake ▷ *vb* old form of survey
MERED *adj* forming a boundary
MEREL, -S *same as* ▸ **meril**
MERELL *same as* ▸ **meril**
MERELLS *same as* ▸ **merils**
MERELS ▸ **merel**
MERELY *adv* only
MERER ▸ **mere**
MERES ▸ **mere**
MEREST ▸ **mere**
MERFOLK *n* mermaids and mermen
MERGE, -D, -S *vb*
MERGEE, -S *n* business taken over by merger
MERGER, -S *n* combination of business firms into one
MERGES ▸ **merge**
MERGING ▸ **merge**
MERGUEZ *n* heavily spiced N African sausage
MERI, -S *n* Māori war club
MERIL *n* counter used in merils
MERILS *n* old board game
MERING, -S ▸ **mere**
MERINO, -S *n* breed of sheep with fine soft wool
MERIS ▸ **meri**
MERISIS, MERISES *n* growth by division of cells
MERISM, -S *n* duplication of biological parts
MERIT, -ED, -S *n* excellence or worth ▷ *vb* deserve
MERK, -S *n* old Scots coin
MERL, -S *same as* ▸ **merle**
MERLE, -S *adj* (of a dog, esp a collie) having a bluish-grey coat with speckles or streaks of black ▷ *n* dog with this coat
MERLIN, -S *n*
MERLING *n* whiting
MERLINS ▸ **merlin**
MERLON, -S *n* solid upright section in a crenellated battlement
MERLOT, -S *n* type of black grape
MERLS ▸ **merl**
MERMAID *n*
MERMAN, MERMEN *n* male counterpart of the mermaid
MEROME, -S *same as* > **merosome**
MERONYM *n* part of something used to refer to the whole
MEROPIA *n* partial blindness
MEROPIC ▸ **meropia**
MERRIE *adj* (archaic) merry
MERRIER ▸ **merry**
MERRIES ▸ **merry**
MERRILY ▸ **merry**
MERRY, MERRIER, MERRIES *adj, n*
MERSE, -S *n* low level ground by a river or shore
MERSION *n* dipping in water

MES ▸ **me**
MESA, -S *n* flat-topped hill found in arid regions
MESAIL, -S *n* visor
MESAL *same as* ▸ **mesial**
MESALLY ▸ **mesal**
MESARCH *adj* having the first-formed xylem surrounded by that formed later
MESAS ▸ **mesa**
MESCAL, -S *n* spineless globe-shaped cactus
MESCLUM *same as* ▸ **mesclun**
MESCLUN *n* type of green salad
MESE, -S *n* middle string on lyre
MESEEMS *vb* it seems to me
MESEL, -S *n* archaic word for a person with leprosy
MESELED *adj* archaic word meaning having leprosy
MESELS ▸ **mesel**
MESES ▸ **mese**
MESETA, -S *n* plateau in Spain
MESH, -ED, -ES *n, vb, adj*
MESHIER ▸ **meshy**
MESHING ▸ **mesh**
MESHUGA *n* crazy person
MESHY, MESHIER ▸ **mesh**
MESIAD *adj* relating to or situated at the middle or centre
MESIAL *another word for* ▸ **medial**
MESIAN *same as* ▸ **mesial**
MESIC ▸ **meson**
MESNE, -S *adj* (in law) intermediate or intervening
MESON, -S *n* elementary atomic particle
MESONIC ▸ **meson**
MESONS ▸ **meson**
MESPIL, -S *n* type of N American tree
MESQUIN *adj* mean
MESQUIT *same as* > **mesquite**
MESS, -ED, -ES, -ING *n, vb*
MESSAGE *n, vb*
MESSAN, -S *Scots word for* ▸ **dog**
MESSED ▸ **mess**
MESSES ▸ **mess**
MESSIAH *n*
MESSIAS *same as* ▸ **messiah**
MESSIER ▸ **messy**
MESSILY ▸ **messy**
MESSING ▸ **mess**
MESSMAN, MESSMEN *n* sailor working in ship's mess
MESSY, MESSIER *adj* dirty, confused, or untidy
MESTER, -S *n* master: used as a term of address for a man who is the head of a house
MESTESO *n* Spanish music genre
MESTO *adj* sad
MESTOM, -S *same as* ▸ **mestome**
MESTOME *n* conducting tissue associated with parenchyma
MESTOMS ▸ **mestom**
MET, -S *n* meteorology
META *adj* in a self-parodying style
METAGE, -S *n* official measuring of weight or contents
METAL, -ED, -S *n, adj, vb*
METALLY *adj* like metal
METALS ▸ **metal**
METAMER *n* any of two or more isomeric compounds exhibiting metamerism
METATAG *n* element of HTML code used by search engines to index pages
METATE, -S *n* stone for grinding grain on
METAYER *n* farmer who pays rent in kind
METAZOA > **metazoan**
METCAST *n* weather forecast
METE, -D, -S, METING *vb* deal out as punishment ▹ *n* measure
METEOR, -S *n*
METEPA, -S *n* type of pesticide
METER, -ED, -S *same as* ▸ **metre**
METES ▸ **mete**
METH *n* methylated spirits
METHANE *n*
METHINK *same as* > **methinks**
METHO, -S *n* methylated spirits
METHOD, -S *n*
METHOS ▸ **metho**
METHOXY *n* steroid drug

METHS *n* methylated spirits
METHYL, -S *n* compound containing a saturated hydrocarbon group of atoms
METIC, -S *n* (in ancient Greece) alien having some rights of citizenship
METICA, -S *n* former proposed monetary unit of Mozambique
METICAL *n* money unit in Mozambique
METICAS ▸ **metica**
METICS ▸ **metic**
METIER, -S *n* profession or trade
METIF, -S *n* person of mixed ancestry
METING ▸ **mete**
METIS *n* person of mixed ancestry
METISSE ▸ **metis**
METOL, -S *n* organic substance used as a photographic developer
METONYM *n* word used in a metonymy
METOPE, METOPAE, -S *n* square space between two triglyphs in a Doric frieze
METOPIC *adj* of or relating to the forehead
METOPON *n* painkilling drug
METRE, -D, -S, METRING *n, vb*
METRIC *adj*
METRICS *n* art of using poetic metre
METRIFY *vb* render into poetic metre
METRING ▸ **metre**
METRIST *n* person skilled in the use of poetic metre
METRO, -S *n*
METS ▸ **met**
METTLE, -S *n*
METTLED *adj* spirited, courageous, or valiant
METTLES ▸ **mettle**
METUMP, -S *n* band for carrying a load or burden
MEU, -S *another name for* ▸ **spignel**
MEUSE, -D, -S, MEUSING *n* gap through which an animal passed ▹ *vb* go through this gap
MEVE, -D, -S, MEVING *same as* ▸ **move**
MEVROU, -S *n* S African title of address
MEW, -ED, -ING *n* cry of a cat ▹ *vb* utter this cry
MEWL, -ED, -ING, -S *vb, n*
MEWLER, -S ▸ **mewl**
MEWLING ▸ **mewl**
MEWLS ▸ **mewl**
MEWS, -ED, -ES, -ING *same as* ▸ **meuse**
MEYNT ▸ **ming**
MEZAIL, -S *same as* ▸ **mesail**
MEZCAL, -S *variant spelling of* ▸ **mescal**
MEZE, -S *n* type of hors d'oeuvre
MEZQUIT *same as* > **mesquite**

A **mezquit** is a kind of American tree, and makes a great bonus to play. Remember also that it takes an E to form the variant spelling **mezquite**.

MEZUZA, -S *same as* ▸ **mezuzah**
MEZUZAH, MEZUZOT *n* piece of parchment inscribed with biblical passages
MEZUZAS ▸ **mezuza**
MEZUZOT ▸ **mezuzah**
MEZZ *same as* > **mezzanine**
MEZZE, -S *same as* ▸ **meze**
MEZZO, -S *adv* moderately ▹ *n* singer with voice between soprano and contralto
MGANGA, -S *n* witch doctor
MHO, -S *former name for* ▸ **siemens**
MHORR, -S *n* African gazelle
MHOS ▸ **mho**
MI, -S *n* (in tonic sol-fa) the third degree of any major scale
MIAOU, -ED, -S *same as* ▸ **meow**
MIAOW, -ED, -S *same as* ▸ **meow**
MIASM, -S *same as* ▸ **miasma**
MIASMA, -S *n*
MIASMAL ▸ **miasma**
MIASMAS ▸ **miasma**
MIASMIC ▸ **miasma**
MIASMS ▸ **miasm**
MIAUL, -ED, -S *same as* ▸ **meow**

MIB, -S *n* marble used in games
MIBUNA, -S *n* type of Japanese leafy vegetable
MIC, -S *n* microphone
MICA, -S *n* glasslike mineral used as an electrical insulator
MICATE, -D, -S *vb* add mica to
MICE ▸ **mouse**
MICELL, -S *same as* ▸ **micelle**
MICELLA *same as* ▸ **micelle**
MICELLE *n* charged aggregate of molecules of colloidal size in a solution
MICELLS ▸ **micell**
MICH, -ED, -ES *same as* ▸ **mitch**
MICHAEL *n* as in **take the michael** teasing
MICHE *same as* ▸ **mich**
MICHED ▸ **mich**
MICHER, -S ▸ **mich**
MICHES ▸ **mich**
MICHING ▸ **mich**
MICHT, -S *n* Scots word for might
MICKERY *n* waterhole, esp in a dry riverbed
MICKEY, -S *n* young bull ▹ *vb* drug a person's drink
MICKIES ▸ **micky**
MICKLE, -R, -S *adj* large or abundant ▹ *adv* much ▹ *n* great amount
MICKY, MICKIES *same as* ▸ **mickey**
MICO, -S *n* marmoset
MICRA ▸ **micron**
MICRIFY *vb* make very small
MICRO, -S *n*
MICROBE *n*
MICROHM *n* millionth of an ohm
MICRON, MICRA, -S *n* unit of length equal to one millionth of a metre
MICROS ▸ **micro**
MICS ▸ **mic**
MICTION *n* urination
MID, -S *adj* intermediate, middle ▹ *n* middle ▹ *prep* amid
MIDAIR, -S *n*
MIDBAND *adj* using a range of frequencies between narrowband and broadband
MIDCALF *n* garment reaching to middle of the calf
MIDCAP *adj* (of investments) involving medium-sized amounts of capital
MIDCULT *n* middlebrow culture
MIDDAY, -S *n*
MIDDEN, -S *n*
MIDDEST *adj* in middle
MIDDIE *same as* ▸ **middy**
MIDDIES ▸ **middy**
MIDDLE, -D, -S *adj, n, vb*
MIDDLER *n* pupil in middle years at school
MIDDLES ▸ **middle**
MIDDY, MIDDIES *n* middle-sized glass of beer
MIDGE, -S *n*
MIDGET, -S *n, adj*
MIDGIE, -S *n* informal word for a midge
MIDGIER ▸ **midgy**
MIDGIES ▸ **midgie**
MIDGUT, -S *n* middle part of the digestive tract
MIDGY, MIDGIER *adj* characterized by midges
MIDI, -S *adj* (of a skirt, coat, etc) reaching to below the knee or midcalf ▹ *n* skirt, coat, etc reaching to below the knee or midcalf
MIDIBUS *n* medium-sized bus
MIDIRON *n* golf club used for medium-length approach shots
MIDIS ▸ **midi**
MIDLAND *n*
MIDLEG, -S *n* middle of leg
MIDLIFE *n*
MIDLINE *n* line at middle of something
MIDLIST *n* books in publisher's range that sell reasonably well
MIDMOST *adv* in the middle or midst ▹ *n* the middle or midst
MIDNOON *n* noon
MIDPAY *adj* paying more than an unskilled job but less than a high-income one
MIDRASH *n* homily on a Jewish scriptural passage
MIDRIB, -S *n* main vein of a leaf
MIDRIFF *n*
MIDS ▸ **mid**

MIDSHIP *adj* in, of, or relating to the middle of a vessel ▷ *n* middle of a vessel
MIDSIZE *adj* medium-sized
MIDSOLE *n* layer between the inner and the outer sole of a shoe
MIDST, -S *n* middle
MIDTERM *n*
MIDTOWN *n* centre of a town
MIDWAY, -S *adv, adj, n*
MIDWEEK *n*
MIDWIFE *n, vb*
MIDWIVE *vb* act as midwife
MIDYEAR *n* middle of the year
MIELIE, -S *same as* ▸ **mealie**
MIEN, -S *n* person's bearing, demeanour, or appearance
MIEVE, -D, -S, MIEVING *same as* ▸ **move**
MIFF, -ED, -ING, -S *vb, n*
MIFFIER ▸ **miffy**
MIFFILY ▸ **miffy**
MIFFING ▸ **miff**
MIFFS ▸ **miff**
MIFFY, MIFFIER *adj* easily upset
MIFTY *same as* ▸ **miffy**
MIG, -S *n* marble used in games
MIGAWD *interj* interjection used to express surprise
MIGG, -S *same as* ▸ **mig**
MIGGLE, -S *n* US word for playing marble
MIGGS ▸ **migg**
MIGHT, -S *n* physical strength
MIGHTST ▸ **may**
MIGHTY *adj* powerful ▷ *adv* very
MIGNON, -S *adj* small and pretty ▷ *n* tender boneless cut of meat
MIGRANT *n, adj*
MIGRATE *vb*
MIGS ▸ **mig**
MIHA, -S *n* young fern frond which has not yet opened
MIHI, -ED, -ING, -S *n* Māori ceremonial greeting ▷ *vb* greet
MIHRAB, -S *n* niche in a mosque showing the direction of Mecca
MIKADO, -S *n* Japanese emperor
MIKE, -D, -S, MIKING *n* microphone ▷ *vb* supply with a microphone
MIKRON, MIKRA, -S *same as* ▸ **micron**
MIKVA, -S *n* place for ritual bathing by Orthodox Jews
MIKVAH, -S, MIKVOTH *n* pool used for ritual purification
MIKVAS ▸ **mikva**
MIKVEH, -S, MIKVOS, MIKVOT *same as* ▸ **mikvah**
MIKVOTH ▸ **mikvah**
MIL, -S *n* unit of length equal to one thousandth of an inch
MILADI, -S *same as* ▸ **milady**
MILADY *n* (formerly) a continental title for an English gentlewoman
MILAGE, -S *same as* ▸ **mileage**
MILCH *adj* (of a cow) giving milk
MILCHIG *same as* ▸ **milchik**
MILCHIK *adj* containing or used in the preparation of milk products
MILD, -ED, -ER, -EST, -ING, -S *adj, n, vb*
MILDEN, -S *vb* make or become mild or milder
MILDER ▸ **mild**
MILDEST ▸ **mild**
MILDEW, -S *same as* ▸ **mould**
MILDEWY *adj* covered with mildew
MILDING ▸ **mild**
MILDISH *adj* rather mild
MILDLY ▸ **mild**
MILDS ▸ **mild**
MILE, -S *n*
MILEAGE *n* distance travelled in miles
MILER, -S *n* athlete, horse, etc, that specializes in races of one mile
MILES ▸ **mile**
MILFOIL *same as* ▸ **yarrow**
MILIA ▸ **milium**
MILIARY *adj* resembling or relating to millet seeds
MILIEU, -S, -X *n* environment or surroundings
MILING, -S *n* activity of running one mile
MILITAR *same as* ▸ **military**
MILITIA *n* military force of trained citizens
MILIUM, MILIA *n* pimple

MILK, -ED, -ING, -S *n, vb*
MILKEN *adj* of or like milk
MILKER, -S *n* cow, goat, etc, that yields milk
MILKIER ▸ **milky**
MILKILY ▸ **milky**
MILKING ▸ **milk**
MILKMAN, MILKMEN *n*
MILKO, -S *informal name for* ▸ **milkman**
MILKS ▸ **milk**
MILKSOP *n* feeble man
MILKY, MILKIER *adj* of or like milk
MILL, -S *n, vb*
MILLAGE *adj* American tax rate calculated in thousandths per dollar
MILLDAM *n* dam built to raise the water level to turn a millwheel
MILLE, -S *French word for* > **thousand**
MILLED *adj* crushed or ground in a mill
MILLER, -S *n*
MILLES ▸ **mille**
MILLET, -S *n* type of cereal grass
MILLIE, -S *n* insulting name for a young working-class woman
MILLIER *n* metric weight of million grams
MILLIES ▸ **millie**
MILLIME *same as* > **millieme**
MILLINE *n* measurement of advertising space
MILLING *n* act or process of grinding, cutting, pressing, or crushing in a mill
MILLION *n* one thousand thousands
MILLRUN *same as* > **millrace**
MILLS ▸ **mill**
MILNEB, -S *n* type of pesticide
MILO, -S *n* variety of sorghum with heads of yellow or pinkish seeds
MILOR, -S *same as* ▸ **milord**
MILORD, -S *n* (formerly) a continental title used for an English gentleman
MILORS ▸ **milor**
MILOS ▸ **milo**
MILPA, -S *n* form of subsistence agriculture in Mexico
MILREIS *n* former monetary unit of Portugal and Brazil
MILS ▸ **mil**
MILSEY, -S *n* milk strainer
MILT, -ED, -ING, -S *n* reproductive fluid of male fish ▹ *vb* fertilize (the roe of a female fish) with milt
MILTER, -S *n* male fish that is mature and ready to breed
MILTIER ▸ **milty**
MILTING ▸ **milt**
MILTS ▸ **milt**
MILTY, MILTIER *adj* full of milt
MILTZ, -ES *same as* ▸ **milt**
MILVINE *adj* of kites and related birds
MIM, -MER, -MEST *adj* prim, modest, or demure
MIMBAR, -S *n* pulpit in mosque
MIME, -D, -S, MIMING *n, vb*
MIMEO, -ED, -S *vb* mimeograph
MIMER, -S ▸ **mime**
MIMES ▸ **mime**
MIMESIS, MIMESES *n* imitative representation of nature or human behaviour
MIMETIC *adj* imitating or representing something
MIMIC, -S *vb, n, adj*
MIMICAL ▸ **mimic**
MIMICRY *n* act or art of copying or imitating closely
MIMICS ▸ **mimic**
MIMING ▸ **mime**
MIMMER ▸ **mim**
MIMMEST ▸ **mim**
MIMMICK *same as* ▸ **minnick**
MIMOSA, -E, -S *n* shrub with fluffy yellow flowers and sensitive leaves
MIMSEY *same as* ▸ **mimsy**
MIMSY, MIMSIER *adj* prim, underwhelming, and ineffectual
MIMULUS *n* plants cultivated for their yellow or red flowers
MINA, -E, -S *n* ancient unit of weight and money, used in Asia Minor
MINABLE ▸ **mine**
MINAE ▸ **mina**
MINAR, -S *n* tower

MINARET *n* tall slender tower of a mosque
MINARS ▸ **minar**
MINAS ▸ **mina**
MINBAR, -S *same as* ▸ **mimbar**
MINCE, -D, -S *vb, n*
MINCER, -S *n* machine for mincing meat
MINCES ▸ **mince**
MINCEUR *adj* (of food) low-fat
MINCIER ▸ **mincy**
MINCING *adj* affectedly elegant in manner
MINCY, MINCIER *adj* excessively particular or fussy
MIND, -S *n, vb*
MINDED *adj* having an inclination as specified
MINDER, -S *n* aide or bodyguard
MINDFUL *adj* heedful
MINDING ▸ **mind**
MINDS ▸ **mind**
MINDSET *n* ideas and attitudes with which a person approaches a situation
MINE, -D, -S *pron, n, vb*
MINEOLA *same as* > **minneola**
MINER, -S *n* person who works in a mine
MINERAL *n, adj*
MINERS ▸ **miner**
MINES ▸ **mine**
MINETTE *n* type of rock
MINEVER *same as* ▸ **miniver**
MING, MEYNT, -ED, -S *vb* mix
MINGER, -S *n* insulting word for an unattractive person
MINGIER ▸ **mingy**
MINGILY *adv* in a miserly manner
MINGING *adj* unattractive or unpleasant
MINGLE, -D, -S *vb*
MINGLER ▸ **mingle**
MINGLES ▸ **mingle**
MINGS ▸ **ming**
MINGY, MINGIER *adj* miserly
MINI, -S *same as* > **minidress**
MINIATE *vb* paint with minium
MINIBAR *n* selection of drinks and confectionery provided in a hotel room
MINIBUS *n* small bus
MINICAB *n* ordinary car used as a taxi
MINICAM *n* portable television camera
MINICAR *n* small car
MINICOM *n* device allowing typed telephone messages to be sent and received
MINIER ▸ **miny**
MINIEST ▸ **miny**
MINIFY *vb* minimize or lessen the size or importance of (something)
MINIKIN *n* small, dainty, or affected person or thing ▹ *adj* dainty, prim, or affected
MINILAB *n* equipment for processing photographic film
MINIM, -S *n, adj*
MINIMA ▸ **minimum**
MINIMAL *adj, n*
MINIMAX *n* lowest of a set of maximum values ▹ *vb* make maximum as low as possible
MINIMS ▸ **minim**
MINIMUM, MINIMA *n, adj*
MINIMUS *adj* youngest: used after the surname of a schoolboy with elder brothers at the same school
MINING, -S *n* act, process, or industry of extracting coal or ores from the earth
MINION, -S *n, adj*
MINIS ▸ **mini**
MINISH *vb* diminish
MINISKI *n* short ski
MINIUM, -S *n* bright red poisonous insoluble oxide of lead
MINIVAN *n* small van, esp one with seats in the back for carrying passengers
MINIVER *n* white fur, used in ceremonial costumes
MINIVET *n* brightly coloured tropical Asian cuckoo shrike
MINK, -S *n*
MINKE, -S *n* as in **minke whale** type of small whalebone whale or rorqual
MINKS ▸ **mink**
MINNICK *vb* behave in fussy way
MINNIE, -S *n* mother
MINNOCK *same as* ▸ **minnick**

MINNOW, -S *n* small freshwater fish
MINNY *same as* ▶ **minnie**
MINO, -S *same as* ▶ **mynah**
MINOR, -ED, -S *adj, n, vb*
MINORCA *n* breed of light domestic fowl
MINORED ▶ **minor**
MINORS ▶ **minor**
MINOS ▶ **mino**
MINSTER *n* cathedral or large church
MINT, -ED, -ING, -S *n, vb*
MINTAGE *n* process of minting
MINTED ▶ **mint**
MINTER, -S ▶ **mint**
MINTIER ▶ **minty**
MINTING ▶ **mint**
MINTS ▶ **mint**
MINTY, MINTIER ▶ **mint**
MINUEND *n* number from which another number is to be subtracted
MINUET, -S *n, vb*
MINUS, -ES *adj, n, prep*
MINUTE, -D, -R *n, vb, adj*
MINUTES *pl n* official record of the proceedings of a meeting or conference
MINUTIA *singular noun of* > **minutiae**
MINX, -ES *n* bold girl
MINXISH ▶ **minx**
MINY, MINIER, MINIEST *adj* of or like mines
MINYAN, -S *n* number of persons required by Jewish law to be present for a religious service
MIOCENE *adj* of, denoting, or formed in the fourth epoch of the Tertiary period
MIOMBO, -S *n* (in E Africa) a dry wooded area with sparse deciduous growth
MIOSIS, MIOSES *n* excessive contraction of the pupil of the eye
MIOTIC, -S ▶ **miosis**
MIPS *n* unit used to express the speed of a computer's central processing unit
MIR, -I, -S *n* peasant commune in prerevolutionary Russia
MIRABLE *adj* wonderful
MIRACLE *n*
MIRADOR *n* window, balcony, or turret
MIRAGE, -S *n*
MIRBANE *n* substance used in perfumes
MIRCHI *Indian English word for* ▶ **hot**
MIRE, -D, -S, MIRING *n, vb*
MIREX, -ES *n* type of insecticide
MIRI ▶ **mir**
MIRID, -S *n* variety of leaf bug
MIRIER ▶ **miry**
MIRIEST ▶ **miry**
MIRIFIC *adj* achieving wonderful things
MIRIN, -S *n* Japanese rice wine
MIRING ▶ **mire**
MIRINS ▶ **mirin**
MIRITI, -S *n* South American palm
MIRK, -ER, -EST, -S *same as* ▶ **murk**
MIRKIER ▶ **mirky**
MIRKILY ▶ **mirk**
MIRKS ▶ **mirk**
MIRKY, MIRKIER ▶ **mirk**
MIRLY, MIRLIER *same as* ▶ **marly**
MIRO, -S *n* tall New Zealand tree
MIRROR, -S *n, vb*
MIRS ▶ **mir**
MIRTH, -S *n*
MIRV, -ED, -ING, -S *n* missile with several warheads ▷ *vb* arm with mirvs
MIRY, MIRIER, MIRIEST ▶ **mire**
MIRZA, -S *n* title of respect placed before the surname of a distinguished man
MIS ▶ **mi**
MISACT, -S *vb* act wrongly
MISADD, -S *vb* add badly
MISAIM, -S *vb* aim badly
MISALLY *vb* form unsuitable alliance
MISATE ▶ **miseat**
MISAVER *vb* claim wrongly
MISBIAS *vb* prejudice wrongly
MISBILL *vb* present inaccurate bill
MISBIND *vb* bind wrongly
MISBORN *adj* born prematurely
MISCALL *vb* call by the wrong name
MISCAST *vb* cast (a role or actor) inappropriately

MISCH *adj* as in **misch metal** alloy of cerium and other rare earth metals
MISCITE *vb* cite wrongly
MISCODE *vb* code wrongly
MISCOIN *vb* coin wrongly
MISCOOK *vb* cook badly
MISCOPY *vb* copy badly
MISCUE, -D, -S *n* faulty stroke in snooker, etc ▷ *vb* make a miscue
MISCUT, -S *vb* cut wrongly
MISDATE *vb* date (a letter, event, etc) wrongly
MISDEAL *vb* deal out cards incorrectly ▷ *n* faulty deal
MISDEED *n* wrongful act
MISDEEM *vb* form bad opinion of
MISDIAL *vb* dial telephone number incorrectly
MISDID ▶ **misdo**
MISDIET *n* wrong diet ▷ *vb* diet or eat improperly
MISDO, MISDID, -ES *vb* do badly or wrongly
MISDOER ▶ **misdo**
MISDOES ▶ **misdo**
MISDONE *adj* done badly
MISDRAW, MISDREW *vb* draw poorly
MISE, -S *n* issue in the obsolete writ of right
MISEASE *n* unease
MISEAT, MISATE, -S *vb* eat unhealthy food
MISEDIT *vb* edit badly
MISER, -S *n*
MISERE, -S *n* call in solo whist and other card games declaring a hand that will win no tricks
MISERLY *adj* of or resembling a miser
MISERS ▶ **miser**
MISERY *n*
MISES ▶ **mise**
MISFALL, MISFELL *vb* happen as piece of bad luck
MISFARE *vb* get on badly
MISFEED, MISFED *vb* feed wrongly
MISFELL ▶ **misfall**
MISFILE *vb* file (papers, records, etc) wrongly
MISFIRE *vb, n*
MISFIT, -S *n, vb*
MISFOLD *vb* fold wrongly
MISFORM *vb* form badly
MISGAGE *vb* gage wrongly
MISGIVE, MISGAVE *vb* make or be apprehensive or suspicious
MISGO, -ES, -NE *vb* go wrong way
MISGROW, MISGREW *vb* grow in unsuitable way
MISHAP, -S *n, vb*
MISHAPT *same as* **> misshapen**
MISHEAR *vb* hear (what someone says) wrongly
MISHIT, -S *n* faulty shot, kick, or stroke ▷ *vb* hit or kick a ball with a faulty stroke
MISHMEE *n* root of Asian plant
MISHMI, -S *n* evergreen perennial plant
MISJOIN *vb* join badly
MISKAL, -S *n* unit of weight in Iran
MISKEEP, MISKEPT *vb* keep wrongly
MISKEN, -S, -T *vb* be unaware of
MISKEPT ▶ **miskeep**
MISKEY, -S *vb* key wrongly
MISKICK *vb* fail to kick properly
MISKNOW, MISKNEW *vb* have wrong idea about
MISLAY, MISLAID, MISLAIN, -S *vb*
MISLEAD, MISLED *vb*
MISLIE, -S *vb* lie wrongly
MISLIKE *vb* dislike ▷ *n* dislike or aversion
MISLIT > mislight
MISLIVE *vb* live wickedly
MISLUCK *vb* have bad luck
MISMAKE, MISMADE *vb* make badly
MISMARK *vb* mark wrongly
MISMATE *vb* mate wrongly
MISMEET, MISMET *vb* fail to meet
MISMOVE *vb* move badly
MISNAME *vb* name badly

MISO, -S *n* thick brown salty paste made from soya beans
MISPAGE *vb* page wrongly
MISPART *vb* part wrongly
MISPEN, -S *vb* write wrongly
MISPLAN *vb* plan badly or wrongly
MISPLAY *vb* play badly or wrongly in games or sports ▷ *n* wrong or unskilful play
MISPLED > **misplead**
MISRATE *vb* rate wrongly
MISREAD *vb* misinterpret (a situation etc)
MISRELY *vb* rely wrongly
MISRULE *vb* govern inefficiently or unjustly ▷ *n* inefficient or unjust government
MISS, -ED, -ES *vb, n*
MISSA, -E *n* Roman Catholic mass
MISSAID ▸ **missay**
MISSAL, -S *n* book containing the prayers and rites of the Mass
MISSAW ▸ **missee**
MISSAY, MISSAID, -S *vb* say wrongly
MISSEAT *vb* seat wrongly
MISSED ▸ **miss**
MISSEE, MISSAW, -N, -S *vb* see wrongly
MISSEEM *vb* be unsuitable for
MISSEEN ▸ **missee**
MISSEES ▸ **missee**
MISSEL, -S *adj* as in **missel thrush** large European thrush
MISSELL, MISSOLD *vb* sell (a product, esp a financial one) misleadingly
MISSELS ▸ **missel**
MISSEND, MISSENT *vb* send wrongly
MISSES ▸ **miss**
MISSET, -S *vb* set wrongly
MISSHOD *adj* badly shod
MISSIER ▸ **missy**
MISSIES ▸ **missy**
MISSILE *n*
MISSING *adj*
MISSION *n, vb*
MISSIS *same as* ▸ **missus**
MISSISH *adj* like a schoolgirl
MISSIVE *n* letter ▷ *adj* sent or intended to be sent
MISSOLD ▸ **missell**
MISSORT *vb* sort wrongly
MISSOUT *n* someone who has been overlooked
MISSTEP *n* false step ▷ *vb* take a false step
MISSTOP *vb* stop wrongly
MISSUIT *vb* be unsuitable for
MISSUS *n* one's wife or the wife of the person addressed or referred to
MISSY, MISSIER, MISSIES *n* affectionate or disparaging form of address to a girl ▷ *adj* missish
MIST, -ED, -S *n, vb*
MISTAKE *n, vb*
MISTAL, -S *n* cow shed
MISTBOW *same as* ▸ **fogbow**
MISTED ▸ **mist**
MISTELL, MISTOLD *vb* tell wrongly
MISTEND *vb* tend wrongly
MISTER, -S *n, vb*
MISTERM *vb* term badly
MISTERS ▸ **mister**
MISTERY *same as* ▸ **mystery**
MISTEUK *Scots variant of* ▸ **mistook**
MISTFUL ▸ **mist**
MISTICO *n* small Mediterranean sailing ship
MISTIER ▸ **misty**
MISTILY ▸ **misty**
MISTIME *vb* do (something) at the wrong time
MISTING *n* application of a fake suntan by spray
MISTLE, -D, -S *same as* ▸ **mizzle**
MISTOLD ▸ **mistell**
MISTOOK *past tense of* ▸ **mistake**
MISTRAL *n* strong dry northerly wind of S France
MISTS ▸ **mist**
MISTUNE *vb* fail to tune properly
MISTY, MISTIER *adj*
MISTYPE *vb* type badly
MISUSE, -D, -S, MISUST *n, vb*

MISUSER *n* abuse of some right, privilege, office, etc
MISUSES ▸ **misuse**
MISUST ▸ **misuse**
MISWEEN *vb* assess wrongly
MISWEND, MISWENT *vb* become lost
MISWORD *vb* word badly
MISWRIT > **miswrite**
MISYOKE *vb* join wrongly
MITCH, -ED, -ES *vb* play truant from school
MITE, -S *n*
MITER, -ED, -S *same as* ▸ **mitre**
MITERER ▸ **miter**
MITERS ▸ **miter**
MITES ▸ **mite**
MITHER, -S *vb* fuss over or moan about something
MITIER ▸ **mity**
MITIEST ▸ **mity**
MITIS, -ES *n* malleable iron
MITOGEN *n* any agent that induces mitosis
MITOSIS, MITOSES *n* type of cell division
MITOTIC ▸ **mitosis**
MITRAL *adj* of or like a mitre
MITRE, -D, -S, MITRING *n* bishop's pointed headdress ▹ *vb* join with a mitre joint
MITSVAH *same as* ▸ **mitzvah**
MITT, -S *same as* ▸ **mitten**
MITTEN, -S *n*
MITTS ▸ **mitt**
MITUMBA *n* used clothes imported for sale in African countries
MITY, MITIER, MITIEST *adj* having mites
MITZVAH *n* commandment or precept, esp one found in the Bible
MIURUS *n* type of rhythm in poetry
MIX, -ES, -T *vb, n*
MIXABLE ▸ **mix**
MIXDOWN *n* (in sound recording) the transfer of a multitrack master mix to two-track stereo tape
MIXED *adj*
MIXEDLY ▸ **mixed**
MIXEN, -S *n* dunghill
MIXER, -S *n*
MIXES ▸ **mix**
MIXIBLE ▸ **mix**
MIXIER ▸ **mixy**
MIXIEST ▸ **mixy**
MIXING, -S *n*
MIXT ▸ **mix**
MIXTAPE *n* compilation of songs from various sources
MIXTE *adj* of a type of bicycle frame
MIXTION *n* amber-based mixture used in making gold leaf
MIXTURE *n*
MIXUP, -S *n* something that is mixed up
MIXY, MIXIER, MIXIEST *adj* mixed
MIZ, -ZES *shortened form of* ▸ **misery**

> **Miz** is an informal short form of **misery**, very useful as a Z word. But you'll need a blank tile for the second Z if you want to form the plural **mizzes**.

MIZEN, -S *same as* ▸ **mizzen**
MIZMAZE *n* maze
MIZUNA, -S *n* Japanese variety of lettuce
MIZZ *same as* ▸ **miz**
MIZZEN, -S *n* sail set on a mizzenmast ▹ *adj* of or relating to any kind of gear used with a mizzenmast
MIZZES ▸ **miz**
MIZZLE, -D, -S *vb* decamp
MIZZLY ▸ **mizzle**
MIZZY *adj* as in **mizzy maze** dialect expression meaning state of confusion
MM *interj* expression of enjoyment of taste or smell
MMM *interj* interjection expressing agreement or enjoyment
MNA, -S *same as* ▸ **mina**
MNEME, -S *n* ability to retain memory
MNEMIC ▸ **mneme**
MNEMON, -S *n* unit of memory
MO, -S *n* moment
MOA, -S *n* large extinct flightless New Zealand bird
MOAI *n* any of the gigantic carved stone

figures found on Easter Island (Rapa Nui)
MOAN, -ED, -S *n, vb*
MOANER, -S ▸ **moan**
MOANFUL ▸ **moan**
MOANING ▸ **moan**
MOANS ▸ **moan**
MOAS ▸ **moa**
MOAT, -ED, -ING, -S *n, vb*
MOB, -BED, -S *n, vb*
MOBBER, -S ▸ **mob**
MOBBIE *same as* ▸ **mobby**
MOBBIES ▸ **mobby**
MOBBING ▸ **mob**
MOBBISH ▸ **mob**
MOBBISM *n* behaviour as mob
MOBBLE, -D, -S *same as* ▸ **moble**
MOBBY, MOBBIES *n* (formerly) drink fermented from sweet potatoes or ginger
MOBCAP, -S *n* woman's 18th-century cotton cap
MOBCAST *vb*
MOBE, -S *n* mobile phone
MOBEY, -S *same as* ▸ **moby**
MOBIE *same as* ▸ **moby**
MOBIES ▸ **moby**
MOBILE, -S *adj, n*
MOBLE, -D, -S, MOBLING *vb* muffle
MOBLOG, -S *n* blog recorded in the form of mobile phone calls, text messages, and photographs
MOBS ▸ **mob**
MOBSMAN, MOBSMEN *n* person in mob
MOBSTER *n* member of a criminal organization
MOBY, MOBIES *n* mobile phone
MOC, -S *shortening of* > **moccasin**
MOCCIES *pl n* informal Australian word for moccasins
MOCH, -ED, -ING, -S *n* spell of humid weather ▹ *vb* (of foods) become musty or spoiled
MOCHA, -S *n* kind of strong dark coffee
MOCHED ▸ **moch**
MOCHELL *same as* ▸ **much**
MOCHI, -S *n* confection made with rice flour and sweetened bean paste
MOCHIE, -R *adj* damp or humid
MOCHILA *n* South American shoulder bag
MOCHING ▸ **moch**
MOCHIS ▸ **mochi**
MOCHS ▸ **moch**
MOCHY *same as* ▸ **mochie**
MOCK, -ED, -S *vb, adj, n*
MOCKADO *n* imitation velvet
MOCKAGE *same as* ▸ **mockery**
MOCKED ▸ **mock**
MOCKER, -S *vb* dress up
MOCKERY *n* derision
MOCKING ▸ **mock**
MOCKNEY *n* person who affects a cockney accent ▹ *adj* denoting an affected cockney accent or a person who has one
MOCKS ▸ **mock**
MOCKUP, -S *n* working full-scale model of a machine, apparatus, etc, for testing, research, etc
MOCOCK, -S *n* Native American birchbark container
MOCS ▸ **moc**
MOCUCK, -S *same as* ▸ **mocock**
MOD, -DED, -S *n* member of a group of fashionable young people, orig in the 1960s ▹ *vb* modify (a piece of software or hardware)
MODAL, -S *adj* of or relating to mode or manner ▹ *n* modal word
MODALLY ▸ **modal**
MODALS ▸ **modal**
MODDED ▸ **mod**
MODDER, -S *n* person who modifies a piece of hardware or software
MODDING *n* practice of modifying a car to alter its appearance or performance
MODE, -S *n*
MODEL, -ED, -S *n, adj, vb*
MODELER ▸ **model**
MODELLO, MODELLI *n* artist's preliminary sketch or model
MODELS ▸ **model**
MODEM, -ED, -S *n, vb*
MODENA, -S *n* popular variety of domestic fancy pigeon

MODER, -S *n* intermediate layer in humus
MODERN, -S *adj, n*
MODERNE *n* style of architecture and design of the late 1920s and 1930s ▷ *adj* of or relating to this style of architecture and design
MODERNS ▸ **modern**
MODERS ▸ **moder**
MODES ▸ **mode**
MODEST *adj*
MODESTY *n*
MODGE, -D, -S, MODGING *vb* do shoddily
MODI ▸ **modus**
MODICUM, MODICA *n*
MODIFY *vb*
MODII ▸ **modius**
MODIOLI > **modiolus**
MODISH *adj* in fashion
MODIST, -S *n* follower of fashion
MODISTE *n* fashionable dressmaker or milliner
MODISTS ▸ **modist**
MODIUS, MODII *n* ancient Roman quantity measure
MODS ▸ **mod**
MODULAR *adj* of, consisting of, or resembling a module or modulus ▷ *n* thing comprised of modules
MODULE, -S *n*
MODULI ▸ **modulus**
MODULO *adv* with reference to modulus
MODULUS, MODULI *n* coefficient expressing a specified property
MODUS, MODI *n* way of doing something
MOE, -S *adv* more ▷ *n* wry face
MOELLON *n* rubble
MOES ▸ **moe**
MOFETTE *n* opening in a region of nearly extinct volcanic activity, through which gases pass
MOG, -GED, -GING, -S *vb* go away
MOGGAN, -S *n* stocking without foot
MOGGED ▸ **mog**
MOGGIE *same as* ▸ **moggy**
MOGGIES ▸ **moggy**
MOGGING ▸ **mog**
MOGGY, MOGGIES *n* cat
MOGHUL, -S *same as* ▸ **mogul**
MOGS ▸ **mog**
MOGUL, -S *n*
MOGULED *adj* having moguls
MOGULS ▸ **mogul**
MOHAIR, -S *n*
MOHALIM *same as* ▸ **mohelim**
MOHAWK, -S *n* half turn from either edge of either skate to the corresponding edge of the other skate
MOHEL, -IM, -S *n* man qualified to conduct circumcisions
MOHICAN *n* punk hairstyle
MOHO, -S *n* boundary between the earth's crust and mantle
MOHR, -S *same as* ▸ **mhorr**
MOHUA, -S *n* small New Zealand bird
MOHUR, -S *n* former Indian gold coin worth 15 rupees
MOI *pron* (used facetiously) me
MOIDER, -S *same as* ▸ **moither**
MOIDORE *n* former Portuguese gold coin
MOIETY *n* half
MOIL, -ED, -ING, -S *vb* moisten or soil or become moist, soiled, etc ▷ *n* toil
MOILE, -S *n* type of rice pudding made with almond milk
MOILED ▸ **moil**
MOILER, -S ▸ **moil**
MOILES ▸ **moile**
MOILING ▸ **moil**
MOILS ▸ **moil**
MOINEAU *n* small fortification

> Meaning a type of small fortification, this is another of those very useful 7-letter vowel dumps.

MOIRA, -I *n* fate
MOIRE, -S *adj* having a watered or wavelike pattern ▷ *n* any fabric that has such a pattern
MOISER, -S *n* informer
MOIST, -ED, -ER, -S *adj, vb*
MOISTEN *vb*
MOISTER ▸ **moist**
MOISTLY ▸ **moist**
MOISTS ▸ **moist**
MOIT, -S *same as* ▸ **mote**
MOITHER *vb* bother or bewilder

MOITS ▸ **moit**
MOJARRA *n* tropical American sea fish
MOJITO, -S *n* rum-based cocktail
MOJO, -ES, -S *n*
MOKE, -S *n* donkey
MOKI, -S *n* edible sea fish of New Zealand
MOKIHI, -S *n* Māori raft
MOKIS ▸ **moki**
MOKO, -S *n* Māori tattoo or tattoo pattern
MOKORO, -S *n* (in Botswana) the traditional dugout canoe of the people of the Okavango Delta
MOKOS ▸ **moko**
MOKSHA, -S *n* freedom from the endless cycle of transmigration into a state of bliss
MOL, -S *n* the SI unit mole
MOLA, -S *another name for* ▸ **sunfish**
MOLAL *adj* of a solution containing one mole of solute per thousand grams of solvent
MOLAR, -S *n, adj*
MOLAS ▸ **mola**
MOLASSE *n* sediment from the erosion of mountain ranges
MOLD, -ED, -S *same as* ▸ **mould**
MOLDER, -S *same as* ▸ **moulder**
MOLDIER ▸ **moldy**
MOLDING *same as* > **moulding**
MOLDS ▸ **mold**
MOLDY, MOLDIER *same as* ▸ **mouldy**
MOLE, -D, -S, MOLING *n, vb*
MOLEST, -S *vb*
MOLIES ▸ **moly**
MOLIMEN *n* effort needed to perform bodily function
MOLINE, -S *adj* (of a cross) having arms of equal length, forked and curved back at the ends ▷ *n* moline cross
MOLINET *n* stick for whipping chocolate
MOLING ▸ **mole**
MOLL, -S *n* gangster's female accomplice
MOLLA, -S *same as* ▸ **mollah**
MOLLAH, -S *same as* ▸ **mullah**
MOLLAS ▸ **molla**
MOLLIE *same as* ▸ **molly**
MOLLIES ▸ **molly**
MOLLIFY *vb*
MOLLS ▸ **moll**
MOLLUSC *n*
MOLLUSK *same as* ▸ **mollusc**
MOLLY, MOLLIES *n* American freshwater fish
MOLOCH, -S *n* spiny Australian desert-living lizard
MOLOSSI > **molossus**
MOLS ▸ **mol**
MOLT, -ED, -ING, -S *same as* ▸ **moult**
MOLTEN ▸ **melt**
MOLTER, -S ▸ **molt**
MOLTING ▸ **molt**
MOLTO *adv* very
MOLTS ▸ **molt**
MOLY, MOLIES, -S *n* mythical magic herb
MOM, -S *same as* ▸ **mother**
MOME, -S *n* fool
MOMENT, -S *n*
MOMENTA > **momentum**
MOMENTO *same as* ▸ **memento**
MOMENTS ▸ **moment**
MOMES ▸ **mome**
MOMI *same as* ▸ **mom**
MOMISM, -S *n* excessive domination of a child by his or her mother
MOMMA, -S *same as* ▸ **mamma**
MOMMET, -S *same as* ▸ **mammet**
MOMMY, MOMMIES *same as* ▸ **mom**
MOMOIR, -S *n* memoir written by a woman about motherhood
MOMS ▸ **mom**
MOMUS, -ES *n* person who ridicules
MON, -S *dialect variant of* ▸ **man**
MONA *n* W African guenon monkey
MONACID *same as* > **monoacid**
MONACT, -S *n* sponge spicule with a single ray
MONAD, -S *n* any fundamental singular metaphysical entity
MONADAL ▸ **monad**
MONADES ▸ **monas**
MONADIC *adj* being or relating to a monad
MONADS ▸ **monad**

MONAL, -S *n* S Asian pheasant
MONARCH *n*
MONARDA *n* mintlike N American plant
MONAS, MONADES, -ES *same as* ▸ **monad**
MONAUL, -S *same as* ▸ **monal**
MONAXON *n* type of sponge
MONDAIN *n* man who moves in fashionable society ▹ *adj* characteristic of fashionable society
MONDE, -S *n* French word meaning world or society
MONDIAL *adj* of or involving the whole world
MONDO, -S *n* Buddhist questioning technique
MONEME, -S *less common word for* > **morpheme**
MONER, -A *n* hypothetical simple organism
MONERAN *n* type of bacterium
MONERON *same as* ▸ **moner**
MONETH, -S *same as* ▸ **month**
MONEY, -S, MONIES *n*
MONEYED *adj* rich
MONEYER *n* person who coins money
MONEYS ▸ **money**
MONG, -S *n* Australian shortening of mongrel
MONGER, -S *n* trader or dealer ▹ *vb* deal in
MONGERY ▸ **monger**
MONGO, -S *same as* ▸ **mungo**
MONGOE, -S *same as* ▸ **mongo**
MONGOS ▸ **mongo**
MONGREL *n, adj*
MONGS ▸ **mong**
MONGST *short for* ▸ **amongst**
MONIAL, -S *n* mullion
MONIC *adj* denoting a type of polynomial
MONIE *Scots word for* ▸ **many**
MONIED *same as* ▸ **moneyed**
MONIES ▸ **money**
MONIKER *n* person's name or nickname
MONILIA *n* type of fungus
MONISH *same as* > **admonish**
MONISM, -S *n* doctrine that reality consists of only one basic substance or element
MONIST, -S ▸ **monism**
MONITOR *n, vb*
MONK, -S *n*
MONKEY, -S *n, vb*
MONKISH *adj* of, relating to, or resembling a monk or monks
MONKS ▸ **monk**
MONO, -S *n* monophonic sound
MONOAO, -S *n* New Zealand plant with rigid leaves
MONOCLE *n*
MONOCOT *n* type of flowering plant with a single embryonic seed leaf
MONODIC ▸ **monody**
MONODY *n* (in Greek tragedy) an ode sung by a single actor
MONOECY *same as* > **monoecism**
MONOFIL *n* synthetic thread or yarn composed of a single strand rather than twisted fibres
MONOLOG *same as* > **monologue**
MONOMER *n* compound whose molecules can join together to form a polymer
MONONYM *n* person who is famous enough to be known only by one name
MONOPOD *same as* > **monopode**
MONOS ▸ **mono**
MONOSIS, MONOSES *n* abnormal separation
MONOSKI *n* wide ski on which the skier stands with both feet ▹ *vb* ski on a monoski
MONOSY *same as* ▸ **monosis**
MONS ▸ **mon**
MONSOON *n*
MONSTER *n, adj, vb*
MONTAGE *n, vb*
MONTAN *adj* as in **montan wax** hard wax obtained from lignite and peat
MONTANE *n* area of mountain dominated by vegetation ▹ *adj* of or inhabiting mountainous regions

MONTANT *n* vertical part in woodwork
MONTE, -S *n* gambling card game of Spanish origin
MONTEM, -S *n* former money-raising practice at Eton school
MONTERO *n* round cap with a flap at the back worn by hunters
MONTES ▶ **monte**
MONTH, -S *n*
MONTHLY *adj, adv, n*
MONTHS ▶ **month**
MONTIES ▶ **monty**
MONTRE, -S *n* pipes of organ
MONTURE *n* mount or frame
MONTY, MONTIES *n* complete form of something
MONURON *n* type of weedkiller
MONY *Scot word for* ▶ **many**
MOO, -ED, -ING, -S *n, vb, interj*
MOOCH, -ED, -ES *vb*
MOOCHER ▶ **mooch**
MOOCHES ▶ **mooch**
MOOD, -S *n*
MOODIED ▶ **moody**
MOODIER ▶ **moody**
MOODIES ▶ **moody**
MOODILY ▶ **moody**
MOODS ▶ **mood**
MOODY, MOODIED, MOODIER, MOODIES *adj, vb*
MOOED ▶ **moo**
MOOI *adj* pleasing or nice
MOOING ▶ **moo**
MOOK, -S *n* person regarded with contempt, esp a stupid person
MOOKTAR *same as* ▶ **mukhtar**
MOOL, -ED, -ING, -S *same as* ▶ **mould**
MOOLA, -S *same as* ▶ **moolah**
MOOLAH, -S *slang word for* ▶ **money**
MOOLAS ▶ **moola**
MOOLED ▶ **mool**
MOOLEY, -S *same as* ▶ **mooly**
MOOLI, -S *n* type of large white radish
MOOLIES ▶ **mooly**
MOOLING ▶ **mool**
MOOLIS ▶ **mooli**
MOOLOO, -S *n* person from the Waikato
MOOLS ▶ **mool**
MOOLVI, -S *same as* ▶ **moolvie**
MOOLVIE *n* (esp in India) Muslim learned man
MOOLVIS ▶ **moolvi**
MOOLY, MOOLIES *same as* ▶ **muley**
MOON, -ING, -S *n, vb*
MOONBOW *n* rainbow made by moonlight
MOONDOG *n* bright spot in the sky caused by moonlight
MOONED *adj* decorated with a moon
MOONER, -S ▶ **moon**
MOONEYE *n* N American large-eyed freshwater fish
MOONG *n* as in **moong bean** kind of bean
MOONIER ▶ **moony**
MOONIES ▶ **moony**
MOONILY ▶ **moony**
MOONING ▶ **moon**
MOONISH ▶ **moon**
MOONLET *n* small moon
MOONLIT *adj* illuminated by the moon
MOONS ▶ **moon**
MOONSET *n* moment when the moon disappears below the horizon
MOONY, MOONIER, MOONIES *adj* dreamy or listless ▷ *n* foolish person
MOOP, -ED, -ING, -S *same as* ▶ **moup**
MOOR, -ED, -S *n, vb*
MOORAGE *n* place for mooring a vessel
MOORED ▶ **moor**
MOORHEN *n*
MOORIER ▶ **moory**
MOORILL *n* disease of cattle on moors
MOORING *n*
MOORISH *adj* denoting a style of architecture in Spain
MOORLOG *n* rotted wood below the surface of a moor
MOORMAN, MOORMEN *n* person living on a moor
MOORS ▶ **moor**
MOORVA, -S *same as* ▶ **murva**
MOORY, MOORIER ▶ **moor**
MOOS ▶ **moo**
MOOSE *n*

MOOT, -ED, -EST, -S *adj, vb, n*
MOOTER, -S ▸ **moot**
MOOTEST ▸ **moot**
MOOTING ▸ **moot**
MOOTMAN, MOOTMEN *n* person taking part in a moot
MOOTS ▸ **moot**
MOOVE, -D, -S, MOOVING *same as* ▸ **move**
MOP, -PED, -PING, -S *n, vb*
MOPANE, -S *same as* ▸ **mopani**
MOPANI, -S *n* S African tree that is highly resistant to drought
MOPE, -S, MOPING *vb, n*
MOPED, -S *n*
MOPER, -S ▸ **mope**
MOPERY *n* gloominess
MOPES ▸ **mope**
MOPEY *same as* ▸ **mopy**
MOPHEAD *n* person with shaggy hair
MOPIER ▸ **mopy**
MOPIEST ▸ **mopy**
MOPILY ▸ **mopy**
MOPING ▸ **mope**
MOPISH ▸ **mope**
MOPOKE, -S *n* species of owl
MOPPED ▸ **mop**
MOPPER, -S ▸ **mop**
MOPPET, -S *same as* ▸ **poppet**
MOPPIER ▸ **moppy**
MOPPING ▸ **mop**
MOPPY, MOPPIER *adj* (of hair) thick, dishevelled
MOPS ▸ **mop**
MOPSY, MOPSIES *n* untidy or dowdy person
MOPUS, -ES *n* person who mopes
MOPY, MOPIER, MOPIEST ▸ **mope**
MOR, -S *n* layer of acidic humus formed in cool moist areas
MORA, -E, -S *n* quantity of a short syllable in verse
MORAINE *n* accumulated mass of debris deposited by a glacier
MORAL, -S *adj, n, vb*
MORALE, -S *n*
MORALL, -S *same as* ▸ **mural**
MORALLY ▸ **moral**
MORALS ▸ **moral**
MORAS ▸ **mora**
MORASS *n*
MORASSY *adj* swampy
MORAT, -S *n* drink containing mulberry juice
MORAY, -S *n* large voracious eel
MORBID *adj*
MORBUS *n* disease
MORCEAU *n* fragment or morsel
MORCHA, -S *n* (in India) hostile demonstration
MORDANT *adj, n, vb*
MORDENT *n* melodic ornament in music
MORE *adj, adv, pron*
MOREEN, -S *n* heavy, usually watered, fabric of wool or wool and cotton
MOREISH *adj* (of food) causing a desire for more
MOREL, -S *n* edible mushroom with a pitted cap
MORELLE *n* nightshade
MORELLO *n* variety of small very dark sour cherry
MORELS ▸ **morel**
MORENDO *adv* (in music) dying away ▹ *n* gentle decrescendo at the end of a musical strain
MORES *pl n* customs and conventions embodying the fundamental values of a community
MORGAN, -S *n* American breed of small compact saddle horse
MORGAY, -S *n* small dogfish
MORGEN, -S *n* South African unit of area
MORGUE, -S *same as* > **mortuary**
MORIA, -S *n* folly
MORICHE *same as* ▸ **miriti**
MORION, -S *n* 16th-century helmet with a brim and wide comb
MORISCO *n* morris dance
MORISH *same as* ▸ **moreish**
MORKIN, -S *n* animal dying in accident
MORLING *n* sheep killed by disease

MORMAOR *n* former high-ranking Scottish nobleman
MORN, -S *n* morning
MORNAY, -S *n* dish served with a cheese sauce
MORNE, -D, -S *same as* ▸ **mourn**
MORNING *n*
MORNS ▸ **morn**
MOROCCO *n* goatskin leather
MORON, -S *n*
MORONIC ▸ **moron**
MORONS ▸ **moron**
MOROSE, -R *adj*
MORPH, -ED, -S *n* phonological representation of a morpheme ▹ *vb* undergo or cause to undergo morphing
MORPHEW *n* blemish on skin
MORPHIA *same as* > **morphine**
MORPHIC *adj* as in **morphic resonance** idea that an event can lead to similar events in the future through a telepathic effect
MORPHIN *variant form of* > **morphine**
MORPHO, -S *n* type of butterfly
MORPHS ▸ **morph**
MORRA, -S *same as* ▸ **mora**
MORRELL *n* tall SW Australian eucalyptus with pointed buds
MORRHUA *n* cod
MORRICE *same as* ▸ **morris**
MORRION *same as* ▸ **morion**
MORRIS *vb* perform morris dance
MORRO, -S *n* rounded hill or promontory
MORROW, -S *n* next day
MORS ▸ **mor**
MORSAL, -S *same as* ▸ **morsel**
MORSE, -S *n* clasp or fastening on a cope
MORSEL, -S *n, vb*
MORSES ▸ **morse**
MORSURE *n* bite
MORT, -S *n* call blown on a hunting horn to signify the death of the animal hunted
MORTAL, -S *adj, n*
MORTAR, -S *n, vb*
MORTARY *adj* of or like mortar
MORTICE *same as* ▸ **mortise**
MORTIFY *vb*
MORTISE *n* slot cut into a piece of wood, stone, etc ▹ *vb* cut a slot in (a piece of wood, stone, etc)
MORTS ▸ **mort**
MORULA, -E, -S *n* solid ball of cells resulting from the splitting of a fertilized ovum
MORULAR ▸ **morula**
MORULAS ▸ **morula**
MORWONG *n* food fish of Australasian coastal waters
MORYAH *interj* exclamation of annoyance, disbelief, etc
MOS ▸ **mo**
MOSAIC, -S *n*
MOSCATO *n* type of sweet dessert wine
MOSE, -D, -S, MOSING *vb* have glanders
MOSELLE *n* German white wine from the Moselle valley
MOSES ▸ **mose**
MOSEY, -ED, -S *vb* walk in a leisurely manner
MOSH, -ED, -ES *n* dance performed to loud rock music ▹ *vb* dance in this manner
MOSHAV *n* cooperative settlement in Israel
MOSHED ▸ **mosh**
MOSHER, -S ▸ **mosh**
MOSHES ▸ **mosh**
MOSHING ▸ **mosh**
MOSING ▸ **mose**
MOSK, -S *same as* ▸ **mosque**
MOSQUE, -S *n*
MOSS, -ED, -ES, -ING *n, vb*
MOSSER, -S ▸ **moss**
MOSSES ▸ **moss**
MOSSIE, -S *n* common sparrow
MOSSIER ▸ **mossy**
MOSSIES ▸ **mossie**
MOSSING ▸ **moss**
MOSSO *adv* to be performed with rapidity
MOSSY, MOSSIER ▸ **moss**
MOST, -S *n, adj, adv*
MOSTE ▸ **mote**
MOSTEST ▸ **most**
MOSTLY *adv*
MOSTS ▸ **most**
MOT, -S *n* girl or young woman, esp one's girlfriend

MOTE, MOSTE, -N, -S *n* tiny speck ▷ *vb* may or might
MOTED *adj* containing motes
MOTEL, -S *n*
MOTEN ▶ **mote**
MOTES ▶ **mote**
MOTET, -S *n* short sacred choral song
MOTETT, -S *same as* ▶ **motet**
MOTEY, -S, MOTIER, MOTIEST *adj* containing motes ▷ *n* pigment made from earth
MOTH, -S *n*
MOTHED *adj* damaged by moths
MOTHER, -S *n, adj, vb*
MOTHERY *adj* like mother of vinegar
MOTHIER ▶ **mothy**
MOTHS ▶ **moth**
MOTHY, MOTHIER *adj* ragged
MOTIER ▶ **motey**
MOTIEST ▶ **motey**
MOTIF, -S *n*
MOTIFIC *adj* causing motion
MOTIFS ▶ **motif**
MOTILE, -S *adj* capable of independent movement ▷ *n* person whose mental imagery strongly reflects movement
MOTION, -S *n, vb*
MOTIVE, -D, -S *n, adj, vb*
MOTIVIC *adj* of musical motif
MOTLEY, -S, MOTLIER *adj, n*
MOTMOT, -S *n* tropical American bird with a long tail and blue and brownish-green plumage
MOTOR, -ED, -S *n, vb, adj*
MOTORIC *n* person trained in the muscular causes of vocal changes ▷ *adj* pertaining to motion
MOTORS ▶ **motor**
MOTORY ▶ **motor**
MOTS ▶ **mot**
MOTSER, -S *n* large sum of money, esp a gambling win
MOTT, -S *n* clump of trees
MOTTE, -S *n* mound on which a castle was built
MOTTIER ▶ **motty**
MOTTIES ▶ **motty**
MOTTLE, -D, -S *vb* colour with streaks or blotches of different shades ▷ *n* mottled appearance, as of the surface of marble
MOTTLER *n* paintbrush for mottled effects
MOTTLES ▶ **mottle**
MOTTO, -ES, -S *n*
MOTTOED *adj* having motto
MOTTOES ▶ **motto**
MOTTOS ▶ **motto**
MOTTS ▶ **mott**
MOTTY, MOTTIER, MOTTIES *n* target at which coins are aimed in pitch-and-toss ▷ *adj* containing motes
MOTUCA, -S *n* Brazilian fly
MOTZA, -S *same as* ▶ **motser**
MOU, -S *Scots word for* ▶ **mouth**
MOUCH, -ED, -ES *same as* ▶ **mooch**
MOUCHER ▶ **mouch**
MOUCHES ▶ **mouch**
MOUE, -S *n* disdainful or pouting look
MOUFLON *n* wild mountain sheep of Corsica and Sardinia
MOUGHT ▶ **may**
MOUILLE *adj* palatalized, as in the sounds represented by Spanish *ll* or *ñ*
MOUJIK, -S *same as* ▶ **muzhik**
MOULAGE *n* mould making
MOULD, -ED, -S *n, vb*
MOULDER *vb* decay into dust ▷ *n* person who moulds or makes moulds
MOULDS ▶ **mould**
MOULDY *adj*
MOULIN, -S *n* vertical shaft in a glacier
MOULS *Scots word for* ▶ **mould**
MOULT, -ED, -S *vb, n*
MOULTEN *adj* having moulted
MOULTER ▶ **moult**
MOULTS ▶ **moult**
MOUND, -ED, -S *n, vb*
MOUNT, -S *vb, n*
MOUNTED *adj* riding horses
MOUNTER ▶ **mount**
MOUNTS ▶ **mount**
MOUP, -ED, -ING, -S *vb* nibble

MOURN, -ED, -S *vb*
MOURNER *n*
MOURNS ▶ **mourn**
MOUS ▶ **mou**
MOUSAKA *same as* > **moussaka**
MOUSE, MICE, -D, -S *n*, *vb*
MOUSER, -S *n* cat used to catch mice
MOUSERY *n* place infested with mice
MOUSES ▶ **mouse**
MOUSEY *same as* ▶ **mousy**
MOUSIE, -S *n* little mouse
MOUSIER ▶ **mousy**
MOUSIES ▶ **mousie**
MOUSILY ▶ **mousy**
MOUSING *n* device for closing off a hook
MOUSLE, -D, -S *vb* handle roughly
MOUSME, -S *n* Japanese girl or young woman
MOUSMEE *same as* ▶ **mousme**
MOUSMES ▶ **mousme**
MOUSSE, -D, -S *n*, *vb*
MOUST, -ED, -S *same as* ▶ **must**
MOUSY, MOUSIER *adj* like a mouse, esp in hair colour
MOUTAN, -S *n* variety of peony
MOUTER, -S *same as* ▶ **multure**
MOUTH, -ED, -S *n*, *vb*
MOUTHER ▶ **mouth**
MOUTHS ▶ **mouth**
MOUTHY *adj* bombastic
MOUTON, -S *n* sheepskin processed to resemble the fur of another animal
MOVABLE *adj*, *n*
MOVABLY ▶ **movable**
MOVANT, -S *n* person who applies to a court of law
MOVE, -D, -S *vb*, *n*
MOVER, -S *n* person or animal that moves in a particular way
MOVES ▶ **move**
MOVIE, -S *n* cinema film
MOVING *adj*
MOVIOLA *n* viewing machine used in cutting and editing film
MOW, -ED, -N, -S *vb*, *n*
MOWA, -S *same as* ▶ **mahua**
MOWBURN *vb* heat up in mow
MOWDIE, -S *Scot word for* ▶ **mole**
MOWED ▶ **mow**
MOWER, -S ▶ **mow**
MOWING, -S ▶ **mow**
MOWN ▶ **mow**
MOWRA, -S *same as* ▶ **mahua**
MOWS ▶ **mow**
MOXA, -S *n* downy material obtained from various plants
MOXIE, -S *n* courage, nerve, or vigour
MOY, -S *n* coin
MOYA, -S *n* mud emitted from a volcano
MOYITY *same as* ▶ **moiety**
MOYL, -S *same as* ▶ **moyle**
MOYLE, -D, -S, MOYLING *vb* toil
MOYLS ▶ **moyl**
MOYS ▶ **moy**
MOZ, -ES *n* hex

> This unusual word, Australian slang for bad luck, is another of the very useful short words that use the Z, and it can be extended to **moze** or **mozo**.

MOZE, -D, MOZING *vb* give nap to
MOZES ▶ **moz**
MOZETTA, MOZETTE *same as* > **mozzetta**
MOZING ▶ **moze**
MOZO, -S *n* porter in southwest USA
MOZZ, -ES *same as* ▶ **moz**
MOZZIE, -S *same as* ▶ **mossie**
MOZZLE, -D, -S *n* luck ▷ *vb* hamper or impede (someone)
MPRET, -S *n* former Albanian ruler
MRIDANG *n* drum used in Indian music
MU, -S *n* twelfth letter in the Greek alphabet
MUCATE, -S *n* salt of mucic acid
MUCH, -ES *adj*, *n*, *adv*
MUCHEL, -S *same as* ▶ **much**
MUCHELL *same as* ▶ **much**
MUCHELS ▶ **muchel**
MUCHES ▶ **much**
MUCHLY ▶ **much**
MUCHO *adv* Spanish for very

MUCIC *adj* as in **mucic acid** colourless crystalline solid carboxylic acid
MUCID *adj* mouldy, musty, or slimy
MUCIGEN *n* substance present in mucous cells that is converted into mucin
MUCIN, -S *n* any of a group of nitrogenous mucoproteins occurring in saliva, skin, tendon, etc
MUCK, -ED, -ING, -S *n*
MUCKER, -S *n* person who shifts broken rock or waste ▹ *vb* hoard
MUCKIER ▸ **mucky**
MUCKILY ▸ **mucky**
MUCKING ▸ **muck**
MUCKLE, -R, -S *adj* large
MUCKS ▸ **muck**
MUCKY, MUCKIER *adj*
MUCLUC, -S *same as* ▸ **mukluk**
MUCOID, -S *adj* of the nature of or resembling mucin ▹ *n* substance like mucin
MUCOR, -S *n* type of fungus
MUCOSA, -E, -S *n* mucus-secreting membrane that lines body cavities
MUCOSAL ▸ **mucosa**
MUCOSAS ▸ **mucosa**
MUCOSE *same as* ▸ **mucous**
MUCOUS *adj* of, resembling, or secreting mucus
MUCRO, -S *n* short pointed projection from certain parts or organs
MUCUS, -ES *n*
MUD, -DED, -DING, -S *n, vb*
MUDBANK *n* sloping area of mud beside a body of water
MUDBATH *n* medicinal bath in heated mud
MUDBUG, -S *n* crayfish
MUDCAP, -S *vb* use explosive charge in blasting
MUDCAT, -S *n* any of several large North American catfish
MUDDED ▸ **mud**
MUDDER, -S *n* horse that runs well in mud
MUDDIED ▸ **muddy**
MUDDIER ▸ **muddy**
MUDDIES ▸ **muddy**
MUDDILY ▸ **muddy**
MUDDING ▸ **mud**
MUDDLE, -D, -S *vb* confuse ▹ *n* state of confusion
MUDDLER *n* person who muddles or muddles through
MUDDLES ▸ **muddle**
MUDDLY ▸ **muddle**
MUDDY, MUDDIED, MUDDIER, MUDDIES *adj, vb*
MUDEJAR *n* Spanish Moor ▹ *adj* of or relating to a style of architecture
MUDEYE, -S *n* larva of the dragonfly
MUDFISH *n* fish that lives at the muddy bottoms of rivers, lakes, etc
MUDFLAP *n* flap above wheel to deflect mud
MUDFLAT *n* tract of low muddy land
MUDFLOW *n* flow of soil mixed with water down a steep unstable slope
MUDGE, -D, -S, MUDGING *vb* speak vaguely
MUDGER, -S ▸ **mudge**
MUDGES ▸ **mudge**
MUDGING ▸ **mudge**
MUDHEN, -S *n* water bird living in muddy place
MUDHOLE *n* hole with mud at bottom
MUDHOOK *n* anchor
MUDIR, -S *n* local governor
MUDIRIA *n* province of mudir
MUDIRS ▸ **mudir**
MUDLARK *n* street urchin ▹ *vb* play in mud
MUDPACK *n* cosmetic paste applied to the face
MUDPIE, -S *n* small mass of mud moulded into a pie shape
MUDRA, -S *n* hand movement in Hindu religious dancing
MUDROCK *n* type of sedimentary rock
MUDROOM *n* room where muddy shoes may be left
MUDS ▸ **mud**

MUDSCOW *n* boat for travelling over mudflats
MUDSILL *n* support for building at or below ground
MUDWORT *n* plant growing in mud
MUEDDIN *same as* ▸ **muezzin**
MUESLI, -S *n*
MUEZZIN *n* official who summons Muslims to prayer
MUFF, -ED, -ING, -S *n* tube-shaped covering to keep the hands warm ▹ *vb* bungle (an action)
MUFFIN, -S *n*
MUFFING ▸ **muff**
MUFFINS ▸ **muffin**
MUFFISH ▸ **muff**
MUFFLE, -D, -S *vb, n*
MUFFLER *n* scarf
MUFFLES ▸ **muffle**
MUFFS ▸ **muff**
MUFLON, -S *same as* > **moufflon**
MUFTI, -S *n* civilian clothes worn by a person who usually wears a uniform
MUG, -GED, -S *n, vb*
MUGFUL, -S *same as* ▸ **mug**
MUGG, -S *same as* ▸ **mug**
MUGGA, -S *n* Australian eucalyptus tree
MUGGAR, -S *same as* ▸ **mugger**
MUGGAS ▸ **mugga**
MUGGED ▸ **mug**
MUGGEE, -S *n* mugged person
MUGGER, -S *n* person who commits robbery with violence
MUGGIER ▸ **muggy**
MUGGILY ▸ **muggy**
MUGGING ▸ **mug**
MUGGINS *n* stupid or gullible person
MUGGISH *same as* ▸ **muggy**
MUGGLE, -S *n* person who does not possess supernatural powers
MUGGS ▸ **mugg**
MUGGUR, -S *same as* ▸ **mugger**
MUGGY, MUGGIER *adj*
MUGHAL, -S *same as* ▸ **mogul**
MUGS ▸ **mug**
MUGSHOT *n* police photograph of person's face
MUGWORT *n* N temperate herbaceous plant with aromatic leaves
MUGWUMP *n* neutral or independent person
MUHLY, MUHLIES *n* American grass
MUID, -S *n* former French measure of capacity
MUIL, -S *same as* ▸ **mule**
MUIR, -S *same as* ▸ **moor**
MUIST, -ED, -S *same as* ▸ **must**
MUJIK, -S *same as* ▸ **muzhik**
MUKHTAR *n* lawyer in India
MUKLUK, -S *n* soft boot, usually of sealskin
MUKTUK, -S *n* thin outer skin of the beluga, used as food
MULCH, -ED, -ES *n, vb*
MULCT, -ED, -S *vb* cheat or defraud ▹ *n* fine or penalty
MULE, -D, MULING *n, vb*
MULES, -ED, -ES *vb* surgically remove folds of skin from a sheep
MULETA, -S *n* small cape attached to a stick used by a matador
MULEY, -S *adj* (of cattle) having no horns ▹ *n* any hornless cow
MULGA, -S *n* Australian acacia shrub growing in desert regions
MULIE, -S *n* type of N American deer
MULING ▸ **mule**
MULISH *adj* obstinate
MULL, -ED, -ING, -S *vb, n*
MULLA, -S *same as* ▸ **mullah**
MULLAH, -S *n* Muslim scholar, teacher, or religious leader
MULLAS ▸ **mulla**
MULLED ▸ **mull**
MULLEIN *n* type of European plant
MULLEN, -S *same as* ▸ **mullein**
MULLER, -S *n* flat heavy implement used to grind material ▹ *vb* beat up or defeat thoroughly
MULLET, -S *n* edible sea fish
MULLEY, -S *same as* ▸ **muley**

MULLING ▸ **mull**
MULLION *n* vertical dividing bar in a window ▹ *vb* furnish with mullions
MULLITE *n* colourless mineral
MULLOCK *n* waste material from a mine
MULLS ▸ **mull**
MULMUL, -S *n* muslin
MULMULL *same as* ▸ **mulmul**
MULMULS ▸ **mulmul**
MULSE, -S *n* drink containing honey
MULSH, -ED, -ES *same as* ▸ **mulch**
MULTUM, -S *n* substance used in brewing
MULTURE *n* fee formerly paid to a miller for grinding grain ▹ *vb* take multure
MUM, -MED, -S *n, vb*
MUMBLE, -D, -S *vb, n*
MUMBLER ▸ **mumble**
MUMBLES ▸ **mumble**
MUMBLY ▸ **mumble**
MUMM, -S *same as* ▸ **mum**
MUMMED ▸ **mum**
MUMMER, -S *n* actor in a traditional English folk play ▹ *vb* perform as a mummer
MUMMERY *n* performance by mummers
MUMMIA, -S *n* mummified flesh used as medicine
MUMMIED ▸ **mummy**
MUMMIES ▸ **mummy**
MUMMIFY *vb* preserve a body as a mummy
MUMMING ▸ **mum**
MUMMOCK *same as* ▸ **mammock**
MUMMS ▸ **mumm**
MUMMY, MUMMIED, MUMMIES *n, vb*
MUMP, -ED, -ING *vb* be silent
MUMPER, -S ▸ **mump**
MUMPING ▸ **mump**
MUMPISH ▸ **mumps**
MUMPS *n* infectious disease with swelling in the glands of the neck
MUMS ▸ **mum**
MUMSY, MUMSIER, MUMSIES *adj* (of a woman) wearing clothes that are old-fashioned and unflattering ▹ *n* mother
MUMU, -S *n* oven in Papua New Guinea
MUN, -S *same as* ▸ **maun**
MUNCH, -ED, -ES *vb*
MUNCHER ▸ **munch**
MUNCHES ▸ **munch**
MUNCHIE *n* small amount of food eaten between meals
MUNCHY *adj* suitable for snacking
MUNDANE *adj*
MUNDIC, -S *n* iron pyrites
MUNDIFY *vb* cleanse
MUNG, -ED, -ING, -S *vb* process (computer data)
MUNGA, -S *n* army canteen
MUNGE, -S *vb* modify a password into an unguessable state
MUNGED ▸ **mung**
MUNGES ▸ **munge**
MUNGING ▸ **mung**
MUNGO, -ES, -S *n* cheap felted fabric made from waste wool
MUNGS ▸ **mung**
MUNI, -S *n* municipal radio broadcast
MUNIFY *vb* fortify
MUNIS ▸ **muni**
MUNITE, -D, -S *vb* strengthen
MUNNION *archaic word for* ▸ **mullion**
MUNS ▸ **mun**
MUNSHI, -S *n* secretary in India
MUNSTER *variant of* ▸ **muenster**
MUNTED *adj* destroyed or ruined
MUNTER, -S *n* insulting word for an unattractive person
MUNTIN, -S *n* supporting or strengthening bar
MUNTING *same as* ▸ **muntin**
MUNTINS ▸ **muntin**
MUNTJAC *n* small Asian deer
MUNTJAK *same as* ▸ **muntjac**
MUNTRIE *n* Australian shrub with green-red edible berries
MUON, -S *n* elementary particle with a mass 207 times that of an electron
MUONIC ▸ **muon**

MUONIUM *n* form of hydrogen
MUONS ▶ **muon**
MUPPET, -S *n*
MURA, -S *n* group of people living together in Japanese countryside
MURAENA *n* moray eel
MURAGE, -S *n* tax levied for the construction or maintenance of town walls
MURAL, -S *n, adj*
MURALED *same as* > **muralled**
MURALS ▶ **mural**
MURAS ▶ **mura**
MURDER, -S *n, vb*
MURE, -D, -S, MURING *archaic or literary word for* ▶ **immure**
MUREIN, -S *n* polymer found in cells
MURENA, -S *same as* ▶ **muraena**
MURES ▶ **mure**
MUREX, -ES, MURICES *n* marine gastropod formerly used as a source of purple dye
MURGEON *vb* grimace at
MURIATE *obsolete name for a* > **chloride**
MURICES ▶ **murex**
MURID, -S *n* animal of the mouse family
MURINE, -S *n* animal belonging to the family that includes rats and mice
MURING ▶ **mure**
MURK, -ED, -ER, -EST, -ING, -S *n* thick darkness ▷ *adj* dark or gloomy ▷ *vb* murder (a person)
MURKIER ▶ **murky**
MURKILY ▶ **murky**
MURKING ▶ **murk**
MURKISH ▶ **murk**
MURKLY ▶ **murk**
MURKS ▶ **murk**
MURKY, MURKIER *adj* dark or gloomy
MURL, -ED, -ING, -S *vb* crumble
MURLAIN *n* type of basket
MURLAN, -S *same as* ▶ **murlain**
MURLED ▶ **murl**
MURLIER ▶ **murly**
MURLIN, -S *same as* ▶ **murlain**
MURLING ▶ **murl**
MURLINS ▶ **murlin**
MURLS ▶ **murl**
MURLY, MURLIER ▶ **murl**
MURMUR, -S *vb* speak or say in a quiet indistinct way ▷ *n* continuous low indistinct sound
MURPHY *dialect or informal word for* ▶ **potato**
MURR, -S *n* former name for a cold
MURRA, -S *same as* > **murrhine**
MURRAGH *n* type of large caddis fly
MURRAIN *n* cattle plague
MURRAM, -S *n* type of gravel
MURRAS ▶ **murra**
MURRAY, -S *n* large Australian freshwater fish
MURRE, -S *n* type of guillemot
MURREE, -S *n* native Australian
MURREN, -S *same as* ▶ **murrain**
MURRES ▶ **murre**
MURREY, -S *adj* mulberry colour
MURRHA, -S *same as* ▶ **murra**
MURRI, -S *same as* ▶ **murree**
MURRIES ▶ **murry**
MURRIN, -S *same as* ▶ **murrain**
MURRINE *same as* > **murrhine**
MURRINS ▶ **murrin**
MURRION *same as* ▶ **murrain**
MURRIS ▶ **murri**
MURRS ▶ **murr**
MURRY, MURRIES *same as* ▶ **moray**
MURSHID *n* Sufi master or guide
MURTHER *same as* ▶ **murder**
MURTI, -S *n* image of a deity, which itself is considered divine
MURVA, -S *n* type of hemp
MUS ▶ **mu**
MUSANG, -S *n* catlike animal of Malaysia
MUSAR, -S *n* rabbinic literature concerned with ethics
MUSCA, -E *n* small constellation in the S hemisphere
MUSCAT, -S *same as* > **muscatel**
MUSCID, -S *n* type of fly

MUSCLE, -D, -S *n, vb*
MUSCLEY *adj* of a muscular build
MUSCLY *same as* ▸ **muscley**
MUSCOID *adj* moss-like ▹ *n* moss-like plant
MUSCONE *same as* ▸ **muskone**
MUSCOSE *adj* like moss
MUSCOVY *adj* as in **muscovy duck** a kind of duck
MUSE, -D, -S *vb, n*
MUSEFUL ▸ **muse**
MUSER, -S ▸ **muse**
MUSES ▸ **muse**
MUSET, -S *same as* ▸ **musit**
MUSETTE *n* type of bagpipe formerly popular in France
MUSEUM, -S *n*
MUSH, -ED, -ES *n, interj, vb*
MUSHA *interj* Irish exclamation of surprise
MUSHED ▸ **mush**
MUSHER, -S ▸ **mush**
MUSHES ▸ **mush**
MUSHIE, -S *n* mushroom
MUSHIER ▸ **mushy**
MUSHIES ▸ **mushie**
MUSHILY ▸ **mushy**
MUSHING *n* act of mushing
MUSHRAT *same as* ▸ **muskrat**
MUSHY, MUSHIER *adj*
MUSIC, -S *n, vb*
MUSICAL *adj, n*
MUSICK, -S *same as* ▸ **music**
MUSICS ▸ **music**
MUSIMON *same as* > **moufflon**
MUSING, -S ▸ **muse**
MUSIT, -S *n* gap in fence
MUSIVE *adj* mosaic
MUSJID, -S *same as* ▸ **masjid**
MUSK, -ED, -ING, -S *n, vb*
MUSKEG, -S *n* area of undrained boggy land
MUSKET, -S *n*
MUSKIE, -S *n* large North American freshwater game fish
MUSKIER ▸ **musky**
MUSKIES ▸ **muskie**
MUSKILY ▸ **musky**
MUSKING ▸ **musk**
MUSKIT, -S *same as* > **mesquite**
MUSKLE, -S *same as* ▸ **mussel**
MUSKONE *n* substance in musk
MUSKOX *n* large Canadian mammal
MUSKRAT *n* N American beaver-like rodent
MUSKS ▸ **musk**
MUSKY, MUSKIER *adj* smelling of musk
MUSLIN, -S *n*
MUSMON, -S *same as* ▸ **musimon**
MUSO, -S *n* musician who is concerned with technique rather than content or expression
MUSPIKE *n* Canadian freshwater fish
MUSROL, -S *n* part of bridle
MUSS, -ED, -ES, -ING *vb* make untidy ▹ *n* state of disorder
MUSSE *same as* ▸ **muss**
MUSSED ▸ **muss**
MUSSEL, -S *n* edible shellfish with a dark hinged shell
MUSSES ▸ **muss**
MUSSIER ▸ **mussy**
MUSSILY ▸ **mussy**
MUSSING ▸ **muss**
MUSSY, MUSSIER *adj* untidy or disordered
MUST, -ED, -ING, -S *vb, n*
MUSTANG *n*
MUSTARD *n, adj*
MUSTED ▸ **must**
MUSTER, -S *vb, n*
MUSTH, -S *n* state of frenzied excitement in the males of certain large mammals
MUSTIER ▸ **musty**
MUSTILY ▸ **musty**
MUSTING ▸ **must**
MUSTS ▸ **must**
MUSTY, MUSTIER *adj*
MUT, -S *another word for* ▸ **em**
MUTABLE *adj* liable to change
MUTABLY ▸ **mutable**
MUTAGEN *n* any substance that can induce genetic mutation
MUTANDA > **mutandum**
MUTANT, -S *n* mutated animal, plant, etc ▹ *adj* of or resulting from mutation
MUTASE, -S *n* type of enzyme
MUTATE, -D, -S *vb* (cause to) undergo mutation
MUTATOR *n* something that causes a mutation

MUTCH, -ED, -ES *n* close-fitting linen cap ▷ *vb* cadge
MUTE, -R, -S, -ST, MUTING *adj, vb*
MUTED *adj*
MUTEDLY ▶ **muted**
MUTELY ▶ **mute**
MUTER ▶ **mute**
MUTES ▶ **mute**
MUTEST ▶ **mute**
MUTI, -S *n* medicine, esp herbal medicine
MUTINE, -D, -S *vb* mutiny
MUTING ▶ **mute**
MUTINY *n, vb*
MUTIS ▶ **muti**
MUTISM, -S *n* state of being mute
MUTON, -S *n* part of gene
MUTS ▶ **mut**
MUTT, -S *n*
MUTTER, -S *vb* utter or speak indistinctly ▷ *n* muttered sound or grumble
MUTTON, -S *n* flesh of sheep, used as food
MUTTONY *adj* like mutton
MUTTS ▶ **mutt**
MUTUAL, -S *adj, n*
MUTUCA, -S *same as* ▶ **motuca**
MUTUEL, -S *n* system of betting
MUTULAR ▶ **mutule**
MUTULE, -S *n* flat block in a Doric cornice
MUTUUM, -S *n* contract for loan of goods
MUUMUU, -S *n* loose brightly coloured dress worn by women in Hawaii
MUX, -ED, -ES, -ING *vb* spoil

> This word meaning to spoil or botch is very useful not only because it contains an X, but because its verb forms can enable you to clear your rack of unpromising letters.

MUZAK, -S *n* piped background music
MUZAKY *adj* having a bland sound
MUZHIK, -S *n* Russian peasant, esp under the tsars
MUZJIK, -S *same as* ▶ **muzhik**

> Meaning a Russian peasant, this is a wonderful high-scoring word, combining Z, J and K, and if you can play the plural using all of your tiles, you'll get a bonus of 50 points.

MUZZ, -ED, -ES, -ING *vb* make (something) muzzy
MUZZIER ▶ **muzzy**
MUZZILY ▶ **muzzy**
MUZZING ▶ **muzz**
MUZZLE, -D, -S *n, vb*
MUZZLER ▶ **muzzle**
MUZZLES ▶ **muzzle**
MUZZY, MUZZIER *adj* confused or muddled
MVULE, -S *n* tropical African tree
MWAH *interj* representation of the sound of a kiss
MWALIMU *n* teacher
MY *adj, interj*
MYAL ▶ **myalism**
MYALGIA *n* pain in a muscle or a group of muscles
MYALGIC ▶ **myalgia**
MYALISM *n* kind of witchcraft
MYALIST ▶ **myalism**
MYALL, -S *n* Australian acacia with hard scented wood
MYASIS, MYASES *same as* ▶ **myiasis**
MYC, -S *n* oncogene that aids the growth of tumorous cells
MYCELE, -S *n* microscopic spike-like structure in mucus
MYCELIA > **mycelium**
MYCELLA *n* blue-veined Danish cream cheese
MYCETES *n* fungus
MYCOSIS, MYCOSES *n* any infection or disease caused by fungus
MYCOTIC ▶ **mycosis**
MYCS ▶ **myc**
MYELIN, -S *n* white tissue forming an insulating sheath around certain nerve fibres
MYELINE *same as* ▶ **myelin**
MYELINS ▶ **myelin**
MYELOID *adj* of or relating to the spinal cord or the bone marrow
MYELOMA *n* tumour of the bone marrow
MYELON, -S *n* spinal cord

MYGALE, -S *n* large American spider
MYIASIS, MYIASES *n* infestation of the body by the larvae of flies
MYLAR, -S *n* tradename for a kind of strong polyester film
MYLODON *n* prehistoric giant sloth
MYNA, -S *same as* ▸ **mynah**
MYNAH, -S *n* tropical Asian starling which can mimic human speech
MYNAS ▸ **myna**
MYNHEER *n* Dutch title of address
MYOGEN, -S *n* albumin found in muscle
MYOGRAM *n* tracings of muscular contractions
MYOID, -S *adj* like muscle ▹ *n* section of a retinal cone or rod which is sensitive to changes in light intensity
MYOLOGY *n* study of the structure and diseases of muscles
MYOMA, -S, -TA *n* benign tumour composed of muscle tissue
MYOMERE *n* part of a vertebrate embryo
MYOPE, -S *n* a person with myopia
MYOPIA, -S *n*
MYOPIC, -S *n* shortsighted person
MYOPIES ▸ **myopy**
MYOPS, -ES *same as* ▸ **myope**
MYOPY, MYOPIES *same as* ▸ **myopia**
MYOSES ▸ **myosis**
MYOSIN, -S *n* protein found in muscle
MYOSIS, MYOSES *same as* ▸ **miosis**
MYOSOTE *same as* > **myosotis**
MYOTIC, -S ▸ **miosis**
MYOTOME *n* any segment of embryonic mesoderm that develops into skeletal muscle
MYOTUBE *n* cylindrical cell in muscle
MYRBANE *same as* ▸ **mirbane**
MYRIAD, -S *adj, n*
MYRICA, -S *n* dried root bark of the wax myrtle
MYRINGA *n* eardrum
MYRRH, -S *n*
MYRRHIC ▸ **myrrh**
MYRRHOL *n* oil of myrrh
MYRRHS ▸ **myrrh**
MYRRHY *adj* of or like myrrh
MYRTLE, -S *n*
MYSELF *pron*
MYSID, -S *n* small shrimplike crustacean
MYSOST, -S *n* Norwegian cheese
MYSPACE *vb*
MYSTERY *n*
MYSTIC, -S *n, adj*
MYSTIFY *vb*
MYTH, -S *n*
MYTHI ▸ **mythus**
MYTHIC *same as* > **mythical**
MYTHIER ▸ **mythy**
MYTHISE *same as* ▸ **mythize**
MYTHISM *same as* > **mythicism**
MYTHIST ▸ **mythism**
MYTHIZE *same as* > **mythicize**
MYTHOS, MYTHOI *n* beliefs of a specific group or society
MYTHS ▸ **myth**
MYTHUS, MYTHI *same as* ▸ **mythos**
MYTHY, MYTHIER *adj* of or like myth
MYXO, -S *n* viral disease of rabbits
MYXOID *adj* containing mucus
MYXOMA, -S *n* tumour composed of mucous connective tissue
MYXOS ▸ **myxo**
MZEE, -S *n* old person ▹ *adj* advanced in years
MZUNGU, -S *n* (in E Africa) White person

Nn

NA *same as* ▸ **nae**
NAAM, -S *same as* ▸ **nam**
NAAN, -S *n* slightly leavened flat Indian bread
NAARTJE *same as* > **naartjie**
NAB, -BED, -BING, -S *vb*
NABBER, -S *n* thief
NABBING ▸ **nab**
NABE, -S *n* Japanese hotpot
NABIS *n* Parisian art movement
NABK, -S *n* edible berry
NABLA, -S *another name for* ▸ **del**
NABOB, -S *n* rich, powerful, or important man
NABS ▸ **nab**
NACARAT *n* red-orange colour
NACELLE *n* streamlined enclosure on an aircraft
NACH *n* Indian dance
NACHAS *n* pleasure
NACHE, -S *n* rump
NACHO, -S *n* snack of a piece of tortilla with a topping
NACKET, -S *n* light lunch, snack
NACRE, -S *n* mother of pearl
NACRED ▸ **nacre**
NACRES ▸ **nacre**
NACRITE *n* mineral
NACROUS ▸ **nacre**
NADA, -S *n* nothing
NADIR, -S *n*
NADIRAL ▸ **nadir**
NADIRS ▸ **nadir**
NAE, -S *Scot word for* ▸ **no**
NAEBODY *Scots variant of* ▸ **nobody**
NAES ▸ **nae**
NAEVE, -S *n* birthmark
NAEVI ▸ **naevus**
NAEVOID ▸ **naevus**
NAEVUS, NAEVI *n* birthmark or mole
NAFF, -ED, -ER, -EST, -ING, -S *adj, vb*
NAFFLY ▸ **naff**
NAFFS ▸ **naff**
NAG, -GED, -GING, -S *vb, n*
NAGA, -S *n* cobra
NAGANA, -S *n* disease of all domesticated animals of central and southern Africa
NAGAPIE *n* bushbaby
NAGARI, -S *n* scripts for writing several languages of India
NAGAS ▸ **naga**
NAGGED ▸ **nag**
NAGGER, -S ▸ **nag**
NAGGIER ▸ **naggy**
NAGGING ▸ **nag**
NAGGY, NAGGIER ▸ **nag**
NAGMAAL *n* Communion
NAGOR, -S *another name for* > **reedbuck**
NAGS ▸ **nag**
NAGWARE *n* software that is initially free and then requires payment
NAH *same as* ▸ **no**
NAHAL, -S *n* agricultural settlement run by an Israeli military youth organization
NAIAD, -ES, -S *n* nymph living in a lake or river
NAIANT *adj* swimming
NAIF, -ER, -EST, -S *less common word for* ▸ **naive**
NAIFLY ▸ **naif**
NAIFS ▸ **naif**
NAIK, -S *n* chief
NAIL, -ED, -S *n, vb*
NAILER, -S ▸ **nail**
NAILERY *n* nail factory
NAILING ▸ **nail**
NAILS ▸ **nail**
NAILSET *n* punch for driving down the head of a nail

NAIN *adj* own
NAIRA, -S *n* standard monetary unit of Nigeria, divided into 100 kobo
NAIRU, -S *n* Non-Accelerating Inflation Rate of Unemployment
NAIVE, -R, -S, -ST *adj, n*
NAIVELY ▸ **naive**
NAIVER ▸ **naive**
NAIVES ▸ **naive**
NAIVEST ▸ **naive**
NAIVETE *variant of* ▸ **naivety**
NAIVETY *n*
NAIVIST ▸ **naive**
NAKED, -ER *adj*
NAKEDLY ▸ **naked**
NAKER, -S *n* small kettledrum used in medieval music
NAKFA, -S *n* standard currency unit of Eritrea
NALA, -S *n* ravine
NALED, -S *n* type of insecticide
NALLA, -S *n* ravine
NALLAH, -S *same as* ▸ **nalla**
NALLAS ▸ **nalla**
NAM, -S *n* distraint
NAMABLE ▸ **name**
NAMASTE *n* Indian greeting
NAME, -D, -S *n, vb*
NAMELY *adv*
NAMER, -S ▸ **name**
NAMES ▸ **name**
NAMETAG *n*
NAMING, -S ▸ **name**
NAMMA *adj* as in **namma hole** Australian word for a natural well in rock
NAMS ▸ **nam**
NAMU, -S *n* black New Zealand sandfly
NAN, -S *n* grandmother
NANA, -S *same as* ▸ **nan**
NANDIN, -S *same as* ▸ **nandina**
NANDINA *n* type of shrub
NANDINE *n* African palm civet
NANDINS ▸ **nandin**
NANDOO, -S *same as* ▸ **nandu**
NANDU, -S *n* type of ostrich
NANE *Scot word for* ▸ **none**
NANG *adj* excellent; cool
NANISM, -S *n* dwarfism
NANITE, -S *n* microscopically small machine or robot
NANKEEN *n* hard-wearing buff-coloured cotton fabric
NANKIN, -S *same as* ▸ **nankeen**
NANNA, -S *same as* ▸ **nan**
NANNIE *same as* ▸ **nanny**
NANNY, NANNIED, NANNIES *n, vb*
NANO, -S *n* science concerned with materials on a molecular scale
NANOBE, -S *n* microbe that is smaller than the smallest known bacterium
NANOBEE *n* artificial nanoparticle
NANOBES ▸ **nanobe**
NANOBOT *n* microscopically small robot
NANODOT *n* microscopic cluster of atoms used to store data in a computer chip
NANOOK, -S *n* polar bear
NANOS ▸ **nano**
NANS ▸ **nan**
NANUA, -S *same as* ▸ **moki**
NAOS, NAOI, -ES *n* ancient classical temple
NAP, -PED, -PING, -S *n, vb*
NAPA, -S *n* type of leather
NAPALM, -S *n* highly inflammable jellied petrol, used in bombs ▹ *vb* attack (people or places) with napalm
NAPAS ▸ **napa**
NAPE, -D, -S, NAPING *n* back of the neck ▹ *vb* attack with napalm
NAPERY *n* household linen, esp table linen
NAPES ▸ **nape**
NAPHTHA *n* liquid mixture used as a solvent and in petrol
NAPHTOL *same as* > **naphthol**
NAPING ▸ **nape**
NAPKIN, -S *same as* ▸ **nappy**
NAPLESS *adj* threadbare
NAPOO, -ED, -S *vb* military slang meaning kill

NAPPA, -S *n* soft leather
NAPPE, -S *n* mass of rock that has been thrust from its original position by earth movements
NAPPED ▶ **nap**
NAPPER, -S *n* person or thing that raises the nap on cloth
NAPPES ▶ **nappe**
NAPPIE *same as* ▶ **nappy**
NAPPIER ▶ **nappy**
NAPPIES ▶ **nappy**
NAPPING ▶ **nap**
NAPPY, NAPPIER, NAPPIES *n, adj*
NAPRON, -S *same as* ▶ **apron**
NAPS ▶ **nap**
NARAS, -ES *same as* ▶ **narras**
NARCEEN *same as* > **narceine**
NARCEIN *same as* > **narceine**
NARCISM *n* exceptional admiration for oneself
NARCIST *n* narcissist
NARCOMA *n* coma caused by intake of narcotic drugs
NARCOSE *same as* > **narcosis**
NARD, -ED, -ING, -S *n* any of several plants with aromatic roots ▷ *vb* anoint with nard oil
NARDINE ▶ **nard**
NARDING ▶ **nard**
NARDOO, -S *n* cloverlike fern which grows in swampy areas
NARDS ▶ **nard**
NARES, NARIS *pl n* nostrils
NARGILE *same as* > **narghile**
NARGILY *same as* > **narghile**
NARIAL *adj* of or relating to the nares
NARIC ▶ **nares**
NARINE *same as* ▶ **narial**
NARIS ▶ **nares**
NARK, -ED, -ING, -S *vb* annoy ▷ *n* informer or spy
NARKIER ▶ **narky**
NARKING ▶ **nark**
NARKS ▶ **nark**
NARKY, NARKIER *adj*
NARRAS *n* type of shrub
NARRATE *vb*
NARRE *adj* nearer
NARROW *adj, vb*
NARROWS *pl n* narrow part of a strait, river, or current
NARTHEX *n* portico at the west end of a basilica or church
NARTJIE *same as* > **naartjie**

This word for a small sweet orange is one to look out for when you have the J with the good letters of 'retain'. And it has alternative spellings **naartje** and **naartjie**.

NARWAL, -S *same as* ▶ **narwhal**
NARWHAL *n* Arctic whale with a long spiral tusk
NARY *adv* not
NAS *vb* has not
NASAL, -S *adj, n*
NASALLY ▶ **nasal**
NASALS ▶ **nasal**
NASARD, -S *n* organ stop
NASCENT *adj* starting to grow or develop
NASHGAB *n* chatter
NASHI, -S *n* fruit of the Japanese pear
NASIAL ▶ **nasion**
NASION, -S *n* craniometric point where the top of the nose meets the ridge of the forehead
NASTIC *adj* (of movement of plants) independent of the direction of the external stimulus
NASTIER ▶ **nasty**
NASTIES ▶ **nasty**
NASTILY ▶ **nasty**
NASTY, NASTIER, NASTIES *adj, n*
NASUTE, -S *n* type of termite
NAT, -S *n* supporter of nationalism
NATAL *adj*
NATANT *adj* (of aquatic plants) floating on the water
NATCH, -ES *sentence substitute* naturally ▷ *n* notch
NATES, NATIS *pl n* buttocks
NATHEMO *same as* > **nathemore**
NATION, -S *n*
NATIS ▶ **nates**
NATIVE, -S *adj, n*

NATRIUM *obsolete name for* ▸ **sodium**
NATRON, -S *n* whitish or yellow mineral
NATS ▸ **nat**
NATTER, -S *vb, n*
NATTERY *adj* irritable
NATTIER ▸ **natty**
NATTILY ▸ **natty**
NATTY, NATTIER *adj*
NATURA, -E *n* nature
NATURAL *adj, n*
NATURE, -S *n*
NATURED *adj* having a certain disposition
NATURES ▸ **nature**
NAUCH, -ES *same as* ▸ **nautch**
NAUGHT, -S *n, adv*
NAUGHTY *adj*
NAUNT, -S *n* aunt
NAUPLII > **nauplius**
NAUSEA, -S *n*
NAUTCH *n* intricate traditional Indian dance
NAUTIC *same as* > **nautical**
NAUTICS *n* science of navigation
NAUTILI > **nautilus**
NAV, -S *n* (short for) navigation
NAVAID, -S *n* navigational aid
NAVAL *adj*
NAVALLY ▸ **naval**
NAVAR, -S *n* system of air navigation
NAVARCH *n* admiral
NAVARHO *n* aircraft navigation system
NAVARIN *n* stew of mutton or lamb with root vegetables
NAVARS ▸ **navar**
NAVE, -S *n* long central part of a church
NAVEL, -S *n*
NAVES ▸ **nave**
NAVETTE *n* gem cut
NAVEW, -S *another name for* ▸ **turnip**
NAVIES ▸ **navy**
NAVS ▸ **nav**
NAVVY, NAVVIED, NAVVIES *n* labourer employed on a road or a building site ▷ *vb* work as a navvy
NAVY, NAVIES *n, adj*
NAW *same as* ▸ **no**
NAWAB, -S *n* (formerly) a Muslim ruler or landowner in India
NAY, -S *interj, n, adv, sentence substitute*
NAYSAY, NAYSAID, -S *vb* say no
NAYWARD *n* as in *to the nayward* towards denial
NAYWORD *n* proverb
NAZE, -S *n* flat marshy headland
NAZI, -S *n*
NAZIFY *vb* make nazi in character
NAZIR, -S *n* Muslim official
NAZIS ▸ **nazi**
NDUJA, -S *n* spicy pork paste
NE *conj* nor
NEAFE, -S *same as* ▸ **nieve**
NEAFFE, -S *same as* ▸ **nieve**
NEAL, -ED, -ING, -S *same as* ▸ **anneal**
NEANIC *adj* of or relating to the early stages in a life cycle
NEAP, -ED, -ING, -S *adj* of, relating to, or constituting a neap tide ▷ *vb* be grounded by a neap tide
NEAR, -ED, -ER, -EST, -ING, -S *adj, vb, prep, adv, n*
NEARBY *adj, adv*
NEARED ▸ **near**
NEARER ▸ **near**
NEAREST ▸ **near**
NEARING ▸ **near**
NEARISH *adj* quite near
NEARLY *adv*
NEARS ▸ **near**
NEAT, -ER, -EST, -S *adj, n*
NEATEN, -S *vb* make neat
NEATER ▸ **neat**
NEATEST ▸ **neat**
NEATH *short for* ▸ **beneath**
NEATLY ▸ **neat**
NEATNIK *n* very neat and tidy person
NEATS ▸ **neat**
NEB, -BED, -BING, -S *n* beak of a bird or the nose of an animal ▷ *vb* look around nosily
NEBBICH *same as* ▸ **nebbish**
NEBBING ▸ **neb**
NEBBISH *n* timid person
NEBBUK, -S *n* type of shrub
NEBECK, -S *same as* ▸ **nebbuk**
NEBEK, -S *same as* ▸ **nebbuk**
NEBEL, -S *n* Hebrew musical instrument
NEBISH *same as* ▸ **nebbish**

NEBRIS *n* fawn-skin
NEBS ▸ **neb**
NEBULA, -E, -S *n* hazy cloud of particles and gases
NEBULAR ▸ **nebula**
NEBULAS ▸ **nebula**
NEBULE, -S *n* cloud
NEBULY *adj* wavy
NECK, -ED, -S *n, vb*
NECKER, -S ▸ **neck**
NECKING *n* activity of kissing and embracing passionately
NECKLET *n* ornament worn round the neck
NECKS ▸ **neck**
NECKTIE *same as* ▸ **tie**
NECROSE *vb* cause or undergo necrosis
NECTAR, -S *n*
NECTARY *n* structure secreting nectar in a plant
NED, -S *n* derogatory name for an adolescent hooligan
NEDDIER ▸ **neddy**
NEDDIES ▸ **neddy**
NEDDISH ▸ **ned**
NEDDY, NEDDIER, NEDDIES *n* donkey ▹ *adj* of or relating to neds
NEDETTE *n* derogatory name for a female adolescent hooligan
NEDS ▸ **ned**
NEE *prep* indicating the maiden name of a married woman ▹ *adj* indicating the maiden name of a married woman
NEED, -ED, -ING *vb, n*
NEEDER, -S ▸ **need**
NEEDFUL *adj* necessary or required
NEEDIER ▸ **needy**
NEEDILY ▸ **needy**
NEEDING ▸ **need**
NEEDLE, -D, -S *n, vb*
NEEDLER *n* needle maker
NEEDLES ▸ **needle**
NEEDLY *adj* like or full of needles
NEEDS *adv* necessarily ▹ *pl n* what is required
NEEDY, NEEDIER *adj*
NEELD, -S *same as* ▸ **needle**
NEELE, -S *same as* ▸ **needle**
NEEM, -S *n* type of large Indian tree
NEEMB, -S *same as* ▸ **neem**
NEEMS ▸ **neem**
NEEP, -S *dialect name for* ▸ **turnip**
NEESE, -D, -S, NEESING *same as* ▸ **neeze**
NEEZE, -D, -S, NEEZING *vb* sneeze
NEF, -S *n* church nave
NEFAST *adj* wicked
NEFS ▸ **nef**
NEG, -S *n* photographic negative
NEGATE, -D, -S *vb*
NEGATER ▸ **negate**
NEGATES ▸ **negate**
NEGATON *same as* > **negatron**
NEGATOR ▸ **negate**
NEGLECT *vb, n*
NEGLIGE *variant of* > **negligee**
NEGRONI *n* type of cocktail
NEGS ▸ **neg**
NEGUS, -ES *n* hot drink of port and lemon juice
NEIF, -S *same as* ▸ **nieve**
NEIGH, -ED, -S *n, vb*
NEINEI, -S *n* type of plant
NEIST *Scots variant of* ▸ **next**
NEITHER *pron, adj*
NEIVE, -S *same as* ▸ **nieve**
NEK, -S *n* mountain pass
NEKTON, -S *n* free-swimming animals in the middle depths of a sea or lake
NELIES *same as* ▸ **nelis**
NELIS *n* type of pear
NELLIE, -S *n* type of albatross
NELLY *n* as in **not on your nelly** not under any circumstances
NELSON, -S *n* type of wrestling hold
NELUMBO *n* type of aquatic plant
NEMA, -S *n* filament
NEMATIC *n* substance having a mesomorphic state
NEMESES ▸ **nemesis**
NEMESIA *n* type of southern African plant
NEMESIS, NEMESES *n*
NEMN, -ED, -ING, -S *vb* name
NEMORAL *adj* of a wood
NEMPT *adj* named
NENE, -S *n* rare black-and-grey short-winged Hawaiian goose
NEOCON, -S *n* supporter of neoconservative politics

NEOGENE *adj* of, denoting, or formed during the Miocene and Pliocene epochs
NEOLITH *n* Neolithic stone implement
NEOLOGY *same as* > **neologism**
NEON, -S *n, adj*
NEONATE *n* newborn child
NEONED *adj* lit with neon
NEONS ▶ **neon**
NEOSOUL *n* soul music combined with other genres
NEOTENY *n* persistence of larval or fetal features in the adult form of an animal
NEOTYPE *n* specimen selected to replace a type specimen that has been lost or destroyed
NEP, -S *n* catmint
NEPER, -S *n* unit expressing the ratio of two quantities
NEPETA, -S *same as* ▶ **catmint**
NEPHEW, -S *n*
NEPHRIC *adj* renal
NEPHRON *n* urine-secreting tubule in the kidney
NEPIT, -S *n* unit of information equal to 1.44 bits
NEPOTIC > **nepotism**
NEPS ▶ **nep**
NERAL, -S *n* isomer of citral
NERD, -S *n*
NERDIC, -S *same as* > **geekspeak**
NERDIER ▶ **nerdy**
NERDISH ▶ **nerd**
NERDS ▶ **nerd**
NERDY, NERDIER *adj*
NEREID, -S *n* sea nymph in Greek mythology
NEREIS *n* type of marine worm
NERINE, -S *n* type of S African plant related to the amaryllis
NERITE, -S *n* type of sea snail
NERITIC *adj* of or formed in shallow seas near a coastline
NERK, -S *n* fool
NERKA, -S *n* type of salmon
NERKS ▶ **nerk**
NEROL, -S *n* scented liquid
NEROLI, -S *n* brown oil used in perfumery
NEROLS ▶ **nerol**
NERTS *interj* nuts
NERTZ *same as* ▶ **nerts**
NERVAL ▶ **nerve**
NERVATE *adj* (of leaves) with veins
NERVE, -D, -S *n, vb*
NERVER, -S *n* someone or something which nerves
NERVES ▶ **nerve**
NERVIER ▶ **nervy**
NERVILY ▶ **nervy**
NERVINE *adj* having a soothing effect upon the nerves ▷ *n* nervine drug or agent
NERVING ▶ **nerve**
NERVOUS *adj*
NERVULE *n* small vein
NERVURE *n* stiff rod in an insect's wing
NERVY, NERVIER *adj*
NESH, -ER, -EST *adj* sensitive to the cold
NESS, -ES *n* headland, cape
NEST, -ED, -S *n, vb*
NESTER, -S ▶ **nest**
NESTFUL *n* the contents of a nest
NESTING ▶ **nest**
NESTLE, -D, -S *vb*
NESTLER ▶ **nestle**
NESTLES ▶ **nestle**
NESTOR, -S *n* wise old man
NESTS ▶ **nest**
NET, -S, -TED *n* fabric of meshes of string, thread, or wire with many openings ▷ *vb* catch (a fish or animal) in a net ▷ *adj* left after all deductions
NETBALL *n* team game in which a ball has to be thrown through a high net
NETBOOK *n* type of small laptop computer
NETE, -S *n* lyre string
NETFUL, -S *n* the contents of a net
NETHEAD *n* expert on the internet
NETHER *adj*
NETIZEN *n* person who regularly uses the internet
NETLESS *adj* without a net
NETLIKE *adj* resembling a net
NETOP, -S *n* friend
NETROOT *n* activist who promotes a cause via the internet

NETS ▸ **net**
NETSUKE *n* (in Japan) a carved ornamental toggle
NETSURF *vb* browse the internet for information
NETT, -S *same as* ▸ **net**
NETTED ▸ **net**
NETTER, -S *n* person that makes nets
NETTIE *n* enthusiastic user of the internet
NETTIER ▸ **netty**
NETTIES ▸ **netty**
NETTING ▸ **net**
NETTLE, -D, -S *n, vb*
NETTLER *n* one that nettles
NETTLES ▸ **nettle**
NETTLY *adj* like a nettle
NETTS ▸ **nett**
NETTY, NETTIER, NETTIES *n* lavatory ▹ *adj* resembling a net
NETWORK *n* system of intersecting lines, roads, etc ▹ *vb* broadcast (a programme) over a network
NEUK, -S *Scot word for* ▸ **nook**
NEUM, -S *same as* ▸ **neume**
NEUME, -S *n* notational symbol
NEUMIC ▸ **neume**
NEUMS ▸ **neum**
NEURAL *adj*
NEURINE *n* poisonous alkaloid
NEURISM *n* nerve force
NEURITE *n* biological cell component
NEUROID *adj* resembling a nerve ▹ *n* either of the halves of a neural arch
NEUROMA *n* any tumour composed of nerve tissue
NEURON, -S *same as* ▸ **neurone**
NEURONE *n* cell specialized to conduct nerve impulses
NEURONS ▸ **neuron**
NEURULA *n* stage of embryonic development
NEUSTIC *n* part of a sentence that differs with mood
NEUSTON *n* organisms that float on the surface of open water
NEUTER, -S *adj* belonging to a particular class of grammatical inflections in some languages ▹ *vb* castrate (an animal) ▹ *n* neuter gender
NEUTRAL *adj, n*
NEUTRON *n*
NEVE, -S *n* mass of porous ice, formed from snow
NEVEL, -S *vb* beat with the fists
NEVER *adv, sentence substitute, interj*
NEVES ▸ **neve**
NEVI ▸ **nevus**
NEVOID ▸ **naevus**
NEVUS, NEVI *same as* ▸ **naevus**
NEW, -ED, -ER, -EST, -ING *adj* not existing before ▹ *adv* recently ▹ *vb* make new
NEWB, -S *n* newbie
NEWBIE, -S *n* person new to a job, club, etc
NEWBORN *adj, n*
NEWBS ▸ **newb**
NEWCOME *adj* recently arrived
NEWED ▸ **new**
NEWEL, -S *n* post at the top or bottom of a flight of stairs
NEWELL, -S *n* new thing
NEWELS ▸ **newel**
NEWER ▸ **new**
NEWEST ▸ **new**
NEWIE, -S *n* fresh idea or thing
NEWING ▸ **new**
NEWISH *adj* fairly new
NEWLY *adv*
NEWMOWN *adj* freshly cut
NEWNESS ▸ **new**
NEWS, -ED, -ES, -ING *n* important or interesting new happenings ▹ *vb* report
NEWSBOY *n* boy who sells or delivers newspapers
NEWSED ▸ **news**
NEWSES ▸ **news**
NEWSIE *same as* ▸ **newsy**
NEWSIER ▸ **newsy**
NEWSIES ▸ **newsy**
NEWSING ▸ **news**
NEWSMAN, NEWSMEN *n* male newsreader or reporter
NEWSY, NEWSIER, NEWSIES *adj* full of news ▹ *n* newsagent

NEWT, -S *n*
NEWTON, -S *n* unit of force
NEWTS ▸ **newt**
NEXT, -S *adv, n*
NEXTLY ▸ **next**
NEXTS ▸ **next**
NEXUS, -ES *n* connection or link
NGAI *n* clan or tribe
NGAIO, -S *n* small New Zealand tree
NGANA, -S *same as* ▸ **nagana**
NGARARA *n* lizard found in New Zealand
NGATI, -S *n* (occurring as part of the tribe name) a tribe or clan
NGOMA, -S *n* type of drum
NGWEE, -S *n* Zambian monetary unit
NHANDU, -S *n* type of spider
NIACIN, -S *n* vitamin of the B complex
NIAGARA *n* deluge or outpouring
NIB, -BED, -BING, -S *n* writing point of a pen ▹ *vb* provide with a nib
NIBBLE, -D, -S *vb, n*
NIBBLER *n* person, animal, or thing that nibbles
NIBBLES ▸ **nibble**
NIBBLY *n* small item of food
NIBLET, -S *n* very small piece of food
NIBLICK *n* former golf club giving a great deal of lift
NIBLIKE ▸ **nib**
NIBS ▸ **nib**
NICAD, -S *n* rechargeable dry-cell battery
NICE, -R, -ST *adj*
NICEISH ▸ **nice**
NICELY ▸ **nice**
NICER ▸ **nice**
NICEST ▸ **nice**
NICETY *n*
NICHE, -D, -S, NICHING *n, adj, vb*
NICHER, -S *vb* snigger
NICHES ▸ **niche**
NICHING ▸ **niche**
NICHT, -S *Scot word for* ▸ **night**
NICISH ▸ **nice**
NICK, -ED, -ING, -S *vb, n*
NICKAR, -S *n* hard s eed
NICKED ▸ **nick**
NICKEL, -S *n, vb*
NICKER, -S *n* pound sterling ▹ *vb* (of a horse) to neigh softly
NICKING ▸ **nick**
NICKLE, -D, -S *same as* ▸ **nickel**
NICKS ▸ **nick**
NICKUM, -S *n* mischievous person
NICOISE *adj* prepared with tomatoes, black olives, garlic and anchovies
NICOL, -S *n* device for producing plane-polarized light
NICOTIN *same as* > **nicotine**
NICTATE *same as* > **nictitate**
NID, -S *same as* ▸ **nide**
NIDAL ▸ **nidus**
NIDATE, -D, -S *vb* undergo nidation
NIDDICK *n* nape of the neck
NIDE, -D, -S *vb* nest
NIDGET, -S *n* type of hoe ▹ *vb* assist a woman in labour
NIDI ▸ **nidus**
NIDIFY *vb* (of a bird) to make or build a nest
NIDING, -S *n* coward
NIDOR, -S *n* cooking smell
NIDS ▸ **nid**
NIDUS, NIDI, -ES *n* nest in which insects or spiders deposit their eggs
NIE, -D, -S *archaic spelling of* ▸ **nigh**
NIECE, -S *n*
NIED ▸ **nie**
NIEF, -S *same as* ▸ **nieve**
NIELLO, NIELLI, -S *n* black compound of sulphur and silver, lead, or copper ▹ *vb* decorate or treat with niello
NIENTE *adv* softly fading away
NIES ▸ **nie**
NIEVE, -S *n* closed hand
NIFE, -S *n* earth's core
NIFF, -ED, -ING, -S *n* stink ▹ *vb* stink
NIFFER, -S *vb* barter
NIFFIER ▸ **niffy**
NIFFING ▸ **niff**
NIFFS ▸ **niff**
NIFFY, NIFFIER ▸ **niff**
NIFTIER ▸ **nifty**
NIFTIES ▸ **nifty**
NIFTILY ▸ **nifty**
NIFTY, NIFTIER, NIFTIES *adj, n*

NIGELLA *n* type of Mediterranean plant
NIGGARD *n* stingy person ▷ *adj* miserly ▷ *vb* act in a niggardly way
NIGGLE, -D, -S *vb, n*
NIGGLER ▶ **niggle**
NIGGLES ▶ **niggle**
NIGGLY ▶ **niggle**
NIGH, -ED, -ER, -EST, -ING, -S *prep* near ▷ *adv* nearly ▷ *adj* near ▷ *vb* approach
NIGHLY ▶ **nigh**
NIGHS ▶ **nigh**
NIGHT *n, adj*
NIGHTED *adj* darkened
NIGHTIE *n* nightgown
NIGHTLY *adv, adj*
NIGHTS *adv* at night or on most nights
NIGHTY *same as* ▶ **nightie**
NIGIRI, -S *n* small oval block of cold rice, wasabi and fish
NIGRIFY *vb* blacken
NIHIL, -S *n* nil
NIHONGA *n* Japanese form of painting
NIKAB, -S *same as* ▶ **niqab**
NIKAH, -S *n* Islamic marriage contract
NIKAU, -S *n* palm tree native to New Zealand
NIL, -S *n*
NILGAI, -S *n* large Indian antelope
NILGAU, -S *same as* ▶ **nilghau**
NILGHAI *same as* ▶ **nilgai**
NILGHAU *same as* ▶ **nilgai**
NILL, -ED, -ING, -S *vb* be unwilling
NILS ▶ **nil**
NIM, -MED, -MING, -S *n* game involving removing one or more small items from several rows or piles ▷ *vb* steal
NIMB, -S *n* halo
NIMBED ▶ **nimb**
NIMBI ▶ **nimbus**
NIMBLE, -R *adj*
NIMBLY ▶ **nimble**
NIMBS ▶ **nimb**
NIMBUS, NIMBI *n*
NIMIETY *rare word for* ▶ **excess**
NIMIOUS ▶ **nimiety**
NIMMED ▶ **nim**
NIMMER, -S ▶ **nim**
NIMMING ▶ **nim**
NIMONIC *adj* as in **nimonic alloy** type of nickel-based alloy
NIMPS *adj* easy
NIMROD, -S *n* hunter
NIMS ▶ **nim**
NINCOM, -S *same as* > **nicompoop**
NINCUM, -S *same as* > **nicompoop**
NINE, -S *n*
NINEPIN *n* skittle used in ninepins
NINER, -S *n* (US) student in the ninth grade
NINES ▶ **nine**
NINETY *n*
NINJA, -S *n* person skilled in ninjutsu
NINNY, NINNIES *n* stupid person
NINON, -S *n* fine strong silky fabric
NINTH, -S *n, adj*
NINTHLY *adv* in the ninth place or position
NINTHS ▶ **ninth**
NIOBATE *n* type of salt crystal
NIOBIC *adj* of or containing niobium in the pentavalent state
NIOBITE *another name for* > **columbite**
NIOBIUM *n* white metallic element
NIOBOUS *adj* of or containing niobium in the trivalent state
NIP, -PED, -PING, -S *vb, n*
NIPA, -S *n* palm tree of S and SE Asia
NIPPED ▶ **nip**
NIPPER *n, vb*
NIPPERS *pl n* instrument or tool for pinching or squeezing
NIPPIER ▶ **nippy**
NIPPILY ▶ **nippy**
NIPPING ▶ **nip**
NIPPLE, -D, -S *n, vb*
NIPPY, NIPPIER *adj*
NIPS ▶ **nip**
NIPTER, -S *n* type of religious ceremony
NIQAAB, -S *same as* ▶ **niqab**
NIQAB, -S *n* type of veil worn by some Muslim women

One of those invaluable words allowing you to play the Q without a U. It can also be spelt **niqaab** or **nikab**.

NIRL, -ED, -ING, -IT, -S *vb* shrivel

NIRLIE *variant of* ▶ **nirly**
NIRLIER ▶ **nirly**
NIRLING ▶ **nirl**
NIRLIT ▶ **nirl**
NIRLS ▶ **nirl**
NIRLY, NIRLIER *adj* shrivelled
NIRVANA *n* absolute spiritual enlightenment and bliss
NIS *n* friendly goblin
NISEI, -S *n* native-born citizen of the US or Canada whose parents were Japanese
NISGUL, -S *n* smallest and weakest bird in a brood of chickens
NISH, -ES *n* nothing
NISI *adj* (of a court order) coming into effect on a specified date
NISSE, -S *same as* ▶ **nis**
NISUS *n* impulse towards or striving after a goal
NIT, -S *n*
NITE, -S *variant of* ▶ **night**
NITER, -S *same as* ▶ **nitre**
NITERIE *n* nightclub
NITERS ▶ **niter**
NITERY ▶ **niter**
NITES ▶ **nite**
NITHER, -S *vb* shiver
NITHING *n* coward
NITID *adj* bright
NITINOL *n* metal alloy
NITON, -S *less common name for* ▶ **radon**
NITPICK *vb* criticize unnecessarily
NITRATE *n, vb*
NITRE, -S *n* potassium nitrate
NITRIC *adj* of or containing nitrogen
NITRID, -S *same as* ▶ **nitride**
NITRIDE *n* compound of nitrogen ▷ *vb* make into a nitride
NITRIDS ▶ **nitrid**
NITRIFY *vb* treat or cause to react with nitrogen
NITRIL, -S *same as* ▶ **nitrile**
NITRILE *n* any one of a particular class of organic compounds
NITRILS ▶ **nitril**
NITRITE *n* salt or ester of nitrous acid
NITRO, -S *n* nitroglycerine
NITROSO *adj* of a particular monovalent group
NITROUS *adj* derived from or containing nitrogen in a low valency state
NITROX *n* mixture of nitrogen and oxygen used in diving
NITRY *adj* nitrous
NITRYL, -S *n* chemical compound
NITS ▶ **nit**
NITTY, NITTIER *adj* infested with nits
NITWIT, -S *n* stupid person
NIVAL *adj* of or growing in or under snow
NIVEOUS *adj* resembling snow, esp in colour
NIX, -ED, -ES, -ING *sentence substitute* be careful! watch out! ▷ *n* rejection or refusal ▷ *vb* veto, deny, reject, or forbid (plans, suggestions, etc)

This is a handy little word, combining X with two of the most common tiles in the game.

NIXE *n* water sprite
NIXED ▶ **nix**
NIXER, -S *n* spare-time job
NIXES ▶ **nix**
NIXIE, -S *n* female water sprite, usually unfriendly to humans
NIXING ▶ **nix**
NIXY *same as* ▶ **nixie**
NIZAM, -S *n* (formerly) a Turkish regular soldier
NKOSI, -S *n* term of address to a superior
NO, -ES, -S *interj, adj, adv, n*
NOAH, -S *n* shark
NOB, -S *n* person of wealth or social distinction
NOBBIER ▶ **nobby**
NOBBILY ▶ **nob**
NOBBLE, -D, -S *vb* attract the attention of
NOBBLER ▶ **nobble**
NOBBLES ▶ **nobble**
NOBBUT *adv* nothing but
NOBBY, NOBBIER ▶ **nob**
NOBLE, -R, -S, -ST *adj, n*
NOBLY ▶ **noble**
NOBODY *pron, n*
NOBS ▶ **nob**

NOCAKE, -S *n* Indian meal made from dried corn
NOCEBO, -S *n* harmless substance that causes harmful effects in patients who expect it to be harmful
NOCENT, -S *n* guilty person
NOCHEL, -S *same as* ▶ **notchel**
NOCK, -ED, -ING, -S *n* notch on an arrow or a bow for the bowstring ▷ *vb* fit (an arrow) on a bowstring
NOCKET, -S *same as* ▶ **nacket**
NOCKING ▶ **nock**
NOCKS ▶ **nock**
NOCTUA, -S *n* type of moth
NOCTUID *n* type of nocturnal moth ▷ *adj* of or relating to this type of moth
NOCTULE *n* any of several large Old World insectivorous bats
NOCTURN *n* any of the main sections of the office of matins
NOCUOUS *adj* harmful
NOD, -DED, -S *vb*, *n*
NODAL *adj* of or like a node
NODALLY ▶ **nodal**
NODATED *adj* knotted
NODDED ▶ **nod**
NODDER, -S ▶ **nod**
NODDIER ▶ **noddy**
NODDIES ▶ **noddy**
NODDING ▶ **nod**
NODDLE, -D, -S *n* head ▷ *vb* nod (the head), as through drowsiness
NODDY, NODDIER, NODDIES *n* tropical tern with a dark plumage ▷ *adj* very easy to use or understand
NODE, -S *n*
NODI ▶ **nodus**
NODICAL *adj* of or relating to the nodes of a celestial body
NODOSE *adj* having nodes or knotlike swellings
NODOUS *same as* ▶ **nodose**
NODS ▶ **nod**
NODULAR ▶ **nodule**
NODULE, -S *n*
NODULED ▶ **nodule**
NODULES ▶ **nodule**
NODUS, NODI *n* problematic idea, situation, etc
NOEL, -S *n* Christmas
NOES ▶ **no**
NOESIS, NOESES *n* exercise of reason
NOETIC *adj* of or relating to the mind
NOG, -S *same as* ▶ **nogging**
NOGAKU *n* Japanese style of drama
NOGG, -S *same as* ▶ **nog**
NOGGED *adj* built with timber and brick
NOGGIN, -S *n*
NOGGING *n* short horizontal timber member
NOGGINS ▶ **noggin**
NOGGS ▶ **nogg**
NOGS ▶ **nog**
NOH *n* stylized classic drama of Japan
NOHOW *adv* under any conditions
NOIL, -S *n* short or knotted fibres that are separated from the long fibres by combing
NOILIER ▶ **noily**
NOILIES ▶ **noily**
NOILS ▶ **noil**
NOILY, NOILIER, NOILIES *n* dry white vermouth drink from France ▷ *adj* resembling a noil
NOINT, -ED, -S *vb* anoint
NOINTER *n* mischievous child
NOINTS ▶ **noint**
NOIR, -S *adj* (of a film) showing characteristics of a *film noir*, in plot or style ▷ *n* film noir
NOIRISH ▶ **noir**
NOIRS ▶ **noir**
NOISE, -D, -S, NOISING *n*, *vb*
NOISIER ▶ **noisy**
NOISILY ▶ **noisy**
NOISING ▶ **noise**
NOISOME *adj* (of smells) offensive
NOISY, NOISIER *adj*
NOLE, -S *same as* ▶ **noll**
NOLL, -S *n* head
NOLO, -S *n* as in **nolo contendere** plea indicating that the defendant does not wish to contest the case
NOM, -S *n* name
NOMA, -S *n* gangrenous inflammation of the mouth

NOMAD, -S *n* member of a tribe with no fixed dwelling place
NOMADE, -S *same as* ▸ **nomad**
NOMADIC *adj* relating to or characteristic of nomads
NOMADS ▸ **nomad**
NOMADY *n* practice of living like nomads
NOMARCH *n* head of an ancient Egyptian nome
NOMAS ▸ **noma**
NOMBLES *variant spelling of* ▸ **numbles**
NOMBRIL *n* point on a shield
NOME, -S *n* any of the former provinces of modern Greece
NOMEN, -S, NOMINA *n* ancient Roman's second name
NOMES ▸ **nome**
NOMIC *adj* normal or habitual
NOMINA ▸ **nomen**
NOMINAL *adj, n*
NOMINEE *n*
NOMISM, -S *n* adherence to laws as a primary exercise of religion
NOMOS, NOMOI *n* convention
NOMS ▸ **nom**
NON *adv* not
NONA *n* sleeping sickness
NONACID *adj* not acid ▹ *n* nonacid substance
NONAGE, -D, -S *n* state of being under full legal age
NONAGON *n* geometric figure with nine sides
NONANE, -S *n* type of chemical compound
NONART, -S *n* something that does not constitute art
NONARY *n* set or group of nine
NONAS *same as* ▸ **nones**
NONBANK *n* business or institution that is not a bank but provides similar services
NONBODY *n* nonphysical nature of a person
NONBOOK *n* book with little substance
NONCASH *adj* other than cash
NONCE, -S *n* present time or occasion
NONCOLA *n* soft drink other than cola
NONCOM, -S *n* person not involved in combat
NONCORE *adj* not central or essential
NONDRIP *adj* (of paint) specially formulated to minimize dripping during application
NONDRUG *adj* not involving the use of drugs
NONE *pron*
NONEGO, -S *n* everything that is outside one's conscious self
NONES *n* (in the Roman calendar) the ninth day before the ides of each month
NONET, -S *n* piece of music composed for a group of nine instruments
NONETTE *same as* ▸ **nonet**
NONETTO, NONETTI *same as* ▸ **nonet**
NONFACT *n* event or thing not provable
NONFAN, -S *n* person who is not a fan
NONFARM *adj* not connected with a farm
NONFAT *adj* fat free
NONFOOD *n* item that is not food ▹ *adj* relating to items other than food
NONFUEL *adj* not relating to fuel ▹ *n* energy not used for generating heat, power, or electricity
NONG, -S *n* stupid or incompetent person
NONGAME *adj* not pursued for competitive sport purposes
NONGAY, -S *n* person who is not gay
NONGS ▸ **nong**
NONHEME *adj* of dietary iron, obtained from vegetable foods
NONHERO *n* person who is not a hero
NONHOME *adj* not of the home
NONI, -S *n* tree of SE Asia and the Pacific islands
NONIRON *adj* not requiring ironing
NONIS ▸ **noni**

NONJURY *n* trial without a jury
NONKIN, -S *n* those who are not related to a person
NONLIFE *n* matter which is not living
NONMAN, NONMEN *n* being that is not a man
NONMEAT *n* substance that does not contain meat ▷ *adj* not containing meat
NONMEN ▶ **nonman**
NONNEWS *adj* not concerned with news
NONNY, NONNIES *n* meaningless word
NONOILY *adj* not oily
NONORAL *adj* not oral
NONPAID *adj* without payment
NONPAR *adj* nonparticipating
NONPAST *n* any grammatical tense that is not the past tense
NONPEAK *n* period of low demand
NONPLAY *n* social behaviour that is not classed as play
NONPLUS *vb* put at a loss ▷ *n* state of utter perplexity prohibiting action or speech
NONPOOR *adj* not poor ▷ *n* person who is not poor
NONPROS *vb* enter a judgment of non prosequitur
NONRUN *adj* (of tights) not laddering
NONSELF *n* foreign molecule in the body
NONSKED *n* non-scheduled aeroplane
NONSKID *adj* designed to reduce skidding
NONSLIP *adj* designed to prevent slipping
NONSTOP *adv, adj, n*
NONSUCH *same as* > **nonesuch**
NONSUIT *n* order of a judge dismissing a suit ▷ *vb* order the dismissal of the suit of (a person)
NONTAX *n* tax that has little real effect
NONUPLE *adj* ninefold ▷ *n* ninefold number
NONUSE, -S *n* failure to use
NONUSER ▶ **nonuse**
NONUSES ▶ **nonuse**
NONWAGE *adj* not part of wages
NONWAR, -S *n* state of nonviolence
NONWOOL *adj* not wool
NONWORD *n* series of letters not recognised as a word
NONWORK *adj* not involving work ▷ *n* part of life which does not involve work
NONYL, -S *n* type of chemical
NONZERO *adj* not equal to zero
NOO *n* type of Japanese musical drama
NOOB, -S *same as* ▶ **newbie**
NOODGE, -D, -S *vb* annoy persistently
NOODLE, -D, -S *n, vb*
NOOGIE, -S *n* act of inflicting pain by rubbing head hard
NOOIT *interj* South African exclamation of surprise
NOOK, -S *n*
NOOKIER ▶ **nooky**
NOOKS ▶ **nook**
NOOKY, NOOKIER *adj* resembling a nook
NOOLOGY *n* study of intuition
NOON, -ED, -S *n, vb*
NOONDAY *adj* happening at noon ▷ *n* middle of the day
NOONED ▶ **noon**
NOONER, -S *n* event taking place in the middle of the day
NOONING *n* midday break for rest or food
NOONS ▶ **noon**
NOOP, -S *n* point of the elbow
NOOSE, -D, -S, NOOSING *n, vb*
NOOSER, -S *n* person who uses a noose
NOOSES ▶ **noose**
NOOSING ▶ **noose**
NOPAL, -ES, -S *n* type of cactus
NOPE *interj*
NOPLACE *same as* ▶ **nowhere**
NOR *prep*
NORDIC *adj* of competitions in cross-country racing and ski-jumping

NORI, -S *n* edible seaweed
NORIA, -S *n* water wheel with buckets attached to its rim
NORIMON *n* Japanese passenger vehicle
NORIS ▸ **nori**
NORITE, -S *n* variety of igneous rock
NORITIC ▸ **norite**
NORLAND *n* north part of a country or the earth
NORM, -S *n*
NORMA, -S *n* norm or standard
NORMAL, -S *adj, n*
NORMAN, -S *n* post used for winding on a ship
NORMAS ▸ **norma**
NORMED *adj* having been normalized
NORMS ▸ **norm**
NORSEL, -S *vb* fit with short lines for fastening hooks
NORTENA *same as* ▸ **norteno**
NORTENO *n* type of Mexican music
NORTH, -ED, -S *n, adj, adv, vb*
NORTHER *n* wind or storm from the north ▹ *vb* move north
NORTHS ▸ **north**
NORWARD *same as* > **northward**
NOS ▸ **no**
NOSE, -D, -S *n, vb*
NOSEAN, -S *n* type of mineral
NOSEBAG *n* bag containing feed fastened round a horse's head
NOSED ▸ **nose**
NOSEGAY *n* small bunch of flowers
NOSER, -S *n* strong headwind
NOSES ▸ **nose**
NOSEY, -S *adj, n*
NOSH, -ED, -ES, -ING *n* food ▹ *vb* eat
NOSHER, -S ▸ **nosh**
NOSHERY *n* restaurant or other place where food is served
NOSHES ▸ **nosh**
NOSHING ▸ **nosh**
NOSIER ▸ **nosy**
NOSIES ▸ **nosy**
NOSIEST ▸ **nosy**
NOSILY ▸ **nosy**
NOSING, -S *n* edge of a step or stair tread
NOSODE, -S *n* homeopathic remedy
NOSTOC, -S *n* type of bacterium occurring in moist places
NOSTOS, NOSTOI *n* story of a return home
NOSTRIL *n*
NOSTRO *adj* as in **nostro account** bank account conducted by a British bank with a foreign bank
NOSTRUM *n* quack medicine
NOSY, NOSIER, NOSIES, NOSIEST *adj, n*
NOT *adv*
NOTA ▸ **notum**
NOTABLE *adj, n*
NOTABLY *adv*
NOTAEUM *n* back of a bird's body
NOTAIRE *n* (in France) notary
NOTAL ▸ **notum**
NOTANDA > **notandum**
NOTARY *n*
NOTATE, -D, -S *vb* write (esp music) in notation
NOTATOR *n* person who notates
NOTCH, -ED, -ES *n, vb*
NOTCHEL *vb* refuse to pay another person's debts
NOTCHER *n* person who cuts notches
NOTCHES ▸ **notch**
NOTCHY *adj* (of a motor vehicle gear mechanism) requiring careful gear-changing
NOTE, -S, NOTING *n, vb*
NOTED *adj*
NOTEDLY ▸ **noted**
NOTELET *n* small folded card with a design on the front
NOTEPAD *n* number of sheets of paper fastened together
NOTER, -S *n* person who takes notes
NOTES ▸ **note**
NOTHER *same as* ▸ **other**
NOTHING *pron, adv, n*
NOTICE, -D, -S *n, vb*
NOTICER *n* person who takes notice
NOTICES ▸ **notice**
NOTIFY *vb*
NOTING ▸ **note**
NOTION, -S *n*
NOTITIA *n* register or list, esp of ecclesiastical districts
NOTOUR *adj* notorious

NOTT *same as* ▸ **not**
NOTUM, NOTA *n* cuticular plate on an insect
NOUGAT, -S *n*
NOUGHT, -S *n*
NOUL, -S *same as* ▸ **noll**
NOULD *vb* would not
NOULDE *same as* ▸ **nould**
NOULE, -S *same as* ▸ **noll**
NOULS ▸ **noul**
NOUMENA > **noumenon**
NOUN, -S *n*
NOUNAL ▸ **noun**
NOUNIER ▸ **nouny**
NOUNS ▸ **noun**
NOUNY, NOUNIER *adj* like a noun
NOUP, -S *n* steep headland
NOURICE *n* nurse
NOURISH *vb*
NOURSLE *vb* nurse
NOUS, -ES *n* common sense
NOUSELL *vb* foster
NOUSES ▸ **nous**
NOUSLE, -D, -S *vb* nuzzle
NOUT *same as* ▸ **nought**
NOUVEAU *adj*
NOVA, -E, -S *n*
NOVALIA *n* newly reclaimed land
NOVAS ▸ **nova**
NOVATE, -S *vb* substitute one thing in place of another
NOVATED *adj* as in **novated lease** Australian system of employer-aided car purchase
NOVATES ▸ **novate**
NOVEL, -S *n, adj*
NOVELLA, NOVELLE *n*
NOVELLY ▸ **novel**
NOVELS ▸ **novel**
NOVELTY *n*
NOVENA, -E, -S *n* set of prayers or services on nine consecutive days
NOVICE, -S *n*
NOVITY *n* novelty
NOVUM, -S *n* game played with dice
NOW, -S *adv, n*
NOWAY *adv* in no manner
NOWAYS *same as* ▸ **noway**
NOWCAST *n* report on current weather conditions
NOWED *adj* knotted
NOWHERE *adv, n*
NOWISE *another word for* ▸ **noway**
NOWL, -S *n* crown of the head
NOWN *same as* ▸ **own**
NOWNESS ▸ **nown**
NOWS ▸ **now**
NOWT, -S *n*
NOWTIER ▸ **nowty**
NOWTS ▸ **nowt**
NOWTY, NOWTIER *adj* bad-tempered
NOWY *adj* having a small projection at the centre (of a cross)
NOX, -ES *n* nitrogen oxide

Meaning nitrogen oxide, this is another of those very useful short words containing X.

NOXAL *adj* relating to damage done by something belonging to another
NOXES ▸ **nox**
NOXIOUS *adj*
NOY, -ED, -ING, -S *vb* harass
NOYADE, -S *n* execution by drowning
NOYANCE *n* nuisance
NOYAU, -S, -X *n* brandy-based liqueur
NOYED ▸ **noy**
NOYES, -ES *archaic form of* ▸ **noise**
NOYING ▸ **noy**
NOYOUS ▸ **noy**
NOYS ▸ **noy**
NOYSOME ▸ **noy**
NOZZER, -S *n* new recruit (in the Navy)
NOZZLE, -S *n*
NTH *adj* of an unspecified number

A good word to remember for awkward situations on the board, as it's one of very few 3-letter words that doesn't contain a vowel.

NU, -S *n* 13th letter in the Greek alphabet
NUANCE, -D, -S *n, vb*
NUB, -BED, -S *n* point or gist (of a story etc) ▷ *vb* hang from the gallows
NUBBER, -S *n* weakly hit ball in baseball
NUBBIER ▸ **nubby**
NUBBIN, -S *n* something small or undeveloped, esp a fruit or ear of corn

NUBBING *n* act of hanging (a criminal)
NUBBINS ▶ **nubbin**
NUBBLE, -D, -S *n* small lump ▷ *vb* dialect word for beat or pound using one's fists
NUBBLY ▶ **nubble**
NUBBY, NUBBIER *adj* having small lumps or protuberances
NUBIA, -S *n* fleecy scarf for the head, worn by women
NUBILE *adj*
NUBS ▶ **nub**
NUBUCK, -S *n* type of leather with a velvety finish
NUCELLI > **nucellus**
NUCHA, -E *n* back or nape of the neck
NUCHAL, -S *n* scale on a reptile's neck
NUCLEAL ▶ **nucleus**
NUCLEAR *adj*
NUCLEI ▶ **nucleus**
NUCLEIC *adj* as in **nucleic acid** type of complex compound that is a vital constituent of living cells
NUCLEIN *n* protein that occurs in the nuclei of living cells
NUCLEON *n* proton or neutron
NUCLEUS, NUCLEI *n*
NUCLIDE *n* species of atom characterized by its atomic number and its mass number
NUCULE, -S *n* small seed
NUDDY, NUDDIES *n* as in **in the nuddy** in the nude
NUDE, -R, -S, -ST *adj, n*
NUDELY ▶ **nude**
NUDER ▶ **nude**
NUDES ▶ **nude**
NUDEST ▶ **nude**
NUDGE, -D, -S, NUDGING *vb, n*
NUDGER, -S ▶ **nudge**
NUDGES ▶ **nudge**
NUDGING ▶ **nudge**
NUDISM, -S *n* practice of not wearing clothes
NUDIST, -S ▶ **nudism**
NUDITY *n*
NUDNICK *same as* ▶ **nudnik**
NUDNIK, -S *n* boring person
NUDZH, -ED, -ES *same as* ▶ **nudge**
NUFF, -S *slang form of* ▶ **enough**
NUFFIN, -S *slang form of* ▶ **nothing**
NUFFS ▶ **nuff**
NUG, -S *n* lump of wood sawn from a log
NUGAE *pl n* jests
NUGGAR, -S *n* sailing boat used to carry cargo on the Nile
NUGGET, -S *n, vb*
NUGGETY *adj* of or resembling a nugget
NUGS ▶ **nug**
NUKE, -D, -S, NUKING *vb, n*
NULL, -S *adj, vb*
NULLA, -S *same as* ▶ **nullah**
NULLAH, -S *n* stream or drain
NULLAS ▶ **nulla**
NULLED ▶ **null**
NULLIFY *vb*
NULLING *n* knurling
NULLITY *n* state of being null
NULLS ▶ **null**
NUMB, -ED, -EST, -ING, -S *adj, vb*
NUMBAT, -S *n* small Australian marsupial
NUMBED ▶ **numb**
NUMBER, -S *n, vb*
NUMBEST ▶ **numb**
NUMBING ▶ **numb**
NUMBLES *pl n* animal organs, cooked for food
NUMBLY ▶ **numb**
NUMBNUT *n* insulting word for a stupid person
NUMBS ▶ **numb**
NUMDAH, -S *n* coarse felt made esp in India
NUMEN *n* deity or spirit presiding over a thing or place
NUMERAL *n, adj*
NUMERIC *n*
NUMINA *plural of* ▶ **numen**
NUMMARY *adj* of or relating to coins
NUMMY, NUMMIER *adj* delicious
NUMNAH, -S *same as* ▶ **numdah**
NUMPKIN *n* stupid person
NUMPTY *n*
NUN, -S *n*
NUNATAK *n* isolated mountain peak projecting through glacial ice

NUNCHUK *n* throwing weapon used in martial arts
NUNCIO, -S *n* pope's ambassador
NUNCLE, -S *archaic or dialect word for* ▸ **uncle**
NUNDINE *n* market day
NUNHOOD *n* condition, practice, or character of a nun
NUNLIKE ▸ **nun**
NUNNERY *n* convent
NUNNISH ▸ **nun**
NUNNY *n* as in **nunny bag** small sealskin haversack used in Canada
NUNS ▸ **nun**
NUNSHIP ▸ **nun**
NUPTIAL *adj* relating to marriage
NUR, -S *n* wooden ball
NURAGHE, NURAGHI *n* Sardinian round tower
NURD, -S *same as* ▸ **nerd**
NURDIER ▸ **nurdy**
NURDISH ▸ **nerd**
NURDLE, -D, -S *vb* score runs in cricket by soft deflections
NURDS ▸ **nurd**
NURDY, NURDIER ▸ **nurd**
NURHAG, -S *n* Sardinian round tower
NURL, -ED, -ING, -S *variant of* ▸ **knurl**
NURR, -S *n* wooden ball
NURS ▸ **nur**
NURSE, -D, -S *n, vb*
NURSER, -S *n* person who treats something carefully
NURSERY *n*
NURSES ▸ **nurse**
NURSING *n*
NURSLE, -D, -S *vb* nuzzle
NURTURE *n, vb*
NUS ▸ **nu**
NUT, -S, -TED *n, vb*
NUTANT *adj* having the apex hanging down
NUTATE, -D, -S *vb* nod
NUTBAR, -S *n* bar made from chopped nuts
NUTCASE *n* slang word for a foolish or reckless person
NUTGALL *n* nut-shaped gall caused by gall wasps on the oak and other trees
NUTHIN *n* nothing
NUTJOB, -S *n* slang word for a foolish or reckless person
NUTLET, -S *n* portion of a fruit that fragments when mature
NUTLIKE ▸ **nut**
NUTLOAF *n* savoury loaf made from nuts
NUTMEAL *n* type of grain
NUTMEAT *n* kernel of a nut
NUTMEG, -S *n, vb*
NUTPICK *n* tool used to dig the meat from nuts
NUTRIA, -S *n* fur of the coypu
NUTS ▸ **nut**
NUTSIER ▸ **nutsy**
NUTSO, -S *n* slang word for a foolish or reckless person
NUTSY *adj* slang word for foolish or reckless
NUTTED ▸ **nut**
NUTTER, -S *n* slang word for a foolish or reckless person
NUTTERY *n* place where nut trees grow
NUTTIER ▸ **nutty**
NUTTILY ▸ **nutty**
NUTTING *n* act of gathering nuts
NUTTY, NUTTIER *adj*
NUTWOOD *n* any of various nut-bearing trees, such as walnut
NUZZER, -S *n* present given to a superior in India
NUZZLE, -D, -S *vb*
NUZZLER *n* person or thing that nuzzles
NUZZLES ▸ **nuzzle**
NY, -S *same as* ▸ **nigh**
NYAFF, -ED, -S *n* small or contemptible person ▹ *vb* yelp like a small dog
NYAH *interj* interjection used to express contempt
NYALA, -S *n* spiral-horned southern African antelope
NYANZA, -S *n* (in E Africa) a lake
NYAS, -ES *n* young hawk
NYBBLE, -S *n* small byte
NYE, -D, -S, NYING *n* flock of pheasants ▹ *vb* near
NYLGHAI *same as* ▸ **nilgai**
NYLGHAU *same as* ▸ **nilgai**

NYLON *n*
NYLONED *adj* wearing nylons
NYLONS *pl n* stockings made of nylon
NYM *adj* as in **nym war** dispute about publishing material online under a pseudonym
NYMPH, -ED, -S *n, vb*
NYMPHA, -E *n* either one of the labia minora
NYMPHAL ▸ **nymph**
NYMPHED ▸ **nymph**
NYMPHIC ▸ **nymph**
NYMPHLY *adj* resembling a nymph
NYMPHS ▸ **nymph**
NYS ▸ **ny**
NYSSA, -S *n* type of tree

Oo

OAF, -S, OAVES *n* stupid or clumsy person
OAFISH ▸ **oaf**
OAFS ▸ **oaf**
OAK, -S *n*
OAKED *adj* relating to wine that is stored for a time in oak barrels prior to bottling
OAKEN *adj* made of the wood of the oak
OAKER, -S *same as* ▸ **ochre**
OAKIER ▸ **oaky**
OAKIES ▸ **oaky**
OAKIEST ▸ **oaky**
OAKLEAF *n* the leaf of the oak
OAKLIKE ▸ **oak**
OAKLING *n* young oak
OAKMOSS *n* type of lichen
OAKS ▸ **oak**
OAKUM, -S *n* fibre obtained by unravelling old rope
OAKWOOD *n* the wood of the oak
OAKY, OAKIER, OAKIES, OAKIEST *adj* hard like the wood of an oak ▹ *n* ice cream
OAR, -ING, -S *n, vb*
OARAGE, -S *n* use or number of oars
OARED *adj* equipped with oars
OARFISH *n* very long ribbonfish with long slender ventral fins
OARIER ▸ **oary**
OARIEST ▸ **oary**
OARING ▸ **oar**
OARLESS ▸ **oar**
OARLIKE ▸ **oar**
OARLOCK *n* swivelling device that holds an oar in place
OARS ▸ **oar**
OARSMAN, OARSMEN *n* man who rows a boat
OARWEED *n* type of brown seaweed
OARY, OARIER, OARIEST *adj* of or like an oar
OASIS, OASES *n*
OAST, -S *n* oven for drying hops
OAT, -S *n*
OATCAKE *n* thin flat biscuit of oatmeal
OATEN *adj* made of oats or oat straw
OATER, -S *n* film about the American Wild West
OATH, -S *n*
OATIER ▸ **oaty**
OATIEST ▸ **oaty**
OATLIKE ▸ **oat**
OATMEAL *n, adj*
OATS ▸ **oat**
OATY, OATIER, OATIEST *adj* of, like, or containing oats
OAVES ▸ **oaf**
OB, -S *n* expression of opposition
OBA, -S *n* (in W Africa) a Yoruba chief or ruler
OBANG, -S *n* former Japanese coin
OBAS ▸ **oba**
OBCONIC *adj* shaped like a cone and attached at the pointed end
OBDURE, -D, -S *vb* make obdurate
OBE, -S *n* ancient Laconian village
OBEAH, -ED, -S *vb* cast spell on
OBECHE, -S *n* African tree
OBEISM, -S *n* belief in obeah
OBELI ▸ **obelus**
OBELIA, -S *n* type of jellyfish
OBELION *n* area of skull
OBELISE *same as* ▸ **obelize**
OBELISK *n*
OBELISM *n* practice of marking passages in text

OBELIZE *vb* mark (a word or passage) with an obelus
OBELUS, OBELI *n* mark used to indicate spurious words or passages
OBENTO, -S *n* Japanese lunch box
OBES ▸ **obe**
OBESE, -R, -ST *adj*
OBESELY ▸ **obese**
OBESER ▸ **obese**
OBESEST ▸ **obese**
OBESITY ▸ **obese**
OBEY, -ED, -ING, -S *vb*
OBEYER, -S ▸ **obey**
OBEYING ▸ **obey**
OBEYS ▸ **obey**
OBI, -ED, -ING, -S *n* broad sash tied in a large flat bow at the back ▹ *vb* bewitch
OBIA, -S *same as* ▸ **obeah**
OBIED ▸ **obi**
OBIING ▸ **obi**
OBIISM, -S ▸ **obi**
OBIIT *vb* died
OBIS ▸ **obi**
OBIT, -S *n* memorial service
OBITAL *adj* of obits
OBITER *adv* by the way
OBITS ▸ **obit**
OBITUAL *adj* of obits
OBJECT, -S *n, vb*
OBJET, -S *n* object
OBJURE, -D, -S *vb* put on oath
OBLAST, -I, -S *n* administrative division of the constituent republics of Russia
OBLATE, -S *adj* (of a sphere) flattened at the poles ▹ *n* person dedicated to a monastic or religious life
OBLIGE, -D, -S *vb*
OBLIGEE *n* person in whose favour an obligation, contract, or bond is created
OBLIGER ▸ **oblige**
OBLIGES ▸ **oblige**
OBLIGOR *n* person who binds themself by contract
OBLIQUE *adj, n, vb*
OBLONG, -S *adj, n*
OBLOQUY *n* verbal abuse
OBO, -S *n* ship carrying oil and ore
OBOE, -S *n*
OBOIST, -S ▸ **oboe**
OBOL, -S *same as* ▸ **obolus**
OBOLARY *adj* very poor
OBOLE, -S *n* former weight unit in pharmacy
OBOLI ▸ **obolus**
OBOLS ▸ **obol**
OBOLUS, OBOLI *n* Greek unit of weight
OBOS ▸ **obo**
OBOVATE *adj* shaped like the longitudinal section of an egg
OBOVOID *adj* (of a fruit) egg-shaped with the narrower end at the base
OBS ▸ **ob**
OBSCENE *adj*
OBSCURE *adj, vb*
OBSEQUY *singular of* > **obsequies**
OBSERVE *vb*
OBSESS *vb*
OBSIGN, -S *vb* confirm
OBTAIN, -S *vb*
OBTECT *adj* (of a pupa) encased in a hardened secretion
OBTEND, -S *vb* put forward
OBTEST, -S *vb* beg (someone) earnestly
OBTRUDE *vb* push oneself or one's ideas on others
OBTUND, -S *vb* deaden or dull
OBTUSE, -R *adj*
OBVERSE *n* opposite way of looking at an idea ▹ *adj* facing or turned towards the observer
OBVERT, -S *vb* deduce the obverse of (a proposition)
OBVIATE *vb* make unnecessary
OBVIOUS *adj*
OBVS *adv* obviously
OCA, -S *n* any of various South American herbaceous plants
OCARINA *n* small oval wind instrument
OCAS ▸ **oca**
OCCAM, -S *n* computer programming language
OCCAMY *n* type of alloy
OCCIES ▸ **occy**
OCCIPUT *n* back of the head
OCCLUDE *vb* obstruct
OCCULT, -S *adj, vb*
OCCUPY *vb*
OCCUR, -S *vb*

OCCY, OCCIES *n* as in **all over the occy** dialect expression meaning in every direction
OCEAN, -S *n*
OCEANIC *adj* of or relating to the ocean
OCEANID *n* ocean nymph in Greek mythology
OCEANS ▶ **ocean**
OCELLAR ▶ **ocellus**
OCELLUS, OCELLI *n* simple eye of insects and some other invertebrates
OCELOID *adj* of or like an ocelot
OCELOT, -S *n* American wild cat with a spotted coat
OCH *interj* expression of surprise, annoyance, or disagreement
OCHE, -S *n* (in darts) mark behind which a player must stand
OCHER, -ED, -S *same as* ▶ **ochre**
OCHERY *same as* ▶ **ochry**
OCHES ▶ **oche**
OCHONE *interj* expression of sorrow or regret
OCHRE, -D, -S, OCHRING *n, adj, vb*
OCHREA, -E, -S *n* cup-shaped structure that sheathes the stems of certain plants
OCHRED ▶ **ochre**
OCHRES ▶ **ochre**
OCHREY ▶ **ochre**
OCHRIER ▶ **ochry**
OCHRING ▶ **ochre**
OCHROID ▶ **ochre**
OCHROUS ▶ **ochre**
OCHRY, OCHRIER *adj* containing or resembling ochre
OCICAT, -S *n* breed of cat with a spotted coat
OCKER, -S *n* uncultivated or boorish Australian
OCREA, -E, -S *same as* ▶ **ochrea**
OCREATE *adj* possessing an ocrea
OCTA, -S *same as* ▶ **okta**
OCTAD, -S *n* group or series of eight
OCTADIC ▶ **octad**
OCTADS ▶ **octad**
OCTAGON *n*
OCTAL, -S *n* number system with a base 8
OCTAN, -S *n* illness that occurs weekly
OCTANE, -S *n*
OCTANOL *n* alcohol containing eight carbon atoms
OCTANS ▶ **octan**
OCTANT, -S *n* any of the eight parts into which the three planes containing the Cartesian coordinate axes divide space
OCTAPLA *n* book with eight texts
OCTAS ▶ **octa**
OCTAVAL ▶ **octave**
OCTAVE, -S *n, adj*
OCTAVO, -S *n* book size in which the sheets are folded into eight leaves
OCTET, -S *n* group of eight performers
OCTETT, -S *same as* ▶ **octet**
OCTETTE *same as* ▶ **octet**
OCTETTS ▶ **octett**
OCTOFID *adj* divided into eight
OCTOPI ▶ **octopus**
OCTOPOD *n* type of mollusc ▷ *adj* of these molluscs
OCTOPUS, OCTOPI *n*
OCTROI, -S *n* duty on various goods brought into certain European towns
OCTUOR, -S *n* octet
OCTUPLE *n* quantity or number eight times as great as another ▷ *adj* eight times as much or as many ▷ *vb* multiply by eight
OCTUPLY *adv* by eight times
OCTYL, -S *n* group of atoms
OCULAR, -S *adj* relating to the eyes or sight ▷ *n* lens in an optical instrument
OCULATE *adj* possessing eyes
OCULI ▶ **oculus**
OCULIST *n* ophthalmologist
OCULUS, OCULI *n* round window
OD, -S *n* hypothetical force
ODA, -S *n* room or chamber
ODAH, -S *same as* ▶ **oda**
ODAL, -S *same as* ▶ **udal**
ODALLER ▶ **odal**
ODALS ▶ **odal**

ODAS ▸ **oda**
ODD, -ER, -EST *adj*
ODDBALL *n* eccentric person ▹ *adj* strange or peculiar
ODDER ▸ **odd**
ODDEST ▸ **odd**
ODDISH ▸ **odd**
ODDITY *n*
ODDLY ▸ **odd**
ODDMENT *n* odd piece or thing
ODDNESS ▸ **odd**
ODDS *pl n* probability of something happening
ODDSMAN, ODDSMEN *n* umpire
ODE, -S *n*
ODEA ▸ **odeum**
ODEON, -S *same as* ▸ **odeum**
ODES ▸ **ode**
ODEUM, ODEA, -S *n* ancient building for musical performances
ODIC ▸ **od**
ODIOUS *adj*
ODISM, -S ▸ **od**
ODIST, -S ▸ **od**
ODIUM, -S *n* widespread dislike
ODONATA *pl n* insects of an order that includes dragonflies
ODONATE *n* dragonfly or related insect
ODONTIC *adj* of teeth
ODOR, -S *same as* ▸ **odour**
ODORANT *n* something with a strong smell
ODORATE *adj* having a strong smell
ODORED *same as* ▸ **odoured**
ODORFUL *same as* > **odourful**
ODORISE *same as* ▸ **odorize**
ODORIZE *vb* give an odour to
ODOROUS *adj* having or emitting a characteristic smell
ODORS ▸ **odor**
ODOUR, -S *n*
ODOURED *adj* having an odour
ODOURS ▸ **odour**
ODS ▸ **od**
ODSO *n* cry of surprise
ODYL, -S *same as* ▸ **od**
ODYLE, -S *same as* ▸ **od**
ODYLISM ▸ **odyl**
ODYLS ▸ **odyl**
ODYSSEY *n*
ODZOOKS *interj* cry of surprise
OE, -S *n* grandchild
OECIST, -S *n* colony founder
OEDEMA, -S *n* abnormal swelling
OEDIPAL *adj* relating to a complex whereby a male child wants to replace his father
OENOMEL *n* drink made of wine and honey
OERSTED *n* cgs unit of magnetic field strength
OES ▸ **oe**
OESTRAL ▸ **oestrus**
OESTRIN *obsolete term for* > **oestrogen**
OESTRUM *same as* ▸ **oestrus**
OESTRUS *n* regularly occurring period of fertility in female mammals
OEUVRE, -S *n* work of art, literature, music, etc
OF *prep*
OFF, -ED, -S *prep, adv, adj, n, vb*
OFFA *prep* off
OFFAL, -S *n*
OFFBEAT *adj* unusual or eccentric ▹ *n* any of the normally unaccented beats in a bar
OFFCAST *n* cast-off
OFFCUT, -S *n* piece remaining after the required parts have been cut out
OFFED ▸ **off**
OFFENCE *n*
OFFEND, -S *vb*
OFFENSE *same as* ▸ **offence**
OFFER, -ED, -S *vb, n*
OFFEREE *n* person to whom an offer is made
OFFERER ▸ **offer**
OFFEROR ▸ **offer**
OFFERS ▸ **offer**
OFFHAND *adj, adv*
OFFICE, -S *n*
OFFICER *n, vb*
OFFICES ▸ **office**
OFFIE, -S *n* off-licence
OFFING, -S *n*
OFFISH *adj* aloof or distant in manner
OFFKEY *adj* out of tune
OFFLINE *adj*
OFFLOAD *vb*
OFFPEAK *adj* relating to times outside periods of intensive use
OFFPUT, -S *n* act of putting off

OFFRAMP *n* road allowing traffic to leave a motorway
OFFS ▸ **off**
OFFSCUM *n* scum
OFFSET, -S *vb, n*
OFFSIDE *adv, n*
OFFTAKE *n* act of taking off
OFFY *same as* ▸ **offie**
OFLAG, -S *n* prisoner-of-war camp for officers in World War II
OFT, -ER, -EST *adv* often
OFTEN, -ER *adv*
OFTER ▸ **oft**
OFTEST ▸ **oft**
OGAM, -S *same as* ▸ **ogham**
OGAMIC ▸ **ogam**
OGAMS ▸ **ogam**
OGDOAD, -S *n* group of eight
OGEE, -S *n* moulding having a cross section in the form of a letter S
OGEED *adj* (of an arch or moulding) having an ogee
OGEES ▸ **ogee**
OGGIN, -S *n* sea
OGHAM, -S *n* ancient writing system used by the Celts
OGHAMIC ▸ **ogham**
OGHAMS ▸ **ogham**
OGIVAL ▸ **ogive**
OGIVE, -S *n* diagonal rib or groin of a Gothic vault
OGLE, -D, -S *vb, n*
OGLER, -S ▸ **ogle**
OGLES ▸ **ogle**
OGLING, -S ▸ **ogle**
OGMIC ▸ **ogam**
OGRE, -S *n*
OGREISH ▸ **ogre**
OGREISM ▸ **ogre**
OGRES ▸ **ogre**
OGRESS ▸ **ogre**
OGRISH ▸ **ogre**
OGRISM, -S ▸ **ogre**
OH, -ED, -ING, -S *interj, vb*
OHIA, -S *n* Hawaiian plant
OHING ▸ **oh**
OHM, -S *n* unit of electrical resistance
OHMAGE, -S *n* electrical resistance in ohms
OHMIC *adj* of or relating to a circuit element
OHMS ▸ **ohm**
OHO *interj* exclamation expressing surprise, exultation, or derision
OHONE *same as* ▸ **ochone**
OHS ▸ **oh**
OI, -S *interj* shout to attract attention ▹ *n* grey-faced petrel
OIDIA ▸ **oidium**
OIDIOID ▸ **oidium**
OIDIUM, OIDIA *n* type of fungal spore
OIK, -S *n* insulting word for person regarded as inferior because ignorant or lower-class
OIKIST, -S *same as* ▸ **oecist**
OIKS ▸ **oik**
OIL, -ED, -ING, -S *n, vb*
OILBIRD *n* type of nocturnal gregarious cave-dwelling bird
OILCAMP *n* camp for oil workers
OILCAN, -S *n* container with a long nozzle for applying oil to machinery
OILCUP, -S *n* cup-shaped oil reservoir in a machine providing continuous lubrication for a bearing
OILED ▸ **oil**
OILER, -S *n* person, device, etc, that lubricates or supplies oil
OILERY *n* oil business
OILGAS *n* gaseous mixture of hydrocarbons used as a fuel
OILHOLE *n* hole for oil
OILIER ▸ **oily**
OILIEST ▸ **oily**
OILILY ▸ **oily**
OILING ▸ **oil**
OILLET, -S *same as* ▸ **eyelet**
OILMAN, OILMEN *n* person who owns or operates oil wells
OILNUT, -S *n* nut from which oil is extracted
OILPAN, -S *n* sump
OILS ▸ **oil**
OILSEED *n* seed from which oil is extracted
OILSKIN *n* (garment made from) waterproof material
OILWAY, -S *n* channel for oil
OILY, OILIER, OILIEST *adj*
OINK, -ED, -ING, -S *n, interj, vb*
OINOMEL *same as* ▸ **oenomel**

OINT, -ED, -ING, -S *vb* anoint
OIS ▸ **oi**
OJIME, -S *n* Japanese bead used to secure cords
OK *interj* expression of approval
OKA, -S *n* unit of weight used in Turkey
OKAPI, -S *n* African animal related to the giraffe but with a shorter neck
OKAS ▸ **oka**
OKAY, -ED, -ING, -S *adj, vb, n, interj*
OKE, -S *same as* ▸ **oka**
OKEH, -S *variant of* ▸ **okay**
OKES ▸ **oke**
OKIMONO *n* Japanese ornamental item
OKRA, -S *n*
OKTA, -S *n* unit used in meteorology to measure cloud cover
OLD, -EST, -S *adj, n*
OLDE *adj*
OLDEN, -ED, -S *adj* old ▹ *vb* grow old
OLDER ▸ **old**
OLDEST ▸ **old**
OLDIE, -S *n*
OLDISH ▸ **old**
OLDNESS ▸ **old**
OLDS ▸ **old**
OLDSTER *n* older person
OLDWIFE *n* any of various fishes, esp the menhaden or the alewife
OLDY *same as* ▸ **oldie**
OLE, -S *interj* exclamation of approval or encouragement customary at bullfights ▹ *n* cry of olé
OLEA ▸ **oleum**
OLEARIA *n* daisy bush
OLEATE, -S *n* any salt or ester of oleic acid
OLEFIN, -S *same as* ▸ **olefine**
OLEFINE *another name for* ▸ **alkene**
OLEFINS ▸ **olefin**
OLEIC *adj* as in **oleic acid** colourless oily liquid used in making soap
OLEIN, -S *another name for* ▸ **triolein**
OLEINE, -S *same as* ▸ **olein**
OLEINS ▸ **olein**
OLENT *adj* having smell
OLEO, -S *n* as in **oleo oil** oil extracted from beef fat
OLES ▸ **ole**
OLESTRA *n* trademark term for an artificial fat
OLEUM, OLEA, -S *n* type of sulphuric acid
OLFACT, -S *vb* smell something
OLICOOK *n* doughnut
OLID *adj* foul-smelling
OLIGIST *n* type of iron ore
OLINGO, -S *n* South American mammal
OLIO, -S *n* dish of many different ingredients
OLITORY *n* kitchen garden
OLIVARY *adj* shaped like an olive
OLIVE, -S *n, adj*
OLIVER, -S *n* as in **Bath oliver** type of unsweetened biscuit
OLIVES ▸ **olive**
OLIVET, -S *n* button shaped like olive
OLIVINE *n* olive-green mineral of the olivine group
OLLA, -S *n* cooking pot
OLLAMH, -S *n* old Irish term for a wise man
OLLAS ▸ **olla**
OLLAV, -S *same as* ▸ **ollamh**
OLLER, -S *n* waste ground
OLLIE, -D, -S *n* type of skateboarding jump ▹ *vb* perform an ollie
OLM, -S *n* pale blind eel-like salamander
OLOGIES ▸ **ology**
OLOGIST *n* scientist
OLOGOAN *vb* complain loudly without reason
OLOGY, OLOGIES *n* science or other branch of knowledge
OLOROSO *n* golden-coloured sweet sherry
OLPE, OLPAE, -S *n* ancient Greek jug
OLYCOOK *same as* ▸ **olykoek**
OLYKOEK *n* American type of doughnut
OM, -S *n* sacred syllable in Hinduism
OMA, -S *n* grandmother
OMASA ▸ **omasum**
OMASAL ▸ **omasum**
OMASUM, OMASA *n* compartment in the stomach of a ruminant animal

OMBER, -S *same as* ▸ **ombre**
OMBRE, -S *n* 18th-century card game
OMBU, -S *n* South American tree
OMEGA, -S *n* last letter in the Greek alphabet
OMELET, -S *same as* > **omelette**
OMEN, -ED, -ING, -S *n, vb*
OMENTA ▸ **omentum**
OMENTAL ▸ **omentum**
OMENTUM, OMENTA *n* double fold of the peritoneum
OMER, -S *n* ancient Hebrew unit of dry measure
OMERTA, -S *n* conspiracy of silence
OMICRON *n* 15th letter in the Greek alphabet
OMIKRON *same as* ▸ **omicron**
OMINOUS *adj*
OMIT, -S, -TED *vb*
OMITTER ▸ **omit**
OMLAH, -S *n* staff team in India
OMMATEA > **ommateum**
OMNEITY *n* state of being all
OMNIANA *n* miscellaneous collection
OMNIBUS *n, adj*
OMNIETY *same as* ▸ **omneity**
OMNIFIC *adj* creating all things
OMNIFY *vb* make something universal
OMNIUM, -S *n* total value
OMOV, -S *n* voting system in which each voter has one vote to cast
OMPHALI > **omphalos**
OMRAH, -S *n* Muslim noble
OMS ▸ **om**
ON, -NED, -NING, -S *prep, adv, adj, n, vb*
ONAGER, -S, ONAGRI *n* wild ass of Persia
ONBEAT, -S *n* first and third beats in a bar of four-four time
ONBOARD *vb*
ONCE, -S *adv, n*
ONCER, -S *n* (formerly) a one-pound note
ONCES ▸ **once**
ONCET *dialect form of* ▸ **once**
ONCOGEN *n* substance causing tumours to form
ONCOME, -S *n* act of coming on
ONCOST, -S *same as* > **overheads**
ONCUS *same as* ▸ **onkus**
ONDATRA *same as* > **musquash**
ONDINE, -S *same as* ▸ **undine**
ONDING, -S *Scots word for* ▸ **onset**
ONE, -S *adj, n, pron*
ONEFOLD *adj* simple
ONEIRIC *adj* of or relating to dreams
ONELY *same as* ▸ **only**
ONENESS *n* unity
ONER, -S *n* single continuous action
ONERIER ▸ **onery**
ONEROUS *adj*
ONERS ▸ **oner**
ONERY, ONERIER *same as* ▸ **ornery**
ONES ▸ **one**
ONESELF *pron*
ONESIE, -S *n* one-piece garment combining a top with trousers
ONETIME *adj*
ONEYER, -S *old form of* ▸ **one**
ONEYRE, -S *same as* ▸ **oneyer**
ONFALL, -S *n* attack or onset
ONFLOW, -S *n* flowing on
ONGOING *adj*
ONIE *variant spelling of* ▸ **ony**
ONION, -ED, -S *n, vb*
ONIONY ▸ **onion**
ONIRIC *same as* ▸ **oneiric**
ONIUM, -S *n* as in **onium compound** type of chemical salt
ONKUS *adj* bad
ONLAY, -S *n* artificial veneer for a tooth
ONLIEST *same as* ▸ **only**
ONLINE *adj*
ONLINER *n* person who uses the internet regularly
ONLOAD, -S *vb* load files on to a computer
ONLY *adj, adv*
ONNED ▸ **on**
ONNING ▸ **on**
ONO, -S *n* Hawaiian fish
ONOMAST *n* person who studies proper names

ONOS ▸ **ono**
ONRUSH *n* forceful forward rush or flow
ONS ▸ **on**
ONSET, -S *n*
ONSHORE *adv*
ONSIDE, -S *adv, adj, n*
ONST *same as* ▸ **once**
ONSTAGE *adj*
ONSTEAD *Scots word for* > **farmstead**
ONTIC *adj* having real existence
ONTO *prep* a position on
ONUS, -ES *n*
ONWARD *same as* ▸ **onwards**
ONWARDS *adv*
ONY *Scots word for* ▸ **any**
ONYCHA, -S *n* part of mollusc
ONYCHIA *n* inflammation of the nails or claws of animals
ONYMOUS *adj* (of a book) bearing its author's name
ONYX, -ES *n* type of quartz with coloured layers
OO, -S *Scots word for* ▸ **wool**
OOBIT, -S *n* hairy caterpillar
OOCYST, -S *n* type of zygote
OOCYTE, -S *n* immature female germ cell that gives rise to an ovum
OODLES *pl n*
OODLINS *same as* ▸ **oodles**
OOF, -S *n* money
OOFIER ▸ **oofy**
OOFIEST ▸ **oofy**
OOFS ▸ **oof**
OOFTISH *n* money
OOFY, OOFIER, OOFIEST ▸ **oof**
OOGAMY *n* type of reproduction
OOGENY *same as* > **oogenesis**
OOGONIA > **oogonium**
OOH, -ED, -S *interj, vb*
OOHING, -S *n* act of exclaiming 'ooh'
OOHS ▸ **ooh**
OOIDAL *adj* shaped like an egg
OOLAKAN *same as* > **eulachon**
OOLITE, -S *n* limestone made up of tiny grains of calcium carbonate
OOLITH, -S *n* tiny spherical grain of sedimentary rock
OOLITIC ▸ **oolite**
OOLOGIC ▸ **oology**
OOLOGY *n* study of birds' eggs
OOLONG, -S *n* kind of dark tea
OOM, -S *n* title of respect used to refer to an elderly man
OOMIAC, -S *same as* ▸ **umiak**
OOMIACK *same as* ▸ **umiak**
OOMIACS ▸ **oomiac**
OOMIAK, -S *same as* ▸ **umiak**
OOMPAH, -S *n* representation of the sound made by a deep brass instrument ▹ *vb* make the noise of a brass instrument
OOMPH, -S *n*
OOMS ▸ **oom**
OON, -S *Scots word for* ▸ **oven**
OONT, -S *n* camel
OOP, -ED, -ING *vb* Scots word meaning to bind
OOPHYTE *n* gametophyte in mosses, liverworts, and ferns
OOPING ▸ **oop**
OOPS *interj*
OOR *Scots form of* ▸ **our**
OORALI, -S *n* member of Indian people
OORIAL, -S *n* Himalayan sheep
OORIE, -R, -ST *adj* Scots word meaning shabby

This Scots word is one of the classic 5-letter vowel dumps. It has almost equally useful variants **ourie** and **owrie**.

OOS ▸ **oo**
OOSE, -S *n* dust
OOSIER ▸ **oosy**
OOSIEST ▸ **oosy**
OOSPERM *n* fertilized ovum
OOSPORE *n* thick-walled spore developed from a fertilized oosphere
OOSY, OOSIER, OOSIEST ▸ **oose**
OOT, -S *Scots word for* ▸ **out**
OOTHECA *n* capsule containing eggs
OOTID, -S *n* immature female gamete that develops into an ovum

OOTS ▸ **oot**
OOZE, -D, -S, OOZING *vb, n*
OOZIER ▸ **oozy**
OOZIEST ▸ **oozy**
OOZILY ▸ **oozy**
OOZING ▸ **ooze**
OOZY, OOZIER, OOZIEST *adj*
OP, -S *n* operation
OPA, -S *n* grandfather
OPACIFY *vb* become or make opaque
OPACITY *n* state or quality of being opaque
OPACOUS *same as* ▸ **opaque**
OPAH, -S *n* large soft-finned deep-sea fish
OPAL, -S *n*
OPALED *adj* made like opal
OPALINE *adj* opalescent ▹ *n* opaque or semiopaque whitish glass
OPALS ▸ **opal**
OPAQUE, -D, -R, -S *adj, n, vb*
OPAS ▸ **opa**
OPCODE, -S *n* computer code containing operating instructions
OPE, -D, -S, OPING *archaic or poetic word for* ▸ **open**
OPEN, -ED, -EST, -S *adj, vb, n*
OPENER, -S *n*
OPENEST ▸ **open**
OPENING *n, adj*
OPENLY ▸ **open**
OPENS ▸ **open**
OPEPE, -S *n* African tree
OPERA, -S *n*
OPERAND *n* quantity, variable, or function upon which an operation is performed
OPERANT *adj* producing effects ▹ *n* person or thing that operates
OPERAS ▸ **opera**
OPERATE *vb*
OPERON, -S *n* group of adjacent genes in bacteria
OPEROSE *adj* laborious
OPES ▸ **ope**
OPHITE, -S *n* any of several greenish mottled rocks
OPHITIC *adj* having small elongated feldspar crystals enclosed
OPHIURA *n* sea creature like a starfish
OPIATE, -D, -S *n, adj, vb*
OPINE, -D, -S, OPINING *vb* express an opinion
OPING ▸ **ope**
OPINING ▸ **opine**
OPINION *n*
OPIOID, -S *n* substance that resembles morphine
OPIUM, -S *n*
OPORICE *n* former medicine made from fruit
OPOSSUM *n*
OPPIDAN *adj* of a town ▹ *n* person living in a town
OPPO, -S *n* counterpart in another organization
OPPOSE, -D, -S *vb*
OPPOSER ▸ **oppose**
OPPOSES ▸ **oppose**
OPPRESS *vb*
OPPUGN, -S *vb* call into question
OPS ▸ **op**
OPSIN, -S *n* type of protein
OPSONIC ▸ **opsonin**
OPSONIN *n* constituent of blood serum
OPT, -ED, -ING, -S *vb*
OPTANT, -S *n* person who opts
OPTED ▸ **opt**
OPTER, -S ▸ **opt**
OPTIC *adj*
OPTICAL *adj*
OPTICS *n*
OPTIMA ▸ **optimum**
OPTIMAL *adj*
OPTIME, -S *n* mathematics student at Cambridge University
OPTIMUM, OPTIMA *n, adj*
OPTING ▸ **opt**
OPTION, -S *n, vb*
OPTS ▸ **opt**
OPULENT *adj*
OPULUS *n* flowering shrub
OPUNTIA *n* type of cactus
OPUS, -ES *n*
OPUSCLE *same as* > **opuscule**
OPUSES ▸ **opus**
OQUASSA *n* American trout
OR, -S *prep, adj, n*
ORA ▸ **os**
ORACH *same as* ▸ **orache**

ORACHE, -S *n* type of plant
ORACIES ▸ **oracy**
ORACLE, -D, -S *n, vb*
ORACY, ORACIES *n* capacity to use speech
ORAD *adv* towards the mouth
ORAL, -S *adj, n*
ORALISM *n* oral method of communicating with deaf people
ORALIST ▸ **oralism**
ORALITY *n* state of being oral
ORALLY ▸ **oral**
ORALS ▸ **oral**
ORANG, -S *n* orangutan
ORANGE, -R, -S *n, adj*
ORANGEY ▸ **orange**
ORANGS ▸ **orang**
ORANGY ▸ **orange**
ORANT, -S *n* artistic representation of worshipper
ORARIA ▸ **orarium**
ORARIAN *n* person who lives on the coast
ORARION *n* garment worn by Greek clergyman
ORARIUM, ORARIA *n* handkerchief
ORATE, -D, -S, ORATING *vb* make or give an oration
ORATION *n*
ORATOR, -S *n*
ORATORY *n*
ORATRIX *n* female orator
ORATURE *n* oral forms of literature
ORB, -ED, -ING, -S *n, vb*
ORBIER ▸ **orby**
ORBIEST ▸ **orby**
ORBING ▸ **orb**
ORBIT, -ED, -S *n, vb*
ORBITA, -S *same as* ▸ **orbit**
ORBITAL *adj, n*
ORBITAS ▸ **orbita**
ORBITED ▸ **orbit**
ORBITER *n*
ORBITS ▸ **orbit**
ORBITY *n* bereavement
ORBLESS ▸ **orb**
ORBLIKE *adj* like an orb
ORBS ▸ **orb**
ORBY, ORBIER, ORBIEST *adj* orb-shaped
ORC, -S *n* any of various whales, such as the killer and grampus
ORCA, -S *n* killer whale
ORCEIN, -S *n* brown crystalline material
ORCHARD *n*
ORCHAT, -S *same as* ▸ **orchard**
ORCHEL, -S *same as* ▸ **orchil**
ORCHID, -S *n*
ORCHIL, -S *n* any of various lichens
ORCHIS *n* type of orchid
ORCIN, -S *same as* ▸ **orcinol**
ORCINE, -S *same as* ▸ **orcinol**
ORCINOL *n* colourless crystalline water-soluble solid
ORCINS ▸ **orcin**
ORCS ▸ **orc**
ORD, -S *n* pointed weapon
ORDAIN, -S *vb*
ORDEAL, -S *n*
ORDER, -ED, -S *n, vb*
ORDERER ▸ **order**
ORDERLY *adj, n, adv*
ORDERS ▸ **order**
ORDINAL *adj* denoting a certain position in a sequence of numbers ▹ *n* book containing the forms of services for the ordination of ministers
ORDINAR *Scots word for* > **ordinary**
ORDINEE *n* person being ordained
ORDO, ORDINES, -S *n* religious order
ORDS ▸ **ord**
ORDURE, -S *n* excrement
ORE, -S *n*
OREAD, -ES, -S *n* mountain nymph
OREBODY *n* mass of ore in a mine
ORECTIC *adj* of or relating to the desires
OREGANO *n*
OREIDE, -S *same as* ▸ **oroide**
ORES ▸ **ore**
OREWEED *n* seaweed
OREXIN, -S *n* hormone that promotes wakefulness and stimulates the appetite
OREXIS *n* appetite
ORF, -S *n* infectious disease of sheep
ORFE, -S *n* small slender European fish
ORFRAY, -S *same as* ▸ **orphrey**
ORFS ▸ **orf**
ORG, -S *n* organization
ORGAN, -S *n*

ORGANA ▸ **organon**
ORGANDY *same as* > **organdie**
ORGANIC *adj, n*
ORGANON, ORGANA *n* system of logical or scientific rules
ORGANS ▸ **organ**
ORGANUM *same as* ▸ **organon**
ORGANZA *n* thin stiff fabric of silk, cotton, or synthetic fibre
ORGEAT, -S *n* drink made with orange flower water
ORGIA, -S *same as* ▸ **orgy**
ORGIAC ▸ **orgy**
ORGIAS ▸ **orgia**
ORGIAST *n* person who indulges immoderately in an activity
ORGIC ▸ **orgy**
ORGIES ▸ **orgy**
ORGONE, -S *n* substance claimed to be needed for mental health
ORGS ▸ **org**
ORGUE, -S *n* number of stakes lashed together
ORGY, ORGIES *n*
ORIBI, -S *n* small African antelope
ORIEL, -S *n* type of bay window
ORIENCY *n* state of being iridescent
ORIENT, -S *vb, n, adj*
ORIFEX *same as* ▸ **orifice**
ORIFICE *n*
ORIGAMI *n*
ORIGAN, -S *another name for* > **marjoram**
ORIGANE *same as* ▸ **origan**
ORIGANS ▸ **origan**
ORIGIN, -S *n*
ORIHOU, -S *n* small New Zealand tree
ORIOLE, -S *n* tropical or American songbird
ORISHA, -S *n* any of the minor gods or spirits of traditional Yoruba religion
ORISON, -S *another word for* ▸ **prayer**
ORIXA, -S *same as* ▸ **orisha**
ORLE, -S *n* border around a shield
ORLEANS *n* type of fabric
ORLES ▸ **orle**
ORLON, -S *n* crease-resistant acrylic fibre or fabric
ORLOP, -S *n* (in a vessel with four or more decks) the lowest deck
ORMER, -S *n* edible marine mollusc
ORMOLU, -S *n* gold-coloured alloy used for decoration
ORNATE, -R *adj*
ORNERY *adj*
ORNIS, -ES *less common word for* > **avifauna**
OROGEN, -S *n* part of earth subject to orogeny
OROGENY *n* formation of mountain ranges
OROIDE, -S *n* alloy containing copper, tin, and other metals
OROLOGY *same as* > **orography**
OROPESA *n* float used in minesweeping
OROTUND *adj* (of the voice) resonant and booming
ORPHAN, -S *n, vb*
ORPHIC *adj* mystical or occult
ORPHISM *n* style of abstract art
ORPHREY *n* richly embroidered band or border
ORPIN, -S *same as* ▸ **orpine**
ORPINE, -S *n* type of plant
ORPINS ▸ **orpin**
ORRA *adj* odd or unmatched
ORRAMAN, ORRAMEN *n* man who does odd jobs
ORRERY *n* mechanical model of the solar system
ORRICE, -S *same as* ▸ **orris**
ORRIS, -ES *n* kind of iris
ORS ▸ **or**
ORT *n* fragment
ORTHIAN *adj* having high pitch
ORTHO, -S *n* type of photographic plate
ORTHROS *n* canonical hour in the Greek Church
ORTOLAN *n* small European songbird eaten as a delicacy
ORTS *pl n* scraps or leavings
ORVAL, -S *n* plant of sage family

ORYX, -ES *n* large African antelope
ORZO, -S *n* pasta in small grain shapes
OS, ORA, -AR, -SA *n* mouth or mouthlike part or opening
OSCAR, -S *n* cash
OSCHEAL *adj* of the scrotum
OSCINE, -S *n* songbird ▷ *adj* of songbirds
OSCULA ▶ **osculum**
OSCULAR *adj* of or relating to an osculum
OSCULE, -S *n* small mouth or opening
OSCULUM, OSCULA *n* mouthlike aperture
OSE, -S *same as* ▶ **esker**
OSETRA, -S *n* type of caviar
OSHAC, -S *n* plant smelling of ammonia
OSIER, -S *n* willow tree
OSIERED *adj* covered with osiers
OSIERS ▶ **osier**
OSIERY *n* work done with osiers
OSMATE, -S *n* salt of osmic acid
OSMATIC *adj* relying on sense of smell
OSMIATE *same as* ▶ **osmate**
OSMIC *adj* of or containing osmium in a high valence state
OSMICS *n* science of smell
OSMIOUS *same as* ▶ **osmous**
OSMIUM, -S *n* heaviest known metallic element
OSMOL, -S *same as* ▶ **osmole**
OSMOLAL ▶ **osmole**
OSMOLAR *adj* containing one osmole per litre
OSMOLE, -S *n* unit of osmotic pressure
OSMOLS ▶ **osmol**
OSMOSE, -D, -S *vb* undergo or cause to undergo osmosis
OSMOSIS *n*
OSMOTIC ▶ **osmosis**
OSMOUS *adj* of or containing osmium in a low valence state
OSMUND, -S *same as* ▶ **osmunda**
OSMUNDA *n* type of fern
OSMUNDS ▶ **osmund**
OSPREY, -S *n*
OSSA ▶ **os**
OSSEIN, -S *n* protein that forms the organic matrix of bone
OSSELET *n* growth on knee of horse
OSSEOUS *adj* consisting of or like bone
OSSETER *n* sturgeon
OSSETRA *same as* ▶ **osetra**
OSSIA, -S *n* alternate version or passage ▷ *conj* or
OSSICLE *n* small bone, esp one of those in the middle ear
OSSIFIC *adj* making something turn to bone
OSSIFY *vb*
OSSUARY *n* any container for the burial of human bones, such as an urn or vault
OSTEAL *adj* of or relating to bone or to the skeleton
OSTENT, -S *n* appearance ▷ *vb* display boastfully
OSTEOID *adj* of or resembling bone ▷ *n* bony deposit
OSTEOMA *n* tumour composed of bone or bonelike tissue
OSTIA ▶ **ostium**
OSTIAL ▶ **ostium**
OSTIARY *another word for* ▶ **porter**
OSTIATE *adj* having ostium
OSTIOLE *n* pore in the reproductive bodies of certain algae and fungi
OSTIUM, OSTIA *n* pore in sponges through which water enters the body
OSTLER, -S *n* stableman at an inn
OSTMARK *n* currency of the former East Germany
OSTOMY *n* surgically made opening
OSTOSIS, OSTOSES *n* formation of bone
OSTRACA > **ostracon**
OSTRAKA > **ostrakon**
OSTRICH *n*
OTAKU, -S *n* Japanese computer geek
OTALGIA *technical name for* ▶ **earache**
OTALGIC ▶ **otalgia**

OTALGY *same as* ▶ **otalgia**
OTARID *adj* of or like an otary, an eared seal
OTARIES ▶ **otary**
OTARINE ▶ **otary**

This means like an otary or eared seal, and is perhaps the most commonly played of all 7-letter bonus words, so well worth learning for that extra 50 points it can give you.

OTARY, OTARIES *n* seal with ears
OTHER, -ED, -S *vb*
OTIC *adj* of or relating to the ear
OTIOSE *adj* not useful
OTITIC ▶ **otitis**
OTITIS *n* inflammation of the ear
OTOCYST *n* embryonic structure in vertebrates that develops into the inner ear
OTOLITH *n* granule of calcium carbonate in the inner ear of vertebrates
OTOLOGY *n* branch of medicine concerned with the ear
OTTAR, -S *variant of* ▶ **attar**
OTTAVA, -S *n* interval of an octave
OTTER, -ED, -S *n, vb*
OTTO, -S *another name for* ▶ **attar**
OTTOMAN *n*
OTTOS ▶ **otto**
OU, -ENS, -S *interj* expressing concession ▷ *n* man, bloke, or chap
OUABAIN *n* poisonous white crystalline glycoside
OUAKARI *n* South American monkey
OUBAAS *n* man in authority
OUBIT, -S *n* hairy caterpillar
OUCH, -ED, -ES, -ING *interj, n, vb*
OUCHT, -S *Scots word for* > **anything**
OUD, -S *n* Arabic stringed musical instrument
OUENS ▶ **ou**
OUGHLY *variant of* ▶ **ugly**
OUGHT, -ED, -S *vb, n*
OUGIYA, -S *n* standard monetary unit of Mauritania
OUGLIE, -D, -S *variant of* ▶ **ugly**
OUGUIYA *n* standard monetary unit of Mauritania
OUIJA, -S *n* tradename for a board through which spirits supposedly answer questions
OUK, -S *Scots word for* ▶ **week**
OULAKAN *same as* > **eulachon**
OULD, -ER, -EST *Scots or Irish form of* ▶ **old**
OULK, -S *Scots form of* ▶ **week**
OULONG, -S *same as* ▶ **oolong**
OUMA, -S *n* grandmother, often as a title with a surname
OUNCE, -S *n*
OUNDY, OUNDIER *adj* wavy
OUP, -ED, -ING, -S *same as* ▶ **oop**
OUPA, -S *n* grandfather, often as a title with a surname
OUPED ▶ **oup**
OUPH, -S *same as* ▶ **oaf**
OUPHE, -S *same as* ▶ **oaf**
OUPHS ▶ **ouph**
OUPING ▶ **oup**
OUPS ▶ **oup**
OUR *adj, determiner*
OURALI, -S *n* plant from which curare comes
OURANG, -S *same as* ▶ **orang**
OURARI, -S *same as* ▶ **ourali**
OUREBI, -S *same as* ▶ **oribi**
OURIE, -R, -ST *same as* ▶ **oorie**
OURN *dialect form of* ▶ **our**
OURS *pron*
OURSELF *pron* formal word for *myself* used by monarchs
OUS ▶ **ou**
OUSEL, -S *same as* ▶ **ouzel**
OUST, -ED, -ING, -S *vb*
OUSTER, -S *n* act of forcing someone out of a position
OUSTING ▶ **oust**
OUSTITI *n* device for opening locked door
OUSTS ▶ **oust**
OUT, -ED, -S *adj, vb*

OUTA *prep* informal contraction of out of
OUTACT, -S *vb* surpass in acting
OUTADD, -S *vb* beat or surpass at adding
OUTAGE, -S *n*
OUTASK, -S *vb* declare wedding banns
OUTATE ▸ **outeat**
OUTBACK *n*
OUTBAKE *vb* bake more or better than
OUTBAR, -S *vb* keep out
OUTBARK *vb* bark more or louder than
OUTBARS ▸ **outbar**
OUTBAWL *vb* bawl more or louder than
OUTBEAM *vb* beam more or brighter than
OUTBEG, -S *vb* beg more or better than
OUTBID, -S *vb*
OUTBOX *vb* surpass in boxing
OUTBRAG *vb* brag more or better than
OUTBRED > **outbreed**
OUTBULK *vb* exceed in bulk
OUTBURN *vb* burn longer or brighter than
OUTBUY, -S *vb* buy more than
OUTBY *adv* outside
OUTBYE *same as* ▸ **outby**
OUTCALL *n* visit to customer's home by professional ▹ *vb* bid higher than another player in a card game
OUTCAST *n, adj*
OUTCHID > **outchide**
OUTCITY *n* anywhere outside a city's confines
OUTCOME *n*
OUTCOOK *vb* cook more or better than
OUTCROP *n, vb*
OUTCROW *vb* exceed in crowing
OUTCRY *n, vb*
OUTDARE *vb* be more brave than
OUTDATE *vb* make or become old-fashioned or obsolete
OUTDO, OUTDID, -ES, -NE *vb*
OUTDOER ▸ **outdo**
OUTDOES ▸ **outdo**
OUTDONE ▸ **outdo**
OUTDOOR *adj*
OUTDRAG *vb* beat in drag race
OUTDRAW, OUTDREW *vb* draw (a gun) faster than
OUTDROP *same as* ▸ **outcrop**
OUTDUEL *vb* defeat in duel
OUTDURE *vb* last longer than
OUTEARN *vb* earn more than
OUTEAT, OUTATE, -S *vb* eat more than
OUTECHO *vb* echo more than
OUTED ▸ **out**
OUTEDGE *n* furthest limit
OUTER, -S *adj, n*
OUTFACE *vb* subdue or disconcert by staring
OUTFALL *n* mouth of a river or drain
OUTFAST *vb* fast longer than
OUTFAWN *vb* exceed in fawning
OUTFEEL, OUTFELT *vb* exceed in feeling
OUTFIND *vb* exceed in finding
OUTFIRE *vb* exceed in firing
OUTFISH *vb* catch more fish than
OUTFIT, -S *n, vb*
OUTFLEW ▸ **outfly**
OUTFLOW *n, vb*
OUTFLY, OUTFLEW *vb* fly better or faster than
OUTFOOL *vb* be more foolish than
OUTFOOT *vb* (of a boat) to go faster than (another boat)
OUTFOX *vb* defeat or foil by being more cunning
OUTGAIN *vb* gain more than
OUTGAS *vb* undergo the removal of adsorbed or absorbed gas from solids
OUTGATE *n* way out
OUTGAVE ▸ **outgive**
OUTGAZE *vb* gaze beyond
OUTGIVE, OUTGAVE *vb* exceed in giving
OUTGLOW *vb* glow more than
OUTGNAW *vb* exceed in gnawing
OUTGO, -ES, -NE, OUTWENT *vb* exceed or outstrip ▹ *n* cost
OUTGOER ▸ **outgo**
OUTGOES ▸ **outgo**

OUTGONE ▸ **outgo**
OUTGREW ▸ **outgrow**
OUTGRIN *vb* exceed in grinning
OUTGROW, OUTGREW *vb*
OUTGUN, -S *vb* surpass in fire power
OUTGUSH *vb* gush out
OUTHAUL *n* line or cable for tightening the foot of a sail
OUTHEAR *vb* exceed in hearing
OUTHER *same as* ▸ **other**
OUTHIRE *vb* hire out
OUTHIT, -S *vb* hit something further than (someone else)
OUTHOWL *vb* exceed in howling
OUTHUNT *vb* exceed in hunting
OUTHYRE *same as* ▸ **outhire**
OUTING, -S *n*
OUTJEST *vb* exceed in jesting
OUTJET, -S *n* projecting part
OUTJINX *vb* exceed in jinxing

If someone else plays **jinx**, you can outjinx them by adding O, U and T! And if you can form the whole word using all of your letters, you'll get a 50-point bonus.

OUTJUMP *vb* jump higher or farther than
OUTJUT, -S *vb* jut out ▹ *n* projecting part
OUTKEEP, OUTKEPT *vb* beat or surpass at keeping
OUTKICK *vb* exceed in kicking
OUTKILL *vb* exceed in killing
OUTKISS *vb* exceed in kissing
OUTLAID ▸ **outlay**
OUTLAIN ▸ **outlie**
OUTLAND *adj* outlying or distant ▹ *n* outlying areas of a country or region
OUTLASH *n* sudden attack ▹ *vb* shed tears
OUTLAST *vb*
OUTLAW, -S *n, vb*
OUTLAY, OUTLAID, -S *n, vb*
OUTLEAD, OUTLED *vb* be better leader than
OUTLEAP *vb* leap higher or farther than
OUTLED ▸ **outlead**
OUTLER, -S *n* farm animal kept out of doors
OUTLET, -S *n*
OUTLIE, OUTLAIN, -D, -S *vb* lie outside a particular place
OUTLIER *n*
OUTLIES ▸ **outlie**
OUTLINE *n, vb*
OUTLIVE *vb*
OUTLOOK *n, vb*
OUTLOVE *vb* exceed in loving
OUTMAN, -S *vb* surpass in manpower
OUTMODE *vb* make unfashionable
OUTMOST *another word for* ▸ **outermost**
OUTMOVE *vb* move faster or better than
OUTNAME *vb* be more notorious than
OUTNESS *n* state or quality of being external
OUTPACE *vb* go faster than (someone)
OUTPART *n* remote region
OUTPASS *vb* exceed in passing
OUTPEEP *vb* peep out
OUTPEER *vb* surpass
OUTPITY *vb* exceed in pitying
OUTPLAN *vb* exceed in planning
OUTPLAY *vb* perform better than one's opponent
OUTPLOD *vb* exceed in plodding
OUTPLOT *vb* exceed in plotting
OUTPOLL *vb* win more votes than
OUTPORT *n* isolated fishing village, esp in Newfoundland
OUTPOST *n*
OUTPOUR *n* act of flowing or pouring out ▹ *vb* pour or cause to pour out freely or rapidly
OUTPRAY *vb* exceed in praying
OUTPULL *vb* exceed in pulling
OUTPUSH *vb* exceed in pushing
OUTPUT, -S *n* amount produced ▹ *vb* produce (data) at the end of a process

OUTRACE *vb* surpass in racing
OUTRAGE *n*, *vb*
OUTRAN ▸ **outrun**
OUTRANG ▸ **outring**
OUTRANK *vb*
OUTRATE *vb* offer better rate than
OUTRAVE *vb* outdo in raving
OUTRE *adj*
OUTREAD *vb* outdo in reading
OUTRED, -S *vb* be redder than
OUTRIDE, OUTRODE *vb* outdo by riding faster, farther, or better than ▹ *n* extra unstressed syllable within a metrical foot
OUTRIG, -S *vb* supply with outfit
OUTRING, OUTRANG, OUTRUNG *vb* exceed in ringing
OUTRO, -S *n* instrumental passage that concludes a piece of music
OUTROAR *vb*
OUTROCK *vb* outdo in rocking
OUTRODE ▸ **outride**
OUTROLL *vb* exceed in rolling
OUTROOP *n* auction
OUTROOT *vb* root out
OUTROPE *same as* ▸ **outroop**
OUTROS ▸ **outro**
OUTROW, -S *vb* outdo in rowing
OUTRUN, OUTRAN, -S *vb*
OUTRUNG ▸ **outring**
OUTRUNS ▸ **outrun**
OUTRUSH *n* flowing or rushing out ▹ *vb* rush out
OUTS ▸ **out**
OUTSAID ▸ **outsay**
OUTSAIL *vb* sail better than
OUTSANG ▸ **outsing**
OUTSAT ▸ **outsit**
OUTSAW ▸ **outsee**
OUTSAY, OUTSAID, -S *vb* say something out loud
OUTSEE, OUTSAW, -N, -S *vb* exceed in seeing
OUTSELL, OUTSOLD *vb*
OUTSERT *another word for* > **wrapround**
OUTSET, -S *n*
OUTSHOT *n* projecting part
OUTSIDE *adv*, *adj*, *n*
OUTSIN, -S *vb* sin more than
OUTSING, OUTSANG, OUTSUNG *vb* sing better or louder than
OUTSINS ▸ **outsin**
OUTSIT, OUTSAT, -S *vb* sit longer than
OUTSIZE *adj*, *n*
OUTSOAR *vb* fly higher than
OUTSOLD ▸ **outsell**
OUTSOLE *n* outermost sole of a shoe
OUTSPAN *vb* relax
OUTSPED > **outspeed**
OUTSTAY *vb* overstay
OUTSTEP *vb* step farther than
OUTSULK *vb* outdo in sulking
OUTSUM, -S *vb* add up to more than
OUTSUNG ▸ **outsing**
OUTSWIM, OUTSWAM, OUTSWUM *vb* outdo in swimming
OUTTA *prep* informal contraction of out of
OUTTAKE, OUTTOOK *n* unreleased take from a recording session, film, or TV programme ▹ *vb* take out
OUTTALK *vb* talk more, longer, or louder than (someone)
OUTTASK *vb* assign task to staff outside organization
OUTTELL, OUTTOLD *vb* make known
OUTTOOK ▸ **outtake**
OUTTOP, -S *vb* rise higher than
OUTTROT *vb* exceed at trotting
OUTTURN *same as* ▸ **output**
OUTVIE, -D, -S *vb* outdo in competition
OUTVOTE *vb* defeat by getting more votes than
OUTWAIT *vb* wait longer than
OUTWALK *vb* walk farther or longer than
OUTWAR, -S *vb* surpass or exceed in warfare
OUTWARD *same as* > **outwards**
OUTWARS ▸ **outwar**
OUTWASH *n* gravel carried and deposited by water from melting glaciers
OUTWEAR, OUTWORE *vb* use up or destroy by wearing

OUTWEED *vb* root out
OUTWEEP, OUTWEPT *vb* outdo in weeping
OUTWELL *vb* pour out
OUTWENT ▸ **outgo**
OUTWEPT ▸ **outweep**
OUTWICK *vb* move one curling stone by striking with another
OUTWILE *vb* surpass in cunning
OUTWILL *vb* demonstrate stronger will than
OUTWIN, -S, OUTWON *vb* get out of
OUTWIND *vb* unwind
OUTWING *vb* surpass in flying
OUTWINS ▸ **outwin**
OUTWISH *vb* surpass in wishing
OUTWIT, -S *vb*
OUTWITH *prep*
OUTWITS ▸ **outwit**
OUTWON ▸ **outwin**
OUTWORE ▸ **outwear**
OUTWORK *n* defences which lie outside main defensive works ▹ *vb* work better, harder, etc, than
OUTWORN *adj* no longer in use
OUTWRIT > **outwrite**
OUTYELL *vb* outdo in yelling
OUTYELP *vb* outdo in yelping
OUVERT *adj* open
OUVERTE *feminine form of* ▸ **ouvert**
OUVRAGE *n* work
OUVRIER *n* worker
OUZEL, -S *n* type of bird
OUZO, -S *n* strong aniseed-flavoured spirit from Greece
OVA ▸ **ovum**
OVAL, -S *adj, n*
OVALITY ▸ **oval**
OVALLY ▸ **oval**
OVALS ▸ **oval**
OVARIAL ▸ **ovary**
OVARIAN ▸ **ovary**
OVARY, OVARIES *n*
OVATE, -D, -S, OVATING *adj* shaped like an egg ▹ *vb* give ovation
OVATELY ▸ **ovate**
OVATES ▸ **ovate**
OVATING ▸ **ovate**
OVATION *n*
OVATOR, -S ▸ **ovate**
OVEL, -S *n* mourner, esp during the first seven days after a death
OVEN, -ED, -ING, -S *n, vb*
OVER, -ED, -ING, -S *adv, adj, n, vb*
OVERACT *vb*
OVERAGE *adj* beyond a specified age ▹ *n* amount beyond given limit
OVERALL *adv, n, adj*
OVERAPT *adj* tending excessively
OVERARM *adv* with the arm above the shoulder ▹ *adj* bowled, thrown, or performed with the arm raised above the shoulder ▹ *vb* throw (a ball) overarm
OVERATE ▸ **overeat**
OVERAWE *vb* affect (someone) with an overpowering sense of awe
OVERBED *adj* fitting over bed
OVERBET *vb* bet too much
OVERBID *vb* bid for more tricks than one can expect to win ▹ *n* bid higher than someone else's bid
OVERBIG *adj* too big
OVERBUY *vb* buy too much or too many
OVERBY *adv* Scots expression meaning over the road or across the way
OVERCOY *adj* too modest
OVERCUT *vb* cut too much
OVERDO, OVERDID *vb*
OVERDOG *n* person or side in an advantageous position
OVERDRY *vb* dry too much
OVERDUB *vb, n*
OVERDUE *adj*
OVERDYE *vb* dye (a fabric, yarn, etc) excessively
OVEREAT, OVERATE *vb*
OVERED ▸ **over**
OVEREGG *vb* exaggerate absurdly
OVEREYE *vb* survey
OVERFAR *adv* too far
OVERFAT *adj* too fat
OVERFED > **overfeed**
OVERFIT *adj* too fit
OVERFLY *vb* fly over (a territory) or past (a point)
OVERGET, OVERGOT *vb* overtake
OVERGO *vb* go beyond

OVERGOT ▸ **overget**
OVERHIT *vb* hit too strongly
OVERHOT *adj* too hot
OVERING ▸ **over**
OVERJOY *vb*
OVERLAP *vb, n*
OVERLAX *adj* too lax
OVERLAY *vb* cover with a thin layer ▹ *n* something that is laid over something else
OVERLET *vb* let to too many
OVERLIE *vb* lie on or cover (something or someone)
OVERLIT > **overlight**
OVERLY *adv*
OVERMAN, OVERMEN *vb* provide with too many workers ▹ *n* man who oversees others
OVERMIX *vb* mix too much
OVERNET *vb* cover with net
OVERNEW *adj* too new
OVERPAY *vb*
OVERPLY *vb* ply too much
OVERRAN ▸ **overrun**
OVERRED *vb* paint over in red
OVERREN *same as* ▸ **overrun**
OVERRUN, OVERRAN *vb, n*
OVERS ▸ **over**
OVERSAD *adj* too sad
OVERSAW ▸ **oversee**
OVERSEA *same as* > **overseas**
OVERSEE, OVERSAW *vb*
OVERSET *vb* disturb or upset
OVERSEW *vb* sew (two edges) with stitches that pass over them both
OVERSOW *vb* sow again after first sowing
OVERSUP *vb* sup too much
OVERT *adj*
OVERTAX *vb* put too great a strain on
OVERTIP *vb* give too much money as a tip
OVERTLY ▸ **overt**
OVERTOP *vb* exceed in height
OVERUSE *vb, n*
OVERWET *vb* make too wet
OVIBOS *n* type of ox
OVICIDE *n* killing of sheep
OVIDUCT *n* tube through which eggs are conveyed
OVIFORM *adj* shaped like an egg
OVINE, -S *adj* of or like a sheep ▹ *n* member of sheep family
OVIPARA *n* all oviparous animals
OVISAC, -S *n* capsule or sac in which egg cells are produced
OVIST, -S *n* person believing ovum contains all subsequent generations
OVOID, -S *adj* egg-shaped ▹ *n* something that is ovoid
OVOIDAL *adj* ovoid ▹ *n* something that is ovoid
OVOIDS ▸ **ovoid**
OVOLO, OVOLI, -S *n* type of convex moulding

Two Os on your rack can normally be dealt with; three is a bit much, but this word for a moulding can handle them. Note that the plural can be **ovolos** or **ovoli**.

OVONIC *adj* using particular electronic storage batteries
OVONICS *n* science of ovonic equipment
OVULAR ▸ **ovule**
OVULARY ▸ **ovule**
OVULATE *vb*
OVULE, -S *n* plant part that contains the egg cell
OVUM, OVA *n* unfertilized egg cell
OW *interj* exclamation of pain
OWCHE, -S *same as* ▸ **ouch**
OWE, -D, -S, OWING *vb*
OWELTY *n* equality, esp in financial transactions
OWER *Scots word for* ▸ **over**
OWERBY *adv* over there
OWES ▸ **owe**
OWIE, -S *n* minor injury
OWING ▸ **owe**
OWL, -ED, -ING, -S *n, vb*
OWLER, -S *n* smuggler

OWLERY *n* place where owls live
OWLET, -S *n* young or nestling owl
OWLIER ▸ **owly**
OWLIEST ▸ **owly**
OWLING ▸ **owl**
OWLISH *adj* like an owl
OWLLIKE ▸ **owl**
OWLS ▸ **owl**
OWLY, OWLIER, OWLIEST *same as* ▸ **owlish**
OWN, -ED, -ING, -S *adj, pron, vb*
OWNABLE *adj* able to be owned
OWNED ▸ **own**
OWNER, -S *n*
OWNING ▸ **own**
OWNS ▸ **own**
OWNSOME *n* solitary state
OWRE, -S *same as* ▸ **ower**
OWRELAY *Scots form of* ▸ **overlay**
OWRES ▸ **owre**
OWRIE, -R, -ST *same as* ▸ **oorie**
OWSE *Scots form of* ▸ **ox**
OWSEN *Scots word for* ▸ **oxen**
OWT, -S *dialect word for* > **anything**
OX, -EN, -ES *n*
OXALATE *n* salt or ester of oxalic acid ▹ *vb* treat with oxalate
OXALIC *adj* as in **oxalic acid** poisonous acid found in many plants
OXALIS *n* type of plant
OXAZINE *n* type of chemical compound
OXAZOLE *n* type of liquid chemical compound
OXBLOOD *n* dark reddish-brown colour ▹ *adj* of this colour
OXBOW, -S *n* piece of wood fitted around the neck of a harnessed ox
OXCART, -S *n* cart pulled by ox
OXEN ▸ **ox**
OXER, -S *n* high fence
OXES ▸ **ox**
OXEYE, -S *n* daisy-like flower
OXFORD, -S *n* type of stout laced shoe with a low heel
OXGANG, -S *n* old measure of farmland
OXGATE, -S *same as* ▸ **oxgang**
OXHEAD, -S *n* head of an ox
OXHEART *n* heart-shaped cherry
OXHERD, -S *n* person who tends oxen
OXHIDE, -S *n* leather made from the hide of an ox
OXIC *adj* involving oxygen
OXID, -S *same as* ▸ **oxide**
OXIDANT *n* substance that acts or is used as an oxidizing agent
OXIDASE *n* enzyme that brings about oxidation
OXIDATE *another word for* ▸ **oxidize**
OXIDE, -S *n*
OXIDIC ▸ **oxide**
OXIDISE *same as* ▸ **oxidize**
OXIDIZE *vb*
OXIDS ▸ **oxid**
OXIES ▸ **oxy**
OXIM, -S *same as* ▸ **oxime**
OXIME, -S *n* type of chemical compound
OXIMS ▸ **oxim**
OXLAND, -S *same as* ▸ **oxgang**
OXLIKE ▸ **ox**
OXLIP, -S *n* type of woodland plant
OXO *n* as in **oxo acid** acid that contains oxygen
OXONIUM *n* as in **oxonium compound** type of salt derived from an organic ether
OXSLIP, -S *same as* ▸ **oxlip**
OXTAIL, -S *n*
OXTER, -ED, -S *n, vb*
OXY, OXIES ▸ **ox**
OXYACID *n* any acid that contains oxygen
OXYGEN, -S *n*
OXYMEL, -S *n* mixture of vinegar and honey
OXYMORA > **oxymoron**
OXYNTIC *adj* of or denoting stomach cells that secrete acid
OXYPHIL *n* type of cell found in glands
OXYSALT *n* any salt of an oxyacid
OXYSOME *n* group of molecules
OXYTONE *adj* having an accent on the final syllable ▹ *n* oxytone word

OY, -S *n* grandchild
OYE *same as* ▸ **oy**
OYER, -S *n* (in the 13th century) an assize
OYES, -ES, -SES *same as* ▸ **oyez**
OYEZ, -ES *interj* shouted three times by a public crier calling for attention ▹ *n* such a cry
OYS ▸ **oy**
OYSTER, -S *n, vb*
OZAENA, -S *n* inflammation of nasal mucous membrane
OZALID, -S *n* method of duplicating writing or illustrations
OZEKI, -S *n* sumo wrestling champion
OZONATE *vb* add ozone to
OZONE, -S *n*
OZONIC ▸ **ozone**
OZONIDE *n* type of unstable explosive compound
OZONISE *same as* ▸ **ozonize**
OZONIZE *vb* convert (oxygen) into ozone
OZONOUS ▸ **ozone**
OZZIE, -S *n* hospital

Pp

PA *n* (formerly) fortified Māori settlement
PAAL, -S *n* stake driven into the ground
PAAN, -S *n* leaf of the betel tree
PABLUM, -S *same as* ▸ **pabulum**
PABULAR ▸ **pabulum**
PABULUM *n* food
PAC, -S *n* soft shoe
PACA, -S *n* large burrowing rodent
PACABLE *adj* easily appeased
PACAS ▸ **paca**
PACE, -D, -S *n, vb, prep*
PACEMAN, PACEMEN *n* (in cricket) fast bowler
PACER, -S *n*
PACES ▸ **pace**
PACEWAY *n* racecourse for trotting and pacing
PACEY *adj* fast-moving, quick, lively
PACHA, -S *same as* ▸ **pasha**
PACHAK, -S *n* fragrant roots of Asian plant
PACHAS ▸ **pacha**
PACHISI *n* Indian game resembling backgammon
PACHUCO *n* young Mexican living in the US
PACIER ▸ **pacy**
PACIEST ▸ **pacy**
PACIFIC *adj*
PACIFY *vb*
PACING, -S *n*
PACK, -S *vb, n*
PACKAGE *same as* ▸ **packet**
PACKED *adj*
PACKER, -S *n*
PACKET, -S *n, vb*
PACKING *n*
PACKMAN, PACKMEN *n* man carrying a pack
PACKS ▸ **pack**
PACKWAX *n* neck ligament
PACKWAY *n* path for pack animals
PACO, -S *n* S American mammal
PACS ▸ **pac**
PACT, -S *n* formal agreement
PACTA ▸ **pactum**
PACTION *vb* concur with
PACTS ▸ **pact**
PACTUM, PACTA *n* pact
PACY, PACIER, PACIEST *same as* ▸ **pacey**
PACZKI, -S *n* round filled doughnut
PAD, -DED, -S *n, vb*
PADANG, -S *n* (in Malaysia) playing field
PADAUK, -S *n* tropical African or Asian tree
PADDED ▸ **pad**
PADDER, -S *n* highwayman who robs on foot
PADDIES ▸ **paddy**
PADDING ▸ **pad**
PADDLE, -D, -S *n, vb*
PADDLER ▸ **paddle**
PADDLES ▸ **paddle**
PADDOCK *n, vb*
PADDY, PADDIES *n* fit of temper
PADELLA *n* type of candle
PADI, -S *same as* ▸ **paddy**
PADKOS *n* snacks and provisions for a journey
PADLE, -S *another name for* ▸ **lumpfish**
PADLOCK *n, vb*
PADMA, -S *n* type of lotus
PADNAG, -S *n* ambling horse
PADOUK, -S *same as* ▸ **padauk**
PADRE, -S, PADRI *n* chaplain to the armed forces
PADRONA *n* female boss or employer
PADRONE, PADRONI *n* owner or proprietor of an inn, esp in Italy

PADS ▸ **pad**
PADSAW, -S *n* small narrow saw used for cutting curves
PADSHAH *same as* > **padishah**
PAEAN, -S *n* song of triumph or thanksgiving
PAELLA, -S *n* Spanish dish of rice, chicken, shellfish, and vegetables
PAENULA *n* ancient Roman cloak
PAEON, -S *n* metrical foot of four syllables
PAEONIC ▸ **paeon**
PAEONS ▸ **paeon**
PAEONY *same as* ▸ **peony**
PAESAN, -S *n* fellow countryman
PAESANO, PAESANI *n* Italian-American man
PAESANS ▸ **paesan**
PAGAN, -S *adj, n*
PAGE, -D, -S *n, vb*
PAGEANT *n*
PAGEBOY *n* type of hairstyle
PAGED ▸ **page**
PAGEFUL *n* amount (of text, etc) that a page will hold
PAGER, -S *n*
PAGES ▸ **page**
PAGINAL *adj* page-for-page
PAGING, -S ▸ **page**
PAGLE, -S *same as* ▸ **paigle**
PAGOD, -S *same as* ▸ **pagoda**
PAGODA, -S *n* pyramid-shaped Asian temple or tower
PAGODS ▸ **pagod**
PAGRI, -S *n* type of turban
PAGURID *same as* > **pagurian**
PAH, -S *same as* ▸ **pa**
PAHLAVI *n* former Iranian coin
PAHS ▸ **pah**
PAID ▸ **pay**
PAIDLE, -S *Scots variant of* ▸ **paddle**
PAIGLE, -S *n* cowslip
PAIK, -ED, -ING, -S *vb* thump or whack
PAIL, -S *n* bucket
PAILFUL *same as* ▸ **pail**
PAILLON *n* thin leaf of metal
PAILS ▸ **pail**
PAIN, -ING *n, vb*
PAINCH *Scots variant of* ▸ **paunch**
PAINED *adj*
PAINFUL *adj*
PAINIM, -S *n* heathen or pagan
PAINING ▸ **pain**
PAINS *pl n*
PAINT, -ED, -S *n, vb*
PAINTER *n*
PAINTS ▸ **paint**
PAINTY ▸ **paint**
PAIOCK, -S *obsolete word for* ▸ **peacock**
PAIOCKE *obsolete word for* ▸ **peacock**
PAIOCKS ▸ **paiock**
PAIR, -ED, -ER, -EST, -S *n, vb*
PAIRE, -S *obsolete spelling of* ▸ **pair**
PAIRED ▸ **pair**
PAIRER ▸ **pair**
PAIRES ▸ **paire**
PAIREST ▸ **pair**
PAIRIAL *variant of* ▸ **prial**
PAIRING ▸ **pair**
PAIRS ▸ **pair**
PAIS *n* country
PAISA, -S, PAISE *n* monetary unit of Bangladesh, Bhutan, India, Nepal, and Pakistan
PAISAN, -S *n* fellow countryman
PAISANA *n* female peasant
PAISANO *n* friend
PAISANS ▸ **paisan**
PAISAS ▸ **paisa**
PAISE ▸ **paisa**
PAISLEY *n* pattern of small curving shapes with intricate detailing
PAJAMA, -S *same as* ▸ **pyjama**
PAJOCK, -S *obsolete word for* ▸ **peacock**
PAJOCKE *obsolete word for* ▸ **peacock**
PAJOCKS ▸ **pajock**
PAK, -S *n* pack
PAKAHI, -S *n* acid land that is unsuitable for cultivation
PAKAPOO *n* Chinese lottery
PAKEHA, -S *n* person of European descent, as distinct from a Māori
PAKFONG *same as* > **packfong**
PAKIHI, -S *n* area of swampy infertile land
PAKKA *variant of* ▸ **pukka**
PAKOKO, -S *n* small freshwater fish

PAKORA, -S *n* fried battered pieces of vegetable, chicken, etc
PAKS ▸ **pak**
PAKTONG *same as* > **pakthong**
PAL, -S *n, vb*
PALABRA *n* word
PALACE, -S *n*
PALACED *adj* having palaces
PALACES ▸ **palace**
PALADIN *n*
PALAGI, -S *n* (in Samoa) European
PALAIS *n* dance hall
PALAMA, -E *n* webbing on bird's feet
PALAPA, -S *n* open-sided tropical building
PALAS, -ES *n* East Indian tree
PALATAL *adj* of or relating to the palate ▹ *n* bony plate that forms the palate
PALATE, -D, -S *n, vb*
PALAVER *n, vb*
PALAY, -S *n* type of rubber
PALAZZO, PALAZZI *n* Italian palace
PALE, -D, -R, -S, -ST *adj, vb, n*
PALEA, -E *n* bract in a grass spikelet
PALEAL ▸ **palea**
PALEATE *adj* having scales
PALED ▸ **pale**
PALELY ▸ **pale**
PALER ▸ **pale**
PALES ▸ **pale**
PALEST ▸ **pale**
PALET, -S *n* perpendicular band on escutcheon
PALETOT *n* loose outer garment
PALETS ▸ **palet**
PALETTE *n*
PALFREY *n* light saddle horse, esp ridden by women
PALI, -S *n* cliff in Hawaii
PALIER ▸ **paly**
PALIEST ▸ **paly**
PALIKAR *n* Greek soldier
PALING, -S *n* wooden or metal post used in fences
PALINKA *n* type of apricot brandy
PALIS ▸ **pali**
PALISH *adj* rather pale
PALKEE, -S *n* (formerly, in S Asia) covered litter carried on the shoulders
PALKI, -S *same as* ▸ **palkee**
PALL, -ED, -ING, -S *n, vb*
PALLA, -E *n* ancient Roman cloak
PALLAH, -S *n* S African antelope
PALLED ▸ **pall**
PALLET, -S *same as* ▸ **palette**
PALLIA ▸ **pallium**
PALLIAL *adj* relating to cerebral cortex
PALLID *adj*
PALLIED ▸ **pally**
PALLIER ▸ **pally**
PALLIES ▸ **pally**
PALLING ▸ **pall**
PALLIUM, PALLIA *n* garment worn by men in ancient Greece or Rome
PALLONE *n* Italian ball game
PALLOR, -S *n*
PALLS ▸ **pall**
PALLY, PALLIED, PALLIER, PALLIES *adj* on friendly terms ▹ *vb* as in **pally up** become friends with
PALM, -ED, -ING, -S *n, vb*
PALMAR *adj* of or relating to the palm of the hand
PALMARY *adj* worthy of praise
PALMATE *adj* shaped like an open hand
PALMED ▸ **palm**
PALMER, -S *n* medieval pilgrim
PALMFUL *n* amount that can be held in the palm of a hand
PALMIE, -S *n* palmtop computer
PALMIER *n* type of French pastry
PALMIES ▸ **palmie**
PALMIET *n* South African rush
PALMING ▸ **palm**
PALMIST > **palmistry**
PALMS ▸ **palm**
PALMTOP *adj* small enough to be held in the hand ▹ *n* computer small enough to be held in the hand
PALMY *adj* successful, prosperous and happy
PALMYRA *n* tall tropical Asian palm

PALOLO, -S *n* polychaete worm of the S Pacific Ocean
PALOOKA *n* stupid or clumsy boxer or other person
PALP, -ED, -ING, -S *n, vb*
PALPAL ▸ **palp**
PALPATE *vb* examine (an area of the body) by touching ▹ *adj* of, relating to, or possessing a palp or palps
PALPED ▸ **palp**
PALPI ▸ **palpus**
PALPING ▸ **palp**
PALPS ▸ **palp**
PALPUS, PALPI *same as* ▸ **palp**
PALS ▸ **pal**
PALSA, -S *n* landform of subarctic regions
PALSHIP *n* state of being pals
PALSIED ▸ **palsy**
PALSY, PALSIER, PALSIES *n, vb, adj*
PALTER, -S *vb* act or talk insincerely
PALTRY *adj*
PALUDAL *adj* of, relating to, or produced by marshes
PALUDIC *adj* of malaria
PALY, PALIER, PALIEST *adj* vertically striped
PAM, -S *n* knave of clubs
PAMPA *n* grassland area
PAMPAS *pl n* vast grassy plains in S America
PAMPEAN ▸ **pampas**
PAMPER, -S *vb*
PAMPERO *n* dry cold wind in South America
PAMPERS ▸ **pamper**
PAMPOEN *n* pumpkin
PAMS ▸ **pam**
PAN, -NED, -S *n, vb*
PANACEA *n* remedy for all diseases or problems
PANACHE *n*
PANADA, -S *n* mixture used as a thickening in cookery
PANAMA, -S *n* hat made of plaited leaves
PANARY *n* storehouse for bread
PANAX, -ES *n* genus of perennial herbs
PANCAKE *n, vb*
PANCE, -S *n* pansy
PANCHAX *n* brightly coloured tropical Asian cyprinodont fish
PAND, -S *n* valance
PANDA, -S *n*
PANDAN, -S *n* type of palm of S E Asia
PANDANI *n* tropical tree
PANDANS ▸ **pandan**
PANDAR, -S *rare variant of* ▸ **pander**
PANDAS ▸ **panda**
PANDECT *n* treatise covering all aspects of a particular subject
PANDER, -S *vb, n*
PANDIED ▸ **pandy**
PANDIES ▸ **pandy**
PANDIT, -S *same as* ▸ **pundit**
PANDOOR *same as* ▸ **pandour**
PANDORA *n*
PANDORE *another word for* ▸ **bandore**
PANDOUR *n* one of an 18th-century force of Croatian soldiers
PANDROP *n* hard mint-flavoured sweet
PANDS ▸ **pand**
PANDURA *n* ancient stringed instrument
PANDY, PANDIED, PANDIES *n, vb*
PANE, -D, -S, PANING *n, adj*
PANEER, -S *n* soft white cheese, used in Indian cookery
PANEITY *n* state of being bread
PANEL, -ED, -S *n, vb, adj*
PANES ▸ **pane**
PANFISH *n* small food fish ▹ *vb* fish for panfish
PANFRY *vb* fry in a pan
PANFUL, -S *n* the contents of a pan
PANG, -ED, -ING, -S *n, vb*
PANGA, -S *n* broad heavy knife of E Africa, used as a tool or weapon
PANGAMY *n* unrestricted mating
PANGAS ▸ **panga**
PANGED ▸ **pang**
PANGEN, -S *same as* ▸ **pangene**
PANGENE *n* hypothetical particle of protoplasm
PANGENS ▸ **pangen**
PANGING ▸ **pang**
PANGRAM *n* sentence incorporating all the letters of the alphabet
PANGS ▸ **pang**
PANIC, -S *n, vb, adj*
PANICK, -S *old word for* ▸ **panic**
PANICKY ▸ **panic**

PANICLE *n* loose, irregularly branched cluster of flowers
PANICS ▶ **panic**
PANICUM *n* type of grass
PANIER, -S *same as* ▶ **pannier**
PANIM, -S *n* heathen or pagan
PANING ▶ **pane**
PANINO, PANINI *n* Italian sandwich
PANISC, -S *n* faun; attendant of Pan
PANISK, -S *same as* ▶ **panisc**
PANKO, -S *n* flaky breadcrumbs used in Japanese cookery
PANLIKE *adj* resembling a pan
PANNAGE *n* pasturage for pigs, esp in a forest
PANNE, -S *n* lightweight velvet fabric
PANNED ▶ **pan**
PANNER, -S ▶ **pan**
PANNES ▶ **panne**
PANNI ▶ **pannus**
PANNICK *old spelling of the noun* ▶ **panic**
PANNIER *n* bag fixed on the back of a cycle
PANNING ▶ **pan**
PANNIST *n* person who plays a steel drum
PANNOSE *adj* like felt
PANNUS, PANNI *n* inflammatory fleshy lesion on the surface of the eye
PANOCHA *n* coarse grade of sugar made in Mexico
PANOCHE *n* type of dark sugar
PANOPLY *n* magnificent array
PANPIPE *n* wind instrument
PANS ▶ **pan**
PANSIED *adj* covered with pansies
PANSY, PANSIES *n*
PANT, -ED *vb, n*
PANTER, -S *n* person who pants
PANTHER *n*
PANTIE *same as* ▶ **panty**
PANTIES *pl n*
PANTILE *n* roofing tile with an S-shaped cross section ▷ *vb* tile roof with pantiles
PANTINE *n* pasteboard puppet
PANTING ▶ **pant**
PANTLEG *n*
PANTLER *n* pantry servant
PANTO, -S *same as* > **pantomime**
PANTON, -S *n* type of horseshoe
PANTOS ▶ **panto**
PANTOUM *n* verse form
PANTRY *n*
PANTS *pl n*
PANTUN, -S *n* Malayan poetry
PANTY *n* woman's undergarment
PANZER, -S *n* German tank
PAOLO, PAOLI *n* former Italian coin
PAP, -PED, -PING, -S *n, vb*
PAPA, -S *n* father
PAPABLE *adj* suitable for papacy
PAPACY *n*
PAPADAM *variant of* > **poppadom**
PAPADOM *variant of* > **poppadom**
PAPADUM *variant of* > **poppadom**
PAPAIN, -S *n* enzyme in the unripe fruit of the papaya
PAPAL *adj*
PAPALLY ▶ **papal**
PAPAS ▶ **papa**
PAPASAN *n* bowl-shaped chair
PAPAUMA *n* New Zealand word for broadleaf
PAPAVER *n* genus of poppies
PAPAW, -S *same as* ▶ **papaya**
PAPAYA, -S *n* large sweet tropical fruit
PAPAYAN ▶ **papaya**
PAPAYAS ▶ **papaya**
PAPE, -S *n* spiritual father
PAPER, -ED, -S *n, vb*
PAPERER ▶ **paper**
PAPERS ▶ **paper**
PAPERY *adj*
PAPES ▶ **pape**
PAPILIO *n* butterfly
PAPILLA *n* small projection of tissue
PAPOOSE *n*
PAPPED ▶ **pap**
PAPPI ▶ **pappus**
PAPPIER ▶ **pappy**
PAPPIES ▶ **pappy**
PAPPING ▶ **pap**
PAPPOSE ▶ **pappus**
PAPPOUS ▶ **pappus**
PAPPUS, PAPPI *n* ring of hairs surrounding

the fruit in composite plants
PAPPY, PAPPIER, PAPPIES *adj* resembling pap
PAPRICA *same as* ▸ **paprika**
PAPRIKA *n*
PAPS ▸ **pap**
PAPULA, -E, -S *same as* ▸ **papule**
PAPULAR ▸ **papule**
PAPULAS ▸ **papula**
PAPULE, -S *n* small solid usually round elevation of the skin
PAPYRAL ▸ **papyrus**
PAPYRUS, PAPYRI *n*
PAR, -RED, -RING, -S *n, vb*
PARA, -S *n* paratrooper
PARABEN *n* carcinogenic ester
PARABLE *n, vb*
PARACME *n* phase where fever lessens
PARADE, -D, -S *n, vb*
PARADER ▸ **parade**
PARADES ▸ **parade**
PARADOR *n* state-run hotel in Spain
PARADOS *n* bank behind a trench or other fortification
PARADOX *n*
PARAE *n* type of fish
PARAFLE *same as* > **paraffle**
PARAGE, -S *n* type of feudal land tenure
PARAGON *n, vb*
PARAMO, -S *n* high plateau in the Andes
PARANG, -S *n* knife used by the Dyaks of Borneo
PARANYM *n* euphemism
PARAPET *n, vb*
PARAPH, -S *n* flourish after a signature ▹ *vb* embellish signature
PARAS ▸ **para**
PARASOL *n*
PARATHA *n* (in Indian cookery) flat unleavened bread
PARAZOA > **parazoan**
PARBAKE *vb* partially bake
PARBOIL *vb*
PARCEL, -S *n, vb*
PARCH, -ED, -ES *vb*
PARD, -S *n* leopard or panther
PARDAH, -S *same as* ▸ **purdah**
PARDAL, -S *variant spelling of* ▸ **pardale**
PARDALE *n* leopard
PARDALS ▸ **pardal**
PARDED *adj* having spots
PARDEE *adv* certainly
PARDI *same as* ▸ **pardee**
PARDIE *same as* ▸ **pardee**
PARDINE *adj* spotted
PARDNER *n* friend or partner: used as a term of address
PARDON, -S *vb, n, interj, sentence substitute*
PARDS ▸ **pard**
PARDY *same as* ▸ **pardee**
PARE, -D, -S *vb*
PAREIRA *n* root of a South American climbing plant
PARELLA *n* type of lichen
PARELLE *same as* ▸ **parella**
PAREN, -S *n* parenthesis
PARENT, -S *n, vb*
PAREO, -S *same as* ▸ **pareu**
PARER, -S ▸ **pare**
PARERA, -S *n* New Zealand duck
PARERGA > **parergon**
PARERS ▸ **parer**
PARES ▸ **pare**
PARESIS, PARESES *n* incomplete or slight paralysis of motor functions
PARETIC ▸ **paresis**
PAREU, -S *n* Polynesian skirt or loincloth
PAREV *adj* containing neither meat nor milk products
PAREVE *same as* ▸ **parev**
PARFAIT *n* dessert consisting of layers of ice cream, fruit, and sauce
PARGANA *n* Indian sub-district
PARGE, -D, -S *vb* coat with plaster
PARGET, -S *n* plaster, mortar, etc, used to line chimney flues or cover walls ▹ *vb* cover or decorate with parget
PARGING ▸ **parge**
PARGO, -ES, -S *n* sea bream
PARIAH, -S *n*
PARIAL, -S *n* pair royal of playing cards
PARIAN, -S *n* type of marble or porcelain
PARIES *n* wall of an organ or bodily cavity
PARING, -S *n*

PARIS, -ES *n* type of herb
PARISH *n*
PARISON *n* unshaped mass of glass
PARITOR *n* official who summons witnesses
PARITY *n*
PARK, -ED, -S *n, vb*
PARKA, -S *n*
PARKADE *n* building used as a car park
PARKAS ▶ **parka**
PARKED ▶ **park**
PARKEE, -S *n* Inuit outer garment
PARKER, -S ▶ **park**
PARKI, -S *variant of* ▶ **parka**
PARKIE, -S *n* park keeper
PARKIER ▶ **parky**
PARKIES ▶ **parkie**
PARKIN, -S *n* moist spicy ginger cake
PARKING ▶ **park**
PARKINS ▶ **parkin**
PARKIS ▶ **parki**
PARKISH *adj* like a park
PARKLY *adj* having many parks or resembling a park
PARKOUR *n* sport of running in urban areas over obstacles
PARKS ▶ **park**
PARKWAY *n*
PARKY, PARKIER *adj* (of the weather) chilly
PARLAY, -S *vb* stake (winnings from one bet) on a subsequent wager ▷ *n* bet in which winnings are parlayed
PARLE, -D, -S, PARLING *vb* speak
PARLEY, -S *n, vb*
PARLIES *pl n* small Scottish biscuits
PARLING ▶ **parle**
PARLOR, -S *same as* ▶ **parlour**
PARLOUR *n*
PARLOUS *adj* dire ▷ *adv* extremely
PARLY *n* short form of parliament
PARMA, -S *n* breaded chicken dish
PARODIC ▶ **parody**
PARODOI *n* path leading to Greek theatre
PARODOS *n* ode sung by Greek chorus
PARODY *n, vb*
PAROL, -S *n* (formerly) pleadings in an action when presented by word of mouth ▷ *adj* (of a contract, lease, etc) not made under seal
PAROLE, -D, -S *n, vb*
PAROLEE ▶ **parole**
PAROLES ▶ **parole**
PAROLS ▶ **parol**
PARONYM *n* cognate word
PARORE, -S *n* type of fish found around Australia and New Zealand
PAROTIC *adj* situated near the ear
PAROTID *adj* relating to or situated near the parotid gland ▷ *n* parotid gland
PAROTIS *n* parotid gland
PAROUS *adj* having given birth
PARP, -ED, -ING, -S *vb* make a honking sound
PARPANE *n* parapet on bridge
PARPED ▶ **parp**
PARPEN, -S *same as* ▶ **parpend**
PARPEND *same as* ▶ **perpend**
PARPENS ▶ **parpen**
PARPENT *n* parapet on bridge
PARPING ▶ **parp**
PARPS ▶ **parp**
PARQUET *n* floor covering made of wooden blocks ▷ *vb* cover with parquet
PARR, -S *n* salmon up to two years of age
PARRA, -S *n* tourist or non-resident on a beach
PARRAL, -S *same as* ▶ **parrel**
PARRAS ▶ **parra**
PARRED ▶ **par**
PARREL, -S *n* ring that holds the jaws of a boom to the mast
PARRIED ▶ **parry**
PARRIER ▶ **parry**
PARRIES ▶ **parry**
PARRING ▶ **par**
PARROCK *vb* put (an animal) in a small field
PARROT, -S *n, vb*
PARROTY *adj*
PARRS ▶ **parr**
PARRY, PARRIED, PARRIES *vb, n*
PARS ▶ **par**
PARSE, -D, -S *vb*
PARSEC, -S *n*

PARSED ▶ **parse**
PARSER, -S *n* program that interprets input to a computer
PARSES ▶ **parse**
PARSING ▶ **parse**
PARSLEY *n, vb*
PARSNEP *same as* ▶ **parsnip**
PARSNIP *n*
PARSON, -S *n*
PART *n, vb*
PARTAKE, PARTOOK *vb*
PARTAN, -S *Scottish word for* ▶ **crab**
PARTED *adj*
PARTER, -S *n* thing that parts
PARTI, -S *n* concept of architectural design
PARTIAL *adj, n, vb*
PARTIED ▶ **party**
PARTIER *n* person who parties
PARTIES ▶ **party**
PARTIM *adv* in part
PARTING *same as* ▶ **part**
PARTIS ▶ **parti**
PARTITA *n* type of suite
PARTITE *adj* composed of or divided into a specified number of parts
PARTLET *n* woman's garment
PARTLY *adv*
PARTNER *n, vb*
PARTON, -S *n* hypothetical elementary particle
PARTOOK ▶ **partake**
PARTS *pl n*
PARTURE *n* departure
PARTWAY *adv* some of the way
PARTY, PARTIED, PARTIES *n, vb, adj*
PARTYER *n* person who parties
PARULIS *another name for* ▶ **gumboil**
PARURA, -S *same as* ▶ **parure**
PARURE, -S *n* set of jewels or other ornaments
PARVE *same as* ▶ **parev**
PARVENU *n, adj*
PARVIS *n* court or portico in front of a building, esp a church
PARVISE *same as* ▶ **parvis**
PARVO, -S *n* disease of cattle and dogs
PAS *n* dance step or movement, esp in ballet
PASCAL, -S *n* unit of pressure
PASCHAL *adj* of the Passover or Easter ▷ *n* Passover or Easter
PASCUAL *adj* relating to pasture ▷ *n* plant that grows in pasture
PASE, -S *n* movement of the cape or muleta by a matador
PASEAR, -S *vb* go for a rambling walk
PASELA, -S *same as* ▶ **bonsela**
PASEO, -S *n* bullfighters' procession
PASES ▶ **pase**
PASH, -ED, -ES, -ING *n* infatuation ▷ *vb* throw or be thrown and break or be broken to bits
PASHA, -S *n* high official of the Ottoman Empire
PASHED ▶ **pash**
PASHES ▶ **pash**
PASHIM, -S *same as* ▶ **pashm**
PASHING ▶ **pash**
PASHKA, -S *n* rich Russian dessert
PASHM, -S *n* underfur of various Tibetan animals, esp goats, used for cashmere shawls
PASKA, -S *same as* ▶ **paskha**
PASKHA, -S *n* Russian dessert eaten at Easter
PASPY, PASPIES *n* piece of music in triple time
PASQUIL *n* abusive lampoon or satire ▷ *vb* ridicule with pasquil
PASS, -ED, -ES *vb, n*
PASSADE *n* act of moving back and forth in the same place
PASSADO *n* forward thrust with sword
PASSAGE *n, vb*
PASSANT *adj* (of a heraldic beast) walking
PASSATA *n* sauce made from sieved tomatoes
PASSE *adj* out-of-date
PASSED ▶ **pass**
PASSEE *adj* out-of-date
PASSEL, -S *n* group or quantity of no fixed number
PASSER, -S *n* person or thing that passes
PASSES ▶ **pass**
PASSIM *adv* everywhere, throughout
PASSING *adj, n*
PASSION *n, vb*

PASSIVE *adj, n*
PASSKEY *n* private key
PASSMAN, PASSMEN *n* student who passes without honours
PASSOUT *n* (in ice hockey) pass by an attacking player from behind the opposition goal line
PASSUS *n* division or section of a poem, story, etc
PAST, -S *adj, n, adv, prep*
PASTA, -S *n*
PASTE, -D, -S *n, vb*
PASTEL, -S *n, adj*
PASTER, -S *n* person or thing that pastes
PASTERN *n* part of a horse's foot
PASTERS ▶ **paster**
PASTES ▶ **paste**
PASTEUP *n* material pasted on a sheet of paper or board
PASTIER ▶ **pasty**
PASTIES ▶ **pasty**
PASTIL, -S *same as* > **pastille**
PASTILY ▶ **pasty**
PASTIME *n*
PASTINA *n* small pieces of pasta
PASTING *n* heavy defeat
PASTIS *n* anise-flavoured alcoholic drink
PASTOR, -S *n, vb*
PASTRY *n* baking dough made of flour, fat, and water
PASTS ▶ **past**
PASTURE *n, vb*
PASTY, PASTIER, PASTIES *adj, n*
PAT, -S, -TED, -TEST, -TING *vb, n, adj*
PATACA, -S *n* monetary unit of Macao
PATAGIA > **patagium**
PATAKA, -S *n* building on stilts, used for storing provisions
PATAMAR *n* type of boat
PATBALL *n* game like squash but using hands
PATCH, -ED, -ES *n, vb*
PATCHER ▶ **patch**
PATCHES ▶ **patch**
PATCHY *adj*
PATE, -S *n* head
PATED ▶ **pate**
PATELLA *n*
PATEN, -S *n* plate used for the bread at Communion
PATENCY *n* condition of being obvious
PATENS ▶ **paten**
PATENT, -S *n, adj, vb*
PATER, -S *n* father
PATERA, -E *n* shallow ancient Roman bowl
PATERS ▶ **pater**
PATES ▶ **pate**
PATH, -ED, -ING, -S *n, vb*
PATHIC, -S *n* person who suffers ▷ *adj* of or relating to suffering
PATHING ▶ **path**
PATHOS *n*
PATHS ▶ **path**
PATHWAY *n*
PATIBLE *adj* endurable
PATIENT *adj, n, vb*
PATIKI, -S *n* New Zealand sand flounder or dab
PATIN, -S *same as* ▶ **paten**
PATINA, -E, -S *n* fine layer on a surface
PATINE, -D, -S *vb* cover with patina
PATINS ▶ **patin**
PATIO, -S *n*
PATKA, -S *n* head covering worn by Sikh men
PATLY *adv* fitly
PATNESS *n* appropriateness
PATOIS *n*
PATONCE *adj* (of cross) with limbs which broaden from centre
PATOOT, -S *same as* > **patootie**
PATRIAL *n* (in Britain, formerly) person with a right to live in the United Kingdom
PATRICK *n* former Irish coin
PATRICO *n* fraudulent priest
PATRIOT *n*
PATROL, -S *n, vb*
PATRON, -S *n*
PATROON *n* Dutch land-holder in New Netherland and New York
PATS ▶ **pat**
PATSY, PATSIES *n*
PATTE, -S *n* band keeping belt in place
PATTED ▶ **pat**
PATTEE *adj* (of a cross) having triangular arms widening outwards
PATTEN, -S *n* wooden clog or sandal ▷ *vb* wear pattens
PATTER, -S *vb, n*
PATTERN *n, vb*

PATTERS ▸ **patter**
PATTES ▸ **patte**
PATTEST ▸ **pat**
PATTIE *same as* ▸ **patty**
PATTIES ▸ **patty**
PATTING ▸ **pat**
PATTLE, -S *dialect for* ▸ **paddle**
PATTY, PATTIES *n*
PATU, -S *n* short Māori club, now used ceremonially
PATULIN *n* toxic antibiotic
PATUS ▸ **patu**
PATY *adj* (of cross) having arms of equal length
PATZER, -S *n* novice chess player
PAUA, -S *n* edible shellfish of New Zealand
PAUCAL, -S *n* grammatical number for words in contexts where a few of their referents are described ▹ *adj* relating to or inflected for this number
PAUCITY *n*
PAUGHTY *Scots word for* ▸ **haughty**
PAUL, -S *same as* ▸ **pawl**
PAULIN, -S *n* tarpaulin
PAULS ▸ **paul**
PAUNCE, -S *n* pansy
PAUNCH *n, vb*
PAUNCHY *adj* having a protruding belly or abdomen
PAUPER, -S *n, vb*
PAUSAL ▸ **pause**
PAUSE, -D, -S *vb, n*
PAUSER, -S ▸ **pause**
PAUSES ▸ **pause**
PAUSING ▸ **pause**
PAV, -S *short for* ▸ **pavlova**
PAVAGE, -S *n* tax towards paving streets
PAVAN, -S *same as* ▸ **pavane**
PAVANE, -S *n* slow and stately dance
PAVANS ▸ **pavan**
PAVE, -D, -S *vb, n*
PAVEED *adj* (of jewels) set close together
PAVEN, -S *same as* ▸ **pavane**
PAVER, -S ▸ **pave**
PAVES ▸ **pave**
PAVID *adj* fearful
PAVIN, -S *same as* ▸ **pavane**
PAVING, -S *n, adj*
PAVINS ▸ **pavin**
PAVIOR, -S *same as* ▸ **paviour**
PAVIOUR *n* person who lays paving
PAVIS *n* large square shield
PAVISE, -S *same as* ▸ **pavis**
PAVISER *n* soldier holding a pavis
PAVISES ▸ **pavise**
PAVISSE *same as* ▸ **pavis**
PAVLOVA *n*
PAVONE, -S *n* peacock
PAVS ▸ **pav**
PAW, -ED, -ING, -S *n, vb*
PAWA, -S *old word for* ▸ **peacock**
PAWAW, -ED, -S *vb* recite N American incantation
PAWED ▸ **paw**
PAWER, -S *n* person or animal that paws
PAWING ▸ **paw**
PAWK, -S *Scots word for* ▸ **trick**
PAWKIER ▸ **pawky**
PAWKILY ▸ **pawky**
PAWKS ▸ **pawk**
PAWKY, PAWKIER *adj* having or characterized by a dry wit
PAWL, -S *n* pivoted lever shaped to engage with a ratchet
PAWN, -ED, -ING, -S *vb, n*
PAWNAGE ▸ **pawn**
PAWNCE, -S *old word for* ▸ **pansy**
PAWNED ▸ **pawn**
PAWNEE, -S *n* one who accepts goods in pawn
PAWNER, -S *n* one who pawns his or her possessions
PAWNING ▸ **pawn**
PAWNOR, -S *same as* ▸ **pawner**
PAWNS ▸ **pawn**
PAWPAW, -S *same as* ▸ **papaw**
PAWS ▸ **paw**
PAX, -ES *n, interj*

> Latin for peace, this is yet another of those very useful short words containing X.

PAXIUBA *n* tropical tree
PAXWAX *n* strong ligament in the neck of many mammals
PAY, PAID, -ED, -S *vb, n*
PAYABLE *adj, n*
PAYABLY ▸ **payable**
PAYBACK *n*
PAYDAY, -S *n*
PAYDOWN *n* reduction of debt through repayment

OTON *n* main field riders in a bicycle ad race

LS ▸ **pel**

LT, -ED, -S *vb, n*

LTA, -E, -S *n* small ncient shield

ELTAST *n* (in ancient Greece) lightly armed foot soldier

PELTATE *adj* (of leaves) having the stalk attached to the centre of the lower surface

PELTED ▸ **pelt**

PELTER, -S *vb* rain heavily

PELTING ▸ **pelt**

PELTRY *n* pelts of animals collectively

PELTS ▸ **pelt**

PELVES ▸ **pelvis**

PELVIC, -S *adj, n*

PELVIS, PELVES *n*

PEMBINA *n* type of cranberry

PEMICAN *same as* > **pemmican**

PEMPHIX *n* type of crustacean

PEN, -NED, -NING, -S *n, vb*

PENAL *adj*

PENALLY ▸ **penal**

PENALTY *n*

PENANCE *n, vb*

PENANG, -S *variant of* ▸ **pinang**

PENATES *pl n* household gods

PENCE ▸ **penny**

PENCEL, -S *n* small pennon

PENCIL, -S *n, vb*

PEND, -ED, -S *vb* await judgment or settlement ▷ *n* archway or vaulted passage

PENDANT *n* ornament worn on a chain round the neck

PENDED ▸ **pend**

PENDENT *adj* hanging ▷ *n* pendant

PENDING *prep, adj*

PENDS ▸ **pend**

PENDU *adj* in informal Indian English, culturally backward

PENDULE *n* type of climbing manoeuvre

PENE, -D, PENING *variant of* ▸ **peen**

PENES ▸ **penis**

PENFOLD *same as* ▸ **pinfold**

PENFUL, -S *n* contents of pen

PENGO, -S *n* former monetary unit of Hungary

PENGUIN *n*

PENI *old spelling of* ▸ **penny**

PENIAL ▸ **penis**

PENICIL *n* small pad for wounds

PENIE, -S *old spelling of* ▸ **penny**

PENILE *adj*

PENILL > **penillion**

PENING ▸ **pene**

PENIS, PENES, -ES *n*

PENK, -S *n* small fish

PENLIKE *adj* like a pen

PENLITE *same as* > **penlight**

PENMAN, PENMEN *n* person skilled in handwriting

PENNA, -E *n* large feather

PENNAL, -S *n* first-year student of Protestant university

PENNAME *n*

PENNANT *same as* ▸ **pendant**

PENNATE *adj* having feathers, wings, or winglike structures

PENNE, -S *n*

PENNED ▸ **pen**

PENNER, -S *n* person who writes

PENNES ▸ **penne**

PENNI, -A, -S *n* former Finnish monetary unit

PENNIED *adj* having money

PENNIES ▸ **penny**

PENNILL *n* stanza in a Welsh poem

PENNINE *n* mineral found in the Pennine Alps

PENNING ▸ **pen**

PENNIS ▸ **penni**

PENNON, -S *n* triangular or tapering flag

PENNY, PENCE, PENNIES *n*

PENOCHE *n* type of fudge

PENS ▸ **pen**

PENSEE, -S *n* thought put down on paper

PENSEL, -S *same as* ▸ **pencel**

PENSIL, -S *same as* ▸ **pencel**

PENSILE *adj* designating or building a hanging nest

PENSILS ▸ **pensil**

PENSION *n, vb*

PENSIVE *adj*

PAYED ▸ **pay**

PAYEE, -S *n*

PAYER, -S *n* person who pays

PAYESS *pl n* uncut sideburns worn by some Jewish men

PAYFONE *US spelling of* > **payphone**

PAYING, -S ▸ **pay**

PAYLIST *n* list of people to be paid

PAYLOAD *n*

PAYMENT *n*

PAYNIM, -S *n* heathen or pagan

PAYOFF, -S *n*

PAYOLA, -S *n*

PAYOR, -S *same as* ▸ **payer**

PAYOUT, -S *n* sum of money paid out

PAYROLL *n*

PAYS ▸ **pay**

PAYSAGE *n* landscape

PAYSD *Spenserian form of* ▸ **poised**

PAYSLIP *n*

PAYWALL *n* system that denies access to a website unless a payment is made

PAZAZZ *same as* ▸ **pizzazz**

PAZZAZZ *same as* ▸ **pizzazz**

PE *n* 17th letter of the Hebrew alphabet, transliterated as *p*

PEA, -S *n* climbing plant with seeds growing in pods

PEACE, -D, -S, PEACING *n*

PEACH, -ED, -ES *n, adj, vb*

PEACHER ▸ **peach**

PEACHES ▸ **peach**

PEACHY *adj*

PEACING ▸ **peace**

PEACOAT *n* woollen jacket

PEACOCK *n, vb*

PEACOD, -S *same as* ▸ **peascod**

PEAFOWL *n* peacock or peahen

PEAG, -S *n* (formerly) money used by Native Americans

PEAGE, -S *same as* ▸ **peag**

PEAGS ▸ **peag**

PEAHEN, -S ▸ **peacock**

PEAK, -S *n, vb, adj*

PEAKED *adj*

PEAKIER ▸ **peaky**

PEAKING *n*

PEAKISH *adj* sickly

PEAKS ▸ **peak**

PEAKY, PEAKIER ▸ **peak**

PEAL, -ED, -ING, -S *n, vb*

PEALIKE ▸ **pea**

PEALING ▸ **peal**

PEALS ▸ **peal**

PEAN, -ED, -ING, -S *same as* ▸ **peen**

PEANUT, -S *n*

PEAPOD, -S *n* pod of the pea plant

PEAR, -S *n*

PEARCE, -D, -S *old spelling of* ▸ **pierce**

PEARE, -S *obsolete spelling of* ▸ **pear**

PEARL, -ED, -S *same as* ▸ **purl**

PEARLER *n* person who dives for or trades in pearls ▷ *adj* excellent

PEARLIN *n* type of lace used to trim clothes

PEARLS ▸ **pearl**

PEARLY *adj, n*

PEARS ▸ **pear**

PEARST *archaic variant of* ▸ **pierced**

PEART, -ER *adj* lively

PEARTLY ▸ **peart**

PEAS ▸ **pea**

PEASANT *n*

PEASCOD *n* pod of a pea plant

PEASE, -D, -S, PEASING *n* archaic or dialect word for pea ▷ *vb* appease

PEASEN *obsolete plural of* ▸ **pease**

PEASES ▸ **pease**

PEASING ▸ **pease**

PEASON *obsolete plural of* ▸ **pease**

PEAT, -S *n*

PEATARY *n* area covered with peat

PEATERY *same as* ▸ **peatary**

PEATIER ▸ **peaty**

PEATMAN, PEATMEN *n* person who collects peat

PEATS ▸ **peat**

PEATY, PEATIER ▸ **peat**

PEAVEY, -S *n* wooden lever used for handling logs

PEAVY, PEAVIES *same as* ▸ **peavey**

PEAZE, -D, -S, PEAZING *same as* ▸ **pease**

PEBA, -S *n* type of armadillo

PEBBLE, -D, -S *n, vb*

PEBBLY ▸ **pebble**

PEBRINE *n* disease of silkworms

PEC *n* pectoral muscle

PECAN, -S *n*

PECCANT *adj* guilty of an offence
PECCARY *n* piglike animal of American forests
PECCAVI *n* confession of guilt
PECH, -ED, -ING, -S *Scottish word for* ▶ **pant**
PECHAN, -S *Scots word for* ▶ **stomach**
PECHED ▶ **pech**
PECHING ▶ **pech**
PECHS ▶ **pech**
PECK, -ED, -S *vb, n*
PECKE, -S *n* quarter of bushel
PECKED ▶ **peck**
PECKER, -S *n* short for woodpecker
PECKES ▶ **pecke**
PECKIER ▶ **pecky**
PECKING ▶ **peck**
PECKISH *adj* slightly hungry
PECKS ▶ **peck**
PECKY, PECKIER *adj* discoloured
PECS *pl n*
PECTASE *n* enzyme occurring in certain ripening fruits
PECTATE *n* salt or ester of pectic acid
PECTEN, -S *n* comblike structure in the eye of birds and reptiles
PECTIC ▶ **pectin**
PECTIN, -S *n*
PECTISE *same as* ▶ **pectize**
PECTIZE *vb* change into a jelly
PECTOSE *n* insoluble carbohydrate found in unripe fruit
PECULIA > **peculium**
PED, -S *n* pannier
PEDAGOG *same as* > **pedagogue**
PEDAL, -ED, -S *n, vb, adj*
PEDALER ▶ **pedal**
PEDALO, -S *n*
PEDALS ▶ **pedal**
PEDANT, -S *n*
PEDATE *adj* (of a plant leaf) divided into several lobes arising at a common point
PEDDER, -S *old form of* ▶ **pedlar**
PEDDLE, -D, -S *vb*
PEDDLER *same as* ▶ **pedlar**
PEDDLES ▶ **peddle**
PEDES ▶ **pes**
PEDESIS, PEDESES *n* random motion of small particles
PEDETIC *adj* of feet
PEDI, -S *n* pedicure
PEDICAB *n* pedal-operated tricycle, available for hire
PEDICEL *n* stalk bearing a single flower of an inflorescence
PEDICLE *n* any small stalk
PEDIS ▶ **pedi**
PEDLAR, -S *n* person who sells goods from door to door
PEDLARY *same as* ▶ **pedlery**
PEDLER, -S *same as* ▶ **pedlar**
PEDLERY *n* business of pedler
PEDOCAL *n* type of soil that is rich in lime
PEDRAIL *n* device replacing wheel on rough surfaces
PEDRERO *n* type of cannon
PEDRO, -S *n* card game
PEDS ▶ **ped**
PEDWAY, -S *n* walkway for pedestrians only
PEE, -D, -ING, -S *vb, n*
PEEBEEN *n* type of large evergreen
PEECE, -S *obsolete variant of* ▶ **piece**
PEED ▶ **pee**
PEEING ▶ **pee**
PEEK, -ED, -ING, -S *n, vb*
PEEKABO *same as* > **peekaboo**
PEEKED ▶ **peek**
PEEKING ▶ **peek**
PEEKS ▶ **peek**
PEEL, -ED, -S *vb, n*
PEELER, -S *n*
PEELING *n*
PEELS ▶ **peel**
PEEN, -ED, -S *n* end of a hammer head opposite the striking face ▷ *vb* strike with the peen of a hammer
PEENGE, -D, -S *vb* complain
PEENING *n* act of peening
PEENS ▶ **peen**
PEEOY, -S *n* homemade firework
PEEP, -ED, -ING, -S *vb, n*
PEEPBO, -S *n* game of peekaboo
PEEPE *old spelling of* ▶ **pip**
PEEPED ▶ **peep**
PEEPER, -S *n*
PEEPES *archaic spelling of* ▶ **peeps**
PEEPING ▶ **peep**
PEEPS ▶ **peep**
PEEPTOE *adj* of a shoe in which the toe is not covered
PEEPUL, -S *n* Indian moraceous tree
PEER, -ED, -ING, -S *n, vb*
PEERAGE *n*
PEERED ▶ **peer**
PEERESS *n* (in Britain) woman holding the rank of a peer
PEERIE, -R, -S *n* spinning top ▷ *adj* small
PEERING ▶ **peer**
PEERS ▶ **peer**
PEERY *n* child's spinning top
PEES ▶ **pee**
PEEVE, -S, PEEVING *vb, n*
PEEVED ▶ **peeve**
PEEVER, -S *n* hopscotch
PEEVES ▶ **peeve**
PEEVING ▶ **peeve**
PEEVISH *adj*
PEEWEE, -S *same as* ▶ **pewee**
PEEWIT, -S *same as* ▶ **lapwing**
PEG, -GED, -S *n, vb*
PEGASUS *n*
PEGBOX *n* part of stringed instrument that holds tuning pegs
PEGGED ▶ **peg**
PEGGIER ▶ **peggy**
PEGGIES ▶ **peggy**
PEGGING ▶ **peg**
PEGGY, PEGGIER, PEGGIES *n* type of small warbler ▷ *adj* resembling a peg
PEGH, -ED, -ING, -S *variant of* ▶ **pech**
PEGLESS ▶ **peg**
PEGLIKE ▶ **peg**
PEGS ▶ **peg**
PEGTOP, -S *n* type of spinning top
PEH, -S *same as* ▶ **pe**
PEIN, -ED, -ING, -S *same as* ▶ **peen**
PEINCT, -S *vb* paint
PEINED ▶ **pein**
PEINING ▶ **pein**
PEINS ▶ **pein**
PEISE, -D, -S, PEISING *same as* ▶ **peize**
PEISHWA *n* Indian leader
PEISING ▶ **peise**
PEIZE, -D, -S, PEIZING *vb* weight or poise
PEKAN, -S *n* large North American marten
PEKE, -S *n* Pekingese dog
PEKEPOO *same as* > **peekapoo**
PEKES ▶ **peke**
PEKIN, -S *n* silk fabric
PEKOE, -S *n* high-quality tea
PEL, -S *n* pixel
PELA, -S *n* insect living on wax
PELAGE, -S *n* coat of a mammal, consisting of hair, wool, fur, etc
PELAGIC *adj* of or relating to the open sea ▷ *n* any pelagic creature
PELAS ▶ **pela**
PELAU, -S *n* dish made with meat, rice, and pigeon peas
PELE, -S *Spenserian variant of* ▶ **peal**
PELF, -S *n* m… wealth
PELHAM, -S *n* … bit for a doubl…
PELICAN *n*
PELISSE *n* cloak … coat which is us… fur-trimmed
PELITE, -S *n* any argillaceous rock su… as shale
PELITIC ▶ **pelite**
PELL, -ED, -ING, -S *n* hide of an animal ▷ *vb* hit violently
PELLACH *same as* ▶ **pellack**
PELLACK *n* porpoise
PELLED ▶ **pell**
PELLET, -S *n, vb*
PELLING ▶ **pell**
PELLOCK *n* porpoise
PELLS ▶ **pell**
PELLUM, -S *n* dust
PELMA, -S *n* sole of the foot
PELMET, -S *n* ornamental drapery or board, concealing a curtain rail
PELOID, -S *n* mud used therapeutically
PELON, -S *adj* hairless ▷ *n* hairless person or animal
PELORIA *n* abnormal production of flowers in a plant
PELORIC ▶ **peloria**
PELORUS *n* sighting device
PELORY *n* floral mutation
PELOTA, -S *n* game where players propel a ball against a wall

PENSTER *n* writer
PENSUM, -S *n* school exercise
PENT, -S *n* penthouse
PENTACT *n* sponge spicule with five rays
PENTAD, -S *n* group or series of five
PENTANE *n* alkane hydrocarbon with three isomers
PENTEL, -S *n* type of pen
PENTENE *n* colourless flammable liquid alkene
PENTHIA *n* child born fifth
PENTICE *vb* accommodate in a penthouse
PENTISE *same as* ▸ **pentice**
PENTITO, PENTITI *n* criminal who offers information to the police
PENTODE *n* electronic valve having five electrodes
PENTOSE *n* monosaccharide containing five atoms of carbon per molecule
PENTS ▸ **pent**
PENTYL, -S *n* one of a particular chemical group
PENUCHE *same as* ▸ **panocha**
PENUCHI *same as* ▸ **panocha**
PENULT, -S *n* last syllable but one in a word
PENURY *n* extreme poverty
PEON, -ES, -S *n* Spanish-American farm labourer or unskilled worker
PEONAGE *n* state of being a peon
PEONES ▸ **peon**
PEONIES ▸ **peony**
PEONISM *same as* ▸ **peonage**
PEONS ▸ **peon**
PEONY, PEONIES *n* garden plant
PEOPLE, -D, -S *pl n, vb*
PEOPLER *n* settler
PEOPLES ▸ **people**
PEP, -PED, -PING, -S *n, vb*
PEPFUL *adj* full of vitality
PEPINO, -S *n* purple-striped yellow fruit
PEPITA, -S *n* edible dried seed of a squash
PEPLA ▸ **peplum**
PEPLOS *n* part of a woman's attire in ancient Greece
PEPLUM, PEPLA, -S *same as* ▸ **peplos**
PEPLUS *same as* ▸ **peplos**
PEPO, -S *n* fruit such as the melon, squash, cucumber, or pumpkin
PEPPED ▸ **pep**
PEPPER, -S *n* sharp hot condiment ▹ *vb* season with pepper
PEPPERY *adj* tasting of pepper
PEPPIER ▸ **peppy**
PEPPILY ▸ **peppy**
PEPPING ▸ **pep**
PEPPY, PEPPIER *adj* full of vitality
PEPS ▸ **pep**
PEPSI, -S *n* (tradename) brand of soft drink
PEPSIN, -S *n* enzyme produced in the stomach
PEPSINE *same as* ▸ **pepsin**
PEPSINS ▸ **pepsin**
PEPSIS ▸ **pepsi**
PEPTALK *n, vb*
PEPTIC, -S *adj, n*
PEPTID, -S *variant of* ▸ **peptide**
PEPTIDE *n* organic chemical compound
PEPTIDS ▸ **peptid**
PEPTISE *same as* ▸ **peptize**
PEPTIZE *vb* disperse into a colloidal state
PEPTONE *n* any of a group of organic compounds
PER *prep* for each
PERACID *n* acid in which the element forming the acid radical exhibits its highest valency
PERAEON, PERAEA *same as* ▸ **pereion**
PERAI, -S *another name for* ▸ **piranha**
PERC, -S *n* perchloride
PERCALE *n* close-textured woven cotton fabric
PERCASE *adv* perchance
PERCE, -D, -N, -S, PERCING *obsolete word for* ▸ **pierce**
PERCENT *n*
PERCEPT *n* concept that depends on

recognition of some external object or phenomenon
PERCES ▸ **perce**
PERCH, -ED, -ES *n, vb*
PERCHER ▸ **perch**
PERCHES ▸ **perch**
PERCID, -S *n* type of freshwater fish
PERCINE *adj* of perches ▹ *n* type of perch-like fish
PERCING ▸ **perce**
PERCOCT *adj* well-cooked ▹ *vb* cook thoroughly
PERCOID *n* type of spiny-finned teleost fish
PERCS ▸ **perc**
PERCUSS *vb* strike sharply, rapidly, or suddenly
PERDIE *adv* certainly
PERDU, -S *adj* (of a soldier) placed on hazardous sentry duty ▹ *n* soldier placed on hazardous sentry duty
PERDUE, -S *same as* ▸ **perdu**
PERDURE *vb* last for long time
PERDUS ▸ **perdu**
PERDY *adv* certainly
PERE, -S *n* addition to a French surname to specify the father
PEREA ▸ **pereon**
PEREGAL *adj* equal ▹ *n* equal
PEREION, PEREIA *n* thorax of some crustaceans
PEREIRA *n* bark of a South American apocynaceous tree
PERENTY *same as* > **perentie**
PEREON, PEREA, -S *same as* ▸ **pereion**
PERES ▸ **pere**
PERFAY *interj* by my faith
PERFECT *adj, n, vb*
PERFET *obsolete variant of* ▸ **perfect**
PERFIDY *n* perfidious act
PERFIN, -S *former name for* ▸ **spif**
PERFING *n* practice of taking early retirement from the police force
PERFINS ▸ **perfin**
PERFORM *vb*
PERFUME *n, vb*
PERFUMY *adj* like perfume
PERFUSE *vb* permeate through or over
PERGOLA *n* framework of trellis supporting climbing plants
PERHAPS *adv, sentence substitute, n*
PERI, -S *n* (in Persian folklore) one of a race of beautiful supernatural beings
PERIAPT *n* charm or amulet
PERICON *n* Argentinian dance
PERIDIA > **peridium**
PERIDOT *n* pale green transparent gemstone
PERIGEE *n* point in the orbit of the moon or a satellite that is nearest the earth
PERIGON *n* angle of 360°
PERIL, -ED, -S *n, vb*
PERILLA *n* type of mint
PERILS ▸ **peril**
PERINEA > **perineum**
PERIOD, -S *n, adj, vb*
PERIOST *n* thick fibrous two-layered membrane covering the surface of bones
PERIQUE *n* strong highly flavoured tobacco
PERIS ▸ **peri**
PERISH *vb*
PERITUS, PERITI *n* Catholic theology consultant
PERIWIG *same as* ▸ **peruke**
PERJINK *adj* prim or finicky
PERJURE *vb*
PERJURY *n*
PERK, -ED, -ING, -S *n, adj, vb*
PERKIER ▸ **perky**
PERKILY ▸ **perky**
PERKIN, -S *same as* ▸ **parkin**
PERKING ▸ **perk**
PERKINS ▸ **perkin**
PERKISH *adj* perky
PERKS ▸ **perk**
PERKY, PERKIER *adj*
PERLITE *n* variety of obsidian
PERLOUS *same as* > **perilous**
PERM, -ED, -ING, -S *n, vb*
PERMIAN *adj* of, denoting, or formed in the last period of the Palaeozoic era
PERMIE, -S *n* person, esp an office worker, employed by a firm on a permanent basis

PERMING ▸ **perm**
PERMIT, -S *vb, n*
PERMS ▸ **perm**
PERMUTE *vb* change the sequence of
PERN, -ED, -ING, -S *n* type of buzzard ▹ *vb* spin
PERNIO *n* chilblain
PERNOD, -S *n* aniseed-flavoured aperitif from France
PERNS ▸ **pern**
PEROG, -EN, -S *same as* ▸ **pirog**
PEROGI, -S *n* type of Polish dumpling
PEROGIE *same as* ▸ **perogi**
PEROGIS ▸ **perogi**
PEROGS ▸ **perog**
PEROGY *same as* ▸ **perogi**
PERONE, -S *n* fibula
PERONEI > **peroneus**
PERONES ▸ **perone**
PERORAL *adj* administered through mouth
PEROXID *variant of* > **peroxide**
PEROXO *n* type of acid
PEROXY *adj* containing the peroxide group
PERP, -S *n* someone who has committed a crime
PERPEND *n* large stone that passes through a wall from one side to the other ▹ *vb* ponder
PERPENT *same as* ▸ **perpend**
PERPLEX *vb*
PERPS ▸ **perp**
PERRIER *n* short mortar
PERRIES ▸ **perry**
PERRON, -S *n* external flight of steps
PERRY, PERRIES *n* alcoholic drink made from fermented pears
PERSALT *n* any salt of a peracid
PERSANT *adj* piercing
PERSE, -S, PERSING *old variant of* ▸ **pierce**
PERSICO *same as* > **persicot**
PERSING ▸ **perse**
PERSIST *vb*
PERSON, -S *n*
PERSONA *n*
PERSONS ▸ **person**
PERSPEX *n* any of various clear acrylic resins
PERST *adj* perished
PERSUE, -D, -S *obsolete form of* ▸ **pursue**
PERT, -ER, -EST, -S *adj, n*
PERTAIN *vb*
PERTAKE, PERTOOK *obsolete form of* ▸ **partake**
PERTER ▸ **pert**
PERTEST ▸ **pert**
PERTLY ▸ **pert**
PERTOOK ▸ **pertake**
PERTS ▸ **pert**
PERTURB *vb*
PERTUSE *adj* having holes
PERUKE, -S *n* wig for men worn in the 17th and 18th centuries
PERUKED *adj* wearing wig
PERUKES ▸ **peruke**
PERUSAL ▸ **peruse**
PERUSE, -D, -S *vb*
PERUSER ▸ **peruse**
PERUSES ▸ **peruse**
PERVADE *vb*
PERVERT *vb*
PES, PEDES *n* animal part corresponding to the foot
PESADE, -S *n* position in which the horse stands on the hind legs with the forelegs in the air
PESANT, -S *obsolete spelling of* ▸ **peasant**
PESANTE *adv* to be performed clumsily
PESANTS ▸ **pesant**
PESAUNT *obsolete spelling of* ▸ **peasant**
PESETA, -S *n* former monetary unit of Spain
PESEWA, -S *n* Ghanaian monetary unit
PESHWA, -S *same as* ▸ **peishwa**
PESKIER ▸ **pesky**
PESKILY ▸ **pesky**
PESKY, PESKIER *adj*
PESO, -S *n* monetary unit of Argentina, Mexico, etc
PESSIMA *n* lowest point
PEST, -S *n*
PESTER, -S *vb*
PESTFUL *adj* causing annoyance
PESTIER ▸ **pesty**
PESTLE, -D, -S *n, vb*
PESTO, -S *n* sauce for pasta
PESTS ▸ **pest**
PESTY, PESTIER *adj* persistently annoying
PET, -S, -TED *n, adj, vb*
PETAL, -S *n* one of the brightly coloured outer parts of a flower
PETALED ▸ **petal**

PETALS ▸ **petal**
PETAR, -S *obsolete variant of* ▸ **petard**
PETARA, -S *n* clothes basket
PETARD, -S *n* device containing explosives
PETARS ▸ **petar**
PETARY *n* weapon for hurling stones
PETASOS *same as* ▸ **petasus**
PETASUS *n* broad-brimmed hat worn by the ancient Greeks
PETCOCK *n* small valve
PETER, -ED, -S *vb* fall (off) in volume, intensity, etc, and finally cease ▹ *n* act of petering
PETHER, -S *old variant of* ▸ **pedlar**
PETIOLE *n* stalk which attaches a leaf to a plant
PETIT *adj* of little or lesser importance
PETITE, -S *adj, n*
PETITIO *n* as in petitio principii, a form of fallacious reasoning
PETNAP, -S *vb* steal pet
PETRALE *n* type of sole
PETRARY *n* weapon for hurling stones
PETRE, -S *same as* > **saltpetre**
PETREL, -S *n* sea bird with a hooked bill and tubular nostrils
PETRES ▸ **petre**
PETRI *n* as in **petri dish** shallow glass dish used for cultures of bacteria
PETRIFY *vb*
PETROL, -S *n, vb*
PETROUS *adj* denoting the dense part of the temporal bone around the inner ear
PETS ▸ **pet**
PETSAI, -S *n* Chinese cabbage
PETTED ▸ **pet**
PETTER, -S ▸ **pet**
PETTI, -ES, -S *n* petticoat
PETTIER ▸ **petty**
PETTIES ▸ **petti**
PETTILY ▸ **petty**
PETTING ▸ **pet**
PETTIS ▸ **petti**
PETTISH *adj* peevish or fretful
PETTLE, -D, -S *vb* pat animal
PETTO *n* breast of an animal
PETTY, PETTIER *adj*
PETUNIA *n*
PEW, -S *n*
PEWEE, -S *n* small N American flycatcher
PEWIT, -S *another name for* ▸ **lapwing**
PEWS ▸ **pew**
PEWTER, -S *n*
PEWTERY *adj* of or like pewter
PEYOTE, -S *another name for* ▸ **mescal**
PEYOTL, -S *same as* ▸ **peyote**
PEYSE, -D, -S, PEYSING *vb* weight or poise
PEYTRAL *same as* ▸ **peytrel**
PEYTREL *n* breastplate of horse's armour
PEZANT, -S *obsolete spelling of* ▸ **peasant**
PFENNIG *n* former German monetary unit
PFFT *interj* sound indicating sudden disappearance of something
PFUI *interj* phooey
PHABLET *n* type of handheld personal computer
PHACOID *adj* lentil- or lens-shaped
PHAEIC *adj* (of animals) having dusky coloration
PHAEISM ▸ **phaeic**
PHAETON *n* light four-wheeled horse-drawn carriage
PHAGE, -S *n* parasitic virus that destroys its host
PHALANX *n*
PHALLI ▸ **phallus**
PHALLIC *adj*
PHALLIN *n* poisonous substance from mushroom
PHALLUS, PHALLI *n*
PHANG, -ED, -S *old variant spelling of* ▸ **fang**
PHANTOM *n, adj*
PHARAOH *n*
PHARE, -S *n* beacon tower
PHARM, -ED, -S *vb* redirect (a website user) to another, bogus website
PHARMA, -S *n* pharmaceutical companies considered together as an industry
PHARMED ▸ **pharm**
PHARMER *n* person who pharms

PHARMS ▸ **pharm**
PHAROS *n* lighthouse
PHARYNX *n* cavity forming the back part of the mouth
PHASE, -D, -S *n, vb*
PHASEAL ▸ **phase**
PHASED ▸ **phase**
PHASER, -S *n* type of science-fiction weapon
PHASES ▸ **phase**
PHASIC ▸ **phase**
PHASING *n* effect achieved by varying the phase relationship of two similar audio signals
PHASIS *another word for* ▸ **phase**
PHASMID *n* stick insect or leaf insect
PHASOR, -S *n* rotating vector representing a quantity that varies sinusoidally
PHAT, -TER *adj* terrific
PHATIC *adj* (of speech) used to express sociability rather than specific meaning
PHATTER ▸ **phat**
PHEAZAR *old variant of* ▸ **vizier**
PHEER, -S *same as* ▸ **fere**
PHEERE, -S *same as* ▸ **fere**
PHEERS ▸ **pheer**
PHEESE, -D, -S *vb* worry
PHEEZE, -D, -S *same as* ▸ **pheese**
PHELLEM *technical name for* ▸ **cork**
PHENATE *n* ester or salt of phenol
PHENE, -S *n* genetically determined characteristic of organism
PHENIC *adj* of phenol
PHENIX *same as* ▸ **phoenix**
PHENOL, -S *n* chemical used in disinfectants and antiseptics
PHENOM, -S *n* person or thing of outstanding abilities
PHENOME *n* full complement of phenotypical traits of an organism, species, etc
PHENOMS ▸ **phenom**
PHENOXY *modifier* as in **phenoxy resin** any of a class of resins derived from polyhydroxy ethers
PHENYL, -S *n* chemical substance
PHEON, -S *n* barbed iron head of dart
PHESE, -D, -S, PHESING *same as* ▸ **pheese**
PHEW *interj* exclamation of relief, surprise, etc
PHI, -S *n* 21st letter in the Greek alphabet
PHIAL, -S *n* small bottle for medicine etc ▹ *vb* put in phial
PHILTER *same as* ▸ **philtre**
PHILTRA > **philtrum**
PHILTRE *n* magic drink supposed to arouse love in the person who drinks it ▹ *vb* mix with love potion
PHIS ▸ **phi**
PHISH, -ED, -ES *vb* engage in phishing
PHISHER *n* person who phishes
PHISHES ▸ **phish**
PHIZ, -ES, -ZES *n* face or a facial expression
PHIZOG, -S *same as* ▸ **phiz**
PHIZZ *n* face
PHIZZES ▸ **phiz**
PHLEGM, -S *n*
PHLEGMY ▸ **phlegm**
PHLOEM, -S *n* plant tissue that acts as a path for the distribution of food
PHLOMIS *n* plant of Phlomis genus
PHLOX, -ES *n* flowering garden plant
PHO, -S *n* Vietnamese noodle soup
PHOBIA, -S *n*
PHOBIC, -S *adj, n*
PHOBISM *n* phobia
PHOBIST ▸ **phobism**
PHOCA, -E, -S *n* genus of seals
PHOCINE *adj* of, relating to, or resembling a seal
PHOEBE, -S *n* greyish-brown North American flycatcher
PHOEBUS *n* sun
PHOENIX *n*
PHOH *variant of* ▸ **foh**
PHOLAS *n* type of bivalve mollusc
PHON, -S *n* unit of loudness
PHONAL *adj* relating to voice
PHONATE *vb* articulate speech sounds
PHONE, -D, -S, PHONING *vb, n*

PHONEME *n*
PHONER, -S *n* person making a telephone call
PHONES ▸ **phone**
PHONEY, -S *adj* not genuine ▹ *n* phoney person or thing ▹ *vb* fake
PHONIC ▸ **phonics**
PHONICS *n*
PHONIED ▸ **phony**
PHONIER ▸ **phony**
PHONIES ▸ **phony**
PHONILY ▸ **phony**
PHONING ▸ **phone**
PHONO, -S *n* phonograph
PHONON, -S *n* quantum of vibrational energy
PHONOS ▸ **phono**
PHONS ▸ **phon**
PHONY, PHONIED, PHONIER, PHONIES *vb* fake
PHOOEY *interj* exclamation of scorn or contempt
PHORATE *n* type of insecticide
PHORESY *n* association in which one animal clings to another to ensure movement from place to place
PHOS ▸ **pho**
PHOSSY *adj* as in **phossy jaw** gangrenous condition of the lower jawbone
PHOT, -S *n* unit of illumination
PHOTIC *adj* of or concerned with light
PHOTICS *n* science of light
PHOTINO *n* hypothetical elementary particle
PHOTISM *n* sensation of light or colour caused by stimulus of another sense
PHOTO, -ED, -S *n, vb*
PHOTOG, -S *n* photograph
PHOTON, -S *n*
PHOTOS ▸ **photo**
PHOTS ▸ **phot**
PHPHT *interj* expressing irritation or reluctance
PHRASAL *adj* of, relating to, or composed of phrases
PHRASE, -D, -S *n, vb*
PHRASER ▸ **phrase**
PHRASES ▸ **phrase**
PHRASY *adj* containing phrases
PHRATRY *n* group of people within a tribe who have a common ancestor
PHREAK, -S *vb* hack into a telecommunications system
PHRENIC *adj* of or relating to the diaphragm ▹ *n* (a nerve, blood vessel, etc) located in the diaphragm
PHRENSY *obsolete spelling of* ▸ **frenzy**
PHT *same as* ▸ **phpht**

> It is easy to overlook this little word, that may offer a way out when your rack seems hopelessly clogged with consonants.

PHUT, -S, -TED *vb* make muffled explosive sound
PHWOAH *same as* ▸ **phwoar**
PHWOAR *interj* expression of attraction
PHYLA ▸ **phylum**
PHYLAE ▸ **phyle**
PHYLAR ▸ **phylum**
PHYLE, PHYLAE *n* tribe or clan of an ancient Greek people
PHYLIC ▸ **phyle**
PHYLLID *n* leaf of a liverwort or moss
PHYLLO, -S *variant of* ▸ **filo**
PHYLON *n* tribe
PHYLUM, PHYLA *n* major taxonomic division of animals and plants
PHYSED, -S *n* physical education
PHYSES ▸ **physis**
PHYSIC *n* medicine or drug, esp a cathartic or purge ▹ *vb* treat (a patient) with medicine
PHYSICS *n*
PHYSIO, -S *n*
PHYSIS, PHYSES *n* part of bone responsible for lengthening
PHYTANE *n* hydrocarbon found in fossilised plant remains
PHYTIN, -S *n* substance from plants used as an energy supplement
PHYTOID *adj* resembling plant
PHYTOL, -S *n* alcohol used to synthesize some vitamins

PHYTON, -S *n* unit of plant structure
PI, -ED, -ING, -S *n* sixteenth letter in the Greek alphabet ▷ *vb* spill and mix (set type) indiscriminately
PIA, -S *n* innermost of the three membranes that cover the brain and the spinal cord
PIAFFE, -D, -S *n* passage done on the spot ▷ *vb* strut on the spot
PIAFFER ▶ **piaffe**
PIAFFES ▶ **piaffe**
PIAL *adj* relating to pia mater
PIAN, -S *n* contagious tropical skin disease
PIANI ▶ **piano**
PIANIC *adj* of piano
PIANINO *n* small upright piano
PIANISM *n* technique, skill, or artistry in playing the piano
PIANIST *n*
PIANO, PIANI, -S *n, adv*
PIANOLA *n*
PIANOS ▶ **piano**
PIANS ▶ **pian**
PIARIST *n* member of a Roman religious order
PIAS ▶ **pia**
PIASABA *same as* > **piassava**
PIASAVA *same as* > **piassava**
PIASTER *same as* ▶ **piastre**
PIASTRE *n* fractional monetary unit of Egypt, Lebanon, Sudan, South Sudan, and Syria
PIAZZA, -S, PIAZZE *n* square or marketplace, esp in Italy
PIBAL, -S *n* method of measuring wind
PIBROCH *n* form of bagpipe music
PIC, -S *n* photograph or illustration
PICA, -S *n* abnormal craving to ingest substances
PICACHO *n* pointed solitary mountain
PICADOR *n* mounted bullfighter with a lance
PICAL *adj* relating to pica
PICAMAR *n* hydrocarbon extract of beechwood tar
PICANTE *adj* spicy
PICARA, -S *n* female adventurer
PICARO, -S *n* roguish adventurer
PICAS ▶ **pica**
PICCATA *adj* sautéed and served in a lemon sauce ▷ *n* dish of food sautéed and served in a lemon sauce
PICCIES ▶ **piccy**
PICCOLO *n* small flute
PICCY, PICCIES *n* picture or photograph
PICE *n* former Indian coin worth one sixty-fourth of a rupee
PICENE, -S *n* type of hydrocarbon
PICEOUS *adj* of, relating to, or resembling pitch
PICINE *adj* relating to woodpeckers
PICK, -ED, -ING, -S *vb, n*
PICKAX *same as* ▶ **pickaxe**
PICKAXE *n, vb*
PICKED ▶ **pick**
PICKEER *vb* make raid for booty
PICKER, -S *n* person or thing that picks
PICKERY *n* petty theft
PICKET, -S *n, vb*
PICKIER ▶ **picky**
PICKILY ▶ **picky**
PICKIN, -S *n* small child
PICKING ▶ **pick**
PICKINS ▶ **pickin**
PICKLE, -S *n, vb*
PICKLED *adj*
PICKLER ▶ **pickle**
PICKLES ▶ **pickle**
PICKMAW *n* type of gull
PICKOFF *n* baseball play
PICKS ▶ **pick**
PICKUP, -S *n*
PICKY, PICKIER *adj*
PICNIC, -S *n, vb*
PICOLIN *variant of* > **picoline**
PICONG, -S *n* any teasing or satirical banter
PICOT, -ED, -S *n* any of pattern of small loops, as on lace ▷ *vb* decorate material with small loops
PICOTE *adj* (of material) picoted
PICOTED ▶ **picot**
PICOTEE *n* type of carnation
PICOTS ▶ **picot**
PICQUET *vb* provide early warning of attack
PICRA, -S *n* powder of aloes and canella

PICRATE *n* any salt or ester of picric acid
PICRIC *adj* as in **picric acid** toxic sparingly soluble crystalline yellow acid
PICRITE *n* coarse-grained ultrabasic igneous rock
PICS ▸ **pic**
PICTURE *n* drawing or painting ▹ *vb* visualize, imagine
PICUL, -S *n* unit of weight, used in China, Japan, and SE Asia
PICULET *n* small tropical woodpecker with a short tail
PICULS ▸ **picul**
PIDDLE, -D, -S *vb*
PIDDLER ▸ **piddle**
PIDDLES ▸ **piddle**
PIDDLY *adj* trivial
PIDDOCK *n* marine bivalve that bores into rock, clay, or wood
PIDGEON *variant of* ▸ **pidgin**
PIDGIN, -S *n* language made up of elements of other languages
PIE, -S *n*
PIEBALD *adj, n*
PIECE, -D, -S *n*
PIECEN, -S *vb* join broken threads
PIECER, -S *n* person who mends, repairs, or joins something
PIECES ▸ **piece**
PIECING ▸ **piece**
PIED ▸ **pi**
PIEDISH *n* container for baking pies
PIEFORT *same as* > **piedfort**
PIEHOLE *n* person's mouth
PIEING, -S *n* act of pushing a pie into a person's face
PIEMAN, PIEMEN *n* seller of pies
PIEND, -S *n* salient angle
PIER, -S *n*
PIERAGE *n* accommodation for ships at piers
PIERCE, -D, -S *vb*
PIERCER ▸ **pierce**
PIERCES ▸ **pierce**
PIERID, -S *n* type of butterfly
PIERIS *n* American or Asiatic shrub
PIEROG, -S *same as* ▸ **pirog**
PIEROGI *n* Polish dumpling
PIEROGS ▸ **pierog**
PIERROT *n* male clown or masquerader with a whitened face
PIERS ▸ **pier**
PIERST *archaic spelling of* ▸ **pierced**
PIERT, -S *n* small plant with small greenish flowers
PIES ▸ **pie**
PIET, -S *n* magpie
PIETA, -S *n* sculpture, painting, or drawing of the dead Christ, supported by the Virgin Mary
PIETIES ▸ **piety**
PIETISM *n* exaggerated piety
PIETIST ▸ **pietism**
PIETS ▸ **piet**
PIETY, PIETIES *n*
PIEZO *adj* piezoelectric
PIFFERO *n* small rustic flute
PIFFLE, -D, -S *n* nonsense ▹ *vb* talk or behave feebly
PIFFLER *n* talker of nonsense
PIFFLES ▸ **piffle**
PIG, -GED, -S *n, vb*
PIGBOAT *n* submarine
PIGEON, -S *n, vb*
PIGFACE *n* creeping succulent plant
PIGFEED *n* food for pigs
PIGFISH *n* grunting fish of the North American Atlantic coast
PIGGED ▸ **pig**
PIGGERY *n* place for keeping and breeding pigs
PIGGIE *same as* ▸ **piggy**
PIGGIER ▸ **piggy**
PIGGIES ▸ **piggy**
PIGGIN, -S *n* small wooden bucket or tub
PIGGING ▸ **pig**
PIGGINS ▸ **piggin**
PIGGISH *adj* like a pig, esp in appetite or manners
PIGGY, PIGGIER, PIGGIES *n, adj*
PIGHT, -ED, -S *vb* pierce
PIGHTLE *n* small enclosure
PIGHTS ▸ **pight**
PIGLET, -S *n*
PIGLIKE ▸ **pig**
PIGLING *n* young pig
PIGMAN, PIGMEN *n* male pig farmer
PIGMEAN *same as* > **pygmaean**

PIGMEAT *less common name for* ▸ **pork**
PIGMEN ▸ **pigman**
PIGMENT *n, vb*
PIGMIES ▸ **pigmy**
PIGMOID *adj* of pygmies ▹ *n* pygmy
PIGMY, PIGMIES *same as* ▸ **pygmy**
PIGNOLI *same as* > **pignolia**
PIGNUS, PIGNORA *n* pawn or pledge
PIGNUT, -S *n* bitter nut of hickory trees
PIGOUT, -S *n* binge
PIGPEN, -S *same as* ▸ **pigsty**
PIGS ▸ **pig**
PIGSKIN *n* skin of the domestic pig ▹ *adj* made of pigskin
PIGSNEY *same as* ▸ **pigsny**
PIGSNIE *same as* ▸ **pigsny**
PIGSNY *n* archaic pet name for a girl or woman
PIGSTY *n* enclosure for pigs
PIGTAIL *n*
PIGWASH *n* wet feed for pigs
PIGWEED *n* coarse North American weed
PIING ▸ **pi**
PIKA, -S *n* burrowing mammal
PIKAKE, -S *n* type of Asian vine
PIKAS ▸ **pika**
PIKAU, -S *n* pack, knapsack, or rucksack
PIKE, -D, -S *n, vb, adj*
PIKELET *n* small thick pancake
PIKEMAN, PIKEMEN *n* (formerly) soldier armed with a pike
PIKER, -S *n* shirker
PIKES ▸ **pike**
PIKI, -S *n* bread made from blue cornmeal
PIKING, -S ▸ **pike**
PIKIS ▸ **piki**
PIKUL, -S *same as* ▸ **picul**
PILA, -E *n* pillar-like anatomical structure
PILAF, -S *same as* ▸ **pilau**
PILAFF, -S *same as* ▸ **pilau**
PILAFS ▸ **pilaf**
PILAO, -S *same as* ▸ **pilau**
PILAR *adj* relating to hair
PILAU, -S *n* Middle Eastern dish
PILAW, -S *same as* ▸ **pilau**
PILCH, -ES *n* outer garment, originally one made of skin
PILCHER *n* scabbard for sword
PILCHES ▸ **pilch**
PILCORN *n* type of oat
PILCROW *n* paragraph mark
PILE, -D *n, vb*
PILEA, -S *n* plant which releases a cloud of pollen when shaken
PILEATE *adj* (of birds) having a crest
PILED ▸ **pile**
PILEI ▸ **pileus**
PILEOUS *adj* hairy
PILER, -S *n* placer of things on pile
PILES *pl n*
PILEUM *n* top of a bird's head
PILEUP, -S *n* multiple collision of vehicles
PILEUS, PILEI *n* upper cap-shaped part of a mushroom
PILFER, -S *vb* steal in small quantities
PILFERY *n* theft
PILGRIM *n, vb*
PILI, -S, PILUS *n* Philippine tree with edible seeds resembling almonds
PILIER ▸ **pily**
PILIEST ▸ **pily**
PILING, -S *n* act of driving piles
PILINUT *n* type of nut found in the Philippines
PILIS ▸ **pili**
PILL, -ED, -S *n, vb*
PILLAGE *vb, n*
PILLAR, -S *n, vb*
PILLAU, -S *same as* ▸ **pilau**
PILLBOX *n* small box for pills
PILLBUG *n*
PILLED ▸ **pill**
PILLIE, -S *n* pilchard
PILLING ▸ **pill**
PILLION *n* seat for a passenger behind the rider of a motorcycle ▹ *adv* on a pillion ▹ *vb* ride pillion
PILLOCK *n* stupid or annoying person
PILLORY *n, vb*
PILLOW, -S *n, vb*
PILLOWY *adj* like a pillow
PILLS ▸ **pill**
PILOSE *adj* covered with fine soft hairs

PILOT, -ED, -S *n, adj, vb*
PILOTIS *pl n* posts raising a building up from the ground
PILOTS ▸ **pilot**
PILOUS *same as* ▸ **pilose**
PILOW, -S *same as* ▸ **pilau**
PILSNER *n*
PILULA, -E, -S *n* pill
PILULAR ▸ **pilule**
PILULAS ▸ **pilula**
PILULE, -S *n* small pill
PILUM *n* ancient Roman javelin
PILUS ▸ **pili**
PILY, PILIER, PILIEST *adj* like wool or pile
PIMA, -S *n* type of cotton
PIMENT, -S *n* wine flavoured with spices
PIMENTO *same as* > **pimiento**
PIMENTS ▸ **piment**
PIMP, -ED, -ING, -S *vb*
PIMPLE, -S *n*
PIMPLED ▸ **pimple**
PIMPLES ▸ **pimple**
PIMPLY ▸ **pimple**
PIMPS ▸ **pimp**
PIN, -NED, -S *n, vb*
PINA, -S *n* cone of silver amalgam
PINANG, -S *n* areca tree
PINAS ▸ **pina**
PINATA, -S *n* papier-mâché party decoration filled with sweets
PINBALL *vb*
PINBONE *n* part of sirloin
PINCASE *n* case for holding pins
PINCER *vb*
PINCERS *pl n*
PINCH, -ED, -ES *vb, n*
PINCHER ▸ **pinch**
PINCHES ▸ **pinch**
PINCURL *n* curl secured by a hairpin
PINDAN, -S *n* desert region of Western Australia
PINDARI *n* former irregular Indian horseman
PINDER, -S *n* person who impounds
PINDOWN *n* wrestling manoeuvre
PINE, -D, -S, PINING *n, vb*
PINEAL, -S *adj* resembling a pine cone ▹ *n* pineal gland
PINED ▸ **pine**
PINENE, -S *n* isomeric terpene found in many essential oils
PINERY *n* place, esp a hothouse, where pineapples are grown
PINES ▸ **pine**
PINESAP *n* red herb of N America
PINETUM, PINETA *n* area of land where pine trees are grown
PINEY ▸ **pine**
PINFALL *another name for* ▸ **fall**
PINFISH *n* small porgy of the Atlantic
PINFOLD *n* pound for stray cattle ▹ *vb* gather or confine in or as if in a pinfold
PING, -ED, -S *n, vb*
PINGER, -S *n* device, esp a timer, that makes a pinging sound
PINGING ▸ **ping**
PINGLE, -D, -S *vb* enclose small area of ground
PINGLER ▸ **pingle**
PINGLES ▸ **pingle**
PINGO, -ES, -S *n* mound of earth or gravel formed in Arctic regions
PINGS ▸ **ping**
PINGUID *adj* fatty, oily, or greasy
PINGUIN *same as* ▸ **penguin**
PINHEAD *n* head of a pin
PINHOLE *n* small hole made with or as if with a pin
PINIER ▸ **piny**
PINIES ▸ **piny**
PINIEST ▸ **piny**
PINING ▸ **pine**
PINION, -S *n* bird's wing ▹ *vb* immobilize (someone) by tying or holding his or her arms
PINITE, -S *n* greyish-green or brown mineral
PINITOL *n* compound found in pinewood
PINK, -ED, -EST, -S *n, adj, vb*
PINKEN, -S *vb* turn pink
PINKER, -S *n* something that pinks
PINKEST ▸ **pink**
PINKEY, -S *n* type of ship
PINKEYE *n*
PINKEYS ▸ **pinkey**
PINKIE, -S *n*
PINKIER ▸ **pinky**
PINKIES ▸ **pinkie**

PINKING ▶ **pink**
PINKISH ▶ **pink**
PINKLY ▶ **pink**
PINKO, -ES, -S *n* person regarded as mildly left-wing
PINKS ▶ **pink**
PINKY, PINKIER *adj* of a pink colour
PINLESS *adj* without a pin
PINNA, -E, -S *n* external part of the ear
PINNACE *n* ship's boat
PINNAE ▶ **pinna**
PINNAL ▶ **pinna**
PINNAS ▶ **pinna**
PINNATE *adj* (of compound leaves) having leaflets growing opposite each other in pairs
PINNED ▶ **pin**
PINNER, -S *n* person or thing that pins
PINNET, -S *n* pinnacle
PINNIE, -S *same as* ▶ **pinny**
PINNING ▶ **pin**
PINNOCK *n* small bird
PINNOED *adj* held or bound by the arms
PINNULA *same as* ▶ **pinnule**
PINNULE *n* lobe of a leaflet of a pinnate compound leaf
PINNY *informal or child's name for* > **pinafore**
PINOCLE *same as* > **pinochle**
PINOLE, -S *n* flour made in the southwestern United States
PINON, -ES, -S *n* low-growing pine
PINOT, -S *n* any of several grape varieties
PINS ▶ **pin**
PINSPOT *vb* illuminate with a small spotlight
PINT, -S *n*
PINTA, -S *n* pint of milk
PINTADA *same as* ▶ **pintado**
PINTADO *n* species of seagoing petrel
PINTAIL *n* greyish-brown duck with a pointed tail
PINTANO *n* tropical reef fish
PINTAS ▶ **pinta**
PINTLE, -S *n* pin or bolt forming the pivot of a hinge
PINTO, -ES, -S *adj* marked with patches of white ▷ *n* pinto horse
PINTS ▶ **pint**
PINTUCK *vb* tuck with a narrow fold of fabric
PINUP, -S *n*
PINWALE *n* fabric with narrow ridges
PINWEED *n* herb with tiny flowers
PINWORK *n* (in needlepoint lace) fine raised stitches
PINWORM *n* parasitic nematode worm
PINXIT *vb* (he or she) painted (it)
PINY, PINIER, PINIES, PINIEST *variant of* ▶ **peony**
PINYIN, -S *n* system of romanized spelling for the Chinese language
PINYON, -S *n* low-growing pine
PIOLET, -S *n* type of ice axe
PION, -S *n* type of subatomic particle
PIONED *adj* abounding in marsh marigolds
PIONEER *n, vb*
PIONER, -S *obsolete spelling of* ▶ **pioneer**
PIONEY, -S *same as* ▶ **peony**
PIONIC ▶ **pion**
PIONIES ▶ **piony**
PIONING *n* work of pioneers
PIONS ▶ **pion**
PIONY, PIONIES *same as* ▶ **peony**
PIOPIO, -S *n* New Zealand thrush, thought to be extinct
PIOSITY *n* grandiose display of piety
PIOTED *adj* pied
PIOUS *adj*
PIOUSLY ▶ **pious**
PIOY, -S *variant of* ▶ **peeoy**
PIOYE, -S *variant of* ▶ **peeoy**
PIOYS ▶ **pioy**
PIP, -PED, -PING, -S *n, vb*
PIPA, -S *n* tongueless S American toad
PIPAGE, -S *n* pipes collectively
PIPAL, -S *same as* ▶ **peepul**
PIPAS ▶ **pipa**
PIPE, -D, -S *n, vb*
PIPEAGE *same as* ▶ **pipage**
PIPED ▶ **pipe**
PIPEFUL *n* as much tobacco, etc as will fill a pipe

PIPER, -S *n*
PIPERIC > **piperine**
PIPERS ▸ **piper**
PIPES ▸ **pipe**
PIPET, -S *same as* ▸ **pipette**
PIPETTE *n* slender glass tube used to transfer or measure fluids ▹ *vb* transfer or measure out (a liquid) using a pipette
PIPI, -S *n* edible mollusc often used as bait
PIPIER ▸ **pipy**
PIPIEST ▸ **pipy**
PIPING, -S *n* system of pipes
PIPIS ▸ **pipi**
PIPIT, -S *n* small brownish songbird
PIPKIN, -S *same as* ▸ **piggin**
PIPLESS ▸ **pip**
PIPPED ▸ **pip**
PIPPIER ▸ **pippy**
PIPPIN, -S *n* type of eating apple
PIPPING ▸ **pip**
PIPPINS ▸ **pippin**
PIPPY, PIPPIER *adj* containing many pips
PIPS ▸ **pip**
PIPUL, -S *n* Indian fig tree
PIPY, PIPIER, PIPIEST ▸ **pipe**
PIQUANT *adj* having a pleasant spicy taste
PIQUE, -D, -S, PIQUING *n, vb*
PIQUET, -S *n* card game for two ▹ *vb* play game of piquet
PIQUING ▸ **pique**
PIR, -S *n* Sufi master
PIRACY *n*
PIRAGUA *same as* ▸ **pirogue**
PIRAI, -S *n* large S American fish
PIRANA, -S *same as* ▸ **piranha**
PIRANHA *n*
PIRATE, -D, -S *n, vb*
PIRATIC ▸ **pirate**
PIRAYA, -S *same as* ▸ **pirai**
PIRL, -S *n* ripple in water
PIRN, -S *n* reel or bobbin
PIRNIE, -S *n* stripy nightcap
PIRNIT *adj* striped
PIRNS ▸ **pirn**
PIROG, -HI, -I *n* type of large Russian pie
PIROGEN *n* turnovers made from kneaded dough
PIROGHI ▸ **pirog**
PIROGI ▸ **pirog**
PIROGUE *n* any of various kinds of dugout canoes
PIROJKI *same as* > **piroshki**
PIROQUE *same as* ▸ **pirogue**
PIRS ▸ **pir**
PIS ▸ **pi**
PISCARY *n* place where fishing takes place
PISCINA *n* stone basin where water used at Mass is poured away
PISCINE *n* pond or pool
PISCO, -S *n* S American brandy
PISE, -S *n* rammed earth or clay used to make floors or walls
PISH, -ED, -ES, -ING *interj, vb*
PISHEOG *same as* > **pishogue**
PISHER, -S *n* Yiddish term for small boy
PISHES ▸ **pish**
PISHING ▸ **pish**
PISHOGE *same as* > **pishogue**
PISKY, PISKIES *n* Cornish fairy
PISMIRE *archaic or dialect word for* ▸ **ant**
PISO, -S *n* peso of the Philippines
PISTE, -S *n* ski slope
PISTED *adj* marked off into pistes
PISTES ▸ **piste**
PISTIL, -S *n* seed-bearing part of a flower
PISTOL, -S *n, vb*
PISTOLE *n* gold coin formerly used in Europe
PISTOLS ▸ **pistol**
PISTON, -S *n*
PISTOU, -S *n* French sauce
PIT, -S, -TED *n, vb*
PITA, -S *n* any of several agave plants yielding a strong fibre
PITAPAT *adv* with quick light taps ▹ *n* such taps ▹ *vb* make quick light taps or beats
PITARA, -S *variant of* ▸ **petara**
PITARAH *variant of* ▸ **petara**
PITARAS ▸ **pitara**
PITAS ▸ **pita**
PITAYA, -S *same as* > **pitahaya**

PITCH, -ED, -ES *vb, n*
PITCHER *n*
PITCHES ▸ **pitch**
PITCHY *adj* full of or covered with pitch
PITEOUS *adj*
PITFALL *n*
PITH, -ED, -ING, -S *n, vb*
PITHEAD *n* top of a mine shaft and the buildings and hoisting gear around it
PITHED ▸ **pith**
PITHFUL ▸ **pith**
PITHIER ▸ **pithy**
PITHILY ▸ **pithy**
PITHING ▸ **pith**
PITHOS, PITHOI *n* large ceramic container for oil or grain
PITHS ▸ **pith**
PITHY, PITHIER *adj*
PITIED ▸ **pity**
PITIER, -S ▸ **pity**
PITIES ▸ **pity**
PITIETH *vb* as in **it pitieth me** archaic inflection of 'pity'
PITIFUL *adj*
PITLIKE *adj* like a pit
PITMAN, -S, PITMEN *n* coal miner ▹ *n* connecting rod (in a machine)
PITON, -S *n* metal spike used in climbing to secure a rope
PITOT, -S *n* tube used to measure the pressure of a liquid stream
PITPROP *n* support beam in mine shaft
PITS ▸ **pit**
PITSAW, -S *n* large saw formerly used for cutting logs into planks
PITTA, -S *n* small brightly coloured ground-dwelling tropical bird
PITTED ▸ **pit**
PITTEN *adj* having been put
PITTER, -S *vb* make pattering sound
PITTING ▸ **pit**
PITTITE *n* occupant of a theatre pit
PITUITA *n* thick nasal secretion
PITUITE *n* mucus
PITURI, -S *n* Australian solanaceous shrub
PITY, PITIED, PITIES *n* sympathy or sorrow for others' suffering ▹ *vb* feel pity for
PITYING ▸ **pity**
PIU *adv* more (quickly, softly, etc)
PIUM, -S *n* stinging insect
PIUPIU, -S *n* skirt worn by Māoris on ceremonial occasions
PIVOT, -ED, -S *n, vb*
PIVOTAL *adj*
PIVOTED ▸ **pivot**
PIVOTER ▸ **pivot**
PIVOTS ▸ **pivot**
PIX, -ES *less common spelling of* ▸ **pyx**
PIXEL, -S *n*
PIXES ▸ **pix**
PIXIE *n*
PIXY, PIXIES *same as* ▸ **pixie**
PIXYISH ▸ **pixy**
PIZAZZ *same as* ▸ **pizzazz**
PIZAZZY *adj* exciting and lively
PIZE, -D, -S, PIZING *vb* strike (someone a blow)
PIZZA, -S *n*
PIZZAZ *same as* ▸ **pzazz**
PIZZAZZ *n*
PIZZLE, -S *n* archaic word for the penis of an animal
PLAAS, -ES *n* farm
PLACARD *n, vb*
PLACATE *vb*
PLACCAT *variant of* ▸ **placket**
PLACE, -D, -S *n, vb*
PLACEBO *n*
PLACED ▸ **place**
PLACER, -S *n* surface sediment containing particles of gold or some other valuable mineral
PLACES ▸ **place**
PLACET, -S *n* vote or expression of assent
PLACID *adj*
PLACING *n* method of issuing securities to the public using an intermediary
PLACIT, -S *n* decree or dictum
PLACITA > **placitum**
PLACITS ▸ **placit**
PLACK, -S *n* small former Scottish coin
PLACKET *n* opening at the waist of a dress or skirt
PLACKS ▸ **plack**
PLACOID *adj* platelike or flattened ▹ *n* fish with placoid scales
PLAFOND *n* ceiling, esp one having ornamentation

PLAGAL *adj* (of a cadence) progressing from the subdominant to the tonic chord
PLAGE, -S *n* bright patch in the sun's chromosphere
PLAGIUM *n* crime of kidnapping
PLAGUE, -D, -S *n, vb*
PLAGUER ▶ **plague**
PLAGUES ▶ **plague**
PLAGUEY *same as* ▶ **plaguy**
PLAGUY *adj* disagreeable or vexing ▷ *adv* disagreeably or annoyingly
PLAICE, -S *n* edible European flatfish
PLAID, -ED, -S *n, vb*
PLAIN, -ED, -ER *adj, n, adv, vb*
PLAINLY ▶ **plain**
PLAINS *pl n*
PLAINT, -S *n* complaint or lamentation
PLAIT, -ED, -S *n, vb*
PLAITER ▶ **plait**
PLAITS ▶ **plait**
PLAN, -NED, -S *n, vb*
PLANAR *adj*
PLANATE *adj* having been flattened
PLANCH *vb* cover with planks
PLANCHE *same as* ▶ **planch**
PLANE, -D, -S, PLANING *n, adj, vb*
PLANER, -S *n* machine with a cutting tool that makes repeated horizontal strokes
PLANES ▶ **plane**
PLANET, -S *n* large body in space that revolves round the sun or another star
PLANING ▶ **plane**
PLANISH *vb* give a smooth surface to (a metal)
PLANK, -ED, -S *n, vb*
PLANNED ▶ **plan**
PLANNER *n*
PLANS ▶ **plan**
PLANT, -ED, -S *n, vb*
PLANTA, -E, -S *n* sole of foot
PLANTAR *adj* of, relating to, or occurring on the sole of the foot
PLANTAS ▶ **planta**
PLANTED ▶ **plant**
PLANTER *n*
PLANTS ▶ **plant**
PLANULA *n* free-swimming larva of hydrozoan coelenterates
PLANURY *another name for* ▶ **planuria**
PLANXTY *n* Celtic melody for harp
PLAP, -PED, -S *same as* ▶ **plop**
PLAQUE, -S *n*
PLASH, -ED, -ES *same as* ▶ **pleach**
PLASHER *n* type of farm tool
PLASHES ▶ **plash**
PLASHET *n* small pond
PLASHY *adj* wet or marshy
PLASM, -S *same as* ▶ **plasma**
PLASMA, -S *n*
PLASMIC ▶ **plasma**
PLASMID *n* small circle of bacterial DNA
PLASMIN *n* proteolytic enzyme that causes fibrinolysis in blood clots
PLASMON *n* sum total of plasmagenes in a cell
PLASMS ▶ **plasm**
PLAST *archaic past participle of* ▶ **place**
PLASTE *archaic past participle of* ▶ **place**
PLASTER *n, vb*
PLASTIC *n, adj*
PLASTID *n* small particle in the cells of plants and some animals
PLAT, -S, -TED *n* small area of ground
PLATAN, -S *n* plane tree
PLATANE *same as* ▶ **platan**
PLATANS ▶ **platan**
PLATE, -S *n, vb*
PLATEAU *n, vb*
PLATED *adj* coated with a layer of metal
PLATEN, -S *n* roller of a typewriter, against which the paper is held
PLATER, -S *n* person or thing that plates
PLATES ▶ **plate**
PLATIER ▶ **platy**
PLATIES ▶ **platy**
PLATINA *n* alloy of platinum and several other metals
PLATING *n* coating of metal
PLATOON *n, vb*
PLATS ▶ **plat**
PLATT *adj* as in **scale and platt** denoting a

straight staircase with landings, as opposed to a spiral staircase
PLATTED ▶ **plat**
PLATTER *n*
PLATY, PLATIER, PLATIES, -S *adj* of or designating rocks the constituents of which occur in flaky layers ▷ *n* brightly coloured freshwater fish
PLATYPI > **platypus**
PLATYS ▶ **platy**
PLAUDIT *n* expression of enthusiastic approval
PLAY, -ED, -S *vb, n*
PLAYA, -S *n* (in the US) temporary lake in a desert basin
PLAYACT *vb* pretend or make believe
PLAYAS ▶ **playa**
PLAYBOY *n*
PLAYBUS *n* mobile playground in a bus
PLAYDAY *n* day given to play
PLAYED ▶ **play**
PLAYER, -S *n*
PLAYFUL *adj*
PLAYING *n*
PLAYLET *n* short play
PLAYOFF *n*
PLAYPEN *n*
PLAYS ▶ **play**
PLAYSET *n*
PLAZA, -S *n*
PLEA, -ED, -ING, -S *n* serious or urgent request, entreaty ▷ *vb* entreat
PLEACH *vb* interlace the stems or boughs of (a tree or hedge)
PLEAD, -ED, -S, PLED *vb*
PLEADER ▶ **plead**
PLEADS ▶ **plead**
PLEAED ▶ **plea**
PLEAING ▶ **plea**
PLEAS ▶ **plea**
PLEASE, -S *vb, adv*
PLEASED ▶ **please**
PLEASER ▶ **please**
PLEASES ▶ **please**
PLEAT, -ED, -S *n, vb*
PLEATER *n* attachment on a sewing machine that makes pleats
PLEATS ▶ **pleat**
PLEB *n* common vulgar person
PLEBBY *adj* common or vulgar
PLEBE, -S *n* member of the lowest class at the US Naval Academy or Military Academy
PLEBEAN *old variant of* > **plebeian**
PLEBES ▶ **plebe**
PLEBIFY *vb* make plebeian
PLEBS *n* common people
PLECTRA > **plectrum**
PLECTRE *variant of* > **plectrum**
PLED ▶ **plead**
PLEDGE, -D, -S *n, vb*
PLEDGEE *n* person to whom a pledge is given
PLEDGER *same as* ▶ **pledgor**
PLEDGES ▶ **pledge**
PLEDGET *n* small flattened pad of wool, cotton, etc
PLEDGOR *n* person who gives or makes a pledge
PLEIAD, -S *n* brilliant or talented group, esp one with seven members
PLENA ▶ **plenum**
PLENARY *adj, n*
PLENCH *n* tool combining wrench and pliers
PLENIPO *n* plenipotentiary diplomat
PLENISH *vb* fill, stock, or resupply
PLENISM *n* philosophical theory
PLENIST ▶ **plenism**
PLENTY *n, adj, adv*
PLENUM, PLENA, -S *n* enclosure containing gas at a high pressure
PLEON, -S *n* abdomen of crustacean
PLEONAL *adj* of the abdomen of a crustacean
PLEONIC ▶ **pleon**
PLEONS ▶ **pleon**
PLEOPOD *another name for* > **swimmeret**
PLERION *n* filled-centre supernova remnant
PLEROMA *n* abundance
PLEROME *n* central column in growing stem or root
PLESH, -ES *n* small pool
PLESSOR *same as* ▶ **plexor**
PLEUCH, -S *same as* ▶ **pleugh**
PLEUGH, -S *Scottish word for* ▶ **plough**
PLEURA, -E, -S *n* membrane covering the lungs

PLEURAL ▸ **pleura**
PLEURAS ▸ **pleura**
PLEURON *n* part of the cuticle of arthropods
PLEW, -S *n* (formerly in Canada) beaver skin used as a standard unit of value in the fur trade
PLEX, -ED, -ES, -ING *n* shortening of multiplex ▹ *vb* make a plexus
PLEXAL ▸ **plexus**
PLEXED ▸ **plex**
PLEXES ▸ **plex**
PLEXING ▸ **plex**
PLEXOR, -S *n* small hammer with a rubber head
PLEXURE *n* act of weaving together
PLEXUS *n* complex network of nerves or blood vessels
PLIABLE *adj*
PLIABLY ▸ **pliable**
PLIANCY ▸ **pliant**
PLIANT *adj*
PLICA, -E, -S *n* folding over of parts, such as a fold of skin, muscle, peritoneum, etc
PLICAL ▸ **plica**
PLICAS ▸ **plica**
PLICATE *adj* having or arranged in parallel folds or ridges ▹ *vb* arrange into parallel folds
PLIE *n* classic ballet practice posture with back erect and knees bent
PLIED ▸ **ply**
PLIER *n* person who plies a trade
PLIERS *pl n*
PLIES ▸ **ply**
PLIGHT, -S *vb* pledge
PLIM, -MED, -S *vb* swell with water
PLIMSOL *same as* ▸ **plimsoll**
PLING, -ED, -S *n* (in computer jargon) an exclamation mark ▹ *vb* beg from
PLINK, -ED, -S *n* short sharp often metallic sound ▹ *vb* make such a noise
PLINKER ▸ **plink**
PLINKS ▸ **plink**
PLINKY *adj* (of a sound) short, sharp, and often metallic
PLINTH, -S *n*
PLISKIE *n* practical joke ▹ *adj* tricky or mischievous
PLISKY *same as* ▸ **pliskie**
PLISSE, -S *n* fabric with a wrinkled finish, achieved by treatment involving caustic soda
PLOAT, -ED, -S *vb* thrash
PLOD, -DED, -S *vb, n*
PLODDER *n* person who plods
PLODGE, -D, -S *vb* wade in water, esp the sea ▹ *n* act of wading
PLODS ▸ **plod**
PLOIDY *n* number of copies of set of chromosomes in cell
PLONG, -D, -S *obsolete variant of* ▸ **plunge**
PLONGE, -D, -S *same as* ▸ **plunge**
PLONGS ▸ **plong**
PLONK, -ED, -S *vb, n, interj*
PLONKER *n* stupid person
PLONKO, -S *n* alcoholic, esp one who drinks wine
PLONKS ▸ **plonk**
PLONKY ▸ **plonk**
PLOOK, -S *same as* ▸ **plouk**
PLOOKIE *same as* ▸ **plouky**
PLOOKS ▸ **plook**
PLOOKY ▸ **plook**
PLOP, -PED, -S *n, vb, interj*
PLOSION *n* sound of an abrupt break or closure, esp the audible release of a stop
PLOSIVE *adj* pronounced with a sudden release of breath ▹ *n* plosive consonant
PLOT, -S, -TED *n, vb*
PLOTFUL ▸ **plot**
PLOTS ▸ **plot**
PLOTTED ▸ **plot**
PLOTTER *same as* ▸ **plouter**
PLOTTIE *n* hot spiced drink
PLOTTY *adj* intricately plotted
PLOTZ, -ED, -ES *vb* faint or collapse
PLOUGH, -S *n* agricultural tool for turning over soil ▹ *vb* turn over (earth) with a plough
PLOUK, -S *n* pimple
PLOUKIE ▸ **plouk**
PLOUKS ▸ **plouk**
PLOUKY ▸ **plouk**

PLOUTER *same as* ▸ **plowter**
PLOVER, -S *n* shore bird with a straight bill and long pointed wings
PLOVERY *adj* characterized by plovers
PLOW, -ED, -S *same as* ▸ **plough**
PLOWBOY *same as* > **ploughboy**
PLOWED ▸ **plow**
PLOWER, -S ▸ **plow**
PLOWING > **ploughing**
PLOWMAN, PLOWMEN *same as* > **ploughman**
PLOWS ▸ **plow**
PLOWTER *vb* work or play in water or mud ▹ *n* act of plowtering
PLOY, -ED, -ING, -S *n, vb*
PLOYE, -S *n* buckwheat pancake
PLOYED ▸ **ploy**
PLOYES ▸ **ploye**
PLOYING ▸ **ploy**
PLOYS ▸ **ploy**
PLU *same as* ▸ **plew**
PLUCK, -ED, -S *vb, n*
PLUCKER ▸ **pluck**
PLUCKS ▸ **pluck**
PLUCKY *adj*
PLUE, -S *same as* ▸ **plew**
PLUFF, -ED, -S *vb* expel in puffs
PLUFFY ▸ **pluff**
PLUG, -GED, -S *n, vb*
PLUGGER ▸ **plug**
PLUGOLA *n* plugging of products on television
PLUGS ▸ **plug**
PLUM, -MER, -S *n, adj*
PLUMAGE *n*
PLUMATE *adj* of, relating to, or possessing one or more feathers or plumes
PLUMB, -ED, -S *vb, adv, n*
PLUMBER *n*
PLUMBIC *adj* of or containing lead in the tetravalent state
PLUMBS ▸ **plumb**
PLUMBUM *n* obsolete name for lead (the metal)
PLUMCOT *n* hybrid of apricot and plum
PLUME, -D, -S, PLUMING *n, vb*
PLUMERY *n* plumes collectively
PLUMES ▸ **plume**
PLUMIER ▸ **plumy**
PLUMING ▸ **plume**
PLUMIST *n* person who makes plumes
PLUMMER ▸ **plum**
PLUMMET *vb, n*
PLUMMY *adj* of, full of, or like plums
PLUMOSE *same as* ▸ **plumate**
PLUMOUS *adj* having plumes or feathers
PLUMP, -ED, -S *adj, vb, n, adv*
PLUMPEN *vb* make or become plump
PLUMPER *n*
PLUMPIE *same as* ▸ **plumpy**
PLUMPLY ▸ **plump**
PLUMPS ▸ **plump**
PLUMPY *adj* plump
PLUMS ▸ **plum**
PLUMULA *n* down feather
PLUMULE *n* embryonic shoot of seed-bearing plants
PLUMY, PLUMIER *adj* like a feather
PLUNDER *vb, n*
PLUNGE, -D, -S *vb, n*
PLUNGER *n*
PLUNGES ▸ **plunge**
PLUNK, -ED, -S *vb, n, interj, adv*
PLUNKER ▸ **plunk**
PLUNKS ▸ **plunk**
PLUNKY *adj* sounding like plucked banjo string
PLUOT, -S *n* hybrid fruit of the plum and apricot
PLURAL, -S *adj, n*
PLURRY *euphemism for* ▸ **bloody**
PLUS, -ED, -ES, -ING, -SED, -SES *vb*
PLUSAGE *same as* > **plussage**
PLUSED ▸ **plus**
PLUSES ▸ **plus**
PLUSH, -ER, -ES *n, adj*
PLUSHED *adj* showily luxurious
PLUSHER ▸ **plush**
PLUSHES ▸ **plush**
PLUSHLY ▸ **plush**
PLUSHY *same as* ▸ **plush**
PLUSING ▸ **plus**
PLUSSED ▸ **plus**
PLUSSES ▸ **plus**
PLUTEAL ▸ **pluteus**
PLUTEUS, PLUTEI *n* larva of sea urchin
PLUTO, -ED, -ES, -S *vb* reduce in importance
PLUTOID *n* dwarf planet whose orbit is beyond Neptune's
PLUTON, -S *n* any mass of igneous rock that has solidified below the surface of the earth

PLUTOS ▸ **pluto**
PLUVIAL *n* period of high rainfall
PLUVIAN *n* crocodile bird
PLUVIUS *adj* as in **pluvius insurance** insurance against rain
PLY, PLIED, PLIES, -ING *vb, n*
PLYER, -S *n* person who plies trade
PLYING ▸ **ply**
PLYWOOD *n*
PNEUMA, -S *n* person's vital spirit, soul, or creative energy
PO, -S *n* chamberpot
POA, -S *n* type of grass
POACH, -ED, -ES *vb*
POACHER *n*
POACHES ▸ **poach**
POACHY *adj* (of land) wet and soft
POAKA, -S *n* type of stilt (bird) native to New Zealand
POAKE, -S *n* waste matter from tanning of hides
POAS ▸ **poa**
POBLANO *n* variety of chilli pepper
POBOY, -S *n* New Orleans sandwich
POCHARD *n* European diving duck
POCHAY, -S *n* closed horse-drawn four-wheeled coach ▹ *vb* transport by pochay
POCHOIR *n* print made from stencils
POCK, -ED, -ING, -S *n, vb*
POCKARD *variant of* ▸ **pochard**
POCKED ▸ **pock**
POCKET, -S *n, vb, adj*
POCKIER ▸ **pocky**
POCKIES *pl n* woollen mittens
POCKILY ▸ **pock**
POCKING ▸ **pock**
POCKPIT *n* mark left on skin after a pock has gone
POCKS ▸ **pock**
POCKY, POCKIER ▸ **pock**
POCO *adv* little
POCOSEN *same as* ▸ **pocosin**
POCOSIN *n* swamp in US upland coastal region
POCOSON *same as* ▸ **pocosin**
POD, -DED, -DING, -S *n, vb*
PODAGRA *n* gout of the foot or big toe
PODAL *adj* relating to feet
PODALIC *adj* relating to feet
PODCAST *n, vb*
PODDED ▸ **pod**
PODDIE *n* user of or enthusiast for the iPod, a portable digital music player
PODDIER ▸ **poddy**
PODDIES ▸ **poddy**
PODDING ▸ **pod**
PODDLE, -D, -S *vb* move or travel in a leisurely manner
PODDY, PODDIER, PODDIES *n* handfed calf or lamb ▹ *adj* fat
PODESTA *n* (in modern Italy) subordinate magistrate in some towns
PODEX, -ES *n* posterior
PODGE, -S *n* chubby person
PODGIER ▸ **podgy**
PODGILY ▸ **podgy**
PODGY, PODGIER *adj*
PODIA ▸ **podium**
PODIAL ▸ **podium**
PODITE, -S *n* crustacean leg
PODITIC *adj* similar to the limb segment of an arthropod
PODIUM, PODIA, -S *n, vb*
PODLEY, -S *n* young coalfish
PODLIKE ▸ **pod**
PODS ▸ **pod**
PODSOL, -S *same as* ▸ **podzol**
PODUNK, -S *adj* small or unimportant ▹ *n* small or unimportant thing
PODZOL, -S *n* type of soil characteristic of coniferous forest regions
POEM, -S *n*
POEP, -ED, -ING, -S *n* emission of gas from the anus ▹ *vb* break wind
POESY, POESIED, POESIES *n* poetry ▹ *vb* write poems
POET, -S *n*
POETESS *n* female poet
POETIC *adj*
POETICS *n*
POETISE *same as* > **poeticize**
POETIZE *same as* > **poeticize**

POETRY *n*
POETS ▸ **poet**
POFFLE, -S *n* small piece of land
POGEY, -S *n* financial or other relief given to the unemployed by the government
POGGE, -S *n* European marine scorpaenoid fish
POGIES ▸ **pogy**
POGO, -ED, -ES, -ING, -S *vb* jump up and down on one spot
POGOER, -S ▸ **pogo**
POGOES ▸ **pogo**
POGOING ▸ **pogo**
POGONIA *n* orchid with pink or white fragrant flowers
POGONIP *n* icy winter fog
POGOS ▸ **pogo**
POGROM, -S *n, vb*
POGY, POGIES *same as* ▸ **pogey**
POH, -ED, -ING, -S *interj* exclamation expressing contempt or disgust ▹ *vb* reject contemptuously
POHIRI, -S *variant spelling of* ▸ **powhiri**
POHS ▸ **poh**
POI, -S *n* ball of woven flax swung rhythmically by Māori women during poi dances
POILU, -S *n* infantryman in the French Army
POINADO *old variant of* ▸ **poniard**
POIND, -ED, -S *vb* take (property of a debtor) in execution or by way of distress
POINDER ▸ **poind**
POINDS ▸ **poind**
POINT, -S *n, vb*
POINTE, -S *n* tip of the toe
POINTED *adj*
POINTEL *n* engraver's tool
POINTER *n*
POINTES ▸ **pointe**
POINTS ▸ **point**
POINTY *adj*
POIS ▸ **poi**
POISE, -S, POISING *n, vb*
POISED *adj*
POISER, -S *n* balancing organ of some insects
POISES ▸ **poise**
POISHA, -S *n* monetary unit of Bangladesh
POISING ▸ **poise**
POISON, -S *n, vb*
POISSON *n* fish
POITIN, -S *variant spelling of* ▸ **poteen**
POITREL *n* breastplate of horse's armour
POKABLE ▸ **poke**
POKAL, -S *n* tall drinking cup
POKE, -D, -S, POKING *vb, n*
POKEFUL *n* contents of small bag
POKER, -S *n*
POKES ▸ **poke**
POKEY, -S *same as* ▸ **pokie**
POKIE *n* poker machine
POKIER ▸ **poky**
POKIES ▸ **poky**
POKIEST ▸ **poky**
POKILY ▸ **poky**
POKING ▸ **poke**
POKY, POKIER, POKIES, POKIEST *adj* small and cramped
POL, -S *n* political campaigner
POLACCA *same as* ▸ **polacre**
POLACRE *n* three-masted sailing vessel
POLAR, -S *adj, n*
POLARON *n* kind of electron
POLARS ▸ **polar**
POLDER, -S *n* land reclaimed from the sea, esp in the Netherlands ▹ *vb* reclaim land from the sea
POLE, -D, -S *n, vb*
POLEAX *same as* ▸ **poleaxe**
POLEAXE *vb, n*
POLECAT *n*
POLED ▸ **pole**
POLEIS ▸ **polis**
POLEMIC *n, adj*
POLENTA *n*
POLER, -S *n* person or thing that poles, esp a punter
POLES ▸ **pole**
POLEY, -S *adj* (of cattle) hornless or polled ▹ *n* animal with horns removed
POLEYN, -S *n* piece of armour for protecting the knee
POLEYS ▸ **poley**
POLICE, -D, -S *n, vb*
POLICER *n* computer device controlling use
POLICES ▸ **police**
POLICY *n*

POLIES ▸ **poly**
POLING, -S ▸ **pole**
POLIO, -S *n*
POLIS, POLEIS, -ES *n* ancient Greek city-state
POLISH *vb, n*
POLITE, -R *adj*
POLITIC *adj*
POLITY *n*
POLJE, -S *n* large elliptical depression in karst regions
POLK, -ED, -ING, -S *vb* dance a polka
POLKA, -ED, -S *n, vb*
POLKED ▸ **polk**
POLKING ▸ **polk**
POLKS ▸ **polk**
POLL, -S *n, vb*
POLLACK *n* food fish related to the cod, found in northern seas
POLLAN, -S *n* whitefish that occurs in lakes in Northern Ireland
POLLARD *n* animal that has shed its horns or has had them removed ▹ *vb* cut off the top of (a tree) to make it grow bushy
POLLAXE *same as* ▸ **poleaxe**
POLLED *adj*
POLLEE, -S ▸ **poll**
POLLEN, -S *n, vb*
POLLENT *adj* strong
POLLER, -S ▸ **poll**
POLLEX *n* first digit of the forelimb of amphibians, reptiles, birds, and mammals
POLLICY *obsolete spelling of* ▸ **policy**
POLLIES ▸ **polly**
POLLING *n*
POLLIST *n* one advocating the use of polls
POLLMAN, POLLMEN *n* one passing a degree without honours
POLLOCK *same as* ▸ **pollack**
POLLS ▸ **poll**
POLLUTE *vb*
POLLY, POLLIES *n* politician
POLO, -S *n*
POLOIST *n* devotee of polo
POLONIE *same as* ▸ **polony**
POLONY *n* bologna sausage
POLOS ▸ **polo**
POLS ▸ **pol**
POLT, -ED, -ING, -S *n* thump or blow ▹ *vb* strike
POLY, POLIES, -S *n* polytechnic
POLYACT *adj* (of a sea creature) having many tentacles or limb-like protrusions
POLYBAG *vb*
POLYCOT *n* plant that has or appears to have more than two cotyledons
POLYENE *n* organic chemical compound
POLYGAM *n* plant of the Polygamia class
POLYGON *n*
POLYMER *n*
POLYNIA *same as* ▸ **polynya**
POLYNYA, POLYNYI *n* stretch of open water surrounded by ice
POLYOL, -S *n* type of alcohol
POLYOMA *n* type of tumour caused by virus
POLYP, -S *n* small simple sea creature with a hollow cylindrical body
POLYPE, -S *variant of* ▸ **polyp**
POLYPED *same as* ▸ **polypod**
POLYPES ▸ **polype**
POLYPI ▸ **polypus**
POLYPOD *adj* (esp of insect larvae) having many legs or similar appendages ▹ *n* animal of this type
POLYPS ▸ **polyp**
POLYPUS, POLYPI *same as* ▸ **polyp**
POLYS ▸ **poly**
POLYZOA *n* small mosslike aquatic creatures
POM, -S *same as* ▸ **pommy**
POMACE, -S *n* apple pulp left after pressing for juice
POMADE, -D, -S *n* perfumed oil put on the hair to make it smooth and shiny ▹ *vb* put pomade on
POMATO *n* hybrid of tomato and potato
POMATUM *n* pomade ▹ *vb* put pomatum on
POMBE, -S *n* any alcoholic drink
POME, -S *n* fleshy fruit of the apple and related plants

POMELO, -S *n* edible yellow fruit, like a grapefruit
POMEROY *n* bullet used to down airships
POMES ▶ **pome**
POMFRET *n* small black rounded liquorice sweet
POMMEE *adj* (of cross) having end of each arm ending in disk
POMMEL, -S *same as* ▶ **pummel**
POMMELE *adj* having a pommel
POMMELS ▶ **pommel**
POMMIE *same as* ▶ **pommy**
POMMY, POMMIES *n* word used by Australians and New Zealanders for a British person
POMO, -S *n* postmodernist
POMP, -S *n*
POMPANO *n* deep-bodied carangid food fish
POMPELO *n* large Asian citrus fruit
POMPEY, -S *vb* mollycoddle
POMPIER *adj* slavishly conventional ▷ *n* conventional or imitative artist
POMPION *n* pumpkin
POMPOM, -S *n*
POMPON, -S *same as* ▶ **pompom**
POMPOON *variant of* ▶ **pompom**
POMPOSO *adj* (of music) to be played in a ceremonial manner
POMPOUS *adj*
POMPS ▶ **pomp**
POMROY, -S *variant of* ▶ **pomeroy**
POMS ▶ **pom**
PONCE, -D, -S, PONCING *vb* act stupidly or waste time
PONCEAU *n* scarlet red
PONCED ▶ **ponce**
PONCES ▶ **ponce**
PONCEY, PONCIER *adj*
PONCHO, -S *n* loose circular cloak with a hole for the head
PONCIER ▶ **poncey**
PONCING ▶ **ponce**
PONCY *same as* ▶ **poncey**
POND, -ED, -ING, -S *n, vb*
PONDAGE *n* water held in reservoir
PONDED ▶ **pond**
PONDER, -S *vb*
PONDING ▶ **pond**
PONDOK, -S *n* (in southern Africa) crudely made house or shack
PONDS ▶ **pond**
PONE, -S *n* bread made of maize
PONENT, -S *adj* westerly ▷ *n* the west
PONES ▶ **pone**
PONEY, -S *same as* ▶ **pony**
PONG, -ED, -ING, -S *n* strong unpleasant smell ▷ *vb* give off a strong unpleasant smell
PONGA, -S *n* tall New Zealand tree fern
PONGAL, -S *n* Indian dish of cooked rice
PONGAS ▶ **ponga**
PONGED ▶ **pong**
PONGEE, -S *n* thin plain-weave silk fabric
PONGID, -S *n* primate of the family which includes the gibbons and the great apes
PONGIER ▶ **pongy**
PONGING ▶ **pong**
PONGO, -ES, -S *n* anthropoid ape, esp an orang-utan or (formerly) a gorilla
PONGS ▶ **pong**
PONGY, PONGIER ▶ **pong**
PONIARD *n* small slender dagger ▷ *vb* stab with a poniard
PONIED ▶ **pony**
PONIES ▶ **pony**
PONK, -ED, -ING, -S *n* evil spirit ▷ *vb* stink
PONS, PONTES *n* bridge of connecting tissue
PONT, -S *n* (in South Africa) river ferry
PONTAGE *n* tax paid for repairing bridge
PONTAL *adj* of or relating to the pons
PONTES ▶ **pons**
PONTIC *adj* of or relating to the pons
PONTIE *same as* ▶ **ponty**
PONTIES ▶ **ponty**
PONTIFF *n*
PONTIFY *vb* speak or behave in a pompous or dogmatic manner
PONTIL, -S *same as* ▶ **punty**
PONTILE *adj* relating to pons ▷ *n* metal bar used in glass-making

PONTILS ▸ **pontil**
PONTINE *adj* of or relating to bridges
PONTON, -S *variant of* ▸ **pontoon**
PONTOON *n, vb*
PONTS ▸ **pont**
PONTY, PONTIES *n* rod used for shaping molten glass
PONY, PONIED, PONIES, -ING *n, vb*
PONZU, -S *n* type of Japanese dipping sauce
POO, -ED, -ING, -S *vb*
POOBAH, -S *n* influential person
POOCH, -ED, -ES *n, vb*
POOD, -S *n* unit of weight, used in Russia
POODLE, -S *n*
POODS ▸ **pood**
POOED ▸ **poo**
POOGYE, -S *n* Hindu nose-flute
POOH, -ED, -ING, -S *interj* exclamation of disdain, contempt, or disgust ▹ *vb* make such an exclamation
POOING ▸ **poo**
POOJA, -S *variant of* ▸ **puja**
POOJAH, -S *variant of* ▸ **puja**
POOJAS ▸ **pooja**
POOK, -ING, -IT, -S *vb* pluck
POOKA, -S *n* malevolent Irish spirit
POOKING ▸ **pook**
POOKIT ▸ **pook**
POOKS ▸ **pook**
POOL, -ED, -ING *n, vb*
POOLER, -S *n* person taking part in pool
POOLING ▸ **pool**
POOLS *pl n* organized nationwide gambling pool
POON, -S *n* SE Asian tree
POONAC, -S *n* coconut residue
POONCE, -D, -S *vb* act stupidly or waste time
POONS ▸ **poon**
POOP, -ED, -ING, -S *n, vb*
POOPER, -S *n*
POOPIER ▸ **poopy**
POOPING ▸ **poop**
POOPS ▸ **poop**
POOPY, POOPIER *adj*
POOR, -ER, -EST *adj*
POORBOX *n* box used for the collection of money for the poor
POORER ▸ **poor**
POOREST ▸ **poor**
POORI, -S *n* unleavened Indian bread
POORISH ▸ **poor**
POORLY *adv, adj*
POORT, -S *n* (in South Africa) steep narrow mountain pass
POOS ▸ **poo**
POOT, -ED, -ERS, -ING, -S *vb* break wind
POOTER *vb* hurry away
POOTERS ▸ **poot**
POOTING ▸ **poot**
POOTLE, -D, -S *vb* travel or go in a relaxed or leisurely manner
POOTS ▸ **poot**
POP, -PED, -PING, -S *vb, n, adj*
POPADUM *same as* > **poppadom**
POPCORN *n*
POPE, -S *n*
POPEDOM *n* office or dignity of a pope
POPERA, -S *n* pop music drawing on opera or classical music
POPERIN *n* kind of pear
POPES ▸ **pope**
POPETTE *n* young female fan or performer of pop music
POPEYED *adj* staring in astonishment
POPGUN, -S *n* toy gun that fires a pellet or cork by means of compressed air
POPINAC *n* type of thorny shrub
POPJOY, -S *vb* amuse oneself
POPLAR, -S *n*
POPLIN, -S *n* ribbed cotton material
POPOUT, -S *n*
POPOVER *n*
POPPA, -S *same as* ▸ **papa**
POPPED ▸ **pop**
POPPER, -S *n*
POPPET, -S *n*
POPPIED *adj* covered with poppies
POPPIER ▸ **poppy**
POPPIES ▸ **poppy**
POPPING ▸ **pop**
POPPISH *adj* like pop music
POPPIT, -S *n* bead used to form necklace
POPPLE, -D, -S *vb* (of boiling water or a choppy sea) to heave or toss
POPPLY *adj* covered in small bumps

POPPY, POPPIER, POPPIES *n, adj*
POPRIN *same as* ▸ **poperin**
POPS ▸ **pop**
POPSIE *same as* ▸ **popsy**
POPSIES ▸ **popsy**
POPSOCK *n*
POPSTER *n* pop star
POPSY, POPSIES *n* attractive young woman
POPULAR *adj, n*
PORAE, -S *n* large edible sea fish of New Zealand waters
PORAL *adj* relating to pores
PORANGI *adj* crazy
PORCH, -ES *n*
PORCHED *adj* having a porch
PORCHES ▸ **porch**
PORCINE *adj* of or like a pig
PORCINO, PORCINI *n* edible woodland fungus
PORE, -D, -S, PORING *n, vb*
PORER, -S *n* person who pores
PORES ▸ **pore**
PORGE, -D, -S, PORGING *vb* cleanse (slaughtered animal) ceremonially
PORGIE *same as* ▸ **porgy**
PORGIES ▸ **porgy**
PORGING ▸ **porge**
PORGY, PORGIES *n* any of various sparid fishes
PORIER ▸ **pory**
PORIEST ▸ **pory**
PORIFER *n* type of invertebrate
PORIN, -S *n* protein through which molecules can pass
PORINA, -S *n* moth the larva of which causes damage to grassland
PORING ▸ **pore**
PORINS ▸ **porin**
PORISM, -S *n* type of mathematical proposition
PORK, -ED, -ING, -S *vb, n*
PORKER, -S *n* pig raised for food
PORKIER ▸ **porky**
PORKIES ▸ **porky**
PORKING ▸ **pork**
PORKPIE *n*
PORKS ▸ **pork**
PORKY, PORKIER, PORKIES *adj, n*
PORLOCK *vb* interrupt or intrude at an awkward moment
POROSE *adj* pierced with small pores
POROSIS, POROSES *n* porous condition of bones
POROUS *adj*
PORPESS *n* type of fish
PORRECT *adj* extended forwards ▹ *vb* stretch forward
PORRIGO *n* disease of the scalp
PORT, -ED, -ING, -S *vb* turn (a boat) towards its left side
PORTA, -S *n* aperture in an organ
PORTAGE *n* (route for) transporting boats overland ▹ *vb* transport (boats) in this way
PORTAL, -S *n*
PORTAS ▸ **porta**
PORTATE *adj* diagonally athwart escutcheon
PORTED ▸ **port**
PORTEND *vb*
PORTENT *n*
PORTER, -S *n, vb*
PORTESS *variant of* > **portesse**
PORTHOS *same as* > **portesse**
PORTICO *n*
PORTIER ▸ **porty**
PORTING ▸ **port**
PORTION *n, vb*
PORTLY *adj*
PORTMAN, PORTMEN *n* inhabitant of a port
PORTOUS *variant of* > **portesse**
PORTRAY *vb*
PORTS ▸ **port**
PORTY, PORTIER *adj* like port
PORY, PORIER, PORIEST *adj* containing pores
POS ▸ **po**
POSABLE ▸ **pose**
POSADA, -S *n* inn in a Spanish-speaking country
POSAUNE *n* organ chorus reed
POSE, -D, -S *vb, n*
POSER, -S *n*
POSES ▸ **pose**
POSEUR, -S *n* person who behaves in an affected way
POSEUSE *n* female poseur
POSEY *adj*
POSH, -ED, -ER, -ES, -EST, -ING *adj, adv, vb*
POSHLY ▸ **posh**
POSHO, -S *n* corn meal

POSIER ▶ **posy**
POSIES ▶ **posy**
POSIEST ▶ **posy**
POSING, -S ▶ **pose**
POSIT, -ED, -S *vb* lay down as a basis for argument ▷ *n* fact, idea, etc, that is posited
POSITIF *n* (on older organs) manual controlling soft stops
POSITON *n* part of chromosome
POSITS ▶ **posit**
POSNET, -S *n* small basin or dish
POSOLE, -S *n* Central American stew
POSS, -ED, -ING *vb* wash (clothes) by agitating them with a long rod, pole, etc
POSSE, -S *n* group of people organized to maintain law and order
POSSED ▶ **poss**
POSSER, -S *n* short stick used for stirring clothes in a washtub
POSSES ▶ **posse**
POSSESS *vb* have as one's property
POSSET, -S *n* drink of hot milk curdled with ale, beer, etc, flavoured with spices ▷ *vb* treat with a posset
POSSIE, -S *n* place
POSSING ▶ **poss**
POSSUM, -S *vb*
POST, -ED, -S *n, vb*
POSTAGE *n*
POSTAL, -S *adj, n*
POSTBAG *n*
POSTBOX *n*
POSTBOY *n* man or boy who brings the post round to offices
POSTBUS *n* vehicle carrying the mail that also carries passengers
POSTDOC *n* postdoctoral degree
POSTED ▶ **post**
POSTEEN *n* Afghan leather jacket
POSTER, -S *n, vb*
POSTERN *n, adj*
POSTERS ▶ **poster**
POSTFIX *vb* add or append at the end of something
POSTIE, -S *n*
POSTIL, -S *n* commentary or marginal note, as in a Bible ▷ *vb* annotate (a biblical passage)
POSTIN, -S *variant of* ▶ **posteen**
POSTING *n*
POSTINS ▶ **postin**
POSTMAN, POSTMEN *n*
POSTOP, -S *n* person recovering from surgery
POSTS ▶ **post**
POSTTAX *adj* of the period after tax is paid
POSTURE *n, vb*
POSTWAR *adj*
POSY, POSIER, POSIES, POSIEST *n* small bunch of flowers
POT, -S, -TED, -TING *n, vb*
POTABLE *adj, n*
POTAE, -S *n* hat
POTAGE, -S *n*
POTAGER *n* small kitchen garden
POTAGES ▶ **potage**
POTALE, -S *n* residue from a grain distillery, used as animal feed
POTAMIC *adj* of or relating to rivers
POTASH *n, vb*
POTASS *abbreviated form of* ▶ **potassium**
POTASSA *n* potassium oxide
POTATO *n*
POTBOIL *vb* boil in a pot
POTBOY, -S *n* (esp formerly) youth or man employed at a public house to serve beer, etc
POTCH, -ES *n* inferior quality opal used in jewellery for mounting precious opals
POTCHE, -D *vb* stab
POTCHER ▶ **potche**
POTCHES ▶ **potch**
POTE, -D, -S, POTING *vb* push
POTEEN, -S *n* (in Ireland) illegally made alcoholic drink
POTENCE *same as* ▶ **potency**
POTENCY *n*
POTENT, -S *adj, n*
POTES ▶ **pote**
POTFUL, -S *n* amount held by a pot
POTGUN, -S *n* pot-shaped mortar
POTHEEN *rare variant of* ▶ **poteen**
POTHER, -S *n* fuss or commotion ▷ *vb* make or be troubled or upset
POTHERB *n* plant whose leaves, flowers, or stems are used in cooking

POTHERS ▶ **pother**
POTHERY *adj* stuffy
POTHOLE *n*
POTHOOK *n* S-shaped hook for suspending a pot over a fire
POTHOS *n* climbing plant
POTICHE *n* tall vase or jar that narrows towards the neck
POTIN, -S *n* bronze alloy with high tin content
POTING ▶ **pote**
POTINS ▶ **potin**
POTION, -S *n*
POTJIE, -S *n* three-legged iron pot used for cooking
POTLACH *same as* > **potlatch**
POTLIKE ▶ **pot**
POTLINE *n* row of electrolytic cells for reducing metals
POTLUCK *n*
POTMAN, POTMEN *same as* ▶ **potboy**
POTOO, -S *n* nocturnal tropical bird
POTOROO *n* Australian leaping rodent
POTPIE, -S *n* meat and vegetable stew with a pie crust on top
POTS ▶ **pot**
POTSHOP *n* public house
POTSHOT *n*
POTSIE *same as* ▶ **potsy**
POTSY, POTSIES *n* hopscotch
POTT, -S *old variant of* ▶ **pot**
POTTAGE *n*
POTTED ▶ **pot**
POTTEEN *same as* ▶ **poteen**
POTTER, -S *same as* ▶ **putter**
POTTERY *n*
POTTIER ▶ **potty**
POTTIES ▶ **potty**
POTTING ▶ **pot**
POTTLE, -S *n* liquid measure equal to half a gallon
POTTO, -S *n* short-tailed prosimian primate
POTTS ▶ **pott**
POTTY, POTTIER, POTTIES *adj, n*
POTZER, -S *same as* ▶ **patzer**
POUCH, -ED, -ES *n, vb*
POUCHY ▶ **pouch**
POUDER, -S *obsolete spelling of* ▶ **powder**
POUDRE, -S *old spelling of* ▶ **powder**
POUF, -ED, -ING, -S *n* large solid cushion used as a seat ▷ *vb* pile up hair into rolled puffs
POUFF, -S *same as* ▶ **pouf**
POUFFE, -D, -S *same as* ▶ **pouf**
POUFFS ▶ **pouff**
POUFFY *adj* (of hair) puffed out
POUFING ▶ **pouf**
POUFS ▶ **pouf**
POUK, -ING, -S *Scots variant of* ▶ **poke**
POUKE, -S *n* mischievous spirit
POUKING ▶ **pouk**
POUKIT ▶ **pouk**
POUKS ▶ **pouk**
POULARD *n* hen that has been spayed for fattening
POULDER *obsolete spelling of* ▶ **powder**
POULDRE *archaic spelling of* ▶ **powder**
POULE, -S *n* fowl suitable for slow stewing
POULP, -S *n* octopus
POULPE, -S *variant of* ▶ **poulp**
POULPS ▶ **poulp**
POULT, -S *n* young of a gallinaceous bird
POULTER *n* poultry dealer
POULTRY *n*
POULTS ▶ **poult**
POUNCE, -D, -S *vb, n*
POUNCER ▶ **pounce**
POUNCES ▶ **pounce**
POUNCET *n* box with a perforated top used for perfume
POUND, -ED, -S *n, vb*
POUNDAL *n* fps unit of force
POUNDED ▶ **pound**
POUNDER ▶ **pound**
POUNDS ▶ **pound**
POUPE, -D, -S, POUPING, POUPT *vb* make sudden blowing sound
POUR, -ED, -S *vb*
POURER, -S ▶ **pour**
POURIE, -S *n* jug
POURING ▶ **pour**
POURS ▶ **pour**
POURSEW *obsolete spelling of* ▶ **pursue**
POURSUE *obsolete spelling of* ▶ **pursue**
POUSADA *n* traditional Portuguese hotel
POUSSE, -S *same as* ▶ **pease**

POUSSIE *old variant of* ▶ **pussy**
POUSSIN *n* young chicken reared for eating
POUT, -ED, -S *vb, n*
POUTER, -S *n* pigeon that can puff out its crop
POUTFUL *adj* tending to pout
POUTHER *Scots variant of* ▶ **powder**
POUTIER ▶ **pouty**
POUTINE *n* dish of chipped potatoes topped with cheese and sauce
POUTING ▶ **pout**
POUTS ▶ **pout**
POUTY, POUTIER ▶ **pout**
POVERTY *n*
POW, -S *interj* exclamation to indicate that a collision or explosion has taken place ▷ *n* head or a head of hair
POWAN, -S *n* type of freshwater whitefish occurring in some Scottish lakes
POWDER, -S *n, vb*
POWDERY ▶ **powder**
POWER, -ED, -S *n, vb*
POWHIRI *n* Māori ceremony of welcome, esp to a marae
POWIN, -S *n* peacock
POWN, -S *variant of* ▶ **powin**
POWND, -ED, -S *obsolete spelling of* ▶ **pound**
POWNEY, -S *old Scots spelling of* ▶ **pony**
POWNIE, -S *old Scots spelling of* ▶ **pony**
POWNS ▶ **pown**
POWNY *old Scots spelling of* ▶ **pony**
POWRE, -D, -S, POWRING *obsolete spelling of* ▶ **power**
POWS ▶ **pow**
POWTER, -S *vb* scrabble about
POWWAW *interj* expression of disbelief or contempt
POWWOW, -S *n* talk or conference ▷ *vb* hold a powwow
POX, -ED, -ES, -ING *n, vb*
POXIER ▶ **poxy**
POXIEST ▶ **poxy**
POXING ▶ **pox**
POXY, POXIER, POXIEST *adj*
POYNANT *old variant of* > **poignant**
POYNT, -ED, -S *obsolete spelling of* ▶ **point**
POYOU, -S *n* type of armadillo
POYSE, -D, -S, POYSING *obsolete variant of* ▶ **poise**
POYSON, -S *obsolete spelling of* ▶ **poison**
POZ *adj* positive

Poz is an old-fashioned short form of **positive**, and one of the most frequently played short Z words.

POZOLE, -S *same as* ▶ **posole**
POZZ *adj* positive
POZZY, POZZIES *same as* ▶ **possie**
PRAAM, -S *same as* ▶ **pram**
PRABBLE *variant of* ▶ **brabble**
PRACTIC *adj* practical ▷ *n* practice ▷ *vb* put (a theory) into practice
PRAD, -S *n* horse
PRADHAN *n* (in India) chief or leader
PRADS ▶ **prad**
PRAESES *n* Roman governor
PRAETOR *n*
PRAHU, -S *same as* ▶ **proa**
PRAIRIE *n*
PRAISE, -D, -S *vb, n*
PRAISER ▶ **praise**
PRAISES ▶ **praise**
PRAJNA, -S *n* wisdom or understanding
PRALINE *n*
PRAM, -S *n*
PRANA, -S *n* cosmic energy believed to come from the sun
PRANCE, -D, -S *vb, n*
PRANCER ▶ **prance**
PRANCES ▶ **prance**
PRANCK, -S *obsolete variant of* ▶ **prank**
PRANCKE *obsolete variant of* ▶ **prank**
PRANCKS ▶ **pranck**
PRANG, -ED, -S *n* crash in a car or aircraft ▷ *vb* crash or damage (an aircraft or car)
PRANK, -ED, -S *n, vb*
PRANKLE *obsolete variant of* ▶ **prance**
PRANKS ▶ **prank**
PRANKY ▶ **prank**
PRAO, -S *same as* ▶ **proa**

PRASE, -S *n* light green translucent variety of chalcedony
PRAT, -S *n* stupid person
PRATE, -D, -S *vb* talk idly and at length ▷ *n* chatter
PRATER, -S ▶ **prate**
PRATES ▶ **prate**
PRATIE, -S *n* potato
PRATING ▶ **prate**
PRATS ▶ **prat**
PRATT, -ED, -S *n* buttocks ▷ *vb* hit on the buttocks
PRATTLE *vb*, *n*
PRATTS ▶ **pratt**
PRATY *obsolete variant of* ▶ **pretty**
PRAU, -S *same as* ▶ **proa**
PRAUNCE *obsolete variant of* ▶ **prance**
PRAUS ▶ **prau**
PRAVITY *n* moral degeneracy
PRAWLE, -S *n* Shakespearian spelling of 'brawl'
PRAWLIN *variant of* ▶ **praline**
PRAWN, -ED, -S *n*, *vb*
PRAWNER ▶ **prawn**
PRAWNS ▶ **prawn**
PRAXIS, PRAXES *n* practice as opposed to theory
PRAY, -ED, -S *vb*, *adv*, *interj*
PRAYER, -S *n*
PRAYING ▶ **pray**
PRAYS ▶ **pray**
PRE *prep*
PREACE, -D, -S *obsolete variant of* ▶ **press**
PREACH *vb*
PREACHY *adj*
PREACT, -S *vb* act beforehand
PREAGED *adj* treated to appear older
PREAMP, -S *n* electronic amplifier
PREANAL *adj* situated in front of anus
PREARM, -S *vb* arm beforehand
PREASE, -D, -S *vb* crowd or press
PREASSE *obsolete spelling of* ▶ **press**
PREAVER *vb* aver in advance
PREBADE ▶ **prebid**
PREBAKE *vb* bake before further cooking
PREBEND *n* allowance paid to a canon or member of the cathedral chapter
PREBID, PREBADE, -S *vb* bid beforehand
PREBILL *vb* issue an invoice before the service has been provided
PREBIND *vb* bind a book in a hard-wearing binding
PREBOIL *vb* boil beforehand
PREBOOK *vb* book well in advance
PREBOOM *adj* of the period before an economic boom
PREBORN *adj* unborn
PREBUY, -S *vb* buy in advance
PRECAST *adj* cast in a particular form before being used ▷ *vb* cast (concrete) in a particular form before use
PRECAVA *n* superior vena cava
PRECEDE *vb*
PRECENT *vb* issue a command or law
PRECEPT *n*
PRECES *pl n* prayers
PRECESS *vb* undergo or cause to undergo precession
PRECIP, -S *n* precipitation
PRECIPE *n* type of legal document
PRECIPS ▶ **precip**
PRECIS *n*, *vb*
PRECISE *adj*
PRECODE *vb* code beforehand
PRECOOK *vb* cook (food) beforehand
PRECOOL *vb* cool in advance
PRECOUP *adj* of the period before a coup
PRECURE *vb* cure in advance
PRECUT, -S *vb* cut in advance
PREDATE *vb*
PREDAWN *n*
PREDIAL *same as* > **praedial**
PREDICT *vb*
PREDIED ▶ **predy**
PREDIES ▶ **predy**
PREDIVE *adj* happening before a dive
PREDOOM *vb* pronounce (someone or something's) doom beforehand
PREDRY *vb* dry beforehand

PREDUSK *n* period before dusk
PREDY, PREDIED, PREDIES *vb* prepare for action
PREE, -D, -ING, -S *vb* try or taste
PREEDIT *vb* edit beforehand
PREEING ▸ **pree**
PREEMIE *n* premature infant
PREEMPT *vb*
PREEN, -ED, -S *vb, n*
PREENER ▸ **preen**
PREENS ▸ **preen**
PREES ▸ **pree**
PREEVE, -D, -S *old form of* ▸ **prove**
PREFAB, -S *n, vb*
PREFACE *n, vb*
PREFADE *vb* fade beforehand
PREFARD *vb* old form of preferred
PREFECT *n*
PREFER, -S *vb*
PREFILE *vb* file beforehand
PREFIRE *vb* fire beforehand
PREFIX *n, vb*
PREFORM *vb* form beforehand
PREFUND *vb* pay for in advance
PREGAME *vb*
PREGGO *adj* slang word for pregnant
PREGGY *informal word for* > **pregnant**
PREHAB, -S *n* any programme of training designed to prevent sports injury
PREHEAT *vb*
PREHEND *vb* take hold of
PREIF, -S *old form of* ▸ **proof**
PREIFE, -S *old form of* ▸ **proof**
PREIFS ▸ **preif**
PREJINK *variant of* ▸ **perjink**
PRELACY *n* office or status of a prelate
PRELATE *n*
PRELATY *n* prelacy
PRELAW *adj*
PRELECT *vb* lecture or discourse in public
PRELIFE *n* life lived before one's life on earth
PRELIM *n*
PRELIMS *pl n*
PRELOAD *vb* load beforehand
PRELUDE *n, vb*
PRELUDI > **preludio**
PREM, -S *n* informal word for a premature infant
PREMADE *adj*
PREMAKE *vb* make beforehand
PREMAN, PREMEN *n* hominid
PREMEAL *adj* of the period before a meal
PREMED, -S *n*
PREMEET *adj* happening before a meet
PREMEN ▸ **preman**
PREMIA ▸ **premium**
PREMIE, -S *same as* ▸ **preemie**
PREMIER *n, adj*
PREMIES ▸ **premie**
PREMISE *n, vb*
PREMISS *same as* ▸ **premise**
PREMIUM, PREMIA *n*
PREMIX, -T *vb* mix beforehand
PREMOLD *same as* > **premould**
PREMOLT *same as* > **premoult**
PREMOVE *vb* prompt to action
PREMS ▸ **prem**
PREMUNE *adj* having immunity to a disease as a result of latent infection
PREMY *variant of* ▸ **preemie**
PRENAME *n* forename
PRENEED *adj* arranged in advance of eventual requirements
PRENOON *adj* of the period before noon
PRENT, -ED, -S *Scots variant of* ▸ **print**
PRENUP, -S *n* prenuptial agreement
PRENZIE *adj* Shakespearian word supposed by some to mean 'princely'
PREON, -S *n* (in particle physics) hypothetical subcomponent of a quark
PREOP, -S *n* patient being prepared for surgery
PREORAL *adj* situated in front of mouth
PREP, -PED, -S *vb*
PREPACK *vb*
PREPAID ▸ **prepay**
PREPARE *vb*
PREPAVE *vb* pave beforehand

PREPAY, PREPAID, -S *vb*
PREPLAN *vb* plan beforehand
PREPONE *vb* bring forward to an earlier time
PREPOSE *vb* place before
PREPPED ▸ **prep**
PREPPIE *same as* ▸ **preppy**
PREPPY *adj, n*
PREPREG *n* material already impregnated with synthetic resin
PREPS ▸ **prep**
PREPUCE *n* foreskin
PREPUPA *n* insect in stage of life before pupa
PREQUEL *n*
PRERACE *adj* of the period before a race
PRERIOT *adj* of the period before a riot
PREROCK *adj* of the era before rock music
PRERUPT *adj* abrupt
PRESA, PRESE *n* musical sign or symbol to indicate the entry of a part
PRESAGE *vb* be a sign or warning of ▹ *n* omen
PRESALE *n* practice of arranging the sale of a product before it is available
PRESE ▸ **presa**
PRESELL, PRESOLD *vb* promote in advance of appearance
PRESENT *adj, n, vb*
PRESES *variant of* ▸ **praeses**
PRESET, -S *vb, adj, n*
PRESHIP *vb* ship in advance
PRESHOW *vb* show in advance
PRESIDE *vb* be in charge, esp of a meeting
PRESIFT *vb* sift beforehand
PRESOAK *vb* soak beforehand
PRESOLD ▸ **presell**
PRESONG *adj* of the period before a song is sung
PRESORT *vb* sort in advance
PRESS, -ED, -ES *vb, n*
PRESSER ▸ **press**
PRESSES ▸ **press**
PRESSIE *informal word for* ▸ **present**
PRESSOR *n* something that produces an increase in blood pressure
PRESSY *same as* ▸ **pressie**
PREST, -ED, -S *adj* prepared for action or use ▹ *n* loan of money ▹ *vb* give as a loan
PRESTER ▸ **prest**
PRESTO, -S *adv, n*
PRESTS ▸ **prest**
PRESUME *vb*
PRETAPE *vb* (formerly) tape in advance
PRETAX *adj*
PRETEEN *n*
PRETELL, PRETOLD *vb* predict
PRETEND *vb, adj*
PRETERM *n* premature baby
PRETEST *vb* test (something) before presenting it ▹ *n* act or instance of pretesting
PRETEXT *n, vb*
PRETOLD ▸ **pretell**
PRETOR, -S *same as* ▸ **praetor**
PRETRIM *vb* trim in advance
PRETTY *adj, adv, vb*
PRETYPE *vb* type in advance
PRETZEL *n, vb*
PREVAIL *vb*
PREVE, -D, -S, PREVING *vb* prove
PREVENE *vb* come before
PREVENT *vb*
PREVERB *n* particle preceding root of verb
PREVES ▸ **preve**
PREVIEW *n, vb*
PREVING ▸ **preve**
PREVISE *vb* predict or foresee
PREVUE, -D, -S *same as* ▸ **preview**
PREWAR *adj*
PREWARM *vb* warm beforehand
PREWARN *vb* warn in advance
PREWASH *vb, n*
PREWIRE *vb* wire beforehand
PREWORK *vb* work in advance
PREWORN *adj*
PREWRAP *vb* wrap in advance
PREWYN, -S *obsolete spelling of* ▸ **prune**
PREX, -ES *same as* ▸ **prexy**

PREXIE *same as* ▸ **prexy**
PREXY, PREXIES *n* US college president
PREY, -ED, -ING, -S *n, vb*
PREYER, -S ▸ **prey**
PREYFUL *adj* rich in prey
PREYING ▸ **prey**
PREYS ▸ **prey**
PREZ, -ES *n* president
PREZZIE *same as* ▸ **pressie**
PRIAL, -S *n* pair royal of cards
PRIAPI ▸ **priapus**
PRIAPIC *adj*
PRIAPUS, PRIAPI *n* representation of the penis
PRIBBLE *variant of* ▸ **prabble**
PRICE, -D, -S *n, vb*
PRICER, -S ▸ **price**
PRICES ▸ **price**
PRICEY *adj*
PRICIER ▸ **pricy**
PRICILY ▸ **pricey**
PRICING ▸ **price**
PRICK, -ED, -S *vb, n*
PRICKER *n* person or thing that pricks
PRICKET *n* male deer in the second year of life
PRICKLE *n, vb*
PRICKLY *adj*
PRICKS ▸ **prick**
PRICKY *adj*
PRICY, PRICIER *same as* ▸ **pricey**
PRIDE, -D, -S, PRIDING *n*
PRIDIAN *adj* relating to yesterday
PRIDING ▸ **pride**
PRIED ▸ **pry**
PRIEF, -S *obsolete variant of* ▸ **proof**
PRIEFE, -S *obsolete variant of* ▸ **proof**
PRIEFS ▸ **prief**
PRIER, -S *n* person who pries
PRIES ▸ **pry**
PRIEST, -S *n, vb*
PRIEVE, -D, -S *obsolete variant of* ▸ **proof**
PRIG, -GED, -S *n*
PRIGGER *n* thief
PRIGS ▸ **prig**
PRILL, -ED, -S *vb* convert (a material) into a granular free-flowing form ▹ *n* prilled material
PRIM, -MED, -S *adj, vb*
PRIMA, -S *same as* ▸ **primo**
PRIMACY *n*
PRIMAGE *n* tax added to customs duty
PRIMAL *adj*
PRIMARY *adj, n*
PRIMAS ▸ **prima**
PRIMATE *n*
PRIME, -D, -S *adj, n, vb*
PRIMELY ▸ **prime**
PRIMER, -S *n*
PRIMERO *n* 16th- and 17th-century card game
PRIMERS ▸ **primer**
PRIMES ▸ **prime**
PRIMEUR *n* anything (esp fruit) produced early
PRIMI ▸ **primo**
PRIMINE *n* integument surrounding an ovule or the outer of two such integuments
PRIMING *same as* ▸ **primer**
PRIMLY ▸ **prim**
PRIMMED ▸ **prim**
PRIMMER *n* elementary textbook
PRIMO, PRIMI, -S *n* upper or right-hand part in a piano duet
PRIMP, -ED, -S *vb* tidy (one's hair or clothes) fussily
PRIMS ▸ **prim**
PRIMSIE *Scots variant of* ▸ **prim**
PRIMULA *n* type of primrose with brightly coloured flowers
PRIMUS *n* presiding bishop in the Synod
PRIMY *adj* prime
PRINCE, -D, -S *n, vb*
PRINCOX *n* pert youth
PRINK, -ED, -S *vb* dress (oneself) finely
PRINKER ▸ **prink**
PRINKS ▸ **prink**
PRINT, -ED, -S *vb, n*
PRINTER *n*
PRINTS ▸ **print**
PRION, -S *n* dovelike petrel with a serrated bill
PRIOR, -S *adj, n*
PRIORLY ▸ **prior**
PRIORS ▸ **prior**
PRIORY *n*
PRISAGE *n* customs duty levied until 1809 upon wine imported into England
PRISE, -D, -S, PRISING *same as* ▸ **pry**
PRISER, -S ▸ **prise**
PRISERE *n* primary sere or succession from bare ground to the community climax
PRISERS ▸ **priser**
PRISES ▸ **prise**

PRISING ▸ **prise**
PRISM, -S *n*
PRISMY ▸ **prism**
PRISON, -S *n, vb*
PRISS, -ED, -ES *n, vb*
PRISSY *adj, n*
PRITHEE *interj* pray thee
PRIVACY *n*
PRIVADO *n* close friend
PRIVATE *adj, n*
PRIVET, -S *n*
PRIVIER ▸ **privy**
PRIVIES ▸ **privy**
PRIVILY *adv* in a secret way
PRIVITY *n* legally recognized relationship between two parties
PRIVY, PRIVIER, PRIVIES *adj, n*
PRIZE, -D, -S, PRIZING *n, adj, vb*
PRIZER, -S *n* contender for prize
PRIZES ▸ **prize**
PRIZING ▸ **prize**
PRO, -S *prep, n, adv*
PROA, -S *n* canoe-like boat used in the South Pacific
PROB, -S *n* problem
PROBALL *adj* believable
PROBAND *n* first patient to be investigated in a family study
PROBANG *n* long flexible rod used to apply medication
PROBATE *n, vb*
PROBE, -D, -S *vb, n*
PROBER, -S ▸ **probe**
PROBES ▸ **probe**
PROBING *n*
PROBIT, -S *n* statistical measurement
PROBITY *n* honesty, integrity
PROBLEM *n, adj*
PROBS ▸ **prob**
PROCARP *n* female reproductive organ in red algae
PROCEED *vb*
PROCESS *n, vb*
PROCTAL *adj* relating to the rectum
PROCTOR *n* university worker who enforces discipline ▹ *vb* invigilate (an examination)
PROCURE *vb*
PROD, -DED, -S *vb, n*
PRODDER ▸ **prod**
PRODIGY *n*
PRODRUG *n* compound that is metabolized in the body to produce an active drug
PRODS ▸ **prod**
PRODUCE *vb, n*
PRODUCT *n*
PROEM, -S *n* introduction or preface
PROETTE *n* female golfing professional
PROF, -S *short for* > **professor**
PROFACE *interj* much good may it do you
PROFANE *adj, vb*
PROFESS *vb*
PROFFER *vb, n*
PROFILE *n, vb*
PROFIT, -S *n, vb*
PROFS ▸ **prof**
PROFUSE *adj*
PROG, -GED, -S *vb* prowl about for or as if for food or plunder ▹ *n* food obtained by begging
PROGENY *n*
PROGGED ▸ **prog**
PROGGER *n* fan of progressive rock
PROGRAM *n* sequence of coded instructions for a computer ▹ *vb* write a computer program
PROGS ▸ **prog**
PROGUN *adj* in favour of public owning firearms
PROIGN, -S *same as* ▸ **proin**
PROIN, -ED, -S *vb* trim or prune
PROINE, -S *same as* ▸ **proin**
PROINED ▸ **proin**
PROINES ▸ **proine**
PROINS ▸ **proin**
PROJECT *n, vb*
PROJET, -S *n* draft of a proposed treaty
PROKE, -D, -S, PROKING *vb* thrust or poke
PROKER, -S ▸ **proke**
PROKES ▸ **proke**
PROKING ▸ **proke**
PROLAN, -S *n* constituent of human pregnancy urine
PROLATE *adj* having a polar diameter which is longer than the equatorial diameter ▹ *vb* pronounce or utter
PROLE, -D, -S, PROLING *old form of* ▸ **prowl**
PROLEG, -S *n* appendage on abdominal segment of a caterpillar
PROLER, -S *n* prowler

PROLES ▸ **prole**
PROLINE *n* nonessential amino acid that occurs in protein
PROLING ▸ **prole**
PROLIX *adj* (of speech or a piece of writing) overlong and boring
PROLL, -ED, -S *vb* prowl or search
PROLLER ▸ **proll**
PROLLS ▸ **proll**
PROLLY *adv* probably
PROLOG, -S *same as* > **prologue**
PROLONG *vb* make (something) last longer
PROM, -S *n*
PROMINE *n* substance promoting cell growth
PROMISE *vb, n*
PROMMER *n* spectator at promenade concert
PROMO, -ED, -S *vb*
PROMOTE *vb*
PROMPT, -S *vb, adj, adv, n*
PROMS ▸ **prom**
PRONAOS, PRONAOI *n* inner area of the portico of a classical temple
PRONATE *vb* turn (a limb, hand, or foot) so that the palm or sole is directed downwards
PRONE, -R, -S, -ST *n, adj*
PRONELY ▸ **prone**
PRONER ▸ **prone**
PRONES ▸ **prone**
PRONEST ▸ **prone**
PRONEUR *n* flatterer
PRONG, -ED, -S *n, vb*
PRONK, -ED, -S *vb* jump straight up
PRONOTA > **pronotum**
PRONOUN *n*
PRONTO *adv*
PROO *interj* (to a horse) stop!
PROOF, -ED, -S *n, adj, vb*
PROOFER *n* reader of proofs
PROOFS ▸ **proof**
PROOTIC *n* bone in front of ear
PROP, -PED, -S *vb, n*
PROPAGE *vb* propagate
PROPALE *vb* publish (something)
PROPANE *n*
PROPEL, -S *vb*
PROPEND *vb* be inclined or disposed
PROPENE *n* colourless gaseous alkene obtained by cracking petroleum
PROPER, -S *adj, n*
PROPHET *n*
PROPINE *vb* drink a toast to
PROPJET *another name for* > **turboprop**
PROPMAN, PROPMEN *n* member of the stage crew in charge of the stage props
PROPONE *vb* propose or put forward, esp before a court
PROPOSE *vb*
PROPPED ▸ **prop**
PROPRIA > **proprium**
PROPS ▸ **prop**
PROPYL, -S *n* type of monovalent radical
PROPYLA > **propylon**
PROPYLS ▸ **propyl**
PROPYNE *n* type of gaseous methyl acetylene
PRORATE *vb* divide, assess, or distribute (something) proportionately
PRORE, -S *n* forward part of ship
PROS ▸ **pro**
PROSAIC *adj*
PROSE, -D, -S *n, vb*
PROSECT *vb* dissect a cadaver for a public demonstration
PROSED ▸ **prose**
PROSER, -S *n* writer of prose
PROSES ▸ **prose**
PROSIER ▸ **prosy**
PROSIFY *vb*
PROSILY ▸ **prosy**
PROSING ▸ **prose**
PROSIT *interj* good health! cheers!
PROSO, -S *n* millet
PROSODY *n*
PROSOMA *n* head and thorax of an arachnid
PROSOS ▸ **proso**
PROSPER *vb*
PROST *same as* ▸ **prosit**
PROSY, PROSIER *adj*
PROTEA, -S *n* African shrub with showy flowers
PROTEAN *adj, n*
PROTEAS ▸ **protea**
PROTECT *vb*
PROTEGE *n*
PROTEI ▸ **proteus**
PROTEID *n* protein
PROTEIN *n*
PROTEND *vb* hold out or stretch
PROTEST *n, vb*
PROTEUS, PROTEI *n* aerobic bacterium

PROTHYL *variant of* ▸ **protyle**
PROTIST *n* organism belonging to the protozoans, unicellular algae, and simple fungi
PROTIUM *n* most common isotope of hydrogen
PROTO *adj* as in **proto team** team of people trained to deal with underground rescues, etc
PROTON, -S *n*
PROTORE *n* primary mineral deposit
PROTYL, -S *same as* ▸ **protyle**
PROTYLE *n* hypothetical primitive substance
PROTYLS ▸ **protyl**
PROUD, -ER *adj*
PROUDLY ▸ **proud**
PROUL, -ED, -S *variant of* ▸ **prowl**
PROULER *Scots variant of* ▸ **prowler**
PROULS ▸ **proul**
PROVAND *n* food
PROVANT *adj* supplied with provisions ▹ *vb* supply with provisions
PROVE, -D, -N, -S *vb*
PROVEND *same as* ▸ **provand**
PROVER, -S ▸ **prove**
PROVERB *n, vb*
PROVERS ▸ **prover**
PROVES ▸ **prove**
PROVIDE *vb*
PROVINE *vb* plant branch of vine in ground for propagation
PROVING ▸ **prove**
PROVISO *n*
PROVOKE *vb*
PROVOST *n*
PROW, -ER, -EST, -S *n, adj*
PROWAR *adj* in favour of or supporting war
PROWER ▸ **prow**
PROWESS *n*
PROWEST ▸ **prow**
PROWL, -ED, -S *vb, n*
PROWLER ▸ **prowl**
PROWLS ▸ **prowl**
PROWS ▸ **prow**
PROXIES ▸ **proxy**
PROXIMO *adv* in or during the next or coming month
PROXY, PROXIES *n*
PROYN, -ED, -S *obsolete spelling of* ▸ **prune**
PROYNE, -S *obsolete spelling of* ▸ **prune**
PROYNED ▸ **proyn**
PROYNES ▸ **proyne**
PROYNS ▸ **proyn**
PRUDE, -S *n*
PRUDENT *adj*
PRUDERY ▸ **prude**
PRUDES ▸ **prude**
PRUDISH ▸ **prude**
PRUH *variant of* ▸ **proo**
PRUINA, -S *n* woolly white covering on some lichens
PRUINE, -S *obsolete spelling of* ▸ **prune**
PRUNE, -D, -S *n, vb*
PRUNER, -S ▸ **prune**
PRUNES ▸ **prune**
PRUNEY, PRUNIER *adj* resembling a prune
PRUNING ▸ **prune**
PRUNT, -S *n* glass ornamentation
PRUNTED ▸ **prunt**
PRUNTS ▸ **prunt**
PRUNUS *n* type of ornamental tree or shrub
PRURIGO *n* chronic inflammatory disease of the skin
PRUSIK, -S *n* sliding knot used in climbing ▹ *vb* climb (up a rope) using prusiks
PRUSSIC *adj* as in **prussic acid** weakly acidic extremely poisonous aqueous solution of hydrogen cyanide
PRUTA *same as* ▸ **prutah**
PRUTAH, PRUTOT, PRUTOTH *n* former Israeli coin
PRY, PRIED, PRIES *vb, n*
PRYER, -S *same as* ▸ **prier**
PRYING, -S ▸ **pry**
PRYS *old variant of* ▸ **price**
PRYSE, -D, -S, PRYSING *old variant of* ▸ **price**
PRYTHEE *same as* ▸ **prithee**
PSALM, -ED, -S *n, vb*
PSALMIC ▸ **psalm**
PSALMS ▸ **psalm**
PSALTER *n*
PSALTRY *same as* > **psaltery**
PSAMMON *n* microscopic life forms living between grains of sand
PSCHENT *n* ancient Egyptian crown
PSEUD, -S *n* pretentious person

PSEUDO, -S *n*
PSEUDS ▶ **pseud**
PSHAW, -ED, -S *n* exclamation of disgust, impatience, disbelief, etc ▷ *vb* make this exclamation
PSI, -S *n* 23rd letter of the Greek alphabet
PSION, -S *n* type of elementary particle
PSIONIC > **psionics**
PSIONS ▶ **psion**
PSIS ▶ **psi**
PSOAS, PSOAE, PSOAI, -ES *n* either of two muscles of the loins that aid in flexing and rotating the thigh
PSOATIC ▶ **psoas**
PSOCID, -S *n* tiny wingless insect
PSORA, -S *n* itching skin complaint
PSORIC ▶ **psora**
PSST *interj* sound made to attract someone's attention
PST *interj* sound made to attract someone's attention

You would need to be fairly desperate to use good letters to play this exclamation, but sometimes with no vowels on your rack things can be that desperate.

PSYCH, -ED, -ES, -S *vb*
PSYCHE *same as* ▶ **psych**
PSYCHED ▶ **psych**
PSYCHES ▶ **psych**
PSYCHIC *adj, n*
PSYCHS ▶ **psych**
PSYLLA, -S *same as* ▶ **psyllid**
PSYLLID *n* type of insect of the family which comprises the jumping plant lice
PSYOP, -S *n* psychological operation
PSYWAR, -S *n* psychological warfare
PTARMIC *n* material that causes sneezing
PTERIA ▶ **pterion**
PTERIN, -S *n* compound such as folic acid
PTERION, PTERIA *n* point on the side of the skull where a number of bones meet
PTEROIC *adj* as in **pteroic acid** a kind of acid found in spinach
PTERYLA *n* any of the tracts of skin that bear contour feathers
PTISAN, -S *n* grape juice drained off without pressure
PTOMAIN *same as* > **ptomaine**
PTOOEY *interj* imitation of the sound of spitting
PTOSIS, PTOSES *n* prolapse or drooping of a part, esp the eyelid
PTOTIC ▶ **ptosis**
PTUI *same as* ▶ **ptooey**
PTYALIN *n* amylase secreted in the saliva of human beings and other animals
PTYXIS, PTYXES *n* folding of a leaf in a bud
PUB, -BED, -BING, -S *n, vb*
PUBCO, -S *n* company operating a chain of pubs
PUBERAL *adj* relating to puberty
PUBERTY *n*
PUBIC *adj*
PUBIS, -ES *n*
PUBLIC, -S *adj, n*
PUBLISH *vb*
PUBS ▶ **pub**
PUCAN, -S *n* traditional Connemara open sailing boat
PUCCOON *n* N American plant that yields a red dye
PUCE, -R, -S, -ST *adj, n*
PUCELLE *n* maid or girl
PUCER ▶ **puce**
PUCES ▶ **puce**
PUCEST ▶ **puce**
PUCK, -ED, -ING, -S *n* mischievous or evil spirit ▷ *vb* strike (the ball) in hurling
PUCKA *same as* ▶ **pukka**
PUCKED ▶ **puck**
PUCKER, -S *vb, n*
PUCKERY *adj* tending to pucker ▷ *n* puckishness
PUCKING ▶ **puck**
PUCKISH ▶ **puck**
PUCKLE, -S *n* early type of machine gun
PUCKOUT *n* (in hurling) free hit made by the goalkeeper
PUCKS ▶ **puck**
PUD, -S *short for* ▶ **pudding**
PUDDEN, -S *dialect spelling of* ▶ **pudding**
PUDDER, -S *vb* make bother or fuss

PUDDIER ▶ **puddy**
PUDDIES ▶ **puddy**
PUDDING *n*
PUDDLE, -D, -S *n, vb*
PUDDLER ▶ **puddle**
PUDDLES ▶ **puddle**
PUDDLY ▶ **puddle**
PUDDOCK *same as* ▶ **paddock**
PUDDY, PUDDIER, PUDDIES *n* paw ▷ *adj* short and podgy
PUDENCY *n* modesty, shame, or prudishness
PUDENDA > **pudendum**
PUDENT *adj* lacking in ostentation; humble
PUDEUR, -S *n* sense of shame or embarrassment
PUDGE, -S *same as* ▶ **podge**
PUDGIER ▶ **pudgy**
PUDGILY ▶ **pudgy**
PUDGY, PUDGIER *adj*
PUDIC *adj* relating to the pudenda
PUDOR, -S *n* sense of shame
PUDS ▶ **pud**
PUDSEY *variant of* ▶ **pudsy**
PUDSY, PUDSIER, PUDSIES *adj* plump ▷ *n* plump person
PUDU, -S *n* diminutive Andean antelope
PUEBLO, -S *n* communal village of flat-roofed houses
PUER, -ED, -ING, -S *vb* steep hides in an alkaline substance from the dung of dogs
PUERILE *adj*
PUERING ▶ **puer**
PUERS ▶ **puer**
PUFF, -ED, -S *n, vb*
PUFFA *adj* type of quilted and padded jacket
PUFFED ▶ **puff**
PUFFER, -S *n* person or thing that puffs
PUFFERY *n* exaggerated praise, esp in publicity or advertising
PUFFIER ▶ **puffy**
PUFFILY ▶ **puffy**
PUFFIN, -S *n*
PUFFING ▶ **puff**
PUFFINS ▶ **puffin**
PUFFS ▶ **puff**
PUFFY, PUFFIER *adj*
PUG, -GED, -S *n, vb*
PUGAREE *same as* ▶ **puggree**
PUGGED ▶ **pug**
PUGGERY *same as* ▶ **puggree**
PUGGIE, -S *n* Scottish word for fruit machine
PUGGIER ▶ **puggy**
PUGGIES ▶ **puggie**
PUGGING ▶ **pug**
PUGGISH ▶ **pug**
PUGGLE, -D, -S *vb* stir up by poking
PUGGREE *n* scarf, usually pleated, around the crown of some hats, esp sun helmets
PUGGRY *same as* ▶ **puggree**
PUGGY, PUGGIER *adj* sticky, claylike ▷ *n* term of endearment
PUGH *interj* exclamation of disgust
PUGIL, -S *n* pinch or small handful
PUGMARK *n* trail of an animal
PUGREE, -S *same as* ▶ **puggree**
PUGS ▶ **pug**
PUH *interj* exclamation expressing contempt or disgust
PUHA, -S *n* sow thistle
PUIR, -ER, -EST *Scottish word for* ▶ **poor**
PUISNE, -S *adj* (esp of a subordinate judge) of lower rank ▷ *n* judge of lower rank
PUISNY *adj* younger or inferior
PUJA, -S *n* ritual in honour of the gods, performed either at home or in the mandir (temple)
PUJAH, -S *same as* ▶ **puja**
PUJARI, -S *n* Hindu priest
PUJAS ▶ **puja**
PUKA, -S *in New Zealand English, same as* > **broadleaf**
PUKATEA *n* aromatic New Zealand tree
PUKE, -D, -S, PUKING *vb, n*
PUKEKO, -S *n* brightly coloured New Zealand wading bird
PUKER, -S *n* person who vomits
PUKES ▶ **puke**
PUKEY, PUKIER, PUKIEST *adj* of or like vomit
PUKING ▶ **puke**
PUKKA *adj* properly done, constructed, etc

PUKKAH *adj* genuine
PUKU, -S *n* belly or stomach
PUKY *same as* ▸ **pukey**
PUL, -IK, -S *n* Afghan monetary unit
PULA, -S *n* standard monetary unit of Botswana
PULAO, -S *same as* ▸ **pilau**
PULAS ▸ **pula**
PULDRON *same as* > **pauldron**
PULE, -D, -S *vb* whine or whimper
PULER, -S ▸ **pule**
PULES ▸ **pule**
PULI, -S *n* Hungarian sheepdog
PULIER ▸ **puly**
PULIEST ▸ **puly**
PULIK ▸ **pul**
PULING, -S ▸ **pule**
PULIS ▸ **puli**
PULK, -S *same as* ▸ **pulka**
PULKA, -S *n* reindeer-drawn sleigh
PULKHA, -S *same as* ▸ **pulka**
PULKS ▸ **pulk**
PULL, -ED, -ING, -S *vb, n*
PULLER, -S ▸ **pull**
PULLET, -S *n* young hen
PULLEY, -S *n, vb*
PULLI ▸ **pullus**
PULLIES ▸ **pully**
PULLING ▸ **pull**
PULLMAN *n*
PULLOUT *n* removable section of a magazine, etc
PULLS ▸ **pull**
PULLUP, -S *n* exercise in which the body is raised by the arms pulling on a horizontal bar
PULLUS, PULLI *n* technical term for a chick or young bird
PULLY, PULLIES *n* pullover
PULMO *n* lung
PULP, -ED, -S *n, vb*
PULPAL ▸ **pulp**
PULPED ▸ **pulp**
PULPER, -S ▸ **pulp**
PULPIER ▸ **pulpy**
PULPIFY *vb* reduce to pulp
PULPILY ▸ **pulpy**
PULPING *n* act of pulping
PULPIT, -S *n*
PULPOUS *adj* soft and yielding
PULPS ▸ **pulp**
PULPY, PULPIER *adj* having a soft or soggy consistency
PULQUE, -S *n* light alcoholic drink from Mexico
PULS ▸ **pul**
PULSANT *adj* vibrant
PULSAR, -S *n*
PULSATE *vb*
PULSE, -D, -S, PULSING *n, vb*
PULSER, -S *n* thing that pulses
PULSES ▸ **pulse**
PULSING ▸ **pulse**
PULSION *n* act of driving forward
PULTAN, -S *n* native Indian regiment
PULTON, -S *same as* ▸ **pultan**
PULTOON *same as* ▸ **pultan**
PULTUN, -S *same as* ▸ **pultan**
PULTURE *n* food and drink claimed by foresters
PULU, -S *n* substance used for stuffing cushions
PULVER, -S *vb* make into powder
PULVIL, -S *vb* apply perfumed powder
PULVINI > **pulvinus**
PULWAR, -S *n* light Indian river boat
PULY, PULIER, PULIEST *adj* whiny
PUMA, -S *n*
PUMELO, -S *same as* ▸ **pomelo**
PUMICE, -D, -S *n, vb*
PUMICER ▸ **pumice**
PUMICES ▸ **pumice**
PUMIE, -S *n* small stone
PUMMEL, -S *vb* strike repeatedly with or as if with the fists
PUMMELO *same as* ▸ **pomelo**
PUMMELS ▸ **pummel**
PUMP, -ED, -ING, -S *n, vb*
PUMPER, -S ▸ **pump**
PUMPING ▸ **pump**
PUMPION *archaic word for* ▸ **pumpkin**
PUMPKIN *n*
PUMPS ▸ **pump**
PUMY *adj* large and round
PUN, -NED, -S *n, vb*
PUNA, -S *n* high cold dry plateau, esp in the Andes
PUNALUA *n* marriage between the sisters of one family to the brothers of another

PUNAS ▶ **puna**
PUNCE, -D, -S, PUNCING *n* kick ▷ *vb* kick
PUNCH, -ED, -ES *vb, n*
PUNCHER ▶ **punch**
PUNCHES ▶ **punch**
PUNCHY *adj*
PUNCING ▶ **punce**
PUNCTA ▶ **punctum**
PUNCTO, -S *n* tip of a fencing sword
PUNCTUM, PUNCTA *n* tip or small point
PUNDIT, -S *n*
PUNG, -S *n* horse-drawn sleigh with a boxlike body on runners
PUNGA, -S *variant spelling of* ▶ **ponga**
PUNGENT *adj* having a strong sharp bitter flavour
PUNGLE, -D, -S *vb* make payment
PUNGS ▶ **pung**
PUNIER ▶ **puny**
PUNIEST ▶ **puny**
PUNILY ▶ **puny**
PUNISH *vb*
PUNJI, -ED, -ES, -S *n* sharpened bamboo stick ▷ *vb* fortify with punjis
PUNK, -ER, -ERS, -EST, -S *n, adj*
PUNKA, -S *n* fan made of a palm leaf or leaves
PUNKAH, -S *same as* ▶ **punka**
PUNKAS ▶ **punka**
PUNKER ▶ **punk**
PUNKERS ▶ **punk**
PUNKEST ▶ **punk**
PUNKEY, -S *n* small winged insect
PUNKIE, -S *same as* ▶ **punkey**
PUNKIER ▶ **punky**
PUNKIES ▶ **punkie**
PUNKIN, -S *same as* ▶ **pumpkin**
PUNKISH ▶ **punk**
PUNKS ▶ **punk**
PUNKY, PUNKIER *adj*
PUNNED ▶ **pun**
PUNNER, -S ▶ **pun**
PUNNET, -S *n*
PUNNIER ▶ **punny**
PUNNING ▶ **pun**
PUNNY, PUNNIER *adj* of puns
PUNS ▶ **pun**
PUNSTER *n* person who is fond of making puns
PUNT, -ED, -ING, -S *n, vb*
PUNTEE, -S *same as* ▶ **punty**
PUNTER, -S *n*
PUNTIES ▶ **punty**
PUNTING ▶ **punt**
PUNTO, -S *n* hit in fencing
PUNTS ▶ **punt**
PUNTY, PUNTIES *n* long iron rod used in the finishing process of glass-blowing
PUNY, PUNIER, PUNIEST *adj*
PUP, -PED, -PING, -S *n, vb*
PUPA, -E, -S *n*
PUPAL ▶ **pupa**
PUPARIA > **puparium**
PUPAS ▶ **pupa**
PUPATE, -D, -S *vb* (of an insect larva) to develop into a pupa
PUPFISH *n* type of small fish
PUPIL, -S *n*
PUPILAR ▶ **pupil**
PUPILS ▶ **pupil**
PUPPED ▶ **pup**
PUPPET, -S *n*
PUPPIED ▶ **puppy**
PUPPIES ▶ **puppy**
PUPPING ▶ **pup**
PUPPY, PUPPIED, PUPPIES *n, vb*
PUPS ▶ **pup**
PUPU, -S *n* Hawaiian dish
PUPUNHA *n* fruit of a type of palm tree
PUPUS ▶ **pupu**
PUR, -S *same as* ▶ **purr**
PURANA, -S *n* type of Sanskrit sacred writing
PURANIC ▶ **purana**
PURDA, -S *same as* ▶ **purdah**
PURDAH, -S *n* Muslim and Hindu custom of keeping women in seclusion
PURDAS ▶ **purda**
PURE, -D, -R, -S, -ST, PURING *adj, vb*
PUREE, -D, -S *n* smooth thick pulp of cooked and sieved fruit, vegetables, meat, or fish ▷ *vb* make (cooked foods) into a puree
PURELY *adv*
PURER ▶ **pure**
PURES ▶ **pure**
PUREST ▶ **pure**
PURFLE, -D, -S *n* ruffled or curved ornamental band ▷ *vb* decorate with such a band or bands
PURFLER ▶ **purfle**
PURFLES ▶ **purfle**
PURFLY ▶ **purfle**

PURGE, -D, -S *vb, n*
PURGER, -S ▸ **purge**
PURGES ▸ **purge**
PURGING ▸ **purge**
PURI, -S *n* unleavened flaky Indian bread, that is deep-fried in ghee and served hot
PURIFY *vb*
PURIN, -S *same as* ▸ **purine**
PURINE, -S *n* colourless crystalline solid that can be prepared from uric acid
PURING ▸ **pure**
PURINS ▸ **purin**
PURIRI, -S *n* forest tree of New Zealand
PURIS ▸ **puri**
PURISM, -S *n* strict insistence on the correct usage or style
PURIST, -S ▸ **purism**
PURITAN *n, adj*
PURITY *n*
PURL, -ED, -S *n* stitch made by knitting a plain stitch backwards ▹ *vb* knit in purl
PURLER, -S *n* headlong or spectacular fall
PURLIEU *n* land on the edge of a royal forest
PURLIN, -S *n* horizontal beam that supports the rafters of a roof
PURLINE *same as* ▸ **purlin**
PURLING ▸ **purl**
PURLINS ▸ **purlin**
PURLOIN *vb*
PURLS ▸ **purl**
PURPIE, -S *old Scots word for* > **purslane**
PURPLE, -D, -R, -S *n, adj, vb*
PURPLY ▸ **purple**
PURPORT *vb, n*
PURPOSE *n*
PURPURA *n* blood disease causing purplish spots
PURPURE *n* purple
PURPY *variant of* ▸ **purpie**
PURR, -ED, -S *vb, n*
PURRING ▸ **purr**
PURRS ▸ **purr**
PURS ▸ **pur**
PURSE, -D, -S, PURSING *n, vb*
PURSER, -S *n* ship's officer who keeps the accounts
PURSES ▸ **purse**
PURSEW, -S *archaic spelling of* ▸ **pursue**
PURSIER ▸ **pursy**
PURSILY ▸ **pursy**
PURSING ▸ **purse**
PURSUAL *n* act of pursuit
PURSUE, -D, -S *vb*
PURSUER ▸ **pursue**
PURSUES ▸ **pursue**
PURSUIT *n*
PURSY, PURSIER *adj* short-winded
PURTY, PURTIER *adj* pretty
PURVEY, -S *vb* supply (provisions) ▹ *n* food and drink laid on at a wedding reception, etc
PURVIEW *n* scope or range of activity or outlook
PUS, -ES *n*
PUSH, -ES *vb, n*
PUSHED *adj* short of
PUSHER, -S *n* person who or thing that pushes
PUSHES ▸ **push**
PUSHFUL ▸ **push**
PUSHIER ▸ **pushy**
PUSHILY ▸ **pushy**
PUSHING *prep, adj, adv*
PUSHPIN *n* pin with a small ball-shaped head
PUSHPIT *n* safety rail at the stern of a boat
PUSHROD *n* metal rod transmitting motion in an engine
PUSHUP, -S *n* exercise in which the body is raised and lowered to the floor by the arms
PUSHY, PUSHIER *adj*
PUSLE, -D, -S, PUSLING *old spelling of* ▸ **puzzle**
PUSLEY, -S *same as* > **purslane**
PUSLIKE ▸ **pus**
PUSLING ▸ **pusle**
PUSS, -ES *same as* ▸ **pussy**
PUSSEL, -S *n* maid or girl
PUSSER, -S *n* naval purser
PUSSES ▸ **puss**
PUSSIER ▸ **pussy**
PUSSIES ▸ **pussy**
PUSSLEY *n* weedy trailing herb
PUSSLY *variant of* ▸ **pussley**
PUSSY, PUSSIER, PUSSIES *n, adj*
PUSTULE *n* pimple containing pus
PUT, -S *vb, n*
PUTAMEN *n* hard endocarp or stone of fruit

PUTCHER *n* trap for catching salmon
PUTCHUK *same as* ▸ **pachak**
PUTDOWN *n*
PUTEAL, -S *n* enclosure around a well
PUTELI, -S *n* (in India) type of boat
PUTID *adj* having an unpleasant odour
PUTLOCK *same as* ▸ **putlog**
PUTLOG, -S *n* short horizontal beam that with others supports the floor planks of a scaffold
PUTOFF, -S *n* pretext or delay
PUTOIS *n* brush to paint pottery
PUTON, -S *n* hoax or piece of mockery
PUTOUT, -S *n* baseball play in which the batter or runner is put out
PUTREFY *vb*
PUTRID *adj*
PUTS ▸ **put**
PUTSCH *n* sudden violent attempt to remove a government from power
PUTT, -ED, -S *n, vb*
PUTTEE, -S *n* strip of cloth worn wound around the leg
PUTTEN *old Scots past participle of* ▸ **put**
PUTTER, -S *n, vb*
PUTTI ▸ **putto**
PUTTIE *same as* ▸ **puttee**
PUTTIED ▸ **putty**
PUTTIER *n* glazier
PUTTIES ▸ **putty**
PUTTING ▸ **put**
PUTTO, PUTTI *n* representation of a small boy
PUTTOCK *n* type of bird of prey
PUTTS ▸ **putt**
PUTTY, PUTTIED, PUTTIES *n, vb*
PUTURE, -S *n* claim of foresters for food
PUTZ, -ED, -ES, -ING *n, vb*
PUY, -S *n* small volcanic cone
PUZEL, -S *same as* ▸ **pucelle**
PUZZEL, -S *same as* ▸ **pucelle**
PUZZLE, -D, -S *vb, n*
PUZZLER *n* person or thing that puzzles
PUZZLES ▸ **puzzle**
PWN, -ED, -ING, -S *vb* defeat (an opponent) in conclusive and humiliating fashion
PYA, -S *n* monetary unit of Myanmar worth one hundredth of a kyat
PYAEMIA *n* type of blood poisoning
PYAEMIC ▸ **pyaemia**
PYAS ▸ **pya**
PYAT, -S *n* magpie ▹ *adj* pied
PYCNIC *same as* ▸ **pyknic**
PYCNITE *n* variety of topaz
PYCNON, -S *old word for* > **semitone**
PYE, -ING, -S *same as* ▸ **pie**
PYEBALD *same as* ▸ **piebald**
PYEING ▸ **pye**
PYEMIA, -S *same as* ▸ **pyaemia**
PYEMIC ▸ **pyaemia**
PYES ▸ **pye**
PYET, -S *same as* ▸ **pyat**
PYGAL, -S *n* rear part
PYGARG, -S *n* type of horned mammal
PYGIDIA > **pygidium**
PYGMEAN ▸ **pygmy**
PYGMIES ▸ **pygmy**
PYGMOID *adj* of or like pygmies ▹ *n* pygmy
PYGMY, PYGMIES *n, adj*
PYIC *adj* relating to pus
PYIN, -S *n* constituent of pus
PYJAMA *same as* ▸ **pyjamas**
PYJAMAS *pl n*
PYKNIC, -S *adj* characterized by a broad squat fleshy physique ▹ *n* person with this physical type
PYLON, -S *n*
PYLORI ▸ **pylorus**
PYLORIC ▸ **pylorus**
PYLORUS, PYLORI *n* small circular opening at the base of the stomach
PYNE, -D, -S, PYNING *archaic variant of* ▸ **pine**
PYOID *adj* resembling pus
PYONER, -S *old variant of* ▸ **pioneer**
PYOSIS, PYOSES *n* formation of pus
PYOT, -S *same as* ▸ **pyat**

PYRAL ▶ **pyre**
PYRALID *n* tropical moth
PYRALIS *same as* ▶ **pyralid**
PYRAMID *n, vb*
PYRAMIS *n* pyramid-shaped structure
PYRAN, -S *n* unsaturated heterocyclic organic compound
PYRE, -S *n*
PYRENE, -S *n* solid polynuclear aromatic hydrocarbon extracted from coal tar
PYRES ▶ **pyre**
PYRETIC *adj* of, relating to, or characterized by fever
PYREX, -ES *n*
PYREXIA *technical name for* ▶ **fever**
PYREXIC ▶ **pyrexia**
PYRIC *adj* of or relating to burning
PYRIDIC > **pyridine**
PYRITE *n*
PYRITES *same as* ▶ **pyrite**
PYRITIC ▶ **pyrite**
PYRO, -S *n* pyromaniac
PYROGEN *n* any of a group of substances that cause a rise in temperature in an animal body
PYROGY *same as* ▶ **pierogi**
PYROHY *same as* ▶ **perogi**
PYROLA, -S *n* evergreen perennial
PYRONE, -S *n* type of heterocyclic compound
PYRONIN *n* red dye used as a biological stain
PYROPE, -S *n* deep yellowish-red garnet used as a gemstone
PYROPUS *variant of* ▶ **pyrope**
PYROS ▶ **pyro**
PYROSIS, PYROSES *technical name for* > **heartburn**
PYRRHIC *n, adj*
PYRROL, -S *same as* ▶ **pyrrole**
PYRROLE *n* colourless insoluble toxic liquid
PYRROLS ▶ **pyrrol**
PYRUVIC *adj* as in **pyruvic acid** colourless pleasant-smelling liquid
PYSANKA, PYSANKY *n* hand-painted Ukrainian Easter egg
PYTHIUM *n* type of fungi
PYTHON, -S *n*
PYURIA, -S *n* any condition characterized by the presence of pus in the urine
PYX, -ED, -ES, -ING *n* any receptacle for the Eucharistic Host ▷ *vb* put (something) in a pyx

This word can also be spelt **pix**. It's a great word to know as it can earn a good score from a rack that is short of vowels.

PYXIDES ▶ **pyxis**
PYXIDIA > **pyxidium**
PYXIE, -S *n* creeping evergreen shrub of the eastern US
PYXING ▶ **pyx**
PYXIS, PYXIDES *same as* > **pyxidium**
PZAZZ, -ES *same as* ▶ **pizzazz**

Qq

QABALA, -S *same as* **> kabbalah**
QABALAH *same as* **> kabbalah**
QABALAS ▶ qabala
QADI, -S *variant spelling of* **▶ cadi**
QAID, -S *n* chief

An Arabic word, this and its variant **qadi** are two of the most frequently played words in Scrabble. There are also alternative spellings **cadi, caid, kadi** and **kaid**.

QAJAQ, -S *n* kayak
QAMUTIK *n* sledge with wooden runners
QANAT, -S *n* underground irrigation channel

This word comes up many times as one of the words allowing you to play the Q without a U.

QAPIK, -S *n* monetary unit of Azerbaijan
QASIDA, -S *n* Arabic verse form
QAT, -S *variant spelling of* **▶ khat**

The leaves of this shrub are chewed as a stimulant, and it's certainly been a stimulus for Scrabble, being one of the three 3-letter words that can be played without a U: the others are **qin** and **qis**.

QAWWAL, -S *n* qawwali singer
QAWWALI *n* Islamic religious song, esp in Asia
QAWWALS ▶ qawwal
QI, -S *n* vital energy
QIBLA, -S *variant of* **▶ kiblah**

The direction in which Muslims turn to pray, a useful word allowing the Q to be played without the U. It can also be spelt **keblah, kibla** and **kiblah**.

QIGONG, -S *n* system of breathing and exercise
QIN, -S *n* Chinese stringed instrument related to the zither

This Chinese musical instrument is another indispensable word as, like **qat**, it combines Q with two of the most common letters in the game.

QINDAR, -S *n* Albanian monetary unit
QINS ▶ qin
QINTAR, -S *same as* **▶ qindar**
QIS ▶ qi
QIVIUT, -S *n* soft muskox wool
QOPH, -S *variant of* **▶ koph**

A letter of the Hebrew alphabet, also spelt **koph**. The Hebrew alphabet, like the Greek alphabet, is well worth studying from the Scrabble point of view, as it gives us many other useful short words like **ayin, beth, heth, kaph** and **lamedh**.

QORMA, -S *variant spelling of* **▶ korma**
QUA *prep* in the capacity of

This is the only three-letter word beginning with Q that needs a U. It is played so often that it is well worth mastering all the hooks to this: it takes A at the front to make **aqua** and D, G, I, T and Y at the back to make **quad, quag, quai, quat** and **quay**.

QUACK, -ED, -S *vb, n*
QUACKER ▸ **quack**
QUACKLE *same as* ▸ **quack**
QUACKS ▸ **quack**
QUACKY ▸ **quack**
QUAD, -S *n*
QUADDED *adj* formed of multiple quads
QUADRAT *n*
QUADRIC *adj* having or characterized by an equation of the second degree ▹ *n* quadric curve or surface
QUADS ▸ **quad**
QUAERE, -D, -S *n* query or question ▹ *interj* ask or inquire ▹ *vb* ask
QUAFF, -ED, -S *vb*
QUAFFER ▸ **quaff**
QUAFFS ▸ **quaff**
QUAG, -S *another word for* ▸ **quagmire**
QUAGGA, -S *n* recently extinct zebra
QUAGGY *adj* resembling a marsh or quagmire
QUAGS ▸ **quag**
QUAHAUG *same as* ▸ **quahog**
QUAHOG, -S *n* edible clam
QUAI, -S *same as* ▸ **quay**
QUAICH, -S *n* small shallow drinking cup
QUAIGH, -S *same as* ▸ **quaich**
QUAIL, -ED, -S *n, vb*
QUAINT *adj*
QUAIR, -S *n* book
QUAIS ▸ **quai**
QUAKE, -D, -S, QUAKING *vb, n*
QUAKER, -S ▸ **quake**
QUAKES ▸ **quake**
QUAKIER ▸ **quaky**
QUAKILY ▸ **quaky**
QUAKING ▸ **quake**
QUAKY, QUAKIER *adj* inclined to quake
QUALE, QUALIA *n* essential property or quality
QUALIFY *vb*
QUALITY *n, adj*
QUALM, -S *n*
QUALMY ▸ **qualm**
QUAMASH *another name for* ▸ **camass**
QUANGO, -S *n*
QUANNET *n* flat file with handle at one end
QUANT, -ED, -S *n* long pole for propelling a boat ▹ *vb* propel (a boat) with a quant
QUANTA ▸ **quantum**
QUANTAL *adj* of or relating to a quantum or an entity that is quantized
QUANTED ▸ **quant**
QUANTIC *n* mathematical function
QUANTS ▸ **quant**
QUANTUM, QUANTA *n, adj*
QUARE, -R, -ST *adj* remarkable or strange
QUARK, -S *n*

This subatomic particle appears in the Scrabble cloud-chamber fairly often, and when it does, remember that you can put an S on the front of it to make **squark**.

QUARREL *n, vb*
QUARRY *n, vb*
QUART, -S *n*
QUARTAN *adj* (esp of a malarial fever) occurring every third day ▹ *n* quartan malaria
QUARTE, -S *n* fourth of eight basic positions from which a parry or attack can be made in fencing
QUARTER *n, vb, adj*
QUARTES ▸ **quarte**
QUARTET *n*
QUARTIC *n* biquadratic equation
QUARTO, -S *n* book size in which the sheets are folded into four leaves
QUARTS ▸ **quart**
QUARTZ *n*
QUARTZY ▸ **quartz**
QUASAR, -S *n*
QUASH, -ED, -ES *vb*
QUASHER ▸ **quash**
QUASHES ▸ **quash**
QUASI *adv*
QUASS, -ES *variant of* ▸ **kvass**
QUASSIA *n* tropical American tree
QUASSIN *n* bitter crystalline substance

QUAT, -S, -TED *n* spot ▷ *vb* beat down or squash
QUATCH *vb* move
QUATE, -S *n* fortune
QUATRE, -S *n* playing card with four pips
QUATS ▶ **quat**
QUATTED ▶ **quat**
QUAVER, -S *vb, n*
QUAVERY ▶ **quaver**
QUAY, -S *n*
QUAYAGE *n* system of quays
QUAYD *archaic past participle of* ▶ **quail**

Meaning daunted, this Spenserian word makes a surprising hook for **quay**.

QUAYS ▶ **quay**
QUAZZY *adj* unwell
QUBIT, -S *n*
QUBYTE, -S *n* unit of eight qubits
QUEACH *n* thicket
QUEACHY *adj* unwell
QUEAN, -S *n*
QUEASY *adj*
QUEAZY *same as* ▶ **queasy**
QUEBEC, -S *n* code word for the letter Q
QUEECHY *same as* ▶ **queachy**
QUEEN, -ED, -S *n, vb*
QUEENIE *n* scallop
QUEENLY *adj, adv*
QUEENS ▶ **queen**
QUEENY *adj* resembling a queen
QUEER, -ED, -ER, -S *adj, vb*
QUEERLY ▶ **queer**
QUEERS ▶ **queer**
QUEEST, -S *n* wood pigeon
QUEINT *same as* ▶ **quaint**
QUELCH *same as* ▶ **squelch**
QUELEA, -S *n* East African weaver bird
QUELL, -ED, -S *vb*
QUELLER ▶ **quell**
QUELLS ▶ **quell**
QUEME, -D, -S, QUEMING *vb* please
QUENA, -S *n* Andean flute
QUENCH *vb*
QUEP *interj* expression of derision
QUERIDA *n* sweetheart
QUERIED ▶ **query**
QUERIER ▶ **query**
QUERIES ▶ **query**
QUERIST *n* person who makes inquiries or queries
QUERN, -S *n* stone hand mill for grinding corn
QUERY, QUERIED, QUERIES *n, vb*
QUEST, -ED, -S *n, vb*
QUESTER ▶ **quest**
QUESTOR *same as* > **quaestor**
QUESTS ▶ **quest**
QUETCH *vb* move
QUETHE, -S *vb* say
QUETSCH *n* plum brandy
QUETZAL *n* crested bird of Central and N South America

This is a great word if you can get the tiles for it, so it's well worth remembering both spellings – it can also be **quezal** – and the four plural forms, which are **quetzals** or **quetzales** and **quezals** or **quezales**.

QUEUE, -D, -S, QUEUING *n, vb*
QUEUER, -S ▶ **queue**
QUEUES ▶ **queue**
QUEUING ▶ **queue**
QUEY, -S *n* young cow
QUEYN, -S *n* girl or young woman
QUEYNIE *same as* ▶ **queyn**
QUEYNS ▶ **queyn**
QUEYS ▶ **quey**
QUEZAL, -S *same as* ▶ **quetzal**
QUIBBLE *vb, n*
QUIBLIN *same as* ▶ **quibble**
QUICH, -ED *vb* move
QUICHE, -S *n*
QUICHED ▶ **quich**
QUICHES ▶ **quiche**
QUICK, -ER, -S *adj, n, adv*
QUICKEN *vb, n*
QUICKER ▶ **quick**
QUICKIE *n, adj*
QUICKLY ▶ **quick**
QUICKS ▶ **quick**
QUICKY *same as* ▶ **quickie**
QUID, -S *n*
QUIDAM, -S *n* specified person
QUIDDIT *same as* > **quiddity**
QUIDDLE *vb* waste time
QUIDS ▶ **quid**

QUIESCE *vb*
QUIET, -ED, -ER, -S *adj, n, vb*
QUIETEN *vb*
QUIETER ▸ **quiet**
QUIETLY ▸ **quiet**
QUIETS ▸ **quiet**
QUIETUS *n* release from life
QUIFF, -S *n*
QUIFFED *adj* having a quiff
QUIFFS ▸ **quiff**
QUIGHT, -S *vb* quit
QUILL, -ED, -S *n, vb*
QUILLAI *another name for* > **soapbark**
QUILLED ▸ **quill**
QUILLET *n* quibble or subtlety
QUILLON *n* either half of the extended crosspiece of a sword or dagger
QUILLOW *n* quilt folded to make a pillow
QUILLS ▸ **quill**
QUILT, -ED, -S *n, vb*
QUILTER ▸ **quilt**
QUILTS ▸ **quilt**
QUIN, -S *n* short for quintuplet
QUINA, -S *n* quinine
QUINARY *adj* consisting of fives or by fives ▷ *n* set of five
QUINAS ▸ **quina**
QUINATE *adj* arranged in or composed of five parts
QUINCE, -S *n*
QUINCHE *vb* move
QUINE, -S *variant of* ▸ **quean**
QUINELA *same as* > **quinella**
QUINES ▸ **quine**
QUINIC *adj* as in **quinic acid** white crystalline soluble optically active carboxylic acid
QUINIE, -S *n* girl or young woman
QUININ, -S *same as* ▸ **quinine**
QUININA *same as* ▸ **quinine**
QUININE *n*
QUININS ▸ **quinin**
QUINNAT *n* Pacific salmon
QUINO, -S *same as* ▸ **keno**
QUINOA, -S *n*
QUINOID *same as* > **quinonoid**
QUINOL, -S *n* white crystalline soluble phenol used as a photographic developer
QUINONE *n* yellow crystalline water-soluble unsaturated ketone
QUINOS ▸ **quino**
QUINS ▸ **quin**
QUINSY *n* inflammation of the throat or tonsils
QUINT, -S *same as* ▸ **quin**
QUINTA, -S *n* Portuguese vineyard where grapes for wine or port are grown
QUINTAL *n* unit of weight
QUINTAN *adj* (of a fever) occurring every fourth day ▷ *n* quintan fever
QUINTAR *n* Albanian unit of currency
QUINTAS ▸ **quinta**
QUINTE, -S *n* fifth of eight basic positions from which a parry or attack can be made in fencing
QUINTET *n*
QUINTIC *adj* of or relating to the fifth degree ▷ *n* mathematical function
QUINTIN *same as* > **quintain**
QUINTS ▸ **quint**
QUINZE, -S *n* card game where players aim to score 15

Deriving from the French word for fifteen, this makes a high-scoring word that you may well get to play, and if you can use all your tiles to form the plural, you'll get a 50-point bonus.

QUINZIE *same as* > **quinzhee**
QUIP, -PED, -S *n, vb*
QUIPO, -S *same as* ▸ **quipu**
QUIPPED ▸ **quip**
QUIPPER ▸ **quip**
QUIPPU, -S *same as* ▸ **quipu**
QUIPPY ▸ **quip**
QUIPS ▸ **quip**
QUIPU, -S *n* device of the Incas used to record information using knotted cords
QUIRE, -D, -S, QUIRING *n* set of 24 or 25 sheets

of paper ▷ *vb* arrange in quires
QUIRK, -ED, -S *n, vb*
QUIRKY ▶ **quirk**
QUIRT, -ED, -S *n* whip with a leather thong at one end ▷ *vb* strike with a quirt
QUIST, -S *n* wood pigeon
QUIT, -S, -TED *vb, adj*
QUITCH *vb* move
QUITE, -D, -S, QUITING *archaic form of* ▶ **quit**
QUITS ▶ **quit**
QUITTAL *n* repayment of an action with a similar action
QUITTED ▶ **quit**
QUITTER *n*
QUITTOR *n* infection of the cartilages on the side of a horse's foot
QUIVER, -S *vb, n*
QUIVERY ▶ **quiver**
QUIXOTE *n*

Using the Q and X, this word for an impractical dreamer has a reasonable chance of coming up, so keeping an eye open for it is not that quixotic!

QUIZ, -ZED, -ZES *n, vb*
QUIZZER ▶ **quiz**
QUIZZES ▶ **quiz**
QULLIQ, -S *n* type of oil lamp used by Inuit people
QUOAD *adv* as far as
QUOD, -DED, -S *n* jail ▷ *vb* say
QUODLIN *n* cooking apple
QUODS ▶ **quod**
QUOHOG, -S *n* edible clam
QUOIF, -ED, -S *vb* arrange (the hair)
QUOIN, -ED, -S *n* external corner of a building ▷ *vb* wedge
QUOIST, -S *n* wood pigeon
QUOIT, -ED *n, vb*
QUOITER ▶ **quoit**
QUOITS *n*
QUOKKA, -S *n* small Australian wallaby
QUOLL, -S *n* Australian catlike carnivorous marsupial
QUOMODO *n* manner
QUONDAM *adj* of an earlier time
QUONK, -ED, -S *vb* make an accidental noise while broadcasting
QUOOKE *archaic past participle of* ▶ **quake**
QUOP, -PED, -S *vb* pulsate or throb
QUORATE *adj* having or being a quorum
QUORUM, -S *n*
QUOTA, -S *n*
QUOTE, -D, -S, QUOTING *vb, n, interj*
QUOTER, -S ▶ **quote**
QUOTES ▶ **quote**
QUOTH *vb*
QUOTHA *interj* expression of mild sarcasm, used in picking up a word or phrase used by someone else
QUOTING ▶ **quote**
QUOTUM, -S *same as* ▶ **quota**
QURSH, -ES *same as* ▶ **qurush**
QURUSH *n* former Saudi Arabian currency unit
QUYTE, -D, -S, QUYTING *same as* ▶ **quit**
QWERTY, -S *n*

Rr

RABANNA *n* Madagascan woven raffia
RABASKA *n* large canoe
RABAT, -S *vb* rotate so that the plane rotated coincides with another
RABATO, -S *n* wired or starched collar
RABATS ▸ **rabat**
RABATTE *same as* ▸ **rabat**
RABBET, -S *n* recess cut into a surface ▹ *vb* cut or form a rabbet in (timber)
RABBI, -ES, -S *n*
RABBIN, -S *same as* ▸ **rabbi**
RABBIS ▸ **rabbi**
RABBIT, -S *n, vb*
RABBITO *same as* > **rabbitoh**
RABBITS ▸ **rabbit**
RABBITY *adj*
RABBLE, -D, -S *n, vb*
RABBLER *n* device for stirring, mixing, or skimming a molten charge in a furnace
RABBLES ▸ **rabble**
RABBONI *n* very respectful Jewish title or form of address
RABI, -S *n* (in Pakistan, India, etc) a crop that is harvested at the end of winter
RABIC ▸ **rabies**
RABID, -ER *adj*
RABIDLY ▸ **rabid**
RABIES *n*
RABIS ▸ **rabi**
RABONA, -S *n* method of kicking a football
RACA *adj* biblical word meaning worthless or empty-headed
RACCOON *n*
RACE, -D, -S *n, vb*
RACEME, -S *n* cluster of flowers along a central stem, as in the foxglove
RACEMED *adj* with or in racemes
RACEMES ▸ **raceme**
RACEMIC *adj* being a mixture of equal amounts of enantiomers
RACER, -S *n*
RACES ▸ **race**
RACEWAY *n*
RACH, -ES *n* scent hound
RACHE *same as* ▸ **rach**
RACHES ▸ **rach**
RACHET, -S *same as* ▸ **ratchet**
RACHIAL ▸ **rachis**
RACHIS *n* main axis or stem of an inflorescence or compound leaf
RACIAL *adj*
RACIER ▸ **racy**
RACIEST ▸ **racy**
RACILY ▸ **racy**
RACING, -S *adj, n*
RACINO, -S *n* combined racetrack and casino
RACISM, -S *n*
RACIST, -S ▸ **racism**
RACK, -ED, -ING, -S *n, vb*
RACKER, -S ▸ **rack**
RACKET, -S *n, vb*
RACKETT *n* early double-reeded wind instrument
RACKETY *adj* involving noise, commotion and excitement
RACKFUL ▸ **rack**
RACKING ▸ **rack**
RACKLE, -S *n* (Scot) chain
RACKS ▸ **rack**
RACLOIR *n* scraper
RACON, -S *n* radar beacon
RACOON, -S *same as* ▸ **raccoon**
RACQUET *same as* ▸ **racket**
RACY, RACIER, RACIEST *adj*
RAD, -DED, -DER, -DEST, -DING, -S *n, vb, adj*
RADAR, -S *n*
RADDED ▸ **rad**

RADDER ▸ **rad**
RADDEST ▸ **rad**
RADDING ▸ **rad**
RADDLE, -S *same as* ▸ **ruddle**
RADDLED *adj* (of a person) unkempt or run-down in appearance
RADDLES ▸ **raddle**
RADE *(in Scots dialect) past tense of* ▸ **ride**
RADGE, -R, -S, -ST *adj* angry or uncontrollable ▹ *n* person acting in such a way
RADIAL, -S *adj, n*
RADIALE *n* bone in the wrist
RADIALS ▸ **radial**
RADIAN, -S *n* unit for measuring angles, equal to 57.296°
RADIANT *adj, n*
RADIATA *n* type of pine tree
RADIATE *vb, adj*
RADICAL *adj, n*
RADICEL *n* very small root
RADICES ▸ **radix**
RADICLE *n* small or developing root
RADII ▸ **radius**
RADIO, -ED, -S *n, vb, adj*
RADIOES *less common spelling of* ▸ **radios**
RADIOS ▸ **radio**
RADISH *n*
RADIUM, -S *n*
RADIUS, RADII *n, vb*
RADIX, RADICES, -ES *n* any number that is the base of a number system or of a system of logarithms
RADOME, -S *n* protective housing for a radar antenna
RADON, -S *n* radioactive gaseous element
RADS ▸ **rad**
RADULA, -E, -S *n* horny tooth-bearing strip on the tongue of molluscs
RADULAR ▸ **radula**
RADULAS ▸ **radula**
RAFALE, -S *n* burst of artillery fire
RAFF, -S *n* rubbish
RAFFIA, -S *n*
RAFFISH *adj* slightly disreputable
RAFFLE, -D, -S *n, vb*
RAFFLER ▸ **raffle**
RAFFLES ▸ **raffle**
RAFFS ▸ **raff**
RAFT, -ED, -S *n, vb*
RAFTER, -S *n, vb*
RAFTING ▸ **raft**
RAFTMAN, RAFTMEN *same as* > **raftsman**
RAFTS ▸ **raft**
RAG, -S *n, vb, adj*
RAGA, -S *n* pattern of melody and rhythm in Indian music
RAGBAG, -S *n* confused assortment, jumble
RAGBOLT *n* bolt that has angled projections on it
RAGDE *archaic past form of* ▸ **rage**
RAGDOLL *n* breed of cat
RAGE, -D, -S *n, vb*
RAGEE, -S *same as* ▸ **ragi**
RAGEFUL ▸ **rage**
RAGER, -S ▸ **rage**
RAGES ▸ **rage**
RAGG, -S *same as* > **ragstone**
RAGGA, -S *n* dance-oriented style of reggae
RAGGED *adj*
RAGGEDY *adj*
RAGGEE, -S *same as* ▸ **ragi**
RAGGERY *n* rags
RAGGIER ▸ **raggy**
RAGGIES ▸ **raggy**
RAGGING ▸ **rag**
RAGGLE, -D, -S *n* thin groove cut in stone or brickwork ▹ *vb* cut a raggle in
RAGGS ▸ **ragg**
RAGGY, RAGGIER, RAGGIES *adj* ragged ▹ *n* cereal grass cultivated in Africa and Asia for its edible grain
RAGI, -S *n* cereal grass cultivated in Africa and Asia for its edible grain
RAGING, -S ▸ **rage**
RAGINI, -S *n* Indian musical form related to a raga
RAGIS ▸ **ragi**
RAGLAN, -S *adj* (of a sleeve) joined to a garment from the neck to the underarm ▹ *n* coat with sleeves that continue to the collar
RAGMAN, -S, RAGMEN *n* rag-and-bone man
RAGMENT *n* statute, roll, or list
RAGOUT, -S *n* richly seasoned stew of meat and vegetables ▹ *vb* make into a ragout
RAGS ▸ **rag**

RAGTAG, -S *n*
RAGTAIL *adj* ragged; shabby
RAGTIME *n*
RAGTOP, -S *n* informal word for a car with a folding or removable roof
RAGU, -S *n* Italian meat and tomato sauce
RAGULED *same as* ▸ **raguly**
RAGULY *adj* (in heraldry) having toothlike projections
RAGUS ▸ **ragu**
RAGWEED *n* any of several plants
RAGWORK *n* weaving or needlework using rags
RAGWORM *n* type of worm that lives chiefly in burrows in sand or mud
RAGWORT *n* plant with ragged leaves and yellow flowers
RAH, -ED, -ING, -S *informal US word for* ▸ **cheer**
RAHUI, -S *n* Māori prohibition
RAI, -S *n* type of Algerian popular music
RAIA, -S *same as* ▸ **rayah**
RAID, -ED, -S *n, vb*
RAIDER, -S ▸ **raid**
RAIDING ▸ **raid**
RAIDS ▸ **raid**
RAIK, -ED, -ING, -S *n* wander ▷ *vb* wander
RAIL, -ED, -S *n, vb*
RAILAGE *n* cost of transporting goods by rail
RAILBED *n* ballast layer supporting the sleepers of a railway track
RAILBUS *n* bus-like vehicle for use on railway lines
RAILCAR *n* passenger-carrying railway vehicle consisting of a single coach
RAILE, -S *archaic spelling of* ▸ **rail**
RAILED ▸ **rail**
RAILER, -S ▸ **rail**
RAILES ▸ **raile**
RAILING *n*
RAILLY *old word for* ▸ **mock**
RAILMAN, RAILMEN *n* railway employee
RAILS ▸ **rail**
RAILWAY *n*
RAIMENT *n*
RAIN, -ED, -ING, -S *n, vb*
RAINBOW *n*
RAINE, -S *archaic spelling of* ▸ **reign**
RAINED ▸ **rain**
RAINES ▸ **raine**
RAINIER ▸ **rainy**
RAINILY ▸ **rainy**
RAINING ▸ **rain**
RAINOUT *n* radioactive fallout or atmospheric pollution carried to the earth by rain
RAINS ▸ **rain**
RAINY, RAINIER *adj*
RAIRD, -S *same as* ▸ **reird**
RAIS ▸ **rai**
RAISE, -D, -S *vb, n*
RAISER, -S ▸ **raise**
RAISES ▸ **raise**
RAISIN, -S *n*
RAISING *n*
RAISINS ▸ **raisin**
RAISINY *adj* tasting of raisins
RAIT, -ED, -ING, -S *same as* ▸ **ret**
RAITA, -S *n* Indian dish of chopped cucumber, mint, etc in yogurt
RAITED ▸ **rait**
RAITING ▸ **rait**
RAITS ▸ **rait**
RAIYAT, -S *same as* ▸ **ryot**
RAJ, -ES *n* (in India) government

> This Indian word for rule or empire is one of the essential short words that use a J. Remember that it can be extended to **raja**.

RAJA, -S *same as* ▸ **rajah**
RAJAH, -S *n* Indian ruler
RAJAS ▸ **raja**
RAJES ▸ **raj**
RAKE, -D, -S *n, vb*
RAKEE, -S *same as* ▸ **raki**
RAKEOFF *n* share of profits, esp one that is illegal or given as a bribe
RAKER, -S *n* person who rakes
RAKERY *n* rakish behaviour
RAKES ▸ **rake**
RAKI, -S *n* strong spirit distilled from grain
RAKIA, -S *n* strong fruit-based alcoholic

drink popular in the Balkans
RAKIJA, -S *same as* ▸ **rakia**
RAKING, -S *n*
RAKIS ▸ **raki**
RAKISH *adj*
RAKSHAS *same as* > **rakshasa**
RAKU, -S *n* type of Japanese pottery
RALE, -S *n* abnormal coarse crackling sound heard on auscultation of the chest
RALLIED ▸ **rally**
RALLIER ▸ **rally**
RALLIES ▸ **rally**
RALLINE *adj* relating to a family of birds that includes the rails, crakes, and coots
RALLY, RALLIED, RALLIES *n, vb*
RALLYE, -S *US variant of* ▸ **rally**
RALPH, -ED, -S *vb* slang word meaning vomit
RAM, -MED, -MING, -S *n, vb*
RAMADA, -S *n* outdoor eating area with roof but open sides
RAMAKIN *same as* ▸ **ramekin**
RAMAL *adj* relating to a branch or branches
RAMATE *adj* with branches
RAMBLA, -S *n* dried-up riverbed
RAMBLE, -D, -S *vb, n*
RAMBLER *n*
RAMBLES ▸ **ramble**
RAMCAT, -S *n* dialect word for a male cat
RAMEAL *same as* ▸ **ramal**
RAMEE, -S *same as* ▸ **ramie**
RAMEKIN *n* small ovenproof dish for a single serving of food
RAMEN, -S *n* Japanese dish consisting of a clear broth containing thin white noodles
RAMENTA > **ramentum**
RAMEOUS *same as* ▸ **ramal**
RAMET, -S *n* any of the individuals in a group of clones
RAMI, -S *same as* ▸ **ramie**
RAMIE, -S *n* woody Asian shrub with broad leaves
RAMIFY *vb* become complex
RAMILIE *same as* > **ramillie**
RAMIN, -S *n* swamp-growing tree found in Malaysia and Indonesia
RAMIS ▸ **rami**
RAMJET, -S *n* type of jet engine
RAMMED ▸ **ram**
RAMMEL, -S *n* discarded or waste matter
RAMMER, -S ▸ **ram**
RAMMIER ▸ **rammy**
RAMMIES ▸ **rammy**
RAMMING ▸ **ram**
RAMMISH *adj* like a ram, esp in being foul-smelling
RAMMLE, -S *n* collection of items saved in case they become useful
RAMMY, RAMMIER, RAMMIES *n* Scots word for a noisy disturbance or free-for-all ▹ *adj* like a ram
RAMONA, -S *same as* > **sagebrush**
RAMOSE *adj* having branches
RAMOUS *same as* ▸ **ramose**
RAMP, -ED, -S *n, vb*
RAMPAGE *vb*
RAMPANT *adj*
RAMPART *n, vb*
RAMPED ▸ **ramp**
RAMPER, -S ▸ **ramp**
RAMPICK *same as* ▸ **rampike**
RAMPIKE *n* US or dialect word for a dead tree
RAMPING ▸ **ramp**
RAMPION *n* European and Asian plant with an edible root
RAMPIRE *archaic variant of* ▸ **rampart**
RAMPOLE *same as* ▸ **rampike**
RAMPS ▸ **ramp**
RAMROD, -S *n* long thin rod used for cleaning the barrel of a gun ▹ *adj* (of someone's posture) very straight and upright ▹ *vb* drive
RAMS ▸ **ram**
RAMSON, -S *n* type of garlic
RAMSTAM *adv* headlong ▹ *adj* headlong

RAMTIL, -S *n* African plant grown in India esp for its oil
RAMULAR *adj* relating to a branch or branches
RAMULUS, RAMULI *n* small branch
RAMUS *n* barb of a bird's feather
RAN ▸ **run**
RANA, -S *n* genus of frogs
RANCE, -D, -S, RANCING *Scots word for* ▸ **prop**
RANCEL, -S *vb* (in Shetland and Orkney) carry out a search
RANCES ▸ **rance**
RANCH, -ED, -ES *n, vb*
RANCHER *n*
RANCHES ▸ **ranch**
RANCHO, -S *n* hut or group of huts for housing ranch workers
RANCID *adj*
RANCING ▸ **rance**
RANCOR, -S *same as* ▸ **rancour**
RANCOUR *n*
RAND, -ED, -ING, -S *n, vb*
RANDAN, -S *n* boat rowed by three people
RANDED ▸ **rand**
RANDEM, -S *adv* with three horses harnessed together as a team ▹ *n* carriage or team of horses so driven
RANDIE *same as* ▸ **randy**
RANDIER ▸ **randy**
RANDIES ▸ **randy**
RANDILY ▸ **randy**
RANDING ▸ **rand**
RANDOM, -S *adj, n*
RANDON, -S *old variant of* ▸ **random**
RANDS ▸ **rand**
RANDY, RANDIER, RANDIES *adj, n*
RANEE, -S *same as* ▸ **rani**
RANG, -S *n* (Scot) rank
RANGE, -D, -S *n, vb*
RANGER, -S *n*
RANGES ▸ **range**
RANGI, -S *n* sky
RANGIER ▸ **rangy**
RANGILY ▸ **rangy**
RANGING ▸ **range**
RANGIS ▸ **rangi**
RANGOLI *n* traditional Indian ground decoration
RANGS ▸ **rang**
RANGY, RANGIER *adj* having long slender limbs
RANI, -S *n* wife or widow of a rajah
RANID, -S *n* frog
RANINE *adj* relating to frogs
RANIS ▸ **rani**
RANK, -ED, -EST, -S *n, vb, adj*
RANKE, -S *archaic variant of* ▸ **rank**
RANKED ▸ **rank**
RANKER, -S *n* soldier in the ranks
RANKES ▸ **ranke**
RANKEST ▸ **rank**
RANKING *adj, n*
RANKISH *adj* old word meaning rather rank
RANKISM *n* discrimination against people on the grounds of rank
RANKIST *n* person who discriminates on the grounds of rank
RANKLE, -D, -S *vb*
RANKLY ▸ **rank**
RANKS ▸ **rank**
RANPIKE *same as* ▸ **rampike**
RANSACK *vb*
RANSEL, -S *same as* ▸ **rancel**
RANSOM, -S *n, vb*
RANT, -ED, -S *vb, n*
RANTER, -S ▸ **rant**
RANTING ▸ **rant**
RANTS ▸ **rant**
RANULA, -S *n* saliva-filled cyst that develops under the tongue
RANULAR *adj* of a cyst under the tongue
RANULAS ▸ **ranula**
RANZEL, -S *same as* ▸ **rancel**
RAOULIA *n* flowering plant of New Zealand
RAP, -PED, -S *vb, n*
RAPE *n*
RAPHE, RAPHAE, -S *n* elongated ridge of conducting tissue along the side of certain seeds
RAPHIA, -S *same as* ▸ **raffia**
RAPHIDE *n* needle-shaped crystal that occurs in many plant cells
RAPHIS *same as* ▸ **raphide**
RAPID, -ER *adj*
RAPIDLY ▸ **rapid**
RAPIDS *pl n*

RAPIER, -S *n*
RAPINE, -S *n* pillage or plundering
RAPINI, -S *n* type of leafy vegetable
RAPLOCH *n* Scots word for homespun woollen material ▷ *adj* Scots word meaning coarse or homemade
RAPPE, -S *n* Arcadian dish of grated potatoes and pork or chicken
RAPPED ▸ **rap**
RAPPEE, -S *n* moist English snuff of the 18th and 19th centuries
RAPPEL, -S *n* (formerly) a drumbeat to call soldiers to arms ▷ *vb* abseil
RAPPEN *n* Swiss coin equal to one hundredth of a franc
RAPPER, -S *n* something used for rapping, such as a knocker on a door
RAPPES ▸ **rappe**
RAPPING ▸ **rap**
RAPPINI *same as* ▸ **rapini**
RAPPORT *n*
RAPS ▸ **rap**
RAPT *adj*
RAPTLY ▸ **rapt**
RAPTOR, -S *n* any bird of prey
RAPTURE *n, vb*
RARE, -D, -R, -S, -ST *adj, vb*
RAREBIT *n* as in **Welsh rarebit** dish made from melted cheese served on toast
RARED ▸ **rare**
RAREE *n* as in **raree show** street show or carnival
RAREFY *vb* make or become rarer or less dense
RARELY *adv*
RARER ▸ **rare**
RARES ▸ **rare**
RAREST ▸ **rare**
RARIFY *same as* ▸ **rarefy**
RARING *adj*
RARITY *n*
RARK, -ED, -ING, -S *vb* as in **rark up** informal New Zealand expression meaning reprimand severely
RAS *n* headland
RASBORA *n* often brightly coloured tropical fish
RASCAL, -S *n, adj*
RASCHEL *n* type of loosely knitted fabric
RASE, -D, -S, RASING *same as* ▸ **raze**
RASER, -S ▸ **rase**
RASES ▸ **rase**
RASH, -ED, -ES, -EST, -ING *adj, n, vb*
RASHER, -S *n*
RASHES ▸ **rash**
RASHEST ▸ **rash**
RASHIE, -S *n* protective shirt worn by surfers
RASHING ▸ **rash**
RASHLY ▸ **rash**
RASING ▸ **rase**
RASP, -ED, -S *n, vb*
RASPER, -S ▸ **rasp**
RASPIER ▸ **raspy**
RASPING *adj* (esp of a noise) harsh or grating
RASPISH ▸ **rasp**
RASPS ▸ **rasp**
RASPY, RASPIER *same as* ▸ **rasping**
RASSE, -S *n* small S Asian civet
RASSLE, -D, -S *dialect variant of* ▸ **wrestle**
RASSLER *n* wrestler
RASSLES ▸ **rassle**
RAST *archaic past form of* ▸ **race**
RASTA *adj* rastafarian
RASTER, -S *n* image consisting of rows of pixel information ▷ *vb* turn a digital image into a large picture
RASTRUM *n* pen for drawing the five lines of a musical stave simultaneously
RASURE, -S *n* scraping
RAT, -S, -TED *n, vb*
RATA, -S *n* New Zealand hardwood forest tree
RATABLE *adj* able to be rated or evaluated ▷ *n* something that can be rated or evaluated
RATABLY ▸ **ratable**
RATAFEE *same as* ▸ **ratafia**
RATAFIA *n* liqueur made from fruit
RATAL, -S *n* amount on which rates are assessed ▷ *adj* of or relating to rates (local taxation)
RATAN, -S *same as* ▸ **rattan**
RATANY *n* flowering desert shrub
RATAS ▸ **rata**
RATATAT *n* sound of knocking on a door

RATBAG, -S *n* insulting term for an eccentric or unreliable person
RATBITE *n* as in **ratbite fever** acute infectious disease that can be caught from rats
RATCH, -ED, -ES *same as* ▶ **ratchet**
RATCHET *n, vb*
RATE, -D *n, vb*
RATEEN, -S *same as* ▶ **ratine**
RATEL, -S *n* large African and S Asian musteline mammal
RATER, -S ▶ **rate**
RATES *pl n*
RATFINK *n* contemptible or undesirable person
RATFISH *n* deep-sea fish with a whiplike tail
RATH, -S *same as* ▶ **rathe**
RATHA, -S *n* (in India) a four-wheeled carriage drawn by horses or bullocks
RATHE *adj* blossoming or ripening early in the season
RATHER *adv, interj*
RATHEST *adv* dialect or archaic word meaning soonest
RATHOLE *n* rat's hiding place or burrow
RATHS ▶ **rath**
RATIFY *vb*
RATINE, -S *n* coarse loosely woven cloth
RATING, -S *n*
RATIO, -S *n*
RATION *n, vb*
RATIONS *pl n*
RATIOS ▶ **ratio**
RATITE, -S *adj* (of flightless birds) having a breastbone that lacks a keel ▷ *n* bird that belongs to this group
RATLIKE ▶ **rat**
RATLIN, -S *same as* ▶ **ratline**
RATLINE *n* light line tied across the shrouds of a sailing vessel
RATLING *n* young rat
RATLINS ▶ **ratlin**
RATO, -S *n* rocket-assisted take-off
RATOO, -S *same as* ▶ **ratu**
RATOON, -S *n* new shoot that grows from near the root or crown of crop plants ▷ *vb* propagate by such a growth
RATOOS ▶ **ratoo**
RATOS ▶ **rato**
RATPACK *n* members of the press who pursue celebrities
RATS ▶ **rat**
RATTAIL *n*
RATTAN, -S *n*
RATTED ▶ **rat**
RATTEEN *same as* ▶ **ratine**
RATTEN, -S *vb* sabotage or steal tools in order to disrupt the work of
RATTER, -S *n* dog or cat that catches and kills rats
RATTERY *n* rats' dwelling area
RATTIER ▶ **ratty**
RATTILY ▶ **ratty**
RATTING ▶ **rat**
RATTISH *adj* of, resembling, or infested with rats
RATTLE, -D, -S *vb, n*
RATTLER *n* something that rattles
RATTLES ▶ **rattle**
RATTLIN *same as* ▶ **ratline**
RATTLY *adj* having a rattle
RATTON, -S *n* dialect word for a little rat
RATTOON *same as* ▶ **ratoon**
RATTRAP *n* device for catching rats
RATTY, RATTIER *adj*
RATU, -S *n* title used by Fijian chiefs or nobles
RAUCID *adj* raucous
RAUCITY ▶ **raucous**
RAUCLE, -R *adj* Scots word for rough or tough
RAUCOUS *adj*
RAUGHT *archaic past form of* ▶ **reach**
RAUN, -S *n* fish roe or spawn
RAUNCH *n* lack of polish or refinement ▷ *vb* behave in a raunchy manner
RAUNCHY *adj*
RAUNGE, -D, -S *archaic word for* ▶ **range**
RAUNS ▶ **raun**
RAUPATU *n* confiscation or seizure of land
RAUPO, -S *n* New Zealand bulrush

RAURIKI *n* any of various plants with prickly leaves
RAV, -S *n* Hebrew word for rabbi
RAVAGE, -D, -S *vb, n*
RAVAGER ▸ **ravage**
RAVAGES ▸ **ravage**
RAVE, -D, -S *vb, n*
RAVEL, -ED, -S *vb* tangle or become entangled ▹ *n* tangle or complication
RAVELER ▸ **ravel**
RAVELIN *n* outwork having two embankments at a salient angle
RAVELLY *adj* tangled
RAVELS ▸ **ravel**
RAVEN, -ED, -S *n, adj, vb*
RAVENER ▸ **raven**
RAVENS ▸ **raven**
RAVER, -S *n* person who leads a wild or uninhibited social life
RAVES ▸ **rave**
RAVEY, RAVIER, RAVIEST *adj* characteristic of a rave
RAVIN, -ED, -S *archaic spelling of* ▸ **raven**
RAVINE, -S *n*
RAVINED ▸ **ravin**
RAVINES ▸ **ravine**
RAVING, -S *adj, n*
RAVINS ▸ **ravin**
RAVIOLI *n*
RAVISH *vb*
RAVS ▸ **rav**
RAW, -ER, -EST, -S *n, adj*
RAWARU, -S *n* New Zealand name for blue cod
RAWBONE *archaic variant of* > **rawboned**
RAWER ▸ **raw**
RAWEST ▸ **raw**
RAWHEAD *n* bogeyman
RAWHIDE *n* untanned hide ▹ *vb* whip
RAWIN, -S *n* monitoring of winds in the upper atmosphere using radar and a balloon
RAWING, -S *(in dialect) same as* ▸ **rowen**
RAWINS ▸ **rawin**
RAWISH ▸ **raw**
RAWLY ▸ **raw**
RAWN, -S *(in dialect) same as* ▸ **rowen**
RAWNESS ▸ **raw**
RAWNS ▸ **rawn**
RAWS ▸ **raw**
RAX, -ED, -ES, -ING *vb* stretch or extend ▹ *n* act of stretching or straining

A dialect word meaning to stretch or strain, and one of the essential short words to know for using the X.

RAY, -ED, -ING, -S *n, vb*
RAYA, -S *same as* ▸ **rayah**
RAYAH, -S *n* (formerly) a non-Muslim subject of the Ottoman Empire
RAYAS ▸ **raya**
RAYED ▸ **ray**
RAYING ▸ **ray**
RAYLE, -D, -S, RAYLING *archaic spelling of* ▸ **rail**
RAYLESS *adj* dark
RAYLET, -S *n* small ray
RAYLIKE *adj* resembling a ray
RAYLING ▸ **rayle**
RAYNE, -S *archaic spelling of* ▸ **reign**
RAYON, -S *n* (fabric made of) a synthetic fibre
RAYS ▸ **ray**
RAZE, -D, -S, RAZING *vb* destroy (buildings or a town) completely
RAZEE, -D, -S *n* sailing ship that has had its upper deck or decks removed ▹ *vb* remove the upper deck or decks of (a sailing ship)
RAZER, -S ▸ **raze**
RAZES ▸ **raze**
RAZING ▸ **raze**
RAZOO, -S *n* imaginary coin
RAZOR, -ED, -S *n, vb*
RAZURE, -S *same as* ▸ **rasure**
RAZZ, -ED, -ES *vb* make fun of
RAZZIA, -S *n* raid for plunder or slaves
RAZZING *n* act of making fun of someone
RAZZLE, -S *n* as in **on the razzle** out enjoying oneself or celebrating
RE *prep* concerning ▹ *n* the second note of the musical scale
REACH, -ED, -ES *vb, n*
REACHER ▸ **reach**
REACHES ▸ **reach**
REACT, -ED, -S *vb*
REACTOR *n*
REACTS ▸ **react**
READ, -S *vb, n*
READAPT *vb* adapt again

READD, -ED, -S *vb* add again
READER, -S *n*
READIED ▸ **ready**
READIER ▸ **ready**
READIES *pl n* ready money
READILY *adv*
READING ▸ **read**
README, -S *n* document which accompanies computer files or software
READMIT *vb* let (a person, country, etc) back into a place or organization
READOPT *vb* adopt again
READORN *vb* adorn again
READOUT *n*
READS ▸ **read**
READY, READIED, READIER *adj, vb*
REAFFIX *vb* affix again
REAGENT *n*
REAGIN, -S *n* type of antibody that is formed against an allergen
REAIS ▸ **real**
REAK, -ED, -ING, -S *same as* ▸ **reck**
REAL, REAIS, -ER, -ES, -EST, -S *adj, n*
REALGAR *n* rare orange-red soft mineral
REALIA *pl n* real-life facts and material used in teaching
REALIGN *vb* change or put back to a new or former place or position
REALISE *same as* ▸ **realize**
REALISM *n*
REALIST *n*
REALITY *n*
REALIZE *vb*
REALLIE *old or dialect variant of* ▸ **really**
REALLOT *vb* allot again
REALLY *adv, interj, vb*
REALM, -S *n*
REALO, -S *n* member of the German Green party with moderate views

A **realo** is a member of the less radical section of the German Green party. It is important to know not because it scores well, but because it provides an easily overlooked hook by allowing you to add O to **real**.

REALS ▸ **real**
REALTER *vb* alter again
REALTIE *n* archaic word meaning sincerity
REALTOR *n* estate agent
REALTY *n* immovable property
REAM, -ED, -ING, -S *n* twenty quires of paper, generally 500 sheets ▹ *vb* enlarge (a hole) by use of a reamer
REAME, -S *archaic variant of* ▸ **realm**
REAMED ▸ **ream**
REAMEND *vb* amend again
REAMER, -S *n* tool used for smoothing the bores of holes accurately to size
REAMES ▸ **reame**
REAMIER ▸ **reamy**
REAMING ▸ **ream**
REAMS ▸ **ream**
REAMY, REAMIER *Scots for* ▸ **creamy**
REAN, -S *same as* ▸ **reen**
REANNEX *vb* annex again
REANS ▸ **rean**
REAP, -ED, -S *vb*
REAPER, -S *n* person who reaps or machine for reaping
REAPING *n*
REAPPLY *vb*
REAPS ▸ **reap**
REAR, -ED, -S *n, vb*
REARER, -S ▸ **rear**
REARGUE *vb* argue again
REARING *n* act of rearing
REARISE, REAROSE *vb* arise again
REARLY *old word for* ▸ **early**
REARM, -ED, -S *vb* arm again
REAROSE ▸ **rearise**
REARS ▸ **rear**
REASON, -S *n, vb*
REAST, -ED, -S *same as* ▸ **reest**
REASTY *adj* (in dialect) rancid
REATA, -S *n* lasso
REATE, -S *n* type of crowfoot
REAVAIL *vb* avail again
REAVE, -D, -S, REAVING, REFT *vb* carry off (property, prisoners, etc) by force

REAVER, -S ▸ **reave**
REAVES ▸ **reave**
REAVING ▸ **reave**
REAVOW, -S *vb* avow again
REAWAKE, REAWOKE *vb* awake again
REB, -S *n* Confederate soldier in the American Civil War
REBACK, -S *vb* provide with a new back, backing, or lining
REBADGE *vb* relaunch (a product) under a new name, brand, or logo
REBAIT, -S *vb* bait again
REBAR, -S *n* rod providing reinforcement in concrete structures
REBASE, -D, -S *vb* set on a new foundation
REBATE, -D, -S *n, vb*
REBATER ▸ **rebate**
REBATES ▸ **rebate**
REBATO, -S *same as* ▸ **rabato**
REBBE, -S *n* individual's chosen spiritual mentor
REBEC, -S *n* medieval stringed instrument resembling the violin
REBECK, -S *same as* ▸ **rebec**
REBECS ▸ **rebec**
REBEGIN, REBEGAN, REBEGUN *vb* begin again
REBEL, -S *vb, n, adj*
REBID, -S *vb* bid again
REBILL, -S *vb* bill again
REBIND, -S *vb* bind again
REBIRTH *n*
REBITE, REBIT, -S *vb* (in printing) to give another application of acid
REBLEND *vb* blend again
REBLENT *same as* ▸ **reblend**
REBLOOM *vb* bloom again
REBOANT *adj* resounding or reverberating
REBOARD *vb* board again
REBODY *vb* give a new body to
REBOIL, -S *vb* boil again
REBOOK, -S *vb* book again
REBOOT, -S *vb*
REBOP, -S *same as* ▸ **bebop**
REBORE, -D, -S *n* boring of a cylinder to restore its true shape ▹ *vb* carry out this process
REBORN *adj*
REBOUND *vb, n*
REBOZO, -S *n* long scarf covering the shoulders and head
REBRACE *vb* brace again
REBRAND *vb* change or update the image of (an organization or product)
REBREED, REBRED *vb* breed again
REBS ▸ **reb**
REBUFF, -S *vb, n*
REBUILD, REBUILT *vb*
REBUKE, -D, -S *vb, n*
REBUKER ▸ **rebuke**
REBUKES ▸ **rebuke**
REBURY *vb* bury again
REBUS, -ES *n* puzzle consisting of pictures and symbols representing words or syllables
REBUT, -S *vb*
REBUY, -S *vb* buy again
REC, -S *n* short for recreation
RECAL, -S *same as* ▸ **recall**
RECALL, -S *vb, n*
RECALS ▸ **recal**
RECANE, -D, -S *vb* cane again
RECANT, -S *vb*
RECAP, -S *vb, n*
RECARRY *vb* carry again
RECAST, -S *vb* organize or set out in a different way
RECATCH *vb* catch again
RECCE, -D, -ED, -S *vb, n*
RECCIED ▸ **reccy**
RECCIES ▸ **reccy**
RECCO, -S *same as* ▸ **recce**
RECCY, RECCIED, RECCIES *same as* ▸ **recce**
RECEDE, -D, -S *vb*
RECEIPT *n, vb*
RECEIVE *vb*
RECENCY ▸ **recent**
RECENSE *vb* revise
RECENT *adj*
RECEPT, -S *n* idea or image formed in the mind by repeated experience
RECESS *n, vb*
RECHART *vb* chart again

RECHATE *same as* ▸ **recheat**
RECHEAT *n* (in a hunt) sounding of the horn to call back the hounds ▹ *vb* sound the horn to call back the hounds
RECHECK *vb* check again
RECHEW, -S *vb* chew again
RECHIE *adj* smoky
RECHIP, -S *vb* put a new chip into (a stolen mobile phone) so it can be reused
RECHOSE > **rechoose**
RECIPE, -S *n*
RECIT, -S *n* narrative
RECITAL *n*
RECITE, -D, -S *vb*
RECITER ▸ **recite**
RECITES ▸ **recite**
RECITS ▸ **recit**
RECK, -ED, -ING, -S *vb* mind or care about (something)
RECKAN, -S *adj* strained, tormented, or twisted ▹ *n* chain or hook for hanging a pot over a fire
RECKED ▸ **reck**
RECKING ▸ **reck**
RECKON, -S *vb*
RECKS ▸ **reck**
RECLAD, -S *vb* cover in a different substance
RECLAIM *vb, n*
RECLAME *n* public acclaim or attention
RECLASP *vb* clasp again
RECLEAN *vb* clean again
RECLIMB *vb* climb again
RECLINE *vb*
RECLOSE *vb* close again
RECLUSE *n, adj*
RECOAL, -S *vb* supply or be supplied with fresh coal
RECOAT, -S *vb* coat again
RECOCK, -S *vb* cock again
RECODE, -D, -S *vb* put into a new code
RECOIL, -S *vb, n*
RECOIN, -S *vb* coin again
RECOLOR *same as* > **recolour**
RECOMB, -S *vb* comb again
RECON, -S *vb* make a preliminary survey
RECOOK, -S *vb* cook again
RECOPY *vb* copy again
RECORD, -S *n, vb*
RECORK, -S *vb* cork again
RECOUNT *vb*
RECOUP, -S *vb*
RECOUPE *vb* (in law) keep back or withhold
RECOUPS ▸ **recoup**
RECOURE *archaic variant of* ▸ **recover**
RECOVER *vb*
RECOWER *archaic variant of* ▸ **recover**
RECOYLE *archaic spelling of* ▸ **recoil**
RECRATE *vb* crate again
RECROSS *vb* move or go across (something) again
RECROWN *vb* crown again
RECRUIT *vb, n*
RECS ▸ **rec**
RECTA ▸ **rectum**
RECTAL *adj*
RECTI ▸ **rectus**
RECTIFY *vb*
RECTION *n* (in grammar) the determination of the form of one word by another word
RECTO, -S *n* right-hand page of a book
RECTOR, -S *n*
RECTORY *n*
RECTOS ▸ **recto**
RECTRIX *n* any of the large stiff feathers of a bird's tail
RECTUM, RECTA, -S *n*
RECTUS, RECTI *n* straight muscle
RECUILE *archaic variant of* ▸ **recoil**
RECULE, -D, -S *archaic variant of* ▸ **recoil**
RECUR, -S *vb*
RECURE, -D, -S *vb* archaic word for cure or recover
RECURS ▸ **recur**
RECURVE *vb* curve or bend (something) back or down
RECUSAL *n*
RECUSE, -D, -S *vb* (in law) object to or withdraw (a judge)
RECUT, -S *vb* cut again
RECYCLE *vb, n*
RED, -DEST, -S *adj, n*
REDACT, -S *vb*
REDAN, -S *n* fortification of two parapets at a salient angle
REDATE, -D, -S *vb* change date of

REDBACK *n* small venomous Australian spider
REDBAIT *vb* harass those with leftwing leanings
REDBAY, -S *n* type of tree
REDBIRD *n* type of bird, the male of which has bright red plumage
REDBONE *n* type of American dog
REDBUD, -S *n* American tree with heart-shaped leaves
REDBUG, -S *another name for* ▸ **chigger**
REDCAP, -S *n* member of the military police
REDCOAT *n* (formerly) a British soldier
REDD, -ED, -S *vb* bring order to ▹ *n* act or an instance of redding
REDDEN, -S *vb* make or become red
REDDER, -S ▸ **redd**
REDDEST ▸ **red**
REDDIER ▸ **reddy**
REDDING ▸ **redd**
REDDISH *adj*
REDDLE, -D, -S *same as* ▸ **ruddle**
REDDS ▸ **redd**
REDDY, REDDIER *adj* reddish
REDE, -D, -S, REDING *n* advice or counsel ▹ *vb* advise
REDEAL, -S, -T *vb* deal again
REDEAR, -S *n* variety of sunfish with a red flash above the gills
REDED ▸ **rede**
REDEEM, -S *vb*
REDEFY *vb* defy again
REDENY *vb* deny again
REDES ▸ **rede**
REDEYE, -S *n* inferior whiskey
REDFIN, -S *n* any of various small fishes with reddish fins that are popular aquarium fishes
REDFISH *n* male salmon that has recently spawned
REDFOOT *n* fatal disease of newborn lambs
REDHEAD *n*
REDIA, -E, -S *n* parasitic larva of flukes
REDIAL, -S *vb*
REDIAS ▸ **redia**
REDID ▸ **redo**
REDING ▸ **rede**
REDIP, -S *vb* dip again
REDIPT *archaic past form of* ▸ **redip**
REDLEG, -S *n* bird with red legs
REDLINE *vb* refuse a loan to (a person or country) because of the presumed risks involved
REDLY ▸ **red**
REDNESS ▸ **red**
REDO, REDID, -ES, -ING, -NE, -S *vb* do over again in order to improve ▹ *n* instance of redoing something
REDOCK, -S *vb* dock again
REDOES ▸ **redo**
REDOING ▸ **redo**
REDON, -S *vb* don again
REDONE ▸ **redo**
REDONS ▸ **redon**
REDOS ▸ **redo**
REDOUBT *n* small fort defending a hilltop or pass ▹ *vb* fear
REDOUND *vb* cause advantage or disadvantage (to)
REDOUT, -S *n* reddened vision caused by a rush of blood to the head
REDOWA, -S *n* Bohemian folk dance similar to the waltz
REDOX, -ES *n* chemical reaction in which one substance is reduced and the other is oxidized
REDPOLL *n* mostly grey-brown finch with a red crown and pink breast
REDRAFT *vb* write a second copy of (a letter, proposal, essay, etc) ▹ *n* second draft
REDRAW, -N, -S, REDREW *vb* draw or draw up (something) again or differently
REDREAM *vb* dream again
REDRESS *vb, n*
REDREW ▸ **redraw**
REDRIED ▸ **redry**
REDRIES ▸ **redry**
REDRILL *vb* drill again
REDRIVE, REDROVE *vb* drive again
REDROOT *n* yellow-flowered bog plant whose roots yield a red dye
REDROVE ▸ **redrive**

REDRY, REDRIED, REDRIES *vb* dry again
REDS ▸ **red**
REDSEAR *same as* > **redshort**
REDTAIL *n* variety of bird with red colouring on its tail
REDTOP, -S *n* sensationalist tabloid newspaper
REDUB, -S *vb* fix or repair
REDUCE, -D, -S *vb*
REDUCER *n* chemical solution used to lessen the density of a negative or print
REDUCES ▸ **reduce**
REDUIT, -S *n* fortified part from which a garrison may fight on once an enemy has taken outworks
REDUX *adj* brought back or returned
REDWARE *another name for* ▸ **kelp**
REDWING *n* small European thrush
REDWOOD *n*
REDYE, -D, -S *vb* dye again
REE, -S *n* Scots word for walled enclosure
REEARN, -S *vb* earn again
REEBOK, -S *same as* ▸ **rhebok**
REECH, -ED, -ES *vb* (in dialect) smoke
REECHIE *same as* ▸ **reechy**
REECHO *vb* echo again
REECHY *adj* (in dialect) smoky
REED, -ED, -S *n*
REEDBED *n* area of wetland with reeds growing in it
REEDE, -S *obsolete variant of* ▸ **red**
REEDED ▸ **reed**
REEDEN *adj* of or consisting of reeds
REEDER, -S *n* thatcher
REEDES ▸ **reede**
REEDIER ▸ **reedy**
REEDIFY *vb* edify again or rebuild
REEDILY ▸ **reedy**
REEDING *n* set of small semicircular architectural mouldings
REEDIT, -S *vb* edit again
REEDMAN, REEDMEN *n* musician who plays a wind instrument that has a reed
REEDS ▸ **reed**
REEDY, REEDIER *adj*
REEF, -ED, -S *n, vb*
REEFER, -S *n*
REEFIER ▸ **reefy**
REEFING ▸ **reef**
REEFS ▸ **reef**
REEFY, REEFIER *adj* with reefs
REEJECT *vb* eject again
REEK, -ED, -S *vb, n*
REEKER, -S ▸ **reek**
REEKIE *same as* ▸ **reeky**
REEKIER ▸ **reeky**
REEKING ▸ **reek**
REEKS ▸ **reek**
REEKY, REEKIER *adj*
REEL, -ED, -S *n, vb*
REELECT *vb*
REELED ▸ **reel**
REELER, -S ▸ **reel**
REELING ▸ **reel**
REELMAN, REELMEN *n* (formerly) member of a beach life-saving team operating a winch
REELS ▸ **reel**
REEMIT, -S *vb* emit again
REEN, -S *n* ditch, esp a drainage channel
REENACT *vb*
REENDOW *vb* endow again
REENJOY *vb* enjoy again
REENS ▸ **reen**
REENTER *vb*
REENTRY *n*
REEQUIP *vb* equip again
REERECT *vb* erect again
REES ▸ **ree**
REEST, -ED, -S *vb* (esp of horses) to be noisily uncooperative
REESTY *same as* ▸ **reasty**
REEVE, -D, -S, REEVING *n, vb*
REEVOKE *vb* evoke again
REEXPEL *vb* expel again
REF, -FED, -S *n* referee in sport ▹ *vb* referee
REFACE, -D, -S *vb* repair or renew the facing of (a wall)
REFALL, -S, REFELL *vb* fall again
REFECT, -S *vb* archaic word for restore or refresh with food and drink
REFEED, REFED, -S *vb* feed again
REFEEL, -S, REFELT *vb* feel again

REFEL, -S *vb* refute
REFELL ▸ **refall**
REFELS ▸ **refel**
REFELT ▸ **refeel**
REFENCE *vb* fence again
REFER, -S *vb*
REFEREE *n, vb*
REFERS ▸ **refer**
REFFED ▸ **ref**
REFFING *n* act or instance of refereeing a sports match
REFI, -S *n* refinancing of a debt
REFIGHT *vb* fight again ▹ *n* second or new fight
REFILE, -D, -S *vb* file again
REFILL, -S *vb, n*
REFILM, -S *vb* film again
REFIND, -S *vb* find again
REFINE, -S *vb*
REFINED *adj*
REFINER *n* person, device, or substance that removes impurities, etc
REFINES ▸ **refine**
REFIRE, -D, -S *vb* fire again
REFIS ▸ **refi**
REFIT, -S *vb, n*
REFIX, -ED, -ES *vb* fix again
REFLAG, -S *vb* flag again
REFLATE *vb* inflate or be inflated again
REFLECT *vb*
REFLET, -S *n* iridescent glow or lustre, as on ceramic ware
REFLEW ▸ **refly**
REFLEX *n, adj, vb*
REFLIES ▸ **refly**
REFLOAT *vb* float again
REFLOOD *vb* flood again
REFLOW, -S *vb* flow again
REFLOWN ▸ **refly**
REFLOWS ▸ **reflow**
REFLUX *vb, n*
REFLY, REFLEW, REFLIES, REFLOWN *vb* fly again
REFOCUS *vb* focus again or anew
REFOLD, -S *vb* fold again
REFOOT, -S *vb* foot again
REFORGE *vb* forge again
REFORM, -S *n, vb*
REFOUND *vb* found again
REFRACT *vb* change the course of (light etc) passing from one medium to another
REFRAIN *n, vb*
REFRAME *vb* support or enclose (a picture, photograph, etc) in a new or different frame
REFRESH *vb*
REFRIED ▸ **refry**
REFRIES ▸ **refry**
REFRONT *vb* put a new front on
REFROZE > **refreeze**
REFRY, REFRIED, REFRIES *vb* fry again
REFS ▸ **ref**
REFT ▸ **reave**
REFUEL, -S *vb*
REFUGE, -D, -S *n, vb*
REFUGEE *n*
REFUGES ▸ **refuge**
REFUGIA > **refugium**
REFUND, -S *vb, n*
REFURB, -S *vb, n*
REFUSAL *n*
REFUSE, -D, -S *vb, n*
REFUSER ▸ **refuse**
REFUSES ▸ **refuse**
REFUTAL *n* act or process of refuting
REFUTE, -D, -S *vb*
REFUTER ▸ **refute**
REFUTES ▸ **refute**
REG, -S *n* large expanse of stony desert terrain
REGAIN, -S *vb, n*
REGAL, -S *adj, n*
REGALE, -D, -S *vb, n*
REGALER ▸ **regale**
REGALES ▸ **regale**
REGALIA *pl n*
REGALLY ▸ **regal**
REGALS ▸ **regal**
REGAR, -S *same as* ▸ **regur**
REGARD, -S *vb, n*
REGARS ▸ **regar**
REGATTA *n* meeting for yacht or boat races
REGAUGE *vb* gauge again
REGAVE ▸ **regive**
REGEAR, -S *vb* readjust
REGENCE *old variant of* ▸ **regency**
REGENCY *n*
REGENT, -S *n, adj*
REGES ▸ **rex**
REGEST, -S *n* archaic word for register ▹ *vb* register
REGGAE, -S *n*
REGGO, -S *same as* ▸ **rego**
REGIE, -S *n* government-directed management

or government monopoly
REGIFT, -S *vb* give (a previously received gift) to someone else
REGILD, -S *vb* gild again
REGILT *archaic past form of* ▸ **regild**
REGIME, -S *n*
REGIMEN *n* prescribed system of diet etc
REGIMES ▸ **regime**
REGINA, -E, -S *n* queen
REGINAL *adj* queenly
REGINAS ▸ **regina**
REGION, -S *n*
REGIUS *adj* as in **regius professor** Crown-appointed holder of a university chair
REGIVE, REGAVE, -N, -S *vb* give again or back
REGLAZE *vb* glaze again
REGLET, -S *n* flat narrow architectural moulding
REGLOSS *vb* gloss again or give a new gloss to
REGLOW, -S *vb* glow again
REGLUE, -D, -S *vb* glue again
REGMA, -TA *n* type of fruit with cells that break open and break away when ripe
REGNA ▸ **regnum**
REGNAL *adj*
REGNANT *adj* reigning
REGNUM, REGNA *n*
REGO, -S *n* registration of a motor vehicle
REGORGE *vb* vomit up
REGOS ▸ **rego**
REGOSOL *n* type of azonal soil
REGRADE *vb* grade again
REGRAFT *vb* graft again
REGRANT *vb* grant again
REGRATE *vb* buy up (commodities) in advance so as to raise their price for resale
REGREDE *vb* go back
REGREEN *vb* green again
REGREET *vb* greet again or return greetings of
REGRESS *vb, n*
REGRET, -S *vb, n*
REGREW ▸ **regrow**
REGRIND *vb* grind again
REGROOM *vb* groom again
REGROUP *vb*
REGROW, REGREW, -N, -S *vb* grow or be grown again after having been cut or having died or withered
REGS ▸ **reg**
REGULA, -E *n* rule
REGULAR *adj, n*
REGULI ▸ **regulus**
REGULO, -S *n* any of a number of temperatures to which a gas oven may be set
REGULUS, REGULI *n* impure metal forming beneath the slag during the smelting of ores
REGUR, -S *n* black loamy Indian soil
REH, -S *n* (in India) salty surface crust on the soil
REHAB, -S *vb, n*
REHANG, -S, REHUNG *vb* hang again
REHASH *vb, n*
REHEAR, -D, -S *vb* hear again
REHEAT, -S *vb*
REHEEL, -S *vb* put a new heel or new heels on
REHEM, -S *vb* hem again
REHINGE *vb* put a new hinge or new hinges on
REHIRE, -D, -S *vb* hire again
REHOME, -D, -S *vb* find a new home for (esp a pet)
REHOUSE *vb* provide with a new (and better) home
REHS ▸ **reh**
REHUNG ▸ **rehang**
REI *n* name for a former Portuguese coin
REIF, -S *n* Scots word meaning robbery or plunder
REIFIED ▸ **reify**
REIFIER ▸ **reify**
REIFIES ▸ **reify**
REIFS ▸ **reif**
REIFY, REIFIED, REIFIES *vb* consider or make (an abstract idea or concept) real or concrete
REIGN, -ED, -S *n, vb*
REIK, -S *Scots word for* ▸ **smoke**

REIKI, -S *n* form of therapy to encourage healing or restore wellbeing
REIKS ▸ **reik**
REIMAGE *vb* image again
REIN, -ED, -ING *vb*
REINCUR *vb* incur again
REINDEX *vb* index again
REINED ▸ **rein**
REINING ▸ **rein**
REINK, -ED, -S *vb* ink again
REINS *pl n*
REINTER *vb* inter again
REIRD, -S *Scots word for* ▸ **din**
REIS, -ES *n* small branch
REISHI, -S *n* type of mushroom with a shiny cap
REISSUE *n, vb*
REIST, -ED, -S *same as* ▸ **reest**
REITBOK *same as* > **reedbuck**
REITER, -S *n* soldier in the German cavalry ▹ *vb* repeat something
REIVE, -D, -S *vb* go on a plundering raid
REIVER, -S ▸ **reive**
REIVES ▸ **reive**
REIVING *n* act of going on a plundering raid
REJECT, -S *vb, n*
REJIG, -S *vb, n*
REJOICE *vb*
REJOIN, -S *vb*
REJON, -ES *n* bullfighting lance
REJONEO *n* bullfighting activity in which a mounted bullfighter spears the bull with lances
REJONES ▸ **rejon**
REJOURN *vb* archaic word meaning postpone or adjourn
REJUDGE *vb* judge again
REKE, -D, -S, REKING *same as* ▸ **reck**
REKEY, -ED, -S *vb* key again
REKING ▸ **reke**
REKNIT, -S *vb* knit again
REKNOT, -S *vb* knot again
RELABEL *vb* label again
RELACE, -D, -S *vb* lace again
RELACHE *n* break
RELAID ▸ **relay**
RELAND, -S *vb* land again
RELAPSE *vb, n*
RELATA ▸ **relatum**
RELATE, -S *vb*
RELATED *adj*
RELATER ▸ **relate**
RELATES ▸ **relate**
RELATOR *n* person who relates a story
RELATUM, RELATA *n* one of the objects between which a relation is said to hold
RELAX, -ES *vb*
RELAXED ▸ **relax**
RELAXER *n* person or thing that relaxes
RELAXES ▸ **relax**
RELAXIN *n* hormone secreted during pregnancy
RELAY, RELAID, -ED, -S *n, vb*
RELEARN *vb* learn (something previously known) again
RELEASE *vb, n*
RELEND, -S *vb* lend again
RELENT, -S *vb*
RELET, -S *vb* let again
RELEVE, -S *n* dance move in which heels are off the ground
RELIANT > **reliance**
RELIC, -S *n*
RELICT, -S *n* relic
RELIDE *archaic past form of* ▸ **rely**
RELIE *archaic spelling of* ▸ **rely**
RELIED ▸ **rely**
RELIEF, -S *n*
RELIER, -S ▸ **rely**
RELIES ▸ **rely**
RELIEVE *vb*
RELIEVO *same as* ▸ **relief**
RELIGHT, RELIT *vb* ignite or cause to ignite again
RELINE, -D, -S *vb* line again or anew
RELINK, -S *vb* link again
RELIQUE *archaic spelling of* ▸ **relic**
RELISH *vb, n*
RELIST, -S *vb* list again
RELIT ▸ **relight**
RELIVE, -D, -S *vb*
RELIVER *vb* deliver up again
RELIVES ▸ **relive**
RELLENO *n* Mexican dish of stuffed vegetable
RELLIE, -S *n* informal word for a relative

RELLISH *(in music) variant of* ▸ **relish**
RELLO, -S *n* informal Australian word for a relative
RELOAD, -S *vb*
RELOAN, -S *vb* loan again
RELOCK, -S *vb* lock again
RELOOK, -S *vb* look again
RELUCT, -S *vb* struggle or rebel
RELUME, -D, -S *vb* light or brighten again
RELY, RELIED, RELIES, -ING *vb*
REM, -S *n* dose of ionizing radiation
REMADE, -S *n* reconstructed object
REMAIL, -S *vb* mail again
REMAIN *vb*
REMAINS *pl n*
REMAKE, -S *vb, n*
REMAKER ▸ **remake**
REMAKES ▸ **remake**
REMAN, -S *vb* man again or afresh
REMAND, -S *vb*
REMANET *n* something left over
REMANIE *n* fragments and fossils of older origin found in a more recent deposit
REMANS ▸ **reman**
REMAP, -S *vb* map again
REMARK, -S *vb, n*
REMARRY *vb*
REMATCH *n, vb*
REMATE, -D, -S *vb* mate (animals) again ▹ *n* finishing pass in bullfighting
REMBLAI *n* earth used for an embankment or rampart
REMBLE, -D, -S *dialect word for* ▸ **remove**
REMEAD, -S *archaic or dialect word for* ▸ **remedy**
REMEDE, -D, -S *archaic or dialect word for* ▸ **remedy**
REMEDY *n, vb*
REMEET, -S, REMET *vb* meet again
REMEID, -S *archaic or dialect word for* ▸ **remedy**
REMELT, -S *vb* melt again
REMEN, -S *n* ancient Egyptian measurement unit
REMEND, -S *vb* mend again
REMENS ▸ **remen**
REMERCY *vb* archaic word for thank
REMERGE *vb* merge again
REMET ▸ **remeet**
REMEX, REMIGES *n* any of the large flight feathers of a bird's wing
REMIND, -S *vb*
REMINT, -S *vb* mint again
REMISE, -D, -S *vb* give up or relinquish (a right, claim, etc) ▹ *n* second thrust made on the same lunge after the first has missed
REMISS *adj*
REMIT, -S *vb, n*
REMIX, -ED, -ES *vb, n*
REMIXER *n* person who remixes a recording
REMIXES ▸ **remix**
REMIXT *informal past form of* ▸ **remix**
REMNANT *n, adj*
REMODEL *vb, n*
REMOLD, -S *US spelling of* ▸ **remould**
REMORA, -S *n* spiny-finned fish
REMORID ▸ **remora**
REMORSE *n*
REMOTE, -R, -S *adj, n*
REMOUD *Spenserian variant of* ▸ **removed**
REMOULD *vb* change completely ▹ *n* renovated tyre
REMOUNT *vb* get on (a horse, bicycle, etc) again ▹ *n* fresh horse
REMOVAL *n*
REMOVE, -S *vb, n*
REMOVED *adj*
REMOVER ▸ **remove**
REMOVES ▸ **remove**
REMS ▸ **rem**
REMUAGE *n* process of turning wine bottles to let the sediment out
REMUDA, -S *n* stock of horses enabling riders to change mounts
REMUEUR *n* person carrying out remuage
REN, -NED, -S *archaic variant of* ▸ **run**
RENAGUE *same as* ▸ **renege**
RENAIL, -S *vb* nail again
RENAL *adj*
RENAME, -D, -S *vb*

RENAY, -ED, -S *vb* archaic word meaning renounce
REND, -ED, -ING, -S *vb*
RENDANG *n* spicy Indonesian meat dish
RENDED ▸ **rend**
RENDER, -S *vb, n*
RENDING ▸ **rend**
RENDS ▸ **rend**
RENEGE, -D, -S *vb*
RENEGER ▸ **renege**
RENEGES ▸ **renege**
RENEGUE *same as* ▸ **renege**
RENEST, -S *vb* nest again or form a new nest
RENEW, -ED, -S *vb*
RENEWAL *n*
RENEWED ▸ **renew**
RENEWER ▸ **renew**
RENEWS ▸ **renew**
RENEY, -ED, -S *same as* ▸ **renay**
RENGA, -S *n* type of collaborative poetry found in Japan
RENIED ▸ **reny**
RENIES ▸ **reny**
RENIG, -S *same as* ▸ **renege**
RENIN, -S *n* enzyme secreted by the kidneys
RENK, -ER, -EST *adj* unpleasant
RENNASE *same as* ▸ **rennin**
RENNE, -S *archaic variant of* ▸ **run**
RENNED ▸ **ren**
RENNES ▸ **renne**
RENNET, -S *n*
RENNIN, -S *n* enzyme that occurs in gastric juice
RENNING ▸ **ren**
RENNINS ▸ **rennin**
RENO, -S *n* renovated house
RENOWN, -S *n, vb*
RENS ▸ **ren**
RENT, -ED, -S *n, vb*
RENTAL, -S *n, adj*
RENTE, -S *n* annual income from capital investment
RENTED ▸ **rent**
RENTER, -S *n*
RENTES ▸ **rente**
RENTIER *n* person who lives off unearned income such as rents or interest
RENTING ▸ **rent**
RENTS ▸ **rent**
RENVOI, -S *n* referring of a dispute to a jurisdiction other than that in which it arose
RENVOY, -S *old variant of* ▸ **renvoi**
RENY, RENIED, RENIES, -ING *same as* ▸ **renay**
REO, -S *n* New Zealand language
REOCCUR *vb* happen, take place, or come about again
REOFFER *vb* offer again
REOIL, -ED, -S *vb* oil again
REOPEN, -S *vb*
REORDER *vb*
REORG, -ED, -S *vb* reorganize
REOS ▸ **reo**
REP, -PED, -S *n, vb*
REPACK, -S *vb* place or arrange (articles) in (a container) again or in a different way
REPAID ▸ **repay**
REPAINT *vb*
REPAIR, -S *vb, n*
REPAND *adj* having a wavy margin
REPANEL *vb* panel again or anew
REPAPER *vb* paper again or afresh
REPARK, -S *vb* park again
REPASS *vb* pass again
REPAST, -S *n, vb*
REPATCH *vb* patch again
REPAVE, -D, -S *vb* pave again
REPAY, REPAID, -S *vb*
REPEAL, -S *vb, n*
REPEAT, -S *vb, n*
REPEG, -S *vb* peg again
REPEL, -S *vb*
REPENT, -S *vb, adj*
REPERK, -S *vb* perk again
REPIN, -S *vb* pin again
REPINE, -D, -S *vb* fret or complain
REPINER ▸ **repine**
REPINES ▸ **repine**
REPINS ▸ **repin**
REPIQUE *n* score of 30 in the card-game piquet ▹ *vb* score a repique against (someone)
REPLA ▸ **replum**
REPLACE *vb*
REPLAN, -S *vb* plan again
REPLANT *vb* plant again
REPLATE *vb* plate again
REPLAY, -S *n, vb*

REPLEAD, REPLED *vb* plead again
REPLETE *adj, vb*
REPLEVY *vb* recover possession of (goods) by replevin
REPLICA *n*
REPLIED ▸ **reply**
REPLIER ▸ **reply**
REPLIES ▸ **reply**
REPLOT, -S *vb* plot again
REPLOW, -S *vb* plow again
REPLUM, REPLA *n* internal separating wall in some fruits
REPLUMB *vb* plumb again
REPLY, REPLIED, REPLIES *vb, n*
REPO, -S *n* act of repossessing
REPOINT *vb* repair the joints of (brickwork, masonry, etc) with mortar or cement
REPOLL, -S *vb* poll again
REPOMAN, REPOMEN *n* man employed to repossess goods in cases of non-payment
REPONE, -D, -S *vb* restore (someone) to his or her former status, office, etc
REPORT, -S *vb, n*
REPOS ▸ **repo**
REPOSAL *n* repose
REPOSE, -D, -S *n, vb*
REPOSER ▸ **repose**
REPOSES ▸ **repose**
REPOSIT *vb* put away, deposit, or store up
REPOST, -S *vb* post again
REPOT, -S *vb* put (a house plant) into a new usually larger pot
REPOUR, -S *vb* pour back or again
REPOWER *vb* put new engine in
REPP, -S *same as* ▸ **rep**
REPPED ▸ **rep**
REPPING ▸ **rep**
REPPS ▸ **repp**
REPRESS *vb*
REPRICE *vb* price again
REPRIME *vb* prime again
REPRINT *vb, n*
REPRISE *n, vb*
REPRIVE *archaic spelling of* ▸ **reprieve**
REPRIZE *archaic spelling of* ▸ **reprise**
REPRO, -S *n* imitation or facsimile of a work of art; reproduction
REPROBE *vb* probe again
REPROOF *n, vb*
REPROS ▸ **repro**
REPROVE *vb*
REPRYVE *archaic spelling of* ▸ **reprieve**
REPS ▸ **rep**
REPTANT *adj* creeping, crawling, or lying along the ground
REPTILE *n, adj*
REPUGN, -S *vb*
REPULP, -S *vb* pulp again
REPULSE *vb, n*
REPUMP, -S *vb* pump again
REPUNIT *n* any number that consists entirely of the same repeated digits
REPURE, -D, -S *vb* archaic word meaning make pure again
REPUTE, -S *n, vb*
REPUTED *adj*
REPUTES ▸ **repute**
REQUERE *archaic variant of* ▸ **require**
REQUEST *vb, n*
REQUIEM *n*
REQUIN, -S *vb* type of shark
REQUIRE *vb*
REQUIT, -S *vb* quit again
REQUITE *vb* return to someone (the same treatment or feeling as received)
REQUITS ▸ **requit**
REQUOTE *vb* quote again
RERACK, -S *vb* rack again
RERAIL, -S *vb* put back on a railway line
RERAISE *vb* raise again
RERAN ▸ **rerun**
REREAD, -S *vb* read (something) again
REREDOS *n* ornamental screen behind an altar
REREMAI *n* New Zealand word for the basking shark
RERENT, -S *vb* rent again
RERIG, -S *vb* rig again
RERISE, -N, -S, REROSE *vb* rise again
REROLL, -S *vb* roll again
REROOF, -S *vb* put a new roof or roofs on
REROSE ▸ **rerise**
REROUTE *vb*

RERUN, RERAN, -S *n, vb*
RES, -ES *informal word for* > **residence**
RESAID ▸ **resay**
RESAIL, -S *vb* sail again
RESALE, -S *n* selling of something purchased earlier
RESAT ▸ **resit**
RESAW, -ED, -N, -S *vb* saw again
RESAY, RESAID, -S *vb* say again or in response
RESCALE *vb* resize
RESCIND *vb* annul or repeal
RESCORE *vb* score afresh
RESCUE, -D, -S *vb, n*
RESCUEE *n* person who is rescued
RESCUER ▸ **rescue**
RESCUES ▸ **rescue**
RESEAL, -S *vb* close or secure tightly again
RESEAT, -S *vb* show (a person) to a new seat
RESEAU, -S, -X *n* mesh background to a lace or other pattern
RESECT, -S *vb* cut out part of (a bone, an organ, or other structure or part)
RESEDA, -S *n* plant that has small spikes of grey-green flowers ▹ *adj* of a greyish-green colour
RESEE, -N, -S *vb* see again
RESEED, -S *vb* form seed and reproduce naturally, forming a constant plant population
RESEEK, -S *vb* seek again
RESEEN ▸ **resee**
RESEES ▸ **resee**
RESEIZE *vb* seize again
RESELL, -S, RESOLD *vb*
RESEND, -S *vb*
RESENT, -S *vb*
RESERVE *vb, n*
RESES ▸ **res**
RESET, -S *vb, n*
RESEW, -ED, -N, -S *vb* sew again
RESH, -ES *n* 20th letter of the Hebrew alphabet
RESHAPE *vb* shape (something) again or differently
RESHAVE *vb* shave again
RESHES ▸ **resh**
RESHINE, RESHONE *vb* shine again
RESHIP, -S *vb* ship again
RESHOE, RESHOD, -D, -S *vb* put a new shoe or shoes on
RESHONE ▸ **reshine**
RESHOOT, RESHOT *vb* shoot again
RESHOW, -N, -S *vb* show again
RESIANT *archaic word for* > **resident**
RESID, -S *n* residual oil left over from the petroleum distillation process
RESIDE, -D, -S *vb*
RESIDER ▸ **reside**
RESIDES ▸ **reside**
RESIDS ▸ **resid**
RESIDUA > **residuum**
RESIDUE *n*
RESIFT, -S *vb* sift again
RESIGHT *vb* sight again
RESIGN, -S *vb*
RESILE, -D, -S *vb* spring or shrink back
RESILIN *n* substance found in insect bodies
RESIN, -ED, -S *n, vb*
RESINER *n* applier or collector of resin
RESINS ▸ **resin**
RESINY *adj* resembling, containing or covered with resin
RESIST, -S *vb, n*
RESIT, RESAT, -S *vb, n*
RESITE, -D, -S *vb* move to a different site
RESITS ▸ **resit**
RESIZE, -D, -S *vb*
RESKEW, -S *archaic spelling of* ▸ **rescue**
RESKILL *vb*
RESKIN, -S *vb* replace the outermost layer of an aircraft
RESKUE, -D, -S *archaic spelling of* ▸ **rescue**
RESLATE *vb* slate again
RESMELT *vb* smelt again
RESOAK, -S *vb* soak again
RESOD, -S *vb* returf
RESOJET *n* type of jet engine
RESOLD ▸ **resell**
RESOLE, -D, -S *vb* put a new sole or new soles on
RESOLVE *vb, n*
RESORB, -S *vb* absorb again
RESORT, -S *vb, n*
RESOUND *vb*
RESOW, -ED, -N, -S *vb* sow again

RESPACE *vb* change the spacing of
RESPADE *vb* dig over
RESPEAK, RESPOKE *vb* speak further
RESPECT *n, vb*
RESPELL, RESPELT *vb* spell again
RESPIRE *vb*
RESPITE *n, vb*
RESPLIT *vb* split again
RESPOKE ▸ **respeak**
RESPOND *vb, n*
RESPOOL *vb* rewind onto spool
RESPOT, -S *vb* (in billiards) replace (a ball) on one of the spots
RESPRAY *n* new coat of paint applied to a car, van, etc ▹ *vb* spray (a car, wheels, etc) with a new coat of paint
REST, -ED, -S *n, vb*
RESTACK *vb* stack again
RESTAFF *vb* staff again
RESTAGE *vb* produce or perform a new production of (a play)
RESTAMP *vb* stamp again
RESTART *vb, n*
RESTATE *vb* state or affirm (something) again or in a different way
RESTED ▸ **rest**
RESTEM, -S *vb* stem again
RESTER, -S ▸ **rest**
RESTFUL *adj* relaxing or soothing
RESTIER ▸ **resty**
RESTIFF *same as* ▸ **restive**
RESTING ▸ **rest**
RESTIVE *adj* restless or impatient
RESTO, -S *n* restored antique, vintage car, etc
RESTOCK *vb*
RESTOKE *vb* stoke again
RESTORE *vb*
RESTOS ▸ **resto**
RESTS ▸ **rest**
RESTUDY *vb* study again
RESTUFF *vb* put new stuffing in
RESTUMP *vb* provide with new stumps
RESTY, RESTIER *adj* restive
RESTYLE *vb* style again
RESULT, -S *n, vb*
RESUME, -D, -S *vb, n*
RESUMER ▸ **resume**
RESUMES ▸ **resume**
RESURGE *vb*
RESUS, -ES *n* (short for) resuscitation room
RET, -S, -TED, -TING *vb* moisten or soak (flax, hemp, jute, etc) to facilitate separation of fibres
RETABLE *n* ornamental screenlike structure above and behind an altar
RETABLO *n* shelf for panels behind an altar
RETACK, -S *vb* tack again
RETAG, -S *vb* tag again
RETAIL, -S *n, adj, adv, vb*
RETAIN, -S *vb*

> Perhaps the most important word in Scrabble, because its letters combine with every other letter apart from A, Q, V, X, Y and Z to form a 7-letter bonus word that will score you an extra 50 points, so if you have these six letters on your rack you know that a bonus is either available or very close. And if you have an S as well, so much the better, because not only does this rack offer you 11 different words to choose from, but if none of those can be fitted in then **retains** combines with every other letter except for Q, V, X, Y and Z to form at least one 8-letter word.

RETAKE, -N, -S, RETOOK *vb* recapture ▹ *n* act of rephotographing a scene
RETAKER ▸ **retake**
RETAKES ▸ **retake**
RETALLY *vb* count up again
RETAMA, -S *n* type of shrub
RETAPE, -D, -S *vb* tape again
RETARD, -S *vb*
RETASTE *vb* taste again
RETAX, -ED, -ES *vb* tax again
RETCH, -ED, -ES *vb, n*

RETE, RETIA *n* any network of nerves or blood vessels
RETEACH *vb* teach again
RETEAM, -S *vb* team up again
RETEAR, -S, RETORE, RETORN *vb* tear again
RETELL, -S, RETOLD *vb*
RETEM, -S *n* type of shrub
RETENE, -S *n* yellow crystalline hydrocarbon found in tar oils
RETEST, -S *vb* test (something) again or differently
RETHINK *vb, n*
RETIA ▸ **rete**
RETIAL ▸ **rete**
RETIARY *adj* of, relating to, or resembling a net or web
RETICLE *n* network of fine lines, wires, etc, used in optical instruments
RETIE, -D, -S, RETYING *vb* tie again
RETILE, -D, -S *vb* put new tiles in or on
RETIME, -D, -S *vb* time again or alter time of
RETINA, -E, -S *n*
RETINAL *adj, n*
RETINAS ▸ **retina**
RETINE, -S *n* chemical found in body cells that slows cell growth and division
RETINOL *n* another name for vitamin A and rosin oil
RETINT, -S *vb* tint again or change tint of
RETINUE *n*
RETIRAL *n* act of retiring from office, one's work, etc
RETIRE, -S *vb*
RETIRED *adj*
RETIREE *n*
RETIRER ▸ **retire**
RETIRES ▸ **retire**
RETITLE *vb* give a new title to
RETOLD ▸ **retell**
RETOOK ▸ **retake**
RETOOL, -S *vb*
RETORE ▸ **retear**
RETORN ▸ **retear**
RETORT, -S *vb, n*
RETOTAL *vb* add up again
RETOUCH *vb, n*
RETOUR, -S *vb* (in Scottish law) to return as heir
RETOX, -ED, -ES *vb* embark on a binge of something unhealthy after a period of abstinence
RETRACE *vb*
RETRACK *vb* track again
RETRACT *vb*
RETRAIN *vb*
RETRAIT *archaic form of* ▸ **retreat**
RETRAL *adj* at, near, or towards the back
RETRATE *archaic form of* ▸ **retreat**
RETREAD, RETROD *n* remould ▹ *vb* remould
RETREAT *vb, n*
RETREE, -S *n* imperfectly made paper
RETRIAL *n*
RETRIED ▸ **retry**
RETRIES ▸ **retry**
RETRIM, -S *vb* trim again
RETRO, -S *adj, n*
RETROD ▸ **retread**
RETROS ▸ **retro**
RETRY, RETRIED, RETRIES *vb*
RETS ▸ **ret**
RETSINA *n* Greek wine flavoured with resin
RETTED ▸ **ret**
RETTERY *n* flax-retting place
RETTING ▸ **ret**
RETUND, -S *vb* weaken or blunt
RETUNE, -D, -S *vb*
RETURF, -S *vb* turf again
RETURN, -S *vb, n, adj*
RETUSE *adj* having a rounded apex and a central depression
RETWEET *vb* post (another user's post) on the Twitter website for one's own followers
RETWIST *vb* twist again
RETYING ▸ **retie**
RETYPE, -D, -S *vb*
REUNIFY *vb*
REUNION *n*
REUNITE *vb*
REURGE, -D, -S *vb* urge again
REUSE, -D, -S, REUSING *vb, n*
REUTTER *vb* utter again
REV, -S, -VED, -VING *n* revolution (of an engine) ▹ *vb* increase the speed of revolution of (an engine)

REVALUE *vb* adjust the exchange value of (a currency) upwards
REVAMP, -S *vb, n*
REVEAL, -S *vb, n*
REVEL, -ED, -S *vb, n*
REVELER ▸ **revel**
REVELRY *n*
REVELS ▸ **revel**
REVENGE *n, vb*
REVENUE *n*
REVERB, -S *n, vb*
REVERE, -D, -S *vb*
REVERER ▸ **revere**
REVERES ▸ **revere**
REVERIE *n* absent-minded daydream
REVERS *n* turned back part of a garment, such as a lapel
REVERSE *vb, n, adj*
REVERSI *n* game played on a draughtboard
REVERSO *another name for* ▸ **verso**
REVERT, -S *vb*
REVERY *same as* ▸ **reverie**
REVEST, -S *vb* restore (former power, authority, status, etc, to a person)
REVET, -S *vb* face (a wall or embankment) with stones
REVEUR, -S *n* daydreamer
REVEUSE *n* female daydreamer
REVIE, -D, -S, REVYING *vb* archaic cards term meaning challenge by placing a larger stake
REVIEW, -S *n, vb*
REVILE, -D, -S *vb*
REVILER ▸ **revile**
REVILES ▸ **revile**
REVISAL ▸ **revise**
REVISE, -D, -S *vb, n*
REVISER ▸ **revise**
REVISES ▸ **revise**
REVISIT *vb*
REVISOR ▸ **revise**
REVIVAL *n*
REVIVE, -D, -S *vb*
REVIVER ▸ **revive**
REVIVES ▸ **revive**
REVIVOR *n* means of reviving a lawsuit that has been suspended
REVOICE *vb* utter again
REVOKE, -D, -S *vb, n*
REVOKER ▸ **revoke**
REVOKES ▸ **revoke**
REVOLT, -S *n, vb*
REVOLVE *vb, n*
REVOTE, -D, -S *vb* decide or grant again by a new vote
REVS ▸ **rev**
REVUE, -S *n*
REVUIST ▸ **revue**
REVVED ▸ **rev**
REVVING ▸ **rev**
REVYING ▸ **revie**
REW, -S *archaic spelling of* ▸ **rue**
REWAKE, -D, -S, REWOKE, REWOKEN *vb* awaken again
REWAKEN *vb* awaken again
REWAKES ▸ **rewake**
REWAN *archaic past form of* ▸ **rewin**
REWARD, -S *n, vb*
REWARM, -S *vb* warm again
REWASH *vb* wash again
REWATER *vb* water again
REWAX, -ED, -ES *vb* wax again
REWEAR, -S, REWORE, REWORN *vb* wear again
REWEAVE, REWOVE, REWOVEN *vb* weave again
REWED, -S *vb* wed again
REWEIGH *vb* weigh again
REWELD, -S *vb* weld again
REWET, -S *vb* wet again
REWIDEN *vb* widen again
REWILD, -S *vb*
REWIN, -S, REWON *vb* win again
REWIND, -S, REWOUND *vb*
REWINS ▸ **rewin**
REWIRE, -D, -S *vb*
REWOKE ▸ **rewake**
REWOKEN ▸ **rewake**
REWON ▸ **rewin**
REWORD, -S *vb*
REWORE ▸ **rewear**
REWORK, -S *vb*
REWORN ▸ **rewear**
REWOUND ▸ **rewind**
REWOVE ▸ **reweave**
REWOVEN ▸ **reweave**
REWRAP, -S, -T *vb* wrap again
REWRITE, REWROTE *vb, n*
REWS ▸ **rew**
REWTH, -S *archaic variant of* ▸ **ruth**
REX, REGES, -ES *n* king

Rex is a Latin word for **king**, a very commonly played X word.

REXINE, -S *n* tradename for a form of artificial leather
REYNARD *n* fox
REZ, -ES, -ZES *n* informal word for an instance of reserving; reservation

Rez is a short informal word for **reservation**, and is one of the most commonly played Z words.

REZERO, -S *vb* reset to zero
REZES ▸ **rez**
REZONE, -D, -S *vb* zone again
REZZES ▸ **rez**
RHABDOM *n* rodlike structure found in the eye of insects
RHABDUS *n* sponge spicule
RHACHIS *same as* ▸ **rachis**
RHAMNUS *n* buckthorn
RHAPHE, RHAPHAE, -S *same as* ▸ **raphe**
RHAPHIS *same as* ▸ **raphide**
RHATANY *n* S American leguminous shrub
RHEA, -S *n* S American three-toed ostrich
RHEBOK, -S *n* woolly brownish-grey southern African antelope
RHEME, -S *n* constituent of a sentence that adds most new information
RHENIUM *n* silvery-white metallic element with a high melting point
RHESUS *n* macaque monkey
RHETOR, -S *n* teacher of rhetoric
RHEUM, -S *n* watery discharge from the eyes or nose
RHEUMED *adj* rheumy
RHEUMIC *adj* of or relating to rheum
RHEUMS ▸ **rheum**
RHEUMY *adj* of the nature of rheum
RHEXIS, RHEXES *n* rupture
RHIES ▸ **rhy**
RHIME, -S *old spelling of* ▸ **rhyme**
RHINAL *adj* of or relating to the nose
RHINE, -S *n* dialect word for a ditch
RHINO, -S *n*
RHIZIC *adj* of or relating to the root of an equation
RHIZINE *same as* ▸ **rhizoid**
RHIZOID *n* hairlike structure in mosses, ferns, and related plants
RHIZOMA *same as* ▸ **rhizome**
RHIZOME *n* thick underground stem producing new plants
RHIZOPI > **rhizopus**
RHO, -S *n* 17th letter in the Greek alphabet

It's useful to remember words that start with RH, as they can come in useful. If you or someone else plays **rho**, which is a Greek letter, remember that it can be expanded to, for example, **rhody, rhomb, rhodium, rhombus** or **rhomboid**.

RHODIC *adj* of or containing rhodium, esp in the tetravalent state
RHODIE *same as* ▸ **rhody**
RHODIES ▸ **rhody**
RHODIUM *n* hard metallic element
RHODORA *n* type of shrub
RHODOUS *adj* of or containing rhodium (but proportionally more than a rhodic compound)
RHODY, RHODIES *n* rhododendron
RHOMB, -S *same as* ▸ **rhombus**
RHOMBI ▸ **rhombus**
RHOMBIC *adj* relating to or having the shape of a rhombus
RHOMBOS, RHOMBOI *n* wooden slat attached to a thong that makes a roaring sound when the thong is whirled
RHOMBS ▸ **rhomb**
RHOMBUS, RHOMBI *n* diamond-shaped figure
RHONCHI > **rhonchus**

RHONCUS *n* respiratory sound resembling snoring
RHONE, -S *same as* ▸ **rone**
RHOS ▸ **rho**
RHOTIC *adj* denoting or speaking a dialect of English in which postvocalic rs are pronounced
RHUBARB *n, interj, vb*
RHUMB, -S *n* imaginary line on the surface of a sphere that intersects all meridians at the same angle
RHUMBA, -S *same as* ▸ **rumba**
RHUMBS ▸ **rhumb**
RHUS, -ES *n* genus of shrubs and small trees
RHY, RHIES *archaic spelling of* ▸ **rye**

This alternative spelling of **rye** can come in useful when you are short of vowels.

RHYME, -D, -S, RHYMING *n, vb*
RHYMER, -S *same as* > **rhymester**
RHYMES ▸ **rhyme**
RHYMING ▸ **rhyme**
RHYMIST ▸ **rhyme**
RHYNE, -S *same as* ▸ **rhine**
RHYTA ▸ **rhyton**
RHYTHM, -S *n*
RHYTHMI > **rhythmus**
RHYTHMS ▸ **rhythm**
RHYTINA *n* type of sea cow
RHYTON, RHYTA, -S *n* (in ancient Greece) horn-shaped drinking vessel
RIA, -S *n* long narrow inlet of the seacoast
RIAD, -S *n* traditional Moroccan house with an interior garden
RIAL, -S *n* standard monetary unit of Iran
RIALTO, -S *n* market or exchange
RIANCY ▸ **riant**
RIANT *adj* laughing
RIANTLY ▸ **riant**
RIAS ▸ **ria**
RIATA, -S *same as* ▸ **reata**
RIB, -BED, -S *n, vb*
RIBA, -S *n* (in Islam) interest or usury
RIBALD, -S *adj, n*
RIBAND, -S *n* ribbon awarded for some achievement
RIBAS ▸ **riba**
RIBAUD, -S *archaic variant of* ▸ **ribald**
RIBBAND *same as* ▸ **riband**
RIBBED ▸ **rib**
RIBBER, -S *n* someone who ribs
RIBBIE, -S *n* baseball run batted in
RIBBIER ▸ **ribby**
RIBBIES ▸ **ribbie**
RIBBING ▸ **rib**
RIBBIT, -S *n* sound a frog makes
RIBBON, -S *n, vb*
RIBBONY *adj* resembling ribbons
RIBBY, RIBBIER *adj* with noticeable ribs
RIBCAGE *n*
RIBES *n* genus of shrubs that includes currants
RIBEYE, -S *n*
RIBIBE, -S *n* rebeck
RIBIBLE *same as* ▸ **ribibe**
RIBIER, -S *n* variety of grape
RIBLESS ▸ **rib**
RIBLET, -S *n* small rib
RIBLIKE ▸ **rib**
RIBOSE, -S *n* pentose sugar that occurs in RNA and riboflavin
RIBS ▸ **rib**
RIBSTON *n* variety of apple
RIBWORK *n* work or structure involving ribs
RIBWORT *n* Eurasian plant with lancelike ribbed leaves
RICE, -D, -S, RICING *n, vb*
RICER, -S *n* kitchen utensil through which soft foods are pressed to form a coarse mash
RICES ▸ **rice**
RICEY *adj* resembling or containing rice
RICH, -ED, -ER, -EST, -ING *adj, vb*
RICHEN, -S *vb* enrich
RICHER ▸ **rich**
RICHES *pl n*
RICHEST ▸ **rich**
RICHING ▸ **rich**
RICHLY *adv*
RICHT, -ED, -ER, -S *Scots variant of* ▸ **right**
RICIER ▸ **ricy**
RICIEST ▸ **ricy**
RICIN, -S *n* highly toxic protein, a lectin,

derived from castor-oil seeds
RICING ▶ **rice**
RICINS ▶ **ricin**
RICINUS *n* genus of plants
RICK, -ED, -ING, -S *n* stack of hay etc ▷ *vb* wrench or sprain (a joint)
RICKER, -S *n* young kauri tree of New Zealand
RICKET *n*
RICKETS *n*
RICKETY *adj*
RICKEY, -S *n* cocktail consisting of gin or vodka, lime juice, and soda water, served iced
RICKING ▶ **rick**
RICKLE, -S *n* unsteady or shaky structure
RICKLY *adj* archaic word for run-down or rickety
RICKS ▶ **rick**
RICKSHA *same as* > **rickshaw**
RICOTTA *n* soft white unsalted Italian cheese made from sheep's milk
RICRAC, -S *same as* > **rickrack**
RICTAL ▶ **rictus**
RICTUS *n* gape or cleft of an open mouth or beak
RICY, RICIER, RICIEST *same as* ▶ **ricey**
RID, -DED, -DING, -S *vb*
RIDABLE ▶ **ride**
RIDDED ▶ **rid**
RIDDEN ▶ **ride**
RIDDER, -S ▶ **rid**
RIDDING ▶ **rid**
RIDDLE, -D, -S *n, vb*
RIDDLER ▶ **riddle**
RIDDLES ▶ **riddle**
RIDE, RIDDEN, -S *vb, n*
RIDENT *adj* laughing, smiling, or happy
RIDER, -S *n*
RIDERED ▶ **rider**
RIDERS ▶ **rider**
RIDES ▶ **ride**
RIDGE, -D, -S *n, vb*
RIDGER, -S *n* plough used to form furrows and ridges
RIDGES ▶ **ridge**
RIDGIER ▶ **ridgy**
RIDGING ▶ **ridge**
RIDGY, RIDGIER ▶ **ridge**
RIDIC *adj* ridiculous
RIDING, -S ▶ **ride**
RIDLEY, -S *n* marine turtle
RIDOTTO *n* entertainment with music and dancing, often in masquerade
RIDS ▶ **rid**
RIEL, -S *n* standard monetary unit of Cambodia
RIEM, -S *n* strip of hide
RIEMPIE *n* leather thong or lace used mainly to make chair seats
RIEMS ▶ **riem**
RIEVE, -D, -S, RIEVING *vb* archaic word for rob or plunder
RIEVER, -S *n* archaic word for robber or plunderer
RIEVES ▶ **rieve**
RIEVING ▶ **rieve**
RIF, -S *vb* lay off
RIFE, -R, -ST *adj*
RIFELY ▶ **rife**
RIFER ▶ **rife**
RIFEST ▶ **rife**
RIFF, -ED, -ING, -S *n, vb*
RIFFAGE *n* (in jazz or rock music) act or an instance of playing a short series of chords
RIFFED ▶ **riff**
RIFFING ▶ **riff**
RIFFLE, -D, -S *vb* flick through (pages etc) quickly ▷ *n* rapid in a stream
RIFFLER *n* file with a curved face for filing concave surfaces
RIFFLES ▶ **riffle**
RIFFOLA *n* use of an abundance of dominant riffs
RIFFS ▶ **riff**
RIFLE, -D, -S *n, vb*
RIFLER, -S ▶ **rifle**
RIFLERY *n* rifle shots
RIFLES ▶ **rifle**
RIFLING *n*
RIFLIP, -S *n* genetic difference between two individuals
RIFS ▶ **rif**
RIFT, -ED, -ING, -S *n, vb*
RIFTE *archaic word for* ▶ **rift**
RIFTED ▶ **rift**
RIFTIER ▶ **rifty**
RIFTING ▶ **rift**
RIFTS ▶ **rift**
RIFTY, RIFTIER ▶ **rift**
RIG, -GED, -S *vb, n*
RIGG, -S *n* type of fish
RIGGED ▶ **rig**
RIGGER, -S *n* person who rigs vessels, etc
RIGGING ▶ **rig**

RIGGS ▸ **rigg**
RIGHT, -ED, -S *adj, adv, n, vb*
RIGHTEN *vb* set right
RIGHTER ▸ **right**
RIGHTLY *adv*
RIGHTO *interj* expression of agreement or compliance
RIGHTS ▸ **right**
RIGHTY *n, adj*
RIGID, -ER, -S *adj, adv, n*
RIGIDLY ▸ **rigid**
RIGIDS ▸ **rigid**
RIGLINS ▸ **riglin**
RIGOL, -S *n* (in dialect) ditch or gutter
RIGOLL, -S *same as* ▸ **rigol**
RIGOLS ▸ **rigol**
RIGOR, -S *same as* ▸ **rigour**
RIGOUR, -S *n*
RIGOUT, -S *n* person's clothing
RIGS ▸ **rig**
RIKISHA *same as* > **rickshaw**
RIKISHI *n* sumo wrestler
RIKSHAW *same as* > **rickshaw**
RILE, -D, -S, RILING *vb*
RILEY, RILIER, RILIEST *adj* cross or irritable
RILIEVO, RILIEVI *same as* ▸ **relief**
RILING ▸ **rile**
RILL, -ED, -ING, -S *n* small stream ▹ *vb* trickle
RILLE, -S *same as* ▸ **rill**
RILLED ▸ **rill**
RILLES ▸ **rille**
RILLET, -S *n* little rill
RILLING ▸ **rill**
RILLS ▸ **rill**
RIM, -MED, -S *n, vb*
RIMA, -E *n* long narrow opening
RIMAYE, -S *n* crevasse at the head of a glacier
RIME, -D, -S, RIMING *same as* ▸ **rhyme**
RIMER, -S *same as* > **rhymester**
RIMES ▸ **rime**
RIMFIRE *adj* (of a cartridge) having the primer in the rim of the base ▹ *n* cartridge of this type
RIMIER ▸ **rimy**
RIMIEST ▸ **rimy**
RIMING ▸ **rime**
RIMLAND *n* area situated on the outer edges of a region
RIMLESS ▸ **rim**
RIMMED ▸ **rim**
RIMMER, -S *n* tool for shaping the edge of something
RIMMING ▸ **rim**
RIMOSE *adj* (esp of plant parts) having the surface marked by a network of intersecting cracks
RIMOUS *same as* ▸ **rimose**
RIMPLE, -D, -S *vb* crease or wrinkle
RIMROCK *n* rock forming the boundaries of a sandy or gravelly alluvial deposit
RIMS ▸ **rim**
RIMSHOT *n* deliberate simultaneous striking of skin and rim of drum
RIMU, -S *n* New Zealand tree
RIMY, RIMIER, RIMIEST *adj* coated with rime
RIN, -NING, -S *Scots variant of* ▸ **run**
RIND, -ED, -ING, -S *n, vb*
RINDIER ▸ **rindy**
RINDING ▸ **rind**
RINDS ▸ **rind**
RINDY, RINDIER *adj* with a rind or rindlike skin
RINE, -S *archaic variant of* ▸ **rind**
RING, -ED, -S *vb, n*
RINGBIT *n* type of bit worn by a horse
RINGED ▸ **ring**
RINGENT *adj* (of the corolla of plants) consisting of two gaping lips
RINGER, -S *n*
RINGGIT *n* standard monetary unit of Malaysia
RINGING ▸ **ring**
RINGLET *n*
RINGMAN, RINGMEN *n* (in dialect) ring finger
RINGS ▸ **ring**
RINGTAW *n* game in which the aim is to knock marbles out of a ring
RINGWAY *n* bypass
RINK, -ED, -ING, -S *n, vb*
RINNING ▸ **rin**
RINS ▸ **rin**
RINSE, -D, -S *vb, n*
RINSER, -S ▸ **rinse**
RINSES ▸ **rinse**
RINSING ▸ **rinse**
RIOJA, -S *n* red or white Spanish wine with a

vanilla bouquet and flavour
RIOT, -ED, -S *n, vb*
RIOTER, -S ▸ **riot**
RIOTING ▸ **riot**
RIOTISE *n* archaic word for riotous behaviour and excess
RIOTIZE *same as* ▸ **riotise**
RIOTOUS *adj*
RIOTRY *n* riotous behaviour
RIOTS ▸ **riot**
RIP, -PED, -PING, -S *vb, n*
RIPCORD *n*
RIPE, -D, -S, -ST, RIPING *adj, vb*
RIPECK, -S *same as* ▸ **ryepeck**
RIPED ▸ **ripe**
RIPELY ▸ **ripe**
RIPEN, -ED, -S *vb*
RIPENER ▸ **ripen**
RIPENS ▸ **ripen**
RIPER, -S *adj* more ripe ▹ *n* old Scots word meaning plunderer
RIPES ▸ **ripe**
RIPEST ▸ **ripe**
RIPIENO, RIPIENI *n* (in baroque concertos and concerti grossi) the full orchestra
RIPING ▸ **ripe**
RIPOFF, -S *n*
RIPOST, -S *same as* ▸ **riposte**
RIPOSTE *n, vb*
RIPOSTS ▸ **ripost**
RIPP, -S *n* old Scots word for a handful of grain
RIPPED ▸ **rip**
RIPPER, -S *n*
RIPPIER *n* archaic word for fish seller
RIPPING ▸ **rip**
RIPPLE, -D, -S *n, vb*
RIPPLER ▸ **ripple**
RIPPLES ▸ **ripple**
RIPPLET *n*
RIPPLY ▸ **ripple**
RIPPS ▸ **ripp**
RIPRAP, -S *vb* deposit broken stones in or on
RIPS ▸ **rip**
RIPSAW, -N, -S *n* handsaw for cutting along the grain of timber ▹ *vb* saw with a ripsaw
RIPSTOP *n* tear-resistant cloth
RIPT *archaic past form of* ▸ **rip**
RIPTIDE *n*
RISE, -N, -S *vb, n*
RISER, -S *n*
RISES ▸ **rise**
RISHI, -S *n* Indian seer or sage
RISIBLE *adj*
RISIBLY ▸ **risible**
RISING, -S ▸ **rise**
RISK, -ED, -ING, -S *n, vb*
RISKER, -S ▸ **risk**
RISKFUL ▸ **risk**
RISKIER ▸ **risky**
RISKILY ▸ **risky**
RISKING ▸ **risk**
RISKS ▸ **risk**
RISKY, RISKIER *adj*
RISORII > **risorius**
RISOTTO *n*
RISP, -ED, -S *vb* Scots word meaning rasp
RISPING ▸ **risp**
RISPS ▸ **risp**
RISQUE, -S *same as* ▸ **risk**
RISSOLE *n* cake of minced meat, coated with breadcrumbs and fried
RISTRA, -S *n* string of dried chilli peppers
RISUS, -ES *n* involuntary grinning expression
RIT, -S, -TED, -TING *vb* Scots word for cut or slit
RITARD, -S *n* (in music) a slowing down
RITE, -S *n*
RITS ▸ **rit**
RITT, -S *same as* ▸ **rit**
RITTED ▸ **rit**
RITTER, -S *n* knight or horseman/ horsewoman
RITTING ▸ **rit**
RITTS ▸ **ritt**
RITUAL, -S *n, adj*
RITZ, -ES *n* ostentatious display
RITZIER ▸ **ritzy**
RITZILY ▸ **ritzy**
RITZY, RITZIER *adj* luxurious or elegant
RIVA, -S *n* rock cleft
RIVAGE, -S *n* bank, shore, or coast
RIVAL, -ED, -S *n, adj, vb*
RIVALRY *n*
RIVALS ▸ **rival**
RIVAS ▸ **riva**
RIVE, -D, -N, -S, RIVING *vb* split asunder
RIVEL, -S *vb* archaic word meaning wrinkle
RIVEN ▸ **rive**
RIVER, -S *n*
RIVERED *adj* with a river or rivers
RIVERET *n* archaic word for rivulet or stream

RIVERS ▸ **river**
RIVERY *adj* riverlike
RIVES ▸ **rive**
RIVET, -ED, -S *n, vb*
RIVETER ▸ **rivet**
RIVETS ▸ **rivet**
RIVIERA *n*
RIVIERE *n* necklace of diamonds which gradually increase in size
RIVING ▸ **rive**
RIVLIN, -S *n* Scots word for rawhide shoe
RIVO *interj* (in the past) an informal toast
RIVULET *n* small stream
RIVULUS *n* type of small tropical American fish
RIYAL, -S *n* standard monetary unit of Qatar, divided into 100 dirhams
RIZ *(in some dialects) past form of* ▸ **rise**

This unusual past tense of **rise** is one of the essential Z words.

RIZA, -S *n* partial icon cover made from precious metal
RIZARD, -S *n* redcurrant
RIZAS ▸ **riza**
RIZZAR, -S *n* Scots word for redcurrant ▹ *vb* Scots word for sun-dry
RIZZART *n* Scots word for redcurrant
RIZZER, -S *same as* ▸ **rizzar**
RIZZOR, -S *vb* dry
ROACH, -ES *n, vb*
ROACHED *adj* arched convexly, as the back of certain breeds of dog, such as the whippet
ROACHES ▸ **roach**
ROAD, -S *n*
ROADBED *n* material used to make a road
ROADEO, -S *n* competition testing driving skills
ROADHOG *n* selfish or aggressive driver
ROADIE, -S *n* person who transports and sets up equipment for a band
ROADING *n* road building
ROADMAN, ROADMEN *n* someone involved in road repair or construction
ROADS ▸ **road**
ROADWAY *n*
ROAM, -ED, -S *vb, n*
ROAMER, -S ▸ **roam**
ROAMING ▸ **roam**
ROAMS ▸ **roam**
ROAN, -S *adj* (of a horse) having a brown or black coat sprinkled with white hairs ▹ *n* roan horse
ROAR, -ED, -S *vb, n*
ROARER, -S ▸ **roar**
ROARIE *Scots word for* ▸ **noisy**
ROARIER ▸ **roary**
ROARING ▸ **roar**
ROARS ▸ **roar**
ROARY, ROARIER *adj* sounding like a roar or tending to roar
ROAST, -ED, -S *vb, n, adj*
ROASTER *n* person or thing that roasts
ROASTIE *n* roast potato
ROASTS ▸ **roast**
ROATE, -D, -S, ROATING *archaic form of* ▸ **rote**
ROB, -BED, -BING, -S *vb*
ROBALO, -S *n* tropical fish
ROBAND, -S *n* piece of marline used for fastening a sail to a spar
ROBATA, -S *n* grill used for Japanese cooking
ROBBED ▸ **rob**
ROBBER, -S ▸ **rob**
ROBBERY *n*
ROBBIN, -S *same as* ▸ **roband**
ROBBING ▸ **rob**
ROBBINS ▸ **robbin**
ROBE, -D, -S *n, vb*
ROBIN, -S *n*
ROBING, -S ▸ **robe**
ROBINIA *n* type of leguminous tree
ROBINS ▸ **robin**
ROBLE, -S *n* oak tree
ROBOT, -S *n*
ROBOTIC ▸ **robot**
ROBOTRY ▸ **robot**
ROBOTS ▸ **robot**
ROBS ▸ **rob**
ROBUST *adj*
ROBUSTA *n* species of coffee tree
ROC, -S *n* monstrous bird of Arabian mythology
ROCH, -ES *same as* ▸ **rotch**
ROCHET, -S *n* white surplice with tight sleeves, worn by Church dignitaries
ROCK, -ED, -S *n, vb, adj*
ROCKABY *same as* > **rockabye**

ROCKED ▸ **rock**
ROCKER, -S *n*
ROCKERY *n* garden featuring rocks
ROCKET, -S *n, vb*
ROCKIER *n*
ROCKILY ▸ **rocky**
ROCKING ▸ **rock**
ROCKLAY *same as* ▸ **rokelay**
ROCKOON *n* rocket fired from a balloon at high altitude
ROCKS ▸ **rock**
ROCKY *adj*
ROCOCO, -S *adj* (of furniture, architecture, etc) having much elaborate decoration ▹ *n* style of architecture and decoration characterized by elaborate ornamentation
ROCQUET *n* another name for the salad plant rocket
ROCS ▸ **roc**
ROD, -DED, -S *n, vb*
RODDING ▸ **rod**
RODE, -D, -S *vb*
RODENT, -S *n*
RODEO, -ED, -S *n, vb*
RODES ▸ **rode**
RODEWAY *archaic spelling of* ▸ **roadway**
RODING, -S ▸ **rode**
RODLESS ▸ **rod**
RODLIKE ▸ **rod**
RODMAN, RODMEN *n* someone who uses or fishes with a rod
RODNEY, -S *n* type of small fishing boat used in Canada
RODS ▸ **rod**
RODSMAN, RODSMEN *same as* ▸ **rodman**
RODSTER *n* angler
ROE, -S *n*
ROEBUCK *n* male of the roe deer
ROED *adj* with roe inside
ROEMER, -S *n* drinking glass, typically having an ovoid bowl on a short stem
ROES ▸ **roe**
ROESTI, -S *same as* ▸ **rosti**
ROGALLO *n* flexible fabric delta wing
ROGER, -ED, -S *interj* (used in signalling) message received ▹ *vb* acknowledge a received message
ROGNON, -S *n* isolated rock outcrop on a glacier
ROGUE, -D, -S, ROGUING *n, adj, vb*
ROGUER, -S *n* rogue
ROGUERY *n* dishonest or immoral behaviour
ROGUES ▸ **rogue**
ROGUIER ▸ **roguy**
ROGUING ▸ **rogue**
ROGUISH *adj*
ROGUY, ROGUIER *adj* roguish
ROHE, -S *n* territory of a Māori tribal group
ROID, -S *n* short form of steroid
ROIL, -ED, -ING, -S *vb* make (a liquid) cloudy or turbid by stirring up dregs or sediment
ROILIER ▸ **roily**
ROILING ▸ **roil**
ROILS ▸ **roil**
ROILY, ROILIER *adj* cloudy or muddy
ROIN, -ED, -ING, -S *same as* ▸ **royne**
ROINISH *same as* ▸ **roynish**
ROINS ▸ **roin**
ROIST, -ED, -S *archaic variant of* ▸ **roister**
ROISTER *vb* make merry noisily or boisterously
ROISTS ▸ **roist**
ROJAK, -S *n* (in Malaysia) a salad dish served in chilli sauce
ROJI, -S *n* Japanese tea garden or its path of stones
ROK, -S *same as* ▸ **roc**

Rok is an alternative spelling of **roc**, the mythical bird. Other spellings are **ruc** and **rukh**.

ROKE, -D, -S, ROKING *vb* (in dialect) steam or smoke
ROKELAY *n* type of cloak
ROKER, -S *n* variety of ray
ROKES ▸ **roke**
ROKIER ▸ **roky**
ROKIEST ▸ **roky**
ROKING ▸ **roke**
ROKKAKU *n* hexagonal Japanese kite
ROKS ▸ **rok**
ROKY, ROKIER, ROKIEST *adj* (in dialect) steamy or smoky

ROLAG, -S *n* roll of carded wool ready for spinning
ROLE, -S *n*
ROLF, -ED, -ING, -S *vb* massage following a particular technique
ROLFER, -S ▸ **rolf**
ROLFING ▸ **rolf**
ROLFS ▸ **rolf**
ROLL, -ED, -S *vb, n*
ROLLBAR *n* bar that reinforces the frame of a car
ROLLED ▸ **roll**
ROLLER, -S *n*
ROLLICK *vb, n*
ROLLIE, -S *n* hand-rolled cigarette
ROLLING ▸ **roll**
ROLLMOP *n* herring fillet rolled round onion slices and pickled
ROLLOCK *same as* ▸ **rowlock**
ROLLOUT *n*
ROLLS ▸ **roll**
ROLLTOP *n* as in **rolltop desk** desk having a slatted wooden panel that can be pulled down over the writing surface
ROLLUP, -S *n* something rolled into a tube shape
ROLLWAY *n* incline down which logs are rolled
ROM, -S *n* member of a European nomadic people
ROMA *n* member of a European nomadic people
ROMAGE, -S *archaic variant of* ▸ **rummage**
ROMAIKA *n* Greek dance
ROMAINE *n* cos (lettuce)
ROMAJI, -S *n* Roman alphabet as used to write Japanese
ROMAL, -S *same as* ▸ **rumal**
ROMAN, -S *adj* in or relating to the vertical style of printing type used for most printed matter ▹ *n* roman type
ROMANCE *n, vb*
ROMANO, -S *n* hard light-coloured sharp-tasting cheese
ROMANS ▸ **roman**
ROMANZA *n* short instrumental piece of song-like character
ROMAUNT *n* verse romance
ROMCOM, -S *n* comedy based around the romantic relationships of the characters
ROMEO, -S *n* male sweetheart
ROMNEYA *n* bushy type of poppy
ROMP, -ED, -ING, -S *vb, n*
ROMPER *n* playful or boisterous child
ROMPERS *pl n* child's overalls
ROMPING ▸ **romp**
ROMPISH *adj* inclined to romp
ROMPS ▸ **romp**
ROMS ▸ **rom**
RONDE, -S *n* round dance
RONDEAU *n* poem with the opening words of the first line used as a refrain
RONDEL, -S *n* rondeau with a two-line refrain appearing twice or three times
RONDES ▸ **ronde**
RONDINO *n* short rondo
RONDO, -S *n* piece of music with a leading theme continually returned to
RONDURE *n* circle or curve
RONE, -S *n* Scots word for a gutter carrying rainwater from a roof
RONEO, -ED, -S *vb* duplicate (a document) from a stencil ▹ *n* document reproduced by this process
RONES ▸ **rone**
RONG *archaic past participle of* ▸ **ring**
RONIN, -S *n* lordless samurai, esp one whose feudal lord had been deprived of his territory
RONNE, RONNING *archaic form of* ▸ **run**
RONNEL, -S *n* type of pesticide
RONNIE, -S *n* Dublin slang word for moustache
RONNING ▸ **ronne**
RONT, -S *archaic variant of* ▸ **runt**
RONTE, -S *archaic variant of* ▸ **runt**
RONTGEN *variant spelling of* > **roentgen**
RONTS ▸ **ront**

RONZ *n* rest of New Zealand (in relation to Auckland)
RONZER, -S *n* New Zealander not from Auckland
ROO, -S *n* kangaroo
ROOD, -S *n* crucifix
ROOF, -ED, -S *n, vb*
ROOFER, -S ▶ **roof**
ROOFIE, -S *n* tablet of sedative drug
ROOFIER ▶ **roofy**
ROOFIES ▶ **roofie**
ROOFING *n*
ROOFS ▶ **roof**
ROOFTOP *n*
ROOFY, ROOFIER *adj* with roofs
ROOIBOS *n* tea prepared from the dried leaves of an African plant
ROOIKAT *n* South African lynx
ROOK, -ED, -ING, -S *n* Eurasian bird of the crow family ▷ *vb* swindle
ROOKERY *n* colony of rooks, penguins, or seals
ROOKIE, -S *n*
ROOKIER ▶ **rooky**
ROOKIES ▶ **rookie**
ROOKING ▶ **rook**
ROOKISH ▶ **rook**
ROOKS ▶ **rook**
ROOKY, ROOKIER *adj* abounding in rooks
ROOM, -ED, -ING, -S *n, vb*
ROOMER, -S ▶ **room**
ROOMFUL *n* number or quantity sufficient to fill a room
ROOMIE, -S *n* roommate
ROOMIER ▶ **roomy**
ROOMIES ▶ **roomie**
ROOMILY ▶ **roomy**
ROOMING ▶ **room**
ROOMS ▶ **room**
ROOMY, ROOMIER *adj*
ROON, -S *n* Scots word for shred or strip
ROOP, -ED, -ING, -S *same as* ▶ **roup**
ROOPIER ▶ **roopy**
ROOPING ▶ **roop**
ROOPIT *same as* ▶ **roopy**
ROOPS ▶ **roop**
ROOPY, ROOPIER *adj* (in dialect) hoarse
ROOS ▶ **roo**
ROOSA, -S *n* type of grass
ROOSE, -D, -S, ROOSING *vb* flatter
ROOSER, -S ▶ **roose**
ROOSES ▶ **roose**
ROOSING ▶ **roose**
ROOST, -ED, -S *n, vb*
ROOSTER *n*
ROOSTS ▶ **roost**
ROOT, -ED *n, vb*
ROOTAGE *n* root system
ROOTCAP *n* layer of cells at root tip
ROOTED ▶ **root**
ROOTER, -S ▶ **root**
ROOTIER ▶ **rooty**
ROOTIES ▶ **rooty**
ROOTING ▶ **root**
ROOTKIT *n* set of programs used to gain unauthorized access to a computer system
ROOTLE, -D, -S *vb* search unsystematically
ROOTLET *n* small root or branch of a root
ROOTS *adj*
ROOTSY ▶ **roots**
ROOTY, ROOTIER, ROOTIES *adj* rootlike ▷ *n* (in military slang) bread
ROPABLE *adj* capable of being roped
ROPE, -D, -S *n, vb*
ROPER, -S *n* someone who makes ropes
ROPERY *n* place where ropes are made
ROPES ▶ **rope**
ROPEWAY *n* type of aerial lift
ROPEY *adj*
ROPIER ▶ **ropy**
ROPIEST ▶ **ropy**
ROPILY ▶ **ropey**
ROPING, -S ▶ **rope**
ROPY, ROPIER, ROPIEST *same as* ▶ **ropey**
ROQUE, -S *n* game developed from croquet
ROQUET, -S *vb* drive one's ball against (another person's ball) in croquet ▷ *n* act of roqueting
RORAL *archaic word for* ▶ **dewy**
RORE, -S *archaic spelling of* ▶ **roar**
RORIC *same as* ▶ **roral**
RORID *same as* ▶ **roral**
RORIE *same as* ▶ **roary**
RORIER ▶ **rory**
RORIEST ▶ **rory**
RORQUAL *n* toothless whale with a dorsal fin
RORT, -ED, -ING, -S *n* dishonest scheme ▷ *vb*

take unfair advantage of something
RORTER, -S *n* small-scale confidence trickster
RORTIER ▸ **rorty**
RORTING ▸ **rort**
RORTS ▸ **rort**
RORTY, RORTIER ▸ **rort**
RORY, RORIER, RORIEST *adj* dewy
ROSACE, -S *another name for* ▸ **rosette**
ROSACEA *n* chronic inflammatory disease affecting the skin of the face
ROSACES ▸ **rosace**
ROSAKER *archaic word for* ▸ **realgar**
ROSALIA *n* melody which is repeated but at a higher pitch each time
ROSARIA > **rosarium**
ROSARY *n*
ROSBIF, -S *n* term used in France for an English person
ROSCID *adj* dewy
ROSCOE, -S *slang word for* ▸ **gun**
ROSE, -D, -S, ROSING *n, vb*
ROSEAL *adj* rosy or roselike
ROSEATE *adj* rose-coloured
ROSEBAY *n* perennial plant with spikes of deep pink flowers
ROSEBED *n* part of a garden where roses grow
ROSEBUD *n*
ROSED ▸ **rose**
ROSEHIP *n*
ROSELLA *n* type of Australian parrot
ROSELLE *n* Indian flowering plant
ROSEOLA *n* feverish condition of young children caused by a virus
ROSERY *n* bed or garden of roses
ROSES ▸ **rose**
ROSET, -ED, -S *n* Scots word meaning rosin ▹ *vb* rub rosin on
ROSETTE *n* rose-shaped ornament
ROSETTY ▸ **roset**
ROSETY ▸ **roset**
ROSHI, -S *n* teacher of Zen Buddhism
ROSIED ▸ **rosy**
ROSIER, -S *archaic word for* > **rosebush**
ROSIERE *archaic word for* > **rosebush**
ROSIERS ▸ **rosier**
ROSIES ▸ **rosy**
ROSIEST ▸ **rosy**
ROSILY ▸ **rosy**
ROSIN, -ED, -S *n* resin used for treating the bows of violins etc ▹ *vb* apply rosin to
ROSINER *n* strong alcoholic drink
ROSING ▸ **rose**
ROSINOL *n* yellowish fluorescent oily liquid obtained from certain resins
ROSINS ▸ **rosin**
ROSINY *adj* resembling rosin
ROSIT, -ED, -S *same as* ▸ **roset**
ROSOLIO *n* type of cordial
ROSSER, -S *n* bark-removing machine
ROST, -ED, -ING, -S *archaic spelling of* ▸ **roast**
ROSTER, -S *n, vb*
ROSTI, -S *n* Swiss dish of fried grated potato
ROSTING ▸ **rost**
ROSTIS ▸ **rosti**
ROSTRA ▸ **rostrum**
ROSTRAL *adj* of or like a beak or snout
ROSTRUM, ROSTRA *n* platform or stage
ROSTS ▸ **rost**
ROSULA, -S *n* rosette
ROSY, ROSIED, ROSIES, ROSIEST, -ING *adj* pink-coloured ▹ *vb* redden or make pink
ROT, -S, -TED, -TING *vb, n*
ROTA, -S *n*
ROTAL *adj* of or relating to wheels or rotation
ROTAN, -S *another name for* ▸ **rattan**
ROTARY *adj, n*
ROTAS ▸ **rota**
ROTATE, -D, -S *vb*
ROTATOR *n* person, device, part, or muscle that rotates or causes rotation
ROTCH, -ES *n* little auk
ROTCHE *same as* ▸ **rotch**
ROTCHES ▸ **rotch**
ROTCHIE *same as* ▸ **rotch**
ROTE, -D, -S, ROTING *n, vb*
ROTELY *adv* by rote
ROTES ▸ **rote**

ROTGUT, -S *n* alcoholic drink of inferior quality
ROTHER, -S *dialect word for* ▸ **ox**
ROTI, -S *n* (in India and the Caribbean) a type of unleavened bread
ROTIFER *n* minute aquatic multicellular invertebrate
ROTING ▸ **rote**
ROTINI, -S *n* type of small spiral-shaped pasta
ROTIS ▸ **roti**
ROTL, -S *n* unit of weight used in Muslim countries
ROTO, -S *n* printing process using a cylinder etched with many small recesses in a rotary press
ROTOLO, ROTOLI, -S *n* (in Italian cuisine) a roll
ROTON, -S *n* quantum of vortex motion
ROTOR, -S *n*
ROTOS ▸ **roto**
ROTS ▸ **rot**
ROTTAN, -S *n* (in dialect) a rat
ROTTE, -S *n* ancient stringed instrument
ROTTED ▸ **rot**
ROTTEN, -S *adj* decaying ▹ *n* (in dialect) a rat
ROTTER, -S *n*
ROTTES ▸ **rotte**
ROTTING ▸ **rot**
ROTULA, -E, -S *n* kneecap
ROTUND, -S *adj* round and plump ▹ *vb* make round
ROTUNDA *n* circular building or room, esp with a dome
ROTUNDS ▸ **rotund**
ROUBLE, -S *n*
ROUCHE, -S *same as* ▸ **ruche**
ROUCHED *adj* trimmed with a rouche
ROUCHES ▸ **rouche**
ROUCOU, -S *another name for* ▸ **annatto**
ROUE, -S *n* man given to immoral living
ROUEN, -S *n* breed of duck
ROUES ▸ **roue**
ROUGE, -D, -S, ROUGING *n, vb*
ROUGH, -ED, -S *adj, vb, n*
ROUGHEN *vb*
ROUGHER *n* person that does the rough preparatory work on something ▹ *adj* more rough
ROUGHIE *n* small food fish found in Australian waters
ROUGHLY *adv*
ROUGHS ▸ **rough**
ROUGHT *archaic past form of* ▸ **reach**
ROUGHY *spelling variant of* ▸ **roughie**
ROUGING ▸ **rouge**
ROUILLE *n* kind of sauce
ROUL, -S *archaic form of* ▸ **roll**
ROULADE *n* slice of meat rolled and cooked
ROULE, -S *archaic form of* ▸ **roll**
ROULEAU *n* roll of paper containing coins
ROULES ▸ **roule**
ROULS ▸ **roul**
ROUM, -S *archaic spelling of* ▸ **room**
ROUMING *n* portion of common pastureland
ROUMS ▸ **roum**
ROUNCE, -S *n* handle that is turned to move paper and plates on a printing press
ROUNCY *archaic word for* ▸ **horse**
ROUND, -S *adj, prep, vb, n*
ROUNDED *adj*
ROUNDEL *same as* > **roundelay**
ROUNDER *n*
ROUNDLE *same as* ▸ **roundel**
ROUNDLY *adv*
ROUNDS ▸ **round**
ROUNDUP *n*
ROUP, -ED, -ING, -S *n* any of various chronic respiratory diseases of birds, esp poultry ▹ *vb* sell by auction
ROUPET *adj* Scots word meaning hoarse or croaky
ROUPIER ▸ **roupy**
ROUPILY ▸ **roup**
ROUPING ▸ **roup**
ROUPIT *same as* ▸ **roupet**
ROUPS ▸ **roup**
ROUPY, ROUPIER ▸ **roup**
ROUSANT *adj* (in heraldry) rising
ROUSE, -D, -S *vb* provoke or excite
ROUSER, -S *n* person or thing that rouses people

ROUSES ▸ **rouse**
ROUSING *adj*
ROUST, -ED, -S *vb* rout or stir, as out of bed
ROUSTER *n* unskilled labourer on an oil rig
ROUSTS ▸ **roust**
ROUT, -S *n, vb*
ROUTE, -D, -S *n, vb*
ROUTER, -S *n*
ROUTES ▸ **route**
ROUTH, -S *n* abundance ▹ *adj* abundant
ROUTHIE *adj* abundant, plentiful, or well filled
ROUTHS ▸ **routh**
ROUTINE *n, adj*
ROUTING ▸ **rout**
ROUTOUS ▸ **rout**
ROUTS ▸ **rout**
ROUX *n* fat and flour cooked together as a basis for sauces
ROVE, -D, -N, -S, ROVING, ROVINGS *vb* wander about
ROVER, -S *n*
ROVES ▸ **rove**
ROVING ▸ **rove**
ROVINGS ▸ **rove**
ROW, -ED, -S *n, vb*
ROWABLE ▸ **row**
ROWAN, -S *n* tree producing bright red berries; mountain ash
ROWBOAT *n* small boat propelled by one or more pairs of oars
ROWDIER ▸ **rowdy**
ROWDIES ▸ **rowdy**
ROWDILY ▸ **rowdy**
ROWDY, ROWDIER, ROWDIES *adj, n*
ROWED ▸ **row**
ROWEL, -ED, -S *n* small spiked wheel on a spur ▹ *vb* goad (a horse) using a rowel
ROWEN, -S *another word for* ▸ **aftermath**
ROWER, -S ▸ **row**
ROWIE, -S *n* Scottish bread roll made with butter and fat
ROWING, -S ▸ **row**
ROWLOCK *n* device on a boat that holds an oar in place
ROWME, -S *archaic variant of* ▸ **room**
ROWND, -ED, -S *archaic variant of* ▸ **round**
ROWOVER *n* act of winning a rowing race unopposed
ROWS ▸ **row**
ROWT, -ED, -ING, -S *archaic variant of* ▸ **rout**
ROWTH, -S *same as* ▸ **routh**
ROWTING ▸ **rowt**
ROWTS ▸ **rowt**
ROYAL, -S *adj, n*
ROYALET *n* minor king
ROYALLY ▸ **royal**
ROYALS ▸ **royal**
ROYALTY *n*
ROYNE, -D, -S, ROYNING *archaic word for* ▸ **gnaw**
ROYNISH *archaic word for* ▸ **mangy**
ROYST, -ED, -S *same as* ▸ **roist**
ROYSTER *same as* ▸ **roister**
ROYSTS ▸ **royst**
ROZELLE *same as* ▸ **roselle**
ROZET, -ED, -S *same as* ▸ **roset**
ROZIT, -ED, -S *same as* ▸ **roset**
ROZZER, -S *n* slang word for a police officer
RUANA, -S *n* woollen wrap resembling a poncho
RUB, -BED, -S *vb, n*
RUBABOO *n* soup or stew made by boiling pemmican
RUBACE, -S *same as* ▸ **rubasse**
RUBAI, -S *n* verse form of Persian origin consisting of four-line stanzas
RUBASSE *n* type of quartz containing red haematite
RUBATO, RUBATI, -S *n* expressive flexibility of tempo ▹ *adv* with a flexible tempo
RUBBED ▸ **rub**
RUBBER, -S *n, adj, vb*
RUBBERY *adj*
RUBBET *old Scots past form of* ▸ **rob**
RUBBIDY *same as* ▸ **rubbity**
RUBBIES ▸ **rubby**
RUBBING ▸ **rub**
RUBBISH *n, vb*
RUBBIT *old Scots past form of* ▸ **rob**
RUBBITY *n* pub
RUBBLE, -D, -S *n, vb*
RUBBLY ▸ **rubble**
RUBBY, RUBBIES *n* slang word for rubbing alcohol
RUBDOWN *n* act of drying or cleaning vigorously
RUBE, -S *n* unsophisticated countryman

RUBEFY *vb* make red
RUBEL, -S *n* currency unit of Belarus
RUBELLA *n*
RUBELS ▸ **rubel**
RUBEOLA *technical name for* ▸ **measles**
RUBES ▸ **rube**
RUBICON *n* point of no return ▹ *vb* (in bezique) to beat before the loser has managed to gain as many as 1000 points
RUBIDIC > **rubidium**
RUBIED ▸ **ruby**
RUBIER ▸ **ruby**
RUBIES ▸ **ruby**
RUBIEST ▸ **ruby**
RUBIFY *same as* ▸ **rubefy**
RUBIN, -S *archaic word for* ▸ **ruby**
RUBINE, -S *archaic word for* ▸ **ruby**
RUBINS ▸ **rubin**
RUBIOUS *adj* of the colour ruby
RUBLE, -S, RUBLI *same as* ▸ **rouble**
RUBOFF, -S *n* resulting effect on something else; consequences
RUBRIC, -S *n* set of rules for behaviour ▹ *adj* written, printed, or marked in red
RUBS ▸ **rub**
RUBUS, -ES *n* fruit-bearing genus of shrubs
RUBY, RUBIED, RUBIER, RUBIES, RUBIEST, -ING *n, adj, vb*
RUC, -S *same as* ▸ **roc**
RUCHE, -D, -S *n* pleat or frill of lace etc as a decoration ▹ *vb* put a ruche on
RUCHING *n* material used for a ruche
RUCK, -ED, -ING, -S *n* rough crowd of common people ▹ *vb* wrinkle or crease
RUCKLE, -D, -S *another word for* ▸ **ruck**
RUCKMAN, RUCKMEN *n* person who plays in a ruck
RUCKS ▸ **ruck**
RUCKUS *n* uproar
RUCOLA, -S *n* another name for the salad plant rocket
RUCS ▸ **ruc**
RUCTION *n* uproar
RUD, -DED, -DING, -S *n* red or redness ▹ *vb* redden
RUDAS, -ES *n* Scots word for a coarse, rude old woman
RUDD, -S *n* European freshwater fish
RUDDED ▸ **rud**
RUDDER, -S *n*
RUDDIED ▸ **ruddy**
RUDDIER ▸ **ruddy**
RUDDIES ▸ **ruddy**
RUDDILY ▸ **ruddy**
RUDDING ▸ **rud**
RUDDLE, -D, -S *n* red ochre, used esp to mark sheep ▹ *vb* mark (sheep) with ruddle
RUDDOCK *dialect name for the* ▸ **robin**
RUDDS ▸ **rudd**
RUDDY, RUDDIED, RUDDIER, RUDDIES *adj, adv, vb*
RUDE, -R, -S, -ST *adj* insulting or impolite ▹ *n* archaic spelling of rood (crucifix)
RUDELY ▸ **rude**
RUDER ▸ **rude**
RUDERAL *n* plant that grows on waste ground ▹ *adj* growing in waste places
RUDERY ▸ **rude**
RUDES ▸ **rude**
RUDESBY *n* archaic word for rude person
RUDEST ▸ **rude**
RUDI, -S *same as* ▸ **rudie**
RUDIE, -S *n* member of a youth movement originating in the 1960s
RUDIS ▸ **rudi**
RUDISH *adj* somewhat rude
RUDIST, -S *n* cone-shaped extinct mollusc
RUDS ▸ **rud**
RUDY *same as* ▸ **rudie**
RUE, -D, -S *vb, n*
RUEDA, -S *n* type of Cuban round dance
RUEFUL *adj* regretful or sorry
RUEING, -S ▸ **rue**
RUELLE, -S *n* area between bed and wall
RUELLIA *n* genus of plants
RUER, -S ▸ **rue**
RUES ▸ **rue**
RUFF, -ED, -ING, -S *n, vb*
RUFFE, -S *n* European freshwater fish
RUFFED ▸ **ruff**
RUFFES ▸ **ruffe**
RUFFIAN *n, vb*
RUFFIN, -S *archaic name for* ▸ **ruffe**
RUFFING ▸ **ruff**
RUFFINS ▸ **ruffin**

RUFFLE, -D, -S *vb, n*
RUFFLER *n* person or thing that ruffles
RUFFLES ▶ **ruffle**
RUFFLY *adj* ruffled
RUFFS ▶ **ruff**
RUFIYAA *n* standard monetary unit of the Maldives
RUFOUS *n* reddish-brown colour
RUG, -S *n, vb*
RUGA, -E *n* fold, wrinkle, or crease
RUGAL *adj* (in anatomy) with ridges or folds
RUGATE *same as* ▶ **rugose**
RUGBY, RUGBIES *n*
RUGGED *adj*
RUGGER, -S *same as* ▶ **rugby**
RUGGIER ▶ **ruggy**
RUGGING ▶ **rug**
RUGGY, RUGGIER *adj* (in dialect) rough or rugged
RUGLIKE ▶ **rug**
RUGOLA, -S *n* another name for the salad plant rocket
RUGOSA, -S *n* any of various shrubs descended from a particular type of wild rose
RUGOSE *adj* wrinkled
RUGOUS *same as* ▶ **rugose**
RUGRAT, -S *n* informal word for a young child
RUGS ▶ **rug**
RUIN, -ED, -S *vb, n*
RUINATE *vb* archaic word for bring or come to ruin
RUINED ▶ **ruin**
RUINER, -S ▶ **ruin**
RUING, -S ▶ **rue**
RUINING ▶ **ruin**
RUINOUS *adj*
RUINS ▶ **ruin**
RUKH, -S *same as* ▶ **roc**
RULABLE ▶ **rule**
RULE, -D, -S *n, vb*
RULER, -ED, -S *n* person who governs ▷ *vb* punish by hitting with a ruler
RULES ▶ **rule**
RULESSE *adj* archaic word meaning ruleless or without rules
RULIER ▶ **ruly**
RULIEST ▶ **ruly**
RULING, -S *n, adj*
RULLION *n* Scots word for rawhide shoe
RULLOCK *same as* ▶ **rowlock**
RULY, RULIER, RULIEST *adj* orderly
RUM, -MEST, -S *n, adj*
RUMAKI, -S *n* savoury of chicken liver and sliced water chestnut wrapped in bacon
RUMAL, -S *n* handkerchief or type of cloth
RUMBA, -ED, -S *n* lively ballroom dance of Cuban origin ▷ *vb* dance the rumba
RUMBLE, -D, -S *vb, n*
RUMBLER ▶ **rumble**
RUMBLES ▶ **rumble**
RUMBLY *adj* rumbling or liable to rumble
RUMBO, -S *n* rum-based cocktail
RUMDUM, -S *n* alcoholic
RUME, -S *archaic form of* ▶ **rheum**
RUMEN, -S, RUMINA *n* first compartment of the stomach of ruminants
RUMES ▶ **rume**
RUMINA ▶ **rumen**
RUMINAL ▶ **rumen**
RUMKIN, -S *n* archaic term for a drinking vessel
RUMLY ▶ **rum**
RUMMAGE *vb, n*
RUMMER, -S *n* drinking glass
RUMMEST ▶ **rum**
RUMMIER ▶ **rummy**
RUMMIES ▶ **rummy**
RUMMILY ▶ **rummy**
RUMMISH *adj* rather strange, peculiar, or odd ▷ *vb* roar or protest
RUMMY, RUMMIER, RUMMIES *n, adj*
RUMNESS ▶ **rum**
RUMOR, -ED, -S *same as* ▶ **rumour**
RUMORER *n* person given to spreading rumours
RUMORS ▶ **rumor**
RUMOUR, -S *n, vb*
RUMP, -ED, -ING, -S *n* buttocks ▷ *vb* turn back on
RUMPIER ▶ **rumpy**
RUMPIES ▶ **rumpy**
RUMPING ▶ **rump**
RUMPLE, -D, -S *vb, n*
RUMPLY ▶ **rumple**
RUMPOT, -S *n* alcoholic
RUMPS ▶ **rump**
RUMPUS *n*

RUMPY, RUMPIER, RUMPIES *n* tailless Manx cat ▷ *adj* with a large or noticeable rump
RUMS ▸ **rum**
RUN, RAN, -S *vb, n*
RUNANGA *n* Māori assembly or council
RUNAWAY *n*
RUNBACK *n* (in tennis) the areas behind the baselines of the court
RUNCH, -ES *n* another name for white charlock
RUND, -S *same as* ▸ **roon**
RUNDALE *n* system of land tenure in Ireland
RUNDLE, -S *n* rung of a ladder
RUNDLED *adj* rounded
RUNDLES ▸ **rundle**
RUNDLET *n* liquid measure, generally about 15 gallons
RUNDOWN *adj, n*
RUNDS ▸ **rund**
RUNE, -S *n*
RUNED *adj* with runes on
RUNES ▸ **rune**
RUNFLAT *adj* having a safety feature that prevents tyres becoming dangerous when flat
RUNG, -S *n*
RUNGED *adj*
RUNGS ▸ **rung**
RUNIC ▸ **rune**
RUNKLE, -D, -S *vb* (in dialect) crease or wrinkle
RUNLESS ▸ **run**
RUNLET, -S *n* cask for wine, beer, etc
RUNNEL, -S *n* small brook
RUNNER, -S *n*
RUNNET, -S *dialect word for* ▸ **rennet**
RUNNIER ▸ **runny**
RUNNING ▸ **run**
RUNNY, RUNNIER *adj*
RUNOFF, -S *n*
RUNOUT, -S *n* dismissal of a batsman by running them out
RUNOVER *n* incident in which someone is run over by a vehicle
RUNRIG, -S *same as* ▸ **rundale**
RUNS ▸ **run**
RUNT, -S *n*
RUNTED *adj* stunted
RUNTIER ▸ **runty**
RUNTISH ▸ **runt**
RUNTS ▸ **runt**
RUNTY, RUNTIER ▸ **runt**
RUNWAY, -S *n*
RUPEE, -S *n*
RUPIA, -S *n* type of skin eruption
RUPIAH, -S *n*
RUPIAS ▸ **rupia**
RUPTURE *n, vb*
RURAL, -S *adj, n*
RURALLY ▸ **rural**
RURALS ▸ **rural**
RURBAN *adj* part country, part urban
RURP, -S *n* very small piton
RURU, -S *another name for* ▸ **mopoke**
RUSA, -S *n* type of deer with a mane
RUSALKA *n* water nymph or spirit
RUSAS ▸ **rusa**
RUSCUS *n* type of shrub
RUSE, -S *n*
RUSH, -ED *vb, n, adj*
RUSHEE, -S *n* someone interested in gaining fraternity or sorority membership
RUSHEN *adj* made of rushes
RUSHER, -S ▸ **rush**
RUSHES *pl n*
RUSHIER ▸ **rushy**
RUSHING ▸ **rush**
RUSHY, RUSHIER *adj* full of rushes
RUSINE *adj* of or relating to rusa deer
RUSK, -S *n*
RUSMA, -S *n* Turkish depilatory
RUSSE *adj* as in **charlotte russe** cold dessert made from cream, etc, surrounded by sponge fingers
RUSSEL, -S *n* type of woollen fabric
RUSSET, -S *adj, n, vb*
RUSSETY *adj* of a russet colour
RUSSIA, -S *n* Russia leather
RUSSIFY *vb* cause to become Russian in character
RUSSULA *n* type of fungus, typically of toadstool shape
RUST, -ED, -S *n, adj, vb*
RUSTIC, -S *adj, n*
RUSTIER ▸ **rusty**
RUSTILY ▸ **rusty**
RUSTING ▸ **rust**
RUSTLE, -D, -S *n, vb*
RUSTLER *n*
RUSTLES ▸ **rustle**

RUSTRE, -S *n* (in heraldry) lozenge with a round hole in the middle showing the background colour
RUSTRED ▸ **rustre**
RUSTRES ▸ **rustre**
RUSTS ▸ **rust**
RUSTY, RUSTIER *adj*
RUT, -S, -TED *n, vb*
RUTH, -S *n*
RUTHER *adv* rather
RUTHFUL *adj* full of or causing sorrow or pity
RUTHS ▸ **ruth**
RUTILE, -S *n* black, yellowish, or reddish-brown mineral
RUTIN, -S *n* bioflavonoid found in various plants including rue
RUTS ▸ **rut**
RUTTED ▸ **rut**
RUTTER, -S *n* (in history) type of cavalry soldier
RUTTIER ▸ **rutty**
RUTTILY ▸ **rutty**
RUTTING ▸ **rut**
RUTTISH *adj* (of an animal) in a condition of rut
RUTTY, RUTTIER *adj* full of ruts or holes
RYA, -S *n* type of rug originating in Scandinavia
RYAL, -S *n* one of several old coins
RYAS ▸ **rya**
RYBAT, -S *n* polished stone piece forming the side of a window or door
RYE, -S *n*
RYEPECK *n* punt-mooring pole
RYES ▸ **rye**
RYFE *archaic variant of* ▸ **rife**
RYKE, -D, -S, RYKING *Scots variant of* ▸ **reach**
RYMME, -D, -S, RYMMING *same as* ▸ **rim**
RYND, -S *n* (in milling) crossbar piece forming part of the support structure of the upper millstone
RYOKAN, -S *n* traditional Japanese inn
RYOT, -S *n* (in India) a peasant or tenant farmer
RYPE, -R *n* ptarmigan
RYPECK, -S *same as* ▸ **ryepeck**
RYPER ▸ **rype**
RYU, -S *n* school of Japanese martial arts

Ss

SAAG, -S *n* (in Indian cookery) spinach
SAB, -BED, -BING, -S *n* person engaged in direct action to prevent a targeted activity taking place ▷ *vb* take part in such action
SABAL, -S *n* variety of palm tree
SABATON *n* foot covering in suit of armour
SABAYON *n* dessert or sweet sauce made with egg yolks, sugar, and wine
SABBAT, -S *n* midnight meeting of witches
SABBATH *n* period of rest
SABBATS ▶ **sabbat**
SABBED ▶ **sab**
SABBING ▶ **sab**
SABE, -D, -ING, -S *n* very informal word meaning sense or savvy ▷ *vb* very informal word meaning know or savvy
SABELLA *n* marine worm
SABER, -ED, -S *same as* ▶ **sabre**
SABES ▶ **sabe**
SABHA, -S *n* set of Muslim prayer beads
SABICU, -S *n* type of Caribbean tree
SABIN, -S *n* unit of acoustic absorption
SABINE, -S *variant of* ▶ **savin**
SABINS ▶ **sabin**
SABIR, -S *n* member of ancient Turkic people
SABKHA, -S *n* flat coastal plain with a salt crust, common in Arabia
SABKHAH *n* sabkha
SABKHAS ▶ **sabkha**
SABKHAT *n* sabkha
SABLE, -D, -R, -S, -ST, SABLING *n* dark fur from a small weasel-like Arctic animal ▷ *adj* black
SABOT, -S *n* wooden shoe traditionally worn by peasants in France
SABOTED *adj* wearing sabots
SABOTS ▶ **sabot**
SABRA, -S *n* native-born Israeli Jew
SABRE, -D, -S, SABRING *n* curved cavalry sword ▷ *vb* injure or kill with a sabre
SABREUR *n* person wielding sabre
SABRING ▶ **sabre**
SABS ▶ **sab**
SABURRA *n* granular deposit
SAC, -S *n* pouchlike structure in an animal or plant
SACATON *n* coarse grass of the southwestern US and Mexico
SACBUT, -S *n* medieval trombone
SACCADE *n* movement of the eye when it makes a sudden change of fixation, as in reading
SACCATE *adj* in the form of a sac
SACCOS, SACCOI *n* bishop's garment in the Orthodox Church
SACCULE *n* small sac
SACCULI > **sacculus**
SACELLA > **sacellum**
SACHEM, -S *same as* > **sagamore**
SACHET, -S *n* small envelope or bag containing a single portion
SACK, -ED, -S *n* large bag made of coarse material ▷ *vb* dismiss

SACKAGE *n* act of sacking a place ▷ *vb* sack or plunder
SACKBUT *n* medieval form of trombone
SACKED ▶ **sack**
SACKER, -S ▶ **sack**
SACKFUL ▶ **sack**
SACKING *n* rough woven material used for sacks
SACKS ▶ **sack**
SACLESS *adj* old word meaning unchallengeable
SACLIKE ▶ **sac**
SACQUE, -S *same as* ▶ **sack**
SACRA ▶ **sacrum**
SACRAL, -S *adj* of or associated with sacred rites ▷ *n* sacral vertebra
SACRED *adj* holy
SACRIFY *vb* old form of sacrifice
SACRING *n* act or ritual of consecration
SACRIST *same as* > **sacristan**
SACRUM, SACRA, -S *n* wedge-shaped bone at the base of the spine
SACS ▶ **sac**
SAD, -DED, -DER, -DEST, -DING, -S *adj* sorrowful, unhappy ▷ *vb* New Zealand word meaning express sadness or displeasure strongly
SADDEN, -S *vb* make (someone) sad
SADDER ▶ **sad**
SADDEST ▶ **sad**
SADDHU, -S *same as* ▶ **sadhu**
SADDIE, -S *same as* ▶ **saddo**
SADDING ▶ **sad**
SADDISH ▶ **sad**
SADDLE, -D, -S *n* rider's seat on a horse or bicycle ▷ *vb* put a saddle on (a horse)
SADDLER *n* maker or seller of saddles
SADDLES ▶ **saddle**
SADDO, -ES, -S *vb* make sad ▷ *n* socially inadequate or pathetic person
SADE, -S *same as* ▶ **sadhe**
SADHANA *n* one of a number of spiritual practices which lead to perfection
SADHE, -S *n* 18th letter in the Hebrew alphabet
SADHU, -S *n* Hindu wandering holy man
SADI, -S *variant of* ▶ **sadhe**
SADIRON *n* heavy iron pointed at both ends, for pressing clothes
SADIS ▶ **sadi**
SADISM, -S *n* gaining of pleasure from inflicting suffering
SADIST, -S ▶ **sadism**
SADLY ▶ **sad**
SADNESS ▶ **sad**
SADO, -S *variant of* ▶ **chado**
SADS ▶ **sad**
SADZA, -S *n* southern African porridge
SAE *Scot word for* ▶ **so**
SAECULA > **saeculum**
SAETER, -S *n* upland pasture in Norway
SAFARI, -S *n* expedition to hunt or observe wild animals, esp in Africa ▷ *vb* go on safari
SAFE, -D, -R, -S, -ST, SAFING *adj* secure, protected ▷ *n* strong lockable container ▷ *vb* make safe
SAFELY ▶ **safe**
SAFER ▶ **safe**
SAFES ▶ **safe**
SAFEST ▶ **safe**
SAFETY *n* state of being safe ▷ *vb* make safe
SAFFIAN *n* leather tanned with sumach and usually dyed a bright colour
SAFFRON *n* orange-coloured flavouring obtained from a crocus ▷ *adj* orange
SAFING ▶ **safe**
SAFROL, -S *n* oily liquid obtained from sassafras
SAFROLE *n* colourless or yellowish oily water-insoluble liquid
SAFROLS ▶ **safrol**
SAFT, -ER, -EST *Scot word for* ▶ **soft**
SAG, -GED, -S *vb* sink in the middle ▷ *n* droop
SAGA, -S *n* legend of Norse heroes
SAGAMAN, SAGAMEN *n* person reciting Norse sagas
SAGAS ▶ **saga**

SAGATHY *n* type of light fabric
SAGBUT, -S *n* medieval trombone
SAGE, -R, -S, -ST *n* very wise person ▷ *adj* wise
SAGELY ▶ **sage**
SAGENE, -S *n* fishing net
SAGER ▶ **sage**
SAGES ▶ **sage**
SAGEST ▶ **sage**
SAGGAR, -S *n* box in which fragile ceramic wares are placed for protection ▷ *vb* put in a saggar
SAGGARD *n* saggar
SAGGARS ▶ **saggar**
SAGGED ▶ **sag**
SAGGER, -S *same as* ▶ **saggar**
SAGGIER ▶ **saggy**
SAGGING ▶ **sag**
SAGGY, SAGGIER *adj* tending to sag
SAGIER ▶ **sagy**
SAGIEST ▶ **sagy**
SAGITTA *n* sine of an arc
SAGO, -S *n* starchy cereal from the powdered pith of the sago palm tree
SAGOIN, -S *n* South American monkey
SAGOS ▶ **sago**
SAGOUIN *n* South American monkey
SAGRADA *adj* as in **cascara sagrada** dried bark of the cascara buckthorn
SAGS ▶ **sag**
SAGUARO *n* giant cactus of desert regions
SAGUIN, -S *n* South American monkey
SAGUM *n* Roman soldier's cloak
SAGY, SAGIER, SAGIEST *adj* like or containing sage
SAHEB, -S *same as* ▶ **sahib**
SAHIB, -S *n* Indian term of address placed after a man's name as a mark of respect
SAHIBA, -S *n* respectful Indian term of address for woman
SAHIBAH *n* sahiba
SAHIBAS ▶ **sahiba**
SAHIBS ▶ **sahib**
SAHIWAL *n* breed of cattle in India
SAHUARO *same as* ▶ **saguaro**
SAI, -S *n* South American monkey
SAIC, -S *n* boat of eastern Mediterranean
SAICE, -S *same as* ▶ **syce**
SAICK, -S *n* boat of eastern Mediterranean
SAICS ▶ **saic**
SAID, -S *same as* ▶ **sayyid**
SAIDEST ▶ **say**
SAIDS ▶ **said**
SAIDST ▶ **say**
SAIGA, -S *n* either of two antelopes of the plains of central Asia
SAIKEI, -S *n* Japanese ornamental miniature landscape
SAIL, -ED, -S *n* sheet of fabric stretched to catch the wind for propelling a sailing boat ▷ *vb* travel by water
SAILER, -S *n* vessel, esp one equipped with sails, with specified sailing characteristics
SAILING *n* practice, art, or technique of sailing a vessel
SAILOR, -S *n* member of a ship's crew
SAILS ▶ **sail**
SAIM, -S *Scots word for* ▶ **lard**
SAIMIN, -S *n* Hawaiian dish of noodles
SAIMIRI *n* South American monkey
SAIMS ▶ **saim**
SAIN, -ED, -ING, -S *vb* make the sign of the cross over so as to bless or protect from evil or sin
SAINE *vb* old form of say
SAINED ▶ **sain**
SAINING ▶ **sain**
SAINS ▶ **sain**
SAINT, -S *n* person venerated after death as specially holy ▷ *vb* canonize
SAINTED *adj* formally recognized by a Christian Church as a saint
SAINTLY *adj* behaving in a very good, patient, or holy way
SAINTS ▶ **saint**
SAIQUE, -S *n* boat in eastern Mediterranean
SAIR, -ED, -ER, -EST, -ING, -S *Scot word for* ▶ **sore**

SAIS ▸ **sai**
SAIST ▸ **say**
SAITH, -S *form of the present tense (indicative mood) of* ▸ **say**
SAITHE, -S *n* dark-coloured food fish found in northern seas
SAITHS ▸ **saith**
SAIYID, -S *n* Muslim descended from Muhammad's grandson
SAJOU, -S *n* South American monkey
SAKE, -S *n* benefit
SAKER, -S *n* large falcon of E Europe and central Asia
SAKERET *n* male saker
SAKERS ▸ **saker**
SAKES ▸ **sake**
SAKI, -S *n* small arboreal monkey
SAKIA, -S *n* water wheel in Middle East
SAKIEH, -S *same as* ▸ **sakia**
SAKIS ▸ **saki**
SAKIYEH *same as* ▸ **sakia**
SAKKOS, SAKKOI *n* bishop's garment in Orthodox Church
SAKSAUL *n* Asian tree
SAKTI, -S *n* wife of a Hindu god
SAL, -S *pharmacological term for* ▸ **salt**
SALAAM, -S *n* low bow of greeting among Muslims ▹ *vb* make a salaam
SALABLE *same as* > **saleable**
SALABLY > **saleably**
SALAD, -S *n* dish of raw vegetables, eaten as a meal or part of a meal
SALADE, -S *same as* ▸ **sallet**
SALADS ▸ **salad**
SALAL, -S *n* North American shrub
SALAMI, -S *n* highly spiced sausage
SALAMON *n* word used in old oaths
SALARY *n* fixed regular payment, usu monthly, to an employee ▹ *vb* pay a salary to
SALAT, -S *n* obligatory series of Islamic prayers facing towards Mecca
SALBAND *n* coating of mineral
SALCHOW *n* type of figure-skating jump
SALE, -S *n* exchange of goods for money
SALEP, -S *n* dried ground starchy tubers of various orchids
SALES ▸ **sale**
SALET, -S *same as* ▸ **sallet**
SALEWD ▸ **salue**
SALFERN *n* plant of borage family
SALIC *adj* (of rocks and minerals) having a high content of silica and alumina
SALICES ▸ **salix**
SALICET *n* soft-toned organ stop
SALICIN *n* colourless or white crystalline water-soluble glucoside
SALIENT *adj* prominent, noticeable ▹ *n* projecting part of a front line
SALIFY *vb* treat, mix with, or cause to combine with a salt
SALIGOT *n* water chestnut
SALINA, -S *n* salt marsh, lake, or spring
SALINE, -S *adj* containing salt ▹ *n* solution of sodium chloride and water
SALIVA, -S *n* liquid that forms in the mouth, spittle
SALIVAL ▸ **saliva**
SALIVAS ▸ **saliva**
SALIX, SALICES *n* plant or tree of willow family
SALL *archaic form of* ▸ **shall**
SALLAD, -S *old spelling of* ▸ **salad**
SALLAL, -S *n* North American shrub
SALLE, -S *n* hall
SALLEE, -S *n* SE Australian eucalyptus
SALLES ▸ **salle**
SALLET, -S *n* light round helmet
SALLIED ▸ **sally**
SALLIER ▸ **sally**
SALLIES ▸ **sally**
SALLOW, -S *adj* of an unhealthy pale or yellowish colour ▹ *vb* make sallow ▹ *n* any of several small willow trees
SALLOWY *adj* full of sallows

SALLY, SALLIED, SALLIES *n, vb*
SALMI *n* ragout of game stewed in a rich brown sauce
SALMIS *same as* ▸ **salmi**
SALMON, -S *n, adj*
SALMONY *adj* of or like a salmon
SALOL, -S *n* white sparingly soluble crystalline compound
SALON, -S *n*
SALOON, -S *n*
SALOOP, -S *n* infusion of aromatic herbs or other plant parts formerly used as a tonic or cure
SALOP, -S *variant of* ▸ **saloop**
SALP, -S *n* minute animal floating in sea
SALPA, -E, -S *n* any of various minute floating animals of warm oceans
SALPIAN *n* minute animal floating in sea
SALPID, -S *n* minute animal floating in sea
SALPINX *n* Fallopian tube or Eustachian tube
SALPS ▸ **salp**
SALS ▸ **sal**
SALSA, -ED, -S *n, vb*
SALSE, -S *n* volcano expelling mud
SALSIFY *n*
SALT, -EST, -S *n, vb*
SALTANT *adj* (of an organism) differing from others of its species because of a saltation ▹ *n* saltant organism
SALTATE *vb* go through saltation
SALTATO *n* staccato piece of violin playing
SALTBOX *n* box for salt with a sloping lid
SALTCAT *n* salty medicine for pigeons
SALTED *adj*
SALTER, -S *n* person who deals in or manufactures salt
SALTERN *n* place where salt is obtained from pools of evaporated sea water
SALTERS ▸ **salter**
SALTERY *n* factory where fish is salted for storage
SALTEST ▸ **salt**
SALTIE, -S *n* saltwater crocodile
SALTIER *same as* ▸ **saltire**
SALTIES ▸ **saltie**
SALTILY ▸ **salty**
SALTINE *n* salty biscuit
SALTING *n* area of low ground regularly inundated with salt water
SALTIRE *n* diagonal cross on a shield
SALTISH ▸ **salt**
SALTLY ▸ **salt**
SALTO, -ED, -S *n* daring jump ▹ *vb* perform a daring jump
SALTPAN *n* shallow basin containing salt from an evaporated salt lake
SALTS ▸ **salt**
SALTUS *n* break in the continuity of a sequence
SALTY *adj*
SALUE, SALEWD, -D, -S, SALUING *vb* old word meaning salute
SALUKI, -S *n* type of tall hound with a smooth coat
SALUT *interj* cheers!
SALUTE, -D, -S *n* motion of the arm as a formal military sign of respect ▹ *vb* greet with a salute
SALUTER ▸ **salute**
SALUTES ▸ **salute**
SALVAGE *n, vb*
SALVE, -D, -S *n, vb*
SALVER, -S *same as* ▸ **salvor**
SALVES ▸ **salve**
SALVETE *n* Latin greeting
SALVIA, -S *n* plant with blue or red flowers
SALVING ▸ **salve**
SALVO, -ED, -ES, -S *n* simultaneous discharge of guns etc ▹ *vb* attack with a salvo
SALVOR, -S *n* person instrumental in salvaging a vessel or its cargo
SALVOS ▸ **salvo**
SALWAR, -S *n* pair of loose-fitting trousers narrowing around the ankles
SAM, -MED, -MING, -S *vb* collect
SAMA, -S *n* Japanese title of respect
SAMAAN, -S *n* South American tree

SAMADHI *n* state of deep meditative contemplation
SAMAN, -S *n* South American tree
SAMARA, -S *n* dry indehiscent one-seeded fruit
SAMAS ▸ **sama**
SAMBA, -ED, -S *n* lively Brazilian dance ▹ *vb* perform such a dance
SAMBAL, -S *n* Malaysian dish
SAMBAR, -S *n* S Asian deer with three-tined antlers
SAMBAS ▸ **samba**
SAMBHAR *n* Indian dish
SAMBHUR *n* Asian deer
SAMBO, -ES, -S *n* type of wrestling based on judo
SAMBUCA *n* Italian liqueur
SAMBUKE *n* ancient Greek stringed instrument
SAMBUR, -S *same as* ▸ **sambar**
SAME, -S *adj, n*
SAMECH, -S *n* letter in Hebrew alphabet
SAMEK, -S *variant of* ▸ **samekh**
SAMEKH, -S *n* 15th letter in the Hebrew alphabet
SAMEKS ▸ **samek**
SAMEL *adj* of brick, not sufficiently fired
SAMELY *adj* the same
SAMEN *old Scots form of* ▸ **same**
SAMES ▸ **same**
SAMEY, SAMIER, SAMIEST *adj*
SAMFOO, -S *n* style of casual dress worn by Chinese women
SAMFU, -S *same as* ▸ **samfoo**
SAMIEL, -S *same as* ▸ **simoom**
SAMIER ▸ **samey**
SAMIEST ▸ **samey**
SAMISEN *n* Japanese plucked stringed instrument with a long neck
SAMITE, -S *n* heavy fabric of silk used in the Middle Ages
SAMITHI *same as* ▸ **samiti**
SAMITI, -S *n* (in India) an association, esp one formed to organize political activity
SAMLET, -S *n* young salmon
SAMLOR, -S *n* motor vehicle in Thailand
SAMMED ▸ **sam**
SAMMIE *n* sandwich
SAMMIES ▸ **sammy**
SAMMING ▸ **sam**
SAMMY, SAMMIES *n* (in South Africa) an Indian fruit and vegetable vendor
SAMOSA, -S *n* (in Indian cookery) a small fried triangular spiced meat or vegetable pasty
SAMOVAR *n* Russian tea urn
SAMOYED *n* Siberian breed of dog with a tightly curled tail
SAMP, -S *n* crushed maize used for porridge
SAMPAN, -S *n* small boat with oars used in China
SAMPI, -S *n* old Greek number character
SAMPIRE *n* samphire
SAMPIS ▸ **sampi**
SAMPLE, -D, -S *n, vb*
SAMPLER *n*
SAMPLES ▸ **sample**
SAMPS ▸ **samp**
SAMS ▸ **sam**
SAMSARA *n* endless cycle of birth, death, and rebirth
SAMSHOO *same as* ▸ **samshu**
SAMSHU, -S *n* alcoholic drink made from fermented rice
SAMURAI *n*
SAN *n* sanatorium
SANCAI, -S *n* glaze in Chinese pottery
SANCHO, -S *n* African stringed instrument
SANCTUM, SANCTA *n* sacred place
SAND, -ED, -S *n, vb*
SANDAL, -S *n, vb*
SANDBAG *n, vb*
SANDBAR *n*
SANDBOX *n*
SANDBOY *n* as in **happy as a sandboy** very happy or high-spirited
SANDBUR *n* variety of wild grass
SANDDAB *n* type of small Pacific flatfish
SANDED ▸ **sand**

SANDEK, -S *n* man who holds a baby being circumcised
SANDER, -S *n* power tool for smoothing surfaces
SANDFLY *n*
SANDHI, -S *n* modification of a word under the influence of an adjacent word
SANDHOG *n* person who works in underground or underwater construction projects
SANDIER ▸ **sandy**
SANDING ▸ **sand**
SANDLOT *n* area of vacant ground used for children's games
SANDMAN, SANDMEN *n*
SANDPIT *n*
SANDS ▸ **sand**
SANDY, SANDIER *adj*
SANE, -D, -R, -S, -ST, SANING *adj, vb*
SANELY ▸ **sane**
SANER ▸ **sane**
SANES ▸ **sane**
SANEST ▸ **sane**
SANG, -S *Scots word for* ▸ **song**
SANGA, -S *n* Ethiopian ox
SANGAR, -S *n* breastwork of stone or sods
SANGAS ▸ **sanga**
SANGEET *n* Indian pre-wedding celebration
SANGER, -S *n* sandwich
SANGH, -S *n* Indian union or association
SANGHA, -S *n* Buddhist monastic order or community
SANGHAT *n* local Sikh community or congregation
SANGHS ▸ **sangh**
SANGO, -S *same as* ▸ **sanger**
SANGOMA *n* witch doctor or herbalist
SANGOS ▸ **sango**
SANGRIA *n* Spanish drink of red wine and fruit
SANGS ▸ **sang**
SANICLE *n* type of plant with clusters of small white flowers
SANIES *n* thin greenish foul-smelling discharge from a wound, etc
SANIFY *vb* make healthy
SANING ▸ **sane**
SANIOUS ▸ **sanies**
SANITY *n*
SANJAK, -S *n* (in the Turkish Empire) a subdivision of a vilayet
SANK ▸ **sink**
SANKO, -S *n* African stringed instrument
SANNIE, -S *Scots word for* > **sandshoe**
SANNOP, -S *n* Native American married man
SANNUP, -S *n* Native American married man
SANPAN, -S *n* sampan
SANPRO, -S *n* sanitary-protection products collectively
SANS *archaic word for* ▸ **without**
SANSA, -S *n* African musical instrument
SANSAR, -S *n* name of a wind that blows in Iran
SANSAS ▸ **sansa**
SANSEI, -S *n* American whose parents were Japanese immigrants
SANT, -S *n* devout person in India
SANTAL, -S *n* sandalwood
SANTERA *n* priestess of santeria
SANTERO *n* priest of santeria
SANTIM, -I, -S, -U *n* former money unit in Latvia
SANTIR, -S *n* Middle Eastern stringed instrument
SANTO, -S *n* saint or representation of one
SANTOKU *n* type of Japanese knife
SANTOL, -S *n* fruit from Southeast Asia
SANTON, -S *n* French figurine
SANTOOR *same as* ▸ **santir**
SANTOS ▸ **santo**
SANTOUR *n* Middle Eastern stringed instrument
SANTS ▸ **sant**
SANTUR, -S *n* Middle Eastern stringed instrument
SANYASI *same as* > **sannyasi**
SAOLA, -S *n* small, very rare bovine mammal of Vietnam and Laos

SAOUARI *n* tropical American tree
SAP, -PED, -S *n, vb*
SAPAJOU *n* capuchin monkey
SAPAN, -S *n* tropical tree
SAPEGO *n* skin disease
SAPELE, -S *n* type of W African tree
SAPFUL *adj* full of sap
SAPHEAD *n* idiot or fool
SAPHENA *n* either of two large superficial veins of the legs
SAPID, -ER *adj* having a pleasant taste
SAPIENS *adj* relating to or like modern human beings
SAPIENT *adj* wise, shrewd ▷ *n* wise person
SAPLESS ▸ **sap**
SAPLING *n*
SAPONIN *n* any of a group of plant glycosides
SAPOR, -S *n* quality in a substance that is perceived by the sense of taste
SAPOTA, -S *same as* > **sapodilla**
SAPOTE, -S *n* Central American tree
SAPOUR, -S *variant of* ▸ **sapor**
SAPPAN, -S *n* tropical tree
SAPPED ▸ **sap**
SAPPER, -S *n* soldier in an engineering unit
SAPPHIC *adj* lesbian ▷ *n* verse written in a particular form
SAPPIER ▸ **sappy**
SAPPILY ▸ **sappy**
SAPPING *n* act of sapping
SAPPLE, -D, -S *vb* Scots word meaning wash in water
SAPPY, SAPPIER *adj*
SAPROBE *n* organism that lives on decaying organisms
SAPS ▸ **sap**
SAPSAGO *n* hard greenish Swiss cheese
SAPWOOD *n* soft wood, just beneath the bark in tree trunks, that consists of living tissue
SAR, -ED, -ING, -S *n* marine fish ▷ *vb* Scots word meaning savour
SARAFAN *n* Russian woman's cloak
SARAN, -S *n* any one of a class of thermoplastic resins
SARANGI *n* stringed instrument of India played with a bow
SARANS ▸ **saran**
SARAPE, -S *n* serape
SARCASM *n*
SARCINA *n* type of bacterium
SARCODE *n* material making up living cell
SARCOID *adj* of, relating to, or resembling flesh ▷ *n* tumour resembling a sarcoma
SARCOMA *n* malignant tumour beginning in connective tissue
SARCOUS *adj* (of tissue) muscular or fleshy
SARD, -S *n* orange, red, or brown variety of chalcedony
SARDANA *n* Catalan dance
SARDAR, -S *n* title used before the name of Sikh men
SARDEL, -S *n* small fish
SARDINE *n, vb*
SARDIUS *same as* ▸ **sard**
SARDS ▸ **sard**
SARED ▸ **sar**
SAREE, -S *same as* ▸ **sari**
SARGE, -S *n* sergeant
SARGO *same as* ▸ **sargus**
SARGOS *variant of* ▸ **sargus**
SARGUS *n* species of sea fish
SARI, -S *n* long piece of cloth draped around the body and over one shoulder
SARIN, -S *n* chemical used in warfare as a lethal nerve gas producing asphyxia
SARING ▸ **sar**
SARINS ▸ **sarin**
SARIS ▸ **sari**
SARK, -S *n* shirt or (formerly) chemise
SARKIER ▸ **sarky**
SARKILY ▸ **sarky**
SARKING *n* flat planking supporting the roof cladding of a building
SARKS ▸ **sark**
SARKY, SARKIER *adj* sarcastic
SARMENT *n* thin twig

SARMIE, -S *n* sandwich
SARNEY, -S *n* sandwich
SARNIE, -S *n*
SAROD, -S *n* Indian stringed musical instrument
SARODE, -S *n* Indian stringed instrument
SARODS ▸ **sarod**
SARONG, -S *n*
SARONIC ▸ **saros**
SAROS, -ES *n* cycle in which eclipses of the sun and moon occur in the same sequence
SARS ▸ **sar**
SARSAR, -S *same as* ▸ **sansar**
SARSDEN *n* sarsen
SARSEN, -S *n* boulder of silicified sandstone
SARSNET *n* type of silk
SARTOR, -S *humorous or literary word for* ▸ **tailor**
SARUS, -ES *n* Indian bird of crane family
SASER, -S *n* device for amplifying ultrasound
SASH, -ED, -ES, -ING *n, vb*
SASHAY, -S *vb*
SASHED ▸ **sash**
SASHES ▸ **sash**
SASHIMI *n* Japanese dish of thin fillets of raw fish
SASHING ▸ **sash**
SASIN, -S *another name for* > **blackbuck**
SASINE, -S *n* granting of legal possession of feudal property
SASINS ▸ **sasin**
SASS, -ED, -ES, -ING *n, vb*
SASSABY *n* African antelope of grasslands and semideserts
SASSE *n* old word meaning canal lock
SASSED ▸ **sass**
SASSES ▸ **sass**
SASSIER ▸ **sassy**
SASSIES ▸ **sassy**
SASSILY ▸ **sassy**
SASSING ▸ **sass**
SASSY, SASSIER, SASSIES *adj, n*
SASTRA, -S *same as* ▸ **shastra**
SAT ▸ **sit**
SATAI, -S *same as* ▸ **satay**
SATANG, -S *n* monetary unit of Thailand worth one hundredth of a baht
SATANIC *adj*
SATARA, -S *n* type of cloth
SATAY, -S *n*
SATCHEL *n*
SATCOM, -S *n* satellite communications
SATE, -D, -S, SATING *vb*
SATEEN, -S *n* glossy linen or cotton fabric, woven in such a way that it resembles satin
SATEM *adj* denoting or belonging to a particular group of Indo-European languages
SATES ▸ **sate**
SATI, -S *n* Indian widow suicide
SATIATE *vb*
SATIETY *n*
SATIN, -ED, -S *n, adj, vb*
SATINET *n* thin or imitation satin
SATING ▸ **sate**
SATINS ▸ **satin**
SATINY *adj* like satin
SATIRE, -S *n*
SATIRIC *same as* > **satirical**
SATIS ▸ **sati**
SATISFY *vb*
SATIVE *adj* old word meaning cultivated
SATNAV, -S *n*
SATORI, -S *n* state of sudden indescribable intuitive enlightenment
SATRAP, -S *n* (in ancient Persia) a provincial governor or subordinate ruler
SATRAPY *n* province, office, or period of rule of a satrap
SATSANG *n* sacred gathering in Hinduism
SATSUMA *n*
SATYR, -S *n*
SATYRA, -S *n* female satyr
SATYRAL *n* mythical beast in heraldry
SATYRAS ▸ **satyra**
SATYRE, -S *n* as in **sea satyre** sea creature mentioned in Spenser's poetry
SATYRIC ▸ **satyr**
SATYRID *n* butterfly with typically brown or dark wings with paler markings
SATYRS ▸ **satyr**
SAU *archaic past tense of* ▸ **see**
SAUBA, -S *n* South American ant
SAUCE, -D, -S, SAUCING *n, vb*
SAUCER, -S *n*

SAUCES ▶ **sauce**
SAUCH, -S *n* sallow or willow
SAUCIER *n* chef who makes sauces
SAUCILY ▶ **saucy**
SAUCING ▶ **sauce**
SAUCY *adj*
SAUGER, -S *n* small North American pikeperch
SAUGH, -S *same as* ▶ **sauch**
SAUGHY *adj* Scots word meaning made of willow
SAUL, -S *Scots word for* ▶ **soul**
SAULGE, -S *n* old word for sage plant
SAULIE, -S *n* Scots word meaning professional mourner
SAULS ▶ **saul**
SAULT, -S *n* waterfall in Canada
SAUNA, -ED, -S *n, vb*
SAUNT, -ED, -S *Scots form of* ▶ **saint**
SAUNTER *vb, n*
SAUNTS ▶ **saunt**
SAUREL, -S *n* type of mackerel
SAURIAN *n* lizard
SAURIES ▶ **saury**
SAUROID *adj* like a lizard ▷ *n* type of fish
SAURY, SAURIES *n* type of fish of tropical and temperate seas
SAUSAGE *n*
SAUT, -ED, -ING, -S *Scot word for* ▶ **salt**
SAUTE, -ED, -S *vb* fry quickly in a little fat ▷ *n* dish of sautéed food ▷ *adj* sautéed until lightly brown
SAUTED ▶ **saut**
SAUTEED ▶ **saute**
SAUTES ▶ **saute**
SAUTING ▶ **saut**
SAUTOIR *n* long necklace or pendant
SAUTS ▶ **saut**
SAV, -S *short for* ▶ **saveloy**
SAVABLE ▶ **save**
SAVAGE, -D, -R, -S *adj* wild, untamed ▷ *n* uncivilized person ▷ *vb* attack ferociously
SAVANNA *n*
SAVANT, -S *n* learned person
SAVANTE ▶ **savant**
SAVANTS ▶ **savant**
SAVARIN *n* type of cake
SAVATE, -S *n* form of boxing in which blows may be delivered with the feet
SAVE, -D, -S *vb, n, prep*
SAVELOY *n* spicy smoked sausage
SAVER, -S ▶ **save**
SAVES ▶ **save**
SAVEY, -ED, -S *vb* understand
SAVIN, -S *n* small spreading juniper bush of Europe, N Asia, and North America
SAVINE, -S *same as* ▶ **savin**
SAVING, -S *n, prep, adj*
SAVINS ▶ **savin**
SAVIOR, -S *same as* ▶ **saviour**
SAVIOUR *n*
SAVOR, -ED, -S *same as* ▶ **savour**
SAVORER ▶ **savor**
SAVORS ▶ **savor**
SAVORY *same as* ▶ **savoury**
SAVOUR, -S *vb, n*
SAVOURY *adj, n*
SAVOY, -S *n* variety of cabbage
SAVS ▶ **sav**
SAVVEY, -S *vb* understand
SAVVIED ▶ **savvy**
SAVVIER ▶ **savvy**
SAVVIES ▶ **savvy**
SAVVILY ▶ **savvy**
SAVVY, SAVVIED, SAVVIER, SAVVIES *vb, n, adj*
SAW, -ED, -S *n, vb*
SAWAH, -S *n* paddy field
SAWBILL *n* type of hummingbird
SAWBUCK *n* structure for supporting wood that is being sawn
SAWDER, -S *n* flattery ▷ *vb* flatter
SAWDUST *n, vb*
SAWED ▶ **saw**
SAWER, -S ▶ **saw**
SAWFISH *n* fish with a long toothed snout
SAWFLY *n* any of various hymenopterous insects
SAWING, -S ▶ **saw**
SAWLIKE ▶ **saw**
SAWLOG, -S *n* log suitable for sawing
SAWMILL *n*
SAWN *past participle of* ▶ **saw**
SAWNEY, -S *n* derogatory word for a fool

SAWPIT, -S *n* pit above which a log is sawn into planks
SAWS ▸ **saw**
SAWYER, -S *n* person who saws timber for a living
SAX, -ES *same as* > **saxophone**
SAXAUL, -S *n* Asian tree
SAXE *adj* as in **saxe blue** light greyish-blue colour
SAXES ▸ **sax**
SAXHORN *n* valved brass instrument used chiefly in brass and military bands
SAXIST, -S *n* saxophone player
SAXMAN, SAXMEN *n* saxophone player
SAXONY *n* fine three-ply yarn
SAXTUBA *n* bass saxhorn
SAY, SAIDEST, SAIDST, SAIST, -EST, -NE, -S, -ST *vb, n*
SAYABLE *n* anything that can be said
SAYED, -S *same as* ▸ **sayyid**
SAYER, -S ▸ **say**
SAYEST ▸ **say**
SAYID, -S *same as* ▸ **sayyid**
SAYING, -S ▸ **say**
SAYNE ▸ **say**
SAYON, -S *n* type of tunic
SAYS ▸ **say**
SAYST ▸ **say**
SAYYID, -S *n* Muslim descended from Muhammad's grandson
SAZ, -ES, -ZES *n* Middle Eastern stringed instrument

> This musical instrument is one of the most frequently played Z words.

SAZERAC *n* mixed drink of whisky, Pernod, syrup, bitters, and lemon
SAZES ▸ **saz**
SAZHEN, -S *n* Russian measure of length
SAZZES ▸ **saz**
SBIRRO, SBIRRI *n* Italian police officer
SCAB, -BED, -S *n, vb*
SCABBLE *vb* shape (stone) roughly
SCABBY *adj*
SCABIES *n*
SCABRID *adj* having a rough or scaly surface
SCABS ▸ **scab**
SCAD *n* any of various carangid fishes
SCADS *pl n* large amount or number
SCAFF, -ED, -S *n* Scots word meaning food ▹ *vb* ask for (food) in a mean or rude manner
SCAFFIE *n* Scots word meaning street cleaner
SCAFFS ▸ **scaff**
SCAFFY *adj* having little value, cheap
SCAG, -GED, -S *n* tear in a garment or piece of cloth ▹ *vb* make a tear in (cloth)
SCAGLIA *n* type of limestone
SCAGS ▸ **scag**
SCAIL, -ED, -S *vb* Scots word meaning disperse
SCAITH, -S *vb* old word meaning injure
SCALA, -E *n* passage inside the cochlea
SCALADE *short for* > **escalade**
SCALADO *same as* ▸ **scalade**
SCALAE ▸ **scala**
SCALAGE *n* percentage deducted from the price of goods liable to shrink or leak
SCALAR, -S *adj* having magnitude but no direction ▹ *n* quantity that has magnitude but not direction
SCALARE *another name for* > **angelfish**
SCALARS ▸ **scalar**
SCALD, -ED, -S *vb* burn with hot liquid ▹ *n* (in ancient Scandinavia) a bard or minstrel
SCALDER ▸ **scald**
SCALDIC ▸ **scald**
SCALDS ▸ **scald**
SCALE, -D, -S *n, vb*
SCALENE *n* triangle with three unequal sides
SCALENI > **scalenus**
SCALER, -S *n* person or thing that scales
SCALES ▸ **scale**
SCALEUP *n* increase
SCALIER ▸ **scaly**
SCALING ▸ **scale**
SCALL, -S *n* disease of the scalp characterized by itching and scab formation
SCALLED ▸ **scall**

SCALLOP *n, vb*
SCALLS ▶ **scall**
SCALLY *n* rascal
SCALP, -ED, -S *n, vb*
SCALPEL *n*
SCALPER ▶ **scalp**
SCALPS ▶ **scalp**
SCALY, SCALIER *adj*
SCAM, -MED, -S *n, vb*
SCAMBLE *vb* scramble
SCAMEL, -S *n* Shakespearian word of uncertain meaning
SCAMMED ▶ **scam**
SCAMMER *n*
SCAMP, -ED, -S *n, vb*
SCAMPER *vb, n*
SCAMPI, -S *pl n*
SCAMPS ▶ **scamp**
SCAMS ▶ **scam**
SCAMTO, -S *n* argot of urban Black people in South Africa
SCAN, -D, -NED, -S *vb, n*
SCANDAL *n, vb*
SCANDIA *n* scandium oxide
SCANDIC *adj* of or containing scandium
SCANNED ▶ **scan**
SCANNER *n*
SCANS ▶ **scan**
SCANT, -ED, -ER, -S *adj, vb, adv*
SCANTLE *vb* stint
SCANTLY ▶ **scant**
SCANTS ▶ **scant**
SCANTY *adj*
SCAPA, -ED, -S *variant of* ▶ **scarper**
SCAPE, -D, -S, SCAPING *n* leafless stalk in plants ▷ *vb* archaic word for escape
SCAPI ▶ **scapus**
SCAPING ▶ **scape**
SCAPOSE ▶ **scape**
SCAPPLE *vb* shape roughly
SCAPULA *n*
SCAPUS, SCAPI *n* flower stalk
SCAR, -RED, -S *n, vb*
SCARAB, -S *n*
SCARCE, -R *adj*
SCARE, -S, SCARING *vb, n, adj*
SCARED ▶ **scare**
SCAREDY *n*
SCARER, -S ▶ **scare**
SCARES ▶ **scare**
SCAREY *adj* frightening
SCARF, -ED, -S, SCARVES *n, vb*
SCARFER ▶ **scarf**
SCARFS ▶ **scarf**
SCARIER ▶ **scary**
SCARIFY *vb*
SCARILY ▶ **scary**
SCARING ▶ **scare**
SCARLET *n, adj, vb*
SCARP, -ED, -S *n* steep slope ▷ *vb* wear or cut so as to form a steep slope
SCARPA, -S *vb* run away
SCARPED ▶ **scarp**
SCARPER *vb* run away ▷ *n* hasty departure
SCARPH, -S *vb* join with scarf joint
SCARPS ▶ **scarp**
SCARRE, -S *n* Shakespearian word of unknown meaning
SCARRED ▶ **scar**
SCARRES ▶ **scarre**
SCARRY ▶ **scar**
SCARS ▶ **scar**
SCART, -ED, -S *vb* scratch or scrape ▷ *n* scratch or scrape
SCARTH, -S *Scots word for* ▶ **cormorant**
SCARTS ▶ **scart**
SCARVED *adj* wearing a scarf
SCARVES ▶ **scarf**
SCARY, SCARIER *adj*
SCAT, -S, -TED *vb* go away ▷ *n* jazz singing using improvised vocal sounds instead of words
SCATCH *same as* ▶ **stilt**
SCATH, -S *vb* old word meaning injure
SCATHE, -D, -S *vb* attack with severe criticism ▷ *n* harm
SCATHS ▶ **scath**
SCATOLE *n* substance found in coal
SCATS ▶ **scat**
SCATT, -S *n* old word meaning tax ▷ *vb* tax
SCATTED ▶ **scat**
SCATTER *vb, n*
SCATTS ▶ **scatt**
SCATTY *adj* empty-headed
SCAUD, -ED, -S *Scot word for* ▶ **scald**
SCAUP, -ED, -S *variant of* ▶ **scalp**
SCAUPER *same as* ▶ **scorper**
SCAUPS ▶ **scaup**
SCAUR, -ED, -S *same as* ▶ **scar**
SCAURY *n* young seagull
SCAVAGE *n* old word meaning toll ▷ *vb* scavenge
SCAW, -S *n* headland
SCAZON, -S *n* metre in poetry

SCEAT, -S, -TS *n* Anglo-Saxon coin
SCEATT *same as* ▸ **sceat**
SCEATTS ▸ **sceat**
SCEDULE *old spelling of* > **schedule**
SCENA, -S *n* scene in an opera, usually longer than a single aria
SCENARY *n* scenery
SCENAS ▸ **scena**
SCEND, -ED, -S *vb* (of a vessel) to surge upwards in a heavy sea ▹ *n* upward heaving of a vessel pitching
SCENE, -D, -S, SCENING *n, vb*
SCENERY *n*
SCENES ▸ **scene**
SCENIC, -S *adj, n*
SCENING ▸ **scene**
SCENT, -S *n, vb*
SCENTED ▸ **scent**
SCENTS ▸ **scent**
SCEPSIS *n* doubt
SCEPTER *same as* ▸ **sceptre**
SCEPTIC *n, adj*
SCEPTRE *n, vb*
SCEPTRY *adj* having sceptre
SCERNE, -D, -S *vb* old word meaning discern
SCHANSE > **schantze**
SCHANZE *same as* > **schantze**
SCHAPPE *n* yarn or fabric made from waste silk
SCHAV, -S *n* Polish soup
SCHELLY *n* freshwater whitefish of the English Lake District
SCHELM, -S *n* South African word meaning rascal
SCHEMA, -S *n*
SCHEME, -D, -S *n, vb*
SCHEMER ▸ **scheme**
SCHEMES ▸ **scheme**
SCHEMIE *n* insulting Scots word for a resident of a housing scheme
SCHERZO, SCHERZI *n* brisk lively piece of music
SCHISM, -S *n*
SCHISMA *n* short musical interval of half a comma
SCHISMS ▸ **schism**
SCHIST, -S *n* crystalline rock which splits into layers
SCHLEP, -S *vb* drag or lug (oneself or an object) with difficulty ▹ *n* arduous journey or procedure
SCHLEPP *vb* schlep
SCHLEPS ▸ **schlep**
SCHLICH *n* finely crushed ore
SCHLOCK *n* goods of cheap or inferior quality ▹ *adj* cheap, inferior, or trashy
SCHLOSS *n* German castle
SCHLUB, -S *n* coarse or contemptible person
SCHLUMP *vb* move in lazy way
SCHMALZ *same as* > **schmaltz**
SCHMEAR *n* situation, matter, or affair ▹ *vb* spread or smear
SCHMECK *n* taste ▹ *vb* taste good
SCHMEER *same as* ▸ **schmear**
SCHMELZ *n* ornamental glass
SCHMICK *adj* (in Australia) excellent, elegant, or stylish
SCHMO, -S *n* dull, stupid, or boring person
SCHMOCK *n* stupid person
SCHMOE, -S *same as* ▸ **schmo**
SCHMOOS *variant of* > **schmoose**
SCHMOOZ *n* chat
SCHMOS ▸ **schmo**
SCHMUCK *n, vb*
SCHMUTZ *n* dirt; grime
SCHNAPS *same as* > **schnapps**
SCHNEID *n* succession of losses
SCHNELL *adj* German word meaning quick
SCHNOOK *n* stupid or gullible person
SCHNORR *vb* beg
SCHNOZ *n* nose
SCHNOZZ *n* nose
SCHOLAR *n*
SCHOLIA > **scholium**
SCHOOL, -S *n, vb*
SCHOOLE *n* old form of shoal
SCHOOLS ▸ **school**
SCHORL, -S *n* type of black tourmaline
SCHOUT, -S *n* council officer in Netherlands
SCHRIK, -S *variant of* ▸ **skrik**
SCHROD, -S *n* young cod

SCHTICK *same as* ▸ **shtick**
SCHTIK, -S *n* schtick
SCHTOOK *n* trouble
SCHTOOM *adj* silent
SCHTUCK *n* trouble
SCHTUM *adj* silent
SCHUIT, -S *n* Dutch boat with flat bottom
SCHUL, -N, -S *same as* ▸ **shul**
SCHUSS *n* straight high-speed downhill run ▹ *vb* perform a schuss
SCHUYT, -S *n* Dutch boat with flat bottom
SCHVITZ *same as* ▸ **shvitz**
SCHWA, -S *n* vowel representing the sound in unstressed syllables
SCHWAG, -S *n* promotional material given away for free
SCHWAS ▸ **schwa**
SCIARID *n* small fly
SCIATIC *adj* of the hip ▹ *n* sciatic part of the body
SCIENCE *n*
SCIENT *adj* old word meaning scientific
SCILLA, -S *n* plant with small bell-shaped flowers
SCIOLTO *adv* musical direction meaning freely
SCION, -S *n*
SCIROC, -S > scirocco
SCIRRHI > scirrhus
SCISSEL *n* waste metal left over from sheet metal after discs have been punched out of it
SCISSIL *n* scissel
SCISSOR *vb*
SCIURID *n* squirrel or related rodent
SCLAFF, -S *vb* cause (the club) to hit (the ground behind the ball) when making a stroke ▹ *n* sclaffing stroke or shot
SCLATE, -D, -S *vb* (Scots) slate ▹ *n* (Scots) slate
SCLAVE, -S *n* old form of slave
SCLERA, -E, -S *n* tough white substance that forms the outer covering of the eyeball
SCLERAL ▸ **sclera**
SCLERAS ▸ **sclera**
SCLERE, -S *n* supporting anatomical structure
SCLIFF, -S *n* Scots word for small piece
SCLIM, -S *vb* Scots word meaning climb
SCODY, SCODIER *adj* unkempt
SCOFF, -ED, -S *vb, n*
SCOFFER ▸ **scoff**
SCOFFS ▸ **scoff**
SCOG, -GED, -S *vb* shelter
SCOLD, -ED, -S *vb, n*
SCOLDER ▸ **scold**
SCOLDS ▸ **scold**
SCOLEX *n* headlike part of a tapeworm
SCOLION, SCOLIA *n* ancient Greek drinking song
SCOLLOP *variant of* ▸ **scallop**
SCONCE, -D, -S *n* bracket on a wall for holding candles or lights ▹ *vb* challenge (a fellow student) to drink a large quantity of beer
SCONE, -S *n*
SCOOBY *n* slang for a clue, notion
SCOOCH *vb* compress one's body into smaller space
SCOOG, -ED, -S *vb* shelter
SCOOP, -ED, -S *n, vb*
SCOOPER ▸ **scoop**
SCOOPS ▸ **scoop**
SCOOSH *vb* squirt ▹ *n* squirt or rush of liquid
SCOOT, -ED, -S *vb, n*
SCOOTCH *same as* ▸ **scooch**
SCOOTED ▸ **scoot**
SCOOTER *n, vb*
SCOOTS ▸ **scoot**
SCOP, -S *n* (in Anglo-Saxon England) a bard or minstrel
SCOPA, -E, -S *n* tuft of hairs on the abdomen or hind legs of a bee
SCOPATE *adj* having tuft-type hairs
SCOPE, -D, -S, SCOPING *n, vb*
SCOPS ▸ **scop**
SCOPULA *n* small tuft of dense hairs on the legs and chelicerae of some spiders
SCORCH *vb, n*
SCORE, -D, -S *n, vb*
SCORER, -S ▸ **score**
SCORES ▸ **score**

SCORIA, -E *n* mass of solidified lava containing many cavities
SCORIAC ▸ **scoria**
SCORIAE ▸ **scoria**
SCORIFY *vb* remove (impurities) from metals by forming scoria
SCORING *n*
SCORN, -ED, -S *n, vb*
SCORNER ▸ **scorn**
SCORNS ▸ **scorn**
SCORPER *n* kind of fine chisel with a square or curved tip
SCORSE, -D, -S *vb* exchange
SCORSER ▸ **scorse**
SCORSES ▸ **scorse**
SCOT, -S *n* payment or tax
SCOTCH *vb, n*
SCOTER, -S *n* type of sea duck
SCOTIA, -S *n* deep concave moulding
SCOTOMA *n* blind spot
SCOTOMY *n* dizziness
SCOTS ▸ **scot**
SCOTTIE *n* type of small sturdy terrier
SCOUG, -ED, -S *vb* shelter
SCOUP, -ED, -S *vb* Scots word meaning jump
SCOUR, -ED, -S *vb, n*
SCOURER ▸ **scour**
SCOURGE *n, vb*
SCOURIE *n* young seagull
SCOURS ▸ **scour**
SCOURSE *vb* exchange
SCOUSE, -S *n* stew made from left-over meat
SCOUSER *n* inhabitant of Liverpool
SCOUSES ▸ **scouse**
SCOUT, -ED, -S *n, vb*
SCOUTER ▸ **scout**
SCOUTH, -S *n* Scots word meaning plenty of scope
SCOUTS ▸ **scout**
SCOW, -ED, -ING, -S *n* unpowered barge used for carrying freight ▹ *vb* transport by scow
SCOWDER *vb* Scots word meaning scorch
SCOWED ▸ **scow**
SCOWING ▸ **scow**
SCOWL, -ED, -S *vb*
SCOWLER *n* person who scowls
SCOWLS ▸ **scowl**
SCOWP, -ED, -S *vb* Scots word meaning jump
SCOWRER *n* old word meaning hooligan
SCOWRIE *n* young seagull
SCOWS ▸ **scow**
SCOWTH, -S *n* Scots word meaning plenty of scope
SCOZZA, -S *n* rowdy person, esp one who drinks a lot of alcohol
SCRAB, -S *vb* scratch
SCRAE, -S *Scots word for* ▸ **scree**
SCRAG, -S *n* thin end of a neck of mutton ▹ *vb* wring the neck of
SCRAGGY *adj* thin, bony
SCRAGS ▸ **scrag**
SCRAICH *vb* Scots word meaning scream
SCRAIGH *same as* ▸ **scraich**
SCRAM, -S *vb, n*
SCRAMB, -S *vb* scratch with nails or claws
SCRAMS ▸ **scram**
SCRAN, -S *n* food
SCRANCH *vb* crunch
SCRANNY *adj* scrawny
SCRANS ▸ **scran**
SCRAP, -S *n, vb*
SCRAPE, -D, -S *vb, n*
SCRAPER ▸ **scrape**
SCRAPES ▸ **scrape**
SCRAPIE *n* disease of sheep and goats
SCRAPPY *adj*
SCRAPS ▸ **scrap**
SCRAT, -S *vb* scratch
SCRATCH *vb, n, adj*
SCRATS ▸ **scrat**
SCRAUCH *vb* squawk
SCRAUGH *vb* squawk
SCRAVEL *vb* move quickly
SCRAW, -S *n* sod from the surface of a peat bog or from a field
SCRAWB, -S *same as* ▸ **scrob**
SCRAWL, -S *vb, n*
SCRAWLY ▸ **scrawl**
SCRAWM, -S *vb* dialect word meaning scratch
SCRAWNY *adj*
SCRAWP, -S *vb* scratch (the skin) to relieve itching
SCRAWS ▸ **scraw**
SCRAY, -S *n* tern
SCRAYE, -S *n* tern
SCRAYS ▸ **scray**
SCREAK, -S *vb* screech or creak ▹ *n* screech or creak
SCREAKY ▸ **screak**

SCREAM, -S *vb, n*
SCREAMO *n* type of emo music featuring screaming vocals
SCREAMS ▸ **scream**
SCREE, -S *n* slope of loose shifting stones
SCREECH *n, vb*
SCREED, -S *n* long tedious piece of writing ▹ *vb* rip
SCREEN, -S *n, vb*
SCREES ▸ **scree**
SCREET, -S *vb* shed tears ▹ *n* act or sound of crying
SCREEVE *vb* write
SCREICH *same as* ▸ **screigh**
SCREIGH *Scot word for* ▸ **screech**
SCREW, -S *n, vb*
SCREWED *adj*
SCREWER ▸ **screw**
SCREWS ▸ **screw**
SCREWUP *n*
SCREWY *adj*
SCRIBAL ▸ **scribe**
SCRIBE, -D, -S *n, vb*
SCRIBER *n* pointed steel tool used to score materials as a guide to cutting, etc
SCRIBES ▸ **scribe**
SCRIECH *vb* Scots word meaning screech
SCRIED ▸ **scry**
SCRIENE *n* old form of screen
SCRIES ▸ **scry**
SCRIEVE *vb* Scots word meaning write
SCRIKE, -D, -S *vb* old word meaning shriek
SCRIM, -S *n* open-weave muslin or hessian fabric
SCRIMP, -S *vb*
SCRIMPY ▸ **scrimp**
SCRIMS ▸ **scrim**
SCRINE, -S *n* old form of shrine
SCRIP, -S *n* certificate representing a claim to stocks or shares
SCRIPT, -S *n, vb*
SCRITCH *vb* screech
SCRIVE, -D, -S *Scots word for* ▸ **write**
SCROB, -S *vb* scrape with claws
SCROBE, -S *n* groove
SCROBS ▸ **scrob**
SCROD, -S *n* young cod or haddock
SCROG, -S *n* Scots word meaning small tree
SCROGGY *variant of* > **scroggie**
SCROGS ▸ **scrog**
SCROLL, -S *n, vb*
SCROME, -D, -S *vb* crawl or climb
SCROOCH *vb* scratch (the skin) to relieve itching
SCROOGE *variant of* ▸ **scrouge**
SCROOP, -S *vb* emit a grating or creaking sound ▹ *n* such a sound
SCRORP, -S *n* deep scratch or weal
SCROTA ▸ **scrotum**
SCROTAL ▸ **scrotum**
SCROTUM, SCROTA *n*
SCROUGE *vb* crowd or press
SCROW, -S *n* scroll
SCROWL, -S *vb* old form of scroll
SCROWLE *vb* old form of scroll
SCROWLS ▸ **scrowl**
SCROWS ▸ **scrow**
SCROYLE *n* old word meaning wretch
SCRUB, -S *vb, n, adj*
SCRUBBY *adj* covered with scrub
SCRUBS ▸ **scrub**
SCRUFF, -S *same as* ▸ **scum**
SCRUFFY *adj*
SCRUM, -S *n, vb*
SCRUMMY *adj* delicious
SCRUMP, -S *vb* steal (apples) from an orchard or garden
SCRUMPY *n*
SCRUMS ▸ **scrum**
SCRUNCH *vb* crumple or crunch or be crumpled or crunched ▹ *n* act or sound of scrunching
SCRUNT, -S *n* Scots word meaning stunted thing
SCRUNTY ▸ **scrunt**
SCRUPLE *n, vb*
SCRUTO, -S *n* trapdoor on stage
SCRUZE, -D, -S *vb* old word meaning squeeze
SCRY, SCRIED, SCRIES, -DE *vb* divine, esp by crystal gazing
SCRYER, -S ▸ **scry**
SCRYING ▸ **scry**
SCRYNE, -S *n* old form of shrine
SCUBA, -ED, -S *n, vb*
SCUCHIN *n* old form of scutcheon
SCUD, -DED, -S *vb* move along swiftly ▹ *n* act of scudding

SCUDDER ▸ **scud**
SCUDDLE *vb* scuttle
SCUDI ▸ **scudo**
SCUDLER *n* Scots word meaning leader of festivities
SCUDO, SCUDI *n* any of several former Italian coins
SCUDS ▸ **scud**
SCUFF, -ED, -S *vb* drag (the feet) while walking ▹ *n* mark caused by scuffing
SCUFFER *n* type of sandal
SCUFFLE *vb, n*
SCUFFS ▸ **scuff**
SCUFT, -S *n* dialect word meaning nape of neck
SCUG, -GED, -S *vb* shelter
SCUL, -S *n* old form of school
SCULCH *n* rubbish
SCULK, -ED, -S *vb* old form of skulk
SCULKER ▸ **sculk**
SCULKS ▸ **sculk**
SCULL, -ED, -S *n, vb*
SCULLE, -S *n* old form of school
SCULLED ▸ **scull**
SCULLER ▸ **scull**
SCULLES ▸ **sculle**
SCULLS ▸ **scull**
SCULP, -ED, -S *variant of* > **sculpture**
SCULPIN *n* type of fish of the family which includes bullheads and sea scorpions
SCULPS ▸ **sculp**
SCULPT, -S *same as* > **sculpture**
SCULS ▸ **scul**
SCULTCH *same as* ▸ **sculch**
SCUM, -MED, -S *n, vb*
SCUMBER *vb* old word meaning defecate
SCUMBLE *vb* soften or blend (an outline or colour) with a thin upper coat of opaque colour ▹ *n* upper layer of colour applied in this way
SCUMMED ▸ **scum**
SCUMMER ▸ **scum**
SCUMMY *adj*
SCUMS ▸ **scum**
SCUNGE, -D, -S *vb* borrow ▹ *n* dirty or worthless person
SCUNGY *adj* sordid or dirty
SCUNNER *vb, n*
SCUP, -S *n* common sparid fish of American coastal regions of the Atlantic
SCUPPER *vb, n*
SCUPS ▸ **scup**
SCUR, -RED, -S *n* small unattached growth of horn at the site of a normal horn in cattle
SCURF, -S *n* flaky skin on the scalp
SCURFY ▸ **scurf**
SCURRED ▸ **scur**
SCURRIL *adj* old word meaning vulgar
SCURRY *vb, n*
SCURS ▸ **scur**
SCURVY *n, adj*
SCUSE, -D, -S, SCUSING *shortened form of* ▸ **excuse**
SCUT, -S *n* short tail of the hare, rabbit, or deer
SCUTA ▸ **scutum**
SCUTAGE *n* payment to a lord from his vassal in lieu of military service
SCUTAL ▸ **scute**
SCUTATE *adj* (of animals) having or covered with large bony or horny plates
SCUTCH *vb* separate the fibres from the woody part of (flax) by pounding ▹ *n* tool used for this
SCUTE, -S *n* horny or chitinous plate that makes up part of the exoskeleton in armadillos, etc
SCUTS ▸ **scut**
SCUTTER *informal word for* ▸ **scurry**
SCUTTLE *n* fireside container for coal ▹ *vb* run with short quick steps
SCUTUM, SCUTA *n* middle of three plates into which the notum of an insect's thorax is divided
SCUZZ, -ES *n* dirt
SCUZZY *adj* unkempt, dirty, or squalid
SCYBALA > **scybalum**
SCYE, -S *n* Scots word meaning sleeve-hole
SCYPHUS, SCYPHI *n* ancient Greek two-handled drinking cup
SCYTALE *n* coded message in ancient Sparta

SCYTHE, -D, -S *n* long-handled tool with a curved blade for cutting grass ▷ *vb* cut with a scythe
SCYTHER ▶ **scythe**
SCYTHES ▶ **scythe**
SDAINE, -D, -S *vb* old form of disdain
SDAYN, -ED, -S *vb* old form of disdain
SDEIGN, -S *vb* old form of disdain
SDEIGNE *vb* old form of disdain
SDEIGNS ▶ **sdeign**
SDEIN, -ED, -S *vb* old form of disdain
SEA, -S *n*
SEABAG, -S *n* canvas bag for holding a sailor's belongings
SEABANK *n* sea shore
SEABED, -S *n*
SEABIRD *n* bird that lives on the sea
SEABOOT *n* sailor's waterproof boot
SEACOCK *n* valve in the hull of a vessel below the water line
SEADOG, -S *another word for* ▶ **fogbow**
SEAFOAM *n* foam formed on the sea
SEAFOLK *n* people who sail the sea
SEAFOOD *n*
SEAFOWL *n* seabird
SEAGIRT *adj* surrounded by the sea
SEAGULL *n*
SEAHAWK *n*
SEAHOG, -S *n* porpoise
SEAKALE *n* European coastal plant
SEAL, -S *n, vb*
SEALANT *n*
SEALCH, -S *Scots word for* ▶ **seal**
SEALED *adj*
SEALER, -S *n*
SEALERY *n* occupation of hunting seals
SEALGH, -S *Scots word for* ▶ **seal**
SEALIFT *vb* transport by ship
SEALINE *n* company running regular sailings
SEALING ▶ **seal**
SEALS ▶ **seal**
SEALWAX *n* sealing wax
SEAM, -ED, -ING, -S *n, vb*
SEAMAID *n* mermaid
SEAMAN, SEAMEN *n*
SEAMARK *n* conspicuous object on a shore used as a guide
SEAME, -S *n* old word meaning grease
SEAMED ▶ **seam**
SEAMEN ▶ **seaman**
SEAMER, -S *n* bowler who makes the ball bounce on its seam
SEAMES ▶ **seame**
SEAMIER ▶ **seamy**
SEAMING ▶ **seam**
SEAMS ▶ **seam**
SEAMSET *n* tool for flattening seams in metal
SEAMY, SEAMIER *adj* sordid
SEAN, -ED, -ING, -S *vb* fish with seine net
SEANCE, -S *n*
SEANED ▶ **sean**
SEANING ▶ **sean**
SEANS ▶ **sean**
SEAPORT *n*
SEAR, -ED, -ER, -EST, -S *vb, n, adj*
SEARAT, -S *n* pirate
SEARCE, -D, -S *vb* sift
SEARCH *vb, n*
SEARE *adj* old word meaning dry and withered
SEARED ▶ **sear**
SEARER ▶ **sear**
SEAREST ▶ **sear**
SEARING ▶ **sear**
SEARS ▶ **sear**
SEAS ▶ **sea**
SEASE, -D, -S, SEASING *vb* old form of seize
SEASICK *adj*
SEASIDE *n*
SEASING ▶ **sease**
SEASON, -S *n, vb*
SEASURE *n* old form of seizure
SEAT, -ED, -S *n, vb*
SEATER, -S *n*
SEATING *n, adj*
SEATS ▶ **seat**
SEAWALL *n*
SEAWAN, -S *n* shell beads used by certain Native Americans as money
SEAWANT *n* Native American name for silver coins
SEAWARD *same as* > **seawards**
SEAWARE *n* any of numerous large coarse seaweeds
SEAWAY, -S *n* waterway giving access to an inland port
SEAWEED *n*

SEAWIFE *n* variety of sea fish
SEAWORM *n* marine worm
SEAZE, -D, -S, SEAZING *vb* old form of seize
SEBACIC *adj* derived from sebacic acid, a white crystalline acid
SEBASIC *same as* ▸ **sebacic**
SEBATE, -S *n* salt of sebacic acid
SEBIFIC *adj* producing fat
SEBUM, -S *n* oily substance secreted by the sebaceous glands
SEBUNDY *n* irregular soldier in India
SEC, -S *same as* ▸ **secant**
SECANT, -S *n* the ratio of the length of the hypotenuse to the length of the adjacent side
SECCO, -S *n* wall painting done on dried plaster with tempera
SECEDE, -D, -S *vb*
SECEDER ▸ **secede**
SECEDES ▸ **secede**
SECERN, -S *vb* (of a gland or follicle) to secrete
SECESH *n* secessionist in US Civil War
SECH, -S *n* hyperbolic secant
SECKEL, -S *variant of* ▸ **seckle**
SECKLE, -S *n* type of pear
SECLUDE *vb*
SECO *adj* (of wine) dry
SECONAL *n* tradename for secobarbital
SECOND, -S *adj, n, vb*
SECONDE *n* second of eight positions from which a parry or attack can be made in fencing
SECONDO, SECONDI *n* left-hand part in a piano duet
SECONDS ▸ **second**
SECPAR, -S *n* distance unit in astronomy
SECRECY *n*
SECRET, -S *adj, n*
SECRETA *n* secretions
SECRETE *vb*
SECRETS ▸ **secret**
SECS ▸ **sec**
SECT, -S *n*
SECTARY *n* member of a sect
SECTILE *adj* able to be cut smoothly
SECTION *n, vb*
SECTOR, -S *n, vb*
SECTS ▸ **sect**
SECULA ▸ **seculum**
SECULAR *adj, n*
SECULUM, SECULA *n* age in astronomy
SECUND *adj* having or designating parts arranged on or turned to one side of the axis
SECURE, -D, -S *adj, vb*
SECURER ▸ **secure**
SECURES ▸ **secure**
SED *old spelling of* ▸ **said**
SEDAN, -S *same as* ▸ **saloon**
SEDARIM ▸ **seder**
SEDATE, -D, -R, -S *adj, vb*
SEDENT *adj* seated
SEDER, SEDARIM, -S *n* Jewish ceremonial meal held on the first night or first two nights of Passover
SEDES *Latin word for* ▸ **seat**
SEDGE, -S *n* coarse grasslike plant growing on wet ground
SEDGED *adj* having sedge
SEDGES ▸ **sedge**
SEDGY, SEDGIER ▸ **sedge**
SEDILE *n* seat for clergy in church
SEDILIA *n* group of three seats where the celebrant and ministers sit during High Mass
SEDUCE, -D, -S *vb*
SEDUCER *n*
SEDUCES ▸ **seduce**
SEDUM, -S *n* rock plant
SEE, -N, -S *vb, n*
SEEABLE ▸ **see**
SEED, -ED, -S *n, vb*
SEEDBED *n* area of soil prepared for the growing of seedlings before they are transplanted
SEEDBOX *n* part of plant that contains seeds
SEEDED ▸ **seed**
SEEDER, -S *n* person or thing that seeds
SEEDIER ▸ **seedy**
SEEDILY ▸ **seedy**
SEEDING ▸ **seed**
SEEDLIP *n* basket holding seeds to be sown
SEEDMAN, SEEDMEN *n* seller of seeds

SEEDPOD *n*
SEEDS ▸ **seed**
SEEDY, SEEDIER *adj*
SEEING, -S ▸ **see**
SEEK, -ING, -S, SOUGHT *vb*
SEEKER, -S ▸ **seek**
SEEKING ▸ **seek**
SEEKS ▸ **seek**
SEEL, -ED, -S *vb* sew up the eyelids of (a hawk or falcon) so as to render it tame
SEELD *adj* old word meaning rare
SEELED ▸ **seel**
SEELIE *pl n* good benevolent fairies
SEELIER ▸ **seely**
SEELING ▸ **seel**
SEELS ▸ **seel**
SEELY, SEELIER *adj* old word meaning happy
SEEM, -ED, -S *vb*
SEEMER, -S ▸ **seem**
SEEMING *adj, n*
SEEMLY *adj, adv*
SEEMS ▸ **seem**
SEEN ▸ **see**
SEEP, -ED, -ING, -S *vb, n*
SEEPAGE *n*
SEEPED ▸ **seep**
SEEPIER ▸ **seepy**
SEEPING ▸ **seep**
SEEPS ▸ **seep**
SEEPY, SEEPIER *adj* tending to seep
SEER, -S *n*
SEERESS ▸ **seer**
SEERS ▸ **seer**
SEES ▸ **see**
SEESAW, -S *n, vb*
SEETHE, -D, -S *vb, n*
SEETHER ▸ **seethe**
SEETHES ▸ **seethe**
SEEWING *n* suing
SEFER, SIFREI *n* scrolls of the Law
SEG, -S *n* metal stud on shoe sole
SEGAR, -S *n* cigar
SEGETAL *adj* (of weeds) growing amongst crops
SEGGAR, -S *n* box in which pottery is baked
SEGHOL, -S *n* pronunciation mark in Hebrew
SEGMENT *n, vb*
SEGNO, SEGNI, -S *n* sign at the beginning or end of a section directed to be repeated
SEGO, -S *n* American variety of lily
SEGOL, -S *variant of* ▸ **seghol**
SEGOS ▸ **sego**
SEGS ▸ **seg**
SEGUE, -D, -S *vb* proceed from one section or piece of music to another without a break ▹ *n* practice or an instance of playing music in this way
SEGUGIO *n* Italian breed of dog
SEHRI, -S *n* meal eaten before sunrise by Muslims fasting during Ramadan
SEI, -S *n* type of rorqual
SEICHE, -S *n* periodic oscillation of the surface of an enclosed or partially enclosed body of water
SEIDEL, -S *n* vessel for drinking beer
SEIF, -S *n* long ridge of blown sand in a desert
SEIK, -ER, -EST *Scot word for* ▸ **sick**
SEIL, -ED, -ING, -S *vb* dialect word meaning strain
SEINE, -D, -S *n* large fishing net that hangs vertically from floats ▹ *vb* catch (fish) using this net
SEINER, -S ▸ **seine**
SEINES ▸ **seine**
SEINING ▸ **seine**
SEIR, -S *n* fish of Indian seas
SEIS ▸ **sei**
SEISE, -D, -S *vb* put into legal possession of (property, etc)
SEISER, -S ▸ **seise**
SEISES ▸ **seise**
SEISIN, -S *n* feudal possession of an estate in land
SEISING ▸ **seise**
SEISINS ▸ **seisin**
SEISM, -S *n* earthquake
SEISMAL *adj* of earthquakes
SEISMIC *adj*
SEISMS ▸ **seism**
SEISOR, -S *n* person who takes seisin
SEISURE *n*
SEITAN, -S *same as* ▸ **seiten**
SEITEN, -S *n* gluten from wheat
SEITY, SEITIES *n* selfhood
SEIZA, -S *n* traditional Japanese kneeling position
SEIZE, -D, -S *vb*

SEIZER, -S ▶ **seize**
SEIZES ▶ **seize**
SEIZIN, -S *same as* ▶ **seisin**
SEIZING *n* binding used for holding together two ropes, two spars, etc
SEIZINS ▶ **seizin**
SEIZOR, -S *n* person who takes seisin
SEIZURE *n*
SEJANT *adj* (of a beast) shown seated
SEJEANT *same as* ▶ **sejant**
SEKOS, -ES *n* holy place
SEKT, -S *n* German sparkling wine
SEL, -S *Scot word for* ▶ **self**
SELAH, -S *n* Hebrew word of unknown meaning occurring in the Old Testament psalms
SELD *adj* old word meaning rare
SELDOM *adv*
SELE, -S *n* old word meaning happiness
SELECT, -S *vb, adj*
SELECTA *n* disc jockey
SELECTS ▶ **select**
SELENIC *adj* of or containing selenium, esp in the hexavalent state
SELES ▶ **sele**
SELF, -ED, -S, SELVES *n, pron, vb*
SELFDOM *n* selfhood
SELFED ▶ **self**
SELFIE, -S *n*
SELFING ▶ **self**
SELFISH *adj*
SELFISM *n* emphasis on self
SELFIST ▶ **selfism**
SELFS ▶ **self**
SELKIE, -S *same as* ▶ **silkie**
SELL, -S *vb, n*
SELLA, -E, -S *n* area of bone in body
SELLE, -S *n* old word meaning seat
SELLER, -S *n*
SELLES ▶ **selle**
SELLING *n*
SELLOFF *n* act of selling cheaply
SELLOUT *n*
SELLS ▶ **sell**
SELS ▶ **sel**
SELSYN, -S *same as* ▶ **synchro**
SELTZER *n* natural effervescent water containing minerals
SELVA, -S *n* dense equatorial forest
SELVAGE *n* edge of cloth, woven so as to prevent unravelling ▷ *vb* edge or border
SELVAS ▶ **selva**
SELVES ▶ **self**
SEMATIC *adj* acting as a warning, esp to potential predators
SEMBLE, -D, -S *vb* seem
SEME, -S *adj* dotted (with)
SEMEE *variant of* ▶ **seme**
SEMEED *adj* seme
SEMEION, SEMEIA *n* unit of metre in ancient poetry
SEMEME, -S *n* meaning of a morpheme
SEMEMIC ▶ **sememe**
SEMEN, -S, SEMINA *n*
SEMES ▶ **seme**
SEMI *n* semidetached house
SEMIDRY *adj* partly dry
SEMIE, -S *n* historical name for a student in second year at a Scottish university
SEMIFIT *adj* not fully fit
SEMILOG *adj* semilogarithmic
SEMIMAT *adj* semimatt
SEMINA ▶ **semen**
SEMINAL *adj*
SEMINAR *n*
SEMIPED *n* measure in poetic metre
SEMIPRO *n* semiprofessional
SEMIRAW *adj* not fully cooked or processed
SEMIS, -ES *n* ancient Roman coin
SEMITAR *old spelling of* > **scimitar**
SEMMIT, -S *n* Scots word meaning a vest
SEMPER *adv* Latin word meaning always
SEMPLE, -R *adj* Scots word meaning simple
SEMPRE *adv* (preceding a tempo or dynamic marking) always
SEMSEM, -S *n* sesame
SEN, -S *n* monetary unit of Brunei, Cambodia, Indonesia, and Malaysia
SENA, -S *n* (in India) the army
SENARII > **senarius**
SENARY *adj* of or relating to the number six

SENAS ▸ **sena**
SENATE, -S *n*
SENATOR *n*
SEND, -S *vb*
SENDAL, -S *n* fine silk fabric used for ceremonial clothing, etc
SENDED *vb* old word meaning sent
SENDER, -S ▸ **send**
SENDING ▸ **send**
SENDOFF *n, vb*
SENDS ▸ **send**
SENDUP, -S *n*
SENE, -S *n* money unit in Samoa
SENECA, -S *variant of* ▸ **senega**
SENECIO *n* type of plant of the genus which includes groundsels and ragworts
SENEGA, -S *n* milkwort plant of the eastern US
SENES ▸ **sene**
SENESCE *vb* grow old
SENGI, -S *n* African shrew
SENHOR, -S *n* Portuguese term of address for man
SENHORA *n* Portuguese term of address for woman
SENHORS ▸ **senhor**
SENILE, -S *adj, n*
SENIOR, -S *adj, n*
SENITI, -S *n* money unit in Tonga
SENNA, -S *n* tropical plant
SENNET, -S *n* fanfare: used as a stage direction in Elizabethan drama
SENNIT, -S *n* flat braided cordage used on ships
SENOPIA *n* short-sightedness in old age
SENOR, -ES, -S *n* Spanish term of address equivalent to *sir* or *Mr*
SENORA, -S *n* Spanish term of address equivalent to *madam* or *Mrs*
SENORES ▸ **senor**
SENORS ▸ **senor**
SENRYU *n* Japanese short poem
SENS ▸ **sen**
SENSA ▸ **sensum**
SENSATE *adj* perceived by the senses ▹ *vb* make sensate
SENSE, -D, -S *n, vb*
SENSEI, -S *n* martial arts teacher
SENSES ▸ **sense**
SENSI, -S *same as* ▸ **sensei**
SENSILE *adj* capable of feeling
SENSING ▸ **sense**
SENSIS ▸ **sensi**
SENSISM *n* theory that ideas spring from senses
SENSIST ▸ **sensism**
SENSOR, -S *n*
SENSORY *adj*
SENSUAL *adj*
SENSUM, SENSA *n* sensation detached from the information it conveys
SENT, -ED, -I, -ING, -S *n, vb*
SENTE, LISENTE *n* money unit in Lesotho
SENTED ▸ **sent**
SENTI ▸ **sent**
SENTIMO *n* money unit in Philippines
SENTING ▸ **sent**
SENTRY *n*
SENTS ▸ **sent**
SENVY, SENVIES *n* mustard
SENZA *prep* without
SEPAD, -S *vb* suppose
SEPAL, -S *n* leaflike division of the calyx of a flower
SEPALED ▸ **sepal**
SEPALS ▸ **sepal**
SEPHEN, -S *n* stingray
SEPIA, -S *n, adj*
SEPIC *adj* of sepia
SEPIOST *n* cuttlefish bone
SEPIUM, -S *n* cuttlefish bone
SEPMAG *adj* designating a film, etc for which the sound is recorded on separate magnetic material
SEPOY, -S *n* (formerly) Indian soldier in the service of the British
SEPPUKU *n* Japanese ritual suicide
SEPS *n* species of lizard
SEPSIS, SEPSES *n* poisoning caused by pus-forming bacteria
SEPT, -S *n* clan, esp in Ireland or Scotland
SEPTA ▸ **septum**
SEPTAGE *n* waste removed from septic tank

SEPTAL *adj* of or relating to a septum
SEPTATE *adj* divided by septa
SEPTET, -S *n* group of seven performers
SEPTIC, -S *adj, n*
SEPTIME *n* seventh of eight basic positions from which a parry can be made in fencing
SEPTS ▶ **sept**
SEPTUM, SEPTA, -S *n* dividing partition between two cavities in the body
SEPTUOR *n* group of seven musicians
SEQUEL, -S *n*
SEQUELA *n* disease related to or arising from a pre-existing disease
SEQUELS ▶ **sequel**
SEQUENT *adj* following in order or succession ▷ *n* something that follows
SEQUIN, -S *n, vb*
SEQUOIA *n*

This word for a redwood tree is one of the most frequently played bonuses using the Q, a great one to remember as it also clears out a surplus of vowels.

SER, -S *n* unit of weight used in India
SERA ▶ **serum**
SERAC, -S *n* pinnacle of ice among crevasses on a glacier, usually on a steep slope
SERAFIN *n* old silver coin of Goa
SERAI, -S *n* caravanserai or inn
SERAIL, -S *same as* > **seraglio**
SERAIS ▶ **serai**
SERAL ▶ **sere**
SERANG, -S *n* captain of a crew of sailors in SE Asia
SERAPE, -S *n* blanket-like shawl often of brightly-coloured wool
SERAPH, -S *n*
SERDAB, -S *n* secret chamber in an ancient Egyptian tomb
SERE, -D, -R, -S, -ST, SERING *adj* dried up or withered ▷ *n* series of changes occurring in the ecological succession of a particular community ▷ *vb* sear
SEREIN, -S *n* fine rain falling from a clear sky after sunset
SERENE, -D, -R, -S *adj, vb*
SERER ▶ **sere**
SERES ▶ **sere**
SEREST ▶ **sere**
SERF, -S *n*
SERFAGE ▶ **serf**
SERFDOM ▶ **serf**
SERFISH ▶ **serf**
SERFS ▶ **serf**
SERGE, -S *n* strong woollen fabric
SERGED *adj* with sewn seam
SERGER, -S *n* sewing machine attachment for finishing seams
SERGES ▶ **serge**
SERGING *n* type of sewing
SERIAL, -S *n, adj*
SERIATE *adj* forming a series ▷ *vb* form into a series
SERIC *adj* of silk
SERICIN *n* gelatinous protein found on the fibres of raw silk
SERICON *n* solution used in alchemy
SERIEMA *n* either of two cranelike South American birds
SERIES *n*
SERIF, -S *n* small line at the extremities of a main stroke in a type character
SERIFED *adj* having serifs
SERIFS ▶ **serif**
SERIN, -S *n* any of various small yellow-and-brown finches
SERINE, -S *n* sweet-tasting amino acid
SERING ▶ **sere**
SERINGA *n* any of several trees that yield rubber
SERINS ▶ **serin**
SERIOUS *adj*
SERIPH, -S *same as* ▶ **serif**
SERK, -S *Scots word for* ▶ **shirt**
SERKALI *n* government in Africa
SERKS ▶ **serk**
SERMON, -S *n, vb*

SEROMA, -S *n* abnormal pocket of clear fluid in the body
SERON, -S *n* crate
SEROON, -S *n* crate
SEROPUS *n* liquid consisting of serum and pus
SEROSA, -E, -S *n* one of the thin membranes surrounding the embryo in an insect's egg
SEROSAL ▸ serosa
SEROSAS ▸ serosa
SEROUS *adj* of, containing, or like serum
SEROVAR *n* subdivision of species
SEROW, -S *n* either of two antelopes of mountainous regions of S and SE Asia
SERPENT *n*
SERPIGO *n* any progressive skin eruption
SERPULA *n* type of marine mollusc
SERR, -S *vb* press close together
SERRA, -E, -S *n* sawlike part or organ
SERRAN, -S *n* species of fish
SERRANO *n* type of Spanish ham
SERRANS ▸ serran
SERRAS ▸ serra
SERRATE *adj* (of leaves) having a margin of forward pointing teeth ▹ *vb* make serrate
SERRATI > serratus
SERRE, -D, -S, SERRING *vb* press close together
SERRIED *adj* in close formation
SERRIES ▸ serry
SERRING ▸ serre
SERRS ▸ serr
SERRY, SERRIES *vb* close together
SERS ▸ ser
SERUEWE *vb* old word meaning survey
SERUM, SERA, -S *n*
SERUMAL ▸ serum
SERUMS ▸ serum
SERVAL, -S *n* feline African mammal
SERVANT *n, vb*
SERVE, -D, -S *vb, n*
SERVER, -S *n*
SERVERY *n* room from which food is served
SERVES ▸ serve
SERVEWE *vb* old word meaning survey
SERVICE *n, adj, vb*
SERVILE *adj, n*
SERVING *n*
SERVLET *n* small program that runs on a web server
SERVO, -S *n* servomechanism ▹ *adj* of a servomechanism
SESAME, -S *n*
SESE *interj* exclamation found in Shakespeare
SESELI, -S *n* garden plant
SESEY *interj* exclamation found in Shakespeare
SESH, -ES *short for* **▸ session**
SESS, -ED, -ES, -ING *n* old word meaning tax ▹ *vb* assess or impose (a tax)
SESSA *interj* exclamation found in Shakespeare
SESSED ▸ sess
SESSES ▸ sess
SESSILE *adj* (of flowers or leaves) having no stalk
SESSING ▸ sess
SESSION *n*
SESTET, -S *n* last six lines of a sonnet
SESTETT *n* group of six
SESTINA *n* elaborate verse form of Italian origin
SESTINE *n* poem of six lines
SESTON, -S *n* type of plankton
SET, -S *vb, n, adj*
SETA, -E *n* bristle or bristle-like appendage
SETAL ▸ seta
SETBACK *n*
SETLINE *n* any of various types of fishing line
SETNESS ▸ set
SETOFF, -S *n* counterbalance
SETON, -S *n* surgical thread inserted below the skin
SETOSE *adj* covered with setae
SETOUS ▸ seta
SETOUT, -S *n* beginning or outset
SETS ▸ set
SETT, -S *n* badger's burrow
SETTEE, -S *n*
SETTER, -S *n, vb*

SETTING ▸ **set**
SETTLE, -D, -S *vb, n*
SETTLER *n*
SETTLES ▸ **settle**
SETTLOR *n* person who settles property on someone
SETTS ▸ **sett**
SETUALE *n* valerian
SETULE, -S *n* small bristle
SETUP, -S *n*
SETWALL *n* valerian
SEV, -S *n* Indian snack of deep-fried noodles
SEVEN *n*
SEVENS *n* Rugby Union match or series of matches played with seven players on each side
SEVENTH *n, adj*
SEVENTY *n*
SEVER, -ED, -S *vb*
SEVERAL *adj, n*
SEVERE, -R *adj*
SEVERED ▸ **sever**
SEVERER ▸ **severe**
SEVERS ▸ **sever**
SEVERY *n* part of vaulted ceiling
SEVICHE *n* Mexican fish dish
SEVRUGA *n* species of sturgeon
SEVS ▸ **sev**
SEW, -ED, -N, -S *vb*
SEWABLE ▸ **sew**
SEWAGE, -S *n*
SEWAN, -S *same as* ▸ **seawan**
SEWAR, -S *n* Asian dagger
SEWED ▸ **sew**
SEWEL, -S *n* scarecrow
SEWEN, -S *same as* ▸ **sewin**
SEWER, -ED, -S *n, vb*
SEWIN, -S *n* sea trout
SEWING, -S ▸ **sew**
SEWINS ▸ **sewin**
SEWN ▸ **sew**
SEWS ▸ **sew**
SEX, -ED, -ES, -ING *n, vb*
SEXER, -S *n* person who determines the sex of chickens
SEXES ▸ **sex**
SEXFID *adj* split into six
SEXFOIL *n* flower with six petals or leaves
SEXIER ▸ **sexy**
SEXIEST ▸ **sexy**
SEXILY ▸ **sexy**
SEXING, -S ▸ **sex**
SEXISM, -S *n*
SEXIST, -S ▸ **sexism**
SEXLESS *adj* neither male nor female
SEXTAIN *same as* ▸ **sestina**
SEXTAN *adj* (of a fever) marked by paroxysms that recur after an interval of five days
SEXTANS *n* ancient Roman coin
SEXTANT *n*
SEXTET, -S *n*
SEXTETT *n* sextet
SEXTILE *n* value of a variable dividing its distribution into six groups with equal frequencies
SEXTO, -S *same as* ▸ **sixmo**
SEXTON, -S *n*
SEXTOS ▸ **sexto**
SEXTUOR *n* sextet
SEXUAL *adj*
SEXY, SEXIER, SEXIEST *adj*
SEY, -S *n* Scots word meaning part of a cow carcase
SEYEN, -S *n* old form of scion
SEYS ▸ **sey**
SEYSURE *n* old form of seizure
SEZ *vb* informal spelling of 'says'

> **Sez** is a short informal form of **says**, very useful for disposing of the Z.

SFERICS *same as* ▸ **spherics**
SFUMATO *n* gradual transition between areas of different colour in painting
SH *interj* hush
SHA *interj* be quiet
SHABASH *interj* (in Indian English) bravo or well done
SHABBLE *n* Scots word meaning old sword
SHABBY *adj*
SHACK, -ED, -S *n, vb*
SHACKLE *n, vb*
SHACKO, -S *same as* ▸ **shako**
SHACKS ▸ **shack**
SHACKY *adj* resembling a shack; dilapidated
SHAD, -S *n* herring-like fish
SHADDUP *interj* shut up
SHADE, -D *n, vb*
SHADER, -S ▸ **shade**
SHADES *pl n*
SHADFLY *American name for* ▸ **mayfly**
SHADIER ▸ **shady**

SHADILY ▶ **shady**
SHADING *n*
SHADOOF *n* mechanism for raising water
SHADOW, -S *n, vb*
SHADOWY *adj*
SHADS ▶ **shad**
SHADUF, -S *same as* ▶ **shadoof**
SHADY, SHADIER *adj*
SHAFT, -ED, -S *n, vb*
SHAFTER ▶ **shaft**
SHAFTS ▶ **shaft**
SHAG, -S *n* cormorant ▷ *adj* (of a carpet) having a long pile ▷ *vb* make shaggy
SHAGGED *adj* shaggy
SHAGGY *adj*
SHAGS ▶ **shag**
SHAH, -S *n* formerly, ruler of Iran
SHAHADA *n* Islamic declaration of faith
SHAHDOM ▶ **shah**
SHAHEED *same as* ▶ **shahid**
SHAHID, -S *n* Muslim martyr
SHAHS ▶ **shah**
SHAIKH, -S *n* sheikh
SHAIRD, -S *n* Scots word meaning shred
SHAIRN, -S *Scots word for* ▶ **dung**
SHAITAN *n* (in Muslim countries) an evil spirit
SHAKE, -N, -S *vb, n*
SHAKED *vb* old form of shook
SHAKEN ▶ **shake**
SHAKER, -S *n*
SHAKES ▶ **shake**
SHAKEUP *n*
SHAKIER ▶ **shaky**
SHAKILY ▶ **shaky**
SHAKING ▶ **shake**
SHAKO, -ES, -S *n* tall cylindrical peaked military hat with a plume
SHAKT *vb* old form of shook
SHAKUDO *n* Japanese alloy of copper and gold
SHAKY, SHAKIER *adj*
SHALE, -D, -S, SHALING *n*
SHALEY ▶ **shale**
SHALIER ▶ **shaly**
SHALING ▶ **shale**
SHALL, SHOULD *vb*
SHALLI, -S *n* type of fabric
SHALLON *n* American shrub
SHALLOP *n* light boat used for rowing in shallow water
SHALLOT *n*
SHALLOW *adj, n, vb*
SHALM, -S *n* old woodwind instrument
SHALOM, -S *n* Jewish greeting meaning 'peace be with you'
SHALOT, -S *n* shallot
SHALT *singular form of the present tense (indicative mood) of* ▶ **shall**
SHALWAR *n* pair of loose-fitting trousers narrowing around the ankles
SHALY, SHALIER ▶ **shale**
SHAM, -MED, -S *n, adj, vb*
SHAMA, -S *n* Indian songbird
SHAMAL, -S *n* hot northwesterly wind
SHAMAN, -S *n* priest of shamanism
SHAMAS ▶ **shama**
SHAMBA, -S *n* (in E Africa) any field used for growing crops
SHAMBLE *vb, n*
SHAMBLY ▶ **shamble**
SHAME, -D, -S *n, vb*
SHAMER, -S *n* cause of shame
SHAMES ▶ **shame**
SHAMINA *n* wool blend of pashm and shahtoosh
SHAMING *n* act or attempt to embarrass someone
SHAMMAS *same as* ▶ **shammes**
SHAMMED ▶ **sham**
SHAMMER ▶ **sham**
SHAMMES *n* official acting as the beadle, sexton, and caretaker of a synagogue
SHAMMOS *same as* ▶ **shammes**
SHAMMY *n* piece of chamois leather ▷ *vb* rub with a shammy
SHAMOIS *n* chamois ▷ *vb* clean with shamois
SHAMOS *same as* ▶ **shammes**
SHAMOY, -S *n* chamois ▷ *vb* rub with a shamoy
SHAMPOO *n, vb*
SHAMS ▶ **sham**
SHAMUS *n* police or private detective

SHAN, -S *variant of* ▸ **shand**
SHAND, -S *n* old word meaning fake coin
SHANDRY *n* light horse-drawn cart
SHANDS ▸ **shand**
SHANDY *n*
SHANK, -ED, -S *n, vb*
SHANNY *n* European blenny of rocky coastal waters
SHANS ▸ **shan**
SHANTEY *same as* ▸ **shanty**
SHANTI, -S *n* peace
SHANTIH *same as* ▸ **shanti**
SHANTIS ▸ **shanti**
SHANTY *n*
SHAPE, -D, -S *n, vb*
SHAPELY *adj*
SHAPEN, -S *vb* shape
SHAPER, -S ▸ **shape**
SHAPES ▸ **shape**
SHAPEUP *n* system of hiring dockers for a day's work
SHAPING ▸ **shape**
SHAPS *n* leather over-trousers worn by cowboys
SHARD, -S *n*
SHARDED *adj* old word meaning hidden under dung
SHARDS ▸ **shard**
SHARE, -D, -S *n, vb*
SHARER, -S ▸ **share**
SHARES ▸ **share**
SHARIA, -S *n* body of doctrines that regulate the lives of Muslims
SHARIAH *same as* ▸ **sharia**
SHARIAS ▸ **sharia**
SHARIAT *n* Islamic religious law
SHARIF, -S *same as* ▸ **sherif**
SHARING ▸ **share**
SHARK, -ED, -S *n, vb*
SHARKER *n* shark hunter
SHARKS ▸ **shark**
SHARN, -S *Scots word for* ▸ **dung**
SHARNY *n* (Scot) person who cleans a cow-house ▹ *adj* (Scot) covered in dung
SHARON *n* as in **sharon fruit** persimmon
SHARP, -ED, -S *adj, adv, n, vb*
SHARPEN *vb*
SHARPER *n* person who cheats
SHARPIE *n* member of a teenage group having short hair and distinctive clothes
SHARPLY ▸ **sharp**
SHARPS ▸ **sharp**
SHARPY *n* swindler
SHASH, -ED, -ES *vb* old form of sash
SHASLIK *n* type of kebab
SHASTA, -S *n* plant of the daisy family
SHASTER *same as* ▸ **shastra**
SHASTRA *n* any of the sacred writings of Hinduism
SHATTER *vb, n*
SHAUGH, -S *n* old word meaning small wood
SHAUL, -ED, -S *vb* old form of shawl
SHAVE, -D, -S *vb, n*
SHAVEN *adj*
SHAVER, -S *n*
SHAVES ▸ **shave**
SHAVIE, -S *n* Scots word meaning trick
SHAVING ▸ **shave**
SHAW, -ED, -ING, -S *n* small wood ▹ *vb* show
SHAWL, -ED, -S *n, vb*
SHAWLEY *same as* ▸ **shawlie**
SHAWLIE *n* insulting term for a working-class woman who wears a shawl
SHAWLS ▸ **shawl**
SHAWM, -S *n* medieval form of the oboe with a conical bore and flaring bell
SHAWN *variant of* ▸ **shawm**
SHAWS ▸ **shaw**
SHAY, -S *dialect word for* ▸ **chaise**
SHAYA, -S *n* Indian plant
SHAYKH, -S *same as* ▸ **sheikh**
SHAYS ▸ **shay**
SHAZAM *interj* magic slogan
SHCHI, -S *n* Russian cabbage soup
SHE, -S *pron, n*
SHEA, -S *n* tropical African tree
SHEAF, -ED, -S, SHEAVES *n, vb*
SHEAFY ▸ **sheaf**
SHEAL, -ED, -S *vb* old word meaning shell
SHEAR, -ED, -S *vb, n*
SHEARER ▸ **shear**
SHEARS ▸ **shear**
SHEAS ▸ **shea**

SHEATH, -S *n*
SHEATHE *vb* put into a sheath
SHEATHS ▸ **sheath**
SHEATHY ▸ **sheathe**
SHEAVE, -D *vb* gather or bind into sheaves ▹ *n* wheel with a grooved rim
SHEAVES ▸ **sheaf**
SHEBANG *n* situation, matter, or affair
SHEBEAN *same as* ▸ **shebeen**
SHEBEEN *n* place where alcohol is sold illegally ▹ *vb* run a shebeen
SHED, -DED, -S *n, vb*
SHEDDER *n* person or thing that sheds
SHEDFUL *n* quantity or amount contained in a shed
SHEDS ▸ **shed**
SHEEL, -ED, -S *vb* old word meaning shell
SHEEN, -ED, -S *n, adj, vb*
SHEENY ▸ **sheen**
SHEEP *n*
SHEEPLE *n* group of people who follow the majority in matters of opinion, taste, etc
SHEEPO, -S *n* person employed to bring sheep to the catching pen in a shearing shed
SHEEPY ▸ **sheep**
SHEER, -ED, -ER, -S *adj, adv, vb, n*
SHEERLY ▸ **sheer**
SHEERS ▸ **sheer**
SHEESH *interj* exclamation of surprise or annoyance
SHEESHA *n* water-pipe for smoking tobacco
SHEET, -ED, -S *n, vb*
SHEETER ▸ **sheet**
SHEETS ▸ **sheet**
SHEETY ▸ **sheet**
SHEEVE, -S *n* part of mine winding gear
SHEHITA *n* slaughter of animals according to Jewish religious law
SHEHNAI *n* Indian wind instrument
SHEIK, -S *same as* ▸ **sheikh**
SHEIKH, -S *n*
SHEIKHA *n* chief wife of a sheikh
SHEIKHS ▸ **sheikh**
SHEIKS ▸ **sheik**
SHEILA, -S *n* girl or woman
SHEITAN *n* Muslim demon
SHEITEL *n* traditional wig worn by Orthodox Jewish women
SHEKEL, -S *n* monetary unit of Israel
SHELF, -ED, -S, SHELVES *n, vb*
SHELFY ▸ **shelf**
SHELL, -ED, -S *n, vb*
SHELLAC *n, vb*
SHELLED ▸ **shell**
SHELLER ▸ **shell**
SHELLS ▸ **shell**
SHELLY ▸ **shell**
SHELTA, -S *n* secret language used by some travelling people in Britain and Ireland
SHELTER *n, vb*
SHELTIE *n* small dog similar to a collie
SHELTY *same as* ▸ **sheltie**
SHELVE, -D *vb*
SHELVER ▸ **shelve**
SHELVES ▸ **shelf**
SHELVY *adj* having shelves
SHEN *n* (in Chinese thought) spiritual element of the psyche
SHENAI, -S *same as* ▸ **shehnai**
SHEND, -S, SHENT *vb* put to shame
SHEOL, -S *n* hell
SHEQEL, -S *same as* ▸ **shekel**
SHERANG *n* person in charge
SHERBET *n*
SHERD, -S *same as* ▸ **shard**
SHERE *old spelling of* ▸ **sheer**
SHEREEF *same as* ▸ **sherif**
SHERIA, -S *same as* ▸ **sharia**
SHERIAT *n* Muslim religious law
SHERIF, -S *n* descendant of Muhammad through his daughter Fatima
SHERIFF *n*
SHERIFS ▸ **sherif**
SHERO, -ES *n* woman considered a hero
SHEROOT *n* cheroot
SHERPA, -S *n*
SHERRIS *n* old form of sherry
SHERRY *n*
SHES ▸ **she**
SHET, -S *vb* old form of shut

SHEUCH, -S *n* ditch or trough ▷ *vb* dig
SHEUGH, -S *same as* ▸ **sheuch**
SHEVA, -S *n* mark in Hebrew writing
SHEW, -ED, -ING, -N, -S *archaic spelling of* ▸ **show**
SHEWEL, -S *n* old word meaning scarecrow
SHEWER, -S ▸ **shew**
SHEWING ▸ **shew**
SHEWN ▸ **shew**
SHEWS ▸ **shew**
SHH *interj* sound made to ask for silence
SHHH *interj* used to request quietness
SHIAI, -S *n* judo contest
SHIATSU *n* type of massage
SHIATZU *n* shiatsu
SHIBAH, -S *n* Jewish period of mourning
SHICKER *n* alcoholic drink
SHIDDER *n* old word meaning a female animal
SHIED ▸ **shy**
SHIEL, -ED, -S *vb* sheal
SHIELD, -S *n, vb*
SHIELED ▸ **shiel**
SHIELS ▸ **shiel**
SHIER, -S *n* horse that shies habitually
SHIES ▸ **shy**
SHIEST ▸ **shy**
SHIFT, -ED, -S *vb, n*
SHIFTER ▸ **shift**
SHIFTS ▸ **shift**
SHIFTY *adj*
SHIKAR, -S *n* hunting, esp big-game hunting ▷ *vb* hunt (game, esp big game)
SHIKARA *n* (in Kashmir) light, flat-bottomed boat
SHIKARI *n* (in India) a hunter
SHIKARS ▸ **shikar**
SHIKKER *n* Yiddish term for drunk person
SHIKRA, -S *n* small Asian sparrowhawk
SHILL, -ED, -S *n* confidence trickster's assistant ▷ *vb* act as a shill
SHILPIT *adj* puny
SHILY ▸ **shy**
SHIM, -MED, -S *n* thin strip of material placed between two close surfaces to fill a gap ▷ *vb* fit or fill up with a shim
SHIMAAL *n* hot Middle Eastern wind
SHIMMED ▸ **shim**
SHIMMER *n, vb*
SHIMMEY *n* chemise
SHIMMY *n* American ragtime dance ▷ *vb* dance the shimmy
SHIMS ▸ **shim**
SHIN, -NED, -S *n, vb*
SHINDIG *n*
SHINDY, -S *n* quarrel or commotion
SHINE, -D, -S, SHINING, SHONE *vb, n*
SHINER, -S *n*
SHINES ▸ **shine**
SHINESS ▸ **shy**
SHINGLE *n, vb*
SHINGLY ▸ **shingle**
SHINIER ▸ **shiny**
SHINIES ▸ **shiny**
SHINILY ▸ **shiny**
SHINING ▸ **shine**
SHINKIN *n* worthless person
SHINNE, -S *n* old form of chin
SHINNED ▸ **shin**
SHINNES ▸ **shinne**
SHINNEY *vb* climb with hands and legs
SHINNY *same as* ▸ **shinty**
SHINOLA *n* tradename of a kind of boot polish
SHINS ▸ **shin**
SHINTY *n* game like hockey ▷ *vb* play shinty
SHINY, SHINIER, SHINIES *adj*
SHIP, -PED, -S *n, vb*
SHIPFUL *n* amount carried by ship
SHIPLAP *n* method of constructing ship hull
SHIPMAN, SHIPMEN *n* master or captain of a ship
SHIPPED ▸ **ship**
SHIPPEN *n* dialect word for cattle shed
SHIPPER *n*
SHIPPO, -S *n* Japanese enamel work
SHIPPON *n* dialect word for cattle shed
SHIPPOS ▸ **shippo**
SHIPS ▸ **ship**
SHIPWAY *n* structure on which a vessel is built, then launched
SHIR, -S *n* gathering in material
SHIRAZ *n*
SHIRE, -D, -S, SHIRING *n, vb*
SHIRK, -ED, -S *vb, n*
SHIRKER ▸ **shirk**

SHIRKS ▸ **shirk**
SHIRR, -ED, -S *vb* gather (fabric) into parallel rows to decorate a dress, etc ▹ *n* series of gathered rows decorating a dress, etc
SHIRRA, -S *old Scots word for* ▸ **sheriff**
SHIRRED ▸ **shirr**
SHIRRS ▸ **shirr**
SHIRS ▸ **shir**
SHIRT, -ED, -S *n, vb*
SHIRTY *adj* bad-tempered or annoyed
SHISH *adj* as in **shish kebab** dish of meat and vegetables grilled on skewers
SHISHA, -S *n* water-pipe for smoking tobacco
SHISO, -S *n* Asian plant with aromatic leaves
SHIST, -S *n* schist
SHITAKE *same as* > **shiitake**
SHITTAH, SHITTIM *n* tree mentioned in the Old Testament
SHITZU, -S *n* breed of small dog with long, silky fur
SHIUR, -IM *n* lesson in which a passage of the Talmud is studied
SHIV, -S, -VED *variant spelling of* ▸ **chiv**
SHIVA, -S *variant of* ▸ **shivah**
SHIVAH, -S *n* Jewish period of formal mourning
SHIVAS ▸ **shiva**
SHIVE, -S *n* flat cork or bung for wide-mouthed bottles
SHIVER, -S *vb, n*
SHIVERY *adj* inclined to shiver or tremble
SHIVES ▸ **shive**
SHIVITI *n* Jewish decorative plaque with religious message
SHIVOO, -S *n* Australian word meaning rowdy party
SHIVS ▸ **shiv**
SHIVVED ▸ **shiv**
SHIZZLE *n* form of US rap slang
SHLEP, -S *vb* schlep
SHLEPP, -S *vb* schlep
SHLEPPY *adj* dingy, shabby, or rundown
SHLEPS ▸ **shlep**
SHLOCK, -S *n* something of poor quality
SHLOCKY ▸ **shlock**
SHLUB, -S *same as* ▸ **schlub**
SHLUMP, -S *vb* move in lazy way
SHLUMPY ▸ **shlump**
SHMALTZ *n* schmaltz
SHMATTE *n* rag
SHMEAR, -S *same as* ▸ **schmear**
SHMEER, -S *same as* ▸ **schmear**
SHMEK, -S *n* smell
SHMO, -ES *same as* ▸ **schmo**
SHMOCK, -S *n* despicable person
SHMOE *same as* ▸ **schmoe**
SHMOES ▸ **shmo**
SHMOOSE *variant of* > **schmooze**
SHMOOZE *variant of* > **schmooze**
SHMOOZY *adj* talking casually, gossipy
SHMUCK, -S *n*
SHMUCKY *same as* > **schmucky**
SHNAPPS *same as* > **schnapps**
SHNAPS *n*
SHNOOK, -S *n* stupid person
SHO *adj* sure, as pronounced in southern US
SHOAL, -ED, -ER, -S *n, vb, adj*
SHOALY *adj* shallow
SHOAT, -S *n* piglet that has recently been weaned
SHOCHET *n* (in Judaism) a person licensed to slaughter animals and birds
SHOCHU, -S *n* type of Japanese alcoholic spirit
SHOCK, -ED, -S *vb, n, adj*
SHOCKER *n*
SHOCKS ▸ **shock**
SHOD ▸ **shoe**
SHODDEN *vb* old form of shod
SHODDY *adj, n*
SHODER, -S *n* skins used in making gold leaf
SHOE, SHOD, -D, -S *n, vb*
SHOEBOX *n*
SHOED ▸ **shoe**
SHOEING ▸ **shoe**
SHOEPAC *n* waterproof boot
SHOER, -S *n* person who shoes horses

SHOES ▸ **shoe**
SHOFAR, -S *n* ram's horn sounded in Jewish synagogue
SHOG, -GED, -S *vb* shake
SHOGGLE *vb* shake
SHOGGLY ▸ **shoggle**
SHOGI, -S *n* Japanese chess
SHOGS ▸ **shog**
SHOGUN, -S *n*
SHOJI, -S *n* Japanese rice-paper screen in a sliding wooden frame
SHOJO *n* genre of Japanese comics intended for girls
SHOLA, -S *n* Indian plant
SHOLOM, -S *n* Hebrew greeting
SHONE ▸ **shine**
SHONEEN *n* Irishman who imitates English ways
SHONKY *adj*
SHOO, -ED, -ING, -S *interj* go away! ▹ *vb* drive away as by saying 'shoo'
SHOOFLY *n* as in **shoofly pie** US dessert similar to treacle tart
SHOOGIE *vb* Scots word meaning swing
SHOOGLE *vb* shake, sway, or rock back and forth ▹ *n* rocking motion
SHOOGLY ▸ **shoogle**
SHOOING ▸ **shoo**
SHOOK, -S *n*
SHOOL, -ED, -S *dialect word for* ▸ **shovel**
SHOOLE, -S *dialect word for* ▸ **shovel**
SHOOLED ▸ **shool**
SHOOLES ▸ **shoole**
SHOOLS ▸ **shool**
SHOON *plural of* ▸ **shoe**
SHOORA, -S *same as* ▸ **shura**
SHOOS ▸ **shoo**
SHOOSH *vb* make a rushing sound when moving
SHOOT, -S *vb, n*
SHOOTER *n*
SHOOTIE *n* type of shoe that covers the ankle
SHOOTS ▸ **shoot**
SHOP, -PED, -S *n, vb*
SHOPBOT *n* price-comparison website
SHOPBOY *n* boy working in shop
SHOPE *n* old form of shape
SHOPFUL *n* amount stored in shop
SHOPHAR *same as* ▸ **shofar**
SHOPMAN, SHOPMEN *n* man working in shop
SHOPPE, -S *old-fashioned spelling of* ▸ **shop**
SHOPPED ▸ **shop**
SHOPPER *n*
SHOPPES ▸ **shoppe**
SHOPPY *adj* of a shop ▹ *n* shop assistant
SHOPS ▸ **shop**
SHORAN, -S *n* short-range radar system
SHORE, -D, -S *n, vb*
SHORER, -S ▸ **shore**
SHORES ▸ **shore**
SHORING ▸ **shore**
SHORL, -S *n* black mineral
SHORN *past participle of* ▸ **shear**
SHORT, -ED, -ER *adj, adv, n, vb*
SHORTEN *vb*
SHORTER ▸ **short**
SHORTIA *n* American flowering plant
SHORTIE *n* person or thing that is extremely short
SHORTLY *adv*
SHORTS *pl n*
SHORTY *same as* ▸ **shortie**
SHOT, -S, -TED *vb*
SHOTE, -S *same as* ▸ **shoat**
SHOTGUN *n, adj, vb*
SHOTS ▸ **shot**
SHOTT, -S *n* shallow temporary salt lake or marsh in the North African desert
SHOTTE, -S *n* old form of shoat
SHOTTED ▸ **shot**
SHOTTEN *adj* (of fish, esp herring) having recently spawned
SHOTTES ▸ **shotte**
SHOTTLE *n* small drawer
SHOTTS ▸ **shott**
SHOUGH, -S *n* old word meaning lapdog
SHOULD ▸ **shall**
SHOUSE, -S *n* toilet ▹ *adj* unwell or in poor spirits
SHOUT, -ED, -S *n, vb*
SHOUTER ▸ **shout**
SHOUTS ▸ **shout**
SHOUTY *adj*

SHOVE, -D, -S *vb, n*
SHOVEL, -S *n, vb*
SHOVER, -S ▸ **shove**
SHOVES ▸ **shove**
SHOVING *n*
SHOW, -ED, -N, -S *vb, n*
SHOWBIZ *n*
SHOWBOX *n* box containing showman's material
SHOWD, -ED, -S *vb* rock or sway to and fro ▹ *n* rocking motion
SHOWED ▸ **show**
SHOWER, -S *n, vb*
SHOWERY ▸ **shower**
SHOWGHE *n* old word meaning lapdog
SHOWIER ▸ **showy**
SHOWILY ▸ **showy**
SHOWING ▸ **show**
SHOWMAN, SHOWMEN *n*
SHOWN ▸ **show**
SHOWOFF *n*
SHOWS ▸ **show**
SHOWY, SHOWIER *adj*
SHOYU, -S *n* Japanese variety of soy sauce
SHRANK ▸ **shrink**
SHRED, -S *n, vb*
SHREDDY ▸ **shred**
SHREDS ▸ **shred**
SHREEK, -S *old spelling of* ▸ **shriek**
SHREIK, -S *old spelling of* ▸ **shriek**
SHREW, -ED, -S *n, vb*
SHREWD *adj*
SHREWED ▸ **shrew**
SHREWS ▸ **shrew**
SHRI, -S *n* Indian title of respect
SHRIECH *old spelling of* ▸ **shriek**
SHRIEK, -S *n, vb*
SHRIEKY ▸ **shriek**
SHRIEVE *archaic word for* ▸ **sheriff**
SHRIFT, -S *n*
SHRIGHT *n* old word meaning shriek
SHRIKE, -D, -S *n* songbird with a heavy hooked bill ▹ *vb* archaic word for shriek
SHRILL, -S *adj, vb*
SHRILLY ▸ **shrill**
SHRIMP, -S *n, vb*
SHRIMPY ▸ **shrimp**
SHRINAL ▸ **shrine**
SHRINE, -D, -S *n, vb*
SHRINK, SHRANK, -S, SHRUNK *vb, n*
SHRIS ▸ **shri**
SHRITCH *vb* old word meaning shriek
SHRIVE, -D, -N, -S *vb*
SHRIVEL *vb*
SHRIVEN ▸ **shrive**
SHRIVER ▸ **shrive**
SHRIVES ▸ **shrive**
SHROFF, -S *n* (in China and Japan) expert employed to identify counterfeit money ▹ *vb* test (money) and separate out the counterfeit and base
SHROUD, -S *n, vb*
SHROUDY ▸ **shroud**
SHROVE, -D, -S *vb*
SHROW, -ED, -S *vb* old form of shrew
SHROWD *adj*
SHROWED ▸ **shrow**
SHROWS ▸ **shrow**
SHRUB, -S *n, vb*
SHRUBBY *adj* consisting of, planted with, or abounding in shrubs
SHRUBS ▸ **shrub**
SHRUG, -S *vb, n*
SHRUNK ▸ **shrink**
SHTCHI, -S *n* Russian cabbage soup
SHTETEL *same as* ▸ **shtetl**
SHTETL, -S *n* Jewish community in Eastern Europe
SHTICK, -S *n*
SHTICKY ▸ **shtick**
SHTIK, -S *n* shtick
SHTOOK, -S *n* trouble
SHTOOM *adj* silent
SHTUCK, -S *n* trouble
SHTUM *adj*
SHTUMM *adj* silent
SHUCK, -ED *n, vb*
SHUCKER ▸ **shuck**
SHUCKS *pl n, interj*
SHUDDER *vb, n*
SHUFFLE *vb, n*
SHUFTI, -S *same as* ▸ **shufty**
SHUFTY *n* look
SHUGGY *n* swing, as at a fairground
SHUL, -N, -S *Yiddish word for* > **synagogue**
SHULE, -D, -S, SHULING *vb* saunter
SHULN ▸ **shul**
SHULS ▸ **shul**
SHUMAI *pl n* (in Japan) small stuffed dumplings
SHUN, -NED, -S *vb*
SHUNNER ▸ **shun**
SHUNS ▸ **shun**
SHUNT, -ED, -S *vb, n*
SHUNTER *n* small railway locomotive used for manoeuvring coaches
SHUNTS ▸ **shunt**

SHURA, -S *n* consultative council or assembly
SHUSH, -ED, -ES *interj, vb*
SHUSHER ▸ **shush**
SHUSHES ▸ **shush**
SHUT, -S *vb*
SHUTE, -D, -S, SHUTING *variant of* ▸ **chute**
SHUTEYE *n*
SHUTING ▸ **shute**
SHUTOFF *n* device that shuts something off
SHUTOUT *n* game in which the opposing team does not score
SHUTS ▸ **shut**
SHUTTER *n, vb*
SHUTTLE *n, vb*
SHVITZ *vb* sweat
SHWA, -S *same as* ▸ **schwa**
SHY, SHIED, SHIES, SHIEST, -EST, -ING *adj, vb, n*
SHYER, -S ▸ **shy**
SHYEST ▸ **shy**
SHYING ▸ **shy**
SHYISH ▸ **shy**
SHYLOCK *vb* lend money at an exorbitant rate of interest
SHYLY ▸ **shy**
SHYNESS ▸ **shy**
SHYPOO, -S *n* liquor of poor quality
SHYSTER *n*
SI *same as* ▸ **te**
SIAL, -S *n* silicon-rich and aluminium-rich rocks of the earth's continental upper crust
SIALIC ▸ **sial**
SIALID, -S *n* species of fly
SIALOID *adj* resembling saliva
SIALON, -S *n* type of ceramic
SIALS ▸ **sial**
SIAMANG *n* large black gibbon
SIAMESE *variant of* ▸ **siameze**
SIAMEZE *vb* join together
SIB, -S *n* blood relative
SIBB, -S *n* sib
SIBLING *n*
SIBS ▸ **sib**
SIBSHIP *n* group of children of the same parents
SIBYL, -S *n* (in ancient Greece and Rome) prophetess
SIBYLIC ▸ **sibyl**
SIBYLS ▸ **sibyl**
SIC, -CED, -CING, -S *adv, vb*
SICARIO *n* hired gunman, esp in Latin America
SICCAN *adj* Scots word meaning such
SICCAR *adj* sure
SICCED ▸ **sic**
SICCING ▸ **sic**
SICCITY *n* dryness
SICE, -S *same as* ▸ **syce**
SICH *adj* old form of such
SICHT, -ED, -S *Scot word for* ▸ **sight**
SICK, -ED, -ER, -EST, -ING, -S *adj, n, vb*
SICKBAY *n*
SICKBED *n*
SICKED ▸ **sick**
SICKEE, -S *n* person off work through illness
SICKEN, -S *vb*
SICKER ▸ **sick**
SICKEST ▸ **sick**
SICKIE, -S *n*
SICKING ▸ **sick**
SICKISH ▸ **sick**
SICKLE, -D, -S *n, vb*
SICKLY *adj, adv, vb*
SICKOUT *n* industrial action in which all workers report sick simultaneously
SICKS ▸ **sick**
SICKY *n* day off work due to illness
SICLIKE *adj* Scots word meaning suchlike
SICS ▸ **sic**
SIDA, -S *n* Australian hemp plant
SIDDHA, -S *n* (in Hinduism) person who has achieved perfection
SIDDHI, -S *n* (in Hinduism) power attained with perfection
SIDDUR, -S *n* Jewish prayer book
SIDE, -D, -S *n, adj*
SIDEARM *n, vb*
SIDEBAR *n*
SIDECAR *n*
SIDED ▸ **side**
SIDEDLY *adv* pertaining to given number of sides
SIDEMAN, SIDEMEN *n* member of a dance band or a jazz group other than the leader
SIDER, -S *n* one who sides with another
SIDERAL *adj*
SIDERS ▸ **sider**

SIDES ▸ **side**
SIDEWAY *variant of* ▸ **sideways**
SIDH *pl n* fairy people
SIDHA, -S *n* (in Hinduism) person who has achieved perfection
SIDHE *pl n* inhabitants of fairyland
SIDING, -S *n*
SIDLE, -D, -S, SIDLING *vb, n*
SIDLER, -S ▸ **sidle**
SIDLES ▸ **sidle**
SIDLING ▸ **sidle**
SIECLE, -S *n* century, period, or era
SIEGE, -D, -S, SIEGING *n, vb*
SIEGER, -S *n* person who besieges
SIEGES ▸ **siege**
SIEGING ▸ **siege**
SIELD *adj* (archaic) provided with a ceiling
SIEMENS *n* SI unit of electrical conductance
SIEN, -S *n* old word meaning scion
SIENITE *n* type of igneous rock
SIENNA, -S *n* reddish- or yellowish-brown pigment made from natural earth
SIENS ▸ **sien**
SIENT, -S *n* old word meaning scion
SIERRA, -S *n* range of mountains in Spain or America with jagged peaks
SIERRAN ▸ **sierra**
SIERRAS ▸ **sierra**
SIES *interj* in South Africa, an exclamation of disgust
SIESTA, -S *n*
SIETH, -S *n* old form of scythe
SIEUR, -S *n* French word meaning lord
SIEVE, -D, -S, SIEVING *n* utensil with mesh through which a substance is sifted or strained ▷ *vb* sift or strain through a sieve
SIEVERT *n* derived SI unit of dose equivalent, equal to 1 joule per kilogram
SIEVES ▸ **sieve**
SIEVING ▸ **sieve**
SIF *adj* South African slang for disgusting
SIFAKA, -S *n* either of two large rare arboreal lemuroid primates
SIFFLE, -D, -S *vb* whistle
SIFREI ▸ **sefer**
SIFT, -ED, -ING, -S *vb*
SIFTER, -S ▸ **sift**
SIFTING ▸ **sift**
SIFTS ▸ **sift**
SIG, -S *n* short for signature
SIGANID *n* tropical fish
SIGH, -ED, -S *n, vb*
SIGHER, -S ▸ **sigh**
SIGHFUL ▸ **sigh**
SIGHING *n*
SIGHS ▸ **sigh**
SIGHT, -S *n, vb*
SIGHTED *adj*
SIGHTER *n* any of six practice shots allowed to each competitor in a tournament
SIGHTLY *adj* pleasing or attractive to see
SIGHTS ▸ **sight**
SIGIL, -S *n*
SIGLA, -S *n* list of symbols used in a book
SIGLOS, SIGLOI *n* silver coin of ancient Persia
SIGLUM *n* symbol used in book
SIGMA, -S *n* 18th letter in the Greek alphabet
SIGMATE *adj* shaped like the Greek letter sigma or the Roman S ▷ *n* sigmate thing ▷ *vb* add a sigma
SIGMOID *adj* shaped like the letter S ▷ *n* S-shaped bend in the final portion of the large intestine
SIGN, -ED, -S *n, vb*
SIGNA *pl n* symbols
SIGNAGE *n*
SIGNAL, -S *n, adj, vb*
SIGNARY *n* set of symbols
SIGNED ▸ **sign**
SIGNEE, -S *n*
SIGNER, -S *n*
SIGNET, -S *n, vb*
SIGNEUR *old spelling of* ▸ **senior**
SIGNIFY *vb*
SIGNING *n*
SIGNIOR *same as* ▸ **signor**
SIGNOR, -S *n* Italian term of address equivalent to *sir* or *Mr*
SIGNORA *n* Italian term of address equivalent to *madam* or *Mrs*
SIGNORE, SIGNORI *n* Italian man: a title of

respect equivalent to *sir*
SIGNORS ▸ **signor**
SIGNORY *same as* > **seigniory**
SIGNS ▸ **sign**
SIGS ▸ **sig**
SIJO, -S *n* Korean poem
SIK *adj* excellent
SIKA, -S *n* Japanese forest-dwelling deer
SIKE, -S *n* small stream
SIKER *adj* old spelling of sicker
SIKES ▸ **sike**
SIKSIK, -S *n* Arctic ground squirrel
SILAGE, -D, -S *n, vb*
SILANE, -S *n* gas containing silicon
SILD, -S *n* any of various small young herrings
SILE, -D, -S, SILING *vb* pour with rain
SILEN, -S *n* god of woodland
SILENCE *n, vb*
SILENE, -S *n* type of plant with mostly red or pink flowers, often grown as a garden plant
SILENI ▸ **silenus**
SILENS ▸ **silen**
SILENT, -S *adj, n*
SILENUS, SILENI *n* woodland deity
SILER, -S *n* strainer
SILES ▸ **sile**
SILESIA *n* twill-weave fabric of cotton or other fibre
SILEX, -ES *n* type of heat-resistant glass made from fused quartz
SILICA, -S *n*
SILICIC *adj* of, concerned with, or containing silicon or an acid obtained from silicon
SILICLE *same as* > **silicula**
SILICON *n, adj*
SILING ▸ **sile**
SILIQUA *n* long dry dehiscent fruit of cruciferous plants such as the wallflower
SILIQUE *same as* ▸ **siliqua**
SILK, -ED, -ING, -S *n, vb*
SILKEN, -S *adj, vb*
SILKIE, -S *n* Scots word for a seal
SILKIER ▸ **silky**
SILKIES ▸ **silkie**
SILKILY ▸ **silky**
SILKING ▸ **silk**
SILKS ▸ **silk**
SILKY, SILKIER *adj*
SILL, -S *n*
SILLER, -S *n* silver ▹ *adj* silver
SILLIER ▸ **silly**
SILLIES ▸ **silly**
SILLILY ▸ **silly**
SILLOCK *n* young coalfish
SILLS ▸ **sill**
SILLY, SILLIER, SILLIES *adj, n*
SILO, -ED, -ING, -S *n, vb*
SILPHIA > **silphium**
SILT, -ED, -ING, -S *n, vb*
SILTIER ▸ **silty**
SILTING ▸ **silt**
SILTS ▸ **silt**
SILTY, SILTIER ▸ **silt**
SILURID *n* type of freshwater fish of the family which includes catfish
SILVA, -E, -S *same as* ▸ **sylva**
SILVAN, -S *same as* ▸ **sylvan**
SILVAS ▸ **silva**
SILVER, -S *n, adj, vb*
SILVERN *adj* silver
SILVERS ▸ **silver**
SILVERY *adj*
SILVEX *n* type of weedkiller
SILVICS *n* study of trees
SIM, -S *n* computer game that simulates an activity
SIMA, -S *n* silicon-rich and magnesium-rich rocks of the earth's oceanic crust
SIMAR, -S *variant spelling of* ▸ **cymar**
SIMARRE *n* woman's loose gown
SIMARS ▸ **simar**
SIMAS ▸ **sima**
SIMATIC ▸ **sima**
SIMBA, -S *E African word for* ▸ **lion**
SIMCHA, -S *n* Jewish celebration or festival
SIMI, -S *n* East African sword
SIMIAL *adj* of apes
SIMIAN, -S *n, adj*
SIMILAR *adj*
SIMILE, -S *n*
SIMILOR *n* alloy used in cheap jewellery
SIMIOID *adj* of apes
SIMIOUS *adj* of apes
SIMIS ▸ **simi**
SIMITAR *same as* > **scimitar**

SIMKIN, -S *word used in India for* > **champagne**
SIMLIN, -S *n* American variety of squash plant
SIMMER, -S *vb, n*
SIMNEL, -S *n* fruit cake with marzipan eaten at Easter
SIMONY *n*
SIMOOM, -S *n* hot suffocating sand-laden desert wind
SIMOON, -S *same as* ▶ **simoom**
SIMORG, -S *n* bird in Persian myth
SIMP, -S *short for* > **simpleton**
SIMPAI, -S *n* Indonesian monkey
SIMPER, -S *vb, n*
SIMPKIN *word used in India for* > **champagne**
SIMPLE, -D, -S *adj* easy to understand or do ▷ *vb* archaic word meaning to look for medicinal herbs
SIMPLER ▶ **simple**
SIMPLES ▶ **simple**
SIMPLEX *adj, n*
SIMPLY *adv*
SIMPS ▶ **simp**
SIMS ▶ **sim**
SIMUL, -S *adj* simultaneous ▷ *n* simultaneous broadcast
SIMULAR *n* person or thing that simulates or imitates ▷ *adj* fake
SIMULS ▶ **simul**
SIMURG, -S *same as* ▶ **simurgh**
SIMURGH *n* bird in Persian myth
SIMURGS ▶ **simurg**
SIN, -NED, -NING, -S *n, vb*
SINCE *prep, adv*
SINCERE *adj*
SIND, -ED, -S *variant of* ▶ **syne**
SINDING ▶ **sind**
SINDON, -S *n* type of cloth
SINDS ▶ **sind**
SINE, -D, -S, SINING *same as* ▶ **syne**
SINEW, -S *n, vb*
SINEWED *adj* having sinews
SINEWS ▶ **sinew**
SINEWY *adj*
SINFUL *adj*
SING, -S, SUNG *vb, n*
SINGE, -D, -S *vb, n*
SINGER, -S *n*
SINGES ▶ **singe**
SINGING ▶ **sing**
SINGLE, -D, -S *adj, n, vb*
SINGLET *n* sleeveless vest
SINGLY *adv*
SINGS ▶ **sing**
SINGULT *n* old word meaning sob
SINH, -S *n* hyperbolic sine
SINICAL ▶ **sine**
SINING ▶ **sine**
SINK, SANK, -S *vb, n*
SINKAGE *n* act of sinking or degree to which something sinks or has sunk
SINKER, -S *n*
SINKFUL *n* amount that can be held in a sink
SINKIER ▶ **sinky**
SINKING ▶ **sink**
SINKS ▶ **sink**
SINKY, SINKIER *adj* giving underfoot
SINLESS *adj* free from sin or guilt
SINNED ▶ **sin**
SINNER, -S *n, vb*
SINNET, -S *n* braided rope
SINNING ▶ **sin**
SINOPIA, SINOPIE *n* pigment made from iron ore
SINOPIS *n*
SINS ▶ **sin**
SINSYNE *adv* Scots word meaning since
SINTER, -S *n* whitish porous incrustation deposited from hot springs ▷ *vb* form large particles from (powders) by heating or pressure
SINTERY *adj* consisting of sinter
SINUATE *vb* wind
SINUOSE *adj* sinuous
SINUOUS *adj* full of turns or curves
SINUS, -ES *n*
SIP, -PED, -PING, -S *vb, n*
SIPE, -D, -S, SIPING *vb* soak
SIPHON, -S *n, vb*
SIPING ▶ **sipe**
SIPPED ▶ **sip**
SIPPER, -S ▶ **sip**
SIPPET, -S *n* small piece of toast eaten with soup or gravy
SIPPING ▶ **sip**
SIPPLE, -D, -S *vb* sip
SIPPY *adj*
SIPS ▶ **sip**
SIR, -RED, -RING, -S *n, vb*

SIRCAR, -S *n* government in India
SIRDAR, -S *same as* ▸ **sardar**
SIRE, -D, -S, SIRING *n, vb*
SIREE, -S *emphasized form of* ▸ **sir**
SIREN, -S *n*
SIRENIC ▸ **siren**
SIRENS ▸ **siren**
SIRES ▸ **sire**
SIRGANG *n* Asian bird
SIRI, -S *n* betel
SIRIH, -S *n* betel
SIRING, -S ▸ **sire**
SIRIS ▸ **siri**
SIRKAR, -S *n* government in India
SIRLOIN *n*
SIRNAME *vb* old form of surname
SIROC, -S *n* sirocco
SIROCCO *n* hot wind blowing from N Africa into S Europe
SIROCS ▸ **siroc**
SIROSET *adj* of the chemical treatment of woollen fabrics to give a permanent-press effect
SIRRA, -S *disrespectful form of* ▸ **sir**
SIRRAH, -S *n* contemptuous term used in addressing a man or boy
SIRRAS ▸ **sirra**
SIRRED ▸ **sir**
SIRREE, -S *n* form of 'sir' used for emphasis
SIRRING ▸ **sir**
SIRS ▸ **sir**
SIRTUIN *n* protein that regulates cell metabolism and ageing
SIRUP, -ED, -S *same as* ▸ **syrup**
SIRUPY ▸ **sirup**
SIS, -ES *n*
SISAL, -S *n*
SISES ▸ **sis**
SISKIN, -S *n* yellow-and-black finch
SISS, -ES *shortening of* ▸ **sister**
SISSIER ▸ **sissy**
SISSIES ▸ **sissy**
SISSOO, -S *n* Indian tree
SISSY, SISSIER, SISSIES *n, adj*
SIST, -ED, -ING, -S *vb* Scottish law term meaning stop
SISTER, -S *n, adj, vb*
SISTING ▸ **sist**
SISTRUM, SISTRA *n* musical instrument of ancient Egypt consisting of a metal rattle
SISTS ▸ **sist**
SIT, SAT, -S *vb*
SITAR, -S *n*
SITCOM, -S *n*
SITE, -D, -S *n, vb*
SITELLA *n* type of small generally black-and-white bird
SITES ▸ **site**
SITFAST *n* sore on a horse's back caused by rubbing of the saddle
SITH *archaic word for* ▸ **since**
SITHE, -D, -S, SITHING *vb* old form of scythe
SITHEE *interj* look here! listen!
SITHEN *adv* old word meaning since
SITHENS *adv* old word meaning since
SITHES ▸ **sithe**
SITHING ▸ **sithe**
SITING, -S *n* act of siting
SITKA *modifier* as in **sitka spruce** tall North American spruce tree
SITREP, -S *n* military situation report
SITS ▸ **sit**
SITTAR, -S *n* sitar
SITTEN *adj* dialect word for in the saddle
SITTER, -S *n*
SITTINE *adj* of nuthatch bird family ▹ *n* type of nuthatch
SITTING ▸ **sit**
SITUATE *vb, adj*
SITULA, -E *n* bucket-shaped container
SITUP, -S *n*
SITUS, -ES *n* position or location
SITZ *n* as in **sitz bath** bath in which the buttocks and hips are immersed in hot water
SIVER, -S *same as* ▸ **syver**
SIWASH *vb* (in the Pacific Northwest) to camp out with only natural shelter
SIX, -ES *n*
SIXAIN, -S *n* stanza or poem of six lines
SIXAINE *n* six-line stanza of poetry
SIXAINS ▸ **sixain**
SIXER, -S *same as* ▸ **six**
SIXES ▸ **six**
SIXFOLD *adj, adv*
SIXISH *adj*

SIXMO, -S *n* book size resulting from folding a sheet of paper into six leaves
SIXTE, -S *n* sixth of eight basic positions from which a parry or attack can be made in fencing
SIXTEEN *n*
SIXTES ▸ **sixte**
SIXTH, -S *n, adj*
SIXTHLY *adv* in the sixth place or position
SIXTHS ▸ **sixth**
SIXTY, SIXTIES *n*
SIZABLE *adj*
SIZABLY ▸ **sizable**
SIZAR, -S *n* undergraduate receiving a maintenance grant from the college
SIZE, -S *n, vb*
SIZED *adj*
SIZEISM *n* discrimination on the basis of a person's size
SIZEIST ▸ **sizeism**
SIZEL, -S *n* scrap metal clippings
SIZER, -S ▸ **size**
SIZES ▸ **size**
SIZIER ▸ **sizy**
SIZIEST ▸ **sizy**
SIZING, -S ▸ **size**
SIZISM, -S *n* discrimination against people because of weight
SIZIST, -S ▸ **sizism**
SIZY, SIZIER, SIZIEST ▸ **size**
SIZZLE, -D, -S *vb, n*
SIZZLER *n*
SIZZLES ▸ **sizzle**
SJAMBOK *n* whip or riding crop made of hide ▹ *vb* beat with a sjambok
SJOE *interj* South African exclamation of surprise, admiration, exhaustion, etc
SKA, -S *n*
SKAG, -S *same as* ▸ **scag**
SKAIL, -ED, -S *vb* Scots word meaning disperse
SKAITH, -S *vb* Scots word meaning injure
SKALD, -S *n* (in ancient Scandinavia) a bard or minstrel
SKALDIC ▸ **skald**
SKALDS ▸ **skald**
SKANGER *n* insulting Irish word for a young working-class person who wears casual sports clothes
SKANK, -ED, -S *n* fast dance to reggae music ▹ *vb* perform this dance
SKANKER ▸ **skank**
SKANKS ▸ **skank**
SKANKY *adj* dirty or unattractive
SKART, -S *Scots word for* > **cormorant**
SKARTH, -S *Scots word for* > **cormorant**
SKARTS ▸ **skart**
SKAS ▸ **ska**
SKAT, -S *n* three-handed card game using 32 cards
SKATE, -D, -S *n, vb*
SKATER, -S *n*
SKATES ▸ **skate**
SKATING ▸ **skate**
SKATOL, -S *n* skatole
SKATOLE *n* white or brownish crystalline solid
SKATOLS ▸ **skatol**
SKATS ▸ **skat**
SKATT, -S *n* dialect word meaning throw
SKAW, -S *variant of* ▸ **scaw**
SKEAN, -S *n* kind of double-edged dagger
SKEANE, -S *same as* ▸ **skein**
SKEANS ▸ **skean**
SKEAR, -ED, -S *dialect form of* ▸ **scare**
SKEARY *dialect form of* ▸ **scary**
SKED, -DED, -S *vb* short for schedule
SKEE, -D, -ING, -S *variant spelling of* ▸ **ski**
SKEEF *adj* South African slang for at an oblique angle
SKEEING ▸ **skee**
SKEELY *adj* Scots word meaning skilful
SKEEN, -S *n* type of ibex
SKEER, -ED, -S *dialect form of* ▸ **scare**
SKEERY *dialect form of* ▸ **scary**
SKEES ▸ **skee**
SKEET, -S *n* form of clay-pigeon shooting
SKEETER *informal word for* > **mosquito**
SKEETS ▸ **skeet**
SKEEVY *adj* repulsive
SKEG, -S *n* reinforcing brace between the after end of a keel and the rudderpost
SKEGG, -S *n* skeg

SKEGGER *n* young salmon
SKEGGS ▸ **skegg**
SKEGS ▸ **skeg**
SKEIGH *adj* Scots word meaning shy
SKEIN, -ED, -S *n* yarn wound in a loose coil ▹ *vb* wind into a skein
SKELDER *vb* beg
SKELF, -S *n* splinter of wood, esp when embedded accidentally in the skin
SKELL, -S *n* homeless person
SKELLIE *adj* skelly
SKELLS ▸ **skell**
SKELLUM *n* rogue
SKELLY *n* whitefish of certain lakes in the Lake District ▹ *vb* look sideways or squint ▹ *adj* cross-eyed
SKELM, -S *n* villain or crook
SKELP, -ED, -S *vb* slap ▹ *n* slap
SKELPIT *vb* Scots word meaning skelped
SKELPS ▸ **skelp**
SKELTER *vb* scurry
SKELUM, -S *n* Scots word meaning rascal
SKEN, -NED, -S *vb* squint or stare
SKENE, -S *n* Scots word meaning dagger
SKENNED ▸ **sken**
SKENS ▸ **sken**
SKEO, -ES, -S *n* Scots dialect word meaning hut
SKEP, -PED, -S *n* beehive, esp one constructed of straw ▹ *vb* gather into a hive
SKEPFUL *n* amount skep will hold
SKEPPED ▸ **skep**
SKEPS ▸ **skep**
SKEPSIS *n* doubt
SKEPTIC *same as* ▸ **sceptic**
SKER, -RED, -S *vb* scour
SKERRY *n* rocky island or reef
SKERS ▸ **sker**
SKET, -S, -TED *vb* splash (water)
SKETCH *n, vb*
SKETCHY *adj*
SKETS ▸ **sket**
SKETTED ▸ **sket**
SKEW, -ED, -EST, -ING, -S *vb, adj, n*
SKEWER, -S *n, vb*
SKEWEST ▸ **skew**
SKEWING ▸ **skew**
SKEWS ▸ **skew**
SKI, -S *n, vb*
SKIABLE ▸ **ski**
SKIBOB, -S *n* vehicle made of two short skis for gliding down snow slopes
SKID, -DED, -S *vb, n*
SKIDDER ▸ **skid**
SKIDDOO *vb* go away quickly
SKIDDY ▸ **skid**
SKIDLID *n* crash helmet
SKIDOO, -S *n* snowmobile ▹ *vb* travel on a skidoo
SKIDPAD *n* area of road used to test skidding
SKIDPAN *n* area made slippery so that vehicle drivers can practise controlling skids
SKIDS ▸ **skid**
SKIDWAY *n* platform on which logs ready for sawing are piled
SKIED ▸ **sky**
SKIER, -S ▸ **ski**
SKIES ▸ **sky**
SKIEY, -ER *adj* of the sky
SKIFF, -ED, -S *n, vb*
SKIFFLE *n* style of popular music of the 1950s ▹ *vb* play this style of music
SKIFFS ▸ **skiff**
SKIING, -S ▸ **ski**
SKILFUL *adj*
SKILL, -S *n*
SKILLED *adj*
SKILLET *n*
SKILLS ▸ **skill**
SKILLY *n* thin soup or gruel ▹ *adj* skilled
SKIM, -MED, -S *vb, n*
SKIMMER *n*
SKIMMIA *n* shrub of S and SE Asia
SKIMP, -ED, -S *vb*
SKIMPY *adj*
SKIMS ▸ **skim**
SKIN, -NED, -S *n, vb*
SKINFUL *n* sufficient alcoholic drink to make one drunk
SKINK, -ED, -S *n* type of lizard with reduced limbs and smooth scales ▹ *vb* serve a drink
SKINKER ▸ **skink**
SKINKS ▸ **skink**
SKINNED ▸ **skin**
SKINNER *n* person who prepares or deals in animal skins
SKINNY *adj, n*
SKINS ▸ **skin**

SKINT, -ER *adj*
SKIO, -ES, -S *n* Scots dialect word meaning hut
SKIORER *n* one who engages in the sport of skioring
SKIOS ▶ **skio**
SKIP, -PED, -S *vb, n*
SKIPPER *vb, n*
SKIPPET *n* small round box for preserving a document or seal
SKIPPY *adj* in high spirits
SKIPS ▶ **skip**
SKIRL, -ED, -S *n* sound of bagpipes ▷ *vb* (of bagpipes) to give out a shrill sound
SKIRR, -ED, -S *vb* move, run, or fly rapidly ▷ *n* whirring or grating sound, as of the wings of birds in flight
SKIRRET *n* umbelliferous Old World plant
SKIRRS ▶ **skirr**
SKIRT, -ED, -S *n, vb*
SKIRTER *n* person who skirts fleeces
SKIRTS ▶ **skirt**
SKIS ▶ **ski**
SKIT, -S *n*
SKITCH *vb* (of a dog) to attack
SKITE, -D, -S, SKITING *n* boast ▷ *vb* boast
SKITS ▶ **skit**
SKITTER *vb* move or run rapidly or lightly
SKITTLE *n, vb*
SKIVE, -D, -S *vb*
SKIVER, -S *n, vb*
SKIVES ▶ **skive**
SKIVIE, -R *adj* old Scots word meaning disarranged
SKIVING ▶ **skive**
SKIVVY *n* female servant who does menial work ▷ *vb* work as a skivvy
SKIVY ▶ **skive**
SKIWEAR *n* clothes for skiing in
SKLATE, -D, -S *Scots word for* ▶ **slate**
SKLENT, -S *Scots word for* ▶ **slant**
SKLIFF, -S *n* Scots word meaning little piece ▷ *vb* shuffle (the feet)
SKLIM, -S *vb* Scots word meaning climb
SKOAL, -ED, -S *same as* ▶ **skol**
SKODY, SKODIER *adj* dirty, unkempt
SKOFF, -ED, -S *vb* eat greedily
SKOG, -GED, -S *same as* ▶ **scog**
SKOL, -ED, -ING, -LED, -S *sentence substitute* good health! (a drinking toast) ▷ *vb* down (an alcoholic drink) in one go
SKOLIA ▶ **skolion**
SKOLING ▶ **skol**
SKOLION, SKOLIA *n* ancient Greek drinking song
SKOLLED ▶ **skol**
SKOLLIE *same as* ▶ **skolly**
SKOLLY *n* hooligan, usually one of a gang
SKOLS ▶ **skol**
SKOOKUM *adj* strong or brave ▷ *n* strong or brave person
SKOOL, -S *childish spelling of* ▶ **school**
SKOOSH *vb* Scots word meaning squirt
SKORT, -S *n* pair of shorts with a front panel which gives the appearance of a skirt
SKOSH, -ES *n* little bit
SKRAN, -S *n* food
SKREEGH *same as* ▶ **skreigh**
SKREEN, -S *n* screen
SKREIGH *vb* Scots word meaning screech
SKRIECH *same as* ▶ **skreigh**
SKRIED ▶ **skry**
SKRIEGH *same as* ▶ **skreigh**
SKRIES ▶ **skry**
SKRIK, -S *n* South African word meaning fright
SKRIKE, -D, -S *vb* cry
SKRIKS ▶ **skrik**
SKRIMP, -S *vb* steal apples
SKRONK, -S *n* type of dissonant, grating popular music
SKRUMP, -S *vb* steal apples
SKRY, SKRIED, SKRIES, -ING *vb* try to tell future
SKRYER, -S ▶ **skry**
SKRYING ▶ **skry**
SKUA, -S *n* large predatory gull
SKUDLER *n* Scots word meaning leader of festivities

SKUG, -GED, -S *vb* shelter
SKULK, -ED, -S *vb, n*
SKULKER ▸ **skulk**
SKULKS ▸ **skulk**
SKULL, -ED, -S *n, vb*
SKULPIN *n* North American fish
SKUMMER *same as* ▸ **scumber**
SKUNK, -ED, -S *n, vb*
SKUNKY ▸ **skunk**
SKURRY *vb* scurry
SKUTTLE *vb* scuttle
SKY, SKIED, SKIES, -ED, -ING *n, vb*
SKYBORN *adj* born in heaven
SKYBOX *n* luxurious suite high up in the stand of a sports stadium
SKYCAP, -S *n* luggage porter at American airport
SKYCLAD *adj* naked
SKYDIVE, SKYDOVE *vb*
SKYED ▸ **sky**
SKYER, -S *n* cricket ball hit up into air
SKYEY, -ER, SKYIER, SKYIEST *adj* of the sky
SKYF, -ED, -ING, -S *n* South African slang for a cigarette or substance for smoking ▹ *vb* smoke a cigarette
SKYGLOW *n* glow in the night sky caused by urban lights
SKYHOME *n* Australian word for a sub-penthouse flat in a tall building
SKYHOOK *n* hook hung from a helicopter
SKYIER ▸ **skyey**
SKYIEST ▸ **skyey**
SKYING ▸ **sky**
SKYISH ▸ **sky**
SKYJACK *vb* hijack (an aircraft)
SKYLAB, -S *n* orbiting space station
SKYLARK *n* lark that sings while soaring at a great height ▹ *vb* play or frolic
SKYLESS *adj* having no sky
SKYLIKE ▸ **sky**
SKYLINE *n*
SKYLIT *adj* having skylight
SKYMAN, SKYMEN *n* paratrooper
SKYPHOS, SKYPHOI *n* ancient Greek drinking cup
SKYR, -S *n* Scandinavian cheese
SKYRE, -D, -S, SKYRING *vb* Scots word meaning shine
SKYRS ▸ **skyr**
SKYSAIL *n* square sail set above the royal on a square-rigger
SKYSURF *vb* perform freefall aerobatics
SKYTE, -D, -S, SKYTING *vb* Scots word meaning slide
SKYWALK *n* tightrope walk at great height
SKYWARD *adj* towards the sky ▹ *adv* towards the sky
SKYWAY, -S *n* air route
SLAB, -BED, -S *n, vb*
SLABBER *vb* dribble from the mouth
SLABBY *n* person who works with slabs of timber
SLABS ▸ **slab**
SLACK, -ED *same as* ▸ **slake**
SLACKEN *vb*
SLACKER *n*
SLACKLY ▸ **slack**
SLACKS *pl n*
SLADANG *n* Malayan tapir
SLADE, -S *n* little valley
SLAE, -S *Scots word for* ▸ **sloe**
SLAG, -GED, -S *n, vb*
SLAGGY ▸ **slag**
SLAGS ▸ **slag**
SLAHAL, -S *same as* ▸ **lahal**
SLAID, -S *vb* (Scot) sledge
SLAIN ▸ **slay**
SLAINTE *interj* cheers!
SLAIRG, -S *Scots word for* ▸ **spread**
SLAKE, -D, -S, SLAKING *vb*
SLAKER, -S ▸ **slake**
SLAKES ▸ **slake**
SLAKING ▸ **slake**
SLALOM, -S *n, vb*
SLAM, -MED, -S *vb, n*
SLAMMER *n*
SLAMS ▸ **slam**
SLANDER *n, vb*
SLANE, -S *n* spade for cutting turf
SLANG, -ED, -S *n, vb*
SLANGER *n* street vendor
SLANGS ▸ **slang**
SLANGY ▸ **slang**
SLANK *dialect word for* ▸ **lank**
SLANT, -ED, -S *vb, n*

SLANTER *same as* ▸ **slinter**
SLANTLY ▸ **slant**
SLANTS ▸ **slant**
SLANTY *adj*
SLAP, -PED, -S *n, vb*
SLAPPER ▸ **slap**
SLAPS ▸ **slap**
SLART, -ED, -S *vb* spill (something)
SLASH, -ED, -ES *vb, n*
SLASHER *n*
SLASHES ▸ **slash**
SLAT, -S, -TED *n, vb*
SLATCH *n* slack part of rope
SLATE, -D, -S *n, vb, adj*
SLATER, -S *n* person trained in laying roof slates
SLATES ▸ **slate**
SLATEY *adj* slightly mad
SLATHER *vb*
SLATIER ▸ **slaty**
SLATING *n* act or process of laying slates
SLATS ▸ **slat**
SLATTED ▸ **slat**
SLATTER *vb* be slovenly
SLATY, SLATIER *adj* consisting of or resembling slate
SLAVE, -D, -S, SLAVING *n, vb*
SLAVER, -S *n* person or ship engaged in the slave trade ▹ *vb* dribble saliva from the mouth
SLAVERY *n*
SLAVES ▸ **slave**
SLAVEY, -S *n* female general servant
SLAVING ▸ **slave**
SLAVISH *adj*
SLAW, -S *short for* > **coleslaw**
SLAY, SLAIN, -ED, -S *vb*
SLAYER, -S ▸ **slay**
SLAYING *n*
SLAYS ▸ **slay**
SLEAVE, -D, -S *n* tangled thread ▹ *vb* disentangle (twisted thread, etc)
SLEAZE, -D, -S *n, vb*
SLEAZY *adj*
SLEB, -S *n* celebrity
SLED, -DED, -ED, -S *same as* ▸ **sledge**
SLEDDER ▸ **sled**
SLEDED ▸ **sled**
SLEDGE, -D, -S *n, vb*
SLEDGER ▸ **sledge**
SLEDGES ▸ **sledge**
SLEDS ▸ **sled**
SLEE, -R, -ST *Scots word for* ▸ **sly**
SLEECH *n* slippery mud
SLEECHY ▸ **sleech**
SLEEK, -ED, -S *adj, vb*
SLEEKEN *vb* make sleek
SLEEKER ▸ **sleek**
SLEEKIT *adj* smooth
SLEEKLY ▸ **sleek**
SLEEKS ▸ **sleek**
SLEEKY ▸ **sleek**
SLEEP, -S, SLEPT *n, vb*
SLEEPER *n*
SLEEPRY *Scots word for* ▸ **sleepy**
SLEEPS ▸ **sleep**
SLEEPY *adj*
SLEER ▸ **slee**
SLEEST ▸ **slee**
SLEET, -ED, -S *n, vb*
SLEETY ▸ **sleet**
SLEEVE, -D, -S *n*
SLEEVER *n* old beer measure
SLEEVES ▸ **sleeve**
SLEEZY *adj* sleazy
SLEIDED *adj* old word meaning separated
SLEIGH, -S *same as* ▸ **sledge**
SLEIGHT *n*
SLENDER *adj*
SLENTER *same as* ▸ **slinter**
SLEPT ▸ **sleep**
SLEUTH, -S *n, vb*
SLEW, -ED, -ING, -S *vb*
SLEY, -S *n* weaver's tool for separating threads
SLICE, -D, -S *n, vb*
SLICER, -S ▸ **slice**
SLICES ▸ **slice**
SLICING ▸ **slice**
SLICK, -ED, -S *adj, n, vb*
SLICKEN *vb* make smooth
SLICKER *n*
SLICKLY ▸ **slick**
SLICKS ▸ **slick**
SLID ▸ **slide**
SLIDDEN ▸ **slide**
SLIDDER *vb* slip
SLIDE, SLID, SLIDDEN, -D, -S *vb, n*
SLIDER, -S ▸ **slide**
SLIDES ▸ **slide**
SLIDING ▸ **slide**
SLIER ▸ **sly**
SLIEST ▸ **sly**
SLIEVE, -S *n* Irish mountain
SLIGHT, -S *adj, n, vb*
SLILY ▸ **sly**
SLIM, -MED, -S *adj, vb*
SLIME, -D, -S, SLIMING *n, vb*
SLIMIER ▸ **slimy**
SLIMILY ▸ **slimy**
SLIMING ▸ **slime**
SLIMLY ▸ **slim**
SLIMMED ▸ **slim**
SLIMMER ▸ **slim**

SLIMPSY *adj* thin and flimsy
SLIMS ▸ **slim**
SLIMSY *adj* frail
SLIMY, SLIMIER *adj*
SLING, -S, SLUNG *n, vb*
SLINGER ▸ **sling**
SLINGS ▸ **sling**
SLINGY *adj* resembling the act of using a sling
SLINK, -ED, -S, SLUNK *vb, n*
SLINKER ▸ **slink**
SLINKS ▸ **slink**
SLINKY *adj*
SLINTER *n* dodge, trick, or stratagem
SLIOTAR *n* ball used in hurling
SLIP, -PED, -S *vb, n*
SLIPE, -D, -S, SLIPING *n* wool removed from the pelt of a slaughtered sheep ▹ *vb* remove skin
SLIPOUT *n* instance of slipping out
SLIPPED ▸ **slip**
SLIPPER *n, vb*
SLIPPY *adj*
SLIPS ▸ **slip**
SLIPT *vb* old form of slipped
SLIPUP, -S *n* mistake or mishap
SLIPWAY *n* launching slope on which ships are built or repaired
SLISH, -ES *n* old word meaning cut
SLIT, -S, -TED *n, vb*
SLITHER *vb, n*
SLITS ▸ **slit**
SLITTED ▸ **slit**
SLITTER ▸ **slit**
SLITTY ▸ **slit**
SLIVE, -D, -N, -S, SLIVING, SLOVE *vb* slip
SLIVER, -S *n, vb*
SLIVES ▸ **slive**
SLIVING ▸ **slive**
SLOAN, -S *n* severe telling-off
SLOB, -BED, -S *n, vb*
SLOBBER *vb, n*
SLOBBY ▸ **slob**
SLOBS ▸ **slob**
SLOCKEN *vb* Scots word meaning slake
SLOE, -S *n*
SLOG, -GED, -S *vb, n*
SLOGAN, -S *n*
SLOGGED ▸ **slog**
SLOGGER ▸ **slog**
SLOGS ▸ **slog**
SLOID, -S *n* Swedish woodwork
SLOJD, -S *same as* ▸ **sloid**
SLOKEN, -S *vb* Scots word meaning slake
SLOMO, -S *n* slow-motion sequence in a film
SLOOM, -ED, -S *vb* slumber
SLOOMY ▸ **sloom**
SLOOP, -S *n*
SLOOSH *vb* wash with water
SLOOT, -S *n* ditch for irrigation or drainage
SLOP, -PED, -S *vb, n*
SLOPE, -D, -S *vb, n*
SLOPER, -S ▸ **slope**
SLOPES ▸ **slope**
SLOPIER ▸ **slopy**
SLOPING ▸ **slope**
SLOPPED ▸ **slop**
SLOPPY *adj*
SLOPS ▸ **slop**
SLOPY, SLOPIER ▸ **slope**
SLORM, -ED, -S *vb* wipe carelessly
SLOSH, -ED, -ES *vb, n*
SLOSHY ▸ **slosh**
SLOT, -S, -TED *n, vb*
SLOTH, -ED, -S *n, vb*
SLOTS ▸ **slot**
SLOTTED ▸ **slot**
SLOTTER ▸ **slot**
SLOUCH *vb, n*
SLOUCHY *adj*
SLOUGH, -S *n, vb*
SLOUGHI *n* N African breed of dog resembling a greyhound
SLOUGHS ▸ **slough**
SLOUGHY ▸ **slough**
SLOVE ▸ **slive**
SLOVEN, -S *n*
SLOW, -ED, -ER, -EST, -S *adj, adv, vb*
SLOWING ▸ **slow**
SLOWISH ▸ **slow**
SLOWLY ▸ **slow**
SLOWS ▸ **slow**
SLOYD, -S *n* Swedish woodwork
SLUB, -BED, -S *n* lump in yarn or fabric ▹ *vb* draw out and twist (a sliver of fibre) before spinning ▹ *adj* (of material) having an irregular appearance
SLUBB, -S *same as* ▸ **slub**
SLUBBED ▸ **slub**
SLUBBER *vb* smear
SLUBBS ▸ **slubb**
SLUBBY ▸ **slub**
SLUBS ▸ **slub**
SLUDGE, -D, -S *n, vb*
SLUDGY *adj*
SLUE, -D, -ING, -S, SLUING *same as* ▸ **slew**

SLUFF, -ED, -S *same as* ▸ **slough**
SLUG, -GED, -S *n, vb*
SLUGGER *n*
SLUGS ▸ **slug**
SLUICE, -D, -S *n, vb*
SLUICY ▸ **sluice**
SLUING ▸ **slue**
SLUIT, -S *n* water channel in South Africa
SLUM, -MED, -S *n, vb*
SLUMBER *n, vb*
SLUMBRY *same as* ▸ **slumbery**
SLUMGUM *n* material left after wax is extracted from honeycomb
SLUMISM *n* existence of slums
SLUMMED ▸ **slum**
SLUMMER ▸ **slum**
SLUMMY ▸ **slum**
SLUMP, -ED, -S *vb, n*
SLUMPY *adj*
SLUMS ▸ **slum**
SLUNG ▸ **sling**
SLUNK ▸ **slink**
SLUR, -RED, -S *vb, n*
SLURB, -S *n* suburban slum
SLURBAN ▸ **slurb**
SLURBS ▸ **slurb**
SLURP, -ED, -S *vb, n*
SLURPER ▸ **slurp**
SLURPS ▸ **slurp**
SLURPY *adj*
SLURRED ▸ **slur**
SLURRY *n, vb*
SLURS ▸ **slur**
SLURVE, -S *n* pitch in baseball combining elements of the slider and the curveball
SLUSE, -S *same as* ▸ **sluice**
SLUSH, -ED, -ES *n, vb*
SLUSHY *adj, n*
SLUTCH *n* mud
SLUTCHY ▸ **slutch**
SLY, SLIER, SLIEST, -ER, -EST *adj*
SLYISH ▸ **sly**
SLYLY ▸ **sly**
SLYNESS ▸ **sly**
SLYPE, -S *n* covered passageway in a church
SMA *Scots word for* ▸ **small**
SMAAK, -ED, -S *vb* South African slang for like or love
SMACK, -ED, -S *vb, n, adv*
SMACKER *n* loud kiss
SMACKS ▸ **smack**
SMAIK, -S *n* Scots word meaning rascal
SMALL, -ED, -ER, -S *adj, n, adv, vb*
SMALM, -ED, -S *same as* ▸ **smarm**
SMALMY *same as* ▸ **smarmy**
SMALT, -S *n* type of silica glass coloured deep blue with cobalt oxide
SMALTO, SMALTI, -S *n* coloured glass, etc, used in mosaics
SMALTS ▸ **smalt**
SMARAGD *n* any green gemstone, such as the emerald
SMARM, -ED, -S *vb* bring (oneself) into favour (with) ▹ *n* obsequious flattery
SMARMY *adj*
SMART, -ED, -ER *adj, vb, n, adv*
SMARTEN *vb* make or become smart
SMARTER ▸ **smart**
SMARTIE *same as* ▸ **smarty**
SMARTLY ▸ **smart**
SMARTS *pl n*
SMARTY *n*
SMASH, -ED, -ES *vb, n, adv*
SMASHER *n* attractive person or thing
SMASHES ▸ **smash**
SMASHUP *n* bad collision of cars
SMATCH *less common word for* ▸ **smack**
SMATTER *n* smattering ▹ *vb* prattle
SMAZE, -S *n* smoky haze, less damp than fog
SMEAR, -ED, -S *vb, n*
SMEARER ▸ **smear**
SMEARS ▸ **smear**
SMEARY *adj* smeared, dirty
SMEATH, -S *n* duck
SMECTIC *adj* (of a substance) existing in state in which the molecules are oriented in layers
SMEDDUM *n* any fine powder
SMEE, -S *n* duck
SMEECH *Southwest English dialect form of* ▸ **smoke**
SMEEK, -ED, -S *vb* smoke
SMEES ▸ **smee**
SMEETH, -S *n* duck ▹ *vb* make smooth
SMEGMA, -S *n* whitish sebaceous secretion

that accumulates beneath the prepuce
SMEIK, -ED, -S *same as* ▶ **smeke**
SMEKE, -D, -S, SMEKING *n* smoke ▷ *vb* smoke
SMELL, -ED, -S *vb, n*
SMELLER ▶ **smell**
SMELLS ▶ **smell**
SMELLY *adj*
SMELT, -ED, -S *vb*
SMELTER *n*
SMELTS ▶ **smelt**
SMERK, -ED, -S *same as* ▶ **smirk**
SMEUSE, -S *n* way through hedge
SMEW, -S *n* duck of N Europe and Asia
SMICKER *vb* smirk
SMICKET *n* smock
SMIDDY *Scots word for* ▶ **smithy**
SMIDGE, -S *n*
SMIDGEN *n*
SMIDGES ▶ **smidge**
SMIDGIN *same as* ▶ **smidgen**
SMIGHT, -S *same as* ▶ **smite**
SMILAX *n* type of climbing shrub
SMILE, -D, -S *n, vb*
SMILER, -S ▶ **smile**
SMILES ▶ **smile**
SMILET, -S *n* little smile
SMILEY, -S, SMILIER, SMILIES *n, adj*
SMILING ▶ **smile**
SMIR, -S *n* drizzly rain ▷ *vb* drizzle lightly
SMIRCH *n* stain ▷ *vb* disgrace
SMIRK, -ED, -S *n, vb*
SMIRKER ▶ **smirk**
SMIRKS ▶ **smirk**
SMIRKY ▶ **smirk**
SMIRR, -ED, -S *same as* ▶ **smir**
SMIRRY ▶ **smirr**
SMIRS ▶ **smir**
SMITE, SMIT, -S, SMITING, SMITTEN, SMOTE *vb*
SMITER, -S ▶ **smite**
SMITES ▶ **smite**
SMITH, -ED, -S *n, vb*
SMITHY *n, vb*
SMITING ▶ **smite**
SMITS ▶ **smit**
SMITTED ▶ **smit**
SMITTEN ▶ **smite**
SMITTLE *adj* infectious
SMOCK, -ED, -S *n, vb*
SMOG, -S *n*
SMOGGY ▶ **smog**
SMOGS ▶ **smog**
SMOILE, -D, -S *same as* ▶ **smile**
SMOKE, -D, -S, SMOKING *n, vb*
SMOKEHO *same as* ▶ **smoko**
SMOKER, -S *n*
SMOKES ▶ **smoke**
SMOKEY, -S ▶ **smoky**
SMOKIE *n* smoked haddock
SMOKIER ▶ **smoky**
SMOKIES ▶ **smoky**
SMOKILY ▶ **smoky**
SMOKING ▶ **smoke**
SMOKO, -S *n* short break from work for tea or a cigarette
SMOKY, SMOKIER, SMOKIES *adj, n*
SMOLDER *same as* > **smoulder**
SMOLT, -S *n* young salmon at the stage when it migrates to the sea
SMOOCH *vb, n*
SMOOCHY *adj*
SMOODGE *same as* ▶ **smooch**
SMOOGE, -D, -S *same as* ▶ **smooch**
SMOOR, -ED, -S *vb* Scots word meaning put out fire
SMOOSH *vb* paint to give softened look
SMOOT, -ED, -S *vb* work as printer
SMOOTH, -S *adj, vb, adv, n*
SMOOTHE *same as* ▶ **smooth**
SMOOTHS ▶ **smooth**
SMOOTHY *same as* > **smoothie**
SMOOTS ▶ **smoot**
SMORE, -D, -S, SMORING *same as* ▶ **smoor**
SMORG, -S *n* short for smorgasbord
SMORING ▶ **smore**
SMOTE ▶ **smite**
SMOTHER *vb, n*
SMOUCH *vb* kiss
SMOUSE, -D, -S *vb* South African word meaning peddle
SMOUSER ▶ **smouse**
SMOUSES ▶ **smouse**
SMOUT, -ED, -S *n* child or undersized person ▷ *vb* creep or sneak
SMOWT, -S *same as* ▶ **smout**
SMOYLE, -D, -S *same as* ▶ **smile**
SMRITI, -S *n* class of Hindu sacred literature
SMUDGE, -D, -S *vb, n*
SMUDGER ▶ **smudge**

SMUDGES ▸ **smudge**
SMUDGY *adj*
SMUG, -GED, -GER, -S *adj, vb*
SMUGGLE *vb*
SMUGLY ▸ **smug**
SMUGS ▸ **smug**
SMUR, -RED, -S *same as* ▸ **smir**
SMURRY ▸ **smur**
SMURS ▸ **smur**
SMUSH, -ED, -ES *vb* crush
SMUT, -S, -TED *n, vb*
SMUTCH *vb* smudge ▹ *n* mark
SMUTCHY ▸ **smutch**
SMUTS ▸ **smut**
SMUTTED ▸ **smut**
SMUTTY ▸ **smut**
SMYTRIE *n* Scots word meaning collection
SNAB, -S *same as* ▸ **snob**
SNABBLE *same as* ▸ **snaffle**
SNABS ▸ **snab**
SNACK, -ED, -S *n, vb*
SNACKER ▸ **snack**
SNACKS ▸ **snack**
SNACKY *adj* of the nature of a snack
SNAFFLE *n* jointed bit for a horse ▹ *vb* steal
SNAFU, -ED, -S *n, adj, vb*
SNAG, -GED, -S *n, vb*
SNAGGER *n* type of fishing hook
SNAGGLE *n*
SNAGGY *adj* having sharp protuberances
SNAGS ▸ **snag**
SNAIL, -ED, -S *n, vb*
SNAILY ▸ **snail**
SNAKE, -D, -S, SNAKING *n, vb*
SNAKEY *same as* ▸ **snaky**
SNAKIER ▸ **snaky**
SNAKILY ▸ **snaky**
SNAKING ▸ **snake**
SNAKISH ▸ **snake**
SNAKY, SNAKIER *adj*
SNAP, -PED, -S *vb, n, adj, adv*
SNAPPER *n, vb*
SNAPPY *adj*
SNAPS ▸ **snap**
SNAPTIN *n* container for food
SNAR, -RED, -S *same as* ▸ **snarl**
SNARE, -D, -S *n, vb*
SNARER, -S ▸ **snare**
SNARES ▸ **snare**
SNARF, -ED, -S *vb* eat or drink greedily
SNARFLE *vb* (of an animal) grunt and snort while rooting for food
SNARFS ▸ **snarf**
SNARIER ▸ **snary**
SNARING ▸ **snare**
SNARK, -S *n* imaginary creature in Lewis Carroll's poetry
SNARKY *adj*
SNARL, -ED, -S *vb, n*
SNARLER ▸ **snarl**
SNARLS ▸ **snarl**
SNARLY ▸ **snarl**
SNARRED ▸ **snar**
SNARS ▸ **snar**
SNARY, SNARIER ▸ **snare**
SNASH, -ED, -ES *vb* Scots word meaning speak cheekily
SNASTE, -S *n* candle wick
SNATCH *vb, n*
SNATCHY *adj* disconnected or spasmodic
SNATH, -S *n* handle of a scythe
SNATHE, -S *same as* ▸ **snath**
SNATHS ▸ **snath**
SNAW, -ED, -ING, -S *Scots variant of* ▸ **snow**
SNAZZY *adj*
SNEAD, -S *n* scythe handle
SNEAK, -ED, -S *vb, n, adj*
SNEAKER *n*
SNEAKS ▸ **sneak**
SNEAKY ▸ **sneak**
SNEAP, -ED, -S *vb* nip
SNEATH, -S *same as* ▸ **snath**
SNEB, -BED, -S *same as* ▸ **snib**
SNEBBE, -S *same as* ▸ **snub**
SNEBBED ▸ **sneb**
SNEBBES ▸ **snebbe**
SNEBS ▸ **sneb**
SNECK, -ED, -S *n* small squared stone used in a rubble wall to fill spaces between stones ▹ *vb* fasten (a latch)
SNED, -DED, -S *vb* prune or trim
SNEE, -D, -ING, -S *vb* cut
SNEER, -ED, -S *n, vb*
SNEERER ▸ **sneer**
SNEERS ▸ **sneer**
SNEERY *adj* contemptuous or scornful
SNEES ▸ **snee**
SNEESH *n* Scots word meaning pinch of snuff ▹ *vb* take snuff
SNEEZE, -D, -S *vb, n*

SNEEZER ▸ **sneeze**
SNEEZES ▸ **sneeze**
SNEEZY ▸ **sneeze**
SNELL, -ED, -ER, -S *adj* biting ▹ *vb* attach hook to fishing line
SNELLY ▸ **snell**
SNIB, -BED, -S *n* catch of a door or window ▹ *vb* bolt or fasten (a door)
SNICK, -ED, -S *n* small cut or notch ▹ *vb* make a small cut or notch in (something)
SNICKER *same as* ▸ **snigger**
SNICKET *n* passageway between walls or fences
SNICKS ▸ **snick**
SNIDE, -D, -R, -S, -ST, SNIDING *adj, n, vb*
SNIDELY ▸ **snide**
SNIDER ▸ **snide**
SNIDES ▸ **snide**
SNIDEST ▸ **snide**
SNIDEY, SNIDIER *same as* ▸ **snide**
SNIDING ▸ **snide**
SNIES ▸ **sny**
SNIFF, -ED, -S *vb, n*
SNIFFER *n*
SNIFFLE *vb, n*
SNIFFLY ▸ **sniffle**
SNIFFS ▸ **sniff**
SNIFFY *adj*
SNIFT, -ED, -S *same as* ▸ **sniff**
SNIFTER *n, vb*
SNIFTS ▸ **snift**
SNIFTY *adj* slang word meaning excellent
SNIG, -GED, -S *vb* drag (a felled log) by a chain or cable
SNIGGER *n, vb*
SNIGGLE *vb* fish for eels by dangling or thrusting a baited hook into cavities ▹ *n* baited hook used for sniggling eels
SNIGLET *n* invented word
SNIGS ▸ **snig**
SNIP, -PED, -S *vb, n, interj*
SNIPE, -D, -S *n, vb*
SNIPER, -S *n*
SNIPES ▸ **snipe**
SNIPIER ▸ **snipy**
SNIPING ▸ **snipe**
SNIPPED ▸ **snip**
SNIPPER ▸ **snip**
SNIPPET *n*
SNIPPY *adj*
SNIPS ▸ **snip**
SNIPY, SNIPIER *adj* like a snipe
SNIRT, -ED, -S *n* Scots word meaning suppressed laugh ▹ *vb* to snigger
SNIRTLE *vb* Scots word meaning snicker
SNIRTS ▸ **snirt**
SNIT, -S *n* fit of temper
SNITCH *vb, n*
SNITCHY *adj* bad-tempered or irritable
SNITS ▸ **snit**
SNITTY *adj* cross or irritable
SNIVEL, -S *vb, n*
SNIVELY *adj* tending to snivel
SNOB, -S *n*
SNOBBY ▸ **snob**
SNOBS ▸ **snob**
SNOD, -DED, -DER, -DIT, -S *adj* Scots word meaning tidy ▹ *vb* make tidy
SNOEK, -S *n* edible marine fish
SNOEP *adj* mean or tight-fisted
SNOG, -GED, -S *vb, n*
SNOGGER *n* person who snogs
SNOGS ▸ **snog**
SNOKE, -D, -S, SNOKING *same as* ▸ **snook**
SNOOD, -ED, -S *n, vb*
SNOOK, -ED, -S *n* any of several large game fishes ▹ *vb* lurk
SNOOKER *n, vb*
SNOOKS ▸ **snook**
SNOOL, -ED, -S *vb* Scots word meaning dominate
SNOOP, -ED, -S *vb, n*
SNOOPER *n*
SNOOPS ▸ **snoop**
SNOOPY ▸ **snoop**
SNOOSE, -S *n* snuff
SNOOT, -ED, -S *n* nose ▹ *vb* look contemptuously at
SNOOTY *adj*
SNOOZE, -D, -S *vb, n*
SNOOZER ▸ **snooze**
SNOOZES ▸ **snooze**
SNOOZLE *vb* cuddle and sleep
SNOOZY ▸ **snooze**
SNORE, -D, -S *vb, n*
SNORER, -S ▸ **snore**
SNORES ▸ **snore**
SNORING ▸ **snore**
SNORKEL *n, vb*
SNORT, -ED, -S *vb, n*
SNORTER *n* person or animal that snorts

SNORTS ▸ **snort**
SNORTY ▸ **snort**
SNOT, -S, -TED *n, vb*
SNOTRAG *n*
SNOTS ▸ **snot**
SNOTTED ▸ **snot**
SNOTTER *vb* breathe through obstructed nostrils
SNOTTIE *n* midshipman
SNOTTY *adj*
SNOUT, -S *n, vb*
SNOUTED ▸ **snout**
SNOUTS ▸ **snout**
SNOUTY ▸ **snout**
SNOW, -ED, -ING, -S *n, vb*
SNOWCAP *n* cap of snow on top of a mountain
SNOWCAT *n* tracked vehicle for travelling over snow
SNOWED ▸ **snow**
SNOWIER ▸ **snowy**
SNOWILY ▸ **snowy**
SNOWING ▸ **snow**
SNOWISH *adj* like snow
SNOWK, -ED, -S *same as* ▸ **snook**
SNOWMAN, SNOWMEN *n*
SNOWS ▸ **snow**
SNOWY, SNOWIER *adj*
SNUB, -BED, -S *vb, n, adj*
SNUBBE, -S *n* stub
SNUBBED ▸ **snub**
SNUBBER ▸ **snub**
SNUBBES ▸ **snubbe**
SNUBBY ▸ **snub**
SNUBFIN *adj* as in **snubfin dolphin** Australian dolphin with a small dorsal fin
SNUBS ▸ **snub**
SNUCK *past tense and past participle of* ▸ **sneak**
SNUDGE, -D, -S *vb* be miserly
SNUFF, -ED, -S *n, vb*
SNUFFER ▸ **snuff**
SNUFFLE *vb, n*
SNUFFLY ▸ **snuffle**
SNUFFS ▸ **snuff**
SNUFFY *adj* of, relating to, or resembling snuff
SNUG, -GED, -GER, -S *adj, n, vb*
SNUGGLE *vb, n*
SNUGGLY *adj*
SNUGLY ▸ **snug**
SNUGS ▸ **snug**
SNUSH, -ED, -ES *vb* take snuff
SNUZZLE *vb* root in ground
SNY, SNIES *same as* ▸ **snye**

> A side channel of a river, that can be useful when you are short of vowels. And note that it can be extended to form **snye**.

SNYE, -S *n* side channel of a river
SO, -S *adv, interj, n*
SOAK, -ED, -EN, -S *vb, n*
SOAKAGE *n* process or a period in which a permeable substance is soaked in a liquid
SOAKED ▸ **soak**
SOAKEN ▸ **soak**
SOAKER, -S ▸ **soak**
SOAKING ▸ **soak**
SOAKS ▸ **soak**
SOAP, -ED, -ING, -S *n, vb*
SOAPBOX *n, vb*
SOAPED ▸ **soap**
SOAPER, -S *n* soap opera
SOAPIE, -S *n* soap opera
SOAPIER ▸ **soapy**
SOAPIES ▸ **soapie**
SOAPILY ▸ **soapy**
SOAPING ▸ **soap**
SOAPS ▸ **soap**
SOAPY, SOAPIER *adj*
SOAR, -ED, -S *vb, n*
SOARE, -S *n* young hawk
SOARED ▸ **soar**
SOARER, -S ▸ **soar**
SOARES ▸ **soare**
SOARING ▸ **soar**
SOARS ▸ **soar**
SOAVE, -S *n* dry white Italian wine
SOB, -BED, -S *vb, n*
SOBA, -S *n* (in Japanese cookery) noodles made from buckwheat flour
SOBBED ▸ **sob**
SOBBER, -S ▸ **sob**
SOBBING ▸ **sob**
SOBEIT *conj* provided that
SOBER, -ED, -ER, -S *adj, vb*
SOBERLY ▸ **sober**
SOBERS ▸ **sober**
SOBFUL *adj* tearful
SOBOLE, -S *n* creeping underground stem that produces roots and buds
SOBS ▸ **sob**
SOC, -ES, -S *n* feudal right to hold court
SOCA, -S *n* mixture of soul and calypso music
SOCAGE, -S *n* tenure of land by certain services

SOCAGER ▸ **socage**
SOCAGES ▸ **socage**
SOCAS ▸ **soca**
SOCCAGE *same as* ▸ **socage**
SOCCER, -S *n*
SOCES ▸ **soc**
SOCIAL, -S *adj, n*
SOCIATE *n* associate
SOCIETY *n*
SOCK, -ED, -ING, -S *n, vb*
SOCKET, -S *n, vb*
SOCKEYE *n* Pacific salmon with red flesh
SOCKING ▸ **sock**
SOCKMAN, SOCKMEN *same as* ▸ **socman**
SOCKO *adj* excellent
SOCKS ▸ **sock**
SOCLE, -S *another name for* ▸ **plinth**
SOCMAN, SOCMEN *n* tenant holding land by socage
SOCS ▸ **soc**
SOD, -DED, -S *n, vb*
SODA, -S *n*
SODAIC *adj* containing soda
SODAIN *same as* ▸ **sudden**
SODAINE *same as* ▸ **sudden**
SODAS ▸ **soda**
SODDED ▸ **sod**
SODDEN, -S *adj, vb*
SODDIE, -S *n* house made of sod
SODDIER ▸ **soddy**
SODDIES ▸ **soddie**
SODDING ▸ **sod**
SODDY, SODDIER *adj* covered with turf
SODGER, -S *dialect variant of* ▸ **soldier**
SODIC *adj* containing sodium
SODIUM, -S *n*
SODS ▸ **sod**
SOEVER *adv* in any way at all
SOFA, -S *n*
SOFABED *n*
SOFAR, -S *n* system for determining a position at sea
SOFAS ▸ **sofa**
SOFFIT, -S *n* underside of a part of a building or a structural component
SOFT, -ED, -ER, -EST, -ING, -S *adj, adv, vb*
SOFTA, -S *n* Muslim student of divinity and jurisprudence
SOFTED ▸ **soft**
SOFTEN, -S *vb*
SOFTER ▸ **soft**
SOFTEST ▸ **soft**
SOFTIE *n*
SOFTIES ▸ **softy**
SOFTING ▸ **soft**
SOFTISH ▸ **soft**
SOFTLY ▸ **soft**
SOFTS ▸ **soft**
SOFTY, SOFTIES *same as* ▸ **softie**
SOG, -GED, -S *vb* soak
SOGER, -S *same as* ▸ **sodger**
SOGGED ▸ **sog**
SOGGIER ▸ **soggy**
SOGGILY ▸ **soggy**
SOGGING ▸ **sog**
SOGGY, SOGGIER *adj*
SOGS ▸ **sog**
SOH, -S *n* (in tonic sol-fa) fifth degree of any major scale
SOHO *interj* exclamation announcing the sighting of a hare
SOHS ▸ **soh**
SOHUR, -S *same as* ▸ **suhur**
SOIGNE *adj* well-groomed, elegant
SOIGNEE *variant of* ▸ **soigne**
SOIL, -ED, -S *n, vb*
SOILAGE *n* green fodder
SOILED ▸ **soil**
SOILIER ▸ **soily**
SOILING ▸ **soil**
SOILS ▸ **soil**
SOILURE *n* act of soiling or the state of being soiled
SOILY, SOILIER ▸ **soil**
SOIREE, -S *n*
SOJA, -S *same as* ▸ **soya**
SOJOURN *n, vb*
SOJU, -S *n* type of Korean vodka
SOKAH, -S *same as* ▸ **soca**
SOKAIYA *n* Japanese extortionist
SOKE, -S *n* right to hold a local court
SOKEMAN, SOKEMEN *same as* ▸ **socman**
SOKEN, -S *n* feudal district
SOKES ▸ **soke**
SOKOL, -S *n* Czech gymnastic association
SOL, -S *n* liquid colloidal solution
SOLA, -S *n* Indian plant
SOLACE, -D, -S *vb, n*
SOLACER ▸ **solace**
SOLACES ▸ **solace**
SOLAH, -S *n* Indian plant

SOLAN, -S *archaic name for* ▸ **gannet**
SOLAND, -S *n* solan goose
SOLANIN *same as* > **solanine**
SOLANO, -S *n* hot wind in Spain
SOLANS ▸ **solan**
SOLANUM *n* any plant of the genus that includes the potato
SOLAR, -S *adj, n*
SOLARIA > **solarium**
SOLARS ▸ **solar**
SOLAS ▸ **sola**
SOLATE, -D, -S *vb* change from gel to liquid
SOLATIA > **solatium**
SOLD, -S *n*
SOLDADO *n* soldier
SOLDAN, -S *archaic word for* ▸ **sultan**
SOLDE, -S *n* wages
SOLDER, -S *n, vb*
SOLDES ▸ **solde**
SOLDI ▸ **soldo**
SOLDIER *n, vb*
SOLDO, SOLDI *n* former Italian copper coin
SOLDS ▸ **sold**
SOLE, -D, -S, SOLING *adj, n, vb*
SOLEI ▸ **soleus**
SOLEIN *same as* ▸ **sullen**
SOLELY *adv*
SOLEMN *adj*
SOLER, -S *same as* ▸ **sole**
SOLERA, -S *n* system for ageing sherry and other fortified wines
SOLERET *n* armour for foot
SOLERS ▸ **soler**
SOLES ▸ **sole**
SOLEUS, SOLEI *n* muscle in calf of leg
SOLFEGE *variant of* > **solfeggio**
SOLGEL *adj* changing between sol and gel
SOLI *adv* to be performed by or with soloists
SOLICIT *vb*
SOLID, -ER, -S *adj, n*
SOLIDI ▸ **solidus**
SOLIDLY ▸ **solid**
SOLIDS ▸ **solid**
SOLIDUM *n* part of pedestal
SOLIDUS, SOLIDI *same as* ▸ **slash**
SOLING ▸ **sole**
SOLION, -S *n* amplifier used in chemistry
SOLIPED *n* animal whose hooves are not cloven
SOLITO *adv* musical instruction meaning play in usual manner
SOLITON *n* type of isolated particle-like wave
SOLIVE, -S *n* type of joist
SOLLAR, -S *n* archaic word meaning attic ▹ *vb* put in a sollar
SOLLER, -S *same as* ▸ **sollar**
SOLO, -ED, -ES, -ING, -S *n, adj, adv, vb*
SOLOIST *n*
SOLON, -S *n* US congressperson
SOLOS ▸ **solo**
SOLS ▸ **sol**
SOLUBLE *adj, n*
SOLUBLY ▸ **soluble**
SOLUM, -S *n* upper layers of the soil profile
SOLUNAR *adj* relating to sun and moon
SOLUS, -ES *n* advert printed or published separately from others
SOLUTAL *adj* relating to a solute
SOLUTE, -S *n* substance in a solution that is dissolved ▹ *adj* loose or unattached
SOLVATE *vb* undergo, cause to undergo, or partake in solvation
SOLVE, -D, -S, SOLVING *vb*
SOLVENT *adj, n*
SOLVER, -S ▸ **solve**
SOLVES ▸ **solve**
SOLVING ▸ **solve**
SOM, -S, -Y *n* currency of Kyrgyzstan and Uzbekistan
SOMA, -S, -TA *n* body of an organism as distinct from the germ cells
SOMAN, -S *n* compound developed as a nerve gas
SOMAS ▸ **soma**
SOMATA ▸ **soma**
SOMATIC *adj*
SOMBER, -S *adj, vb*
SOMBRE, -D, -R, -S *adj, vb*
SOME *pron, adv*
SOMEDAY *adv*
SOMEHOW *adv*
SOMEONE *pron, n*
SOMEWAY *adv*
SOMEWHY *adv* for some reason
SOMITAL ▸ **somite**

SOMITE, -S *n* segment of mesoderm in vertebrate embryos
SOMITIC ▸ **somite**
SOMNIAL *adj* of dreams
SOMONI, -S *n* monetary unit of Tajikistan
SOMS ▸ **som**
SOMY ▸ **som**
SON, -S *n* male offspring
SONANCE ▸ **sonant**
SONANCY ▸ **sonant**
SONANT, -S *n* voiced sound able to form a syllable or syllable nucleus ▹ *adj* denoting a voiced sound like this
SONAR, -S *n*
SONATA, -S *n*
SONCE, -S *n* Scots word meaning good luck
SONDAGE *n* deep trial trench for inspecting stratigraphy
SONDE, -S *n* rocket, balloon, or probe used for observing in the upper atmosphere
SONDELI *n* Indian shrew
SONDER, -S *n* yacht category
SONDES ▸ **sonde**
SONE, -S *n* subjective unit of loudness
SONERI, -S *n* Indian cloth of gold
SONES ▸ **sone**
SONG, -S *n*
SONGFUL *adj* tuneful
SONGKOK *n* (in Malaysia and Indonesia) a kind of oval brimless hat, resembling a skull
SONGMAN, SONGMEN *n* singer
SONGS ▸ **song**
SONHOOD ▸ **son**
SONIC *adj*
SONICS *n* study of mechanical vibrations in matter
SONLESS ▸ **son**
SONLIER ▸ **sonly**
SONLIKE ▸ **son**
SONLY, SONLIER *adj* like a son
SONNE, -S *same as* ▸ **son**
SONNET, -S *n, vb*
SONNY, SONNIES *n* term of address to a boy
SONOVOX *n* device used to alter sound of human voice in music recordings
SONS ▸ **son**
SONSE, -S *same as* ▸ **sonce**
SONSHIP ▸ **son**
SONSIE *same as* ▸ **sonsy**
SONSY, SONSIER *adj* plump
SONTAG, -S *n* type of knitted women's cape
SONTIES *n* Shakespearian oath
SOOEY *interj* call used to summon pigs
SOOGEE, -D, -S *vb* clean a ship using a special solution
SOOGIE, -D, -S *same as* ▸ **soogee**
SOOJEY, -S *same as* ▸ **soogee**
SOOK, -ED, -ING, -S *n* baby ▹ *vb* suck
SOOKIER ▸ **sooky**
SOOKING ▸ **sook**
SOOKS ▸ **sook**
SOOKY, SOOKIER *adj* tending to complain peevishly
SOOL, -ED, -ING, -S *vb* incite (a dog) to attack
SOOLE, -S *same as* ▸ **sool**
SOOLED ▸ **sool**
SOOLER, -S *n* person who incites a dog to attack
SOOLES ▸ **soole**
SOOLING ▸ **sool**
SOOLS ▸ **sool**
SOOM, -ED, -ING, -S *Scots word for* ▸ **swim**
SOON *adv*
SOONER, -S *adv, n*
SOONEST *adv*
SOONISH *adj*
SOOP, -ED, -S *Scots word for* ▸ **sweep**
SOOPING ▸ **soop**
SOOPS ▸ **soop**
SOOT, -ED, -ES, -S *n, vb*
SOOTE *n* sweet
SOOTED ▸ **soot**
SOOTES ▸ **soot**
SOOTH, -S *n* truth or reality ▹ *adj* true or real
SOOTHE, -D, -S *vb*
SOOTHER *vb*
SOOTHES ▸ **soothe**
SOOTHLY ▸ **sooth**
SOOTHS ▸ **sooth**
SOOTIER ▸ **sooty**
SOOTILY ▸ **sooty**
SOOTING *n* state of becoming covered with soot
SOOTS ▸ **soot**
SOOTY, SOOTIER *adj*

SOP, -PED, -S *n* concession to pacify someone ▷ *vb* mop up or absorb (liquid)
SOPH, -S *shortened form of* > **sophomore**
SOPHIES ▶ **sophy**
SOPHISM *n* argument that seems reasonable but is actually false and misleading
SOPHIST *n* person who uses clever but invalid arguments
SOPHS ▶ **soph**
SOPHY, SOPHIES *n* title of the Persian monarchs
SOPITE, -D, -S *vb* lull to sleep
SOPOR, -S *n* abnormally deep sleep
SOPPED ▶ **sop**
SOPPIER ▶ **soppy**
SOPPILY ▶ **soppy**
SOPPING ▶ **sop**
SOPPY, SOPPIER *adj* over-sentimental
SOPRA *adv* musical instruction meaning above
SOPRANO, SOPRANI *n, adj*
SOPS ▶ **sop**
SORA, -S *n* North American rail with a yellow bill
SORAGE, -S *n* first year in hawk's life
SORAL ▶ **sorus**
SORAS ▶ **sora**
SORB, -ED, -ING, -S *n* any of various related trees, esp the mountain ash ▷ *vb* absorb or adsorb
SORBATE *n* salt of sorbic acid
SORBED ▶ **sorb**
SORBENT ▶ **sorb**
SORBET, -S *same as* ▶ **sherbet**
SORBIC ▶ **sorb**
SORBING ▶ **sorb**
SORBITE *n* mineral found in steel
SORBO *n* as in **sorbo rubber** spongy form of rubber
SORBOSE *n* sugar derived from the berries of the mountain ash
SORBS ▶ **sorb**
SORBUS *n* rowan or related tree
SORCERY *n*
SORD, -ED, -ING, -S *n* flock of mallard ducks ▷ *vb* ascend in flight
SORDA *n* deaf woman
SORDED ▶ **sord**
SORDES *pl n* dark incrustations on the lips and teeth of patients with prolonged fever
SORDID *adj*
SORDINE *same as* ▶ **sordino**
SORDING ▶ **sord**
SORDINO, SORDINI *n* mute for a stringed or brass musical instrument
SORDO *n* deaf man
SORDOR, -S *n* sordidness
SORDS ▶ **sord**
SORE, -D, -R, -S, -ST *adj, n, adv, vb*
SOREDIA > **soredium**

This is the plural of **soredium**, a reproductive body in lichens. It is a very frequently played bonus, and it has a 'twin': **roadies**. It is a good idea to become familiar with at least the higher probability twin sevens and eights, since the thought of one will often prompt the other, and it may well be that one twin will fit on the board where the other would not.

SOREE, -S *same as* ▶ **sora**
SOREHON *n* old Irish feudal right
SOREL, -S *variant of* ▶ **sorrel**
SORELL, -S *same as* ▶ **sorrel**
SORELS ▶ **sorel**
SORELY *adv*
SORER ▶ **sore**
SORES ▶ **sore**
SOREST ▶ **sore**
SOREX, -ES *n* shrew or related animal
SORGHO, -S *same as* ▶ **sorgo**
SORGHUM *n*
SORGO, -S *n* any of several varieties of sorghum that have watery sweet juice
SORI ▶ **sorus**
SORING, -S ▶ **sore**
SORITES *n* type of syllogism in which only the final conclusion is stated
SORITIC ▶ **sorites**

SORN, -ED, -S *vb* obtain food, etc, from another person by presuming on his or her generosity
SORNER, -S ▸ **sorn**
SORNING ▸ **sorn**
SORNS ▸ **sorn**
SOROBAN *n* Japanese abacus
SOROCHE *n* altitude sickness
SORORAL *adj* of sister
SOROSIS, SOROSES *n*
SORRA, -S *Irish word for* ▸ **sorrow**
SORREL, -S *n*
SORRIER ▸ **sorry**
SORRILY ▸ **sorry**
SORROW, -S *n, vb*
SORRY, SORRIER *adj, interj*
SORT, -S *n, vb*
SORTA *adv*
SORTAL, -S *n* type of logical or linguistic concept
SORTED *interj, adj*
SORTER, -S ▸ **sort**
SORTES *pl n* divination by opening book at random
SORTIE, -D, -S *n, vb*
SORTING ▸ **sort**
SORTS ▸ **sort**
SORUS, SORI *n* cluster of sporangia on the undersurface of certain fern leaves
SOS ▸ **so**
SOSATIE *n* skewer of curried meat pieces
SOSS, -ED, -ES *vb* make dirty or muddy
SOSSING ▸ **soss**
SOT, -S, -TED *n, adv, vb*
SOTH, -S *archaic variant of* ▸ **sooth**
SOTOL, -S *n* American plant related to agave
SOTS ▸ **sot**
SOTTED ▸ **sot**
SOTTING ▸ **sot**
SOTTISH ▸ **sot**
SOU, -S *n* former French coin
SOUARI, -S *n* tree of tropical America
SOUBISE *n* purée of onions mixed into a thick white sauce and served over eggs, fish, etc
SOUCAR, -S *n* Indian banker
SOUCE, -D, -S, SOUCING, SOUCT *same as* ▸ **souse**
SOUDAN, -S *obsolete variaint of* ▸ **sultan**
SOUFFLE *n, adj*
SOUGH, -ED, -S *vb* (of the wind) make a sighing sound ▹ *n* soft continuous murmuring sound
SOUGHT ▸ **seek**
SOUK, -ED, -ING, -S *same as* ▸ **sook**
SOUKOUS *n* style of African popular music
SOUKS ▸ **souk**
SOUL, -S *n*
SOULDAN *same as* ▸ **soldan**
SOULED *adj* having soul
SOULFUL *adj*
SOULS ▸ **soul**
SOUM, -ED, -S *vb* decide how many animals can graze particular pasture
SOUMING ▸ **soum**
SOUMS ▸ **soum**
SOUND, -ED, -S *n, vb, adj, adv*
SOUNDER *n* device formerly used to convert electric signals into sounds
SOUNDLY ▸ **sound**
SOUNDS ▸ **sound**
SOUP, -ED, -ING, -S *n, vb*
SOUPCON *n* small amount
SOUPED ▸ **soup**
SOUPER, -S *n* person dispensing soup
SOUPFIN *n* Pacific requiem shark valued for its fins
SOUPIER ▸ **soupy**
SOUPILY *adv* in a soupy manner
SOUPING ▸ **soup**
SOUPLE, -D, -S *same as* ▸ **supple**
SOUPS ▸ **soup**
SOUPY, SOUPIER *adj*
SOUR, -ED, -ER, -EST, -S *adj, vb*
SOURCE, -D, -S *n, vb*
SOURED ▸ **sour**
SOURER ▸ **sour**
SOUREST ▸ **sour**
SOURGUM *n* tree of eastern N America
SOURING ▸ **sour**
SOURISH ▸ **sour**
SOURLY ▸ **sour**
SOUROCK *n* Scots word for sorrel plant
SOURS ▸ **sour**
SOURSE, -S *same as* ▸ **source**
SOURSOP *n* small tropical American tree
SOUS ▸ **sou**

SOUSE, -D, -S *vb, n*
SOUSER, -S *n* person who frequently gets drunk
SOUSES ▶ **souse**
SOUSING ▶ **souse**
SOUSLIK *same as* ▶ **suslik**
SOUT, -S *same as* ▶ **soot**
SOUTANE *n*
SOUTAR, -S *same as* ▶ **souter**
SOUTER, -S *n* shoemaker or cobbler
SOUTH, -ED, -S *n, adj, adv, vb*
SOUTHER *n* strong wind or storm from the south ▷ *vb* turn south
SOUTHS ▶ **south**
SOUTS ▶ **sout**
SOV, -S *shortening of* > **sovereign**
SOVIET, -S *n, adj*
SOVKHOZ *n* large mechanized farm in former USSR
SOVRAN, -S *literary word for* > **sovereign**
SOVS ▶ **sov**
SOW, -ED, -N, -S *vb, n*
SOWABLE ▶ **sow**
SOWANS *same as* ▶ **sowens**
SOWAR, -S *n* Indian cavalryman
SOWARRY *same as* > **sowarree**
SOWARS ▶ **sowar**
SOWBACK *another name for* ▶ **hogback**
SOWBUG, -S *n* (in N America) woodlouse
SOWCAR, -S *same as* ▶ **soucar**
SOWCE, -D, -S, SOWCING *same as* ▶ **souse**
SOWDER, -S *same as* ▶ **sawder**
SOWED ▶ **sow**
SOWENS *n* pudding made from oatmeal husks steeped and boiled
SOWER, -S ▶ **sow**
SOWF, -ED, -ING, -S *same as* ▶ **sowth**
SOWFF, -ED, -S *same as* ▶ **sowth**
SOWFING ▶ **sowf**
SOWFS ▶ **sowf**
SOWING, -S ▶ **sow**
SOWL, -ED, -ING, -S *same as* ▶ **sole**
SOWLE, -S *same as* ▶ **sole**
SOWLED ▶ **sowl**
SOWLES ▶ **sowle**
SOWLING ▶ **sowl**
SOWLS ▶ **sowl**
SOWM, -ED, -ING, -S *same as* ▶ **soum**
SOWN ▶ **sow**
SOWND, -ED, -S *vb* wield
SOWNE, -S *same as* ▶ **sound**
SOWP, -ED, -ING, -S *n* spoonful ▷ *vb* soak
SOWS ▶ **sow**
SOWSE, -D, -S, SOWSING *same as* ▶ **souse**
SOWSSE, -D, -S *same as* ▶ **souse**
SOWTER, -S *same as* ▶ **souter**
SOWTH, -ED, -S *vb* Scots word meaning whistle
SOX *pl n* informal spelling of 'socks'

This informal word for **socks** is one of the key short words to remember for using the X.

SOY, -S *n*
SOYA, -S *n*
SOYBEAN *n*
SOYLE, -D, -S, SOYLING *n* body ▷ *vb* elucidate
SOYMEAL *n* foodstuff made from soybeans
SOYMILK *n* milk substitute made from soya
SOYS ▶ **soy**
SOYUZ, -ES *n* Russian spacecraft
SOZ *interj* (slang) sorry
SOZIN, -S *n* form of protein
SOZINE, -S *same as* ▶ **sozin**
SOZINS ▶ **sozin**
SOZZLE, -S *vb* make wet
SOZZLED *adj* drunk
SOZZLES ▶ **sozzle**
SOZZLY *adj* wet
SPA, -S *n, vb*
SPACE, -D, -S *n, vb*
SPACER, -S *n* piece of material used to create or maintain a space between two things
SPACES ▶ **space**
SPACEY, SPACIER *adj*
SPACIAL *same as* ▶ **spatial**
SPACIER ▶ **spacey**
SPACING *n*
SPACKLE *vb* fill holes in plaster
SPACY *same as* ▶ **spacey**
SPADE, -D, -S, SPADING *n*

SPADER, -S ▶ **spade**
SPADES ▶ **spade**
SPADGER *n* sparrow
SPADING ▶ **spade**
SPADIX *n* spike of small flowers on a fleshy stem
SPADO, -ES, -S *n* neutered animal
SPAE, -D, -S *vb* foretell (the future)
SPAEING ▶ **spae**
SPAEMAN, SPAEMEN *n* man who can supposedly foretell the future
SPAER, -S ▶ **spae**
SPAES ▶ **spae**
SPAG, -GED, -S *vb* (of a cat) to scratch (a person) with the claws
SPAHEE, -S *same as* ▶ **spahi**
SPAHI, -S *n* (formerly) an irregular cavalryman in the Turkish armed forces
SPAIL, -S *Scots word for* ▶ **spall**
SPAIN, -ED, -S *variant of* ▶ **spane**
SPAING, -S ▶ **spa**
SPAINS ▶ **spain**
SPAIRGE *Scots word for* ▶ **sparge**
SPAIT, -S *same as* ▶ **spate**
SPAKE *past tense of* ▶ **speak**
SPALD, -S *same as* ▶ **spauld**
SPALE, -S *Scots word for* ▶ **spall**
SPALL, -ED, -S *n* splinter or chip of ore, rock, or stone ▷ *vb* split or cause to split into such fragments
SPALLE, -S *same as* ▶ **spauld**
SPALLED ▶ **spall**
SPALLER ▶ **spall**
SPALLES ▶ **spalle**
SPALLS ▶ **spall**
SPALT, -ED, -S *vb* split
SPAM, -MED, -S *vb, n*
SPAMBOT *n* computer program that sends spam
SPAMMED ▶ **spam**
SPAMMER ▶ **spam**
SPAMMIE *n* love bite
SPAMMY *adj* bland
SPAMS ▶ **spam**
SPAN, -NED, -S *n, vb*
SPANCEL *n* length of rope for hobbling an animal ▷ *vb* hobble (an animal) with a loose rope
SPANDEX *n*
SPANE, -D, -S, SPANING *vb* Scots word meaning wean
SPANG, -ED, -S *adv* exactly, firmly, or straight ▷ *vb* dash
SPANGLE *n, vb*
SPANGLY ▶ **spangle**
SPANGS ▶ **spang**
SPANIEL *n*
SPANING ▶ **spane**
SPANK, -ED, -S *vb, n*
SPANKER *n* fore-and-aft sail or a mast that is aftermost in a sailing vessel
SPANKS ▶ **spank**
SPANNED ▶ **span**
SPANNER *n*
SPANS ▶ **span**
SPAR, -RED, -S *n, vb*
SPARE, SPARD, -D, -S, -ST *adj, n, vb*
SPARELY ▶ **spare**
SPARER, -S ▶ **spare**
SPARES ▶ **spare**
SPAREST ▶ **spare**
SPARGE, -D, -S *vb* sprinkle or scatter (something)
SPARGER ▶ **sparge**
SPARGES ▶ **sparge**
SPARID, -S *n* type of marine percoid fish ▷ *adj* of or belonging to this family of fish
SPARING *adj*
SPARK, -ED *n, vb*
SPARKE, -S *n* weapon
SPARKED ▶ **spark**
SPARKER ▶ **spark**
SPARKES ▶ **sparke**
SPARKIE *n* electrician
SPARKLE *vb, n*
SPARKLY *adj, n*
SPARKS *n*
SPARKY *adj* lively
SPAROID *same as* ▶ **sparid**
SPARRE, -S *same as* ▶ **spar**
SPARRED ▶ **spar**
SPARRER ▶ **spar**
SPARRES ▶ **sparre**
SPARROW *n*
SPARRY *adj* (of minerals) containing, relating to, or resembling spar
SPARS ▶ **spar**
SPARSE, -R *adj*
SPART, -S *n* esparto
SPARTAN *adj, n*
SPARTH, -S *n* type of battle-axe
SPARTHE *same as* ▶ **sparth**

SPARTHS ▸ **sparth**
SPARTS ▸ **spart**
SPAS ▸ **spa**
SPASM, -ED, -S *n, vb*
SPASMIC ▸ **spasm**
SPASMS ▸ **spasm**
SPASTIC *adj*
SPAT, -S, -TED *vb*
SPATE, -S *n*
SPATHAL ▸ **spathe**
SPATHE, -S *n* large sheathlike leaf enclosing a flower cluster
SPATHED ▸ **spathe**
SPATHES ▸ **spathe**
SPATHIC *adj* (of minerals) resembling spar
SPATIAL *adj*
SPATS ▸ **spat**
SPATTED ▸ **spat**
SPATTEE *n* type of gaiter
SPATTER *vb, n*
SPATULA *n*
SPATULE *n* spatula
SPATZLE *same as* > **spaetzle**
SPAUL, -S *same as* ▸ **spauld**
SPAULD, -S *n* shoulder
SPAULS ▸ **spaul**
SPAVIE, -S *Scots variant of* ▸ **spavin**
SPAVIET *adj* Scots word meaning spavined
SPAVIN, -S *n* enlargement of the hock of a horse by a bony growth
SPAW, -S *same as* ▸ **spa**
SPAWL, -ED, -S *vb* spit
SPAWN, -ED, -S *n, vb*
SPAWNER ▸ **spawn**
SPAWNS ▸ **spawn**
SPAWNY *adj* like spawn
SPAWS ▸ **spaw**
SPAY, -ED, -ING, -S *vb*
SPAYAD, -S *n* male deer
SPAYD, -S *same as* ▸ **spayad**
SPAYED ▸ **spay**
SPAYING ▸ **spay**
SPAYS ▸ **spay**
SPAZA *adj* as in **spaza shop** South African slang for a small shop in a township
SPEAK, -S, SPOKEN *vb*
SPEAKER *n*
SPEAKS ▸ **speak**
SPEAL, -S *same as* ▸ **spule**
SPEAN, -ED, -S *same as* ▸ **spane**
SPEAR, -ED, -S *n, vb*
SPEARER ▸ **spear**
SPEARS ▸ **spear**
SPEARY ▸ **spear**
SPEAT, -S *same as* ▸ **spate**
SPEC, -CED *vb*
SPECCY *n, adj*
SPECIAL *adj, n, vb*
SPECIE *n* coins as distinct from paper money
SPECIES *n*
SPECIFY *vb*
SPECK, -ED, -S *n, vb*
SPECKLE *n, vb*
SPECKS ▸ **speck**
SPECKY *same as* ▸ **speccy**
SPECS *pl n*
SPECT, -ED, -S *vb* expect
SPECTER *same as* ▸ **spectre**
SPECTRA > **spectrum**
SPECTRE *n*
SPECTS ▸ **spect**
SPECULA > **speculum**
SPED ▸ **speed**
SPEECH *n, vb*
SPEED, SPED, -ED, -S *n, vb*
SPEEDER ▸ **speed**
SPEEDO, -S *n* speedometer
SPEEDS ▸ **speed**
SPEEDUP *n* acceleration
SPEEDY *adj*
SPEEL, -ED, -S *n* splinter of wood ▹ *vb* Scots word meaning climb
SPEELER ▸ **speel**
SPEELS ▸ **speel**
SPEER, -ED, -S *same as* ▸ **speir**
SPEIL, -ED, -S *dialect word for* ▸ **climb**
SPEIR, -ED, -S *vb* ask
SPEISE, -S *same as* ▸ **speiss**
SPEISS *n* compounds formed when ores containing arsenic or antimony are smelted
SPEK, -S *n* bacon, fat, or fatty pork used for larding venison or other game
SPELD, -ED, -S *vb* Scots word meaning spread
SPELDER *same as* ▸ **speld**
SPELDIN *n* fish split and dried
SPELDS ▸ **speld**
SPELEAN *same as* > **spelaean**
SPELK, -S *n* splinter of wood
SPELL, -ED, -S *vb, n*
SPELLER *n*
SPELLS ▸ **spell**

SPELT, -S *n*
SPELTER *n* impure zinc, usually containing about 3 per cent of lead and other impurities
SPELTS ▸ **spelt**
SPELTZ *n* wheat variety
SPELUNK *vb*
SPENCE, -S *n* larder or pantry
SPENCER *n* short fitted coat or jacket
SPENCES ▸ **spence**
SPEND, -S, SPENT *vb*
SPENDER *n*
SPENDS ▸ **spend**
SPENDY *adj* expensive
SPENSE, -S *same as* ▸ **spence**
SPENT ▸ **spend**
SPEOS, -ES *n* (esp in ancient Egypt) a temple or tomb cut into a rock face
SPERM, -S *n*
SPERMIC *same as* > **spermatic**
SPERMS ▸ **sperm**
SPERRE, -D, -S *vb* bolt
SPERSE, -D, -S, SPERST *vb* disperse
SPERTHE *same as* ▸ **sparth**
SPET, -S *same as* ▸ **spit**
SPETCH *n* piece of animal skin
SPETS ▸ **spet**
SPEUG, -S *n* Scots word for sparrow
SPEW, -ED, -ING, -S *vb, n*
SPEWER, -S ▸ **spew**
SPEWIER ▸ **spewy**
SPEWING ▸ **spew**
SPEWS ▸ **spew**
SPEWY, SPEWIER *adj* marshy
SPHAER, -S *same as* ▸ **sphere**
SPHAERE *same as* ▸ **sphere**
SPHAERS ▸ **sphaer**
SPHEAR, -S *same as* ▸ **sphere**
SPHEARE *same as* ▸ **sphere**
SPHEARS ▸ **sphear**
SPHENE, -S *n* brown, yellow, green, or grey lustrous mineral
SPHENIC *adj* having the shape of a wedge
SPHERAL *adj* of or shaped like a sphere
SPHERE, -D, -S *n, vb*
SPHERIC *same as* > **spherical**
SPHERY *adj* resembling a sphere
SPHINX *n*
SPHYNX *n*
SPIAL, -S *n* observation
SPICA, -E, -S *n* spiral bandage formed by a series of overlapping figure-of-eight turns
SPICATE *adj* having, arranged in, or relating to spikes
SPICE, -D, -S, SPICING *n, vb*
SPICER, -S ▸ **spice**
SPICERY *n* spices collectively
SPICES ▸ **spice**
SPICEY *same as* ▸ **spicy**
SPICIER ▸ **spicy**
SPICILY ▸ **spicy**
SPICING ▸ **spice**
SPICULA *same as* > **spiculum**
SPICULE *n* small slender pointed structure or crystal
SPICY, SPICIER *adj*
SPIDE, -S *n* insulting Irish word for a young working-class man who dresses in casual sports clothes
SPIDER, -S *n, vb*
SPIDERY *adj*
SPIDES ▸ **spide**
SPIE *same as* ▸ **spy**
SPIED ▸ **spy**
SPIEGEL *n* manganese-rich pig iron
SPIEL, -ED, -S *n, vb*
SPIELER ▸ **spiel**
SPIELS ▸ **spiel**
SPIER, -ED, -S *variant of* ▸ **speir**
SPIES ▸ **spy**
SPIF, -S *n* postage stamp perforated with the initials of a firm to avoid theft by employees
SPIFF, -ED, -S *vb* make smart
SPIFFY *adj* smart ▹ *n* smart thing or person ▹ *vb* smarten
SPIFS ▸ **spif**
SPIGHT, -S *same as* ▸ **spite**
SPIGNEL *n* European umbelliferous plant
SPIGOT, -S *n*
SPIKE, -D, -S, SPIKING *n, vb*
SPIKER, -S ▸ **spike**
SPIKERY *n* High-Church Anglicanism
SPIKES ▸ **spike**
SPIKEY *same as* ▸ **spiky**
SPIKIER ▸ **spiky**
SPIKILY ▸ **spiky**
SPIKING ▸ **spike**

SPIKY, SPIKIER *adj*
SPILE, -D, -S *n* heavy timber stake or pile ▷ *vb* provide or support with a spile
SPILING ▶ **spile**
SPILITE *n* type of igneous rock
SPILL, -ED, -S, SPILT *vb, n*
SPILLER ▶ **spill**
SPILLS ▶ **spill**
SPILT ▶ **spill**
SPILTH, -S *n* something spilled
SPIM, -S *n* spam sent and received via an instant-messaging system
SPIMMER *n* person who sends spam via an instant-messaging system
SPIMS ▶ **spim**
SPIN, -S, SPUN *vb, n*
SPINA, -E, -S *n* spine
SPINACH *n*
SPINAE ▶ **spina**
SPINAGE *same as* ▶ **spinach**
SPINAL, -S *adj, n*
SPINAR, -S *n* fast-spinning star
SPINAS ▶ **spina**
SPINATE *adj* having a spine
SPINDLE *n, vb*
SPINDLY *adj*
SPINE, -S *n*
SPINED ▶ **spine**
SPINEL, -S *n* any of a group of hard glassy minerals of variable colour
SPINES ▶ **spine**
SPINET, -S *n* small harpsichord
SPINIER ▶ **spiny**
SPINK, -ED, -S *n* finch ▷ *vb* (of a finch) chirp
SPINNER *n*
SPINNET *same as* ▶ **spinet**
SPINNEY *n* small wood
SPINNY *adj* crazy
SPINODE *another name for* ▶ **cusp**
SPINOFF *n*
SPINONE, SPINONI *n* as in **Italian spinone** wiry-coated gun dog
SPINOR, -S *n* type of mathematical object
SPINOSE *adj* (esp of plants) bearing many spines
SPINOUS *adj* resembling a spine or thorn
SPINOUT *n* spinning skid that causes a car to run off the road
SPINS ▶ **spin**
SPINTO, -S *n* lyrical singing voice
SPINULA *n* small spine
SPINULE *n* very small spine, thorn, or prickle
SPINY, SPINIER *adj*
SPIRAEA *n* plant with small white or pink flowers
SPIRAL, -S *n, vb, adj*
SPIRANT *n* fricative consonant
SPIRE, -D, -S, SPIRING *n, vb*
SPIREA, -S *same as* ▶ **spiraea**
SPIRED ▶ **spire**
SPIREM, -S *same as* ▶ **spireme**
SPIREME *n* tangled mass of chromatin threads
SPIREMS ▶ **spirem**
SPIRES ▶ **spire**
SPIRIC, -S *n* type of curve
SPIRIER ▶ **spiry**
SPIRING ▶ **spire**
SPIRIT, -S *n, vb*
SPIRITY *adj* spirited
SPIROID *adj* resembling a spiral or displaying a spiral form
SPIRT, -ED, -S *same as* ▶ **spurt**
SPIRTLE *same as* ▶ **spurtle**
SPIRTS ▶ **spirt**
SPIRULA *n* tropical cephalopod mollusc
SPIRY, SPIRIER ▶ **spire**
SPIT, -S, -TED, -TEN *vb, n*
SPITAL, -S *n* obsolete word for hospital
SPITE, -D, -S, SPITING *n, vb*
SPITS ▶ **spit**
SPITTED ▶ **spit**
SPITTEN ▶ **spit**
SPITTER ▶ **spit**
SPITTLE *n*
SPITTLY *adj* covered with spittle
SPITTY *adj* covered with saliva
SPITZ, -ES *n* stockily built dog with a tightly curled tail
SPIV, -S *n* smartly dressed man who makes a living by shady dealings
SPIVVY ▶ **spiv**
SPLAKE, -S *n* type of hybrid trout bred by Canadian zoologists

SPLASH *vb, n*
SPLASHY *adj*
SPLAT, -S *n, vb*
SPLATCH *vb* splash
SPLATS ▶ **splat**
SPLAY, -ED, -S *vb, adj, n*
SPLEEN, -S *n*
SPLEENY ▶ **spleen**
SPLENIA > **splenium**
SPLENIC *adj* of, relating to, or in the spleen
SPLENII > **splenius**
SPLENT, -S *same as* ▶ **splint**
SPLICE, -D, -S *vb*
SPLICER ▶ **splice**
SPLICES ▶ **splice**
SPLINE, -D, -S *n* type of narrow key around a shaft that fits into a corresponding groove ▷ *vb* provide (a shaft, part, etc) with splines
SPLINT, -S *n, vb*
SPLISH *vb*
SPLIT, -S *vb, n*
SPLODGE *n, vb*
SPLODGY ▶ **splodge**
SPLOG, -S *n* spam blog
SPLOOSH *vb, n*
SPLORE, -S *n* revel
SPLOSH *vb, n*
SPLOTCH *vb* splash, daub
SPLURGE *vb, n*
SPLURGY ▶ **splurge**
SPLURT, -S *vb* gush out
SPOD, -S *adj* boring, unattractive, or overly studious
SPODDY ▶ **spod**
SPODE, -S *n* type of English china or porcelain
SPODIUM *n* black powder
SPODS ▶ **spod**
SPOFFY *same as* > **spoffish**
SPOIL, -ED, -S, -T *vb*
SPOILER *n*
SPOILS ▶ **spoil**
SPOILT ▶ **spoil**
SPOKE, -D, -S, SPOKING *n, vb*
SPOKEN ▶ **speak**
SPOKES ▶ **spoke**
SPOKING ▶ **spoke**
SPONDEE *n* metrical foot of two long syllables
SPONDYL *n* vertebra
SPONGE, -D, -S *n, vb*
SPONGER *n*
SPONGES ▶ **sponge**
SPONGIN *n* fibrous horny protein in sponges
SPONGY *adj*
SPONSAL *n* marriage
SPONSON *n* outboard support for a gun enabling it to fire fore and aft
SPONSOR *n, vb*
SPOOF, -ED, -S *n, vb*
SPOOFER ▶ **spoof**
SPOOFS ▶ **spoof**
SPOOFY ▶ **spoof**
SPOOK, -ED, -S *n, vb*
SPOOKY *adj*
SPOOL, -ED, -S *n, vb*
SPOOLER ▶ **spool**
SPOOLS ▶ **spool**
SPOOM, -ED, -S *vb* sail fast before wind
SPOON, -ED, -S *n, vb*
SPOONER *n* person who engages in spooning
SPOONEY *same as* ▶ **spoony**
SPOONS ▶ **spoon**
SPOONY *adj* foolishly or stupidly in love ▷ *n* fool or silly person, esp one in love
SPOOR, -ED, -S *n* trail of an animal ▷ *vb* track (an animal) by following its trail
SPOORER ▶ **spoor**
SPOORS ▶ **spoor**
SPOOT, -S *n* razor shell
SPORAL ▶ **spore**
SPORE, -D, -S, SPORING *n, vb*
SPORK, -S *n* spoon-shaped piece of cutlery with tines like a fork
SPOROID *adj* of or like a spore
SPORRAN *n* pouch worn in front of a kilt
SPORT, -ED *n, vb*
SPORTER ▶ **sport**
SPORTIF *adj* sporty ▷ *n* sporty person
SPORTS *adj, n*
SPORTY *adj, n*
SPORULE *n* spore, esp a very small spore
SPOSH, -ES *n* slush
SPOSHY ▶ **sposh**
SPOT, -S, -TED *n, vb*
SPOTLIT > **spotlight**
SPOTS ▶ **spot**
SPOTTED ▶ **spot**
SPOTTER *n* person who notes numbers or types of trains or planes
SPOTTIE *n* young deer of up to three months of age
SPOTTY *adj*
SPOUSAL *n, adj*

SPOUSE, -D, -S *n, vb*
SPOUT, -ED, -S *vb, n*
SPOUTER ▸ **spout**
SPOUTS ▸ **spout**
SPOUTY ▸ **spout**
SPRACK *adj* vigorous
SPRAD ▸ **spread**
SPRAG, -S *n* device used to prevent a vehicle from running backwards on an incline ▷ *vb* use sprag to prevent vehicle from moving
SPRAID *vb* chapped
SPRAIN, -S *vb, n*
SPRAINT *n* piece of otter's dung
SPRANG, -S *n*
SPRAT, -S *n* small sea fish
SPRAWL, -S *vb, n*
SPRAWLY ▸ **sprawl**
SPRAY, -ED, -S *n, vb*
SPRAYER ▸ **spray**
SPRAYEY ▸ **spray**
SPRAYS ▸ **spray**
SPREAD, SPRAD, -S *vb, n, adj*
SPREAGH *n* cattle raid
SPREAZE *same as* > **spreathe**
SPRED, -S *same as* ▸ **spread**
SPREDD, -S *same as* ▸ **spread**
SPREDDE *same as* ▸ **spread**
SPREDDS ▸ **spredd**
SPREDS ▸ **spred**
SPREE, -D, -S *n, vb*
SPREEZE *same as* > **spreathe**
SPRENT, -S *adj* sprinkled ▷ *vb* leap forward in an agile manner
SPREW, -S *same as* ▸ **sprue**
SPRIER ▸ **spry**
SPRIEST ▸ **spry**
SPRIG, -S *n, vb*
SPRIGGY ▸ **sprig**
SPRIGHT *same as* ▸ **sprite**
SPRIGS ▸ **sprig**
SPRING, -S, SPRONG, SPRUNG *vb, n*
SPRINGE *n* type of snare for catching small wild animals or birds ▷ *vb* set such a snare
SPRINGS ▸ **spring**
SPRINGY *adj*
SPRINT, -S *n, vb*
SPRIT, -S *n* small spar set diagonally across a sail to extend it
SPRITE, -S *n*
SPRITS ▸ **sprit**
SPRITZ *vb*
SPRITZY *adj* fizzy
SPROD, -S *n* young salmon
SPROG, -S *n*
SPRONG ▸ **spring**
SPROUT, -S *vb, n*
SPRUCE, -D, -R, -S *n, adj*
SPRUCY ▸ **spruce**
SPRUE, -S *n* vertical channel in a mould
SPRUG, -S *n* sparrow
SPRUIK, -S *vb* old word meaning speak in public
SPRUIT, -S *n* small tributary stream or watercourse
SPRUNG ▸ **spring**
SPRUSH *Scots form of* ▸ **spruce**
SPRY, SPRIER, SPRIEST, -ER, -EST *adj* active or nimble
SPRYLY ▸ **spry**
SPUD, -DED, -S *n, vb*
SPUDDER *same as* ▸ **spud**
SPUDDLE *n* feeble movement
SPUDDY *adj* short and fat
SPUDGEL *n* bucket on a long handle
SPUDS ▸ **spud**
SPUE, -D, -ING, -S, SPUING *same as* ▸ **spew**
SPUER, -S ▸ **spue**
SPUES ▸ **spue**
SPUG, -S *same as* ▸ **spuggy**
SPUGGY *n* house sparrow
SPUGS ▸ **spug**
SPUING ▸ **spue**
SPULE, -S *Scots word for* > **shoulder**
SPULYE, -D, -S *same as* > **spuilzie**
SPULYIE *same as* > **spuilzie**
SPULZIE *same as* > **spuilzie**
SPUME, -D, -S, SPUMING *vb* froth ▷ *n* foam or froth on the sea
SPUMIER ▸ **spumy**
SPUMING ▸ **spume**
SPUMONE *n* creamy Italian ice cream
SPUMONI *same as* ▸ **spumone**
SPUMOUS ▸ **spume**
SPUMY, SPUMIER ▸ **spume**
SPUN ▸ **spin**

SPUNGE, -S *same as* ▶ **sponge**
SPUNK, -ED, -S *n* courage, spirit ▷ *vb* catch fire
SPUNKIE *n* will-o'-the-wisp
SPUNKS ▶ **spunk**
SPUNKY ▶ **spunk**
SPUR, -RED, -S *n* stimulus or incentive ▷ *vb* urge on, incite (someone)
SPURDOG *n* the dogfish
SPURGE, -S *n* plant with milky sap
SPURIAE *n* type of bird feathers
SPURN, -ED, -S *vb, n*
SPURNE, -S *vb* spur
SPURNED ▶ **spurn**
SPURNER ▶ **spurn**
SPURNES ▶ **spurne**
SPURNS ▶ **spurn**
SPURRED ▶ **spur**
SPURRER ▶ **spur**
SPURREY *n* any of several low-growing European plants
SPURRY *n* spurrey ▷ *adj* resembling a spur
SPURS ▶ **spur**
SPURT, -ED, -S *vb, n*
SPURTER ▶ **spurt**
SPURTLE *n* wooden spoon for stirring porridge
SPURTS ▶ **spurt**
SPURWAY *n* path used by riders
SPUTA ▶ **sputum**
SPUTNIK *n* early Soviet artificial satellite
SPUTTER *n, vb*
SPUTUM, SPUTA, -S *n* mass of spittle ejected from the mouth
SPY, SPIED, SPIES *n, vb*
SPYAL, -S *n* spy
SPYCAM, -S *n* camera used for covert surveillance
SPYHOLE *n* small hole in a door, etc through which one may watch secretly
SPYING, -S ▶ **spy**
SPYRE, -S *same as* ▶ **spire**
SPYWARE *n*
SQUAB, -S *n* young bird yet to leave the nest ▷ *adj* (of birds) recently hatched and still unfledged ▷ *vb* fall
SQUABBY ▶ **squab**
SQUABS ▶ **squab**
SQUACCO *n* S European heron
SQUAD, -S *n, vb*
SQUADDY *same as* > **squaddie**
SQUADS ▶ **squad**
SQUAIL, -S *vb* throw sticks at
SQUALID *adj*
SQUALL, -S *n, vb*
SQUALLY ▶ **squall**
SQUALOR *n*
SQUAMA, -E *n* scale or scalelike structure
SQUAME, -S *same as* ▶ **squama**
SQUARE, -D, -S *n, adj, vb, adv*
SQUARER ▶ **square**
SQUARES ▶ **square**
SQUARK, -S *n* hypothetical boson partner of a quark
SQUASH *vb, n*
SQUASHY *adj*
SQUAT, -S *vb, n, adj*
SQUATLY ▶ **squat**
SQUATS ▶ **squat**
SQUATTY *adj* short and broad
SQUAWK, -S *n, vb*
SQUAWKY ▶ **squawk**
SQUEAK, -S *n, vb*
SQUEAKY ▶ **squeak**
SQUEAL, -S *n, vb*
SQUEEZE *vb, n*
SQUEEZY ▶ **squeeze**
SQUEG, -S *vb* oscillate
SQUELCH *vb, n*
SQUIB, -S *n*
SQUID, -S *n, vb*
SQUIDGE *vb*
SQUIDGY *adj*
SQUIDS ▶ **squid**
SQUIER, -S *same as* ▶ **squire**
SQUIFF *same as* ▶ **squiffy**
SQUIFFY *adj* slightly drunk
SQUILL, -S *n* Mediterranean plant of the lily family
SQUILLA *n* type of mantis shrimp
SQUILLS ▶ **squill**
SQUINCH *n* small arch across an internal corner of a tower ▷ *vb* squeeze
SQUINNY *vb* squint ▷ *adj* squint
SQUINT, -S *vb, n, adj*
SQUINTY ▶ **squint**
SQUINY *same as* ▶ **squinny**
SQUIRE, -D, -S *n, vb*
SQUIRL, -S *n*
SQUIRM, -S *vb, n*

SQUIRMY *adj*
SQUIRR, -S *same as* ▸ **skirr**
SQUIRT, -S *vb, n*
SQUISH *n, vb*
SQUISHY *adj*
SQUIT, -S *n* insignificant person
SQUITCH *n* couch grass
SQUITS ▸ **squit**
SQUIZ *n* look or glance, esp an inquisitive one

The word **quiz** comes up surprisingly often, so it is useful to remember that you can put an S on the front of it to form this Australian slang word for a quick look.

SQUOOSH *vb* squash
SQUUSH *same as* ▸ **squoosh**
SRADDHA *n* Hindu offering to ancestor
SRADHA, -S *same as* ▸ **sraddha**
SRI, -S *n* title of respect used when addressing a Hindu
ST *interj* exclamation to attract attention
STAB, -BED, -S *vb, n*
STABBER ▸ **stab**
STABILE *n* stationary abstract construction, usually of wire, metal, wood, etc ▹ *adj* fixed
STABLE, -D, -S *n, vb, adj*
STABLER *n* stable owner
STABLES ▸ **stable**
STABLY ▸ **stable**
STABS ▸ **stab**
STACHYS *n* type of plant of the genus which includes lamb's ears and betony
STACK, -ED, -S *n, vb*
STACKER ▸ **stack**
STACKET *n* fence of wooden posts
STACKS ▸ **stack**
STACKUP *n* number of aircraft waiting to land
STACTE, -S *n* one of several sweet-smelling spices used in incense
STADDA, -S *n* type of saw
STADDLE *n* type of support or prop
STADE, -S *same as* ▸ **stadium**
STADIA, -S *n* instrument used in surveying
STADIAL *n* stage in development of glacier
STADIAS ▸ **stadia**
STADIUM *n*
STAFF, -ED, -S *n, vb*
STAFFER *n*
STAFFS ▸ **staff**
STAG, -GED, -S *n, adv, vb*
STAGE, -D, -S *n, vb*
STAGER, -S *n* person of experience
STAGERY *n* theatrical effects or techniques
STAGES ▸ **stage**
STAGEY *same as* ▸ **stagy**
STAGGED ▸ **stag**
STAGGER *vb, n*
STAGGIE *n* little stag
STAGGY ▸ **stag**
STAGIER ▸ **stagy**
STAGILY ▸ **stagy**
STAGING *n*
STAGS ▸ **stag**
STAGY, STAGIER *adj* too theatrical or dramatic
STAID, -ER *adj*
STAIDLY ▸ **staid**
STAIG, -S *Scots variant of* ▸ **stag**
STAIN, -ED, -S *vb, n*
STAINER ▸ **stain**
STAINS ▸ **stain**
STAIR *n*
STAIRED *adj* having stairs
STAIRS *pl n*
STAITH, -S *same as* ▸ **staithe**
STAITHE *n* wharf
STAITHS ▸ **staith**
STAKE, -D, -S, STAKING *n, vb*
STAKER, -S *n* person who marks off an area with stakes
STAKES ▸ **stake**
STAKING ▸ **stake**
STALAG, -S *n* German prisoner-of-war camp
STALE, -D, -R, -S, -ST, STALING *adj, vb, n*
STALELY ▸ **stale**
STALER ▸ **stale**
STALES ▸ **stale**
STALEST ▸ **stale**
STALING ▸ **stale**
STALK, -ED, -S *n, vb*
STALKER ▸ **stalk**
STALKO, -S *n* idle gentleman
STALKS ▸ **stalk**
STALKY *adj* like a stalk
STALL, -ED, -S *n, vb*
STAMEN, -S *n*
STAMINA *n*
STAMMEL *n* coarse woollen cloth in former use for undergarments
STAMMER *vb, n*

STAMNOS, STAMNOI *n* ancient Greek jar
STAMP, -ED, -S *n, vb*
STAMPER ▸ **stamp**
STAMPS ▸ **stamp**
STANCE, -S *n*
STANCH *vb* stem the flow of (a liquid, esp blood) ▹ *adj* loyal and dependable
STANCK *adj* faint
STAND, -EN, -S, STOOD, STOODEN, STUDDEN *vb, n*
STANDBY *n*
STANDEE *n* person who stands
STANDEN ▸ **stand**
STANDER ▸ **stand**
STANDS ▸ **stand**
STANDUP *n*
STANE, -D, -S, STANING *Scot word for* ▸ **stone**
STANG, -ED, -S *vb* sting
STANIEL *n* kestrel
STANINE *n* scale of nine levels
STANING ▸ **stane**
STANK, -ED, -S *vb* dam
STANNEL *same as* ▸ **staniel**
STANNIC *adj* of or containing tin, esp in the tetravalent state
STANNUM *n* tin (the metal)
STANOL, -S *n* drug taken to prevent heart disease
STANYEL *same as* ▸ **staniel**
STANZA, -S *n*
STANZE, -S *same as* ▸ **stanza**
STANZO, -S *same as* ▸ **stanza**
STAP, -PED, -S *same as* ▸ **stop**
STAPES *n* stirrup-shaped bone in the middle ear of mammals
STAPH, -S *n* staphylococcus
STAPLE, -D, -S *n, vb, adj*
STAPLER *n*
STAPLES ▸ **staple**
STAPPED ▸ **stap**
STAPPLE *same as* ▸ **stopple**
STAPS ▸ **stap**
STAR, -RED, -S *n, vb, adj*
STARCH *n, vb, adj*
STARCHY *adj*
STARDOM *n*
STARE, -D, -S *vb, n*
STARER, -S ▸ **stare**
STARES ▸ **stare**
STARETS, STARTSY *n* Russian holy man
STARETZ *same as* ▸ **starets**
STARING ▸ **stare**
STARK, -ED, -ER, -S *adj, adv, vb*
STARKEN *vb* become or make stark
STARKER ▸ **stark**
STARKLY ▸ **stark**
STARKS ▸ **stark**
STARLET *n*
STARLIT *same as* > **starlight**
STARN, -ED, -S *same as* ▸ **stern**
STARNIE *n* Scots word for little star
STARNS ▸ **starn**
STARR, -S *n* (in Judaism) release from a debt
STARRED ▸ **star**
STARRS ▸ **starr**
STARRY *adj*
STARS ▸ **star**
START, -ED, -S *vb, n*
STARTER *n*
STARTLE *vb*
STARTLY *adj* (of a horse) prone to starting
STARTS ▸ **start**
STARTSY ▸ **starets**
STARTUP *n*
STARVE, -D, -S *vb*
STARVER ▸ **starve**
STARVES ▸ **starve**
STASES ▸ **stasis**
STASH, -ED, -ES *vb, n*
STASHIE *same as* ▸ **stushie**
STASIMA > **stasimon**
STASIS, STASES *n*
STAT, -S *n*
STATAL *adj* of a federal state
STATANT *adj* (of an animal) in profile with all four feet on the ground
STATE, -S, STATING *n, adj, vb*
STATED *adj*
STATELY *adj, adv*
STATER, -S *n* any of various usually silver coins of ancient Greece
STATES ▸ **state**
STATIC *adj, n*
STATICE *n* plant name formerly used for both thrift and sea lavender
STATICS *n* study of the forces producing a state of equilibrium
STATIM *adv* right away
STATIN, -S *n* type of drug that lowers the levels of low-density

lipoproteins in the blood
STATING ▸ **state**
STATINS ▸ **statin**
STATION *n, vb*
STATISM *n* theory or practice of concentrating economic and political power in the state
STATIST *n* advocate of statism ▹ *adj* of, characteristic of, advocating, or relating to statism
STATIVE *adj* denoting a verb describing a state rather than an activity, act, or event ▹ *n* stative verb
STATOR, -S *n* stationary part of a rotary machine or device
STATS ▸ **stat**
STATTO, -S *n* person preoccupied with the facts and figures of a subject
STATUA, -S *same as* ▸ **statue**
STATUE, -S *n*
STATUED *adj* decorated with or portrayed in a statue or statues
STATUES ▸ **statue**
STATURE *n*
STATUS *n*
STATUSY *adj* conferring or having status
STATUTE *n*
STAUN, -S *Scot word for* ▸ **stand**
STAUNCH *same as* ▸ **stanch**
STAUNS ▸ **staun**
STAVE, -D, -S, STAVING *same as* ▸ **staff**
STAW, -ED, -ING, -S *Scots form of* ▸ **stall**
STAY, -ED, -ING *vb, n*
STAYER, -S *n* person or thing that stays
STAYING ▸ **stay**
STAYNE, -D, -S *same as* ▸ **stain**
STAYRE, -S *same as* ▸ **stair**
STAYS *pl n* old-fashioned corsets with bones in them
STEAD, -ED, -S *n, vb*
STEADY *adj, vb, adv*
STEAK, -S *n*
STEAL, -ED, -S, -T, STOLEN, STOLN, STOWN *vb*
STEALE, -S *n* handle
STEALED ▸ **steal**
STEALER *n* person who steals something
STEALES ▸ **steale**
STEALS ▸ **steal**
STEALT ▸ **steal**
STEALTH *n, adj, vb*
STEAM, -ED, -S *n, vb*
STEAMER *n, vb*
STEAMIE *n* public wash house
STEAMS ▸ **steam**
STEAMY *adj*
STEAN, -S *n* earthenware vessel
STEANE, -D, -S *same as* ▸ **steen**
STEANS ▸ **stean**
STEAR, -D, -S *same as* ▸ **steer**
STEARE, -D, -S *same as* ▸ **steer**
STEARIC *adj* of or relating to suet or fat
STEARIN *n* colourless crystalline ester of glycerol and stearic acid
STEARS ▸ **stear**
STED, -DED, -S *same as* ▸ **stead**
STEDD, -S *same as* ▸ **stead**
STEDDE, -S *same as* ▸ **stead**
STEDDED ▸ **sted**
STEDDES ▸ **stedde**
STEDDS ▸ **stedd**
STEDDY *same as* ▸ **steady**
STEDE, -D, -S, STEDING *same as* ▸ **stead**
STEDS ▸ **sted**
STEED, -ED, -S *same as* ▸ **stead**
STEEDY *same as* ▸ **steady**
STEEK, -ED, -IT, -S *vb* Scots word meaning shut
STEEL, -D, -ED *n, vb*
STEELIE *n* steel ball bearing used as marble
STEELS *pl n* shares and bonds of steel companies
STEELY ▸ **steel**
STEEM, -ED, -S *variant of* ▸ **esteem**
STEEN, -ED, -S *vb* line with stone
STEEP, -ED, -S *adj, vb, n*
STEEPEN *vb* become steep or steeper
STEEPER ▸ **steep**
STEEPLE *same as* ▸ **spire**
STEEPLY ▸ **steep**
STEEPS ▸ **steep**
STEEPUP *adj* very steep
STEEPY *same as* ▸ **steep**

STEER, -ED, -S *vb, n*
STEERER ▸ **steer**
STEERS ▸ **steer**
STEERY *n* commotion ▹ *adj* busy or bustling
STEEVE, -D, -R, -S *n* spar having a pulley block at one end ▹ *vb* stow (cargo) securely in the hold of a ship
STEIL, -S *same as* ▸ **steal**
STEIN, -ED, -S *same as* ▸ **steen**
STELA, -E, -I *same as* ▸ **stele**
STELAR ▸ **stele**
STELE, -S *n* upright stone slab or column decorated with figures or inscriptions
STELENE ▸ **stele**
STELES ▸ **stele**
STELIC ▸ **stele**
STELL, -ED, -S *n* shelter for cattle or sheep built on moorland or hillsides ▹ *vb* position or place
STELLA, -S *n* star or something star-shaped
STELLAR *adj*
STELLAS ▸ **stella**
STELLED ▸ **stell**
STELLIO *n* as in **stellio lizard** type of lizard
STELLS ▸ **stell**
STEM, -MED, -S *vb, n*
STEMBOK *same as* > **steenbok**
STEME, -D, -S, STEMING *same as* ▸ **steam**
STEMLET *n* little stem
STEMMA, -S *n* family tree
STEMME, -S *archaic variant of* ▸ **stem**
STEMMED ▸ **stem**
STEMMER ▸ **stem**
STEMMES ▸ **stemme**
STEMMY *adj* (of wine) young and raw
STEMPEL *n* timber support
STEMPLE *same as* ▸ **stempel**
STEMS ▸ **stem**
STEMSON *n* curved timber at the bow of a wooden vessel
STEN, -NED, -S *vb* stride
STENCH *n, vb*
STENCHY ▸ **stench**
STENCIL *n, vb*
STEND, -ED, -S *vb* Scots word meaning bound
STENGAH *same as* ▸ **stinger**
STENNED ▸ **sten**
STENO, -S *n* stenographer
STENOKY *n* survival dependent on conditions remaining within a narrow range of variables
STENOS ▸ **steno**
STENS ▸ **sten**
STENT, -ED, -S *n* surgical implant used to keep an artery open ▹ *vb* assess
STENTOR *n* person with an unusually loud voice
STENTS ▸ **stent**
STEP, -PED, -S, -T *vb, n*
STEPDAD *n*
STEPMOM *n*
STEPNEY *n*
STEPPE, -S *n*
STEPPED ▸ **step**
STEPPER *n* person who or animal that steps, esp a horse or a dancer
STEPPES ▸ **steppe**
STEPS ▸ **step**
STEPSON *n*
STEPT ▸ **step**
STERANE *n* any of a class of hydrocarbons found in crude oils
STERE, -S *n* unit used to measure volumes of stacked timber
STEREO, -S *n, adj, vb*
STERES ▸ **stere**
STERIC *adj* of or caused by the spatial arrangement of atoms in a molecule
STERILE *adj*
STERLET *n* small sturgeon of N Asia and E Europe
STERN, -ED, -ER, -S *adj, n, vb*
STERNA ▸ **sternum**
STERNAL ▸ **sternum**
STERNED ▸ **stern**
STERNER ▸ **stern**
STERNLY ▸ **stern**
STERNS ▸ **stern**
STERNUM, STERNA *n*
STEROID *n*
STEROL, -S *n* natural insoluble alcohol such as cholesterol and ergosterol
STERTOR *n* laborious or noisy breathing
STERVE, -D, -S *same as* ▸ **starve**
STET, -S, -TED *interj, vb, n*
STETSON *n*
STETTED ▸ **stet**
STEVEN, -S *n* voice

STEVIA, -S *n* any of a genus of plant with sweet leaves
STEW, -S *n, vb*
STEWARD *n, vb*
STEWED *adj*
STEWER, -S ▶ **stew**
STEWIER ▶ **stewy**
STEWING ▶ **stew**
STEWPAN *n* pan used for making stew
STEWPOT *n* pot used for making stew
STEWS ▶ **stew**
STEWY, STEWIER ▶ **stew**
STEY, -ER, -EST, -S *adj* (Scots) steep ▷ *n* ladder
STHENIA *n* abnormal strength
STHENIC *adj* abounding in energy or bodily strength
STIBBLE *Scots form of* ▶ **stubble**
STIBIAL ▶ **stibium**
STIBINE *n* colourless slightly soluble poisonous gas
STIBIUM *obsolete name for* > **antimony**
STICH, -S *n* line of poetry
STICHIC ▶ **stich**
STICHOS, STICHOI *n* line of poem
STICHS ▶ **stich**
STICK, -ED, -S *n, vb*
STICKER *n, vb*
STICKIE *n* notepaper with an adhesive strip
STICKIT *Scots form of* ▶ **stuck**
STICKLE *vb*
STICKS ▶ **stick**
STICKUM *n* adhesive
STICKUP *n*
STICKY *adj, vb, n*
STIDDIE *same as* ▶ **stithy**
STIE *same as* ▶ **sty**
STIED ▶ **sty**
STIES ▶ **sty**
STIEVE, -R *same as* ▶ **steeve**
STIFF, -ED, -ER, -S *adj, n, adv, vb*
STIFFEN *vb*
STIFFER ▶ **stiff**
STIFFLY ▶ **stiff**
STIFFS ▶ **stiff**
STIFLE, -D, -S *vb, n*
STIFLER ▶ **stifle**
STIFLES ▶ **stifle**
STIGMA, -S *n*
STIGMAL *adj* of part of insect wing
STIGMAS ▶ **stigma**
STIGME, -S *n* dot in Greek punctuation
STILB, -S *n* unit of luminance
STILE, -D, -S, STILING *same as* ▶ **style**
STILET, -S *same as* ▶ **stylet**
STILING ▶ **stile**
STILL, -ED, -S *adv, adj, n, vb*
STILLER ▶ **still**
STILLS ▶ **still**
STILLY *adv* quietly or calmly ▷ *adj* still, quiet, or calm
STILT, -S *n, vb*
STILTED *adj*
STILTER ▶ **stilt**
STILTS ▶ **stilt**
STILTY ▶ **stilt**
STIM, -S *n* very small amount
STIME, -D, -S, STIMING *same as* ▶ **styme**
STIMIE, -D, -S *same as* ▶ **stymie**
STIMING ▶ **stime**
STIMS ▶ **stim**
STIMULI > **stimulus**
STIMY *same as* ▶ **stymie**
STING, -ED, -S, STONG, STUNG *vb, n*
STINGE, -S *n* stingy or miserly person
STINGED ▶ **sting**
STINGER *n*
STINGES ▶ **stinge**
STINGO, -S *n* strong alcohol
STINGS ▶ **sting**
STINGY *adj, n*
STINK, -S, STUNK *n, vb*
STINKER *n*
STINKO *adj* drunk
STINKS ▶ **stink**
STINKY *adj*
STINT, -ED, -S *vb, n*
STINTER ▶ **stint**
STINTS ▶ **stint**
STINTY ▶ **stint**
STIPA, -S *n* variety of grass
STIPE *n* stalk in plants that bears reproductive structures
STIPED *same as* > **stipitate**
STIPEL, -S *n* small paired leaflike structure at the base of certain leaflets
STIPEND *n*
STIPES *n* second maxillary segment in insects and crustaceans
STIPPLE *vb* paint, draw, or engrave using dots

▷ *n* technique of stippling
STIPULE *n* small paired usually leaflike outgrowth occurring at the base of a leaf or its stalk
STIR, -RED, -S *vb, n*
STIRE, -D, -S, STIRING *same as* ▶ **steer**
STIRK, -S *n* heifer of 6 to 12 months old
STIRP *same as* ▶ **stirps**
STIRPS, STIRPES *n* line of descendants from an ancestor
STIRRA, -S *same as* ▶ **sirra**
STIRRAH *same as* ▶ **sirrah**
STIRRAS ▶ **stirra**
STIRRE, -S *same as* ▶ **steer**
STIRRED ▶ **stir**
STIRRER *n*
STIRRES ▶ **stirre**
STIRRUP *n*
STIRS ▶ **stir**
STISHIE *same as* ▶ **stushie**
STITCH *n, vb*
STITHY *n* forge or anvil ▷ *vb* forge on an anvil
STIVE, -D, -S, STIVING *vb* stifle
STIVER, -S *n* former Dutch coin
STIVES ▶ **stive**
STIVIER ▶ **stivy**
STIVING ▶ **stive**
STIVY, STIVIER *adj* stuffy
STOA, -E, -I, -S *n* covered walk that has a colonnade on one or both sides
STOAT, -S *n*
STOB, -BED, -S *same as* ▶ **stab**
STOBIE *adj* as in **stobie pole** steel and concrete pole for supporting electricity wires
STOBS ▶ **stob**
STOCK, -ED *n, adj, vb*
STOCKER ▶ **stock**
STOCKS *pl n*
STOCKY *adj*
STODGE, -D, -S *n, vb*
STODGER *n* dull person
STODGES ▶ **stodge**
STODGY *adj*
STOEP, -S *n* verandah
STOGEY, -S *same as* ▶ **stogy**
STOGIE *same as* ▶ **stogy**
STOGY, STOGIES *n* any long cylindrical inexpensive cigar
STOIC, -S *n, adj*
STOICAL *adj* suffering great difficulties without showing one's feelings
STOICS ▶ **stoic**
STOIT, -ED, -S *vb* bounce
STOITER *vb* stagger
STOITS ▶ **stoit**
STOKE, STOKING *vb*
STOKED *adj*
STOKER, -S *n*
STOKES *n* cgs unit of kinematic viscosity
STOKING ▶ **stoke**
STOKVEL *n* (in S Africa) informal savings pool or syndicate
STOLE, -S *n*
STOLED *adj* wearing a stole
STOLEN ▶ **steal**
STOLES ▶ **stole**
STOLID *adj*
STOLLEN *n* rich sweet bread containing nuts, raisins, etc
STOLN ▶ **steal**
STOLON, -S *n* long horizontal stem that grows along the surface of the soil
STOMA, -S, -TA *n* pore in a plant leaf that controls the passage of gases
STOMACH *n, vb*
STOMACK *n* as in **have a stomack** (in E Africa) be pregnant
STOMAL ▶ **stoma**
STOMAS ▶ **stoma**
STOMATA ▶ **stoma**
STOMATE *n* opening on leaf through which water evaporates
STOMIUM, STOMIA *n* part of the sporangium of ferns that ruptures to release the spores
STOMP, -ED, -S *vb, n*
STOMPER *n* song with a strong beat
STOMPIE *n* cigarette butt
STOMPS ▶ **stomp**
STOMPY *adj* (of music) encouraging stomping of the feet
STOND, -S *same as* ▶ **stand**
STONE, -D, -S *n, vb*
STONEN *adj* of stone
STONER, -S *n*
STONERN *same as* ▶ **stonen**
STONERS ▶ **stoner**

STONES ▸ stone
STONEY *same as* ▸ stony
STONG ▸ sting
STONIED ▸ stony
STONIER ▸ stony
STONIES ▸ stony
STONILY ▸ stony
STONING ▸ stone
STONISH *same as* > astonish
STONK, -ED, -S *vb* bombard (soldiers, buildings, etc) with artillery ▹ *n* concentrated bombardment
STONKER *vb*
STONKS ▸ stonk
STONN, -S *same as* ▸ stun
STONNE, -D, -S *same as* ▸ stun
STONNS ▸ stonn
STONY, STONIED, STONIER, STONIES *adj, vb*
STOOD ▸ stand
STOODEN ▸ stand
STOOGE, -D, -S *n, vb*
STOOK, -ED, -S *n* number of sheaves set upright in a field to dry ▹ *vb* set up (sheaves) in stooks
STOOKER ▸ stook
STOOKIE *n* stucco
STOOKS ▸ stook
STOOL, -ED, -S *n, vb*
STOOLIE *n* police informer
STOOLS ▸ stool
STOOLY *n* (US) informant for the police
STOOP, -ED, -S *vb*
STOOPE, -S *same as* ▸ stoup
STOOPED ▸ stoop
STOOPER ▸ stoop
STOOPES ▸ stoope
STOOPS ▸ stoop
STOOR, -S *same as* ▸ stour
STOOZE, -D, -S *vb* borrow money cheaply and invest it to make a profit
STOOZER *n* person who stoozes
STOOZES ▸ stooze
STOP, -PED, -S, -T *vb, n*
STOPE, -D, -S *n* steplike excavation made in a mine to extract ore ▹ *vb* mine (ore, etc) by cutting stopes
STOPER, -S *n* drill used in mining
STOPES ▸ stope
STOPGAP *n*
STOPING *n* process by which country rock is broken up and engulfed by magma
STOPOFF *n*
STOPPED ▸ stop
STOPPER *n, vb*
STOPPLE *same as* ▸ stopper
STOPS ▸ stop
STOPT ▸ stop
STORAGE *n*
STORAX *n* type of tree or shrub with white flowers
STORE, -D, STORING *vb, n*
STORER, -S ▸ store
STORES *pl n*
STOREY, -S *n*
STORGE, -S *n* affection
STORIED ▸ story
STORIES ▸ story
STORING ▸ store
STORK, -S *n*
STORM, -ED, -S *n, vb*
STORMER *n* outstanding example of its kind
STORMS ▸ storm
STORMY *adj*
STORY, STORIED, STORIES *n, vb*
STOSS, -ES *adj* (of the side of a hill) facing the onward flow of a glacier ▹ *n* hillside facing glacier flow
STOT, -S, -TED *n* bullock ▹ *vb* bounce or cause to bounce
STOTIN, -S *n* former monetary unit of Slovenia
STOTS ▸ stot
STOTT, -S *same as* ▸ stot
STOTTED ▸ stot
STOTTER *same as* ▸ stot
STOTTIE *n* wedge of bread cut from a flat round loaf
STOTTS ▸ stott
STOTTY *same as* ▸ stottie
STOUN, -S *same as* ▸ stun
STOUND, -S *n* short while ▹ *vb* ache
STOUNS ▸ stoun
STOUP, -S *n* small basin for holy water
STOUR, -S *n* turmoil or conflict
STOURE, -S *same as* ▸ stour
STOURIE *same as* ▸ stoury

STOURS ▸ **stour**
STOURY *adj* dusty
STOUSH *vb* hit or punch (someone) ▹ *n* fighting or violence
STOUT, -ER, -S *adj, n*
STOUTEN *vb* make or become stout
STOUTER ▸ **stout**
STOUTH, -S *n* Scots word meaning theft
STOUTLY ▸ **stout**
STOUTS ▸ **stout**
STOVE, -D, -S *n, vb*
STOVER, -S *n* fodder
STOVES ▸ **stove**
STOVIES *pl n* potatoes stewed with onions
STOVING ▸ **stove**
STOW, -ED, -S *vb*
STOWAGE *n* space or charge for stowing goods
STOWED ▸ **stow**
STOWER, -S ▸ **stow**
STOWING ▸ **stow**
STOWN ▸ **steal**
STOWND, -S *same as* ▸ **stound**
STOWP, -S *same as* ▸ **stoup**
STOWRE, -S *same as* ▸ **stour**
STOWS ▸ **stow**
STRACK *vb* archaic past tense form of strike
STRAD, -S *n* violin made by Stradivarius
STRAE, -S *Scots form of* ▸ **straw**
STRAFE, -D, -S *vb, n*
STRAFER ▸ **strafe**
STRAFES ▸ **strafe**
STRAFF, -S *same as* ▸ **strafe**
STRAG, -S *n* straggler
STRAIK, -S *Scots word for* ▸ **stroke**
STRAIN, -S *vb, n*
STRAINT *n* pressure
STRAIT, -S *n, adj, vb*
STRAK *vb* archaic past tense form of strike
STRAKE, -S *n* curved metal plate forming part of the metal rim on a wooden wheel
STRAKED *adj* having a strake
STRAKES ▸ **strake**
STRAMP, -S *Scots variant of* ▸ **tramp**
STRAND, -S *vb, n*
STRANG *dialect variant of* ▸ **strong**
STRANGE *adj, n*
STRAP, -S *n, vb*
STRAPPY *adj*
STRAPS ▸ **strap**
STRASS *another word for* ▸ **paste**
STRATA ▸ **stratum**
STRATAL ▸ **stratum**
STRATH, -S *n* flat river valley
STRATI ▸ **stratus**
STRATUM, STRATA *n* layer, esp of rock
STRATUS, STRATI *n* grey layer cloud
STRAW, -ED, -S *n, vb*
STRAWEN *adj* of straw
STRAWN ▸ **strew**
STRAWS ▸ **straw**
STRAWY *adj* containing straw, or like straw in colour or texture
STRAY, -ED, -S *vb, adj, n*
STRAYER ▸ **stray**
STRAYS ▸ **stray**
STRAYVE *vb* wander aimlessly
STREAK, -S *n, vb*
STREAKY *adj*
STREAM, -S *n, vb*
STREAMY *adj* (of an area, land, etc) having many streams
STREEK, -S *Scots word for* ▸ **stretch**
STREEL, -S *vb* trail
STREET, -S *n, vb*
STREETY *adj* of streets
STRENE, -S *same as* ▸ **strain**
STREP, -S *n* streptococcus
STRESS *n, vb*
STRESSY *adj* characterized by stress
STRETCH *vb, n*
STRETTA, STRETTE *same as* ▸ **stretto**
STRETTO, STRETTI *n* (in a fugue) the close overlapping of two parts or voices
STREW, STRAWN, -ED, -N, -S *vb*
STREWER ▸ **strew**
STREWN ▸ **strew**
STREWS ▸ **strew**
STREWTH *interj* expression of surprise or alarm
STRIA, -E *n* scratch or groove on the surface of a rock crystal
STRIATA > **striatum**
STRIATE *adj* marked with striae ▹ *vb* mark with striae
STRICH *n* screech owl
STRICK, -S *n* any bast fibres preparatory to being made into slivers
STRICT *adj*
STRIDE, -S, STRODE *vb, n*

STRIDER ▸ **stride**
STRIDES ▸ **stride**
STRIDOR *n* high-pitched whistling sound made during respiration
STRIFE, -S *n*
STRIFT, -S *n* struggle
STRIG, -S *vb* remove stalk from
STRIGA, -E *same as* ▸ **stria**
STRIGIL *n* curved blade used to scrape the body after bathing
STRIGS ▸ **strig**
STRIKE, -S, STROKEN, STROOK, STRUCK *vb, n*
STRIKER *n*
STRIKES ▸ **strike**
STRIM, -S *vb* cut (grass) using an electric trimmer
STRINE, -S *n* informal name for Australian English
STRING, -S, STRUNG *n, vb*
STRINGY *adj*
STRIP, -S, -T *vb, n*
STRIPE, -S *n, vb*
STRIPED *adj*
STRIPER *n* officer who has a stripe or stripes on his or her uniform
STRIPES ▸ **stripe**
STRIPEY *same as* ▸ **stripy**
STRIPS ▸ **strip**
STRIPT ▸ **strip**
STRIPY *adj*
STRIVE, -D, -N, -S, STROVE *vb*
STRIVER ▸ **strive**
STRIVES ▸ **strive**
STROAM, -S *vb* wander
STROBE, -D, -S *n, vb*
STROBIC *adj* spinning or appearing to spin
STROBIL *n* scaly multiple fruit
STRODE ▸ **stride**
STRODLE *same as* ▸ **straddle**
STROKE, -D, -S *vb, n*
STROKEN ▸ **strike**
STROKER ▸ **stroke**
STROKES ▸ **stroke**
STROLL, -S *vb, n*
STROMA *n* gel-like matrix of chloroplasts and certain cells
STROMAL ▸ **stroma**
STROMB, -S *n* shellfish like a whelk
STROND, -S *same as* ▸ **strand**
STRONG *adj*
STROOK ▸ **strike**
STROOKE *n* stroke
STROP, -S *n* leather strap for sharpening razors ▹ *vb* sharpen (a razor, etc) on a strop
STROPHE *n* movement made by chorus during a choral ode
STROPPY *adj*
STROPS ▸ **strop**
STROUD, -S *n* coarse woollen fabric
STROUP, -S *Scots word for* ▸ **spout**
STROUT, -S *vb* bulge
STROVE ▸ **strive**
STROW, -ED, -N, -S *archaic variant of* ▸ **strew**
STROWER ▸ **strow**
STROWN ▸ **strow**
STROWS ▸ **strow**
STROY, -ED, -S *archaic variant of* ▸ **destroy**
STROYER ▸ **stroy**
STROYS ▸ **stroy**
STRUCK ▸ **strike**
STRUDEL *n*
STRUM, -S *vb*
STRUMA, -E, -S *n* abnormal enlargement of the thyroid gland
STRUMS ▸ **strum**
STRUNG ▸ **string**
STRUNT, -S *Scots word for* ▸ **strut**
STRUT, -S *vb, n*
STUB, -BED, -S *n, vb*
STUBBIE *same as* ▸ **stubby**
STUBBLE *n*
STUBBLY ▸ **stubble**
STUBBY *adj, n*
STUBS ▸ **stub**
STUCCO, -S *n, vb*
STUCK, -S *n*
STUD, -DED, -S *n, vb*
STUDDEN ▸ **stand**
STUDDIE *Scots word for* ▸ **anvil**
STUDDLE *n* post
STUDE *vb* past tense and past participle of staun (Scots form of stand)
STUDENT *n*
STUDIED *adj*
STUDIER ▸ **study**
STUDIES ▸ **study**
STUDIO, -S *n*
STUDLY *adj*
STUDS ▸ **stud**
STUDY, STUDIES *vb, n*
STUFF, -ED, -S *n, vb*
STUFFER ▸ **stuff**
STUFFS ▸ **stuff**
STUFFY *adj*
STUGGY *adj* stout

STUIVER *same as* ▸ **stiver**
STULL, -S *n* timber prop or platform in a stope
STULM, -S *n* shaft
STUM, -MED, -S *n* partly fermented wine added to fermented wine as a preservative ▹ *vb* preserve (wine) by adding stum
STUMBLE *vb, n*
STUMBLY *adj* tending to stumble
STUMER, -S *n* forgery or cheat
STUMM *same as* ▸ **shtoom**
STUMMED ▸ **stum**
STUMMEL *n* bowl of a smoker's pipe
STUMP, -ED, -S *n, vb*
STUMPER ▸ **stump**
STUMPS ▸ **stump**
STUMPY *adj, n*
STUMS ▸ **stum**
STUN, -NED, -S *vb, n*
STUNG ▸ **sting**
STUNK ▸ **stink**
STUNNED ▸ **stun**
STUNNER *n*
STUNS ▸ **stun**
STUNT, -S *vb, n*
STUNTED ▸ **stunt**
STUNTS ▸ **stunt**
STUPA, -S *n* domed edifice housing Buddhist or Jain relics
STUPE, -D, -S, STUPING *n* hot damp cloth applied to the body to relieve pain ▹ *vb* treat with a stupe
STUPEFY *vb*
STUPENT *adj* astonished
STUPES ▸ **stupe**
STUPID, -S *adj, n*
STUPING ▸ **stupe**
STUPOR, -S *n*
STURDY *adj, n*
STURE *same as* ▸ **stoor**
STURMER *n* type of eating apple with pale green skin
STURNUS *n* bird of starling family
STURT, -ED, -S *vb* bother
STUSHIE *n* commotion, rumpus, or row
STUTTER *vb, n*
STY, STIED, STIES, -ING *vb*
STYE, -D, -S *n* inflammation at the base of an eyelash
STYGIAN *adj*
STYING ▸ **sty**
STYLAR ▸ **stylus**
STYLATE *adj* having style
STYLE, -D, -S *n, vb*
STYLEE, -S *same as* ▸ **style**
STYLER, -S ▸ **style**
STYLES ▸ **style**
STYLET, -S *n* wire to stiffen a flexible cannula or catheter
STYLI ▸ **stylus**
STYLIE, -R *adj* fashion-conscious
STYLING ▸ **style**
STYLISE *same as* ▸ **stylize**
STYLISH *adj*
STYLIST *n*
STYLITE *n* one of a class of recluses who in ancient times lived on the top of high pillars
STYLIZE *vb*
STYLO, -S *n* type of fountain pen
STYLOID *adj* resembling a stylus ▹ *n* spiny growth
STYLOPS *n* type of insect that lives as a parasite in other insects
STYLOS ▸ **stylo**
STYLUS, STYLI *n*
STYME, -D, -S, STYMING *vb* peer
STYMIE *vb*
STYMIED ▸ **stymy**
STYMIES ▸ **stymy**
STYMING ▸ **styme**
STYMY, STYMIED, STYMIES *same as* ▸ **stymie**
STYPSIS *n* action, application, or use of a styptic
STYPTIC *adj* (drug) used to stop bleeding ▹ *n* styptic drug
STYRAX *n* type of tropical or subtropical tree
STYRE, -D, -S, STYRING *same as* ▸ **stir**
STYRENE *n* colourless flammable liquid
STYRES ▸ **styre**
STYRING ▸ **styre**
STYTE, -D, -S, STYTING *vb* bounce
SUABLE *adj* liable to be sued in a court
SUABLY ▸ **suable**
SUASION *n* persuasion
SUASIVE ▸ **suasion**
SUASORY ▸ **suasion**
SUAVE, -R, -ST *adj*

SUAVELY ▸ **suave**
SUAVER ▸ **suave**
SUAVEST ▸ **suave**
SUAVITY ▸ **suave**
SUB, -BED, -S *n, vb*
SUBA, -S *n* shepherd's cloak
SUBACID *adj* (esp of some fruits) moderately acid or sour
SUBACT, -S *vb* subdue
SUBADAR *n* chief native officer of a company of Indian soldiers in the British service
SUBAH, -S *same as* ▸ **subadar**
SUBALAR *adj* below a wing
SUBAQUA *adj* of or relating to underwater sport
SUBAREA *n* area within a larger area
SUBARID *adj* receiving slightly more rainfall than arid regions
SUBAS ▸ **suba**
SUBATOM *n* part of an atom
SUBBASE *same as* ▸ **subbass**
SUBBASS *another name for* ▸ **bourdon**
SUBBED ▸ **sub**
SUBBIE, -S *n* subcontractor
SUBBING ▸ **sub**
SUBBY *same as* ▸ **subbie**
SUBCELL *n* cell within a larger cell
SUBCLAN *n* clan within a larger clan
SUBCODE *n* computer tag identifying data
SUBCOOL *vb* make colder
SUBCULT *n* cult within larger cult
SUBDEAN *n* deputy of dean
SUBDEB, -S *n* young woman who is not yet a debutante
SUBDEW, -S *same as* ▸ **subdue**
SUBDUAL ▸ **subdue**
SUBDUCE *vb* withdraw
SUBDUCT *vb* draw or turn (the eye, etc) downwards
SUBDUE, -S *vb*
SUBDUED *adj*
SUBDUER ▸ **subdue**
SUBDUES ▸ **subdue**
SUBECHO *n* echo resonating more quietly than another echo
SUBEDAR *same as* ▸ **subadar**
SUBEDIT *vb* edit and correct (written or printed material)
SUBER, -S *n* cork
SUBERIC *same as* > **suberose**
SUBERIN *n* fatty or waxy substance that is present in the walls of cork cells
SUBERS ▸ **suber**
SUBFEU, -S *vb* grant feu or land rights to a vassal
SUBFILE *n* file within another file
SUBFIX *n* suffix
SUBFUSC *adj* devoid of brightness or appeal ▷ *n* (at Oxford University) formal academic dress
SUBFUSK *same as* ▸ **subfusc**
SUBGOAL *n* secondary goal
SUBGUM, -S *n* Chinese dish
SUBHA, -S *n* string of beads used in praying and meditating
SUBHEAD *n* heading of a subsection in a printed work
SUBIDEA *n* secondary idea
SUBITEM *n* item that is less important than another item
SUBITO *adv*
SUBJECT *n, adj, vb*
SUBJOIN *vb* add or attach at the end of something spoken, written, etc
SUBLATE *vb* deny
SUBLET, -S *vb, n*
SUBLIME *adj, vb*
SUBLINE *n* secondary headline
SUBLOT, -S *n* subdivision of a lot
SUBMAN, SUBMEN *n* primitive form of human
SUBMENU *n*
SUBMISS *adj* old word meaning docile or submissive
SUBMIT, -S *vb*
SUBNET, -S *n* part of network
SUBORAL *adj* not quite oral

SUBORN, -S *vb* bribe or incite (a person) to commit a wrongful act
SUBOVAL *adj* not quite oval
SUBPAR *adj*
SUBPART *n* part within another part
SUBPENA *same as* **> subpoena**
SUBPLOT *n*
SUBRACE *n* subdivision of a race
SUBRENT *n* rent paid to renter who rents to another ▷ *vb* rent out (a property that is already rented)
SUBRING *n* mathematical ring that is a subset of another ring
SUBRULE *n* rule within another rule
SUBS ▶ **sub**
SUBSALE *n* sale carried out within the process of a larger sale
SUBSEA *adj* undersea
SUBSECT *n* sect within a larger sect
SUBSERE *n* secondary sere arising when the progress of a sere has been interrupted
SUBSET, -S *n*
SUBSIDE *vb*
SUBSIDY *n*
SUBSIST *vb*
SUBSITE *n* location within a website
SUBSOIL *n* earth just below the surface soil ▷ *vb* plough (land) to a depth below the normal ploughing level
SUBSONG *n* subdued form of birdsong modified from the full territorial song
SUBSUME *vb* include (an idea, case, etc) under a larger classification or group
SUBTACK *Scots word for* **> sublease**
SUBTASK *n* task that is part of a larger task
SUBTAXA > subtaxon
SUBTEEN *n* young person who has not yet become a teenager
SUBTEND *vb* be opposite (an angle or side)
SUBTEST *n* test that is part of larger test
SUBTEXT *n*
SUBTIL *same as* ▶ **subtle**
SUBTILE *rare spelling of* ▶ **subtle**
SUBTLE, -R *adj*
SUBTLY ▶ **subtle**
SUBTONE *n* subdivision of a tone
SUBTYPE *n* secondary or subordinate type or genre
SUBUNIT *n* distinct part or component of something larger
SUBURB, -S *n*
SUBVENE *vb* happen in such a way as to be of assistance
SUBVERT *vb*
SUBWAY, -S *n, vb*
SUBZERO *adj*
SUBZONE *n* subdivision of a zone
SUCCADE *n* piece of candied fruit
SUCCAH, -S *same as* ▶ **sukkah**
SUCCEED *vb*
SUCCES *French word for* ▶ **success**
SUCCESS *n*
SUCCI ▶ **succus**
SUCCISE *adj* ending abruptly, as if cut off
SUCCOR, -S *same as* ▶ **succour**
SUCCORY *another name for* ▶ **chicory**
SUCCOS *same as* ▶ **succoth**
SUCCOSE ▶ **succus**
SUCCOT *same as* ▶ **sukkoth**
SUCCOTH *variant of* ▶ **sukkoth**
SUCCOUR *n, vb*
SUCCOUS ▶ **succus**
SUCCUMB *vb*
SUCCUS, SUCCI *n* fluid
SUCCUSS *vb* shake (a patient) to detect the sound of fluid in a cavity
SUCH *adj, pron*
SUCK, -ED *vb, n*
SUCKEN, -S *Scots word for* **> district**
SUCKER, -S *n, vb*
SUCKET, -S *same as* ▶ **succade**
SUCKIER ▶ **sucky**
SUCKING *adj*
SUCKLE, -D, -S *vb*
SUCKLER ▶ **suckle**
SUCKLES ▶ **suckle**
SUCKS *interj*
SUCKY, SUCKIER *adj*
SUCRASE *another name for* **> invertase**
SUCRE, -S *n* former standard monetary unit of Ecuador

SUCRIER *n* small container for sugar at table
SUCROSE *same as* ▸ **sugar**
SUCTION *n, vb*
SUD *singular of* ▸ **suds**
SUDAMEN *n* small cavity in the skin
SUDARIA > **sudarium**
SUDARY *same as* > **sudarium**
SUDATE, -D, -S *vb* sweat
SUDD, -S *n* floating masses of reeds and weeds on the White Nile
SUDDEN, -S *adj*
SUDDER, -S *n* supreme court in India
SUDDS ▸ **sudd**
SUDOKU, -S *n*
SUDOR, -S *technical name for* ▸ **sweat**
SUDORAL ▸ **sudor**
SUDORS ▸ **sudor**
SUDS, -ED, -ES, -ING *pl n, vb*
SUDSER, -S *n* soap opera
SUDSES ▸ **suds**
SUDSIER ▸ **sudsy**
SUDSING ▸ **suds**
SUDSY, SUDSIER ▸ **suds**
SUE, -D, -S *vb*
SUEABLE ▸ **sue**
SUED ▸ **sue**
SUEDE, -D, -S, SUEDING *n, vb*
SUENT *adj* smooth
SUER, -S ▸ **sue**
SUES ▸ **sue**
SUET, -S *n*
SUETE, -S *n* southeasterly wind in Cape Breton Island
SUETIER ▸ **suety**
SUETS ▸ **suet**
SUETTY ▸ **suet**
SUETY, SUETIER ▸ **suet**
SUFFARI *same as* ▸ **safari**
SUFFECT *adj* additional ▹ *n* additional consul in ancient Rome
SUFFER, -S *vb*
SUFFETE *n* official in ancient Carthage
SUFFICE *vb*
SUFFIX *n, vb*
SUFFUSE *vb*
SUG, -GED, -S *vb* sell a product while pretending to conduct market research
SUGAN, -S *n* straw rope
SUGAR, -S *n, vb*
SUGARED *adj*
SUGARER ▸ **sugar**
SUGARS ▸ **sugar**
SUGARY *adj*
SUGGED ▸ **sug**
SUGGEST *vb*
SUGGING *n* practice of selling products under the pretence of conducting market research
SUGH, -ED, -ING, -S *same as* ▸ **sough**
SUGO, -S *n* Italian pasta sauce
SUGS ▸ **sug**
SUHUR, -S *n* meal eaten before sunrise by Muslims fasting during Ramadan
SUI *adj* of itself
SUICIDE *n, vb*
SUID, -S *n* pig or related animal
SUIDIAN ▸ **suid**
SUIDS ▸ **suid**
SUING, -S ▸ **sue**
SUINT, -S *n* water-soluble substance found in the fleece of sheep
SUIPLAP *n* South African slang for a drunkard
SUIT, -ED, -S *n, vb*
SUITE, -S *n*
SUITED ▸ **suit**
SUITER, -S *n* piece of luggage for carrying suits and dresses
SUITES ▸ **suite**
SUITING *n* fabric used for suits
SUITOR, -S *n, vb*
SUITS ▸ **suit**
SUIVEZ *vb* musical direction meaning follow
SUJEE, -S *same as* ▸ **soogee**
SUK, -S *same as* ▸ **suq**
SUKH, -S *same as* ▸ **suq**
SUKKAH, -S *n* structure in which orthodox Jews eat and sleep during Sukkoth
SUKKOS *same as* ▸ **sukkoth**
SUKKOT *same as* ▸ **sukkoth**
SUKKOTH *n* eight-day Jewish harvest festival
SUKS ▸ **suk**
SUKUK, -S *n* financial certificate conforming to Islam lending principles
SULCAL ▸ **sulcus**
SULCATE *adj* marked with longitudinal parallel grooves

SULCUS, SULCI *n* linear groove, furrow, or slight depression
SULDAN, -S *same as* ▶ **sultan**
SULFA, -S *same as* ▶ **sulpha**
SULFATE *same as* > **sulphate**
SULFID, -S *same as* > **sulphide**
SULFIDE *same as* > **sulphide**
SULFIDS ▶ **sulfid**
SULFITE *same as* > **sulphite**
SULFO *same as* > **sulphonic**
SULFONE *same as* > **sulphone**
SULFUR, -S *variant of* ▶ **sulphur**
SULFURY *adj* containing sulfur
SULK, -ED, -ING, -S *vb, n*
SULKER, -S *same as* ▶ **sulk**
SULKIER ▶ **sulky**
SULKIES ▶ **sulky**
SULKILY ▶ **sulky**
SULKING ▶ **sulk**
SULKS ▶ **sulk**
SULKY, SULKIER, SULKIES *adj, n*
SULLAGE *n* filth or waste, esp sewage
SULLEN, -S *adj, n*
SULLY, SULLIED, SULLIES *vb, n*
SULPHA, -S *n* any of a group of sulphonamides that prevent the growth of bacteria
SULPHID *same as* > **sulphide**
SULPHUR *n, vb*
SULTAN, -S *n*
SULTANA *n*
SULTANS ▶ **sultan**
SULTRY *adj*
SULU, -S *n* type of sarong worn in Fiji
SUM, -MED, -S *n, vb*
SUMAC, -S *same as* ▶ **sumach**
SUMACH, -S *n* type of temperate or subtropical shrub or small tree
SUMACS ▶ **sumac**
SUMATRA *n* violent storm blowing from the direction of Sumatra
SUMI, -S *n* type of black ink used in Japan
SUMLESS *adj* uncountable
SUMMA, -E, -S *n* compendium of theology, philosophy, or canon law
SUMMAND *n* number or quantity forming part of a sum
SUMMAR *Scots variant of* ▶ **summer**
SUMMARY *n, adj*
SUMMAS ▶ **summa**
SUMMAT, -S *pron* something ▷ *n* impressive or important person or thing
SUMMATE *vb* add up
SUMMATS ▶ **summat**
SUMMED ▶ **sum**
SUMMER, -S *n, vb*
SUMMERY ▶ **summer**
SUMMING ▶ **sum**
SUMMIST *n* writer of summae
SUMMIT, -S *n, vb*
SUMMON *vb*
SUMMONS *n, vb*
SUMO, -S *n* Japanese style of wrestling
SUMOIST ▶ **sumo**
SUMOS ▶ **sumo**
SUMP, -S *n* container in an internal-combustion engine into which oil can drain
SUMPH, -S *n* stupid person
SUMPIT, -S *n* Malay blowpipe
SUMPS ▶ **sump**
SUMPTER *n* packhorse, mule, or other beast of burden
SUMS ▶ **sum**
SUMY *pl n* the monetary units of Uzbekistan
SUN, -NED, -NING, -S *n, vb*
SUNBACK *adj* (of dress) cut low at back
SUNBAKE *vb* sunbathe, esp in order to become tanned ▷ *n* period of sunbaking
SUNBATH *n* exposure of the body to the sun to get a suntan
SUNBEAM *n*
SUNBEAT *adj* exposed to sun
SUNBED, -S *n*
SUNBELT *n* southern states of the US
SUNBIRD *n* type of small songbird with a bright plumage in the males
SUNBOW, -S *n* bow of colours produced

when sunlight shines through spray
SUNBURN *n, vb*
SUNCARE *n* use of products in protecting skin from the sun
SUNDAE, -S *n*
SUNDARI *n* Indian tree
SUNDECK *n* upper open deck on a passenger ship
SUNDER, -S *vb*
SUNDEW, -S *n* type of bog plant with leaves covered in sticky hairs
SUNDIAL *n*
SUNDOG, -S *n* small rainbow or halo near the horizon
SUNDOWN *same as* ▶ **sunset**
SUNDRA, -S *same as* ▶ **sundari**
SUNDRI, -S *same as* ▶ **sundari**
SUNDRY *adj*
SUNFAST *adj* not fading in sunlight
SUNFISH *n* large sea fish with a rounded body
SUNG ▶ **sing**
SUNGAR, -S *same as* ▶ **sangar**
SUNGLOW *n* pinkish glow often seen in the sky before sunrise or after sunset
SUNHAT, -S *n*
SUNI, -S *n* S African dwarf antelope
SUNK, -S *n*
SUNKEN *adj*
SUNKER, -S *n* rock (partially) submerged in shallow water
SUNKET, -S *n* something good to eat
SUNKIE, -S *n* little stool
SUNKS ▶ **sunk**
SUNLAMP *n*
SUNLAND *n* sunny area
SUNLESS *adj* without sun or sunshine
SUNLIKE ▶ **sun**
SUNLIT > **sunlight**
SUNN, -S *n* tropical leguminous plant
SUNNA, -S *n* body of traditional Islamic law
SUNNAH, -S *same as* ▶ **sunna**
SUNNAS ▶ **sunna**
SUNNED ▶ **sun**
SUNNIER ▶ **sunny**
SUNNIES *pl n* pair of sunglasses
SUNNILY ▶ **sunny**
SUNNING ▶ **sun**
SUNNS ▶ **sunn**
SUNNY, SUNNIER *adj*
SUNRAY, -S *n* ray of light from the sun
SUNRISE *n*
SUNROOF *n*
SUNROOM *n* room or glass-enclosed porch designed to display beautiful views
SUNS ▶ **sun**
SUNSET, -S *vb*
SUNSPOT *n*
SUNSTAR *n* type of starfish with up to 13 arms
SUNSUIT *n* child's outfit consisting of a brief top and shorts or a short skirt
SUNTAN, -S *n*
SUNTRAP *n*
SUNUP, -S *same as* ▶ **sunrise**
SUNWARD *same as* > **sunwards**
SUNWISE *adv* moving in the same direction as the sun
SUP, -PED, -PING, -S *same as* ▶ **supine**
SUPAWN, -S *same as* ▶ **suppawn**
SUPE, -S *n* superintendent
SUPER, -ED, -S *adj, n, interj, vb*
SUPERB *adj*
SUPERED ▶ **super**
SUPERS ▶ **super**
SUPES ▶ **supe**
SUPINE, -S *adj, n*
SUPLEX *n* type of wrestling hold
SUPPAWN *n* kind of porridge
SUPPED ▶ **sup**
SUPPER, -S *n, vb*
SUPPING ▶ **sup**
SUPPLE, -D, -R, -S *adj, vb*
SUPPLY *vb, n, adj, adv*
SUPPORT *vb, n*
SUPPOSE *vb*
SUPRA *adv* above, esp referring to earlier parts of a book etc
SUPREMA > **supremum**
SUPREME *adj, n*
SUPREMO *n* person in overall authority
SUPS ▶ **sup**
SUQ, -S *n* open-air marketplace

This unusual word for an Arab marketplace is easy to overlook because we tend not to think of words ending in Q. It can also be spelt **sook, souk, suk** or **sukh**.

SUR *prep* above
SURA, -S *n* any of the 114 chapters of the Koran
SURAH, -S *n* twill-weave fabric of silk or rayon, used for dresses, blouses, etc
SURAL *adj* of or relating to the calf of the leg
SURAMIN *n* drug used in treating sleeping sickness
SURANCE *same as* **> assurance**
SURAS ▸ sura
SURAT, -S *n* cotton fabric from Surat in India
SURBASE *n* uppermost part, such as a moulding, of a pedestal, base, or skirting
SURBATE, SURBET *vb* make feet sore through walking
SURBED, -S *vb* put something on its edge
SURBET ▸ surbate
SURCOAT *n* tunic worn by a knight over their armour
SURCULI > surculus
SURD, -S *n* number that cannot be expressed in whole numbers ▹ *adj* of or relating to a surd
SURDITY *n* deafness
SURDS ▸ surd
SURE, -D, -R, -S, -ST, SURING *adj, interj, vb*
SURELY *adv*
SURER ▸ sure
SURES ▸ sure
SUREST ▸ sure
SURETY *n, vb*
SURF, -ED, -S *n, vb*
SURFACE *n, vb*
SURFED ▸ surf
SURFEIT *n, vb*
SURFER, -S ▸ surfing
SURFIE, -S *n* young person whose main interest is in surfing
SURFIER ▸ surfy
SURFIES ▸ surfie
SURFING *n*
SURFMAN, SURFMEN *n* sailor skilled in sailing through surf
SURFS ▸ surf
SURFY, SURFIER ▸ surf
SURGE, -D, -S *n, vb*
SURGENT ▸ surge
SURGEON *n*
SURGER, -S ▸ surge
SURGERY *n*
SURGES ▸ surge
SURGIER ▸ surgy
SURGING ▸ surge
SURGY, SURGIER ▸ surge
SURIMI, -S *n* blended seafood product made from precooked fish
SURING ▸ sure
SURLIER ▸ surly
SURLILY ▸ surly
SURLOIN *same as* **▸ sirloin**
SURLY, SURLIER *adj*
SURMISE *n, vb*
SURNAME *n, vb*
SURPASS *vb*
SURPLUS *n, adj, vb*
SURRA, -S *n* tropical febrile disease of animals
SURREAL *adj, n*
SURREY, -S *n* light horse-drawn carriage
SURTAX *n, vb*
SURTOUT *n* man's overcoat resembling a frock coat
SURVEIL *same as* **> surveille**
SURVEY, -S *vb, n*
SURVIEW *vb* survey
SURVIVE *vb*
SUS, -ED, -ES, -ING *same as* **▸ suss**
SUSHI, -S *n*
SUSING ▸ sus
SUSLIK, -S *n* central Eurasian ground squirrel
SUSPECT *vb, adj, n*
SUSPEND *vb*
SUSPENS *same as* **> suspense**
SUSPIRE *vb* sigh or utter with a sigh
SUSS, -ED, -ES, -ING *vb, n*
SUSTAIN *vb, n*
SUSU, -S *n* (in the Caribbean) savings fund shared by friends
SUTILE *adj* involving sewing
SUTLER, -S *n* merchant who accompanied an army in order to sell provisions
SUTLERY ▸ sutler
SUTOR, -S *n* cobbler
SUTRA, -S *n* Sanskrit sayings or collections of sayings
SUTTA, -S *n* Buddhist scripture
SUTTEE, -S *n* custom whereby a widow burnt herself on her husband's funeral pyre
SUTTLE, -D, -S *vb* work as a sutler

SUTTLY ▸ **subtle**
SUTURAL ▸ **suture**
SUTURE, -D, -S *n, vb*
SVARAJ *same as* ▸ **swaraj**
SVELTE, -R *adj*
SWAB, -BED, -S *n, vb*
SWABBER *n* person who uses a swab
SWABBIE *same as* ▸ **swabby**
SWABBY *n* seaman
SWABS ▸ **swab**
SWACHH *adj* (in Indian English) clean
SWACK, -ED, -S *adj* flexible ▹ *vb* strike
SWAD, -S *n* loutish person
SWADDIE *same as* ▸ **swaddy**
SWADDLE *vb, n*
SWADDY *n* private soldier
SWADS ▸ **swad**
SWAG, -GED, -S *n* stolen property ▹ *vb* sway from side to side
SWAGE, -D, -S, SWAGING *n* shaped tool or die used in forming cold metal by hammering ▹ *vb* form (metal) with a swage
SWAGER, -S ▸ **swage**
SWAGES ▸ **swage**
SWAGGED ▸ **swag**
SWAGGER *vb, n, adj*
SWAGGIE *same as* ▸ **swagger**
SWAGING ▸ **swage**
SWAGMAN, SWAGMEN *n* tramp who carries their belongings in a bundle on their back
SWAGS ▸ **swag**
SWAIL, -S *same as* ▸ **swale**
SWAIN, -S *n* suitor
SWALE, -D, -S *n* moist depression in a tract of land ▹ *vb* sway
SWALIER ▸ **swaly**
SWALING ▸ **swale**
SWALLET *n* hole where water goes underground
SWALLOW *vb, n*
SWALLY *n* alcoholic drink
SWALY, SWALIER ▸ **swale**
SWAM ▸ **swim**
SWAMI, -ES, -S *n* Hindu religious teacher
SWAMP, -ED, -S *n, vb*
SWAMPER *n* person who lives or works in a swampy region
SWAMPS ▸ **swamp**
SWAMPY ▸ **swamp**
SWAMY *same as* ▸ **swami**
SWAN, -NED, -S *n, vb*
SWANG ▸ **swing**
SWANK, -ED, -S *vb* show off or boast ▹ *n* showing off or boasting
SWANKER ▸ **swank**
SWANKEY *same as* ▸ **swanky**
SWANKIE *same as* ▸ **swanky**
SWANKS ▸ **swank**
SWANKY *adj, n*
SWANNED ▸ **swan**
SWANNIE *n* (in New Zealand) type of heavy woollen shirt
SWANNY *adj* swanlike
SWANPAN *n* Chinese abacus
SWANS ▸ **swan**
SWAP, -PED, -S, -T *vb, n*
SWAPPER ▸ **swap**
SWAPS ▸ **swap**
SWAPT ▸ **swap**
SWARAJ *n* (in British India) self-government
SWARD, -ED, -S *n* stretch of short grass ▹ *vb* cover or become covered with grass
SWARDY *adj* covered with sward
SWARE ▸ **swear**
SWARF, -ED, -S, SWARVED, SWARVES *n* material removed by cutting tools in the machining of metals, stone, etc ▹ *vb* faint
SWARM, -ED, -S *n, vb*
SWARMER ▸ **swarm**
SWARMS ▸ **swarm**
SWART *adj* swarthy
SWARTH, -S *same as* ▸ **swart**
SWARTHY *adj*
SWARTY *adj* swarthy
SWARVE *same as* ▸ **swarf**
SWARVED ▸ **swarf**
SWARVES ▸ **swarf**
SWASH, -ED, -ES *n* rush of water up a beach following each break of the waves ▹ *vb* wash or move with noisy splashing
SWASHER *n* braggart
SWASHES ▸ **swash**
SWASHY *adj* slushy
SWAT, -S, -TED *vb, n*
SWATCH *n* sample of cloth
SWATH, -S *n*
SWATHE, -D, -S *vb, n*

SWATHER ▶ **swathe**
SWATHES ▶ **swathe**
SWATHS ▶ **swath**
SWATHY ▶ **swath**
SWATS ▶ **swat**
SWATTED ▶ **swat**
SWATTER *n* device for killing insects ▷ *vb* splash
SWATTY *same as* ▶ **swotty**
SWAY, -ED, -S *vb, n*
SWAYER, -S ▶ **sway**
SWAYFUL ▶ **sway**
SWAYING ▶ **sway**
SWAYL, -ED, -S *same as* ▶ **sweal**
SWAYS ▶ **sway**
SWAZZLE *n* small metal instrument used to produce a shrill voice
SWEAL, -ED, -S *vb* scorch
SWEAR, SWARE, -S, SWORE, SWORN *vb*
SWEARD, -S *same as* ▶ **sword**
SWEARER ▶ **swear**
SWEARS ▶ **swear**
SWEARY *adj*
SWEAT, -S *n, vb*
SWEATED *adj* made by exploited labour
SWEATER *n*
SWEATS ▶ **sweat**
SWEATY *adj*
SWEDE, -S *n*
SWEDGER *n* Scots dialect word for sweet
SWEE, -D, -ING, -S *vb* sway
SWEEL, -ED, -S *same as* ▶ **sweal**
SWEENEY *n* police flying squad
SWEENY *n* wasting of the shoulder muscles of a horse
SWEEP, -S, SWEPT *vb, n*
SWEEPER *n*
SWEEPS ▶ **sweep**
SWEEPY ▶ **sweep**
SWEER, -ED, -S *variant of* ▶ **sweir**
SWEERT *variant of* ▶ **sweer**
SWEES ▶ **swee**
SWEET, -ED, -ER, -S *adj, n, vb*
SWEETEN *vb*
SWEETER ▶ **sweet**
SWEETIE *n*
SWEETLY ▶ **sweet**
SWEETS ▶ **sweet**
SWEETY *same as* ▶ **sweetie**
SWEIR, -ED, -ER, -S *vb* swear ▷ *adj* lazy
SWEIRT *variant of* ▶ **sweir**
SWELL, -ED, -S, SWOLLEN, SWOLN *vb, n, adj*
SWELLER ▶ **swell**
SWELLS ▶ **swell**
SWELT, -ED, -S *vb* die
SWELTER *vb, n*
SWELTRY *adj* sultry
SWELTS ▶ **swelt**
SWEPT ▶ **sweep**
SWERF, -ED, -S *same as* ▶ **swarf**
SWERVE, -D, -S *vb, n*
SWERVER ▶ **swerve**
SWERVES ▶ **swerve**
SWEVEN, -S *n* vision or dream
SWEY, -ED, -ING, -S *same as* ▶ **swee**
SWIDDEN *n* area of land where slash-and-burn techniques have been used
SWIES ▶ **swy**
SWIFT, -ED, -S *adj, n, adv, vb*
SWIFTER *n* line run around the ends of capstan bars
SWIFTIE *n* trick, ruse, or deception
SWIFTLY ▶ **swift**
SWIFTS ▶ **swift**
SWIFTY *same as* ▶ **swiftie**
SWIG, -GED, -S *n, vb*
SWIGGER ▶ **swig**
SWIGS ▶ **swig**
SWILE, -S *n* seal (the marine animal)
SWILER, -S *n* (in Newfoundland) a seal hunter
SWILES ▶ **swile**
SWILING *n* practice of hunting seals
SWILL, -ED, -S *vb, n*
SWILLER ▶ **swill**
SWILLS ▶ **swill**
SWIM, SWAM, -S, SWUM *vb, n*
SWIMMER ▶ **swim**
SWIMMY *adj* dizzy
SWIMS ▶ **swim**
SWINDGE *same as* ▶ **swinge**
SWINDLE *vb, n*
SWINE, -S *n*
SWINERY *n* pig farm
SWINES ▶ **swine**
SWING, SWANG, -S, SWUNG *vb, n*
SWINGBY *n* act of spacecraft passing close to planet
SWINGE, -D, -S *vb*
SWINGER *n*

SWINGES ▸ **swinge**
SWINGLE *n* flat-bladed wooden instrument used for beating and scraping flax ▹ *vb* use a swingle on
SWINGS ▸ **swing**
SWINGY *adj* lively and modern
SWINISH ▸ **swine**
SWINK, -ED, -S *vb* toil or drudge ▹ *n* toil or drudgery
SWINKER ▸ **swink**
SWINKS ▸ **swink**
SWINNEY *variant of* ▸ **sweeny**
SWIPE, -D, SWIPING *vb, n*
SWIPER, -S ▸ **swipe**
SWIPES *pl n* beer, esp when poor or weak
SWIPEY, SWIPIER *adj* drunk
SWIPING ▸ **swipe**
SWIPLE, -S *same as* ▸ **swipple**
SWIPPLE *n* part of a flail that strikes the grain
SWIRE, -S *n* neck
SWIRL, -ED, -S *vb* turn with a whirling motion ▹ *n* whirling motion
SWIRLY ▸ **swirl**
SWISH, -ED, -ES *vb, n, adj*
SWISHER ▸ **swish**
SWISHES ▸ **swish**
SWISHY *adj*
SWISS, -ES *n* type of muslin
SWITCH *n, vb*
SWITCHY ▸ **switch**
SWITH *adv* swiftly
SWITHE *same as* ▸ **swith**
SWITHER *vb, n*
SWITHLY ▸ **swith**
SWITS, -ES *same as* ▸ **switch**
SWIVEL, -S *vb, n*
SWIVET, -S *n* nervous state
SWIZ *n* swindle or disappointment
SWIZZ, -ED, -ES *same as* ▸ **swiz**
SWIZZLE *vb, n*
SWOB, -BED, -S *less common word for* ▸ **swab**
SWOBBER ▸ **swob**
SWOBS ▸ **swob**
SWOFFER > **swoffing**
SWOLE, -R, -ST *adj* muscular from weight training
SWOLLEN ▸ **swell**
SWOLN ▸ **swell**
SWOON, -ED, -S *n, vb*
SWOONER ▸ **swoon**
SWOONS ▸ **swoon**
SWOONY *adj* romantic
SWOOP, -ED, -S *vb, n*
SWOOPER ▸ **swoop**
SWOOPS ▸ **swoop**
SWOOPY ▸ **swoop**
SWOOSH *vb, n*
SWOP, -PED, -S, -T *same as* ▸ **swap**
SWOPPER ▸ **swop**
SWOPS ▸ **swop**
SWOPT ▸ **swop**
SWORD, -ED, -S *n, vb*
SWORDER *n* fighter with sword
SWORDS ▸ **sword**
SWORE ▸ **swear**
SWORN ▸ **swear**
SWOT, -S, -TED *vb, n*
SWOTTER *same as* ▸ **swot**
SWOTTY *adj* given to studying hard, esp to the exclusion of other activities
SWOUN, -S *same as* ▸ **swoon**
SWOUND *same as* ▸ **swoon**
SWOUNDS *less common spelling of* ▸ **zounds**
SWOUNE, -D, -S *same as* ▸ **swoon**
SWOUNS ▸ **swoun**
SWOWND, -S *same as* ▸ **swoon**
SWOWNE, -S *same as* ▸ **swoon**
SWOZZLE *same as* ▸ **swazzle**
SWUM ▸ **swim**
SWUNG ▸ **swing**
SWY, SWIES *n* Australian gambling game involving two coins

A type of card game, this word can be useful in helping you to clear a difficult rack.

SYBBE, -S *same as* ▸ **sib**
SYBIL, -S *same as* ▸ **sibyl**
SYBO *n* spring onion
SYBOE, -S *same as* ▸ **sybo**
SYBOTIC *adj* of a swineherd
SYBOW, -S *same as* ▸ **sybo**
SYCE, -S *n* (formerly, in India) a servant employed to look after horses, etc
SYCEE, -S *n* silver ingots formerly used as a medium of exchange in China
SYCES ▸ **syce**

SYCON, -S *n* type of sponge
SYCONIA > **syconium**
SYCONS ▸ **sycon**
SYCOSIS, SYCOSES *n* chronic inflammation of the hair follicles
SYE, -D, -ING, -S *vb* strain
SYEN, -S *same as* ▸ **scion**
SYENITE *n* light-coloured coarse-grained plutonic igneous rock
SYENS ▸ **syen**
SYES ▸ **sye**
SYKE, -S *same as* ▸ **sike**
SYKER *adv* surely
SYKES ▸ **syke**
SYLI, -S *n* Finnish unit of volume
SYLLABI > **syllabus**
SYLLOGE *n* collection or summary
SYLPH, -S *n* slender, graceful girl or woman
SYLPHIC ▸ **sylph**
SYLPHID *n* little sylph
SYLPHS ▸ **sylph**
SYLPHY ▸ **sylph**
SYLVA, -E, -S *n* trees growing in a particular region
SYLVAN, -S *adj* relating to woods and trees ▹ *n* inhabitant of the woods, esp a spirit
SYLVAS ▸ **sylva**
SYLVIA, -S *n* songbird
SYLVIN, -S *same as* ▸ **sylvite**
SYLVINE *same as* ▸ **sylvite**
SYLVINS ▸ **sylvin**
SYLVITE *n* soluble colourless, white, or coloured mineral
SYMAR, -S *same as* ▸ **cymar**
SYMBION *same as* > **symbiont**
SYMBIOT *same as* > **symbiont**
SYMBOL, -S *n*, *vb*
SYMBOLE *same as* ▸ **cymbal**
SYMBOLS ▸ **symbol**
SYMITAR *same as* > **scimitar**
SYMPTOM *n*
SYN *Scots word for* ▸ **since**
SYNAGOG *same as* > **synagogue**
SYNANON *n* type of therapy given to drug addicts
SYNAPSE *n*, *vb*
SYNAPTE *n* litany in Greek Orthodox Church
SYNAXIS, SYNAXES *n* early Christian meeting
SYNC, -ED, -ING, -S *n*, *vb*
SYNCARP *n* fleshy multiple fruit
SYNCED ▸ **sync**
SYNCH, -ED, -S *same as* ▸ **sync**
SYNCHRO *n* type of electrical device
SYNCHS ▸ **synch**
SYNCING ▸ **sync**
SYNCOM, -S *n* communications satellite in stationary orbit
SYNCOPE *n* omission of one or more sounds or letters from the middle of a word
SYNCS ▸ **sync**
SYND, -ED, -S *same as* ▸ **syne**
SYNDET, -S *n* synthetic detergent
SYNDIC, -S *n* business or legal agent of some institutions
SYNDING ▸ **synd**
SYNDS ▸ **synd**
SYNE, -D, -S, SYNING *vb* rinse ▹ *n* rinse ▹ *adv* since
SYNERGY *n*
SYNES ▸ **syne**
SYNESIS, SYNESES *n* grammatical construction in which the form of a word is conditioned by the meaning
SYNFUEL *n* synthetic fuel
SYNGAMY *n* reproduction involving the fusion of male and female gametes
SYNGAS *n* mixture of carbon monoxide and hydrogen
SYNING ▸ **syne**
SYNOD, -S *n*
SYNODAL *adj* of or relating to a synod ▹ *n* money paid to a bishop by less senior members of the clergy at a synod
SYNODIC *adj* involving conjunction of the same star, planet, or satellite
SYNODS ▸ **synod**
SYNONYM *n*
SYNOVIA *n* clear thick fluid that lubricates the body joints
SYNROC, -S *n* titanium-ceramic substance that can

incorporate nuclear waste in its crystals

SYNTAGM *same as* > **syntagma**

SYNTAN, -S *n* synthetic tanning substance

SYNTAX *n*

SYNTENY *n* presence of two or more genes on the same chromosome

SYNTH, -S *n*

SYNTHON *n* molecule used in synthesis

SYNTHS ▸ **synth**

SYNTONE *n* person who is syntonic

SYNTONY *n* matching of frequencies

SYNTYPE *n* original specimen by which a new species is described

SYNURA, -E *n* variety of microbe

SYPE, -D, -S, SYPING *same as* ▸ **sipe**

SYPHER, -S *vb* lap (a chamfered edge) in order to form a flush surface

SYPHON, -S *same as* ▸ **siphon**

SYPING ▸ **sype**

SYRAH, -S *n* type of French red wine

SYREN, -S *same as* ▸ **siren**

SYRETTE *n* small disposable syringe

SYRINGA *n* mock orange or lilac

SYRINGE *n, vb*

SYRINX *n* vocal organ of a bird

SYRPHID *n* type of fly

SYRTIS, SYRTES *n* area of quicksand

SYRUP, -ED, -S *n, vb*

SYRUPY *adj*

SYSOP, -S *n* person who runs a system or network

SYSTEM, -S *n*

SYSTOLE *n* regular contraction of the heart as it pumps blood

SYSTYLE *n* building with different types of columns

SYTHE, -S *same as* ▸ **sith**

SYVER, -S *n* street drain or the grating over it

SYZYGAL ▸ **syzygy**

SYZYGY *n* position of a celestial body when sun, earth, and the body are in line

Tt

TA, -S *interj, n*
TAAL, -S *n* language: usually, by implication, Afrikaans
TAATA, -S *n* (in E Africa) father

This East African word for a father is one of those short words that can help you dispose of a surplus of As.

TAB, -BED, -S *n, vb*
TABANID *n* stout-bodied fly
TABARD, -S *n*
TABARET *n* hard-wearing fabric of silk or similar cloth with stripes of satin or moire
TABBED ▸ **tab**
TABBIED ▸ **tabby**
TABBIER ▸ **tabby**
TABBIES ▸ **tabby**
TABBING *n* act of supplying with tabs
TABBIS *n* silken cloth
TABBY, TABBIED, TABBIER, TABBIES *vb* make (a material) appear wavy ▹ *n* female domestic cat ▹ *adj* brindled
TABEFY *vb* emaciate or become emaciated
TABER, -ED, -S *old variant of* ▸ **tabor**
TABERD, -S *same as* ▸ **tabard**
TABERED ▸ **taber**
TABERS ▸ **taber**
TABES *n* wasting of a bodily organ or part
TABETIC ▸ **tabes**
TABI, -S *n* thick-soled Japanese sock, worn with sandals
TABID *adj* emaciated
TABINET *n* type of tabbied fabric
TABIS ▸ **tabi**
TABLA, -S *n* one of a pair of Indian drums played with the hands
TABLE, -D, -S *n, vb*
TABLEAU *n*
TABLED ▸ **table**
TABLES ▸ **table**
TABLET, -S *n, vb*
TABLIER *n* (formerly) part of a dress resembling an apron
TABLING ▸ **table**
TABLOID *n*
TABOO, -ED, -S *n, adj, vb*
TABOR, -ED, -S *n* small drum ▹ *vb* play the tabor
TABORER ▸ **tabor**
TABORET *n* low stool, originally in the shape of a drum
TABORIN *same as* ▸ **taboret**
TABORS ▸ **tabor**
TABOULI *same as* > **tabbouleh**
TABOUR, -S *same as* ▸ **tabor**
TABRERE *same as* ▸ **tabor**
TABRET, -S *n* smaller version of a tabor
TABS ▸ **tab**
TABU, -ED, -ING, -S *same as* ▸ **taboo**
TABULA, -E *n* tablet for writing on
TABULAR *adj*
TABULI, -S *variant of* > **tabbouleh**
TABUN, -S *n* organic compound used as a lethal nerve gas
TABUS ▸ **tabu**
TACAN, -S *n* electronic ultrahigh-frequency navigation system for aircraft
TACE, -S *same as* ▸ **tasset**
TACET *adv* (in a musical direction) indicating that an instrument or singer does not take part
TACH, -S *n* device for measuring speed

TACHE, -S *n* buckle, clasp, or hook
TACHINA *n* as in **tachina fly** bristly fly
TACHISM *same as* > **tachisme**
TACHIST ▸ **tachism**
TACHO, -S *same as* > **tachogram**
TACHS ▸ **tach**
TACHYON *n* hypothetical elementary particle
TACIT *adj*
TACITLY ▸ **tacit**
TACK, -ED, -S *n, vb*
TACKER, -S ▸ **tack**
TACKET, -S *n* nail, esp a hobnail
TACKETY *adj* studded with tackets
TACKEY *same as* ▸ **tacky**
TACKIER ▸ **tacky**
TACKIES *pl n* S African word for plimsolls
TACKIFY *vb* give (eg rubber) a sticky feel
TACKILY ▸ **tacky**
TACKING ▸ **tack**
TACKLE, -D, -S *vb, n*
TACKLER ▸ **tackle**
TACKLES ▸ **tackle**
TACKS ▸ **tack**
TACKY, TACKIER *adj*
TACNODE *n* point at which two branches of a curve have a common tangent
TACO, -S *n*
TACRINE *n* drug used to treat Alzheimer's disease
TACT, -S *n*
TACTFUL ▸ **tact**
TACTIC *n*
TACTICS *n*
TACTILE *adj*
TACTION *n* act of touching
TACTISM *another word for* ▸ **taxis**
TACTS ▸ **tact**
TACTUAL *adj* caused by touch
TAD, -S *n*
TADDIE, -S *short for* ▸ **tadpole**
TADPOLE *n*
TADS ▸ **tad**
TAE, -D, -ING, -S *Scots form of* ▸ **toe**
TAEDIUM *archaic spelling of* ▸ **tedium**
TAEING ▸ **tae**
TAEL, -S *n* unit of weight, used in East Asia
TAENIA, -E, -S *n* (in ancient Greece) a narrow fillet or headband for the hair
TAENITE *n* nickel-iron alloy found in meteorites
TAES ▸ **tae**
TAFFETA *n*
TAFFETY *adj* made of taffeta
TAFFIA, -S *same as* ▸ **tafia**
TAFFY, TAFFIES *same as* ▸ **toffee**
TAFIA, -S *n* type of rum, esp from Guyana or the Caribbean
TAG, -GED, -GING, -S *n, vb*
TAGETES *n* any of a genus of plants with yellow or orange flowers
TAGGANT *n* microscopic material added to substance to identify it
TAGGED ▸ **tag**
TAGGEE, -S *n* one who has been made to wear a tag
TAGGER, -S *n* one who marks with a tag
TAGGIER ▸ **taggy**
TAGGING ▸ **tag**
TAGGY, TAGGIER *adj* (of wool, hair, etc) matted
TAGINE, -S *n* large, heavy N African cooking pot
TAGLESS *adj* having no tag
TAGLIKE *adj* resembling a tag
TAGLINE *n*
TAGMA, -TA *n* distinct region of the body of an arthropod
TAGMEME *n* class of speech elements all of which may fulfil the same grammatical role
TAGRAG, -S *same as* ▸ **ragtag**
TAGS ▸ **tag**
TAGUAN, -S *n* nocturnal flying squirrel
TAHA, -S *n* type of South African bird
TAHINA, -S *same as* ▸ **tahini**
TAHINI, -S *n* paste made from ground sesame seeds
TAHR, -S *n* goatlike mammal of mountainous regions of S and SW Asia

TAHSIL, -S *n* administrative division of a zila in certain states in India
TAI, -S *n* type of sea bream
TAIAHA, -S *n* carved weapon in the form of a staff, now used in Māori ceremonial oratory
TAIGA, -S *n* belt of coniferous forest
TAIGLE, -D, -S *vb* entangle or impede
TAIHOA, -S *vb* in New Zealand English, wait
TAIKO, -S *n* large Japanese drum
TAIL, -ED *n, adj, vb*
TAILARD *n* one having a tail
TAILED ▸ **tail**
TAILER, -S *n* one that tails
TAILFAN *n* fanned structure at the hind end of a lobster
TAILFIN *n*
TAILFLY *n* in angling, the lowest fly on a wet-fly cast
TAILING *n* part of a beam, rafter, projecting brick or stone, etc, embedded in a wall
TAILLE, -S *n* (in France before 1789) a tax levied by a king or overlord on his subjects
TAILLIE *n* (in Scots law) the limitation of an estate or interest to a person and their heirs
TAILOR, -S *n, vb*
TAILS *adv*
TAILYE, -S *same as* ▸ **taillie**
TAILZIE *same as* ▸ **taillie**
TAIN, -S *n* tinfoil used in backing mirrors
TAINT, -ED, -S *vb, n*
TAIPAN, -S *n* large poisonous Australian snake
TAIRA, -S *same as* ▸ **tayra**
TAIS ▸ **tai**
TAISCH *n* (in Scotland) apparition of a person whose death is imminent
TAISH, -ES *same as* ▸ **taisch**
TAIT, -S *same as* ▸ **tate**
TAIVER, -S *same as* ▸ **taver**
TAIVERT *adj* Scots word meaning confused or bewildered
TAJ, -ES *n* tall conical cap worn as a mark of distinction by Muslims

> This is one of the key words to remember for using the J.

TAJINE, -S *same as* ▸ **tagine**
TAK, -S *Scots variant spelling of* ▸ **take**
TAKA, -S *n* standard monetary unit of Bangladesh, divided into 100 paise
TAKABLE ▸ **take**
TAKAHE, -S *n* very rare flightless New Zealand bird
TAKAS ▸ **taka**
TAKE, -N, -S, TOOK *vb, n*
TAKEOFF *n*
TAKEOUT *n*
TAKER, -S *n*
TAKES ▸ **take**
TAKEUP, -S *n*
TAKHI, -S *n* type of wild Mongolian horse
TAKI, -S *same as* ▸ **takhi**
TAKIER ▸ **taky**
TAKIEST ▸ **taky**
TAKIN, -S *n* bovid mammal of mountainous regions of S Asia
TAKING, -S ▸ **take**
TAKINS ▸ **takin**
TAKIS ▸ **taki**
TAKKIES ▸ **takky**
TAKKY *n* S African word for plimsoll
TAKS ▸ **tak**
TAKY, TAKIER, TAKIEST *adj* appealing
TALA, -S *n* standard monetary unit of Samoa, divided into 100 sene
TALAK, -S *same as* ▸ **talaq**
TALANT, -S *old variant of* ▸ **talon**
TALAQ, -S *n* Muslim form of divorce

> In Islamic law, a word for divorce: easy to miss because one tends not to think of words ending in Q.

TALAR, -S *n* ankle-length robe
TALARIA *pl n* winged sandals, such as those worn by Hermes
TALARS ▸ **talar**
TALAS ▸ **tala**

TALAUNT *old variant of* ▸ **talon**
TALAYOT *n* ancient Balearic stone tower
TALBOT, -S *n* ancient breed of large hound
TALC, -ED, -ING, -KED, -S *n, vb, adj*
TALCIER ▸ **talcy**
TALCING ▸ **talc**
TALCKED ▸ **talc**
TALCKY *same as* ▸ **talcy**
TALCOSE ▸ **talc**
TALCOUS ▸ **talc**
TALCS ▸ **talc**
TALCUM, -S *n, vb*
TALCY, TALCIER *adj* like, containing, or covered in talc
TALE *n*
TALEA, -E *n* rhythmic pattern in certain mediaeval choral compositions
TALEFUL *adj* having many tales
TALENT, -S *n*
TALER, -S *same as* ▸ **thaler**
TALES *n*
TALI ▸ **talus**
TALION, -S *n* principle of making punishment correspond to the crime
TALIPAT *same as* ▸ **talipot**
TALIPED *adj* having a club foot ▹ *n* club-footed person
TALIPES *n* congenital deformity of the foot by which it is twisted in any of various positions
TALIPOT *n* palm tree of East India
TALK, -ED, -S *vb, n*
TALKBOX *n* voice box
TALKED ▸ **talk**
TALKER, -S ▸ **talk**
TALKIE, -S *n*
TALKIER ▸ **talky**
TALKIES ▸ **talkie**
TALKING *n*
TALKS ▸ **talk**
TALKY, TALKIER *adj* containing too much dialogue or inconsequential talk
TALL, -ER, -EST, -S *adj*
TALLAGE *n* tax levied on Crown lands and royal towns ▹ *vb* levy a tax (upon)
TALLAT, -S *same as* ▸ **tallet**
TALLBOY *n* high chest of drawers
TALLENT *n* archaic word meaning abundance
TALLER ▸ **tall**
TALLEST ▸ **tall**
TALLET, -S *n* loft
TALLIED ▸ **tally**
TALLIER ▸ **tally**
TALLIES ▸ **tally**
TALLIS *variant of* ▸ **tallith**
TALLISH *adj* quite tall
TALLIT, -S *variant of* ▸ **tallith**
TALLITH *n* shawl worn by Jewish males during religious services
TALLITS ▸ **tallit**
TALLOL, -S *n* oily liquid used for making soaps, lubricants, etc
TALLOT, -S *same as* ▸ **tallet**
TALLOW, -S *n, vb*
TALLOWY *adj* like tallow
TALLS ▸ **tall**
TALLY, TALLIED, TALLIES *vb, n*
TALLYHO *n* cry to encourage hounds when the quarry is sighted ▹ *vb* make the cry of tallyho
TALMA, -S *n* short cloak
TALMUD, -S *n*
TALON, -S *n*
TALONED ▸ **talon**
TALONS ▸ **talon**
TALOOKA *same as* ▸ **taluk**
TALPA, -E, -S *n* sebaceous cyst
TALUK, -S *n* subdivision of a district
TALUKA, -S *same as* ▸ **taluk**
TALUKS ▸ **taluk**
TALUS, TALI, -ES *n* bone of the ankle that articulates with the leg bones to form the ankle joint
TALWEG, -S *same as* ▸ **thalweg**
TAM, -S *n* type of hat
TAMABLE ▸ **tame**
TAMAL, -S *same as* ▸ **tamale**
TAMALE, -S *n* Mexican dish of minced meat wrapped in maize husks and steamed
TAMALS ▸ **tamal**
TAMANDU *same as* > **tamandua**
TAMANU, -S *n* poon tree
TAMARA, -S *n* powder consisting of cloves,

cinnamon, fennel, coriander, etc
TAMARAO *same as* ▸ **tamarau**
TAMARAS ▸ **tamara**
TAMARAU *n* small rare member of a cattle tribe in the Philippines
TAMARI, -S *n* Japanese variety of soy sauce
TAMARIN *n* small monkey of South and Central America
TAMARIS ▸ **tamari**
TAMASHA *n* (in India) a show
TAMBAC, -S *same as* ▸ **tombac**
TAMBAK, -S *same as* ▸ **tombac**
TAMBALA *n* unit of Malawian currency
TAMBER, -S *same as* ▸ **timbre**
TAMBOUR *n* embroidery frame consisting of two hoops ▹ *vb* embroider (fabric or a design) on a tambour
TAMBUR, -S *n* old Turkish stringed instrument
TAMBURA *n* Middle-Eastern stringed instrument with a long neck
TAMBURS ▸ **tambur**
TAME, -D, -S, -ST *adj, vb*
TAMEIN, -S *n* Burmese skirt
TAMELY ▸ **tame**
TAMER, -S ▸ **tame**
TAMES ▸ **tame**
TAMEST ▸ **tame**
TAMIN, -S *n* thin woollen fabric
TAMINE, -S *same as* ▸ **tamin**
TAMING, -S *n*
TAMINS ▸ **tamin**
TAMIS, -ES *same as* ▸ **tammy**
TAMISE *n* type of thin cloth
TAMISES ▸ **tamis**
TAMMAR, -S *n* small scrub wallaby
TAMMIE, -S *n* short for tam-o'shanter, a traditional Scottish hat
TAMMIED ▸ **tammy**
TAMMIES ▸ **tammie**
TAMMY, TAMMIED *n* glazed woollen or mixed fabric ▹ *vb* strain (sauce, soup, etc) through a tammy
TAMP, -ED, -S *vb*
TAMPALA *n* Asian plant, eaten as food
TAMPAN, -S *n* biting mite
TAMPED ▸ **tamp**
TAMPER, -S *vb, n*
TAMPING *adj* very angry ▹ *n* act or instance of tamping
TAMPION *n* plug placed in a gun's muzzle to keep out moisture and dust
TAMPON, -S *n, vb*
TAMPS ▸ **tamp**
TAMS ▸ **tam**
TAN, -NED, -NEST, -S *n, vb, adj*
TANA, -S *n* small Madagascan lemur
TANADAR *n* commanding officer of an Indian police station
TANAGER *n* American songbird with a short thick bill
TANAGRA *n* type of tanager
TANAS ▸ **tana**
TANBARK *n* bark of certain trees, esp the oak and hemlock, used as a source of tannin
TANDEM, -S *n*
TANDOOR *n* type of Indian clay oven
TANE *old Scottish variant of* ▸ **taken**
TANG, -ED, -ING, -S *n, vb*
TANGA, -S *n* triangular loincloth worn by indigenous peoples in tropical America
TANGED ▸ **tang**
TANGELO *n* hybrid produced by crossing a tangerine tree with a grapefruit tree
TANGENT *n*
TANGHIN *n* poison formerly used in Madagascar to determine the guilt of crime suspects
TANGI, -S *n* Māori funeral ceremony
TANGIE, -S *n* water spirit of Orkney, appearing as a figure draped in seaweed, or as a seahorse
TANGIER ▸ **tangy**
TANGIES ▸ **tangie**
TANGING ▸ **tang**
TANGIS ▸ **tangi**
TANGLE, -D, -S *n, vb*
TANGLER ▸ **tangle**
TANGLES ▸ **tangle**
TANGLY ▸ **tangle**

TANGO, -ED, -ES, -S *n, vb*
TANGRAM *n* type of Chinese puzzle
TANGS ▸ **tang**
TANGUN, -S *n* small and sturdy Tibetan pony
TANGY, TANGIER *adj*
TANH, -S *n* hyperbolic tangent
TANIST, -S *n* heir apparent of a Celtic chieftain
TANIWHA *n* mythical Māori monster that lives in water
TANK, -ED, -S *n, vb*
TANKA, -S *n* Japanese verse form consisting of five lines
TANKAGE *n* capacity or contents of a tank or tanks
TANKARD *n*
TANKAS ▸ **tanka**
TANKED ▸ **tank**
TANKER, -S *n, vb*
TANKFUL *n* quantity contained in a tank
TANKIA, -S *n* type of boat used in Canton
TANKIES ▸ **tanky**
TANKING *n*
TANKINI *n* swimming costume consisting of a camisole top and bikini briefs
TANKS ▸ **tank**
TANKY, TANKIES *n* die-hard communist
TANLING *n* suntanned person
TANNA, -S *n* Indian police station or army base
TANNAGE *n* act or process of tanning
TANNAH, -S *same as* ▸ **tanna**
TANNAS ▸ **tanna**
TANNATE *n* any salt or ester of tannic acid
TANNED ▸ **tan**
TANNER, -S ▸ **tan**
TANNERY *n*
TANNEST ▸ **tan**
TANNIC *adj* of, containing, or produced from tannin or tannic acid
TANNIE, -S *n* in S Africa, title of respect used to refer to an elderly woman
TANNIN, -S *n*
TANNING ▸ **tan**
TANNINS ▸ **tannin**
TANNISH ▸ **tan**
TANNOY, -S *n, vb*
TANREC, -S *same as* ▸ **tenrec**
TANS ▸ **tan**
TANSY, TANSIES *n* yellow-flowered plant
TANTARA *n* blast, as on a trumpet or horn
TANTI *adj* old word for worthwhile
TANTIES ▸ **tanty**
TANTIVY *adv* at full speed ▹ *n* hunting cry, esp at full gallop
TANTO, -S *adv* too much ▹ *n* type of Japanese sword
TANTONY *n* runt
TANTOS ▸ **tanto**
TANTRA, -S *n*
TANTRIC ▸ **tantra**
TANTRUM *n*
TANTY, TANTIES *n* tantrum
TANUKI, -S *n* animal similar to a raccoon, found in Japan
TANYARD *n* part of a tannery
TAO, -S *n* (in Confucian philosophy) the correct course of action
TAONGA, -S *n* New Zealand word meaning treasure
TAOS ▸ **tao**
TAP, -PED, -PING, -S *vb, n*
TAPA *n* inner bark of the paper mulberry
TAPALO, -S *n* Latin American scarf, often patterned and brightly coloured
TAPAS *pl n*
TAPE, -D, -S *n, vb*
TAPEN *adj* made of tape
TAPER, -ED, -S ▸ **tape**
TAPERER ▸ **tape**
TAPERS ▸ **taper**
TAPES ▸ **tape**
TAPET, -ED, -S *n* example of tapestry ▹ *vb* decorate with tapestries
TAPETA ▸ **tapetum**
TAPETAL ▸ **tapetum**
TAPETED ▸ **tapet**
TAPETI, -S *n* forest rabbit of Brazil
TAPETS ▸ **tapet**
TAPETUM, TAPETA *n* layer of nutritive cells that surrounds developing spore cells
TAPHOLE *n* hole in a furnace for running off molten metal or slag
TAPING, -S *n*
TAPIOCA *n*

TAPIR, -S *n*
TAPIS, -ES *n* tapestry or carpeting
TAPIST, -S *n* person who records printed matter in an audio format
TAPLASH *n* dregs of beer
TAPLESS *adj* without a tap
TAPPA, -S *same as* ▸ **tapa**
TAPPED ▸ **tap**
TAPPER, -S *n* person who taps
TAPPET, -S *n* short steel rod in an engine, transferring motion from one part to another
TAPPICE *vb* hide
TAPPING ▸ **tap**
TAPPIT *adj* crested; topped
TAPROOM *n*
TAPROOT *n* main root of a plant, growing straight down
TAPS ▸ **tap**
TAPSMAN, TAPSMEN *n* old word for a barman
TAPSTER *n* bartender
TAPSTRY *adj* relating to tapestry ▹ *n* taproom in a public house
TAPU, -ED, -ING, -S *adj* sacred ▹ *n* Māori religious or superstitious restriction on something ▹ *vb* put a tapu on something
TAR, -RED, -RING, -S *n, vb*
TARA, -S *same as* ▸ **taro**
TARAIRE *n* type of New Zealand tree
TARAMA, -S *n* cod roe
TARAMEA *n* variety of New Zealand speargrass
TARAND, -S *n* northern animal of legend, now supposed to have been the reindeer
TARAS ▸ **tara**
TARBOY, -S *n* boy who applies tar to the skin of sheep cut during shearing
TARBUSH *same as* ▸ **tarboosh**
TARCEL, -S *same as* ▸ **tercel**
TARDIED ▸ **tardy**
TARDIER ▸ **tardy**
TARDIES ▸ **tardy**
TARDILY ▸ **tardy**
TARDIVE *adj* tending to develop late
TARDO *adj* (of music) slow; to be played slowly
TARDY, TARDIED, TARDIER, TARDIES *adj, vb*
TARDYON *n* particle travelling more slowly than the speed of light
TARE, -D, -S, TARING, TARINGS *n, vb*
TARGA, -S *n* as in **targa top** denotes removable hard roof on a car
TARGE, -D, -S, TARGING *vb* interrogate
TARGET, -S *n, vb*
TARGING ▸ **targe**
TARIFF, -S *n, vb*
TARING ▸ **tare**
TARINGS ▸ **tare**
TARMAC, -S *same as* ▸ **macadam**
TARN, -S *n*
TARNAL *adj* damned ▹ *adv* extremely
TARNISH *vb, n*
TARNS ▸ **tarn**
TARO, -S *n* plant with a large edible rootstock
TAROC, -S *old variant of* ▸ **tarot**
TAROK, -S *old variant of* ▸ **tarot**
TAROS ▸ **taro**
TAROT, -S *n, adj*
TARP, -S *informal word for* ▸ **tarpaulin**
TARPAN, -S *n* European wild horse common in prehistoric times
TARPON, -S *n* large silvery clupeoid game fish found in warm Atlantic waters
TARPS ▸ **tarp**
TARRAS *same as* ▸ **trass**
TARRE, -S *vb* old word meaning to provoke or goad
TARRED ▸ **tar**
TARRES ▸ **tarre**
TARRIED ▸ **tarry**
TARRIER ▸ **tarry**
TARRIES ▸ **tarry**
TARRING ▸ **tar**
TARROCK *n* seabird
TARROW, -S *vb* exhibit reluctance
TARRY, TARRIED, TARRIES *vb, adj*
TARS ▸ **tar**
TARSAL, -S *adj, n*
TARSEAL *n* bitumen surface of a road
TARSEL, -S *same as* ▸ **tercel**

TARSI ▸ **tarsus**
TARSIA, -S *another term for* > **intarsia**
TARSIER *n* small nocturnal primate
TARSUS, TARSI *n* bones of the heel and ankle collectively
TART, -ED, -ER, -EST, -ING, -S *n* pie or flan with a sweet filling ▹ *adj* sharp or bitter ▹ *vb* (of food, drink, etc) become tart (sour)
TARTAN, -S *n*
TARTANA *n* small Mediterranean sailing boat
TARTANE *same as* ▸ **tartana**
TARTANS ▸ **tartan**
TARTAR, -S *n*
TARTARE *n* mayonnaise sauce mixed with hard-boiled egg yolks, herbs, etc
TARTARS ▸ **tartar**
TARTED ▸ **tart**
TARTER ▸ **tart**
TARTEST ▸ **tart**
TARTINE *n* slice of bread with butter or jam spread on it
TARTING ▸ **tart**
TARTISH ▸ **tart**
TARTLET *n*
TARTLY ▸ **tart**
TARTS ▸ **tart**
TARTUFE *same as* > **tartuffe**
TARTUFO, TARTUFI *n* Italian mousse-like chocolate dessert
TARWEED *n* resinous Californian plant
TARZAN, -S *n* man with great physical strength
TAS ▸ **ta**
TASAR, -S *same as* ▸ **tussore**
TASBIH, -S *n* form of Islamic prayer
TASE, -D, -S, TASING *vb* stun with a taser gun
TASER, -ED, -S *vb*
TASES ▸ **tase**
TASH, -ED, -ES, -ING *vb* stain or besmirch
TASING ▸ **tase**
TASK, -ED, -ING, -S *n, vb*
TASKBAR *n*
TASKED ▸ **task**
TASKER, -S ▸ **task**
TASKING ▸ **task**
TASKS ▸ **task**
TASLET, -S *same as* ▸ **tasset**
TASS *n* cup, goblet, or glass
TASSA, -S *n* type of Indian kettledrum
TASSE, -S *same as* ▸ **tasset**
TASSEL, -S *n, vb*
TASSELL *same as* ▸ **tassel**
TASSELS ▸ **tassel**
TASSELY *adj* decorated with tassels
TASSES ▸ **tasse**
TASSET, -S *n* piece of armour to protect the thigh
TASSIE, -S *same as* ▸ **tass**
TASSO, -S *n* spicy cured pork cut into strips
TASTE, -D, -S, TASTING *n, vb*
TASTER, -S *n* person employed to test the quality of food or drink by tasting it
TASTES ▸ **taste**
TASTIER ▸ **tasty**
TASTILY ▸ **tasty**
TASTING ▸ **taste**
TASTY, TASTIER *adj*
TAT, -S, -TED *n, vb*
TATAMI, -S *n* thick rectangular mat of woven straw
TATAR, -S *n* brutal person
TATE, -S *n* small tuft of fibre
TATER, -S *n* potato
TATES ▸ **tate**
TATH, -ED, -ING, -S *vb* (of cattle) to defecate
TATHATA *n* (in Buddhism) ultimate nature of things
TATHED ▸ **tath**
TATHING ▸ **tath**
TATHS ▸ **tath**
TATIE, -S *same as* ▸ **tattie**
TATLER, -S *old variant of* ▸ **tattler**
TATOU, -S *n* armadillo
TATOUAY *n* large armadillo of South America
TATOUS ▸ **tatou**
TATS ▸ **tat**
TATSOI, -S *n* variety of Chinese cabbage
TATT, -S *same as* ▸ **tat**
TATTED ▸ **tat**
TATTER, -S *vb*
TATTERY *adj* ragged
TATTIE, -S *Scot or dialect word for* ▸ **potato**
TATTIER ▸ **tatty**
TATTIES ▸ **tattie**
TATTILY ▸ **tatty**

TATTING ▶ **tat**
TATTLE, -D, -S *n, vb*
TATTLER *n* person who tattles
TATTLES ▶ **tattle**
TATTOO, -S *n, vb*
TATTOW, -S *old variant of* ▶ **tattoo**
TATTS ▶ **tatt**
TATTY, TATTIER *adj*
TATU, -ED, -ING, -S *old variant of* ▶ **tattoo**
TAU, -S *n* 19th letter in the Greek alphabet
TAUBE, -S *n* type of obsolete German aeroplane
TAUGHT ▶ **teach**
TAUHINU *New Zealand name for* ▶ **poplar**
TAUHOU, -S *same as* > **silvereye**
TAUIWI, -S *n* Māori term for the non-Māori people of New Zealand
TAULD *vb* old Scots variant of told
TAUNT, -ED, -S *vb, n, adj*
TAUNTER ▶ **taunt**
TAUNTS ▶ **taunt**
TAUON, -S *n* negatively charged elementary particle
TAUPATA *n* New Zealand shrub or tree
TAUPE, -S *adj, n*
TAUPIE, -S *same as* ▶ **tawpie**
TAUREAN *adj* born under or characteristic of Taurus
TAURIC *same as* ▶ **taurean**
TAURINE *adj* of, relating to, or resembling a bull ▷ *n* substance obtained from the bile of animals
TAUS ▶ **tau**
TAUT, -ED, -ER, -EST, -ING, -S *adj, vb*
TAUTAUG *same as* ▶ **tautog**
TAUTED ▶ **taut**
TAUTEN, -S *vb* make or become taut
TAUTER ▶ **taut**
TAUTEST ▶ **taut**
TAUTING ▶ **taut**
TAUTIT *adj* Scots word meaning tangled
TAUTLY ▶ **taut**
TAUTOG, -S *n* large dark-coloured wrasse, used as a food fish
TAUTS ▶ **taut**
TAV, -S *n* 23rd and last letter in the Hebrew alphabet
TAVA, -S *n* thick Indian frying pan
TAVAH, -S *variant of* ▶ **tava**
TAVAS ▶ **tava**
TAVER, -ED, -S *vb* wander about
TAVERN, -S *n*
TAVERNA *n* Greek restaurant
TAVERNS ▶ **tavern**
TAVERS ▶ **taver**
TAVERT *adj* bewildered or confused
TAVS ▶ **tav**
TAW, -ED, -ING, -INGS *vb* convert skins into leather
TAWA, -S *n* tall timber tree from New Zealand
TAWAI, -S *n* New Zealand beech
TAWAS ▶ **tawa**
TAWDRY *adj, n*
TAWED ▶ **taw**
TAWER, -S ▶ **taw**
TAWERY *n* place where tawing is carried out
TAWHAI, -S *same as* ▶ **tawai**
TAWHIRI *n* small New Zealand tree with wavy green glossy leaves
TAWIE, -R, -ST *adj* easily persuaded or managed
TAWING ▶ **taw**
TAWINGS ▶ **taw**
TAWNEY, -S *same as* ▶ **tawny**
TAWNIER ▶ **tawny**
TAWNIES ▶ **tawny**
TAWNILY ▶ **tawny**
TAWNY, TAWNIER, TAWNIES *adj, n*
TAWPIE, -S *n* Scottish word for a foolish young woman
TAWS *same as* ▶ **tawse**
TAWSE, -D, -S, TAWSING *n* leather strap with one end cut into thongs ▷ *vb* punish (someone) with or as if with a tawse
TAWT, -ED, -IER, -ING, -S *same as* ▶ **taut**
TAWTIE ▶ **tawt**
TAWTIER ▶ **tawt**
TAWTING ▶ **tawt**
TAWTS ▶ **tawt**
TAX, -ED, -ES, -INGS *n, vb*
TAXA ▶ **taxon**
TAXABLE *adj, n*
TAXABLY ▶ **taxable**
TAXED ▶ **tax**
TAXEME, -S *n* any element of speech that

may differentiate meaning
TAXEMIC ▸ **taxeme**
TAXER, -S ▸ **tax**
TAXES ▸ **tax**
TAXI, -ED, -ES, -ING, TAXYING *n, vb*
TAXICAB *same as* ▸ **taxi**
TAXIED ▸ **taxi**
TAXIES ▸ **taxi**
TAXIING ▸ **taxi**
TAXIMAN, TAXIMEN *n* taxi driver
TAXING *adj*
TAXINGS ▸ **tax**
TAXIS, -ES *n* movement of a cell or organism in response to an external stimulus
TAXITE, -S *n* type of volcanic rock
TAXITIC ▸ **taxite**
TAXIWAY *n* marked path along which aircraft taxi to or from a runway, parking area, etc
TAXLESS ▸ **tax**
TAXMAN, TAXMEN *n*
TAXOL, -S *n* trademarked anti-cancer drug
TAXON, TAXA, -S *n* any taxonomic group or rank
TAXOR, -S ▸ **tax**
TAXPAID *adj* having had the applicable tax paid already
TAXUS *n* genus of conifers
TAXWISE *adv* regarding tax
TAXYING ▸ **taxi**
TAY, -S *Irish dialect word for* ▸ **tea**
TAYRA, -S *n* large arboreal mammal of Central and South America
TAYS ▸ **tay**
TAZZA, -S, TAZZE *n* cup with a shallow bowl and a circular foot
TCHICK, -S *vb* make a clicking noise with the tongue
TE, -S *n* (in tonic sol-fa) seventh degree of any major scale
TEA, -ED, -ING, -S *n, vb*
TEABAG, -S *n*
TEABOWL *n* small bowl used (instead of a teacup) for serving tea
TEABOX *n* box for storing tea
TEACAKE *n*
TEACART *n* trolley from which tea is served
TEACH, TAUGHT, -ES *vb*
TEACHER *n*
TEACHES ▸ **teach**
TEACHIE *old form of* ▸ **tetchy**
TEACUP, -S *n*
TEAD, -S *old word for* ▸ **torch**
TEADE, -S *same as* ▸ **tead**
TEADS ▸ **tead**
TEAED ▸ **tea**
TEAGLE, -D, -S *vb* raise or hoist using a tackle
TEAING ▸ **tea**
TEAK, -S *n*
TEAL, -S *n*
TEALIKE *adj* resembling tea
TEALS ▸ **teal**
TEAM, -ED, -S *n, vb*
TEAMER, -S ▸ **team**
TEAMING ▸ **team**
TEAMS ▸ **team**
TEAPOT, -S *n*
TEAPOY, -S *n* small table or stand with a tripod base
TEAR, -ED, -ING, -S, TORN *n, vb*
TEARER, -S ▸ **tear**
TEARFUL *adj*
TEARGAS *n, vb*
TEARIER ▸ **teary**
TEARILY ▸ **teary**
TEARING ▸ **tear**
TEAROOM *same as* ▸ **teashop**
TEARS ▸ **tear**
TEARY, TEARIER *adj*
TEAS ▸ **tea**
TEASE, -D, -S *vb, n*
TEASEL, -S *n* plant with prickly leaves and flowers ▹ *vb* tease (a fabric)
TEASER, -S *n*
TEASES ▸ **tease**
TEASHOP *n*
TEASING ▸ **tease**
TEAT, -S *n*
TEATED ▸ **teat**
TEATIME *n*
TEATS ▸ **teat**
TEAWARE *n* implements for brewing and serving tea
TEAZE, -D, -S, TEAZING *old variant of* ▸ **tease**
TEAZEL, -S *same as* ▸ **teasel**
TEAZES ▸ **teaze**
TEAZING ▸ **teaze**
TEAZLE, -D, -S *same as* ▸ **teasel**
TEBBAD, -S *n* sandstorm

TEC, -S *short for* > **detective**
TECH, -S *n*
TECHED *adj* slightly mad
TECHIE, -S *n, adj*
TECHIER ▸ **techy**
TECHIES ▸ **techie**
TECHILY ▸ **techy**
TECHNIC *another word for* > **technique**
TECHNO, -S *n*
TECHS ▸ **tech**
TECHY, TECHIER *same as* ▸ **techie**
TECKEL, -S *n* dachshund
TECS ▸ **tec**
TECTA ▸ **tectum**
TECTAL ▸ **tectum**
TECTITE *same as* ▸ **tektite**
TECTRIX *n* small feather on a bird's wing or tail
TECTUM, TECTA, -S *n* any roof-like structure in the body
TED, -DED, -DING, -S *vb* shake out (hay), so as to dry it
TEDDER, -S *n* machine equipped with a series of small rotating forks for tedding hay
TEDDIE *same as* ▸ **teddy**
TEDDIES ▸ **teddy**
TEDDING ▸ **ted**
TEDDY, TEDDIES *n*
TEDIER ▸ **tedy**
TEDIEST ▸ **tedy**
TEDIOUS *adj*
TEDIUM, -S *n*
TEDS ▸ **ted**
TEDY, TEDIER, TEDIEST *same as* ▸ **tedious**
TEE, -D, -ING, -S *n, vb*
TEEK *adj* in Indian English, well
TEEL, -S *same as* ▸ **sesame**
TEEM, -ED, -ING, -S *vb*
TEEMER, -S ▸ **teem**
TEEMFUL ▸ **teem**
TEEMING ▸ **teem**
TEEMS ▸ **teem**
TEEN, -ED, -ING, -S *n* teenager ▹ *vb* set alight
TEENAGE *adj, n*
TEEND, -ED, -S *same as* ▸ **tind**
TEENDOM *n* state of being a teenager
TEENDS ▸ **teend**
TEENE, -S *n* affliction or woe
TEENED ▸ **teen**
TEENER, -S ▸ **teen**
TEENES ▸ **teene**
TEENFUL *adj* troublesome or harmful
TEENIER ▸ **teeny**
TEENING ▸ **teen**
TEENS ▸ **teen**
TEENSY *same as* ▸ **teeny**
TEENTSY *same as* ▸ **teeny**
TEENTY *same as* ▸ **teeny**
TEENY, TEENIER *adj*
TEEPEE, -S *same as* ▸ **tepee**
TEER, -ED, -ING, -S *vb* smear; daub
TEES ▸ **tee**
TEETER, -S *vb*
TEETH ▸ **tooth**
TEETHE, -D, -S *vb*
TEETHER *n*
TEETHES ▸ **teethe**
TEEVEE, -S *n*
TEF, -S *n* annual grass, of NE Africa, grown for its grain
TEFF, -S *same as* ▸ **tef**
TEFLON, -S *n*
TEFS ▸ **tef**
TEG, -S *n* two-year-old sheep
TEGG, -S *same as* ▸ **teg**
TEGMEN, TEGMINA *n* either of the leathery forewings of the cockroach and related insects
TEGS ▸ **teg**
TEGU, -S *n* large South American lizard
TEGUA, -S *n* type of moccasin
TEGULA, -E *n* one of a pair of coverings of the forewings of certain insects
TEGULAR *adj* of, relating to, or resembling a tile or tiles
TEGUMEN *same as* ▸ **tegmen**
TEGUS ▸ **tegu**
TEHR, -S *same as* ▸ **tahr**
TEHSIL, -S *n* administrative region in some S Asian countries
TEIID, -S *n* member of the Teiidae family of lizards
TEIL, -S *n* lime tree
TEIN, -S *n* monetary unit of Kazakhstan
TEIND, -ED, -S *Scot and northern English word for* ▸ **tithe**
TEINS ▸ **tein**

TEKKIE, -S *variant of* ▸ **techie**
TEKTITE *n* small dark glassy object found in several areas around the world
TEL, -S *same as* ▸ **tell**
TELA, -E *n* any delicate tissue or weblike structure
TELAMON *n* column in the form of a male figure
TELARY *adj* capable of spinning a web
TELCO, -S *n* telecommunications company
TELD *same as* ▸ **tauld**
TELE, -S *same as* ▸ **telly**
TELECOM *n*
TELECON *n* (short for) teleconference
TELEDU, -S *n* badger of SE Asia and Indonesia
TELEFAX *another word for* ▸ **fax**
TELEGA, -S *n* rough four-wheeled cart used in Russia
TELEMAN, TELEMEN *n* noncommissioned officer in the US navy
TELEOST *n* bony fish with rayed fins and a swim bladder ▹ *adj* of, relating to, or belonging to this type of fish
TELEPIC *n* feature-length film made for television
TELERAN *n* electronic navigational aid
TELERGY *n* name for the form of energy supposedly transferred during telepathy
TELES ▸ **tele**
TELESIS, TELESES *n* purposeful use of natural and social processes to obtain specific social goals
TELESM, -S *n* talisman
TELETEX *n* international means of communicating text between a variety of terminals
TELEX, -ED, -ES *n, vb*
TELFER, -S *n* overhead transport system
TELFORD *n* road built using a method favoured by Thomas Telford
TELIA ▸ **telium**
TELIAL ▸ **telium**
TELIC *adj* directed or moving towards some goal
TELIUM, TELIA *n* spore-producing body of some rust fungi in which the teliospores are formed
TELL, -ING, -S, TOLD *vb, n*
TELLAR, -S *same as* ▸ **tiller**
TELLEN, -S *same as* ▸ **tellin**
TELLER, -S *n, vb*
TELLIES ▸ **telly**
TELLIN, -S *n* slim marine bivalve molluscs that live in intertidal sand
TELLING ▸ **tell**
TELLINS ▸ **tellin**
TELLS ▸ **tell**
TELLUS *n* earth
TELLY, TELLIES, -S *n*
TELNET, -S *n* system allowing remote access to other computers on the same network ▹ *vb* use a telnet system
TELOGEN *n* phase of hair growth
TELOI ▸ **telos**
TELOME, -S *n* fundamental unit of a plant's structure
TELOMIC ▸ **telome**
TELOS, TELOI *n* objective; ultimate purpose
TELPHER *same as* ▸ **telferage**
TELS ▸ **tel**
TELSON, -S *n* segment of the body of crustaceans and arachnids
TELT *same as* ▸ **tauld**
TEMBLOR *n* earthquake or earth tremor
TEME, -D, -S *old variant of* ▸ **team**
TEMENOS, TEMENE *n* sacred area, esp one surrounding a temple
TEMES ▸ **teme**
TEMP, -ED, -S *vb*
TEMPEH, -S *n* fermented soya beans
TEMPER, -S *n, vb*
TEMPERA *n* painting medium for powdered pigments
TEMPERS ▸ **temper**
TEMPEST *n, vb*
TEMPI ▸ **tempo**
TEMPING *n*

TEMPLAR *n*
TEMPLE, -S *n*
TEMPLED ▸ **temple**
TEMPLES ▸ **temple**
TEMPLET *same as* > **template**
TEMPO, TEMPI, -S *n*
TEMPORE *adv*
TEMPOS ▸ **tempo**
TEMPS ▸ **temp**
TEMPT, -ED, -S *vb*
TEMPTER ▸ **tempt**
TEMPTS ▸ **tempt**
TEMPURA *n*
TEMS *same as* ▸ **temse**
TEMSE, -D, -S, TEMSING *vb* sieve
TEN, -S *n*
TENABLE *adj*
TENABLY ▸ **tenable**
TENACE, -S *n* holding of two nonconsecutive high cards of a suit, such as the ace and queen
TENAIL, -S *same as* > **tenaille**
TENANCY *n*
TENANT, -S *n, vb*
TENCH, -ES *n* freshwater game fish of the carp family
TEND, -ED, -ING, -S *vb*
TENDENZ *same as* > **tendency**
TENDER, -S *adj, vb, n*
TENDING ▸ **tend**
TENDON, -S *n*
TENDRE, -S *n* care
TENDRIL *n*
TENDRON *n* shoot
TENDS ▸ **tend**
TENDU, -S *n* position in ballet
TENE, -S *same as* ▸ **teen**
TENENDA > **tenendum**
TENES ▸ **tene**
TENESI *n* monetary unit of Turkmenistan
TENET, -S *n*
TENFOLD *n*
TENGE, -S *n* standard monetary unit of Kazakhstan
TENIA, -E, -S *same as* ▸ **taenia**
TENIOID ▸ **tenia**
TENNE, -S *n* tawny colour
TENNER, -S *n*
TENNES ▸ **tenne**
TENNESI *same as* ▸ **tenesi**
TENNIES ▸ **tenny**
TENNIS *n*
TENNIST *n* tennis player
TENNO, -S *n* formal title of the Japanese emperor
TENNY, TENNIES *same as* ▸ **tenne**
TENON, -ED, -S *n* projecting end on a piece of wood fitting into a slot in another ▹ *vb* form a tenon on (a piece of wood)
TENONER ▸ **tenon**
TENONS ▸ **tenon**
TENOR, -S *n, adj*
TENOUR, -S *old variant of* ▸ **tenor**
TENPIN, -S *n*
TENREC, -S *n* small mammal resembling hedgehogs or shrews
TENS ▸ **ten**
TENSE, -D, -R, -S, -ST, TENSING *adj, vb, n*
TENSELY ▸ **tense**
TENSER ▸ **tense**
TENSES ▸ **tense**
TENSEST ▸ **tense**
TENSILE *adj*
TENSING ▸ **tense**
TENSION *n, vb*
TENSITY *rare word for* ▸ **tension**
TENSIVE *adj* of or causing tension or strain
TENSON, -S *n* type of French lyric poem
TENSOR, -S *n*
TENT, -ING, -S *n, vb*
TENTAGE *n* tents collectively
TENTED ▸ **tent**
TENTER, -S ▸ **tent**
TENTFUL *n* number of people or objects that can fit in a tent
TENTH, -S *n, adj*
TENTHLY *adv* in the tenth place or position
TENTHS ▸ **tenth**
TENTIE, -R *adj* wary
TENTING ▸ **tent**
TENTS ▸ **tent**
TENTY *same as* ▸ **tentie**
TENUE *n* deportment
TENUIS, TENUES *n* (in the grammar of classical Greek) any of the voiceless stops
TENUITY ▸ **tenuous**
TENUOUS *adj*
TENURE, -S *n, vb*
TENURED *adj*
TENURES ▸ **tenure**
TENUTO, TENUTI, -S *adv* (of a note) to be held for or beyond its full time value ▹ *n* note sustained thus
TENZON, -S *same as* ▸ **tenson**

TEOPAN, -S *n* enclosure surrounding a teocalli
TEPA, -S *n* type of tree native to South America
TEPACHE *n* type of Mexican soft drink
TEPAL, -S *n* subdivisions of a perianth
TEPAS ▸ **tepa**
TEPEE, -S *n* cone-shaped tent, formerly used by Native Americans
TEPEFY *vb* make or become tepid
TEPHRA, -S *n* solid matter ejected during a volcanic eruption
TEPID, -ER *adj*
TEPIDLY ▸ **tepid**
TEPOY, -S *same as* ▸ **teapoy**
TEQUILA *n*
TERAI, -S *n* felt hat with a wide brim worn in subtropical regions
TERAOHM *n* unit of resistance
TERAPH *n* household god or image venerated by ancient Semitic peoples
TERAS, TERATA *n* monstrosity; teratism
TERBIA, -S *n* amorphous white insoluble powder
TERBIC ▸ **terbium**
TERBIUM *n* rare metallic element
TERCE, -S *n* third of the seven canonical hours of the divine office
TERCEL, -S *n* male falcon or hawk, esp as used in falconry
TERCES ▸ **terce**
TERCET, -S *n* group of three lines of verse that rhyme together
TERCIO, -S *n* regiment of Spanish or Italian infantry
TEREBIC *adj* as in **terebic acid** white crystalline carboxylic acid produced by the action of nitric acid on turpentine
TEREBRA *n* ancient Roman device used for boring holes in defensive walls
TEREDO, -S *n* marine mollusc that bores into and destroys submerged timber
TEREFA *same as* ▸ **tref**
TEREFAH *same as* ▸ **tref**
TEREK, -S *n* type of sandpiper
TERES, -ES, TERETES *n* shoulder muscle
TERETE *adj* (esp of plant parts) smooth and usually cylindrical and tapering
TERETES ▸ **teres**
TERF, -S *old variant of* ▸ **turf**
TERFE, -S *old variant of* ▸ **turf**
TERFS ▸ **terf**
TERGA ▸ **tergum**
TERGAL ▸ **tergum**
TERGITE *n* constituent part of a tergum
TERGUM, TERGA *n* cuticular plate covering the dorsal surface of a body segment of an arthropod
TERM, -ED, -ING, -S *n, vb*
TERMER, -S *same as* ▸ **termor**
TERMING ▸ **term**
TERMINI > **terminus**
TERMITE *n*
TERMLY *n* publication issued once a term
TERMOR, -S *n* person who holds an estate for a term of years or until he or she dies
TERMS ▸ **term**
TERN, -S *n* gull-like sea bird with a forked tail and pointed wings
TERNAL ▸ **tern**
TERNARY *adj, n*
TERNATE *adj* (esp of a leaf) consisting of three leaflets or other parts
TERNE, -D, -S, TERNING *n* alloy of lead containing tin and antimony ▹ *vb* coat with this alloy
TERNION *n* group of three
TERNS ▸ **tern**
TERPENE *n* unsaturated hydrocarbon found in the essential oils of many plants
TERPINE *n* type of expectorant
TERRA, -E *n* (in legal contexts) earth or land
TERRACE *n, vb*
TERRAE ▸ **terra**
TERRAIN *same as* ▸ **terrane**
TERRANE *n* series of rock formations
TERRAS *same as* ▸ **trass**

TERREEN *old variant of* ▸ **tureen**
TERRENE *adj* of or relating to the earth ▹ *n* land
TERRET, -S *n* ring on a harness saddle through which the reins are passed
TERRIER *n*
TERRIES ▸ **terry**
TERRIFY *vb*
TERRINE *n* earthenware dish with a lid
TERRIT, -S *same as* ▸ **terret**
TERROIR *n* combination of factors that gives a wine its distinctive character
TERROR, -S *n*
TERRY, TERRIES *n* fabric with small loops covering both sides
TERSE, -R, -ST *adj*
TERSELY ▸ **terse**
TERSER ▸ **terse**
TERSEST ▸ **terse**
TERSION *n* action of rubbing off or wiping
TERTIA, -S *same as* ▸ **tercio**
TERTIAL *same as* > **tertiary**
TERTIAN *adj* (of a fever or the symptoms of a disease) occurring every other day ▹ *n* tertian fever or symptoms
TERTIAS ▸ **tertia**
TERTIUM *adj* as in **tertium quid** unknown or indefinite thing related in some way to two known or definite things, but distinct from both
TERTIUS *n* third (in a group)
TERTS *n* card game using 32 cards
TES ▸ **te**
TESLA, -S *n* derived SI unit of magnetic flux density
TESSERA *n* small square tile used in mosaics
TEST, -ED, -S *vb, n*
TESTA, -E *n* hard outer layer of a seed
TESTACY ▸ **testate**
TESTAE ▸ **testa**
TESTATA > **testatum**
TESTATE *adj* having left a valid will ▹ *n* person who dies and leaves a legally valid will
TESTE *n* witness
TESTED ▸ **test**
TESTEE, -S *n* person subjected to a test
TESTER, -S *n*
TESTERN *vb* give (someone) a teston
TESTERS ▸ **tester**
TESTES ▸ **testis**
TESTIER ▸ **testy**
TESTIFY *vb*
TESTILY ▸ **testy**
TESTING ▸ **test**
TESTIS, TESTES *same as* > **testicle**
TESTON, -S *n* French silver coin of the 16th century
TESTOON *same as* ▸ **teston**
TESTRIL *same as* > **testrill**
TESTS ▸ **test**
TESTUDO *n* protective cover used by the ancient Roman army
TESTY, TESTIER *adj*
TET, -S *same as* ▸ **teth**
TETANAL ▸ **tetanus**
TETANIC *adj* of, relating to, or producing tetanus ▹ *n* tetanic drug or agent
TETANUS *n*
TETANY *n* abnormal increase in the excitability of nerves and muscles
TETCHED *same as* ▸ **teched**
TETCHY *adj*
TETE, -S *n* elaborate hairstyle
TETH, -S *n* ninth letter of the Hebrew alphabet
TETHER, -S *n, vb*
TETHS ▸ **teth**
TETOTUM *same as* > **teetotum**
TETRA, -S *n*
TETRACT *n* sponge spicule with four rays
TETRAD, -S *n* group or series of four
TETRAS ▸ **tetra**
TETRI, -S *n* currency unit of Georgia
TETRODE *n* electronic valve having four electrodes
TETROSE *n* type of sugar
TETRYL, -S *n* yellow crystalline explosive solid used in detonators
TETS ▸ **tet**

TETTER, -S *n* blister or pimple ▷ *vb* cause a tetter to erupt (on)
TETTIX *n* cicada
TEUCH, -ER *Scots variant of* ▸ **tough**
TEUCHAT *Scots variant of* ▸ **tewit**
TEUCHER ▸ **teuch**
TEUGH, -ER *same as* ▸ **teuch**
TEUGHLY ▸ **teugh**
TEW, -ED, -ING, -S *vb* work hard
TEWART, -S *same as* ▸ **tuart**
TEWED ▸ **tew**
TEWEL, -S *n* horse's rectum
TEWHIT, -S *same as* ▸ **tewit**
TEWING ▸ **tew**
TEWIT, -S *n* lapwing
TEWS ▸ **tew**
TEX, -ES *n* unit of weight used to measure yarn density
TEXAS, -ES *n* structure on the upper deck of a paddle-steamer
TEXES ▸ **tex**
TEXT, -ED, -ING, -S *n, vb*
TEXTER, -S *n* person who communicates by text messaging
TEXTILE *n, adj*
TEXTING ▸ **text**
TEXTISM *n* word typically used in a text message
TEXTS ▸ **text**
TEXTUAL *adj*
TEXTURE *n, vb*
THACK, -ED, -S *Scots word for* ▸ **thatch**
THAE *Scots word for* ▸ **those**
THAGI, -S *same as* ▸ **thuggee**
THAIM *Scots variant of* ▸ **them**
THAIRM, -S *n* catgut
THALAMI > **thalamus**
THALE *n* as in **thale cress** cruciferous wall plant
THALER, -S *n* former German, Austrian, or Swiss silver coin
THALI, -S *n* Indian meal consisting of several small dishes
THALIAN *adj* of or relating to comedy
THALIS ▸ **thali**
THALLI ▸ **thallus**
THALLIC *adj* of or containing thallium
THALLUS, THALLI *n* undifferentiated vegetative body of algae, fungi, and lichens
THALWEG *n* longitudinal outline of a riverbed from source to mouth
THAN, -S *prep, n*
THANA, -S *same as* ▸ **tana**
THANAGE *n* state of being a thane
THANAH, -S *same as* ▸ **tana**
THANAS ▸ **thana**
THANE, -S *n* Anglo-Saxon or medieval Scottish nobleman
THANG, -S *n* thing
THANGKA *n* (in Tibetan Buddhism) a religious painting on a scroll
THANGS ▸ **thang**
THANK, -ED *vb*
THANKEE *interj* thank you
THANKER ▸ **thank**
THANKIT *adj* as in **be thankit** thank God
THANKS *pl n, interj*
THANNA, -S *same as* ▸ **tana**
THANNAH *same as* ▸ **tana**
THANNAS ▸ **thanna**
THANS ▸ **than**
THANX *interj* informal spelling of 'thanks'
THAR, -S *same as* ▸ **tahr**
THARM, -S *n* stomach
THARS ▸ **thar**
THAT *pron*
THATCH *n, vb*
THATCHT *old variant of* > **thatched**
THATCHY ▸ **thatch**
THAW, -ED, -ING, -S *vb, n*
THAWER, -S ▸ **thaw**
THAWIER ▸ **thawy**
THAWING ▸ **thaw**
THAWS ▸ **thaw**
THAWY, THAWIER *adj* tending to thaw
THE *determiner*
THEATER *same as* ▸ **theatre**
THEATRE *n*
THEAVE, -S *n* young ewe
THEBE, -S *n* monetary unit of Botswana
THECA, -E *n* enclosing organ, cell, or spore case
THECAL ▸ **theca**
THECATE ▸ **theca**
THEE, -D, -ING, -S *pron, vb*

THEEK, -ED, -S *Scots variant of* ▸ **thatch**
THEELIN *trade name for* ▸ **estrone**
THEELOL *n* estriol
THEES ▸ **thee**
THEFT, -S *n*
THEGN, -S *same as* ▸ **thane**
THEGNLY *adj* like a thegn
THEGNS ▸ **thegn**
THEIC, -S *n* person who drinks excessive amounts of tea
THEIN, -S *old variant of* ▸ **thane**
THEINE, -S *another name for* > **caffeine**
THEINS ▸ **thein**
THEIR *determiner*
THEIRS *pron*
THEISM, -S *n* belief in a God or gods
THEIST, -S ▸ **theism**
THELF, THELVES *n* old contraction of 'the elf'
THEM *pron*
THEMA, -TA *n*
THEME, -D, -S, THEMING *n, vb*
THEN, -S *adv, pron, adj, n*
THENAGE *old variant of* ▸ **thanage**
THENAL *adj* of or relating to the thenar
THENAR, -S *n* palm of the hand ▹ *adj* of or relating to the palm or the region at the base of the thumb
THENCE *adv*
THENS ▸ **then**
THEOCON *n* person who believes that religion should play a greater role in politics
THEOLOG *same as* > **theologue**
THEORBO *n* obsolete form of the lute, having two necks
THEOREM *n*
THEORIC *n* theory; conjecture
THEORY *n*
THEOW, -S *n* slave in Anglo-Saxon Britain
THERAPY *n*
THERE, -S *adv, n*
THEREAT *adv*
THEREBY *adv*
THEREIN *adv*
THEREOF *adv*
THEREON *archaic word for* > **thereupon**
THERES ▸ **there**
THERETO *adv*
THERIAC *n* ointment or potion used as an antidote to a poison
THERIAN *n* animal of the class Theria, a subclass of mammals
THERM, -S *n* unit of measurement of heat
THERMAE *pl n* public baths or hot springs, esp in ancient Greece or Rome
THERMAL *adj, n*
THERME, -S *old variant of* ▸ **therm**
THERMEL *n* type of thermometer using thermoelectric current
THERMES ▸ **therme**
THERMIC *same as* ▸ **thermal**
THERMIT *variant of* > **thermite**
THERMOS *n*
THERMS ▸ **therm**
THEROID *adj* of, relating to, or resembling a beast
THESE *determiner*
THESIS, THESES *n*
THESP, -S *short for* > **thespian**
THETA, -S *n*
THETCH *old variant spelling of* ▸ **thatch**
THETE, -S *n* member of the lowest order of freeman in ancient Athens
THETHER *old variant of* ▸ **thither**
THETIC *adj* (in classical prosody) of, bearing, or relating to a metrical stress
THETRI, -S *n* currency unit of Georgia
THEURGY *n* intervention of a divine or supernatural agency in the affairs of human beings
THEW, -ES, -S *n*
THEWED *adj* strong; muscular
THEWES ▸ **thew**
THEWIER ▸ **thewy**
THEWS ▸ **thew**
THEWY, THEWIER ▸ **thew**
THEY *pron*
THIAMIN *same as* > **thiamine**
THIASUS *n* people gathered to sing and dance in honour of a god
THIAZIN *same as* > **thiazine**
THIAZOL *same as* > **thiazole**

THIBET, -S *n* coloured woollen cloth
THIBLE, -S *n* stick for stirring porridge
THICK, -ED, -ER, -S *adj, vb*
THICKEN *vb*
THICKER ▸ **thick**
THICKET *n*
THICKIE *same as* ▸ **thicko**
THICKLY ▸ **thick**
THICKO, -S *n* insulting word for a stupid person
THICKS ▸ **thick**
THICKY *same as* ▸ **thicko**
THIEF *n*
THIEVE, -D, -S *vb*
THIG, -GED, -S *vb* beg
THIGGER ▸ **thig**
THIGGIT *Scots inflection of* ▸ **thig**
THIGH, -S *n*
THIGHED *adj* having thighs
THIGHS ▸ **thigh**
THIGS ▸ **thig**
THILK *pron* that same
THILL, -S *another word for* ▸ **shaft**
THILLER *n* horse that goes between the thills of a cart
THILLS ▸ **thill**
THIMBLE *n, vb*
THIN, -NED, -S *adj, vb, adv*
THINE *adj, pron*
THING, -S *n*
THINGO, -S *n* thing the name of which is temporarily forgotten
THINGS ▸ **thing**
THINGY *adj, n*
THINK, -S *vb*
THINKER ▸ **think**
THINKS ▸ **think**
THINLY ▸ **thin**
THINNED ▸ **thin**
THINNER ▸ **thin**
THINS ▸ **thin**
THIO *adj* of, or relating to, sulphur
THIOL, -S *n* any of a class of sulphur-containing organic compounds
THIOLIC ▸ **thiol**
THIOLS ▸ **thiol**
THIONIC *adj* of, relating to, or containing sulphur
THIONIN *same as* > **thionine**
THIONYL *n* the divalent group SO
THIR *Scots word for* ▸ **these**
THIRAM, -S *n* antifungal agent
THIRD, -ED, -S *adj, n, vb*
THIRDLY *adv* in the third place or position
THIRDS ▸ **third**
THIRL, -ED, -S *vb* bore or drill
THIRST, -S *n, vb*
THIRSTY *adj*
THIRTY *n*
THIS *pron, adj*
THISTLE *n*
THISTLY ▸ **thistle**
THITHER *adv*
THIVEL, -S *same as* ▸ **thible**
THO *short for* ▸ **though**
THOFT, -S *n* bench (in a boat) upon which a rower sits
THOLE, -D, -S, THOLING *n* wooden pin set in the side of a rowing boat to serve as a fulcrum for rowing ▹ *vb* bear or put up with
THOLI ▸ **tholus**
THOLING ▸ **thole**
THOLOS, THOLOI *n* beehive-shaped tomb associated with Mycenaean Greece
THOLUS, THOLI *n* domed tomb
THON *Scot word for* ▸ **yon**
THONDER *Scot word for* ▸ **yonder**
THONG, -S *n, vb*
THONGED *adj* fastened with a thong
THONGS ▸ **thong**
THONGY *adj* resembling a thong
THORAX *n*
THORIA, -S *n* insoluble white powder
THORIC ▸ **thorium**
THORITE *n* yellow, brownish, or black radioactive mineral
THORIUM *n* radioactive metallic element
THORN, -ED, -S *n, vb*
THORNY *adj*
THORO *(nonstandard) variant spelling of* > **thorough**
THORON, -S *n* radioisotope of radon that is a decay product of thorium
THORP, -S *n* small village
THORPE, -S *same as* ▸ **thorp**

THORPS ▸ **thorp**
THOSE *determiner*
THOTHER *pron* old contraction of *the other*
THOU, -ED, -ING, -S *pron, n, vb*
THOUGH *adv*
THOUGHT *n* concept or opinion
THOUING ▸ **thou**
THOUS ▸ **thou**
THOWEL, -S *old variant of* ▸ **thole**
THOWL, -S *old variant of* ▸ **thole**
THRAE *same as* ▸ **frae**
THRALL, -S *n, vb*
THRANG, -S *n* throng ▹ *vb* throng ▹ *adj* crowded
THRASH *vb, n*
THRASHY *adj* relating to thrash punk
THRAVE, -S *n* twenty-four sheaves of corn
THRAW, -ED, -S *vb* twist (something); make something thrawn
THRAWN *adj* crooked or twisted
THRAWS ▸ **thraw**
THREAD *n, vb*
THREADS *slang word for* ▸ **clothes**
THREADY *adj* of, relating to, or resembling a thread or threads
THREAP, -S *vb* scold
THREAT, -S *n* declaration of intent to harm
THREAVE *same as* ▸ **thrave**
THREE, -S *n*
THREEP, -S *same as* ▸ **threap**
THREES ▸ **three**
THRENE, -S *n* dirge; threnody
THRENOS *n* threnody; lamentation
THRESH *vb, n*
THRETTY *nonstandard variant of* ▸ **thirty**
THREW ▸ **throw**
THRICE *adv*
THRID, -S *old variant of* ▸ **thread**
THRIFT, -S *n*
THRIFTY *adj*
THRILL, -S *n, vb*
THRILLY *adj* causing thrills
THRIMSA *same as* ▸ **thrymsa**
THRIP *same as* ▸ **thrips**
THRIPS *n* small slender-bodied insect with piercing mouthparts that feeds on plant sap
THRIST, -S *old variant of* ▸ **thirst**
THRISTY ▸ **thrist**
THRIVE, -D, -N, -S, THROVE *vb*
THRIVER ▸ **thrive**
THRIVES ▸ **thrive**
THRO *same as* ▸ **through**
THROAT, -S *n, vb*
THROATY *adj*
THROB, -S *vb, n*
THROE, -D *n, vb*
THROES *pl n*
THROMBI > **thrombus**
THRONE, -D, -S *n, vb*
THRONG, -S *vb, n, adj*
THROUGH *prep, adj*
THROVE ▸ **thrive**
THROW, THREW, -N, -S *vb, n*
THROWE, -S *old variant of* ▸ **throe**
THROWER ▸ **throw**
THROWES ▸ **throwe**
THROWN ▸ **throw**
THROWS ▸ **throw**
THRU *same as* ▸ **through**
THRUM, -S *vb, n*
THRUMMY *adj* made of thrums
THRUMS ▸ **thrum**
THRUPUT *n* quantity of raw material or information processed in a given period
THRUSH *n*
THRUST, -S *vb, n*
THRUTCH *n* narrow, fast-moving stream ▹ *vb* thrust
THRUWAY *n* thoroughfare
THRYMSA *n* gold coin used in Anglo-Saxon England
THUD, -DED, -S *n, vb*
THUG, -S *n*
THUGGEE *n* (formerly) the methods of thugs in India
THUGGO, -S *n* tough and violent person
THUGS ▸ **thug**
THUJA, -S *n* coniferous tree of North America and East Asia
THULIA, -S *n* oxide of thulium
THULITE *n* rose-coloured zoisite sometimes incorporated into jewellery

THULIUM *n* malleable ductile silvery-grey element
THUMB, -ED, -S *n, vb*
THUMBY *adj* clumsy; uncoordinated
THUMP, -ED, -S *n, vb*
THUMPER ▸ **thump**
THUMPS ▸ **thump**
THUNDER *n, vb*
THUNK, -ED, -S *another word for* ▸ **thud**
THURIFY *vb* burn incense near or before an altar, shrine, etc
THURL, -S *same as* ▸ **thirl**
THUS, -ES *adv, n*
THUSLY *adv*
THUYA, -S *same as* ▸ **thuja**
THWACK, -S *n, vb, interj*
THWAITE *n* piece of land cleared from forest or reclaimed from wasteland
THWART, -S *vb, n, adj, adv*
THY *adj, determiner*
THYINE *adj* of relating to the sandarac tree
THYLOSE *old variant of* ▸ **tylosis**
THYME, -S *n*
THYMEY ▸ **thyme**
THYMI ▸ **thymus**
THYMIC *adj* of or relating to the thymus
THYMIER ▸ **thymy**
THYMINE *n* white crystalline pyrimidine base found in DNA
THYMOL, -S *n* substance obtained from thyme
THYMOMA *n* type of tumour
THYMUS, THYMI *n* small gland at the base of the neck
THYMY, THYMIER ▸ **thyme**
THYROID *n, adj*
THYRSE, -S *n* type of inflorescence, occurring in the lilac and grape
THYRSUS, THYRSI *same as* ▸ **thyrse**
THYSELF *pron*
TI, -S *same as* ▸ **te**
TIAN, -S *n* traditional French vegetable stew or earthenware dish it is cooked in
TIAR, -S *same as* ▸ **tiara**
TIARA, -S *n*
TIARAED ▸ **tiara**
TIARAS ▸ **tiara**
TIARS ▸ **tiar**
TIBIA, -E, -S *n*
TIBIAL ▸ **tibia**
TIBIAS ▸ **tibia**
TIC, -CED, -CING, -S *n, vb*
TICAL, -S *n* former standard monetary unit of Thailand
TICCA *adj* acquired for temporary use in exchange for payment
TICCED ▸ **tic**
TICCING ▸ **tic**
TICE, -D, -S, TICING *vb* tempt or allure; entice
TICH, -ES *same as* ▸ **titch**
TICHY, TICHIER *same as* ▸ **titchy**
TICING ▸ **tice**
TICK, -ED, -S *n, vb*
TICKEN, -S *same as* ▸ **ticking**
TICKER, -S *n*
TICKET *n, vb*
TICKETS *pl n*
TICKEY, -S *n* former South African threepenny piece
TICKIES ▸ **ticky**
TICKING *n*
TICKLE, -D, -S *vb, n*
TICKLER *n*
TICKLES ▸ **tickle**
TICKLY ▸ **tickle**
TICKS ▸ **tick**
TICKY, TICKIES *same as* ▸ **tickey**
TICS ▸ **tic**
TICTAC, -S *same as* > **ticktack**
TICTOC, -S *same as* > **ticktock**
TID, -S *n*
TIDAL *adj*
TIDALLY ▸ **tidal**
TIDBIT, -S *same as* ▸ **titbit**
TIDDIER ▸ **tiddy**
TIDDIES ▸ **tiddy**
TIDDLE, -D, -S *vb*
TIDDLER *n*
TIDDLES ▸ **tiddle**
TIDDLEY *same as* ▸ **tiddly**
TIDDLY *adj, n*
TIDDY, TIDDIER, TIDDIES *n* four of trumps in the card game gleek
TIDE, -D, -S, TIDING *n, vb*
TIDERIP *same as* ▸ **riptide**
TIDES ▸ **tide**
TIDEWAY *n* strong tidal current or its channel, esp the tidal part of a river
TIDIED ▸ **tidy**
TIDIER ▸ **tidy**
TIDIERS ▸ **tidy**

TIDIES ▸ **tidy**
TIDIEST ▸ **tidy**
TIDILY ▸ **tidy**
TIDING ▸ **tide**
TIDINGS *pl n*
TIDS ▸ **tid**
TIDY, TIDIED, TIDIER, TIDIERS, TIDIES, TIDIEST, -ING *adj, vb, n*
TIE, -D, -S, TYING *vb, n*
TIEBACK *n* length of cord, ribbon, or other fabric used for tying a curtain to one side
TIED ▸ **tie**
TIEING *same as* ▸ **tie**
TIELESS ▸ **tie**
TIEPIN, -S *n* ornamental pin used to pin the two ends of a tie to a shirt
TIER, -ED, -ING, -S *n, vb*
TIERCE, -S *same as* ▸ **terce**
TIERCED *adj* (of a shield) divided into three sections of similar size but different colour
TIERCEL *same as* ▸ **tercel**
TIERCES ▸ **tierce**
TIERCET *same as* ▸ **tercet**
TIERED ▸ **tier**
TIERING ▸ **tier**
TIERS ▸ **tier**
TIES ▸ **tie**
TIETAC, -S *n* fastener for holding a tie in place
TIETACK *same as* ▸ **tietac**
TIETACS ▸ **tietac**
TIFF, -ED, -ING, -S *n* petty quarrel ▹ *vb* have or be in a tiff
TIFFANY *n* sheer fine gauzy fabric
TIFFED ▸ **tiff**
TIFFIN, -S *n, vb*
TIFFING ▸ **tiff**
TIFFINS ▸ **tiffin**
TIFFS ▸ **tiff**
TIFO, -S *n* organized fan display during a football match
TIFOSO, TIFOSI, -S *n* (in sport) a fanatical fan
TIFT, -ED, -ING, -S *Scots variant of* ▸ **tiff**
TIG, -GED, -GING, -S *n*
TIGE, -S *n* trunk of an architectural column
TIGER, -S *n*
TIGERLY *adj* of or like a tiger
TIGERS ▸ **tiger**
TIGERY *adj* like a tiger
TIGES ▸ **tige**
TIGGED ▸ **tig**
TIGGER, -S *vb* damage beyond repair by tinkering
TIGGING ▸ **tig**
TIGHT, -ER *adj, adv*
TIGHTEN *vb*
TIGHTER ▸ **tight**
TIGHTLY ▸ **tight**
TIGHTS *pl n*
TIGLIC *adj* as in **tiglic acid** syrupy liquid or crystalline colourless unsaturated carboxylic acid
TIGLON, -S *same as* ▸ **tigon**
TIGNON, -S *n* type of cloth headdress
TIGON, -S *n* hybrid offspring of a male tiger and a female lion
TIGRESS *n*
TIGRINE *adj* of, characteristic of, or resembling a tiger
TIGRISH ▸ **tiger**
TIGROID *adj* resembling a tiger
TIGS ▸ **tig**
TIKA, -S *same as* ▸ **tikka**
TIKANGA *n* Māori ways or customs
TIKAS ▸ **tika**
TIKE, -S *same as* ▸ **tyke**
TIKI, -ED, -ING, -S *n* small carving of a grotesque person worn as a pendant ▹ *vb* take a scenic tour around an area
TIKKA, -S *adj, n*
TIL, -S *another name for* ▸ **sesame**
TILAK, -S *n* coloured spot or mark worn by Hindus
TILAPIA *n* type of fish
TILBURY *n* light two-wheeled horse-drawn open carriage
TILDE, -S *n* mark used in Spanish to indicate pronunciation
TILE, -D, -S *n, vb*
TILER, -S ▸ **tile**
TILERY *n* place where tiles are produced
TILES ▸ **tile**
TILING, -S *n*
TILL, -ED, -ING, -S *prep, vb, n*
TILLAGE *n* act, process, or art of tilling
TILLED ▸ **till**
TILLER, -S *n, vb*
TILLIER ▸ **tilly**
TILLING ▸ **till**

TILLITE *n* rock formed from hardened till
TILLS ▸ **till**
TILLY, TILLIER ▸ **till**
TILS ▸ **til**
TILT, -ED, -ING, -S *vb, n*
TILTER, -S ▸ **tilt**
TILTH, -S *n* (condition of) land that has been tilled
TILTING ▸ **tilt**
TILTS ▸ **tilt**
TIMARAU *same as* ▸ **tamarau**
TIMBAL, -S *n* type of kettledrum
TIMBALE *n* mixture of meat, fish, etc, in a rich sauce
TIMBALS ▸ **timbal**
TIMBER, -S *n, adj, vb, interj*
TIMBERY *adj* like timber
TIMBO, -S *n* Amazonian vine from which a useful insecticide can be derived
TIMBRAL *adj* relating to timbre
TIMBRE, -S *n*
TIMBREL *n* tambourine
TIMBRES ▸ **timbre**
TIME, -D, -S *n, vb*
TIMELY *adj, adv*
TIMEOUS *adj* in good time
TIMEOUT *n*
TIMER, -S *n*
TIMES ▸ **time**
TIMID, -ER *adj*
TIMIDLY ▸ **timid**
TIMING, -S *n*
TIMIST, -S *n* one concerned with time
TIMOLOL *n* relaxant medicine used (for example) to reduce blood pressure
TIMON, -S *n* apparatus by which a vessel is steered
TIMOTHY *n* perennial grass of temperate regions
TIMOUS *same as* ▸ **timeous**
TIMPANA *n* traditional Maltese baked pasta and pastry dish
TIMPANI *pl n*
TIMPANO *n* kettledrum
TIMPS *same as* ▸ **timpani**
TIN, -NED, -NING, -S *n, vb*
TINAJA, -S *n* large jar for cooling water
TINAMOU *n* type of bird of Central and S America
TINCAL, -S *another name for* ▸ **borax**
TINCHEL *n* in Scotland, a circle of deer hunters who gradually close in on their quarry
TINCT, -ED, -S *vb* tint ▹ *adj* tinted or coloured
TIND, -ED, -ING, -S *vb* set alight
TINDAL, -S *n* petty officer
TINDED ▸ **tind**
TINDER, -S *n*
TINDERY *adj* like tinder
TINDING ▸ **tind**
TINDS ▸ **tind**
TINE, -S, TINING *n, vb*
TINEA, -S *n* any fungal skin disease, esp ringworm
TINEAL ▸ **tinea**
TINEAS ▸ **tinea**
TINED ▸ **tine**
TINEID, -S *n* type of moth of the family which includes the clothes moths
TINES ▸ **tine**
TINFOIL *n*
TINFUL, -S *n* contents of a tin or the amount a tin will hold
TING, -S *same as* ▸ **thing**
TINGE, -D, -S, TINGING *n, vb*
TINGLE, -D, -S *n, vb*
TINGLER ▸ **tingle**
TINGLES ▸ **tingle**
TINGLY ▸ **tingle**
TINGS ▸ **ting**
TINHORN *n* cheap pretentious person ▹ *adj* cheap and showy
TINIER ▸ **tiny**
TINIES *pl n* small children
TINIEST ▸ **tiny**
TINILY ▸ **tiny**
TINING ▸ **tine**
TINK, -ED, -ING, -S *vb* make short sound like a bell
TINKER, -S *n, vb*
TINKING ▸ **tink**
TINKLE, -D, -S *vb, n*
TINKLER *same as* ▸ **tinker**
TINKLES ▸ **tinkle**
TINKLY ▸ **tinkle**
TINKS ▸ **tink**
TINLIKE ▸ **tin**
TINMAN, TINMEN *n* one who works with tin or tin plate
TINNED ▸ **tin**
TINNER, -S *n* tin miner

TINNIE *same as* ▸ **tinny**
TINNIER ▸ **tinny**
TINNIES ▸ **tinny**
TINNILY ▸ **tinny**
TINNING ▸ **tin**
TINNY, TINNIER, TINNIES *adj, n*
TINPOT, -S *adj* worthless or unimportant ▷ *n* pot made of tin
TINS ▸ **tin**
TINSEL, -S *n, adj, vb*
TINSELY *adj* (US) like tinsel
TINSEY, -S *old variant of* ▸ **tinsel**
TINT, -ED, -ING, -S *n, vb*
TINTACK *n* tin-plated tack
TINTED ▸ **tint**
TINTER, -S ▸ **tint**
TINTIER ▸ **tinty**
TINTING ▸ **tint**
TINTS ▸ **tint**
TINTY, TINTIER *adj* having many tints
TINTYPE *another name for* ▸ **ferrotype**
TINWARE *n* objects made of tin plate
TINWORK *n* objects made of tin
TINY, TINIER, TINIEST *adj*
TIP, -PED, -PING, -S, -T *n, vb*
TIPCART *n* cart that can be tipped to empty out its contents
TIPCAT, -S *n* game in which a piece of wood is tipped in the air with a stick
TIPI, -S *variant spelling of* ▸ **tepee**
TIPLESS ▸ **tip**
TIPOFF, -S *n*
TIPPED ▸ **tip**
TIPPEE, -S *n* person who receives a tip, esp regarding share prices
TIPPER, -S *n*
TIPPET, -S *n* fur cape for the shoulders
TIPPIER ▸ **tippy**
TIPPING ▸ **tip**
TIPPLE, -D, -S *vb, n*
TIPPLER ▸ **tipple**
TIPPLES ▸ **tipple**
TIPPY, TIPPIER *adj* extremely fashionable or stylish
TIPS ▸ **tip**
TIPSIER ▸ **tipsy**
TIPSIFY *vb* make tipsy
TIPSILY ▸ **tipsy**
TIPSTER *n* person who sells tips about races
TIPSY, TIPSIER *adj*
TIPT ▸ **tip**
TIPTOE, -D, -S *vb*
TIPTOP, -S *adj, n*
TIPULA, -S *n* crane fly
TIPUNA, -S *n* ancestor
TIRADE, -S *n*
TIRAGE, -S *n* drawing of wine from a barrel prior to bottling
TIRASSE *n* mechanism in an organ connecting two pedals
TIRE, -S *vb*
TIRED, -ER *adj*
TIREDLY ▸ **tired**
TIRES ▸ **tire**
TIRING, -S ▸ **tire**
TIRITI, -S *n* another name for the Treaty of Waitangi

A Māori word for treaty. Any 6-letter word that lets you get rid of three Is can't be bad!

TIRL, -ED, -ING, -S *vb* turn
TIRO, -ES, -S *same as* ▸ **tyro**
TIRONIC *variant of* ▸ **tyronic**
TIROS ▸ **tiro**
TIRR, -ED, -ING, -S *vb* strip or denude
TIRRIT, -S *n* panic; scare
TIRRS ▸ **tirr**
TIS ▸ **ti**
TISANE, -S *n* infusion of dried or fresh leaves or flowers
TISICK, -S *n* splutter; cough
TISSUAL *adj* relating to tissue
TISSUE, -D, -S *n, vb*
TISSUEY *adj* like tissue
TISWAS *n* state of anxiety or excitement
TIT, -S, -TED, -TING *n, vb*
TITAN, -S *n*
TITANIA *n* titanium dioxide
TITANIC *adj*
TITANIS *n* large predatory flightless prehistoric bird
TITANS ▸ **titan**
TITBIT, -S *n*
TITCH, -ES *n* small person
TITCHIE *same as* ▸ **titchy**
TITCHY *adj*
TITE *adj* immediate
TITELY *adv* immediately
TITER, -S *same as* ▸ **titre**

TITFER, -S *n* hat
TITHE, -D, -S, TITHING *n, vb*
TITHER, -S ▸ **tithe**
TITHES ▸ **tithe**
TITHING ▸ **tithe**
TITI, -S *n* small omnivorous monkey
TITIAN, -S *n* reddish gold colour
TITIS ▸ **titi**
TITLARK *another name for* ▸ **pipit**
TITLE, -S, TITLING *n, vb*
TITLED *adj*
TITLER, -S *n* one who writes titles
TITLES ▸ **title**
TITLIKE *adj* like a tit
TITLING ▸ **title**
TITLIST *n* titleholder
TITMAN, TITMEN *n* (of pigs) the runt of a litter
TITMICE > **titmouse**
TITMOSE *old spelling of* > **titmouse**
TITOKI, -S *n* New Zealand evergreen tree with a spreading crown and glossy green leaves
TITRANT *n* solution in a titration that is added to a measured quantity of another solution
TITRATE *vb* measure the volume or concentration of (a solution) by titration
TITRE, -S *n* concentration of a solution as determined by titration
TITS ▸ **tit**
TITTED ▸ **tit**
TITTER, -S *vb, n*
TITTIE, -S *n*
TITTING ▸ **tit**
TITTISH *adj* testy
TITTLE, -D, -S *n, vb*
TITTUP, -S *vb* prance or frolic ▹ *n* caper
TITTUPY *adj* sprightly; lively
TITTY *same as* ▸ **tittie**
TITULAR *adj, n*
TITULE, -D, -S *same as* ▸ **title**
TITULUS, TITULI *n* sign attached to the top of the cross during crucifixion
TITUP, -ED, -S *same as* ▸ **tittup**
TITUPY *same as* ▸ **tittupy**
TIVY *same as* ▸ **tantivy**
TIX *pl n* tickets

> **Tix** is an informal word for **tickets** and one of the key short words for using the X.

TIYIN, -S *n* monetary unit of Uzbekistan and Kyrgyzstan
TIYN, -S *same as* ▸ **tiyin**
TIZ, -ES *n* state of confusion
TIZWAS *same as* ▸ **tiswas**
TIZZ, -ES *same as* ▸ **tizzy**
TIZZY, TIZZIES *n* confused or agitated state
TMESIS, TMESES *n* interpolation of a word between the parts of a compound word
TO *prep, adv*
TOAD, -S *n*
TOADIED ▸ **toady**
TOADIES ▸ **toady**
TOADISH ▸ **toad**
TOADLET *n* small toad
TOADS ▸ **toad**
TOADY, TOADIED, TOADIES *n, vb*
TOAST, -ED, -S *n, vb*
TOASTER ▸ **toast**
TOASTIE *same as* ▸ **toasty**
TOASTS ▸ **toast**
TOASTY *n, adj*
TOAZE, -D, -S, TOAZING *variant spelling of* ▸ **toze**
TOBACCO *n*
TOBY, TOBIES *n* water stopcock at the boundary of a street and house section
TOC, -S *n* in communications code, signal for letter t
TOCCATA, TOCCATE *n* rapid piece of music for a keyboard instrument
TOCHER, -S *n* dowry ▹ *vb* give a dowry to
TOCK, -ED, -ING, -S *n* sound made by a clock ▹ *vb* (of a clock) make such a sound
TOCKIER ▸ **tocky**
TOCKING ▸ **tock**
TOCKS ▸ **tock**
TOCKY, TOCKIER *adj* muddy
TOCO, -S *n* punishment
TOCS ▸ **toc**
TOCSIN, -S *n* warning signal
TOD, -DED, -DING, -S *n* unit of weight, used for wool, etc ▹ *vb* produce a tod
TODAY, -S *n, adv*
TODDE, -S *same as* ▸ **tod**

TODDED ▶ **tod**
TODDES ▶ **todde**
TODDIES ▶ **toddy**
TODDING ▶ **tod**
TODDLE, -D, -S *vb, n*
TODDLER *n*
TODDLES ▶ **toddle**
TODDY, TODDIES *n*
TODIES ▶ **tody**
TODS ▶ **tod**
TODY, TODIES *n* small bird of the Caribbean
TOE, -D, -ING, -S *n, vb*
TOEA, -S *n* monetary unit of Papua New Guinea

This monetary unit of Papua New Guinea is very often played to rid the rack of a surplus of vowels.

TOEBIE, -S *n* South African slang for sandwich
TOECAP, -S *n* strengthened covering for the toe of a shoe
TOECLIP *n* clip on a bicycle pedal for the toes
TOED ▶ **toe**
TOEHOLD *n*
TOEIER ▶ **toey**

This is the comparative of **toey**, Australian slang for nervous or edgy, and can come in useful for dumping a surplus of vowels.

TOEIEST ▶ **toey**
TOEING ▶ **toe**
TOELESS *adj* not having toes
TOELIKE ▶ **toe**
TOENAIL *n, vb*
TOERAG, -S *n* contemptible person
TOES ▶ **toe**
TOESHOE *n* ballet pump with padded toes
TOETOE, -S *same as* ▶ **toitoi**
TOEY, TOEIER, TOEIEST *adj* (of a person) nervous or anxious
TOFF *n*
TOFFEE, -S *n*
TOFFIER ▶ **toffy**
TOFFIES ▶ **toffy**
TOFFISH *adj* belonging to or characteristic of the upper class
TOFFS *adj*
TOFFY, TOFFIER, TOFFIES *same as* ▶ **toffee**
TOFORE *prep* before
TOFT, -S *n* homestead
TOFU, -S *n*
TOFUTTI *n* tradename for nondairy, soya-based food products
TOG, -GED, -GING, -S *n, vb*
TOGA, -E, -S *n, vb*
TOGAED ▶ **toga**
TOGAS ▶ **toga**
TOGATE *adj* clad in a toga
TOGATED *same as* ▶ **togate**
TOGE, -S *old variant of* ▶ **toga**
TOGED ▶ **toge**
TOGES ▶ **toge**
TOGGED ▶ **tog**
TOGGER, -S *vb* play football ▷ *n* football player
TOGGERY *n* clothes
TOGGING ▶ **tog**
TOGGLE, -D, -S *n, vb*
TOGGLER ▶ **toggle**
TOGGLES ▶ **toggle**
TOGROG, -S *n* unit of currency in Mongolia
TOGS ▶ **tog**
TOGUE, -S *n* large North American freshwater game fish
TOHEROA *n* large edible mollusc of New Zealand
TOHO, -S *n* (to a hunting dog) an instruction to stop
TOHUNGA *n* Māori priest
TOIL, -ED, -ING, -S *n, vb*
TOILE, -S *n* transparent linen or cotton fabric
TOILED ▶ **toil**
TOILER, -S ▶ **toil**
TOILES ▶ **toile**
TOILET, -S *n, vb*
TOILFUL *same as* > **toilsome**
TOILING ▶ **toil**
TOILS ▶ **toil**
TOING, -S *n* as in **toing and froing** state of going back and forth
TOISE, -S *n* obsolete French unit of length roughly equal to 2 metres
TOISECH *same as* > **toiseach**
TOISES ▶ **toise**
TOISON, -S *n* fleece
TOIT, -ED, -ING, -S *vb* walk or move in an unsteady manner, as from old age

TOITOI, -S *n* tall grasses with feathery fronds
TOITS ▶ **toit**
TOKAMAK *n* reactor used in thermonuclear experiments
TOKAY, -S *n* small gecko of S and SE Asia, having a retractile claw at the tip of each digit
TOKEN, -ED, -S *n* sign or symbol ▷ *adj* nominal or slight ▷ *vb* act as a symbol
TOKO, -S *same as* ▶ **toco**
TOKOMAK *variant spelling of* ▶ **tokamak**
TOKOS ▶ **toko**
TOLA, -S *n* unit of weight, used in India
TOLAN, -S *n* white crystalline derivative of acetylene
TOLANE, -S *same as* ▶ **tolan**
TOLANS ▶ **tolan**
TOLAR, -JI, -S *n* former monetary unit of Slovenia
TOLAS ▶ **tola**
TOLD ▶ **tell**
TOLE, -D, -S, TOLING, TOLINGS *same as* ▶ **toll**
TOLEDO, -S *n* type of sword originally made in Toledo
TOLES ▶ **tole**
TOLIDIN *same as* > **tolidine**
TOLING ▶ **tole**
TOLINGS ▶ **tole**
TOLL, -ED, -ING, -S *vb*, *n*
TOLLAGE *same as* ▶ **toll**
TOLLBAR *n* bar blocking passage of a thoroughfare, raised on payment of a toll
TOLLED ▶ **toll**
TOLLER, -S ▶ **toll**
TOLLEY, -S *n* large shooting marble used in a game of marbles
TOLLIE *same as* ▶ **tolly**
TOLLIES ▶ **tolly**
TOLLING ▶ **toll**
TOLLMAN, TOLLMEN *n* man who collects tolls
TOLLS ▶ **toll**
TOLLWAY *n*
TOLLY, TOLLIES *n* castrated calf
TOLSEL, -S *n* tolbooth
TOLSEY, -S *n* tolbooth
TOLT, -S *n* type of obsolete English writ
TOLTER, -S *vb* struggle or move with difficulty, as in mud
TOLTS ▶ **tolt**
TOLU, -S *n* sweet-smelling balsam obtained from a South American tree
TOLUATE *n* any salt or ester of any of the three isomeric forms of toluic acid
TOLUENE *n* colourless volatile flammable liquid obtained from petroleum and coal tar
TOLUIC *adj* as in **toluic acid** white crystalline derivative of toluene
TOLUID, -S *n* white crystalline derivative of glycocoll
TOLUIDE *variant of* ▶ **toluid**
TOLUIDS ▶ **toluid**
TOLUOL, -S *another name for* ▶ **toluene**
TOLUOLE *another name for* ▶ **toluene**
TOLUOLS ▶ **toluol**
TOLUS ▶ **tolu**
TOLUYL, -S *n* any of three groups derived from a toluic acid
TOLYL, -S *n* type of monovalent radical
TOLZEY, -S *n* tolbooth
TOM, -S *n* male cat ▷ *adj* (of an animal) male
TOMAN, -S *n* gold coin formerly issued in Persia
TOMATO *n*
TOMB, -ED, -ING, -S *n*, *vb*
TOMBAC, -S *n* any of various brittle alloys containing copper and zinc
TOMBACK *variant spelling of* ▶ **tombac**
TOMBACS ▶ **tombac**
TOMBAK, -S *same as* ▶ **tombac**
TOMBAL *adj* like or relating to a tomb
TOMBED ▶ **tomb**
TOMBIC *adj* of or relating to tombs
TOMBING ▶ **tomb**
TOMBOC, -S *n* weapon
TOMBOLA *n*
TOMBOLO *n* narrow bar linking a small island with another island or the mainland
TOMBOY, -S *n*
TOMBS ▶ **tomb**
TOMCAT, -S *n*
TOMCOD, -S *n* small fish resembling the cod
TOME, -S *n*

TOMENTA > **tomentum**
TOMES ▶ **tome**
TOMFOOL *n, vb*
TOMIA ▶ **tomium**
TOMIAL ▶ **tomium**
TOMIUM, TOMIA *n* sharp edge of a bird's beak
TOMMY, TOMMIED, TOMMIES *n* private in the British Army ▷ *vb* (formerly) to exploit workers by paying them in goods rather than in money
TOMO, -S *n* shaft formed by the action of water on limestone or volcanic rock
TOMPION *same as* ▶ **tampion**
TOMPON, -S *same as* ▶ **tampon**
TOMPOT *adj* as in **tompot blenny** variety of blenny with tentacles over its eyes
TOMS ▶ **tom**
TOMTIT, -S *n* small European bird that eats insects and seeds
TON, -S *n*
TONAL *adj*
TONALLY ▶ **tonal**
TONANT *adj* very loud
TONDI ▶ **tondo**
TONDINO, TONDINI *n* small tondo
TONDO, TONDI, -S *n* circular easel painting or relief carving
TONE, -D, -S, TONING, TONINGS *n, vb*
TONEARM *same as* ▶ **pickup**
TONED ▶ **tone**
TONEME, -S *n* phoneme that is distinguished from another phoneme only by its tone
TONEMIC ▶ **toneme**
TONEPAD *n* keypad used to transmit information
TONER, -S *n*
TONES ▶ **tone**
TONETIC *adj* (of a language) distinguishing words by tone as well as by other sounds
TONETTE *n* small musical instrument resembling a recorder
TONEY *variant spelling of* ▶ **tony**
TONG, -ED, -ING *vb, n*
TONGA, -S *n* light two-wheeled vehicle used in rural areas of India
TONGED ▶ **tong**
TONGER, -S *n* one who uses tongs to gather oysters
TONGING ▶ **tong**
TONGMAN, TONGMEN *another word for* ▶ **tonger**
TONGS *pl n*
TONGUE, -D, -S *n, vb*
TONIC, -S *n, adj*
TONIER ▶ **tony**
TONIES ▶ **tony**
TONIEST ▶ **tony**
TONIFY *vb* give tone to
TONIGHT *n, adv*
TONING ▶ **tone**
TONINGS ▶ **tone**
TONISH *adj* stylish or fashionable
TONITE, -S *n*
TONK, -ED, -ING, -S *vb* strike with a heavy blow
TONKA *n* as in **tonka bean** tall leguminous tree of tropical America
TONKED ▶ **tonk**
TONKER, -S ▶ **tonk**
TONKING ▶ **tonk**
TONKS ▶ **tonk**
TONLET, -S *n* skirt of a suit of armour, consisting of overlapping metal bands
TONNAG, -S *n* type of (usually tartan) shawl
TONNAGE *n*
TONNAGS ▶ **tonnag**
TONNE, -S *same as* ▶ **ton**
TONNEAU *n* detachable cover to protect the rear part of an open car
TONNELL *old spelling of* ▶ **tunnel**
TONNER, -S *n* something that weighs one ton
TONNES ▶ **tonne**
TONNISH *adj* stylish or fashionable
TONS ▶ **ton**
TONSIL, -S *n*
TONSOR, -S *n* barber
TONSURE *n* shaving of all or the top of the head as a religious or monastic practice ▷ *vb* shave the head of
TONTINE *n* type of annuity scheme
TONUS, -ES *n* normal tension of a muscle at rest

TONY, TONIER, TONIES, TONIEST *adj* stylish or distinctive ▷ *n* stylish or distinctive person
TOO *adv*
TOOART, -S *variant spelling of* ▸ **tuart**
TOODLE, -D, -S *vb*
TOOK ▸ **take**
TOOL, -ED, -S *n, vb*
TOOLBAG *n* bag for storing or carrying tools
TOOLBAR *n*
TOOLBOX *n*
TOOLED ▸ **tool**
TOOLER, -S ▸ **tool**
TOOLIE, -S *n* adult who gatecrashes social events for school leavers
TOOLING *n* any decorative work done with a tool
TOOLKIT *n*
TOOLMAN, TOOLMEN *n* person who works with tools
TOOLS ▸ **tool**
TOOLSET *n*
TOOLTIP *n* temporary window containing information about a tool on a computer application
TOOM, -ED, -EST, -ING, -S *vb* empty (something) ▷ *adj* empty
TOOMER ▸ **toom**
TOOMEST ▸ **toom**
TOOMING ▸ **toom**
TOOMS ▸ **toom**
TOON, -S *n*
TOONIE, -S *n* Canadian two-dollar coin
TOONS ▸ **toon**
TOORIE, -S *n* tassel or bobble on a bonnet
TOOSHIE *adj*
TOOT, -ED, -ING *n, vb*
TOOTER, -S ▸ **toot**
TOOTH, TEETH, -S *n*
TOOTHED *adj* having a tooth or teeth
TOOTHS ▸ **tooth**
TOOTHY *adj*
TOOTING ▸ **toot**
TOOTLE, -D, -S *vb, n*
TOOTLER ▸ **tootle**
TOOTLES ▸ **tootle**
TOOTS, -ED, -ES *Scots version of* ▸ **tut**
TOOTSIE *same as* ▸ **tootsy**
TOOTSY *n*
TOP, -PED, -S *n, adj, vb*
TOPARCH *n* ruler of a small state or realm
TOPAZ, -ES *n*
TOPCOAT *n* overcoat
TOPE, -D, -S, TOPING *vb* drink alcohol regularly ▷ *n* small European shark
TOPEE, -S *n* lightweight hat worn in tropical countries
TOPEK, -S *same as* ▸ **tupik**
TOPER, -S ▸ **tope**
TOPES ▸ **tope**
TOPFUL *variant spelling of* ▸ **topfull**
TOPFULL *adj* full to the top
TOPH, -S *n* variety of sandstone
TOPHE, -S *variant spelling of* ▸ **toph**
TOPHI ▸ **tophus**
TOPHS ▸ **toph**
TOPHUS, TOPHI *n* deposit of sodium urate in the helix of the ear or surrounding a joint
TOPI, -S *same as* ▸ **topee**
TOPIARY *n, adj*
TOPIC, -S *n*
TOPICAL *adj, n*
TOPICS ▸ **topic**
TOPING ▸ **tope**
TOPIS ▸ **topi**
TOPKICK *n* (formerly) sergeant
TOPKNOT *n* crest, tuft, decorative bow, etc, on the top of the head
TOPLESS *adj*
TOPLINE *vb* headline; be the main focus of a newspaper story
TOPMAN, TOPMEN *n* sailor positioned in the rigging of the topsail
TOPMAST *n* mast next above a lower mast on a sailing vessel
TOPMEN ▸ **topman**
TOPMOST *adj*
TOPO *n* picture of a mountain with details of climbing routes superimposed on it
TOPOI ▸ **topos**
TOPONYM *n*
TOPOS, TOPOI *n* basic theme or concept
TOPPED ▸ **top**
TOPPER, -S *n*
TOPPIER ▸ **toppy**
TOPPING ▸ **top**
TOPPLE, -D, -S *vb*
TOPPY, TOPPIER *adj* (of audio reproduction) having too many high-frequency sounds

TOPRAIL *n* top rail on something such as a piece of furniture
TOPS ▸ **top**
TOPSAIL *n*
TOPSIDE *n*
TOPSMAN, TOPSMEN *n* chief drover
TOPSOIL *n* surface layer of soil ▹ *vb* spread topsoil on (land)
TOPSPIN *n* spin imparted to make a ball bounce or travel exceptionally far, high, or quickly
TOPWORK *vb* graft shoots or twigs onto the main branches of (a tree)
TOQUE, -S *same as* ▸ **tuque**
TOQUET, -S *same as* ▸ **toque**
TOR, -S *n* high rocky hill
TORA, -S *variant spelling of* ▸ **torah**
TORAH, -S, TOROT, TOROTH *n*
TORAN, -S *n* (in Indian architecture) an archway
TORANA, -S *same as* ▸ **toran**
TORANS ▸ **toran**
TORAS ▸ **tora**
TORC, -S *same as* ▸ **torque**
TORCH, -ED, -ES *n, vb*
TORCHER ▸ **torch**
TORCHES ▸ **torch**
TORCHON *n* coarse linen or cotton lace with a simple openwork pattern
TORCHY *adj* sentimental; maudlin; characteristic of a torch song
TORCS ▸ **torc**
TORDION *n* old triple-time dance for two people
TORE, -S *same as* ▸ **torus**
TORERO, -S *n* bullfighter, esp one on foot
TORES ▸ **tore**
TORGOCH *n* type of char
TORI ▸ **torus**
TORIC, -S *adj* of, relating to, or having the form of a torus
TORIES ▸ **tory**
TORII *n* gateway, esp one at the entrance to a Japanese Shinto temple
TORMENT *vb, n*
TORMINA *pl n* severe stomach pains
TORN ▸ **tear**
TORNADE *same as* ▸ **tornado**
TORNADO *n*
TORO, -S *n* bull
TOROID, -S *n* surface generated by rotating a closed plane curve about a coplanar line that does not intersect it
TOROS ▸ **toro**
TOROSE *adj* (of a cylindrical part) having irregular swellings
TOROT ▸ **torah**
TOROTH ▸ **torah**
TOROUS *same as* ▸ **torose**
TORPEDO *n, vb*
TORPEFY *vb* make torpid
TORPID *adj*
TORPIDS *pl n* series of boat races held at Oxford University
TORPOR, -S *n*
TORQUE, -D *n, vb*
TORQUER ▸ **torque**
TORQUES *n* distinctive band of hair, feathers, skin, or colour around the neck of an animal
TORQUEY *adj* providing torque
TORR, -S *n* unit of pressure
TORREFY *vb* dry (ores, etc) by subjection to intense heat
TORRENT *n, adj*
TORRET, -S *same as* ▸ **terret**
TORRID *adj*
TORRIFY *same as* ▸ **torrefy**
TORRS ▸ **torr**
TORS ▸ **tor**
TORSADE *n* ornamental twist or twisted cord, as on hats
TORSE, -S *same as* ▸ **torso**
TORSEL, -S *n* wooden beam along the top of a wall
TORSES ▸ **torse**
TORSI ▸ **torso**
TORSION *n*
TORSIVE *adj* twisted
TORSK, -S *n* fish with a single long dorsal fin
TORSO, TORSI, -S *n*

TORT, -S *n* civil wrong or injury for which damages may be claimed
TORTA, -S *n* (in mining) a flat circular pile of silver ore
TORTE, -N, -S *n*
TORTIE, -S *n* tortoiseshell cat
TORTILE *adj* twisted or coiled
TORTIVE *adj* twisted
TORTONI *n* rich ice cream often flavoured with sherry
TORTRIX *n* type of moth
TORTS ▸ **tort**
TORTURE *vb, n*
TORULA, -E, -S *n* any of various species of fungal microorganisms
TORULI ▸ **torulus**
TORULIN *n* vitamin found in yeast
TORULUS, TORULI *n* socket in an insect's head in which its antenna is attached
TORUS, TORI, -ES *n* large convex moulding approximately semicircular in cross section
TORY, TORIES *n, adj*
TOSA, -S *n* large reddish dog, originally bred for fighting
TOSE, -D, -S, TOSING *same as* ▸ **toze**
TOSH, -ED, -ES, -ING *n, vb*
TOSHACH *n* military leader of a clan
TOSHED ▸ **tosh**
TOSHER, -S ▸ **tosh**
TOSHES ▸ **tosh**
TOSHIER ▸ **toshy**
TOSHING ▸ **tosh**
TOSHY, TOSHIER *adj* neat; trim
TOSING ▸ **tose**
TOSS, -ED, -ES, -ING *vb, n*
TOSSEN *old past participle of* ▸ **toss**
TOSSES ▸ **toss**
TOSSIER ▸ **tossy**
TOSSILY ▸ **tossy**
TOSSING ▸ **toss**
TOSSPOT *n* habitual drinker
TOSSUP, -S *n*
TOSSY, TOSSIER *adj* impudent
TOST *old past participle of* ▸ **toss**
TOSTADA *n* crispy deep-fried tortilla topped with meat, cheese, and refried beans
TOSTADO *same as* ▸ **tostada**
TOSTONE *n* Mexican dish of fried plantains
TOT, -S, -TED *n, vb*
TOTABLE ▸ **tote**
TOTAL, -ED, -S *n, adj, vb*
TOTALLY ▸ **total**
TOTALS ▸ **total**
TOTANUS *another name for* ▸ **redshank**
TOTARA, -S *n* tall coniferous forest tree of New Zealand
TOTE, -D, -S, TOTING *vb, n*
TOTEM, -S *n*
TOTEMIC ▸ **totem**
TOTEMS ▸ **totem**
TOTER, -S ▸ **tote**
TOTES ▸ **tote**
TOTHER, -S *n* other ▹ *adj* the other
TOTIENT *n* quantity of numbers less than, and sharing no common factors with, a number
TOTING ▸ **tote**
TOTS ▸ **tot**
TOTTED ▸ **tot**
TOTTER, -S *vb, n*
TOTTERY *adj* tending to totter
TOTTIE *adj* very small
TOTTIER ▸ **totty**
TOTTIES ▸ **totty**
TOTTING ▸ **tot**
TOTTY, TOTTIER, TOTTIES *n* small child ▹ *adj* very small
TOUCAN, -S *n*
TOUCH, -ES *vb, n, adj*
TOUCHE *interj* acknowledgment of a remark or witty reply
TOUCHED *adj*
TOUCHER ▸ **touch**
TOUCHES ▸ **touch**
TOUCHUP *n*
TOUCHY *adj*
TOUGH, -ED, -ER, -S *adj, n, vb*
TOUGHEN *vb*
TOUGHER ▸ **tough**
TOUGHIE *n* person who is tough
TOUGHLY ▸ **tough**
TOUGHS ▸ **tough**
TOUGHY *same as* ▸ **toughie**
TOUK, -ED, -ING, -S *same as* ▸ **tuck**
TOULADI *same as* ▸ **tuladi**
TOUN, -S *n* Scots word for a town
TOUPEE, -S *n*

TOUPEED *adj*
TOUPEES ▸ **toupee**
TOUPET, -S *same as* ▸ **toupee**
TOUPIE, -S *n* round boneless smoked ham
TOUR, -ED, -S *n, vb*
TOURACO *n* brightly coloured crested arboreal African bird
TOURED ▸ **tour**
TOURER, -S *n* large open car with a folding top
TOURIE, -S *same as* ▸ **toorie**
TOURING ▸ **tour**
TOURISM *n*
TOURIST *n, adj*
TOURNEY *n* knightly tournament ▹ *vb* engage in a tourney
TOURS ▸ **tour**
TOUSE, -D, -S, TOUSING *vb* tangle, ruffle, or disarrange; treat roughly
TOUSER, -S ▸ **touse**
TOUSES ▸ **touse**
TOUSIER ▸ **tousy**
TOUSING ▸ **touse**
TOUSLE, -D, -S *vb, n*
TOUSTIE *adj* irritable; testy
TOUSY, TOUSIER *adj* tousled
TOUT, -ED, -ING, -S *vb, n*
TOUTER, -S ▸ **tout**
TOUTIE, -R *adj* childishly irritable or sullen
TOUTING ▸ **tout**
TOUTON, -S *n* deep-fried round of bread dough
TOUTS ▸ **tout**
TOUZE, -D, -S, TOUZING *variant spelling of* ▸ **touse**
TOUZIER ▸ **touzy**
TOUZING ▸ **touze**
TOUZLE, -D, -S *rare spelling of* ▸ **tousle**
TOUZY, TOUZIER *variant spelling of* ▸ **tousy**
TOW, -ED, -ING, -INGS, -S *vb, n*
TOWABLE ▸ **tow**
TOWAGE, -S *n* charge made for towing
TOWARD *same as* ▸ **towards**
TOWARDS *prep*
TOWAWAY *n* vehicle which has been towed away
TOWBAR, -S *n* metal bar on a car for towing vehicles
TOWBOAT *n*
TOWED ▸ **tow**
TOWEL, -ED, -S *n, vb*
TOWER, -S *n, vb*
TOWERED *adj*
TOWERS ▸ **tower**
TOWERY *adj* with towers
TOWHEAD *n* person with blond or yellowish hair
TOWHEE, -S *n* N American brownish-coloured sparrow
TOWIE, -S *n* truck used for towing
TOWIER ▸ **towy**
TOWIES ▸ **towie**
TOWIEST ▸ **towy**
TOWING ▸ **tow**
TOWINGS ▸ **tow**
TOWKAY, -S *n* sir
TOWLINE *same as* ▸ **towrope**
TOWMON, -S *same as* ▸ **towmond**
TOWMOND *n* old word for year
TOWMONS ▸ **towmon**
TOWMONT *same as* ▸ **towmond**
TOWN, -S *n*
TOWNEE, -S *same as* ▸ **townie**
TOWNIE *n*
TOWNIER ▸ **towny**
TOWNIES ▸ **towny**
TOWNISH ▸ **town**
TOWNLET *n* small town
TOWNLY *adj* characteristic of a town
TOWNS ▸ **town**
TOWNY, TOWNIER, TOWNIES *adj* characteristic of a town
TOWPATH *n* path beside a canal or river
TOWROPE *n*
TOWS ▸ **tow**
TOWSACK *n* sack made from tow
TOWSE, -D, -S, TOWSING *same as* ▸ **touse**
TOWSER, -S ▸ **towse**
TOWSES ▸ **towse**
TOWSIER ▸ **towsy**
TOWSING ▸ **towse**
TOWSY, TOWSIER *same as* ▸ **tousy**
TOWT, -ED, -ING, -S *vb* sulk
TOWY, TOWIER, TOWIEST ▸ **tow**
TOWZE, -D, -S, TOWZING *same as* ▸ **touse**
TOWZIER ▸ **towzy**

TOWZING ▸ **towze**
TOWZY, TOWZIER *same as* ▸ **tousy**
TOXEMIA *same as* > **toxaemia**
TOXEMIC > **toxaemia**
TOXIC, -S *adj, n*
TOXICAL *adj* toxic
TOXICS ▸ **toxic**
TOXIN, -S *n*
TOXINE, -S *nonstandard variant spelling of* ▸ **toxin**
TOXINS ▸ **toxin**
TOXOID, -S *n* toxin that has been treated to reduce its toxicity
TOY, -ED, -ING, -INGS, -S *n, adj, vb*
TOYBOX *n*
TOYED ▸ **toy**
TOYER, -S ▸ **toy**
TOYETIC *adj* (of a film or television franchise) able to generate revenue via spin-off toys
TOYING ▸ **toy**
TOYINGS ▸ **toy**
TOYISH *adj* resembling a toy
TOYLAND *n* toy industry
TOYLESS ▸ **toy**
TOYLIKE ▸ **toy**
TOYLSOM *old spelling of* > **toilsome**
TOYMAN, TOYMEN *n* man who sells toys
TOYO, -S *n* Japanese straw-like material made out of rice paper and used to make hats
TOYON, -S *n* shrub related to the rose
TOYOS ▸ **toyo**
TOYS ▸ **toy**
TOYSHOP *n*
TOYSOME *adj* playful
TOYTOWN *adj* having an unreal and picturesque appearance ▹ *n* place with an unreal and picturesque appearance
TOZE, -D, -S, TOZING *vb* tease out; (of wool, etc) card
TOZIE, -S *n* type of shawl
TOZING ▸ **toze**
TRABS *pl n* training shoes
TRACE, -D, -S *vb, n*
TRACER, -S *n*
TRACERY *n* pattern of interlacing lines
TRACES ▸ **trace**
TRACEUR *n* parkour participant
TRACHEA *n*
TRACHLE *vb* Scots word meaning make (hair, clothing, etc) untidy
TRACING *n*
TRACK, -ED, -S *n, vb*
TRACKER ▸ **track**
TRACKIE *adj* resembling or forming part of a tracksuit
TRACKS ▸ **track**
TRACT, -ED, -S *n* wide area ▹ *vb* track
TRACTOR *n*
TRACTS ▸ **tract**
TRACTUS *n* anthem sung in some RC masses
TRAD, -S *n* traditional jazz, as revived in the 1950s
TRADE, -D, -S *n, vb, adj*
TRADER, -S *n*
TRADES ▸ **trade**
TRADIE, -S *n* tradesperson
TRADING ▸ **trade**
TRADS ▸ **trad**
TRADUCE *vb*
TRAFFIC *n, vb*
TRAGAL ▸ **tragus**
TRAGEDY *n*
TRAGI ▸ **tragus**
TRAGIC, -S *adj, n*
TRAGULE *n* mouse deer
TRAGUS, TRAGI *n* fleshy projection that partially covers the entrance to the external ear
TRAIK, -ED, -IT, -S *vb* Scots word for trudge
TRAIL, -ED, -S *n, vb*
TRAILER *n, vb*
TRAILS ▸ **trail**
TRAIN, -ED, -S *vb, n*
TRAINEE *n, adj*
TRAINER *n*
TRAINS ▸ **train**
TRAIPSE *vb, n*
TRAIT, -S *n*
TRAITOR *n*
TRAITS ▸ **trait**
TRAJECT *vb*
TRAM, -MED, -S *n* electric public transport vehicle ▹ *vb* adjust (a mechanism) to a fine degree
TRAMCAR *same as* ▸ **tram**
TRAMEL, -S *vb* hinder or restrain
TRAMELL *old variant of* ▸ **trammel**
TRAMELS ▸ **tramel**
TRAMMED ▸ **tram**

TRAMMEL *n, vb*
TRAMMIE *n* conductor or driver of a tram
TRAMP, -ED, -S *vb, n*
TRAMPER *n* person who tramps
TRAMPET *variant spelling of* > **trampette**
TRAMPLE *vb, n*
TRAMPS ▸ **tramp**
TRAMPY *adj* like or characteristic of a tramp
TRAMS ▸ **tram**
TRAMWAY *same as* > **tramline**
TRANCE, -D, -S *n, vb*
TRANCEY *adj* (of music) characteristic of the trance sub-genre
TRANCHE *n*
TRANECT *n* ferry
TRANGAM *n* bauble or trinket
TRANGLE *n* (in heraldry) a small fesse
TRANKUM *same as* ▸ **trangam**
TRANS *n*
TRANSE, -S *n* way through; passage
TRANSIT *n, vb*
TRANSOM *n* horizontal bar across a window
TRANT, -ED, -S *vb* travel from place to place selling goods
TRANTER ▸ **trant**
TRANTS ▸ **trant**
TRAP, -PED, -S *n, vb*
TRAPAN, -S *same as* ▸ **trepan**
TRAPE, -D, TRAPING *same as* ▸ **traipse**
TRAPES *same as* ▸ **traipse**
TRAPEZE *n, vb*
TRAPING ▸ **trape**
TRAPPED ▸ **trap**
TRAPPER *n*
TRAPPY *adj* having many traps
TRAPS ▸ **trap**
TRAPSE, -D, -S *vb* traipse
TRAPT *old past participle of* ▸ **trap**
TRASH, -ED, -ES *n, vb*
TRASHER ▸ **trash**
TRASHES ▸ **trash**
TRASHY *adj*
TRASS, -ES *n* variety of the volcanic rock tuff
TRAT, -S *n* type of fishing line holding a series of baited hooks
TRATT, -S *short for* > **trattoria**
TRAUMA, -S *n*
TRAVAIL *n, vb*
TRAVE, -S *n* stout wooden cage in which difficult horses are shod
TRAVEL, -S *vb, n*
TRAVES ▸ **trave**
TRAVIS *same as* ▸ **treviss**
TRAVOIS *n* sledge used for dragging logs
TRAWL, -ED, -S *n, vb*
TRAWLER *n*
TRAWLEY *same as* ▸ **trolley**
TRAWLS ▸ **trawl**
TRAY, -S *n*
TRAYBIT *n* threepenny bit
TRAYF *adj* not prepared according to Jewish law
TRAYFUL *n* as many or as much as will fit on a tray
TRAYNE, -D, -S *old spelling of* ▸ **train**
TRAYS ▸ **tray**
TREACLE *n, vb*
TREACLY ▸ **treacle**
TREAD, -ED, -S, TRODDEN *vb, n*
TREADER ▸ **tread**
TREADLE *n* lever worked by the foot to turn a wheel ▹ *vb* work (a machine) with a treadle
TREADS ▸ **tread**
TREAGUE *n* agreement to stop fighting
TREASON *n*
TREAT, -ED, -S *vb, n*
TREATER ▸ **treat**
TREATS ▸ **treat**
TREATY *n*
TREBLE, -D, -S *adj, n, vb*
TREBLY *adj* (of music) tinny
TRECK, -ED, -S *same as* ▸ **trek**
TREDDLE *variant spelling of* ▸ **treadle**
TREE, -D, -ING, -S *n, vb*
TREEN, -S *adj* made of wood ▹ *n* art of making treenware
TREES ▸ **tree**
TREETOP *n*
TREEWAX *n* any wax secreted by a tree
TREF *adj* in Judaism, ritually unfit to be eaten
TREFA *same as* ▸ **tref**
TREFAH *same as* ▸ **tref**
TREFOIL *n* plant with a three-lobed leaf

TREHALA *n* edible sugary substance from the cocoon of an Asian weevil
TREIF *same as* ▸ **tref**
TREIFA *same as* ▸ **tref**
TREILLE *another word for* ▸ **trellis**
TREK, -KED, -S *n, vb*
TREKKER ▸ **trek**
TREKS ▸ **trek**
TRELLIS *n, vb*
TREM, -S *n* lever for producing a tremolo on a guitar
TREMA, -S *n* mark placed over vowel to indicate it is to be pronounced separately
TREMBLE *vb, n*
TREMBLY ▸ **tremble**
TREMIE, -S *n* metal hopper and pipe used to distribute freshly mixed concrete underwater
TREMOLO *n*
TREMOR, -S *n, vb*
TREMS ▸ **trem**
TRENAIL *same as* > **treenail**
TRENCH *n, adj, vb*
TREND, -ED, -S *n, vb*
TRENDY *n, adj*
TRENISE *n* one of the figures in a quadrille
TRENTAL *n* mass said in remembrance of a person 30 days after his or her death
TREPAN, -S *same as* > **trephine**
TREPANG *n* any of various large sea cucumbers
TREPANS ▸ **trepan**
TREPID *adj* trembling
TRES *adj* very
TRESS, -ES *n, vb*
TRESSED *adj* having a tress or tresses
TRESSEL *variant spelling of* ▸ **trestle**
TRESSES ▸ **tress**
TRESSY ▸ **tress**
TREST, -S *old variant of* ▸ **trestle**
TRESTLE *n*
TRESTS ▸ **trest**
TRET, -S *n* (formerly) allowance granted for waste due to transportation
TREVET, -S *same as* ▸ **trivet**
TREVIS *variant spelling of* ▸ **treviss**
TREVISS *n* partition in a stable for keeping animals apart
TREW *old variant spelling of* ▸ **true**
TREWS *pl n*
TREY, -S *n* any card or dice throw with three spots
TREYBIT *same as* ▸ **traybit**
TREYF *adj* not prepared according to Jewish law
TREYFA *same as* ▸ **treyf**
TREYS ▸ **trey**
TREZ, -ES *same as* ▸ **trey**
TRIABLE *adj* liable to be tried judicially
TRIAC, -S *n* device for regulating the amount of electric current reaching a circuit
TRIACID *adj* (of a base) capable of reacting with three molecules of a monobasic acid
TRIACS ▸ **triac**
TRIACT, -S *adj* having three rays ▹ *n* sponge spicule with three rays
TRIAD, -S *n*
TRIADIC *n* something that has the characteristics of a triad
TRIADS ▸ **triad**
TRIAGE, -D, -S *n, vb*
TRIAL, -ED, -S *n, vb*
TRIARCH *n* one of three rulers of a triarchy
TRIATIC *n* rope between a ship's mastheads
TRIAXON *another name for* > **triaxial**
TRIAZIN *same as* > **triazine**
TRIBAL, -S *adj, n*
TRIBBLE *n* frame for drying paper
TRIBE, -S *n*
TRIBLET *n* spindle or mandrel used in making rings, tubes, etc
TRIBUNE *n*
TRIBUTE *n*
TRICAR, -S *n* car with three wheels
TRICE, -D, -S, TRICING *n, vb*
TRICEP *same as* ▸ **triceps**
TRICEPS *n*
TRICES ▸ **trice**
TRICING ▸ **trice**
TRICITY *n* area that comprises three adjoining cities
TRICK, -ED, -S *n, vb*

TRICKER ▸ **trick**
TRICKIE *Scots form of* ▸ **tricky**
TRICKLE *vb, n*
TRICKLY ▸ **trickle**
TRICKS ▸ **trick**
TRICKSY *adj*
TRICKY *adj*
TRICLAD *n* type of worm having a tripartite intestine
TRICORN *n, adj*
TRICOT, -S *n* thin rayon or nylon fabric knitted or resembling knitting, used for dresses, etc
TRIDARN *n* sideboard with three levels
TRIDE *old spelling of the past tense of* ▸ **try**
TRIDENT *n, adj*
TRIDUAN *adj* three days long
TRIDUUM *n* period of three days for prayer before a feast
TRIE *old spelling of* ▸ **try**
TRIED ▸ **try**
TRIELLA *n* bet on the winners of three nominated horse races
TRIENE, -S *n* chemical compound containing three double bonds
TRIENS *n* Byzantine gold coin worth one third of a solidus
TRIER, -S *n* person or thing that tries
TRIES ▸ **try**
TRIFF, -ER *adj* terrific; very good indeed
TRIFFIC *adj* terrific; very good indeed
TRIFFID *n*
TRIFID *adj* divided or split into three parts or lobes
TRIFLE, -D, -S *n, vb*
TRIFLER ▸ **trifle**
TRIFLES ▸ **trifle**
TRIFOLD *less common word for* ▸ **triple**
TRIFOLY *same as* ▸ **trefoil**
TRIFORM *adj* having three parts
TRIG, -GED, -S *adj, vb*
TRIGAMY *n* condition of having three spouses
TRIGGED ▸ **trig**
TRIGGER *n, vb*
TRIGLOT *n* person who can speak three languages
TRIGLY ▸ **trig**
TRIGO, -S *n* wheat field
TRIGON, -S *n* (in classical Greece or Rome) a triangular harp or lyre
TRIGOS ▸ **trigo**
TRIGRAM *n* three-letter inscription
TRIGS ▸ **trig**
TRIJET, -S *n* jet with three engines
TRIKE, -S *n*
TRILBY, -S *n*
TRILD *old past tense of* ▸ **trill**
TRILITH *same as* ▸ **trilithon**
TRILL, -ED, -S *n, vb*
TRILLER ▸ **trill**
TRILLO *n* (in music) a trill
TRILLS ▸ **trill**
TRILOBE *n* three-lobed thing
TRILOGY *n*
TRIM, -MED, -S *adj, vb, n*
TRIMER, -S *n* polymer or a molecule of a polymer consisting of three identical monomers
TRIMIX *n* gas mixture of nitrogen, helium and oxygen used by deep-sea divers
TRIMLY ▸ **trim**
TRIMMED ▸ **trim**
TRIMMER ▸ **trim**
TRIMPOT *n* small instrument for adjusting resistance or voltage
TRIMS ▸ **trim**
TRIMTAB *n* small control surface to enable the pilot to balance an aircraft
TRIN, -S *n* triplet
TRINAL ▸ **trine**
TRINARY *adj* made up of three parts
TRINDLE *vb* move heavily on (or as if on) wheels
TRINE, -D, -S, TRINING *n* aspect of 120° between two planets, an orb of 8° being allowed ▹ *adj* of or relating to a trine ▹ *vb* put in a trine aspect
TRINGLE *n* slim rod
TRINING ▸ **trine**
TRINITY *n*
TRINKET *n, vb*
TRINKUM *n* trinket or bauble
TRINS ▸ **trin**
TRIO, -S *n*

TRIODE, -S *n* electronic valve having three electrodes, a cathode, an anode, and a grid
TRIOL, -S *n* any of a class of alcohols that have three hydroxyl groups per molecule
TRIOLET *n* verse form of eight lines
TRIOLS ▸ **triol**
TRIONES *pl n* seven stars of the constellation Ursa Major
TRIONYM *another name for* > **trinomial**
TRIOR, -S *old form of* ▸ **trier**
TRIOS ▸ **trio**
TRIOSE, -S *n* simple monosaccharide produced by the oxidation of glycerol
TRIOXID *same as* > **trioxide**
TRIP, -PED, -S *n, vb*
TRIPACK *n* pack of three
TRIPART *adj* composed of three parts
TRIPE, -S *n*
TRIPERY *n* place where tripe is prepared
TRIPES ▸ **tripe**
TRIPEY ▸ **tripe**
TRIPIER ▸ **tripy**
TRIPLE, -D, -S *adj, vb, n*
TRIPLET *n*
TRIPLEX *n* building divided into three separate dwellings ▹ *vb* separate into three parts
TRIPLY *vb* give a reply to a duply
TRIPMAN, TRIPMEN *n* man working on a trip
TRIPOD, -S *n*
TRIPODY *n* metrical unit consisting of three feet
TRIPOLI *n* lightweight porous siliceous rock
TRIPOS *n* final examinations for an honours degree at Cambridge University
TRIPPED ▸ **trip**
TRIPPER *n*
TRIPPET *n* any mechanism that strikes or is struck at regular intervals, as by a cam
TRIPPLE *vb* canter
TRIPPY *adj*
TRIPS ▸ **trip**
TRIPSIS, TRIPSES *n* act of kneading the body to promote circulation, suppleness, etc
TRIPTAN *n* drug used to treat migraine
TRIPY, TRIPIER ▸ **tripe**
TRIREME *n* ancient Greek warship with three rows of oars on each side
TRISECT *vb* divide into three parts, esp three equal parts
TRISEME *n* metrical foot of a length equal to three short syllables
TRISHAW *another name for* > **rickshaw**
TRISMIC ▸ **trismus**
TRISMUS *n* state of being unable to open the mouth
TRISOME *n* chromosome occurring three times (rather than twice) in a cell
TRISOMY *n*
TRIST *variant spelling of* ▸ **triste**
TRISTE *adj* sad
TRISUL, -S *n* trident symbol of Siva
TRISULA *same as* ▸ **trisul**
TRISULS ▸ **trisul**
TRITE, -R, -S, -ST *adj, n*
TRITELY ▸ **trite**
TRITER ▸ **trite**
TRITES ▸ **trite**
TRITEST ▸ **trite**
TRITIDE *n* tritium compound
TRITIUM *n* radioactive isotope of hydrogen
TRITOMA *another name for* > **kniphofia**
TRITON, -S *n* any of various chiefly tropical marine gastropod molluscs
TRITONE *n* musical interval consisting of three whole tones
TRITONS ▸ **triton**
TRIUMPH *n, vb*
TRIUNE, -S *adj* constituting three things in one ▹ *n* group of three
TRIVET, -S *n* metal stand for a pot or kettle
TRIVIA *pl n*
TRIVIAL *adj*
TRIVIUM *n* (in medieval learning) the lower division of the seven liberal arts
TRIZONE *n* area comprising three zones

TROAD, -S *same as* ▸ **trod**
TROADE, -S *same as* ▸ **trod**
TROADS ▸ **troad**
TROAK, -ED, -S *old form of* ▸ **truck**
TROAT, -ED, -S *vb* (of a rutting buck) to call or bellow
TROCAR, -S *n* surgical instrument for removing fluid from bodily cavities
TROCHAL *adj* shaped like a wheel
TROCHAR *old variant spelling of* ▸ **trocar**
TROCHE, -S *another name for* ▸ **lozenge**
TROCHEE *n* metrical foot of one long and one short syllable
TROCHES ▸ **troche**
TROCHI ▸ **trochus**
TROCHIL *same as* > **trochilus**
TROCHUS, TROCHI *n* hoop (used in exercise)
TROCK, -ED, -S *same as* ▸ **truck**
TROCKEN *adj* dry (used of wine)
TROCKS ▸ **trock**
TROD, -S *vb* past participle of tread ▹ *n* path
TRODDEN ▸ **tread**
TRODE, -S *same as* ▸ **trod**
TRODS ▸ **trod**
TROELIE *same as* ▸ **troolie**
TROELY *same as* ▸ **troolie**
TROFFER *n* fixture for holding and reflecting light from a fluorescent tube
TROG, -GED, -S *vb* walk, esp aimlessly or heavily
TROGGS *n* Scots word meaning fidelity, loyalty
TROGON, -S *n* bird of tropical and subtropical America, Africa, and Asia
TROGS ▸ **trog**
TROIKA, -S *n* Russian vehicle drawn by three horses abreast
TROILUS *n* type of large butterfly
TROIS *Scots form of* ▸ **troy**
TROJAN, -S *n* bug inserted into a computer program
TROKE, -D, -S, TROKING *same as* ▸ **truck**
TROLAND *n* unit of light intensity in the eye
TROLL, -ED, -S *n, vb*
TROLLER ▸ **troll**
TROLLEY *n, vb*
TROLLS ▸ **troll**
TROLLY *same as* ▸ **trolley**
TROMINO *n* shape made from three squares, each joined to the next along one full side
TROMMEL *n* revolving cylindrical sieve used to screen crushed ore
TROMP, -ED, -S *vb* trample
TROMPE, -S *n* apparatus for supplying the blast of air in a forge
TROMPED ▸ **tromp**
TROMPES ▸ **trompe**
TROMPS ▸ **tromp**
TRON, -S *n* public weighing machine
TRONA, -S *n* greyish mineral that occurs in salt deposits
TRONC, -S *n* pool into which waiters, waitresses, hotel workers, etc pay their tips
TRONE, -S *same as* ▸ **tron**
TRONK, -S *n* jail
TRONS ▸ **tron**
TROOLIE *n* large palm leaf
TROOP, -ED, -S *n, vb*
TROOPER *n*
TROOPS ▸ **troop**
TROOZ *same as* ▸ **trews**
TROP *adv* too, too much
TROPE, -D, -S, TROPING *n* figure of speech ▹ *vb* use tropes
TROPHI *pl n* collective term for the mandibles and other parts of an insect's mouth
TROPHIC *adj* of or relating to nutrition
TROPHY *n, adj, vb*
TROPIC, -S *n*
TROPIN, -S *n* adrenal androgen
TROPINE *n* white crystalline poisonous alkaloid
TROPING ▸ **trope**
TROPINS ▸ **tropin**

TROPISM *n* tendency of a plant or animal to turn in response to an external stimulus
TROPIST ▸ **tropism**
TROPPO *adv* too much ▹ *adj* mentally affected by a tropical climate
TROT, -S, -TED *vb, n*
TROTH, -ED, -S *n* pledge of devotion, esp a betrothal ▹ *vb* promise to marry (someone)
TROTS ▸ **trot**
TROTTED ▸ **trot**
TROTTER *n*
TROTYL, -S *n* yellow solid used chiefly as a high explosive
TROU *pl n* trousers
TROUBLE *n, vb*
TROUCH *n* rubbish
TROUGH, -S *n, vb*
TROULE, -D, -S *old variant of* ▸ **troll**
TROUNCE *vb*
TROUPE, -D, -S *n, vb*
TROUPER *n*
TROUPES ▸ **troupe**
TROUSE, -S *pl n* close-fitting breeches worn in Ireland
TROUSER *vb*
TROUSES ▸ **trouse**
TROUT, -S *n, vb*
TROUTER ▸ **trout**
TROUTS ▸ **trout**
TROUTY ▸ **trout**
TROVE, -S *n*
TROVER, -S *n* act of assuming proprietary rights over goods or property belonging to another
TROVES ▸ **trove**
TROW, -ED, -ING, -S *vb*
TROWEL, -S *n, vb*
TROWING ▸ **trow**
TROWS ▸ **trow**
TROWTH, -S *variant spelling of* ▸ **troth**
TROY, -S *n* system of weights used for precious metals and gemstones
TRUANCY ▸ **truant**
TRUANT, -S *n, adj, vb*
TRUCAGE *n* art forgery
TRUCE, -D, -S, TRUCING *n, vb*
TRUCIAL ▸ **truce**
TRUCING ▸ **truce**
TRUCK, -ED, -S *n, vb*
TRUCKER *n*
TRUCKIE *n* truck driver
TRUCKLE *vb* yield weakly or give in ▹ *n* small wheel
TRUCKS ▸ **truck**
TRUDGE, -D, -S *vb, n*
TRUDGEN *n* type of swimming stroke
TRUDGER ▸ **trudge**
TRUDGES ▸ **trudge**
TRUE, -D, -ING, -R, -S, -ST, TRUING *adj*
TRUEMAN, TRUEMEN *n* honest person
TRUER ▸ **true**
TRUES ▸ **true**
TRUEST ▸ **true**
TRUFFE, -S *rare word for* ▸ **truffle**
TRUFFLE *n, vb*
TRUG, -S *n* long shallow basket used by gardeners
TRUGO, -S *n* game similar to croquet
TRUGS ▸ **trug**
TRUING ▸ **true**
TRUISM, -S *n*
TRULY *adv*
TRUMEAU *n* section of a wall or pillar between two openings
TRUMP, -ED, -S *adj, vb*
TRUMPET *n, vb*
TRUMPS ▸ **trump**
TRUNCAL *adj* of or relating to the trunk
TRUNDLE *vb, n*
TRUNK, -ED *n, vb*
TRUNKS *pl n*
TRUNNEL *same as* > **treenail**
TRUSS, -ED, -ES *vb, n*
TRUSSER ▸ **truss**
TRUSSES ▸ **truss**
TRUST, -ED, -S *vb, n, adj*
TRUSTEE *n, vb*
TRUSTER ▸ **trust**
TRUSTOR *n* person who sets up a trust
TRUSTS ▸ **trust**
TRUSTY *adj, n*
TRUTH, -S *n*
TRUTHER *n* person who does not believe official accounts of the 9/11 attacks on the US
TRUTHS ▸ **truth**
TRUTHY *adj* truthful
TRY, TRIED, TRIES, -ING, -INGS *vb, n*
TRYE *adj* very good; select
TRYER, -S *variant of* ▸ **trier**
TRYING ▸ **try**
TRYINGS ▸ **try**
TRYKE, -S *variant spelling of* ▸ **trike**
TRYMA, -TA *n* drupe produced by the walnut and similar plants
TRYOUT, -S *n*

TRYP, -S *n* parasitic protozoan
TRYPAN *modifier* as in **trypan blue** dye used for staining cells in biological research
TRYPS ▸ **tryp**
TRYPSIN *n* enzyme occurring in pancreatic juice
TRYPTIC ▸ **trypsin**
TRYSAIL *n* small fore-and-aft sail on a sailing vessel
TRYST, -ED, -S *n, vb*
TRYSTE, -S *variant spelling of* ▸ **tryst**
TRYSTED ▸ **tryst**
TRYSTER ▸ **tryst**
TRYSTES ▸ **tryste**
TRYSTS ▸ **tryst**
TSADDIK *variant of* ▸ **zaddik**
TSADDIQ *variant of* ▸ **zaddik**
TSADE, -S *variant spelling of* ▸ **sadhe**
TSADI, -S *variant of* ▸ **sadhe**
TSADIK, -S *same as* ▸ **zaddik**
TSADIS ▸ **tsadi**
TSAMBA, -S *n* Tibetan dish made from roasted barley and tea
TSANTSA *n* shrunken head of an enemy kept as a trophy
TSAR, -S *n*
TSARDOM ▸ **tsar**
TSARINA *n*
TSARISM *n* system of government by a tsar
TSARIST *n* supporter of a tsar
TSARS ▸ **tsar**
TSATSKE *variant of* ▸ **tchotchke**
TSETSE, -S *n* any of various bloodsucking African flies
TSIGANE *variant of* ▸ **tzigane**
TSIMMES *variant spelling of* ▸ **tzimmes**
TSK, -ED, -ING, -S *vb*

This can occasionally be useful because it enables you to play K without using vowels.

TSKTSK, -S *same as* ▸ **tsk**
TSOORIS *variant of* ▸ **tsuris**
TSORES *variant of* ▸ **tsuris**
TSORIS *variant of* ▸ **tsuris**
TSOTSI, -S *n* (in South Africa) an urban thug or gang member
TSOURIS *variant of* ▸ **tsuris**
TSUBA, -S *n* sword guard of a Japanese sword
TSUBO, -S *n* unit of area
TSUNAMI *n*
TSURIS *n* grief or strife
TUAN, -S *n* lord
TUART, -S *n* eucalyptus tree of Australia
TUATARA *n* large lizard-like New Zealand reptile
TUATERA *variant spelling of* ▸ **tuatara**
TUATH, -S *n* territory of an ancient Irish tribe
TUATUA, -S *n* edible marine bivalve of New Zealand waters
TUB, -BED, -BING, -S *n, vb*
TUBA, -E, -S *n*
TUBAGE, -S *n* insertion of a tube
TUBAIST ▸ **tuba**
TUBAL *adj* of or relating to a tube
TUBAR *another word for* ▸ **tubular**
TUBAS ▸ **tuba**
TUBATE *less common word for* ▸ **tubular**
TUBBED ▸ **tub**
TUBBER, -S ▸ **tub**
TUBBIER ▸ **tubby**
TUBBING ▸ **tub**
TUBBISH *adj* fat
TUBBY, TUBBIER *adj*
TUBE, -D, -S *n*
TUBEFUL *n* quantity (of something) that a tube can hold
TUBER, -S *n*
TUBES ▸ **tube**
TUBFAST *n* period of fasting and sweating in a tub, intended as a cure for disease
TUBFISH *another name for* ▸ **gurnard**
TUBFUL, -S *n* amount a tub will hold
TUBIFEX *n* type of small reddish freshwater worm
TUBING, -S *n*
TUBIST, -S ▸ **tuba**
TUBLIKE ▸ **tub**
TUBS ▸ **tub**
TUBULAR *adj, n*
TUBULE, -S *n* any small tubular structure
TUBULIN *n* protein forming the basis of microtubules
TUCHIS *n* buttocks

TUCHUN, -S *n* (formerly) a Chinese military governor or warlord
TUCHUS *same as* ▸ **tuchis**
TUCK, -ED, -S *vb, n*
TUCKBOX *n*
TUCKED ▸ **tuck**
TUCKER, -S *n, vb*
TUCKET, -S *n* flourish on a trumpet
TUCKING *n* act of tucking
TUCKS ▸ **tuck**
TUFA, -S *n* porous rock formed as a deposit from springs
TUFF, -S *n* porous rock formed from volcanic dust or ash
TUFFE, -S *old form of* ▸ **tuft**
TUFFET, -S *n*
TUFFS ▸ **tuff**
TUFOLI, -S *n* type of tubular pasta
TUFT, -ING, -S *n, vb*
TUFTED *adj*
TUFTER, -S ▸ **tuft**
TUFTIER ▸ **tufty**
TUFTILY ▸ **tuft**
TUFTING ▸ **tuft**
TUFTS ▸ **tuft**
TUFTY, TUFTIER ▸ **tuft**
TUG, -GED, -GING, -S *vb, n*
TUGBOAT *n* boat used for towing barges, ships, etc
TUGGED ▸ **tug**
TUGGER, -S ▸ **tug**
TUGGING ▸ **tug**
TUGHRA, -S *n* Turkish Sultan's official emblem
TUGHRIK *same as* ▸ **tugrik**
TUGLESS ▸ **tug**
TUGRA, -S *variant of* ▸ **tughra**
TUGRIK, -S *n* standard monetary unit of Mongolia
TUGS ▸ **tug**
TUI, -S *n* New Zealand honeyeater that mimics human speech and the songs of other birds
TUILE, -S *n* type of almond-flavoured dessert biscuit
TUILLE, -S *n*
TUILYIE *vb* fight
TUILZIE *variant form of* ▸ **tuilyie**
TUINA, -S *n* form of massage originating in China
TUIS ▸ **tui**
TUISM, -S *n* practice of putting the interests of another before one's own
TUITION *n*
TUKTOO, -S *same as* ▸ **tuktu**
TUKTU, -S *(in Canada) another name for* ▸ **caribou**
TULADI, -S *n* large trout found in Canada and the northern US
TULBAN, -S *old form of* ▸ **turban**
TULCHAN *n* skin of a calf placed next to a cow to induce it to give milk
TULE, -S *n* type of bulrush found in California
TULIP, -S *n*
TULLE, -S *n* fine net fabric of silk etc
TULPA, -S *n* being or object created through willpower and visualization techniques
TULSI, -S *n* type of basil
TULWAR, -S *n* Indian sabre
TUM, -S *informal or childish word for* ▸ **stomach**
TUMBLE, -D, -S *vb, n*
TUMBLER *n*
TUMBLES ▸ **tumble**
TUMBREL *n* farm cart for carrying manure
TUMBRIL *same as* ▸ **tumbrel**
TUMEFY *vb* make or become tumid
TUMESCE *vb* swell
TUMID *adj* (of an organ or part of the body) enlarged or swollen
TUMIDLY ▸ **tumid**
TUMMIES ▸ **tummy**
TUMMLER *n* entertainer employed to encourage audience participation
TUMMY, TUMMIES *n*
TUMOR, -S *same as* ▸ **tumour**
TUMORAL ▸ **tumour**
TUMORS ▸ **tumor**
TUMOUR, -S *n*
TUMP, -ED, -ING, -S *n* small mound or clump ▹ *vb* make a tump around
TUMPHY *n* dolt; fool
TUMPIER ▸ **tumpy**
TUMPING ▸ **tump**

TUMPS ▶ **tump**
TUMPY, TUMPIER ▶ **tump**
TUMS ▶ **tum**
TUMSHIE *n* turnip
TUMULAR *adj* of, relating to, or like a mound
TUMULI ▶ **tumulus**
TUMULT, -S *n, vb*
TUMULUS, TUMULI *n* burial mound
TUN, -NED, -NING, -S *n* large beer cask ▷ *vb* put into or keep in tuns
TUNA, -S *n*
TUNABLE *adj* able to be tuned
TUNABLY ▶ **tunable**
TUNAS ▶ **tuna**
TUND, -ED, -ING, -S *vb* beat; strike
TUNDISH *n* type of funnel
TUNDRA, -S *n*
TUNDS ▶ **tund**
TUNDUN, -S *n* wooden instrument used by Aboriginal Australians in religious rites
TUNE, -D, -S *n, vb*
TUNEAGE *n* music
TUNED ▶ **tune**
TUNEFUL *adj*
TUNER, -S *n*
TUNES ▶ **tune**
TUNEUP, -S *n*
TUNG, -S *n* fast-drying oil obtained from the seeds of a central Asian tree
TUNIC, -S *n*
TUNICA, -E *n* tissue forming a layer or covering of an organ or part
TUNICIN *n* cellulose-like substance found in tunicates
TUNICLE *n* vestment worn at High Mass and other religious ceremonies
TUNICS ▶ **tunic**
TUNIER ▶ **tuny**
TUNIEST ▶ **tuny**
TUNING, -S *n*
TUNKET, -S *n* hell
TUNNAGE *same as* ▶ **tonnage**
TUNNED ▶ **tun**
TUNNEL, -S *n, vb*
TUNNIES ▶ **tunny**
TUNNING ▶ **tun**
TUNNY, TUNNIES *same as* ▶ **tuna**
TUNS ▶ **tun**
TUNY, TUNIER, TUNIEST *adj* having an easily discernable melody
TUP, -PED, -S *n* male sheep ▷ *vb* cause (a ram) to mate with a ewe
TUPEK, -S *same as* ▶ **tupik**
TUPELO, -S *n* large tree of deep swamps and rivers of the southern US
TUPIK, -S *n* tent of seal or caribou skin used for shelter by Inuit people in summer
TUPLE, -S *n* row of values in a relational database
TUPPED ▶ **tup**
TUPPING *n* act of sheep mating
TUPS ▶ **tup**
TUPUNA, -S *same as* ▶ **tipuna**
TUQUE, -S *n* knitted cap with a long tapering end
TURACIN *n* red pigment found in touraco feathers
TURACO, -S *same as* ▶ **touraco**
TURACOU *variant of* ▶ **touraco**
TURBAN, -S *n*
TURBAND *old variant of* ▶ **turban**
TURBANS ▶ **turban**
TURBANT *old variant of* ▶ **turban**
TURBARY *n* land where peat or turf is cut or has been cut
TURBETH *variant of* ▶ **turpeth**
TURBID *adj*
TURBINE *n*
TURBIT, -S *n* crested breed of domestic pigeon
TURBITH *variant of* ▶ **turpeth**
TURBITS ▶ **turbit**
TURBO, -S *n*
TURBOND *old variant of* ▶ **turban**
TURBOS ▶ **turbo**
TURBOT, -S *n* large European edible flatfish
TURD, -S *n*
TURDINE *adj* of, relating to, or characteristic of thrushes
TURDION *variant of* ▶ **tordion**
TURDOID *same as* ▶ **turdine**

TURDS ▸ **turd**
TUREEN, -S *n*
TURF, -ED, -ING, -S, TURVES *n, vb*
TURFEN *adj* made of turf
TURFIER ▸ **turfy**
TURFING ▸ **turf**
TURFITE *same as* ▸ **turfman**
TURFMAN, TURFMEN *n* person devoted to horse racing
TURFS ▸ **turf**
TURFSKI *n* ski down a grassy hill on skis modified with integral wheels
TURFY, TURFIER *adj* of, covered with, or resembling turf
TURGENT *obsolete word for* ▸ **turgid**
TURGID *adj*
TURGITE *n* red or black mineral consisting of hydrated ferric oxide
TURGOR, -S *n* normal rigid state of a cell
TURION, -S *n* perennating bud produced by many aquatic plants
TURISTA *n* traveller's diarrhoea
TURK, -S *n* as in **young turk** person who agitates for radical reform
TURKEY, -S *n*
TURKIES *old form of* > **turquoise**
TURKIS *old form of* > **turquoise**
TURKOIS *old form of* > **turquoise**
TURKS ▸ **turk**
TURM, -S *n* troop of horsemen
TURME, -S *variant of* ▸ **turm**
TURMOIL *n, vb*
TURMS ▸ **turm**
TURN, -ED, -S *vb, n*
TURNDUN *another name for* ▸ **tundun**
TURNED ▸ **turn**
TURNER, -S *n* person or thing that turns
TURNERY *n* objects made on a lathe
TURNING *n*
TURNIP, -S *n, vb*
TURNIPY *adj* like a turnip
TURNKEY *n, adj*
TURNOFF *n*
TURNOUT *n*
TURNS ▸ **turn**
TURNT *adj* slang word for intoxicated
TURNUP, -S *n* the turned-up fold at the bottom of some trouser legs
TURPETH *n* convolvulaceous plant of India, having roots with purgative properties
TURPS *n* colourless, flammable liquid
TURR, -S *n* Newfoundland name for the guillemot
TURRET, -S *n*
TURRS ▸ **turr**
TURTLE, -D, -S *n, vb*
TURTLER ▸ **turtle**
TURTLES ▸ **turtle**
TURVES ▸ **turf**
TUSCHE, -S *n* substance used in lithography for drawing the design
TUSH, -ED, -ES, -ING *interj* exclamation of disapproval or contempt ▹ *n* small tusk ▹ *vb* utter the interjection 'tush'
TUSHERY *n* use of affectedly archaic language in novels, etc
TUSHES ▸ **tush**
TUSHIE, -S *n* pair of buttocks
TUSHING ▸ **tush**
TUSHKAR *variant of* ▸ **tuskar**
TUSHKER *variant of* ▸ **tuskar**
TUSHY *variant of* ▸ **tushie**
TUSK, -ING, -S *n, vb*
TUSKAR, -S *n* peat-cutting spade
TUSKED ▸ **tusk**
TUSKER, -S *n* any animal with prominent tusks, esp a wild boar or elephant
TUSKIER ▸ **tusky**
TUSKING ▸ **tusk**
TUSKS ▸ **tusk**
TUSKY, TUSKIER ▸ **tusk**
TUSSAC *modifier* as in **tussac grass** kind of grass
TUSSAH, -S *same as* ▸ **tussore**
TUSSAL ▸ **tussis**
TUSSAR, -S *variant of* ▸ **tussore**
TUSSEH, -S *variant of* ▸ **tussore**
TUSSER, -S *same as* ▸ **tussore**
TUSSIS, TUSSES *technical name for a* ▸ **cough**

TUSSIVE ▸ **tussis**
TUSSLE, -D, -S *vb, n*
TUSSOCK *n*
TUSSOR, -S *variant of* ▸ **tussore**
TUSSORE *n* strong coarse brownish Indian silk
TUSSORS ▸ **tussor**
TUSSUCK *variant of* ▸ **tussock**
TUSSUR, -S *variant of* ▸ **tussore**
TUT, -TED, -TING *interj, vb, n*
TUTANIA *n* alloy of low melting point used mostly for decorative purposes
TUTEE, -S *n* one who is tutored, esp in a university
TUTELAR *same as* > **tutelary**
TUTENAG *n* zinc alloy
TUTMAN, TUTMEN *n* one who does tutwork
TUTOR, -ED, -S *n, vb*
TUTOYED *adj* addressed in a familiar way
TUTOYER *vb* speak to someone on familiar terms
TUTRESS *same as* > **tutoress**
TUTRIX *n* female tutor; tutoress
TUTS, -ED, -ES, -ING *Scots version of* ▸ **tut**
TUTSAN, -S *n* woodland shrub of Europe and W Asia
TUTSED ▸ **tuts**
TUTSES ▸ **tuts**
TUTSING ▸ **tuts**
TUTTED ▸ **tut**
TUTTI, -S *adv* to be performed by the whole orchestra or choir ▹ *n* piece of tutti music
TUTTIES ▸ **tutty**
TUTTING ▸ **tut**
TUTTIS ▸ **tutti**
TUTTY, TUTTIES *n* finely powdered impure zinc oxide
TUTU, -S *n*
TUTUED *adj* wearing tutu
TUTUS ▸ **tutu**
TUTWORK *n* work paid using a tut system
TUX, -ES *short for* ▸ **tuxedo**

Tux is a short form of **tuxedo**, and is a very commonly played X word.

TUXEDO, -S *n*
TUXES ▸ **tux**
TUYER, -S *variant of* ▸ **tuyere**
TUYERE, -S *n* water-cooled nozzle through which air is blown into a cupola, blast furnace, or forge
TUYERS ▸ **tuyer**
TUZZ, -ES *n* tuft or clump of hair
TWA, -S *Scots word for* ▸ **two**
TWADDLE *n, vb*
TWADDLY ▸ **twaddle**
TWAE, -S *same as* ▸ **twa**
TWAFALD *Scots variant of* ▸ **twofold**
TWAIN, -S *n*
TWAITE, -S *n* herring-like food fish
TWAL, -S *n* Scots word meaning twelve
TWANG, -ED, -S *n, vb*
TWANGER ▸ **twang**
TWANGLE *vb* make a continuous loose twanging sound
TWANGS ▸ **twang**
TWANGY ▸ **twang**
TWANK, -ED, -S *vb* make a sharply curtailed twang
TWANKAY *n* variety of Chinese green tea
TWANKED ▸ **twank**
TWANKS ▸ **twank**
TWANKY *same as* ▸ **twankay**
TWAS ▸ **twa**
TWASOME *same as* ▸ **twosome**
TWATTLE *rare word for* ▸ **twaddle**
TWAY, -S *old variant of* ▸ **twain**
TWEAK, -ED, -S *vb, n*
TWEAKER *n* engineer's small screwdriver
TWEAKS ▸ **tweak**
TWEAKY ▸ **tweak**
TWEE, -ST *adj*
TWEED, -S *n*
TWEEDLE *vb*
TWEEDS ▸ **tweed**
TWEEDY *adj* of or made of tweed
TWEEL, -ED, -S *variant of* ▸ **twill**
TWEELY ▸ **twee**
TWEEN, -S *same as* ▸ **between**
TWEENER *same as* > **tweenager**
TWEENIE *same as* ▸ **tweeny**
TWEENS ▸ **tween**

TWEENY *n* maid who assists both cook and housemaid
TWEEP, -S *n* person who uses Twitter
TWEEPLE *pl n* people who communicate via the Twitter website
TWEEPS ▸ **tweep**
TWEER, -ED, -S *variant of* ▸ **twire**
TWEEST ▸ **twee**
TWEET, -ED, -S *vb, interj*
TWEETER *n* loudspeaker reproducing high-frequency sounds
TWEETS ▸ **tweet**
TWEETUP *n* online meeting of individuals arranged on the social networking website Twitter
TWEEZE, -D, -S *vb*
TWEEZER *same as* > **tweezers**
TWEEZES ▸ **tweeze**
TWELFTH *n, adj*
TWELVE, -S *n*
TWENTY *n*
TWERK, -ED, -S *vb* dance provocatively by moving the hips rapidly back and forth
TWERP, -S *n*
TWERPY ▸ **twerp**
TWIBIL, -S *same as* ▸ **twibill**
TWIBILL *n* mattock with a blade shaped like an adze at one end and like an axe at the other
TWIBILS ▸ **twibil**
TWICE *adv*
TWICER, -S *n* someone who does something twice
TWIDDLE *vb* fiddle or twirl in an idle way ▹ *n* act or instance of twiddling
TWIDDLY ▸ **twiddle**
TWIER, -S *variant of* ▸ **tuyere**
TWIFOLD *variant of* ▸ **twofold**
TWIG, -GED, -S *n, vb*
TWIGGEN *adj* made of twigs
TWIGGER ▸ **twig**
TWIGGY *adj*
TWIGHT, -S *old variant of* ▸ **twit**
TWIGLET *n* small twig
TWIGLOO *n* temporary shelter made from twigs, branches, leaves, etc
TWIGS ▸ **twig**
TWILIT > **twilight**
TWILL, -ED, -S *n* fabric woven to produce parallel ridges ▹ *adj* of a weave in which the weft yarns are worked around two or more warp yarns ▹ *vb* weave in this fashion
TWILLY *n* machine having revolving spikes for opening and cleaning raw textile fibres
TWILT, -ED, -S *variant of* ▸ **quilt**
TWIN, -NED, -S *n, vb*
TWINE, -D, -S, TWINING *n, vb*
TWINER, -S ▸ **twine**
TWINES ▸ **twine**
TWINGE, -D, -S *n, vb*
TWINIER ▸ **twiny**
TWINING ▸ **twine**
TWINJET *n* jet aircraft with two engines
TWINK, -ED, -S *n* white correction fluid for deleting written text ▹ *vb* twinkle
TWINKIE *n* stupid person
TWINKLE *vb, n*
TWINKLY *adj*
TWINKS ▸ **twink**
TWINKY *n* stupid person
TWINNED ▸ **twin**
TWINS ▸ **twin**
TWINSET *n* matching jumper and cardigan
TWINTER *n* animal that is two years old
TWINY, TWINIER ▸ **twine**
TWIRE, -D, -S, TWIRING *vb* look intently at with (or as if with) difficulty
TWIRL, -ED, -S *vb, n*
TWIRLER ▸ **twirl**
TWIRLS ▸ **twirl**
TWIRLY ▸ **twirl**
TWIRP, -S *same as* ▸ **twerp**
TWIRPY ▸ **twirp**
TWISCAR *variant of* ▸ **tuskar**
TWIST, -ED, -S *vb, n*
TWISTER *n*
TWISTOR *n* variable corresponding to the coordinates of a point in space and time
TWISTS ▸ **twist**
TWISTY ▸ **twist**
TWIT, -S, -TED *vb, n*
TWITCH *vb, n*

TWITCHY *adj*
TWITE, -S *n* N European finch with a brown streaked plumage
TWITS ▸ **twit**
TWITTED ▸ **twit**
TWITTEN *n* narrow alleyway
TWITTER *vb, n*
TWIXT *same as* ▸ **betwixt**
TWIZZLE *vb* spin around
TWO, -S *n*
TWOCCER > **twoccing**
TWOCKER > **twoccing**
TWOER, -S *n* (in a game) something that scores two
TWOFER, -S *n* single ticket allowing the buyer entrance to two events
TWOFOLD *adj, adv, n*
TWONESS *n* state or condition of being two
TWONIE, -S *same as* ▸ **toonie**
TWOONIE *variant of* ▸ **toonie**
TWOS ▸ **two**
TWOSOME *n*
TWP *adj* Welsh dialect word meaning stupid

This Welsh word for stupid is useful because it contains no vowels, and so can help when you have an awkward rack full of consonants.

TWYER, -S *same as* ▸ **tuyere**
TWYERE, -S *variant of* ▸ **tuyere**
TWYERS ▸ **twyer**
TWYFOLD *adj* twofold
TYCHISM *n* theory that chance is an objective reality at work in the universe
TYCOON, -S *n*
TYDE *old variant of the past participle of* ▸ **tie**
TYE, -D, -ING, -S *n* trough used in mining to separate valuable material from dross ▹ *vb* (in mining) isolate valuable material from dross using a tye
TYEE, -S *n* large northern Pacific salmon
TYEING ▸ **tye**
TYER, -S ▸ **tye**
TYES ▸ **tye**
TYG, -S *n* mug with two handles

This old word for a two-handled drinking cup is another key word to know for situations when you are short of vowels.

TYIN *variant of* ▸ **tyiyn**
TYING ▸ **tie**
TYIYN, -S *n* money unit of Kyrgyzstan
TYKE, -S *n*
TYKISH ▸ **tyke**
TYLER, -S *variant of* ▸ **tiler**
TYLOPOD *n* mammal with padded feet, such as a camel or llama
TYLOSES ▸ **tylosis**
TYLOSIN *n* broad spectrum antibiotic
TYLOSIS, TYLOSES *n* bladder-like outgrowth from certain cells in woody tissue
TYLOTE, -S *n* knobbed sponge spicule
TYMBAL, -S *same as* ▸ **timbal**
TYMP, -S *n* blast furnace outlet through which molten metal flows
TYMPAN, -S *same as* > **tympanum**
TYMPANA > **tympanum**
TYMPANI, TYMPANO *same as* ▸ **timpani**
TYMPANS ▸ **tympan**
TYMPANY *n* distention of the abdomen
TYMPS ▸ **tymp**
TYND *variant of* ▸ **tind**
TYNDE *variant of* ▸ **tind**
TYNE, -D, -S, TYNING *variant of* ▸ **tine**
TYPABLE ▸ **type**
TYPAL *rare word for* ▸ **typical**
TYPE, -D, -S *n, vb*
TYPEBAR *n* one of the bars in a typewriter that carry the type and are operated by keys
TYPED ▸ **type**
TYPES ▸ **type**
TYPESET *vb*
TYPEY *variant of* ▸ **typy**
TYPHOID *adj, n*
TYPHON, -S *n* whirlwind
TYPHOON *n*
TYPHOSE *adj* relating to typhoid
TYPHOUS ▸ **typhus**
TYPHUS *n*

TYPIC *same as* ▸ **typical**
TYPICAL *adj*
TYPIER ▸ **typy**
TYPIEST ▸ **typy**
TYPIFY *vb* be typical of
TYPING, -S *n* work or activity of using a typewriter or word processor
TYPIST, -S *n*
TYPO, -S *n*
TYPP, -S *n* unit of thickness of yarn
TYPTO, -ED, -S *vb* learn Greek conjugations
TYPY, TYPIER, TYPIEST *adj* (of an animal) typifying the breed
TYRAN, -ED, -S *vb* act as a tyrant
TYRANNE *variant of* ▸ **tyran**
TYRANNY *n*
TYRANS ▸ **tyran**
TYRANT, -S *n, vb*
TYRE, -D, -S, TYRING *n, vb*
TYRO, -ES, -NES, -S *n*
TYRONIC ▸ **tyro**
TYROS ▸ **tyro**
TYSTIE, -S *n* black guillemot
TYTE *variant spelling of* ▸ **tite**
TYTHE, -D, -S, TYTHING *variant of* ▸ **tithe**
TZADDI, -S *same as* ▸ **sadhe**
TZADDIK *variant of* ▸ **zaddik**
TZADDIQ *variant of* ▸ **zaddik**

An unlikely word from Judaism, meaning a person of great piety, but offering a great score played as a bonus.

TZADDIS ▸ **tzaddi**
TZADIK, -S *same as* ▸ **zaddik**
TZAR, -S *same as* ▸ **tsar**
TZARDOM ▸ **tzar**
TZARINA *variant of* ▸ **tsarina**
TZARISM *variant of* ▸ **tsarism**
TZARIST *variant of* ▸ **tsarist**
TZARS ▸ **tzar**
TZETSE, -S *variant of* ▸ **tsetse**
TZETZE, -S *variant of* ▸ **tsetse**
TZIGANE *n* Romany dance
TZIGANY *variant of* ▸ **tzigane**
TZIMMES *n* traditional Jewish stew
TZITZIS *variant of* > **tsitsith**
TZITZIT *variant of* > **tsitsith**
TZURIS *variant of* ▸ **tsuris**

Uu

UAKARI, -S *n* type of monkey
UBEROUS *adj* abundant
UBERTY *n* abundance
UBIETY *n* condition of being in a particular place
UBIQUE *adv* everywhere
UBUNTU, -S *n* quality of compassion and humanity
UCKERS *n* type of naval game
UDAL, -S *n* form of freehold possession of land used in Orkney and Shetland
UDALLER *n* person possessing a udal
UDALS ▸ **udal**
UDDER, -S *n*
UDDERED ▸ **udder**
UDDERS ▸ **udder**
UDO, -S *n* stout perennial plant of Japan and China
UDON, -S *n*
UDOS ▸ **udo**
UDS *interj* God's or God save
UEY, -S *n* u-turn
UFO, -S *n*
UFOLOGY *n*
UFOS ▸ **ufo**
UG, -GED, -GING, -S *vb* hate
UGALI, -S *n* type of stiff porridge
UGGED ▸ **ug**
UGGING ▸ **ug**
UGH, -S *interj, n*

Together with **uke**, this is the highest-scoring 3-letter word starting with U.

UGLIED ▸ **ugly**
UGLIER ▸ **ugly**
UGLIES ▸ **ugly**
UGLIEST ▸ **ugly**
UGLIFY *vb* make or become ugly or more ugly
UGLILY ▸ **ugly**
UGLY, UGLIED, UGLIER, UGLIES, UGLIEST, -ING *adj, vb*
UGS ▸ **ug**
UGSOME *adj* loathsome
UH *interj*
UHLAN, -S *n* member of a body of lancers first employed in the Polish army
UHURU, -S *n* national independence

You won't often have three Us on your rack, but when you do, this Swahili word for freedom may get you out of trouble. The only other 5-letter word containing three Us is **urubu**, a kind of vulture.

UILLEAN *adj* as in **uillean pipes** bagpipes developed in Ireland
UJAMAA, -S *n* communally organized village in Tanzania
UKASE, -S *n* (in imperial Russia) a decree from the tsar
UKE, -S *short form of* ▸ **ukulele**

Together with **ugh**, this is the highest-scoring 3-letter word starting with U.

UKELELE *same as* ▸ **ukulele**
UKES ▸ **uke**
UKULELE *n*
ULAMA, -S *n* body of Muslim scholars or religious leaders
ULAN, -S *same as* ▸ **uhlan**
ULCER, -ED, -S *n, vb*
ULE, -S *n* rubber tree
ULEMA, -S *same as* ▸ **ulama**
ULES ▸ **ule**
ULEX, -ES, ULICES *n* variety of shrub

ULEXITE *n* type of mineral
ULICES ▸ **ulex**
ULICON, -S *same as* > **eulachon**
ULIKON, -S *same as* > **eulachon**
ULITIS *n* gingivitis
ULLAGE, -S *n* volume by which a liquid container falls short of being full ▹ *vb* create ullage in
ULLAGED ▸ **ullage**
ULLAGES ▸ **ullage**
ULLING, -S *n* process of filling
ULMIN, -S *n* substance found in decaying vegetation
ULNA, -E, -S *n*
ULNAD *adv* towards the ulna
ULNAE ▸ **ulna**
ULNAR ▸ **ulna**
ULNARE, ULNARIA *n* bone in the wrist
ULNAS ▸ **ulna**
ULOSIS, ULOSES *n* formation of a scar
ULPAN, -IM *n* Israeli study centre
ULSTER, -S *n* man's heavy double-breasted overcoat
ULTIMA, -S *n* final syllable of a word
ULTIMO *adv* in or during the previous month
ULTION, -S *n* vengeance
ULTISOL *n* reddish-yellow acid soil
ULTRA, -S *n, adj*
ULU, -S *n* type of knife
ULULANT ▸ **ululate**
ULULATE *vb*
ULUS ▸ **ulu**
ULVA, -S *n* genus of seaweed
ULYIE, -S *Scots variant of* ▸ **oil**
ULZIE, -S *Scots variant of* ▸ **oil**
UM, -MED, -MING, -S *interj, vb*
UMAMI, -S *n*
UMBEL, -S *n* umbrella-like flower cluster
UMBELED *same as* > **umbelled**
UMBELS ▸ **umbel**
UMBER, -S *adj* dark brown to reddish-brown ▹ *n* type of dark brown earth containing ferric oxide (rust) ▹ *vb* stain with umber
UMBERED ▸ **umber**
UMBERS ▸ **umber**
UMBERY *adj* like umber
UMBLE *adj*
UMBLES *another term for* ▸ **numbles**
UMBO, -NES, -S *n* small hump projecting from the centre of the cap in certain mushrooms
UMBONAL ▸ **umbo**
UMBONES ▸ **umbo**
UMBONIC ▸ **umbo**
UMBOS ▸ **umbo**
UMBRA, -E, -S *n* shadow, esp the shadow cast by the moon onto the earth during a solar eclipse
UMBRAGE *n, vb*
UMBRAL ▸ **umbra**
UMBRAS ▸ **umbra**
UMBRE, -S *same as* > **umbrette**
UMBREL, -S *n* umbrella
UMBRERE *n* helmet visor
UMBRES ▸ **umbre**
UMBRIL, -S *same as* ▸ **umbrere**
UMBROSE *same as* ▸ **umbrous**
UMBROUS *adj* shady
UME, -S *n* sour Japanese fruit
UMFAZI, -S *n* African married woman
UMIAC, -S *variant of* ▸ **umiak**
UMIACK, -S *variant of* ▸ **umiak**
UMIACS ▸ **umiac**
UMIAK, -S *n* Inuit boat made of skins
UMIAQ, -S *same as* ▸ **umiak**

An Inuit word for a type of canoe: easy to miss because one tends automatically to put the Q with the U and not think of a word ending in Q. The many variant spellings of this word include **umiac** and **umiak**.

UMLAUT, -S *n* mark (¨) placed over a vowel, esp in German, to indicate a change in its sound ▹ *vb* modify by umlaut
UMM *same as* ▸ **um**
UMMA, -S *n* Muslim community
UMMAH, -S *same as* ▸ **umma**

UMMAS ▸ **umma**
UMMED ▸ **um**
UMMING ▸ **um**
UMP, -ED, -ING, -S *short for* ▸ **umpire**
UMPH, -S *same as* ▸ **humph**
UMPIE *informal word for* ▸ **umpire**
UMPIES ▸ **umpy**
UMPING ▸ **ump**
UMPIRE, -D, -S *n, vb*
UMPS ▸ **ump**
UMPTEEN *adj*
UMPTY, UMPTIER *adj* very many
UMPY, UMPIES *same as* ▸ **umpie**
UMRA, -S *n* pilgrimage to Mecca that can be made at any time of the year
UMRAH, -S *same as* ▸ **umra**
UMRAS ▸ **umra**
UMS ▸ **um**
UMU, -S *n* type of oven
UMWELT, -S *n* environmental factors that affect the behaviour of an animal or individual
UMWHILE *same as* > **umquhile**
UN, -S *pron*
UNABLE *adj* lacking the necessary power, ability, or authority (to do something)
UNACTED *adj* not acted or performed
UNADDED *adj* not added
UNADEPT *adj* not adept ▹ *n* person who is not adept
UNADULT *adj* not mature
UNAGED *adj* not old
UNAGILE *adj* not agile
UNAGING *same as* > **unageing**
UNAI, -S *same as* ▸ **unau**
UNAIDED *adv, adj*
UNAIMED *adj* not aimed or specifically targeted
UNAIRED *adj*
UNAIS ▸ **unai**
UNAKIN *adj* not related
UNAKING *Shakespearean form of* > **unaching**
UNAKITE *n* type of mineral
UNALIKE *adj* not similar
UNALIST *n* priest holding only one benefice
UNALIVE *adj* unaware
UNAPT *adj* not suitable or qualified
UNAPTLY ▸ **unapt**
UNARM, -S *less common word for* ▸ **disarm**
UNARMED *adj*
UNARMS ▸ **unarm**
UNARY *adj* consisting of, or affecting, a single element or component
UNASKED *adv, adj*
UNAU, -S *n* two-toed sloth
UNAWAKE *adj* not awake
UNAWARE *adj, adv*
UNAWED *adj* not awed
UNAXED *adj* not axed
UNBAG, -S *vb* take out of a bag
UNBAKED *adj* not having been baked
UNBALE, -D, -S *vb* remove from bale
UNBAN, -S *vb* stop banning or permit again
UNBAR, -S *vb* take away a bar or bars from
UNBARE, -D, -S *vb* expose
UNBARK, -S *vb* strip bark from
UNBARS ▸ **unbar**
UNBASED *adj* not having a base
UNBATED *adj* (of a sword, lance, etc) not covered with a protective button
UNBE, -EN *vb* make non-existent
UNBEAR, -S *vb* release (horse) from the bearing rein
UNBED, -S *vb* remove from bed
UNBEEN ▸ **unbe**
UNBEGET *vb* deprive of existence
UNBEGOT *adj* unbegotten
UNBEGUN *adj* not commenced
UNBEING *n* non-existence
UNBELT, -S *vb* unbuckle the belt of (a garment)
UNBEND, -S *vb* become less strict or more informal in one's attitudes or behaviour
UNBENT *adj* not bent or bowed
UNBIAS *vb*
UNBID *same as* > **unbidden**

UNBIND, -S *vb* set free from bonds or chains
UNBITT, -S *vb* remove (cable) from the bitts
UNBLENT *same as* > **unblended**
UNBLESS *vb* deprive of a blessing
UNBLEST *same as* > **unblessed**
UNBLIND *vb* rid of blindness
UNBLOCK *vb*
UNBLOWN *adj* (of a flower) still in the bud
UNBOLT, -S *vb* unfasten a bolt of (a door)
UNBONE, -S *vb* remove bone from
UNBONED *adj* (of meat, fish, etc) not having had the bones removed
UNBONES ▸ **unbone**
UNBOOT, -S *vb* remove boots from
UNBORE *adj* unborn
UNBORN *adj*
UNBORNE *adj* not borne
UNBOSOM *vb* relieve (oneself) of (secrets or feelings) by telling someone
UNBOUND *adj*
UNBOWED *adj* not giving in or submitting
UNBOX, -ED, -ES *vb*
UNBRACE *vb* remove tension or strain from
UNBRAID *vb* remove braids from
UNBRAKE *vb* stop reducing speed by releasing brake
UNBRED *adj* not taught or instructed
UNBROKE *same as* > **unbroken**
UNBUILD, UNBUILT *vb*
UNBULKY *adj* not bulky
UNBURNT *adj* not burnt
UNBURY *vb*
UNBUSY *adj* not busy ▹ *vb* make less busy
UNCAGE, -S *vb* release from a cage
UNCAGED *adj* at liberty
UNCAGES ▸ **uncage**
UNCAKE, -D, -S *vb* remove compacted matter from
UNCANNY *adj*
UNCAP, -S *vb* remove a cap or top from (a container)
UNCAPE, -D, -S *vb* remove the cape from
UNCAPS ▸ **uncap**
UNCARED *adj* as in **uncared for** not cared (for)
UNCART, -S *vb* remove from a cart
UNCASE, -D, -S *vb* display
UNCAST, -S *adj* not cast ▹ *vb* undo the process of casting
UNCATE *same as* > **uncinate**
UNCE, -S *same as* ▸ **ounce**
UNCEDED *adj* not ceded
UNCES ▸ **unce**
UNCHAIN *vb*
UNCHAIR *vb* unseat from chair
UNCHARM *vb* disenchant
UNCHARY *adj* not cautious
UNCHECK *vb*
UNCHIC *adj* not chic
UNCHILD *vb* deprive of children
UNCHOKE *vb* unblock
UNCI ▸ **uncus**
UNCIA, -E *n* twelfth part
UNCIAL, -S *adj* of a writing style used in manuscripts of the third to ninth centuries ▹ *n* uncial letter or manuscript
UNCINAL *same as* > **uncinate**
UNCINUS, UNCINI *n* small hooked structure
UNCITED *adj* not quoted
UNCIVIL *adj*
UNCLAD *adj* having no clothes on
UNCLAMP *vb* remove clamp from
UNCLASP *vb* unfasten the clasp of (something)
UNCLE, -S, UNCLING *n, vb*
UNCLEAN *adj* lacking moral, spiritual, or physical cleanliness
UNCLEAR *adj*
UNCLED ▸ **uncle**
UNCLEFT *adj* not cleft
UNCLES ▸ **uncle**
UNCLEW, -S *vb* undo
UNCLING ▸ **uncle**
UNCLIP, -S *vb* remove clip from
UNCLIPT *archaic past form of* ▸ **unclip**
UNCLOAK *vb* remove cloak from

UNCLOG, -S *vb*
UNCLOSE *vb* open or cause to open
UNCLOUD *vb* clear clouds from
UNCO, -ER, -ES, -EST, -S *adj* Scots word meaning unfamiliar or strange ▷ *n* remarkable person or thing
UNCOCK, -S *vb* remove from a cocked position
UNCODED *adj* not coded
UNCOER ▶ **unco**
UNCOES ▶ **unco**
UNCOEST ▶ **unco**
UNCOIL, -S *vb*
UNCOLT, -S *vb* divest of a horse
UNCOMFY *adj*
UNCOMIC *adj* not comical
UNCOOL *adj*
UNCOPE, -D, -S *vb* unmuzzle
UNCORD, -S *vb* release from cords
UNCORK, -S *vb*
UNCOS ▶ **unco**
UNCOUTH *adj*
UNCOVER *vb*
UNCOWL, -S *vb* remove hood from
UNCOY *adj* not modest
UNCRATE *vb* remove from a crate
UNCRAZY *adj* not crazy
UNCROSS *vb* cease to cross
UNCROWN *vb* take the crown from
UNCTION *n*
UNCUFF, -S *vb* remove handcuffs from
UNCURB, -S *vb* remove curbs from (a horse)
UNCURED *adj* not cured
UNCURL, -S *vb*
UNCURSE *vb* remove curse from
UNCUS, UNCI *n* hooked part or process, as in the human cerebrum
UNCUT *adj*
UNCUTE *adj* not cute
UNDAM, -S *vb* free from a dam
UNDATE, -S *vb* remove date from
UNDATED *adj*
UNDATES ▶ **undate**
UNDE *same as* ▶ **undee**
UNDEAD *adj*
UNDEAF, -S *vb* restore hearing to
UNDEALT *adj* not dealt (with)
UNDEAR *adj* not dear
UNDECK, -S *vb* remove decorations from
UNDEE *adj* wavy
UNDEIFY *vb* strip of the status of a deity
UNDER *adv, prep*
UNDERDO *vb* do (something) inadequately
UNDERGO *vb*
UNDERN, -S *n* time between sunrise and noon
UNDID ▶ **undo**
UNDIES *pl n*
UNDIGHT *vb* remove
UNDINE, -S *n* female water spirit
UNDO, UNDID, -ES, -S *vb, n*
UNDOCK, -S *vb* take out of a dock
UNDOER, -S ▶ **undo**
UNDOES ▶ **undo**
UNDOING *n*
UNDONE *adj*
UNDOS ▶ **undo**
UNDRAPE *vb* remove drapery from
UNDRAW, -N, -S, UNDREW *vb* open (curtains)
UNDRESS *vb, n, adj*
UNDREST *same as* > **undressed**
UNDREW ▶ **undraw**
UNDRIED *adj* not dried
UNDRUNK *adj* not drunk
UNDUE *adj*
UNDUG *adj* not having been dug
UNDULAR > **undulate**
UNDULY *adv* excessively
UNDY *same as* ▶ **undee**
UNDYED *adj*
UNDYING *adj*
UNEAGER *adj* nonchalant
UNEARED *adj* not ploughed
UNEARTH *vb*
UNEASE, -S ▶ **uneasy**
UNEASY *adj*
UNEATEN *adj*
UNEATH *adv* not easily
UNEDGE, -D, -S *vb* take the edge off
UNENDED *adj* without end
UNEQUAL *adj, n*
UNETH *same as* ▶ **uneath**
UNEVEN *adj*
UNEYED *adj* unseen
UNFACT, -S *n* event or thing not provable

UNFADED *adj*
UNFAIR, -S *adj, vb*
UNFAITH *n* lack of faith
UNFAKED *adj* not faked
UNFAMED *adj* not famous
UNFANCY *vb* consider (a sportsperson or team) unlikely to win or succeed ▷ *adj* not fancy
UNFAZED *adj*
UNFED *adj*
UNFEED *adj* unpaid
UNFELT *adj*
UNFENCE *vb* remove a fence from
UNFEUED *adj* not feued
UNFILDE *archaic form of* ▶ **unfiled**
UNFILED *adj* not filed
UNFINE *adj* not fine
UNFIRED *adj* not fired
UNFIRM *adj* soft or unsteady
UNFIT, -S *adj, vb*
UNFITLY *adv* in an unfit way
UNFITS ▶ **unfit**
UNFIX, -ES *vb* unfasten, detach, or loosen
UNFIXED *adj* not fixed
UNFIXES ▶ **unfix**
UNFIXT *variant of* ▶ **unfixed**
UNFLESH *vb* remove flesh from
UNFLUSH *vb* lose the colour caused by flushing
UNFOLD, -S *vb*
UNFOND *adj*
UNFOOL, -S *vb* undeceive
UNFORM, -S *vb* make formless
UNFOUND *adj*
UNFREE, -D, -S *vb*
UNFROCK *vb* deprive (a priest in holy orders) of his or her priesthood
UNFROZE > **unfreeze**
UNFUMED *adj* not fumigated
UNFUNNY *adj*
UNFURL, -S *vb*
UNFUSED *adj* not fused
UNFUSSY *adj* not characterized by overelaborate detail
UNGAG, -S *vb* restore freedom of speech to
UNGAIN *adj* inconvenient
UNGATED *adj* without a gate
UNGAZED *adj* as in **ungazed at/ungazed upon** not gazed (at or upon)
UNGEAR, -S *vb* disengage
UNGET, -S *vb* get rid of
UNGILD, -S, UNGILT *vb* remove gilding from
UNGIRD, -S *vb* remove belt from
UNGIRT *adj* not belted
UNGIRTH *vb* release from a girth
UNGLAD *adj* not glad
UNGLOVE *vb* remove a glove or gloves
UNGLUE, -D, -S *vb*
UNGOD, -S *vb* remove status of being a god from
UNGODLY *adj*
UNGODS ▶ **ungod**
UNGORD *same as* ▶ **ungored**
UNGORED *adj* not gored
UNGOT *same as* > **ungotten**
UNGOWN, -S *vb* remove a gown from
UNGREEN *adj* not environmentally friendly
UNGROUP *vb* separate from a group
UNGROWN *adj* not fully developed
UNGUAL *adj* of, relating to, or affecting the fingernails or toenails
UNGUARD *vb* expose (to attack)
UNGUENT *n* ointment
UNGUIS, UNGUES *n* nail, claw, or hoof, or the part of the digit giving rise to it
UNGULA, -E *n* truncated cone, cylinder, etc
UNGULAR ▶ **ungula**
UNGULED *adj* hoofed
UNGUM, -S *vb* remove adhesive from
UNGYVE, -D, -S *vb* release from shackles
UNHABLE *same as* ▶ **unable**
UNHAIR, -S *vb* remove the hair from (a hide)
UNHAND, -S *vb* release from one's grasp
UNHANDY *adj* not skilful with one's hands
UNHANG, -S, UNHUNG *vb* take down from hanging position
UNHAPPY *adj, vb*
UNHARDY *adj* fragile
UNHASP, -S *vb* unfasten
UNHASTY *adj* not speedy

UNHAT, -S *vb* doff one's hat
UNHEAD, -S *vb* remove the head from
UNHEAL, -S *vb* expose
UNHEARD *adj*
UNHEART *vb* discourage
UNHEEDY *adj* not heedful
UNHELE, -D, -S *same as* ▸ **unheal**
UNHELM, -S *vb* remove the helmet of (oneself or another)
UNHERST *archaic past form of* > **unhearse**
UNHEWN *adj* not hewn
UNHINGE *vb*
UNHIP *adj*
UNHIRED *adj* not hired
UNHITCH *vb*
UNHIVE, -D, -S *vb* remove from a hive
UNHOARD *vb* remove from a hoard
UNHOLY *adj*
UNHOOD, -S *vb* remove a hood from
UNHOOK, -S *vb*
UNHOOP, -S *vb* remove a hoop from
UNHOPED *adj* not anticipated
UNHORSE *vb* knock or throw from a horse
UNHOUSE *vb* remove from a house
UNHUMAN *adj* inhuman or not human
UNHUNG ▸ **unhang**
UNHURT *adj*
UNHUSK, -S *vb* remove the husk from
UNI, -S *n*
UNIBODY *adj* of a vehicle in which the frame and body are one unit ▹ *n* vehicle in which the frame and body are one unit
UNIBROW *n*
UNICA ▸ **unicum**
UNICED *adj* not iced
UNICITY *n* oneness
UNICOM, -S *n* designated radio frequency at some airports
UNICORN *n*
UNICUM, UNICA *n* unique example or specimen
UNIDEAL *adj* not ideal
UNIFACE *n* type of tool
UNIFIC *adj* unifying
UNIFIED ▸ **unify**
UNIFIER ▸ **unify**
UNIFIES ▸ **unify**
UNIFORM *n, adj, vb*
UNIFY, UNIFIED, UNIFIES *vb*
UNION, -S *n, adj*
UNIPED, -S *n* person or thing with one foot
UNIPOD, -S *n* one-legged support, as for a camera
UNIQUE, -R, -S *adj, n*
UNIS ▸ **uni**
UNISEX *adj, n*
UNISIZE *adj* in one size only
UNISON, -S *n*
UNIT, -S *n*
UNITAGE ▸ **unit**
UNITAL ▸ **unit**
UNITARD *n* all-in-one skintight suit
UNITARY *adj* consisting of a single undivided whole
UNITE, -S *vb, n*
UNITED *adj*
UNITER, -S ▸ **unite**
UNITES ▸ **unite**
UNITIES ▸ **unity**
UNITING ▸ **unite**
UNITION *n* joining
UNITISE *same as* ▸ **unitize**
UNITIVE *adj* tending to unite or capable of uniting
UNITIZE *vb* convert (an investment trust) into a unit trust
UNITS ▸ **unit**
UNITY, UNITIES *n*
UNJADED *adj* not jaded
UNJAM, -S *vb* remove blockage from
UNJOINT *vb* disjoint
UNJUST *adj*
UNKED *adj* alien
UNKEMPT *adj*
UNKEND *same as* > **unkenned**
UNKENT *same as* > **unkenned**
UNKEPT *adj* not kept
UNKET *same as* ▸ **unked**
UNKID *same as* ▸ **unked**
UNKIND *adj*
UNKING, -S *vb* strip of sovereignty
UNKINK, -S *vb* straighten out
UNKISS *vb* cancel (a previous action) with a kiss
UNKNIT, -S *vb* make or become undone, untied, or unravelled
UNKNOT, -S *vb* disentangle or undo a knot or knots in
UNKNOWN *adj, n*

UNLACE, -S *vb* loosen or undo the lacing of (shoes, garments, etc)
UNLACED *adj* not laced
UNLACES ▸ **unlace**
UNLADE, -D, -S *less common word for* ▸ **unload**
UNLADEN *adj*
UNLADES ▸ **unlade**
UNLAID ▸ **unlay**
UNLASH *vb* untie or unfasten
UNLAST *archaic variant of* ▸ **unlaced**
UNLASTE *archaic variant of* ▸ **unlaced**
UNLATCH *vb*
UNLAW, -ED, -S *vb* penalize
UNLAY, UNLAID, -S *vb* untwist (a rope or cable) to separate its strands
UNLEAD, -S *vb* strip off lead
UNLEAL *adj* treacherous
UNLEARN *vb*
UNLEASH *vb*
UNLED *adj* not led
UNLESS *conj, prep*
UNLET *adj* not rented
UNLEVEL *adj* not level ▹ *vb* make unbalanced
UNLICH *Spenserian form of* ▸ **unlike**
UNLID, -S *vb* remove lid from
UNLIKE, -S *adj, prep, n*
UNLIKED *adj*
UNLIKES ▸ **unlike**
UNLIME, -D, -S *vb* detach
UNLINE, -S *vb* remove the lining from
UNLINED *adj* not having any lining
UNLINES ▸ **unline**
UNLINK, -S *vb*
UNLIT *adj*
UNLIVE, -D, -S *vb* live so as to nullify, undo, or live down (past events or times)
UNLOAD, -S *vb*
UNLOBED *adj* without lobes
UNLOCK, -S *vb*
UNLOOSE *vb* set free or release
UNLORD, -S *vb* remove from position of being lord
UNLOST *adj* not lost
UNLOVE, -S *vb* stop loving
UNLOVED *adj*
UNLOVES ▸ **unlove**
UNLUCKY *adj*
UNMACHO *adj* not macho
UNMADE *adj*
UNMAKE, -S *vb*
UNMAKER ▸ **unmake**
UNMAKES ▸ **unmake**
UNMAN, -S *vb*
UNMANLY *adj*
UNMANS ▸ **unman**
UNMARD *same as* > **unmarred**
UNMARRY *vb* divorce
UNMASK, -S *vb*
UNMATED *adj* not mated
UNMEANT *adj* unintentional
UNMEEK *adj* not submissive
UNMEET *adj* not meet
UNMERRY *adj* not merry
UNMESH *vb* release from mesh
UNMET *adj* unfulfilled
UNMETED *adj* unmeasured
UNMEW, -ED, -S *vb* release from confinement
UNMINED *adj*
UNMIRY *adj* not swampy
UNMITER *same as* ▸ **unmitre**
UNMITRE *vb* divest of a mitre
UNMIX, -ED, -ES *vb*
UNMIXT *same as* ▸ **unmix**
UNMOLD, -S *same as* ▸ **unmould**
UNMOOR, -S *vb* weigh the anchor or drop the mooring of (a vessel)
UNMORAL *adj* outside morality
UNMOULD *vb* change the shape of
UNMOUNT *vb* dismount
UNMOVED *adj*
UNMOWN *adj* not mown
UNNAIL, -S *vb* unfasten by removing nails
UNNAMED *adj*
UNNEATH *adj* archaic word for underneath
UNNERVE *vb*
UNNEST, -S *vb* remove from a nest
UNNOBLE *vb* strip of nobility
UNNOISY *adj* quiet
UNNOTED *adj* not noted
UNOAKED *adj*

UNOFTEN *adv* infrequently
UNOILED *adj* not lubricated with oil
UNOPEN *adj*
UNORDER *vb* cancel an order
UNOWED *same as* ▸ **unowned**
UNOWNED *adj* not owned
UNPACED *adj* without the aid of a pacemaker
UNPACK, -S *vb*
UNPAGED *adj* (of a book) having no page numbers
UNPAID *adj*
UNPAINT *vb*
UNPANEL *vb* unsaddle
UNPAPER *vb* remove paper from
UNPARED *adj* not pared
UNPAVED *adj* not covered in paving
UNPAY, -S *vb* undo
UNPEG, -S *vb* remove a peg or pegs from, esp to unfasten
UNPEN, -S *vb* release from a pen
UNPENT *archaic past form of* ▸ **unpen**
UNPERCH *vb* remove from a perch
UNPICK, -S *vb* undo (the stitches) of (a piece of sewing)
UNPILE, -D, -S *vb* remove from a pile
UNPIN, -S *vb* remove a pin or pins from
UNPINKT *same as* > **unpinked**
UNPINS ▸ **unpin**
UNPLACE *same as* > **displace**
UNPLAIT *vb* remove plaits from
UNPLUG, -S *vb*
UNPLUMB *vb* remove lead from
UNPLUME *vb* remove feathers from
UNPOPE, -D, -S *vb* strip of popedom
UNPOSED *adj* not posed
UNPRAY, -S *vb* withdraw (a prayer)
UNPROP, -S *vb* remove support from
UNPURE *same as* ▸ **impure**
UNPURSE *vb* relax (lips) from pursed position
UNQUEEN *vb* depose from the position of queen
UNQUIET *adj, n, vb*
UNQUOTE *interj, vb*
UNRACED *adj* not raced
UNRAKE, -S *vb* unearth through raking
UNRAKED *adj* not raked
UNRAKES ▸ **unrake**
UNRATED *adj*
UNRAVEL *vb*
UNRAZED *adj* not razed
UNREAD *adj*
UNREADY *adj*
UNREAL *adj*
UNREAVE *vb* unwind
UNRED *same as* ▸ **unread**
UNREDY *same as* ▸ **unready**
UNREEL, -S *vb* unwind from a reel
UNREEVE, UNROVE, UNROVEN *vb* withdraw (a rope) from a block, thimble, etc
UNREIN, -S *vb* free from reins
UNRENT *adj* not torn
UNREST, -S *n*
UNRID *adj* unridden
UNRIG, -S *vb* strip (a vessel) of standing and running rigging
UNRIGHT *n* wrong ▹ *adj* not right or fair ▹ *vb* make wrong
UNRIGS ▸ **unrig**
UNRIMED *same as* > **unrhymed**
UNRIP, -S *vb* rip open
UNRIPE, -R *adj*
UNRIPS ▸ **unrip**
UNRISEN *adj*
UNRIVEN *adj* not torn apart
UNRIVET *vb* remove rivets from
UNROBE, -D, -S *same as* ▸ **disrobe**
UNROLL, -S *vb*
UNROOF, -S *vb* remove the roof from
UNROOST *vb* remove from a perch
UNROOT, -S *less common word for* ▸ **uproot**
UNROPE, -D, -S *vb* release from a rope
UNROUGH *adj* not rough
UNROUND *vb* release (lips) from a rounded position
UNROVE ▸ **unreeve**
UNROVEN ▸ **unreeve**
UNROYAL *adj* not royal
UNRUDE *adj* not rude

UNRUFFE *same as* ▸ **unrough**
UNRULE, -S *n* lack of authority
UNRULED *adj* not ruled
UNRULES ▸ **unrule**
UNRULY *adj*
UNS ▸ **un**
UNSAFE, -R *adj*
UNSAID *adj*
UNSAINT *vb* remove status of being a saint from
UNSATED *adj* not sated
UNSAVED *adj* not saved
UNSAW ▸ **unsee**
UNSAWED *same as* ▸ **unsawn**
UNSAWN *adj* not cut with a saw
UNSAY, -S *vb*
UNSCALE *same as* ▸ **descale**
UNSCARY *adj* not scary
UNSCREW *vb*
UNSEAL, -S *vb* remove or break the seal of
UNSEAM, -S *vb* open or undo the seam of
UNSEAT, -S *vb*
UNSEE, UNSAW, -S *vb* undo the act of seeing something
UNSEEL, -S *vb* undo seeling
UNSEEN, -S *adj, adv, n*
UNSEES ▸ **unsee**
UNSELF, -S *vb* remove self-centredness from ▷ *n* lack of self
UNSELL, -S *vb* speak unfavourably and off-puttingly of (something or someone)
UNSENSE *vb* remove sense from
UNSENT *adj*
UNSET, -S *adj* not yet solidified or firm ▷ *vb* displace
UNSEW, -ED, -N, -S *vb* undo stitching of
UNSEX, -ED, -ES *vb*
UNSEXY *adj*
UNSHALE *vb* expose
UNSHAPE *vb* make shapeless
UNSHARP *adj* not sharp
UNSHED *adj* not shed
UNSHELL *vb* remove from a shell
UNSHENT *adj* undamaged
UNSHEWN *adj* unshown
UNSHIFT *vb* release the shift key on a keyboard
UNSHIP, -S *vb* be or cause to be unloaded, discharged, or disembarked from a ship
UNSHOD *adj*
UNSHOE, -S *vb* remove shoes from
UNSHOED *same as* ▸ **unshod**
UNSHOES ▸ **unshoe**
UNSHOOT *Shakespearean variant of* ▸ **unshout**
UNSHORN *adj*
UNSHOT, -S *adj* not shot ▷ *vb* remove shot from
UNSHOUT *vb* revoke (an earlier statement) by shouting a contrary one
UNSHOWN *adj* not shown
UNSHOWY *adj* not showy
UNSHUT, -S *vb* open
UNSIGHT *vb* obstruct vision of
UNSINEW *vb* weaken
UNSIZED *adj* not made or sorted according to size
UNSLAIN *adj* not killed
UNSLICK *adj* not slick
UNSLING, UNSLUNG *vb* remove or release from a slung position
UNSMART *adj* not smart
UNSMOTE *same as* > **unsmitten**
UNSNAG, -S *vb* remove snags from
UNSNAP, -S *vb* unfasten (the snap or catch) of (something)
UNSNARL *vb* free from a snarl or tangle
UNSNECK *vb* unlatch
UNSOBER *adj* not sober ▷ *vb* make unrefined in manners
UNSOD *same as* > **unsodden**
UNSOFT *adj* hard
UNSOLD *adj*
UNSOLID *adj* not solid
UNSONCY *same as* ▸ **unsonsy**
UNSONSY *adj* unfortunate
UNSOOTE *adj* not sweet
UNSOUL, -S *vb* cause to be soulless
UNSOUND *adj* unhealthy or unstable
UNSOWED *same as* ▸ **unsown**

UNSOWN *adj* not sown
UNSPAR, -S *vb* open
UNSPEAK, UNSPOKE *obsolete word for* ▸ **unsay**
UNSPED *adj* not achieved
UNSPELL *vb* release from a spell
UNSPENT *adj*
UNSPIDE *same as* ▸ **unspied**
UNSPIED *adj* unnoticed
UNSPILT *adj* not spilt
UNSPLIT *adj* not split
UNSPOKE ▸ **unspeak**
UNSPOOL *vb* unwind from spool
UNSPUN *adj*
UNSTACK *vb* remove from a stack
UNSTAID *adj* not staid
UNSTATE *vb* deprive of state
UNSTEEL *vb* make (the heart, feelings, etc) more gentle or compassionate
UNSTEP, -S *vb* remove (a mast) from its step
UNSTICK *vb* free or loosen (something stuck)
UNSTOCK *vb* remove stock from
UNSTOP, -S *vb* remove the stop or stopper from
UNSTOW, -S *vb* remove from storage
UNSTRAP *vb* undo the straps fastening (something) in position
UNSTRIP *vb* strip
UNSTUCK *adj*
UNSTUFT *same as* > **unstuffed**
UNSTUNG *adj* not stung
UNSUIT, -S *vb* make unsuitable
UNSUNG *adj*
UNSUNK *adj* not sunken
UNSUNNY *adj* not sunny
UNSURE, -R *adj*
UNSURED *adj* not assured
UNSURER ▸ **unsure**
UNSWEAR, UNSWORE, UNSWORN *vb* retract or revoke (a sworn oath)
UNSWEET *adj* not sweet
UNSWEPT *adj* not swept
UNSWORE ▸ **unswear**
UNSWORN ▸ **unswear**
UNTACK, -S *vb* remove saddle and harness, etc from
UNTAKEN *adj* not taken
UNTAME, -S *vb* undo the taming of
UNTAMED *adj*
UNTAMES ▸ **untame**
UNTAX, -ES *vb*
UNTAXED *adj*
UNTAXES ▸ **untax**
UNTEACH *vb* cause to disbelieve (teaching)
UNTEAM, -S *vb* disband a team
UNTENT, -S *vb* remove from a tent
UNTENTY *adj* inattentive
UNTHAW, -S *same as* ▸ **thaw**
UNTHINK *vb* reverse one's opinion about
UNTIDY *adj, vb*
UNTIE, -D, -S *vb*
UNTIL *prep*
UNTILE, -D, -S *vb* strip tiles from
UNTIMED *adj* not timed
UNTIN, -S *vb* remove tin from
UNTIRED *adj* not tired
UNTO *prep*
UNTOLD *adj*
UNTOMB, -S *vb* exhume
UNTONED *adj* not toned
UNTORN *adj* not torn
UNTRACE *vb* remove traces from
UNTRACK *vb* remove from a track
UNTREAD, UNTROD *vb* retrace (a course, path, etc)
UNTRIDE *same as* ▸ **untried**
UNTRIED *adj*
UNTRIM, -S *vb* deprive of elegance or adornment
UNTROD ▸ **untread**
UNTRUE, -R *adj*
UNTRULY ▸ **untrue**
UNTRUSS *vb* release from or as if from a truss
UNTRUST *n* mistrust
UNTRUTH *n*
UNTUCK, -S *vb*
UNTUNE, -D, -S *vb* make out of tune
UNTURF, -S *vb* remove turf from
UNTURN, -S *vb* turn in a reverse direction
UNTWINE *vb* untwist, unravel, and separate

UNTWIST *vb* twist apart and loosen
UNTYING ▸ **untie**
UNURGED *adj* not urged
UNUSED *adj*
UNUSUAL *adj*
UNVAIL, -S *same as* ▸ **unveil**
UNVAILE *same as* ▸ **unveil**
UNVAILS ▸ **unvail**
UNVEIL, -S *vb*
UNVEXED *adj* not annoyed
UNVEXT *same as* ▸ **unvexed**
UNVISOR *vb* remove a visor from
UNVITAL *adj* not vital
UNVOCAL *adj* not vocal
UNVOICE *vb* pronounce without vibration of the vocal cords
UNWAGED *adj*
UNWAKED *same as* > **unwakened**
UNWARE *same as* ▸ **unaware**
UNWARES *same as* > **unawares**
UNWARIE *same as* ▸ **unwary**
UNWARY *adj*
UNWATER *vb* dry out
UNWAXED *adj*
UNWAYED *adj* having no routes
UNWEAL, -S *n* ill or sorrow
UNWEARY *adj* not weary ▹ *vb* refresh or energize
UNWEAVE, UNWOVE, UNWOVEN *vb* undo or unravel
UNWED *adj*
UNWELDY *same as* > **unwieldy**
UNWELL *adj*
UNWEPT *adj* not wept for or lamented
UNWET *adj* not wet
UNWHIPT *same as* > **unwhipped**
UNWHITE *adj* not white
UNWILL, -S *vb* will the reversal of (something that has already occurred)
UNWIND, -S *vb*
UNWIPED *adj* not wiped
UNWIRE, -D, -S *vb* remove wiring from
UNWISE, -R *adj*
UNWISH *vb* retract or revoke (a wish)
UNWIST *adj* unknown
UNWIT, -S *vb* divest of wit
UNWITCH *vb* release from witchcraft
UNWITS ▸ **unwit**
UNWITTY *adj* not clever and amusing
UNWIVE, -D, -S *vb* remove a wife from
UNWOMAN *vb* remove womanly qualities from
UNWON *adj* not won
UNWONT *adj* unaccustomed
UNWOOED *adj* not wooed
UNWORK, -S *vb* destroy (work previously done)
UNWORN *adj*
UNWORTH *n* lack of value
UNWOUND *past tense and past participle of* ▸ **unwind**
UNWOVE ▸ **unweave**
UNWOVEN ▸ **unweave**
UNWRAP, -S *vb*
UNWRITE, UNWROTE *vb* cancel (what has been written)
UNWRUNG *adj* not twisted
UNYOKE, -D, -S *vb*
UNYOUNG *adj* not young
UNZIP, -S *vb*
UNZONED *adj* not divided into zones
UP, -PED, -S *adv, adj, vb*
UPALONG *n* location away from a place
UPAS, -ES *n* large Javan tree with whitish bark and poisonous milky sap
UPBEAR, -S, UPBORE *vb* sustain
UPBEAT, -S *adj, n*
UPBIND, -S *vb* bind up
UPBLOW, UPBLEW, -N, -S *vb* inflate
UPBOIL, -S *vb* boil up
UPBORE ▸ **upbear**
UPBORNE *adj* held up
UPBOUND *adj* travelling upwards
UPBOW, -S *n* stroke of the bow from its tip to its nut on a stringed instrument
UPBRAID *vb*
UPBRAST *same as* ▸ **upburst**
UPBRAY, -S *vb* shame
UPBREAK, UPBROKE *vb* escape upwards
UPBRING *vb*

UPBROKE ▸ **upbreak**
UPBUILD, UPBUILT *vb* build up
UPBURST *vb* burst upwards
UPBY *same as* ▸ **upbye**
UPBYE *adv* yonder
UPCAST, -S *n* material cast or thrown up ▹ *adj* directed or thrown upwards ▹ *vb* throw or cast up
UPCATCH *vb* catch up
UPCHEER *vb* cheer up
UPCHUCK *vb* vomit
UPCLIMB *vb* ascend
UPCLOSE *vb* close up
UPCOAST *adv* up the coast
UPCOIL, -S *vb* make into a coil
UPCOME, -S *vb* come up
UPCOURT *adv* (in basketball) away from one's own basket
UPCURL, -S *vb* curl up
UPCURVE *vb* curve upwards
UPCYCLE *vb* recycle a disposable product into an object of greater value
UPDART, -S *vb* dart upwards
UPDATE, -D, -S *vb, n*
UPDATER ▸ **update**
UPDATES ▸ **update**
UPDIVE, -D, -S, UPDOVE *vb* leap upwards
UPDO, -S *n* type of hairstyle
UPDOVE ▸ **updive**
UPDRAFT *n*
UPDRAG, -S *vb* drag up
UPDRAW, -N, -S, UPDREW *vb* draw up
UPDRY, UPDRIED, UPDRIES *vb* dry up
UPEND, -ED, -S *vb*
UPFIELD *adj* in sport, away from the defending team's goal
UPFILL, -S *vb* fill up
UPFLING, UPFLUNG *vb* throw upwards
UPFLOW, -S *vb* flow upwards
UPFLUNG ▸ **upfling**
UPFOLD, -S *vb* fold up
UPFRONT *adj, adv*
UPFURL, -S *vb* roll up
UPGANG, -S *n* climb
UPGAZE, -D, -S *vb* gaze upwards
UPGIRD, -S *vb* support or hold up
UPGIRT, -S *same as* ▸ **upgird**
UPGO, -ES, -ING, -NE, UPWENT *vb* ascend
UPGRADE *vb*
UPGROW, UPGREW, -N, -S *vb* grow up
UPGUSH *vb* flow upwards
UPHAND *adj* lifted by hand
UPHANG, -S, UPHUNG *vb* hang up
UPHAUD, -S *Scots variant of* ▸ **uphold**
UPHEAP, -S *vb* heap or pile up
UPHEAVE, UPHOVE *vb*
UPHELD ▸ **uphold**
UPHILD *archaic past form of* ▸ **uphold**
UPHILL, -S *adj* sloping or leading upwards ▹ *adv* up a slope ▹ *n* difficulty
UPHOARD *vb* hoard up
UPHOIST *vb* raise
UPHOLD, UPHELD, -S *vb*
UPHOORD *vb* heap up
UPHOVE ▸ **upheave**
UPHROE, -S *variant spelling of* ▸ **euphroe**
UPHUNG ▸ **uphang**
UPHURL, -S *vb* throw upwards
UPJET, -S *vb* stream upwards
UPKEEP, -S *n*
UPKNIT, -S *vb* bind
UPLAID ▸ **uplay**
UPLAND, -S *adj, n*
UPLAY, UPLAID, -S *vb* stash
UPLEAD, -S, UPLED *vb* lead upwards
UPLEAN, -S, -T *vb* lean on something
UPLEAP, -S, -T *vb* jump upwards
UPLED ▸ **uplead**
UPLIFT, -S *vb, n*
UPLIGHT, UPLIT *n* lamp or wall light designed or positioned to cast its light upwards ▹ *vb* light in an upward direction
UPLINK, -S *n* transmitter that sends signals up to a communications satellite ▹ *vb* send (data) to a communications satellite
UPLIT ▸ **uplight**
UPLOAD, -S *vb*
UPLOCK, -S *vb* lock up
UPLOOK, -S *vb* look up
UPLYING *adj* raised
UPMAKE, UPMADE, -S *vb* make up

UPMAKER ▸ **upmake**
UPMAKES ▸ **upmake**
UPMOST *another word for* > **uppermost**
UPO *prep* upon
UPON *prep*
UPPED ▸ **up**
UPPER, -S *adj, n*
UPPILE, -D, -S *vb* pile up
UPPING, -S ▸ **up**
UPPISH *adj* snobbish, arrogant, or presumptuous
UPPITY *adj*
UPPROP, -S *vb* support
UPRAISE *vb* lift up
UPRAN ▸ **uprun**
UPRATE, -D, -S *vb* raise the value, rate, or size of, upgrade
UPREACH *vb* reach up
UPREAR, -S *vb* lift up
UPREST, -S *n* uprising
UPRIGHT *adj, adv, n, vb*
UPRISAL ▸ **uprise**
UPRISE, -N, -S, UPROSE *vb*
UPRISER ▸ **uprise**
UPRISES ▸ **uprise**
UPRIST, -S *same as* ▸ **uprest**
UPRIVER *adv* towards or near the source of a river ▹ *n* area located upstream
UPROAR, -S *n, vb*
UPROLL, -S *vb* roll up
UPROOT, -S *vb*
UPROSE ▸ **uprise**
UPROUSE *vb* rouse or stir up
UPRUN, UPRAN, -S *vb* run up
UPRUSH *n* upward rush, as of consciousness ▹ *vb* rush upwards
UPRYST *same as* ▸ **uprest**
UPS ▸ **up**
UPSCALE *adj, vb*
UPSEE, -S *n* drunken revel
UPSELL, -S, UPSOLD *vb*
UPSEND, -S, UPSENT *vb* send up
UPSET, -S *adj, vb, n*
UPSEY, -S *same as* ▸ **upsee**
UPSHIFT *vb*
UPSHOOT *vb* shoot upwards
UPSHOT, -S *n*
UPSIDE, -S *n*
UPSIES ▸ **upsy**
UPSILON *n* 20th letter in the Greek alphabet
UPSIZE, -D, -S *vb*
UPSKILL *vb*
UPSLOPE *adv* up a slope ▹ *n* upward slope
UPSOAR, -S *vb* soar up
UPSOLD ▸ **upsell**
UPSPEAK, UPSPAKE, UPSPOKE *vb* speak with rising intonation
UPSPEAR *vb* grow upwards in a spear-like manner
UPSPOKE ▸ **upspeak**
UPSTAGE *adj, vb, adv, n*
UPSTAIR *same as* > **upstairs**
UPSTAND, UPSTOOD *vb*
UPSTARE *vb* stare upwards
UPSTART *n, vb*
UPSTATE *adv* towards, in, from, or relating to the outlying or northern sections of a state ▹ *n* outlying, esp northern, sections of a state
UPSTAY, -S *vb* support
UPSTEP, -S *n* type of vocal intonation
UPSTIR, -S *vb* stir up ▹ *n* commotion
UPSTOOD ▸ **upstand**
UPSURGE *n* rapid rise or swell ▹ *vb* surge up
UPSWARM *vb* rise or send upwards in a swarm
UPSWAY, -S *vb* swing in the air
UPSWEEP, UPSWEPT *n* curve or sweep upwards ▹ *vb* sweep, curve, or brush or be swept, curved, or brushed upwards
UPSWELL *vb* swell up or cause to swell up
UPSWEPT ▸ **upsweep**
UPSWING, UPSWUNG *n* recovery period in a trade cycle ▹ *vb* swing or move up
UPSY, UPSIES *same as* ▸ **upsee**
UPTA *same as* ▸ **upter**
UPTAK, -S *same as* ▸ **uptake**
UPTAKE, -N, -S, UPTOOK *n, vb*
UPTAKS ▸ **uptak**
UPTALK, -S *n* style of speech in which every sentence ends with a rising tone ▹ *vb* talk in this manner
UPTEAR, -S, UPTORE, UPTORN *vb* tear up
UPTEMPO *adj, n*
UPTER *adj* of poor quality
UPTHROW, UPTHREW *n* upward movement of

rocks on one side of a fault plane relative to rocks on the other side ▷ *vb* throw upwards
UPTICK, -S *n* rise or increase
UPTIE, -D, -S, UPTYING *vb* tie up
UPTIGHT *adj*
UPTILT, -S *vb* tilt up
UPTIME, -S *n* time during which a machine, such as a computer, actually operates
UPTOOK ▶ **uptake**
UPTORE ▶ **uptear**
UPTORN ▶ **uptear**
UPTOSS *vb* throw upwards
UPTOWN, -S *adv, n*
UPTRAIN *vb* train up
UPTREND *n* upward trend
UPTURN, -S *n, vb*
UPTYING ▶ **uptie**
UPVALUE *vb* raise the value of
UPVOTE, -D, -S *vb* publicly approve of a social media post
UPWAFT, -S *vb* waft upwards
UPWARD *same as* ▶ **upwards**
UPWARDS *adv*
UPWELL, -S *vb* well up
UPWENT ▶ **upgo**
UPWHIRL *vb* spin upwards
UPWIND, -S, UPWOUND *adv* into or against the wind ▷ *adj* going against the wind ▷ *vb* wind up
UPWRAP, -S *vb* wrap up
UR *interj* hesitant utterance used to fill gaps in talking
URACHUS, URACHI *n* cord of tissue connected to the bladder
URACIL, -S *n* pyrimidine present in all living cells
URAEI ▶ **uraeus**

This plural of **uraeus**, an Egyptian symbol of kingship, is very useful for dumping a surplus of vowels.

URAEMIA *n* accumulation of waste products in the blood
URAEMIC ▶ **uraemia**
URAEUS, URAEI *n* sacred serpent of ancient Egypt
URALI, -S *n* type of plant
URALITE *n* mineral that replaces pyroxene in some rocks
URANIA, -S *n* uranium dioxide
URANIAN *adj* heavenly
URANIAS ▶ **urania**
URANIC *adj* of or containing uranium, esp in a high valence state
URANIDE *n* any element having an atomic number greater than that of protactinium
URANIN, -S *n* type of alkaline substance
URANISM *n* old word for homosexuality
URANITE *n* any of various minerals containing uranium, esp torbernite or autunite
URANIUM *n*
URANOUS *adj* of or containing uranium, esp in a low valence state
URANYL, -S *n* type of divalent ion
URAO, -S *n* type of mineral
URARE, -S *same as* ▶ **urali**
URARI, -S *same as* ▶ **urali**
URASE, -S *same as* ▶ **urease**
URATE, -S *n* any salt or ester of uric acid
URATIC ▶ **urate**
URB, -S *n* urban area
URBAN *adj*
URBANE, -R *adj*
URBEX, -ES *n* short for urban exploration, the hobby of exploring derelict urban structures
URBIA, -S *n* urban area
URBS ▶ **urb**
URCEOLI > **urceolus**
URCHIN, -S *n*
URD, -S *n* type of plant with edible seeds
URDE *adj* (in heraldry) having points
URDEE *same as* ▶ **urde**
URDS ▶ **urd**
URDY *n* heraldic line pattern
URE, -S *same as* ▶ **aurochs**

UREA, -S *n* white soluble crystalline compound found in urine
UREAL ▸ **urea**
UREAS ▸ **urea**
UREASE, -S *n* enzyme that converts urea to ammonium carbonate
UREDIA ▸ **uredium**
UREDIAL ▸ **uredium**
UREDINE ▸ **uredo**
UREDIUM, UREDIA *n* spore-producing body of some rust fungi in which uredospores are formed
UREDO, -S *less common name for* ▸ **urticaria**
UREIC ▸ **urea**
UREIDE, -S *n* any of a class of organic compounds derived from urea
UREMIA, -S *same as* ▸ **uraemia**
UREMIC ▸ **uremia**
URENA, -S *n* plant genus
URENT *adj* burning
URES ▸ **ure**
URESIS, URESES *n* urination
URETER, -S *n* tube that conveys urine from the kidney to the bladder
URETHAN *same as* ▸ **urethane**
URETHRA *n*
URETIC *adj* of or relating to urine
URGE, -D, -S *n, vb*
URGENCE ▸ **urgent**
URGENCY ▸ **urgent**
URGENT *adj*
URGER, -S ▸ **urge**
URGES ▸ **urge**
URGING, -S ▸ **urge**
URIAL, -S *n* type of sheep
URIC *adj* of or derived from urine
URICASE *n* type of enzyme
URIDINE *n* nucleoside present in all living cells in a combined form, esp in RNA
URINAL, -S *n*
URINANT *adj* having the head downwards
URINARY *adj, n*
URINATE *vb*
URINE, -D, -S, URINING *n, vb*
URINOSE *same as* ▸ **urinous**
URINOUS *adj* of, resembling, or containing urine
URITE, -S *n* part of the abdomen
URMAN, -S *n* forest
URN, -ED, -S *n, vb*
URNAL ▸ **urn**
URNED ▸ **urn**
URNFUL, -S *n* capacity of an urn
URNLIKE ▸ **urn**
URNS ▸ **urn**
URODELE *n* amphibian of the order which includes the salamanders and newts
UROGRAM *n* X-ray of the urinary tract
UROLITH *n* calculus in the urinary tract
UROLOGY *n*
UROMERE *n* part of the abdomen
UROPOD, -S *n* paired appendage that forms part of the tailfan in lobsters
UROSIS, UROSES *n* urinary disease
UROSOME *n* abdomen of arthropods
URP, -ED, -ING, -S *dialect word for* ▸ **vomit**
URSA, -E *n* she-bear
URSID, -S *n* meteor
URSINE *adj* of or like a bear
URSON, -S *n* type of porcupine
URTEXT, -S *n* earliest form of a text
URTEXTE *same as* ▸ **urtexts**
URTEXTS ▸ **urtext**
URTICA, -S *n* type of nettle
URUBU, -S *n* type of bird
URUS, -ES *another name for the* ▸ **aurochs**
URVA, -S *n* Indian mongoose
US *pron*
USABLE *adj*
USABLY ▸ **usable**
USAGE, -S *n*
USAGER, -S *n* person who has the use of something in trust
USAGES ▸ **usage**
USANCE, -S *n* period of time permitted for the redemption of foreign bills of exchange
USAUNCE *same as* ▸ **usance**
USE, -S, USING *vb, n*
USEABLE *same as* ▸ **usable**

USEABLY ▸ **usable**
USED *adj*
USEFUL, -S *adj, n*
USELESS *adj*
USER, -S *n*
USES ▸ **use**
USHER, -ED, -S *n, vb*
USING ▸ **use**
USNEA, -S *n* type of lichen
USQUE, -S *n* whisky
USTION, -S *n* burning
USUAL, -S *adj, n*
USUALLY *adv*
USUALS ▸ **usual**
USUCAPT > **usucapion**
USURE, -D, -S, USURING *vb*
USURER, -S *n*
USURES ▸ **usure**
USURESS *n* female usurer
USURIES ▸ **usury**
USURING ▸ **usure**
USUROUS ▸ **usury**
USURP, -ED, -S *vb*
USURPER ▸ **usurp**
USURPS ▸ **usurp**
USURY, USURIES *n*
USWARD *adv* towards us
USWARDS *same as* ▸ **usward**
UT, -S *n* syllable used in the fixed system of solmization for the note C
UTA *n* side-blotched lizard
UTAS, -ES *n* eighth day of a festival
UTE, -S *n*
UTENSIL *n*
UTERI ▸ **uterus**
UTERINE *adj*
UTERUS, UTERI *n*
UTES ▸ **ute**
UTILE, -S *n* W African tree
UTILISE *same as* ▸ **utilize**
UTILITY *n, adj*
UTILIZE *vb*
UTIS, -ES *n* uproar
UTMOST, -S *n, adj*
UTOPIA, -S *n*
UTOPIAN *adj, n*
UTOPIAS ▸ **utopia**
UTOPISM ▸ **utopia**
UTOPIST ▸ **utopia**
UTRICLE *n* larger of the two parts of the membranous labyrinth of the internal ear
UTS ▸ **ut**
UTTER, -ED, -ER, -S *vb, adj*
UTTERLY *adv*
UTTERS ▸ **utter**
UTU, -S *n* reward
UVA, -E, -S *n* grape or fruit resembling this
UVEA, -S *n* part of the eyeball consisting of the iris, ciliary body, and choroid
UVEAL ▸ **uvea**
UVEAS ▸ **uvea**
UVEITIC ▸ **uveitis**
UVEITIS *n* inflammation of the uvea
UVEOUS ▸ **uvea**
UVULA, -E, -S *n*
UVULAR, -S *adj, n*
UVULAS ▸ **uvula**
UXORIAL *adj*

Vv

VAC, -KED, -KING, -S *vb* clean with a vacuum cleaner

Meaning to clean with a vacuum cleaner, this can be a useful short word for dealing with that awkward letter V.

VACANCE *n* vacant period
VACANCY *n*
VACANT *adj*
VACATE, -D, -S *vb*
VACATUR *n* annulment
VACCINA *same as* > **vaccinia**
VACCINE *n*
VACKED ▶ **vac**
VACKING ▶ **vac**
VACS ▶ **vac**
VACUA ▶ **vacuum**
VACUATE *vb* empty
VACUIST *n* person believing in the existence of vacuums in nature
VACUITY *n*
VACUOLE *n*
VACUOUS *adj*
VACUUM, VACUA, -S *n, vb*
VADE, -S *vb* fade
VADED ▶ **vade**
VADES ▶ **vade**
VADING ▶ **vade**
VADOSE *adj* of or derived from water occurring above the water table
VAE, -S *same as* ▶ **voe**
VAG, -GED, -GING, -S *n* informal Australian word for a vagrant ▷ *vb* arrest someone for vagrancy
VAGAL *adj* of, relating to, or affecting the vagus nerve
VAGALLY ▶ **vagal**
VAGARY *n*
VAGGED ▶ **vag**
VAGGING ▶ **vag**
VAGI ▶ **vagus**
VAGILE *adj* able to move freely
VAGINA, -E, -S *n*
VAGINAL ▶ **vagina**
VAGINAS ▶ **vagina**
VAGITUS *n* newborn baby's cry
VAGRANT *n, adj*
VAGROM *same as* ▶ **vagrant**
VAGS ▶ **vag**
VAGUE, -R, -S, -ST *adj, vb*
VAGUED ▶ **vague**
VAGUELY ▶ **vague**
VAGUER ▶ **vague**
VAGUES ▶ **vague**
VAGUEST ▶ **vague**
VAGUING ▶ **vague**
VAGUISH *adj* rather vague
VAGUS, VAGI *n* tenth cranial nerve, which supplies the heart, lungs, and viscera
VAHANA, -S *n* vehicle
VAHINE, -S *n* Polynesian woman
VAIL, -ED, -ING, -S *vb* lower (something, such as a weapon), esp as a sign of deference or submission
VAIN, -ER, -EST *adj*
VAINLY ▶ **vain**
VAIR, -S *n* fur used to trim robes in the Middle Ages
VAIRE *adj* of Russian squirrel fur
VAIRIER ▶ **vairy**
VAIRS ▶ **vair**
VAIRY, VAIRIER ▶ **vair**
VAIVODE *n* Slavic governor
VAKAS, -ES *n* Armenian priestly collar
VAKASS *n* Armenian priestly collar
VAKEEL, -S *n* (in India) ambassador
VAKIL, -S *same as* ▶ **vakeel**
VALANCE *n, vb*
VALE, -S *n, sentence substitute*
VALENCE *same as* ▶ **valency**

VALENCY *n* power of an atom to make molecular bonds
VALERIC *adj* of, relating to, or derived from valerian
VALES ▸ **vale**
VALET, -ED, -S *n, vb*
VALETA, -S *n* old-time dance in triple time
VALETE, -S *n* farewell
VALETED ▸ **valet**
VALETES ▸ **valete**
VALETS ▸ **valet**
VALGOID ▸ **valgus**
VALGOUS *same as* ▸ **valgus**
VALGUS *adj* denoting a deformity of a limb ▹ *n* abnormal position of a limb
VALI, -S *n* Turkish civil governor
VALIANT *adj, n*
VALID, -ER *adj*
VALIDLY ▸ **valid**
VALINE, -S *n* essential amino acid
VALIS ▸ **vali**
VALISE, -S *n*
VALIUM, -S *n*
VALKYR, -S *variant of* > **valkyrie**
VALLAR, -S *adj* pertaining to a rampart ▹ *n* gold Roman crown awarded to the first soldier who broke into the enemy's camp
VALLARY *same as* ▸ **vallar**
VALLATE *adj* surrounded with a wall
VALLEY, -S *n*
VALLUM, -S *n* Roman rampart or earthwork
VALONEA *same as* ▸ **valonia**
VALONIA *n* acorn cups and unripe acorns of a particular oak
VALOR, -S *same as* ▸ **valour**
VALOUR, -S *n* bravery; brave person
VALSE, -D, -S, VALSING *another word for* ▸ **waltz**
VALUATE *vb* value or evaluate
VALUE, -D, -S, VALUING *n, vb*
VALUER, -S ▸ **value**
VALUES ▸ **value**
VALUING ▸ **value**
VALUTA, -S *n* value of one currency in terms of its exchange rate with another
VALVAL *same as* > **valvular**
VALVAR *same as* > **valvular**
VALVATE *adj* furnished with a valve or valves
VALVE, -S *n, vb*
VALVED ▸ **valve**
VALVES ▸ **valve**
VALVING ▸ **valve**
VALVULA *same as* ▸ **valvule**
VALVULE *n* small valve or a part resembling one
VAMOOSE *vb* leave a place hurriedly
VAMOSE, -S *same as* ▸ **vamoose**
VAMOSED ▸ **vamose**
VAMOSES ▸ **vamose**
VAMP, -ED, -S *n, vb*
VAMPER, -S ▸ **vamp**
VAMPIER ▸ **vampy**
VAMPING ▸ **vamp**
VAMPIRE *n, vb*
VAMPISH ▸ **vamp**
VAMPS ▸ **vamp**
VAMPY, VAMPIER ▸ **vamp**
VAN, -S *n, vb*
VANADIC *adj* of or containing vanadium, esp in a trivalent or pentavalent state
VANDA, -S *n* type of orchid
VANDAL, -S *n*
VANDAS ▸ **vanda**
VANDYKE *n* short pointed beard ▹ *vb* cut with deep zigzag indentations
VANE, -S *n*
VANED ▸ **vane**
VANES ▸ **vane**
VANESSA *n* type of butterfly
VANG, -S *n* type of rope or tackle on a sailing ship
VANILLA *n, adj*
VANISH *vb, n*
VANITAS *n* type of Dutch painting
VANITY *n*
VANLIKE *adj* like a van
VANLOAD *n* amount van will carry
VANMAN, VANMEN *n* man in control of a van
VANNED ▸ **van**
VANNER, -S *n* horse used to pull delivery vehicles
VANNING ▸ **van**
VANPOOL *n* van-sharing group
VANS ▸ **van**
VANT, -S *archaic word for* > **vanguard**

VANTAGE *n, vb*
VANTS ▸ **vant**
VANWARD *adv* in or towards the front
VAPE, -D, -S *vb* inhale nicotine vapour (from an electronic cigarette)
VAPER, -S *n* one who inhales nicotine vapour from an electronic cigarette
VAPES ▸ **vape**
VAPID, -ER *adj*
VAPIDLY ▸ **vapid**
VAPING, -S *n* the practice of inhaling nicotine vapour (from an electronic cigarette)
VAPOR, -ED, -S *same as* ▸ **vapour**
VAPORER ▸ **vapor**
VAPORS ▸ **vapor**
VAPORY *same as* ▸ **vapoury**
VAPOUR, -S *n, vb*
VAPOURY *adj* full of vapours
VAQUERO *n* cattle-hand
VAR, -S *n* unit of reactive power of an alternating current
VARA, -S *n* unit of length used in Spain, Portugal, and South America
VARAN, -S *n* type of lizard
VARAS ▸ **vara**
VARDY, VARDIES *n* verdict
VARE, -S *n* rod
VAREC, -S *n* ash obtained from kelp
VARECH, -S *same as* ▸ **varec**
VARECS ▸ **varec**
VARES ▸ **vare**
VAREUSE *n* type of coat
VARIA, -S *n* collection or miscellany, esp of literary works
VARIANT *adj, n*
VARIAS ▸ **varia**
VARIATE *n* random variable or a numerical value taken by it ▹ *vb* vary
VARICES ▸ **varix**
VARIED ▸ **vary**
VARIER, -S *n* person who varies
VARIES ▸ **vary**
VARIETY *n*
VARIOLA *n* smallpox
VARIOLE *n* any of the rounded masses that make up the rock variolite
VARIOUS *adj*
VARIX, VARICES *n* tortuous dilated vein
VARLET, -S *n* menial servant
VARMENT *same as* ▸ **varmint**
VARMINT *n*
VARNA, -S *n* any of the four Hindu castes
VARNISH *n, vb*
VAROOM *same as* ▸ **vroom**
VAROOMS *same as* ▸ **varoom**
VARROA, -S *n* small parasite
VARS ▸ **var**
VARSAL *adj* universal
VARSITY *n*
VARUS, -ES *adj* denoting a deformity of a limb ▹ *n* abnormal position of a limb
VARVE, -S *n* typically thin band of sediment deposited annually in glacial lakes
VARVED *adj* having layers of sedimentary deposit
VARVEL, -S *n* piece of falconry equipment
VARVES ▸ **varve**
VARY, VARIED, VARIES *vb*
VARYING ▸ **vary**
VAS, -A *n* vessel or tube that carries a fluid
VASAL ▸ **vas**
VASCULA > **vasculum**
VASE, -S *n*
VASEFUL *n* contents of a vase
VASES ▸ **vase**
VASSAIL *archaic variant of* ▸ **vassal**
VASSAL, -S *n, adj, vb*
VAST, -ER, -EST, -S *adj, n*
VASTIER ▸ **vasty**
VASTITY ▸ **vast**
VASTLY ▸ **vast**
VASTS ▸ **vast**
VASTY, VASTIER *archaic or poetic word for* ▸ **vast**
VAT, -S, -TED, -TING *n, vb*
VATABLE *adj* subject to VAT
VATFUL, -S *n* amount enough to fill a vat
VATIC *adj* of or characteristic of a prophet
VATICAL *same as* ▸ **vatic**
VATMAN, VATMEN *n* Customs and Excise employee
VATS ▸ **vat**
VATTED ▸ **vat**
VATTER, -S *n* person who works with vats; blender

VATTING ▸ **vat**
VATU, -S *n* standard monetary unit of Vanuatu
VAU, -S *same as* ▸ **vav**
VAUCH, -ED, -ES *vb* move fast
VAUDOO, -S *same as* ▸ **voodoo**
VAUDOUX *same as* ▸ **voodoo**
VAULT, -ED, -S *n, vb*
VAULTER ▸ **vault**
VAULTS ▸ **vault**
VAULTY *adj* arched
VAUNCE, -D, -S *same as* ▸ **advance**
VAUNT, -ED, -S *vb* describe or display (success or possessions) boastfully ▹ *n* boast
VAUNTER ▸ **vaunt**
VAUNTIE *same as* ▸ **vaunty**
VAUNTS ▸ **vaunt**
VAUNTY *adj* proud
VAURIEN *n* rascal
VAUS ▸ **vau**
VAUT, -S *same as* ▸ **vault**
VAUTE, -D, -S, VAUTING *same as* ▸ **vault**
VAUTS ▸ **vaut**
VAV, -S *n* sixth letter of the Hebrew alphabet

It is surprising how often one wants to get rid of two Vs, and when one does, this word, the name of a Hebrew letter, fits the bill nicely. It has an equally useful variant **vaw**.

VAVASOR *n* (in feudal society) vassal who also has their own vassals
VAVS ▸ **vav**
VAW, -S *same as* ▸ **vav**
VAWARD, -S *n* vanguard
VAWNTIE ▸ **vaunt**
VAWS ▸ **vaw**
VAWTE, -D, -S, VAWTING *same as* ▸ **vault**
VAX, -ES *n* vaccination
VEAL, -ED, -ING, -S *n, vb*
VEALE, -S *Spenserian word for* ▸ **veil**
VEALED ▸ **veal**
VEALER, -S *n* young bovine animal of up to 14 months old grown for veal
VEALES ▸ **veale**
VEALIER ▸ **vealy**
VEALING ▸ **veal**
VEALS ▸ **veal**
VEALY, VEALIER ▸ **veal**
VECTOR, -S *n, vb*
VEDALIA *n* Australian ladybird which is a pest of citrus fruits
VEDETTE *n* small patrol vessel
VEDUTA, -S, VEDUTE *n* painting of a town or city
VEE, -S *n* letter 'v'
VEEJAY, -S *n* video jockey
VEENA, -S *same as* ▸ **vina**
VEEP, -S *n* vice president
VEEPEE, -S *n* vice president
VEEPS ▸ **veep**
VEER, -ED, -ING, -S *vb, n*

VEERIES ▸ **veery**
VEERING ▸ **veer**
VEERS ▸ **veer**
VEERY, VEERIES *n* tawny brown North American thrush
VEES ▸ **vee**
VEG, -ES, -GED, -GES, -GING *n, vb*

Veg is a short form of **vegetable**. If someone plays this, remember that you can add an A or O to it to form **vega** or **vego**.

VEGA, -S *n* tobacco plantation
VEGAN, -S *n, adj*
VEGANIC *adj* farmed without the use of animal products or byproducts
VEGANS ▸ **vegan**
VEGAS ▸ **vega**
VEGES ▸ **veg**
VEGETAL *adj* of or relating to plant life ▹ *n* vegetable
VEGETE *adj* lively
VEGGED ▸ **veg**
VEGGES ▸ **veg**
VEGGIE, -R, -S *n, adj*
VEGGING ▸ **veg**
VEGIE, -R, -S, -ST *n* vegetable ▹ *adj* vegetarian
VEGO, -S *adj* vegetarian ▹ *n* vegetarian
VEHICLE *n*
VEHM, -E *n* type of medieval German court
VEHMIC ▸ **vehm**
VEIL, -S *n, vb*
VEILED *adj*

VEILER, -S ▸ **veil**
VEILIER ▸ **veily**
VEILING *n* veil or the fabric used for veils
VEILS ▸ **veil**
VEILY, VEILIER ▸ **veil**
VEIN, -ED, -S *n, vb*
VEINAL ▸ **vein**
VEINED ▸ **vein**
VEINER, -S *n* wood-carving tool
VEINIER ▸ **veiny**
VEINING *n* pattern or network of veins or streaks
VEINLET *n* any small vein or venule
VEINOUS ▸ **vein**
VEINS ▸ **vein**
VEINULE *less common spelling of* ▸ **venule**
VEINY, VEINIER ▸ **vein**
VELA ▸ **velum**
VELAMEN *n* thick layer of dead cells that covers the aerial roots of certain orchids
VELAR, -S *adj* of, relating to, or attached to a velum ▹ *n* velar sound
VELARIA > **velarium**
VELARIC ▸ **velar**
VELARS ▸ **velar**
VELATE *adj* having or covered with velum
VELATED *same as* ▸ **velate**
VELCRO, -S *n*
VELD, -S *n* high grassland in southern Africa
VELDT, -S *same as* ▸ **veld**
VELE, -S *same as* ▸ **veil**
VELETA, -S *same as* ▸ **valeta**
VELIGER *n* free-swimming larva of many molluscs
VELITES *pl n* light-armed troops in ancient Rome, drawn from the poorer classes
VELL, -S *n* salted calf's stomach, used in cheese making
VELLET, -S *n* velvet
VELLON, -S *n* silver and copper alloy used in old Spanish coins
VELLS ▸ **vell**
VELLUM, -S *n, adj*
VELLUS *n* as in **vellus hair** short fine unpigmented hair covering the human body
VELOCE *adv* to be played rapidly
VELOUR *n*
VELOURS *same as* ▸ **velour**
VELOUTE *n* rich white sauce or soup made from stock, egg yolks, and cream
VELUM, VELA *n* any of various membranous structures
VELURE, -S *n* velvet or a similar fabric ▹ *vb* cover with velure
VELURED ▸ **velure**
VELURES ▸ **velure**
VELVET, -S *n, vb*
VELVETY ▸ **velvet**
VENA, -E *n* vein in the body
VENAL *adj*
VENALLY ▸ **venal**
VENATIC *adj* of, relating to, or used in hunting
VENATOR *n* hunter
VEND, -ED, -S *vb*
VENDACE *n* either of two small whitefish occurring in lakes in Scotland and NW England
VENDAGE *n* vintage
VENDED ▸ **vend**
VENDEE, -S *n* person to whom something, esp real property, is sold
VENDER, -S *same as* ▸ **vendor**
VENDING ▸ **vend**
VENDIS *same as* ▸ **vendace**
VENDISS *same as* ▸ **vendace**
VENDOR, -S *n*
VENDS ▸ **vend**
VENDUE, -S *n* public sale
VENEER, -S *n, vb*
VENEFIC *adj* having poisonous effects
VENENE, -S *n* medicine from snake venom
VENERER *n* hunter
VENEWE, -S *same as* ▸ **venue**
VENEY, -S *n* thrust
VENGE, -D, -S, VENGING *vb*
VENGER, -S ▸ **venge**
VENGES ▸ **venge**
VENGING ▸ **venge**
VENIAL *adj* (of a sin or fault) easily forgiven
VENIN, -S *n* any of the poisonous constituents of animal venoms
VENINE, -S *same as* ▸ **venin**
VENINS ▸ **venin**

VENIRE, -S *n* list from which jurors are selected
VENISON *n*
VENITE, -S *n* musical setting for the 95th psalm
VENNEL, -S *n* lane
VENOM, -ED, -S *n, vb*
VENOMER ▸ **venom**
VENOMS ▸ **venom**
VENOSE *adj* having veins
VENOUS *adj* of veins
VENT, -ED, -ING, -S *n, vb*
VENTAGE *n* small opening
VENTAIL *n* (in medieval armour) a covering for the lower part of the face
VENTANA *n* window
VENTED ▸ **vent**
VENTER, -S ▸ **vent**
VENTIGE *same as* ▸ **ventage**
VENTIL, -S *n* valve on a musical instrument
VENTING ▸ **vent**
VENTOSE *adj* full of wind ▹ *n* apparatus sometimes used to assist the delivery of a baby
VENTRAL *adj* relating to the front of the body ▹ *n* ventral fin
VENTRE, -S *same as* ▸ **venture**
VENTRED ▸ **ventre**
VENTRES ▸ **ventre**
VENTS ▸ **vent**
VENTURE *n, vb*
VENTURI *n* tube used to control the flow of fluid
VENUE, -S *n*
VENULAR ▸ **venule**
VENULE, -S *n* any of the small branches of a vein
VENUS, -ES *n*
VERA *adj* as in **aloe vera** plant substance used in skin and hair preparations
VERANDA *n*
VERB, -S *n*
VERBAL, -S *adj, n, vb*
VERBENA *n* plant with sweet-smelling flowers
VERBID, -S *n* any nonfinite form of a verb or any nonverbal word derived from a verb
VERBIFY *another word for* > **verbalize**
VERBILE *n* person who is best stimulated by words
VERBING *n* use of nouns as verbs
VERBOSE *adj*
VERBS ▸ **verb**
VERD *n* as in **verd antique** dark green mottled impure variety of serpentine marble
VERDANT *adj*
VERDET, -S *n* type of verdigris
VERDICT *n*
VERDIN, -S *n* small W North American tit having grey plumage with a yellow head
VERDIT, -S *same as* ▸ **verdict**
VERDITE *n* type of rock used in jewellery
VERDITS ▸ **verdit**
VERDOY, -S *n* floral or leafy shield decoration
VERDURE *n* flourishing green vegetation
VERGE, -D, -S, VERGING *n, vb*
VERGER, -S *n* church caretaker
VERGES ▸ **verge**
VERGING ▸ **verge**
VERGLAS *n* thin film of ice on rock
VERIDIC *same as* > **veridical**
VERIER ▸ **very**
VERIEST ▸ **very**
VERIFY *vb*
VERILY *adv*
VERISM, -S *n* extreme naturalism in art or literature
VERISMO *n* school of composition that originated in Italian opera
VERISMS ▸ **verism**
VERIST, -S ▸ **verism**
VERITAS *n*
VERITE, -S *adj* involving a high degree of realism or naturalism ▹ *n* this kind of realism in film
VERITY *n* true statement or principle
VERJUS *n* acid juice of unripe grapes, apples, or crab apples
VERLAN, -S *n* variety of French slang in which the syllables are inverted
VERLIG *adj* enlightened
VERMAL ▸ **vermis**
VERMEIL *n* gilded silver, bronze, or other metal, used esp in the 19th century ▹ *vb* decorate

with vermeil ▷ *adj* vermilion
VERMELL *same as* ▶ **vermeil**
VERMES ▶ **vermis**
VERMIAN ▶ **vermis**
VERMIL, -S *same as* ▶ **vermeil**
VERMILY ▶ **vermeil**
VERMIN, -S *n*
VERMINY *adj* full of vermin
VERMIS, VERMES *n* middle lobe connecting the two halves of the cerebellum
VERMUTH *same as* ▶ **vermouth**
VERNAL *adj* occurring in spring
VERNANT ▶ **vernal**
VERNIER *n* movable scale on a measuring instrument for taking readings in fractions
VERNIX *n* white substance covering the skin of a foetus
VERONAL *n* long-acting barbiturate used medicinally
VERRA *Scot word for* ▶ **very**
VERREL, -S *n* ferrule
VERREY *same as* ▶ **vair**
VERRINE *n* starter, dessert, or other dish served in a glass
VERRUCA *n*
VERRUGA *same as* ▶ **verruca**
VERRY *same as* ▶ **vair**
VERS *n* verse
VERSAL, -S *n* embellished letter
VERSANT *n* side or slope of a mountain or mountain range
VERSE, -S *n, vb*
VERSED *adj*
VERSER, -S *n* versifier
VERSES ▶ **verse**
VERSET, -S *n* short, often sacred, verse
VERSIFY *vb*
VERSIN, -S *same as* ▶ **versine**
VERSINE *n* trigonometric function
VERSING ▶ **verse**
VERSINS ▶ **versin**
VERSION *n, vb*
VERSO, -S *n*
VERST, -S *n* unit of length used in Russia
VERSTE, -S *same as* ▶ **verst**
VERSTS ▶ **verst**
VERSUS *prep*
VERSUTE *adj* cunning
VERT, -ED, -ING, -S *n* right to cut green wood in a forest ▷ *vb* turn
VERTEX *n* point on a geometric figure where the sides form an angle
VERTIGO *n*
VERTING ▶ **vert**
VERTS ▶ **vert**
VERTU, -S *same as* ▶ **virtu**
VERTUE, -S *same as* ▶ **virtu**
VERTUS ▶ **vertu**
VERVAIN *n* plant with spikes of blue, purple, or white flowers
VERVE, -S *n*
VERVEL, -S *same as* ▶ **varvel**
VERVEN, -S *same as* ▶ **vervain**
VERVES ▶ **verve**
VERVET, -S *n* variety of South African guenon monkey
VERY, VERIER, VERIEST *adv, adj*
VESICA, -E, -S *n* bladder
VESICAL *adj* of or relating to a vesica, esp the urinary bladder
VESICAS ▶ **vesica**
VESICLE *n* sac or small cavity
VESPA, -S *n* type of wasp
VESPER *n* evening prayer, service, or hymn
VESPERS *pl n* service of evening prayer
VESPID, -S *n* insect of the family that includes the common wasp and hornet ▷ *adj* of or belonging to this family
VESPINE *adj* of, relating to, or resembling a wasp or wasps
VESPOID *adj* like a wasp
VESSAIL *archaic variant of* ▶ **vessel**
VESSEL, -S *n, adj*
VEST, -S *n, vb*
VESTA, -S *n* short friction match, usually of wood
VESTAL, -S *adj, n*
VESTAS ▶ **vesta**
VESTED *adj*
VESTEE, -S *n* person having a vested interest in something

VESTIGE *n*
VESTING ▸ **vest**
VESTRAL ▸ **vestry**
VESTRY *n* room in a church used as an office by the priest or minister
VESTS ▸ **vest**
VESTURE *n* garment or something that seems like a garment ▹ *vb* clothe
VET, -S, -TED *vb, n*
VETCH, -ES *n* climbing plant with a beanlike fruit used as fodder
VETCHY *adj* consisting of vetches
VETERAN *n, adj*
VETIVER *n* tall hairless grass of tropical and subtropical Asia
VETKOEK *n* South African cake
VETO, -ED, -ES, -ING *n, vb*
VETOER, -S ▸ **veto**
VETOES ▸ **veto**
VETOING ▸ **veto**
VETS ▸ **vet**
VETTED ▸ **vet**
VETTER, -S ▸ **vet**
VETTING *n*
VETTURA *n* Italian mode of transport
VEX, -ES *vb*
VEXED *adj*
VEXEDLY ▸ **vexed**
VEXER, -S ▸ **vex**
VEXES ▸ **vex**
VEXIL, -S *same as* > **vexillum**
VEXILLA > **vexillum**
VEXILS ▸ **vexil**
VEXING, -S ▸ **vex**
VEXT *same as* ▸ **vexed**
VEZIR, -S *same as* ▸ **vizier**
VIA, -E, -S *prep, n*
VIABLE *adj*
VIABLY ▸ **viable**
VIADUCT *n*
VIAE ▸ **via**
VIAL, -ED, -ING, -LED, -S *n, vb*
VIALFUL ▸ **vial**
VIALING ▸ **vial**
VIALLED ▸ **vial**
VIALS ▸ **vial**
VIAND, -S *n* type of food, esp a delicacy
VIAS ▸ **via**
VIATIC *same as* > **viatical**
VIATICA > **viaticum**
VIATOR, -S *n* traveller
VIBE *n*
VIBES *pl n*
VIBEX, VIBICES *n* mark under the skin
VIBEY, VIBIER, VIBIEST *adj* lively and vibrant
VIBICES ▸ **vibex**
VIBIER ▸ **vibey**
VIBIEST ▸ **vibey**
VIBIST, -S *n* person who plays a vibraphone in a jazz band or group
VIBRANT *adj, n*
VIBRATE *vb*
VIBRATO *n*
VIBRIO, -S *n* curved or spiral rodlike bacterium
VIBRION *same as* ▸ **vibrio**
VIBRIOS ▸ **vibrio**
VIBS *pl n* type of climbing shoes
VICAR, -S *n*
VICARLY *adj* like a vicar
VICARS ▸ **vicar**
VICARY *n* office of a vicar
VICE, -D, -S, VICING *n, adj, vb, prep*
VICEROY *n* governor of a colony who represented the monarch
VICES ▸ **vice**
VICHY, VICHIES *n* French mineral water
VICIATE *same as* ▸ **vitiate**
VICINAL *adj* neighbouring
VICING ▸ **vice**
VICIOUS *adj*
VICOMTE *n* French nobleman
VICTIM, -S *n*
VICTOR, -S *n*
VICTORY *n*
VICTRIX *same as* > **victress**
VICTUAL *vb*
VICUGNA *same as* ▸ **vicuna**
VICUNA, -S *n* S American animal like the llama
VID, -S *same as* ▸ **video**
VIDALIA *n* type of sweet onion
VIDAME, -S *n* French nobleman
VIDE *interj* look
VIDENDA > **videndum**
VIDEO, -ED, -S *vb, adj, n*
VIDETTE *same as* ▸ **vedette**
VIDICON *n* small television camera tube used in closed-circuit television
VIDIMUS *n* inspection

VIDIOT, -S *n* person who watches a lot of low-quality television
VIDS ▸ **vid**
VIDUAGE *n* widows collectively
VIDUAL *adj* widowed
VIDUITY *n* widowhood
VIDUOUS *adj* empty
VIE, -D, -S *vb*
VIELLE, -S *n* stringed musical instrument
VIENNA *n* as in **vienna loaf, vienna steak** associated with Vienna
VIER, -S ▸ **vie**
VIES ▸ **vie**
VIEW, -ED, -S *n, vb*
VIEWER, -S *n*
VIEWIER ▸ **viewy**
VIEWING *n*
VIEWLY *adj* pleasant on the eye
VIEWS ▸ **view**
VIEWY, VIEWIER *adj* having fanciful opinions or ideas
VIFDA, -S *same as* ▸ **vivda**
VIFF, -ED, -ING, -S *vb* (of an aircraft) change direction abruptly
VIG, -S *n* interest on a loan that is paid to a moneylender
VIGA, -S *n* rafter
VIGIA, -S *n* navigational hazard whose existence has not been confirmed
VIGIL, -S *n*
VIGOR, -S *same as* ▸ **vigour**
VIGORO, -S *n* women's game similar to cricket
VIGORS ▸ **vigor**
VIGOUR, -S *n*
VIGS ▸ **vig**
VIHARA, -S *n* type of Buddhist temple
VIHUELA *n* obsolete plucked stringed instrument of Spain
VIKING, -S *n*
VILAYET *n* major administrative division of Turkey
VILD *same as* ▸ **vile**
VILDE *same as* ▸ **vile**
VILDLY ▸ **vild**
VILE, -R, -ST *adj*
VILELY ▸ **vile**
VILER ▸ **vile**
VILEST ▸ **vile**
VILIACO *n* coward
VILIAGO *same as* ▸ **viliaco**
VILIFY *vb*
VILL, -S *n* township
VILLA, -E, -S *n*
VILLAGE *n*
VILLAIN *n*
VILLAN, -S *same as* ▸ **villein**
VILLANY *same as* > **villainy**
VILLAR ▸ **vill**
VILLAS ▸ **villa**
VILLEIN *n* peasant bound in service to their lord
VILLI ▸ **villus**
VILLOSE *same as* ▸ **villous**
VILLOUS *adj* (of plant parts) covered with long hairs
VILLS ▸ **vill**
VILLUS, VILLI *n* one of the finger-like projections in the small intestine of many vertebrates
VIM, -S *n* force, energy

> This word can be helpful when you're stuck with unpromising letters, and gives a reasonable score for a three-letter word.

VIMANA, -S *n* Indian mythological chariot of the gods
VIMEN, VIMINA *n* long flexible shoot that occurs in certain plants
VIMINAL ▸ **vimen**
VIMS ▸ **vim**
VIN, -S *n* French wine
VINA, -S *n* stringed musical instrument related to the sitar
VINAL, -S *n* type of manmade fibre
VINAS ▸ **vina**
VINASSE *n* residue left in a still after distilling spirits, esp brandy
VINCA, -S *n* type of trailing plant with blue flowers
VINCULA > **vinculum**
VINE, -S *n, vb*
VINEAL *adj* relating to wines
VINED ▸ **vine**
VINEGAR *n, vb*
VINER, -S *n* vinedresser
VINERY *n* hothouse for growing grapes
VINES ▸ **vine**
VINEW, -ED, -S *vb* become mouldy
VINIC *adj* of, relating to, or contained in wine
VINIER ▸ **viny**

VINIEST ▸ **viny**
VINIFY *vb* convert into wine
VINING ▸ **vine**
VINO, -S *n*
VINOUS *adj* of or characteristic of wine
VINS ▸ **vin**
VINT, -ED, -ING, -S *vb* sell (wine)
VINTAGE *n, adj, vb*
VINTED ▸ **vint**
VINTING ▸ **vint**
VINTNER *n*
VINTRY *n* place where wine is sold
VINTS ▸ **vint**
VINY, VINIER, VINIEST ▸ **vine**
VINYL, -S *n, adj*
VINYLIC ▸ **vinyl**
VINYLS ▸ **vinyl**
VIOL, -S *n*
VIOLA, -S *n*
VIOLATE *vb, adj*
VIOLD *archaic or poetic past form of* ▸ **vial**
VIOLENT *adj, vb*
VIOLER, -S *n* person who plays the viol
VIOLET, -S *n, adj*
VIOLIN, -S *n*
VIOLIST *n* person who plays the viola
VIOLONE *n* double-bass member of the viol family
VIOLS ▸ **viol**
VIPER, -S *n*
VIRAGO, -S *n* aggressive woman
VIRAL, -S *adj, n*
VIRALLY ▸ **viral**
VIRALS ▸ **viral**
VIRANDA *same as* ▸ **veranda**
VIRANDO *same as* ▸ **veranda**
VIRE, -D, -S, VIRING *vb* turn
VIRELAI *same as* ▸ **virelay**
VIRELAY *n* old French verse form
VIREMIA *same as* > **viraemia**
VIREMIC ▸ **viremia**
VIRENT *adj* green
VIREO, -S *n* American songbird
VIRES ▸ **vire**
VIRETOT *n* as in **on the viretot** in a rush
VIRGA, -E, -S *n* wisps of rain or snow that evaporate before reaching the earth
VIRGATE *adj* long, straight, and thin ▹ *n* obsolete measure of land area
VIRGE, -S *n* rod
VIRGER, -S *n* rod-bearer
VIRGES ▸ **virge**
VIRGIN, -S *n, adj, vb*
VIRGULE *another name for* ▸ **slash**
VIRID *adj* verdant
VIRILE *adj* having traditional male characteristics
VIRING ▸ **vire**
VIRINO, -S *n* entity postulated to be the causative agent of BSE
VIRION, -S *n* virus in infective form, consisting of an RNA particle within a protein covering
VIRL, -S *same as* ▸ **ferrule**
VIROID, -S *n* any of various infective RNA particles
VIROSE *adj* poisonous
VIROSIS, VIROSES *n* viral disease
VIROUS *same as* ▸ **virose**
VIRTU, -S *n* taste or love for curios or works of fine art
VIRTUAL *adj* having the effect but not the form of
VIRTUE, -S *n*
VIRTUS ▸ **virtu**
VIRUS, -ES *n*
VIS *n* power, force, or strength
VISA, -ED, -ING, -S *n, vb*
VISAGE, -S *n*
VISAGED ▸ **visage**
VISAGES ▸ **visage**
VISAING ▸ **visa**
VISARD, -S *same as* ▸ **vizard**
VISAS ▸ **visa**
VISCERA *pl n*
VISCID *adj* sticky
VISCIN, -S *n* sticky substance found on plants
VISCOID *adj* (of a fluid) somewhat viscous
VISCOSE *same as* ▸ **viscous**
VISCOUS *adj*
VISCUM, -S *n* shrub genus
VISCUS *n* internal organ
VISE, -D, -ING, -S, VISING *n, vb, vb*
VISEED ▸ **vise**
VISEING ▸ **vise**
VISES ▸ **vise**

VISHING *n* telephone scam used to gain access to credit card numbers or bank details
VISIBLE *adj, n*
VISIBLY ▸ **visible**
VISIE, -D, -S *same as* ▸ **vizy**
VISIER, -S ▸ **visie**
VISIES ▸ **visie**
VISILE, -S *n* person best stimulated by vision
VISING ▸ **vise**
VISION, -S *n, vb*
VISIT, -ED, -S *vb, n*
VISITE, -S *n* type of cape
VISITED ▸ **visit**
VISITEE *n* person who is visited
VISITER *variant of* ▸ **visitor**
VISITES ▸ **visite**
VISITOR *n*
VISITS ▸ **visit**
VISIVE *adj* visual
VISNE, -S *n* neighbourhood
VISNOMY *n* method of judging character from facial features
VISON, -S *n* type of mink
VISOR, -ED, -S *n, vb*
VISTA, -S *n, vb*
VISTAED ▸ **vista**
VISTAL ▸ **vista**
VISTAS ▸ **vista**
VISTO, -S *same as* ▸ **vista**
VISUAL, -S *adj, n*
VITA, -E, -S *n*
VITAL *adj*
VITALLY ▸ **vital**
VITALS *pl n*
VITAMER *n* type of chemical
VITAMIN *n*
VITAS ▸ **vita**
VITE *adv* musical direction
VITELLI > **vitellus**
VITESSE *n* speed
VITEX, -ES *n* type of herb
VITIATE *vb* spoil the effectiveness of
VITIOUS *adj* mistaken
VITRAGE *n* light fabric
VITRAIL, VITRAUX *n* stained glass
VITRAIN *n* type of coal
VITRAUX ▸ **vitrail**
VITREUM *n* vitreous body
VITRIC *adj* of, relating to, resembling, or having the nature of glass
VITRICS *pl n* glass products
VITRIFY *vb* change or be changed into glass or a glassy substance
VITRINE *n* glass display case or cabinet for works of art, curios, etc
VITRIOL *n, vb*
VITRO *n* as in **in vitro** (of processes) made to occur in an artificial environment
VITTA, -E *n* tubelike cavity containing oil that occurs in the fruits of certain plants
VITTATE ▸ **vitta**
VITTLE, -D *obsolete or dialect spelling of* ▸ **victual**
VITTLES *obsolete or dialect spelling of* > **victuals**
VITULAR *same as* > **vituline**
VIVA, -ED, -ING, -S *interj, n, vb*
VIVACE, -S *adv* in a lively manner ▹ *n* piece of music to be performed in this way
VIVAED ▸ **viva**
VIVAING ▸ **viva**
VIVARIA > **vivarium**
VIVARY *same as* > **vivarium**
VIVAS ▸ **viva**
VIVAT, -S *interj* long live ▹ *n* expression of acclamation
VIVDA, -S *n* method of drying meat
VIVE *interj* long live
VIVELY *adv* in a lively manner
VIVENCY *n* physical or mental energy
VIVER, -S *n* fish pond
VIVERRA *n* civet genus
VIVERS ▸ **viver**
VIVES *n* disease found in horses
VIVID, -ER *adj* very bright
VIVIDLY ▸ **vivid**
VIVIFIC *adj* giving life
VIVIFY *vb* animate, inspire
VIVO *adv* with life and vigour
VIVRES *pl n* provisions
VIXEN, -S *n*
VIXENLY ▸ **vixen**
VIXENS ▸ **vixen**
VIZARD, -S *n* means of disguise ▹ *vb* conceal by means of a disguise

VIZIED ▸ **vizy**
VIZIER, -S *n*
VIZIES ▸ **vizy**
VIZIR, -S *same as* ▸ **vizier**
VIZOR, -S *same as* ▸ **visor**
VIZORED ▸ **vizor**
VIZORS ▸ **vizor**
VIZSLA, -S *n* breed of Hungarian hunting dog
VIZY, VIZIED, VIZIES, -ING *vb* look
VIZZIE, -D, -S *same as* ▸ **vizy**
VLEI, -S *n* area of low marshy ground
VLIES ▸ **vly**
VLOG, -GED, -S *n, vb*
VLOGGER *n*
VLOGS ▸ **vlog**
VLY, VLIES *same as* ▸ **vlei**

This word for low-lying wet ground can be useful when you are short of vowels. It can also be spelt **vlei**.

VOAR, -S *n* spring
VOCAB, -S *n* vocabulary
VOCABLE *n* word regarded as a sequence of letters or sounds ▹ *adj* capable of being uttered
VOCABLY ▸ **vocable**
VOCABS ▸ **vocab**
VOCAL, -S *adj, n*
VOCALIC *adj* of, relating to, or containing a vowel or vowels
VOCALLY ▸ **vocal**
VOCALS ▸ **vocal**
VOCES ▸ **vox**
VOCODER *n* type of synthesizer that uses the human voice as an oscillator
VOCULAR ▸ **vocule**
VOCULE, -S *n* faint noise made when articulating certain sounds
VODCAST *vb* podcast with video
VODDY, VODDIES *n* informal word for vodka
VODKA, -S *n*
VODOU, -S *variant of* ▸ **voodoo**

This word for a kind of black magic may indeed work magic on an unpromising rack. And it has a host of variants, though few people will remember them all: **vaudoo, vaudoux, vodoun, vodun, voudon, voudou** and **voudoun**!

VODOUN, -S *same as* ▸ **vodun**
VODOUS ▸ **vodou**
VODUN, -S *n* voodoo
VOE, -S *n* (in Orkney and Shetland) a small bay or narrow creek
VOEMA, -S *n* vigour or energy
VOES ▸ **voe**
VOG, -S *n* air pollution caused by volcanic dust
VOGIE, -R, -ST *adj* conceited
VOGS ▸ **vog**
VOGUE, -S, VOGUIER *n, adj, vb*
VOGUED ▸ **vogue**
VOGUER, -S ▸ **vogue**
VOGUES ▸ **vogue**
VOGUEY ▸ **vogue**
VOGUIER ▸ **vogue**
VOGUING *same as* ▹ **vogueing**
VOGUISH ▸ **vogue**
VOICE, -S *n, vb*
VOICED *adj*
VOICER, -S ▸ **voice**
VOICES ▸ **voice**
VOICING ▸ **voice**
VOID, -ING, -S *adj, n, vb*
VOIDED *adj*
VOIDEE, -S *n* light meal eaten before bed
VOIDER, -S ▸ **void**
VOIDING ▸ **void**
VOIDS ▸ **void**
VOILA *interj*
VOILE, -S *n* light semitransparent fabric
VOIP, -S *n* voice over internet protocol
VOITURE *n* type of vehicle
VOIVODE *n* Slavic governor
VOL, -S *n* heraldic wings
VOLA, -E *n* palm of hand or sole of foot
VOLABLE *adj* quick-witted
VOLAE ▸ **vola**
VOLAGE *adj* changeable
VOLANT *adj* in a flying position
VOLANTE *n* Spanish horse carriage
VOLAR *adj* of or relating to the palm of the hand or the sole of the foot

VOLARY *n* large bird enclosure
VOLATIC *adj* flying ▷ *n* creature with wings
VOLCANO *n*
VOLE, -S *n* small rodent ▷ *vb* win by taking all the tricks in a deal
VOLED ▸ **vole**
VOLENS *adj* as in **nolens volens** whether willing or unwilling
VOLERY *same as* ▸ **volary**
VOLES ▸ **vole**
VOLET, -S *n* type of veil
VOLING ▸ **vole**
VOLK, -S *n* people or nation, esp the nation of Afrikaners
VOLLEY, -S *n, vb*
VOLOST, -S *n* (in the former Soviet Union) a rural soviet
VOLPINO *n* Italian breed of dog
VOLS ▸ **vol**
VOLT, -ED, -ING, -S *n, vb*
VOLTA *n* quick-moving Italian dance
VOLTAGE *n*
VOLTAIC *adj* producing an electric current
VOLTE, -S *same as* ▸ **volt**
VOLTED ▸ **volt**
VOLTES ▸ **volte**
VOLTI, -S *n* musical direction meaning turn the page
VOLTING ▸ **volt**
VOLTIS ▸ **volti**
VOLTS ▸ **volt**
VOLUBIL *same as* ▸ **voluble**
VOLUBLE *adj* talking easily and at length
VOLUBLY ▸ **voluble**
VOLUME, -D, -S *n, vb*
VOLUSPA *n* Icelandic mythological poem
VOLUTE, -S *n* spiral or twisting turn, form, or object ▷ *adj* having the form of a volute
VOLUTED ▸ **volute**
VOLUTES ▸ **volute**
VOLUTIN *n* granular substance found in cells
VOLVA, -E, -S *n* cup-shaped structure that sheathes the base of the stalk of certain mushrooms
VOLVATE ▸ **volva**
VOLVE, -D, -S, VOLVING *vb* turn over
VOLVOX *n* freshwater protozoan
VOLVULI > **volvulus**
VOM, -MED, -MING, -S *vb* vomit
VOMER, -S *n* thin flat bone separating the nasal passages in mammals
VOMICA, -E, -S *n* pus-containing cavity
VOMIT, -ED, -S *vb, n*
VOMITER ▸ **vomit**
VOMITO, -S *n* form of yellow fever
VOMITS ▸ **vomit**
VOMITUS *n* matter that has been vomited
VOMITY *adj* resembling or smelling of vomit
VOMMED ▸ **vom**
VOMMING ▸ **vom**
VOMS ▸ **vom**
VONGOLE *pl n* (in Italian cookery) clams
VOODOO, -S *n, adj, vb*
VOR, -RED, -RING, -S *vb* (in dialect) warn
VORAGO, -S *n* chasm
VORANT *adj* devouring
VORLAGE *n* skiing position
VORPAL *adj* sharp
VORRED ▸ **vor**
VORRING ▸ **vor**
VORS ▸ **vor**
VORTEX *n*
VOSTRO *adj* as in **vostro account** bank account held by a foreign bank with a British bank
VOTABLE ▸ **vote**
VOTARY *n, adj*
VOTE, -D, -S *n, vb*
VOTEEN, -S *n* devotee
VOTER, -S *n*
VOTES ▸ **vote**
VOTING, -S ▸ **vote**
VOTIVE, -S *adj* done or given to fulfil a vow ▷ *n* votive offering
VOTRESS > **votaress**
VOUCH, -ED, -ES *vb, n*
VOUCHEE *n* person summoned to court to defend a title
VOUCHER *n, vb*
VOUCHES ▸ **vouch**
VOUDON, -S *variant of* ▸ **voodoo**
VOUDOU, -S *same as* ▸ **voodoo**
VOUDOUN *variant of* ▸ **voodoo**
VOUDOUS ▸ **voudou**
VOUGE, -S *n* form of pike used by foot soldiers in the 14th century and later
VOULGE, -S *n* type of medieval weapon
VOULU *adj* deliberate

VOUVRAY *n* dry white French wine
VOW, -ED, -ING, -S *n, vb*
VOWEL, -S *n, vb*
VOWELED *adj* having vowels
VOWELLY *adj* marked by vowels
VOWELS ▶ **vowel**
VOWER, -S ▶ **vow**
VOWESS *n* nun
VOWING ▶ **vow**
VOWLESS ▶ **vow**
VOWS ▶ **vow**
VOX, VOCES *n* voice or sound

Along with **vex**, this Latin word for voice is the highest-scoring 3-letter word beginning with V.

VOXEL, -S *n* any of a number of very small elements in a 3D image
VOYAGE, -D, -S *n, vb*
VOYAGER ▶ **voyage**
VOYAGES ▶ **voyage**
VOYEUR, -S *n*
VOZHD, -S *n* Russian leader

This unlikely looking word is Russian for a chief or leader, and may provide a great score from an apparently difficult rack.

VRAIC, -S *n* type of seaweed
VRIL, -S *n* life force
VROOM, -ED, -S *interj* exclamation imitative of a car engine revving up ▷ *vb* move noisily and at high speed
VROT *adj* South African slang for rotten
VROU, -S *n* South African word for a woman or wife
VROUW, -S *n* Afrikaner woman

The heart of any Scrabble player sinks to see a combination of U, V and W on the rack, as there are relatively few words that use even two of these letters. But **vrouw**, a word of Dutch origin for a woman or wife, may get you out of the mess.

VROW, -S *same as* ▶ **vrouw**
VUG, -S *n* small cavity in a rock or vein, usually lined with crystals

This unusual word of Cornish origin, meaning a cavity in rock, is another that can be useful when you have an uninspiring combination of letters. And it has a variant **vugh** and can be extended to **vuggy** or **vughy.**

VUGG, -S *same as* ▶ **vug**
VUGGIER ▶ **vuggy**
VUGGS ▶ **vugg**
VUGGY, VUGGIER ▶ **vug**
VUGH, -IER, -S *same as* ▶ **vug**
VUGHY ▶ **vug**
VUGS ▶ **vug**
VUGULAR *adj* relating to vugs
VULCAN, -S *n*
VULGAR, -S *adj, n*
VULGATE *n* commonly recognized text or version
VULGO *adv* generally
VULGUS *n* the common people
VULN, -ED, -S *vb* wound
VULNING ▶ **vuln**
VULNS ▶ **vuln**
VULPINE *adj* of or like a fox
VULTURE *n*
VULTURN *n* type of turkey
VULVA, -E, -S *n*
VULVAL ▶ **vulva**
VULVAR ▶ **vulva**
VULVAS ▶ **vulva**
VULVATE ▶ **vulva**
VUM, -MED, -MING, -S *vb* swear
VUTTY, VUTTIER *adj* dirty
VYING, -S ▶ **vie**
VYINGLY ▶ **vie**
VYINGS ▶ **vying**

Ww

WAAC, -S *n* (formerly) member of the Women's Auxiliary Army Corp
WAAH *interj* interjection used to express wailing
WAB, -S *n* skin web between the digits of certain animals
WABAIN, -S *same as* ▸ **ouabain**
WABBIT *adj* Scots word meaning weary
WABBLE, -D, -S *same as* ▸ **wobble**
WABBLER ▸ **wabble**
WABBLES ▸ **wabble**
WABBLY ▸ **wabble**
WABOOM, -S *another word for* > **wagenboom**
WABS ▸ **wab**
WABSTER *Scots form of* ▸ **webster**
WACK, -EST, -S *n* friend ▹ *adj* bad or inferior
WACKE, -S *n* any of various soft earthy rocks that resemble or are derived from basaltic rocks
WACKED *adj* exhausted
WACKER, -S *same as* ▸ **wack**
WACKES ▸ **wacke**
WACKEST ▸ **wack**
WACKIER ▸ **wacky**
WACKILY ▸ **wacky**
WACKO, -ES, -S *n*
WACKS ▸ **wack**
WACKY, WACKIER *adj*
WACONDA *n* supernatural force in Sioux belief
WAD, -DED, -DING, -S *n* black earthy ore of manganese ▹ *n* small mass of soft material ▹ *vb* form (something) into a wad
WADABLE ▸ **wade**
WADD, -S *same as* ▸ **wad**
WADDED ▸ **wad**
WADDER, -S ▸ **wad**
WADDIE *same as* ▸ **waddy**
WADDIED ▸ **waddy**
WADDIES ▸ **waddy**
WADDING ▸ **wad**
WADDLE, -D, -S *vb, n*
WADDLER ▸ **waddle**
WADDLES ▸ **waddle**
WADDLY ▸ **waddle**
WADDS ▸ **wadd**
WADDY, WADDIED, WADDIES *n* heavy wooden club used by Aboriginal Australians ▹ *vb* hit with a waddy
WADE, -D, -S, WADING, WADINGS *vb, n*
WADER *n*
WADERS *pl n*
WADES ▸ **wade**
WADGE, -S *n* large or roughly cut portion
WADI, -S *n* (in N Africa and Arabia) river which is dry except in the wet season
WADIES ▸ **wady**
WADING ▸ **wade**
WADINGS ▸ **wade**
WADIS ▸ **wadi**
WADMAAL *same as* ▸ **wadmal**
WADMAL, -S *n* coarse thick woollen fabric, formerly woven for outer garments
WADMEL, -S *same as* ▸ **wadmal**
WADMOL, -S *same as* ▸ **wadmal**
WADMOLL *same as* ▸ **wadmal**
WADMOLS ▸ **wadmol**
WADS ▸ **wad**
WADSET, -S *vb* pledge or mortgage
WADSETT *same as* ▸ **wadset**
WADT, -S *same as* ▸ **wad**
WADY, WADIES *same as* ▸ **wadi**
WAE, -S *old form of* ▸ **woe**

WAEFUL *old form of* ▶ **woeful**
WAENESS *n* sorrow
WAES ▶ **wae**
WAESOME *adj* sorrowful
WAESUCK *interj* Scots word meaning alas
WAFER, -ED, -S *n, vb*
WAFERY *adj* like wafer; thin
WAFF, -ED, -ING, -S *n* gust or puff of air ▷ *vb* flutter or cause to flutter
WAFFIE, -S *n* person regarded as having little worth to society
WAFFING ▶ **waff**
WAFFLE, -D, -S *vb, n*
WAFFLER ▶ **waffle**
WAFFLES ▶ **waffle**
WAFFLY ▶ **waffle**
WAFFS ▶ **waff**
WAFT, -ED, -S *vb, n*
WAFTAGE ▶ **waft**
WAFTED ▶ **waft**
WAFTER, -S *n* device that causes a draught
WAFTING ▶ **waft**
WAFTS ▶ **waft**
WAFTURE *n* act of wafting or waving
WAG, -GED, -GING, -S *vb, n*
WAGE, -D, -S, WAGING *n, vb*
WAGER, -ED, -S *vb, n*
WAGERER ▶ **wager**
WAGERS ▶ **wager**
WAGES ▶ **wage**
WAGGA, -S *n* blanket or bed covering made out of sacks stitched together
WAGGED ▶ **wag**
WAGGER, -S ▶ **wag**
WAGGERY *n* quality of being humorous
WAGGING ▶ **wag**
WAGGISH *adj*
WAGGLE, -D, -S *vb, n*
WAGGLER *n* float only the bottom of which is attached to the fishing line
WAGGLES ▶ **waggle**
WAGGLY ▶ **waggle**
WAGGON, -S *same as* ▶ **wagon**
WAGING ▶ **wage**
WAGON, -ED, -S *n, vb*
WAGONER *n* person who drives a wagon
WAGONS ▶ **wagon**
WAGS ▶ **wag**
WAGSOME *another word for* ▶ **waggish**
WAGTAIL *n* small long-tailed bird
WAGYU, -S *n* Japanese breed of beef cattle
WAHINE, -S *n* Māori woman, esp a wife
WAHOO, -S *n* food and game fish of tropical seas
WAI, -S *n* in New Zealand, water
WAIATA, -S *n* Māori song
WAID ▶ **weigh**
WAIDE ▶ **weigh**
WAIF, -ED, -ING, -S *n, vb*
WAIFISH ▶ **waif**
WAIFS ▶ **waif**
WAIFT, -S *n* piece of lost property found by someone other than the owner
WAIL, -ED, -S *vb, n*
WAILER, -S ▶ **wail**
WAILFUL ▶ **wail**
WAILING ▶ **wail**
WAILS ▶ **wail**
WAIN, -ED, -ING, -S *vb* transport ▷ *n* farm wagon
WAINAGE *n* carriages etc for transportation of goods
WAINED ▶ **wain**
WAINING ▶ **wain**
WAINS ▶ **wain**
WAIR, -ED, -ING, -S *vb* spend
WAIRSH *variant spelling of* ▶ **wersh**
WAIRUA, -S *n* in New Zealand, spirit or soul
WAIS ▶ **wai**
WAIST, -S *n*
WAISTED *adj* having a waist or waistlike part
WAISTER *n* sailor performing menial duties
WAISTS ▶ **waist**
WAIT, -ED, -ING, -S *vb, n*
WAITE, -S *old form of* ▶ **wait**
WAITED ▶ **wait**
WAITER, -S *n, vb*
WAITES ▶ **waite**
WAITING ▶ **wait**
WAITRON *n* waiter or waitress
WAITS ▶ **wait**
WAIVE, -D, -S, WAIVING *vb*
WAIVER, -S *n*
WAIVES ▶ **waive**
WAIVING ▶ **waive**
WAIVODE *same as* ▶ **voivode**
WAIWODE *same as* ▶ **voivode**
WAKA, -S *n* Māori canoe

WAKAME, -S *n* edible seaweed
WAKANDA *n* supernatural quality in Native American belief system
WAKANE, -S *n* type of seaweed
WAKAS ▸ **waka**
WAKE, -D, -S, WOKEN *vb, n*
WAKEFUL *adj*
WAKEMAN, WAKEMEN *n* watchman
WAKEN, -ED, -S *vb*
WAKENER ▸ **waken**
WAKENS ▸ **waken**
WAKER, -S ▸ **wake**
WAKES ▸ **wake**
WAKF, -S *same as* ▸ **waqf**
WAKIKI, -S *n* Melanesian shell currency
WAKING, -S ▸ **wake**
WALD, -S *Scots form of* ▸ **weld**
WALDO, -ES, -S *n* gadget for manipulating objects by remote control
WALDS ▸ **wald**
WALE, -D, -R, -RS, -S, WALING *same as* ▸ **weal**
WALI, -S *same as* ▸ **vali**
WALIE *adj* robust or strong
WALIER ▸ **waly**
WALIES ▸ **waly**
WALIEST ▸ **waly**
WALING ▸ **wale**
WALIS ▸ **wali**
WALISE, -S *same as* ▸ **valise**
WALK, -ED, -S *vb, n*
WALKER, -S *n*
WALKIES *pl n*
WALKING *adj, n*
WALKOUT *n*
WALKS ▸ **walk**
WALKUP, -S *n* building with stairs to upper floors
WALKWAY *n*
WALL, -ER, -ERS, -S *n, vb*
WALLA, -S *same as* ▸ **wallah**
WALLABA *n* type of S American tree
WALLABY *n*
WALLAH, -S *n* person involved with or in charge of a specified thing
WALLAS ▸ **walla**
WALLED ▸ **wall**
WALLER ▸ **wall**
WALLERS ▸ **wall**
WALLET, -S *n*
WALLEY, -S *n* type of jump in figure skating
WALLEYE *n* fish with large staring eyes
WALLEYS ▸ **walley**
WALLIE *same as* ▸ **wally**
WALLIER ▸ **wally**
WALLIES ▸ **wally**
WALLING ▸ **wall**
WALLOP, -S *vb, n*
WALLOW, -S *vb, n*
WALLS ▸ **wall**
WALLY, WALLIER, WALLIES *n, adj*
WALNUT, -S *n, adj*
WALRUS *n*
WALTY, WALTIER *adj* (of a ship) likely to roll over
WALTZ, -ED, -ES *n, vb*
WALTZER *n*
WALTZES ▸ **waltz**
WALY, WALIER, WALIES, WALIEST *same as* ▸ **wally**
WAMBLE, -D, -S *vb* move unsteadily ▹ *n* unsteady movement
WAMBLY ▸ **wamble**
WAME, -S *n* belly, abdomen, or womb
WAMED ▸ **wame**
WAMEFOU *Scots variant of* ▸ **wameful**
WAMEFUL *n* bellyful
WAMES ▸ **wame**
WAMMUL, -S *n* dog
WAMMUS *same as* ▸ **wamus**
WAMPEE, -S *n* type of Asian fruit tree
WAMPISH *vb* wave
WAMPUM, -S *n* shells woven together, formerly used by Native Americans as money
WAMPUS *same as* ▸ **wamus**
WAMUS, -ES *n* type of cardigan or jacket
WAN, -NED, -NER, -NEST, -NING, -S *adj, vb*
WAND, -S *n*
WANDER, -S *vb, n*
WANDLE, -D, -S *adj* supple ▹ *vb* walk haltingly
WANDOO, -S *n* eucalyptus tree of W Australia, having white bark and durable wood
WANDS ▸ **wand**
WANE, -D, -S *vb*
WANEY ▸ **wane**
WANG, -S *n* cheekbone
WANGAN, -S *same as* ▸ **wanigan**

WANGLE, -D, -S *vb* get by devious methods ▷ *n* act or an instance of wangling
WANGLER ▶ **wangle**
WANGLES ▶ **wangle**
WANGS ▶ **wang**
WANGUN, -S *same as* ▶ **wanigan**
WANHOPE *n* delusion
WANIER ▶ **wany**
WANIEST ▶ **wany**
WANIGAN *n* provisions for camp
WANING, -S ▶ **wane**
WANION, -S *n* vehemence
WANKLE *adj* unstable
WANLE *same as* ▶ **wandle**
WANLY ▶ **wan**
WANNA *vb* spelling of 'want to' intended to reflect a dialectal or informal pronunciation
WANNABE *adj*, *n*
WANNED ▶ **wan**
WANNEL *same as* ▶ **wandle**
WANNER ▶ **wan**
WANNESS ▶ **wan**
WANNEST ▶ **wan**
WANNING ▶ **wan**
WANNION *same as* ▶ **wanion**
WANNISH *adj* rather wan
WANS ▶ **wan**
WANT, -ED, -S *vb*, *n*
WANTAGE *n* shortage
WANTED ▶ **want**
WANTER, -S ▶ **want**
WANTIES ▶ **wanty**
WANTING *adj*, *prep*
WANTON, -S *adj*, *n*, *vb*
WANTS ▶ **want**
WANTY, WANTIES *n* belt
WANY, WANIER, WANIEST ▶ **wane**
WANZE, -D, -S, WANZING *vb* wane
WAP, -PED, -PING, -S *vb* strike
WAPITI, -S *n* large N American deer
WAPPED ▶ **wap**
WAPPEND *adj* tired
WAPPER, -S *vb* blink
WAPPING ▶ **wap**
WAPS ▶ **wap**
WAQF, -S *n* endowment in Muslim law

> An Arabic word meaning the donation of land, property or money for charitable purposes. As one of the Q words without a U, this comes up surprisingly often. It can also be spelt **wakf**.

WAR, -RED, -RING, -S *n*, *adj*, *vb*
WARAGI, -S *n* Ugandan alcoholic drink made from bananas
WARATAH *n* Australian shrub with crimson flowers
WARB, -S *n* dirty or insignificant person
WARBIER ▶ **warby**
WARBIRD *n*
WARBLE, -D, -S *vb*, *n*
WARBLER *n*
WARBLES ▶ **warble**
WARBLY *adj* said in a quavering manner
WARBOT, -S *n* any robot or unmanned vehicle or device designed for and used in warfare
WARBS ▶ **warb**
WARBY, WARBIER ▶ **warb**
WARD, -ED, -S *n*, *vb*
WARDEN, -S *n*, *vb*
WARDER, -S *vb* guard ▷ *n* prison officer
WARDIAN *n* as in **wardian case** type of glass container for housing delicate plants
WARDING ▶ **ward**
WARDOG, -S *n* veteran warrior
WARDROP *obsolete form of* ▶ **wardrobe**
WARDS ▶ **ward**
WARE, -D, WARING *n*, *vb*
WAREHOU *n* any of several edible saltwater New Zealand fish
WARES *pl n*
WAREZ *pl n* illegally copied computer software
WARFARE *vb*, *n*
WARGAME *vb*
WARHEAD *n*
WARIER ▶ **wary**
WARIEST ▶ **wary**
WARILY ▶ **wary**
WARING ▶ **ware**
WARISON *n* (esp formerly) a bugle note used as an order to a military force to attack
WARK, -ED, -ING, -S *Scots form of* ▶ **work**
WARLESS ▶ **war**
WARLIKE *adj*
WARLING *n* one who is not liked
WARLOCK *n*

WARLORD *n*
WARM, -ED, -EST, -ING, -S *adj, vb, n*
WARMAN, WARMEN *n* one experienced in warfare
WARMED ▶ **warm**
WARMEN ▶ **warman**
WARMER, -S ▶ **warm**
WARMEST ▶ **warm**
WARMING ▶ **warm**
WARMISH ▶ **warm**
WARMIST *n* person who believes global warming results from human activity
WARMLY ▶ **warm**
WARMS ▶ **warm**
WARMTH, -S *n*
WARMUP, -S *n*
WARN, -ED, -S *vb*
WARNER, -S ▶ **warn**
WARNING *n, adj*
WARNS ▶ **warn**
WARP, -ED, -S *vb, n*
WARPAGE ▶ **warp**
WARPATH *n*
WARPED ▶ **warp**
WARPER, -S ▶ **warp**
WARPING ▶ **warp**
WARPS ▶ **warp**
WARRAN, -S *same as* ▶ **warrant**
WARRAND *same as* ▶ **warrant**
WARRANS ▶ **warran**
WARRANT *n, vb*
WARRAY, -S *vb* wage war on
WARRE *same as* ▶ **war**
WARRED ▶ **war**
WARREN, -S *n*
WARREY, -S *same as* ▶ **warray**
WARRING ▶ **war**
WARRIOR *n*
WARS ▶ **war**
WARSAW, -S *n* type of grouper fish
WARSHIP *n*
WARSLE, -D, -S *dialect word for* ▶ **wrestle**
WARSLER ▶ **warsle**
WARSLES ▶ **warsle**
WARST *obsolete form of* ▶ **worst**
WARSTLE *dialect form of* ▶ **wrestle**
WART, -S *n*
WARTED ▶ **wart**
WARTHOG *n*
WARTIER ▶ **warty**
WARTIME *n, adj*
WARTS ▶ **wart**
WARTY, WARTIER ▶ **wart**
WARWOLF *n* Roman engine of war
WARWORK *n* work contributing to war effort
WARWORN *adj* worn down by war
WARY, WARIER, WARIEST *adj*
WARZONE *n*
WAS *vb*
WASABI, -S *n*
WASE, -S *n* pad to relieve pressure of load carried on head
WASH, -ED, -EN, -ES *vb, n*
WASHBAG *n*
WASHDAY *n*
WASHED ▶ **wash**
WASHEN ▶ **wash**
WASHER, -S *n, vb*
WASHERY *n* plant where liquid is used to remove dirt from a mineral
WASHES ▶ **wash**
WASHIER ▶ **washy**
WASHILY ▶ **washy**
WASHIN, -S *n* increase in the angle of attack of an aircraft wing towards the wing tip
WASHING *n*
WASHINS ▶ **washin**
WASHOUT *n*
WASHPOT *n* pot for washing things in
WASHRAG *same as* ▶ **washcloth**
WASHTUB *n*
WASHUP, -S *n*
WASHY, WASHIER *adj* overdiluted or weak
WASM, -S *n* obsolete belief; an out-of-fashion 'ism'
WASP, -S *n*
WASPIE, -S *n* tight-waisted corset
WASPIER ▶ **waspy**
WASPIES ▶ **waspie**
WASPILY ▶ **wasp**
WASPISH *adj*
WASPS ▶ **wasp**
WASPY, WASPIER ▶ **wasp**
WASSAIL *n, vb*
WASSUP *sentence substitute* what is happening?
WAST, -S *singular form of the past tense of* ▶ **be**
WASTAGE *n* loss by wear or waste
WASTE, -D, -S *vb, n, adj*
WASTEL, -S *n* fine bread or cake
WASTER, -S *vb, n*
WASTERY *n* extravagance
WASTES ▶ **waste**

WASTING *adj*
WASTREL *n*
WASTRIE *same as* ▸ **wastery**
WASTRY *n* wastefulness
WASTS ▸ **wast**
WAT, -S, -TER, -TEST *adj* wet
WATAP, -S *n* stringy thread made by Native Americans from the roots of conifers
WATAPE, -S *same as* ▸ **watap**
WATAPS ▸ **watap**
WATCH, -ED, -ES *vb, n*
WATCHA *interj* greeting meaning 'what are you?'
WATCHED ▸ **watch**
WATCHER *n*
WATCHES ▸ **watch**
WATCHET *n* shade of blue
WATE ▸ **wit**
WATER, -ED, -S *n, vb*
WATERER ▸ **water**
WATERS ▸ **water**
WATERY *adj*
WATS ▸ **wat**
WATT, -S *n*
WATTAGE *n*
WATTAPE *same as* ▸ **watap**
WATTER ▸ **wat**
WATTEST ▸ **wat**
WATTLE, -S *n, adj, vb*
WATTLED ▸ **wattle**
WATTLES ▸ **wattle**
WATTS ▸ **watt**
WAUCHT, -S *same as* ▸ **waught**
WAUFF, -ED, -S *same as* ▸ **waff**
WAUGH, -ED, -S *vb* bark
WAUGHT, -S *vb* drink in large amounts
WAUK, -ED, -ING, -S *vb* full (cloth)
WAUKER, -S ▸ **wauk**
WAUKING ▸ **wauk**
WAUKS ▸ **wauk**
WAUL, -ED, -S *vb* cry or wail plaintively like a cat
WAULING ▸ **waul**
WAULK, -ED, -S *same as* ▸ **wauk**
WAULKER ▸ **waulk**
WAULKS ▸ **waulk**
WAULS ▸ **waul**
WAUR, -ED, -ING, -S, -ST *obsolete form of* ▸ **war**
WAVE, -D, -S *vb, n*
WAVELET *n* small wave
WAVEOFF *n* signal or instruction to an aircraft not to land
WAVER, -ED, -S *vb* hesitate or be irresolute ▹ *n* act or an instance of wavering
WAVERER ▸ **waver**
WAVERS ▸ **waver**
WAVERY *adj* lacking firmness
WAVES ▸ **wave**
WAVESON *n* goods floating on waves after shipwreck
WAVEY, -S *n* snow goose or other wild goose
WAVICLE *n* origin of wave
WAVIER ▸ **wavy**
WAVIES ▸ **wavy**
WAVIEST ▸ **wavy**
WAVILY ▸ **wavy**
WAVING, -S ▸ **wave**
WAVY, WAVIER, WAVIES, WAVIEST *adj, n*
WAW, -S *another name for* ▸ **vav**
WAWA, -ED, -ING, -S *n* speech ▹ *vb* speak
WAWE, -S *same as* ▸ **waw**
WAWL, -ED, -S *same as* ▸ **waul**
WAWLING ▸ **wawl**
WAWLS ▸ **wawl**
WAWS ▸ **waw**
WAX, -ED, -ES, WOX, WOXEN *n, vb*
WAXABLE ▸ **wax**
WAXBILL *n* any of various chiefly African finchlike weaverbirds
WAXED ▸ **wax**
WAXEN *adj*
WAXER, -S ▸ **wax**
WAXES ▸ **wax**
WAXEYE, -S *n* small New Zealand bird
WAXIER ▸ **waxy**
WAXIEST ▸ **waxy**
WAXILY ▸ **waxy**
WAXING, -S ▸ **wax**
WAXLIKE ▸ **wax**
WAXWEED *n* type of wild flower
WAXWING *n*
WAXWORK *n*
WAXWORM *n* wax moth larva
WAXY, WAXIER, WAXIEST *adj*
WAY, -ED, -ING, -S *n, vb*
WAYANG, -S *n* type of Indonesian performance with dancers or puppets
WAYBACK *n* area in the rear of a vehicle

WAYBILL *n* document stating the nature, origin, and destination of goods being transported
WAYED ▸ **way**
WAYFARE *vb* travel
WAYGONE *adj* travel-weary
WAYING ▸ **way**
WAYLAY, WAYLAID, -S *vb*
WAYLESS ▸ **way**
WAYMARK *n* symbol or signpost marking the route of a footpath ▹ *vb* mark out with waymarks
WAYMENT *vb* express grief
WAYPOST *n* signpost
WAYS ▸ **way**
WAYSIDE *n* side of a road
WAYWARD *adj*
WAYWODE *n* Slavic governor
WAYWORN *adj* worn or tired by travel
WAZ *same as* ▸ **wazz**
WAZIR, -S *another word for* ▸ **vizier**
WAZOO, -S *n* slang word for person's bottom
WAZZ, -ED, -ES, -ING *vb* urinate ▹ *n* act of urinating
WAZZOCK *n* foolish or annoying person
WE *pron*
WEAK, -ER, -EST *adj*
WEAKEN, -S *vb*
WEAKER ▸ **weak**
WEAKEST ▸ **weak**
WEAKISH ▸ **weak**
WEAKLY *adv, adj*
WEAKON, -S *n* subatomic particle
WEAL, -S *n*
WEALD, -S *n* open or forested country
WEALS ▸ **weal**
WEALTH, -S *n*
WEALTHY *adj*
WEAMB, -S *same as* ▸ **wame**
WEAN, -ED, -S *vb*
WEANEL, -S *n* recently weaned child or animal
WEANER, -S *n* person or thing that weans
WEANING ▸ **wean**
WEANS ▸ **wean**
WEAPON, -S *vb, n*
WEAR, -ED, -S, WORE, WORN *vb, n*
WEARER, -S ▸ **wear**
WEARIED ▸ **weary**
WEARIER ▸ **weary**
WEARIES ▸ **weary**
WEARILY ▸ **weary**
WEARING *adj, n*
WEARISH *adj* withered
WEARS ▸ **wear**
WEARY, WEARIED, WEARIER, WEARIES *adj, vb*
WEASAND *former name for the* ▸ **trachea**
WEASEL, -S *n, vb*
WEASELY *adj* devious, cunning
WEASON, -S *Scots form of* ▸ **weasand**
WEATHER *n, vb*
WEAVE, -D, -S, WOVE *vb*
WEAVER, -S *n*
WEAVES ▸ **weave**
WEAVING ▸ **weave**
WEAZAND *same as* ▸ **weasand**
WEAZEN, -S *same as* ▸ **wizen**
WEB, -BED, -S *n, vb*
WEBAPP, -S *n* application program that is accessed on the internet
WEBBED ▸ **web**
WEBBIE, -S *n* person who is well versed in the use of the World Wide Web
WEBBIER ▸ **webby**
WEBBIES ▸ **webbie**
WEBBING *n*
WEBBY, WEBBIER *adj* of, relating to, resembling, or consisting of a web
WEBCAM, -S *n*
WEBCAST *n, vb*
WEBCHAT *vb* exchange messages via the internet
WEBER, -S *n* SI unit of magnetic flux
WEBFED *adj* (of printing press) printing from rolls of paper
WEBFOOT, WEBFEET *n*
WEBHEAD *n* person who uses the internet a lot
WEBIFY *vb* convert (information) for display on the internet
WEBINAR *n*
WEBLESS ▸ **web**
WEBLIKE ▸ **web**
WEBLISH *n* shorthand form of English that is used in text messaging, chatrooms, etc
WEBLOG, -S *n*
WEBMAIL *n*

WEBPAGE *n*
WEBRING *n* group of websites organized in a circular structure
WEBS ▸ **web**
WEBSITE *n*
WEBSTER *archaic word for* ▸ **weaver**
WEBWORK *n* work done using the World Wide Web
WEBWORM *n* type of caterpillar
WEBZINE *n* magazine published on the internet
WECHT, -ED, -S *n* agricultural tool ▹ *vb* winnow (corn)
WED, -DED, -DING, -S *vb*
WEDDER, -S *dialect form of* ▸ **weather**
WEDDING ▸ **wed**
WEDEL, -ED, -S *variant of* ▸ **wedeln**
WEDELN, -S *n* succession of high-speed turns performed in skiing ▹ *vb* perform a wedeln
WEDELS ▸ **wedel**
WEDGE, -D, -S *n, vb*
WEDGIE, -S *n*
WEDGIER ▸ **wedgy**
WEDGIES ▸ **wedgie**
WEDGING ▸ **wedge**
WEDGY, WEDGIER ▸ **wedge**
WEDLOCK *n*
WEDS ▸ **wed**
WEE, -ING, -R, -S, -ST *adj, n, vb*
WEED, -ED *n, vb*
WEEDBED *n* body of water having lots of weeds
WEEDED ▸ **weed**
WEEDER, -S ▸ **weed**
WEEDERY *n* weed-ridden area
WEEDIER ▸ **weedy**
WEEDILY ▸ **weedy**
WEEDING ▸ **weed**
WEEDS *pl n*
WEEDY, WEEDIER *adj*
WEEING ▸ **wee**
WEEJUNS *pl n* moccasin-style shoes for casual wear
WEEK, -S *n, adv*
WEEKDAY *n*
WEEKE, -S *same as* ▸ **wick**
WEEKEND *n, vb*
WEEKES ▸ **weeke**
WEEKLY *adv, n, adj*
WEEKS ▸ **week**
WEEL, -S *Scot word for* ▸ **well**
WEEM, -S *n* underground home
WEEN, -ED, -ING, -S *vb* think or imagine (something)
WEENIE, -S *adj, n*
WEENIER ▸ **weeny**
WEENIES ▸ **weenie**
WEENING ▸ **ween**
WEENS ▸ **ween**
WEENSY *same as* ▸ **weeny**
WEENY, WEENIER *adj* very small
WEEP, -S, WEPT *vb, n*
WEEPER, -S *n*
WEEPIE *same as* ▸ **weepy**
WEEPIER ▸ **weepy**
WEEPIES ▸ **weepy**
WEEPILY ▸ **weepy**
WEEPING *adj*
WEEPS ▸ **weep**
WEEPY, WEEPIER, WEEPIES *adj, n*
WEER ▸ **wee**
WEES ▸ **wee**
WEEST ▸ **wee**
WEET, -ER, -EST, -ING, -S *dialect form of* ▸ **wet**
WEETE, -D *same as* ▸ **wit**
WEETEN *same as* ▸ **wit**
WEETER ▸ **weet**
WEETEST ▸ **weet**
WEETING ▸ **weet**
WEETS ▸ **weet**
WEEVER, -S *n* type of small fish
WEEVIL, -S *n*
WEEVILY *adj* full of weevils
WEEWEE, -D, -S *vb*
WEFT, -ED, -ING, -S *n, vb*
WEFTAGE *n* texture
WEFTE, -S *n* forsaken child
WEFTED ▸ **weft**
WEFTES ▸ **wefte**
WEFTING ▸ **weft**
WEFTS ▸ **weft**
WEID, -S *n* sudden illness
WEIGELA *n* type of shrub
WEIGH, WAID, WAIDE, -ED, -S *vb*
WEIGHER ▸ **weigh**
WEIGHS ▸ **weigh**
WEIGHT, -S *n, vb*
WEIGHTY *adj*
WEIL, -S *n* whirlpool
WEINER, -S *same as* ▸ **wiener**
WEIR, -ED, -ING, -S *vb, n*
WEIRD, -ED, -ER, -S *adj, vb*
WEIRDIE *same as* ▸ **weirdo**
WEIRDLY ▸ **weird**

WEIRDO, -S *n*
WEIRDS ▸ **weird**
WEIRDY *n* weird person
WEIRED ▸ **weir**
WEIRING ▸ **weir**
WEIRS ▸ **weir**
WEISE, -D, -S, WEISING *same as* ▸ **wise**
WEIZE, -D, -S, WEIZING *same as* ▸ **wise**
WEKA, -S *n* flightless New Zealand rail
WELAWAY *same as* > **wellaway**
WELCH, -ED, -ES *same as* ▸ **welsh**
WELCHER ▸ **welch**
WELCHES ▸ **welch**
WELCOME *vb, n, adj*
WELD, -ED, -S *vb, n*
WELDER, -S ▸ **weld**
WELDING ▸ **weld**
WELDOR, -S ▸ **weld**
WELDS ▸ **weld**
WELFARE *n*
WELK, -ED, -ING, -S *vb*
WELKE, -S *obsolete form of* ▸ **welk**
WELKED ▸ **welk**
WELKES ▸ **welke**
WELKIN, -S *n* sky, heavens, or upper air
WELKING ▸ **welk**
WELKINS ▸ **welkin**
WELKS ▸ **welk**
WELKT *adj* twisted
WELL, -ED, -ING, -S *adv, adj, interj, n, vb*
WELLIE *n* wellington boot
WELLIES ▸ **welly**
WELLING ▸ **well**
WELLS ▸ **well**
WELLY, WELLIES *n*
WELS *n* type of catfish
WELSH, -ED, -ES *vb*
WELSHER ▸ **welsh**
WELSHES ▸ **welsh**
WELT, -ED, -S *same as* ▸ **weal**
WELTER, -S *n, vb*
WELTING ▸ **welt**
WELTS ▸ **welt**
WEM, -S *same as* ▸ **wame**
WEMB, -S *same as* ▸ **wame**
WEMS ▸ **wem**
WEN, -S *n* cyst on the scalp
WENA *pron* South African word for you
WENCH, -ES *n*
WEND, -ED, -ING, -S *vb*
WENDIGO *n* evil spirit or cannibal
WENDING ▸ **wend**
WENDS ▸ **wend**
WENGE, -S *n* type of tree found in central and West Africa
WENNIER ▸ **wenny**
WENNISH ▸ **wen**
WENNY, WENNIER ▸ **wen**
WENS ▸ **wen**
WENT, -S *n*
WEPT ▸ **weep**
WERE *vb*
WERGELD *same as* ▸ **wergild**
WERGELT *same as* ▸ **wergeld**
WERGILD *n* price set on a person's life, to be paid as compensation by their slayer
WERO, -S *n* challenge made by an armed Māori warrior to a visitor to a marae
WERRIS *Australian slang word for* > **urination**
WERSH, -ER *adj* tasteless
WERT *singular form of the past tense of* ▸ **be**
WERWOLF *same as* > **werewolf**
WESAND, -S *same as* ▸ **weasand**
WESKIT, -S *informal word for* > **waistcoat**
WESSAND *same as* ▸ **weasand**
WEST, -ED, -S *n, adj, adv, vb*
WESTER, -S *vb* move or appear to move towards the west ▹ *n* strong wind or storm from the west
WESTERN *adj, n*
WESTERS ▸ **wester**
WESTIE, -S *n* insulting word for a young working-class person from the western suburbs of Sydney
WESTING *n* movement, deviation, or distance covered in a westerly direction
WESTLIN *Scots word for* ▸ **western**
WESTS ▸ **west**
WET, -S, -TED, -TEST, -TING *adj, n, vb*
WETA, -S *n* type of wingless insect
WETHER, -S *n*
WETLAND *n*
WETLY ▸ **wet**
WETNESS *n*
WETS ▸ **wet**
WETSUIT *n*
WETTED ▸ **wet**
WETTER, -S ▸ **wet**
WETTEST ▸ **wet**

WETTIE, -S *n* wetsuit
WETTING ▸ **wet**
WETTISH ▸ **wet**
WETWARE *n* the brain, as opposed to computers
WEX, -ED, -ES, -ING *obsolete form of* ▸ **wax**

Wex is an old word for **wax**, in the sense of grow. It gives a very good score for a 3-letter word, and can be extended to **wexe**.

WEXE *obsolete form of* ▸ **wax**
WEXED ▸ **wex**
WEXES ▸ **wex**
WEXING ▸ **wex**
WEY, -S *n* measurement of weight
WEYARD *obsolete form of* ▸ **weird**
WEYS ▸ **wey**
WEYWARD *obsolete form of* ▸ **weird**
WEZAND, -S *obsolete form of* ▸ **weasand**
WHA *Scot word for* ▸ **who**
WHACK, -ED, -S *vb, n*
WHACKER ▸ **whack**
WHACKO, -S *n*
WHACKS ▸ **whack**
WHACKY *variant spelling of* ▸ **wacky**
WHAE *same as* ▸ **wha**
WHAISLE *Scots form of* ▸ **wheeze**
WHAIZLE *same as* ▸ **whaisle**
WHALE, -D, -S *n, vb*
WHALER, -S *n*
WHALERY *n* whaling
WHALES ▸ **whale**
WHALING *n, adv*
WHALLY *adj* (of eyes) with light-coloured irises
WHAM, -MED, -S *interj, n, vb*
WHAMMO, -S *n* sound of a sudden collision
WHAMMY *n*
WHAMO *same as* ▸ **whammo**
WHAMPLE *n* strike
WHAMS ▸ **wham**
WHANAU, -S *n* (in Māori societies) a family, esp an extended family
WHANG, -ED, -S *vb* strike or be struck so as to cause a resounding noise ▷ *n* resounding noise produced by a heavy blow
WHANGAM *n* imaginary creature
WHANGED ▸ **whang**
WHANGEE *n* tall woody grass grown for its stems, which are used for bamboo canes
WHANGS ▸ **whang**
WHAP, -PED, -S *same as* ▸ **whop**
WHAPPER *same as* ▸ **whopper**
WHAPS ▸ **whap**
WHARE, -S *n* Māori hut or dwelling place
WHARF, -ED, -S *n, vb*
WHARFIE *n* person employed to load and unload ships
WHARFS ▸ **wharf**
WHARVE, -S *n* wooden disc or wheel on a shaft serving as a flywheel or pulley
WHAT, -S *pron, interj, adv, n*
WHATA, -S *n* building on stilts or a raised platform for storing provisions
WHATCHA *interj*
WHATEN *adj* what; what kind of
WHATEVS *interj* whatever
WHATNA *another word for* ▸ **whaten**
WHATNOT *n*
WHATS ▸ **what**
WHATSIS *US form of* ▸ **whatsit**
WHATSIT *n*
WHATSO *adj* of whatever kind
WHATTEN *same as* ▸ **whaten**
WHAUP, -S *n* curlew
WHAUR, -S *Scot word for* ▸ **where**
WHEAL, -S *same as* ▸ **weal**
WHEAR *obsolete variant of* ▸ **where**
WHEARE *obsolete variant of* ▸ **where**
WHEAT, -S *n*
WHEATEN *n* type of dog ▷ *adj* made of the grain or flour of wheat
WHEATS ▸ **wheat**
WHEATY *adj*
WHEE *interj* exclamation of joy, thrill, etc
WHEECH, -S *vb* Scots word meaning move quickly
WHEEDLE *vb*

WHEEL, -S *n, vb*
WHEELED *adj*
WHEELER *n*
WHEELIE *n*
WHEELS ▸ **wheel**
WHEELY *adj* resembling a wheel
WHEEN, -S *n* few
WHEENGE *Scots form of* ▸ **whinge**
WHEENS ▸ **wheen**
WHEEP, -ED, -S *vb* fly quickly and lightly
WHEEPLE *vb* whistle weakly
WHEEPS ▸ **wheep**
WHEESH *vb* Scots word meaning silence (a person, noise, etc)
WHEESHT *same as* ▸ **wheesh**
WHEEZE, -D, -S *vb, n*
WHEEZER ▸ **wheeze**
WHEEZES ▸ **wheeze**
WHEEZLE *vb* make hoarse breathing sound
WHEEZY ▸ **wheeze**
WHEFT, -S *same as* ▸ **waft**
WHELK, -S *n*
WHELKED *adj* having or covered with whelks
WHELKS ▸ **whelk**
WHELKY ▸ **whelk**
WHELM, -ED, -S *vb* engulf entirely with or as if with water
WHELP, -ED, -S *n, vb*
WHEMMLE *vb* overturn
WHEN, -S *adv, pron, n*
WHENAS *conj* while; inasmuch as
WHENCE, -S *n, adv, pron*
WHENS ▸ **when**
WHENUA, -S *n* land
WHENWE, -S *n* White immigrant to South Africa from Zimbabwe
WHERE, -S *adv, pron, n*
WHEREAS *n*
WHEREAT *adv*
WHEREBY *pron, adv*
WHEREIN *adv, pron*
WHEREOF *adv, pron*
WHEREON *adv, pron*
WHERES ▸ **where**
WHERESO *adv* in or to an unspecified place
WHERETO *adv, pron*
WHERRET *vb* strike (someone) a blow ▹ *n* blow, esp a slap on the face
WHERRIT *vb* worry or cause to worry
WHERRY *n* any of certain kinds of half-decked commercial boats ▹ *vb* travel in a wherry
WHERVE, -S *same as* ▸ **wharve**
WHET, -S, -TED *vb, n*
WHETHER *conj*
WHETS ▸ **whet**
WHETTED ▸ **whet**
WHETTER ▸ **whet**
WHEUGH, -S *same as* ▸ **whew**
WHEW, -ED, -ING, -S *interj, vb*
WHEY, -IER, -S *n*
WHEYEY ▸ **whey**
WHEYIER ▸ **whey**
WHEYISH ▸ **whey**
WHEYS ▸ **whey**
WHICH *pron, adj*
WHICKER *vb* (of a horse) to whinny or neigh
WHID, -DED, -S *vb* move quickly
WHIDAH, -S *same as* ▸ **whydah**
WHIDDED ▸ **whid**
WHIDDER *vb* move with force
WHIDS ▸ **whid**
WHIFF, -ED, -S *n, vb*
WHIFFER ▸ **whiff**
WHIFFET *n* insignificant person
WHIFFLE *vb* think or behave in an erratic or unpredictable way
WHIFFS ▸ **whiff**
WHIFFY *adj*
WHIFT, -S *n* brief emission of air
WHIG, -GED, -S *vb* go quickly
WHILE, -D, WHILING *n, vb*
WHILERE *adv* a while ago
WHILES *adv* at times
WHILING ▸ **while**
WHILK *archaic and dialect word for* ▸ **which**
WHILLY *vb* influence by flattery
WHILOM *adv* formerly ▹ *adj* one-time
WHILST *same as* ▸ **while**
WHIM, -MED, -S *n, vb*
WHIMMY *adj* having whims
WHIMPER *vb, n*
WHIMPLE *same as* ▸ **wimple**
WHIMS ▸ **whim**
WHIMSEY *same as* ▸ **whimsy**
WHIMSY *n, adj*
WHIN, -S *n* gorse
WHINE, -D, -S *n, vb*
WHINER, -S ▸ **whine**

WHINES ▸ **whine**
WHINEY *same as* ▸ **whiny**
WHINGE, -D, -S *vb, n*
WHINGER ▸ **whinge**
WHINGES ▸ **whinge**
WHINGY *adj*
WHINIER ▸ **whiny**
WHINING ▸ **whine**
WHINNY *vb, n, adj*
WHINS ▸ **whin**
WHINY, WHINIER *adj* high-pitched and plaintive
WHIO, -S *n* New Zealand mountain duck with blue plumage
WHIP, -PED, -S *n, vb*
WHIPCAT *n* tailor
WHIPPED ▸ **whip**
WHIPPER ▸ **whip**
WHIPPET *n*
WHIPPIT *n* small canister of nitrous oxide
WHIPPY *adj*
WHIPRAY *n* stingray
WHIPS ▸ **whip**
WHIPSAW *n* any saw with a flexible blade, such as a bandsaw ▹ *vb* saw with a whipsaw
WHIPT *old past tense of* ▸ **whip**
WHIR, -RED, -S *n* prolonged soft swish or buzz ▹ *vb* make or cause to make a whir
WHIRL, -ED, -S *vb, n*
WHIRLER ▸ **whirl**
WHIRLS ▸ **whirl**
WHIRLY *adj*
WHIRR, -S *same as* ▸ **whir**
WHIRRA *interj* exclamation of sorrow or deep concern
WHIRRED ▸ **whir**
WHIRRET *vb* strike with sharp blow
WHIRRS ▸ **whirr**
WHIRRY *vb* move quickly ▹ *adj* characteristic of a whir
WHIRS ▸ **whir**
WHIRTLE *same as* ▸ **wortle**
WHISH, -ED, -ES *less common word for* ▸ **swish**
WHISHT, -S *interj* hush!, be quiet! ▹ *adj* silent or still ▹ *vb* make or become silent
WHISK, -ED, -S *vb, n*
WHISKER *n*
WHISKET *same as* ▸ **wisket**
WHISKEY *n*
WHISKS ▸ **whisk**
WHISKY *n*
WHISPER *vb, n*
WHISS, -ED, -ES *vb* hiss
WHIST, -ED, -S *same as* ▸ **whisht**
WHISTLE *vb, n*
WHISTS ▸ **whist**
WHIT, -S *n*
WHITE, -R, -ST *adj, n*
WHITED *adj* as in **whited sepulchre** hypocrite
WHITELY ▸ **white**
WHITEN, -S *vb*
WHITER ▸ **white**
WHITES *pl n*
WHITEST ▸ **white**
WHITEY *same as* ▸ **whity**
WHITHER *same as* ▸ **wuther**
WHITIER ▸ **whity**
WHITING *n* edible sea fish
WHITISH ▸ **white**
WHITLOW *n* inflamed sore on a finger or toe, esp round a nail
WHITRET *same as* > **whittret**
WHITS ▸ **whit**
WHITTAW *same as* > **whittawer**
WHITTER *variant spelling of* ▸ **witter**
WHITTLE *vb, n*
WHITY, WHITIER *adj* of a white colour
WHIZ *same as* ▸ **whizz**
WHIZZ, -ED, -ES *vb, n*
WHIZZER ▸ **whizz**
WHIZZES ▸ **whizz**
WHIZZO *same as* ▸ **whizzy**
WHIZZY *adj* using sophisticated technology
WHO *pron*
WHOA *interj*
WHOEVER *pron*
WHOLE, -S *adj, n*
WHOLISM *same as* ▸ **holism**
WHOLIST *same as* ▸ **holist**
WHOLLY *adv*
WHOM *pron*
WHOMBLE *same as* ▸ **whemmle**
WHOMMLE *same as* ▸ **whemmle**
WHOMP, -ED, -S *vb* strike; thump
WHOMSO *pron* whom; whomever

WHOOBUB *same as* ▸ **hubbub**
WHOOF, -ED, -S *same as* ▸ **woof**
WHOOMP, -S *n* sudden loud sound
WHOOMPH *same as* ▸ **whoomp**
WHOOMPS ▸ **whoomp**
WHOOP, -ED *n, vb*
WHOOPEE *n*
WHOOPER *n* type of swan
WHOOPIE *same as* ▸ **whoopee**
WHOOPLA *n* commotion; fuss
WHOOPS *interj*
WHOOSH *n, vb*
WHOOSIS *n* thingamajig
WHOOT, -ED, -S *obsolete variant of* ▸ **hoot**
WHOP, -PED, -S *vb* strike, beat, or thrash
WHOPPER *n*
WHOPS ▸ **whop**
WHORL, -S *n, vb*
WHORLED ▸ **whorl**
WHORLS ▸ **whorl**
WHORT, -S *n* small shrub bearing blackish edible sweet berries
WHORTLE *n* whortleberry
WHORTS ▸ **whort**
WHOSE *pron, determiner*
WHOSESO *adj* possessive form of whoso
WHOSIS *n* thingamajig
WHOSIT, -S *n* object or person whose name is not known
WHOSO *archaic word for* ▸ **whoever**
WHOT *obsolete variant of* ▸ **hot**
WHOW, -ED, -ING, -S *interj* wow ▹ *vb* to wow
WHUMMLE *same as* ▸ **whemmle**
WHUMP, -ED, -S *vb* make a dull thud ▹ *n* dull thud
WHUP, -PED, -S *vb* defeat totally
WHY, -S *adv, pron, n*
WHYDA, -S *same as* ▸ **whydah**
WHYDAH, -S *n* type of black African bird
WHYDAS ▸ **whyda**
WHYEVER *adv* for whatever reason
WHYS ▸ **why**
WIBBLE, -D, -S *vb* wobble
WICCA, -S *n* cult or practice of witchcraft
WICCAN, -S *n* practitioner of wicca
WICCAS ▸ **wicca**
WICE *Scots form of* ▸ **wise**
WICH, -ES *n* variant of wych
WICK, -S *n, adj, vb*
WICKAPE *same as* ▸ **wicopy**
WICKED, -S *adj, n*
WICKEN, -S *same as* ▸ **quicken**
WICKER, -S *adj, n*
WICKET, -S *n*
WICKIES ▸ **wicky**
WICKING ▸ **wick**
WICKIUP *n* crude shelter made of brushwood, mats, or grass and having an oval frame
WICKS ▸ **wick**
WICKY, WICKIES *same as* ▸ **quicken**
WICKYUP *same as* ▸ **wickiup**
WICOPY *n* any of various North American trees, shrubs, or herbaceous plants
WIDDER, -S *same as* ▸ **widow**
WIDDIE *same as* ▸ **widdy**
WIDDIES ▸ **widdy**
WIDDLE, -D, -S *vb, n*
WIDDY, WIDDIES *vb* rope made of twigs
WIDE, -R, -S, -ST *adj, adv, n*
WIDELY ▸ **wide**
WIDEN, -ED, -S *vb*
WIDENER ▸ **widen**
WIDENS ▸ **widen**
WIDEOUT *n* (in American football) player who catches passes from the quarterback
WIDER ▸ **wide**
WIDES ▸ **wide**
WIDEST ▸ **wide**
WIDGEON *same as* ▸ **wigeon**
WIDGET, -S *n*
WIDGIE, -S *n* Australian word for a female hooligan
WIDISH ▸ **wide**
WIDOW, -ED, -S *n, vb*
WIDOWER *n*
WIDOWS ▸ **widow**
WIDTH, -S *n*
WIEL, -S *same as* ▸ **weel**
WIELD, -ED, -S *vb*

WIELDER ▸ **wield**
WIELDS ▸ **wield**
WIELDY *adj* easily handled, used, or managed
WIELS ▸ **wiel**
WIENER, -S *n*
WIENIE, -S *same as* ▸ **wiener**
WIFE, -D, -S, WIFING, WIVES *n, vb*
WIFEDOM *n* state of being a wife
WIFELY ▸ **wife**
WIFES ▸ **wife**
WIFEY, -S *n*
WIFIE, -S *n* woman
WIFING ▸ **wife**
WIFTY, WIFTIER *adj* scatterbrained
WIG, -GING, -S *n, vb*
WIGAN, -S *n* stiff fabric
WIGEON, -S *n* duck found in marshland
WIGGED ▸ **wig**
WIGGERY *n* wigs
WIGGIER ▸ **wiggy**
WIGGING ▸ **wig**
WIGGLE, -D, -S *vb, n*
WIGGLER ▸ **wiggle**
WIGGLES ▸ **wiggle**
WIGGLY ▸ **wiggle**
WIGGY, WIGGIER *adj* eccentric
WIGHT, -ED, -S *vb, n, adj*
WIGHTLY *adv* swiftly
WIGHTS ▸ **wight**
WIGLESS ▸ **wig**
WIGLET, -S *n* small wig
WIGLIKE ▸ **wig**
WIGS ▸ **wig**
WIGWAG, -S *vb* move (something) back and forth ▹ *n* system of communication by flag semaphore
WIGWAM, -S *n* Native American's tent
WIKI, -S *n* website consisting mainly of user-generated content
WIKIUP, -S *same as* ▸ **wickiup**
WILCO *interj* expression indicating that the message just received will be complied with
WILD, -ED, -EST, -S *same as* ▸ **wield**
WILDCAT *n* European wild animal like a large domestic cat ▹ *adj* risky and financially unsound ▹ *vb* drill for petroleum or natural gas in an area having no known reserves
WILDED ▸ **wild**
WILDER, -S *vb* lead or be led astray
WILDEST ▸ **wild**
WILDING *n* uncultivated plant
WILDISH ▸ **wild**
WILDLY ▸ **wild**
WILDMAN, WILDMEN *n* man who lives in the wild
WILDS ▸ **wild**
WILE, -D, -S, WILING *n, vb*
WILEFUL *adj* deceitful
WILES ▸ **wile**
WILFUL *adj* headstrong or obstinate
WILGA, -S *n* small drought-resistant tree of Australia
WILI, -S *n* spirit
WILIER ▸ **wily**
WILIEST ▸ **wily**
WILILY ▸ **wily**
WILING ▸ **wile**
WILIS ▸ **wili**
WILJA, -S *same as* ▸ **wiltja**
WILL, -EST, -S, WOULD *vb, n*
WILLED *adj*
WILLER, -S ▸ **will**
WILLEST ▸ **will**
WILLET, -S *n* large American shore bird
WILLEY, -S *same as* ▸ **willy**
WILLFUL *same as* ▸ **wilful**
WILLIAM *n* as in **sweet william** flowering plant
WILLIE *n*
WILLIED ▸ **willy**
WILLIES ▸ **willy**
WILLING *adj*
WILLOW, -S *n, vb*
WILLOWY *adj* slender and graceful
WILLS ▸ **will**
WILLY, WILLIED, WILLIES *vb* clean in a willowing-machine
WILT, -ED, -ING, -S *vb, n*
WILTJA, -S *n* Aboriginal Australian shelter
WILTS ▸ **wilt**
WILY, WILIER, WILIEST *adj*
WIMBLE, -D, -S *n* any of a number of hand tools used for boring holes ▹ *vb* bore (a hole) with or as if with a wimble
WIMBREL *same as* > **whimbrel**
WIMMIN *pl n* intentional non-standard spelling of 'women'

WIMP, -ED, -ING, -S *n, vb*
WIMPIER ▶ **wimpy**
WIMPING ▶ **wimp**
WIMPISH ▶ **wimp**
WIMPLE, -D, -S *n, vb*
WIMPS ▶ **wimp**
WIMPY, WIMPIER ▶ **wimp**
WIN, -NED, -S *vb, vb, n*
WINCE, -D, -S *vb, n*
WINCER, -S ▶ **wince**
WINCES ▶ **wince**
WINCEY, -S *n* plain- or twill-weave cloth
WINCH, -ED, -ES *n, vb*
WINCHER ▶ **winch**
WINCHES ▶ **winch**
WINCING ▶ **wince**
WIND, -ED, -ING, -S *n, vb*
WINDAC, -S *same as* ▶ **windas**
WINDAGE *n* deflection of a projectile as a result of the effect of the wind
WINDAS *n* windlass
WINDBAG *n*
WINDED ▶ **wind**
WINDER, -S *n* person or device that winds, as an engine for hoisting the cages in a mine shaft
WINDGUN *n* air gun
WINDIER ▶ **windy**
WINDIGO *same as* ▶ **wendigo**
WINDILY ▶ **windy**
WINDING ▶ **wind**
WINDLE, -D, -S *vb* wind something round continuously
WINDOCK *same as* ▶ **winnock**
WINDORE *n* window
WINDOW, -S *n, vb*
WINDOWY *adj* having many windows
WINDROW *n* long low ridge or line of hay or a similar crop ▷ *vb* put (hay or a similar crop) into windrows
WINDS ▶ **wind**
WINDSES *pl n* ventilation shafts within mines
WINDUP, -S *n* prank or hoax
WINDWAY *n* part of wind instrument
WINDY, WINDIER *adj*
WINE, -D, -S, WINING *n, adj, vb*
WINERY *n*
WINES ▶ **wine**
WINESAP *n* variety of apple
WINESOP *n* old word for an alcoholic
WINEY *adj* having the taste or qualities of wine
WING, -ING, -S *n, vb*
WINGBOW *n* distinctive band of colour marking the wing of a bird
WINGE, -S *same as* ▶ **whinge**
WINGED *adj*
WINGER, -S *n* player positioned on a wing
WINGES ▶ **winge**
WINGIER ▶ **wingy**
WINGING ▶ **wing**
WINGLET *n* small wing
WINGMAN, WINGMEN *n*
WINGNUT *n*
WINGS ▶ **wing**
WINGTIP *n*
WINGY, WINGIER *adj* having wings
WINIER ▶ **winy**
WINIEST ▶ **winy**
WINING ▶ **wine**
WINISH ▶ **wine**
WINK, -ED, -S *vb, n*
WINKER, -S *n* person or thing that winks
WINKING ▶ **wink**
WINKLE, -D, -S *n, vb*
WINKLER *n* one who forces a person or thing out
WINKLES ▶ **winkle**
WINKS ▶ **wink**
WINLESS *adj* not having won anything
WINN, -S *n* penny
WINNA *vb* will not
WINNARD *n* heron
WINNED ▶ **win**
WINNER, -S *n*
WINNING *adj*
WINNLE, -S *n* machine for winding thread or yarn
WINNOCK *n* window
WINNOW, -S *vb, n*
WINNS ▶ **winn**
WINO, -ES, -S *n*
WINS ▶ **win**
WINSEY, -S *same as* ▶ **wincey**
WINSOME *adj*
WINTER, -S *n, vb*
WINTERY *same as* ▶ **wintry**
WINTLE, -D, -S *vb* reel; stagger
WINTRY *adj*
WINY, WINIER, WINIEST *same as* ▶ **winey**
WINZE, -S *n* steeply inclined shaft, as for ventilation between levels
WIPE, -D, -S *vb, n*

WIPEOUT *n*
WIPER, -S *n*
WIPES ▸ **wipe**
WIPING, -S ▸ **wipe**
WIPPEN, -S *n* part of the hammer action in a piano
WIRABLE *adj* that can be wired
WIRE, -S *n, vb*
WIRED *adj*
WIREMAN, WIREMEN *n* person who installs and maintains electric wiring, cables, etc
WIRER, -S *n* person who sets or uses wires to snare rabbits and similar animals
WIRES ▸ **wire**
WIRETAP *vb*
WIREWAY *n* tube for electric wires
WIRIER ▸ **wiry**
WIRIEST ▸ **wiry**
WIRILDA *n* SE Australian acacia tree with edible seeds
WIRILY ▸ **wiry**
WIRING, -S *n* system of wires ▹ *adj* used in wiring
WIRRA *interj* exclamation of sorrow or deep concern
WIRRAH, -S *n* Australian saltwater fish with bright blue spots
WIRY, WIRIER, WIRIEST *adj*
WIS, -SED, -SES, -SING *vb* know or suppose (something)
WISARD, -S *obsolete spelling of* ▸ **wizard**
WISDOM, -S *n*
WISE, -D, -R, -S, -ST, WISING *vb* guide ▹ *adj* having wisdom ▹ *n* manner
WISEGUY *n*
WISELY ▸ **wise**
WISENT, -S *n* European bison
WISER ▸ **wise**
WISES ▸ **wise**
WISEST ▸ **wise**
WISH, -ED, -ES *vb, n*
WISHA *interj* expression of surprise
WISHED ▸ **wish**
WISHER, -S ▸ **wish**
WISHES ▸ **wish**
WISHFUL *adj*
WISHING ▸ **wish**
WISHT *variant of* ▸ **whisht**
WISING ▸ **wise**
WISKET, -S *n* basket
WISP, -ED, -ING, -S *n, vb*
WISPIER ▸ **wispy**
WISPILY ▸ **wispy**
WISPING ▸ **wisp**
WISPISH ▸ **wisp**
WISPS ▸ **wisp**
WISPY, WISPIER *adj*
WISS *vb* urinate
WISSED ▸ **wis**
WISSES ▸ **wis**
WISSING ▸ **wis**
WIST, -ED, -ING, -S *vb* know
WISTFUL *adj*
WISTING ▸ **wist**
WISTITI *n* marmoset
WISTLY *adv* intently
WISTS ▸ **wist**
WIT, WATE, -S *vb, n*
WITAN, -S *n* Anglo-Saxon assembly that met to counsel the king
WITCH, -ED, -ES *n, vb*
WITCHEN *n* rowan tree
WITCHES ▸ **witch**
WITCHY *adj*
WITE, -D, -S, WITING *vb* blame
WITGAT, -S *n* type of S African tree
WITH, -S *prep, n*
WITHAL *adv*
WITHE, -D, -S, WITHING *n* strong flexible twig suitable for binding things together ▹ *vb* bind with withes
WITHER *vb*
WITHERS *pl n*
WITHES ▸ **withe**
WITHIER ▸ **withy**
WITHIES ▸ **withy**
WITHIN, -S *adv, prep, n*
WITHING ▸ **withe**
WITHINS ▸ **within**
WITHOUT *prep, adv, n*
WITHS ▸ **with**
WITHY, WITHIER, WITHIES *n* willow tree, esp an osier ▹ *adj* (of people) tough and agile
WITING ▸ **wite**
WITLESS *adj*
WITLING *n* person who thinks themself witty
WITLOOF *n* chicory
WITNESS *n, vb*
WITNEY, -S *n* type of blanket; heavy cloth
WITS ▸ **wit**
WITTED *adj* having wit
WITTER, -S *vb, n*
WITTIER ▸ **witty**
WITTILY ▸ **witty**
WITTING *adj, n*
WITTY, WITTIER *adj*

WITWALL *n* golden oriole
WIVE, -D, WIVING *vb*
WIVER, -S *another word for* ▸ **wivern**
WIVERN, -S *same as* ▸ **wyvern**
WIVERS ▸ **wiver**
WIVES ▸ **wife**
WIVING ▸ **wive**
WIZ, -ES, -ZES *shortened form of* ▸ **wizard**

Wiz is a short form of **wizard**. This is the highest-scoring 3-letter word beginning with W, and can be especially useful when there isn't much room to manoeuvre.

WIZARD, -S *n, adj*
WIZEN, -ER, -S *vb* make or become shrivelled ▹ *n* archaic word for 'weasand' (the gullet) ▹ *adj* wizened
WIZENED *adj*
WIZENER ▸ **wizen**
WIZENS ▸ **wizen**
WIZES ▸ **wiz**
WIZIER, -S *same as* ▸ **vizier**
WIZZEN, -S *same as* ▸ **wizen**
WIZZES ▸ **wiz**
WO, -S *archaic spelling of* ▸ **woe**
WOAD, -S *n* blue dye obtained from a plant
WOADED *adj* coloured blue with woad
WOADS ▸ **woad**
WOADWAX *same as* > **woadwaxen**
WOAH *same as* ▸ **whoa**
WOALD, -S *same as* ▸ **weld**
WOBBLE, -D, -S *vb, n*
WOBBLER ▸ **wobble**
WOBBLES ▸ **wobble**
WOBBLY *adj, n*
WOCK, -S *same as* ▸ **wok**
WODGE, -S *n* thick lump or chunk
WOE, -S *n*
WOEFUL *adj*
WOENESS ▸ **woe**
WOES ▸ **woe**
WOESOME *adj* woeful
WOF, -S *n* fool
WOFUL *same as* ▸ **woeful**
WOFULLY ▸ **woful**
WOGGLE, -S *n* ring of leather through which a Scout neckerchief is threaded
WOIWODE *same as* ▸ **voivode**
WOJUS *adj* (Irish) of a poor quality
WOK, -S *n*
WOKE, -R, -ST *adj* alert to social and political injustice
WOKEN ▸ **wake**
WOKER ▸ **woke**
WOKEST ▸ **woke**
WOKKA *modifier* as in **wokka board** piece of fibreboard used as a musical instrument
WOKS ▸ **wok**
WOLD, -S *same as* ▸ **weld**
WOLF, -ED, -S, WOLVES *n, vb*
WOLFER, -S *same as* ▸ **wolver**
WOLFING ▸ **wolf**
WOLFISH ▸ **wolf**
WOLFKIN *n* young wolf
WOLFRAM *another name for* > **tungsten**
WOLFS ▸ **wolf**
WOLLY, WOLLIES *n* pickled cucumber or olive
WOLVE, -D *vb* hunt for wolves
WOLVER, -S *n* person who hunts wolves
WOLVES ▸ **wolf**
WOLVING ▸ **wolve**
WOLVISH *same as* ▸ **wolfish**
WOMAN, -ED, -S, WOMEN *n, adj, vb*
WOMANLY *adj*
WOMANS ▸ **woman**
WOMB, -ING, -S *vb, n*
WOMBAT, -S *n*
WOMBED ▸ **womb**
WOMBIER ▸ **womby**
WOMBING ▸ **womb**
WOMBS ▸ **womb**
WOMBY, WOMBIER *adj* hollow; spacious
WOMEN ▸ **woman**
WOMERA, -S *same as* ▸ **woomera**
WOMMERA *same as* ▸ **woomera**
WOMMIT, -S *n* foolish person
WOMYN *n* intentional non-standard spelling of 'women'
WON, -NED, -S *n* standard monetary unit of North Korea ▹ *vb* live or dwell
WONDER, -S *vb, n, adj*
WONDRED *adj* splendid
WONGA, -S *n* money

WONGI, -ED, -S *vb* talk informally
WONING, -S ▶ **won**
WONK, -S *n*
WONKERY *n* activities of a wonk
WONKIER ▶ **wonky**
WONKILY *adv* in a wonky manner
WONKISH *adj* like a wonk
WONKS ▶ **wonk**
WONKY, WONKIER *adj*
WONNED ▶ **won**
WONNER, -S ▶ **won**
WONNING ▶ **won**
WONS ▶ **won**
WONT, -ING, -S *adj, n, vb*
WONTED *adj*
WONTING ▶ **wont**
WONTON, -S *n* dumpling filled with spiced minced pork
WONTS ▶ **wont**
WOO, -ED, -S *vb*
WOOABLE *adj* able to be wooed
WOOBUT, -S *same as* ▶ **woubit**
WOOD, -ING *n, adj, vb*
WOODBIN *n* box for firewood
WOODBOX *n* box for firewood
WOODCUT *n*
WOODED *adj*
WOODEN, -S *adj, vb*
WOODHEN *another name for* ▶ **weka**
WOODIE, -S *n* gallows rope
WOODIER ▶ **woody**
WOODIES ▶ **woodie**
WOODING ▶ **wood**
WOODLOT *n* area restricted to the growing of trees
WOODMAN, WOODMEN *same as* > **woodsman**
WOODRAT *n* pack-rat
WOODS *pl n*
WOODSIA *n* type of small fern with tufted rhizomes and wiry fronds
WOODSY *adj*
WOODWAX *same as* > **woadwaxen**
WOODY, WOODIER *adj*
WOOED ▶ **woo**
WOOER, -S ▶ **woo**
WOOF, -ED, -ING, -S *vb*
WOOFER, -S *n*
WOOFIER ▶ **woofy**
WOOFING ▶ **woof**
WOOFS ▶ **woof**
WOOFY, WOOFIER *adj* with close, dense texture
WOOHOO *interj*
WOOING, -S ▶ **woo**
WOOL, -S *n*
WOOLD, -ED, -S *vb* wind (rope)
WOOLDER *n* stick for winding rope
WOOLDS ▶ **woold**
WOOLED *same as* ▶ **woolled**
WOOLEN, -S *same as* ▶ **woollen**
WOOLER, -S *same as* ▶ **woolder**
WOOLFAT *same as* ▶ **lanolin**
WOOLHAT *n* hat made of wool
WOOLIE *n* wool garment
WOOLIER ▶ **wooly**
WOOLIES ▶ **wooly**
WOOLILY ▶ **wooly**
WOOLLED *adj* (of animals) having wool
WOOLLEN *adj, n*
WOOLLY *adj, n*
WOOLMAN, WOOLMEN *n* wool trader
WOOLS ▶ **wool**
WOOLSEY *n* cotton and wool blend
WOOLY, WOOLIER, WOOLIES *same as* ▶ **woolly**
WOOMERA *n* notched stick used by Aboriginal Australians to aid the propulsion of a spear
WOON, -ED, -ING, -S *same as* ▶ **won**
WOONERF *n* (in the Netherlands) road primarily for cyclists and pedestrians
WOONING ▶ **woon**
WOONS ▶ **woon**
WOOPIE, -S *n* well-off older person
WOOPS, -ED, -ES *vb*
WOOPY *n* well-off older person
WOORALI *less common name for* ▶ **curare**
WOORARA *same as* ▶ **wourali**
WOORARI *same as* ▶ **wourali**
WOOS ▶ **woo**
WOOSE, -S *same as* ▶ **wuss**
WOOSEL, -S *same as* ▶ **ouzel**
WOOSELL *same as* ▶ **ouzel**
WOOSELS ▶ **woosel**
WOOSES ▶ **woose**
WOOSH, -ED, -ES *same as* ▶ **whoosh**

WOOT *interj* (esp used by players in online games) shout of joy, victory, etc
WOOTZ, -ES *n* Middle-Eastern steel
WOOZIER ▸ **woozy**
WOOZILY ▸ **woozy**
WOOZY, WOOZIER *adj*
WOP, -PED, -PING, -S *vb* strike, beat, or thrash
WORD, -ED, -S *n, vb*
WORDAGE *n* words considered collectively, esp a quantity of words
WORDED ▸ **word**
WORDIE, -S *n* person who loves words
WORDIER ▸ **wordy**
WORDIES ▸ **wordie**
WORDILY ▸ **wordy**
WORDING *n*
WORDISH *adj* talkative
WORDS ▸ **word**
WORDY, WORDIER *adj*
WORE ▸ **wear**
WORK, -S *n, adj, vb*
WORKBAG *n* container for implements, tools, or materials
WORKBOX *same as* ▸ **workbag**
WORKDAY *another word for* ▸ **workaday**
WORKED *adj*
WORKER, -S *n*
WORKFUL *adj* hardworking
WORKING *n, adj*
WORKMAN, WORKMEN *n* manual worker
WORKOUT *n*
WORKS ▸ **work**
WORKSHY *adj*
WORKTOP *n*
WORKUP, -S *n* medical examination
WORLD, -S *n, adj*
WORLDED *adj* incorporating worlds
WORLDER *n* person who belongs to a specified class or domain
WORLDIE *n* world-class performance, achievement, person, etc
WORLDLY *adj, adv*
WORLDS ▸ **world**
WORM, -ED, -ING *n, vb*
WORMER, -S ▸ **worm**
WORMERY *n* piece of apparatus in which worms are kept for study
WORMFLY *n* type of lure dressed on a double hook
WORMIER ▸ **wormy**
WORMIL, -S *n* burrowing larva of type of fly
WORMING ▸ **worm**
WORMISH ▸ **worm**
WORMS *n*
WORMY, WORMIER *adj*
WORN ▸ **wear**
WORRAL, -S *n* type of lizard
WORREL, -S *same as* ▸ **worral**
WORRIED ▸ **worry**
WORRIER ▸ **worry**
WORRIES ▸ **worry**
WORRIT, -S *vb* tease or worry
WORRY, WORRIED, WORRIES *vb, n*
WORSE, -D, -S, WORSING *vb*
WORSEN, -S *vb*
WORSER *archaic or nonstandard word for* ▸ **worse**
WORSES ▸ **worse**
WORSET, -S *n* worsted fabric
WORSHIP *vb, n*
WORSING ▸ **worse**
WORST, -S *n, vb*
WORSTED *n*
WORSTS ▸ **worst**
WORT, -S *n* any of various plants formerly used to cure diseases
WORTH, -ED, -S *prep* having a value of ▹ *n* value or price ▹ *vb* happen or betide
WORTHY *adj, n, vb*
WORTLE, -S *n* plate with holes for drawing wire through
WORTS ▸ **wort**
WOS ▸ **wo**
WOST *form of the second person singular of* ▸ **wit**
WOT, -S, -TED, -TEST, -TETH, -TING *form of the present tense of* ▸ **wit**
WOTCHA *same as* ▸ **wotcher**
WOTCHER *sentence substitute* slang term of greeting
WOTS ▸ **wot**
WOTTED ▸ **wot**
WOTTEST ▸ **wot**
WOTTETH ▸ **wot**
WOTTING ▸ **wot**
WOUBIT, -S *n* type of caterpillar
WOULD ▸ **will**
WOULDS *same as* ▸ **wouldst**

WOULDST *singular form of the past tense of* ▸ **will**
WOUND, -S *vb, n*
WOUNDED *adj*
WOUNDER ▸ **wound**
WOUNDS ▸ **wound**
WOUNDY *adj* extreme
WOURALI *n* plant from which curare is obtained
WOVE ▸ **weave**
WOVEN, -S *n*
WOW, -ED, -ING, -S *interj, n, vb*
WOWEE *stronger form of* ▸ **wow**
WOWF, -ER, -EST *adj* mad

This is a Scots word meaning crazy: you are not likely to get the chance to play this very often, but if your opponent plays **wow** and you have an F, you would be wowf to miss the opportunity of the hook!

WOWING ▸ **wow**
WOWS ▸ **wow**
WOWSER, -S *n*
WOX ▸ **wax**

Wox is an old past tense of the verb **wax**, to grow, and is another of the key words using X.

WOXEN ▸ **wax**
WRACK, -ED, -S *n, vb*
WRAITH, -S *n*
WRANG, -ED, -S *Scot word for* ▸ **wrong**
WRANGLE *vb, n*
WRANGS ▸ **wrang**
WRAP, -PED, -S *vb, n*
WRAPPER *vb, n*
WRAPS ▸ **wrap**
WRAPT *same as* ▸ **rapt**
WRASSE, -S *n* colourful sea fish
WRASSLE *same as* ▸ **wrestle**
WRAST, -ED, -S *same as* ▸ **wrest**
WRASTLE *same as* ▸ **wrestle**
WRASTS ▸ **wrast**
WRATE ▸ **write**
WRATH, -ED, -S *n* intense anger ▹ *adj* incensed ▹ *vb* make angry
WRATHY *same as* > **wrathful**
WRAWL, -ED, -S *vb* howl
WRAXLE, -D, -S *vb* wrestle
WREAK, -ED, -S, WROKE, WROKEN *vb*
WREAKER ▸ **wreak**
WREAKS ▸ **wreak**
WREATH, -S *n*
WREATHE *vb* form into or take the form of a wreath by twisting together
WREATHS ▸ **wreath**
WREATHY *adj* twisted into wreath
WRECK, -ED, -S *vb, n*
WRECKER *n* formerly, person who lured ships onto the rocks in order to plunder them
WRECKS ▸ **wreck**
WREN, -S *n*
WRENCH *vb, n*
WRENS ▸ **wren**
WRENTIT *n* type of long-tailed North American bird
WREST, -ED, -S *vb, n*
WRESTER ▸ **wrest**
WRESTLE *vb, n*
WRESTS ▸ **wrest**
WRETCH *n*
WRETHE, -D, -S *same as* ▸ **wreathe**
WRICK, -ED, -S *variant spelling (chiefly Brit) of* ▸ **rick**
WRIED ▸ **wry**
WRIER ▸ **wry**
WRIES ▸ **wry**
WRIEST ▸ **wry**
WRIGGLE *vb, n*
WRIGGLY ▸ **wriggle**
WRIGHT, -S *n*
WRING, -ED, -S, WRUNG *vb*
WRINGER *same as* ▸ **mangle**
WRINGS ▸ **wring**
WRINKLE *n, vb*
WRINKLY ▸ **wrinkle**
WRIST, -ED, -S *n, vb*
WRISTER *n* type of shot in hockey
WRISTS ▸ **wrist**
WRISTY *adj* characterized by considerable movement of the wrist
WRIT, -S *n*
WRITE, WRATE, -S, WRITING, WRITTEN, WROTE *vb*
WRITER, -S *n*
WRITES ▸ **write**
WRITHE, -D, -S *vb, n*
WRITHEN *adj* twisted
WRITHER ▸ **writhe**
WRITHES ▸ **writhe**
WRITING ▸ **write**

WRITS ▸ **writ**
WRITTEN ▸ **write**
WRIZLED *adj* wrinkled
WROATH, -S *n* unforeseen trouble
WROKE ▸ **wreak**
WROKEN ▸ **wreak**
WRONG, -ED, -S *adj, adv, n, vb*
WRONGER ▸ **wrong**
WRONGLY ▸ **wrong**
WRONGS ▸ **wrong**
WROOT, -ED, -S *obsolete form of* ▸ **root**
WROTE ▸ **write**
WROTH *adj* angry
WROUGHT *adj*
WRUNG ▸ **wring**
WRY, WRIED, WRIER, WRIES, WRIEST, -ER, -EST, -ING *adj, vb*
WRYBILL *n* New Zealand plover whose bill is bent to one side
WRYER ▸ **wry**
WRYEST ▸ **wry**
WRYING ▸ **wry**
WRYLY ▸ **wry**
WRYNECK *n* woodpecker that has a habit of twisting its neck round
WRYNESS ▸ **wry**
WRYTHEN *adj* twisted
WUD, -DED, -DING, -S *Scots form of* ▸ **wood**

W and U are a horrible combination to have on your rack, so this Scots word for wood can be a godsend. And remember that it can also be a verb, meaning to load with wood, so you have **wuds, wudding** and **wudded**.

WUDDIES ▸ **wuddy**
WUDDING ▸ **wud**
WUDDY, WUDDIES *n* loop at the end of a rope
WUDS ▸ **wud**
WUDU, -S *n* Muslim practice of ritual washing before daily prayer
WULL, -ED, -ING, -S *obsolete form of* ▸ **will**
WUNNER, -S *same as* ▸ **oner**
WURLEY, -S *n* Aboriginal Australian hut
WURLIE, -S *same as* ▸ **wurley**
WURST, -S *n* large sausage, esp of a type made in Germany, Austria, etc
WURZEL, -S *n* root
WUS, -ES *n* Welsh dialect term of address
WUSHU, -S *n* Chinese martial arts
WUSS, -ES *n*
WUSSY, WUSSIER, WUSSIES *adj, n*
WUTHER, -S *vb* (of wind) blow and roar
WUXIA, -S *n* Chinese fiction concerning the adventures of sword-wielding heroes

This Chinese word for a genre of fiction may get you a decent score from a very difficult-looking rack.

WUZ *vb* nonstandard spelling of was
WUZZLE, -D, -S *vb* mix up
WYCH, -ES *n* type of tree having flexible branches
WYE, -S *n* Y-shaped pipe

If you have W and Y on your rack, look for an E on the board that will allow you to play this name for the letter Y, especially if you can land on a bonus square as a result.

WYLE, -D, -S, WYLING *vb* entice
WYN, -S *n* rune equivalent to English 'w'
WYND, -S *n* narrow lane or alley
WYNN, -S *same as* ▸ **wyn**
WYNS ▸ **wyn**
WYSIWYG *adj*
WYTE, -D, -S, WYTING *vb* blame
WYVERN, -S *n* heraldic beast

Xx

XANTHAM *n* acacia gum
XANTHAN *same as* ▸ **xantham**
XANTHIC *adj* of, containing, or derived from xanthic acid
XANTHIN *n* any of a group of yellow or orange carotene derivatives
XEBEC, -S *n* small three-masted Mediterranean vessel

A kind of small boat, and a good high-scoring word that can easily be missed, as we tend to be slow to consider words beginning with X.

XED *adj* having a cross against
XENIA, -S *n* influence of pollen upon the form of the fruit developing after pollination
XENIAL ▸ **xenia**
XENIAS ▸ **xenia**
XENIC *adj* denoting the presence of bacteria
XENIUM *n* diplomatic gift
XENON, -S *n* colourless odourless gas
XENOPUS *n* African frog
XERAFIN *n* Indian coin
XERARCH *adj* (of a sere) having its origin in a dry habitat
XERASIA *n* dryness of the hair
XERIC *adj* of, relating to, or growing in dry conditions
XEROMA, -S *n* excessive dryness of the cornea
XEROSIS, XEROSES *n* abnormal dryness of bodily tissues
XEROTES *same as* ▸ **xerosis**
XEROTIC ▸ **xerosis**
XEROX, -ED, -ES *n, vb*
XERUS, -ES *n* ground squirrel
XI, -S *n* 14th letter in the Greek alphabet
XIPHOID *adj* shaped like a sword ▹ *n* part of the sternum
XIS ▸ **xi**
XOANON, XOANA *n* primitive image of a god supposed to have fallen from heaven

One of the few words starting with X. But be careful: the plural is **xoana** not **xoanons**.

XRAY, -S *n*
XU *n* Vietnamese currency unit
XYLAN, -S *n* yellow polysaccharide consisting of xylose units
XYLEM, -S *n* plant tissue that conducts water and minerals from the roots to all other parts
XYLENE, -S *n* type of hydrocarbon
XYLENOL *n* synthetic resin made from xylene
XYLIC ▸ **xylem**
XYLIDIN *same as* ▸ **xylidine**
XYLITOL *n* crystalline alcohol used as a sweetener
XYLOGEN *same as* ▸ **xylem**
XYLOID *adj* of, relating to, or resembling wood
XYLOL, -S *another name (not in technical usage) for* ▸ **xylene**
XYLOMA, -S *n* hard growth in fungi
XYLONIC *adj* denoting an acid formed from xylose
XYLOSE, -S *n* white crystalline sugar found in wood and straw

XYLYL, -S *n* group of atoms

XYST, -S *n* long portico, esp one used in ancient Greece for athletics

A kind of court used by ancient Greek athletes for exercises, this is a lovely high-scoring word to play. And if your opponent plays it, remember that you can put an I on it to make **xysti**, as well as an S to make **xysts**.

XYSTER, -S *n* surgical instrument for scraping bone

XYSTI ▶ **xystus**

XYSTOS, XYSTOI *same as* ▶ **xyst**

XYSTS ▶ **xyst**

XYSTUS, XYSTI *same as* ▶ **xyst**

Yy

YA, -S *n*
YAAR, -S *n* in informal Indian English, a friend
YABA, -S *n* informal word for 'yet another bloody acronym'
YABBA, -S *n* form of methamphetamine
YABBER, -S *vb* talk or jabber ▷ *n* talk or jabber
YABBIE *same as* ▶ **yabby**
YABBY, YABBIED, YABBIES *n* small freshwater crayfish ▷ *vb* go out to catch yabbies
YACCA, -S *n* Australian plant with a woody stem
YACHT, -ED, -S *n*; *vb*
YACHTER ▶ **yacht**
YACHTIE *n* yachtsman
YACHTS ▶ **yacht**
YACK, -ED, -ING, -S *same as* ▶ **yak**
YACKA, -S *same as* ▶ **yacca**
YACKED ▶ **yack**
YACKER, -S *same as* ▶ **yakka**
YACKING ▶ **yack**
YACKS ▶ **yack**
YAD, -S *n* hand-held pointer used for reading the sefer torah
YAE *same as* ▶ **ae**
YAFF, -ED, -ING, -S *vb* bark
YAFFLE, -S *n* woodpecker with a green back and wings
YAFFS ▶ **yaff**
YAG, -S *n* artificial crystal
YAGE, -S *n* tropical vine of the Amazon region
YAGER, -S *same as* ▶ **jaeger**
YAGES ▶ **yage**
YAGGER, -S *n* pedlar
YAGI, -S *n* type of highly directional aerial
YAGS ▶ **yag**
YAH, -S *interj* exclamation of derision or disgust ▷ *n* affected upper-class person
YAHOO, -S *n* crude coarse person
YAHS ▶ **yah**
YAIRD, -S *Scots form of* ▶ **yard**
YAK, -KED, -KING, -S *n*, *vb*
YAKHDAN *n* box for carrying ice on a pack animal
YAKKA, -S *n* informal Australian word for work
YAKKED ▶ **yak**
YAKKER, -S *same as* ▶ **yakka**
YAKKING ▶ **yak**
YAKOW, -S *n* animal bred from a male yak and a domestic cow
YAKS ▶ **yak**
YAKUZA *n* Japanese criminal organization
YALD *adj* vigorous
YALE, -S *n* mythical beast with the body of an antelope (or similar animal) and swivelling horns
YAM, -S *n*
YAMALKA *same as* > **yarmulke**
YAMEN, -S *n* (in imperial China) the office or residence of a public official
YAMMER, -S *vb*, *n*
YAMPY, YAMPIES *n* foolish person
YAMS ▶ **yam**
YAMULKA *same as* > **yarmulke**
YAMUN, -S *same as* ▶ **yamen**
YANG, -S *n* (in Chinese philosophy) one of two complementary principles maintaining harmony in the universe

YANK, -ED, -ING, -S *vb, n*
YANKEE, -S *n*
YANKER, -S ▸ **yank**
YANKIE, -S *n* impudent woman
YANKING ▸ **yank**
YANKS ▸ **yank**
YANQUI, -S *n* slang word for American
YANTRA, -S *n* diagram used in meditation
YAOURT, -S *n* yoghurt
YAP, -PED, -S *vb, n, interj*
YAPOCK, -S *same as* ▸ **yapok**
YAPOK, -S *n* type of opossum
YAPON, -S *same as* ▸ **yaupon**
YAPP, -S *n* type of book binding
YAPPED ▸ **yap**
YAPPER, -S ▸ **yap**
YAPPIE, -S *n* young aspiring professional
YAPPIER ▸ **yappy**
YAPPIES ▸ **yappie**
YAPPING *n*
YAPPS ▸ **yapp**
YAPPY, YAPPIER ▸ **yap**
YAPS ▸ **yap**
YAPSTER ▸ **yap**
YAQONA, -S *n* Polynesian shrub
YAR *adj* nimble
YARAK, -S *n* fit condition for hunting
YARCO, -S *n* insulting word for a young working-class person who wears casual sports clothes
YARD, -ED, -S *n, vb*
YARDAGE *n*
YARDANG *n* ridge formed by wind erosion
YARDARM *n*
YARDED ▸ **yard**
YARDER, -S *n* one who drafts animals to a sale yard
YARDING *n* group of animals displayed for sale
YARDMAN, YARDMEN *n* farm overseer
YARDS ▸ **yard**
YARE, -R, -ST *adj* ready, brisk, or eager ▹ *adv* readily or eagerly
YARELY ▸ **yare**
YARER ▸ **yare**
YAREST ▸ **yare**
YARFA, -S *n* peat
YARK, -ED, -ING, -S *vb* make ready
YARN, -ED, -ING, -S *n, vb*
YARNER, -S ▸ **yarn**
YARNING ▸ **yarn**
YARNS ▸ **yarn**
YARPHA, -S *n* peat
YARR, -ED, -ING, -S *n* wild white flower ▹ *vb* growl or snarl
YARRAN, -S *n* type of small hardy tree of inland Australia
YARRED ▸ **yarr**
YARRING ▸ **yarr**
YARROW, -S *n* wild plant with flat clusters of white flowers
YARRS ▸ **yarr**
YARTA, -S *Shetland word for* ▸ **heart**
YARTO, -S *same as* ▸ **yarta**
YAS ▸ **ya**
YASHMAC *same as* ▸ **yashmak**
YASHMAK *n*
YASMAK, -S *same as* ▸ **yashmak**
YATAGAN *same as* > **yataghan**
YATE, -S *n* type of small eucalyptus tree yielding a very hard timber
YATTER, -S *vb* talk at length ▹ *n* continuous chatter
YAUD, -S *Scots word for* ▸ **mare**
YAULD *adj* alert or nimble
YAUP, -ED, -ING, -S *variant spelling of* ▸ **yawp**
YAUPER, -S ▸ **yaup**
YAUPING ▸ **yaup**
YAUPON, -S *n* southern US evergreen holly shrub
YAUPS ▸ **yaup**
YAUTIA, -S *n* Caribbean plant cultivated for its edible leaves and underground stems
YAW, -ED, -ING *vb, n*
YAWEY ▸ **yaws**
YAWIER ▸ **yawy**
YAWIEST ▸ **yawy**
YAWING ▸ **yaw**
YAWL, -ED, -ING, -S *n* two-masted sailing boat ▹ *vb* howl, weep, or scream harshly
YAWN, -ED, -S *vb, n*
YAWNER, -S ▸ **yawn**
YAWNIER ▸ **yawny**
YAWNING ▸ **yawn**
YAWNS ▸ **yawn**
YAWNY, YAWNIER ▸ **yawn**
YAWP, -ED, -ING, -S *vb* gape or yawn, esp audibly ▹ *n* shout, bark, yelp, or cry

YAWPER, -S ▸ **yawp**
YAWPING ▸ **yawp**
YAWPS ▸ **yawp**
YAWS *n* infectious tropical skin disease
YAWY, YAWIER, YAWIEST *adj* having or resembling yaws
YAY, -S *interj, n*
YBET *archaic past participle of* ▸ **beat**
YBLENT *archaic past participle of* ▸ **blend**
YBORE *archaic past participle of* ▸ **bear**
YBOUND *archaic past participle of* ▸ **bind**
YBRENT *archaic past participle of* ▸ **burn**
YCLAD *archaic past participle of* ▸ **clothe**
YCLED *archaic past participle of* ▸ **clothe**
YCLEEPE *archaic form of* ▸ **clepe**
YCLEPED *same as* ▸ **yclept**
YCLEPT *adj* having the name of
YCOND *archaic past participle of* ▸ **con**
YDRAD *archaic past participle of* ▸ **dread**
YDRED *archaic past participle of* ▸ **dread**
YE *pron, adj*
YEA, -S *interj, adv, n*
YEAD, -ING, -S, YODE *vb* proceed
YEAH, -S *n*
YEALDON *n* fuel
YEALING *n* person of the same age as oneself
YEALM, -ED, -S *vb* prepare for thatching
YEAN, -ED, -ING, -S *vb* (of a sheep or goat) to give birth to (offspring)
YEAR, -S *n*
YEARD, -ED, -S *vb* bury
YEAREND *n*
YEARLY *adv, adj, n*
YEARN, -ED, -S *vb*
YEARNER ▸ **yearn**
YEARNS ▸ **yearn**
YEARS ▸ **year**
YEAS ▸ **yea**
YEAST, -ED, -S *n, vb*
YEASTY *adj*
YEBO *interj* yes
YECCH, -S *same as* ▸ **yech**
YECH, -S *n* expression of disgust
YECHIER ▸ **yechy**
YECHS ▸ **yech**
YECHY, YECHIER ▸ **yech**
YEDE, -S, YEDING *same as* ▸ **yead**
YEED, -ING, -S *same as* ▸ **yead**
YEELIN, -S *n* person of the same age as oneself
YEESH *interj* interjection used to express frustration
YEGG, -S *n* burglar or safe-breaker
YEGGMAN, YEGGMEN *same as* ▸ **yegg**
YEGGS ▸ **yegg**
YEH *same as* ▸ **yeah**
YELD *adj* (of an animal) barren or too young to bear young
YELK, -S *n* yolk of an egg
YELL, -ED, -ING, -S *vb, n*
YELLER, -S ▸ **yell**
YELLING ▸ **yell**
YELLOCH *vb* yell
YELLOW *n, adj, vb*
YELLOWS *n* any of various fungal or viral diseases of plants
YELLOWY ▸ **yellow**
YELLS ▸ **yell**
YELM, -ED, -ING, -S *same as* ▸ **yealm**
YELP, -ED, -ING, -S *n, vb*
YELPER, -S ▸ **yelp**
YELPING ▸ **yelp**
YELPS ▸ **yelp**
YELT, -S *n* young sow
YEMMER, -S *southwest English form of* ▸ **ember**
YEN, -NED, -NING, -S *n, vb*
YENTA, -S *n* meddlesome woman
YENTE, -S *same as* ▸ **yenta**
YEOMAN, YEOMEN *n*
YEOW *interj*
YEP, -S *n* answer of yes
YER *adj* informal spelling of 'your'
YERBA, -S *n* stimulating South American drink
YERD, -ED, -ING, -S *vb* bury
YERK, -ED, -ING, -S *vb* tighten stitches
YES, -ES, -SED, -SES, -SING *interj, n, vb*
YESHIVA *n*
YESK, -ED, -ING, -S *vb* hiccup
YESSED ▸ **yes**
YESSES ▸ **yes**
YESSING ▸ **yes**
YESSIR *interj*
YESSUM *interj* expression of assent to a woman
YEST, -S *archaic form of* ▸ **yeast**

YESTER *adj* of or relating to yesterday
YESTERN *same as* ▸ **yester**
YESTS ▸ **yest**
YESTY *archaic form of* ▸ **yeasty**
YET *adv*
YETI, -S *n*
YETT, -S *n* gate or door
YETTIE, -S *n* young, entrepreneurial, and technology-based (person)
YETTS ▸ **yett**
YEUK, -ED, -ING, -S *vb* itch
YEUKIER ▸ **yeuky**
YEUKING ▸ **yeuk**
YEUKS ▸ **yeuk**
YEUKY, YEUKIER ▸ **yeuk**
YEVE, -N, -S, YEVING *vb* give
YEW, -S *n*
YEWEN *adj* made of yew
YEWS ▸ **yew**
YEX, -ED, -ES, -ING *vb* hiccup

> This word meaning to hiccup gives you a good score, and the verb forms offer the chance to expand it if someone else plays it, or if you get the chance later on.

YEZ *interj* yes
YFERE, -S *adv* together ▹ *n* friend or associate
YGO *archaic past participle of* ▸ **go**
YGOE *archaic past participle of* ▸ **go**
YIBBLES *adv* Scots word meaning perhaps
YICKER, -S *vb* squeal or squeak
YIDAKI, -S *n* long wooden wind instrument played by some Australian Aboriginal peoples
YIELD, -ED, -S *vb, n*
YIELDER ▸ **yield**
YIELDS ▸ **yield**
YIKE, -D, YIKING *n* argument, squabble, or fight ▹ *vb* argue, squabble, or fight
YIKES *interj*
YIKING ▸ **yike**
YIKKER, -S *vb* squeal or squeak
YILL, -ED, -ING, -S *n* ale ▹ *vb* entertain with ale
YIN, -S *Scots word for* ▸ **one**
YINCE *Scots form of* ▸ **once**
YINDIE, -S *n* person who combines a lucrative career with non-mainstream tastes
YINS ▸ **yin**
YIP, -PED, -PING, -S *vb* emit a high-pitched bark
YIPE *same as* ▸ **yipes**
YIPES *interj* expression of surprise, fear, or alarm
YIPPED ▸ **yip**
YIPPEE *interj*
YIPPER, -S *n* golfer who has a failure of nerve
YIPPIE, -S *n* young person sharing hippy ideals
YIPPING ▸ **yip**
YIPPY *same as* ▸ **yippie**
YIPS ▸ **yip**
YIRD, -ED, -ING, -S *vb* bury
YIRK, -ED, -ING, -S *same as* ▸ **yerk**
YIRR, -ED, -ING, -S *vb* snarl, growl, or yell
YIRTH, -S *n* earth
YITE, -S *n* European bunting with a yellowish head and body and brown streaked wings and tail
YITIE, -S *same as* ▸ **yite**
YITTEN *adj* frightened
YLEM, -S *n* original matter from which the basic elements are said to have been formed
YLIKE *Spenserian form of* ▸ **alike**
YLKE, -S *archaic spelling of* ▸ **ilk**
YMOLT *Spenserian past participle of* ▸ **melt**
YMOLTEN *Spenserian past participle of* ▸ **melt**
YMPE, -S, YMPING, YMPT *Spenserian form of* ▸ **imp**
YNAMBU, -S *n* South American bird
YO *interj*
YOB, -S *n*
YOBBERY *n* behaviour typical of aggressive surly youths
YOBBIER ▸ **yobby**
YOBBISH *adj*
YOBBISM ▸ **yob**
YOBBO, -ES, -S *same as* ▸ **yob**
YOBBY, YOBBIER *adj* like a yob

YOBS ▸ **yob**
YOCK, -ED, -ING, -S *vb* chuckle
YOD, -S *n* tenth letter in the Hebrew alphabet
YODE ▸ **yead**
YODEL, -ED, -S *vb, n*
YODELER ▸ **yodel**
YODELS ▸ **yodel**
YODH, -S *same as* ▸ **yod**
YODLE, -D, -S, YODLING *variant spelling of* ▸ **yodel**
YODLER, -S ▸ **yodle**
YODLES ▸ **yodle**
YODLING ▸ **yodle**
YODS ▸ **yod**
YOGA, -S *n*
YOGEE, -S *same as* ▸ **yogi**
YOGH, -S *n* character used in Old and Middle English to represent a palatal fricative
YOGHURT *same as* ▸ **yogurt**
YOGI, -S *n*
YOGIC ▸ **yoga**
YOGIN, -S *same as* ▸ **yogi**
YOGINI, -S ▸ **yogi**
YOGINS ▸ **yogin**
YOGIS ▸ **yogi**
YOGISM, -S ▸ **yogi**
YOGOURT *same as* ▸ **yogurt**
YOGURT, -S *n*
YOHIMBE *n* bark used in herbal medicine
YOICK, -ED *vb* urge on foxhounds
YOICKS *interj* cry used by huntsmen to urge on the hounds ▹ *vb* urge on foxhounds
YOJAN, -S *n* Indian unit of distance
YOJANA, -S *same as* ▸ **yojan**
YOJANS ▸ **yojan**
YOK, -KED, -KING, -S *vb* chuckle

A useful short word meaning to laugh, with an alternative spelling **yuk**.

YOKE, -D, -RS, -S, YOKING, YOKINGS *n, vb*
YOKEL, -S *n*
YOKER, -ED *vb* spit
YOKERS ▸ **yoke**
YOKES ▸ **yoke**
YOKING ▸ **yoke**
YOKINGS ▸ **yoke**
YOKKED ▸ **yok**
YOKKING ▸ **yok**
YOKS ▸ **yok**
YOKUL *Shetland word for* ▸ **yes**
YOLD *archaic past participle of* ▸ **yield**
YOLK, -S *n*
YOLKED ▸ **yolk**
YOLKIER ▸ **yolky**
YOLKS ▸ **yolk**
YOLKY, YOLKIER ▸ **yolk**
YOM, -IM *n* day
YOMP, -ED, -ING, -S *vb* walk or trek laboriously
YON *adj* that or those over there ▹ *adv* yonder ▹ *pron* that person or thing
YOND *same as* ▸ **yon**
YONDER, -S *adv, adj, determiner, n*
YONI, -S *n* female genitalia
YONIC *adj* resembling a vulva
YONIS ▸ **yoni**
YONKER, -S *same as* ▸ **younker**
YONKS *pl n* very long time
YONNIE, -S *n* stone
YONT *same as* ▸ **yon**
YOOF, -S *n* non-standard spelling of youth
YOOP, -S *n* sob
YOPPER, -S *n* young person employed on a former UK government training programme
YORE, -S *n, adv*
YORK, -ED, -ING, -S *vb* bowl or try to bowl (a batsman) by pitching the ball under or just beyond the bat
YORKER, -S *n* (in cricket) ball that pitches just under the bat
YORKIE, -S *n* Yorkshire terrier
YORKING ▸ **york**
YORKS ▸ **york**
YORLING *n* as in **yellow yorling** yellowhammer
YORP, -ED, -ING, -S *vb* shout
YOU *pron, n*
YOUK, -ED, -ING, -S *vb* itch
YOUNG, -ER, -S *adj, n*
YOUNGLY *adv* youthfully
YOUNGS ▸ **young**
YOUNGTH *n* youth
YOUNKER *n* young man

YOUPON, -S *same as* ▸ **yaupon**
YOUR *adj*
YOURN *dialect form of* ▸ **yours**
YOURS *pron*
YOURT, -S *same as* ▸ **yurt**
YOUS *pron*
YOUSE *same as* ▸ **yous**
YOUTH, -S *n*
YOUTHEN *vb* render more youthful-seeming
YOUTHLY *adj* young
YOUTHS ▸ **youth**
YOUTHY *Scots word for* ▸ **young**
YOW, -ED, -ING, -S *vb* howl
YOWE, -S *Scot word for* ▸ **ewe**
YOWED ▸ **yow**
YOWES ▸ **yowe**
YOWIE, -S *n* legendary Australian apelike creature
YOWING ▸ **yow**
YOWL, -ED, -S *n, vb*
YOWLER, -S ▸ **yowl**
YOWLEY, -S *n* yellowhammer (bird)
YOWLING ▸ **yowl**
YOWLS ▸ **yowl**
YOWS ▸ **yow**
YOWZA *interj* exclamation of enthusiasm
YPERITE *n* mustard gas
YPIGHT *archaic past participle of* ▸ **pitch**
YPLAST *archaic past participle of* ▸ **place**
YPLIGHT *archaic past participle of* ▸ **plight**
YPSILON *same as* ▸ **upsilon**
YRAPT *Spenserian form of* ▸ **rapt**
YRENT *archaic past participle of* ▸ **rend**
YRIVD *archaic past participle of* ▸ **rive**
YRNEH, -S *n* unit of reciprocal inductance
YSAME *Spenserian word for* ▸ **together**
YSHEND, -S, YSHENT *Spenserian form of* ▸ **shend**
YSLAKED *archaic past participle of* ▸ **slake**
YTOST *archaic past participle of* ▸ **toss**
YTTRIA, -S *n* insoluble solid used mainly in incandescent mantles
YTTRIC ▸ **yttrium**
YTTRIUM *n* silvery metallic element used in various alloys
YU, -S *n* jade
YUAN, -S *n* standard monetary unit of the People's Republic of China
YUCA, -S *same as* ▸ **yucca**
YUCCA, -S *n*
YUCCH *interj* expression of disgust
YUCH *interj* expression of disgust
YUCK, -ED, -ING, -S *interj, vb*
YUCKER, -S ▸ **yuck**
YUCKIER ▸ **yucky**
YUCKING ▸ **yuck**
YUCKO *adj* disgusting ▹ *interj* exclamation of disgust
YUCKS ▸ **yuck**
YUCKY, YUCKIER *adj*
YUFT, -S *n* Russia leather
YUG, -S *same as* ▸ **yuga**
YUGA, -S *n* (in Hindu cosmology) one of the four ages of mankind
YUGARIE *variant spelling of* ▸ **eugarie**
YUGAS ▸ **yuga**
YUGS ▸ **yug**
YUK, -KED, -KING, -S *same as* ▸ **yuck**
YUKATA, -S *n* light kimono
YUKE, -D, -S, YUKING *vb* itch
YUKIER ▸ **yuky**
YUKIEST ▸ **yuky**
YUKING ▸ **yuke**
YUKKED ▸ **yuk**
YUKKIER ▸ **yukky**
YUKKING ▸ **yuk**
YUKKY, YUKKIER *same as* ▸ **yucky**
YUKO, -S *n* score of five points in judo
YUKS ▸ **yuk**
YUKY, YUKIER, YUKIEST *adj* itchy
YULAN, -S *n* Chinese magnolia with white flowers
YULE, -S *n*
YUM *interj*
YUMMIER ▸ **yummy**
YUMMIES ▸ **yummy**
YUMMO *adj* tasty ▹ *interj* exclamation of delight or approval
YUMMY, YUMMIER, YUMMIES *adj, interj, n*
YUMP, -ED, -ING, -S *vb* leave the ground when driving over a ridge

YUMPIE, -S *n* young upwardly mobile person
YUMPING ▸ **yump**
YUMPS ▸ **yump**
YUNX, -ES *n* wryneck
YUP, -S *n* answer of yes
YUPON, -S *same as* ▸ **yaupon**
YUPPIE *n, adj*
YUPPIES ▸ **yuppy**
YUPPIFY *vb* make yuppie in nature
YUPPY, YUPPIES *same as* ▸ **yuppie**
YUPS ▸ **yup**
YUPSTER *same as* ▸ **yindie**
YURT, -S *n* circular tent
YURTA, -S *same as* ▸ **yurt**
YURTS ▸ **yurt**
YUS ▸ **yu**
YUTZ, -ES *n* Yiddish word meaning fool
YUZU, -S *n* type of citrus fruit
YWIS *adv* archaic word meaning certainly
YWROKE *archaic past participle of* ▸ **wreak**

Zz

ZA, -S *n* pizza
ZABETA, -S *n* tariff
ZABRA, -S *n* small sailing vessel
ZABTIEH *n* Turkish police officer
ZACATON *n* coarse grass
ZACK, -S *n* Australian five-cent piece
ZADDICK *adj* righteous ▷ *n* Hasidic Jewish spiritual leader
ZADDIK, -S *n* Hasidic Jewish leader
ZAFFAR, -S *same as* ▶ **zaffer**
ZAFFER, -S *n* impure cobalt oxide, used to impart a blue colour to enamels
ZAFFIR, -S *same as* ▶ **zaffer**
ZAFFRE, -S *same as* ▶ **zaffer**
ZAFTIG *adj* ripe or curvaceous
ZAG, -GED, -GING, -S *vb*
ZAIDA, -S *n* grandfather
ZAIDEH, -S *same as* ▶ **zaida**
ZAIDY, ZAIDIES *same as* ▶ **zaida**
ZAIKAI, -S *n* Japanese business community
ZAIRE, -S *n* currency used in the former Zaïre
ZAITECH *n* investment in financial markets by a company to supplement its main income
ZAKAT, -S *n* annual tax on Muslims to aid the poor in the Muslim community
ZAKUSKI, ZAKUSKA *pl n* Russian hors d'oeuvres consisting of tiny sandwiches
ZAMAN, -S *n* tropical tree
ZAMANG, -S *same as* ▶ **zaman**
ZAMANS ▶ **zaman**
ZAMARRA *n* sheepskin coat
ZAMARRO *same as* ▶ **zamarra**
ZAMBUCK *n* informal word for a St John ambulance attendant
ZAMBUK, -S *same as* ▶ **zambuck**
ZAMIA, -S *n* type of plant of tropical and subtropical America
ZAMOUSE *n* West African buffalo
ZAMPONE, ZAMPONI *n* sausage made from pig's trotters
ZANANA, -S *same as* ▶ **zenana**
ZANDER, -S *n* European freshwater pikeperch, valued as a food fish
ZANELLA *n* twill fabric
ZANIED ▶ **zany**
ZANIER ▶ **zany**
ZANIES ▶ **zany**
ZANIEST ▶ **zany**
ZANILY ▶ **zany**
ZANJA, -S *n* irrigation canal

An irrigation canal in Spanish America, notable for combining the J and Z.

ZANJERO *n* irrigation supervisor

Someone who supervises the distribution of water in a **zanja** or irrigation canal. This has a fair chance of coming up in actual play, and would make a great bonus.

ZANTE, -S *n* type of wood
ZANY, ZANIED, ZANIER, ZANIES, ZANIEST, -ING *adj* comical in an endearing way ▷ *n* clown or buffoon who imitated other performers ▷ *vb* clown

ZANYISH ▸ **zany**
ZANYISM ▸ **zany**
ZANZA, -S *same as* ▸ **zanze**
ZANZE, -S *n* African musical instrument
ZAP, -PED, -PING, -S *vb, n, interj*
ZAPATA *adj* (of a moustache) drooping
ZAPATEO *n* Cuban folk dance
ZAPPED ▸ **zap**
ZAPPER, -S *n* remote control for a television, etc
ZAPPIER ▸ **zappy**
ZAPPING ▸ **zap**
ZAPPY, ZAPPIER *adj* energetic
ZAPS ▸ **zap**
ZAPTIAH *same as* ▸ **zaptieh**
ZAPTIEH *n* Turkish police officer

Watch out for this Turkish police officer, who can also be spelt **zabtieh** or **zaptiah**.

ZARAPE, -S *n* blanket-like shawl
ZAREBA, -S *n* (in NE Africa) enclosure of thorn bushes around a village or campsite
ZAREEBA *same as* ▸ **zareba**
ZARF, -S *n* (esp in the Middle East) a holder, usually ornamental, for a hot coffee cup
ZARI, -S *n* thread made from fine gold or silver wire
ZARIBA, -S *same as* ▸ **zareba**
ZARIS ▸ **zari**
ZARNEC, -S *n* sulphide of arsenic
ZARNICH *same as* ▸ **zarnec**
ZAS ▸ **za**
ZATI, -S *n* type of macaque
ZAX, -ES *n* tool for cutting roofing slate

A chopper for trimming slate, and a great word combining X and Z. It has a variant **zex**.

ZAYIN, -S *n* seventh letter of the Hebrew alphabet
ZAZEN, -S *n* deep meditation undertaken whilst sitting upright with legs crossed
ZE *pron* gender-neutral pronoun
ZEA, -S *n* corn silk
ZEAL, -S *n*
ZEALANT *archaic variant of* ▸ **zealot**
ZEALFUL ▸ **zeal**
ZEALOT, -S *n*
ZEALOUS *adj*
ZEALS ▸ **zeal**
ZEAS ▸ **zea**
ZEATIN, -S *n* cytokinin derived from corn
ZEBEC, -S *variant spelling of* ▸ **xebec**
ZEBECK, -S *same as* ▸ **zebec**
ZEBECS ▸ **zebec**
ZEBRA, -S *n*
ZEBRAIC *adj* like a zebra
ZEBRANO *n* type of striped wood
ZEBRAS ▸ **zebra**
ZEBRASS *n* offspring of a male zebra and a female ass
ZEBRINA *n* trailing herbaceous plant
ZEBRINE ▸ **zebra**
ZEBROID ▸ **zebra**
ZEBRULA *n* offspring of a male zebra and a female horse
ZEBRULE *same as* ▸ **zebrula**
ZEBU, -S *n* Asian ox with a humped back and long horns
ZEBUB, -S *n* large African fly
ZEBUS ▸ **zebu**
ZECCHIN *same as* > **zecchino**
ZECHIN, -S *same as* > **zecchino**
ZED, -S *n*

A name for the letter Z, and one of the most commonly played Z words.

ZEDA, -S *n* grandfather
ZEDOARY *n* dried rhizome of a tropical Asian plant
ZEDS ▸ **zed**
ZEE, -S *the US word for* ▸ **zed**

This word can be very useful because E is the most common tile in Scrabble, so keep it in mind if you draw a Z. Zee scores 12 points.

ZEIN, -S *n* protein occurring in maize
ZEK, -S *n* Soviet prisoner

ZEL, -S *n* Turkish cymbal
ZELANT, -S *alternative form of* ▸ **zealant**
ZELATOR *same as* > **zelatrix**
ZELKOVA *n* type of elm tree
ZELOSO *adv* with zeal
ZELS ▸ **zel**
ZEMSTVO, ZEMSTVA *n* council in Tsarist Russia
ZEN, -S *n* calm meditative state
ZENAIDA *n* dove
ZENANA, -S *n* part of Muslim or Hindu home reserved for women and girls
ZENDIK, -S *n* (in Islam) unbeliever or heretic
ZENDO, -S *n* place where Zen Buddhists study
ZENITH, -S *n*
ZENS ▸ **zen**
ZEOLITE *n* any of a large group of glassy secondary minerals
ZEP, -S *n* type of long sandwich
ZEPHYR, -S *n*
ZEPPOLE, ZEPPOLI *n* Italian fritter
ZEPS ▸ **zep**
ZERDA, -S *n* fennec
ZEREBA, -S *same as* ▸ **zareba**
ZERIBA, -S *same as* ▸ **zareba**
ZERK, -S *n* part of a mechanical joint into which grease can be inserted
ZERO, -ED, -ES, -ING, -S *n, adj, vb, determiner*
ZEROTH *adj* denoting a term in a series that precedes the term otherwise regarded as the first term
ZEST, -ED, -ING, -S *n, vb*
ZESTER, -S *n* kitchen utensil used to scrape fine shreds of peel from citrus fruits
ZESTFUL ▸ **zest**
ZESTIER ▸ **zesty**
ZESTILY ▸ **zest**
ZESTING ▸ **zest**
ZESTS ▸ **zest**
ZESTY, ZESTIER ▸ **zest**
ZETA, -S *n*
ZETETIC *adj* proceeding by inquiry ▹ *n* investigation
ZEUGMA, -S *n* figure of speech in which a word is used with two words although appropriate to only one of them
ZEUXITE *n* ferriferous mineral

This mineral, a kind of tourmaline, makes an excellent bonus.

ZEX, -ES *n* tool for cutting roofing slate
ZEZE, -S *n* stringed musical instrument
ZHO, -S *same as* ▸ **zo**

A cross between a yak and a cow; the other forms are **dso, dzo, dzho** and **zo,** and it's worth remembering all of them.

ZHOMO, -S *n* female zho
ZHOOSH *vb* make more exciting or attractive
ZHOS ▸ **zho**
ZIBET, -S *n* large civet of S and SE Asia
ZIBETH, -S *same as* ▸ **zibet**
ZIBETS ▸ **zibet**
ZIFF, -S *n* beard
ZIFFIUS *n* sea monster
ZIFFS ▸ **ziff**
ZIG, -GED, -GING, -S *same as* ▸ **zag**
ZIGAN, -S *n* Romany dance
ZIGANKA *n* Russian dance
ZIGANS ▸ **zigan**
ZIGGED ▸ **zig**
ZIGGING ▸ **zig**
ZIGS ▸ **zig**
ZIGZAG, -S *n, vb, adj, adv*
ZIKURAT *same as* > **ziggurat**
ZILA, -S *n* administrative district in India
ZILCH, -ES *n*
ZILL, -S *n* finger cymbal
ZILLA, -S *same as* ▸ **zila**
ZILLAH, -S *same as* ▸ **zila**
ZILLAS ▸ **zilla**
ZILLION *n*
ZILLS ▸ **zill**
ZIMB, -S *same as* ▸ **zebub**
ZIMBI, -S *n* cowrie shell used as money
ZIMBS ▸ **zimb**
ZIMOCCA *n* bath sponge
ZIN, -S *short form of* > **zinfandel**
ZINC, -ED, -ING, -KED, -S, ZINKED, ZINKING *n, vb*

ZINCATE *n* any of a class of salts derived from the amphoteric hydroxide of zinc
ZINCED ▶ **zinc**
ZINCIC ▶ **zinc**
ZINCIER ▶ **zincy**
ZINCIFY *vb* coat with zinc
ZINCING ▶ **zinc**
ZINCITE *n* red or yellow mineral
ZINCKED ▶ **zinc**
ZINCKY ▶ **zinc**
ZINCO, -S *n* printing plate made from zincography
ZINCODE *n* positive electrode
ZINCOID ▶ **zinc**
ZINCOS ▶ **zinco**
ZINCOUS ▶ **zinc**
ZINCS ▶ **zinc**
ZINCY, ZINCIER ▶ **zinc**
ZINE, -S *n* magazine or fanzine
ZINEB, -S *n* organic insecticide
ZINES ▶ **zine**
ZING, -ED, -ING, -S *n, vb*
ZINGANO, ZINGANI *n* Romany man
ZINGARA, ZINGARE *n* Romany woman
ZINGARO, ZINGARI *n* Romany man
ZINGED ▶ **zing**
ZINGEL, -S *n* small freshwater perch
ZINGER, -S ▶ **zing**
ZINGIER ▶ **zingy**
ZINGING ▶ **zing**
ZINGS ▶ **zing**
ZINGY, ZINGIER *adj* vibrant
ZINKE, -S *n* cornett
ZINKED ▶ **zinc**
ZINKES ▶ **zinke**
ZINKIER ▶ **zinky**
ZINKIFY *vb* coat with zinc
ZINKING ▶ **zinc**
ZINKY, ZINKIER ▶ **zinc**
ZINNIA, -S *n* plant of tropical and subtropical America
ZINS ▶ **zin**
ZIP, -PED, -PING, -S *n, vb*
ZIPLESS ▶ **zip**
ZIPLINE *n*
ZIPLOCK *adj, vb*
ZIPOLA, -S *n* nothing
ZIPPED ▶ **zip**
ZIPPER, -S *same as* ▶ **zip**
ZIPPIER ▶ **zippy**
ZIPPILY *adv* in a zippy manner
ZIPPING ▶ **zip**
ZIPPO, -S *n* nothing
ZIPPY, ZIPPIER *adj*
ZIPS ▶ **zip**
ZIPTOP *adj* (of a bag) closed with a zip
ZIPWIRE *same as* ▶ **zipline**
ZIRAM, -S *n* industrial fungicide
ZIRCON, -S *n*
ZIT, -S *n*

> This little word for a pimple can be very useful for disposing of the Z.

ZITE *same as* ▶ **ziti**
ZITHER, -S *n*
ZITHERN *same as* ▶ **zither**
ZITHERS ▶ **zither**
ZITI, -S *n* type of pasta

> Another very useful word for disposing of the Z, **ziti** is a type of pasta. It has a variant **zite**. Remember that **ziti** takes an S to form **zitis**, but **zite** does not take an S.

ZITS ▶ **zit**
ZIZ *same as* ▶ **zizz**
ZIZANIA *n* aquatic grass
ZIZEL, -S *n* chipmunk
ZIZIT *same as* ▶ **zizith**
ZIZITH *variant spelling of* > **tsitsith**
ZIZZ, -ED, -ES, -ING *n* short sleep ▷ *vb* take a short sleep, snooze
ZIZZLE, -D, -S *vb* sizzle
ZLOTY, ZLOTE, ZLOTIES, -S *n*
ZLOTYCH *same as* ▶ **zloty**
ZLOTYS ▶ **zloty**
ZO, -S *n* Tibetan breed of cattle
ZOA ▶ **zoon**
ZOAEA, -E, -S *same as* ▶ **zoea**
ZOARIA ▶ **zoarium**
ZOARIAL ▶ **zoarium**
ZOARIUM, ZOARIA *n* colony of zooids
ZOBO, -S *same as* ▶ **zo**
ZOBU, -S *same as* ▶ **zo**
ZOCALO, -S *n* plaza in Mexico
ZOCCO, -S *n* plinth
ZOCCOLO *same as* ▶ **zocco**
ZOCCOS ▶ **zocco**
ZODIAC, -S *n*
ZOEA, -E, -S *n* free-swimming larva

of a crab or related crustacean

One of the most frequently played words in Scrabble, along with its friends **zoaea** and **zooea** and the various inflections: remember that these words can take an E in the plural as well as S, giving **zoeae, zoaeae** and **zooeae**.

ZOEAL ▸ **zoea**
ZOEAS ▸ **zoea**
ZOECIUM, ZOECIA *same as* > **zooecium**
ZOEFORM ▸ **zoea**
ZOETIC *adj* pertaining to life
ZOFTIG *adj* ripe or curvaceous
ZOIC *adj* relating to or having animal life
ZOISITE *n* grey, brown, or pink mineral
ZOISM, -S *n* belief in magical animal powers
ZOIST, -S ▸ **zoism**
ZOMBI, -S *same as* ▸ **zombie**
ZOMBIE, -S *n*
ZOMBIFY *vb*
ZOMBIS ▸ **zombi**
ZOMBOID *adj* like a zombie
ZONA, -E *n* zone or belt
ZONAL *adj*
ZONALLY ▸ **zonal**
ZONARY *same as* ▸ **zonal**
ZONATE *adj* marked with, divided into, or arranged in zones
ZONATED *same as* ▸ **zonate**
ZONDA, -S *n* South American wind
ZONE, -D, -S *n, vb*
ZONER, -S *n* something which divides other things into zones
ZONES ▸ **zone**
ZONING, -S ▸ **zone**
ZONK, -ED, -ING, -S *vb* strike resoundingly
ZONOID, -S *adj* resembling a zone ▹ *n* finite vector sum of line segments
ZONULA, -E, -S *n* small zone or belt
ZONULAR ▸ **zonule**
ZONULAS ▸ **zonula**
ZONULE, -S *n* small zone, band, or area
ZONULET *n* small belt
ZONURE, -S *n* lizard with a ringed tail
ZOO, -IER, -IEST, -S *n*
ZOOEA, -E, -S *same as* ▸ **zoea**
ZOOEAL ▸ **zooea**
ZOOEAS ▸ **zooea**
ZOOECIA > **zooecium**
ZOOEY ▸ **zoo**
ZOOGAMY *n* reproduction involving zoosperm
ZOOGENY *n* doctrine of the formation of animals
ZOOGLEA *same as* > **zoogloea**
ZOOGONY *same as* ▸ **zoogeny**
ZOOID, -S *n* any independent animal body, such as an individual of a coral colony
ZOOIDAL ▸ **zooid**
ZOOIDS ▸ **zooid**
ZOOIER ▸ **zoo**
ZOOIEST ▸ **zoo**
ZOOKS *short form of* > **gadzooks**
ZOOLITE *n* fossilized animal
ZOOLITH *n* fossilized animal
ZOOLOGY *n*
ZOOM, -ED, -ING, -S *vb, n*
ZOON, ZOA, -ED, -ING, -S *vb* zoom ▹ *n* zooid
ZOONAL ▸ **zoon**
ZOONED ▸ **zoon**
ZOONIC *adj* concerning animals
ZOONING ▸ **zoon**
ZOONITE *n* segment of an articulated animal
ZOONOMY *n* science of animal life
ZOONS ▸ **zoon**
ZOOPERY *n* experimentation on animals
ZOOS ▸ **zoo**
ZOOT *n* as in **zoot suit** man's suit consisting of baggy trousers and a long jacket
ZOOTAXY *n* science of the classification of animals

The science of classifying animals. An unlikely word to appear on your rack, but you never know, and it would make an impressive bonus!

ZOOTIER ▸ **zooty**
ZOOTOMY *n* branch of zoology concerned

with the dissection and anatomy of animals
ZOOTY, ZOOTIER *adj* showy
ZOOTYPE *n* animal figure used as a symbol
ZOOZOO, -S *n* wood pigeon
ZOPPA *adj* syncopated
ZOPPO *same as* ▸ **zoppa**
ZORBING *n* activity of travelling downhill inside a large air-filled ball
ZORGITE *n* copper-lead selenide
ZORI, -S *n* Japanese sandal
ZORIL, -S *same as* ▸ **zorilla**
ZORILLA *n* skunk-like African musteline mammal having a long black-and-white coat
ZORILLE *same as* ▸ **zorilla**
ZORILLO *same as* ▸ **zorilla**
ZORILS ▸ **zoril**
ZORINO, -S *n* skunk fur
ZORIS ▸ **zori**
ZORRO, -S *n* hoary fox
ZOS ▸ **zo**
ZOSTER, -S *n* shingles; herpes zoster
ZOUAVE, -S *n* (formerly) member of a body of French infantry composed of Algerian recruits
ZOUK, -S *n* style of dance music that combines African and Latin American rhythms
ZOUNDS *interj*
ZOWEE *same as* ▸ **zowie**
ZOWIE *interj* expression of pleasurable surprise
ZOYSIA, -S *n* type of grass with short stiffly pointed leaves, often used for lawns
ZUFFOLO, ZUFFOLI *same as* ▸ **zufolo**
ZUFOLO, ZUFOLI, -S *n* small flute
ZULU, -S *n*
ZUPA, -S *n* confederation of Serbian villages
ZUPAN, -S *n* head of a zupa
ZUPAS ▸ **zupa**
ZUPPA, -S *n* Italian soup
ZURF, -S *same as* ▸ **zarf**
ZUZ, -IM, -ZIM *n* ancient Hebrew silver coin
ZYDECO, -S *n* type of Black Cajun music
ZYGA ▸ **zygon**
ZYGAL ▸ **zygon**
ZYGOID *same as* ▸ **diploid**
ZYGOMA, -S *n* slender arch of bone on each side of the skull of mammals
ZYGON, ZYGA *n* brain fissure
ZYGOSE, -S ▸ **zygosis**
ZYGOSIS *n* direct transfer of DNA between two cells that are temporarily joined
ZYGOTE, -S *n* fertilized egg cell
ZYGOTIC ▸ **zygote**
ZYMASE, -S *n* mixture of enzymes that is obtained as an extract from yeast and ferments sugars
ZYME, -S *n* ferment
ZYMIC ▸ **zyme**
ZYMITE, -S *n* priest who uses leavened bread during communion
ZYMOGEN *n* any of various inactive precursors of enzymes activated by a kinase
ZYMOID *adj* relating to a ferment
ZYMOME, -S *n* glutinous substance that is insoluble in alcohol
ZYMOSAN *n* insoluble carbohydrate found in yeast
ZYMOSIS, ZYMOSES *same as* ▸ **zymolysis**
ZYMOTIC *adj* of, relating to, or causing fermentation ▷ *n* disease caused by an enzyme
ZYMURGY *n* study of fermentation processes
ZYTHUM, -S *n* ancient Egyptian beer
ZYZZYVA *n* American weevil
ZZZ, -S *n* informal word for sleep